INDEX TO CRITICAL FILM REVIEWS

IN BRITISH AND AMERICAN FILM PERIODICALS

Together With:
INDEX TO CRITICAL REVIEWS OF BOOKS ABOUT FILM

Compiled and Edited by Stephen E. Bowles
University of Northern Colorado

VOLUME II: CRITICAL FILM REVIEWS N–Z
VOLUME III: CRITICAL REVIEWS OF BOOKS ABOUT FILM A–Z
AND INDEXES

Burt Franklin & Co., Inc.   NEW YORK

To my parents,
for their constant faith,
And to my wife,
for her many contributions.

©1975 Burt Franklin & Co., Inc., 235 E. 44 St., N.Y. 10017

Library of Congress Cataloging in Publication Data

Bowles, Stephen E., 1943-
  Index to critical film reviews in British and American film periodicals, together with: Index to critical reviews of books about film, 1930-1972.

  CONTENTS: v. 1. Critical film reviews A-M.— v. 2. Critical film reviews N-Z.— v. 3. Critical reviews of books about film A-Z.
  1. Moving-pictures—Reviews—Indexes. 2. Moving-pictures—Periodicals —Indexes. 3. Moving-pictures—Book reviews—Indexes. I. Bowles, Stephen E., 1943- Index to critical reviews of books about film. 1974. II. Title.
Z5784.M9B64   791.43'01'6   74-12109
ISBN 0-89102-040-3 (lib. bdg.) (Formerly 0-8337-4596-3)

INDEX TO CRITICAL FILM REVIEWS
In British and American Film Periodicals
Together With
INDEX TO CRITICAL REVIEWS OF BOOKS ABOUT FILM

Volume II: Critical Film Reviews N–Z
Volume III: Critical Reviews of Books About Film A–Z
            And Indexes

CONTENTS

Volume II

Explanation of Entries.   i
Bibliographical Abbreviations   i
Periodical Abbreviations   ii
Index to Critical Film Reviews N–Z 347

Volume III

Index to Critical Reviews of Books About Film A–Z . . .591

Indexes

Index to Directors 687
Index to Film Reviewers 717
Index to Authors 741
Index to Book Reviewers 751
Subject Index to Books About Film 759
Union List of Film Periodical Locations 767

EXPLANATION OF ENTRIES

Names

For each main title entry, the director's/author's name is given (in parentheses) following the title. In some cases — where the director's name is not known or applicable — the name is either omitted or the appropriate staff member cited (producer or editor).

The name of the reviewer is given in the context of the bibliographical citations. An omission signifies that no one was credited as reviewer.

Alphabetical ordering

The alphabetical ordering of the Index follows (with only slight deviation) the conventions established by the American Library Association. It is an alphabetical listing by word rather than letter, exclusive of both domestic and foreign articles.

When more than one title is listed with an alphabetical equivalency, the subsequent ordering is based upon year of production or publication. *The Star* (1953) for example, precedes *Star!* (1968).

BIBLIOGRAPHICAL ABBREVIATIONS

v	volume
n	number
p(p)	page(s)
wds.	(approximate number of) words
comp.	compiler or compilation
prod.	producer
ed.	editor
cr.	credits (This refers to the film's cast and production credits listed in in the review.)
cp. cr.	complete credits (provided in the review)
pt. cr.	partial credits
no cr.	no credits
pub.	publisher or publication information
cp. pub.	complete publication information (provided in the review)
pt. pub.	partial publication information
no pub.	no publication information
var. sp.	variant spelling
pseud.	pseudonym(s)
*	published in a foreign language

PERIODICAL ABBREVIATIONS

Am Cinematog   American Cinematographer
                            monthly; Los Angeles [Hollywood]
                            v. 39, n. 1 (Jan., 1950) ———

Cahiers in Eng   Cahiers du Cinema in English
                            defunct; New York
                            n. 1 (Jan., 1966) to n. 12 (Dec., 1967)

Cineaste   Cineaste
                            quarterly; New York
                            v. 1, n. 1 (Fall, 1967) ———

Cinema   Cinema
                            3 issues/year; Beverly Hills, Calif.
                            v. 1, n. 1 (1962) ———

Cinema J   Cinema Journal
                            formerly: Society of Cinematologists
                            2 issues/year; [Bridgewater] Boston, Mass.
                            v. 1, n. 1 (1961-1962) ———

Cinema Studies   Cinema Studies
                            Society for Film History Research
                            defunct; London
                            v. I, n. 1 (Mar., 1960) to v. II, n. 3 (Mar., 1967)

Film   Film
                            British Federation of Film Societies
                            quarterly; [London] Sheffield
                            n. 1 (Oct., 1954) ———

F Comment   Film Comment
                            formerly: Vision (first two issues)
                            quarterly; New York
                            v. 1, n. 1 (Spring, 1962) ———

F Culture   Film Culture
                            quarterly; New York
                            v. 1, n. 1 (Jan., 1955) ———

F Heritage   Film Heritage
                            quarterly; Dayton, Ohio
                            v. 1, n. 1 (Autumn, 1965) ———

F Journal   Film Journal
                            New Melbourne Film Group
                            quarterly; Mont Albert, Australia
                            n. 9 (Feb., 1958) to n. 23 (July, 1964) ———

F Lib Quarterly   Film Library Quarterly
                            (Film Library Information Council)
                            quarterly; Greenwich, Conn.
                            v. 1, n. 1 (Winter, 1967-1968) ———

h   **Film Q**   Film Quarterly
                               formerly: Hollywood Quarterly; formerly: Quarterly
                                  of Film, Radio and Television
                               quarterly; Berkeley, Calif.
                               v. 12, n. 1 (Fall, 1958) ———

○   **F Soc Rev**   Film Society Review
                               American Federation of Film Societies
                               monthly (Sept.-May); New York
                               1964 ———

○   **Filmf**   Filmfacts
                               24 issues/year; New York
                               v. 1 (1958) ———

○   **Films**   Films: A Quarterly of Discussion and Analysis
                               defunct; New York
                               v. 1, n. 1 (Nov., 1939) to v. 1, n. 4 (Summer, 1940)

○   **Films & F**   Films and Filming
                               monthly; London
                               v. 1, n. 1 (Oct., 1954) ———

○   **Films in R**   Films in Review
                               National Board of Review of Motion Pictures
                               10 issues/year; New York
                               v. 1, n. 1 (Feb., 1950) ———

○   **Focus**   Focus!
                               Documentary Film Group
                               irregular; Chicago
                               n. 1 (Feb., 1967) ———

○   **Focus on F**   Focus on Film
                               quarterly; London
                               n. 1 (Jan.-Feb., 1970) ———

h   **Hollywood Q**   Hollywood Quarterly; *see* Film Quarterly
1946-51   later: Quarterly of Film, Radio and Television; later:
                                  Film Quarterly
                               v. 1, n. 1 (Oct., 1945) to v. 5, n. 4 (Summer, 1951)

○   **Interntl F G**   International Film Guide
                               annual; London
                               v. 1 (1964) ———

h   **J of Pop Cul**   Journal of Popular Culture
                               Modern Language Association of America
                               quarterly; Bowling Green, Ohio
                               v. 1, n. 1 (Summer, 1967) ———

∂   **Movie**   Movie
                               irregular/quarterly; London
                               n. 1 (June, 1962) — n. 18 (Winter, 1970-1971)

N Y Rev of Books   New York Review of Books
                            24 issues/year; New York
                            v. 1, n. 1 (Jan., 1963) ———

Quarterly of F R TV   Quarterly of Film, Radio and Television
                            formerly: Hollywood Quarterly; *see* Film Quarterly
                            v. 6, n. 1 (Fall, 1951), to v. 11, n. 4 (Summer, 1957)

Screen   Screen
                            formerly: Screen Education
                            Society for Education in Film and Television
                            quarterly; London
                            v. 10, n. 1 (Jan.-Feb., 1969) ———

Sequence   Sequence
                            defunct; London
                            n. 1 (Dec., 1946) — n. 14 (New Year, 1952)

Sight & S   Sight and Sound
                            British Film Institute
                            quarterly; London
                            v. 15, n. 58 (Summer, 1946) ———

Take One   Take One: The Canadian Film Magazine
                            bi-monthly; Montreal, Canada
                            v. 1, n. 2 (Sept., 1966) ———

Views & R   Views & Reviews
                            quarterly; Milwaukee, Wisc.
                            v. 1, n. 1 (Summer, 1969) ———

CRITICAL FILM REVIEWS N–Z

N

NACHTLOKAL ZUM SILBERMOND, DAS (see: Five Sinners)

NACKT UNTER WOLFEN (see: Naked Among the Wolves)

NACKTE UND DER SATAN, DIE (see: The Head)

4349 NAICA AND THE SQUIRREL (Elisabeta Bostan)
    F Lib Quarterly: v. 4, n. 4 (Fall, 1971), p. 54; Hannah Hyatt, 225 wds., pt.
        cr.

4350 NAISENKUVIA (Jorn Donner)
    (also: Portraits of Women)
    Interntl F.G.: v. 8 (1971), pp. 136-137; Peter Cowie, 200 wds., pt. cr.

4351 NAKED ALIBI (Gerry Hopper)
    Films & F: v. I, n. I (Oct., 1954), pp. 25-26; Clayton Cole, 125 wds., cp. cr.

4352 NAKED AMONG THE WOLVES (Frank Beyer)
    Filmf: v. X (1967), p. 126; comp., cp. cr.
    Films & F: v. II, n. I (Oct., 1964), p. 31; Peter Cowie, 500 wds., cp. cr.

4353 NAKED AND THE DEAD, THE (Raoul Walsh)
    F Quarterly: v. XII, n. I (Fall, 1958), pp. 45-50; Colin Young, 2100 wds., no
        cr.
    Filmf: v. I (1958), p. 143; comp., cp. cr.
    Films & F: v. 5, n. 2 (Nov., 1958), pp. 21-22; Peter G. Baker, 400 wds., cp.
        cr.
    Films in R: v. IX, n. 8 (Oct., 1958), pp. 455-456; B. T. Saintsbury, 125 wds.,
        no cr.

4354 NAKED AND THE WICKED, THE (Guido Brignone)
    (also: Noi Peccatori)
    Filmf: v. III (1960), p. 359; comp., cp. cr.

4355 NAKED AUTUMN (Francois Leterrier)
    (also: Les Mauvais Coups)
    Filmf: v. VI (1963), p. 285; comp., cp. cr.

4356 NAKED CITY, THE (Jules Dassin)
    Sequence: n. 5 (Autumn, 1948), pp. 38-40; Gavin Lambert, 800 wds., no cr.

4357 NAKED EARTH (Vincent Sherman)
    Filmf: v. I (1958), p. 152; comp., cp. cr.
    Films & F: v. 4, n. 6 (Mar., 1958), p. 28; Peter G. Baker, 250 wds., cp. cr.
    Films in r: v. IX n. 7 (Aug.-Sept., 1958), p. 403; Louise Corbin, 150 wds., no
        cr.

4358 NAKED EDGE, THE (Michael Anderson)
    Film: n. 30 (Winter, l96l), p. l2; Roderic Allen, 300 wds., no cr.
    F Quarterly: v. XV, n. l (Fall, l96l), p. 56; R. M. Hodgens, l50 wds., no cr.
    Filmf: v. IV (l96l), p. l69; comp., cp. cr.
    Films & F: v. 8, n. l (Oct., l96l), p. 24; John Cutts, 325 wds., cp. cr.
    Films in R: v. XII, n. 7 (Aug.-Sept., l96l), pp. 427-428; Flavia Wharton, l00
        wds., no cr.

4359 NAKED EYE, THE (Louis Clyde Stoumen)
    Films in R: v. VIII, n. 5 (May, l957), pp. 226-227; George Lord, 250 wds.,
        no cr.

4360 NAKED HEARTS (Edouard Luntz)
    Films & F: v. l4, n. 4 (Jan., l968), pp. 2l-22; Peter Davelle, 400 wds., cp. cr.

4361 NAKED HOURS, THE (Marco Vicario)
    (also: Le Ore Nude)
    Films & F: v. l2, n. 2 (Nov., l965), p. 26; Robin Bean, 350 wds., cp. cr.

4362 NAKED IN THE NIGHT (Kurt Meisel)
    (also: Madeleine -- TE. l362ll)
    Filmf: v. IV (l96l), p. 365; comp., cp. cr.

4363 NAKED KISS, THE (Samuel Fuller)
    Cahiers in Eng: n. 4, pp. 57-58; Michel Delahaye, 950 wds., cp. cr.
    Cinema: v. 3, n. 5 (Summer, l967), p. 50; Curtis Lee Hanson, 300 wds., no
        cr.
    F Quarterly: v. XVIII, n. l (Fall, l964), p. 62; R. M. Hodgens, l00 wds., no
        cr.
    Filmf: v. VIII (l965), p. 3l; comp., cp. cr.
    Films & F: v. l6, n. l0 (July, l970), pp. 39-40; Margaret Tarratt, l000 wds.,
        cp. cr.

4364 NAKED MAJA, THE (Henry Koster)
    Filmf: v. II (l959), p. l07; comp., cp. cr.
    Films & F: v. 5, n. ll (Aug., l959), p. 24; Peter Baker, 225 wds., cp. cr.
    Films in R: v. X, n. 5 (May, l959), pp. 302-303; Louise Corbin, 200 wds.,
        no. cr.

    NAKED NIGHT, THE (see: Sawdust and Tinsel)

4365 NAKED PREY, THE (Cornel Wilde)
    Cinema: v. 3, n. 3 (July, l966), p. 49; Rory Guy, 400 wds., pt. cr.
    F Quarterly: v. XX, n. l (Fall, l966), p. 59; R. M. Hodgens, l50 wds., no cr.
    Filmf: v. IX (l966), p. l6l; comp., cp. cr.
    Films & F: v. l3, n. l (Oct., l966), pp. 7, 9; Peter Davalle, 550 wds., cp. cr.
    Films in R: v. XVII, n. 4 (Apr., l966), pp. 248-249; Eloise Hart Carpenter,
        200 wds., no cr.

4366 NAKED RUNNER, THE (Sidney J. Furie)
    Filmf: v. X (l967), p. 2ll; comp., cp. cr.
    Films & F: v. l3, n. l2 (Sept., l967), pp. 20-2l; Gordon Gow, 650 wds., cp.
        cr.

4367 NAKED SEA (Allen H. Miner)
    Films & F: v. 2, n. 3 (Dec., l955), p. l7; Peter G. Baker, 225 wds., cp. cr.
    Films in R: v. VI, n. l0 (Dec., l955), p. 530; l25 wds., no cr.
    Sight & S: v. 25, n. 3 (Winter, l955-l956), p. l5l; Gavin Lambert, l25 wds.,
        no cr.

4368 NAKED TERROR (Joseph Brenner, prod.)
    Filmf: v. IV (l96l), p. 365; comp., cp. cr.

    NAKED TRUTH, THE (see: Your Past Is Showing)

    NAKED UNDER LEATHER (see: The Girl on a Motorcycle)

4369 NAKED YOUTH (Nagisa Oshima)
    (also: Seishun Zankoku Monagatari; A Story of Cruelty)
    Film: n. 58 (Spring, l970), p. 4; 25 wds., pt. cr.

4370 NAME OF THE GAME IS KILL, THE (Gunnar Hellstrom)
Filmf: v. XI (1968), p. 214; comp., cp. cr.

4371 NAMU, THE KILLER WHALE (Laslo Benedek)
Filmf: v. IX (1966), p. 196; comp., cp. cr.
Films in R: v. XVII, n. 8 (Oct., 1966), p. 525; 125 wds., no cr.

4372 NANA (Christian-Jaque)
Films & F: v. 2, n. 10 (July, 1956), p. 26; R. L. Mannock, 250 wds., cp. cr.
Films in R: v. VIII, n. 5 (May, 1957), p. 227; Louise Corbin, 100 wds., no cr.

4373 NANA (Mac Ahlberg)
Filmf: v. XIV (1971), p. 151; comp., cp. cr.

4374 NANAMI (Susumu Hani)
(also: Inferno of First Love; Hatsukoi Jigokuhen)
Filmf: v. XII (1969), p. 367; comp., cp. cr.
Interntl F.G: v. 6 (1969), p. 114; Donald Richie, 200 wds., pt. cr.

NANKAI NO DAIKETTO (see: Ebirah, Horror of the Deep)

4375 NANNY, THE (Seth Holt)
F Quarterly: v. XIX, n. 3 (Spring, 1966), p. 53; R. M. Hodgens, 100 wds., no
cr.
Films & F: v. 12, n. 2 (Nov., 1965), p. 30; Allen Eyles, 225 wds., cp. cr.
Films in R: v. XVI, n. 9 (Nov., 1965), pp. 578-579; 175 wds., no cr.

NARA LIVET (see: Brink of Life)

NARAYAMA BUSHIKO (see: The Ballad of Narayama)

4376 NARCO MEN, THE (Julio Coll)
(also: Persecucion Hasta Valencia; Il Sapore Della Vendetta)
Filmf: v. XIV (1971), p. 717; comp., cp. cr.

4377 NARROW MARGIN, THE (Richard Fleischer)
Sight & S: v. 22, n. 2 (Oct.-Dec., 1952), p. 80; James Morgan, 300 wds., pt.
cr.

4378 NASHVILLE REBEL (Jay J. Sheridan)
Filmf: v. IX (1966), p. 376; comp., cp. cr.

NASILJE NA TRGU (see: Square of Violence)

NATALE CHE QUASI NO FUI, IL (see: The Christmas That Almost Wasn't)

4379 NATCHEZ TRACE (Alan Crosland)
Filmf: v. IV (1961), p. 365; comp., cp. cr.

NATHALIE (see: The Foxiest Girl in Paris)

4380 NATIKA (George Paul Solomos)
Films & F: v. 10, n. 8 (May, 1964), p. 27; Allen Eyles, 250 wds., cp. cr.

4381 NATIONAL FLOWER OF BROOKLYN, THE (Tom McDonough, prod.)
F Lib Quarterly: v. 3, n. 1 (Winter, 1969-1970), p. 38; Don Walker, 450 wds.,
pt. cr.

NATTLEK (see: Night Games)

NATTMARA (see: Nightmare)

NATTVARDSGASTERNA (see: Winter Light)

4382 NATURE GIRL AND THE SLAVER (Hermann Leitner and Gino Talamo)
Filmf: v. IV (1961), p. 374; comp., cp. cr.

4383 NATURE'S PARADISE (Charles Saunders)
(also: Nudist Paradise)
Filmf: v. III (1960), p. 344; comp., cp. cr.
Films & F: v. 5, n. 7 (Apr., 1959), p. 23; Peter Mills, 150 wds., cp. cr.

4384 NAVAJO (Norman Foster)
  Films & F: v. I, n. 6 (Mar., 1955), p. 21; John Pratt, 150 wds., cp. cr.
  Films in R: v. II, n. 10 (Dec., 1951), p. 58; 100 wds., no cr.

4385 NAVAJO JOE (Sergio Corbucci)
  (also: Un Dollaro A Testa; A Dollar A Head)
  Filmf: v. X (1967), p. 396; comp., cp. cr.

4386 NAVAJO RUN (Johnny Seven)
  Filmf: v. IX (1966), p. 228; comp., cp. cr.
  Films & F: v. 12, n. 8 (May, 1966), p. 52; Richard Davis, 450 wds., cp. cr.

  NAVRAT ZTRACENEHO SYNA (see: Return of the Prodigal Son)

4387 NAVY LARK, THE (Gordon Parry)
  Films & F: v. 6, n. 2 (Nov., 1959), p. 25; Robin Bean, 250 wds., cp. cr.

4388 NAVY VS. THE NIGHT MONSTERS, THE (Michael Hoey)
  Filmf: v. IX (1966), p. 315; comp., cp. cr.

4389 NAZARIN (Luis Buñuel)
  Film: n. 33 (Autumn, 1962), pp. 20-21; Philip Strick, 450 wds., no cr.
  F Culture: n. 21 (Summer, 1960), pp. 60-62; Octavio Paz, 600 wds., pt. cr.
  F Journal: n. 15 (Mar., 1960), pp. 51-54; Ian Jarvie, 1200 wds., no cr.
  F Journal: n. 18 (Oct., 1961), p. 19; J. R. Burgess, 100 wds., no cr.
  F Quarterly: v. XIII, n. 3 (Spring, 1960), pp. 30-31; Gavin Lambert,
    1100 wds., pt. cr.
  Filmf: v. XI (1968), p. 249; comp., cp. cr.
  Films & F: v. 10, n. 1 (Oct., 1963), p. 23; Gordon Gow, 700 wds., cp. cr.
  Sight & S: v. 32, n. 4 (Autumn, 1963), pp. 194-195; Geoffrey Nowell-Smith,
    800 wds., no cr.

  NAZI TERROR AT NIGHT (see: The Devil Strikes at Night)

  NEAPOLITAN CAROUSEL (see: Neapolitan Fantasy)

4390 NEAPOLITAN FANTASY (Ettore Giannini)
  (also: Carosello Napolitano; Neapolitan Carousel)
  Filmf: v. IV (1961), p. 314; comp., cp. cr.
  Films & F: v. I, n. 3 (Dec., 1954), p. 21; Peter Brinson, 200 wds., cp. cr.

4391 NEARLY A NASTY ACCIDENT (Don Chaffey)
  Filmf: v. V (1962), p. 136; comp., cp. cr.

  NECRONOMICON (see: Succubus)

4392 NED KELLY (Tony Richardson)
  Films & F: v. 16, n. 11 (Aug., 1970), pp. 41-42; Margaret Tarratt, 400 wds.,
    cp. cr.

  NEFERTITI REGINA DEL NILO (see: Queen of the Nile)

4393 NEGATIVES (Peter Medak)
  Filmf: v. XI (1968), p. 431; comp., cp. cr.
  Films & F: v. 16, n. 9 (June, 1970), pp. 88-89; Peter Buckley, 500 wds., cp.
    cr.

  NEIGE ETAIT SALE, LA (see: The Stain on the Snow)

  NELLA CITTA L'INFERNO (see: Caged)

4394 NEON PALACE (Peter Rowe)
  Take One: v. 2, n. 10 (1971), pp. 32, 34; Bruce Pittman, 300 wds., pt. cr.

4395 NERO, IL (Giovanni Vento)
  Interntl F G: v. 5 (1968), p. 103; 250 wds., pt. cr.

  NEST OF GENTLEFOLK, A (see: Dvorianskoye Gniezdo)

4396 NEVADA SMITH (Henry Hathaway)
        Filmf: v. IX (1966), p. 174; comp., cp. cr.
        Films & F: v. 13, n. I (Oct., 1966), pp. 12, 16; Allen Eyles, 500 wds., cp. cr.

4397 NEVER A DULL MOMENT (George Marshall)
        Filmf: v. XI (1968), p. 332; comp., cp. cr.
        Films in R: v. XIX, n. 5 (May, 1968), p. 311; Veronica Ross, 100 wds., no cr.

4398 NEVER LET GO (John Guillermin)
        Filmf: v. VI (1963), p. 190; comp., cp. cr.
        Films & F: v. 6, n. II (Aug., 1960), pp. 21-22; R. E. Durgnat, 300 wds., cp.
            cr.

4399 NEVER LOVE A STRANGER (Robert Stevens)
        Filmf: v. I (1958), p. 204; comp., cp. cr.

4400 NEVER MENTION MURDER (John Nelson Burton)
        Films & F: v. II, n, 8 (May, 1965), p. 34; Richard Davis, 225 wds., cp. cr.

4401 NEVER ON SUNDAY (Jules Dassin)
        (also: Pote Tiu Kyriaki)
        F Quarterly: v. XIV, n. 2 (Winter, 1960), p. 62; 150 wds., no cr.
        Filmf: v. III (1960), p. 263; comp., cp. cr.
        Films & F: v. 7, n. 3 (Dec., 1960), p. 32; John Cutts, 200 wds., cp. cr.
        Films in R: v. XI, n. 9 (Nov., 1960), pp. 558-559; Adelaide Comerford, 150
            wds., no cr.
        Sight & S: v. 30, n. I (Winter, 1960-1961), pp. 37-48; Kenneth Cavander, 450
            wds., pt. cr.

4402 NEVER PUT IT IN WRITING (Andrew L. Stone)
        Filmf: v. VII (1964), p. 154; comp., cp. cr.
        Films & F: v. 10, n. 12 (Sept., 1964), pp. 19-20; Richard Davis, 425 wds., cp.
            cr.

4403 NEVER SO FEW (John Sturges)
        Filmf: v. III (1960), p. 7; comp., cp. cr.
        Films & F: v. 6, n. 6 (Mar., 1960), p. 25; Tony Keniston, 250 wds., cp. cr.

4404 NEVER STEAL ANYTHING SMALL (Charles Lederer)
        Filmf: v. II (1959), p. 31; comp., cp. cr.
        Films & F: v. 5, n. 8 (May, 1959), p. 23; Derek Conrad, 375 wds., cp. cr.

4405 NEVER TAKE CANDY FROM A STRANGER (Cyril Frankel)
        (also: Never Take Sweets from a Stranger)
        Filmf: v. VI (1963), p. 300; comp., cp. cr.
        Films & F: v. 6, n. 8 (May, 1960), p. 26; John Cutts, 225 wds., cp. cr.

      NEVER TAKE SWEETS FROM A STRANGER (see: Never Take Candy from
          a Stranger)

4406 NEVER TOO LATE (Bud Yorkin)
        Films & F: v. 12, n. 6 (Mar., 1965), pp. 10-11; Nicholas Gosling, 300 wds., cp.
            cr.
        Films in R: v. XVI, n. 10 (Dec., 1965), p. 646; Adelaide Comerford, 150
            wds., no cr.

      NEVINOST BEZ ZASTITE (see: Innocence Unprotected)

4407 NEW ANGELS, THE (Ugo Gregoretti)
        (also: I Nuovi Angeli)
        Films & F: v. 10, n. 7 (Apr., 1964), p. 26; Raymond Durgnat, 500 wds., cp.
            cr.
        Sight & S: v. 33, n. 2 (Spring, 1964), pp. 97-98; J. H. Fenwick, 550 wds., no
            cr.

      NEW FACE IN HELL (see: P.J.)

4408 NEW FACES (Harry Horner)
        Films & F: v. 1, n. 3 (Dec., 1954), p. 18; Kenneth Thompson, 100 wds., cp.
            cr.
        Films in R: v. V, n. 4 (Apr., 1954), p. 196; 125 wds., no cr.
        Sight & S: v. 24, n. 3 (Jan.-Mar., 1955), p. 146; Derek Prouse, 275 wds., pt. cr.

4409 NEW INTERNS, THE (John Rich)
       Filmf: v. VII (1964), p. 162; comp., cp. cr.
       Films & F: v. II, n. 5 (Feb., 1965), pp. 35-36; Richard Davis, 425 wds., cp.
         cr.

4410 NEW KIND OF LOVE, A (Melville Shavelson)
       Filmf: v. VI (1963), p. 238; comp., cp. cr.
       Films & F: v. 10, n. 2 (Nov., 1963), p. 23; Gordon Gow, 450 wds., cp. cr.

4411 NEW LEAF, A (Elaine May)
       Filmf: v. XIV (1971), p. 41; comp., cp. cr.
       Films in R: v. XXII, n. 4 (Apr., 1971), pp. 232-233; Elaine Rothschild, 250
         wds., no cr.

4412 NEW NUMBER COMES TO MOSCOW, A (B. Dolin)
       (also: Novi Attraktzion)
       Filmf: v. II (1959), p. 223; comp., cp. cr.

4413 NEW ORLEANS AFTER DARK (John Sledge)
       Filmf: v. I (1958), p. 296; comp., cp. cr.

       NEW TALES OF THE TAIRA CLAN (see: Shin Heike Monogatari)

       NEW YORK CALLING SUPER DRAGON (see: Secret Agent Super Dragon)

       NEW YORK CHIAMA SUPERDRAGO (see: Secret Agent Super Dragon)

4414 NEW YORK CITY—THE MOST (George Pitt)
       Films & F: v. 15, n. 11 (Aug., 1969), p. 48; Ken Gay, 250 wds., cp. cr.

4415 NEW YORK CONFIDENTIAL (Russell Rouse)
       Films & F: v. I, n. 10 (July, 1955), p. 15; Derek Hill, 150 wds., cp. cr.

4416 NEW YORK, NEW YORK (Francis Thompson)
       F Quarterly: v. XII, n. 4 (Summer, 1959), pp. 52-54; Arthur Knight, 1000
         wds., no cr.

       NEW YORK SUR-MER (see: Only One New York)

4417 NEXT₁ (Sergio Martino)
       (also: The Next Victim; Lo Strano Vizio Della Signoro Wardh)
       Filmf: v. XII (1971), p. 390; comp., cp. cr.

4418 NEXT TO NO TIME (Henry Cornelius)
       Filmf: v. III (1960), p. 149; comp., cp. cr.
       Films & F: v. 4, n. 12 (Sept., 1958), p. 21; Peter John Dyer, 600 wds., cp. cr.
       Sight & S: v. 27, n. 6 (Autumn, 1958), p. 319; Kenneth Cavander, 350 wds.,
         pt. cr.

       NEXT VICTIM, THE (see: Next₁)

4419 NEXT VOICE YOU HEAR, THE (William Wellman)
       Films in R: v. I, n. 6 (Sept., 1950), p. 31; Henry Hart, 250 wds., pt. cr.

       NI LIV (see: Nine Lives)

4420 NIAGRA (Henry Hathaway)
       Films in R: v. IV, n. 3 (Mar., 1953), pp. 150-151; 250 wds., pt. cr.

4421 NICE GIRL LIKE ME, A (Desmond Davis)
       Films & F: v. 16, n. 3 (Dec., 1969), pp. 44-45; David Austen, 450 wds., cp.
         cr.

4422 NICE LITTLE BANK THAT SHOULD BE ROBBED, A (Henry Levin)
       Filmf: v. I (1958) p. 275; comp., cp. cr.

4423 NICHOLAS AND ALEXANDRA (Franklin J. Schaffner)
       Filmf: v. XIV (1971), p. 553; comp., cp. cr.

4424 NICHT VERSOHNT (Daniele Huillet and Jean-Marie Straub)
        (also: Not Reconciled; Unreconciled)
        F Quarterly: v. XIX, n. 4 (Summer, 1966), pp. 51-55; Gideon Bachmann,
            2000 wds., pt. cr.

4425 NIEJNOSTI (Elier Ishmuhamedov)
        (also: Tenderness)
        Interntl F.G.: v. 6 (1969), p. 183; Peter Cowie, 150 wds., pt. cr.

      NIEWINNI CZARODZIEJE (see: Innocent Sorcerers)

      NIGHT, THE (see: La Notte)

4426 NIGHT AFFAIR (Gilles Grangier)
        (also: Le Desordre et la Nuit)
        Filmf: v. IV (1961), p. 328; comp., cp. cr.

4427 NIGHT AFTER NIGHT (Archie Mayo)
        Views & R: v. 3, n. 2 (Fall, 1971), pp. 5-9; 1200 wds., cp. cr.

4428 NIGHT AMBUSH (Michael Powell and Emeric Pressburger)
        (also: Ill Met by Moonlight)
        Filmf: v. I (1958), p. 86; comp., cp. cr.
        Films & F: v. 3, n. 6 (Mar., 1957), p. 26; Peter G. Baker, 250 wds., cp. cr.

4429 NIGHT AND FOG (Alain Resnais)
        (also: Nuit et Brouillard)
        F Quarterly: v. XIV, n. 3 (Spring, 1961), pp. 43-44; Roger Sandall, 700 wds.,
            pt. cr.
        F Soc Rev: v. 6, n. 4 (Dec., 1970), pp. 43-47; Leonard Rubenstein, 2000
            wds., pt. cr.
        Films & F: v. 15, n. 3 (Dec., 1968), p. 73; Ken Gay, 300 wds., no cr.

      NIGHT AND FOG IN JAPAN (see: A Foggy Night in Japan)

4430 NIGHT AND THE CITY (Jules Dassin)
        Sequence: n. 12 (Autumn, 1950), pp. 14-15; Lindsay G. Anderson, 850 wds.,
            no cr.

      NIGHT CALLER, THE (see: Blood Beast from Outer Space)

4431 NIGHT CREATURES (Peter Graham Scott)
        (also: Captain Clegg)
        Filmf: v. V (1962), p. 216; comp., cp. cr.
        Films & F: v. 8, n. 11 (Aug., 1962), p. 32; John Cutts, 200 wds., cp. cr.

4432 NIGHT DIGGER, THE (Alastair Reid)
        Filmf: XIV (1971), p. 299; comp., cp. cr.

      NIGHT DOES STRANGE THINGS, THE (see: Paris Does Strange Things)

4433 NIGHT EDITOR (Henry Levin)
        (also: The Trespasser)
        Focus on F: n. 5 (Winter/Nov.-Dec., 1970), p. 44; Don Miller, 250 wds., pt.
            cr.

4434 NIGHT ENCOUNTER (Robert Hossein)
        (also: La Nuit des Espions)
        Filmf: v. VII (1964), p. 62; comp., cp. cr.

4435 NIGHT FIGHTERS, THE (Tay Garnett)
        (also: A Terrible Beauty)
        Filmf: v. III (1960), p. 297; comp., cp. cr.

4436 NIGHT GAMES (Mai Zetterling)
        (Also: Nattlek)
        F Quarterly: v. XX, n. 2 (Winter, 1966-1967), pp. 37-38; Ernest Callenbach,
            500 wds., pt. cr.
        Filmf: v. IX (1966), p. 342; comp., cp. cr.

Films & F: v. 13, n. 5 (Feb., 1967), pp. 29-30; Raymond Durgnat, 950 wds., cp. cr.
Films in R: v. XVIII, n. 1 (Jan., 1967), p. 53; Rene Jordan, 150 wds., no cr.

NIGHT HEAT (see: La Notte Brava)

4437 NIGHT HEAVEN FELL, THE (Roger Vadim)
(also: Les Bijoutiers du Clair de Lune; Heaven Fell That Night)
Filmf: v. I (1958), p. 201; comp., cp. cr.
Films & F: v. 4, n. II (Aug., 1958), p. 25; Derek Conrad, 250 wds., cp. cr.

4438 NIGHT HOLDS TERROR, THE (Andrew L. Stone)
Films & F: v. 2, n. 2 (Nov., 1955), p. 16; P. L. Monnock, 125 wds., cp. cr.

4439 NIGHT IN ROME (Roberto Rossellini)
(also: Era Notte a Roma)
F Quarterly: v. XIV, n. 2 (Winter, 1960), pp. 52-53; Ciotti Miller, 900 wds., pt. cr.

4440 NIGHT IS MY FUTURE (Ingmar Bergman)
(also: Musik I Morker)
Filmf: v. VI (1963), p. 18; comp., cp. cr.
Films & F: v. 8, n. 7 (Apr., 1962), p. 33; Philip Strick, 300 wds., cp. cr.

4441 NIGHT IS NOT FOR SLEEP, THE (Robert Hossein)
(also: Toi le Venin)
Films & F: v. 5, n. 9 (June, 1959), p. 23; S. M. Neufeld, 175 wds., cp. cr.

4442 NIGHT IS THE PHANTOM (John M. Old)
(also: La Frusta e il Corpo)
Films & F: v. 12, n. I (Oct., 1965), p. 32; Raymond Durgnat, 900 wds., cp. cr.

4443 NIGHT MUST FALL (Karel Reisz)
F Quarterly: v. XVII, n. 4 (Summer, 1964), pp. 58-59; Jesse Smith, 200 wds., no cr.
Filmf: v. VII (1964), p. 92; comp., cp. cr.
Films & F: v. 10, n. 9 (June, 1964), pp. 21-22; John Cutts, 650 wds., cp. cr.
Films in R: v. XV, n. 4 (Apr., 1964), p. 245; Wilfred Mifflin, 150 wds., no cr.
Sight & S: v. 33, n. 3 (Summer, 1964), p. 144; Tom Milne, 800 wds., pt. cr.

4444 NIGHT MY NUMBER CAME UP, THE (Leslie Norman)
Films & F: v. I, n. 8 (May, 1955), p. 19; Derek Hill, 200 wds., cp. cr.

NIGHT OF CABIRIA (see: Le Notti di Cabiria)

4445 NIGHT OF COUNTING THE YEARS, THE (Shadi Abdel Salam)
Movie: n. 18 (Winter, 1970-1971), p. 39; Ian Cameron, 150 wds., no cr.
Sight & S: v. 40, n. I (Winter, 1970-1971), p. 17; John Russell Taylor, 400 wds., no cr.

4446 NIGHT OF DARK SHADOWS (Dan Curtis)
Filmf: v. XIV (1971), p. 543; comp., cp. cr.

4447 NIGHT OF LOVE (Mario Bonnard)
(also: Tradita)
Filmf: v. III (1960-1961), p. 356; comp., cp. cr.

NIGHT OF PASSION (see: During One Night)

4448 NIGHT OF THE BIG HEAT (Terence Fisher)
Films & F: v. 14, n. 5 (Feb., 1968), p. 27; Raymond Durgnat, 400 wds., cp. cr.

4449 NIGHT OF THE BLOOD BEAST (Bernard L. Kowalski)
Filmf: v. I (1958), p. 274; comp., cp. cr.

NIGHT OF THE DEMON (see: Curse of the Demon)

NIGHT OF THE EAGLE (see: Burn Witch, Burn)

4450 NIGHT OF THE FOLLOWING DAY, THE (Hubert Cornfield)
       F Quarterly: v. XXIII, n. I (Fall, 1969), pp. 52-53; Foster Hirsch, 450 wds.,
            no cr.
       Filmf: v. XII (1969), p. 56; comp., cp. cr.
       Films & F: v. 15, n. 7 (Apr., 1969), p. 51; Gordon Gow, 450 wds., cp. cr.
       Sight & S: v. 38, n. 2 (Spring, 1969), p. 99; Penelope Houston, 450 wds., pt.
            cr.

4451 NIGHT OF THE GENERALS, THE (Anatole Litvak)
       Cinema: v. 3, n. 5 (Summer, 1967), p. 49; Axel Madsen, 550 wds., pt. cr.
       Filmf: v. X (1967), p. 28; comp., cp. cr.
       Films & F: v. 13, n. 6 (Mar., 1967), p. 28; Mike Sarne, 950 wds., cp. cr.
       Films in R: v. XVIII, n. 2 (Feb., 1967), pp. 112-114; Henry Hart, 475 wds., no
            cr.

4452 NIGHT OF THE GRIZZLY, THE (Joseph Pevney)
       Filmf: v. IX (1966), p. 169; comp., cp. cr.

4453 NIGHT OF THE HUNTER, THE (Charles Laughton)
       Film: n. 16 (Mar.-Apr., 1958), pp. 23-24; Liam O'Laoghaire, 500 wds., no cr.
       F Culture: v. 1, n. 5-6 (Winter, 1955), pp. 32-33; Eugene Archer, 800 wds.,
            pt. cr.
       Films & F: v. 2, n. 4 (Jan., 1956), pp. 22-23; Michael Winner, 225 wds., cp.
            cr.
       Films in R: v. VI, n. 7 (Aug.-Sept., 1955), pp. 337-339; Henry Hart, 750
            wds., pt. cr.
       Sight & S: v. 25, n. 3 (Winter, 1955-1956), pp. 147-148; Gavin Lambert, 1000
            wds., pt. cr.

4454 NIGHT OF THE IGUANA, THE (John Huston)
       Cinema: v. 2, n. 3 (Oct.-Nov., 1964), p. 48; James Silke, 300 wds., pt. cr.
       F Quarterly: v. XVIII, n. 2 (Winter, 1964), pp. 50-52; Stephen Taylor, 850
            wds., pt. cr.
       Filmf: v. VII (1964), p. 146; comp., cp. cr.
       Films & F: v. II, n. I (Oct., 1964), p. 28; Allen Eyles, 1050 wds., cp. cr.
       Films in R: v. XV, n. 7 (Aug.-Sept., 1964), pp. 439-441; Elaine Rothschild,
            350 wds., no cr.
       Sight & S: v. 33, n. 4 (Autumn, 1964), pp. 198-199; Elizabeth Sussex, 500
            wds., pt. cr.

4455 NIGHT OF THE LIVING DEAD, THE (George A. Romero)
       Filmf: v. XI (1968), p. 442; comp., cp. cr.
       Films & F: v. 17, n. 3 (Dec., 1970), pp. 53, 56; Richard Weaver, 700 wds.,
            cp. cr.
       Sight & S: v. 39, n. 2 (Spring, 1970), p. 105; Elliott Stein, 600 wds., pt. cr.

4456 NIGHT OF THE QUARTER MOON (Hugo Haas)
       (also: Flesh and the Flame; The Color of Her Skin)
       Filmf: v. II (1959), p. 49; comp., cp. cr.
       Films & F: v. 5, n. 9 (June, 1959), p. 22; Peter Whitehall, 350 wds., cp. cr.

4457 NIGHT PEOPLE (Nunnally Johnson)
       Films in R: v. V, n. 5 (May, 1954), p. 244; 175 wds., no cr.

4458 NIGHT PLANE TO AMSTERDAM (Ken Hughes)
       Films & F: v. I, n. 6 (Mar., 1955), p. 21; Derek Hill, 150 wds., cp. cr.

4459 NIGHT THEY KILLED RASPUTIN, THE (Pierre Chenal)
       (also: Rasputin L'Ultimo Czar)
       Filmf: v. V (1962), p. 371; comp., cp. cr.

4460 NIGHT THEY RAIDED MINSKY'S, THE (William Friedkin)
       Filmf: v. XI (1968), p. 505; comp., cp. cr.
       Films & F: v. 15, n. 9 (June, 1969), p. 52; Chris Jones, 600 wds., cp. cr.
       Interntl F G: v. 7 (1970), pp. 223-224; Margot S. Kernan, 250 wds., pt. cr.

4461 NIGHT TIDE (Curtis Harrington)
       F Quarterly: v. XVII, n. 4 (Summer, 1964), pp. 54-55; Steven P. Hill, 800
            wds., pt. cr.
       Filmf: v. VI (1963), p. 166; comp., cp. cr.
       Films & F: v. 13, n. 10 (July, 1967), p. 20; Raymond Durgnat, 850 wds., cp.
            cr.

4462 NIGHT TO REMEMBER, A (Roy Baker)
        Filmf: v. I (1958), p. 245; comp., cp. cr.
        Films & F: v. 4, n. II (Aug., 1958), p. 26; Ken Gay, 650 wds., cp. cr.
        Films in R: v. IX, n. 8 (Oct., 1958), pp. 452-453; Henry Hart, 500 wds., no
             cr.

4463 NIGHT TRAIN (Jerry Kawalerowicz)
        (also: Pociag)
        Films & F: v. 10, n. 6 (Mar., 1964), p. 32; Gordon Gow, 450 wds., cp. cr.

4464 NIGHT TRAIN TO PARIS (Robert Douglas)
        Filmf: v. VII (1964), p. 365; comp., cp. cr.

4465 NIGHT VISITOR, THE (Laslo Benedek)
        Filmf: v. XIV (1971), p. 123; comp., cp. cr.
        Films in R: v. XXII, n. 3 (Mar., 1971), pp. 175-176; Gloria Ives, 150 wds., no
             cr.

4466 NIGHT WALKER, THE (William Castle)
        Filmf: v. VIII (1965), p. 5; comp., cp. cr.

4467 NIGHT WATCH, THE (Jacques Becker)
        (also: The Hole; Le Trou)
        F Comment: v. 2, n. 2 (1964), pp. 53-54; Gordon Hitchens, 800 wds., pt. cr.
        Filmf: v. VII (1964), p. 119; comp., cp. cr.
        Films & F: v. 7, n. 6 (Mar., 1961), pp. 25-26; Gordon Gow, 550 wds., cp. cr.
        Films in R: v. XV, n. 4 (Apr., 1964), p. 242; Georges Millau, 150 wds., no cr.
        Sight & S: v. 30, n. 2 (Spring, 1961), pp. 87-88; Robert Vas, 1500 wds., no
             cr.

4468 NIGHTMARE (Maxwell Shane)
        Films & F: v. 2, n. 10 (July, 1956), p. 25; Michael Winner, 200 wds., cp. cr.

4469 NIGHTMARE (Freddie Francis)
        Filmf: v. VII (1964), p. 92; comp., cp. cr.
        Films & F: v. 10, n. 10 (July, 1964), p. 26; Allen Eyles, 125 wds., cp. cr.

4470 NIGHTMARE (Arne Mattsson)
        (also: Nattmara)
        Films & F: v. 15, n. 7 (Apr., 1969), p. 52; David Hutchison, 400 wds., cp. cr.

4471 NIGHTMARE CASTLE (Allan Grunewald)
        (also: Amanti D'Oltre Tomba; Lovers Beyond the Tomb)
        Filmf: v. X (1967), p. 435; comp., cp. cr.

4472 NIGHTMARE IN THE SUN (Marc Lawrence)
        Films & F: v. II, n. 6 (Mar., 1965), p. 38; Allen Eyles, 750 wds., cp. cr.

      NIGHTS OF CABIRIA (see: Le Notti di Cabiria)

4473 NIGHTS OF LUCRETIA BORGIA, THE (Sergio Grieco)
        Filmf: v. III (1960), p. 228; comp., cp. cr.

4474 NIGHTS OF RASPUTIN, THE (Pierre Chenal)
        Films & F: v. 9, n. 2 (Nov., 1962), pp. 40-41; David Rider, 450 wds., cp. cr.

      NIHON NO YORU TO KIRI (see: A Foggy Night in Japan)

4475 NIKKI, WILD DOG OF THE NORTH (Jack Couffer and Don Haldane)
        Filmf: v. IV (1961), p. 202; comp., cp. cr.
        Films & F: v. 8, n. 2 (Nov., 1961), pp. 26-27; Ken Gay, 300 wds., cp. cr.

      NIKUTAI NO GAKKO (see: School for Sex)

4476 NINE DAYS OF ONE YEAR (Mikhail Romm)
        (also: Devyat Dni Odnovo Goda)
        F Soc Rev: Sept. (1966), pp. 21-22; Edwin Jahiel, 300 wds., pt. cr.
        Filmf: v. VII (1964), p. 273; comp., cp. cr.
        Films & F: v. 12, n. 2 (Nov., 1965), pp. 28-29; Kevin Gough-Yates, 900 wds.,
             cp. cr.

Interntl F G: v. 2 (1965), p. 143; 250 wds., pt. cr.
Sight & S: v. 33, n. 3 (Summer, 1964), pp. 145-146; Elizabeth Sussex, 800
    wds., pt. cr.

4477 NINE HOURS TO RAMA (Mark Robson)
F Quarterly: v. XVII, n. I (Fall, 1963), p. 56; R. M. Hodgens, 150 wds., no
    cr.
Filmf: v. VI (1963), p. 67; comp., cp. cr.
Films & F: v. 9, n. 6 (Mar., 1963), pp. 33-34; Robin Bean, 1000 wds., cp. cr.
Films in R: v. XIV, n. 4 (Apr., 1963), pp. 236-237; Henry Hart, 500 wds.,
    no cr.

4478 NINE LIVES (Arne Skouen)
(Also: Ni Liv; We Die Alone)
Filmf: v. II (1959), p. 7; comp., cp. cr.
Films In R: v. X, n. I (Jan., 1959), p. 4I; Henry Hart, 225 wds., no cr.

4479 NINE VARIATIONS ON A DANCE THEME (Hilary Harris)
F Heritage: v. 2, n. 3 (Spring, 1967), pp. 25-27; Robert Steele, 1000 wds., no
    cr.
F. Quarterly: v. XX, n. 2 (Winter, 1966-1967), pp. 53-54; Ernest Callenbach,
    500 wds., pt. cr.

4480 1984 (Michael Anderson)
Films & F: v. 2, n. 6 (Mar., 1956), p. 16; Rodney Giesler, 300 wds., cp. cr.
Films in R: v. VII, n. 9 (Nov., 1956), pp. 463-464; Henry Hart, 275 wds., no
    cr.
Sight & S: v. 25, n. 4 (Spring, 1956), p. 198; Derek Hill, 325 wds., pt. cr.

NINETY (see: 90 Degrees in the Shade)

4481 90 DEGREES IN THE SHADE (Jiri Weiss)
(also: Ninety; Tricetjedna Ve Stinu)
Filmf: v. IX (1966), p. 363; comp., cp. cr.

99 MUJERES (see: 99 Women)

4482 99 WOMEN (Jesus Franco)
(also: 99 Mujeres)
Filmf: v. XII (1969), p. 257; comp., cp. cr.

4483 99 WOMEN (Jess Franco)
Films & F: v. 16, n. 5 (Feb., 1970), pp. 45-46; Richard Davis, 350 wds., cp.
    cr.

4484 NINGEN JOHATSU (Shohei Imamura)
(also: A Man Vanishes)
Interntl F G: v. 6 (1969), pp. 113-114; Donald Richie, 200 wds., pt. cr.

4485 NINGEN NO JOKEN (Masaki Kobayashi)
(also: The Human Condition; No Greater Love; Road to Eternity; a
    Soldier's Prayer)
Filmf: v. II (1959), p. 313; comp., cp. cr.
Sight & S: v. 30, n. 2 (Spring, 1961), pp. 88-89; Peter John Dyer, 1500 wds.,
    no cr.

NINJUTSU (see: Secret Scrolls)

4486 NINTH BULLET, THE (Lima Barreto)
Filmf: v. V (1962), p. 363; comp., cp. cr.

4487 NINTH CIRCLE, THE (France Stiglic)
(also: Deveti Krug)
Filmf: v. IV (1961-1962), p. 279; comp., cp. cr.
Films & F: v. 8, n. 6 (Mar., 1962), p. 34; Philip Strick, 350 wds., cp. cr.

NIPPON KONCHUKI (see: The Insect Woman)

NIPPON NO ICHIBAN NAGAI HI (see: The Emperor and the General)

NO! (see: Ohi)

4488 NO BLADE OF GRASS (Cornell Wilde)
        Films in R: v. XXII, n. I (Jan., 1971), pp. 44-45; Tatiana Balkoff Drowne,
        200 wds., no cr.

4489 NO DOWN PAYMENT (Martin Ritt)
        Films & F: v. 4, n. 3 (Dec., 1957), p. 24; Peter C. Baker, 350 wds., cp. cr.
        Films in R: v. VIII, n. 9 (Nov., 1957), pp. 460-461; Hy Arnold, 350 wds., no
        cr.
        Sight & S: v. 27, n. 4 (Spring, 1958), pp. 200-201; Richard Roud, 750 wds.,
        pt. cr.

4490 NO ESCAPE (Harold Young)
        (also: I Escaped from the Gestapo)
        Filmf: v. II (1959), p. I60; comp., cp. cr.

4491 NO EXIT (Tad Danielewski)
        Filmf: v. V (1962), p. 328; comp., cp. cr.
        Films in R: v. XIV, n. I (Jan., 1963), p. 49; Jean Cambon, I00 wds., no cr.

       NO GREATER LOVE (see: Ningen No Joken)

4492 NO LAUGHING MATTER (Hynek Bocan)
        Films & F: v. I5, n. I2 (Sept., 1969), pp. 57-58; Gordon Gow, 700 wds., cp.
        cr.

4493 NO LOVE FOR JOHNNIE (Ralph Thomas)
        Cinema: v. I. n. I, p. 43; I25 wds., pt. cr.
        Filmf: v. IV (1961), p. 325; comp., cp. cr.
        Films & F: v. 7, n. 6 (Mar., 1961), p. 27; John Cutts, 350 wds., cp. cr.
        Films in R: v. XII, n. 8 (Oct., 1961), pp. 484-486; Henry Hart, 600 wds., no
        cr.

4494 NO MAN IS AN ISLAND (John Monks, Jr. and Richard Goldstone)
        (also: Island Escape)
        Filmf: v. V (1962), p. 231; comp., cp. cr.
        Films & F: v. 9, n. 4 (Jan., 1963), p. 50; Tony Mallerman, 250 wds., cp. cr.

4495 NO MORALS (Andre Pergament)
        (also: M'sieur la Caille)
        Filmf: v. III (1960), p. 354; comp., cp. cr.

4496 NO MORE EXCUSES (Robert Downey)
        Filmf: v. XI (1968), p. I89; comp., cp. cr.

4497 NO, MY DARLING DAUGHTER (Ralph Thomas)
        Filmf: v. VII (1964), p. I05; comp., cp. cr.
        Films & F: v. 8, n. I (Oct., 1961), p. 30; Robin Bean, 300 wds., cp. cr.

4498 NO NAME ON THE BULLET (Jack Arnold)
        Filmf: v. II (1959), p. 74; comp., cp. cr.

4499 NO ORCHIDS FOR LULU (Rolf Thiele)
        (also: Lulu)
        Films & F: v. I4, n. I (Oct., 1967), p. 26; Raymond Durgnat, 700 wds., cp.
        cr.

4500 NO ORCHIDS FOR MISS BLANDISH (St. John L. Clowes)
        Sight & S: v. I7, n. 66 (Summer, 1948), p. I00; Arthur Vesselo, I50 wds., no
        cr.

4501 NO ORDINARY SUMMER (Vladimir Basov)
        (also: Nyeobyknovennoe Lyeto)
        Filmf: v. I (1958), p. 226; comp., cp. cr.

4502 NO PLACE LIKE HOMICIDE (Pat Jackson)
        Filmf: v. V (1962), p. 226; comp., cp. cr.

4503 NO PLACE TO LAND (Albert Gannaway)
        Filmf: v. I (1958), p. 298; comp., cp. cr.

NO QUESTIONS ON SATURDAY (see: Impossible On Saturday)

4504 NO REASON TO STAY (Mort Ransen)
      Interntl F G: v. 4 (1967), p. 57; 100 wds., pt. cr.

4505 NO RESTING PLACE (Paul Rotha)
      Films in R: v. III, n. 5 (May, 1952), pp. 244-245; 275 wds., no cr.
      Sight & S: v. 21, n. I (Aug.-Sept., 1951), pp. 20-21; Gavin Lambert, 1200 wds.,
        pt. cr.

4506 NO ROOM FOR WILD ANIMALS (Dr. Bernhard Grzimek)
      Films & F: v. 4, n. II (Aug., 1958), p. 24; Ken Gay, 350 wds., cp. cr.

4507 NO ROOM TO DIE (Sergio Gerrone)
      (also: Una Lunga Fila di Croci)
      Films & F: v. 16, n. 10 (July, 1970), p. 42; David Austen, 450 wds., cp. cr.

4508 NO SAD SONGS FOR ME (Rudolph Maté)
      Films in R: v. I, n. 5 (July-Aug., 1950), pp. 24, 47; Arthur Knight, 300 wds.,
        pt. cr.

4509 NO SUN IN VENICE (Roger Vadim)
      (also: Sait-On-Jamais)
      Filmf: v. I (1958), p. 134; comp., cp. cr.

4510 NO TIME FOR FLOWERS (Don Siegel)
      Films in R: v. IV, n. 2 (Feb., 1953), p. 98; 175 wds., pt. cr.

4511 NO TIME FOR SERGEANTS (Mervyn LeRoy)
      Filmf: v. I (1958), p. 81; comp., cp. cr.

4512 NO TIME FOR TEARS (Cyril Frankel)
      Films & F: v. 3, n. 12 (Sept., 1957), p. 26; Kay Collier, 150 wds., cp. cr.

NO TIME TO DIE (see: Tank Force!)

4513 NO TIME TO KILL (Tom Younger)
      (also: Med Mord I Bagaget)
      Filmf: v. V(1962), p. 366; comp., cp. cr.

4514 NO TIMES IN THE STREET (J. Lee Thompson)
      Films & F: v. 5, n. 6 (Mar., 1959), pp. 23-24; Peter G. Baker, 400 wds., cp.
        cr.

4515 NO WAY OUT (Joseph L. Mankiewicz)
      Films in R: v. I, n. 7 (Oct., 1950), pp. 24-25; Henry Hart, 500 wds., pt. cr.
      Sequence: n. 12 (Autumn, 1950), pp. 15-16; A.M., 300 wds., no cr.

4516 NO WAY TO TREAT A LADY (Jack Smight)
      Filmf: v. XI (1968), p. 63; comp., cp. cr.
      Films & F: v. 14, n. 9 (June, 1968), pp. 32-33; Stacy Waddy, 500 wds., cp.,
        cr.
      Films in R: v. XIX, n. 4 (Apr., 1968), p. 243; Flavia Wharton, 200 wds., no
        cr.
      Sight & S: v. 37, n. 3 (Summer, 1968), pp. 155-156; Tom Milne, 700 wds., pt.
        cr.

4517 NOAH'S ARK (Michael Curtiz)
      Films & F: v. 7, n. 3 (Dec., 1960), p. 33; Raymond Durgnat, 350 wds., cp.
        cr.

NOBI (see: Fire's on the Plain)

NOBODY RUNS FOREVER (see: The High Commissioner)

4518 NOBODY WAVED GOODBYE (Don Owen)
      Cahiers in Eng: n. 10 (May, 1967), p. 63; Paul-Louis Martin, 1200 wds., pt.
        cr.
      Film: n. 41 (1964), pp. 29-30; L.R., 200 wds., no cr.
      F Soc Rev: Sept. (1966), pp. 23-24; P.C., 375 wds., pt. cr.

Filmf: v. VIII (1965), p. 128; comp., cp. cr.
Films & F: v. 13, n. 5 (Mar., 1967), pp. 28-29; Raymond Durgnat, 850 wds.,
    cp. cr.
Films in R: v. XVI, n. 6 (June-July, 1965), pp. 382-383; Henry Hart, 300
    wds., no cr.
Interntl F G: v. 3 (1966), p. 54; 125 wds., pt. cr.

4519 NOBODY'S PERFECT (Alan Rafkin)
Filmf: v. XI (1968), p. 115; comp., cp. cr.

NOI PECCATORI (see: Naked and the Wicked)

NOIRE DE..., LA (see: Black Girl)

4520 NON-SCHEDULED TRAIN, A (Veljko Bulajic)
F Quarterly: v. XIII, n. 3 (Spring, 1960, pp. 56-57; Joseph Kostolefsky, 500
    wds., pt. cr.

4521 NONE BUT THE BRAVE (Frank Sinatra)
F Quarterly: v. XVIII, n. 3 (Spring, 1965), p. 61; R. M. Hodgens, 150 wds.,
    no cr.
Filmf: v. VIII (1965), p. 24; comp., cp. cr.
Films & F: v. II, n. 8 (May, 1965), p. 33; Robin Bean, 425 wds., cp. cr.
Films in R: v. XVI, n. 4 (Apr., 1965), p. 252; Adelaide Comerford, 200
    wds., no cr.

4522 NOOSE FOR A GUNMAN (Edward L. Cahn)
Filmf: v. III (1960), p. 119; comp., cp. cr.

NOR THE MOON BY NIGHT (see: Elephant Gun)

NORA INU (see: Stray Dog)

4523 NORMAN NORMAL (N. Paul Stookey)
F Lib Quarterly: v. 2, n. 3 (Summer, 1969), p. 41; Penny Jeffery, 200 wds.,
    pt. cr.

4524 NORMANDIE-NIEMEN (Jean Dreville)
Films & F: v. 6, n. 10 (July, 1960), p. 25; R. E. Durgnat, 100 wds., cp. cr.

4525 NORTH BY NORTHWEST (Alfred Hitchcock)
Filmf: v. II (1959), p. 177; comp., cp. cr.
Films & F: v. 5, n. 12 (Sept., 1959), p. 25; Peter Baker, 300 wds., cp. cr.
Films in R: v. X, n. 7 (Aug.-Sept., 1959), pp. 418-419; Ellen Fitzpatrick, 300
    wds., no cr.
Sight & S: v. 28, n. 3 & 4 (Summer-Autumn, 1959), pp. 168-169; 700 wds.,
    pt. cr.

4526 NORTH TO ALASKA (Henry Hathaway)
F Quarterly: v. XIV, n. 2 (Winter, 1960), p. 62; 125 wds., no cr.
Filmf: v. III (1960), p. 312; comp., cp. cr.
Films & F: v. 7, n. 4 (Jan., 1961), p. 35; Dai Vaughan, 300 wds., cp cr.
Films in R: v. XI, n. 10 (Dec., 1960), pp. 615-616; Dudley Boelker, 400 wds.,
    no cr.

NORTH WEST FRONTIER (see: Flame Over India)

4527 NOSE, THE (Alexander Alexeiff)
F Soc Rev: Nov. (1965) pp. 20-22; Cecile Starr, 800 wds., no cr.

4528 NOSTRA SIGNORA DEI TURCHI (Carmelo Bene)
Interntl F G: v. 7 (1970), p. 149; 225 wds., pt. cr.

4529 NOT AS A STRANGER (Stanley Kramer)
F Culture: v. I, n. 5-6 (Winter, 1955), pp. 35-36; Eugene Archer, 400 wds.,
    pt. cr.
Films & F: v. 2, n. I (Oct., 1955), p. 20; Edward Thorpe, 200 wds., cp. cr.
Films in R: v. VI, n. 6 (June-July, 1955), pp. 286-288; Henry Hart, 850
    wds., pt. cr.

4530 NOT MINE TO LOVE (Uri Zohar)
        (also: Shlosha Yamin Ve'yeled; Three Days and a Child)
        Filmf: v. XII (1969), p. 137; comp., cp. cr.

4531 NOT ON YOUR LIFE (Luis Garcia Berlanga)
        (also: The Executioner; El Verdugo)
        F Soc Rev: Apr. (1966), pp. 18-19; Harvey Deneroff, 175 wds., pt. cr.
        Filmf: v. VIII (1965), p. 92; comp., cp. cr.
        Films & F: v. 12, n. 2 (Nov., 1965), pp. 26-27; Raymond Durgnat, 800 wds.,
              cp. cr.

        NOT RECONCILED (see: Nicht Versöhnt)

4532 NOT WITH MY WIFE, YOU DON'T (Norman Panama)
        F Quarterly: v. XX, n. 3 (Spring, 1967), p. 62; Steven Farber, 225 wds., no
              cr.
        Filmf: v. IX (1966), p. 297; comp., cp. cr.
        Films & F: x. 13, n. 5 (Feb., 1967), pp. 31-32; Richard Davis, 350 wds., cp.
              cr.

4533 N:O:T:H:I:N:G (Paul Sharits)
        F Culture: n. 47 (Summer, 1969), pp. 15-16; Paul Sharits, 900 wds., no cr.

4534 NOTHING BUT A MAN (Michael Roemer)
        Film: n. 41 (1964), pp. 25-26; Stanley Crawford, 400 wds., pt. cr.
        F Comment: v. 3, n. 1 (Winter, 1965), pp. 71-72; F. William Howton, 1500
              wds., pt. cr.
        F Soc Rev: Sept. (1966), pp. 23-24; P.C., 375 wds., pt. cr.
        Films in R: v. XV, n. 10 (Dec., 1964), pp. 633-634; Joan Horvath, 350 wds.,
              no cr.

4535 NOTHING BUT THE BEST (Clive Donner)
        Cahiers in Eng: n. 2 (1966), pp. 74-75; Jean-Andre Fieschi, 700 wds., cp. cr.
        F Quarterly: v. XVIII, n. 1 (Fall, 1964), p. 62; William Johnson, 100 wds., no
              cr.
        Filmf: v. VII (1964), p. 361; comp., cp. cr.
        Films & F: v. 10, n. 7 (Apr., 1964), p. 25; Allen Eyles, 750 wds., cp. cr.
        Films in R: v. XV, n. 7 (Aug.-Sept., 1964), p. 441; Brian Sandenbergh, 250
              wds., no cr.
        Interntl F G: v. 2 (1965), p. 85; 225 wds., pt. cr.
        Sight & S: v. 33, n. 2 (Spring, 1964), p. 96; John Russell Taylor, 600 wds.,
              pt. cr.

4536 NOTORIOUS (Alfred Hitchcock)
        F Heritage: v. 4, n. 3 (Spring, 1969), pp. 6-10; David Bordwell, 2000 wds.,
              pt. cr.

4537 NOTORIOUS LANDLADY, THE (Richard Quine)
        Filmf: v. V (1962), p. 171; comp., cp. cr.
        Films & F: v. 9, n. 2 (Nov., 1962), pp. 33-34; John Cutts, 300 wds., cp. cr.
        Movie: n. 4 (Nov., 1962), p. 35; 100 wds., no cr.
        Sight & S: v. 31, n. 3 (Summer, 1962), p. 147; Penelope Houston, 250 wds.,
              pt. cr.

4538 NOTORIOUS MR. MONKS, THE (Joseph Kane)
        Filmf: v. I (1958), p. 45; comp., cp. cr.

4539 NOTTE, LA (Michelangelo Antonioni)
        (also: The Night)
        Cinema: v. I, n. 2, p. 33; 200 wds., pt. cr.
        Film: n. 31 (Spring, 1962), p. 10; Peter Armitage, 250 wds., no cr.
        F Culture: n. 24 (Spring, 1962), pp. 82-83; Guido Aristarco, 1200 wds., no
              cr.
        F Journal: n. 20 (Aug., 1962), p. 84; John R. Burgess, 300 wds., no cr.
        Filmf: v. V (1962), p. 35; comp., cp. cr.
        Films & F: v. 8, n. 5 (Feb., 1962), p. 28; Gordon Gow, 700 wds., cp. cr.
        Films in R: v. XII, n. 10 (Dec., 1961), p. 625; Ellen Fitzpatrick, 400 wds., no
              cr.
        Sight & S: v. 31, n. 1 (Winter, 1961-1962), pp. 28-31; Geoffrey Nowell-Smith,
              1500 wds., pt. cr.

4540 NOTTE BRAVA, LA (Mauro Bolognini)
         (also: Night Heat; On Any Street)
         Filmf: v. V (1962), p. 19; comp., cp. cr.
         Films & F: v. 7, n. 3 (Dec., 1960), p. 31; Raymond Durgnat, 400 wds., cp.
            cr.

      NOTTI BIANCHE (see: White Nights)

4541 NOTTI DI CABIRIA, LE (Federico Fellini)
         (also: Cabiria; Night of Cabiria; Nights of Cabiria)
         F Culture: v. IV, n. I (Jan., 1958), pp. 18-21; Andrew Sarris, 2500 wds., cp.
            cr.
         F Quarterly: v. XII, n. I (Fall, 1958), pp. 43-45; James Kerans, 750 wds., no
            cr.
         Films & F: v. 4, n. 6 (Mar., 1958), p. 23; Peter G. Baker, 600 wds., cp. cr.
         Films in R: v. VIII, n. 10 (Dec., 1957), p. 529; Louise Corbin, 125 wds., no
            cr.

4542 NOURISHEE, THE (Vatroslav Mimica)
         Interntl F G: v. 9 (1972), p. 287; Ron Holloway, 200 wds., pt. cr.

      NOUS SOMMES TOUS DES ASSASSINS (see: We Are All Murderers)

      NOVEL AFFAIR, A (see: The Passionate Stranger)

      NOVI ATTRAKTZION (see: A New Number Comes to Moscow)

4543 NOW ABOUT THESE WOMEN (Ingmar Bergman)
         (also: All These Women; For Att Inte Tala Om Alla Dessa Kvinnor)
         Filmf: v. VII (1964), p. 336; comp., cp. cr.
         Films & F: v. II, n. 9 (June, 1965), p. 28; Ingmar Bergman, 450 wds., cp. cr.
         Films in R: v. XV, n. 10 (Dec., 1964), p. 637; Flavia Wharton, 100 wds., no
            cr.
         Movie: n. 13 (Summer, 1965), pp. 6-9; Ian Cameron, 2400 wds., no cr.
         Sight & S: v. 34, n. 3 (Summer, 1965), pp. 146-147; Tom Milne, 700 wds., pt.
            cr.

4544 NOW AND FOREVER (Mario Zampi)
         Films & F: v. 2, n. 6 (Mar., 1956), p. 16; Rodney Giesler, 150 wds., cp. cr.

4545 NOW BARABBAS (Gordon Perry)
         Sight & S: v. 18, n. 70 (Summer, 1949), p. 90; Arthur Vesselo, 150 wds., no
            cr.

4546 NOW IS THE TIME (Jim Crum)
         F Lib Quarterly: v. 2, n. 2 (Spring, 1969), pp. 29-30; Kenneth W. Axthelm,
            325 wds., pt. cr.

4547 NOW THAT THE BUFFALO'S GONE (Burton Gershfield)
         F Quarterly: v. XXI, n. 3 (Spring, 1968), pp. 49-50; Richard Whitehall, 500
            wds., pt. cr.

4548 NOWHERE TO GO (Seth Holt)
         Filmf: v. II (1953), p. 89; comp., cp. cr.
         Films & F: v. 5, n. 4 (Jan., 1959), p. 25; Peter G. Baker, 125 wds., cp. cr.
         Films in R: v. X, n. 2 (Feb., 1959), pp. 109-110; Ellen Fitzpatrick, 175 wds.,
            no cr.
         Sight & S: v. 28, n. I (Winter, 1958-1959), pp. 38-39; Penelope Houston, 600
            wds., pt. cr.

      NOZ W WODZIE (see: Knife in the Water)

4549 NUDE IN A WHITE CAR (Robert Hossein)
         Filmf: v. III (1960-1961), p. 247; comp., cp. cr.

4550 NUDE ODYSSEY (Franco Rossi)
         (also: Odissea Nuda)
         Filmf: v. V (1962), p. 301; comp., cp. cr.
         Films & F: v. 9, n. 7 (Apr., 1963), p. 32; Raymond Durgnat, 450 wds., cp.
            cr.

4551 NUDE ONES, THE (Werner Kunz)
        Films & F: v. 9, n. 5 (Feb., 1963), pp. 39-40; Tony Mallerman, 600 wds., cp.
            cr.
        Films & F: v. 16, n. 1 (Oct., 1969), p. 54; Claire Johnston, 100 wds., cp. cr.

4552 NUDE RESTAURANT, THE (Andy Warhol)
        Filmf: v. X (1967), p. 354; comp., cp. cr.

      NUDE TEMPTATION, THE (see: Woman and Temptation)

      NUDIST PARADISE (see: Nature's Paradise)

      NUDIST STORY, THE (see: For Members Only)

      NUERNBERGER PROZESS, DER (see: Hitler's Executioners)

      NUIT DES ESPIONS, LA (see: Night Encounter)

      NUIT ET BROUILLARD (see: Night and Fog)

      NUIT INFIDELE, LA (see: The Unfaithful Night)

4553 NUMBER ONE (Tom Gries)
        F Quarterly: v. XXIII, n. 1 (Fall, 1969), pp. 57-58; Stephen Farber, 700
            wds., no cr.

      NUN, THE (see: La Religieuse)

4554 NUN AND THE SERGEANT, THE (Franklin Adreon)
        Filmf: v. V (1962), p. 182; comp., cp. cr.

4555 NUN AT THE CROSSROADS, A (Julio Buchs)
        (also: Encrucijada Para Una Monja)
        Filmf: v. XIV (1971), p. 108; comp., cp. cr.

4556 NUN'S STORY, THE (Fred Zinnemann)
        F Quarterly: v. XII, n. 2 (Winter, 1958), pp. 57-58; Albert Johnson, 700
            wds., no cr.
        Filmf: v. II (1959), p. 129; comp., cp. cr.
        Films & F: v. 5, n. 10 (July, 1959), p. 21; Paul Rotha, 650 wds., cp. cr.
        Films in R: v. X, n. 6 (June-July, 1959), pp. 351-354; Henry Hart, 1300 wds.,
            no cr.
        Sight & S: v. 28, n. 3 & 4 (Summer-Autumn, 1959), p. 170; Kenneth Cavander,
            600 wds., pt. cr.

      NUOVI ANGELI, I (see: The New Angels)

4557 NUREMBERG CHRONICLE, THE (John Frazer and Russell T. Limbach,
            prod.)
        F Lib Quarterly: v. 4, n. 4 (Fall, 1971), pp. 54-55; Marvin Stone, 450 wds.,
            pt. cr.

4558 NURSE ON WHEELS (Gerald Thomas)
        Filmf: v. VI (1963), p. 339; comp., cp. cr.

4559 NUTCRACKER, THE (Kurt Jacob)
        F Lib Quarterly: v. 2, n. 2 (Spring, 1969), p. 30; Sandra R. Abrams, 300
            wds., pt. cr.

4560 NUTTY PROFESSOR, THE (Jerry Lewis)
        Filmf: v. VI (1963), p. 141; comp., cp. cr.
        Films & F: v. 10, n. 1 (Oct., 1963), p. 31; Raymond Durgnat, 800 wds., cp. cr.
        Focus: n. 8 (Autumn, 1972), pp. 45-50; Michael A. Stern, 3800 wds., no cr.
        Movie: n. 11, p. 34; 150 wds., no cr.
        Sight & S: v. 33, n. 3 (Summer, 1964), p. 147; John Gillett, 550 wds., no cr.

      NYEOBYKNOVENNOE LYETO (see: No Ordinary Summer)

      NYEOTPRAVLYENNIYE PISMO (see: The Undelivered Letter)

4561 NYMPHETTES, LES (Henri Zaphiratos)
        Film & F: v. 7, n. 7 (Apr., 1961), pp. 28-29; Robin Bean, 500 wds., cp. cr.

4562 O DEM WATERMELONS (Robert Nelson)
      (also: Watermelons)
          F Culture: n. 48-49 (Winter-Spring, 1970), p. 24; Robert Nelson, 400 wds.,
              pt. cr.
          F Quarterly: v. XIX, n. 2 (Winter, 1965-1966), pp. 53-54; John Seelye, 500
              wds., no cr.
          F Quarterly: v. XX, n. 3 (Spring, 1967), pp. 50-52; Earl Bodien, 1400 wds.,
              no cr.

4563 O. HENRY'S FULL HOUSE (Jean Negulesco, Henry Hathaway, Henry King,
              Howard Hawks, Henry Koster)
      (also: Full House)
          Films in R: v. III, n. 8 (Oct., 1952), pp. 416-417; 350 wds., pt. cr.
          Sight & S: v. 22, n. 2 (Oct.-Dec., 1952), p. 77; Penelope Houston, 600 wds.,
              pt. cr.

4564 O.K. (Michael Verhoeven)
          Cineaste: v. IV, n. 2 (Fall, 1970), pp. 33-35; Bill Nichols, 2100 wds., pt. cr.
          Take One: v. 2, n. 9 (1970), pp. 21-22; Ronald Blumer, 300 wds., pt. cr.

      O.K. CONNERY (see: Operation Kid Brother)

      00-2 AGENTI SEGRETISSIMI (see: Oh! Those Most Secret Agents!)

      00-2 SECRET AGENTS, THE (see! Oh! Those Most Secret Agents!)

4565 O.S.S. 117 IS NOT DEAD (Jean Sacha)
          Filmf: v. III (1960-1961), p. 349; comp., cp. cr.

4566 O.S.S. 117—MISSION FOR A KILLER (Andre Hunebelle)
          (also: Furia a Bahia Pour O.S.S. 117; Trouble in Bahai for O.S.S. 117)
          Filmf: v. IX (1966), p. 266; comp., cp. cr.
          Films & F: v. 10, n. 7 (Apr., 1964), p. 32; David Rider, 250 wds., cp. cr.

      O SALTO (see: Voyage of Silence)

4567 OASIS (Yves Allegret)
          Films & F: v. 2, n. 8 (May, 1956), p. 24; Peter G. Baker, 175 wds., cp. cr.

      OBCHOD NA KORZE (see: The Shop on Main Street)

      OBIKNOVENNII FASHIZM (See: Triumph Over Violence)

4568 OBLONG BOX, THE (Gordon Hessler)
          (also: Edgar Allan Poe's 'The Oblong Box')
          Filmf: v. XII (1969), p. 375; comp., cp. cr.

4569 OBSESSION (Jean Delannoy)
          Films & F: v. 3, n. 9 (June, 1957), p. 25; Kay Collier, 400 wds., cp. cr.

4570 OBSESSION (Gunnar Hogland)
          (also: Kungsleden: Royal Path)
          Filmf: x. XI (1968), p. 414; comp., cp. cr.

4571 OBSESSIONS (Pim De La Parra)
          Films & F: v. 17, n. 4 (Jan., 1971), pp. 53, 56; Margaret Tarratt, 200 wds.,
              cp. cr.

      OCCHIO SELVAGGIO, L' (see: The Wild Eye)

4572 OCCUPE-TOI D'AMELIE (Claude Autant-Lara)
          (also: Keep an Eye on Amelia)
          Sight & S: v. 19, n. 8 (Dec., 1950), p. 334; Gavin Lambert, 250 wds., pt. cr.

OCCURRENCE AT OWL CREEK BRIDGE, AN (see: Incident at Owl Creek Bridge)

4573 OCEAN'S ELEVEN (Lewis Milestone)
F Quarterly: v. XIV, n. I (Fall, 1960), p. 61; 125 wds., no cr.
Filmf: v. III (1960), p. 199; comp., cp. cr.
Films & F: v. 7, n. I (Oct., 1960), p. 27; Richard Whitehall, 350 wds., cp. cr.
Films in R: v. XI, n. 8 (Oct., 1960), p. 493; Shirley Conover, 175 wds., no cr.

OCHTEND VAN ZES WEKEN, EEN (see: Un Printemps en Hollande)

4574 OCTOBER (Sergei Eisenstein)
(also: Ten Days That Shook the World)
Sight & S: v. 21, n. 2 (Oct.-Dec., 1951), pp. 92-94; Derek Grig and Guy Cote, 2000 wds., cp. cr.

4575 OCTOBER MAN, THE (Roy Baker)
Sight & S: v. 16, n. 63 (Autumn, 1947), p. 121; Arthur Vesselo, 250 wds., no cr.

4576 OCTOBRE A PARIS
Movie: n. II, p. 27; Mark Shivas, 250 wds., no cr.

4577 ODD COUPLE, THE (George Saks)
F Quarterly: v. XXII, n. I (Fall, 1968), p. 75; Stephen Farber, 250 wds., no cr.
Filmf: v. XI (1968), p. 143; comp., cp. cr.
Films & F: v. 14, n. II (Aug., 1968), p. 24; Allen Eyles, 450 wds., cp. cr.
Films in R: v. XIX, n. 6 (June-July, 1968), p. 379; Harriet Gibbs, 125 wds., no cr.

4578 ODD OBSESSION (Kon Ichikawa)
(also: Kagi)
Film: n. 31 (Spring, 1962), p. 15; Peter Armitage, 150 wds., no cr.
F Quarterly: v. XV, n. 2 (Winter, 1961-1962), pp. 53-54; Colin Young, 900 wds., pt. cr.
Filmf: v. IV (1961), p. 347; comp., cp. cr.
Films & F: v. 8, n. 5 (Feb., 1962), pp. 33-34; Raymond Durgnat, 550 wds., cp. cr.
Sight & S: v. 31, n. 2 (Spring, 1962), pp. 91-92; John Gillett, 1200 wds., pt. cr.

4579 ODDS AGAINST TOMORROW (Robert Wise)
Filmf: v. II (1959), p. 251; comp., cp. cr.
Films & F: v. 6, n. 2 (Nov., 1959), p. 25; Derek Conrad, 300 wds., cp. cr.

ODER DAS UNWERTE LEBEN (see: Ursula)

ODISSEA NUDA (see: Nude Odyssey)

4580 OEDIPUS REX (Tyrone Guthrie)
Films in R: v. VII, n. 8 (Oct., 1956), p. 416; Courtland Phipps, 200 wds., no cr.

4581 OEDIPUS THE KING (Philip Saville)
Filmf: v. XI (1968), p. 372; comp., cp. cr.
Films & F: v. 14, n. II (Aug., 1968), pp. 24-25; Michael Armstrong, 600 wds., cp. cr.

4582 OEDIPUS REX (Pier Paolo Pasolini)
(also: Edipo Re)
Films & F: v. 15, n. 9 (June, 1969), pp. 39-40; Peter Whitehead, 1100 wds., cp. cr.
Interntl F G: v. 6 (1969), p. 107; Lucio Settimio Caruso, 225 wds., pt. cr.

OEIL DU MALIN, L' (see: The Third Lover)

OEIL POUR OEIL (see: An Eye for An Eye)

OEUFS DE L'AUTRUCHE, LES (see: The Ostrich Has Two Eggs)

Films in R: v. IX, n. 7 (Aug.-Sept., 1958), pp. 396-398; Henry Hart, 1100 wds., no cr..
Sight & S: v. 28, n. I (Winter, 1958-1959), p. 39; Cynthia Granier, 400 wds., pt. cr.

4610 OLD MAN MOTOR CAR (Alfred Radok)
(also: Dedecek Automobil)
Films & F: v. 5, n. 6 (Mar., 1959), p. 23; Bernard Orna, 275 wds., cp. cr.

OLD SHATTERHAND (see: Apache's Last Battle)

OLD SUREHAND (see: Flaming Frontier)

4611 OLD YELLER (Robert Stevenson)
Films in R: v. VIII, n. 10 (Dec., 1957), pp. 528-529; Elspeth Hart, 300 wds., no cr.

4612 OLDEST PROFESSION, THE (Mauro Bolognine, Philippe De Broca, Clause Autant-Lara, Jean-Luc Godard, F. Indovina, M. Pfleghar)
(also: Le Plus Vieux Metier du Monde)
Filmf: v. XI (1968), p. 483; comp., cp. cr.

4613 OLE DOLE DOFF (Jan Troell)
(also: Eeny Meeny Miny Moe; Who Saw Him Die)
Films & F: v. 15, n. 6 (Mar., 1969), p. 42; Claire Johnston, 600 wds., cp. cr.
Interntl F G: v. 6 (1969), p. 158; Peter Cowie, 225 wds., pt. cr.

4614 OLE REX (Robert Hinkle)
Filmf: v. IV (1961-1962), p. 368; comp., cp. cr.

4615 OLIVE TREES OF JUSTICE, THE (James Blue)
(also: Los Oliviers de la Justice)
F Quarterly: v. XVI, n. 4 (Summer, 1963), pp. 48-50; Richard Grenier, 900 wds., pt. cr.
F Soc Rev: May (1966), pp. 14-15; Gordon Hitchens, 450 wds., pt. cr.
Filmf: v. X (1967), p. 184; comp., cp. cr.

4616 OLIVER! (Carol Reed)
F Quarterly: v. XXII, n. 3 (Spring, 1969), p. 62; Stephen Farber, 350 wds., no cr.
Filmf: v. XI (1968), p. 387; comp., cp. cr.
Films & F: v. 15, n. 2 (Nov., 1968), pp. 44-45; David Austen, 700 wds., cp. cr.
Films in R: v. XX, n. I (Jan., 1969), pp. 56-57; Page Cook, 375 wds., no cr.

4617 OLIVER TWIST (David Lean)
Films in R: v. II, n. 7 (Aug.-Sept., 1951), pp. 39-40; Henry Hart, 450 wds., pt. cr.
Sequence: n. 5 (Autumn, 1948), pp. 37-38; Alberta Marlow, 700 wds., no cr.
Sight & S: v. 17, n. 67 (Autumn, 1948), p. 143; Arthur Vesselo, 600 wds., no cr.

OLIVERS DE LA JUSTICE, LES (see: The Olive Trees of Justice)

OLTRAGGIO AL PUDORE (see: All the Other Girls Do)

4618 OLTRO CRISTOBAL, EL (Armand Gatti)
Movie: n. II, p. 25; Mark Shivas, 50 wds., no cr.

4619 OLVIDADOS, LOS (Luis Bunel)
(also: The Forgotten Ones; Pity for Them; The Young and the Damned)
Films in R: v. III, n. 5 (May, 1952), p. 245; 75 wds., no cr.
Sequence: n. 14 (New Year, 1952), pp. 30-32; Gavin Lambert, 2200 wds., pt. cr.
Sight & S: v. 21, n. 4 (Apr.-June, 1952), pp. 167-168; John Maddison, 900 wds., pt. cr.

4620 OLYMPIC ELK, THE (Walt Disney, prod.)
Films in R: v. III, n. 2 (Feb., 1952), p. 89; 200 wds., no cr.

4621 OLYMPICS IN MEXICO, THE (Alberto Isaac)
　　　Films & F: v. 16, n. 7 (Apr., 1970), pp. 52-53; Ken Gay, 750 wds., cp. cr.

4622 OMAR KHAYYAM (William Dieterle)
　　　Films & F: v. 4, n. 2 (Nov., 1957), pp. 25-27; Kay Collier, 300 wds., cp. cr.

　　　OMBRELLONE, L' (see: Weekend, Italian Style)

4623 OMEGA MAN, THE (Boris Sagal)
　　　Filmf: v. XIV (1971), p. 493; comp., cp. cr.

4624 ON A CLEAR DAY YOU CAN SEE FOREVER (Vincente Minnelli)
　　　Films & F: v. 17, n. 12 (Sept., 1971), p. 50; David McGillivray, 650 wds., cp.
　　　　　cr.
　　　Films in R: v. XXI, n. 7 (Aug.-Sept., 1970), pp. 438-439; Page Cook, 450
　　　　　wds., no cr.
　　　Focus: n. 7 (Spring, 1972), pp. 24-26; James Jubak, 2000 wds., no cr.

　　　ON ANY STREET (see: La Notte Brava)

4625 ON ANY SUNDAY (Bruce Brown)
　　　Filmf: v. XIV (1971), p. 503; comp., cp. cr.

　　　ON FRIDAY AT ELEVEN (see: World in My Pocket)

4626 ON HER BED OF ROSES (Albert Zugsmith)
　　　Filmf: v. IX (1966), p. 385; comp., cp. cr.

4627 ON HER MAJESTY'S SECRET SERVICE (Peter Hunt)
　　　Films & F: v. 16, n. 5 (Feb., 1970), p. 38; David Austen, 400 wds., cp. cr.
　　　Films in R: v. XXI, n. 1 (Jan., 1970), pp. 51-52; Arthur B. Clark, 150 wds., no
　　　　　cr.

4628 ON SUCH A NIGHT (Anthony Asquith)
　　　Sight & S: v. 25, n. 3 (Winter, 1955-1956), p. 151; James Morgan, 175 wds.,
　　　　　pt. cr.

4629 ON THE BEACH (Stanley Kramer)
　　　F Quarterly: v. XIII, n. 2 (Winter, 1959), pp. 52-56; Ernest Callenbach, 1900
　　　　　wds., no cr.
　　　Filmf: v. II (1959), p. 299; comp., cp. cr.
　　　Films & F: v. 6, n. 3 (Dec., 1959), p. 21; Peter Baker, 700 wds., cp. cr.
　　　Films in R: v. XI, n. 1 (Jan., 1960), pp. 36-39; Frances Taylor Patterson,
　　　　　1000 wds., no cr.
　　　Films in R: v. XI, n. 2 (Feb., 1960), pp. 124-125; Earl Ubell (quoted), 450
　　　　　wds., no cr.
　　　Sight & S: v. 29, n. 1 (Winter, 1959-1960), p. 37; Penelope Houston, 800
　　　　　wds., pt. cr.

4630 ON THE BEAT (Robert Asher)
　　　Films & F: v. 9, n. 5 (Feb., 1963), p. 40; David Rider, 700 wds., cp. cr.

4631 ON THE BOWERY (Lionel Rogosin)
　　　F Culture: v. 3, n. 2 (1957), pp. 16-17; Gordon Hendricks, 1500 wds., pt. cr.
　　　Films in R: v. VIII, n. 4 (Apr., 1957), p. 174; Henry Hart, 150 wds., no cr.
　　　Sight & S: v. 26, n. 2 (Autumn, 1956), p. 98; Basil Wright, 700 wds., pt. cr.

4632 ON THE DOUBLE (Melville Shavelson)
　　　Filmf: v. IV (1961), p. 125; comp., cp. cr.
　　　Films & F: v. 7, n. 12 (Sept., 1961), pp. 30-31; Phillip Riley, 450 wds., cp. cr.
　　　Films in R: v. XII, n. 6 (June-July, 1961), p. 360; Charles A. Butler, 225
　　　　　wds., no cr.

4633 ON THE RIVIERA (Walter Lang)
　　　Sight & S: v. 21, n. 1 (Aug.-Sept., 1951), p. 29; Frank Hauser, 500 wds., no cr.

4634 ON THE THRESHOLD OF SPACE (Robert D. Webb)
　　　Films & F: v. 2, n. 8 (May, 1956), p. 22; Rodney Giesler, 325 wds., cp. cr.
　　　Films in R: v. VII, (n. 4 (Apr., 1956), pp. 171-172; Henry Hart, 300 wds., no
　　　　　cr.

ORRIBLE SEGRETO DEL DR. HITCHCOCK, L' (see: The Horrible Dr. Hitchcock)

OSAKA-JO MONOGATARI (see: Daredevil in the Castle)

4714 OSCAR, THE (Russell Rouse)
        Filmf: v. IX (1966), p. 51; comp., cp. cr.
        Films & F: v. 12, n. 10 (July, 1966), pp. 52, 56; Richard Davis, 550 wds., cp. cr.
        Films in R: v. XVII, n. 4 (Apr., 1966), pp. 246-247; Henry Hart, 300 wds., no cr.

4715 OSCAR WILDE (Gregory Ratoff)
        Filmf: v. III (1960), p. 184; comp., cp. cr.
        Films & F: v. 6, n. 10 (July, 1960), p. 23; Peter Baker, 1000 wds., cp. cr.
        Films in R: v. XI, n. 7 (Aug.-Sept., 1960), pp. 432-433; Henry Hart, 400 wds., no cr.
        Sight & S: v. 29, n. 3 (Summer, 1960), p. 146; Derek Hill, 750 wds., pt. cr.

OSMY DZIEN TYGODNIA (see: The Eighth Day of the Week)

4716 OSS EMELLAN (Stellan Olsson)
        (also: It's Up To You)
        Interntl F G: v. 7 (1970), p. 207; Peter Cowie, 175 wds., pt. cr.

OSTRE SLEDOVANE VLAKY (see: Closely Watched Trains)

4717 OSTRICH HAS TWO EGGS, THE (Denys de la Patelliere)
        (also: Les Oeufs de L'Autruche)
        Filmf: v. III (1960), p. 245; comp., cp. cr.
        Films in R: v. XI, n. 8 (Oct., 1960), p. 494; Henry Hart, 200 wds., no cr.

OSWALT KOLLE: DAS WUNDER LIEBE SEXUALITAT IN DER EHE (see: The Miracle of Love)

OTETS SOLDATA (see: Father of a Soldier)

4718 OTHELLO (Orson Welles)
        F Culture: v. I, n. 5-6 (Winter, 1955), p. 32; Donald Phelps, 1200 wds., pt. cr.
        F Heritage: v. 5, n. I (Fall, 1969), pp. 9-15; Frederick Plotkin, 1500 wds., no cr.
        F Journal: n. 5 (1956), pp. 1-4; W. E. Mills, 2000 wds., no cr.
        Films & F: v. 2, n. 7 (Apr., 1956), p. 14; John Carroll, 400 wds., cp. cr.
        Films in R: v. VI, n. 7 (Aug.-Sept., 1955), pp. 341-342; Robert Downing, 500 wds., pt. cr.
        Sight & S: v. 25, n. 4 (Spring, 1956), pp. 196-197: David Robinson, 850 wds., pt. cr.

4719 OTHELLO (Sergei Youtkevich)
        Filmf: v. III (1960), p. 133; comp., cp. cr.
        Films & F: v. 3, n. II (Aug., 1957), pp. 28, 32; Peter John Dyer, 400 wds., cp. cr.
        Films in R: v. XI, n. 4 (Apr., 1960), p. 235; Tatiana Balkoff Drowne, 200 wds., no cr.
        Sight & S: v. 26, n. I (Summer, 1956), p. 30; Derek Prouse, 1200 wds., pt. cr.

4720 OTHELLO (Stuart Burge)
        Cinema: v.3, n. 2 (Mar., 1966), p. 47; Richard Whitehall, 450 wds., pt. cr.
        F Heritage: v. 2 n. I (Fall, 1966), pp. 18-22; Harland S. Nelson, 1300 wds., no cr.
        F Quarterly: v. XIX, n. 4 (Summer, 1966), pp. 48-50; Constance Brown, 1200 wds., pt. cr.
        Filmf: v. IX (1966), p. 17; comp., cp. cr.
        Films & F: v. 12, n, 8 (May, 1966), p. 6; Gordon Gow, 750 wds., cp. cr.
        Filmf in R: v. XVII, n. I (Jan., 1966), pp. 52-53; 300 wds., no cr.
        Sight & S: v. 35, n. 3 (Summer, 1966), p. 149; Brenda Davies, 300 wds., pt. cr.

OTHER ONE, THE (see: L'Une et L'Autre)

4721 OTLEY (Dick Clement)
Filmf: v. XII (1969), p. II6; comp., cp. cr.
Films & F: v. I5, n. IO (July, 1969), pp. 39-40; Richard Davis, I000 wds., cp. cr.
Films in R: v. XX, n. 4 (Apr., 1969), p. 253; Eunice Sinkler, I25 wds., no cr.
Sight & S: v. 38, n. 3 (Summer, 1969), p. I58; James Price, 600 wds., pt. cr.

OTTO E MEZZO (see: 8 1/2)

4722 OUR DAILY BREAD (F.W. Murnau)
(also: City Girl)
F Comment: v. 7, n. 2 (Summer, I97I), pp. 20-22; Richard Koszarski, 2000 wds., pt. cr.
Take One: v. 2, n. 9 (L970), pp. 26-27; Mike Goodwin and Naomi Wise, 850 wds., no cr.

4723 OUR LAST SPRING (Michael Cacoyannis)
Filmf & F: v. 8, n. I (Oct., 1961), p. 26; Gordon Gow, 700 wds., cp. cr.
Sight & S v. 30, n. 4 (Autumn, 1961), p. 200; David Robinson, 425 wds., pt. cr.

4724 OUR MAN FLINT (Daniel Mann)
Filmf: v. IX (1966), p. II; comp., cp. cr.

4725 OUR MAN IN HAVANA (Carol Reed)
F Quarterly: v. XIII, n. 3 (Spring, I960), p. 60; 50 wds., no cr.
Filmf: v. III (I960), p. I9; comp., cp. cr.
Films & F: v. 6, n. 5 (Feb., I960), p. 2I; David Robinson, 450 wds., cp. cr.
Films in R: v. XI, n. 3 (Mar., I960), pp. I67-I68; Charles A. Butler, 225 wds., no cr.
Sight & S: v. 29, n. I (Winter, I959-I960), p. 35; Penelope Houston, I000 wds., pt. cr.

OUR MAN IN MARRAKESH (see: Bang! Bang! You're Dead!)

OUR MOTHER'S HOUSE (Jack Clayton)
F Quarterly: v. XXI, n. 3 (Spring, I968), p. 60; Estelle Changas, 350 wds., no cr.
Filmf: v. X (I967), p. 3I0; comp., cp. cr.
Films & F: v. I4, n. 2 (Nov., I967), p. 20; Raymond Durgnat, II00 wds., cp. cr.
Films in R: v. XVIII, n. 9 (Nov., I967), p. 577; Page Cook, 250 wds., no cr.

4727 OUR TRIP TO AFRICA (Peter Kubelka)
F Quarterly: v. XX, n. 2 (Winter, I966-I967), pp. 54-57; Earl Bodine, I600 wds., pt. cr.

4728 OUR VERY OWN (David Miller)
Sight & S: v. I9, n. II (Mar., I95I), pp. 440-44I; Gavin Lambert, 850 wds., pt. cr.

OURS ET LA POUPEE, L' (see: The Bear and The Doll)

OUT OF DARKNESS (see: Black Jesus)

4729 OUT OF IT (Paul Williams)
Films in R: v. XX, n. 9 (Nov., 1969), pp. 574-575; Grenneth Britt, I25 wds., no cr.

4730 OUT OF SIGHT (Len Weinrib)
Filmf: v. IX (1966), p. II3; comp., cp. cr.

4731 OUT OF THE CLOUDS (Michael Relph and Basil Dearden)
Films & F: v. I, n. 7 (Apr., 1955), p. 2I; Derek Hill, I50 wds., cp. cr.

OUT OF THE SHADOW (see: Murder on the Campus)

4732 OUT OF THIS WORLD (Lowell Thomas)
Films in R: v. V, n. 5 (May, I954), p. 243; Ralph Gerstle, I75 wds., no cr.

4733 OUT-OF-TOWNERS, THE (Arthur Hiller)
        Films & F: v. 16, n. 12 (Sept., 1970), p. 68; Margaret Tarratt, 250 wds., cp.
            cr.
        Films in R: v. XXI, n. 6 (June-July, 1970), pp. 377-378; Hubbell Robinson,
            500 wds., no cr.

4734 OUTBACK (Ted Kotcheff)
        Interntl F G: v. 9 (1972), p. 53; David J. Stratton, 200 wds., pt. cr.

4735 OUTCAST OF THE ISLAND (Carol Reed)
        Films in R: v. III, n. 5 (May, 1952), pp. 238-239; Henry Hart, 700 wds., no
            cr.
        Sight & S: v. 21, n. 4 (Apr.-June, 1952), pp. 166-167; Basil Wright, 1000 wds.,
            pt. cr.

4736 OUTCASTS OF THE CITY (Boris Petroff)
        Filmf: v. I (1958), p. 8; comp., cp. cr.

      OUTCRY, THE (see: Il Grido)

4737 OUTDOORSMAN, THE (William A. Bryant)
        Filmf: v. XII (1969), p. 216; comp., cp. cr.

4738 OUTLAWS IS COMING, THE (Norman Maurer)
        Filmf: v. VIII (1965), p. 108; comp., cp. cr.

4739 OUTLAWS OF LOVE, THE (Valentino Orsini)
        (also: I Fuorilegge del Matrimonio)
        Interntl F G: v. 2 (1965), p. 102; Gaetano Strazzulla, 200 wds., pt. cr.

4740 OUTRAGE, THE (Martin Ritt)
        Filmf: v. VII (1964), p. 248; comp., cp. cr.
        Films & F: v. 12, n. I (Oct., 1965), pp. 29-30; Gordon Gow, 850 wds., cp. cr.
        Films in R: v. XV, n. 9 (Nov., 1964), pp. 573-574; Maya Crandall, 300 wds.,
            no cr.

      OUTRAGEOUS PUBLIC BEHAVIOR (see: All the Other Girls Do)

4741 OUTSIDER, THE (Delbert Mann)
        F Quarterly: v. XV, n. 4 (Summer, 1962), p. 64; R. M. Hodgens, 100 wds.,
            no cr.
        Filmf: v. V (1962), p. 50; comp., cp. cr.

      OUTSIDER, THE (Luchino Visconti/see: The Stranger)

      OUTSIDERS, THE (See: Bande à Part)

4742 OVER THERE 1914-1918 (Jean Aurel)
        Filmf: v. VIII (1965), p. 60; comp., cp. cr.

4743 OVERCOAT, THE (Alberto Lattuada)
        (also: Il Cappotte)
        Films & F: v. I, n. 8 (May, 1955), p. 20; Peter Barnes, 150 wds., cp. cr.

4744 OVERCOAT, THE (Aleksei Batalov)
        (also: Shinel)
        Filmf: v. VIII (1965), p. 95; comp., cp. cr.
        Films in R: v. XVI, n. 4 (Apr., 1965), p. 252; 50 wds., no cr.

      OVERGREPPET (see: Le Viol)

4745 OVERLAND WITH KIT CARSON (Sam Nelson and Norman Deming)
        Views and Rev: v. I, n. 4 (Spring, 1970), pp. 22-27; 1200 wds., cp. cr.

4746 OVERLANDERS, THE (Harry Watt)
        Sight & S: v. 15, n. 60 (Winter, 1946-1947), p. 155; Arthur Vesselo, 400 wds.,
            no cr.

      OVERAL, DE (see: The Silent Raid)

OVOCE STROMU RAJSKYCH JIME (see: Le Fruit du Paradis)

4747 OWL AND THE PUSSYCAT, THE (Herbert Ross)
Films & F: v. 17, n. 12 (Sept., 1971), Peter Buckley, 750 wds., cp. cr.
Films in R: v. XXI, n. 10 (Dec., 1970), p. 646; Elaine Rothschild, 125 wds., no cr.

OWL'S DAY, THE (see: Il Giorno della Civetta)

P

4748 P.J. (John Guillermin)
(also: New Face in Hell)
Filmf: v. XI (1968), p. 72; comp., cp. cr.
Films & F: v. 14, n. 7 (Apr., 1968), pp. 27-28; David Austen, 350 wds., cp. cr.

4749 P... RESPECTUEUSE, LA (Marcel Pagliero and Charles Brabant)
Films & F: v. 2, n. 3 (Dec., 1955), p. 19; Peter G. Baker, 100 wds., cp. cr.

4750 PT 109 (Leslie H. Martinson)
F Quarterly: v. XVII, n. 1 (Fall, 1963), p. 56; R. M. Hodgens, 150 wds., no cr.
Filmf: v. VI (1963), p. 145; comp., cp. cr.
Films & F: v. 9, n. 12 (Sept., 1963), pp. 26, 31; Robin Bean, 250 wds., cp. cr.
Films in R: v. XIV, n. 7 (Aug.-Sept., 1963), p. 435; Arthur B. Clark, 225 wds., no cr.

4751 PACIFIC DESTINY (Wolf Rilla)
Films & F: v. 2, n. 10 (July, 1956), p. 22; Peter G. Baker, 250 wds., cp. cr.
Sight & S: v. 26, n. 1 (Summer, 1956), p. 35; Tony Hodgkinson, 300 wds., pt. cr.

4752 PACSIRTA (Laszlo Ranody)
(also: Skylark)
Film: n. 44 (Winter, 1965-1966), p. 25; J.G., 300 wds., no cr.
Interntl F G: v. 2 (1965), p. 92; Peter Graham, 200 wds., pt. cr.

4753 PAD, THE (Brian G. Hutton)
(also: And How to Use It)
Filmf: v. IX (1966), p. 219; comp., cp. cr.

4754 PADDLE TO THE SEA (Bill Mason)
Take One: v. 1, n. 3 (Feb., 1967), p. 26; Mark Blandford, 300 wds., no cr.

PADENIE BERLINA (see: The Fall of Berlin)

PADRE DI FAMIGLIA, IL (see: The Head of the Family)

PADRI E FIGLI (see: The Tailor's Maid)

PAGADOR DE PROMESSAS, O (see: The Given Word)

4755 PAGANS, THE (Ferrucio Cereo and Richard Heinz)
(also: Il Sacco di Roma)
Filmf: v. I (1958), p. 140; comp., cp. cr.

4756 PAINT YOUR WAGON (Joshua Logan)
Films & F: v. 16, n. 6 (Mar., 1970), pp. 46, 51; Gordon Gow, 1100 wds., cp. cr.
Films in R: v. XX, n. 9 (Nov., 1969), pp. 571-572; Eunice Sinkler, 250 wds., no cr.

PAINTED SMILE, THE (see: Murder Can Be Deadly)

4757 PAINTING PEOPLE (Tim Burstall, writer)
Interntl F G: v. 4 (1967), p. 49; 125 wds., pt. cr.

4758 PAIR OF BRIEFS, A (Ralph Thomas)
Filmf: v. VII (1964), p. 54; comp., cp. cr.

4759 PAISA (Roberto Rossellini)
(also: Ordinary People; Paisan)
Sequence: n. 2 (Winter, 1947), pp. 30-31; Lindsay G. Anderson, 800 wds.,
no cr.

PAISAN (see: Paisa)

4760 PAJAMA GAME, THE (George Abbot and Stanley Donen)
Films & F: v. 4, n. 3 (Dec., 1957), pp. 22-23; Peter G. Baker, 350 wds., cp.
cr.
Films in R: v. VIII, n. 8 (Oct., 1957), p. 413; Edward Jablonski, 200 wds.,
no cr.
Sight & S: v. 27, n. 3 (Winter, 1957-1958), pp. 147-148; David Vaughan, 700
wds., pt. cr.

4761 PAL JOEY (George Sidney)
Films & F: v. 4, n. 5 (Feb., 1958), pp. 23-24; Peter John Dyer, 575 wds., cp.
cr.
Films & F: v. 8, n. II (Aug., 1962), p. 35; John Cutts, 125 wds., cp. cr.
Films in R: v. VIII, n. 10 (Dec., 1957), p. 527; Edward Jablonski, 225 wds.,
no cr.

PAL UTCAI FIUK (see: The Boys of Paul Street)

4762 PALACE OF PLEASURE (John Hofsess)
(also: Black Zero; Redpath - 25)
Take One: v. I, n. 5 (June, 1967), pp. 32-33; Tony Rosenfield, 750 wds., pt.
cr.

4763 PALACES OF A QUEEN (Michael Ingrams)
Filmf: v. X (1967), p. 202; comp., cp. cr.
Films & F: v. 13, n. 5 (Feb., 1967), pp. 33-34; Ken Gay, 400 wds., cp. cr.
Films in R: v. XVIII, n. 7 (Aug.-Sept., 1967), p. 446; Constance McLeod,
175 wds., no cr.

4764 PALM SPRINGS WEEKEND (Norman Taurog)
Filmf: v. VI (1963), p. 237; comp., cp. cr.
Films & F: v. 10, n. 5 (Feb., 1964), pp. 29-30; Robin Bean, 650 wds., cp. cr.

4765 PAMELA, PAMELA YOU ARE (William L. Rose)
Filmf: v. XI (1968), p. 460; comp., cp. cr.

PAMPA SALVAJE (see: Savage Pampas)

4766 PAMPOSH (Ezra Mir)
Films & F: v. I, n. 2 (Nov., 1954), p. 21; John Hall, 100 wds., cp. cr.

4767 PAN (Herman van der Horst)
Interntl F G: v. I (1964), p. 110; 50 wds., pt. cr.

PAN WOLODYJOWSKI (see: Colonel Wolodyjowski)

PANE, AMORE, E... (see: Scandal in Sorrento)

4768 PANIC (John Gilling)
Films & F: v. II, n. II (Aug., 1965), p. 32; Richard Davis, 175 wds., cp. cr.

4769 PANIC IN NEEDLE PARK, THE (Jerry Schatzberg)
Filmf: v. XIV (1971), p. 434; comp., cp. cr.
Films in R: v. XXII, n. 7 (Aug.-Sept., 1971), pp. 443-444; Arthur B. Clark,
150 wds., no cr.

4770 PANIC IN THE CITY (Eddie Davis)
Filmf: v. XI (1968), pp. 426, 540; comp., cp. cr.

4771 PANIC IN THE STREETS (Elia Kazan)
      Films in R: v. I, n. 5 (July-Aug., 1950), pp. 17-19; Hermine Rich Isaacs, 700
            wds., pt. cr.
      Sequence: n. 12 (Autumn, 1950), pp. 14-15; L.G.A., 850 wds., no cr.
      Sight & S: v. 19, n. 6 (Aug., 1950), pp. 241-242; Gavin Lambert, 1100 wds.,
            pt. cr.

4772 PANIC IN YEAR ZERO (Ray Milland)
      Filmf: v. V (1962), p. 309; comp., cp. cr.
      Movie: n. II, pp. 28-29; Paul Mayersberg, 1200 wds., no cr.

      PANTALOONS (see: Don Juan)

4773 PAPA, MAMA, THE MAID AND I (J. P. Le Chanois)
      Films & F: v. 2, n. 8 (May, 1956), p. 22; Michael Winner, 150 wds., cp. cr.

4774 PAPA'S DELICATE CONDITION (George Marshall)
      Filmf: v. VI (1963), p. 22; comp., cp. cr.
      Films & F: v. 9, n. 10 (July, 1963), p. 29; Brian O'Brien, 250 wds., cp. cr.

4775 PAPER LION (Alex March)
      Filmf: v. XI (1968), p. 455; comp., cp. cr.

4776 PAPER PEOPLE, THE (David Gardner)
      Interntl F G: v. 7 (1970), p. 81; Gerald Pratley, 100 wds., pt. cr.
      Take One: v. I, n. 8 (1968), p. 27; Joe Medjuck, 300 wds., pt. cr.

4777 PAPER RUN (Malcolm Otten)
      Interntl F G: v. 2 (1965), p. 54; 100 wds., pt. cr.

      PAPRIKA (see: The Iron Flower)

      PAR DNU, O (see: A Matter of Days)

4778 PARADES AND CHANGES II (Charles Ross and Jo Landor)
      F Quarterly: v. XX, n. 2 (Winter, 1966-1967), pp. 53-54; Ernest Callenbach,
            500 wds., pt. cr.

4779 PARADISE, HAWAIIAN STYLE (Michael Moore)
      Filmf: v. IX (1966), p. 178; comp., cp. cr.
      Films & F: v. 12, n. 12 (Sept., 1966), p. 61; David Rider, 300 wds., cp. cr.

      PARADISE LAGOON (see: The Admirable Crichton)

4780 PARADISE LOST (Evelyn Lambart, prod.)
      F Lib Quarterly: v. 4, n. 4 (Fall, 1971), p. 55; Hannah Miller, 150 wds., pt. cr.

      PARADISE TERRESTRE (see: Ritual of Love)

4781 PARANOIA (Adriaan Ditvoorst)
      Interntl F G: v. 5 (1968), p. 115; 200 wds., pt. cr.

4782 PARANOIA (Umberto Lenzi)
      (also: Orgasmo)
      Filmf: v. XII (1969), p. 414; comp., cp. cr.
      Films & F: v. 16, n. 6 (Mar., 1970), p. 44; Richard Davis, 300 wds., cp. cr.

      PARANOIA (Marco Ferreri/see: The Man with the Balloons)

4783 PARANOIAC (Freddie Francis)
      Filmf: v. VI (1963), p. 114; comp., cp. cr.
      Films & F: v. 10, n. 6 (Mar., 1964), pp. 29-30; Gordon Gow, 600 wds., cp.
            cr.

      PARAPLUIES DE CHERBOURG, LES (see: The Umbrellas of Cherbourg)

4784 PARASITES, THE (Andre Pergament)
      Films & F: v. 2, n. 12 (Sept., 1956), p. 26; Peter Baker, 150 wds., cp. cr.

4785 PARATROOP COMMAND (William Witney)
      Filmf: v. II (1959), p. 10; comp., cp. cr.

PARBESZED (see: Dialogue)

PARDON ME, BUT YOUR TEETH ARE IN MY NECK (see: The Fearless Vampire Killers)

PARENT TRAP, THE (David Swift)
Filmf: v. IV (1961-1962), p. 174; comp., cp. cr.

PARIS AU MOIS D'AOUT (see: Paris in the Month of August)

PARIS BELONGS TO US (see: Paris Nous Appartient)

4786 PARIS BLUES (Martin Ritt)
Film: n. 31 (Spring, 1962), pp. 17-18; Douglas McVay, 200 wds., no cr.
F Quarterly: v. XV, n. 3 (Spring, 1962), p. 71; R. M. Hodgens, 25 wds., no cr.
Filmf: v. IV (1961), p. 289; comp., cp. cr.
Films & F: v. 8, n. 3 (Dec., 1961), pp. 31-32; Raymond Durgnat, 400 wds., cp. cr.
Films in R: v. XII, n. 9 (Nov., 1961), p. 558; Justin Hazlitt, 150 wds., no cr.

PARIS BRULE-T-IL? (see: Is Paris Burning)

4787 PARIS DOES STRANGE THINGS (Jean Renoir)
(also: Eléna et les Hommes; The Night Does Strange Things)
Films in R: v. VIII, n. 6 (June-July, 1957), p. 284; Norman Cecil, 100 wds., no cr.

PARIS DOESN'T EXIST (see: Paris N'Existe Pas)

4788 PARIS HOLIDAY (Gerd Oswald)
Filmf: v. I (1958), p. 71; comp., cp. cr.
Films & F: v. 4, n. 7 (Apr., 1958), p. 22; Derek Conrad, 275 wds., cp. cr.
Films in R: v. IX, n. 5 (May, 1958), pp. 269-270; Louise Corbin, 300 wds., no cr.

4789 PARIS HOTEL (Henri Verneuil)
(also: Paris Palace Hotel)
Filmf: v. II (1959), p. 240; comp., cp. cr.

4790 PARIS IN THE MONTH OF AUGUST (Pierre Granier-Deferre)
(also: Paris Au Mois D'Aout)
Filmf: v. XI (1968), p. 342; comp., cp. cr.
Films & F: v. 14, n. 4 (Jan., 1968), pp. 24-25; Peter Davalle, 300 wds., cp. cr.

4791 PARIS IN THE RAW (Claude Lelouch)
Films & F: v. 12, n, 8 (May, 1966), pp. 56-57; Raymond Durgnat, 500 wds., cp. cr.

4792 PARIS N'EXISTENT PAS (Robert Benayoun)
(also: Paris Doesn't Exist)
Film: n. 57 (Winter, 1970), pp. 26-27; Peter Gargin, 100 wds., pt. cr.
F Quarterly: v. XXIII, n. 2 (Winter, 1969-1970), p. 63; Lawrence Loewinger, 350 wds., no cr.

4793 PARIS 1900 (Pierre Braunberger)
Films in R: v. I, n. 7 (Oct., 1950), pp. 22-24; Arthur Knight, 700 wds., pt. cr.

4794 PARIS NOUS APPARTIENT (Jacques Rivette)
(also: Paris Belongs To Us)
Film: n. 33 (Autumn, 1962), pp. 18, 20; Philip Strick, 300 wds., no cr.
F Culture: n. 25 (Summer, 1962), pp. 23-24; Parker Tyler, 1200 wds., no cr.
Filmf: v. V (1962), p. 305; comp., cp. cr.
Movie: n. 2 (Sept., 1962), p. 34; Paul Mayersberg, 1000 wds., pt. cr.
Sight & S: v. 28, n. 1 (Winter, 1958-1959), p. 33; Louis Marcorelles, 1200 wds., pt. cr.
Sight & S: v. 31, n. 1 (Winter, 1961-1962), pp. 38-39; Robert Vas, 1200 wds., pt. cr.

PARIS PALACE HOTEL (see: Paris Hotel)

4795 PARIS PICK-UP (Marcel Bluwal)
       (also: Le Monte-Charge)
       Filmf: v. VI (1963), p. 326; comp., cp. cr.

PARIS UNDERWORLD (see: Grisbi)

4796 PARIS VU PAR (Jean-Daniel Pollet, Jean Rouch, Jean Douchet,
       Jean-Luc Godard, Eric Rohmer, Claude Chabrol)
       (also: Les Quartiers des Paris; Six in Paris)
       Filmf: v. XII (1969), p. 119; comp., cp. cr.
       Filmf & F: v. 12, n. 8 (May, 1966), pp. 53-54; Peter Whitehead, 1300 wds.,
            cp. cr.
       Movie: n. 14 (Autumn, 1965), pp. 39-40; Mark Shivas, 1400 wds., no cr.
       Sight & S: v. 35, n. 2 (Spring, 1966), pp. 91-92; Michael Kustow, 1000 wds.,
            no cr.

4797 PARIS WHEN IT SIZZLES (Richard Quine)
       F Quarterly: v. XVII, n. 4 (Summer, 1964), p. 59; R. M. Hodgens, 75 wds.,
            no cr.
       Filmf: v. VII (1964), p. 45; comp., cp. cr.
       Films in R. V. XV, n. 5 (May, 1964), p. 305; 150 wds., no cr.

4798 PARISIENNE, LA (Michel Boisrond)
       Filmf: v. I (1958), p. 147; comp., cp. cr.
       Films in R: v. IX, n. 8 (Oct., 1958), p. 458; Ellen Fitzpatrick, 125 wds., no
            cr.

4799 PARRISH (Delmer Daves)
       Film: n. 29 (Summer, 1961), p. 11; Mark Shivas, 100 wds., no cr.
       F Quarterly: v. XV, n. 1 (Fall, 1961), p. 56; R. M. Hodgens, 50 wds., no cr.
       Filmf: v. IV (1961), p. 95; comp., cp. cr.
       Films & F: v. 7, n. 12 (Sept., 1961), p. 30; Robin Bean, 300 wds., cp. cr.
       Films in R: v. XII, n. 6 (June-July, 1961), pp. 355-356; Robert C. Roman,
            225 wds., no cr.

4800 PARTIE DE CAMPAGNE, UNE (Jean Renoir)
       F Journal: n. 23 (July, 1964), p. 38; R. G. Howard, 800 wds., no cr.

PARTINGS (see: Lydia Ate the Apple)

4801 PARTNER (Bernardo Bertolucci)
       Films & F: v. 17, n. 4 (Jan., 1971), p. 53; Gordon Gow, 550 wds., cp. cr.
       Interntl F G: v. 7 (1970), p. 148; Lino Micciche, 200 wds., pt. cr.
       Sight & S: v. 38, n. 1 (Winter, 1968-1969), p. 34; Geoffrey Nowell Smith,
            500 wds., no cr.

4802 PARTY, THE (Blake Edwards)
       Filmf: v. XI (1968), p. 116; comp., cp. cr.
       Films & F: v. 15, n. 9 (June, 1969), pp. 44-45; Richard Davis, 850 wds., cp.
            cr.
       Movie: n. 17 (Winter, 1969-1970), pp. 34-35; Charles Barr, 1100 wds., no cr.

PARTY, THE (Paul Verhoven/see: Het Feest)

PARTY AND GUESTS, THE (see: A Report on the Party and Guests)

4803 PARTY CRASHERS, THE (Bernard Girard)
       Filmf: v. I (1958), p. 240; comp., cp. cr.

4804 PARTY GIRL (Nicholas Ray)
       Filmf: v. I (1958), p. 212; comp., cp. cr.
       Films & F: v. 5, n. 6 (Mar., 1959), p. 23; Ken Gay, 200 wds., cp. cr.

PARTY IS OVER, THE (Torre Nilsson/see: Fin de Fiesta)

4805 PARTY'S OVER, THE (Guy Hamilton)
       Filmf: v. X (1967), p. 322; comp., cp. cr.
       Films & F: v. 11, n. 9 (June, 1965), pp. 30-31; Allen Eyles, 750 wds., cp. cr.

4806 PAS DE DEUX (Norman McLaren)
        F Lib Quarterly: v. 3, n. I (Winter, 1969-1970), pp. 38-39; Philip C. Levering,
            350 wds., pt. cr.
        Take One: v. I, n. 10 (1968), p. 28; Ronald Blumer, 250 wds., pt. cr.

      PAS QUESTION LE SAMEDI (see: Impossible on Saturday)

      PASAZERKA (see: The Passenger)

      PASS, THE (see: The Story of a Three Day Pass)

4807 PASSAGE DU RHIN, LE (Andre Cayatte)
        (also: The Crossing of the Rhine)
        Films & F: v. 7, n. 10 (July, 1961), p. 29; Raymond Durgnat, 550 wds., cp.
            cr.

4808 PASSAGE HOME (Roy Baker)
        Films & F: v. I, n. 9 (June, 1955), p. 20; Derek Hill, 175 wds., cp. cr.

4809 PASSAGE OF LOVE (Desmond Davis)
        Films & F: v. II, n. 12 (Sept., 1965), pp. 43-46; Robin Bean, 2400 wds., no
            cr.

      PASSAGER DE LA PLUIE, LE (see: Rider on the Rain)

      PASSAGES FROM JAMES JOYCE'S FINNEGANS WAKE (see: Finnegans
          Wake)

4810 PASSENGER, THE (Andrzej Munk and Witold Lesiewicz)
        (also: Pasazerka)
        F Quarterly: v. XVIII, n. I (Fall, 1964), pp. 42-46; James Price, 2400 wds.,
            pt. cr.
        Films & F: v. 10, n. II (Aug., 1964), p. 22; Peter Cowie, 400 wds., cp. cr.
        Interntl F G: v. 2 (1965), pp. 125-126; 300 wds., pt. cr.

4811 PASSION (Yasuzo Masumura)
        Films & F: v. 13, n. 9 (June, 1967), pp. 22-23; Richard Davis, 350 wds., cp.
            cr.

      PASSION, A (see: The Passion of Anna)

      PASSION, EN (see: The Passion of Anna)

      PASSION DE JEANNE D'ARC, LA (see: The Passion of Joan of Arc)

4812 PASSION OF ANNA, THE (Ingmar Bergman)
        (also: L 182; A Passion; En Passion)
        Cinema: v. 6, n. 2 (Fall, 1970), pp. 32-39; Peter Harcourt, 5600 wds., no cr.
        Film: n. 57 (Winter, 1970), p. 18; Arne Svensson, 500 wds., no cr.
        Films & F: v. 17, n. I (Oct., 1970), pp. 41-42; Gordon Gow, 800 wds., cp. cr.
        Films in R: v. XXI, n. 7 (Aug.- Sept., 1970), pp. 443; Helen Weldon Kuhn,
            225 wds., no cr.
        Interntl F G: v. 8 (1971), p. 247; Peter Cowie, 350 wds., pt. cr.
        Sight & S: v. 39, n. 4 (Autumn, 1970), pp. 216-217; Philip Strick, 1000 wds.,
            pt. cr.

4813 PASSION OF JOAN OF ARC, THE (Carl Dreyer)
        (also: La Passion de Jeanne D'Arc)
        F Journal: n. 2 (1956), p. 3; Garth Buckner, 450 wds., no cr.
        Films & F: v. 7, n. 9 (June, 1961), pp. II-13, 40-41; Alan Stanbrook, 4500
            wds., cp. cr.
        Films in R: v. III, n. I (Jan. 1952), p. 42; Frank Ward, 175 wds., no cr.
        Sight & S: v. 19, n. 8 (Dec., 1950), p. 337; Roger Manvell, 1700 wds., cp. cr.

4814 PASSION OF SLOW FIRE, THE (Edward Molinaro)
        Filmf: v. V (1962), p. 320; comp., cp. cr.

4815 PASSIONATE DEMONS, THE (Nils Reinhardt Christensen)
        (also: Line)
        Filmf: v. VI (1963), p. 315; comp., cp. cr.

4816 PASSIONATE STRANGER, THE (Peter Rogers)
    (also: A Novel Affair)
    Films & F: v. 3, n. 7 (Apr., 1957), p. 27; Peter G. Baker, 325 wds., cp. cr.
    Films in R: v. VIII, n. 9 (Nov., 1957), p. 464; William K. Everson, 250 wds.,
        no cr.

4817 PASSIONATE SUMMER (Charles Brabant)
    (also: Les Possedes; The Possessed)
    F Culture: v. 3, n. 3 (1957), p. 16; John Gilchrist, 150 wds., pt. cr.
    Films & F: v. 5, n. 10 (July, 1959), p. 25; Brenda Davies, 225 wds., cp. cr.
    Films in R: v. VIII, n. 9 (Nov., 1957), p. 466; R. V. Tozzi, 250 wds., no cr.

4818 PASSIONATE SUMMER (Rudolph Cartier)
    Films & F: v. 5, n. 2 (Nov., 1958), p. 24; Peter John Dyer, 400 wds., cp. cr.

4819 PASSPORT TO CHINA (Michael Carreras)
    Filmf: v. IV (1961), p. 50; comp., cp. cr.

4820 PASSPORT TO PIMLICO (Henry Cornelius)
    Sight & S: v. 18, n. 70 (Summer, 1949), p. 90; Arthur Vesselo, 150 wds., no
        cr.

    PASSPORT TO SHAME (see: Room 43)

4821 PASSWORD IS COURAGE, THE (Andrew L. Stone)
    Filmf: v. V (1962), p. 321; comp., cp. cr.
    Films & F: v. 9, n. 3 (Dec., 1962), p. 46-47; Michael Ratcliffe, 400 wds., cp.
        cr.
    Movie: n. 4 (Nov., 1962), p. 30; Mark Shivas, 600 wds., pt. cr.

4822 PAT AND MIKE (George Cukor)
    Films in R: v. III, n. 6 (June-July, 1952), p. 292; 80 wds., pt. cr.
    Sight & S: v. 22, n. 1 (July-Sept., 1952), p. 29; Penelope Houston, 250 wds.,
        pt. cr.

4823 PATCH OF BLUE, A (Guy Green)
    Cinema: v. 3, n. 2 (Mar., 1966), p. 45; Rory Guy, 650 wds., pt. cr.
    F Quarterly: v. XIX, n. 4 (Summer, 1966), p. 68; Ernest Callenbach, 100
        wds., no cr.
    Films & F: v. 12, n. 12 (Sept., 1966), pp. 60-61; Richard Davis, 700 wds., cp.
        cr.
    Films in R: v. XVII, n. 1 (Jan., 1966), pp. 49-50; Elaine Rothschild, 350
        wds., no cr.

4824 PATHER PANCHALI (Satyajit Ray)
    (also: Song of the Road)
    Film: n. 24 (Mar.-Apr., 1960), pp. 20-24; Douglas McVay, 1200 wds., no cr.
    F Culture: n. 19, pp. 44-50; Arlene Croce, 2500 wds., no cr.
    Filmf: v. I (1958), p. 203; comp., cp. cr.
    Films & F: v. 4, n. 5 (Feb., 1958), p. 23; Peter John Dyer, 875 wds., cp. cr.
    Films in R: v. IX, n. 2 (Feb., 1958), pp. 86-87; Henry Hart, 450 wds., no cr.

4825 PATHS OF GLORY (Stanley Kubrick)
    F Culture: v. IV, n. 2 (Feb., 1958), p. 15; Jonathan Baumbach, 600 wds., cp.
        cr.
    Films & F: v. 4, n. 5 (Feb., 1958), p. 26; Peter G. Baker, 400 wds., cp. cr.
    Films in R: v. IX, n. 1 (Jan., 1958), pp. 30-31; Louise Bruce, 300 wds., no cr.
    Sight & S: v. 27, n. 3 (Winter, 1957-1958), pp. 144-145; Gavin Lambert, 1000
        wds., pt. cr.

    PATROUILLE ANDERSON, LA (see: The Anderson Platoon)

4826 PATSY, THE (Jerry Lewis)
    Filmf: v. VII (1964), p. 222; comp., cp. cr.
    Films & F: v. 11, n. 5 (Feb., 1965), p. 31; Gordon Gow, 725 wds., cp. cr.
    Movie: n. 13 (Summer, 1965), p. 39; Richard H. Bedford, 600 wds., no cr.

    PATTERNS (see: Patterns of Power)

4827 PATTERNS OF POWER (Fielder Cook)
      (also: Patterns)
      Films & F: v. 2, n. 10 (July, 1956), p. 24, Michael Winner, 350 wds., cp. cr.
      Films & F: v. 15, n. 7 (Apr., 1969), p. 86; Kingsley Canham, 400 wds., no cr.
      Films in R: v. VII, n. 4 (Apr., 1956), p. 176; Hobart M. Farquhar, 200 wds.,
          no cr.
      Sight & S: v. 26, n. 1 (Summer, 1956), p. 33; John Cutts, 600 wds., pt. cr.

4828 PATTON (Franklin J. Schaffner)
      (also: Lust for Glory)
      F Heritage: v. 5, n. 4 (Summer, 1970), pp. 21-27; Robert Steele, 1300 wds.,
          no cr.
      F Quarterly: v. XXIII, n. 4 (Summer, 1970), p. 61; Bernard Weiner, 250
          wds., no cr.
      F Soc Rev: v. 5, n. 7, pp. 25-32; Michael Sragow, 3500 wds., cp. cr.
      Films & F: v. 16, n. 10 (July, 1970), pp. 35-36; Gordon Gow, 750 wds., cp.
          cr.
      Films in R: v. XXI, n. 2 (Feb., 1970), pp. 116-117; Henry Hart, 350 wds., no
          cr.
      Focus on F: n. 3 (May-Aug., 1970), pp. 12-15; Gerald Pratley and Allen
          Eyles, 1900 wds., cp. cr.
      Interntl F G: v. 9 (1972), pp. 265-266; Susan Rice, 250 wds., pt. cr.
      Sight & S: v. 39, n. 3 (Summer, 1970), pp. 160-161; David Wilson, 750 wds.,
          pt. cr.

      PATY JEZDEC JE STRACH, A (see: The Fifth Horseman Is Fear)

4829 PAUL (Diurka Medveczky)
      Take One: v. 2, n. 4 (1969), pp. 21-22; Joseph Kostolefsky, 350 wds., pt. cr.

4830 PAUL TAYLOR AND HIS COMPANY (Ted Steeg)
      F Lib Quarterly: v. 2, n. 1 (Winter, 1968-1969), p. 49; Naomi Weiss, 500
          wds., pt. cr.

4831 PAW (Astrid and Bjarne Henning-Jensen)
      F Journal: n. 18 (Oct., 1961), p. 20; Brian J. Davies, 100 wds., no cr.

4832 PAWNBROKER, THE (Sidney Lumet)
      F Heritage: v. 1, n. 3 (Sept., 1966), pp. 3-11; Alan Casty, 300 wds., pt. cr.
      Filmf: v. VIII (1965), p. 111; comp., cp. cr.
      Films & F: v. 11, n. 1 (Oct., 1964), pp. 17-20; Sidney Lumet, 1800 wds., no cr.
      Films & F: v. 13, n. 3 (Dec., 1966), p. 6; Peter G. Baker, 950 wds., cp. cr.
      Films in R: v. XVI, n. 5 (May, 1965), pp. 314-315; Henry Hart, 325 wds., no
          cr.

4833 PAY OR DIE (Richard Wilson)
      Filmf: v. III (1960), p. 137; comp., cp. cr.
      Films & F: v. 7, n. 3 (Dec., 1960), p. 32; Richard Whitehall, 450 wds., cp.
          cr.
      Films in R: v. XI, n. 8 (Oct., 1960), p. 494; 125 wds., no cr.

      PAY THE DEVIL (see: Man in the Shadow)

4834 PAYMENT IN BLOOD (E. G. Rowland)
      (also: Sette Winchester Per Un Massacro; Seven Winchesters for a Massacre)
      Filmf: v. XI (1968), p. 482; comp., cp. cr.

4835 PAYROLL (Sidney Hayers)
      Filmf: v. V (1962), p. 304; comp., cp. cr.
      Films & F: v. 7, n. 8 (May, 1961), pp. 27-28; Richard Whitehall, 150 wds., cp.
          cr.

      PEACE GAME, THE (see: The Gladiators)

4836 PEACE KILLERS, THE (Douglas Schwartz)
      Filmf: v. XIV (1971), p. 406; comp., cp. cr.

4837 PEACE TO HIM WHO ENTERS (A. Alov and V. Naumov)
      F Soc Rev: Dec. (1966), p. 24; Edwin Jahiel, 350 wds., pt. cr.

4838 PEACH THIEF, THE (Veulo Radev)
      (also: Kradezat Na Praskovi)
      Filmf: v. XII (1969), p. 461; comp., cp. cr.
      Films & F: v. 12, n. 4 (Jan., 1966), pp. 26-27; Peter Cowie, 350 wds., cp. cr.
      Sight & S: v. 35, n. I (Winter, 1965-1966), p. 43; Brenda Davies, 500 wds.,
            pt. cr.

4839 PEARLS OF THE DEEP (Jiri Menzel, Jan Nĕmec, Ewald Schorm, Vera
            Chytilova, Jaromil Jires)
      (also: Perlicky Na Dne)
      Films & F: v. 15, n. 3 (Dec., 1968), pp. 44-45; Gordon Gow, 1000 wds., cp.
            cr.

      PEAU DO BANANE (see: Banana Peel)

4840 PEAU DOUCE, LA (Francois Truffaut)
      (also: Silken Skin; The Soft Skin)
      F Comment: v. 3, n. 3 (Summer, 1965), p. 31; Frederick Wellington, 450
            wds., pt. cr.
      Filmf: v. VII (1964), p. 245; comp., cp. cr.
      Films & F: v. II, n. 4 (Jan., 1965), p. 32; Gordon Gow, 650 wds., cp. cr.
      Interntl F G: v. 2 (1965), p. 72; Peter Graham, 200 wds., pt. cr.
      Sight & S: v. 33, n. 4 (Autumn, 1964), p. 194; Gilles Jacob, 800 wds., pt. cr.

      PECCATO DI ANNA, IL (see: Anna's Sin)

      PECHE DE JEUNESSE (see: Sins of Youth)

4841 PEEPING TOM (Michael Powell)
      F Soc Rev: Jan. (1966), p. 13; P.C., 200 wds., pt. cr.
      Filmf: v. V (1962), p. 339; comp., cp. cr.
      Films & F: v. 6, n. 8 (May, 1960), p. 26; Peter G. Baker, 400 wds., cp. cr.

      PEKING MEDALLION, THE (see: The Corrupt Ones)

      PELO NEL MONDO, IL (see: Go! Go! Go! World!)

4842 PENDULUM (George Schaefer)
      Filmf: v. XII (1969), p. 141; comp., cp. cr.
      Films & F: v. 15, n. 9 (June, 1969), p. 50; David Rider, 450 wds., cp. cr.
      Films in R: v. XX, n. 4 (Apr., 1969), pp. 252-253; Flavia Wharton, 250
            wds., no cr.

4843 PENELOPE (Arthur Hiller)
      Filmf: v. IX (1966), p. 305; comp., cp. cr.

4844 PENNY BRIGHT AND JIMMY WITHERSPOON (Robert Nelson)
      F Culture: n. 48-49 (Winter-Spring, 1970), p. 27; Robert Nelson, 350 wds.,
            pt. cr.

4845 PENNY FOR YOUR THOUGHTS, OR, BIRDS, DOLLS AND SCRATCHES
            — ENGLISH STYLE, A (Donovan Winter)
      Films & F: v. 13, n. 4 (Jan., 1967), p. 32; Raymond Durgnat, 900 wds., cp.
            cr.

4846 PENTHOUSE, THE (Peter Collinson)
      Filmf: v. X (1967), p. 286; comp., cp. cr.
      Films & F: v. 14, n. 2 (Nov., 1967), p. 25; 375 wds., cp. cr.

      PENTHOUSE (George Lautner/see: Crooks in Clover)

4847 PEOPLE ARISE, THE (Newsreel)
      (also: El Pueblo Se Levanta)
      Cineaste: v. IV, n. 4 (Spring, 1971), pp. 24-26; Ruth McCormick, 1500 wds.,
            pt. cr.

4848 PEOPLE IN THE CITY (Arne Sucksdorff)
      (also: Manniskor i Stad)
      Sequence: n. 3 (Spring, 1948), pp. 27-28; Peter Ericsson, 450 wds., no cr.

4849 PEOPLE MEET AND SWEET MUSIC FILLS THE HEART (Henning Carlsen)
      (also: Mennesker Modes Og Sod Musik Opstaar I Hjertet)
      Filmf: v. XII (1969), p. 253; comp., cp. cr.

4850 PEOPLE ON THE ROAD (Kazimierz Karabasz)
      (also: Ludzie na Drodzie)
      F Quarterly: v. XV, n. 9 (Fall, 1961), pp. 51-54; Roger Sandall, 1250 wds., no
      cr.

4851 PEOPLE WILL TALK (Joseph L. Mankiewicz)
      Films in R: v. II, n. 8 (Oct., 1951), pp. 46-48; Henry Hart, 800 wds., pt. cr.
      Sight & S: v. 21, n. 2 (Oct.-Dec., 1951), p. 81; Penelope Houston, 800 wds.,
      pt. cr.

      PEP QUALCHE DOLLARO IN PIU (see: For A Few Dollars More)

4852 PEPE (George Sidney)
      Filmf: v. III (1960), p. 337; comp., cp. cr.
      Films & F: v. 7, n. 7 (Apr., 1961), p. 29; John Cutts, 325 wds., cp. cr.
      Films in R: v. XII, n. 2 (Feb., 1961), pp. 108-109; Ellen Fitzpatrick, 400 wds.,
      no cr.

4853 PEPOTE (Ladislao Vajda)
      Filmf: v. I (1958), p. 267; comp., cp. cr.
      Films & F: v. 3, n. 9 (June, 1957), pp. 24-25; Peter John Dyer, 350 wds., cp.
      cr.

      PER UN PUGNO DI DOLLARI (see: A Fistful of Dollars)

4854 PERCE ON THE ROCKS (National Film Board of Canada)
      F Lib Quarterly: v. I, n. 2 (Spring, 1968), p. 38; William Speed, 200 wds., pt.
      cr.

4855 PERCY (Ralph Thomas)
      Filmf: v. XIV (1971), p. 201; comp., cp. cr.
      Films & F: v. 17, n. 9 (June, 1971), pp. 78, 80; Eric Braun, 650 wds., cp. cr.

4856 PERFECT FRIDAY (Peter Hall)
      Films & F: v. 17, n. 5 (Feb., 1971), p. 49; Gordon Gow, 550 wds., cp. cr.
      Films in R: v. XXII, n. I (Jan., 1971), pp. 43-44; Eunice Sinkler, 100 wds., no
      cr.

4857 PERFECT FURLOUGH, THE (Blake Edwards)
      (also: Strictly for Pleasure)
      Filmf: v. II (1959), p. 9; comp., cp. cr.

4858 PERFORMANCE (Nicolas Roeg and Donald Cammell)
      Cinema: v. 6, n. 2 (Fall, 1970), pp. 16-20; Stephen Farber, 3000 wds., no cr.
      F Heritage: v. 6, n. 3 (Spring, 1971), pp. 1-6; Foster Hirsch, 2000 wds., pt. cr.
      Films & F: v. 17, n. 7 (Apr., 1971), pp. 48-49; Gordon Gow, 1000 wds., cp.
      cr.
      Interntl F G: v. 9 (1972), p. 103; Gordon Gow, 200 wds., pt. cr.
      Sight & S: v. 40, n. 2 (Spring, 1971), pp. 67-69; Philip French, 2000 wds., pt.
      cr.

4859 PERILS OF PAULINE, THE (Herbert B. Leonard and Joshua Shelley)
      Filmf: v. X (1967), p. 226; comp., cp. cr.

4860 PERIOD OF ADJUSTMENT (George Roy Hill)
      Filmf: v. V (1962), p. 280; comp., cp. cr.
      Films & F: v. 9, n. 6 (Mar., 1963), p. 38; Richard Whitehall, 500 wds., cp.
      cr.
      Films in R: v. XIII, n. 10 (Dec., 1962), p. 627; Adelaide Comerford, 125
      wds., no cr.
      Sight & S: v. 32, n. 2 (Spring, 1963), p. 93; Brenda Davies, 700 wds., pt. cr.

      PERLICKY NA DNE (see: Pearls of the Deep)

      PERMISSION, LA (see: The Story of a Three Day Pass)

4861 PERRI (N. Paul Kenworth, Jr. and Ralph Wright)
        Films & F: v. 4, n. 4 (Jan., 1958), pp. 24-25; Ropert Butler, 375 wds., cp.
        cr.

        PERSECUCION HASTA VALENCIA (see: The Narco Men)

        PERSECUTION AND ASSASSINATION OF JEAN—PAUL MARAT AS
             PERFORMED BY THE INMATES OF THE ASYLUM OF
             CHARENTON UNDER THE DIRECTION OF THE MARQUIS
             DE SADE, THE (see: Marat/Sade)

4862 PERSONA (Ingmar Bergman)
        Cahiers in Eng: n. II (Sept., 1967), pp. 30-33; Jean Louis Comolli, 800 wds.,
             pt. cr.
        F Comment: v. IV, n. 2 & 3 (Fall-Winter, 1967), pp. 63-65; Erwin Leiser,
             1000 wds., no cr.
        F Culture; n. 48-49 (Winter-Spring, 1970), pp. 56-60; Kirk Bond, 2600 wds.,
             no cr.
        F Heritage: v. 2, n. 3 (Spring, 1967), pp. 28-32; F. A. Macklin, 1500 wds., no
             cr.
        F Quarterly: v. XX, n. 4 (Summer, 1967), pp. 52-54; Richard Corliss, 1200
             wds., pt. cr.
        Filmf: v. X (1967), p. 59; comp., cp. cr.
        Films & F: v. 14, n. 3 (Dec., 1967), p. 20; Raymond Durgnat, 1100 wds., cp.
             cr.
        Films in R: v. XVIII, n. 4 (Apr., 1967), pp. 244-246; Henry Hart, 800 wds.,
             no cr.
        Interntl F G: v. 5 (1968), pp. 137-138; 275 wds., pt. cr.
        Movie: n. 15 (Spring, 1968), pp. 22-24; Robin Wood, 2000 wds., no cr.
        Sight & S: v. 36, n. 4 (Autumn, 1967), pp. 186-191; Susan Sontag, 5000 wds.,
             pt. cr.
        Take One: v. I, n. 8 (1968), pp. 24-26; Michael Harris, 900 wds., pt. cr.

4863 PERSONAL AFFAIR (Anthony Pelissier)
        Films in R: v. V, n. 4 (Apr., 1954), pp. 194-195; 175 wds., no cr.

        PERSONNES GRANDES, LES (see: Time Out for Love)

4864 PERSONS IN HIDING (Louis King)
        Focus on F: n. 5 (Winter/Nov.-Dec., 1970), p. 34; Don Miller, 300 wds., pt.
             cr.

        PERSONS UNKNOWN (see: I Soliti Ignoti)

        PERVY DEN MIRA (see: The Day the War Ended)

4865 PETE KELLY'S BLUES (Jack Webb)
        Films & F: v. 2, n. 2 (Nov., 1955), p. 16; P. L. Mannock, 250 wds., cp. cr.
        Films in R: v. VI, n. 8 (Oct., 1955), pp. 410-411; Edward Jablonski, 450 wds.,
             pt. cr.

        PETER AND PAULA (see: Black Peter)

        PETER GUNN (see: Gunn)

4866 PETER PAN (Walt Disney)
        Films in R: v. IV, n. 2 (Feb., 1953), pp. 94-95; Elspeth Chapin, 750 wds., no
             cr.

4867 PETER RABBIT AND TALES OF BEATRIX POTTER (Reginald Mills)
        (also: Tales of Beatrix Potter)
        Filmf: v. XIV (1971), p. 308; comp., cp. cr.
        Films & F: v. 17, n. 9 (June 1971), p. 80; Margaret Tarratt, 300 wds., cp. cr.
        Films in R: v. XXII, n. 7 (Aug.-Sept., 1971), p. 439; Tatiana Balkoff
             Drowne, 225 wds., no cr.
        Sight & S: v. 40, n. 3 (Summer, 1971), pp. 167-168; James Monahan, 1000
             wds., pt. cr.

4868 PETIT À PETIT (Jean Rouch)
        Movie: n. 18 (Winter, 1970-1971), p. 39; Ian Cameron, 450 wds., no cr.

PETIT MONDE DE DON CAMILLO, LE (see: The Little World of Don Camillo)

4869 PETIT SOLDAT, LE (Jean-Luc Godard)
(also: The Little Soldier)
F Soc Rev: May (1968), pp. 19-22; Patrick McFadden, 1700 wds., cp. cr.
Filmf: v. X (1967), p. 164; comp., cp. cr.
Films & F: v. 9, n. II (Aug., 1963), pp. 23-24; Raymond Durgnat, 600 wds., cp. cr.
Movie: n. II, pp. 18-19; Barry Boys, 1500 wds., no cr.
Sight & S: v. 32, n. 4 (Autumn, 1963), pp. 195-196; Peter John Dyer, 1200 wds., pt. cr.

PETITS MARTINS, LES (see: Girl on the Road)

4870 PETULIA (Richard Lester)
F Quarterly: v. XXII, n. I (Fall, 1968), pp. 67-70; Stephen Farber, 2300 wds., pt. cr.
Filmf: v. XI (1968), p. 159; comp., cp. cr.
Films & F: v. 14, n. 12 (Sept., 1968), pp. 33-34; David Austen, 800 wds., cp. cr.
Films in R: v. XIX, n. 6 (June-July, 1968), pp. 380-381; Rachel Weisbrod, 150 wds., no cr.
Sight & S: v. 37, n. 3 (Summer, 1968), pp. 154-155; James Price, 700 wds., pt. cr.

4871 PEYTON PLACE (Mark Robson)
Filmf & F: v. 4, n. 7 (Apr., 1958), p. 22; Peter G. Baker, 700 wds., cp. cr.
Films & F: v. 12, n. 5 (Feb., 1966), p. 52; Robin Bean, 500 wds., cp. cr.
Films in R: v. IX, n. I (Jan., 1958), pp. 26-28; Elspeth Hart, 400 wds., no cr.

PEZZO, CAPOPEZZO E CAPITANO (see: Always Victorious)

4872 PHAEDRA (Jules Dassin)
Filmf: v. V (1962), p. 288; comp., cp. cr.
Films & F: v. 9, n. 4 (Jan., 1963), pp. 46-47; Robin Bean, 1000 wds., cp. cr.
Films in R: v. XIII, n. 9 (Nov., 1962), pp. 559-560; Flavia Wharton, 225 wds., no cr.
Sight & S: v. 32, n. 2 (Spring, 1963), p. 95; Peter John Dyer, 400 wds., pt. cr.

4873 PHANTOM LOVERS (Antonio Pietrangeli)
(also: Fantasmi A Roma)
Films & F: v. II, n. I (Oct., 1964), pp. 32-33; Allen Eyles, 400 wds., cp. cr.

4874 PHANTOM OF SOHO, THE (Franz Josef Gottlieb)
(also: Das Phantom von Soho)
Filmf: v. X (1967), p. 341; comp., cp. cr.

4875 PHANTOM OF THE OPERA, THE (Terence Fisher)
Filmf: v. V (1962), p. 191; comp., cp. cr.
Films & F: v. 8, n. II (Aug., 1962), p. 31; John Cutts, 225 wds., cp. cr.
Films in R: v. XIII, n. 8 (Oct., 1962), pp. 505-508; Rudy Behlmer, 1500 wds., no cr.

4876 PHANTOM PLANET, THE (William Marshall)
Filmf: v. V (1962), p. 369; comp., cp. cr.
Films & F: v. 9, n. 4 (Jan., 1963), p. 54; Tony Mallerman, 300 wds., cp. cr.

4877 PHANTOM TOLLBOOTH, THE (Chuck Jones and Abe Levitow)
Filmf: v. XIV (1971), p. 253; comp., cp. cr.

PHANTOM VON SOHO, DAS (see: The Phantom of Soho)

4878 PHARAOH (Jerzy Kawalerowicz)
F Quarterly: v. XX, n. 3 (Spring, 1967), pp. 33-37; Albert Johnson, 1700 wds., pt. cr.
Films & F: v. 16, n. I (Oct., 1969), pp. 56-57; Michael Armstrong, 400 wds., cp. cr.

4879 PHARAOH'S WOMAN, THE (Giorgio Rivalta)
      Filmf: v. IV (1961), p. 116; comp., cp. cr.

4880 PHENIX CITY STORY, THE (Phil Karlson)
      F Culture: v. I, n. 5-6 (Winter, 1955), p. 34; George N. Fenin, 450 wds., pt.
        cr.
      Films in R: v. VI, n. 8 (Oct., 1955), pp. 413-414; 250 wds., pt. cr.

4881 PHENOMENA (Jordan Belson)
      F Culture: n. 48-49 (Winter-Spring, 1970), pp. 16-17; Gene Youngblood, 800
        wds., no cr.
      F Quarterly: v. XXI, n. 3 (Spring, 1968), pp. 48-49; Ernest Callenbach, 700
        wds., no cr.

4882 PHFFFT (Mark Robson)
      Films & F: v. I, n. 4 (Jan., 1955), p. 20; Jill Hardy, 150 wds., cp. cr.

4883 PHILADELPHIA STORY, THE (George Cukor)
      Films & F: v. 8, n. 10 (July, 1962), pp. 24-25; John Cutts, 5000 wds., cp. cr.

PHILADELPHIANS, THE (see: The Young Philadelphians)

PHILOSOPHIE DANS LE BOUDOIR, LA (see: Beyond Love and Evil)

PHILOSOPHY OF THE BEDROOM (see: Beyond Love and Evil)

4884 PHOBE (George Kaczender)
      Interntl F G: v. 3 (1966), p. 55; 100 wds., pt. cr.

4885 PHONY AMERICAN, THE (Akos von Rathony)
      (also: It's a Great Life; Toller Hecht auf Krummer Tour)
      Filmf: v. VII (1964), p. 328; comp., cp. cr.
      Films & F: v. 8, n. 10 (July, 1962), p. 36; Robin Bean, 250 wds., cp. cr.

4886 PHYLLIS AND TERRY (Eugene and Carol Marner)
      F Quarterly: v. XXI, n. 2 (Winter, 1967-1968), pp. 52-55; Ernest Callenbach,
        1600 wds., pt. cr.

PIANETA DEGLI UOMINI, IL (see: Battle of the Worlds)

PIANOS MECANICOS, LOS (wee: The Uninhibited)

PIATKA Z ULICY BARSKIEJ (see: Five Boys from Barska Street)

4887 PICASSO (Luciano Emmer)
      Films & F: v. I, n. 4 (Jan., 1955), p. 21; Jill Hardy, 200 wds., cp. cr.
      Sight & S: v. 25, n. I (Summer, 1955), p. 34; Basil Taylor, 575 wds., pt. cr.

4888 PICASSO MYSTERY, THE (Henri-Georges Clouzot)
      (also: Le Mystère Picasso)
      Films & F: v. 4, n. 6 (Mar., 1968), pp. 24-25; Gordon Gow, 475 wds., cp. cr.

4889 PICCADILLY THIRD STOP (Wolf Rilla)
      Films & F: v. 7, n. I (Oct., 1960), p. 28; Richard Whitehall, 200 wds., cp. cr.

4890 PICKPOCKET (Robert Bresson)
      Filmf: v. XII (1969), p. 18; comp., cp. cr.
      Films & F: v. 7, n. I (Oct., 1960), p. 25; Raymond Durgnat, 800 wds., cp. cr.
      Films in R: v. XIV, n. 6 (June-July, 1963), pp. 366-367; Henry Hart, 400
        wds., no cr.
      Sight & F: v. 29, n. 4 (Autumn, 1960), pp. 193-194; Eric Rhoda, 1200 wds.,
        no cr.

PICKUP ALLEY (see: Interpol)

4891 PICKWICK PAPERS, THE (Noel Langley)
      Sight & S: v. 22, n. 3 (Jan.-Mar., 1953), p. 131; Clarissa Bowen, 400 wds., pt.
        cr.

4892 PICNIC (Joshua Logan)
      F Culture: v. 2, n. I (1956), pp. 26-27; Andrew Sarris, 1500 wds., pt. cr.

Films & F: v. 2, n. 6 (Mar., 1956), pp. 16-17; P. L. Mannock, 225 wds., cp. cr.
Films in R: v. VII, n. I (Jan., 1956), pp. 32-33; John Springer, 475 wds., no
cr.
Sight & S: v. 25, n. 4 (Spring, 1956), pp. 194-196; Derek Prouse, 2000 wds.,
pt. cr.

PICNIC ON THE GRASS (see: Le Déjeuner sur l'Herbe)

4893 PICTURA (6 shorts)
Films in R: v. III, n. 5 (May, 1952), p. 245; 150 wds., no cr.

4894 PICTURE MOMMY DEAD (Bert I. Gordon)
Filmf: v. IX (1966), p. 326; comp., cp. cr.

PIE IN THE SKY (see: Terror in the City)

4895 PIECE MANDALA (Paul Sharits)
F Culture: n. 47 (Summer, 1969), pp. 14-15; Paul Sharits, 400 wds., no cr.

4896 PIECES OF DREAMS (Daniel Haller)
Films in R: v. XXI, n. 8 (Oct., 1970), pp. 509-510; Eunice Sinkler, 250 wds.,
no cr.

PIEL DE VERANO (see: Summer Skin)

4897 PIER 5 HAVANA (Edward L. Cahn)
Filmf: v. II (1959), p. 256; comp., cp. cr.

4898 PIERROT LE FOU (Jean-Luc Godard)
(also: Crazy Pete)
Cahiers in Eng: n. 2 (1966), p. 74; Michel Caen, 1400 wds., cp. cr.
Cinema: v. 4, n. 4 (Dec., 1968), p. 37; Allan Aaron Adrian, 1000 wds., no cr.
F Quarterly: v. XIX, n. 3 (Spring, 1966), pp. 46-48; Michael Klein, 1100
wds., pt. cr.
F Soc Rev: v. 4, n. 6, pp. 18-28; A. D. Malmfelt, 2800 wds., pt. cr.
Filmf: v. XII (1969), p. I; comp., cp. cr.
Films & F: v. 12, n. 3 (Dec., 1965), pp. 16, 51-52; Peter Whitehead, 1300 wds.,
cp. cr.
Sight & S v. 35, n. I (Winter, 1965-1966), pp. 6-7; Tom Milne, 500 wds., pt.
cr.

PIERWSZY DZIEN WOLNOSCI (see: The First Day of Freedom)

PIG ACROSS PARIS (see: La Traversée de Paris)

PIG HUNT, THE (see: Grisjakten)

4899 PIG TALES (Gerry Levy)
Films & F: v. 8, n. 12 (Sept., 1962), p. 37; David Gerrard, 200 wds., cp. cr.

4900 PIGEON THAT TOOK ROME, THE (Melville Shavelson)
Filmf: v. V (1962), p. 192; comp., cp. cr.
Films & F: v. 9, n. I (Oct., 1962), pp. 33-34; Gordon Gow, 700 wds., cp. cr.

4901 PIGEONS (John Dexter)
(also: The Sidelong Glances of a Pigeon Kicker)
Filmf: v. XIV (1971), p. 125; comp., cp. cr.

4902 PIGS (Carroll Ballard)
F Lib Quarterly: v. I, n. 3 (Summer, 1968), pp. 49-50; Betty Steinberg, 350
wds., pt. cr.

4903 PIGSTY (Pier Paolo Pasolini)
(also: Porcile)
Film: n. 57 (Winter, 1970), pp. 31-33; Langdon Dewey, 400 wds., pt. cr.
Films & F: v. 16, n. 6 (Mar., 1970), p. 38; Gordon Gow, 900 wds., cp. cr.
Movie: n. 17 (Winter, 1969-1970), p. 37; Ian Cameron, 250 wds., no cr.
Sight & S: v. 39, n. 2 (Spring, 1970), pp. 99-100; Philip Strick, 900 wds., pt.
cr.

PIKOVAYA DAMA (see: The Queen of Spades)

4904 PILGRIM, THE (Charles Chaplin)
Sight & S: v. 29, n. 3 (Summer, 1960), p. 144; Jay Leyda, 650 wds., no cr.

4905 PILLOW TALK (Michael Gordon)
Filmf: v. II (1959), p. 227; comp., cp. cr.
Films & F: v. 6, n. 6 (Mar., 1960), pp. 24-25; Gordon Gow, 400 wds., cp. cr.

4906 PINK ANGELS, THE (Lawrence Brown)
Filmf: v. XIV (1971), p. 758; comp., cp. cr.

4907 PINK JUNGLE, THE (Delbert Mann)
Filmf: v. XI (1968), p. 394; comp., cp. cr.
Films & F: v. 14, n. II (Aug., 1968), pp. 26-27; David Austen, 250 wds., cp. cr.

4908 PINK NARCISSUS
Filmf: v. XIV (1971), p. 336; comp., cp. cr.

4909 PINK PANTHER, THE (Blake Edwards)
F Quarterly: v. XVIII, n. I (Fall, 1964), p. 62; R. M. Hodgens, 175 wds., no cr.
Filmf: v. VII (1964), p. 75; comp., cp. cr.
Films & F: v. 10, n. 5 (Feb., 1964), pp. 30-31; John Cutts, 800 wds., cp. cr.
Films in R: v. XV, n. 5 (May, 1964), pp. 304-305; Georges Millau, 200 wds., no cr.
Sight & S: v. 33, n. 2 (Spring, 1964), pp. 95-96; David Robinson, 700 wds., pt. cr.

4910 PINK PUSSY CAT, THE (Alberto Du Bois)
(also: Acosada Harassed)
Filmf: v. X (1967), p. 441; comp., cp. cr.

4911 PINKY (Elia Kazan)
Sequence: n. 10 (New Year, 1950), pp. 179-183; Lindsay Anderson, 2600 wds., pt. cr.

4912 PIPES, THE (Vojtech Jasny)
Interntl F G: v. 4 (1967), p. 64; 250 wds., pt. cr.

4913 PIRATE, THE (Vincente Minnelli)
Sequence: n. 6 (Winter, 1948-1949), pp. 44-46; Peter Ericsson, 1000 wds., pt. cr.

4914 PIRATE AND THE SLAVE GIRL, THE (Piero Pierotti)
Filmf: v. IV (1961), p. 373; comp., cp. cr.

4915 PIRATE OF THE BLACK HAWK, THE (Sergio Grieco)
Filmf: v. IV (1961), p. 362; comp., cp. cr.

4916 PIRATES OF BLOOD RIVER, THE (John Gilling)
Filmf: v. V (1962), p. 263; comp., cp. cr.

4917 PIRATES OF TORTUGA (Robert Webb)
Filmf: v. IV (1961), p. 344; comp., cp. cr.

PISCINE, LA (see: The Sinners)

4918 PISTOL FOR RINGO, A (Duccio Tessari)
(also: Una Pistola Per Ringo)
Filmf: v. IX (1966), p. 290; comp., cp. cr.

PISTOLA PER RINGO, UNA (see: A Pistol for Ringo)

PISTOLERO (see: The Last Challenge)

PISTOLERO OF RED RIVER, THE (see: The Last Challenge)

4919 PIT AND THE PENDULUM, THE (Roger Corman)
         Filmf: v. IV (1961), p. 212; comp., cp. cr.
         Films & F: v. 8, n. 5 (Feb., 1952), p. 33; John Cutts, 250 wds., cp. cr.

      PITY FOR THEM (see: Los Olvidados)

4920 PLACE CALLED GLORY, A (Sheldon Reynolds)
         (also: The Hell of Manitoba; Die Hoelle von Manitoba)
         Filmf: v. IX (1966), p. 241; comp., cp. cr.

4921 PLACE FOR LOVERS, A (Vittorio De Sica)
         (also: Gli Amanti; Lovers)
         Filmf: v. XII (1969), p. 425; comp., cp. cr.
         Films & F: v. 15, n. 12 (Sept., 1969), p. 60; Richard Combs, 350 wds., cp. cr.

4922 PLACE IN THE SUN, A (George Stevens)
         Films in R: v. II, n. 8 (Oct., 1951), pp. 38-42; Stephen Lewis, 1600 wds., pt.
            cr.
         Sight & S: v. 21, n. 3 (Jan.-Mar., 1952), pp. 120-122; Karel Reisz, 1200 wds.,
            pt. cr.

4923 PLACE TO GO, A (Basil Deardon)
         Films & F: v. 10, n. 8 (May, 1964), pp. 27-28; Raymond Durgnat, 500 wds.,
            cp. cr.

4924 PLAGUE OF THE ZOMBIES (John Gilling)
         Filmf: v. IX (1966), p. 48; comp., cp. cr.

4925 PLAINSMAN, THE (David Lowell Rich)
         Filmf: v. IX (1966), p. 323; comp., cp. cr.
         Films & F: v. 13, n. 7 (Apr., 1967), pp. 7-8; Raymond Durgnat, 850 wds.,
            cp. cr.

4926 PLAISIR, LE (Max Ophuls)
         Sight & S: v. 22, n. 4 (Apr.-June, 1953), pp. 195-196; Simon Harcourt-Smith,
            1000 wds., pt. cr.

4927 PLAN 9 FROM OUTER SPACE (Edward Wood)
         Filmf: v. I (1958), p. 295; comp., cp. cr.

      PLANET OF BLOOD (see: Planet of the Vampires)

4928 PLANET OF THE APES (Franklin J. Schaffner)
         F Quarterly: v. XXI, n. 4 (Summer, 1968), p. 60; Stephen Farber, 500 wds.,
            no cr.
         F Quarterly: v. XXII, n. I (Fall, 1968), pp. 56-62; Judith Shatnoff, 3900
            wds., pt. cr.
         Filmf: v. XI (1968), p. 15; comp., cp. cr.
         Films & F: v. 14, n, 8 (Apr., 1968), pp. 24-25; David Austen, 900 wds., cp.
            cr.
         Films in R: v. XIX, n. 3 (Mar., 1968), pp. 172-174; Henry Hart, 700 wds., no
            cr.
         Sight & S: v. 37, n. 3 (Summer, 1968), p. 156; David Wilson, 500 wds., pt.
            cr.

4929 PLANET OF THE VAMPIRES (Mario Bava)
         (also: Planet of Blood; Terrore Nello Spazio)
         Films & F: v. 15, n. 4 (Jan., 1969), p. 52; Richard David, 350 wds., cp. cr.

      PLANQUE, LA (see: The Hideout)

4930 PLANTS FROM DUNES (Yasushi Nakahira)
         Cinema: v. 3, n. 3 (July, 1966), p. 50; Curtis Lee Hanson, 150 wds., no cr.

4931 PLASTIC HAIRCUT (Robert Nelson)
         F Culture: n. 48-49 (Winter-Spring, 1970), pp. 23-24; Robert Nelson, 400
            wds., pt. cr.
         F Quarterly: v. XX, n. 3 (Spring, 1967), pp. 50-52; Earl Bodien, 1400 wds.,
            no cr.

4932 PLATINUM HIGH SCHOOL (Charles Haas)
(also: Trouble at Sixteen)
Filmf: v. III (1960), p. 120; comp., cp. cr.

4933 PLAY DIRTY (Andre De Toth)
Filmf: v. XII (1969), p. 90; comp., cp. cr.
Films & F: v. 15, n. 5 (Feb., 1969), pp. 36-37; Richard Davis, 300 wds., cp.
cr.
Focus: n. 5 (Oct., 1969), p. 34; Charles Flynn, 150 wds., no cr.

4934 PLAY IT COOL (Michael Winner)
Filmf: v. VI (1963), p. 202; comp., cp. cr.
Films & F: v. 8, n. 11 (Aug., 1962), p. 29; Raymond Durgnat, 425 wds., cp.
cr.

4935 PLAY MISTY FOR ME (Clint Eastwood)
Filmf: v. XIV (1971), p. 534; comp., cp. cr.

4936 PLAYBACK (Quentin Lawrence)
Films & F: v. 9, n. 2 (Nov., 1962), p. 42; David Rider, 250 wds., cp. cr.

4937 PLAYBOY OF THE WESTERN WORLD, THE (Brian Desmond-Hurst)
Filmf: v. VI (1963), p. 75; comp., cp. cr.
Films in R: v. XIV, n. 6 (June-July, 1963), pp. 368-370; Robert C. Roman,
300 wds., no cr.

PLAYER PIANOS, THE (see: The Uninhibited)

4938 PLAYGIRL AFTER DARK (Terence Young)
(also: Too Hot To Handle)
Filmf: v. V (1962), p. 198; comp., cp. cr.
Films & F: v. 7, n. 2 (Nov., 1960), pp. 31-32; John Cutts, 300 wds., cp. cr.

PLAYGIRL AND THE WAR MINISTER, THE (see: The Amorous Pawn)

4939 PLAYGIRLS AND THE VAMPIRE (Piero Regnoli)
(also: Ultima Preda del Vampiro)
Filmf: v. VII (1964), p. 322; comp., cp. cr.

PLAYING AT LOVE (see: The Love Game)

4940 PLAYTIME (Jacques Tati)
Filmf: v. VI (1963), p. 34; comp., cp. cr.
Films & F: v. 15, n. 1 (Oct., 1968), pp. 43-44; Allen Eyles, 750 wds., cp. cr.
Interntl F G: v. 6 (1969), pp. 72-73; Peter Cowie, 200 wds., pt. cr.
Sight & S: v. 37, n. 4 (Autumn, 1968), p. 205; Penelope Houston, 800 wds.,
no cr.

4941 PLAZA SUITE (Arthur Hiller)
Filmf: v. XIV (1971), p. 138; comp., cp. cr.
Films in R: v. XXII, n. 6 (June-July, 1971), pp. 372-373; Elaine Rothschild,
175 wds., no cr.

PLEA FOR PASSION, A (see: The Bigamist)

4942 PLEASE DON'T EAT THE DAISIES (Charles Walters)
F Quarterly: v. XIII, n. 4 (Summer, 1960), p. 60; 50 wds., no cr.
Filmf: v. III (1960), p. 61; comp., cp. cr.
Films & F: v. 6, n. 8 (May, 1960), pp. 25-26; Tony Keniston, 225 wds., cp.
cr.
Films in R: v. XI, n. 4 (Apr., 1960), pp. 236-237; Penelope Clark, 200 wds.,
no cr.

4943 PLEASE, MR. BALZAC (Marc Allégret)
Films in R: v. IX, n. 1 (Jan., 1958), p. 28; Charles A. Butler, 25 wds., no cr.

4944 PLEASE, NOT NOW! (Roger Vadim)
(also: Le Bride sur le Cou)
Filmf: v. VI (1963), p. 328; comp., cp. cr.
Films & F: v. 10, n. 2 (Nov., 1963), p. 25; Ian Johnson, 275 wds., cp. cr.

4949 PLEASE TURN OVER (Gerald Thomas)
       Filmf: v. IV (1961), p. 135; comp., cp. cr.
       Films & F: v. 6, n. 5 (Feb., 1960), p. 24; Robin Bean, 100 wds., cp. cr.

4946 PLEASURE GARDEN, THE (James Broughton)
       Films & F: v. I, n. 2 (Nov., 1954), p. 20; Peter Barnes, 100 wds., cp. cr.
       Films in R: v. V, n. 2 (Feb., 1954), pp. 95-96; Henry Hart, 425 wds., no cr.
       Sight & S: v. 23, n. 3 (Jan.-Mar., 1954), p. 147; William Whitebait, 450
       |wds., no cr.

4947 PLEASURE GIRLS, THE (Gerry O'Hara)
       Filmf: v. IX (1966), p. 108; comp., cp. cr.
       Films & F: v. II, n. 10 (July, 1965), p. 29; David Rider, 450 wds., cp. cr.

4948 PLEASURE IS MUTUAL, THE
       F Lib Quarterly: v. I, n. 3 (Summer, 1968), pp. 50-56; Rachel Smith, 300
       wds., pt. cr.

4949 PLEASURE OF HIS COMPANY, THE (George Seaton)
       Filmf: v. IV (1961), p. 123; comp., cp. cr.
       Films & F: v. 7, n. II (Aug., 1961), p. 28; John Cutts, 300 wds., cp. cr.

4950 PLEASURE PALACE, THE (John Hofsess)
       Take One: v. I, n. 6 (1967), pp. 9-11; John Hofsess, 1800 wds., no cr.

4951 PLEASURE SEEKERS, THE (Jean Negulesco)
       Films & F: v. II, n. 6 (Mar., 1965), pp. 36-37; David Rider, 525 wds., cp. cr.
       Films in R: v. XVI, n. 2 (Feb., 1965), pp. 116-117; Flavia Wharton, 250 wds.,
       no cr.

4952 PLEASURES OF THE BATH, THE (Werner Kunz)
       Films & F: v. 15, n. I (Oct., 1968), p. 49; Allen Eyles, 200 wds., cp. cr.

4953 PLEASURES OF THE FLESH, THE (Nagisa Oshima)
       (also: Etsuraku)
       Filmf: n. 58 (Spring, 1970), p. 5; 50 wds., pt. cr.

       PLEIN SOLEIL (see: Purple Noon)

4954 PLOTZLICHE REICHTUM DER ARMEN LEUTE VON KROMBACH, DER
              (Volker Schlondorff)
       Interntl F G: v. 9 (1972), p. 144; Ulrich von Thüna, 150 wds., pt. cr.

4955 PLUNDERERS, THE (Joseph Pevney)
       Filmf: v. III (1960), p. 348; comp., cp. cr.
       Films & F: v. 7, n. 4 (Jan., 1961), pp. 34-35; Robin Bean, 300 wds., cp. cr.

4956 PLUNDERS OF PAINTED FLATS (Albert Gannaway)
       Filmf: v. II (1959), p. 342; comp., cp. cr.

       PLUS BELLES ESCROQUERIES DU MONDE, LES (see: The Beautiful
              Swindlers)

       PLUS VIEUX METIER DU MONDE, LE (see: The Oldest Profession)

4957 POACHER'S DAUGHTER, THE (George Pollock)
       Filmf: v. III (1960), p. 27; comp., cp. cr.

       POCIAG (see: Night Train)

4958 POCKETFUL OF MIRACLES (Frank Capra)
       Film: n. 31 (Spring, 1962), p. 13; Peter Armitage, 150 wds., no cr.
       Filmf: v. IV (1961), p. 322; comp., cp. cr.
       Films & F: v. 8, n. 4 (Jan., 1962), p. 29; John Cutts, 700 wds., cp. cr.
       Films in R: v. XII, n. 10 (Dec., 1961), p. 624; Elaine Rothschild, 125 wds., no
              cr.
       Sight & S: v. 31, n. I (Winter, 1961-1962), p. 42; Penelope Houston, 350 wds.,
              pt. cr.

       POIKA ELI KESAANSA (see: Young Love)

4959 POINT BLANK (John Boorman)
      F Quarterly: v. XXI, n. 2 (Winter, 1967-1968), p. 63; Dan Bates, 250 wds.,
           no cr.
      F Quarterly: v. XXI, n. 4 (Summer, 1968), pp. 40-43; James Michael Martin,
           1600 wds., pt. cr.
      Filmf: v. X (1967), p. 276; comp., cp. cr.
      Films & F: v. 14, n. 6 (Mar., 1968), pp. 25-26; David Austen, 1100 wds., cp.
           cr.
      Films in R: v. XVIII, n. 8 (Oct., 1967), p. 508; Arthur B. Clark, 175 wds., no
           cr.
      Sight & S: v. 37, n. 2 (Spring, 1968), p. 98; Philip French, 800 wds., pt. cr.

4960 POINT OF ORDER (Emile de Antonio)
      F Comment: v. 2, n. 1 (Winter, 1964), pp. 31-33; Edward Crawford, 1400
           wds., no cr.
      F Comment: v. 2, n. 1 (Winter, 1964), pp. 33-35; David T. Bazelon, 1400
           wds., pt. cr.
      F Comment: v. 2, n. 1 (Winter, 1964), pp. 35-36; Emile de Antonio, 600
           wds., no cr.
      F Quarterly: v. XVII, n. 4 (Summer, 1964), pp. 56-57; Ernest Callenbach,
           600 wds., pt. cr.
      F Soc Rev: Oct. (1966), pp. 16-17; Gordon Hitchens, 475 wds., pt. cr.
      F Soc Rev: Oct. (1966), pp. 17-18; John Thomas, 375 wds., pt. cr.
      Filmf: v. VII (1964), p. 14; comp., cp. cr.
      Films in R: v. XV, n. 2 (Feb., 1964), pp. 116-117; L.W., 350 wds., no cr.
      Take One: v. 1, n. 5 (June, 1967), pp. 31-32; Patrick MacFadden, 1500 wds.,
           pt. cr.

      POISON (see: Venom)

4961 POJKEN I TRADET (Arne Sucksdorff)
      (also: The Boy in the Trees)
      F Quarterly: v. XV, n. 4 (Summer, 1962), pp. 50-53; Vernon Young, 1400
           wds., pt. cr.

4962 POKKERS UNGER, DE (Astrid and Bjarne Henning-Jensen)
      (also: The Mischievous Imps; Those Blasted Kids)
      Sight & S: v. 16, n. 63 (Autumn, 1947), p. 110; Ragna Jackson, 150 wds., no
           cr.

      POKOLENIE (see: A Generation)

4963 POLICE DOG STORY (Edward L. Cahn)
      Filmf: v. IV (1961), p. 40; comp., cp. cr.

4964 POLICE NURSE (Maury Dexter)
      Filmf: v. VI (1963), p. 342; comp., cp. cr.

4965 POLLYANA (David Swift)
      Filmf: v. III (1960), p. 103; comp., cp. cr.
      Films & F: v. 6, n. 12 (Sept., 1960), p. 21; Dai Vaughan, 300 wds., cp. cr.
      Filmf in R: v. XI, n. 5 (May, 1960), pp. 297-298; Elspeth Hart, 450 wds., no
           cr.

      POOKIE (see: The Sterile Cuckoo)

4966 POOL OF LONDON (Basil Dearden)
      Sight & S: v. 19, n. 12 (Apr., 1951), pp. 474-475; Philip Hope-Wallace, 750
           wds., pt. cr.

4967 POOR BUT BEAUTIFUL (Dino Risi)
      (also: Belle Ma Povere)
      Filmf: v. 1 (1958), p. 108; comp., cp. cr.

      POOR BUT HANDSOME (see: Girl in a Bikini)

4968 POOR COW (Kenneth Loach)
      Filmf: v. XI (1968), p. 26; comp., cp. cr.
      Films & F: v. 14, n. 7 (Apr., 1968), pp. 26-27; Michael Armstrong, 800 wds.,
           cp. cr.

Films in R: v. XIX, n. 3 (Mar., 1968), pp. 181-182; Flavia Wharton, 300 wds.,
no cr.
Sight & S: v. 37, n. I (Winter, 1967-1968), p. 43; Brenda Davies, 500 wds.,
pt. cr.

POOR OUTLAWS, THE (see: The Round-Up)

4969 POOR PAY MORE, THE
F Lib Quarterly: v. 2, n. I (Winter, 1968-1969), pp. 50-51; Arthur S. Meyers,
500 wds., pt. cr.

4970 POP GEAR (Frederick Goods)
(also: Go Go Mania)
Filmf: v. VIII (1965), p. 120; comp., cp. cr.
Films & F: v. 12, n. I (Oct., 1965), pp. 30-31; David Rider, 450 wds., cp. cr.

4971 POPI (Arthur Hiller)
F Quarterly: v. XXIII, n. I (Fall, 1969), p. 53; David Denby, 400 wds., no cr.
Filmf: v. XII (1969), p. 258; comp., cp. cr.
Films & F: v. 16, n, 8 (May, 1970), p. 52; John Walker, 350 wds., cp. cr.

POPIOL I DIAMENT (see: Ashes and Diamonds)

POPIOLY (see: Ashes)

4972 POPPY IS ALSO A FLOWER, THE (Terence Young)
(also: Danger Grows Wild)
Filmf: v. X (1967), p. 410; comp., cp. cr.
Films & F: v. 13, n. 5 (Feb., 1967), pp. 30-31; Allen Eyles, 500 wds., cp. cr.

POPRIGUNYA (see: The Grasshopper)

PORCILE (see: Pigsty)

4973 PORGY AND BESS (Otto Preminger)
Filmf: v. II (1959), p. 149; comp., cp. cr.
Films & F: v. 9, n. 2 (Nov., 1962), pp. 35-36; John Cutts, 600 wds., cp. cr.
Films in R: v. X, n. 7 (Aug.-Sept., 1959), pp. 419-420; Henry Hart, 600 wds.,
no cr.
Movie: n. 3 (Oct., 1962), p. 36; 75 wds., no cr.
Movie: n. 4 (Nov., 1962), pp. 21-23; Paul Mayersberg, 2250 wds., no cr.

4974 PORK CHOP HILL (Lewis Milestone)
Filmf: v. II (1959), p. III; comp., cp. cr.
Films & F: v. 5, n. 10 (July, 1959), p. 24; Peter John Dyer, 450 wds., cp. cr.
Films in R: v. X, n. 5 (May, 1959), pp. 300-301; Archie Burroughs, 300 wds.,
no cr.

4975 PORNOGRAPHER, THE (Shohei Imamura)
(also: An Introduction To Anthropology; Jinruigaku Nyumon)
Films & F: v. 13, n. II (Aug., 1967), pp. 27-28; Raymond Durgnat, 700 wds.,
cp. cr.
Interntl F G: v. 4 (1967), pp. 114-115; Donald Richie, 375 wds., pt. cr.

PORT DE DESIR (see: The House on the Waterfront)

4976 PORT OF CALL (Ingmar Bergman)
(also: Hamnstad)
Films & F: v. 6, n. I (Oct., 1959), p. 25; Max Neufeld, 200 wds., cp. cr.

4977 PORT OF DESIRE (Yves Allegret)
(also: La Fille de Hambourg; The Girl from Hamburg)
Filmf: v. III (1960), p. 274; comp., cp. cr.

4978 PORTE DES LILAS (Rene Clair)
(Also: Gates of Paris)
Films & F: v. 4, n. 3 (Dec., 1957), p. 21; Peter John Dyer, 850 wds., cp. cr.
Films in R: v. IX, n. 2 (Feb., 1958), p. 92; Louise Corbin, 400 wds., no cr.
Sight & S: v. 27, n. 3 (Winter, 1957-1958), pp. 145-146; Louis Marcorelles,
1000 wds., pt. cr.

4979 PORTRAIT IN BLACK (Michael Gordon)
  Filmf: v. III (1960), p. 182; comp., cp. cr.
  Films & F: v. 7, n. 2 (Nov., 1960), p. 34; Robin Bean, 350 wds., cp. cr.

  PORTRAIT OF A BOY (see: Once There Was a War)

4980 PORTRAIT OF A MOBSTER (Joseph Pevney)
  Filmf: v. IV (1961), p. 74; comp., cp. cr.

4981 PORTRAIT OF A SINNER (Robert Siodmak)
  (also: The Rough and the Smooth)
  Filmf: v. IV (1961), p. 160; comp., cp. cr.
  Films & F: v. 6, n. 2 (Nov., 1959), p. 22; Derek Conrad, 200 wds., cp. cr.

4982 PORTRAIT OF AN UNKNOWN WOMAN (Helmut Kautner)
  Filmf: v. I (1958), p. 164; comp., cp. cr.

4983 PORTRAIT OF FRANS HAL (Frans Dupont)
  Interntl F G: v. 2 (1965), p. 116; 75 wds., pt. cr.

4984 PORTRAIT OF JASON (Shirley Clarke)
  Cinema: v. 4, n. I (Spring, 1968), p. 48; Quentin Guerlain, 550 wds., pt. cr.
  Film: n. 50 (Winter, 1967), pp. 32-33; Langdon Dewey, 250 wds., no cr.
  F Quarterly: v. XXII, n. I (Fall, 1968), pp. 75-77; Ernest Callenbach, 350
      wds., no cr.
  Filmf: v. X (1967), p. 295; comp., cp. cr.
  Take One: v. I, n. 7 (1967), p. 24; John Hofsess, 200 wds., pt. cr.

4985 PORTRAIT OF QUEENIE (Michael Orrom)
  Films & F: v. II, n. 6 (Mar., 1965), p. 34; David Rider, 350 wds., cp. cr.

  PORTRAITS OF WOMEN (see: Naisenkuvia)

4986 POSSE FROM HELL (Herbert Coleman)
  F Quarterly: v. XV, n. I (Fall, 1961), p. 56; R. M. Hodgens, 100 wds., no cr.
  Filmf: v. IV (1961), p. 98; comp., cp. cr.

  POSSEDES, LES (see: Passionate Summer)

  POSSESSED, THE (see: Passionate Summer)

4987 POSSESSORS, THE (Denys De La Patelliere)
  (also: Les Grandes Familles)
  Filmf: v. II (1959), p. 187; comp., cp. cr.
  Films & F: v. 6, n. II (Aug., 1960), p. 24; Gordon Gow, 450 wds., cp. cr.
  Films in R: v. X, n. 7 (Aug.-Sept., 1959), pp. 416-417; Louise Corbin, 225
      wds., no cr.

  POSTO, IL (see: The Sound of Trumpets)

  POSTZUG-UEBERSALL, DER (see: The Great British Train Robbery)

4988 POT BOUILLE (Julien Duvivier)
  (also: The House of Lovers; The Lovers of Paris)
  F Quarterly: v. XII, n. 2 (Winter, 1958), pp. 55-56; Mark Sufrin, 650 wds.,
      no cr.
  Filmf: v. I (1958), p. 229; comp., cp. cr.
  Films & F: v. 5, n. 5 (Fall, 1959), pp. 23-24; Derek Conrad, 225 wds., cp. cr.
  Films in R: v. IX, n. 9 (Nov., 1958), p. 517; Louise Corbin, 100 wds., no cr.

4989 POT CARRIERS, THE (Peter Graham Scott)
  Films & F: v. 8, n. 9 (June, 1962), p. 33; Peter G. Baker, 400 wds., cp. cr.

  POTE TIU KYRIAKI (see: Never on Sunday)

4990 POUPEE, LA (Jacques Baratier)
  (also: He, She or It?)
  Filmf: v. VI (1963), p. 235; comp., cp. cr.
  Films & F: v. 9, n. 8 (May, 1963), p. 29; Gordon Gow, 350 wds., cp. cr.
  Sight & S: v. 32, n. 2 (Spring, 1963), p. 95; David Robinson, 400 wds., pt.
      cr.

4991 POUR LA SUITE DU MONDE (Michel Brault and Pierre Perrault)
(also: The Moontrap)
F Soc Rev: Sept. (1965), p. 25; P.C., 325 wds., no cr.
Interntl F G: v. I (1964), p. 118; 150 wds., pt. cr.
Movie: n. II, p. 25; Mark Shivas, 200 wds., no cr.

4992 POUSSIERE SUR LA VILLE (Arthur Lamothe)
Take One: v. I, n. 10 (1968), pp. 32-33; Gabriel Breton, 1100 wds., pt. cr.

POVERI MA BELLI (see: Girl in a Bikini)

POVEST PLAMENNYKH LET (see: The Flaming Years)

4993 POWER, THE (Byron Haskin)
Filmf: v. XI (1968), p. 53; comp., cp. cr.
Films & F: v. 14, n. 9 (June, 1968), p. 27; David Austen, 450 wds., cp. cr.
Films in R: v. XIX, n. 2 (Feb., 1968), pp. 113-114; Roi Frumkes, 325 wds., no cr.

4994 POWER AMONG MEN (Thorold Dickinson, with Gian Luigi Polidoro and Alexander Hammid)
F Quarterly: v. XII, n. 4 (Summer, 1959), pp. 54-56; Thalia Selz, 700 wds., no cr.
Films & F: v. 6, n. 4 (Jan., 1960), p. 26; Paul Rotha, 250 wds., cp. cr.

4995 POWER AND THE GLORY, THE (Marc Daniels)
Films & F: v. 8, n. II (Aug., 1962), pp. 33-34; John Cutts, 575 wds., cp. cr.

4996 POWER TO FLY (Bob Privett)
Films & F: v. I, n. 4 (Jan., 1955), p. 9; Bernard Orna, 175 wds., cp. cr.

4997 POWER VS. THE PEOPLE (William Greaves, prod.)
F Lib Quarterly: v. 4, n. 4 (Fall, 1971), pp. 48-49; Shirley McPherson, 700 wds., pt. cr.

4998 POWEDERSMIKE RANGE (Wallace Fox)
Journal of P C: v. V, n. I (Summer, 1971), pp. 65-76; Jon Tuska, 3000 wds., cp. cr.
Views & Rev: v. 2, n. I (Summer, 1970), pp. 40-44; 1000 wds., cp. cr.

POZEGNANIA (see: Lydia Ate the Apple)

4999 PRAISE MARX AND PASS THE AMMUNITION (Maurice Hatton)
Films & F: v. 15, n. 12 (Sept., 1969), pp. 62, 64; Brian Murphy, 700 wds., cp. cr.
Sight & S: v. 38, n. 4 (Autumn, 1969), p. 214; Jan Dawson, 500 wds., pt. cr.

5000 PRATIDWANDI (Satyajit Ray)
(also: The Rival; The Adversary; Siddharth and the City)
Interntl F G: v. 9 (1972), pp. 168-169; Chidananda das Gupta, 250 wds., pt. cr.

5001 PREACHERMAN (Albert T. Viola)
Filmf: v. XIV (1971), p. 753; comp., cp. cr.

PRECIO DE UN HOMBRE, EL (see: The Ugly Ones)

5002 PREHISTORIC WOMEN (Michael Carreras)
Filmf: v. X (1967), p. 86; comp., cp. cr.

5003 PRELUDE: Dog Star Man (Stan Brakhage)
F Culture: n. 26 (Fall, 1962), pp. 54-57; P. Adams Sitney, 500 wds., no cr.

5004 PRELUDE TO ECSTASY (Toivo Sarkka)
Filmf: v. VI (1963), p. 344; comp., cp. cr.
Films & F: v. 9, n. 2 (Nov., 1962), pp. 38-39; Raymond Durgnat, 250 wds., cp. cr.

5005 PREMATURE BURIAL, THE (Roger Corman)
Filmf: v. V (1962), p. 117; comp., cp. cr.

Films & F: v. 9, n. 2 (Nov., 1962), p. 41; Robin Bean, 200 wds., cp. cr.
Movie: n. 4 (Nov., 1962), p. 35; 125 wds., no cr.

5006 PREMIER MAY (Luis Saslavsky)
      (also: The First of May)
      Filmf: v. I (1958), p. 254; comp., cp. cr.

      PRESIDENT, LE (see: The President)

5007 PRESIDENT, THE (Henri Verneuil)
      (also: Le President)
      Films & F: v. 9, n. 10 (July, 1963), p. 29; Peter Cowie, 200 wds., cp. cr.

5008 PRESIDENT'S ANALYST, THE (Theodore J. Flicker)
      F Quarterly: v. XXI, n. 3 (Spring, 1968), pp. 60-61; Dennis Hart, 450 wds.,
            no cr.
      Filmf: v. X (1967), p. 426; comp., cp. cr.
      Films & F: v. 15, n. 4 (Jan., 1969), pp. 49-50; Gordon Gow, 650 wds., cp. cr.
      Films in R: v. XIX, n. 2 (Feb., 1968), p. 114; Arthur B. Clark, 150 wds., no
            cr.
      Sight & S: v. 37, n. 3 (Summer, 1968), pp. 155-156; Tom Milne, 700 wds., pt.
            cr.
      Take One: v. I, n. 9 (1968), p. 22; Juan Rodriguez, 450 wds., pt. cr.

5009 PRESIDENT'S LADY, THE (Henry Levin)
      Filmf & F: v. 15, n. 6 (Mar., 1969), pp. 88, 90; Kingsley Canham, 600 wds.,
            no cr.

5010 PRESS FOR TIME (Robert Asher)
      Films & F: v. 13, n. 5 (Feb., 1967), p. 35; Richard Davis, 500 wds., cp. cr.

5011 PRESSURE POINT (Hubert Cornfield)
      F Quarterly: v. XVI, n. 3 (Spring, 1963), p. 59; R. M. Hodgens, 150 wds., no
            cr.
      Filmf: v. V (1962), p. 224; comp., cp. cr.
      Films & F: v. 10, n. 2 (Nov., 1963), p. 21; Peter Baker, 800 wds., cp. cr.

5012 PRETTY BOY FLOYD (Herbert J. Leder)
      Filmf: v. III (1960), p. 254; comp., cp. cr.

5013 PRETTY MAIDS ALL IN A ROW (Roger Vadim)
      Filmf: v. XIV (1971), p. 38; comp., cp. cr.

5014 PRETTY POISON (Noel Black)
      F Quarterly: v. XXII, n. 4 (Summer, 1969), pp. 59-60; Albert Johnson, 450
            wds., no cr.
      Filmf: v. XI (1968), p. 453; comp., cp. cr.
      Films & F: v. 15, n. 8 (May, 1969), p. 39; David Rider, 700 wds., cp. cr.
      Films in R: v. XX, n. 2 (Feb., 1969), pp. 115-116; Page Cook, 200 wds., no cr.
      Sight & S: v. 38, n. 2 (Spring, 1969), p. 99; Jack Ibberson, 600 wds., pt. cr.

      PRETTY POLLY (see: A Matter of Innocence)

5015 PRICE OF SILENCE, THE (Montgomery Tully)
      Filmf: v. IV (1961), p. 371; comp., cp. cr.

5016 PRIDE AND THE PASSION, THE (Stanley Kramer)
      Films & F: v. 4, n. 2 (Nov., 1957), p. 25; Peter John Dyer, 350 wds., cp. cr.
      Films in R: v. VIII, n. 7 (Aug.-Sept., 1957), pp. 349-350; Ellen Fitzpatrick,
            400 wds., no cr.

5017 PRIEST'S WIFE, THE (Dino Risi)
      (also: La Moglie Del Prete)
      Filmf: v. XIV (1971), p. 32; comp., cp. cr.
      Films in R: v. XXII, n. 4 (Apr., 1971), p. 236; William Herron, 150 wds., no
            cr.

      PRIMA DELLA RIVOLUZIONE (see: Before the Revolution)

5018 PRIME OF MISS JEAN BRODIE, THE (Ronald Neame)
 F Quarterly: v. XXII, n. 3 (Spring, 1969), p. 63; Stephen Farber, 500 wds.,
  no cr.
 Filmf: v. XII (1969), p. 25; comp., cp. cr.
 Films & F: v. 15, n. 8 (May, 1969), pp. 54-55; Gordon Gow, 500 wds., cp.
  cr.
 Films in R: v. XX, n. 4 (Apr., 1969), pp. 250-252; Henry Hart, 650 wds., no
  cr.
 Focus: n. 5 (Oct., 1969), p. 34; Myron Meisel, 100 wds., no cr.

5019 PRIME TIME, THE (Gordon Weisenborn)
 Filmf: v. III (1960), p. 60; comp., cp. cr.

5020 PRIMERA CARGA AL MACHETE, LA (Manvel Octavio Gómez)
 (also: The First Assault with Machetes; The First Use of the Machete)
 Interntl F G: v. 8 (1971), pp. 99-100; Mikko Pyhala, 350 wds., pt. cr.
 Take One: v. 2, n. 3 (1969), p. 23; Arlene Gould, 500 wds., pt. cr.

5021 PRIMITIVE LONDON (Arnold Louis Miller)
 Films & F: v. 11, n. 10 (July, 1965), p. 34; Allen Eyles, 400 wds., cp. cr.

5022 PRIMITIVES, THE (Alfred Travers)
 Films & F: v. 9, n. 3 (Dec., 1962), pp. 45-46; Raymond Durgnat, 275 wds.,
  cp. cr.

5023 PRINCE AND THE PAUPER, THE (Don Chaffey)
 Films & F: v. 8, n. 9 (June, 1962), p. 36; Robin Bean, 200 wds., cp. cr.

5024 PRINCE AND THE SHOWGIRL, THE (Laurence Olivier)
 Films & F: v. 3, n. 10 (July, 1957), pp. 21-22; Rupert Butler, 450 wds., cp.
  cr.
 Films in R: v. VIII, n. 7 (Aug.-Sept., 1957), pp. 347-348; Hartley Ramsay,
  275 wds., no cr.
 Sight & S: v. 27, n. 1 (Summer, 1957), pp. 40-41; Penelope Houston, 650
  wds., pt. cr.

5025 PRINCE OF FOXES (Henry King)
 Sight & S: v. 18, n. 71 (Dec., 1949), p. 21; 30 wds., pt. cr.

5026 PRINCE OF PLAYERS (Philip Dunne)
 Films & F: v. 1, n. 6 (Mar., 1955), p. 24; Clayton Cole, 350 wds., cp. cr.
 Films & F: v. 1, n. 12 (Sept., 1955), p. 21; Peter Brinson, 250 wds., cp. cr.
 Films in R: v. VI, n. 2 (Feb., 1955), pp. 79-81; Robert Downing, 1100 wds.,
  pt. cr.
 Sight & S: v. 24, n. 4 (Spring, 1955), pp. 196-197; Gavin Lambert, 1200 wds.,
  pt. cr.

5027 PRINCE VALIANT (Henry Hathaway)
 Films in R: v. V, n. 5 (May, 1954), pp. 241-242; Alexander Singer, 475 wds.,
  no cr.

5028 PRINTEMPS EN HOLLANDE, UN (Nikolai van der Heyde)
 (also: Een Ochtend van Zes Weken)
 Interntl F G: v. 4 (1967), p. 120; 250 wds., pt. cr.

5029 PRIPAD PRO ZACINA-JICIHO KATA (Pavel Jurácek)
 (also: A Case For The New Hangman)
 Interntl F G: v. 8 (1971), pp. 105-106; Jan Zalman, 350 wds., pt. cr.

 PRISE DE POUVOIR PAR LOUIS XIV, LA (see: The Rise of Louis XIV)

 PRISON (see: The Devil's Wanton)

5030 PRISONER, THE (Peter Glenville)
 Films in R: v. VI, n. 10 (Dec., 1955), pp. 521-523; Henry Hart, 800 wds., pt.
  cr.

5031 PRISONER OF THE IRON MASK (Francesco De Feo)
 Filmf: v. V (1962), p. 366; comp., cp. cr.

5032 PRISONER OF THE VOLGA (W. Tourjansky)
        Filmf: v. III (1960), p. 113; comp., cp. cr.

5033 PRISONER OF WAR (Andrew Marton)
        Films in R: v. V, n. 6 (June-July, 1954), pp. 305-306; 150 wds., no cr.

5034 PRISONERS OF THE CONGO (Willy Rozier)
        (also: Prisonniers de la Brousse; Where Vultures Fly)
        Filmf: v. III (1960), p. 357; comp., cp. cr.
        Films & F: v. 8, n. 12 (Sept., 1962), p. 39; Robin Bean, 325 wds., cp. cr.

5035 PRISONNIERE, LA (Henri-Georges Clouzot)
        (also: Women in Chains)
        F Quarterly: v. XXIII, n. I (Fall, 1969), pp. 53-54; Michael Dempsey, 400
                wds., no cr.
        Filmf: v. XII (1969), p. 126; comp., cp. cr.
        Take One: v. 2, n. 7 (1970), pp. 25-26; T. J. Ross, 1700 wds., no cr.

      PRISONNIERS DE LA BROUSSE (see: Prisoners of the Congo)

      PRIVATE EYES, THE (see: The Great Spy Chase)

5036 PRIVATE HURRICANE (Hynek Bocan)
        Films & F: v. 15, n. 10 (July, 1969), pp. 47-48; Brian Murphy, 500 wds., cp.
                cr.

      PRIVATE LESSON, THE (see: The Tender Moment)

5037 PRIVATE LIFE OF SHERLOCK HOLMES, THE (Billy Wilder)
        Cinema: v. 6 n. 3 (Spring, 1971), pp. 49-50; Robert Mundy, 900 wds., no cr.
        F Quarterly: v. XXIV, n. 3 (Spring, 1971), pp. 45-48; Joseph McBride and
                Michael Wilmington, 1350 wds., pt cr.
        Films & F. v. 17, n. 4 (Jan., 1971), p. 47; Margaret Tarratt, 600 wds., cp. cr.
        Films in R. v. XXI, n. 9 (Nov., 1970), pp. 575-576; Arlene Kramborg, 350
                wds., no cr.
        Sight & S: v. 40, n. I (Winter, 1970-1971), pp. 47-48; Peter Ohlin, 1500 wds.,
                pt. cr.

5038 PRIVATE LIVES OF ADAM AND EVE, THE (Albert Zugsmith and Mickey
                Rooney)
        Filmf: v. IV (1961), p. 70; comp., cp. cr.

5039 PRIVATE NAVY OF SGT. O'FARRELL, THE (Frank Tashlin)
        Filmf: v. XI (1968), p. 173; comp., cp. cr.

5040 PRIVATE POTTER (Caspar Wrede)
        Films & F: v. 9, n. 5 (Feb., 1963), p. 34; Roger Manvell, 900 wds., cp. cr.
        Movie: n. 6, p. 36; 100 wds., no cr.
        Sight & S: v. 32, n. I (Winter, 1962-1963), p. 40; Anna Yates, 500 wds., pt.
                cr.

5041 PRIVATE PROPERTY (Leslie Stevens)
        F Quarterly: v. XIV, n. I (Fall, 1960), pp. 45-47; Benjamin T. Jackson, 1200
                wds., pt. cr.
        Filmf: v. III (1960), p. 97; comp., cp. cr.
        Films in R: v. XI, n. 5 (May, 1960), pp. 292-297; Henry Hart, 1600 wds., no
                cr.
        Sight & S: v. 29, n. 4 (Autumn, 1960), pp. 196-197; Kenneth Cavander, 600
                wds., no cr.

5042 PRIVATE RIGHT, THE (Michael Papas)
        F Quarterly: v. XX, n. 4 (Summer, 1967), pp. 65-68; Margot S. Kernan, 1300
                wds., pt. cr.
        Films & F: v. 14, n. 12 (Sept., 1968), pp. 40-42; Raymond Durgnat, 1100
                wds., cp. cr.

5043 PRIVATE WAR OF MAJOR BENSON (Jerry Hopper)
        Films & F: v. I, n. 12 (Sept., 1955), p. 20; Derek Hill, 200 wds., cp. cr.

5044 PRIVATE'S AFFAIR A (Raoul Walsh)
        Filmf: v. II (1959), p. 189; comp., cp. cr.
        Films & F: v. 6, n. I (Oct., 1959), p. 22; 250 wds., cp. cr.

5045 PRIVATE'S PROGRESS (John Boulting)
> Sight & S: v. 25, n. 4 (Spring, 1956), pp. 198-199; Gavin Lambert, 200 wds., no cr.

5046 PRIVILEGE (Peter Watkins)
> Filmf: v. X (1967), p. 212; comp., cp. cr.
> Films & F: v. 13, n. 9 (June, 1967), p. 27; Robin Bean, 1100 wds., cp. cr.
> Films in R: v. XVIII, n. 8 (Oct., 1967), pp. 503-504; Henry Hart, 400 wds., no cr.
> Take One: v. I, n.7 (1967), pp. 24-25; Bruce Martin, 800 wds., pt. cr.

5047 PRIZE, THE (Tim Burstall)
> F Journal: n. 16 (Aug., 1960), pp. 87-88; James Merralls, 400 wds., no cr.

5048 PRIZE, THE (Mark Robson)
> Filmf: v. VII (1964), p. 9; comp., cp. cr.
> Films & F: v. 10, n. 6 (Mar., 1964), p. 24; Richard Whitehall, 950 wds., cp. cr.
> Films in R: v. XV, n. I (Jan., 1964), pp. 50-51; Georges Millau, 125 wds., no cr.
> Sight & S: v. 33, n. 2 (Spring, 1964), p. 98; Penelope Houston, 250 wds., pt. cr.

5049 PRIZE OF ARMS, A (Cliff Owen)
> Films & F: v. 9, n. 4 (Jan., 1963), p. 52; Michael Ratcliffe, 400 wds., cp. cr.

5050 PRIZE OF GOLD, A (Mark Robson)
> Films & F: v. I, n. 8 (May, 1955), p. 21; Dennis Millmore, 200 wds., cp. cr.

PROCÈS, LE (see: The Trial)

PROCÈS DE JEANNE D'ARC, LE (see: The Trial of Joan of Arc)

5051 PRODUCERS, THE (Mel Brooks)
> F Quarterly: v. XXI, n. 4 (Summer, 1968), p. 60; Dan Bates, 200 wds., no cr.
> Filmf: v. XI (1968), p. 79; comp., cp. cr.
> Films & F: v. 16, n. 5 (Feb., 1970), p. 53; Gordon Gow, 400 wds., cp. cr.
> Films in R: v. XIX, n. 4 (Apr., 1968), p. 244; Norman Cecil, 200 wds., no cr.

5052 PROFESSIONALS, THE (Richard Brooks)
> F Quarterly: v. XX, n. 3 (Spring, 1967), p. 62; Ernest Callenbach, 250 wds., no cr.
> Filmf: v. IX (1966), p. 316; comp., cp. cr.
> Films & F: v. 13, n. 10 (July, 1967), pp. 24-25; David Adams, 700 wds., cp. cr.
> Films in R: v. XVII, n. 10 (Dec., 1966), p. 664; Arthur B. Clark, 125 wds., no cr.

5053 PROFESSOR MAMLOCK (Konrad Wolf)
> F Journal: n. 20 (Aug., 1962), p. 84; J. A. Mawdsley, 250 wds., no cr.

PROFETA, IL (see: Mr. Kinky)

PROIE POUR L'OMBRE, LA (see: Shadow of Adultery)

5054 PROJECT X (William Castle)
> Filmf: v. XI (1968), p. 314; comp., cp. cr.

5055 PROJECTED MAN, THE (Ian Curteis)
> Filmf: v. X (1967), p. 176; comp., cp. cr.

5056 PROJECTIONIST, THE (Harry Hurwitz)
> Filmf: v. XIV (1971), p. 420; comp., cp. cr.

5057 PROLOGUE (Robin Spry)
> Films & F: v. 17, n. 4 (Jan., 1971), p. 52; Gordon Gow, 750 wds., cp. cr.
> Movie: n. 17 (Winter, 1969-1970), p. 37; Ian Cameron, 350 wds., no cr.
> Sight & S: v. 39, n. 2 (Spring, 1970), pp. 103-104; Jan Dawson, 750 wds., pt. cr.

5058 PROMENADE (Donovan Winter)
　　　Films & F: v. 14, n. 10 (July, 1968), pp. 35-36; Michael Armstrong, 300 wds.,
　　　　　cp. cr.

　　　PROMESSE, LA (see: Secret World)

　　　PROMESSE DE L'AUBE, LA (see: Promise at Dawn)

5059 PROMISE AT DAWN (Jules Dassin)
　　　(also: La Promesse De L'Aube)
　　　Filmf: v. XIV (1971), p. 26; comp., cp. cr.
　　　Films & F: v. 17, n. 8 (May, 1971), pp. 89-90; Gordon Gow, 850 wds., cp. cr.
　　　Films in R: v. XXII, n. 3 (Mar., 1971), p. 177; Gwenneth Britt, 150 wds., no
　　　　　cr.

5060 PROMISE HER ANYTHING (Arthur Hiller)
　　　Filmf: v. IX (1966), p. 57; comp., cp. cr.
　　　Films & F: v. 13, n. 4 (Jan., 1967), p. 33; Peter Davalle, 350 wds., cp. cr.
　　　Films & R: v. XVII, n. 4 (Apr., 1966), pp. 253-254; Adelaide Comerford,
　　　　　100 wds., no cr.

5061 PROMISE OF HEAVEN (Frans Dupont)
　　　Interntl F G: v. I (1964), p. 112; 100 wds., pt. cr.

5062 PROMISES, PROMISES (King Donovan)
　　　Filmf: v. VII (1964), p. 310; comp., cp. cr.

5063 PROMOTER, THE (Ronald Neame)
　　　(also: The Card)
　　　Films in R: v. III, n. 8 (Oct., 1952), pp. 413-414; Robert Kass, 650 wds., pt.
　　　　　cr.

5064 PROPER TIME, THE (Tom Laughlin)
　　　F Quarterly: v. XIII, n. 3 (Spring, 1960), pp. 54-55; Joseph Kostolefsky,
　　　　　500 wds., pt. cr.

　　　PROUD AND THE BEAUTIFUL, THE (see: Les Orgueilleux)

5065 PROUD AND THE PROFANE, THE (George Seaton)
　　　Films & F: v. 3, n. 1 (Oct., 1956), p. 25; Peter John Dyer, 450 wds., cp. cr.

5066 PROUD ONES, THE (Robert D. Webb)
　　　Films & F: v. 2, n. 11 (Aug., 1956), p. 24; Ken Gay, 300 wds., cp. cr.
　　　Films & F: v. 15, n. 7 (Apr., 1969), p. 88; Kingsley Canham, 400 wds., no cr.

5067 PROUD REBEL (Michael Curtiz)
　　　Filmf: v. I (1958), p. 121; comp., cp. cr.
　　　Films & F: v. 5, n. 1 (Oct., 1958), pp. 24-25; Tony Buck, 150 wds., cp. cr.

　　　PROVINCIALE, LA (see: The Wayward Wife)

5068 PROWLERS OF THE EVERGLADES
　　　Films in R: v. IV, n. 7 (Aug.-Sept., 1953), pp. 366-367; 150 wds., no cr.

5069 PRUDENCE AND THE PILL (Fiedler Cook and Ronald Neame)
　　　Filmf: v. XI (1968), p. 198; comp., cp. cr.
　　　Films & F: v. 15, n. 1 (Oct., 1968), p. 50; David Rider, 400 wds., cp. cr.
　　　Films in R: v. XIX, n. 5 (May, 1968), p. 311; Louis Corbin, 200 wds., no cr.

5070 PSYCH-OUT (Richard Rush)
　　　Filmf: v. XI (1968), p. 93; comp., cp. cr.
　　　Take One: v. 2, n. 7 (1970), p. 24; Ronald Blumer, 75 wds., no cr.

5071 PSYCHE 59 (Alexander Singer)
　　　Filmf: v. VII (1964), p. 101; comp., cp. cr.
　　　Films & F: v. 11, n. 4 (Jan., 1965), pp. 30-31; Richard Davis, 425 wds., cp. cr.

5072 PSYCHO (Alfred Hitchcock)
　　　F Quarterly: v. XIV, n. 1 (Fall, 1960), pp. 47-49; Ernest Callenbach, 900
　　　　　wds., pt. cr.

      Filmf: v. III (1960), p. 153; comp., cp. cr.
      Films & F: v. 6, n. 12 (Sept., 1960), p. 21; Peter Baker, 450 wds., cp. cr.
      Films in R: v. XI, n. 7 (Aug.-Sept., 1960), pp. 426-427; Shirley Conover, 250 wds., no cr.
      Sight & S: v. 29, n. 4 (Autumn, 1960), pp. 195-196; Peter John Dyer, 1200 wds., pt. cr.

5073 PSYCHO-CIRCUS (John Moxey)
      (also: Circus of Fear)
      Filmf: v. X (1967), p. 429; comp., cp. cr.

5074 PSYCHO LOVER, THE (Robert Vincent O'Neil)
      Filmf: v. XIV (1971), p. 538; comp., cp. cr.

5075 PSYCHOPATH, THE (Freddie Francis)
      Filmf: v. IX (1966), p. 254; comp., cp. cr.

5076 PSYCHOUT FOR MURDER (Edward Ross and Ted Kneeland)
      (also: Salvare La Faccia)
      Filmf: v. XIV (1971), p. 25; comp., cp. cr.

5077 PSYCHOSISSIMO (Steno)
      Filmf: v. V (1962), p. 234; comp., cp. cr.

      PUEBLO SE LEVANTA, EL (see: The People Arise)

      PUGNI IN TASCA, I (see: Fist in His Pocket)

      PUITS AUX TROIS VERITES, LE (see: Three Truths in the Well)

5078 PULL MY DAISY (Robert Frank and Alfred Leslie)
      F Culture: n. 24 (Spring, 1962), pp. 28-33; Parker Tyler, 3500 wds., no cr.

5079 PUMPKIN EATER, THE (Jack Clayton)
      Film: n. 41 (1964), pp. 12-13; Douglas McVay, 150 wds., no cr.
      F Quarterly: v. XVIII, n. 3 (Spring, 1965), pp. 45-48; Stephen Taylor, 1400 wds., pt. cr.
      Filmf: v. VII (1964), p. 282; comp., cp. cr.
      Films & F: v. 10, n. 11 (Aug., 1964), pp. 20-21; Peter Baker, 250 wds., cp. cr.
      Films in R: v. XV, n. 10 (Dec., 1964), p. 633; Elaine Rothschild, 175 wds., no cr.
      Interntl F G: v. 2 (1965), p. 86; Peter Graham; 200 wds., pt. cr.

5080 PUNCH AND JUDY MAN, THE (Jeremy Summers)
      Films & F: v. 9, n. 9 (June, 1963), p. 34; Robin Bean, 300 wds., cp. cr.

      PUNISHMENT ISLAND (see: Shokei No Shima)

5081 PUNISHMENT PARK (Peter Watkins)
      F Quarterly: v. XXV, n. 4 (Summer, 1972), pp. 49-52; Bernard Weiner, 1400 wds., pt. cr.
      F Soc Rev: v. 7, n. 3 (Nov., 1971), pp. 25-26; Gary Crowdus, 200 wds., no cr.
      Filmf: v. XIV (1971), p. 628; comp., cp. cr.

5082 PURE HELL OF ST. TRINIAN'S, THE (Frank Launder)
      Filmf: v. IV (1961), p. 335; comp., cp. cr.
      Films & F: v. 7, n. 4 (Jan., 1961), p. 35; Dai Vaughan, 300 wds., cp. cr.

      PURPLE VICTORIOUS (see: Gone Are the Days)

5083 PURPLE GANG, THE (Frank McDonald)
      Filmf: v. III (1960), p. 15; comp., cp. cr.
      Films & F: v. 6, n. 7 (Apr., 1960), p. 25; Robin Bean, 100 wds., cp. cr.

5084 PURPLE HEART, THE (Lewis Milestone)
      Films & F: v. 15, n. 9 (June, 1969), p. 84; Kingsley Canham, 675 wds., no cr.

5085 PURPLE HILLS, THE (Maury Dexter)
      Filmf: v. IV (1961), p. 344; comp., cp. cr.

5086 PURPLE NOON (René Clément)
        (also: Blazing Sun; Plein Soleil)
        Film: n. 29 (Summer, 1961), p. 11; Mark Shivas, 100 wds., no cr.
        Filmf: v. IV (1961), p. 264; comp., cp. cr.
        Films & F: v. 7, n. 10 (July, 1961), pp. 27-28; Robin Bean, 500 wds., cp. cr.
        Filmf in R: v. XII, n. 8 (Oct., 1961), p. 491; Louise Corbin, 125 wds., no cr.
        Sight & S: v. 30, n. 3 (Summer, 1961), pp. 149-150; Peter John Dyer, 350
            wds., pt. cr.

5087 PURPLE PLAIN, THE (Robert Parrish)
        Films & F: v. I, n. 2 (Nov., 1954), p. 19; Peter Barnes, 200 wds., cp. cr.

5088 PURSE, THE
        F Lib Quarterly: v. 2, n. 2 (Spring, 1969), pp. 28-29; Philip Levering, 200
            wds., pt. cr.

5089 PURSUIT OF HAPPINESS, THE (Robert Mulligan)
        Filmf: v. XIV (1971), p. 115; comp., cp. cr.
        Films in R: v. XXII, n. 2 (Feb., 1971), p. 109; Gwenneth Britt, 100 wds., no
            cr.

5090 PURSUIT OF THE GRAF SPEE (Michael Powell and Emeric Pressburger)
        (also: Battle of the River Platt)
        Films & F: v. 3, n. 3 (Dec., 1956), p. 22; Peter G. Baker, 200 wds., cp. cr.
        Films in R: v. VIII, n. 10 (Dec., 1957), pp. 224-225; Henry Hart, 175 wds.,
            no cr.

5091 PUSHER, THE (Gene Milford)
        Filmf: v. III (1960), p. 6; comp., cp. cr.

5092 PUSHOVER (Richard Quine)
        Films & F: v. I, n. 2 (Nov., 1954), pp. 20-21; Graham Shipham, 200 wds., cp.
            cr.
        Sight & S: v. 24, n. 3 (Jan.-Mar., 1955), p. 144; Lindsay Anderson, 650 wds.,
            pt. cr.

      PUSS AND KRAM (see: Hugs and Kisses)

5093 PUSSYCATS, THE (J. L. Bastid)
        Films & F: v. 14, n. 2 (Nov., 1967), pp. 24-25; Raymond Durgnat, 650 wds.,
            cp. cr.

5094 PUTNEY SWOPE (Robert Downey)
        Cineaste: v. III, n. 3 (Winter, 1969-1970), pp. 17-18; 1600 wds., pt. cr.
        Filmf: v. XII (1969), p. 361; comp., cp. cr.
        Take One: v. 2, n. 3 (1969), pp. 22-23; Susan Rice, 600 wds., pt. cr.

      PUTYOVKA V ZHIZN (see: The Road To Life)

5095 PUZZLE OF A DOWNFALL CHILD (Jerry Schatzberg)
        Filmf: v. XIV (1971), p. 270; comp., cp. cr.

5096 PYRAMIDE HUMAINE, LA (Jean Rouch)
        F Quarterly: v. XV, n. 2 (Winter, 1961-1962), pp. 57-59; Roger Sandall, 1200
            wds., pt. cr.

5097 PYRO (Julio Coll)
        Filmf: v. VII (1964), p. 25; comp., cp. cr.

5098 QUAI DES ORFÈVRES (Henry-Georges Clouzot)
        Sequence: n. 4 (Summer, 1948), pp. 35-37; Peter Ericsson, 1250 wds., no cr.

5099 QUAND LES ANGES TOMBENT (Roman Polanski)
        (also: When Angels Fall)
        Cahiers in Eng: n. 4, pp. 59-60; Jacques Bontemps, 800 wds., cp. cr.

5100 QUANTRILL'S RAIDERS (Edward Bernds)
        Filmf: v. I (1958), p. 67; comp., cp. cr.

5101 QUARE FELLOW, THE (Arthur Dreifuss)
        Filmf: v. VI (1963), p. 53; comp., cp. cr.
        Films & F: v. 9, n. 2 (Nov., 1962), p. 34; Raymond Durgnat, 650 wds., cp.
           cr.

        QUARTERMASS AND THE PIT (see: Five Million Years to Earth)

5102 QUARTERMASS EXPERIMENT, THE (Val Guest)
        (also: The Creeping Unknown)
        Films & F: v. 2, n. I (Oct., 1955), p. 19; P. L. Mannock, 150 wds., cp. cr.

5103 QUARTERMASS II (Val Guest)
        (also: Enemy from Space)
        Films & F: v. 3, n. 8 (May, 1957), p. 28; Peter John Dyer, 300 wds., cp. cr.

5104 QUARTET (Ken Annakin, Arthur Crabtree, Harold French, Ralph Smart)
        Films in R: v. I, n. I (Feb., 1950), pp. 34-35; 450 wds., pt. cr.
        Sight & S: v. 17, n. 68 (Winter, 1948-1949), p. 183; Arthur Vesselo, 160 wds.,
           no cr.

        QUARTIERS DES PARIS, LES (see: Paris Vu Par)

        QUATRE CENTS COUPS, LES (see: The 400 Blows)

5105 QUATRE NUITS D'UN REVEUR (Robert Bresson)
        Interntl F G: v. 9 (1972), pp. 136-137; John Gillett, 200 wds., pt. cr.

        QUATRE VÉRITES, LES (see: Three Fables of Love)

        QUATTRA GIORNATE DI NAPOLI, LE (see: The Four Days of Naples)

        QUE LA BETE MEURE (see: This Man Must Die)

5106 QUEEN, THE (Frank Simon)
        F Quarterly: v. XXI, n. 4 (Summer, 1968), pp. 59-60; Claire Clouzot, 600
           wds., no cr.
        Filmf: v. XI (1968), p. 246; comp., cp. cr.
        Films & F: v. 15, n. 5 (Feb., 1969), p. 36; David Austen, 350 wds., cp. cr.

5107 QUEEN BEE (Ranald MacDougall)
        Films & F: v. 2, n. 3 (Dec., 1955), p. 17; Catherine de la Roche, 300 wds.,
           cp. cr.

5108 QUEEN BEE (Marco Ferreri/ see: The Conjugal Bed)

5109 QUEEN CHRISTINA (Rouben Mamoulian)
        F Soc Rev: May (1966), p. 18; P.C., 200 wds., pt. cr.

5110 QUEEN IS CROWNED, A (Castleton Knight, prod.)
        Films in R: v. IV, n. 7 (Aug.-Sept., 1953), pp. 362-363; Henry Hart, 400
           wds., pt. cr.

5111 QUEEN KELLY (Erich von Stroheim)
        F Heritage: v. 2, n. I (Fall, 1966), pp. 24-29; Arthur Lenning, 1700 wds., no
           cr.

5112 QUEEN OF BLOOD (Curtis Harrington)
        F Quarterly: v. XIX, n. 4 (Summer, 1966), p. 68; R. M. Hodgens, 150 wds.,
           no cr.
        Filmf: v. IX (1966), p. 381; comp., cp. cr.

5113 QUEEN OF OUTER SPACE (Edward Bernds)
        Filmf: v. I (1958), p. 257; comp., cp. cr.

5114 QUEEN OF SHEBA MEETS THE ATOM MAN, THE (Ron Rice and Howard
     Everngam)
     F Culture: n. 48-49 (Winter-Spring, 1970), pp. 30-31; Fred Camper, 1100
     wds., pt. cr.

5115 QUEEN OF SPADES, THE (Roman Tikhomirov)
     (also: Pikovaya Dama)
     Filmf: v. IV (1961), p. 244; comp., cp. cr.

5116 QUEEN OF SPADES (Thorold Dickinson)
     Sequence: n. 8 (Summer, 1949), pp. 82-84; Peter Ericsson, 1050 wds., pt. cr.
     Sight & S: v. 18, n. 70 (Summer, 1949), p. 49; Arthur Vesselo, 150 wds., pt.
     cr.

5117 QUEEN OF THE NILE (Fernando Cerchio)
     (also: Nefertiti; Regina del Nilo)
     Films & F: v. 9, n. 10 (July, 1963), p. 29; Ian Johnson, 200 wds., cp. cr.

5118 QUEEN OF THE PIRATES (Mario Costa)
     Filmf: v. IV (1961), p. 210; comp., cp. cr.
     Films & F: v. 10, n. 3 (Dec., 1963), pp. 29-30; Raymond Durgnat, 325 wds.,
     cp. cr.

5119 QUEENS, THE (Luciano Salce, Mario Monicelli, Mauro Bolognini,
     Antonio Pietrangeli)
     (also: The Faries; Le Fate; Sex Quartet)
     Filmf: v. XI (1968), p. 81; comp., cp. cr.
     Films in R: v. XIX, n. 4 (Apr., 1968), p. 246; Adelaide Comerford, 150 wds.,
     no cr.

5120 QUEEN'S WORLD TOUR, A (Castleton Knight, prod.)
     Films In R: v. V, n. 5 (May, 1954), pp. 242-243; 150 wds., no cr.

     QUEI DISPERATI CHE PUZZANO DI SUDORE E DI MORTE (see: A Bullet
     for Sandoval)

     QUEIMIDA! (see: Burn)

     QUELQU'UN DERRIERE LA PORTE (see: Someone Behind the Door)

     QUENTIN DURWARD (see: The Adventures of Quentin Durward)

     QUESTI FANTASMI (see: hosts—Italian Style)

5121 QUESTION OF ADULTERY, A (Don Chaffey)
     Filmf: v. III (1960), p. 51; comp., cp. cr.
     Films & S: v. 4, n. 10 (July, 1958), p. 29; Peter G. Baker, 150 wds., cp. cr.

5122 QUESTION OF COLOR, A (Richard Bartlett)
     F Soc Rev: May (1968), p. 19; William A. Starr, 250 wds., pt. cr.

     QUESTION OF RAPE, A (see: Le Viol)

5123 QUESTION 7 (Stuart Rosenberg)
     Filmf: v. IV (1961), p. 277; comp., cp. cr.
     Films in R: v. XII, n. 3 (Mar., 1961), pp. 168-169; Henry Hart, 450 wds., no
     cr.

     QUI ETES-VOUS POLLY MAGOO? (see: Who Are You, Polly Maggoo?)

     QUI VEUT TUER CARLOS? (see: Christian-Jaque)

5124 QUICK AND THE DEAD, THE (Robert Totten)
     Filmf: v. VI (1963), p. 333; comp., cp. cr.
     Films & F: v. 9, n. 9 (June, 1963), pp. 34-35; Brian O'Brien, 400 wds., cp.
     cr.

5125 QUICK, BEFORE IT MELTS (Delbert Mann)
     Filmf: v. VIII (1965), p. 49; comp., cp. cr.

5126 QUICK BILLY (Bruce Baillie)
         F Quarterly: v. XXIV, n. 3 (Spring, 1971), p. 58; Ernest Callenbach, 200
            wds., no cr.
         Interntl F G: v. 9 (1972), pp. 271-272; Margot S. Kernan, 200 wds., no cr.

5127 QUICK GUN, THE (Sidney Salkow)
         Filmf: v. VII (1964), p. 80; comp., cp. cr.
         Films & F: v. 10, n. 9 (June, 1964), pp. 24-25; Richard Davis, 200 wds., cp.
            cr.

         QUIEN SABE? (see: A Bullet for the General)

5128 QUIET AMERICAN, THE (Joseph L. Mankiewicz)
         Filmf: v. I (1958), p. 13; comp., cp. cr.
         Films in R: v. IX, n. 2 (Feb., 1958), pp. 88-89; Bradford Banning, 500 wds.,
            no cr.
         Sight & S: v. 27, n. 4 (Spring, 1958), p. 201; David Robinson, 700 wds., pt.
            cr.

5129 QUIET FLOWS THE DON (Sergei Gerasimov)
         (also: Tikhii Don)
         F Journal: n. 16 (Aug., 1960), pp. 86-87; R. J. Garlick, 1000 wds., no cr.
         F Quarterly; v. XIV, n. I (Fall, 1960), pp. 49-51; Harriet R. Polt, 1400 wds.,
            pt. cr.
         Filmf: v. III (1960), p. 155; comp., cp. cr.
         Films & F: v. 5, n. I (Oct., 1958), p. 22; Peter John Dyer, 600 wds., cp. cr.
         Films in R: v. XI, n. 6 (June-July, 1960), pp. 366-367; Tatiana Balkoff
            Drowne, 300 wds., no cr.

5130 QUIET MAN, THE (John Ford)
         Films in R: v. III, n. 7 (Aug.-Sept., 1952), pp. 351-355; Henry Hart, 1600
            wds., pt. cr.
         Sight & S: v. 22, n. I (July-Sept., 1952), pp. 24-26; Lindsay Anderson, 2000
            wds., pt. cr.

5131 QUIET ONE, THE (Sidney Meyers)
         Films in R: v. I, n. I (Feb., 1950), pp. 32-33; 225 wds., pt. cr.

5132 QUIET PLACE IN THE COUNTRY, A (Elio Petri)
         (also: Un Tranquillo Posto di Campagna)
         Films & F: v. 17, n. 10 (July, 1971), p. 57; Gordon Gow, 450 wds., cp. cr.

5133 QUILLER MEMORANDUM, THE (Michael Anderson)
         F Quarterly: v. XX, n. 3 (Spring, 1967), pp. 62-63; Steven Farber, 150 wds.,
            no cr.
         Filmf: v. IX (1966), p. 338; comp., cp. cr.
         Films & F: v. 13, n. 4 (Jan., 1967), pp. 29-30; Gordon Gow, 1000 wds., cp.
            cr.
         Films in R: v. XVIII, n. I (Jan., 1967), pp. 54-55; Adelaide Comerford, 150
            wds., no cr.
         Sight & S: v. 36, n. I (Winter, 1966-1967), p. 48; Penelope Houston, 600
            wds., pt. cr.

5134 QUO VADIS (Mervyn LeRoy)
         Films in R: v. II, n. 10 (Dec., 1951), pp. 47-50; Henry Hart, 1000 wds., no. cr.

5135 R.P.M. (Stanley Kramer)
         Films in R: v. XXI, n. 9 (Nov., 1970), pp. 576-577; 250 wds., no cr.

5136 RX MURDER
         Filmf: v. I (1958), p. 194; comp., cp. cr.

5137 RABBIT, RUN (Jack Smight)
         Filmf: v. XIV (1971), p. 491; comp., cp. cr.

5138 RABBIT TRAP, THE (Philip Leacock)
Filmf: v. II (1959), p. 224; comp., cp. cr.
Films & F: v. 6, n. I (Oct., 1959), p. 23; Gordon Gow, 350 wds., cp. cr.
Films in R: v. X, n. 7 (Aug.-Sept., 1959), p. 425; Prudence Ashton, 200
wds., no cr.
Sight & S: v. 28, n. 3 & 4 (Summer-Autumn, 1951), p. 173; Derek Hill, 350
wds., pt. cr.

5139 RABBLE, THE (Hiroshi Inagaki)
(also: Garakuta)
Filmf: v. XI (1968), p. 155; comp., cp. cr.

RACCONTI D'ESTATE (see: Girls for the Summer)

5140 RACE FOR LIFE (Christian-Jaque)
(also: If All the Guys in the World...; Si Tous les Gars du Monde...)
Films & F: v. 2 n. 7 (Apr., 1956), p. 13; Peter G. Baker, 150 wds., cp. cr.
Films in R: v. VIII, n. 6 (June-July, 1957), pp. 283-284; Louise Corbin, 300
wds., no cr.

5141 RACERS, THE (Henry Hathaway)
(also: Such Men Are Dangerous)
Films in R: v. VI, n. 3 (Mar., 1955), pp. 131-132; Hartley Ramsay, 200 wds.,
pt. cr.

5142 RACHEL, RACHEL (Paul Newman)
F Quarterly: v. XXII, n. I (Fall, 1968), p. 77; Leo Braudy, 450 wds., no cr.
Filmf: v. XI (1968), p. 223; comp., cp. cr.
Films & F: v. 15, n. 5 (Feb., 1969), pp. 38-39; Allen Eyles, 550 wds., cp. cr.
Films in R: v. XIX, n. 8 (Oct., 1968), p. 517; Page Cook, 200 wds., no cr.
Movie: n. 16 (Winter, 1968-1969), p. 39; Ian Cameron, 100 wds., no cr.

5143 RACK, THE (Arnold Laven)
Films & F: v. 2, n. 10 (July, 1956), pp. 25-26; Rodney Giesler, 275 wds., cp.
cr.
Films in R: v. VII, n. 5 (May, 1956), pp. 220-221; Eleanor H. Nash, 250
wds., no cr.

RAFFICA DI COLTELLI (see: Knives of the Avenger)

RAFLES SUR LA VILLE (see: Sinners of Paris)

RAG DOLL (see: Young, Willing and Eager)

5144 RAGA (Howard Worth)
Filmf: v. XIV (1971), p. 744; comp., cp. cr.

RAGAZZA CHE SAPEVA TROPPO, LA (see: The Evil Eye)

RAGAZZA CON LA VILIGIA, LA (see: Girl with a Suitcase)

RAGAZZA DEL PALIO, LA (see: The Love Specialist)

RAGAZZA DI BABE, LA (see: Bebo's Girl)

RAGAZZA E IL GENERALE, LA (see: The Girl and the General)

RAGAZZA IN PRESTITO, LE (see: Engagement Italiono)

RAGAZZA IN VETRINA (see: Woman in the Window)

5145 RAGE (Gilberto Gazcon)
(also: El Mal)
Filmf: v. X (1967), p. 269; comp., cp. cr.

5146 RAGE OF THE BUCCANEERS (Mario Costa)
(also: Gordon, Il Pirata Nero)
Filmf: v. VI (1963), p. 344; comp., cp. cr.

5147 RAGE TO LIVE, A (Walter Grauman)
Films & F: v. 12, n. 6 (Mar., 1965), p. 18; Ian Johnson, 450 wds., cp. cr.
Films in R: v. XVI, n. 9 (Nov., 1965), pp. 579-580; Elaine Rothschild, 125 wds., no cr.

RAGING MOON, THE (see: Long Ago, Tomorrow)

5148 RAICES (Benito Alazraki)
(also: The Roots)
F Culture: v. 3, n. 1 (1957), pp. 16-18; Herman G. Weinberg, 1000 wds., pt. cr.
Films & F: v. 4, n. 11 (Aug., 1958), pp. 26-27; Peter John Dyer, 650 wds., cp. cr.
Films in R: v. VIII, n. 9 (Nov., 1957), pp. 464-465; Jose Mantuella, 150 wds., no cr.

5149 RAID ON ROMMEL (Henry Hathaway)
Filmf: v. XIV (1971), p. 182; comp., cp. cr.

5150 RAIDERS FROM BENEATH THE SEA
Filmf: v. VIII (1965), p. 15; comp., cp. cr.

5151 RAIDERS OF LEYTE GULF (Eddie Romero)
Filmf: v. VI (1963), p. 319; comp., cp. cr.
Films & F: v. 10, n. 6 (Mar., 1964), p. 31; David Rider, 300 wds., cp. cr.

5152 RAIL (Edgar Anstey, prod.)
F Lib Quarterly: v. 2, n. 3 (Summer, 1969), pp. 41, 48; Lewis Archibald, 450 wds., pt. cr.

RAILROAD MAN, THE (see: Man of Iron)

5153 RAILRODDER, THE (Gerald Potterton)
F Soc Rev: May (1967), pp. 17-18; John Thomas, 700 wds., pt. cr.

5154 RAILWAY CHILDREN, THE (Lionel Jeffries)
Filmf: v. XIV (1971), p. 634; comp., cp. cr.
Films & F: v. 17, n. 5 (Feb., 1971), pp. 51-52; Margaret Tarratt, 550 wds., cp. cr.
Films in R: v. XXII, n. 10 (Dec., 1971), pp. 638-639; Flavia Wharton Rhawn, 150 wds., no cr.
Sight & S: v. 40, n. 1 (Winter, 1970-1971), pp. 51-52; Richard Combs, 500 wds., pt. cr.

5155 RAIN (Lewis Milestone)
View & R: v. 3, n. 4 (Spring, 1972), pp. 4-14; Jon Tuska, 2800 wds., no cr.

5156 RAIN PEOPLE, THE (Francis Ford Coppola)
Filmf: v. XII (1969), p. 443; comp., cp. cr.
Films in R: v. XX, n. 8 (Oct., 1969), p. 515; William Herron, 150 wds., no cr.
Focus: n. 5 (Oct., 1969), pp. 20-21; Charles Flynn, 1000 wds., no cr.

5157 RAINMAKER, THE (Joseph Anthony)
Films & F: v. 3, n. 6 (Mar., 1957), p. 23; Peter G. Baker, 400 wds., cp. cr.
Films in R: v. VIII, n. 1 (Jan., 1957), p. 32; Ellen Fitzpatrick, 200 wds., no cr.

5158 RAINS OF RANCHIPUR, THE (Jean Negulesco)
Films & F: v. 2, n. 6 (Mar., 1956), p. 18; Peter G. Baker, 250 wds., cp. cr.

5159 RAINTREE COUNTY (Edward Dmytryk)
Films in R: v. IX, n. 1 (Jan., 1958), pp. 31-33; Courtland Phipps, 500 wds., no cr.

5160 RAISIN IN THE SUN, A (Daniel Petrie)
F Quarterly: v. XV, n. 1 (Fall, 1961), p. 56; R. M. Hodgens, 150 wds., no cr.
Filmf: v. IV (1961), p. 77; comp., cp. cr.
Films & F: v. 7, n. 10 (July, 1961), p. 27; John Cutts, 400 wds., cp. cr.
Films in R: v. XII, n. 5 (May, 1961), p. 298; 250 wds., no cr.

5161 RAISING THE WIND (Gerald Thomas)
        Films & F: v. 8, n. I (Oct., 1961), p. 30; Phillip Riley, 500 wds., cp. cr.

        RALLY (see: Bensaa Suonissa)

5162 RALLY ROUND THE FLAG, BOYS! (Leo McCarey)
        Filmf: v. I (1958), p. 287; comp., cp. cr.
        Films & F: v. 5, n. 6 (Mar., 1959), p. 23; Brenda Davies, 250 wds., cp. cr.
        Films in R: v. X, n. I (Jan., 1959), pp. 38-39; Charles A. Butler, 225 wds., no
            cr.

5163 RAMPAGE (Phil Karlson)
        Cinema: v. I, n. 6 (Nov.-Dec., 1963), p. 46; Rory Guy, 200 wds., pt. cr.
        F Quarterly: v. XVII, n. 2 (Winter, 1963-1964), p. 62; R. M. Hodgens, 100
            wds., no cr.
        Filmf: v. VI (1963), p. 221; comp., cp. cr.
        Films & F: v. I0, n. 2 (Nov., 1963), pp. 25-26; John Cutts, 425 wds., cp. cr.

5164 RAMPARTS OF CLAY (Jean-Louis Bertucelli)
        (also: Remparts D'Argile)
        F Lib Quarterly: v. 4, n. 4 (Fall, 1971), pp. 29-34; Nadine Covert, 1900 wds.,
            pt. cr.
        F Quarterly: v. XXIV, n. 4 (Summer, 1971), pp. 64, 67; Bill Nichols, 500
            wds., no cr.
        Filmf: v. XIV (1971), p. 478; comp., cp. cr.
        Films in R: v. XXII, n. 4 (Apr., 1971), p. 235; Paul-Etienne Coe, 125 wds., no
            cr.

        RANCUNE, LA (see: The Visit)

        RANSOM, THE (see: High and Low)

5165 RAPE, THE (Dinos Dimopoulos)
        Films & F. v. 13, n. 7 (Apr., 1967), pp. 9-10; Raymond Durgnat, 700 wds.,
            cp. cr.

5166 RAPE (Yoko Ono)
        F Culture: n. 48-49 (Winter-Spring, 1970), p. 33; Yoko Ono, 200 wds., no
            cr.

        RAPE, THE (Jacques Doniol-Valcroze/see: Le Viol)

        RAPE OF MALAYA, THE (see: A Town Like Alice)

5167 RAPTURE (John Guillermin)
        Films in R: v. XVI, n. 8 (Oct., 1965), p. 517; Jerry Vermilye, 175 wds., no cr.

5168 RARE BREED, THE (Andrew V. Mc Laglan)
        Filmf: v. IX (1966), p. 94; comp., cp. cr.
        Films & F: v. 12, n. 12 (Sept., 1966), pp. I0-12; Richard Davis, 250 wds., cp.
            cr.

5169 RASCAL
        Films in R: v. XX, n. 6 (June-July, 1969), p. 379; Tatiana Balkoff Drowne,
            100 wds., no cr.

5170 RASHOMON (Akira Kurosawa)
        F Journal: n. 6 (Dec., 1956), pp. 6-9; William E. Mills, 2000 wds., no cr.
        Films in R: v. III, n. I (Jan., 1952), pp. 34-37; Henry Hart, 1100 wds., no cr.
        Sight & S: v. 22, n. I (July-Sept., 1952), pp. 28-29; Simon Harcourt-Smith,
            1000 wds., pt. cr.

        RASPUTIN L'ULTIMO CZAR (see: The Night They Killed Rasputin)

5171 RASPUTIN - THE MAD MONK (Don Sharp)
        Filmf: v. IX (1966), p. 82; comp., cp. cr.

5172 RAT RACE, THE (Robert Mulligan)
        Filmf: v. III (1960), p. I21; comp., cp. cr.
        Films & F: v. 7, n. 7 (Apr., 1961), p. 30; John Cutts, 300 wds., cp. cr.

        RATS AWAKE, THE (see: The Rats Wake Up)

5173 RATS WAKE UP, THE (Zivojin Pavlović)
      (also: The Rats Awake)
      Films & F: v. 15, n. 12 (Sept., 1969), p. 66; Richard Combs, 400 wds., cp. cr.
      Interntl F G: v. 5 (1968), p. 166; 200 wds., pt. cr.

5174 RATTLE OF A SIMPLE MAN (Muriel Box)
      Films & F: v. 11, n. 2 (Nov., 1964), p. 29; John Cutts, 150 wds., cp. cr.

      RAUBFISCHER IN HELLAS (see: As The Sea Rages)

5175 RAVEN, THE (Roger Corman)
      Filmf: v. VI (1963), p. 3; comp., cp. cr.
      Films & F: v. 10, n. 1 (Oct., 1963), p. 25; Allen Eyles, 375 wds., cp. cr.
      Sight & S: v. 32, n. 4 (Autumn, 1963), p. 198; Peter John Dyer, 350 wds.,
          pt. cr.

5176 RAVEN'S END (Bo Widerberg)
      (also: Kvarteret Korpen)
      Films & F: v. 11, n. 7 (Apr., 1965), p. 30; Mike Sarne, 325 wds., cp. cr.
      Interntl F G: v. 2 (1965), p. 131; Peter Graham, 200 wds., pt. cr.
      Movie: n. 12 (Spring, 1965), p. 45; 75 wds., no cr.
      Sight & S: v. 34, n. 2 (Spring, 1965), pp. 96-97; Elizabeth Sussex, 600 wds.,
          pt. cr.

5177 RAW WIND IN EDEN (Richard Wilson)
      Filmf: v. I (1958), p. 168; comp., cp. cr.

5178 RAWHIDE TRAIL, THE (Robert Gordon)
      Filmf: v. I (1958), p. 11; comp., cp. cr.

5179 RAY GUN VIRUS (Paul Sharits)
      F Culture: n. 47 (Summer, 1969), pp. 13-14; Paul Sharits, 200 wds., no cr.

5180 RAYMIE (Frank McDonald)
      Filmf: v. III (1960), p. 234; comp., cp. cr.

5181 RAZOR BLADES (Paul Sharits)
      F Culture: n. 47 (Summer, 1969), pp. 14-15; Paul Sharits, 400 wds., no cr.

      RAZZIA SUR LA CHNOUF (see: Chnouf)

      RE DEI CRIMINALI, IL (see: Superargo and the Faceless Giants)

5182 REACH FOR GLORY (Philip Leacock)
      Filmf: v. VI (1963), p. 209; comp., cp. cr.
      Films & F: v. 9, n. 2 (Nov., 1962), pp. 34-35; Peter Baker, 650 wds., cp. cr.

5183 REACH FOR THE SKY (Lewis Gilbert)
      Films & F: v. 2, n. 11 (Aug., 1956), p. 22; Rodney Giesler, 250 wds., cp. cr.
      Films in R: v. VIII, n. 6 (June-July, 1957), p. 283; Nigel Ames, 200 wds., no
          cr.
      Sight & S: v. 26, n. 2 (Autumn, 1956), pp. 97-98; John Gillett, 375 wds., pt.
          cr.

5184 REACHING FOR THE STARS (Carl Heinz Schroth)
      (also: Griff Nach den Sternen)
      Filmf: v. I (1958), p. 138; comp., cp. cr.

5185 READING INCENTIVE SERIES (Bank Street College of Education)
      F Lib Quarterly: v. 4, n. 2 (Spring, 1971), pp. 49-40; Hannah Miller and
          Masha R. Porte, 400 wds., pt. cr.

5186 READY FOR THE PEOPLE (Buzz Kulik)
      Filmf: v. VII (1964), p. 281; comp., cp. cr.

5187 REALITY OF KAREL APPEL, THE (Jan Vrijman)
      Interntl F G: v. I (1964), p. 111; 100 wds., pt. cr.

5188 REAR WINDOW (Alfred Hitchcock)
      Films & F: v. I, n. 2 (Nov., 1954), p. 18; Ernest Borneman, 575 wds., cp. cr.

Films in R: v. V, n. 8 (Oct., 1954), pp. 427-429; Steve Sondheim, 725 wds.,
   no cr.
Sight & S: v. 24, n. 2 (Oct.-Dec., 1954), pp. 89-90; Derwent May, 550 wds.,
   pt. cr.
Take One: v. 2, n. 2 (1969), pp. 18-20; Alfred Hitchcock, 3000 wds., no cr.

REBEL, THE (see: Call Me Genius)

5189 REBEL FLIGHT TO CUBA (Gottfried Reinhardt)
Films & F: v. 9, n. 6 (Mar., 1963), p. 38; Robin Bean, 150 wds., cp. cr.

5190 REBEL IN TOWN (Alfred Werker)
Films & F: v. 3, n. 2 (Nov., 1956), p. 25; Peter John Dyer, 150 wds., cp. cr.

5191 REBEL SET, THE (Gene Fowler, Jr.)
Filmf: v. II (1959), p. 188; comp., cp. cr.

REBEL WITH A CAUSE (see: The Loneliness of a Long Distance Runner)

5192 REBEL WITHOUT A CAUSE (Nicholas Ray)
F Culture: v. 2, n. I (1956), pp. 19-21; Eugene Archer, 2500 wds., pt. cr.
Films in R: v. VI, n. 9 (Nov., 1955), pp. 467-468; Courtland Phipps, 500
   wds., pt. cr.

5193 REBELLION (Masaki Kobayashi)
(also: Joi-Uchi)
Filmf: v. XI (1968), p. 456; comp., cp. cr.
Films & F: v. 15, n. 6 (Mar., 1969), p. 86; Kingsley Canham, 400 wds., no cr.
Sight & S: v. 37, n. 2 (Spring, 1968), pp. 97-98; Philip Strick, 1000 wds., pt.
   cr.

REBELS AGAINST THE LIGHT (see: Sands of Beersheba)

RECKLESS AGE, THE (see: Dragstrip Riot)

5194 RECKLESS MOMENT, THE (Max Ophuls)
F Comment: v. 7, n. 2 (Summer, 1971), pp. 65-66; William Paul, 1500 wds.,
   cp. cr.
Sequence: n. 10 (New Year, 1950), p. 156; Lindsay G. Anderson, 200 wds.,
   no cr.
Sight & S: v. 18, n. 72 (Jan., 1950), p. 31; 650 wds., pt. cr.

5195 RECKONING THE (Jack Gold)
Filmf: v. XIV (1971), p. 118; comp., cp. cr.
Films & F: v. 16, n. 5 (Feb., 1970), pp. 36-37; Brenda Davies, 350 wds., cp.
   cr.

5196 RECONSTRUCTION, THE (Lucian Pintilie)
Interntl F G: v. 8 (1971), p. 232; Mirella Georgiadou, 225 wds., pt. cr.

RECONSTRUCTION (Thodoros Anghelopoulos/see: Anaparastasis)

RECORD OF A LIVING BEING (see: I Live in Fear)

5197 RED (Gilles Carle)
Interntl F G: v. 8 (1971), p. 95; Gerald Pratley, 100 wds., pt. cr.
Take One: v. 2, n. 6 (1970), pp. 20-21; Ian Ferguson, 550 wds., pt. cr.

5198 RED AND BLUE (Tony Richardson)
Films & F: v. 15, n. I (Oct., 1968), p. 48; Gordon Gow, 300 wds., cp. cr.

5199 RED AND THE WHITE, THE (Miklos Jancso)
(also: Csillagosok, Katonak; Star-Badges, Soldiers)
Filmf: v. XII (1969), p. 157; comp., cp. cr.
Interntl F G: v. 6 (1969), p. 94; Peter Cowie, 225 wds., pt. cr.

5200 RED ANGEL, THE (Yasuzb Masumura)
Films & F: v. 15, n. 12 (Sept., 1969), pp. 65-66; Brian Murphy, 450 wds., cp.
   cr.

5201 RED BADGE OF COURAGE, THE (John Huston)
        Films in R: v. II, n. 8 (Oct., 1951), pp. 42-43; B. G. Marple, 650 wds., pt. cr.
        Sight & S: v. 21, n. 3 (Jan.-Mar., 1952), p. 123; Gavin Lambert, 750 wds., pt.
        cr.

5202 RED BALLOON, THE (Albert Lamorisse)
        (also: Le Ballon Rouge)
        F Culture: v. 3, n. 3 (1957), p. 15; Arlene Croce, 700 wds., pt. cr.
        Films in R: v. VIII, n. 3 (Mar., 1957), p. 132; Diana Willing, 125 wds., no cr.
        Sight & S: v. 26, n. 3 (Winter, 1956-1957), p. 155; Claude Goretta, 325 wds.,
        no cr.

5203 RED BARON, THE (Roger Corman)
        Focus on F: n. 8 (Oct., 1971), p. II; Richard Combs and Allen Eyles, 400
        wds., cp. cr.
        Sight & S: v. 40, n. 4 (Autumn, 1971), p. 226; Tom Milne, 1000 wds., pt. cr.

5204 RED BEARD (Akira Kurosawa)
        (also: Akahige)
        Film: n. 44 (Winter, 1965-1966), pp. 16-17; Stanley Crawford, 250 wds., no
        cr.
        Filmf: v. XI (1968), p. 516; comp., cp. cr.
        Films & F: v. 15, n. 5 (Feb., 1969) p. 46; 250 wds., Richard Davis, cp. cr.

5205 RED CLOAK, THE (Giuseppe Maria-Scotese)
        (also: Il Mantello Rosso)
        Filmf: v. IV (1961), p. 369; comp., cp. cr.

5206 RED DANUBE, THE (George Sidney)
        Sequence: n. II (Summer, 1950), pp. 10-II; Lindsay G. Anderson, 1000 wds.,
        no cr.

5207 RED DESERT, THE (Michelangelo Antonioni)
        (also: Deserto Rosso)
        F Comment: v. 3, n. I (Winter, 1965), pp. 71-72; Jules Cohen, 1500 wds., pt.
        cr.
        F Culture: n. 41 (Summer, 1966), pp. 24-30; John S. Bragin, 3500 wds., no
        cr.
        F Quarterly: v. XIX, n. I (Fall, 1965), pp. 51-54; Colin Young, 1350 wds., pt.
        cr.
        F Soc Rev: Apr. (1967), pp. 15-17; John Thomas, 600 wds., pt. cr.
        Filmf: v. VIII (1965), p. 33; comp., cp. cr.
        Films & F: v. II, n. 9 (June, 1965), p. 27; Gordon Gow, 1075 wds., cp. cr.
        Films in R: v. XVI, n. 3 (Mar., 1965), pp. 180-181; Henry Hart, 375 wds., no
        cr.
        Interntl F G: v. 3 (1966), pp. 98-99; Gaetano Strazzulla, 250 wds., pt. cr.
        Movie: n. 13 (Summer, 1965), pp. 10-13; Robin Wood, 3000 wds., no cr.

5208 RED DRAGON (Ernst Hofbauer)
        (also: Das Geheimnis Der Drei Dschunken; The Secret of the Three Junks)
        Filmf: v. X (1967), p. 336; comp., cp. cr.
        Films in R: v. V, n. 4 (Apr., 1954), p. 193; 125 wds., no cr.

5209 RED HELL (William D. Faralla)
        Films & F: v. II, n. 4 (Jan., 1965), p. 33; David Rider, 575 wds., cp. cr.

        RED INN, THE (see: L'Auberge Rouge)

5210 RED KITE, THE
        F Lib Quarterly: v. 2, n. 2 (Spring, 1969), pp. 28-29; Philip Levering, 200
        wds., pt. cr.

5211 RED LANTERNS (Vassilis Georgiadis)
        (also: Kokkina Quanapia)
        Films & F: v. II, n. 8 (May, 1965), p. 29; Richard Davis, 525 wds., cp. cr.

5212 RED LINE 7000 (Howard Hawks)
        F Quarterly: v. XIX, n. 3 (Spring, 1966), p. 53; R. M. Hodgens, 175 wds., no
        cr.
        Films in R: v. XVI, n. 10 (Dec., 1965), p. 646; Jerry Vermilye, 175 wds., no
        cr.

5213 RED LIPS (Giuseppe Bennati)
        (also: Labbra Rosse)
        Filmf: v. VII (1964), p. l6; comp., cp. cr.

      RED MANTLE, THE (see: Hagbard and Signe)

5214 RED PLANET MARS (Harry Horner)
        Sight & S: v. 22, n. 2 (Oct.-Dec., 1952), p. 81; Penelope Houston, 900 wds.,
          pt. cr.

5215 RED RAIDERS (Albert Rogell)
        Views & R: v. 3, n. 3 (Winter, 1972), pp. 26-35; 2500 wds., cp. cr.

5216 RED SHOES (Michael Powell and Emeric Pressburger)
        Sight & S: v. 17, n. 67 (Autumn, 1948), pp. 143-144; Arthur Vesselo, 250
          wds., no cr.

5217 RED SKY AT MORNING (James Goldstone)
        F Quarterly: v. XXV, n. 2 (Winter, 1971-1972), pp. 57-58; Foster Hirsh, 500
          wds., no cr.
        Filmf: v. XIV (1971), p. 54; comp., cp. cr.
        Films in R: v. XXII, n. 6 (June-July, 1971), p. 373; Gwenneth Britt, 200
          wds., no cr.

5218 RED TENT, THE (Mikhail K. Kalatozov)
        (also: La Tenda Rossa)
        Filmf: v. XIV (1971), p. 458; comp., cp. cr.
        Films in R: v. XXII, n. 8 (Oct., 1971), pp. 510-511; Sigmund Glaubmann, 200
          wds., no cr.

5219 RED TOMAHAWK (R. G. Springsteen)
        Filmf: v. X (1967), p. 54; comp., cp. cr.

      REDPATH - 25 (see: Palace of Pleasure)

      RE-ENACTMENT (see: Anaparastasis)

5220 RE-ENTRY (Jordan Belson)
        F Culture: n. 48-49 (Winter-Spring, 1970), pp. 15-16; Gene Youngblood, 1400
          wds., no cr.
        F Quarterly: v. XIX, n. 1 (Fall, 1965), pp. 60-61; Ernest Callenbach, 600
          wds., pt. cr.

5221 REFINEMENTS IN LOVE (Carlos Tobalina)
        Filmf: v. XIV (1971), p. 524; comp., cp. cr.

5222 REFINER'S FIRE, THE (Carl Hemenway, Keith Beardsley and Richard
          Grossman)
        F Lib Quarterly: v. 3, n. 4 (Fall, 1970), pp. 26-28; Rodney E. Sheratsky,
          850 wds., pt. cr.

5223 REFLECTIONS IN A GOLDEN EYE (John Huston)
        Cinema: v. 4, n. 1 (Spring, 1968), p. 47; Axel Madsen, 750 wds., no cr.
        F Quarterly: v. XXI, n. 2 (Winter, 1967-1968), p. 63; Margot S. Kernan, 250
          wds., no cr.
        Filmf: v. X (1967), p. 288; comp., cp. cr.
        Films & F: v. 14, n. 8 (April, 1968), p. 24; Allen Eyles, 600 wds., cp. cr.
        Films in R: v. XVIII, n. 9 (Nov., 1967), pp. 576-577; Elaine Rothschild, 175
          wds., no cr.
        Movie: n. 15 (Spring, 1968), pp. 25-26; Paul Mayersberg, 1600 wds., no cr.
        Sight & S: v. 37, n. 2 (Spring, 1968), pp. 99-100; John Russell Taylor, 650
          wds., pt. cr.

5224 REFUGE ENGLAND (Robert Vas)
        Sight & S: v. 28, n. 3-4 (Summer-Autumn, 1959), p. 174; Derek Hill, 250
          wds., no cr.

      REGAIN (see: Harvest)

5225 REGGAE (Horace Ove)
        Take One: v. 2, n. 10 (1971), pp. 35-36; Hal Aigner, 300 wds., no cr.

REGINA DEI TARTARI, LA (see: The Huns)

5226 REGION CENTRALE, LA (Michael Snow)
 F Culture: n. 52 (Spring, 1971), pp. 58-63; Michael Snow, 1300 wds., no cr.

5227 REGLE DU JEU, LE (Jean Renoir)
 (also: Rules of the Game)
 F Journal: n. 23 (July, 1964), pp. 35-37; R. J. Garlick, 1800 wds., no cr.
 Filmf: v. IV (1961), p. 7; comp., cp. cr.
 Films & F: v. 8, n. 2 (Nov., 1961), p. 27; Richard Whitehall, 1100 wds., cp. cr.
 Films in R: v. XII, n. I (Jan., 1961), pp. 40-41; Louise Corbin, 300 wds., no
  cr.
 Screen: v. II, n. I (Jan.-Feb., 1970), pp. 3-13; Suzanne Budgen, 4000 wds., no
  cr.
 Sequence: n. II (Summer, 1950), pp. 41-44; Gavin Lambert, 2400 wds., pt.
  cr.
 Sight & S: v. 15, n. 60 (Winter, 1946-1947), p. 153; Roger Manvell, 150 wds.,
  no cr.
 Take One: v. I, n. 12 (1968), pp. 10-12; Suzanne Budgen, 2000 wds., no cr.

5228 REGNE DU JOUR, LE (Pierre Perrault)
 Interntl F G: v. 5 (1968), p. 53; 120 wds., pt. cr.

5229 REIVERS, THE (Mark Rydell)
 Films & F: v. 17, n. 4 (Jan., 1971), pp. 56, 60; Margaret Tarratt, 300 wds.,
  cp. cr.
 Films in R: v. XXI, n. 2 (Feb., 1970), p. 121; Gwenneth Britt, 150 wds., no
  cr.

5230 REJS (Marek Piwowski)
 (also: A Trip Down the River)
 Interntl F G: v. 9 (1972), p. 220; Ryszard Koniczek, 125 wds., pt. cr.
5231 RELATION (Henry Greenspan)
 Take One: v. 2, n. 5 (1970), p. 30; Joe Medjuck, 400 wds., pt. cr.

5232 RELATIONS (Hans Abramson)
 (also: Tumult)
 Filmf: v. XIV (1971), p. 122; comp., cp. cr.

5233 RELATIVITY (Ed Emshwiller)
 F Quarterly: v. XX, n. 3 (Spring, 1967), pp. 46-50; Richard Whitehall, 2200
  wds., no cr.

5234 RELIGIEUSE, LA (Jacques Rivette)
 (also: The Nun; Suzanne Simonin, La Religieuse de Diderot)
 F Quarterly: v. XXII, n. 3 (Spring, 1969), pp. 44-47; Claire Clouzot, 1300
  wds., pt. cr.
 Filmf: v. XIV (1971), p. 486; comp., cp. cr.
 Films in R: v. XXII, n. 7 (Aug.-Sept., 1971), p. 444; Louise Corbin, 200
  wds., no cr.
 Interntl F G: v. 4 (1967), p. 71; 250 wds., pt. cr.
 Sight & S: v. 37, n. I (Winter, 1967-1968), p. 38; Tom Milne, 750 wds., pt.
  cr.

5235 RELIGION IN RUSSIA (Julien Bryan, prod.)
 F Lib Quarterly: v. 2, n. 2 (Spring, 1969), pp. 18-20; Alan Clark, 1300 wds.,
  pt. cr.

 RELITTO, IL (see: The Wastrell)

5236 RELUCTANT ASTRONAUT, THE (Edward Montagne)
 Filmf: v. X (1967), p. 256; comp., cp. cr.

5237 RELUCTANT DEBUTANTE, THE (Vincente Minnelli)
 Filmf: v. I (1958), p. 149; comp., cp. cr.
 Films & F: v. 5, n. 4 (Jan., 1959), p. 22; Peter G. Baker, 450 wds., cp. cr.

5238 RELUCTANT SAINT, THE (Edward Dmytryk)
 Filmf: v. V (1962), p. 336; comp., cp. cr.
 Films & F: v. II, n. 7 (Apr., 1965), p. 29; Gordon Gow, 350 wds., cp. cr.
 Films in R: v. XIII, n. 10 (Dec., 1962), p. 627; Romano Tozzi, 125 wds., no
  cr.

5239 REMARKABLE MR. PENNYPACKER, THE (Henry Levin)
        (also: Mr. Pennypacker)
        Filmf: v. II (1959), p. 29; comp., cp. cr.
        Films & F: v. 5, n. 4 (Jan., 1959), p. 24; Brenda Davies, 250 wds., cp. cr.

5240 REMEDIAL READING COMPREHENSION (George Landow)
        F Culture: n. 52 (Spring, 1971), pp. 73-77; Fred Camper, 2100 wds., no cr.

5241 REMORGUES (Jean Grémillon)
        Sequence: n. 4 (Summer, 1948), pp. 41-42; Gavin Lambert, 700 wds., no cr.

      REMPARTS D'ARGILE (see: Ramparts of Clay)

5242 RENAISSANCE (Walerian Borowczyk)
        F Quarterly: v. XIX, n. 2 (Winter, 1965-1966), pp. 52-53; Peter Graham, 700
          wds., no cr.

5243 RENDEZVOUS AT MIDNIGHT (Roger Leenhardt)
        (also: Le Rendezvous de Minuit)
        Films & F: v. 9, n. I (Oct., 1962), p. 38; Raymond Durgnat, 550 wds., cp. cr.
        Movie: n. 3 (Oct., 1962), p. 36; 50 wds., no cr.
        Movie: n. 4 (Nov., 1962), p. 34; Paul Mayersberg, 900 wds., pt. cr.
        Sight & S: v. 31, n. 4 (Autumn, 1962), p. 194; John Russell Taylor, 500 wds.,
          no cr.

5244 RENDEZVOUS DE JUILLET (Jacques Becker)
        Films & F: v. I, n. 2 (Nov., 1954), p. 18; Peter Barnes, 150 wds., cp. cr.
        Sight & S: v. 24, n. 2 (Oct.-Dec., 1954), pp. 90-91; Lindsay Anderson, 600
          wds., pt. cr.

      RENDEZVOUS DE MINUIT (see: Rendezvous at Midnight)

      RENDEZVOUS DU DIABLE, LES (see: Volcano)

5245 REPORT (Bruce Conner)
        F Culture: n. 44 (Spring, 1967), pp. 57-59; Carl J. Belz, 1700 wds., no cr.
        F Quarterly: v. XIX, n. 3 (Spring, 1966), pp. 54-56; David Mosen, 750 wds.,
          pt. cr.

5246 REPORT FROM CHINA (Takeji Takamura)
        F Quarterly: v. XXIV, n. 4 (Summer, 1971), p. 67; Ernest Callenbach, 100
          wds., no cr.
        F Soc Rev: v. 7, n. I (Sept., 1971), pp. 36-39; Leonard Rubenstein, 1500
          wds., cp. cr.

5247 REPORT ON THE PARTY AND THE GUESTS, A (Jan Němec)
        (also: The Party and the Guests; O Slavnosti A Hostech)
        Filmf: v. XI (1968), p. 440; comp., cp. cr.
        Films & F: v. 15, n. 6 (Mar., 1969), p. 45; Gordon Gow, 1100 wds., cp. cr.
        Interntl F G: v. 6 (1969), pp. 55-56; Peter Cowie, 250 wds., pt. cr.

      REPOS DU GUERRIER, LE (see: Love on a Pillow)

      REPRIEVE (see: Convicts Four)

5248 REPTILE, THE (John Gilling)
        Filmf: v. IX (1966), p. 381; comp., cp. cr.
        Films & F: v. 12, n. 6 (Mar., 1965), p. 55; Nicholas Gosling, 300 wds., cp. cr.

5249 REPTILICUS (Sidney Pink)
        Filmf: v. V (1962), p. 364; comp., cp. cr.

5250 REPUBLIC OF SIN (Luis Buñuel)
        (also: La Fievre Monte a el Pao)
        Films & F: v. 6, n. 11 (Aug., 1960), p. 22; Peter G. Baker, 350 wds., cp. cr.

5251 REPULSION (Roman Polanski)
        Cahiers in Eng: n. 4, pp. 56-57; Michel Caen, 1200 wds., cp. cr.
        F Quarterly: v. XIX, n. 3 (Spring, 1966), pp. 44-45; Albert Johnson, 1000
          wds., pt. cr.

Films & F: v. II, n. II (Aug., 1965), pp. 28-29; Raymond Durgnat, 1000 wds., cp. cr.
Interntl F G: v. 3 (1966), p. 84; 100 wds., pt. cr.
Movie: n. 13 (Summer, 1965), p. 44; 75 wds., no cr.
Movie: n. 14 (Autumn, 1965), pp. 26-27; Charles Barr, 900 wds., no cr.
Movie: n. 14 (Autumn, 1965), pp. 27-28; Peter von Bagh, 1300 wds., no cr.
Sight & S: v. 34, n. 3 (Summer, 1965), p. 146; Peter John Dyer, 600 wds., pt. cr.

5252 REQUIEM FOR A HEAVYWEIGHT (Ralph Nelson)
(also: Blood Money)
F Quarterly: v. XVI, n. 3 (Spring, 1963), p. 59; R. M. Hodgens, 75 wds., no cr.
Filmf: v. V (1962), p. 249; comp., cp. cr.
Films & F: v. 9, n. 7 (Apr., 1963), p. 30; Gordon Gow, 650 wds., cp. cr.
Films in R: v. XIII, n. 9 (Nov., 1962), p. 560; Wilfred Mifflin, 225 wds., no cr.

RESA DEI CONTI, LA (see: The Big Gundown)

RESIDENCIA, LA (see: The House That Screamed)

5253 REST IS SILENCE, THE (Helmut Käutner)
(also: Der Rest Ist Schweigen)
F Quarterly: v. XV, n. I (Fall, 1961), pp. 44-45; Colin Young, 650 wds., pt. cr.
Filmf: v. III (1960), p. 196; comp., cp. cr.

REST IST SCHWIGEN, DER (see: The Rest Is Silence)

5254 RESTLESS YEARS, THE (Helmut Käutner)
Filmf: v. I (1958), p. 285; comp., cp. cr.

5255 RESURRECTION (Mikhail Schweitzer)
F Soc Rev: Apr. (1966), p. II; Edwin Jahiel, 375 wds., pt. cr.

RETOUR DE DON CAMILLO, LE (see: The Return of Don Camillo)

RETOUR DE MANIVELLE (see: There's Always a Price Tag)

5256 RETURN FROM THE ASHES (J. Lee Thompson)
Films & F: v. 12, n. 6 (Mar., 1965), pp. 14, 18; Richard Davis, 550 wds., cp. cr.
Films in R: v. XVI, n. 10 (Dec., 1965), pp. 645-646; Elaine Rothschild, 200 wds., no cr.

5257 RETURN OF DON CAMILLO, THE (Julien Duvivier)
(also: Le Retour de Don Camillo; Il Ritorno di Don Camillo)
Films & F: v. I, n. I (Oct., 1954), pp. 18, 20; John Minchinton, 400 wds., cp. cr.

5258 RETURN OF DRACULA, THE (Julien Duvivier)
Filmf: v. I (1958), p. 57; comp., cp. cr.

5259 RETURN OF SANDOKAN, THE (Luigi Capuano)
Films & F: v. 12, n. 8 (May, 1966), pp. 52-53; Nicholas Gosling, 250 wds., cp. cr.

5260 RETURN OF THE FLY (Edward L. Bernds)
Filmf: v. II (1959), p. 206; comp., cp. cr.
Films & F: v. 6, n. 3 (Dec., 1959), p. 25; Derek Conrad, 200 wds., cp. cr.

5261 RETURN OF THE GUNFIGHTER (James Neilson)
Films & F: v. XIII, n. 6 (Mar., 1967), p. 34; Allen Eyles, 550 wds., cp. cr.

RETURN OF THE ISLANDER, THE (see: An Toileanach a Dfhill)

5262 RETURN OF THE PRODIGAL SON (Ewald Schorm)
(also: Navrat Ztracheneho Syna)
Films & F: v. 16, n. I (Oct., 1969), pp. 54-55; Brian Murphy, 450 wds., cp. cr.
Interntl F G: v. 5 (1968), p. 56; Peter Cowie, 220 wds., pt. cr.

5263 RETURN OF THE SEVEN (Burt Kennedy)
  Filmf: v. IX (1966), p. 295; comp., cp. cr.
  Films & F: v. 13, n. 5 (Feb., 1967), p. 35; Allen Eyles, 600 wds., cp. cr.

5264 RETURN TO PEYTON PLACE (Jose Ferrer)
  Film: n. 29 (Summer, 1961), pp. 9-10; Ian Cameron, 200 wds., no cr.
  Filmf: v. IV (1961), p. 117; comp., cp. cr.
  Films & F: v. 7, n. 10 (July, 1961), pp. 29-30; John Cutts, 400 wds., cp. cr.
  Films in R: v. XII, n. 6 (June-July, 1961), pp. 360-361; Jerry Vermilye, 325
   wds., no cr.

5265 RETURN TO WARBOW (Ray Nazarro)
  Filmf: v. I (1958-1959), p. 6; comp., cp. cr.

5266 REVENGE OF FRANKENSTEIN, THE (Terence Fisher)
  Filmf: v. I (1958), p. 107; comp., cp. cr.
  Films & F: v. 5, n. I (Oct., 1958), p. 22; Tony Buck, 250 wds., cp. cr.

5267 REVENGE OF THE BLOOD BEAST (Mike Reeves)
  Films & F: v. 13, n. 2 (Nov., 1966), p. 18; Raymond Durgnat, 500 wds., cp.
   cr.

  REVENGE OF THE VAMPIRE (see: Black Sunday)

  REVENGE OF YUKINOJO, THE (see: An Actor's Revenge)

5268 REVOLT IN THE BIG HOUSE (R. G. Springsteen)
  Filmf: v. I (1958), p. 274; comp., cp. cr.

5269 REVOLT OF MAMIE STOVER, THE (Raoul Walsh)
  Films & F: v. 2, n. II (Aug., 1956), p. 24; Peter John Dyer, 275 wds., cp. cr.

5270 REVOLT OF THE SLAVES (Nunzio Malasomma)
  Filmf: v. IV (1961), p. 256; comp., cp. cr.

5271 REVOLUTION (Jack O'Connell)
  Filmf: v. XI (1968), p. 322; comp., cp. cr.
  Films in R: v. XIX, n. 8 (Oct., 1968), pp. 514-515; Louise Bartlett, 225 wds.,
   no cr.

5272 REVOLUTIONARY, THE (Paul Williams)
  F Heritage; v. 6, n. 2 (Winter, 1970-1971), pp. 27-32; Rocco Landesman, 1600
   wds., pt. cr.
  F Quarterly: v. XXIV, n. I (Fall, 1970), p. 61; Ernest Callenbach, 200 wds.,
   no cr.
  Sight & S: v. 40, n. 2 (Spring, 1971), p. 107; Jan Dawson, 700 wds., pt. cr.

5273 REWARD, THE (Serge Bourguignon)
  Cinema: v. 3, n. I (Dec., 1965), p. 49; Rory Guy, 500 wds., pt. cr.
  Films & F: v. 12, n. 4 (Jan., 1966), Gordon Gow, 1000 wds., cp. cr.

5274 RHAPSODY (Charles Vidor)
  Films in R: v. V, n. 4 (Apr., 1954), pp. 192-193; 200 wds., no cr.

5275 RHAPSODY IN BLOOD (J. Antonio Isasi-Isasmendi)
  Films & F: v. 10, n. 7 (Apr., 1964), pp. 29-30; Raymond Durgnat, 500 wds.,
   cp. cr.

5276 RHINO! (Ivan Tors)
  Filmf: v. VII (1964), p. 291; comp., cp. cr.
  Films & F: v. II, n. 4 (Jan., 1965), pp. 33-34; David Rider, 450 wds., cp. cr.
  Films in R: v. XV, n. 6 (June-July, 1964), pp. 370-371; Olive Austin, 125
   wds., no cr.

5277 RHYTHM 'N GREENS (Christopher Miles)
  Films & F: v. II, n. 3 (Dec., 1964), p. 30; Paul Brewer, 225 wds., cp. cr.

5278 RICHARD III (Laurence Olivier)
  F Culture: v. 2, n. I (1956), pp. 21-23; Jay Leyda, 2500 wds., pt. cr.
  Films & F: v. 2, n. 3 (Dec., 1955), p. 16; John Carroll, 750 wds., cp. cr.

Films in R: v. VII, n. 3 (Mar., 1956), pp. 122-123; William W. Appleton, 600 wds., no cr.
Films in R: v. VII, n. 3 (Mar., 1956), pp. 123-124; Robert Downing, 400 wds., no cr.
Films in R: v. VII, n. 3 (Mar., 1956), pp. 124-126; Henry Hart, 550 wds., no cr.
Sight & S: v. 25, n. 3 (Winter, 1955-1956), pp. 144-145; Derek Prouse, 850 wds., pt. cr.

RICHER THAN THE EARTH (see: The Whistle at Eaton Falls)

5279 RIDE A CROOKED TRAIL (Jesse Hibbs)
Filmf: v. I (1958), p. 160; comp., cp. cr.

5280 RIDE BACK, THE (Allen H. Milner)
Films & F: v. 4, n. 6 (Mar., 1958), p. 27; John Cutts, 350 wds., cp. cr.

5281 RIDE BEYOND VENGEANCE (Bernard McEveety)
Filmf: v. IX (1966), p. 253; comp., cp. cr.
Films & F: v. 12, n. 3 (Dec., 1965), pp. 11, 14; David Rider, 450 wds., cp. cr.

5282 RIDE LONESOME (Budd Boetticher)
Filmf: v. II (1959), p. 110; comp., cp. cr.

5283 RIDE OUT FOR REVENGE (Bernard Girard)
Filmf: v. I (1958), p. 8; comp., cp. cr.

5284 RIDE THE HIGH COUNTRY (Sam Peckinpah)
(also: Guns in the Afternoon)
Cinema: v. I, n. 3, p. 33; 250 wds., pt. cr.
Filmf: v. V (1962), p. 137; comp., cp. cr.
Films & F: v. 8, n. 9 (June, 1962), p. 38; John Cutts, 300 wds., cp. cr.
Filmf in R: v. XIII, n. 4 (Apr., 1962), pp. 232-233; Robert Anck, 200 wds., no cr.
Sight & S: v. 31, n. 3 (Summer, 1962), p. 146; Dupre Jones, 700 wds., pt. cr.

5285 RIDE THE HIGH WIND (David Millin)
Filmf: v. XI (1968), p. 538; comp., cp. cr.

5286 RIDE THE WILD SURF (Gordon Taylor)
Filmf: v. VII (1964), p. 180; comp., cp. cr.
Films & F: v. II, n. 6 (Mar., 1965), p. 37; Robin Bean, 175 wds., cp. cr.

5287 RIDE TO HANGMAN'S TREE, THE (Alan Rafkin)
Filmf: v. X (1967), p. 391; comp., cp. cr.

5288 RIDEAU CRAMOISI, LE (Alexandre Astruc)
Sight & F: v. 23, n. 2 (Oct.-Dec., 1953), pp. 91-92; J. A. Wilson, 900 wds., pt. cr.

5289 RIDER ON A DEAD HORSE (Herbert L. Strock)
Filmf: v. V (1962), p. 370; comp., cp. cr.
Films & F: v. 9, n. 2 (Nov., 1962), p. 42; John Cutts, 100 wds., cp. cr.

5290 RIDER ON THE RAIN (René Clement)
(also: Le Passager de la Pluie)
Films & F: v. 17, n. 12 (Sept., 1971), pp. 55-56; Gordon Gow, 800 wds., cp. cr.
Films in R: v. XXI, n. 7 (Aug.-Sept., 1970), p. 444; Eunice Sinkler, 75 wds., no cr.

5291 RIFF RAFF GIRLS (Alex Joffe)
Filmf: v. V (1962), p. 272; comp., cp. cr.

5292 RIFF 65 (Eric Camiel)
F Quarterly: v. XX, n. 4 (Summer, 1967), pp. 73-76; Judith Shatnoff, 1500 wds., no cr.

5293 RIFIFI (Jules Dassin)
(also: Du Rififi Chez des Hommes; Rififi Means Trouble; Rififi Spells Trouble)

Films & F: v. 9, n. 7 (Apr., 1963), p. 35; Ian Johnson, 500 wds., cp. cr.
Films in R: v. VII, n. 6 (June-July, 1956), pp. 289-290; 750 wds., no cr.
Sight & S: v. 25, n. 2 (Autumn, 1955), p. 91; John Wilcox, 350 wds., pt. cr.

RIFIFI A TOKYO (see: Rififi in Tokyo)

5294 RIFIFI AND THE WOMEN (Alex Joffe)
Films & F: v. 6, n. II (Aug., 1960), pp. 25, 32; John Cutts, 150 wds., cp. cr.

RIFIFI IN PARIS (see: The Upper Hand)

5295 RIFIFI IN TOKYO (Jacques Deray)
(also: Rififi a Tokyo)
Filmf: v. VI (1963), p. II3; comp., cp. cr.
Films & F: v. 10, n. 4 (Jan., 1964), pp. 28-29; Gordon Williams, 450 wds.,
cp. cr.

RIFIFI MEANS TROUBLE (see: Rififi)

RIFIFI SPELLS TROUBLE (see: Rififi)

5296 RIGHT APPROACH, THE (David Butler)
Filmf: v. IV (1961), p. 99; comp., cp. cr.

5297 RIGHT ON! (Herbert Danska)
Filmf: v. XIV (1971), p. 718; comp., cp. cr.

5298 RIGHT TO BE BORN, THE (Zacarius Gomez Urquiza)
Films & F: v. 4, n. 3 (Dec., 1957), p. 25; Peter John Dyer, 175 wds., cp. cr.

5299 RIGHT TO BE BORN, THE (David Wechsler)
Films & F: v. I5, n. 8 (May, 1969), p. 46; Ken Gay, 325 wds., cp. cr.

5300 RIGHTS OF AGE, THE
F Lib Quarterly: v. I, n. I (Winter, 1967-1968), p. 45; Hannah Hyatt, 350
wds., pt. cr.

5301 RIKISHA MAN, THE (Hiroshi Inagaki)
(also: Muhomatsu No Issho; Muhomatsu, The Rikisha Man)
Filmf: v. III (1960), p. I05; comp., cp. cr.
F Quarterly: v. XII, n. 2 (Winter, 1958), pp. 59-60; Ernest Callenbach, 300
wds., no cr.
Films & F: v. 5, n. II (Aug., 1959), p. 23; Derek Conrad, 325 wds., cp. cr.

5302 RING, THE (Alfred Hitchcock)
Films & F: v. I5, n. II (Aug., 1969), pp. 79-80; Kingsley Canham, 450 wds.,
no cr.

5303 RING-A-DING RHYTHM (Richard Lester)
(also: It's Trad, Dad!)
Filmf: v. V (1962), p. 362; comp., cp. cr.
Films & F: v. 8, n. 8 (May, 1962), p. 36; John Cutts, 100 wds., cp. cr.

5304 RING AROUND THE CLOCK (Paolo W. Tamburella)
Films in R: v. IV, n. 6 (June-July, 1953), p. 303; 250 wds., no cr.

5305 RING OF BRIGHT WATER (Jack Couffer)
F Quarterly: v. XXIII, n. I (Fall, 1969), p. 54; David Denby, 100 wds., no cr.
Filmf: v. XII (1969), p. 334; comp., cp. cr.
Films & F: v. I5, n. 10 (July, 1969), pp. 53-54; David Adams, 850 wds., cp.
cr.

5306 RING OF FIRE (Andrew L. Stone)
Filmf: v. IV (1961), p. I8I; comp., cp. cr.
Films & F: v. 7, n. 9 (June, 1961), p. 26; Phillip Riley, 350 wds., cp. cr.

RING OF SPIES (see: Ring of Treason)

5307 RING OF TREASON (Robert Tronson)
        (also: Ring of Spies)
        Filmf: v. VII (1964), p. 136; comp., cp. cr.
        Films & F: v. 10, n. 8 (May, 1964), p. 23; Raymond Durgnat, 475 wds., cp. cr.
        Films in R: v. XV, n. 7 (Aug.-Sept., 1964), pp. 442-443; Romano Tozzi, 100 wds., no cr.

5308 RINGER, THE (Guy Hamilton)
        Films & F: v. 9, n. 9 (June, 1963), p. 37; Raymond Durgnat, 150 wds., cp. cr.

5309 RINGS AROUND THE WORLD (Gil Cates)
        Filmf: v. X (1967), p. 400; comp., cp. cr.
        Films in R: v. XVII, n. 9 (Nov., 1966), p. 590; 150 wds., no cr.

5310 RIO BRAVO (Howard Hawks)
        F Quarterly: v. XII, n. 4 (Summer, 1959), pp. 51-52; Raymond Fielding, 300 wds., no cr.
        Filmf: v. II (1959), p. 65; comp., cp. cr.
        Films & F: v. 5, n. 8 (May, 1959), p. 22; Derek Conrad, 225 wds., cp. cr.
        Films in R: v. X, n. 4 (Apr., 1959), p. 239; Romano Tozzi, 200 wds., no cr.
        Focus; n. 8 (Autumn, 1972), pp. 13-18; Judith Bernstein, 2400 wds., cp. cr.
        Movie: n. 5 (Dec., 1962), pp. 25-27; Robin Wood, 1850 wds., no cr.

5311 RIO CONCHOS (Gordon Douglas)
        F Quarterly: v. XVIII, n. 3 (Spring, 1965), p. 61; R. M. Hodgens, 100 wds., no cr.
        Filmf: v. VII (1964), p. 244; comp., cp. cr.
        Films & F: v. II, n. 5 (Feb., 1965), p. 31; Allen Eyles, 550 wds., cp. cr.

5312 RIO GRANDE (John Ford)
        Films in R: v. II, n. 2 (Feb., 1951), pp. 41-42; Thomas T. Foose, 100 wds., pt. cr.

5313 RIO LOBO (Howard Hawks)
        Filmf: v. XIV (1971), p. 17; comp., cp. cr.
        Films & F: v. 17, n. 5 (Feb., 1971), p. 50; Margaret Tarratt, 800 wds., cp. cr.
        Films in R: v. XXII, n. I (Jan., 1971), pp. 45-46; Arthur B. Clark, 200 wds., no cr.
        Focus: n. 8 (Autumn, 1972), pp. 13-18; Judith Bernstein, 2400 wds., cp. cr.

5314 RIOT (Buzz Kulik)
        Filmf: v. XII (1969), p. 8; comp., cp. cr.
        Films & F: v. 16, n. 3 (Dec., 1969), p. 53; David Hutchison, 300 wds., cp. cr.

5315 RIOT IN CELL BLOCK II (Don Siegel)
        Films & F: v. I, n. 2 (Nov., 1954), p. 21; John Minchinton, 250 wds., cp. cr.
        Films & F: v. I, n. 4 (Jan., 1955), p. 9; Jill Hardy, 150 wds., cp. cr.
        Sight & S: v. 24, n. 3 (Jan.-Mar., 1955), p. 143; Karel Reisz, 550 wds., pt. cr.

5316 RIOT IN JUVENILE PRISON (Edward L. Cahn)
        Filmf: v. II (1959), p. 122; comp., cp. cr.

5317 RIOT ON SUNSET STRIP (Arthur Dreifus)
        Filmf: v. X (1967), p. 285; comp., cp. cr.

5318 RIPENING SEED (Claude Autant-Lara)
        (also: Le Ble en Herbe)
        Films & F: v. I, n. 2 (Nov., 1954), p. 20; Louis Marks, 300 wds., cp. cr.

5319 RISE AND FALL OF LEGS DIAMOND, THE (Budd Boetticher)
        Filmf: v. III (1960), p. II; comp., cp. cr.
        Films & F: v. 6, n. 9 (June, 1960), p. 23; Robin Bean, 100 wds., cp. cr.

5320 RISE OF LOUIS XIV, THE (Roberto Rossellini)
        (also: La Prise de Pouvoir par Louis XIV; The Rise To Power of Louis XIV)
        Film: n. 47 (Winter, 1966), p. 42; Douglas McVay, 150 wds., no cr.
        F Culture: n. 47 (Summer, 1969), p. 26-27; Ken Kelman, 1200 wds., no cr.

F Quarterly: v. XXV, n. 2 (Winter, 1971-1972), pp. 20-29; James Roy
MacBean, 5000 wds., no cr.
Films in R: v. XXI, n. 8 (Oct., 1970), pp. 507-508; Yvonne Chautemps, 150
wds., no cr.

RISE TO POWER OF LOUIS XIV, THE (see: The Rise of Louis XIV)

5321 RISING OF THE MOON, THE (John Ford)
F Culture: v. 3, n. 3 (1957), p. 13; Jonas Mekas, 170 wds., pt. cr.
Films & F: v. 3, n. II (Aug., 1957), pp. 24-25; Derek Conrad, 500 wds., cp.
cr.
Films in R: v. VIII, n. 7 (Aug.-Sept., 1957), pp. 344-345; Henry Hart, 500
wds., no cr.

RISING STORM, THE (see: La Tempete Se Leve)

5322 RISK, THE (Roy and John Boulting)
Filmf: v. IV (1961), p. 285; comp., cp. cr.
Films in R: v. XII, n. 9 (Nov., 1961), pp. 552-553; Maude McGlashan, 125
wds., no cr.

RISK, THE (Llya Averbach/see: Stepien Riska)

RISO, AMARO (see: Bitter Rice)

5323 RITE, THE (Ingmar Bergman)
(also: Riten; The Ritual)
Cinema J: v. X, n. I (Fall, 1970), pp. 48-50; Judith Gollub, 1700 wds., no cr.
Films & F: v. 17, n. 10 (July, 1971), pp. 55, 57; Gordon Gow, 700 wds., cp.
cr.
Focus on F: n. 5 (Winter/Nov.-Dec., 1970), pp. 7-13; Peter Cowie, 3100 wds.,
cp. cr.
Sight & S: v. 40, n. 3 (Summer, 1971), pp. 162-163; Philip Strick, 1200 wds.,
pt. cr.

5324 RITE OF LOVE AND DEATH, THE (Mishima)
F Soc Rev: Nov. (1966), pp. 16-17; William Raney, 400 wds., pt. cr.

RITEN (see: The Rite)

RITORNO DI DON CAMILLO, IL (see: The Return of Don Camillo)

RITUAL, THE (see: The Rite)

5325 RITUAL IN TRANSFIGURED TIME (Maya Deren)
F Culture: n. 39 (Winter, 1965), pp. 5-10; Maya Deren, 3000 wds., no cr.

5326 RITUAL OF LOVE (Luciano Emmer)
(also: Paradiso Terrestre)
Filmf: v. IV (1961), p. 373; comp., cp. cr.

RIVAL, THE (see: Pratidwandi)

5327 RIVAL WORLD, THE (Bert Haanstra)
(also: Strijd Zonder Einden)
Sight & S: v. 25, n. 3 (Winter, 1955-1956), pp. 150-151; John Gillett, 200
wds., no cr.

5328 RIVER, THE (Pare Lorenz)
F Journal: n. 12 (Feb., 1959), pp. 21-26; James Merralls, 3000 wds., cp. cr.

5329 RIVER, THE (Jean Renoir)
(also: Le Fleuve)
Films in R: v. II, n. 8 (Oct., 1951), pp. 43-46; Thomas T. Foose, 650 wds.,
pt. cr.
Sight & S: v. 21, n. 3 (Jan.-Mar., 1952), pp. 123-124; Gavin Lambert, 1000
wds., pt. cr.

RIVER OF DOLLARS, A (see: The Hills Run Red)

5330 RIVER OF NO RETURN (Otto Preminger)
      Films & F: v. I, n. I (Oct., 1954), p. 29; Sergio Viotti, 100 wds., cp. cr.
      Films in R: v. V, n. 6 (June-July, 1954), p. 307; Henry Hart, 100 wds., no cr.
      Movie: n. 2 (Spring, 1962), pp. 18-19; V. F. Perkins, 1500 wds., no cr.

5331 RIVERRUN (John Korty)
      F Quarterly: v. XXIII, n. I (Fall, 1969), p. 54; Ernest Callenbach, 200 wds.,
            no cr.
      Films & F: v. 16, n. 12 (Sept., 1970), p. 51; John Walker, 300 wds., cp. cr.
      Films in R: v. XXI, n. 5 (May, 1970), p. 310; Sandra Feigenbaum, 175 wds.,
            no cr.

5332 RIVER'S EDGE, THE (Allan Dwan)
      Films & F: v. 3, n. II (Aug., 1957), p. 24; Rodney Giesler, 250 wds., cp. cr.

      RIVERS OF FIRE AND ICE (see: African Safari)

      RIVIERE DU HIBOU, LA (see: Incident at Owl Creek Bridge)

      RIVOLTA DEL GLADIATORI, LA (see: The Warrior and the Slave Girl)

5333 ROAD A YEAR LONG, THE (Giuseppe De Santis)
      (also: Cesta Duga Godino Dana)
      F Quarterly: v. XII, n. 2 (Winter, 1958), p. 60; Albert Johnson, 250 wds., no
            cr.

5334 ROAD HUSTLERS, THE (Larry E. Jackson)
      Filmf: v. XI (1968), p. 537; comp., cp. cr.

5335 ROAD RACERS
      Filmf: v. II (1959), p. 341; comp., cp. cr.

      ROAD TO ETERNITY (see: Ningen No Joken)

5336 ROAD TO HONG KONG, THE (Norman Panama)
      Filmf: v. V (1962), p. 149; comp., cp. cr.
      Films & F: v. 8, n. 9 (June, 1962), pp. 34-35; Gordon Gow, 500 wds., cp. cr.

5337 ROAD TO LIFE, THE (Nikolai Ekk)
      (also: Putyovka V Zhizn)
      Sequence: n. 8 (Summer, 1949), pp. 89-90; 1100 wds., pt. cr.

5338 ROAD TO SAINT TROPEZ, THE (Michael Sarne)
      F Quarterly: v. XX, n. 3 (Spring, 1967), pp. 53-54; Albert Johnson, 275
            wds., pt. cr.
      Films & F: v. XIII, n. 6 (Mar., 1967), p. 35; Gordon Gow, 350 wds., cp. cr.

5339 ROAD TO SALINA (Georges Lautner)
      (also: Sur La Route De Salina)
      Filmf: v. XIV (1971), p. 268; comp., cp. cr.

5340 ROAD TO SANTIAGO, THE
      F Lib Quarterly: v. I, n. 4 (Fall, 1968), pp. 43, 56; 300 wds., pt. cr.

5341 ROAD TO THE STARS (P. Klushentsev)
      (also: Doroga K Zvyozdam)
      Filmf: v. I (1958), p. 106; comp., cp. cr.

5342 ROB ROY (Harold French)
      Films in R: v. V, n. 4 (Apr., 1954), p. 194; 125 wds., no cr.

      ROB YOUR NEIGHBOR (see: A Fine Pair)

5343 ROBBERY (Peter Yates)
      Filmf: v. X (1967), p. 294; comp., cp. cr.
      Films & F: v. 14, n. 2 (Nov., 1967), p. 21; David Austen, 800 wds., cp. cr.

      ROBBERY, THE (Vangelis Serdaris/see: Listia Stin Athina)

      ROBBERY OF DIAMONDS (see: Run Like a Thief)

5344 ROBBERY UNDER ARMS (Jack Lee)
         Filmf: v. I (1958), p. 264; comp., cp. cr.
         Films & F: v. 4, n. 2 (Nov., 1957), p. 27; Peter G. Baker, 475 wds., cp. cr.

5345 ROBBY (Ralph C. Bluemke)
         Filmf: v. XI (1968), p. 357; comp., cp. cr.

5346 ROBE, THE (Henry Koster)
         Films in R: v. IV, n. 8 (Oct., 1953), pp. 426-428; Henry Hart, 1200 wds., pt.
            cr.
         Sight & S: v. 23, n. 3 (Jan.-Mar., 1954), pp. 143-144; Basil Wright, 1000 wds.,
            pt. cr.

5347 ROBERT FROST: A LOVER'S QUARREL WITH THE WORLD (Robert
            Hughes and Charlotte Zwerin, prods.)
         F Lib Quarterly: v. I, n. 2 (Spring, 1968), p. 35; Sam Bicknell, 325 wds., pt.
            cr.
         F Quarterly: v. XVII, n. 3 (Spring, 1964), pp. 44-46; Colin Young, 1100 wds.,
            cp. cr.

5348 ROBIN AND THE 7 HOODS (Gordon Douglas)
         Filmf: v. VII (1964), p. 218; comp., cp. cr.
         Films & F: v. 10, n. II (Aug., 1964), p. 21; Ian Johnson, 450 wds., cp. cr.

      ROBINSON CRUSOE (see: The Adventures of Robinson Crusoe)

5349 ROBINSON CRUSOE ON MARS (Byron Haskin)
         Filmf: v. VII (1964), p. 288; comp., cp. cr.
         Films & F: v. II, n. 6 (Mar., 1965), p. 36; John Cutts, 225 wds., cp. cr.

      ROBO DE DIAMANTES (see: Run Life a Thief)

5350 ROCCO AND HIS BROTHERS (Luchino Visconti)
         (also: Rocco e I Suoi Fratelli)
         Film: n. 30 (Winter, 1961), pp. 28-34; Peter Armitage, 1200 wds., pt. cr.
         F Journal: n. 20 (Aug., 1962), pp. 69-75; John Flaus, 5000 wds., no cr.
         Filmf: v. IV (1961), p. 143; comp., cp. cr.
         Films & F: v. 8, n. I (Oct., 1961), p. 28; Roger Manvell, 800 wds., cp. cr.
         Films in R: v. XII, n. 7 (Aug.-Sept., 1961), pp. 432-433; Henry Hart, 400
            wds., no cr.
         Sight & S: v. 30, n. I (Winter, 1960-1961), p. 35; Derek Prouse, 750 wds., pt.
            cr.

      ROCCO E I SUOI FRATELLI (see: Rocco and His Brothers)

5351 ROCK-A-BYE BABY (Frank Tashlin)
         Filmf: v. I (1958), p. 136; comp., cp. cr.
         Films & F: v. 4, n. 12 (Sept., 1958), p. 25; Derek Conrad, 150 wds., cp. cr.

      ROCK AROUND THE WORLD (see: The Tommy Steele Story)

5352 ROCKET ATTACK, U.S.A. (Barry Mahon)
         Filmf: v. III (1960), p. 359; comp., cp. cr.

5353 ROCKET FROM CALABUCH, THE (Luis G. Berlanga)
         (also: Calabuch)
         Filmf: v. I (1958), p. 212; comp., cp. cr.
         Films & F: v. 4, n. 9 (June, 1958), pp. 25-26; Derek Conrad, 450 wds., cp.
            cr.
         Films in R: v. IX, n. 9 (Nov., 1958), pp. 518-519; Carlos Clarens, 200 wds.,
            no cr.
         Sight & S: v. 27, n. 4 (Spring, 1958), pp. 201-202; John Gillett, 500 wds., pt.
            cr.

5354 ROCKET TO THE MOON (Don Sharp)
         Films & F: v. 14, n. I (Oct., 1967), pp. 26-27; Richard Davis, 200 wds., cp.
            cr.

      ROCKETS GALORE (see: Mad Little Island)

5355 RODAN (Inoshiro Honda)
         Films & F: v. 4, n. 6 (Mar., 1958), p. 24; Ken Gay, 200 wds., cp. cr.

ROEDE KAPPE, DEN (see: Hagbard and Signe)

5356 ROGUE'S GALLERY (Leonard Horn)
       Films & F: v. 15, n. 1 (Oct., 1968), pp. 50-51; Michael Armstrong, 200 wds.,
       cp. cr.

ROI DE COEUR, LE (see: King of Hearts)

5357 ROMAN HOLIDAY (William Wyler)
       Films in R: v. IV, n. 7 (Aug.-Sept., 1953), pp. 363-364; Ralph Gerstle, 250
       wds., pt. cr.
       Sight & S: v. 23, n. 2 (Oct.-Dec., 1953), p. 91; Penelope Houston, 500 wds.,
       pt. cr.

5358 ROMAN SPRING OF MRS. STONE, THE (José Quintero)
       F Quarterly: v. XV, n. 3 (Spring, 1962), p. 72; R. M. Hodgens, 100 wds., no
       cr.
       Filmf: v. IV (1961), p. 329; comp., cp. cr.
       Films in R: v. XIII, n. 1 (Jan., 1962), pp. 42-43; Ellen Fitzpatrick, 200 wds.,
       no cr.
       Sight & S: v. 31, n. 2 (Spring, 1962), pp. 92-93; Francis Wyndham, 1200
       wds., pt. cr.

5359 ROMANCE OF A HORSETHIEF (Abraham Polonsky)
       Filmf: v. XIV (1971), p. 401; comp., cp. cr.
       Focus: n. 7 (Spring, 1972), pp. 16-19; Terry Curtis Fox, 2800 wds., no cr.

5360 ROMANOFF AND JULIET (Peter Ustinov)
       Filmf: v. IV (1961), p. 153; comp., cp. cr.
       Films & F: v. 7, n. 10 (July, 1961), p. 25; Raymond Durgnat, 700 wds., cp.
       cr.
       Sight & S: v. 30, n. 3 (Summer, 1961), p. 150; John Russell Taylor, 275 wds.,
       pt. cr.

5361 ROME ADVENTURE (Delmer Daves)
       (also: Lovers Must Learn)
       Filmf: v. V (1962), p. 63; comp., cp. cr.
       Films & F: v. 8, n. 10 (July, 1962), p. 37; Robin Bean, 500 wds., cp. cr.

5362 ROMEO AND JULIET (Renato Castellani)
       F Culture: v. I, n. 2 (Mar.-Apr., 1955), pp. 44-45; A. Landsbergis, 1000 wds.,
       cp. cr.
       Films in R: v. V, n. 10 (Dec., 1954), pp. 538-540; Lauro Venturi, 750 wds.,
       no cr.

5363 ROMEO AND JULIET (L. Arnshtam and L. Lavrosky)
       Films & F: v. 2, n. 1 (Oct., 1955), p. 21; Peter Brinson, 350 wds., cp. cr.
       Sight & S: v. 25, n. 2 (Autumn, 1955), pp. 85-86; Gavin Lambert, 700 wds.,
       pt. cr.

5364 ROMEO AND JULIET (Paul Czinner)
       Filmf: v. IX (1966), p. 299; comp., cp. cr.
       Films & F: v. 13, n. 4 (Jan., 1967), pp. 31-32; Peter Whitehead, 700 wds., cp.
       cr.
       Films in R: v. XVII, n. 8 (Oct., 1966), pp. 519-520; Page Cook, 300 wds., no
       cr.

5365 ROMEO AND JULIET (Franco Zeffirelli)
       Cineaste: v. II, n. 3 (Winter, 1968-1969), pp. 17, 21; Gary Crowdus, 1250
       wds., pt. cr.
       Filmf: v. XI (1968), p. 275; comp., cp. cr.
       Films & F: v. 14, n. 10 (July, 1968), pp. 34-35; Michael Armstrong, 1000
       wds., cp. cr.
       Films in R: v. XIX, n. 8 (Oct., 1968), pp. 513-514; Page Cook, 300 wds., no
       cr.
       Movie: n. 15 (Spring, 1968), p. 40; 75 wds., no cr.

ROMEO, JULIE A TMA (see: Romeo, Juliet and Darkness)

5366 ROMEO, JULIET, AND DARKNESS (Jiri Weiss)
(also: Romeo, Julie a Tma; Sweet Light in a Dark Room)
F Quarterly: v. XIV, n. 2 (Winter, 1960), pp. 49-50; Joseph Kostolefsky, 750 wds., pt. cr.
Filmf: v. IX (1966), p. 167; comp., cp. cr.
Films & F: v. 8, n. 5 (Feb., 1962), p. 29; Philip Strick, 350 wds., cp. cr.

ROMMEL—THE DESERT FOX (see: The Desert Fox)

5367 ROMMEL'S TREASURE (Romolo Marcellini)
Filmf: v. IV (1961), p. 370; comp., cp. cr.

ROMPIENDO PUERTAS (see: Break and Enter)

5368 RONDE, LA (Max Ophuls)
Sequence: n. 14 (New Year, 1952), pp. 33-35; Karel Reisz, 2300 wds., pt. cr.
Sight & S: v. 20, n. 2 (June, 1951), p. 47; Richard Winnington, 850 wds., pt. cr.

RONDE, LA (Roger Vadim/see: Circle of Love)

5369 RONDO (Zvonimir Berković)
Film: n. 50 (Winter, 1967), pp. 33-34; Langdon Dewey, 200 wds., no cr.
Interntl F G: v. 5 (1968), p. 168; 250 wds., pt. cr.
Sight & S: v. 37, n. 3 (Summer, 1968), p. 158; David Wilson, 400 wds., no cr.

ROOF, THE (see: Il Tetto)

ROOF GARDEN, THE (see: Terrace)

ROOK, THE (see: Something for Everyone)

5370 ROOKIE, THE (George O'Hanlon)
Filmf: v. III (1960), p. 17; comp., cp. cr.

5371 ROOM AT THE TOP (Jack Clayton)
Filmf: v. II (1959), p. 87; comp., cp. cr.
Films & F: v. 5, n. 5 (Feb., 1959), p. 21; Peter John Dyer, 800 wds., cp. cr.
Films in R: v. X, n. 5 (May, 1959), p. 303; Ellen Fitzpatrick, 400 wds., no cr.

5372 ROOM 43 (Alvin Rakoff)
(also: Passport to Shame)
Filmf: v. II (1959), p. 214; comp., cp. cr.
Films & F: v. 5, n. 6 (Mar., 1959), p. 25; Derek Conrad, 175 wds., cp. cr.

5373 ROOMMATES (Jack Baran)
Filmf: v. XIV (1971), p. 207; comp., cp. cr.

5374 ROONEY (George Pollock)
Filmf: v. I (1958), p. 103; comp., cp. cr.
Films & F: v. 4, n. 7 (Apr., 1958), p. 24; Peter G. Baker, 250 wds., cp. cr.
Filmf in R: v. IX, n. 6 (June-July, 1958), p. 338; Nigel Ames, 175 wds., no cr.

ROOTS, THE (see: Raices)

5375 ROOTS OF HEAVEN, THE (John Huston)
F Quarterly: v. XII, n. 2 (Winter, 1958), pp. 42-45; Arlene Croce, 950 wds., no cr.
Filmf: v. I (1958-1959), p. 191; comp., cp. cr.
Films & F: v. 5, n. 5 (Fall, 1959), pp. 25-26; Gordon Gow, 675 wds., cp. cr.
Films in R: v. IX, n. 9 (Nov., 1958), pp. 513-515; Courtland Phipps, 575 wds., no cr.
Sight & S: v. 28, n. 2 (Spring, 1959), p. 94; Derek Hill, 500 wds., pt. cr.

5376 ROPE (Alfred Hitchcock)
    Films & F: v. 9, n. 6 (Mar., 1963), pp. 41-42; Raymond Durgnat, 650 wds.,
        cp. cr.
    Movie: n. 7, pp. 11-13; V. F. Perkins, 2700 wds., no cr.

ROSA PER TUTTI, UNA (see: A Rose for Everyone)

ROSE BERND (see: The Sins of Rose Bernd)

5377 ROSE FOR EVERYONE, A (Franco Rossi)
    (also: Every Man's Woman; Una Rosa per Tutti)
    Filmf: v. X (1967), p. 192; comp., cp. cr.

5378 ROSE MARIE (Mervyn LeRoy)
    Films & F: v. 1, n. 1 (Oct., 1954), p. 20; Jill Hardy, 175 wds., cp. cr.

5379 ROSE TATTOO, THE (Daniel Mann)
    F Culture: v. 1, n. 5-6 (Winter, 1955), p. 36; Andrew George-Sarris, 400
        wds., pt. cr.
    Films & F: v. 2, n. 6 (Mar., 1956), p. 16; Peter G. Baker, 250 wds., cp. cr.
    Films in R: v. VI, n. 10 (Dec., 1955), pp. 527-528; R.D., 450 wds., pt. cr.
    Sight & S: v. 25, n. 4 (Spring, 1956), pp. 194-196; Derek Prouse, 2000
        wds., pt. cr.

5380 ROSEANNA (Hans Abramson)
    Films & F: v. 15, n. 10 (July, 1969), pp. 42, 44; Peter Buckley, 900 wds.,
        cp. cr.

5381 ROSELAND (C. Fredric Hobbs)
    Filmf: v. XIV (1971), p. 496; comp., cp. cr.

ROSEMARIE (see: The Girl Rosemarie)

5382 ROSEMARY (Erich Kuby and Rolf Thiele)
    F Quarterly: v. XIV, n. 1 (Fall, 1960), pp. 55-56; William Bernhardt,
        700 wds., pt. cr.
    Filmf: v. III (1960), p. 13; comp., cp. cr.
    Films in R: v. X, n. 9 (Nov., 1959), pp. 554-556; Henry Hart, 650 wds., no
        cr.

5383 ROSEMARY'S BABY (Roman Polanski)
    Cinema: v. 4, n. 3 (Fall, 1968), pp. 41-42; Harlan Ellison, 750 wds., pt. cr.
    F Quarterly: v. XXII, n. 3 (Spring, 1969), pp. 35-38; Robert Chappetta,
        2400 wds., pt. cr.
    Filmf: v. XI (1968), p. 175; comp., cp. cr.
    Films & F: v. 15, n. 6 (Mar., 1969), pp. 38-39; Gordon Gow, 1300 wds., cp.
        cr.
    Films in R: v. XIX, n. 7 (Aug.-Sept., 1968), pp. 456-457; Henry Hart, 300
        wds., no cr.
    Interntl F G: v. 6 (1969), pp. 173-174, Margot S. Kernan, 300 wds., pt. cr.
    Journal of P C: v. II, n. 3 (Winter, 1968), pp. 493-502; Maisie K. Pearson,
        3000 wds., no cr.
    Movie: n. 16 (Winter, 1968-1969), p. 39; Mark Shivas, 100 wds., no cr.
    Screen: v. 10, n. 2 (Mar.-Apr., 1969), pp. 90-96; Margaret Tarratt, 2300
        wds., cp. cr.
    Sight & S: v. 38, n. 1 (Winter, 1968-1969), pp. 17-19; Beverle Houston and
        Marsha Kinder, 2000 wds., pt. cr.

ROSEN FURO BETTINA (see: Ballerina)

5384 ROSENKAVALIER, DER (Paul Czinner)
    Films & F: v. 8, n. 10 (July, 1962), p. 38; Michael Reynolds, 325 wds., cp.
        cr.
    Films in R: v. XIII, n. 8 (Oct., 1962), pp. 488-489; Tatiana Balkoff Drowne,
        200 wds., no cr.

5385 ROSES FOR THE PROSECUTOR (Wolfgang Staudte)
    Filmf: v. IV (1961), p. 332; comp., cp. cr.
    Films & F: v. 6, n. 12 (Sept., 1960), p. 22; R. E. Durgnat, 300 wds., cp. cr.
    Sight & S: v. 29, n. 4 (Autumn, 1960), p. 196; Robert Vas, 500 wds., no cr.

5386 ROSIE (David Lowell Rich)
        Filmf: v. XI (1968), p. 45; comp., cp. cr.

      ROSMUND E ALBOINO (see: Sword of the Conqueror)

5387 ROSSANA (Emilio Fernandez)
        Films & F: v. 2, n. 10 (July, 1956), p. 25; John Carroll, 100 wds., cp. cr.

5388 ROSY WORKER ON A GOLDEN STREET (Rosa von Praunheim)
        Film: n. 58 (Spring, 1970), p. 30; 50 wds., pt. cr.

5389 ROTMANAD (Jan Halldoff)
        (also: Dog Days)
        Interntl F G: v. 9 (1972), p. 248; Peter Cowle, 200 wds., pt. cr.

5390 ROTTEN TO THE CORE (John Boulting)
        Films & F: v. 11, n. 12 (Sept., 1965), pp. 32-33; David Rider, 500 wds., cp.
          cr.

      ROUGE AUX LEVRES, LE (see: Daughters of Darkness)

      ROUGE EST MIS, LE (see: Speaking of Murder)

5391 ROUGE ET LE NOIR, LE (Claude Autant-Lara)
        (also: Scarlet and Black)
        Filmf: v. I (1958), p. 75; comp., cp. cr.
        Films & F: v. 2, n. 7 (Apr., 1956), pp. 13-14; Michael Winner, 150 wds., cp.
          cr.
        Films in R: v. IX, n. 5 (May, 1958), pp. 267-268; Henry Hart, 300 wds., no
          cr.

      ROUGH AND THE SMOOTH, THE (see: Portrait of a Sinner)

5392 ROUGH COMPANY (Rudolph Maté)
        (also: The Violent Men)
        Films & F: v. 1, n. 6 (Mar., 1955), p. 20; Jill Hardy, 200 wds., cp. cr.

5393 ROUGH NIGHT IN JERICHO (Arnold Laven)
        Filmf: v. X (1967), p. 353; comp., cp. cr.
        Films & F: v. 14, n. 4 (Jan., 1968), pp. 25-26; Peter Davalle, 400 wds., cp.
          cr.

5394 ROUND TRIP (Pierre Dominique Gaisseau)
        Filmf: v. X (1967), p. 237; comp., cp. cr.

5395 ROUND-UP, THE (Miklós Jancsó)
        (also: The Poor Outlaws, The Hopeless Ones, Szegnylegenyek)
        Filmf: v. XII (1969), p. 225; comp., cp. cr.
        Films & F: v. 13, n. 4 (Jan., 1967), p. 38; Gordon Gow, 650 wds., cp. cr.
        Interntl F G: v. 5 (1968), p. 98; Peter Cowie, 250 wds., pt. cr.

5396 ROUNDERS, THE (Burt Kennedy)
        F Quarterly: v. XVIII, n. 4 (Summer, 1965), p. 60; Ernest Callenbach, 100
          wds., no cr.
        Filmf: v. VIII (1965), p. 102; comp., cp. cr.
        Films & F: v. 11, n. 8 (May, 1965), p. 33; Richard Davis, 200 wds., cp. cr.
        Films in R: v. XVI, n. 2 (Feb., 1965), p. 117; Arthur B. Clark, 100 wds., no
          cr.

5397 ROUSTABOUT (John Rich)
        Filmf: v. VII (1964), p. 258; comp., cp. cr.
        Films & F: v. 11, n. 4 (Jan., 1965), p. 39; Allen Eyles, 400 wds., cp. cr.

5398 ROVER, THE (Terence Young)
        (also: L'Avventuriero)
        Filmf: v. XIV (1971), p. 753; comp., cp. cr.

5399 ROYAL AFFAIRS IN VERSAILLES (Sacha Guitry)
        (also: Si Versailles M'Etait Conté; Versailles)
        Films & F: v. 6, n. 8 (May, 1960), p. 25; Richard Whitehall, 450 wds., cp.
          cr.
        Films in R: v. VIII, n. 3 (Mar., 1957), pp. 128-129; Louise Corbin, 400
          wds., no cr.

5400 ROYAL BALLET, THE (Paul Czinner)
      Filmf: v. III (1960), p. 275; comp., cp. cr.
      Films & F: v. 6, n. 5 (Feb., 1960), pp. 24-25; Peter Williams, 650 wds., cp.
          cr.
      Sight & S: v. 29, n. 1 (Winter, 1959-1960), p. 40; Peter Brinson, 450 wds.,
          no cr.

5401 ROYAL BED (Gregory Ratoff)
      Films in R: v. VII, n. 2 (Feb., 1956), pp. 83-84; Penelope Reeves, 550 wds.,
          no cr.

5402 ROYAL HUNT IN THE SUN, THE (Irving Lerner)
      Films & F: v. 16, n. 3 (Dec., 1969), pp. 53-54; Gordon Gow, 450 wds., cp.
          cr.
      Filmf in R: v. XX, n. 9 (Nov., 1969), p. 576; Jose Aguirre, 200 wds., no cr.

      ROYAL PATH (see: Obsession)

5403 ROYAL SYMPHONY (Castleton Knight, prod.)
      Filmf in R: v. V, n. 5 (May, 1954), p. 243; 150 wds., no cr.

      ROZMARNE LETO (see: Capricious Summer)

5404 RUBENS (Henri Storck)
      Sight & S: v. 17, n. 67 (Autumn, 1948), pp. 141-142; Roger Manvell, 1200
          wds., no cr.

      RUBU AL PROSSIMO TUO (see: A Fine Pair)

5405 RUE DE PARIS (Denys de la Patelliere)
      Filmf: v. III (1960), p. 319; comp., cp. cr.

5406 RUFFIANS, THE (Maurice Labro)
      (also: Les Canailles)
      Filmf: v. VI (1963), p. 345; comp., cp. cr.

5407 RUINED MAP, THE (Hiroshi Teshigahara)
      (also: The Man Without a Map; Moetsukita Chizu)
      F Quarterly: v. XXII, n. 3 (Spring, 1969), pp. 63-64; R. C. Dale, 350 wds.,
          no cr.

      RULES OF THE GAME (see: Le Regle du Jeu)

      RUMMELPLATZ DER LIEBE (see: Circus of Love)

      RUMPO KID, THE (see: Carry On Cowboy)

5408 RUN (Jack Kuper)
      F Lib Quarterly: v. 1, n. 1 (Winter, 1967-1968), p. 45; James L. Limbacher,
          250 wds., pt. cr.

5409 RUN, ANGEL, RUN (Jack Starrett)
      Filmf: v. XII (1969), p. 173; comp., cp. cr.

5410 RUN FOR THE SUN (Roy Boulting)
      Films & F: v. 3, n. 1 (Oct., 1956), p. 27; Peter John Dyer, 200 wds., cp. cr.

5411 RUN FOR YOUR MONEY, A (Charles Frend)
      Sequence: n. 10 (New Year, 1950), p. 155; Lindsay G. Anderson, 200 wds.,
          no cr.

5412 RUN FOR YOUR WIFE (Gian Luigi Polidoro)
      (also: Una Moglie Americana)
      Filmf: v. X (1967), p. 351; comp., cp. cr.

5413 RUN LIKE A THIEF (Bernard Glasser)
      (also: Robo de Diamantes; Robbery of Diamonds)
      Filmf: v. XI (1968), pp. 14, 46; comp., cp. cr.
      Filmf & F: v. 14, n. 1 (Oct., 1967), p. 26; Richard Davis, 150 wds., cp. cr.

5414 RUN OF THE ARROW (Samuel Fuller)
        Films & F: v. 3, n. 10 (July, 1957), pp. 26, 33; Leo Harris, 300 wds., cp. cr.
        Films & F: v. 15, n. 12 (Sept., 1969), pp. 88, 90; Kingsley Canham, 750
        wds., no cr.

      RUN ON GOLD, A (see: Midas Run)

5415 RUN SILENT, RUN DEEP (Robert Wise)
        Filmf: v. I (1958), p. 58; comp., cp. cr.
        Films & F: v. 4, n. 10 (July, 1958), pp. 27-28; John Cutts, 300 wds., cp. cr.

5416 RUN THE WILD RIVER (Jack Currey)
        Filmf: v. XIV (1971), p. 667; comp., cp. cr.

5417 RUN WILD, RUN FREE (Richard Sarafian)
        Filmf: v. XII (1969), p. 394; comp., cp. cr.
        Films & F: v. 15, n. 11 (Aug., 1969), pp. 47-48; Richard Davis, 500 wds.,
        cp. cr.
        Films in R: v. XX, n. 7 (Aug.-Sept., 1969), p. 443; Tatiana Balkoff Drowne,
        175 wds., no cr.

5418 RUN WITH THE DEVIL (Mario Camerini)
        (also: Via Margutta)
        Filmf: v. VI (1963), p. 252; comp., cp. cr.

5419 RUNAWAY, THE (Tapan Sinha)
        Sight & S: v. 38, n. 2 (Spring, 1969), pp. 98-99; David Wilson, 500 wds., no
        cr.

5420 RUNAWAY GIRL (Hamil Petroff)
        Filmf: v. IX (1966), p. 384; comp., cp. cr.

5421 RUNNER (Donald Owen)
        Interntl F G: v. 1 (1964), p. 117; 75 wds., pt. cr.

5422 RUNNING JUMPING AND STANDING STILL FILM (Peter Sellers)
        F Quarterly: v. XIII, n. 3 (Spring, 1960), p. 57; James Broughton, 300 wds.,
        pt. cr.

5423 RUNNING MAN, THE (Carol Reed)
        Cinema: v. 1, n. 6 (Nov.-Dec., 1963), p. 45; James Silke, 300 wds., pt. cr.
        F Quarterly: v. XVII, n. 2 (Winter, 1963-1964), p. 62; R. M. Hodgens, 100
        wds., no cr.
        Filmf: v. VI (1963), p. 208; comp., cp. cr.
        Films & F: v. 9, n. 12 (Sept., 1963), p. 23; John Cutts, 300 wds., cp. cr.

5424 RUPTURE, LA (Claude Chabrol)
        (also: The Break-Up)
        Fucus: n. 7 (Spring, 1972), p. 32; Barbara Bernstein, 400 wds., no cr.
        Sight & S: v. 40, n. 1 (Winter, 1970-1971), pp. 7-9; Tom Milne, 2000 wds.,
        pt. cr.

5425 RUSH TO JUDGMENT (Emile De Antonio)
        F Comment: v. IV, n. 2-3 (Fall-Winter, 1967), p. 19; Louis Marcorelles, 450
        wds., no cr.
        Filmf: v. X (1967), p. 185; comp., cp. cr.
        Films in R: v. XVIII, n. 7 (Aug.-Sept., 1967), p. 443; Arthur B. Clark, 200
        wds., no cr.

5426 RUSS MEYER'S VIXEN (Russ Meyer)
        (also: Vixen)
        Filmf: v. XII (1969), p. 255; comp., cp. cr.
        Focus: n. 5 (Oct., 1969), pp. 14-15; Stephen Manes, 700 wds., no cr.
        Journal of P C: v. IV, n. 1 (Summer, 1970), pp. 286-291; Wayne A. Losano,
        2000 wds., no cr.

5427 RUSSIA TODAY
        Filmf: v. II (1959), p. 59; comp., cp. cr.

5428 RUSSIAN ADVENTURE (Leonid Kristie, Roman Karmen, Boris Dolin, Oleg
Lebedev, Soloman Kogan, Vassily Katanian)
Films & F: v. 12, n. 3 (Dec., 1965), p. 11; Peter Davalle, 400 wds., cp. cr.
Films in R: v. XVII, n. 5 (May, 1966), pp. 313-314; Arthur B. Clark, 200
wds., no cr.

5429 RUSSIAN CONSUMER, THE (Julien Bryan, prod.)
F Lib Quarterly: v. 2, n. 2 (Spring, 1969), pp. 18-20; Alan Clark, 1300
wds., pt. cr.

5430 RUSSIAN MIRACLE, THE (Annelie and Andrew Thorndike)
(also: Das Russische Wunder)
Films & F: v. 11, n. 6 (Mar., 1965), pp. 33-34; Peter Cowie, 450 wds., cp.
cr.

5431 RUSSIAN PEASANT, THE (Julien Bryan, prod.)
F Lib Quarterly: v. 2, n. 2 (Spring, 1969), pp. 18-20; Alan Clark, 1300
wds., pt. cr.

5432 RUSSIANS ARE COMING, THE RUSSIANS ARE COMING, THE (Norman
Jewison)
Filmf: v. IX (1966), p. 121; comp., cp. cr.
Films & F: v. 13, n. 2 (Nov., 1966), p. 16; Allen Eyles, 500 wds., cp. cr.
Films in R: v. XVII, n. 7 (Aug.-Sept., 1966), pp. 446-447; Arthur B. Clark,
300 wds., no cr.

RUSSISCHE WUNDER, DAS (see: The Russian Miracle)

5433 RYAN'S DAUGHTER (David Lean)
Films & F: v. 17, n. 5 (Feb., 1971), pp. 57-48; Gordon Gow, 850 wds., cp.
cr.
Films in R: v. XXI, n. 10 (Dec., 1970), pp. 640-643; Henry Hart, 700 wds.,
no cr.
Take One: v. 2, n. 9 (1970), p. 20; John Hofsess, 1000 wds., pt. cr.

S

5434 S.O.S. PACIFIC (Guy Green)
Filmf: v. III (1960), p. 213; comp., cp. cr.
Films & F: v. 6, n. 2 (Nov., 1959), p. 25; Dai Vaughan, 200 wds., cp. cr.

5435 SABATA (Frank Kramer)
Films & F: v. 17, n. 9 (June, 1971), pp. 76, 78; Eric Braun, 450 wds., cp.
cr.

5436 SABOTAGE (Alfred Hitchcock)
F Soc Rev: Jan. (1966), p. 12; David Stewart Hull, 85 wds., pt. cr.

SABOTEUR — CODE NAME MORITURI, THE (see: Morituri)

SABRINA (see: Sabrina Fair)

5437 SABRINA FAIR (Billy Wilder)
(also: Sabrina)
Films & F: v. 1, n. 1 (Oct., 1954), p. 20; 125 wds., cp. cr.
Films in R: v. V, n. 7 (Aug.-Sept., 1954), pp. 361-362; Henry Hart, 300
wds., no cr.
Sight & S: v. 24, n. 2 (Oct.-Dec., 1954), p. 91; Karel Reisz, 375 wds., pt. cr.

5438 SACCO AND VANZETTI (Giuliano Montaldo)
(also: Sacco E Vanzetti)
Filmf: v. XIV (1971), p. 586; comp., cp. cr.

SACCO DI ROMA, IL (see: The Pagans)

SACCO E VANZETTI (see: Sacco and Vanzetti)

SACRE GRAND PERE, CE (see: The Marriage Came Tumbling Down)

5439 SAD HORSE, THE (James B. Clark)
     Filmf: v. II (1959), p. 170; comp., cp. cr.

5440 SAD SACK, THE (George Marshall)
     Filmf & F: v. 4, n. 5 (Feb., 1958), p. 24; Kay Collier, 200 wds., cp. cr.

5441 SAD SONG OF YELLOW SKIN (Michael Rubbo)
     Cineaste: v. IV, n. 4 (Spring, 1971), p. 29; Lenny Rubenstein, 600 wds., pt.
        cr.

5442 SADDLE THE WIND (Robert Parrish)
     Filmf: v. I (1958), p. 45; comp., cp. cr.

5443 SADISMO (Salvatore Billitteri, prod.)
     Filmf: v. X (1967), p. 408; comp., cp. cr.

5444 SADKO (Alexander Ptushko)
     Films in R: v. IV, n. 7 (Aug.-Sept., 1953), pp. 361-362; Tatiana Balkoff-
        Drowne, 550 wds., pt. cr.

5445 SAFARI (Terence Young)
     Films & F: v. 2, n. 7 (Apr., 1956), p. 13; Rodney Giesler, 200 wds., cp. cr.

5446 SAFE AT HOME (Walter Doniger)
     Filmf: v. V (1962), p. 94; comp., cp. cr.

5447 SAFE PLACE, A (Henry Jaglom)
     F Soc Rev: v. 7, n. 3 (Nov., 1971), p. 25; Gary Crowdus, 300 wds., pt. cr.
     Filmf: v. XIV (1971), p. 565; comp., cp. cr.

5448 SAFECRACKER, THE (Ray Milland)
     Filmf: v. I (1958-1959), p. 38; comp., cp. cr.
     Films in R: v. IX, n. 2 (Feb., 1958), p. 90; Ellen Fitzpatrick, 300 wds., no
        cr.

     SAFFO, VENERE DI LESBO (see: The Warrior Empress)

5449 SAGA OF ANATAHAN, THE (Josef von Sternberg)
     (also: Anatahan)
     Films in R: v. V, n. 2 (Feb., 1954), pp. 93-95; 350 wds., no cr.
     Sight & S: v. 24, n. 1 (July-Sept., 1954), pp. 34-35; Tony Richardson, 700
        wds., pt. cr.

5450 SAGA OF HEMP BROWN, THE (Richard Carlson)
     Filmf: v. I (1958), p. 198; comp., cp. cr.

5451 SAIL A CROOKED SHIP (Irving Brecher)
     Filmf: v. V (1962), p. 21; comp., cp. cr.

5452 SAILING (Hattum Hoving)
     Interntl F G: v. 1 (1964), p. 109; 50 wds., pt. cr.

5453 SAILOR BEWARE (Gordon Parry)
     Films & F: v. 3, n. 2 (Nov., 1956), p. 25; P. L. Mannock, 250 wds., cp. cr.

5454 SAILOR FROM GIBRALTER, THE (Tony Richardson)
     Filmf: v. X (1967), p. 103; comp., cp. cr.
     Films in R: v. XVIII, n. 6 (June-July, 1967), p. 371; Diana Willing Cope,
        125 wds., no cr.

5455 SAILOR FROM THE COMET, THE (Isidore Annensky)
     Filmf: v. II (1959), p. 255; comp., cp. cr.

5456 SAINT JOAN (Otto Preminger)
     Films & F: v. 3, n. 10 (July, 1957), p. 21; Paul Rotha, 700 wds., cp. cr.
     Films in R: v. VIII, n. 6 (June-July, 1957), pp. 280-281; Ellen C. Kennedy,
        350 wds., no cr.

Movie: n. 2 (Sept., 1962), p. 21; Paul Mayersberg, 550 wds., no cr.
Sight & S: v. 27, n. 1 (Summer, 1957), p. 38; Penelope Houston, 750 wds.,
pt. cr.

5457 ST. LOUIS BLUES (Allen Reisner)
Filmf: v. I (1958), p. 64; comp., cp. cr.
Films & F: v. 4, n. 9 (June, 1958), p. 25; Derek Conrad, 375 wds., cp. cr.

5458 SAINT TROPEZ BLUES (Marcel Moussy)
Films & F: v. 7, n. 11 (Aug., 1961), p. 27; John Cutts, 200 wds., cp. cr.

5459 ST. VALENTINE'S DAY MASSACRE, THE (Roger Corman)
Filmf: v. X (1967), p. 222; comp., cp. cr.
Films & F: v. 14, n. 3 (Dec., 1967), p. 25; David Austen, 550 wds., cp. cr.
Films in R: v. XVIII, n. 7 (Aug.-Sept., 1967), pp. 444-445; Wilfred Mifflin,
250 wds., no cr.
Take One: v. 1, n. 6 (1967), pp. 24-25; Jay Cocks, 750 wds., pt. cr.

5460 SAINTLY SINNERS (Jean Yarbrough)
Filmf: v. V (1962), p. 52; comp., cp. cr.
Films & F: v. 8, n. 12 (Sept., 1962), p. 36; David Gerrard, 300 wds., cp. cr.

SAIT-ON-JAMAIS (see: No Sun in Venice)

SALAIRE DE LA PEUR, LE (see: The Wages of Fear)

5461 SALESMAN (David and Albert Maysles and Charlotte Zwerin)
Cinema: v. 5, n. 2, p. 46; Sara Fishko, 650 wds., no cr.
F Quarterly: v. XXIII, n. 1 (Fall, 1969), pp. 54-55; Ernest Callenbach, 550
wds., no cr.
F Soc Rev: v. 4, n. 6, pp. 11-17; Patrick MacFadden, 1500 wds., pt. cr.
Filmf: v. XII (1969), p. 178; comp., cp. cr.
Films in R: v. XX, n. 5 (May, 1969), pp. 318-319; Arthur B. Clark, 400
wds., no cr.
Interntl F G: v. 7 (1970), p. 230; Peter Cowie, 200 wds., pt. cr.
Take One: v. 2, n. 2 (1969), p. 23; Patrick MacFadden, 300 wds., pt. cr.

5462 SALLAH (Ephraim Kishon)
Films & F: v. 13, n. 12 (Sept., 1967), p. 21; Peter Davalle, 500 wds., cp. cr.

5463 SALLY'S IRISH ROGUE (George Pollock)
Films & F: v. 5, n. 4 (Jan., 1959), p. 24; Tony Buck, 300 wds., cp. cr.

5464 SALT AND PEPPER (Richard Donner)
Filmf: v. XI (1968), p. 362; comp., cp. cr.

SALT OF THE BLACK EARTH (see: Sol Ziemi Czarnej)

5465 SALT OF THE EARTH (Herbert Biberman)
F Culture: n. 50-51 (Fall-Winter, 1970), pp. 79-80; Gordon Hitchens, 1300
wds., no cr.
F Lib Quarterly: v. 5, n. 1 (Winter, 1971-1972), pp. 51-53; Judith Eisen-
scher, 450 wds., pt. cr.
Films & F: v. 1, n. 2 (Nov., 1954), p. 20; Frances White, 200 wds., pt. cr.
Films in R: v. V, n. 4 (Apr., 1954), p. 197; 350 wds., no cr.

5466 SALTANAT
Film: n. 14 (Nov.-Dec., 1957), pp. 21-22; Dai Vaughan, 1400 wds., no cr.

5467 SALTO (Thaddeus Konwicki)
F Soc Rev: Feb. (1968), pp. 20-21; Steven P. Hill, 700 wds., no cr.
Filmf: v. IX (1966), p. 284; comp., cp. cr.

SALVARE LA FACCIA (see: Psychout for Murder)

5468 SALVATORE GIULIANO (Francesco Rosi)
(also: Dreaded Mafia)
F Soc Rev: Sept. (1966), pp. 19-21; John Thomas, 650 wds., pt. cr.
F Soc Rev: v. 7, n. 2 (Oct., 1971), pp. 33-38; Maria-Teresa Ravage, 2500
wds., cp. cr.

Filmf: v. VII (1964), p. 301; comp., cp. cr.
Films & F: v. 9, n. 9 (June, 1963), p. 36; Robin Bean, 800 wds., cp. cr.
Sight & S: v. 32, n. 3 (Summer, 1963), pp. 142-143; Geoffrey Nowell-
    Smith, 1000 wds., pt. cr.

5469 SAM WHISKEY (Arnold Laven)
Filmf: v. XII (1969), p. 311; comp., cp. cr.
Films & F: v. 15, n. 12 (Sept., 1969), pp. 60-61; David Rider, 275 wds., cp.
    cr.

5470 SAMADHI (Jordan Belson)
F Culture: n. 48-49 (Winter-Spring, 1970), pp. 17-19; Gene Youngblood,
    1400 wds., no cr.
F Quarterly: v. XXI, n. 3 (Spring, 1968), pp. 48-49; Ernest Callenbach, 700
    wds., no cr.

5471 SAMAR (George Montgomery)
Filmf: v. V (1962), p. 70; comp., cp. cr.

SAMMA NO AJI (see: An Autumn Afternoon)

5472 SAMMY GOING SOUTH (Alexander MacKendrick)
(also: A Boy Ten Feet Tall)
Filmf: v. VIII (1965), p. 59; comp., cp. cr.
Films & F: v. 9, n. 8 (May, 1963), p. 28; John Cutts, 600 wds., cp. cr.
Movie: n. 9, pp. 29-30; Ian Cameron, 1200 wds., pt. cr.

5473 SAMMY — THE WAY OUT SEAL (Norman Tokar)
Films & F: v. 9, n. 9 (June, 1963), p. 33; Ian Johnson, 75 wds., cp. cr.

SAMOURAI, LE (see: The Samurai)

5474 SAMSON AND THE SEVEN MIRACLES OF THE WORLD (Riccardo Freda)
Filmf: v. VI (1963), p. 341; comp., cp. cr.
Films & F: v. 10, n. 1 (Oct., 1963), pp. 24-25; Ian Johnson, 350 wds., cp.
    cr.

5475 SAMSON AND THE SLAVE QUEEN (Umberto Lenzi)
(also: Zorro Contro Maciste)
Filmf: v. VII (1964), p. 20; comp., cp. cr.

5476 SAMURAI, THE (Jean-Pierre Melville)
(also: Le Samourai)
Films & F: v. 17, n. 10 (July, 1971), p. 49; Gordon Gow, 700 wds., cp. cr.
Focus on F: n. 4 (Sept.-Oct., 1970), pp. 3-6; Tom Milne and Allen Eyles,
    1300 wds., cp. cr.
Movie: n. 17 (Winter, 1969-1970), p. 37; Ian Cameron, 50 wds., no cr.

SAMURAI (Kihachi Okamoto/see: Samurai Assassin)

5477 SAMURAI ASSASSIN (Kihachi Okamoto)
(also: Samurai)
Filmf: v. VIII (1965), p. 101; comp., cp. cr.

5478 SAN FERRY ANN (Jeremy Summers)
Films & F: v. 12, n. 2 (Nov., 1965), pp. 29-30; Raymond Durgnat, 400
    wds., cp. cr.

5479 SANCTUARY (Tony Richardson)
F Quarterly: v. XIV, n. 4 (Summer, 1961), p. 63; R. M. Hodgens, 275 wds.,
    no cr.
Filmf: v. IV (1961), p. 41; comp., cp. cr.
Films & F: v. 7, n. 8 (May, 1961), p. 26; Richard Whitehall, 600 wds., cp.
    cr.
Films in R: v. XII, n. 3 (Mar., 1961), pp. 174-175; Arthur B. Clark, 250
    wds., no cr.
Sight & S: v. 30, n. 2 (Spring, 1961), p. 90; Penelope Houston, 800 wds.,
    pt. cr.

5480 SAND CASTLE, THE (Jerome Hill)
        F Journal: n. 20 (Aug., 1962), p. 89; John R. Burgess, 300 wds., no cr.
        F Quarterly: v. XVI, n. 4 (Summer, 1963), pp. 54-55; Ernest Callenbach,
              350 wds., pt. cr.
        Filmf: v. IV (1961), p. 216; comp., cp. cr.
        Films & F: v. 8, n. 9 (June, 1962), pp. 35-36; Ken Gay, 450 wds., cp. cr.
        Films in R: v. XII, n. 2 (Feb., 1961), pp. 112-113; Adelaide Comerford,
              300 wds., no cr.

5481 SAND PEBBLES, THE (Robert Wise)
        Filmf: v. IX (1966), p. 329; comp., cp. cr.
        Films & F: v. 13, n. 10 (July, 1967), pp. 22-23; David Adams, 450 wds., cp.
              cr.
        Films in R: v. XVIII, n. 1 (Jan., 1967), pp. 50-51; Henry Hart, 400 wds., no
              cr.

5482 SAND, OR PETER AND THE WOLF (Caroline Leaf)
        F Lib Quarterly: v. 3, n. 1 (Winter, 1969-1970), pp. 38-39, 41; Irene Porter,
              350 wds., pt. cr.

5483 SANDOKAN THE GREAT (Umberto Lenzi)
        Films & F: v. 11, n. 10 (July, 1965), p. 35; David Rider, 350 wds., cp. cr.

5484 SANDPIPER, THE (Vincente Minnelli)
        F Quarterly: v. XIX, n. 1 (Fall, 1965), pp. 62-63; Ernest Callenbach, 250
              wds., no cr.
        Films & F: v. 12, n. 1 (Oct., 1965), p. 28; Gordon Gow, 250 wds., cp. cr.
        Films in R: v. XVI, n. 7 (Aug.-Sept., 1965), pp. 448-449; Elaine Rothschild,
              400 wds., no cr.
        Movie: n. 14 (Aut., 1965), p. 41; Peter Bogdanovich, 350 wds., no cr.

        SANDRA (see: Of a Thousand Delights)

5485 SANDS OF BEERSHEBA (Alexander Ramati)
        (also: Rebels Against the Light)
        Filmf: v. IX (1966), p. 142; comp., cp. cr.

5486 SANDS OF IWO JIMA (Allan Dwan)
        Films in R: v. I, n. 2 (Mar., 1950), pp. 34-35; McClure M. Howland, 250
              wds., pt. cr.

5487 SANDS OF THE KALAHARI (Cy Enfield)
        F Quarterly: v. XIX, n. 3 (Spring, 1966), p. 53; William Johnson, 75 wds.,
              no cr.
        Films & F: v. 12, n. 5 (Feb., 1966), pp. 12, 16; Gordon Gow, 600 wds., cp.
              cr.

5488 SANDWICH MAN, THE (Robert Hartford-Davis)
        Films & F: v. 13, n. 2 (Nov., 1966), pp. 56-57; Raymond Durgnat, 900
              wds., cp. cr.

5489 SANFTE LAUF, DER (Haro Senft)
        Interntl F G: v. 6 (1969), p. 75; 200 wds., pt. cr.

5490 SANG DES BETES, LE (Georges Frangu)
        (also: The Blood of Beasts)
        F Journal: n. 3 (1956), p. ? ; 100 wds., no cr.

5491 SANJURO (Akira Kurosawa)
        Filmf: v. VI (1963), p. 134; comp., cp. cr.
        Films & F: v. 17, n. 4 (Jan., 1971), p. 56; Gordon Gow, 650 wds., cp. cr.

5492 SANS FAMILLE (André Michel)
        Filmf: v. II (1959), p. 220; comp., cp. cr.

5493 SANSHO DAYU (Kenji Mizoguchi)
        (also: Sansho the Bailiff)
        F Quarterly: v. XVII, n. 4 (Summer, 1964), pp. 53-54; Eileen Bowser, 600
              wds., pt. cr.

SANSHO THE BAILIFF (see: Sansho Dayu)

SANTA CLAUS HAS BLUE EYES (see: Bad Company)

SANTO GUERREIRO CONTRA O DRAGAO DA MALDADE (see: Antonio das Mortes)

SAPORE DELLA VENDETTA, IL (see: The Narco Men)

5494 SAPPHIRE (Basil Dearden)
   Filmf: v. II (1959), p. 265; comp., cp. cr.
   Films & F: v. 5, n. 9 (June, 1959), p. 25; Dai Vaughan, 300 wds., cp. cr.
   Films in R: v. XI, n. 3 (Mar., 1960), p. 172; Charles A. Butler, 100 wds., no cr.

5495 SARABAND FOR DEAD LOVERS (Basil Dearden)
   Sight & S: v. 17, n. 67 (Autumn, 1948), p. 144; Arthur Vesselo, 200 wds., no cr.

5496 SARAGOSSA MANUSCRIPT, THE (Wojciech Has)
   F Quarterly: v. XIX, n. 4 (Summer, 1966), pp. 56-59; John Seelye, 1800 wds., no cr.
   Films & F: v. 13, n. 6 (Mar., 1967), pp. 32-33; Raymond Durgnat, 900 wds., cp. cr.
   Interntl F G: v. 3 (1966), p. 125; 225 wds., pt. cr.
   Movie: n. 14 (Autumn, 1965), p. 41; Ian Cameron, 100 wds., no cr.
   Take One: v. 2, n. 7 (1970), p. 24; Ronald Blumer, 75 wds., pt. cr.

SASAKI KOJIRO (see: Kojiro)

SASOM I EN SPEGEL (see: Through A Glass Darkly)

5497 SATAN BUG, THE (John Sturges)
   F Quarterly: v. XVIII, n. 4 (Summer, 1965), pp. 60-61; R. M. Hodgens, 100 wds., no cr.
   Filmf: v. VIII (1965), p. 82; comp., cp. cr.
   Films & F: v. 11, n. 10 (July, 1965), pp. 27-28; Allen Eyles, 450 wds., cp. cr.

SATAN CONDUIT LE BAL, ET (see: Satan Leads the Dance)

5498 SATAN IN HIGH HEELS (Jerald Intrator)
   Filmf: v. V (1962), p. 156; comp., cp. cr.

5499 SATAN LEADS THE DANCE (Ghisha M. Dabat)
   (also: Et Satan Conduit le Bal)
   Films & F: v. 9, n. 12 (Sept., 1963), p. 26; Robin Bean, 400 wds., cp. cr.

5500 SATAN NEVER SLEEPS (Leo McCarey)
   (also: The Devil Never Sleeps)
   Filmf: v. V (1962), p. 43; comp., cp. cr.
   Films & F: v. 8, n. 7 (Apr., 1962), p. 32; Peter Baker, 250 wds., cp. cr.
   Movie: n. 1 (June, 1962), pp. 31-32; Paul Mayersberg, 1100 wds., pt. cr.

5501 SATAN's SADISTS (Al Adamson)
   Filmf: v. XIV (1971), p. 5; comp., cp. cr.

5502 SATAN'S SATELLITES (Fred Brannon)
   Filmf: v. I (1958), p. 295; comp., cp. cr.

SATAN'S SKIN (see: The Blood on Satan's Claw)

5503 SATCHMO THE GREAT (Edward R. Murrow and Fred W. Friendly, prods.)
   Filmf: v. I (1958), p. 28; comp., cp. cr.
   Films & F: v. 4, n. 9 (June, 1958), p. 25; John Cutts, 300 wds., cp. cr.

5504 SATELLITE IN THE SKY (Paul Dickson)
   Films & F: v. 3, n. 1 (Oct., 1956), p. 27; Ken Gay, 300 wds., cp. cr.

SATURDAY ISLAND (see: Island of Desire)

5505 SATURDAY MORNING (Kent MacKenzie)
 Filmf: v. XIV (1971), p. 304; comp., cp. cr.
 Films in R: v. XXII, n. 5 (May, 1971), pp. 312-313; Daphne Norris, 150
 wds., no cr.

5506 SATURDAY NIGHT AND SUNDAY MORNING (Karel Reisz)
 F Quarterly: v. XIV, n. 4 (Summer, 1961), pp. 58-59; Elizabeth Sutherland,
 1200 wds., pt. cr.
 Filmf: v. IV (1961), p. 71; comp., cp. cr.
 Films & F: v. 7, n. 3 (Dec., 1960), p. 28; Gordon Gow, 900 wds., cp. cr.
 Films in R: v. XII, n. 4 (Apr., 1961), pp. 235-237; Harold Dunham, 650
 wds., no cr.
 Sight & S: v. 30, n. 1 (Winter, 1960-1961), p. 33; Peter John Dyer, 1000
 wds., pt. cr.

5507 SATURDAY NIGHT OUT (Robert Hartford-Davis)
 Films & F: v. 10, n. 7 (Apr., 1964), p. 29; Raymond Durgnat, 400 wds., cp.
 cr.

 SATYRICON (see: Fellini's Satyricon)

5508 SAUL AND DAVID (Marcello Baldi)
 (also: Saul E Davide)
 Filmf: v. XI (1968), p. 432; comp., cp. cr.

 SAUL E DAVIDE (see: Saul and David)

5509 SAVAGE EYE, THE (Ben Maddow, Sidney Meyers, Joseph Strick)
 F Quarterly: v. XIII, n. 4 (Summer, 1960), pp. 53-57; Benjamin T. Jackson,
 1400 wds., pt. cr.
 Filmf: v. III (1960), p. 167; comp., cp. cr.
 Films & F: v. 6, n. 4 (Jan., 1960), p. 21; Paul Rotha, 550 wds., cp. cr.
 Sight & S: v. 29, n. 1 (Winter, 1959-1960), p. 37; Eric Rhods, 800 wds., pt.
 cr.

5510 SAVAGE GUNS, THE (Michael Carreras)
 Filmf: v. V (1962), p. 322; comp., cp. cr.
 Films & F: v. 9, n. 4 (Jan., 1963), pp. 49-50; Raymond Durgnat, 350 wds.,
 cp. cr.

5511 SAVAGE INNOCENTS, THE (Nicholas Ray)
 F Quarterly: v. XIV, n. 2 (Winter, 1960), pp. 43-45; Douglas Cox, 1250
 wds., pt. cr.
 Filmf: v. IV (1961), p. 104; comp., cp. cr.
 Films & F: v. 6, n. 11 (Aug., 1960), p. 21; Richard Whitehall, 300 wds., cp.
 cr.

5512 SAVAGE PAMPAS (Hugo Fregonese)
 (also: Pampa Salvaje)
 Filmf: v. X (1967), p. 432; comp., cp. cr.

5513 SAVAGE SAM (Norman Tokar)
 Filmf: v. VI (1963), p. 144; comp., cp. cr.
 Films & F: v. 9, n. 12 (Sept., 1963), p. 24; Allen Eyles, 250 wds., cp. cr.

5514 SAVAGE SEVEN, THE (Richard Rush)
 Filmf: v. XI (1968), p. 371; comp., cp. cr.

5515 SAVAGES, THE (Alan Gorg, prod.)
 F Lib Quarterly: v. 2, n. 1 (Winter, 1968-1969), p. 61; Philip Levering, 200
 wds., pt. cr.

 SAVE YOUR FACE (see: Psychout For Murder)

5516 SAWDUST AND TINSEL (Ingmar Bergman)
 (also: The Naked Night)
 Films & F: v. 1, n. 11 (Aug., 1955), p. 18; Derek Hill, 175 wds., cp. cr.

5517 SAWDUST RING, THE (B. Dolin)
 Films & F: v. 9, n. 8 (May, 1963), p. 33; Ian Johnson, 200 wds., cp. cr.

5518 SAY HELLO TO YESTERDAY (Alvin Rakoff)
       Filmf: v. XIV (1971), p. 74; comp., cp. cr.
       Films & F: v. 17, n. 6 (Mar., 1971), p. 55; Gordon Gow, 750 wds., cp. cr.

5519 SAY ONE FOR ME (Frank Tashlin)
       Filmf: v. II (1959), p. 139; comp., cp. cr.

5520 SAYONARA (Joshua Logan)
       F Culture: v. IV, n. 2 (Feb., 1958), p. 17; Peter Walsh, 175 wds., cp. cr.
       Films & F: v. 4, n. 4 (Jan., 1958), p. 23; Gordon Gow, 500 wds., cp. cr.
       Films in R: v. VIII, n. 10 (Dec., 1957), pp. 527-528; Ellen Fitzpatrick, 200
            wds., no cr.
       Sight & S: v. 27, n. 3 (Winter, 1957-1958), pp. 149-150; John Cutts, 350
            wds., pt. cr.

       SBARCO DI ANZIO, LO (see: Anzio)

5521 SCALPHUNTERS, THE (Sidney Pollack)
       F Quarterly: v. XXI, n. 4 (Summer, 1968), p. 61; Stephen Farber, 400 wds.,
            no cr.
       Filmf: v. XI (1968), p. 118; comp., cp. cr.
       Films & F: v. 14, n. 7 (Apr., 1968), p. 25; David Austen, 450 wds., cp. cr.

5522 SCAMP, THE (Wolf Rilla)
       Filmf: v. 4, n. 3 (Dec., 1957), pp. 23-24; Kay Collier, 400 wds., cp. cr.

5523 SCAMPOLO (Alfred Weidenmann)
       (also: Das Madchen Scampolo)
       Filmf: v. II (1959), p. 211; comp., cp. cr.

5524 SCANDAL IN SORRENTO (Dino Risi)
       (also: Pane, Amore, E . .)
       Films & F: v. 3, n. 7 (Apr., 1957), pp. 24-25; Peter John Dyer, 250 wds.,
            cp. cr.

       SCANDALE, LE (see: The Champagne Murders)

5525 SCANDALOUS JOHN (Robert Butler)
       Filmf: v. XIV (1971), p. 728; comp., cp. cr.

5526 SCAPEGOAT, THE (Robert Hamer)
       Filmf: v. II (1959), p. 191; comp., cp. cr.
       Films & F: v. 5, n. 12 (Sept., 1959), p. 21; Paul Rotha, 600 wds., cp. cr.
       Films in R: v. X, n. 7 (Aug.-Sept., 1959), pp. 423-424; Louise Corbin, 225
            wds., no cr.
       Sight & S: v. 28, n. 3-4 (Summer-Autumn, 1959), p. 172; David Robinson,
            525 wds., pt. cr.

5527 SCARFACE MOB, THE (Phil Karlson)
       Filmf: v. V (1962), p. 367; comp., cp. cr.
       Films & F: v. 6, n. 6 (Mar., 1960), p. 24; Tony Keniston, 200 wds., cp. cr.

       SCARLET AND BLACK (see: Le Rouge et le Noir)

       SCARLET BLADE, THE (see: The Crimson Blade)

5528 SCARLET EMPRESS, THE (Josef von Sternberg)
       Movie: n. 13 (Summer, 1965), pp. 29-30; O. O. Green, 800 wds., no cr.
       Sight & S: v. 34, n. 2 (Spring, 1965), p. 96; John Gillett, 850 wds., pt. cr.

5529 SCARLET HANGMAN, THE (see: Bloody Pit of Horror)

5530 SCARLET HOUR, THE (Michael Curtiz)
       Films & F: v. 2, n. 8 (May, 1956), p. 21; Michael Winner, 150 wds., cp. cr.

       SCARLET PIMPERNEL, THE (see: Michael Powell)

5531 SCARS OF DRACULA, THE (Roy Ward Baker)
       Filmf: v. XIV (1971), p. 264; comp., cp. cr.
       Films & F: v. 17, n. 3 (Dec., 1970), p. 56; Margaret Tarratt, 150 wds., cp.
            cr.

5532 SCARY TIME, A (Shirley Clarke)
   F Quarterly: v. XIII, n. 4 (Summer, 1960), pp. 57-58; Henry Breitrose, 800
    wds., pt. cr.

5533 SCAVENGERS, THE (Ermanno Olmi)
   (also: City of Sin)
   Filmf: v. III (1960), p. 349; comp., cp. cr.
   Sight & S: v. 40, n. 1 (Winter, 1970-1971), pp. 17-18; Philip Strick 1000
    wds., no cr.

5534 SCENT OF MYSTERY (Jack Cardiff)
   (also: Holiday in Spain)
   Filmf: v. III (1960), p. 31; comp., cp. cr.
   Films & F: v. 12, n. 8 (May, 1966), p. 8; David Rider, 350 wds., cp. cr.

  SCHATTEN WERDEN LAENGER, DIE (see: The Shadows Grow Longer)

  SCHIAVE ESISTONO ANCORA, LE (see: Slave Trade in the World Today)

  SCHLOSS, DAS (see: The Castle)

5535 SCHMEERGUNTZ (Gunvor Nelson and Dorothy Wiley)
   F Quarterly: v. XIX, n. 4 (Summer, 1966), p. 67; Ernest Callenbach, 300
    wds., pt. cr.

  SCHMUTZIGER ENGEL (see: Dirty Angel)

  SCHNACHNOVELLE (see: Brainwashed)

5536 SCHONZEIT FUR FUCHSE (Peter Schamoni)
   (also: Close Time for Foxes)
   Interntl F G: v. 4 (1967), p. 79; 150 wds., pt. cr.

5537 SCHOOL FOR LOVE (Marc Allegret)
   (also: Futures Vedettes)
   Filmf: v. III (1960), p. 359; comp., cp. cr.

5538 SCHOOL FOR SCOUNDRELS (Roger Hamer)
   Filmf: v. III (1960), p. 201; comp., cp. cr.
   Films & F: v. 6, n. 8 (May, 1960), p. 23; R. E. Durgnat, 400 wds., cp. cr.

5539 SCHOOL FOR SECRETS (Peter Ustinov)
   Sight & S: v. 15, n. 60 (Winter, 1946-1947) p. 155; Arthur Vesselo, 200
    wds., no cr.

5540 SCHOOL FOR SEX (Ryo Kinoshita)
   (also: Nikutai No Gakko; School of Flesh)
   Filmf: v. X (1967), p. 412; comp., cp. cr.

  SCHOOL OF FLESH (see: School for Sex)

5541 SCHWECHATER (Peter Kubelka)
   F Quarterly: v. XX, n. 2 (Winter, 1966-1967), pp. 54-57; Earl Bodine, 1600
    wds., pt. cr.

  SCHWEIGENDE STERN, DER (see: First Spaceship on Venus)

5542 SCIUSCIA (Vittorio de Sica)
   (also: Shoeshine)
   Sequence: n. 4 (Summer, 1948), pp. 38-39; Lindsay Anderson, 550 wds.,
    no cr.

5543 SCORPIO RISING (Kenneth Anger)
   F Culture: n. 31 (Winter, 1963-1964), pp. 5-6; Gregory Markopoulos, 400
    wds., no cr.
   F Culture: n. 31 (Winter, 1963-1964), pp. 6-7; Ken Kelman, 1100 wds., no
    cr.
   F Culture: n. 32 (Spring, 1964), pp. 9-10; Carolee Schneemann, 600 wds.,
    no cr.
   F Soc Rev: Apr. (1966), pp. 20-21; Louise Howton, 425 wds., pt. cr.

5544 SCOTCH ON THE ROCKS (John Eldridge)
     Films in R: v. V, n. 7 (Aug.-Sept., 1954), p. 368; 50 wds., no cr.

5545 SCOTLAND YARD DRAGNET (Montgomery Tully)
     Filmf: v. I (1958), p. 70; comp., cp. cr.

5546 SCRAMBLES (Ed Emshwiller)
     F Quarterly: v. XX, n. 3 (Spring, 1967), pp. 46-50; Richard Whitehall, 2200
       wds., no cr.

5547 SCREAM AND SCREAM AGAIN (Gordon Hessler)
     Films & F: v. 16, n. 7 (Apr., 1970), p. 54; Richard Davis, 350 wds., cp. cr.

5548 SCREAM OF FEAR (Seth Holt)
     Filmf: v. IV (1961), p. 257; comp., cp. cr.

5549 SCREAM OF THE DEMON LOVER (Jose Luis Merino)
     (also: Ivanna)
     Filmf: v. XIV (1971), p. 757; comp., cp. cr.

     SCREAMING (see: Carry On Screaming)

5550 SCREAMING MIMI (Gerd Oswald)
     Filmf: v. I (1958), p. 99; comp., cp. cr.

5551 SCREAMING SKULL (Alex Nicol)
     Filmf: v. I (1958), p. 258; comp., cp. cr.

5552 SCREEN TESTS (Andy Warhol)
     F Culture: n. 38 (1965), pp. 62-63; Gregory Battcock, 700 wds., no cr.

5553 SCROOGE (Ronald Neame)
     Films & F: v. 17, n. 4 (Jan., 1971), p. 48; Gordon Gow, 700 wds., cp. cr.
     Films in R: v. XXI, n. 10 (Dec., 1970), pp. 643-644; Tatiana Balkoff
      Drowne, 200 wds., no cr.

     SCROOGE (Brian Desmond Hurst/see: A Christmas Carol)

5554 SCUM OF THE EARTH (Lewis H. Gordon)
     Filmf: v. VI (1963), p. 337; comp., cp. cr.

     SCUSI, FACCIAMO L'AMORE? (see: Listen, Let's Make Love)

     SE PERMETTETE PARLIAMO DI DONNE (see: Let's Talk About Women)

     SE TUTTE LE DONNE DEL MONDO (see: Kiss the Girls and Make Them
      Die)

5555 SEA AROUND US, THE (Irwin Allen, prod.)
     Films in R: v. IV, n. 7 (Aug.-Sept., 1953), p. 366; 200 wds., no cr.

5556 SEA FURY (Cy Endfield)
     Filmf: v. II (1959), p. 309; comp., cp. cr.
     Films & F: v. 5, n. 1 (Oct., 1958), p. 24; Rupert Butler, 175 wds., cp. cr.

5557 SEA GULL, THE (Sidney Lumet)
     (also: Chayka)
     Filmf: v. XI (1968), p. 533; comp., cp. cr.
     Films & F: v. 16, n. 5 (Feb., 1970), p. 39-40; Peter Buckley, 600 wds., cp.
      cr.
     Films in R: v. XX, n. 2 (Feb., 1969), pp. 117-118; Tatiana Balkoff Drowne,
      200 wds., no cr.

     SEA OF SAND (see: Desert Patrol)

5558 SEA PIRATE, THE (Roy Rowland)
     Filmf: v. X (1967), p. 386; comp., cp. cr.

5559 SEA SHALL NOT HAVE THEM, THE (Lewis Gilbert)
     Films & F: v. 1, n. 3 (Dec., 1954), p. 20; Kenneth Thompson, 200 wds., cp.
      cr.

SEA WALL, THE (see: This Angry Age)

5560 SEA WIFE (Bob McNaught)
         Films & F: v. 3, n. 8 (May, 1957), p. 26; Peter G. Baker, 200 wds., cp. cr.

5561 SEANCE ON A WET AFTERNOON (Bryan Forbes)
         F Soc Rev: Feb. (1966), p. 11; Philip Chamberlin, 125 wds., pt. cr.
         Filmf: v. VII (1964), p. 262; comp., cp. cr.
         Films & F: v. 10, n. 10 (July, 1964), p. 21; Raymond Durgnat, 725 wds.,
            cp. cr.
         Films in R: v. XV, n. 10 (Dec., 1964), pp. 635-636; Eunice Sinkler, 325
            wds., no cr.
         Sight & S: v. 33, n. 3 (Summer, 1964), p. 146; Peter John Dyer, 500 wds.,
            pt. cr.

5562 SEARCH, THE (Fred Zinnemann)
         Sequence: n. 10 (New Year, 1950), p. 152; K.R., 200 wds., no cr.
         Sight & S: v. 18, n. 71 (Dec., 1949), p. 21; 150 wds., pt. cr.

5563 SEARCH FOR BRIDEY MURPHY, THE (Noel Langley)
         Films & F: v. 3, n. 4 (Jan., 1957), p. 26; Peter John Dyer, 200 wds., cp. cr.

5564 SEARCH FOR PARADISE (Lowell Thomas)
         Films in R: v. VIII, n. 9 (Nov., 1957), pp. 461-462; Courtland Phipps, 200
            wds., no cr.

5565 SEARCHERS, THE (John Ford)
         F Comment: v. 7, n. 1 (Spring, 1971), pp. 56-61; Andrew Sarris, 1600 wds.,
            cp. cr.
         Films & F: v. 2, n. 12 (Sept., 1956), pp. 25-26; Peter G. Baker, 225 wds.,
            cp. cr.
         Films in R: v. VII, n. 6 (June-July, 1956), pp. 284-285; Courtland Phipps,
            450 wds., no cr.
         Sight & S: v. 26, n. 2 (Autumn, 1956), pp. 94-95; Lindsay Anderson, 950
            wds., pt. cr.

5566 SEARCHING WIND, THE (William Dieterle)
         Sight & S: v. 15, n. 59 (Autumn, 1946), p. 98; Roger Manvell, 350 wds., no
            cr.

5567 SEASON FOR LOVE, THE (Pierre Kast)
         (also: La Morte-Saison des Amours)
         Filmf: v. VI (1963), p. 162; comp., cp. cr.
         Sight & S: v. 35, n. 4 (Autumn, 1966), p. 199; Penelope Houston, 650 wds.,
            pt. cr.

5568 SEASON OF PASSION (Leslie Norman)
         (also: Summer of the Seventeenth Doll)
         Filmf: v. V (1962), p. 7; comp., cp. cr.
         Films & F: v. 6, n. 6 (Mar., 1960), p. 23; Peter G. Baker, 300 wds., cp. cr.
         Films in R: v. XIII, n. 2 (Feb., 1962), pp. 105-106; Helen Carpenter, 200
            wds., no cr.
         Sight & S: v. 29, n. 2 (Spring, 1960), p. 93; Kenneth Cavander, 375 wds.,
            pt. cr.

      SEATED AT HIS RIGHT (see: Black Jesus)

5569 SEBASTIAN (David Greene)
         F Quarterly: v. XXI, n. 3 (Spring, 1968), p. 61; Stephen Farber, 350 wds.,
            no cr.
         Filmf: v. XI (1968), p. 20; comp., cp. cr.
         Films & F: v. 14, n. 9 (June, 1968), p. 30; David Austen, 300 wds., cp. cr.
         Films in R: v. XIX, n. 2 (Feb., 1968), pp. 111-112; Norman Cecil, 250
            wds., no cr.

5570 SECOND BEST SECRET AGENT IN THE WHOLE WIDE WORLD, THE
            (Lindsay Shonteff)
         (also: Licensed to Kill)
         Filmf: v IX (1966), p. 116; comp., cp. cr.

      SECOND BREATH, THE (see: Le Deuxième Souffle)

5571 SECOND TIME AROUND, THE (Vincent Sherman)
        Filmf: v. IV (1961), p. 345; comp., cp. cr.
        Films & F: v. 8, n. 7 (Apr., 1962), p. 32; John Cutts, 300 wds., cp. cr.

      SECOND WIND (see: Le Deuxième Souffle)

5572 SECONDS (John Frankenheimer)
        F Quarterly: v. XX, n. 2 (Winter, 1966-1967), pp. 25-28; Stephen Farber,
            1900 wds., pt. cr.
        Filmf: v. IX (1966), p. 255; comp., cp. cr.
        Films & F: v. 13, n. 4 (Jan., 1967), pp. 28-29; Robin Bean, 1600 wds., cp.
            cr.
        Films in R: v. XVII, n. 9 (Nov., 1966), pp. 585-586; Page Cook, 200 wds.,
            no cr.
        Focus: n. 1 (Feb., 1967), p. 16; Stephen Manes, 200 wds., no cr.
        Interntl F G: v. 4 (1967), pp. 162-163; 225 wds., pt. cr.
        Sight & S: v. 36, n. 1 (Winter, 1966-1967), p. 46; David Wilson, 600 wds.,
            pt. cr.

5573 SECRET AGENT FIREBALL (Mario Donen)
        (also: Le Spie Uccidono A Beirut; The Spy Killed at Beirut)
        Filmf: v. IX (1966), p. 233; comp., cp. cr.

5574 SECRET AGENT SUPER DRAGON (Calvin Jackson Paget)
        (also: New York Calling Super Dragon; New York Chiama Superdrago)
        Filmf: v. IX (1966), p. 154; comp., cp. cr.

5575 SECRET CEREMONY (Joseph Losey)
        F Heritage: v. 5, n. 4 (Summer, 1970), pp. 1-6; Michael Dempsey, 1600
            wds., no cr.
        F Quarterly: v. XXII, n. 3 (Spring, 1969), p. 64; Ernest Callenbach, 200
            wds., no cr.
        Filmf: v. XI (1968), p. 436; comp., cp. cr.
        Films & F: v. 15, n. 11 (Aug., 1969), pp. 32-33; Gordon Gow, 1400 wds.,
            cp. cr.
        Films in R: v. XIX, n. 10 (Dec., 1968), pp. 648-649; Page Cook, 225 wds.,
            no cr.
        Movie: n. 16 (Winter, 1968-1969), p. 39; Mark Shivas, 75 wds., no cr.

5576 SECRET DOOR, THE (Gilbert Kay)
        Filmf: v. VII (1964), p. 341; comp., cp. cr.

5577 SECRET FILE: HOLLYWOOD (Ralph Cushman)
        Filmf: v. IV (1961-1962), p. 367; comp., cp. cr.

      SECRET GAME, THE (see: Jeux Interdits)

5578 SECRET GARDEN, THE (Fred Wilcox)
        Sequence: n. 10 (New Year, 1950), p. 156; A.M., 325 wds., no cr.

5579 SECRET INVASION, THE (Roger Corman)
        Filmf: v. VII (1964), p. 269; comp., cp. cr.
        Films & F: v. 11, n. 6 (Mar., 1965), pp. 35-36; Allen Eyles, 375 wds., cp. cr.
        Sight & S: v. 34, n. 1 (Winter, 1964-1965), p. 41; Peter John Dyer, 500
            wds., pt. cr.

5580 SECRET LIFE OF AN AMERICAN WIFE, THE (George Axelrod)
        Filmf: v. XI (1968), p. 247; comp., cp. cr.
        Films & F: v. 15, n. 10 (July, 1969), p. 48; Claire Johnson, 425 wds., cp. cr.
        Sight & S: v. 38, n. 2 (Spring, 1969), pp. 94-95; Gavin Millar, 800 wds., pt.
            cr.

5581 SECRET MARK OF D'ARTAGNAN, THE (Siro Marcellini)
        Films & F: v. 9, n. 9 (June, 1963), p. 35; Tony Mallerman, 150 wds., cp. cr.

5582 SECRET OF DEEP HARBOR (Edward L. Cahn)
        Filmf: v. IV (1961), p. 248; comp., cp. cr.

5583 SECRET OF MONTE CRISTO, THE (Monty Berman)
        Filmf: v. V (1962), p. 79; comp., cp. cr.

5584 SECRET OF MY SUCCESS, THE (Andrew L. Stone)
Films of F: v. 12, n. 6 (Mar., 1965), p. 53; Allen Eyles, 275 wds., cp. cr.

5585 SECRET OF SANTA VITTORIA, THE (Stanley Kramer)
Films & F: v. 15, n. 2 (Nov., 1968), pp. 65-68; Robin Bean, 1900 wds., no cr.
Films & F: v. 16, n. 10 (July, 1970), p. 32; Gordon Gow, 450 wds., cp. cr.
Films in R: v. XX, n. 9 (Nov., 1969), pp. 575-576; William Herron, 125 wds., no cr.

5586 SECRET OF SUCCESS (Leonid Lavrovsky and Alexander Shelenkov)
Films & F: v. 15, n. 3 (Dec., 1968), p. 40; Gordon Gow, 550 wds., cp. cr.

5587 SECRET OF THE PURPLE REEF, THE (William Witney)
Filmf: v. III (1960), p. 316; comp., cp. cr.

SECRET OF THE THREE JUNKS, THE (see: Red Dragon)

SECRET OF THE YELLOW DAFFODIL, THE (see: The Devil's Daffodil)

5588 SECRET PARIS (Eduord Logerau)
Films & F: v. 12, n. 2 (Nov., 1965), pp. 30-31; Raymond Durgnat, 400 wds., cp. cr.

5589 SECRET PARTNER, THE (Basil Dearden)
Filmf: v. IV (1961), p. 237; comp., cp. cr.
Films & F: v. 7, n. 9 (June, 1961), pp. 24-25; Phillip Riley, 450 wds., cp. cr.

5590 SECRET PEOPLE (Thorold Dickinson)
Sight & S: v. 21, n. 4 (Apr.-June, 1952), pp. 168-169; Gavin Lambert, 1500 wds., pt. cr.

5591 SECRET PLACE, THE (Clive Donner)
Filmf: v. I (1958), p. 277; comp., cp. cr.
Films & F: v. 3, n. 7 (Apr., 1957), pp. 27, 30; P. L. Mannock, 200 wds., cp. cr.

5592 SECRET SCROLLS (Hiroshi Inagaki)
(also: Ninjutsu; Yagya Bugeicho)
Filmf: v. XI (1968), p. 200; comp., cp. cr.

5593 SECRET SEVEN, THE (Alberto De Martino)
(also: Gli Invincible Sette; The Invincible Seven)
Filmf: v. IX (1966), p. 258; comp., cp. cr.
Films & F: v. 10, n. 10 (July, 1964), p. 27; David Rider, 300 wds., cp. cr.

SECRET WAR (see: The Dirty Game)

5594 SECRET WAR OF HARRY FRIGG, THE (Jack Smight)
F Quarterly: v. XXI, n. 4 (Summer, 1968), pp. 60-61; Ernest Callenbach, 175 wds., no cr.
Filmf: v. XI (1968), p. 70; comp., cp. cr.
Films & F: v. 14, n. 6 (Mar., 1968), p. 27; David Austen, 500 wds., cp. cr.
Films in R: v. XIX, n. 4 (Apr., 1968), pp. 243-244; Elaine Rothschild, 150 wds., no cr.

5595 SECRET WAYS, THE (Phil Karlson)
F Quarterly: v. XV, n. 2 (Winter, 1961-1962), p. 62; R. M. Hodgens, 50 wds., no cr.
Filmf: v. IV (1961), p. 128; comp., cp. cr.
Films & F: v. 7, n. 9 (June, 1961), p. 25; Robin Bean, 250 wds., cp. cr.

5596 SECRET WORLD (Robert Freeman)
(also: L'Echelle Blanche; La Promesse; The White Ladder)
Filmf: v. XII (1969), p. 349; comp., cp. cr.

SECRETS D'ALCOVE (see: The Bed)

5597 SECRETS OF THE NAZI CRIMINALS (Tore Sjoberg)
Films & F: v. 10, n. 11 (Aug., 1964), p. 27; Allen Eyles, 400 wds., cp. cr.

5598 SECRETS OF WOMEN (Ingmar Bergman)
      (also: Kvinnors Väntan; Waiting Women)
      F Quarterly: v. XV, n. 1 (Fall, 1961), pp. 45-47; Alfred Appel, Jr., 1100
          wds., pt. cr.
      Filmf: v. IV (1961), p. 221; comp., cp. cr.
      Films & F: v. 6, n. 3 (Dec., 1959), p. 24; Max Neufeld, 150 wds., cp. cr.

      SEDDOK (see: Atom Age Vampire)

      SEDMI KONTINENT (see: The Seventh Continent)

      SEDMIKRASKY (see: Daisies)

      SEDOTTA E ABBANDONATA (see: Seduced and Abandoned)

5599 SEDUCED AND ABANDONED (Pietro Germi)
      (also: Sedotta e Abbandonata)
      Cinema: v. 2, n. 3 (Oct.-Nov., 1964), p. 50; James Silke, 250 wds., pt. cr.
      Filmf: v. VII (1964), p. 227; comp., cp. cr.
      Films & F: v. 11, n. 6 (Mar., 1965), p. 28; Raymond Durgnat, 550 wds., cp.
          cr.
      Films in R: v. XV, n. 7 (Aug.-Sept., 1964), pp. 438-439; Joan Horvath, 325
          wds., no cr.
      Interntl F G: v. 2 (1965), p. 103; Gaetano Strazzulla, 200 wds., pt. cr.

      SEDUCER, THE (see: Man of Straw)

5600 SEDUCERS, THE (Graeme Ferguson)
      Filmf: v. V (1962), p. 355; comp., cp. cr.

5601 SEDUCTION OF THE SOUTH (Marlo Camerini)
      (also: I Briganti Italiano)
      Films & F: v. 9, n. 11 (Aug., 1963), p. 33; Brian O'Brien, 300 wds., cp. cr.

      SEDUTO ALLA SUA DESTRA (see: Black Jesus)

5602 SEE NO EVIL (Richard Fleischer)
      (also: Blind Terror)
      Filmf: v. XIV (1971), p. 283; comp., cp. cr.
      Films in R: v. XXII, n. 8 (Oct., 1971), p. 511; Flavia Wharton Rhawn, 125
          wds., no cr.

      SEE YOU AT MAO (see: British Sounds)

      SEE YOU IN HELL, DARLING (see: An American Dream)

5603 SEE YOU TOMORROW (Janusz Morgenstern)
      F Journal: n. 20 (Aug., 1962), p. 83; Brian J. Davies, 150 wds., no cr.
      F Quarterly: v. XIV, n. 2 (Winter, 1960), pp. 51-52; Norman C. Moser, 800
          wds., pt. cr.
      Films & F: v. 13, n. 7 (Apr., 1967), p. 7; Richard Davis, 350 wds., cp. cr.

      SEGNO DI VENERE, IL (see: The Sign of Venus)

      SEGNO DI ZORRO, IL (see: Duel at the Rio Grande)

      SEIGNEURS DE LA FORET (see: Masters of the Congo Jungle)

      SEISHUN ZANKOKU MONOGATARI (see: Naked Youth)

5604 SEKISHUN (Noboru Nakamura)
      (also: Three Faces of Love)
      Interntl F G: v. 5 (1968), p. 108; 200 wds., pt. cr.

5605 SEKSTET (Annelise Hormand)
      Films & F: v. 10, n. 6 (Mar., 1964), pp. 46-47; Denis Duperley, 1650 wds.,
          no cr.

5606 SELLING OF THE PENTAGON, THE (Peter Davis)
      F Lib Quarterly: v. 4, n. 4 (Fall, 1971), pp. 15-16, 56; Janet Handelman,
          900 wds., pt. cr.

5607 SEMINOLE (Budd Boetticher)
      Films in R: v. IV, n. 4 (Apr., 1953), pp. 197-198; Ethel Cutler Freeman, 475
      wds., pt. cr.

5608 SEND ME NO FLOWERS (Norman Jewison)
      Filmf: v. VII (1964), p. 326; comp., cp. cr.
      Films & F: v. 11, n. 4 (Jan., 1965), pp. 29-30; Allen Eyles, 425 wds., cp. cr.

5609 SENECHAL THE MAGNIFICENT (Jacques Boyer)
      Filmf: v. I (1958), p. 213; comp., cp. cr.

5610 SENILITA (Mauro Bolognini)
      Films & F: v. 9, n. 3 (Dec., 1962), p. 43; Gordon Gow, 900 wds., cp. cr.

5611 SENIOR PROM (David Lowell)
      Filmf: v. II (1959), p. 73; comp., cp. cr.

5612 SENSO (Luchino Visconti)
      (also: The Wanton Countess)
      Filmf: v. XI (1968), p. 328; comp., cp. cr.
      Films & F: v. 4, n. 1 (Oct., 1957), p. 25; Peter G. Baker, 275 wds., cp. cr.
      Sight & S: v. 27, n. 2 (Autumn, 1957), pp. 92-93; Alain Tanner, 800 wds.,
      pt. cr.

      SEPARATE BEDS (see: The Wheeler Dealers)

5613 SEPARATE TABLES (Delbert Mann)
      Filmf: v. I (1958), p. 231; comp., cp. cr.
      Films & F: v. 5, n. 6 (Mar., 1959), p. 24; Derek Conrad, 475 wds., cp. cr.
      Films in R: v. IX, n. 10 (Dec., 1958), pp. 592-593; Claudia Belmont, 300
      wds., no cr.
      Sight & S: v. 28, n. 2 (Spring, 1958), pp. 92-93; Peter John Dyer, 550 wds.,
      pt. cr.

5614 SEPARATION (Jack Bond)
      Filmf: v. XI (1968), p. 105; comp., cp. cr.
      Films & F: v. 14, n. 9 (June, 1968), p. 30; Stacy Waddy, 550 wds., cp. cr.

      SEPOLCRO DEI RE, IL (see: Cleopatra's Daughter)

      SEPPUKU (see: Harakiri)

      SEPT PECHES CAPITAUX, LES (Autant-Lara, Rossellini, Allégret, et al.,/see:
      The Seven Deadly Sins)

      SEPT PECHES CAPITAUX, LES (Godard, Chabrol, Vadim, Demy, et al.,/see:
      The Seven Capital Sins)

5615 SEPTEMBER STORM (Byron Haskin)
      Filmf: v. III (1960), p. 295; comp., cp. cr.
      Films in R: v. XI, n. 9 (Nov., 1960), p. 555; Henry Hart, 100 wds., no cr.

      SEPTIEME JURE, LE (see: The Seventh Juror)

      SEQUESTRATI DI ALTONA, I (see: The Condemned of Altona)

      SERDTSE MATERI (see: Heart of a Mother)

5616 SERENA (Peter Maxwell)
      Films & F: v. 9, n. 4 (Jan., 1963), pp. 52-53; Robin Bean, 400 wds., cp. cr.

5617 SERENADE (Anthony Mann)
      Films & F: v. 2, n. 9 (June, 1956), p. 25; P. L. Mannock, 225 wds., cp. cr.

5618 SERENADE FOR TWO SPIES (Michael Pfleghar)
      (also: Serenade fur Zwei Spione)
      Films & F: v. 16, n. 3 (Dec., 1969), p. 54; David Austen, 200 wds., cp. cr.

      SERENADE FUR ZWEI SPIONE (see: Serenade for Two Spies)

5619 SERENGETI (Bernhard and Michael Grzimek)
     (also: Serengeti Shall Not Die)
     Filmf: v. IV (1961), p. 370; comp., cp. cr.
     Films & F: v. 6, n. 6 (Mar., 1960), pp. 22-23; Ken Gay, 500 wds., cp. cr.

     SERENGETI SHALL NOT DIE (see: Serengeti)

5620 SERGEANT, THE (John Flynn)
     Filmf: v. XI (1968), p. 501; comp., cp. cr.
     Films & F: v. 15, n. 8 (May, 1969), pp. 53-54; Peter White head, 1000 wds.,
         cp. cr.

5621 SERGEANT DEADHEAD (Norman Taurog)
     Films & F: v. 12, n. 3 (Dec., 1965), pp. 15-16; David Shipman, 350 wds.,
         cp. cr.

5622 SERGEANT RUTLEDGE (John Ford)
     (also: The Trial of Sergeant Rutledge)
     F Quarterly: v. XIII, n. 3 (Spring, 1960), p. 60; 75 wds., no cr.
     Filmf: v. III (1960), p. 139; comp., cp. cr.
     Films & F: v. 6, n. 10 (July, 1960), pp. 24-25; Robin Bean, 300 wds., cp.
         cr.
     Films in R: v. XI, n. 5 (May, 1960), p. 297; Adelaide Comerford, 250 wds.,
         no cr.
     Sight & S: v. 29, n. 3 (Summer, 1960), p. 142; Penelope Houston, 900 wds.,
         pt. cr.

5623 SERGEANT RYKER (Buzz Kulik)
     Filmf: v. XI (1968), p. 88; comp., cp. cr.

5624 SERGEANT WAS A LADY, THE (Bernard Glasser)
     Filmf: v. IV (1961), p. 317; comp., cp. cr.

5625 SERGEANTS THREE (John Sturges)
     Film: n. 32 (Summer, 1962), p. 20; Bernard Hrusa, 200 wds., no cr.
     Filmf: v. V (1962), p. 39; comp., cp. cr.
     Films & F: v. 8, n. 8 (May, 1962), pp. 33-34; Richard Whitehall, 600 wds.,
         cp. cr.
     Films in R: v. XIII, n. 3 (Mar., 1962), p. 172; Arthur B. Clark, 150 wds., no
         cr.

5626 SERGEI EISENSTEIN (V. Katanian)
     Films & F: v. 6, n. 10 (July, 1960), p. 24; John Cutts, 100 wds., cp. cr.

5627 SERIOUS CHARGE (Terence Young)
     Films & F: v. 5, n. 9 (June, 1959), p. 24; Peter Baker, 300 wds., cp. cr.

5628 SERPENT, THE (Hans Abramson)
     Films & F: v. 14, n. 6 (Mar., 1968), pp. 28-29; Richard Davis, 400 wds., cp.
         cr.

5629 SERVANT, THE (Joseph Losey)
     F Quarterly: v. XVIII, n. 1 (Fall, 1964), pp. 36-38; Ernest Callenbach, 1000
         wds., pt. cr.
     F Soc Rev: May (1967), pp. 20-22; John Thomas, 650 wds., pt. cr.
     Films & F: v. VII (1964), p. 98; comp., cp. cr.
     Films & F: v. 10, n. 3 (Dec., 1963), pp. 24-25; Peter Baker, 600 wds., cp.
         cr.
     Films in R: v. XV, n. 4 (Apr., 1964), pp. 241-242; Flavia Wharton, 325
         wds., no cr.
     Sight & S: v. 33, n. 1 (Winter, 1963-1964), pp. 38-39; John Russell Taylor,
         1300 wds., pt. cr.

     SERYOZHA (see: The Splendid Days)

     SESSION WITH THE COMMITTEE (see; The Committee)

5630 SESTO CONTINENTO (Folco Quilici)
     (also: Blue Continent; Sixth Continent)
     Films & F: v. 1, n. 3 (Dec., 1954), p. 21; Jill Hardy, 150 wds., cp. cr.

SESTRI (see: Sisters)

5631 SET-UP, THE (Robert Wise)
  Sequence: n. 9 (Autumn, 1949), pp. 132-134; Gavin Lambert, 1300 wds., pt. cr.

SETTE DONNE PER I MacGREGOR (see: Up the MacGregors)

SETTE PISTOLE PER I MacGREGOR (see: Seven Guns for the MacGregors)

SETTE UOMINI D'ORO (see: Seven Golden Men)

SETTE VERGINI PER IL DIAVOLO (see: The Young, the Evil and the Savage)

SETTE WINCHESTER PER UN MASSACRO (see: Payment in Blood)

5632 SEUL OU AVEC D'AUTRES (Michel Brault)
  Movie: n. 11, p. 26; Mark Shivas, 150 wds., no cr.

5633 SEVEN BRIDES FOR SEVEN BROTHERS (Stanley Donen)
  Films & F: v. 1, n. 1 (Oct., 1954), p. 25; Clayton Cole, 200 wds., cp. cr.
  Films & F: v. 1, n. 4 (Jan., 1955), p. 19; Peter Brinson, 250 wds., cp. cr.
  Films & F: v. 15, n. 8 (May, 1969), p. 56; David Rider, 500 wds., cp. cr.
  Films in R: v. V, n. 7 (Aug.-Sept., 1954), p. 364; 125 wds., no cr.
  Sight & S: v. 24, n. 3 (Jan.-Mar., 1955), p. 142; Gavin Lambert, 900 wds., pt. cr.

5634 SEVEN CAPITAL SINS, THE (Claude Chabrol, Edouard Molinaro, Jean-Luc Godard, Roger Vadim, Jacques Demy, Philippe De Broca, Sylvan Dhomme)
  (also: Los Sept Peches Capitaux; Avarice)
  Cinema: v. 1, n. 4, p. 46; 100 wds., pt. cr.
  Filmf: v. VI (1963), p. 31; comp., cp. cr.
  Films in R: v. XIII, n. 10 (Dec., 1962), pp. 625-626; Louise Corbin, 500 wds., no cr.

5635 SEVEN CITIES OF GOLD (Robert D. Webb)
  Films & F: v. 2, n. 4 (Jan., 1956), p. 23; John Carroll, 150 wds., cp. cr.

5636 SEVEN DARING GIRLS (Otto Meyer)
  (also: Insel der Amazonen)
  Filmf: v. VI (1963), p. 342; comp., cp. cr.

5637 SEVEN DAYS IN MAY (John Frankenheimer)
  Cinema: v. 2, n. 1 (Feb., 1964), p. 50; Rory Guy, 300 wds., pt. cr.
  Filmf: v. VII (1964), p. 39; comp., cp. cr.
  Films & F: v. 10, n. 9 (June, 1964), pp. 9-10; John Frankenheimer, 2200 wds., no cr.
  Films & F: v. 10, n. 9 (June, 1964), p. 23; Robin Bean, 600 wds., cp. cr.
  Films in R: v. XV, n. 3 (Mar., 1964), pp. 171-172; Wilfred Mifflin, 450 wds., no cr.
  Interntl F G: v. 2 (1965), p. 138; 250 wds., pt. cr.

SEVEN DAYS — SEVEN NIGHTS (see: Moderato Cantabile)

5638 SEVEN DAYS TO NOON (John and Roy Boulting)
  Films in R: v. II, n. 2 (Feb., 1951), p. 36; 300 wds., pt. cr.
  Sight & S: v. 19, n. 8 (Dec., 1950), p. 332; Penelope Houston, 850 wds., pt. cr.

5639 SEVEN DEADLY SINS, THE (Eduardo De Filippo, Claude Autant-Lara, Roberto Rossellini, Yves Allegret, Georges Lacombe, Carlo-Rim, Jean Dreville)
  (also: Los Sept Peches Capitaux)
  Films in R: v. IV, n. 7 (Aug.-Sept., 1953), pp. 358-360; Henrietta Lehman, 1200 wds., pt. cr.

5640 SEVEN FACES OF DR. LAO (George Pal)
  Filmf: v. VII (1964), p. 173; comp., cp. cr.
  Films & F: v. 12, n. 3 (Dec., 1965), p. 28; David Rider, 225 wds., cp. cr.

5641 SEVEN GOLDEN MEN (Marco Vicario)
     (also: Sette Uomini D'Ord)
     Cinema: v. 3, n. 2 (Mar., 1966), p. 49; Saul Kahan, 400 wds., pt. cr.
     Filmf: v. XII (1969), p. 163; comp., cp. cr.

5642 SEVEN GUNS FOR THE MacGREGORS (Frank Garfield)
     (also: Sette Pistole per I MacGregor)
     Filmf: v. XI (1968), p. 531; comp., cp. cr.

5643 SEVEN GUNS TO MESA (Edward Dein)
     Filmf: v. I (1958), p. 297; comp., cp. cr.

5644 SEVEN HILLS OF ROME (Roy Rowland)
     Filmf: v. I (1958), p. 7; comp., cp. cr.
     Films & F: v. 4, n. 6 (Mar., 1958), pp. 26-27; Peter G. Baker, 100 wds., cp.
          cr.

5645 SEVEN KEYS (Pat Jackson)
     Films & F: v. 8, n. 10 (July, 1962), pp. 37-38; David Gerrard, 500 wds., cp.
          cr.

5646 SEVEN LITTLE FOYS, THE (Melville Shavelson)
     Films & F: v. 1, n. 12 (Sept., 1955), p. 21; Michell Raper, 200 wds., cp. cr.

     SEVEN MAGNIFICENT WOMEN, THE (see: The Tall Women)

5647 SEVEN MINUTES, THE (Russ Meyer)
     Filmf: v. XIV (1971), p. 296; comp., cp. cr.

5648 SEVEN SAMURAI, THE (Akira Kurosawa)
     (also: The Magnificent Seven)
     F Culture: v. 2, n. 4 (1956), pp. 3-5; Jay Leyda, 2000 wds., pt. cr.
     F Journal: n. 6 (Dec., 1956), pp. 6-9; William E. Mills, 2000 wds., no cr.
     Films & F: v. 1, n. 7 (Apr., 1955), p. 23; Peter Barnes, 250 wds., cp. cr.
     Films in R: v. VII, n. 10 (Dec., 1956), p. 526; T. S. Hines, 300 wds., no cr.
     Sight & S: v. 24, n. 4 (Spring, 1955), pp. 195-196; Tony Richardson, 1000
          wds., pt. cr.

5649 SEVEN SEAS TO CALAIS (Rusolph Maté)
     Filmf: v. VI (1963), p. 42; comp., cp. cr.
     Films & F: v. 9, n. 8 (May, 1963), p. 29; Richard Whitehall, 400 wds., cp.
          cr.

5650 SEVEN SURPRIZES (Harvey Chertok and Eric Albertson, prods.)
     F Soc Rev: Dec. (1966), p. 26; Edwin Jahlel, 325 wds., pt. cr.

5651 SEVEN THIEVES (Henry Hathaway)
     Filmf: v. III (1960), p. 45; comp., cp. cr.
     Films & F: v. 6, n. 7 (Apr., 1960), p. 24; R. E. Durgnat, 200 wds., cp. cr.
     Films in R: v. XI, n. 2 (Feb., 1960), pp. 105-106; Shirley Conover, 275
          wds., no cr.

     SEVEN THUNDERS, THE (see: The Beasts of Marseilles)

     SEVEN VIRGINS FOR THE DEVIL (see: The Young, the Evil, and the
          Savage)

5652 SEVEN WAVES AWAY (Richard Sale)
     (also: Abandon Ship)
     Films & F: v. 3, n. 8 (May, 1957), pp. 24-25; Peter G. Baker, 250 wds., cp.
          cr.

5653 SEVEN WAYS FROM SUNDOWN (Harry Keller)
     Filmf: v. III (1960), p. 300; comp., cp. cr.

     SEVEN WINCHESTERS FOR A MASSACRE (see: Payment in Blood)

5654 SEVEN WOMEN (John Ford)
     Cinema: v. 3, n. 1 (Dec., 1965), p. 48; Rory Guy, 550 wds., pt. cr.
     F Comment: v. 7, n. 3 (Fall, 1971), pp. 8-17; Robin Wood, 7000 wds., cp.
          cr.

Filmf: v. IX (1966), p. 119; comp., cp. cr.
Films & F: v. 13, n. 5 (Feb., 1967), p. 31; Gordon Gow, 250 wds., cp. cr.
Films in R: v. XVII, n. 2 (Feb., 1966), pp. 116-117; Arthur B. Clark, 250
    wds., no cr.
Focus: n. 2 (Mar., 1967), pp. 19-22; Richard Thompson, 2100 wds., no cr.
Sight & S: v. 36, n. 1 (Winter, 1966-1967), pp. 43-44; Peter John Dyer, 800
    wds., pt. cr.

5655 SEVEN WOMEN AND SYLVIE
      Film: n. 47 (Winter, 1966), pp. 27, 42; Douglas McVay, 300 wds., no cr.

      SEVEN WOMEN FOR THE MacGREGORS (see: Up the MacGregors)

5656 SEVEN WOMEN FROM HELL (Robert Webb)
      Filmf: v. V (1962), p. 8; comp., cp. cr.

5657 SEVEN WONDERS OF THE WORLD (Tay Garnett, Ted Tetzlaff, Andrew
           Marton)
      Films & F: v. 4, n. 7 (Apr., 1958), p. 25; Peter G. Baker, 600 wds., cp. cr.
      Films in R: v. VII, n. 4 (Apr., 1956), p. 174; Diana Willing, 200 wds., no cr.

5658 SEVEN YEAR ITCH, THE (Billy Wilder)
      F Culture: v. 1, n. 4 (Summer, 1955), pp. 22-23; George N. Fenin, 600
          wds., pt. cr.
      Films & F: v. 2, n. 1 (Oct., 1955), p. 20; Peter Barnes, 350 wds., cp. cr.
      Films in R: v. VI, n. 7 (Aug.-Sept., 1955), p. 345; 200 wds., pt. cr.

      SEVENTEEN (see: Eric Soya's "17")

      17 E PARALLELE — LE VIETNAM EN GUERRE (see: 17th Parallel:
           Vietnam in War)

5659 17TH PARALLEL: VIETNAM IN WAR (Joris Ivens)
      (also: 17 E Parallele — Le Vienam En Guerre)
      Filmf: v. XI (1968), p. 404; comp., cp. cr.

5660 SEVENTH COMMANDMENT, THE (Raymond Bernard)
      Filmf: v. IV (1961), p. 370; comp., cp. cr.
      Films & F: v. 3, n. 11 (Aug., 1957), pp. 25-26; Gordon Gow, 400 wds., cp.
          cr.

5661 SEVENTH CONTINENT, THE (Dusan Vukotic)
      (also: Sedmi Kontinent)
      Filmf: v. XI (1968), p. 320; comp., cp. cr.

5662 SEVENTH DAWN, THE (Lewis Gilbert)
      Filmf: v. VII (1964), p. 199; comp., cp. cr.
      Films & F: v. 10, n. 12 (Sept., 1964), p. 21; Richard Davis, 450 wds., cp. cr.
      Films in R: v. XV, n. 7 (Aug.-Sept., 1964), p. 442; Wilfred Mifflin, 150
          wds., no cr.

5663 SEVENTH JUROR, THE (Georges Lautner)
      (also: Le Septieme Jure)
      Filmf: v. VII (1964), p. 299; comp., cp. cr.

5664 SEVENTH SEAL, THE (Ingmar Bergman)
      (also: Det Sjunde Inseglet)
      Film: n. 14 (Nov.-Dec., 1957), pp. 20-21; Ronald Mason, 600 wds., no cr.
      F Culture: n. 19, pp. 51-61; Andrew Sarris, 4500 wds., pt. cr.
      F Quarterly: v. XII, n. 3 (Spring, 1959), pp. 42-44; Colin Young, 1000
          wds., no cr.
      Filmf: v. I (1958), p. 194; comp., cp. cr.
      Films & F: v. 4, n. 7 (Apr., 1958), pp. 22-23; Peter John Dyer, 750 wds.,
          cp. cr.
      Films & F: v. 9, n. 4 (Jan., 1963), pp. 24-29; Peter Cowie, 4800 wds., cp.
          cr.
      Films in R: v. IX, n. 9 (Nov., 1958), pp. 515-517; Louise Corbin, 625 wds.,
          no cr.
      Sight & S: v. 27, n. 4 (Spring, 1958), pp. 199-200; Peter John Dyer, 850
          wds., pt. cr.

5665 SEVENTH SIN, THE (Ronald Neame)
        Films & F: v. 4, n. 1 (Oct., 1957), p. 22; Derek Conrad, 350 wds., cp. cr.

5666 7th VOYAGE OF SINBAD, THE (Nathan Juran)
        Filmf: v. I (1958), p. 268; comp., cp. cr.
        Films in R: v. X, n. 1 (Jan., 1959), pp. 40-41; Prudence Ashton, 200 wds.,
        no cr.

5667 79 SPRINGTIMES (Santiago Alvarez)
        Cineaste: v. IV, n. 3 (Winter, 1970-1971), pp. 39-40; Lenny Rubenstein,
        400 wds., pt. cr.

5668 SEVERED HEAD, A (Dick Clement)
        Filmf: v. XIV (1971), p. 205; comp., cp. cr.
        Films & F: v. 17, n. 7 (Apr., 1971), pp. 57-58; Gordon Gow, 450 wds., cp.
        cr.

5669 SEX AND THE SINGLE GIRL (Richard Quine)
        Cinema: v. 2, n. 3 (Oct.-Nov., 1964), p. 50; Rory Guy, 200 wds., pt. cr.
        Films & F: v. 11, n. 5 (Feb., 1965), p. 31; John Cutts, 350 wds., cp. cr.

5670 SEX CAN BE DIFFICULT (Sergio Sollima, Alberto Bonucci, and Nino
        Manfredi)
        (also: L'amore Difficile; Of Wayward Love)
        Filmf: v. VII (1964), p. 94; comp., cp. cr.
        Filmf & F: v. 10, n. 6 (Mar., 1964), p. 30; David Rider, 500 wds., cp. cr.
        Sight & S: v. 33, n. 2 (Spring, 1964), pp. 97-98; J. H. Fenwick, 550 wds.,
        no cr.

5671 SEX FROM A STRANGER (Sergio Gobbi)
        (also: L'Etrangère)
        Films & F: v. 14, n. 11 (Aug., 1968), p. 32; David Austen, 250 wds., cp. cr.

5672 SEX KITTENS GO TO COLLEGE (Albert Zugsmith)
        Filmf: v. III (1960), p. 290; comp., cp. cr.

      SEX QUARTET (see: The Queens)

5673 SEXPOT (Mick Roussel)
        (also: Le Desir Mene les Hommes)
        Filmf: v. III (1960), p. 354; comp., cp. cr.

      SFINGE TUTTA D'ORO, UNA (see: The Glass Sphinx)

5674 SHADES AND DRUM-BEATS (Andy Meyer)
        F Culture: n. 35 (Winter, 1964-1965), p. 23; Gregory Markopoulos, 250
        wds., no cr.

      SHADOW ARMY (see: L'Armée des Ombres)

5675 SHADOW IN THE SKY (Fred M. Wilcox)
        Sight & S: v. 21, n. 4 (Apr.-June, 1952), p. 171; Gavin Lambert, 650 wds.,
        pt. cr.

5676 SHADOW OF ADULTERY (Alexandre Astruc)
        (also: La Proie pour L'Ombre)
        Film: n. 29 (Summer, 1961), pp. 10-11; Ian Cameron, 75 wds., no cr.
        Films & F: v. 8, n. 3 (Dec., 1961), p. 32; Gordon Gow, 900 wds., cp. cr.
        Sight & S: v. 30, n. 4 (Autumn, 1961), p. 195; Penelope Houston, 1200
        wds., pt. cr.

5677 SHADOW OF EVIL (André Hunebelle)
        (also: Banco A Bangkok Pour O.S.S. 117; Jackpot in Bangkok for O.S.S.
        117)
        Filmf: v. IX (1966), p. 346; comp., cp. cr.

5678 SHADOW OF THE CAT, THE (John Gilling)
        Filmf: v. IV (1961), p. 110; comp., cp. cr.

5679 SHADOWS (John Cassavetes)
    F Culture: n. 24 (Spring, 1962), pp. 28-33; Parker Tyler, 3500 wds., no cr.
    F Journal: n. 20 (Aug., 1962), p. 82; Adrian Rawlins, 300 wds., no cr.
    F Quarterly: v. XIII, n. 3 (Spring, 1960), pp. 32-34; Albert Johnson, 1300
        wds., pt. cr.
    Filmf: v. IV (1961), p. 59; comp., cp. cr.
    Films & F: v. 7, n. 2 (Nov., 1960), pp. 29-30; Raymond Durgnat, 700 wds.,
        cp. cr.
    Sight & S: v. 29, n. 4 (Autumn, 1960), p. 192; Derek Prouse, 800 wds., pt.
        cr.

5680 SHADOWS GROW LONGER, THE (Ladislao Vajda)
    (also: Defiant Daughters; Die Schatten Werden Laenger)
    Filmf: v. V (1962), p. 158; comp., cp. cr.

5681 SHADOWS OF OUR FORGOTTEN ANCESTORS (Sergey Paradjanov)
    (also: Tini Zabutikh Predkiv)
    F Quarterly: v. XIX, n. 4 (Summer, 1966), pp. 56-59; John Ssslye, 1800
        wds., no cr.
    Filmf: v. X (1967), p. 80; comp., cp. cr.
    Films & F: v. 15, n. 9 (June, 1969), pp. 53-54; Gordon Gow, 900 wds., cp.
        cr.
    Interntl F G: v. 4 (1967), pp. 167, 170; 200 wds., pt. cr.

5682 SHAFT (Gordon Parks)
    Filmf: v. XIV (1971), p. 346; comp., cp. cr.
    Focus on F: n. 8 (Oct., 1971), p. 7; Tom Milne and Allen Eyles, 300 wds.,
        cp. cr.

5683 SHAGGY DOG, THE (Charles Barton)
    Filmf: v. II (1959), p. 61; comp., cp. cr.

5684 SHAKE HANDS WITH THE DEVIL (Michael Anderson)
    Filmf: v. II (1959), p. 127; comp., cp. cr.
    Films & F: v. 5, n. 8 (May, 1959), p. 21; Peter Baker, 800 wds., cp. cr.
    Films in R: v. X, n. 6 (June-July, 1959), p. 359; Robert C. Roman, 250
        wds., no cr.

5685 SHAKEDOWN, THE (John Lemont)
    Filmf: v. IV (1961), p. 46; comp., cp. cr.
    Films & F: v. 6, n. 6 (Mar., 1960), p. 25; Dai Vaughan, 200 wds., cp. cr.

5686 SHAKESPEARE WALLAH (James Ivory)
    Film: n. 44 (Winter, 1965-1966), pp. 18-19; Lang Dewey and Stanley
        Crawford, 500 wds., no cr.
    F Quarterly: v. XX, n. 2 (Winter, 1966-1967), pp. 33-35; Harriet Polt, 1100
        wds., pt. cr.
    F Soc Rev: Jan. (1967), pp. 24-25; Bernard Desch, 575 wds., no cr.
    Filmf: v. IX (1966), p. 90; comp., cp. cr.
    Films in R: v. XVII, n. 5 (May, 1966), pp. 316-317; Henry Hart, 200 wds.,
        no cr.

5687 SHAKIEST GUN IN THE WEST, THE (Alan Rafkin)
    Filmf: v. XI (1968), p. 298; comp., cp. cr.

5688 SHALAKO (Edward Dmytryk)
    Filmf: v. XI (1968), p. 443; comp., cp. cr.
    Films & F: v. 15, n. 4 (Jan., 1969), p. 44; Richard Davis, 350 wds., cp. cr.
    Films in R: v. XIX, n. 10 (Dec., 1968), p. 649; Arthur B. Clark, 275 wds.,
        no cr.

5689 SHAME (Ingmar Bergman)
    (also: Skammen)
    F Heritage: v. 4, n. 3 (Spring, 1969), pp. 1-5; Jonathan H. Hoops, 1700
        wds., pt. cr.
    F Quarterly: v. XXIII, n. 1 (Fall, 1969), pp. 32-34; Ernest Callenbach, 1000
        wds., pt. cr.
    F Soc Rev: v. 4, n. 5, pp. 35-39; A. D. Malmfelt, 1500 wds., cp. cr.
    Filmf: v. XI (1968), p. 427; comp., cp. cr.
    Films & F: v. 15, n. 7 (Apr., 1969), p. 38; Gordon Gow, 750 wds., cp. cr.

Films in R: v. XX, n. 1 (Jan., 1969), pp. 51-52; Henry Hart, 450 wds., no
   cr.
Movie: n. 17 (Winter, 1969-1970), pp. 32-34; Michael Walker, 2400 wds.,
   no cr.
Sight & S: v. 38, n. 2 (Spring, 1969), pp. 89-92; Jan Dawson, 3500 wds., pt.
   cr.

5690 SHAME OF PATTY SMITH, THE (Leo A. Handel)
   Filmf: v. VI (1963), p. 264; comp., cp. cr.

5691 SHAMELESS, THE (Jay Martin)
   Filmf: v. V (1962), p. 367; comp., cp. cr.

5692 SHAMELESS OLD LADY, THE (René Allio)
   (also: La Vieille Dame Indigne; Shocking Old Party)
   F Quarterly: v. XX, n. 3 (Spring, 1967), p. 63; Steven Farber, 125 wds., no
      cr.
   Filmf: v. IX (1966), p. 197; comp., cp. cr.
   Films & F: v. 16, n. 10 (July, 1970), pp. 37-38; Margaret Tarratt, 600 wds.,
      cp. cr.
   Films in R: v. XVII, n. 9 (Nov., 1966), p. 585; Louise Corbin, 150 wds., no
      cr.
   Interntl F G: v. 3 (1966), pp. 68-69; Peter Graham, 200 wds., pt. cr.

5693 SHAN-PO AND YING-TAI (Sang Hu and Huang Sha)
   Films & F: v. 1, n. 11 (Aug., 1955), p. 17; Jill Hardy; 175 wds., cp. cr.

5694 SHANE (George Stevens)
   Films in R: v. IV, n. 4 (Apr., 1953), pp. 195-197; Nina Weiss Stern, 800
      wds., pt. cr.

5695 SHANGHAI GESTURE, THE (Josef von Sternberg)
   Movie: n. 13 (Summer, 1965), p. 31; O. O. Green, 650 wds., no cr.

5696 SHANGRI-LA
   Filmf: v. V (1962), p. 369; comp., cp. cr.

5697 SHARK (Samuel Fuller)
   (also: Caine)
   Cinema: v. 6, n. 3 (Spring, 1971), p. 51; Foster Hirsch, 1000 wds., no cr.

   SHATTERHAND (see: Apache's Last Battle)

5698 SHAWL, THE (Roberto Gavaldon)
   Films & F: v. 2, n. 10 (July, 1956), p. 26; Peter G. Baker, 250 wds., cp. cr.

5699 SHE (Robert Day)
   Films & F: v. 11, n. 9 (June, 1965), p. 30; Raymond Durgnat, 700 wds., cp.
      cr.

5700 SHE AND HE (Susumu Hani)
   (also: Kanojo To Kare)
   Filmf: v. X (1967), p. 109; comp., cp. cr.
   Films & F: v. 12, n. 12 (Sept., 1966), pp. 7-8; Gordon Gow, 450 wds., cp.
      cr.

5701 SHE BEAST, THE (Mike Reeves:
   (also: The Sister of Satan; La Sorella Di Satana)
   Filmf: v. IX (1966), p. 383; comp., cp. cr.

   SHE COULDN'T SAY NO (see: Beautiful But Dangerous)

5702 SHE DEMONS (Richard Cunha)
   Filmf: v. I (1958), p. 41; comp., cp. cr.

5703 SHE DIDN'T SAY NO (Cyril Frankel)
   Filmf: v. VI (1963), p. 323; comp., cp. cr.
   Films & F: v. 4, n. 12 (Sept., 1958), p. 22; John Cutts, 125 wds., cp. cr.

5704 SHE DONE HIM WRONG (Lowell Sherman)
   Views and Rev: v. 2, n. 2 (Fall, 1970), pp. 4-10; 2000 wds., cp. cr.

5705 SHE FREAK (Byron Mabe)
        Filmf: v. X (1967), p. 436; comp., cp. cr.

5706 SHE GODS OF SHARK REEF (Roger Corman)
        Filmf: v. I (1958), p. 278; comp., cp. cr.

5707 SHE GOT WHAT SHE ASKED FOR (Giancarlo Zagni)
        (also: La Bellegza di Ippolita)
        Films & F: v. 10, n. 2 (Nov., 1963), p. 26; Raymond Durgnat, 550 wds., cp.
        cr.

5708 SHE PLAYED WITH FIRE (Sidney Gilliat)
        (also: Fortune Is a Woman)
        Filmf: v. I (1958), p. 259; comp., cp. cr.
        Films & F: v. 3, n. 8 (May, 1957), p. 25; Rupert Butler, 200 wds., cp. cr.

5709 SHE WALKS BY NIGHT (Rudolf Jugert)
        (also: Die Wahrheit Uber Rosemarie)
        Filmf: v. IV (1961), p. 196; comp., cp. cr.

5710 SHE WAS LIKE A WILD CHRYSANTHEMUM (Keisuke Kinoshita)
        Filmf: v. III (1960), p. 23; comp., cp. cr.

      SHE-WOLF, THE (see: The Vixen)

5711 SHE WOLVES, THE (Luis Saslavsky)
        Films & F: v. 4, n. 8 (May, 1958), p. 25; John Cutts, 250 wds., cp. cr.

5712 SHEEP HAS FIVE LEGS, THE (Henri Verneuil)
        (also: Le Mouton a Cinq Pattes)
        Films & F: v. 1, n. 4 (Jan., 1955), p. 19; Oswell Blakeston, 200 wds., cp. cr.

5713 SHEEP IN WOOD (Jacques Hnizdovsky)
        F Lib Quarterly: v. 4, n. 3 (Summer, 1971), pp. 40-41; Roman Sawycky,
        200 wds., pt. cr.

5714 SHEEPMAN, THE (George Marshall)
        Filmf: v. I (1958), p. 78; comp., cp. cr.
        Films & F: v. 4, n. 9 (June, 1958), p. 27; John Cutts, 300 wds., cp. cr.
        Films in R: v. IX, n. 6 (June-July, 1958), p. 337; Albert ("Hap") Turner,
        200 wds., no cr.

      SHE'LL HAVE TO GO (see: Maid for Murder)

5715 SHENANDOAH (Andrew V. McLaglen)
        Films & F: v. 11, n. 12 (Sept., 1965), pp. 25-26; Gordon Gow, 1050 wds.,
        cp. cr.
        Movie: n. 14 (Autumn, 1965), p. 44; 150 wds., no cr.

5716 SHERIFF OF FRACTURED JAW, THE (Raoul Walsh)
        Filmf: v. II (1959), p. 35; comp., cp. cr.
        Films & F: v. 5, n. 3 (Dec., 1958), pp. 24-25; Peter G. Baker, 200 wds., cp.
        cr.

      SHESHEY HAYAMIM (see: Six Days To Eternity)

5717 SHIIKU (Nagisa Oshima)
        (also: The Catch)
        Film: n. 58 (Spring, 1970), p. 5; 75 wds., pt. cr.

5718 SHIN HEIKE MONOGATARI (Kenji Mizoguchi)
        (also: New Tales of the Taira Clan)
        Movie: n. 5 (Dec., 1962), p. 36; Ian Cameron, 650 wds., no cr.

5719 SHINBONE ALLEY (John David Wilson)
        Filmf: v. XIV (1971), p. 466; comp., cp. cr.

      SHINEL (see: The Overcoat)

      SHINJO TEN NO AMIJIMA (see: Double Suicide)

SHINJUKU DOROBO NIKKI (see: Diary of a Shinjuku Thief)

5720 SHIP OF FOOLS (Stanley Kramer)
        Films & F: v. 12, n. 2 (Nov., 1965), p. 24; Robin Bean, 850 wds., cp. cr.
        Films in R: v. XVI, n. 6 (June-July, 1965), pp. 380-382; Henry Hart, 750
            wds., no cr.

5721 SHIP THAT DIED OF SHAME, THE (Michael Relph and Basil Dearden)
        Films & F: v. 1, n. 9 (June, 1955), p. 21; Derek Hill, 175 wds., cp. cr.

      SHIP WAS LOADED, THE (see: Carry On, Admiral)

5722 SHIRALEE, THE (Leslie Norman)
        Films & F: v. 3, n. 10 (July, 1957), pp. 25-26; Peter John Dyer, 550 wds.,
            cp. cr.
        Sight & S: v. 27, n. 1 (Summer, 1957), p. 43; John Cutts, 350 wds., pt. cr.

      SHLOSHA YAMIN VE'YELED (see: Not Mine To Love)

5723 SHOCK CORRIDOR (Samuel Fuller)
        Cinema: v. 1, n. 5, p. 46; R.G., 400 wds., pt. cr.
        F Quarterly: v. XVII, n. 2 (Winter, 1963-1964), p. 62; Robert G. Dickson,
            250 wds., no cr.
        Filmf: v. VI (1963), p. 210; comp., cp. cr.
        Films & F: v. 16, n. 10 (July, 1970), pp. 36-37; Margaret Tarratt, 900 wds.,
            cp. cr.

5724 SHOCK TREATMENT (Denis Sanders)
        F Quarterly: v. XVII, n. 4 (Summer, 1964), p. 59; Jesse Smith 200 wds., no
            cr.
        Filmf: v. VII (1964), p. 120; comp., cp. cr.

5725 SHOCK TROOPS (Costa-Gavras)
        (also: Un Homme de Trop; One Man Too Many)
        F Quarterly: v. XXIII, n. 1 (Fall, 1969), p. 55; Richard T. Jameson, 600
            wds., no cr.
        Filmf: v. XII (1969), p. 77; comp., cp. cr.

      SHOCKING OLD PARTY (see: The Shameless Old Lady)

5726 SHOES OF THE FISHERMAN, THE (Michael Anderson)
        Filmf: v. XI (1968), p. 490; comp., cp. cr.
        Films in R: v. XIX, n. 10 (Dec., 1968), pp. 644-646; Henry Hart, 650 wds.,
            no cr.
        Focus on F: n. 8 (Oct., 1971), pp. 12-14; Derek Elley, 450 wds., cp. cr.

      SHOESHINE (see: Sciuscia)

5727 SHOKEI NO SHIMA (Masahiro Shinoda)
        (also: Punishment Island)
        Interntl F G: v. 5 (1968), p. 107; 230 wds., pt. cr.

      SHONEN (see: Boy)

5728 SHOOT LOUD, LOUDER . . . I DON'T UNDERSTAND (Eduardo de Filippo)
        (also: Spara Forte, Piu Forte . . . Non Capisco)
        Filmf: v. X (1967), p. 273; comp., cp. cr.

5729 SHOOT OUT (Henry Hathaway)
        Filmf: v. XIV (1971), p. 505; comp., cp. cr.

      SHOOT THE PIANIST (see: Shoot the Piano Player)

5730 SHOOT THE PIANO PLAYER (Francois Truffaut)
        (also: Shoot the Pianist; Tirez sur le Pianiste)
        F Culture: n. 27 (Winter, 1962-1963), pp. 14-16; Pauline Kael, 1500 wds.,
            no cr.
        Filmf: v. V (1962), p. 165; comp., cp. cr.
        Films & F: v. 7, n. 5 (Feb., 1961), pp. 29-30; Raymond Durgnat, 850 wds.,
            cp. cr.

5731 SHOOTING STARS (A. V. Bramble)
    Sight & S: v. 19, n. 4 (June, 1950), pp. 172-174; Roger Manvell, 1750 wds.,
      cp. cr.

5732 SHOOTOUT AT BIG SAG (Roger Kay)
    Filmf: v. V (1962), p. 361; comp., cp. cr.

SHOP ON HIGH STREET, THE (see: The Shop on Main Street)

5733 SHOP ON MAIN STREET, THE (Jan Kadar and Elmar Klos)
    (also: Obchod Na Korze; The Shop on High Street)
    F Quarterly: v. XIX, n. 4 (Summer, 1966), pp. 56-59; John Seelye, 1800
      wds., no cr.
    F Soc Rev: Dec. (1967), pp. 19-20; Howard Livingston, 400 wds., pt. cr.
    Filmf: v. IX (1966), p. 1; comp., cp. cr.
    Films & F: v. 11, n. 11 (Aug., 1965), pp. 24-25; Peter Cowie, 600 wds., cp.
      cr.
    Films in R: v. XVII, n. 3 (Mar., 1966), p. 185; Flavia Wharton, 250 wds., no
      cr.
    Interntl F G: v. 3 (1966), p. 60; 225 wds., pt. cr.

5734 SHORT CUT TO HELL (James Cagney)
    Films & F: v. 4, n. 2 (Nov., 1957), p. 24; Gordon Gow, 250 wds., cp. cr.

5735 SHOT IN THE DARK, A (Blake Edwards)
    Filmf: v. VII (1964), p. 149; comp., cp. cr.
    Films & F: v. 11, n. 6 (Mar., 1965), pp. 28-29; Mike Sarne, 775 wds., cp. cr.
    Films in R: v. XV, n. 7 (Aug.-Sept., 1964), pp. 443-444; Louise Corbin, 150
      wds., no cr.
    Movie: n. 12 (Spring, 1965), p. 45; 75 wds., no cr.

SHOT IN THE HEART, A (see: Une Balle au Coeur)

SHOT IN THE MOUNTAINS, A (see: Vistril V. Gorach)

5736 SHOULDER ARMS (Charles Chaplin)
    Sight & S: v. 29, n. 3 (Summer, 1960), p. 144; Jay Leyda, 650 wds., no cr.

5737 SHOWDOWN (R. G. Springsteen)
    Filmf: v. VI (1963), p. 48; comp., cp. cr.

5738 SHOWDOWN AT BOOT HILL (Gene Fowler, Jr.)
    Filmf: v. I (1958), p. 102; comp., cp. cr.

5739 SHOWDOWN FOR ZATOICHI (Kenji Misumi)
    (also: Zatoichi Jigokutabi)
    Filmf: v. XI (1968), p. 410; comp., cp. cr.

5740 SHRIKE, THE (Jose Ferrer)
    Films in R: v. VI, n. 7 (Aug.-Sept., 1955), p. 347; 135 wds., pt. cr.

5741 SHUTTERED ROOM, THE (David Greene)
    Filmf: v. XI (1968), p. 58; comp., cp. cr.

5742 SI JOLIE PETITE PLAGE, UNE (Yves Allegret)
    (also: Such a Pretty Little Beach)
    Sequence: n. 10 (New Year, 1950), p. 153; A.P.H., 275 wds., pt. cr.
    Sight & S: v. 18, n. 71 (Dec., 1949), p. 21; 75 wds., pt. cr.

SI TOUS LES GARS DU MONDE... (see: Race for Life)

SI VERSAILLES M'ETAIT CONTE (see: Royal Affairs in Versailles)

SIAMO DONNE (see: We, The Women)

5743 SIBERIAN LADY MACBETH (Andrzej Wajda)
    (also: Sibirska Ledi Magbet; Lady Macbeth of Siberia)
    F Soc Rev: Feb. (1968), pp. 18-19; Steven P. Hill, 300 wds., no cr.

SIBIRSKA LEDI MAGBET (see: Siberian Lady Macbeth)

5744 SICILIAN CLAN, THE (Henri Verneuil)
         (also: Le Clan des Siciliens)
         Films & F: v. 16, n. 12 (Sept., 1970), p. 52; 700 wds., cp. cr.
         Films in R: v. XXI, n. 4 (Apr., 1970), pp. 244-245; Arthur B. Clark, 100
            wds., no cr.

      SIDDHARTHA AND THE CITY (see: Pratidwandi)

      SIDELONG GLANCES OF A PIGEON KICKER, THE (see: Pigeons)

5745 SIEGE OF HELL STREET, THE (Robert S. Baker and Monty Berman)
         (also: The Siege of Sidney Street)
         Filmf: v. VI (1963), p. 76; comp., cp. cr.
         Films & F: v. 7, n. 2 (Nov., 1960), pp. 33-34; Phillip Riley, 350 wds., cp. cr.

5746 SIEGE OF PINCHGUT (Harry Watt)
         Films & F: v. 6, n. 1 (Oct., 1959), pp. 21-22; Dai Vaughan, 200 wds., cp. cr.

5747 SIEGE OF RED RIVER, THE (Rudolph Maté)
         Films in R: v. V, n. 4 (Apr., 1954), p. 194; 150 wds., no cr.

      SIEGE OF SIDNEY STREET, THE (see: The Siege of Hell Street)

5748 SIEGE OF SYRACUSE (Pietro Francisci)
         Filmf: v. V (1962), p. 76; comp., cp. cr.

5749 SIEGE OF THE SAXONS (Nathan Juran)
         Filmf: v. VI (1963), p. 167; comp., cp. cr.
         Films & F: v. 9, n. 12 (Sept., 1963), p. 24; Raymond Durgnat, 400 wds.,
            cp. cr.

5750 SIEGFRIED (Fritz Lang)
         Sight & S: v. 19, n. 2 (Apr., 1950), pp. 83-85; Roger Manvell, 1500 wds.,
            cp. cr.

5751 SIEGFRIED UND DAS SAGENHAFTE LIEBESLEBEN DER NIBELUNGEN
         (see: The Long Swift Sword of Siegfried)

5752 SIERRA BARON (James B. Clark)
         Filmf: v. I (1958), p. 152; comp., cp. cr.

      SIETE MAGNIFICAS, LAS (see: The Tall Women)

5753 SIGHET SIGHET (Harold Becker)
         F Lib Quarterly: v. 2, n. 2 (Spring, 1969), pp. 24, 26; Lewis Archibald, 250
            wds., pt. cr.

5754 SIGN OF THE CROSS, THE (Cecil B. DeMille)
         Cinema: v. 2, n. 2 (July, 1964), p. 50; James Silke, 350 wds., pt. cr.

5755 SIGN OF THE GLADIATOR (Vittorio Musy)
         Filmf: v. II (1959), p. 280; comp., cp. cr.

5756 SIGN OF THE PAGAN (Douglas Sirk)
         Films & F: v. 1, n. 4 (Jan., 1955), p. 21; Kenneth Thompson, 175 wds., cp.
            cr.

5757 SIGN OF VENUS, THE (Dino Risi)
         (also: Il Segno di Venere)
         Films & F: v. 3, n. 1 (Oct., 1956), p. 24; Peter John Dyer, 300 wds., cp. cr.

5758 SIGN OF ZORRO, THE (Norman Foster and Lewis R. Foster)
         Filmf: v. III (1960), p. 358; comp., cp. cr.

      SIGNALI NAD GRADOM (see: The Fifth Battalion)

5759 SIGNE DU LION, LE (Eric Rohmer)
         Sight & S: v. 29, n. 2 (Spring, 1960), pp. 84-85; Louis Marcorelles, 1200
            wds., pt. cr.
         Sight & S: v. 35, n. 4 (Autumn, 1966), p. 199; Penelope Houston, 650 wds.,
            pt. cr.

SIGNORE E SIGNORI (see: The Birds, the Bees and the Italians)

5760 SIGNPOST TO MURDER (George Englund)
      Films & F: v. 11, n. 6 (Mar., 1965), p. 34; Allen Eyles, 300 wds., cp. cr.

      SIGNS OF LIFE (see: Lebenszeichen)

5761 SILENCE, THE (Ingmar Bergman)
      (also: Tystnaden)
      Cinema: v. 2, n. 2 (July, 1964), p. 48; James Silke, 350 wds., pt. cr.
      F Comment: v. 2, n. 3 (Summer, 1964), pp. 56-58; Stephen Taylor, 1500
          wds., pt. cr.
      F Culture: n. 48-49 (Winter-Spring, 1970), pp. 56-60; Kirk Bond, 2600
          wds., no cr.
      Filmf: v. VII (1964), p. 21; comp., cp. cr.
      Films & F: v. 10, n. 9 (June, 1964), p. 22; Raymond Durgnat, 1400 wds.,
          cp. cr.
      Films in R: v. XV, n. 3 (Mar., 1964), pp. 176-178; Henry Hart, 350 wds.,
          no cr.
      Interntl F G: v. 1 (1964), p. 84; 150 wds., pt. cr.
      Movie: n. 12 (Spring, 1965), p. 38; Robin Wood, 1000 wds., no cr.
      Sight & S: v. 33, n. 3 (Summer, 1964), pp. 142-143; Michael Kustow, 1200
          wds., pt. cr.

5762 SILENCE AND CRY (Miklos Jansco)
      (also: Csend es Kialtas)
      Films & F: v. 15, n. 12 (Sept., 1969), p. 57; Brian Murphy, 550 wds., cp. cr.

5763 SILENCE EST D'OR, LE (René Clair)
      Sequence: n. 4 (Summer, 1948), pp. 42-43; Ruth Partington, 450 wds., no
          cr.

5764 SILENCE HAS NO WINGS (Kazuo Kuroki)
      Interntl F G: v. 4 (1967), pp. 113-114; Christopher Lucas, 30 wds., pt. cr.

5765 SILENCERS, THE (Phil Karlson)
      F Quarterly: v. XIX, n. 4 (Summer, 1966), pp. 68-69; R. M. Hodgens, 150
          wds., no cr.
      Filmf: v. IX (1966), p. 38; comp., cp. cr.
      Films & F: v. 12, n. 8 (May, 1966), pp. 6, 8; Allen Eyles, 800 wds., cp. cr.
      Films in R: v. XVII, n. 3 (Mar., 1966), pp. 184-185; Adelaide Comerford,
          175 wds., no cr.

5766 SILENT CALL, THE (John Bushelman)
      Filmf: v. IV (1961), p. 286; comp., cp. cr.

5767 SILENT ENEMY, THE (William Fairchild)
      Filmf: v. II (1959), p. 114; comp., cp. cr.
      Films in R: v. IX, n. 10 (Dec., 1958), p. 593; Ellen Fitzpatrick, 100 wds.,
          no cr.

5768 SILENT PARTNER (George Blair)
      Focus on F: n. 5 (Winter/Nov.-Dec., 1970), p. 41; Don Miller, 300 wds., pt.
          cr.

5769 SILENT PLAYGROUND, THE (Stanley Goulder)
      Films & F: v. 10, n. 9 (June, 1964), p. 27; Raymond Durgnat, 450 wds., cp.
          cr.

5770 SILENT RAID, THE (Paul Rotha)
      (also: De Overval)
      Films & F: v. 10, n. 6 (Mar., 1964), p. 31; Allen Eyles, 425 wds., cp. cr.

5771 SILENT RUNNING (Douglas Trumbull)
      F Quarterly: v. XXV, n. 4 (Summer, 1972), pp. 52-56; William Johnson,
          2100 wds., pt. cr.

5772 SILENT SNOW, SECRET SNOW (George Kleinsinger)
      F Lib Quarterly: v. 1, n. 2 (Spring, 1968), p. 38; Robert Stenzel, 250 wds.,
          pt. cr.

SILENT STRANGER, THE (see: Step Down To Terror)

5773 SILENT WITNESS, THE (Montgomery Tully)
(also: Secrets of a Co-Ed)
Filmf & F: v. 1, n. 4 (Jan., 1955), p. 19; 100 wds., cp. cr.

5774 SILENT WORLD, THE (Jacques-Yves Cousteau and Louis Malle)
(also: Le Monde du Silence)
Films & F: v. 3, n. 4 (Jan., 1957), p. 24; Peter G. Baker, 125 wds., cp. cr.
Films in R: v. VII, n. 8 (Oct., 1956), pp. 411-413; Ralph Gerstle, 500 wds.,
no cr.

5775 SILK STOCKINGS (Rouben Mamoulian)
Films & F: v. 3, n. 11 (Aug., 1957), p. 28; Peter G. Baker, 300 wds., cp. cr.
Films in R: v. VIII, n. 7 (Aug.-Sept., 1957), pp. 351-352; Edward Jablonski,
500 wds., no cr.

5776 SILKEN AFFAIR, THE (Roy Kellino)
Films & F: v. 3, n. 2 (Nov., 1956), pp. 24-25; Peter John Dyer, 350 wds.,
cp. cr.

SILKEN SKIN (see: La Peau Douce)

5777 SILVER CHALICE, THE (Victor Saville)
Films & F: v. 1, n. 9 (June, 1955), p. 20; Derek Hill, 200 wds., cp. cr.

5778 SIMBA (Brian Desmond Hurst)
Films & F: v. 1, n. 6 (Mar., 1955), p. 19; John Minchinton, 325 wds., cp. cr.

SIMEON DEL DESIERTO (see: Simon of the Desert)

5779 SIMON AND LAURA (Muriel Box)
Films & F: v. 2, n. 4 (Jan., 1956), p. 24; Robert A. Pollock, 275 wds., cp.
cr.

5780 SIMON, KING OF THE WITCHES (Bruce Kessler)
Filmf: v. XIV (1971), p. 520; comp., cp. cr.

5781 SIMON OF THE DESERT (Luis Buñuel)
(also: Simeon del Desierto)
F Quarterly: v. XIX, n. 2 (Winter, 1965-1966), pp. 47-48; Jackson Burgess,
600 wds., pt. cr.
Filmf: v. XII (1969), p. 36; comp., cp. cr.
Filmd & F: v. 15, n. 10 (July, 1969), p. 39; Brian Murphy, 900 wds., cp. cr.
Films in R: v. XX, n. 3 (Mar., 1969), p. 178; Jose Aguirre, 250 wds., no cr.
Sight & S: v. 38, n. 3 (Summer, 1969), pp. 154-155; Ian Leslie Christie, 600
wds., pt. cr.
Take One: v. 1, n. 1 (Sept.-Oct., 1966), p. 26; Joe Medjuck, 300 wds., pt.
cr.

SIMON THE SWISS (see: The Crook)

5782 SIMPLE HISTOIRE, UNE (Marcel Hanoun)
Sight & S: v. 29, n. 2 (Spring, 1960), p. 86; Richard Roud, 700 wds., no cr.

5783 SIN AND DESIRE (Willy Rozier)
(also: L'Epave)
Filmf: v. III (1960), p. 359; comp., cp. cr.

5784 SIN FIN (Clemente de la Cerda)
(also: Without End)
Interntl F G: v. 7 (1970), pp. 279-280; Jacobo Brender, 275 wds., pt. cr.

5785 SIN OF JESUS, THE (Robert Frank)
F Culture: n. 25 (Summer, 1962), pp. 30-32; P. Adams Sitney, 700 wds., no
cr.
Sight & S: v. 30, n. 4 (Autumn, 1961), p. 198; Jonathan Miller, 600 wds.,
no cr.

5786 SIN OF MONA KENT, THE (Charles J. Hundt)
Filmf: v. IV (1961), p. 371; comp., cp. cr.

5787 SIN YOU SINNERS (Anthony Farrar)
      Filmf: v. VI (1963), p. 342; comp., cp. cr.

      SINAIA (see: Clouds Over Israel)

5788 SINCERELY YOURS (Gordon Douglas)
      Films & F: v. 2, n. 4 (Jan., 1956), p. 20; P. L. Mannock, 250 wds., cp. cr.

5789 SINFUL DAVEY (John Huston)
      Filmf: v. XII (1969), p. 302; comp., cp. cr.
      Films & F: v. 15, n. 10 (July, 1969), p. 46; Peter Buckley, 600 wds., cp. cr.
      Films in R: v. XX, n. 5 (May, 1969), pp. 319-320; Wilson Derr, 175 wds.,
          no cr.
      Focus: n. 5 (Oct., 1969), p. 34; Myron Meisel, 150 wds., no cr.

5790 SING AND SWING (Lance Comfort)
      Filmf: v. VII (1964), p. 279; comp., cp. cr.

5791 SING, BOY, SING (Henry Ephron)
      Filmf: v. I (1958), p. 23; comp., cp. cr.
      Films & F: v. 4, n. 6 (Mar., 1958), p. 28; Peter John Dyer, 500 wds., cp. cr.

      SINGE EN HIVER, UN (see: Monkey in Winter)

5792 SINGER NOT THE SONG, THE (Roy Baker)
      Filmf: v. V (1962), p. 79; comp., cp. cr.
      Films & F: v. 7, n. 5 (Feb., 1961), p. 33; John Cutts, 400 wds., cp. cr.

      SINGER'S PARADISE (see: Wonderful Life)

5793 SINGIN' IN THE RAIN (Stanley Donen and Gene Kelly)
      Films in R: v. III, n. 4 (Apr., 1952), pp. 198-199; Edward Jablonski, 500
          wds., pt. cr.
      Sight & S: v. 22, n. 1 (July-Sept., 1952), p. 29; James Morgan, 225 wds., pt.
          cr.

5794 SINGING CITY, THE (Mario Costa)
      Films & F: v. 1, n. 1 (Oct., 1954), p. 29; Patrick Goldring, 150 wds., cp. cr.

5795 SINGING NUN, THE (Henry Koster)
      Filmf: v. IX (1966), p. 73; comp., cp. cr.
      Films & F: v. 12, n. 3 (Dec., 1965), pp. 57-58; David Shipman, 1150 wds.,
          cp. cr.

5796 SINK THE BISMARCK! (Lewis Gilbert)
      Filmf: v. III (1960), p. 34; comp., cp. cr.
      Films & F: v. 6, n. 6 (Mar., 1960), p. 23; Peter G. Baker, 300 wds., cp. cr.
      Films & F: v. 9, n. 7 (Apr., 1963), p. 35; Peter G. Baker, 150 wds., cp. cr.
      Films in R: v. XI, n. 3 (Mar., 1960), p. 174; B. T. Saintsbury, 200 wds., no
          cr.
      Sight & S: v. 29, n. 2 (Spring, 1960), pp. 91-92; John Gillett, 700 wds., pt.
          cr.

5797 SINNERS, THE (Jacques Deray)
      (also: La Piscine)
      Films & F: v. 16, n. 2 (Nov., 1969), pp. 41-42; Gordon Gow, 850 wds., cp.
          cr.

5798 SINNERS OF PARIS (Pierre Chenal)
      (also: Rafles sur la Ville)
      Filmf: v. II (1959), p. 107; comp., cp. cr.

5799 SINNING URGE, THE (Hans Abrahamson)
      (also: Brant Barn; Burnt Child)
      Films & F: v. 15, n. 7 (Apr., 1969), pp. 52-53; David Adams, 450 wds., cp.
          cr.

      SINS OF LOLA MONTES, THE (see: Lola Montes)

5800 SINS OF RACHEL CADE, THE (Gordon Douglas)
        Filmf: v. IV (1961), p. 64; comp., cp. cr.
        Films & F: v. 7, n. 7 (Apr., 1961), p. 27; Richard Whitehall, 650 wds., cp.
            cr.

5801 SINS OF ROSE BERND, THE (Wolfgang Staudte)
        (also: Rose Bernd)
        Filmf: v. II (1959), p. 17; comp., cp. cr.
        Films in R: v. X, n. 2 (Feb., 1959), pp. 112-113; Louise Corbin, 75 wds., no
            cr.

5802 SINS OF YOUTH (Louis Duchesne)
        (also: Peche de Jeunesse)
        Filmf: v. III (1960), p. 321; comp., cp. cr.

      SIRENE DE MISSISSIPPI, LA (see: Mississippi Mermaid)

5803 SIROCCO D'HIVER (Miklos Jancso)
        (also: Sirokko; Winter Wind)
        Movie: n. 17 (Winter, 1969-1970), p. 37; Ian Cameron, 175 wds., no cr.

      SIROKKO (see: Sirocco D'Hiver)

5804 SIRUS REMEMBERED (Stan Brakhage)
        F Quarterly: v. XIV, n. 3 (Spring, 1961), pp. 47-48; Ernest Callenbach,
            1200 wds., no cr.

      SISTA STEGEN, DIE (see: A Matter of Morals)

5805 SISTER KENNY (Dudley Nichols)
        Films & F: v. 15, n. 11 (Aug., 1969), p. 80; Kingsley Canham, 800 wds., no
            cr.

      SISTER OF SATAN, THE (see: The She Beast)

5806 SISTERS (Grigory Roshal)
        (also: Sestri)
        Filmf: v. II (1959), p. 146; comp., cp. cr.

5807 SITTING BULL (Sidney Salkow)
        Films & F: v. 1, n. 6 (Mar., 1955), p. 22; Derek Hill, 150 wds., cp. cr.

5808 SITUATION HOPELESS, BUT NOT SERIOUS (Gottfried Reinhardt)
        Films & F: v. 11, n. 6 (Mar., 1965), pp. 48-49; 400 wds., cp. cr.
        Films & F: v. 16, n. 1 (Oct., 1969), pp. 53-54; Michael Armstrong, 450
            wds., cp. cr.
        Films In R: v. XVI, n. 9 (Nov., 1965), pp. 582-583; Helen Weldon Kuhn,
            125 wds., no cr.

5809 SIX BLACK HORSES (Harry Keller)
        Filmf: v. V (1962), p. 106; comp., cp. cr.

5810 SIX BRIDGES TO CROSS (Joseph Pevney)
        Films & F: v. 1, n. 7 (Apr., 1955), p. 21; Derek Hill, 150 wds., cp. cr.

5811 SIX DAYS TO ETERNITY (Y. Hameiri and I. Herbst)
        (also: Sheshey Hayamim)
        Filmf: v. XI (1968), p. 496; comp., cp. cr.

      SIX IN PARIS (see: Paris Vu Par)

5812 633 SQUADRON (Walter E. Grauman)
        Filmf: v. VII (1964), p. 179; comp., cp. cr.
        Films & F: v. 10, n. 10 (July, 1964), p. 23; John Cutts, 175 wds., cp. cr.

5813 SIXIEME FACE DU PENTAGONE, LA (Chris Marker)
        (also: The Sixth Side of the Pentagon)
        F Quarterly: v. XXII, n. 2 (Winter, 1968-1969), pp. 58-59; Larry
            Loewinger, 400 wds., no cr.

      SIXTH CONTINENT (see: Sesto Continento)

5814 SIXTH DAY OF CREATION, THE (Francis Maziere)
      Films & F: v. 15, n. 12 (Sept., 1969), p. 71; Chris Jones, 300 wds., cp. cr.

      SIXTH SIDE OF THE PENTAGON, THE (see: La Sixème Face du Pentagon)

      SJUNDE INSEGLET, DET (see: The Seventh Seal)

      SKAMMEN (see: Shame)

5815 SKEZAG (Joel E. Freedman and Philip F. Messina)
      Filmf: v. XIV (1971), p. 714; comp., cp. cr.

5816 SKI BUM, THE (Bruce Clark)
      Filmf: v. XIV (1971), p. 722; comp., cp. cr.

5817 SKI ON THE WILD SIDE (Warren Miller)
      Filmf: v. X (1967), p. 241; comp., cp. cr.

5818 SKI TROOP ATTACK (Roger Corman)
      Filmf: v. III (1960), p. 87; comp., cp. cr.

5819 SKID (Zbynek Brynych)
      F Journal: n. 20 (Aug., 1962), p. 84; Sylvia Lawson, 150 wds., no cr.

5820 SKIDOO (Otto Preminger)
      Filmf: v. XII (1969), pp. 105, 168; comp., cp. cr.
      Films & F: v. 15, n. 11 (Aug., 1969), p. 40; Gordon Gow, 500 wds., cp. cr.

      SKIN DEEP (see: L'Une et L'Autre)

5821 SKIN GAME, THE (Arnold L. Miller)
      (also: Kil 1)
      Filmf: v. IX (1966), p. 386; comp., cp. cr.

5822 SKIN GAME, THE (Paul Bogart)
      F Quarterly: v. XXV, n. 2 (Winter, 1971-1972), p. 57; Gregg E. Whitman,
          400 wds., no cr.
      Filmf: v. XIV (1971), p. 606; comp., cp. cr.

5823 SKIN SKIN (Mikko Niskanen)
      Films & F: v. 15, n. 1 (Oct., 1968), pp. 48-49; Michael Armstrong, 150
          wds., cp. cr.

5824 SKY ABOVE — THE MUD BELOW, THE (Pierre-Dominique Gaisseau)
      Cinema: v. 1, n. 3 p. 34; 200 wds., pt. cr.
      Filmf: v. V (1962), p. 169; comp., cp. cr.
      Films & F: v. 10, n. 2 (Nov., 1963), pp. 21-22; Ken Gay, 425 wds., cp. cr.
      Films in R: v. XIII, n. 6 (June-July, 1962), pp. 358-359; Adolph Bruckman,
          275 wds., no cr.

5825 SKY OVER HOLLAND (John Ferno)
      Interntl F G: v. 5 (1968), pp. 120-121; 150 wds., pt. cr.

      SKY WEST AND CROOKED (see: Gypsy Girl)

5826 SKY WITHOUT STARS
      Filmf: v. II (1959), p. 145; comp., cp. cr.

5827 SKYDIVERS, THE (Coleman Francis)
      Filmf: v. VI (1963), p. 341; comp., cp. cr.

      SKYLARK (see: Pacsirta)

5828 SKYSCRAPER (Shirley Clarke)
      F Quarterly: v. XIII, n. 4 (Summer, 1960), pp. 57-58; Henry Breitrose, 800
          wds., pt. cr.

5829 SLANDER (Roy Rowland)
      Films & F: v. 3, n. 6 (Mar., 1957), p. 25; Peter G. Baker, 300 wds., cp. cr.
      Films in R: v. VIII, n. 2 (Feb., 1957), p. 83; Diana Willing, 100 wds., no cr.

5830 SLAVE, THE (Yves Ciampi)
        (also: L'Esclave)
        Films & F: v. 1, n. 6 (Mar., 1955), p. 19; Ivan Pattison, 225 wds., cp. cr.

5831 SLAVE, THE (Sergio Corbucci)
        (also: Il Figlio di Spartacus; Son of Spartacus)
        Filmf: v. VI (1963), p. 87; comp., cp. cr.
        Films & F: v. 9, n. 9 (June, 1963), p. 33; Richard Whitehall, 400 wds., cp.
              cr.

5832 SLAVE GIRLS (Michael Carreras)
        Films & F: v. 14, n. 11 (Aug., 1968), p. 26; Michael Armstrong, 400 wds.,
              cp. cr.

5833 SLAVE MERCHANTS, THE (Anthony Dawson)
        Films & F: v. 11, n. 7 (Apr., 1965), p. 38; Richard Davis, 125 wds., cp. cr.

5834 SLAVE TRADE IN THE WORLD TODAY (Folco Quilici and Roberto
              Malenotti)
        (also: Le Schiave Esistono Ancora)
        Films in R: v. XV, n. 10 (Dec., 1964), p. 637; 100 wds., no cr.

5835 SLAVERY: THE BLACK MAN AND THE MAN (John Chandler)
        F Lib Quarterly: v. 4, n. 3 (Summer, 1971), pp. 41-42; Kenneth W.
              Axthelm, 300 wds., pt. cr.

5836 SLAVES (Herbert Biberman)
        Filmf: v. XII (1969), p. 372; comp., cp. cr.

        SLAVNOSTI A HOSTECH, O (see: A Report on the Party and Guests)

        SLEDGE (see: A Man Called Sledge)

5837 SLEEP (Andy Warhol)
        F Culture: n. 32 (Spring, 1964), p. 13; Henry Geldzahler, 575 wds., no cr.

5838 SLEEPING BEAUTY (Walt Disney and Clyde Geronimi)
        F Quarterly: v. XII, n. 3 (Spring, 1959), p. 49; Raymond Fielding, 100
              wds., no cr.
        Filmf: v. II (1959), p. 25; comp., cp. cr.
        Films & F: v. 5, n. 12 (Sept., 1959), p. 25; Campbell Allen, 250 wds., cp.
              cr.
        Films in R: v. X, n. 2 (Feb., 1959), pp. 113, 115; Elspeth Hart, 225 wds.,
              no cr.

5839 SLEEPING BEAUTY, THE (Apollinariy Dudko and Konstantin Sergeyev)
        (also: Spiachtchai Kracavitsa)
        Filmf: v. IX (1966), p. 117; comp., cp. cr.
        Films & F: v. 12, n. 3 (Dec., 1965), p. 34; Kevin Gough-Yates, 75 wds., cp.
              cr.

5840 SLEEPING CAR MURDERS, THE (Costa-Gavras)
        (also: Compartiment Tueurs)
        F Quarterly: v. XXI, n. 3 (Spring, 1968), pp. 44-46; James Michael Martin,
              1500 wds., pt. cr.
        Filmf: v. IX (1966), p. 65; comp., cp. cr.
        Films & F: v. 13, n. 3 (Dec., 1966), p. 52; Richard Davis, 250 wds., cp. cr.
        Films in R: v. XVII, n. 4 (Apr., 1966), pp. 252-253; Lily N. L. Smith, 150
              wds., no cr.

5841 SLENDER THREAD, THE (Sydney Pollack)
        F Quarterly: v. XIX, n. 4 (Summer, 1966), p. 69; R. M. Hodgens, 100 wds.,
              no cr.
        Films & F: v. 12, n. 8 (May, 1966), pp. 51-52; Allen Eyles, 300 wds., cp. cr.
        Films in R: v. XVII, n. 1 (Jan., 1966), pp. 49-50; Elaine Rothschild, 350
              wds., no cr.

        SLEUTEL, DE (see: The Key)

5842 SLICE OF LIFE, A (Alessandro Blasetti)
          (also: Anatomy of Love; Tempi Nostri)
          Filmf: v. II (1959), p. 317; comp., cp. cr.
          Films & F: v. 1, n. 3 (Dec., 1954), pp. 20-21; John Minchinton, 175 wds.,
              cp. cr.
          Films & F: v. 2, n. 3 (Dec., 1955), p. 19; Peter G. Baker, 325 wds., cp. cr.

5843 SLIME PEOPLE, THE (Robert Hutton)
          Filmf: v. VI (1963), p. 341; comp., cp. cr.

5844 SLIPPERY PEARLS, THE
          Focus on F: n. 1 (Jan.-Feb., 1970), pp. 54-55; Anthony Slide, 1100 wds.,
              pt. cr.

5845 SLOW RUN (Larry Kardish)
          Filmf: v. XI (1968), p. 450; comp., cp. cr.

5846 SMALL HOURS, THE (Norman Chaitin)
          Filmf: v. V (1962), p. 261; comp., cp. cr.

5847 SMALL WORLD OF SAMMY LEE, THE (Ken Hughes)
          Filmf: v. VI (1963), p. 202; comp., cp. cr.
          Films & F: v. 9, n. 9 (June, 1963), pp. 31-32; Raymond Durgnat, 750 wds.,
              cp. cr.

5848 SMALLEST SHOW ON EARTH, THE (Basil Dearden)
          (also: Big Time Operators)
          Films & F: v. 3, n. 9 (June, 1957), p. 23; Peter John Dyer, 350 wds., cp. cr.

5849 SMASHING OF THE REICH (Perry Wolff, prod.)
          Filmf: v. V (1962), p. 318; comp., cp. cr.

5850 SMASHING TIME (Desmond Davis)
          Filmf: v. X (1967), p. 430; comp., cp. cr.
          Films & F: v. 14, n. 5 (Feb., 1968), pp. 21-22; Robin Bean, 700 wds., cp.
              cr.
          Films in R: v. XIX, n. 2 (Feb., 1968), pp. 109-110; Page Cook, 250 wds.,
              no cr.

5851 SMILES OF A SUMMER NIGHT (Ingmar Bergman)
          (also: Sommarnattens Leende)
          Films & F: v. 3, n. 2 (Nov., 1956), p. 26; Peter John Dyer, 600 wds., cp. cr.
          Sight & S: v. 26, n. 2 (Autumn, 1956), p. 98; John Gillett, 350 wds., pt. cr.

5852 SMILEY (Anthony Kimmins)
          Films & F: v. 2, n. 11 (Aug., 1956), pp. 21-22; Michael Winner, 300 wds.,
              cp. cr.

5853 SMILEY GETS A GUN (Anthony Kimmins)
          Filmf: v. II (1959), p. 54; comp., cp. cr.
          Films & F: v. 4, n. 9 (June, 1958), pp. 26-27; Gordon Gow, 450 wds., cp.
              cr.

5854 SMOKY (George Sherman)
          Filmf: v. IX (1966), p. 350; comp., cp. cr.
          Films in R: v. XVII, n. 7 (Aug.-Sept., 1966), pp. 452-453; Wilfred Mifflin,
              125 wds., no cr.

5855 SMUGGLERS, THE (Luc Moullet)
          (also: Les Contrebandieres)
          Filmf: v. XII (1969), p. 149; comp., cp. cr.

      SMULTRONSTALLET (see: Wild Strawberries)

5856 SNAKE PIT, THE (Anatole Litvak)
          Sequence: n. 9 (Autumn, 1949), pp. 134-135; Peter Ericsson, 750 wds., pt.
              cr.

5857 SNAKE WOMAN, THE (Sidney J. Furie)
          Filmf: v. IV (1961), p. 166; comp., cp. cr.
          Films & F: v. 8, n. 12 (Sept., 1962), p. 37; Raymond Durgnat, 475 wds.,
              cp. cr.

5858 SNIPER'S RIDGE (John Bushelman)
      Filmf: v. IV (1961), p. 20; comp., cp. cr.
      Films & F: v. 9, n. 8 (May, 1963), pp. 29-30; Ian Johnson, 300 wds., cp. cr.

5859 SNOBS, THE (Jean-Pierre Mocky)
      Films & F: v. 8, n. 8 (May, 1962), pp. 34-35; Raymons Durgnat, 700 wds.,
          cp. cr.
      Sight & S: v. 31, n. 2 (Spring, 1962), p. 96; Richard Roud, 450 wds., no cr.

5860 SNORKEL, THE (Guy Green)
      Filmf: v. I (1958), p. 153; comp., cp. cr.

5861 SNOW QUEEN, THE (Soyuzmultfilm, prod.)
      Filmf: v. III (1960), p. 76; comp., cp. cr.

5862 SNOW WHITE AND THE SEVEN DWARFS (David Herd and Walt Disney)
      Films & F: v. 11, n. 8 (May, 1965), p. 36; David Rider, 400 wds., cp. cr.

5863 SNOW WHITE AND THE THREE STOOGES (Walter Lang)
      Filmf: v. IV (1961), p. 161; comp., cp. cr.

5864 SNOWFIRE (Dorrell and Stuart McGowan)
      Filmf: v. I (1958), p. 228; comp., cp. cr.

5865 SNOWS OF KILIMANJARO, THE (Henry King)
      Films in R: v. III, n. 8 (Oct., 1952), pp. 410-412; Henry Hart, 1200 wds.,
          pt. cr.

      SO CLOSE TO LIFE (see: Brink of Life)

5866 SO DARK THE NIGHT (Joseph H. Lewis)
      Focus on F: n. 5 (Winter/Nov.-Dec., 1970), pp. 44-45; Don Miller, 350
          wds., pt. cr.

5867 SO LITTLE TIME (Compton Bennett)
      Films in R: v. IV, n. 8 (Oct., 1953), p. 433; 200 wds., pt. cr.

5868 SO THIS IS PARIS (Richard Quine)
      Films & F: v. 1, n. 5 (Feb., 1955), p. 24; Clayton Cole, 300 wds., cp. cr.
      Sight & S: v. 24, n. 4 (Spring, 1955), p. 200; Gavin Lambert, 450 wds., pt.
          cr.

5869 SO WELL REMEMBERED (Edward Dmytryk)
      Sight & S: v. 16, n. 63 (Autumn, 1947), p. 120; Arthur Vesselo, 200 wds.,
          no cr.

5870 SOCRATE, LE (Roberto Rossellini)
      (also: Socrates)
      F Quarterly: v. XXIII, n. 1 (Fall, 1969), pp. 29-32; George Lellis, 900 wds.,
          pt. cr.
      Filmf: v. XIV (1971), p. 745; comp., cp. cr.
      Movie: n. 18 (Winter, 1970-1971), pp. 39-40; Ian Cameron, 500 wds., no cr.

      SOCRATES (see: Le Socrate)

5871 SODOM AND GOMORRAH (Robert Aldrich)
      Cinema: v. 1, n. 4, p. 43, 250 wds., pt. cr.
      Filmf: v. VI (1963), p. 6; comp., cp. cr.
      Films & F: v. 9, n. 3 (Dec., 1962), pp. 39-40; Peter Baker, 750 wds., cp. cr.
      Movie: n. 4 (Nov., 1962), p. 35; 175 wds., no cr.

5872 SOFI (Robert Carlisle)
      Filmf: v. XI (1968), p. 148; comp., cp. cr.

      SOFT SKIN, THE (see: La Peau Douce)

5873 SOL MADRID (Brian Hutton)
      Filmf: v. XI (1968), p. 212; comp., cp. cr.

5874 SOL ZIEMI CZARNEJ (Kazimierz Kutz)
      (also: Salt of the Black Earth)
      Interntl F G: v. 8 (1971), pp. 225-226; Ryszard Koniczek, 225 wds., pt. cr.

5875 SOLDATESSE, LE (Valerio Zurlini)
      F Quarterly: v. XIX, n. 3 (Spring, 1966), pp. 48-50; Peter Graham, 1100
      wds., pt. cr.

5876 SOLDIER BLUE (Ralph Nelson)
      Films & F: v. 17, n. 9 (June, 1971), pp. 65-66; Peter Buckley, 800 wds., cp.
      cr.

5877 SOLDIER IN THE RAIN (Ralph Nelson)
      Cinema: v. 2, n. 1 (Feb., 1964), p. 48; James Silke, 225 wds., pt. cr.
      Filmf: v. VI (1963), p. 262; comp., cp. cr.
      Films & F: v. 11, n. 12 (Sept., 1965), p. 34; Richard Davis, 500 wds., cp. cr.
      Films in R: v. XV, n. 1 (Jan., 1964), pp. 52-53; Karl Biberman, 250 wds.,
      no cr.

      SOLDIERS, THE (see: Les Carabiniers)

5878 SOLDIER'S FATHER, A
      F Quarterly: v. XIX, n. 4 (Summer, 1966), pp. 56-59; John Seelye, 1800
      wds., no cr.

      SOLDIER'S PRAYER, A (see: Ningen No Joken)

5879 SOLID GOLD CADILLAC, THE (Richard Quine)
      Films & F: v. 3, n. 2 (Nov., 1956), pp. 25-26; P. L. Mannock, 200 wds., cp.
      cr.
      Sight & S: v. 26, n. 2 (Autumn, 1956), p. 99; Penelope Houston, 300 wds.,
      pt. cr.

5880 SOLITI IGNOTI, I (Mario Monicelli)
      (also: The Big Deal: Big Deal on Madonna Street; Persons Unknown)
      F Quarterly: v. XII, n. 4 (Summer, 1959), pp. 49-50; Henry Goodman, 550
      wds., no cr.
      Filmf: v. III (1960), p. 306; comp., cp. cr.
      Films & F: v. 6, n. 4 (Jan., 1960), pp. 23-24; Gordon Gow, 250 wds., cp. cr.
      Films in R: v. XII, n. 1 (Jan., 1961), pp. 39-40; Shirley Conover, 175 wds.,
      no cr.
      Sight & S: v. 29, n. 1 (Winter, 1959-1960), p. 39; John Gillett, 350 wds., pt.
      cr.

5881 SOLO (Jean-Pierre Mocky)
      Take One: v. 2, n. 7 (1970), p. 24; Geoffrey Minish, 450 wds., pt. cr.

      SOLO CONTRO ROMA (see: Alone Against Rome)

5882 SOLOMON AND SHEBA (King Vidor)
      F Quarterly: v. XIII, n. 3 (Spring, 1960), p. 60; 50 wds., no cr.
      Filmf: v. II (1959), p. 336; comp., cp. cr.
      Films & F: v. 6, n. 2 (Nov., 1959), p. 23; Peter G. Baker, 225 wds., cp. cr.
      Films in R: v. XI, n. 2 (Feb., 1960), p. 106; James K. Loutzenhiser, 150
      wds., no cr.

      SOM NATT OCH DAG (see: Like Night and Day)

5883 SOME CAME RUNNING (Vincente Minnelli)
      Filmf: v. II (1959), p. 1; comp., cp. cr.
      Films & F: v. 5, n. 8 (May, 1959), pp. 23-24; Peter G. Baker, 200 wds., cp.
      cr.
      Films in R: v. X, n. 2 (Feb., 1959), pp. 111-112; Courtland Phipps, 200
      wds., no cr.

5884 SOME GIRLS DO (Ralph Thomas)
      Filmf: v. XIV (1971), p. 105; comp., cp. cr.
      Films & F: v. 15, n. 7 (Apr., 1969), pp. 47, 50; David Adams, 600 wds., cp.
      cr.

5885 SOME LIKE IT HOT (Billy Wilder)
        Filmf: v. II (1959), p. 51; comp., cp. cr.
        Films & F: v. 5, n. 9 (June, 1959), pp. 23-24; Peter G. Baker, 300 wds., cp.
            cr.
        Films in R: v. X, n. 4 (Apr., 1959), pp. 240-241; Ellen Fitzpatrick, 425
            wds., no cr.
        Sight & S: v. 28, n. 3-4 (Summer-Autumn, 1959), p. 173; Peter John Dyer,
            500 wds., pt. cr.

5886 SOME OF MY BEST FRIENDS ARE . . . (Mervyn Nelson)
        Filmf: v. XIV (1971), p. 558; comp., cp. cr.

5887 SOME OF MY BEST FRIENDS ARE WHITE (BBC, prod.)
        F Lib Quarterly: v. 2, n. 2 (Spring, 1969), pp. 30, 52; Philip Levering, 550
            wds., pt. cr.

5888 SOME PEOPLE (Clive Donner)
        Films & F: v. 8, n. 12 (Sept., 1962), p. 32; Gordon Gow, 625 wds., cp. cr.
        Movie: n. 3 (Oct., 1962), pp. 23-25; V. F. Perkins, 2650 wds., pt. cr.

5889 SOMEBODY UP THERE LIKES ME (Robert Wise)
        F Culture: v. 2, n. 3 (1956), pp. 28-30; Eugene Archer, 1500 wds., pt. cr.
        Films & F: v. 3, n. 3 (Dec., 1956), p. 24; Martin Gray, 150 wds., cp. cr.
        Films in R: v. VII, n. 7 (Aug.-Sept., 1956), pp. 344-345; Jim Scovotti, 600
            wds., no cr.

5890 SOMEONE BEHIND THE DOOR (Nicolas Gessner)
        (also: Quelqu'un Derrière La Porte)
        Filmf: v. XIV (1971), p. 677; comp., cp. cr.

5891 SOMETHING FOR EVERYONE (Harold Prince)
        (also: Black Flowers for the Bride; The Cook; The Rook)
        Films & F: v. 17, n. 11 (Aug., 1971), pp. 59-60; Gordon Gow, 650 wds., cp.
            cr.
        Films in R: v. XXI, n. 8 (Oct., 1970), pp. 506-507; Hubbell Robinson, 325
            wds., no cr.
        Sight & S: v. 40, n. 3 (Summer, 1971), pp. 166-167; Tom Milne, 850 wds.,
            pt. cr.
        Take One: v. 2, n. 8 (1970), p. 20; John Hofsess, 500 wds., pt. cr.

5892 SOMETHING OF VALUE (Richard Brooks)
        Films & F: v. 3, n. 10 (July, 1957), pp. 24-25; Ken Gay, 300 wds., cp. cr.
        Films in R: v. VIII, n. 7 (Aug.-Sept., 1957), p. 350; Hy Arnold, 100 wds.,
            no cr.

5893 SOMETHING WILD (Jack Garfein)
        Filmf: v. IV (1961), p. 358; comp., cp. cr.
        Films & F: v. 9, n. 1 (Oct., 1962), p. 33; John Cutts, 450 wds., cp. cr.
        Films in R: v. XIII, n. 2 (Feb., 1962), pp. 109-110; Flavia Wharton, 350
            wds., no cr.

      SOMMAREN MED MONIKA (see: Summer with Monika)

      SOMMARLEK (see: Summer Interlude)

      SOMMARNATTENS LEENDE (see: Smiles of a Summer Night)

      SOMMERSPROSSEN (see: Beyond Control)

5894 SON OF A GUNFIGHTER (Paul Landres)
        (also: El Hijo de Pistolero)
        Filmf: v. IX (1966), p. 308; comp., cp. cr.

5895 SON OF CAPTAIN BLOOD, THE (Tulio Demichelli)
        (also: Il Figlio del Capitano Blood)
        Filmf: v. VII (1964), p. 185; comp., cp. cr.
        Films & F: v. 10, n. 1 (Oct., 1963), p. 26; Robin Bean, 200 wds., cp. cr.

5896 SON OF FLUBBER (Robert Stevenson)
        Filmf: v. VI (1963), p. 17; comp., cp. cr.
        Films & F: v. 9, n. 6 (Mar., 1963), pp. 38-39; John Cutts, 250 wds., cp. cr.

5897 SON OF GODZILLA (Jun Fukuda)
        (also: Godzilla No Musuko)
        Films & F: v. 16, n. 1 (Oct., 1969), p. 56; David Austen, 200 wds., cp. cr.

5898 SON OF ROBIN HOOD (George Sherman)
        Filmf: v. II (1959), p. 206; comp., cp. cr.

5899 SON OF SAMSON (Carlo Campogalliani)
        Filmf: v. V (1962), p. 206; comp., cp. cr.

        SON OF SPARTACUS (see: The Slave)

        SON TORNATA PER TE (see: Heidi)

5900 SONG AND THE SILENCE, THE (Nathan Cohen)
        Filmf: v. XII (1969), p. 47; comp., cp. cr.

5901 SONG OF NORWAY (Andrew L. Stone)
        Films & F: v. 17, n. 6 (Mar., 1971), pp. 56-57; Margaret Tarratt, 400 wds.,
            cp. cr.
        Films in R: v. XXI, n. 10 (Dec., 1970), pp. 646-647; Penelope Graham, 225
            wds., no cr.

5902 SONG OF THE LAND (Henry S. Kesler, prod.)
        Films in R: v. V, n. 2 (Feb., 1954), pp. 97-98; Bradner Lacey, 250 wds., no
            cr.

        SONG OF THE ROAD (see: Pather Panchali)

        SONG XXIII (see: 23rd Psalm)

5903 SONG WITHOUT END (Charles Vidor)
        Filmf: v. III (1960), p. 187; comp., cp. cr.
        Films & F: v. 6, n. 11 (Aug., 1960), p. 23; David Hunt, 400 wds., cp. cr.

5904 SONGS OVER THE DNIEPER (A. Mishurin and A. Vronsky)
        (also: Tantsi I Pyesni Nad Dneprom)
        Filmf: v. I (1958), p. 145; comp., cp. cr.

        SONIDO PREHISTORICO, EL (see: Sound of Horror)

5905 SONS AND DAUGHTERS (Jerry Stoll)
        (also: Days of Protest)
        F Quarterly: v. XX, n. 4 (Summer, 1967), pp. 69-73; Randall Conrad, 1800
            wds., pt. cr.

5906 SONS AND LOVERS (Jack Cardiff)
        F Quarterly: v. XIV, n. 1 (Fall, 1960), pp. 41-42; John Gillett, 700 wds., pt.
            cr.
        Filmf: v. III (1960), p. 179; comp., cp. cr.
        Films & F: v. 6, n. 10 (July, 1960), p. 22; W. G. Smith, 45 wds., cp. cr.
        Films in R: v. XI, n. 7 (Aug.-Sept., 1960), pp. 422-424; Henry Hart, 850
            wds., no cr.
        Sight & S: v. 29, n. 3 (Summer, 1960), p. 145; Kenneth Cavander, 625
            wds., pt. cr.

        SONS AND MOTHERS (see: Heart of a Mother)

5907 SONS OF KATIE ELDER, THE (Henry Hathaway)
        Films & F: v. 12, n. 3 (Dec., 1965), p. 25; Richard Davis, 500 wds., cp. cr.

5908 SONS OF THUNDER (Duccio Tessari)
        (also: I Titani)
        Films & F: v. 9, n. 10 (July, 1963), p. 26; Brian O'Brien, 250 wds., cp. cr.

        SOPHIE ET LE CRIME (see: Girl on the Third Floor)

        SOPHIE'S PLACE (see: Crooks and Coronets)

5909 SORCERERS, THE (Michael Reeves)
    Filmf: v. XI (1968), p. 471; comp., cp. cr.
    Films & F: v. 14, n. 1 (Oct., 1967), pp. 25-26; David Austen 500 wds., cp.
        cr.

5910 SORCERER'S VILLAGE, THE (Hassoldt Davis)
    Filmf: v. I (1958), p. 232; comp., cp. cr.

5911 SORCIERE, LA (André Michel)
    Films in R: v. VIII, n. 1 (Jan., 1957), pp. 30-31; Betty Swyker, 300 wds.,
        no cr.

    SORCIERES DE SALEM, LES (see: The Witches of Salem)

    SORDID AFFAIR, A (see: Man of Straw)

    SORELLA DI SATANA, LA (see: The She Beast)

    SORPASSO, IL (see: The Easy Life)

5912 SORROW AND THE PITY, THE (Marcel Ophuls)
    (also: Le Chagrin et la Pitié)
    Cineaste: v. 1 (Winter, 1971-1972), pp. 15-18; Lenny Rubenstein, 1700
        wds., pt. cr.
    F Quarterly: v. XXV, n. 4 (Summer, 1972), pp. 56-59; Michael Silverman,
        1700 wds., pt. cr.
    F Soc Rev: v. 7, n. 3 (Nov., 1971), pp. 26-28; Gary Crowdus, 450 wds., no
        cr.

5913 SORTILEGES (Christian-Jaque)
    Sight & S: v. 15, n. 60 (Winter, 1946-1947), p. 149; Peter Streuli, 200 wds.,
        no cr.

5914 SOTTO IL SEGNO DELLO SCORPIONE (Paolo and Vittorio Taviani)
    Movie: n. 17 (Winter, 1969-1970), p. 37; Ian Cameron, 175 wds., no cr.

    SOUFFLE AU COEUR, LE (see: Murmur of the Heart)

5915 SOUL TO SOUL (Denis Sanders)
    Filmf: v. XIV (1971), p. 541; comp., cp. cr.

5916 SOUND AND THE FURY, THE (Martin Ritt)
    F Quarterly: v. XII, n. 4 (Summer, 1959), pp. 47-49; Joseph Kostolefsky,
        750 wds., no cr.
    Filmf: v. II (1959), p. 57; comp., cp. cr.
    Films & F: v. 5, n. 8 (May, 1959), p. 24; Brenda Davies, 400 wds., cp. cr.
    Films in R: v. X, n. 4 (Apr., 1959), pp. 234-237; Prudence Ashton, 750
        wds., no cr.

    SOUND BARRIER, THE (see: Breaking the Sound Barrier)

5917 SOUND OF FURY, THE (Cy Endfield)
    Films in R: v. II, n. 3 (Mar., 1951), p. 39; Joseph R. Collidge, 225 wds., pt.
        cr.
    Sight & S: v. 21, n. 1 (Aug.-Sept., 1951), p. 23; James Morgan, 500 wds.,
        pt. cr.

5918 SOUND OF HORROR (Jose Antonio Nieves-Conde)
    (also: El Sonido Prehistorico)
    Filmf: v. X (1967), p. 441; comp., cp. cr.

5919 SOUND OF LAUGHTER, THE (John O'Shaughnesey)
    Filmf: v. VI (1963), p. 311; comp., cp. cr.
    Films in R: v. XV, n. 1 (Jan., 1964), p. 46; Romano Tozzi, 325 wds., no cr.

5920 SOUND OF MUSIC, THE (Robert Wise)
    F Quarterly: v. XX, n. 2 (Winter, 1966-1967), p. 63; R. M. Hodgens, 75
        wds., no cr.
    Filmf: v. VIII (1965), p. 51; comp., cp. cr.

471

Films & F: v. 11, n. 8 (May, 1965), pp. 25-26; Mike Sarne, 1450 wds., cp. cr.

Films in R: v. XVI, n. 3 (Mar., 1965), pp. 176-177; Romano Tozzi, 350 wds., no cr.

5921 SOUND OF TRUMPETS, THE (Ermanno Olmi)
(also: The Job; Il Posto)
Cinema: v. 2, n. 2 (July, 1964), p. 47; Rory Guy, 275 wds., pt. cr.
Film: n. 32 (Summer, 1962), p. 19; Douglas McVay, 150 wds., no cr.
F Comment: v. 1, n. 6 (Fall, 1963), pp. 34-38; Robert Connelly, 2800 wds., no cr.
F Quarterly: v. XVII, n. 4 (Summer, 1964), pp. 44-45; Ernest Callenbach, 700 wds., pt. cr.
Filmf: v. VI (1963), p. 261; comp., cp. cr.
Films & F: v. 8, n. 7 (Apr., 1962), p. 31; Roger Manvell, 800 wds., cp. cr.
Films in R: v. XIV, n. 10 (Dec., 1963), p. 629; Wilfred Miffin, 200 wds., no cr.

SOUPIRANT, LE (see: The Suitor)

SOUS LE CIEL DE PROVENCE (see: Virtuous Bigamist)

5922 SOUTH PACIFIC (Joshua Logan)
Filmf: v. I (1958), p. 47; comp., cp. cr.
Films & F: v. 4, n. 9 (June, 1958), pp. 24-25; Peter G. Baker, 750 wds., cp. cr.
Films in R: v. IX, n. 4 (Apr., 1958), pp. 202-204; Edward Jablonski, 400 wds., no cr.
Sight & S: v. 27, n. 5 (Summer, 1958), pp. 250-251; David Vaughan, 650 wds., pt. cr.

5923 SOUTH SEAS ADVENTURE (Francis D. Lyon, Walter Thompson, Basil Wrangell, Richard Goldstone, Carl Dudley)
Filmf: v. I (1958), p. 131; comp., cp. cr.
Films & F: v. 6, n. 3 (Dec., 1959), p. 25; Peter G. Baker, 75 wds., cp. cr.
Films in R: v. IX, n. 7 (Aug.-Sept., 1958), p. 403; Elsa Von Clemnitz, 175 wds., no cr.

5924 SOUTHERN STAR, THE (Sidney Hayers)
(also: L'Etoile de Sud)
Filmf: v. XII (1969), p. 276; comp., cp. cr.

SOUTHWEST TO SONORA (see: The Appaloosa)

SOUVENIR D'ITALIE (see: It Happened in Rome)

5925 SOUVENIRS PERDUS (Christian-Jaque)
(also: Lost Property)
Sight & S: v. 22, n. 3 (Jan.-Mar., 1953), pp. 130-131; Elizabeth Russell, 500 wds., pt. cr.

SPACE AMOEBA (see: Yog — Monster from Space)

5926 SPACE CHILDREN, THE (Jack Arnold)
Filmf: v. I (1958), p. 171; comp., cp. cr.

5927 SPACE MASTER X-7 (Edward Bernds)
Filmf: v. I (1958), p. 148; comp., cp. cr.

5928 SPANISH AFFAIR (Donald Siegel)
Filmf: v. I (1958), p. 9; comp., cp. cr.

5929 SPANISH GARDNER, THE (Philip Leacock)
Films & F: v. 3, n. 4 (Jan., 1957), p. 26; Peter G. Baker, 300 wds., cp. cr.
Sight & S: v. 26, n. 3 (Winter, 1956-1957), p. 155; Derek Hill, 300 wds., pt. cr.

5930 SPARA FORTE, PIU FORTE . . . NON CAPISCO (see: Shoot Loud, Louder . . . I Don't Understand)

5931 SPARE THE ROD (Leslie Norman)
    Film: n. 29 (Summer, 1961), p. 11; Philip Crick, 150 wds., no cr.
    Films & F: v. 7, n. 10 (July, 1961), p. 26; Peter G. Baker, 500 wds., cp. cr.

5932 SPARROWS CAN'T SING (Joan Littlewood)
    Filmf: v. VI (1963), p. 94; comp., cp. cr.
    Films & F: v. 9, n. 6 (Mar., 1963), pp. 32-33; Gordon Gow, 850 wds., cp. cr.
    Movie: n. 7, p. 36; 100 wds., no cr.
    Sight & S: v. 32, n. 2 (Spring, 1963), pp. 92-93; Tom Milne, 850 wds., pt. cr.

5933 SPARTACUS (Stanley Kubrick)
    F Quarterly: v. XIV, n. 1 (Fall, 1960), pp. 61-62; 200 wds., no cr.
    Filmf: v. III (1960), p. 241; comp., cp. cr.
    Films & F: v. 7, n. 4 (Jan., 1961), pp. 32-33; John Cutts, 700 wds., cp. cr.
    Films in R: v. XI, n. 9 (Nov., 1960), pp. 553-554; 400 wds., no cr.
    Sight & S: v. 30, n. 1 (Winter, 1960-1961), p. 38; Peter John Dyer, 325 wds., pt. cr.

5934 SPARTAN GLADIATORS, THE (Alberto de Martino)
    Films & F: v. 12, n. 6 (Mar., 1965), p. 55; Allen Eyles, 150 wds., cp. cr.

5935 SPEAKING OF MURDER (Gilles Grangier)
    (also: Le Rouge Est Mis)
    Filmf: v. II (1959), p. 269; comp., cp. cr.

    SPECTRE, THE (see: The Ghost)

5936 SPEED CRAZY (William Hole, Jr.)
    Filmf: v. I (1958), p. 299; comp., cp. cr.

5937 SPEEDWAY (Norman Taurog)
    Filmf: v. XI (1968), p. 288; comp., cp. cr.
    Films & F: v. 14, n. 12 (Sept., 1968), p. 40; David Rider, 300 wds., cp. cr.

5938 SPENCER'S MOUNTAIN (Delmer Daves)
    Cinema: v. 1, n. 4, p. 46; John Schrader, 250 wds., pt. cr.
    Filmf: v. VI (1963), p. 88; comp., cp. cr.
    Films & F: v. 9, n. 11 (Aug., 1963), pp. 24-25; Robin Bean, 950 wds., cp. cr.
    Films in R: v. XIV, n. 5 (May, 1963), pp. 309-310; Emily Loeb, 100 wds., no cr.

5939 SPESSART INN, THE (Kurt Hossmann)
    (also: Das Wirtshaus Im Spessart)
    Filmf: v. IV (1961), p. 45; comp., cp. cr.

    SPETTRO, LO (see: The Ghost)

    SPIACHTCHAI KRACAVITSA (see: The Sleeping Beauty)

    SPIAGGIA, LA (see: The Beach)

5940 SPICE OF LIFE (Jean Dreville)
    Films in R: v. V, n. 2 (Feb., 1954), p. 98; N. Hope Wilson, 150 wds., no cr.

5941 SPIDER, THE
    Filmf: v. I (1958), p. 236; comp., cp. cr.

5942 SPIDER AND THE FLY, THE (Robert Hamer)
    Sequence: n. 10 (New Year, 1950), p. 154; Lindsay Anderson, 250 wds., no cr.

    SPIDER'S STRATEGY, THE (see: La Strategia del Ragno)

5943 SPIDER'S WEB, THE (Godfrey Grayson)
    Films & F: v. 7, n. 4 (Jan., 1961), p. 35; Phillip Riley, 250 wds., cp. cr.

    SPIE UCCIDONO A BEIRUT, LE (see: Secret Agent Fireball!)

SPIN OF A COIN (see: The George Raft Story)

SPINA DORSALE DEL DIAVOLO, LA (see: The Deserter)

5944 SPINOUT (Norman Taurog)
      (also: California Holiday)
      Filmf: v. IX (1966), p. 349; comp., cp. cr.
      Films & F: v. 13, n. 3 (Dec., 1966), p. 53; Richard Davis, 300 wds., cp. cr.

SPINSTER (see: Two Loves)

5945 SPIRAL ROAD, THE (Robert Mulligan)
      Filmf: v. V (1962), p. 187; comp., cp. cr.
      Films & F: v. 8, n. 12 (Sept., 1962), p. 34; Robin Bean, 375 wds., cp. cr.
      Films in R: v. XIII, n. 7 (Aug.-Sept., 1962), p. 425; Adelaide Comerford,
          175 wds., no cr.
      Movie: n. 2 (Sept., 1962), p. 35; 100 wds., no cr.

5946 SPIRIT IS WILLING, THE (William Castle)
      Filmf: v. XI (1968), p. 238; comp., cp. cr.
      Films & F: v. 15, n. 1 (Oct., 1968), pp. 52-53; Michael Armstrong, 150
          wds., cp. cr.

5947 SPIRIT OF ST. LOUIS, THE (Billy Wilder)
      Films & F: v. 3, n. 9 (June, 1957), p. 24; Rupert Butler, 400 wds., cp. cr.
      Films in R: v. VIII, n. 3 (Mar., 1957), pp. 126-128; Henry Hart, 700 wds.,
          no cr.
      Sight & S: v. 27, n. 1 (Summer, 1957), pp. 38-39; John Gillett, 900 wds.,
          pt. cr.

SPIRITS OF THE DEAD (see: Tales of Mystery and Imagination)

5948 SPLENDID DAYS, THE (Igor Talankin and Georgy Daniela)
      (also: Seryozha)
      Films & F: v. 8, n. 11 (Aug., 1962), pp. 30-31; Raymond Durgnat, 600
          wds., cp. cr.

5949 SPLENDOR IN THE GRASS (Elia Kazan)
      Film: n. 31 (Spring, 1962), p. 13; Peter Armitage, 200 wds., no cr.
      F Quarterly: v. XV, n. 2 (Winter, 1961-1962), p. 61; R. M. Hodgens, 200
          wds., no cr.
      Filmf: v. IV (1961), p. 239; comp. cp. cr.
      Films & F: v. 8, n. 5 (Feb., 1962), pp. 29-30; Robin Bean, 600 wds., cp. cr.
      Films in R: v. XII, n. 9 (Nov., 1961), pp. 555-556; Arthur B. Clark, 350
          wds., no cr.

5950 SPLIT, THE (Gordon Flemyng)
      Filmf: v. XI (1968), p. 429; comp., cp. cr.
      Films & F: v. 15, n. 5 (Feb., 1969), p. 46; Chris Jones, 200 wds., cp. cr.

5951 SPLIT SECOND (Dick Powell)
      Films & F: v. 15, n. 4 (Jan., 1969), pp. 82; Kingsley Canham, 350 wds., no
          cr.
      Films in R: v. IV, n. 5 (May, 1953), p. 242; 175 wds., pt. cr.

5952 SPORTING CLUB, THE (Larry Peerce)
      Filmf: v. XIV (1971), p. 407; comp., cp. cr.

SPOSA BELLA, LA (see: The Angel Wore Red)

5953 SPREE (Mitchell Leisen and Walon Green)
      Filmf: v. X (1967), p. 380; comp., cp. cr.

5954 SPRING AND PORT WINE (Peter Hammond)
      Films & F: v. 16, n. 6 (Mar., 1970), p. 51; Gordon Gow, 300 wds., cp. cr.

5955 SPRING IN PARK LANE (Herbert Wilcox)
      Sight & S: v. 17, n. 66 (Summer, 1948), p. 100; Arthur Vesselo, 200 wds.,
          pt. cr.

5956 SPRING REUNION (Jerry Bresler)
      Films & F: v. 3, n. 5 (Feb., 1957), p. 25; Peter John Dyer, 100 wds., cp. cr.

5957 SPUD'S SUMMER: INTERRACIAL UNDERSTANDING (CBS News)
      F Lib Quarterly: v. 1, n. 2 (Spring, 1968), pp. 35-36; Naomi S. Weiss, 500
          wds., pt. cr.

5958 SPY IN THE GREEN HAT, THE (Joseph Sargent)
      Films & F: v. XIII, n. 6 (Mar., 1967), p. 34; David Adams, 400 wds., cp. cr.

5959 SPY IN THE SKY (W. Lee Wilder)
      Filmf: v. I (1958), p. 202; comp., cp. cr.

5960 SPY IN YOUR EYE (Vittorio Sala)
      (also: Belino, Appuntamento Per Le Spie; Berlin, Appointment for the
          Spies)
      Filmf: v. IX (1966), p. 111; comp., cp. cr.
      Films & F: v. 13, n. 1 (Oct., 1966), p. 16; David McGillivray, 150 wds., cp.
          cr.

      SPY KILLED AT BEIRUT, THE (see: Secret Agent Fireball)

5961 SPY WHO CAME IN FROM THE COLD, THE (Martin Ritt)
      Cinema: v. 3, n. 2 (Mar., 1966), p. 50; Rory Guy, 475 wds., pt. cr.
      F Quarterly: v. XIX, n. 4 (Summer, 1966), pp. 60-64; Elinor Halprin, 1700
          wds., pt. cr.
      Films in R: v. XVII, n. 1 (Jan., 1966), pp. 47-48; Wilfred Mifflin, 225 wds.,
          no cr.
      Sight & S: v. 35, n. 2 (Spring, 1966), p. 94; James Price, 1000 wds., pt. cr.

5962 SPY WITH A COLD NOSE, THE (Daniel Petrie)
      Filmf: v. IX (1966), p. 347; comp., cp. cr.

5963 SPY WITH MY FACE, THE (John Newland)
      Filmf: v. IX (1966), p. 77; comp., cp. cr.

      SPYLARKS (see: The Intelligence Men)

5964 SQUAD CAR (Ed Leftwich)
      Filmf: v. III (1960), p. 351; comp., cp. cr.

5965 SQUARE OF VIOLENCE (Leonardo Bercovici)
      (also: Nasilje Na Trgu)
      Filmf: v. VI (1963), p. 277; comp., cp. cr.
      Films & F: v. 9, n. 8 (May, 1963), p. 33; Tony Mallerman, 350 wds., cp. cr.

5966 SQUARE PEG, THE (John Paddy Carstairs)
      Films & F: v. 5, n. 5 (Feb., 1959), p. 24; Peter John Dyer, 200 wds., cp. cr.

      STACHKA (see: Strike)

      STADION (see: The Stadium)

5967 STADIUM, THE (Stanislaw Jedryko)
      (also: Stadion)
      F Quarterly: v. XV, n. 1 (Fall, 1961), pp. 51-54; Roger Sandall, 1250 wds.,
          no cr.

      STADT OHNE MITLEID (see: Town Without Pity)

5968 STAGE FRIGHT (Alfred Hitchcock)
      F Comment: v. 6, n. 3 (Fall, 1970), pp. 49-50; Molly Haskell, 1200 wds.,
          cp. cr.
      Films in R: v. I, n. 3 (Apr., 1950), pp. 23-25; Arthur Knight, 650 wds., pt.
          cr.
      Sight & S: v. 19, n. 5 (July, 1950), pp. 207-208; Simon Harcourt-Smith,
          1100 wds., pt. cr.

5969 STAGE STRUCK (Sidney Lumet)
      Filmf: v. I (1958), p. 62; comp., cp. cr.

Films & F: v. 4, n. 10 (July, 1958), pp. 26-27; Richard Roud, 375 wds., cp. cr.

Films in R: v. IX, n. 3 (Mar., 1958), pp. 142-143; Courtland Phipps, 350 wds., no cr.

Sight & S: v. 27, n. 5 (Summer, 1958), p. 253; John Cutts, 400 wds., pt. cr.

5970 STAGE TO THUNDER ROCK (William F. Claxton)
Filmf: v. VII (1964), p. 253; comp., cp. cr.
Films & F: v. 10, n. 12 (Sept., 1964), pp. 18-19; Allen Eyles, 450 wds., cp. cr.

5971 STAGECOACH (Gordon Douglas)
Filmf: v. IX (1966), p. 156; comp., cp. cr.
Films & F: v. 12, n. 10 (July, 1966), p. 12; Gordon Gow, 650 wds., cp. cr.

5972 STAGECOACH TO DANCERS' ROCK (Earl Bellamy)
Filmf: v. V (1962), p. 368; comp., cp. cr.

5973 STAIN ON THE SNOW, THE (Luis Saslavsky)
(also: La Neige Etait Sale)
Films & F: v. 5, n. 4 (Jan., 1959), p. 25; Richard Roud, 375 wds., cp. cr.

5974 STAINED GLASS AT FAIRFORD, THE (Basil Wright)
Sight & S: v. 26, n. 3 (Winter, 1956-1957), p. 155; John Gillett, 150 wds., pt. cr.

5975 STAIRCASE (Stanley Donen)
Filmf: v. XII (1969), p. 446; comp., cp. cr.
Films & F: v. 16, n. 3 (Dec., 1969), pp. 42-43; David Austen, 600 wds., cp. cr.
Films in R: v. XX, n. 8 (Oct., 1969), pp. 512-513; Eunice Sinkler, 150 wds., no cr.
Focus: n. 5 (Oct., 1969), pp. 25-26; Charles Flynn, 1100 wds., no cr.

STAIRWAY TO HEAVEN (see: A Matter of Life and Death)

5976 STAKEOUT (James Landis)
Filmf: v. V (1962), p. 361; comp., cp. cr.

5977 STAKEOUT ON DOPE STREET (Irvin Kershner)
Filmf: v. I (1958), p. 79; comp., cp. cr.
Films & F: v. 5, n. 6 (Mar., 1959), p. 22; Peter G. Baker, 250 wds., cp. cr.
Sight & S: v. 28, n. 3-4 (Summer-Autumn, 1959), p. 174; Peter John Dyer, 300 wds., pt. cr.

5978 STALAG 17 (Billy Wilder)
Films in R: v. IV, n. 6 (June-July, 1953), pp. 302-303; 170 wds., pt. cr.

5979 STALKING MOON, THE (Robert Mulligan)
Filmf: v. XII (1969), p. 4; comp., cp. cr.
Films & F: v. 15, n. 6 (Mar., 1969), pp. 51-52; Gordon Gow, 700 wds., cp. cr.
Films in R: v. XX, n. 3 (Mar., 1969), pp. 177-178; Page Cook, 325 wds., no cr.
Sight & S: v. 38, n. 2 (Spring, 1969), pp. 96-97; Philip French, 900 wds., pt. cr.

5980 STAMPEDED (Gordon Douglas)
(also: The Big Land)
Films & F: v. 3, n. 9 (June, 1957), pp. 23-24; Rupert Butler, 350 wds., cp. cr.

5981 STAR, THE (Stuart Heisler)
Sight & S: v. 22, n. 4 (Apr.-June, 1953), pp. 193-194; James Morgan, 1200 wds., pt. cr.

5982 STAR! (Robert Wise)
Filmf: v. XI (1968), p. 295; comp., cp. cr.
Films & F: v. 14, n. 12 (Sept., 1968), pp. 37, 40; Gordon Gow, 650 wds., cp. cr.

Films in R: v. XIX, n. 10 (Dec., 1968), pp. 646-647; Elaine Rothschild, 275
wds., no cr.
Movie: n. 16 (Winter, 1968-1969), p. 39; Mark Shivas, 100 wds., no cr.

STAR-BADGES, SOLDIERS (see: The Red and the White)

5983 STAR IN THE NIGHT (Don Siegel)
Films & F: v. 15, n. 9 (June, 1969), pp. 85-86; Kingsley Canham, 575 wds.,
no cr.

5984 STAR IS BORN, A (George Cukor)
Films in R: v. V, n. 9 (Nov., 1954), pp. 479-482; Henry Hart, 750 wds., no
cr.
Sight & S: v. 24, n. 4 (Spring, 1955), pp. 194-195; Penelope Houston, 900
wds., pt. cr.

5985 STAR SPANGLED GIRL (Jerry Paris)
Filmf: v. XIV (1971), p. 670; comp., cp. cr.

STARI KHOTTABYCH (see: The Flying Carpet)

5986 STARK FEAR (Ned Hockman)
Filmf: v. V (1962), p. 361; comp., cp. cr.

5987 STARK LOVE (Karl Brown)
Film: n. 53 (Winter, 1968-1969), pp. 15-18; Kevin Brownlow, 600 wds., no
cr.

5988 STARS (Konrad Wolf)
Films & F: v. 7, n. 8 (May, 1961), p. 28; Phillip Riley, 550 wds., cp. cr.

5989 STARS IN MY CROWN (Jacques Tourneur)
Films in R: v. II, n. 2 (Feb., 1951), p. 41; Thomas T. Foose, 250 wds., pt.
cr.

5990 STARS LOOK DOWN, THE (Carol Reed)
Films & F: v. 8, n. 4 (Jan., 1962), pp. 22-23; Richard Whitehall, 3000 wds.,
cp. cr.

START, THE (see: Le Départe)

5991 STATE FAIR (Jose Ferrer)
Filmf: v. V (1962), p. 75; comp., cp. cr.
Films & F: v. 8, n. 9 (June, 1962), p. 36; John Cutts, 425 wds., cp. cr.
Films in R: v. XIII, n. 4 (Apr., 1962), pp. 234-235; Romano Tozzi, 400
wds., no cr.

5992 STATE SECRET (Sidney Gilliat)
(also: The Great Manhunt)
Films in R: v. I, n. 9 (Dec., 1950), p. 41; Thomas T. Foose, 125 wds., pt. cr.

5993 STATION SIX — SAHARA (Seth Holt)
(also: Endstation 13 Sahara)
Filmf: v. VII (1964), p. 310; comp., cp. cr.
Films & F: v. 10, n. 2 (Nov., 1963), p. 31, 33; Gordon Gow, 425 wds., cp.
cr.
Movie: n. 11, p. 34; 150 wds., no cr.

5994 STATUE, THE (Rod Amateau)
Filmf: v. XIV (1971), p. 65; comp., cp. cr.
Films & F: v. 17, n. 9 (June, 1971), p. 72; Margaret Tarratt, 300 wds., cp.
cr.

5995 STAY AWAY, JOE (Peter Tewksbury)
Filmf: v. XI (1968), p. 269; comp., cp. cr.
Filmd & F: v. 15, n. 12 (Sept., 1969), p. 66; David Austen, 400 wds., cp. cr.

STAZIONE TERMINI (see: Indiscretion of an American Wife)

5996 STEAGLE, THE (Paul Sylbert)
Filmf: v. XIV (1971), p. 539; comp., cp. cr.

5997 STEEL BAYONET (Michael Carreras)
 Filmf: v. I (1958), p. 32; comp., cp. cr.
 Films & F: v. 3, n. 10 (July, 1957), p. 25; Derek Conrad, 200 wds., cp. cr.

5998 STEEL CLAW, THE (George Montgomery)
 Filmf: v. IV (1961), p. 104; comp., cp. cr.

5999 STEFANIA (Yiannis Dalianidis)
 (also: Stephania)
 Filmf: v. XI (1968), p. 474; comp., cp. cr.

6000 STEFANIE (Josef von Baky)
 Filmf: v. II (1959), p. 174; comp., cp. cr.

6001 STELLA (Michael Cacoyannis)
 F Culture: v. 3, n. 3 (1957), p. 17; Andrew Sarris, 350 wds., pt. cr.
 Films & F: v. 3, n. 1 (Oct., 1956), pp. 26-27; Peter John Dyer, 450 wds.,
  cp. cr.
 Films in R: v. VIII, n. 4 (Apr., 1957), pp. 173-174; R. V. Tozzi, 300 wds.,
  no cr.
 Sight & S: v. 26, n. 2 (Autumn, 1956), p. 96; Penelope Houston, 475 wds.,
  pt. cr.

6002 STEM VAN HET WATER, DE (Bert Haanstra)
 (also: The Voice In The Water)
 Interntl F G: v. 5 (1968), p. 111; 200 wds., pt. cr.

 STEO SAM CAK I SRECNE CIGANE (see: I Even Met Happy Gypsies)

6003 STEP DOWN TO TERROR (Harry Keller)
 (also: The Silent Stranger)
 Filmf: v. II (1959), p. 42; comp., cp. cr.

 STEPHANIA (see: Stefania)

6004 STEPIEN RISKA (Llya Averbach)
 (also: The Risk)
 Interntl F G: v. 7 (1970), p. 240; Nina Hibbin, 250 wds., pt. cr.

6005 STEPMOTHER, THE (Manuel Mur Oti)
 Films & F: v. 4, n. 5 (Feb., 1958), pp. 24-25; Rupert Butler, 200 wds., cp.
  cr.

 STEPPA, LA (see: The Steppe)

6006 STEPPE, THE (Alberto Lattuada)
 (also: La Steppa)
 Filmf: v. VI (1963), p. 253; comp., cp. cr.
 Films & F: v. 9, n. 10 (July, 1963), p. 25; Gordon Gow, 350 wds., cp. cr.

6007 STEREO (David Cronenberg)
 Take One: v. 2, n. 3 (1969), p. 22; Joe Medjuck, 300 wds., pt. cr.

6008 STERILE CUCKOO, THE (Alan J. Paluka)
 (also: Pookie)
 F Quarterly: v. XXIII, n. 3 (Spring, 1970), pp. 52-54; Paul Warshow, 1600
  wds., pt. cr.
 F Quarterly: v. XXIII, n. 3 (Spring, 1970), pp. 55-58; Stephen Farber, 1700
  wds., no cr.
 Filmf: v. XII (1969), p. 433; comp., cp. cr.
 Films & F: v. 16, n. 6 (Mar., 1970), pp. 39, 42; Gordon Gow, 1000 wds.,
  cp. cr.
 Films in R: v. XX, n. 9 (Nov., 1969), p. 572; Louise Bartlett, 150 wds., no
  cr.
 Sight & S: v. 39, n. 1 (Winter, 1969-1970), p. 51; Tom Milne, 300 wds., pt.
  cr.

6009 STILETTO (Bernard Kowalski)
 Filmf: v. XII (1969), p. 427; comp., cp. cr.

6010 STILL LIFE (Robert Beavers)
        F Culture: n. 52 (Spring, 1971), pp. 56-57; Gregory Markopoulos, 450
            wds., no cr.

6011 STING OF DEATH (William Grefe)
        Films & F: v. 15, n. 1 (Oct., 1968), p. 52; David Austen, 200 wds., cp. cr.
        Filmf: v. X (1967), p. 438; comp., cp. cr.

6012 STITCH IN TIME, A (Robert Asher)
        Films & F: v. 10, n. 4 (Jan., 1964), pp. 30-31; Allen Eyles, 300 wds., cp. cr.

6013 STOLEN HOURS (Daniel Petrie)
        Filmf: v. VI (1963), p. 215; comp., cp. cr.
        Films & F: v. 10, n. 7 (Apr., 1964), p. 32; Richard Whitehall, 200 wds., cp.
            cr.

6014 STOLEN KISSES (Francois Truffaut)
        (also: Baisers Volés)
        F Heritage: v. 5, n. 2 (Winter, 1969-1970), pp. 11-16; William Paul, 1600
            wds., no cr.
        F Quarterly: v. XXII, n. 4 (Summer, 1969), pp. 56-59; Gary Carey, 2100
            wds., pt. cr.
        Filmf: v. XII (1969), p. 49; comp., cp. cr.
        Films & F: v. 15, n. 9 (June, 1969), p. 44; Gordon Gow, 800 wds., cp. cr.
        Films in R: v. XX, n. 2 (Feb., 1969), pp. 116-117; Louise Corbin, 150 wds.,
            no cr.
        Interntl F G: v. 7 (1970), pp. 121-122; Peter Cowie, 275 wds., pt. cr.
        Screen: v. 10, n. 3 (May-June, 1969), pp. 90-95; Donald Allen, 2000 wds.,
            cp. cr.
        Sight & S: v. 38, n. 3 (Summer, 1969), pp. 153-154; Gavin Millar, 1200
            wds., pt. cr.

6015 STOP! LOOK! AND LAUGH! (Jules White)
        Filmf: v. III (1960), p. 288; comp., cp. cr.

6016 STOP ME BEFORE I KILL! (Val Guest)
        (also: The Full Treatment)
        Filmf: v. IV (1961), p. 142; comp., cp. cr.
        Films & F: v. 7, n. 5 (Feb., 1961), p. 31; Phillip Riley, 350 wds., cp. cr.

6017 STOP THE WORLD — I WANT TO GET OFF (Philip Saville)
        Cinema: v. 3, n. 3 (July, 1966), p. 48; John Cutts, 300 wds., pt. cr.
        Filmf: v. IX (1966), p. 128; comp., cp. cr.
        Films in R: v. XVII, n. 6 (June-July, 1966), p. 379; Henry Hart, 250 wds.,
            no cr.

6018 STOP TRAIN 349 (Rolf Haedrich)
        (also: Verspäting in Marienborn)
        Filmf: v. VII (1964), p. 334; comp., cp. cr.
        Films in R: v. XV, n. 6 (June-July, 1964), pp. 371-371; Arthur B. Clark,
            250 wds., no cr.

      STORA AVENTYRET, DET (see: The Great Adventure)

      STORIA DI UNA DONNA (see: Story of a Woman)

      STORIA MODERNA: L'APE REGINA, UNA (see: The Conjugal Bed)

6019 STORK TALK (Michael Forlong)
        Filmf: v. VII (1964), p. 363; comp., cp. cr.
        Films & F: v. 8, n. 8 (May, 1962), p. 34; Philip Strick, 300 wds., cp. cr.

6020 STORM CENTER (Daniel Taradash)
        F Culture: v. 2, n. 3 (1956), pp. 25-26; George N. Fenin, 1200 wds., pt. cr.
        Films & F: v. 2, n. 10 (July, 1956), pp. 23-24; Peter G. Baker, 300 wds., cp.
            cr.
        Films in R: v. VII, n. 8 (Oct., 1956), p. 417; 300 wds., no cr.
        Sight & S: v. 26, n. 1 (Summer, 1956), p. 34; Penelope Houston, 375 wds.,
            pt. cr.

6021 STORM OVER THE NILE (Terence Young and Zoltan Korda)
      Films & F: v. 2, n. 3 (Dec., 1955), p. 18; Peter G. Baker, 300 wds., cp. cr.

6022 STORM WARNING (Richard Brooks)
      Sight & S: v. 19, n. 11 (Mar., 1951), pp. 439-440; Penelope Houston, 900
      wds., pt. cr.

6023 STORY IN SAND (Dennis Hill)
      Interntl F G: v. 2 (1965), p. 54; 75 wds., pt. cr.

6024 STORY OF A THREE DAY PASS, THE (Melvin Van Peebles)
      (also: The Pass; La Permission)
      Filmf: v. XI (1968), p. 278; comp., cp. cr.
      Journal of P C: v. IV, n. 3 (Winter, 1971), pp. 678-679; Charles D. Peavy,
      600 wds., no cr.

6025 STORY OF A WOMAN (Leonardo Bercovici)
      (also: Storia di una Donna)
      Filmf: v. XIV (1971), p. 427; comp., cp. cr.

      STORY OF CRUELTY, A (see: Naked Youth)

6026 STORY OF DR. SCHWEITZER (Andre Haguet)
      Films & F: v. 4, n. 7 (Apr., 1958), p. 24; Ken Gay, 500 wds., cp. cr.

6027 STORY OF ESTHER COSTELLO, THE (David Miller)
      (also: The Golden Virgin)
      Films & F: v. 3, n. 12 (Sept., 1957), p. 24; Peter G. Baker, 400 wds., cp. cr.

6028 STORY OF GILBERT AND SULLIVAN, THE (Sidney Gilliat)
      (also: The Great Gilbert and Sullivan)
      Sight & S: v. 23, n. 1 (July-Sept., 1953), pp. 32-33; Philip Hope-Wallace,
      600 wds., pt. cr.

6029 STORY OF JOSEPH AND HIS BRETHREN, THE (Irving Rapper and Luciano
      Ricci)
      Filmf: v. V (1962), p. 325; comp., cp. cr.

      STORY OF LENNY BRUCE — DIRTYMOUTH, THE (see: Dirtymouth)

6030 STORY OF MANDY, THE (Alexander Mackendrick)
      Films in R: v. IV, n. 3 (Mar., 1953), p. 154; 125 wds., pt. cr.

6031 STORY OF MANKIND, THE (Irwin Allen)
      Filmf & F: v. 4, n. 4 (Jan., 1958), p. 27; Peter G. Baker, 300 wds., cp. cr.
      Films in R: v. VIII, n. 10 (Dec., 1957), pp. 525-527; Hugh de Sola Day, 450
      wds., no cr.

      STORY OF OSAKA CASTLE, THE (see: Daredevil in the Castle)

6032 STORY OF PRIVATE POOLEY, THE (Kurt Jung-Alsen)
      Films & F: v. 9, n. 5 (Feb., 1963), p. 37; Tony Mallerman, 400 wds., cp. cr.

6033 STORY OF ROBIN HOOD, THE (Ken Annakin)
      Films in R: v. III, n. 4 (Apr., 1952), p. 200; 150 wds., pt. cr.

6034 STORY OF RUTH, THE (Henry Koster)
      Filmf: v. III (1960), p. 141; comp., cp. cr.
      Films & F: v. 6, n. 12 (Sept., 1960), p. 22; Richard Whitehall, 200 wds., cp.
      cr.
      Films in R: v. XI, n. 7 (Aug.-Sept., 1960), pp. 428-429; Justin Hazlitt, 300
      wds., no cr.

6035 STORY OF THE COUNT OF MONTE CRISTO, THE (Claude Autant-Lara)
      Filmf: v. V (1962), p. 255; comp., cp. cr.

6036 STORY OF THREE LOVES, THE (Vincente Minnelli and Gorrfried Rein-
      hardt)
      Films in R: v. IV, n. 4 (Apr., 1953), p. 198; 150 wds., pt. cr.

6037 STORY OF VICKIE, THE (Ernst Marischka)
(also: Maedchenjahre Einer Koenigin)
Filmf: v. I (1958), p. 34; comp., cp. cr.
Films in R: v. IX, n. 3 (Mar., 1958), p. 145; Charles A. Butler, 150 wds., no cr.

6038 STORY ON PAGE ONE, THE (Clifford Odets)
Filmf: v. III (1960), p. 1; comp., cp. cr.
Films & F: v. 6, n. 7 (Apr., 1960), p. 23; Richard Whitehall, 250 wds., cp. cr.
Films in R: v. XI, n. 2 (Feb., 1960), pp. 103-105; Ellen Fitzpatrick, 350 wds., no cr.

STOWAWAY GIRL (see: Manuela)

6039 STOWAWAY IN THE SKY (Albert Lamorisse)
Filmf: v. V (1962), p. 359; comp., cp. cr.
Films in R: v. 7 (Aug.-Sept., 1962), pp. 425-426; Louise Corbin, 150 wds., no cr.

6040 STRADA, LA (Federico Fellini)
F Culture: v. 2, n. 1 (1956), pp. 11-14; Edouard de Laurot, 3500 wds., pt. cr.
Films & F: v. 1, n. 3 (Dec., 1954), p. 20; Ernest Borneman, 325 wds., cp. cr.
Films & F: v. 2, n. 4 (Jan., 1956), p. 22; P. L. Mannock, 250 wds., cp. cr.
Films & F: v. 16, n. 1 (Oct., 1969), p. 58; Gordon Gow, 1050 wds., cp. cr.
Films in R: v. VII, n. 7 (Aug.-Sept., 1956), pp. 351-352; Diana Willing, 500 wds., no cr.

6041 STRAFBATALLION 999 (Harold Philipp)
Films & F: v. 9, n. 6 (Mar., 1963), p. 40; Robin Bean, 600 wds., cp. cr.

6042 STRAIT-JACKET (William Castle)
Filmf: v. VII (1964), p. 1; comp., cp. cr.
Films & F: v. 10, n. 12 (Sept., 1964), pp. 20-21; Raymond Durgnat, 500 wds., cp. cr.
Films in R: v. XV, n. 2 (Feb., 1964), pp. 115-116; Elaine Rothschild, 100 wds., no cr.

6043 STRANGE AFFAIR, THE (David Greene)
F Quarterly: v. XXII, n. 4 (Summer, 1969), p. 60; Stephen Farber, 300 wds., no cr.
Filmf: v. XI (1968), p. 300; comp., cp. cr.
Films & F: v. 15, n. 1 (Oct., 1968), pp. 41-42; Raymond Durgnat, 1400 wds., cp. cr.
Sight & S: v. 37, n. 4 (Autumn, 1968), pp. 208-209; Jack Ibberson, 500 wds., pt. cr.

6044 STRANGE BEDFELLOWS (Melvin Frank)
Filmf: v. VIII (1965), p. 73; comp., cp. cr.
Films & F: v. 11, n. 7 (Apr., 1965), p. 28; Allen Eyles, 600 wds., cp. cr.

6045 STRANGE CASE OF BLONDIE, THE (Ken Hughes)
Films & F: v. 1, n. 4 (Jan., 1955), p. 19; Graham Shipham, 150 wds., cp. cr.

6046 STRANGE CASE OF DR. MANNING (Arthur Crabtree)
Filmf: v. I (1958), p. 300; comp., cp. cr.

STRANGE DECEPTION (see: Il Cristo Probito)

STRANGE OBSESSION, THE (see: The Witch in Love)

STRANGE ONE (see: End As a Man)

6047 STRANGER, THE (Orson Welles)
Sight & S: v. 15, n. 59 (Autumn, 1946), p. 98; Roger Manvell, 350 wds., no cr.

6048 STRANGER, THE (Luchino Visconti)
        (also: L'Etranger; II Straniero; The Outsider)
        F Quarterly: v. XXI, n. 4 (Summer, 1968), pp. 43-45; Neal Oxenhandler,
            1250 wds., pt. cr.
        Filmf: v. X (1967), p. 393; comp., cp. cr.
        Films & F: v. 15, n. 2 (Nov., 1968), pp. 38-39; Raymond Durgnat, 2100
            wds., cp. cr.
        Films in R: v. XIX, n. 2 (Feb., 1968), pp. 110-111; Tatiana Balkoff
            Drowne, 200 wds., no cr.
        Screen: v. 10, n. 1 (Jan.-Feb., 1969), pp. 99-104; Margaret Tarratt, 1600
            wds., cp. cr.
        Sight & S: v. 37, n. 3 (Summer, 1968), pp. 148-150; Max Kozloff, 2000
            wds., pt. cr.

      STRANGER, THE (Roger Corman/see: The Intruder)

6049 STRANGER IN MY ARMS (Helmut Kautner)
        Filmf: v. II (1959), p. 44; comp., cp. cr.

      STRANGER IN THE HOUSE (see: Cop-Out)

6050 STRANGER IN TOWN, A (Vance Lewis)
        (also: Un Dollaro Tra I Denti; A Dollar Between the Teeth; For a Dollar in
            the Teeth)
        Filmf: v. XI (1968), p. 149; comp., cp. cr.
        Films & F: v. 15, n. 8 (May, 1969), pp. 45-46; David Hutchison, 350 wds.,
            cp. cr.

6051 STRANGER KNOCKS, A (Johan Jacobsen)
        (also: En Fremmed Banker Paa)
        F Quarterly: v. XIV, n. 2 (Winter, 1960), pp. 53-55; Albert Johnson, 600
            wds., pt. cr.
        Filmf: v. VIII (1965), p. 104; comp., cp. cr.
        Films in R: v. XVI, n. 5 (May, 1965), p. 315; Helen Weldon Kuhn, 125
            wds., no cr.

6052 STRANGER ON THE PROWL (Joseph Losey)
        (also: Encounter; Imbraco a Mezzanotte)
        Films in R: v. V, n. 1 (Jan., 1954), p. 37; 200 wds., no cr.

6053 STRANGER ON THE THIRD FLOOR (Boris Ingster)
        Focus on F: n. 5 (Winter/Nov.-Dec., 1970), p. 36; Don Miller, 300 wds., pt.
            cr.

6054 STRANGER RETURNS, THE (Vance Lewis)
        (also: Un Uomo, Un Cavallo, E Una Pistola; A Man, A Horse and A Pistol)
        Filmf: v. XI (1968), p. 370; comp., cp. cr.

6055 STRANGERS IN THE CITY (Rick Carrier)
        F Quarterly: v. XVII, n. 1 (Fall, 1963), p. 47; James Stoller, 250 wds., no
            cr.
        Filmf: v. V (1962), p. 293; comp., cp. cr.

6056 STRANGERS ON A TRAIN (Alfred Hitchcock)
        Films in R: v. II, n. 6 (June-July, 1951), pp. 36-38; Henry Hart, 950 wds.,
            pt. cr.
        Sight & S: v. 21, n. 1 (Aug.-Sept., 1951), pp. 21-22; Richard Winnington,
            1000 wds., pt. cr.

6057 STRANGERS WHEN WE MEET (Richard Quine)
        Filmf: v. III (1960), p. 151; comp., cp. cr.
        Films & F: v. 7, n. 2 (Nov., 1960), p. 33; Robin Bean, 250 wds., cp. cr.

6058 STRANGLER, THE (Burt Topper)
        Filmf: v. VII (1964), p. 139; comp., cp. cr.

6059 STRANGLERS OF BOMBAY, THE (Anthony Hinds)
        Filmf: v. III (1960), p. 119; comp., cp. cr.
        Films & F: v. 6, n. 5 (Feb., 1960), p. 23; Peter G. Baker, 250 wds., cp. cr.

6060 STRANGLER'S WEB (John Moxey)
         Films & F: v. 13, n. 3 (Dec., 1966), pp. 52-53; David McGillivray, 100 wds.,
            cp. cr.

      STRANIERO, IL (see: The Stranger)

      STRANO VIZIO DELLA SIGNORO WARH, LO (see: Next!)

6061 STRATEGIA DEL RAGNO, LA (Bernardo Bertolucci)
         (also: The Spider's Strategy)
         Movie: n. 18 (Winter, 1970-1971), p. 40; Ian Cameron, 200 wds., no cr.

6062 STRATEGIC AIR COMMAND (Anthony Mann)
         F Culture: v. 1, n. 4 (Summer, 1955), p. 26; Andrew George Sarris, 125
            wds., pt. cr.
         Films & F: v. 1, n. 11 (Aug., 1955), p. 17; Derek Hill, 125 wds., cp. cr.
         Films in R: v. VI, n. 5 (May, 1955), p. 237; Henry Hart, 475 wds., pt. cr.

6063 STRATEGY OF TERROR (Jack Smight)
         (also: In Darkness Waiting)
         Filmf: v. XII (1969), p. 182; comp., cp. cr.

6064 STRAWBERRY STATEMENT, THE (Stuart Hagmann)
         F Quarterly: v. XXIV, n. 1 (Fall, 1970), p. 62; Robert Michaels, 350 wds.,
            no cr.
         F Soc Rev: v. 5, n. 8, pp. 31-36; Gary Crowdus, 2200 wds., cp. cr.
         Sight & S: v. 39, n. 3 (Summer, 1970), p. 160; Russell Campbell, 700 wds.,
            pt. cr.

6065 STRAY DOG (Akira Kurosawa)
         (also: Nora Inu)
         Cinema: v. 1, n. 4, p. 46; John Schrader, 450 wds., pt. cr.
         F Comment: v. 2, n. 1 (Winter, 1964), pp. 38-39; Sally Sherwin, 450 wds.,
            pt. cr.
         Filmf: v. VII (1964), p. 137; comp., cp. cr.
         Films in R: v. XV, n. 4 (Apr., 1964), pp. 240-241; James M. Beck, 100
            wds., no cr.

6066 STREET IS MY BEAT, THE (Irvin Berwick)
         Filmf: v. IX (1966), p. 180; comp., cp. cr.

6067 STREET OF DARKNESS (Robert Walker)
         Filmf: v. I (1958), p. 298; comp., cp. cr.

6068 STREET OF SHAME (Kenji Mizoguchi)
         Filmf: v. II (1959), p. 121; comp., cp. cr.
         Films & F: v. 4, n. 7 (Apr., 1958), p. 25; Peter John Dyer, 200 wds., cp. cr.
         Sight & S: v. 27, n. 4 (Spring, 1958), pp. 198-199; John Gillett, 700 wds.,
            pt. cr.

6069 STREET WITH NO NAME, THE (William Keighley)
         Films & F: v. 10, n. 9 (June, 1964), p. 28; Allen Eyles, 275 wds., cp. cr.

6070 STREETCAR NAMED DESIRE, A (Elia Kazan)
         Films in R: v. II, n. 10 (Dec., 1951), pp. 51-52; Hermine Rich Isaacs, 450
            wds., no cr.
         Films in R: v. II, n. 10 (Dec., 1951), pp. 52-54; Francis Taylor Patterson,
            750 wds., no cr.
         Films in R: v. II, n. 10 (Dec., 1951), pp. 54-55; Eleanor H. Nash, 500 wds.,
            no cr.
         Sight & S: v. 21, n. 4 (Apr.-June, 1952), pp. 170-171; Karel Reisz, 750
            wds., pt. cr.

      STREGA IN AMORE, LA (see: The Witch in Love)

      STREGHE, LE (see: The Witches)

      STRICTLY FOR PLEASURE (see: The Perfect Furlough)

6071 STRICTLY FOR THE BIRDS (Vernon Sewell)
         Films & F: v. 10, n. 7 (Apr., 1964), p. 29; David Rider, 300 wds., cp. cr.

STRIJD ZONDER EINDEN (see: The Rival World)

6072 STRIKE (Sergei Eisenstein)
(also: Stachka)
Cinema J: v. III (1963), pp. 7-16; John B. Kuiper, 1800 wds., no cr.
Films & F: v. 7, n. 6 (Mar., 1961), pp. 17-19, 38; John Cutts, 300 wds., cp. cr.
Sight & S: v. 26, n. 2 (Autumn, 1956), pp. 105-108; Ivor Montagu, 2000 wds., pt. cr.

STRIKERS, THE (see: The Organizer)

6073 STRIP (Peter Davis, Staffan Lemm and Don de Fina)
Films & F: v. 16, n. 1 (Oct., 1969), pp. 52-53; Brian Murphy, 550 wds., cp. cr.

6074 STRIP POKER (Pete Walker)
Films & F: v. 15, n. 3 (Dec., 1968), p. 45; David Austen, 150 wds., cp. cr.

STRIP-TEASE (see: Sweet Skin)

6075 STRIPPER, THE (Franklin J. Schaffner)
(also: Woman of Summer)
Filmf: v. VI (1963), p. 118; comp., cp. cr.
Films & F: v. 9, n. 9 (June, 1963), pp. 28-29; Robin Bean, 700 wds., cp. cr.
Films in R: v. XIV, n. 5 (May, 1963), p. 310; Adelaide Comerford, 300 wds., no cr.
Movie: n. 9, p. 35; 150 wds., no cr.
Sight & S: v. 32, n. 3 (Summer, 1963), p. 146; Elizabeth Sussex, 400 wds., pt. cr.

6076 STROMBOLI (Roberto Rossellini)
Films in R: v. I, n. 2 (Mar., 1950), pp. 27-28; John B. Turner, 350 wds., pt. cr.

STRONGER THAN FEAR (see: Edge of Doom)

6077 STRONGROOM (Vernon Sewell)
Filmf: v. VI (1963), p. 84; comp., cp. cr.

6078 STRUGGLE, THE (D. W. Griffith)
Movie: n. 14 (Autumn, 1965), pp. 43-44; Andrew Sarris, 650 wds., no cr.

6079 STRUGGLE IN ITALY (Jean-Luc Godard)
(also: Lotte in Italia)
F Quarterly: v. XXV, n. 1 (Fall, 1971), pp. 56-57; Bill Nichols, 600 wds., no cr.

6080 STRUKTURA KRYSZTALV (Krysztof Zanvssi)
(also: Crystal's Structure)
Interntl F G: v. 8 (1971), p. 225; Ryszard Koniczek, 175 wds., pt. cr.

6081 STUDENT PRINCE, THE (Richard Thorpe)
Films & F: v. 1, n. 1 (Oct., 1954), p. 24; Clayton Cole, 300 wds., cp. cr.

6082 STUDS LONIGAN (Irving Lerner)
F Quarterly: v. XV, n. 4 (Summer, 1962), pp. 60-61; Lawrence Grauman, Jr., 700 wds., pt. cr.
Filmf: v. III (1960), p. 298; comp., cp. cr.
Films & F: v. 10, n. 2 (Nov., 1963), pp. 24-25; John Cutts, 800 wds., cp. cr.
Films in R: v. XI, n. 8 (Oct., 1960), pp. 491-492; Robert C. Roman, 300 wds., no cr.

6083 STUDY IN TERROR, A (James Hill)
Filmf: v. IX (1966), p. 314; comp., cp. cr.
Films & F: v. 12, n. 4 (Jan., 1966), p. 29; Kevin Gough-Yates, 250 wds., cp. cr.
Films in R: v. XVII, n. 7 (Aug.-Sept., 1966), p. 453; 50 wds., no cr.
Sight & S: v. 35, n. 1 (Winter, 1965-1966), p. 44; John Russell Taylor, 500 wds., pt. cr.

6084 STUMP RUN (Edward Dew)
        Filmf: v. III (1960), p. 352; comp., cp. cr.

6085 STUNTMAN (Marcello Baldi)
        Films & F: v. 16, n. 9 (June, 1970), pp. 89-90; David Hutchison, 350 wds.,
            cp. cr.

6086 SUBJECT WAS ROSES, THE (Ula Grosbard)
        Filmf: v. XI (1968), p. 404; comp., cp. cr.
        Films in R: v. XIX, n. 9 (Nov., 1968), p. 579; Janet Hall, 200 wds., no cr.

6087 SUBMARINE SEAHAWK (Spencer B. Bennet)
        Filmf: v. II (1959), p. 13; comp., cp. cr.

6088 SUBMARINE X-1 (William Graham)
        Filmf: v. XII (1969), p. 249; comp., cp. cr.
        Films & F: v. 15, n. 8 (May, 1969), pp. 44-45; David Adams, 500 wds., cp.
            cr.

6089 SUBTERRANEANS, THE (Ranald McDougall)
        F Quarterly: v. XIV, n. 1 (Fall, 1960), p. 62; 150 wds., no cr.
        Filmf: v. III (1960), p. 190; comp., cp. cr.
        Films & F: v. 6, n. 11 (Aug., 1960), p. 25; Dal Vaughan, 400 wds., cp. cr.
        Films in R: v. XI, n. 7 (Aug.-Sept., 1960), pp. 430-431; Ellen Fitzpatrick,
            300 wds., no cr.

6090 SUBURBAN ROULETTE (Herschell Gordon Lewis)
        Filmf: v. XI (1968), p. 372; comp., cp. cr.

6091 SUBURBIA CONFIDENTIAL (A. C. Stephen)
        Filmf: v. IX (1966), p. 386; comp., cp. cr.

6092 SUBWAY IN THE SKY (Muriel Box)
        Filmf: v. II (1959), p. 341; comp., cp. cr.
        Films & F: v. 5, n. 7 (Apr., 1959), p. 23; Derek Conrad, 200 wds., cp. cr.

6093 SUCCESSO, IL (Mauro Morassi)
        Filmf: v. VIII (1965), p. 113; comp., cp. cr.

6094 SUCCUBUS (Jesus Franco)
        (also: Necronomicon)
        Filmf: v. XII (1969), p. 207; comp., cp. cr.

      SUCH A PRETTY LITTLE BEACH (see: Une Si Jolie Petite Plage)

6095 SUCH GOOD FRIENDS (Otto Preminger)
        Filmf: v. XIV (1971), p. 704; comp., cp. cr.
        Focus: n. 8 (Autumn, 1972), pp. 57-58; Myron Meisel, 1100 wds., no cr.

      SUCH MEN ARE DANGEROUS (see: The Racers)

6096 SUCKER, THE (Gerard Oury)
        (also: Le Corniaud)
        Filmf: v. X (1967), p. 303; comp., cp. cr.
        Films & F: v. 12, n. 3 (Dec., 1965), pp. 10-11; Kevin Gough-Yates, 300
            wds., cp. cr.

      SUDBA CHELOVEKA (see: Fate of a Man)

6097 SUDDEN TERROR (John Hough)
        (also: Eyewitness)
        Filmf: v. XIV (1971), p. 52; comp., cp. cr.
        Films & F: v. 17, n. 2 (Nov., 1970), pp. 50-51; Richard Davis, 500 wds., cp.
            cr.

6098 SUDDENLY (Lewis Allen)
        Films in R: v. V, n. 8 (Oct., 1954), p. 434; 50 wds., no cr.

6099 SUDDENLY, A WOMAN! (Anker)
        (also: Gudrun)
        Filmf: v. XI (1968), p. 488; comp., cp. cr.

6100 SUDDENLY, LAST SUMMER (Joseph Mankiewicz)
         F Quarterly: v. XIII, n. 3 (Spring, 1960), pp. 40-42; Albert Johnson, 1000
              wds., pt. cr.
         Filmf: v. II (1959), p. 319; comp., cp. cr.
         Films & F: v. 6, n. 9 (June, 1960), p. 21; Peter Baker, 800 wds., cp. cr.
         Films in R: v. XI, n. 1 (Jan., 1960), pp. 39-41; Henry Hart, 1000 wds., no
              cr.

6101 SUICIDE BATTALION (Edward L. Cahn)
         Filmf: v. I (1958), p. 46; comp., cp. cr.

6102 SUICIDE PILOTS (Perry Wolff)
         Films & F: v. 9, n. 2 (Nov., 1962), p. 39; Ken Gay, 500 wds., cp. cr.

      SUITABLE CASE FOR TREATMENT, A (see: Morgan)

6103 SUITOR, THE (Pierre Etaix)
         (also: Le Soupirant)
         F Quarterly: v. XVII, n. 3 (Spring, 1964), p. 63; Ernest Callenbach, 150
              wds., no cr.
         Filmf: v. VI (1963), p. 224; comp., cp. cr.
         Films & F: v. 10, n. 5 (Feb., 1964), p. 32; Raymond Durgnat, 600 wds., cp.
              cr.
         Films in R: v. XIV, n. 8 (Oct., 1963), pp. 491-492; Flavia Wharton, 450
              wds., no cr.
         Interntl F G: v. 1 (1964), p. 62; Peter Graham, 160 wds., pt. cr.
         Sight & S: v. 33, n. 2 (Spring, 1964), pp. 95-96; David Robinson, 700 wds.,
              no cr.

6104 SULLIVAN'S EMPIRE (Harvey Hart and Thomas Carr)
         Filmf: v. X (1967), p. 373; comp., cp. cr.

      SULT (see: Hunger)

6105 SUMMER AND SMOKE (Peter Glenville)
         Film: n. 32 (Summer, 1962), p. 22; Peter Armitage, 100 wds., no cr.
         Filmf: v. IV (1961), p. 275; comp., cp. cr.
         Films & F: v. 8, n. 8 (May, 1962), pp. 31-32; Peter Baker, 400 wds., cp. cr.
         Films in R: v. XII, n. 10 (Dec., 1961), p. 621; Flavia Wharton, 275 wds., no
              cr.
         Sight & S: v. 31, n. 2 (Spring, 1962), p. 95; Eric Rhods, 400 wds., pt. cr.

6106 SUMMER HOLIDAY (Rouben Mamoulian)
         Film: n. 44 (Winter, 1965-1966), pp. 26-27; Douglas McVay, 500 wds., no
              cr.
         Sequence: n. 6 (Winter, 1948-1949), pp. 44-46; Peter Ericsson, 1000 wds.,
              pt. cr.

6107 SUMMER HOLIDAY (Peter Yates)
         Filmf: v. VI (1963), p. 290; comp., cp. cr.
         Films & F: v. 9, n. 6 (Mar., 1963), p. 37; Raymond Durgnat, 350 wds., cp.
              cr.

6108 SUMMER INTERLUDE (Ingmar Bergman)
         (also: Illicit Interlude; Sommarlek; Summer Interlude)
         Films & F: v. 6, n. 3 (Dec., 1959), p. 25; Max Neufeld, 200 wds., cp. cr.

6109 SUMMER LOVE (Charles Haas)
         Filmf: v. I (1958), p. 95; comp., cp. cr.

      SUMMER MADNESS (see: Summertime)

6110 SUMMER MAGIC (James Nielson)
         Filmf: v. VI (1963), p. 160; comp., cp. cr.
         Films & F: v. 9, n. 10 (July, 1963), p. 27; Ian Johnson, 300 wds., cp. cr.

      SUMMER MANOEUVRES (see: Les Grandes Manoeuvres)

6111 SUMMER OF '42 (Robert Mulligan)
         F Quarterly: v. XXV, n. 2 (Winter, 1971-1972), pp. 57-58; Foster Hirsh,
              500 wds., no cr.

Filmf: v. XIV (1971), p. 133; comp., cp. cr.
Films & F: v. 17, n. 12 (Sept., 1971), pp. 54-55; Gordon Gow, 1050 wds.,
    cp. cr.
Films in R: v. XXII, n. 5 (May, 1971), pp. 310-311; Henry Hart, 425 wds.,
    no cr.
Sight & S: v. 40, n. 3 (Summer, 1971), pp. 166-167; Richard Combs, 600
    wds., pt. cr.

SUMMER OF THE SEVENTEENTH DOLL (see: Season of Passion)

6112 SUMMER PLACE, A (Delmer Daves)
Filmf: v. II (1959), p. 263; comp., cp. cr.
Films & F: v. 6, n. 4 (Jan., 1960), p. 23; Dai Vaughan, 250 wds., cp. cr.
Films in R: v. X, n. 9 (Nov., 1959), p. 562; Ellen Fitzpatrick, 200 wds., no
    cr.

SUMMER REBELLION (see: Kesakapina)

6113 SUMMER SKIN (Leopoldo Torre Nilsson)
(also: Piel de Verano)
F Quarterly: v. XV, n. 2 (Winter, 1961-1962), pp. 56-57; Ernest Callenbach,
    500 wds., pt. cr.
F Soc Rev: Jan. (1966), pp. 14-15; John Thomas, 900 wds., pt. cr.
Filmf: v. V (1962), p. 203; comp., cp. cr.
Films & F: v. 9, n. 6 (Mar., 1963), pp. 35-36; 800 wds., cp. cr.

6114 SUMMER TO REMEMBER, A (Georgy Danelia and Igor Talankin)
Filmf: v. IV (1961), p. 315; comp., cp. cr.
Films in R: v. XII, n. 10 Dec., 1961), pp. 623-624; Tatiana Balkoff Drowne,
    250 wds., no cr.

SUMMER TRAIL (see: Muurahaispolku)

6115 SUMMER WITH MONIKA (Ingmar Bergman)
(also: Monika; Sommaren Med Monika)
F Quarterly: v. XIII, n. 4 (Summer, 1960), pp. 60-61; 75 wds., no cr.
Films & F: v. 5, n. 5 (Fall, 1959), p. 25; Peter John Dyer, 500 wds., cp. cr.
Films in R: v. XI, n. 3 (Mar., 1960), pp. 173-174; Romano Tozzi, 175 wds.,
    no cr.

SUMMERPLAY (see: Summer Interlude)

6116 SUMMERTIME (David Lean)
(also: Summer Madness)
F Culture: v. 1, n. 4 (Summer, 1955), pp. 23-24; A. Landsbergis, 550 wds.,
    pt. cr.
Films & F: v. 2, n. 2 (Nov., 1955), p. 16; John Carroll, 150 wds., cp. cr.
Films in R: v. VI, n. 7 (Aug.-Sept., 1955), p. 342; Diana Willing, 200 wds.,
    pt. cr.
Sight & S: v. 25, n. 2 (Autumn, 1955), pp. 88-89; Gavin Lambert, 1500
    wds., pt. cr.

6117 SUMMERTREE (Anthony Newley)
Filmf: v. XIV (1971), p. 316; comp., cp. cr.

6118 SUMMONING OF EVERYMAN, THE (Richard L. Hilliard)
Films in R: v. VII, n. 1 (Jan., 1957), p. 81; 150 wds., no cr.

SUMURU (see: The Million Eyes of Su-Muru)

6119 SUN ALSO RISES, THE (Henry King)
F Culture: v. 3, n. 4 (Oct., 1957), pp. 17-18, Peter Walsh, 600 wds., pt. cr.
Films & F: v. 4, n. 3 (Dec., 1957), p. 23; Peter G. Baker, 350 wds., cp. cr.
Films in R: v. VIII, n. 8 (Oct., 1957), pp. 405-406; Henry Hart, 550 wds.,
    no cr.

6120 SUN LOVERS HOLIDAY (Konstantin Tratzcenko)
Filmf: v. IV (1961), p. 363; comp., cp. cr.

6121   SUN SHINES BRIGHT, THE (John Ford)
          Films in R: v. IV, n. 6 (June-July, 1953), pp. 300-301; 125 wds., pt. cr.
          Sight & S: v. 23, n. 2 (Oct.-Dec., 1953), pp. 88-89; Lindsay Anderson, 750
             wds., pt. cr.

          SUNA NO ONNA (see: Woman of the Dunes)

6122   SUNDAY (Dan Drasin)
          F Quarterly: v. XV, n. 4 (Summer, 1962), pp. 49-50; Ernest Callenbach,
             200 wds., no cr.

6123   SUNDAY, BLOODY SUNDAY (John Schlesinger)
          F Lib Quarterly: v. 5, n. 1 (Winter, 1971-1972), pp. 14-21; Lillian Gerard,
             4000 wds., no cr.
          Filmf: v. XIV (1971), p. 273; comp., cp. cr.
          Films & F: v. 17, n. 11 (Aug., 1971), pp. 50-51; Gordon Gow, 900 wds., cp.
             cr.
          Films in R: v. XXII, n. 8 (Oct., 1971), pp. 512-513; 150 wds., no cr.
          Interntl F G: v. 9 (1972), pp. 105-106; Gordon Gow, 150 wds., pt. cr.
          Sight & S: v. 40, n. 3 (Summer, 1971), p. 164; Jan Dawson, 1100 wds., pt.
             cr.
          Take One: v. 2, n. 12 (1971), pp. 18-19; John Hofsess, 750 wds., pt. cr.

6124   SUNDAY BY THE SEA (Anthony Simmons)
          Films in R: v. V, n. 4 (Apr., 1954), p. 196; R.K., 100 wds., no cr.

          SUNDAY IN AUGUST (see: Domenica d'Agosto)

6125   SUNDAY IN NEW YORK (Peter Tewksbury)
          Cinema: v. 2, n. 1 (Feb., 1964), p. 46; James Silke, 250 wds., pt. cr.
          F Quarterly: v. XVII, n. 4 (Summer, 1964), p. 59; R. M. Hodgens, 50 wds.,
             no cr.
          Filmf: v. VII (1964), p. 17; comp., cp. cr.
          Films & F: v. 10, n. 10 (July, 1964), pp. 21-22; Richard Whitehall, 650
             wds., cp. cr.
          Films in R: v. XV, n. 1 (Jan., 1964), p. 45; Emily Loeb, 150 wds., no cr.
          Movie: n. 12 (Spring, 1965), p. 37; Mark Shivas, 600 wds., no cr.
          Sight & S: v. 34, n. 1 (Winter, 1964-1965), p. 41; Elizabeth Sussex, 275
             wds., pt. cr.

6126   SUNDAY OF LIFE, THE (Jean Herman)
          Films & F: v. 13, n. 5 (Feb., 1967), pp. 32-33; Gordon Gow, 650 wds., cp.
             cr.

6127   SUNDAY ON THE ISLAND OF GRAND JATTE, OR, SEVEN AUTHORS IN
          SEARCH OF A READER, A (Frans Weisz)
          F Quarterly: v. XXI, n. 2 (Winter, 1967-1968), pp. 63-64; Albert Johnson,
             250 wds., no cr.

6128   SUNDAY ROMANCE, A (Imre Fehér)
          (also: Bakaruhaban)
          Films & F: v. 5, n. 10 (July, 1959), p. 25; Peter John Dyer, 300 wds., cp.
             cr.
          Sight & S: v. 28, n. 2 (Spring, 1958), p. 92; Robert Vas, 650 wds., pt. cr.

6129   SUNDAY SUN (Jan van der Hoeven)
          Interntl F G: v. 2 (1965), p. 113; 75 wds., pt. cr.

6130   SUNDAYS AND CYBELE (Serge Bourguignon)
          (also: Cybele ou les Dimanches de Ville D'Avray; Dimanches de Ville
             D'Avray)
          Cineaste: v. I, n. 1 (Summer, 1967), pp. 18-25, 28; Gary Crowdus, 4500
             wds., pt. cr.
          Cinema: v. 1, n. 4, p. 44; John Schrader, 350 wds., pt. cr.
          F Quarterly: v. XVI, n. 3 (Spring, 1963), pp. 52-53; Neal Oxenhandler, 650
             wds., pt. cr.
          F Soc Rev: Sept. (1967), pp. 13-15; Martius L. Elmore, 800 wds., cp. cr.
          Filmf: v. V (1962), p. 307; comp., cp. cr.
          Films & F: v. 9, n. 5 (Feb., 1963), pp. 34-35; Robin Bean, 600 wds., cp. cr.
          Films in R: v. XIII, n. 10 (Dec., 1962), pp. 623-624; Ellen Fitzpatrick, 450
             wds., no cr.

6131 SUNDOWNERS, THE (Fred Zinnemann)
    Filmf: v. III (1960), p. 317; comp., cp. cr.
    Films & F: v. 7, n. 5 (Feb., 1961), p. 30; Peter G. Baker, 350 wds., cp. cr.
    Films in R: v. XII, n. 1 (Jan., 1961), pp. 34-35; Henry Hart, 600 wds., no
       cr.
    Sight & S: v. 30, n. 1 (Winter, 1960-1961), pp. 36-37; Penelope Houston,
       600 wds., pt. cr.

6132 SUNFLOWER (Vittorio De Sica)
    (also: I Girasoli)
    Films in R: v. XXI, n. 9 (Nov., 1970), pp. 574-575; Henry Hart, 400 wds.,
       no cr.

    SUNO NO ONNA (see: Woman in the Dunes)

6133 SUNRISE (F. W. Murnau)
    F Comment: v. 7, n. 2 (Summer, 1971), pp. 16-19; Molly Haskell, 2200
       wds., cp. cr.

6134 SUNRISE AT CAMPOBELLO (Vincent J. Donehue)
    F Quarterly: v. XIV, n. 2 (Winter, 1960), p. 62; 150 wds., no cr.
    Filmf: v. III (1960), p. 229; comp., cp. cr.
    Films & F: v. 7, n. 10 (July, 1961), p. 28; John Cutts, 400 wds., cp. cr.
    Films in R: v. XI, n. 8 (Oct., 1960), pp. 488-489; Griswold Banning, 450
       wds., no cr.
    Sight & S: v. 30, n. 2 (Spring, 1961), p. 89; Arlene Croce, 750 wds., pt. cr.

6135 SUN'S BURIAL, THE (Nagisa Oshima)
    (also: Taiyo No Hakaba)
    Film: n. 58 (Spring, 1970), p. 4; 50 wds., pt. cr.

6136 SUNSCORCHED (Mark Stevens)
    Filmf: v. XI (1968), p. 538; comp., cp. cr.

6137 SUNSET BOULEVARD (Billy Wilder)
    Films in R: v. I, n. 4 (May-June, 1950), pp. 28-33; James Agee, 1900 wds.,
       pt. cr.
    Sequence: n. 12 (Autumn, 1950), pp. 16-17; L.G.A., 500 wds., no cr.
    Sight & S: v. 19, n. 7 (Nov., 1950), pp. 283-285; James Agee, 2000 wds.,
       pt. cr.

    SUOR LETIZIA (see: The Last Temptation)

6138 SUPERARGO AND THE FACELESS GIANTS (Paul Maxwell)
    (also: The King of the Criminals; Il Re Del Criminali; Superargo el Gigante)
    Filmf: v. XIV (1971), p. 757; comp., cp. cr.

    SUPERARGO EL GIGANTE (see: Superargo and the Faceless Giants)

6139 SUPERSPREAD (Robert Nelson)
    F Culture: n. 48-49 (Winter-Spring, 1970), p. 28; Robert Nelson, 300 wds.,
       pt. cr.

6140 SUPPORT YOUR LOCAL GUNFIGHTER (Burt Kennedy)
    Filmf: v. XIV (1971), p. 100; comp., cp. cr.

6141 SUPPORT YOUR LOCAL SHERIFF (Burt Kennedy)
    Filmf: v. XII (1969), p. 166; comp., cp. cr.
    Films & F: v. 16, n. 1 (Oct., 1969), p. 52; Richard Davis, 300 wds., cp. cr.
    Films in R: v. XX, n. 5 (May, 1969), pp. 314-315; Henry Hart, 275 wds., no
       cr.
    Sight & S: v. 38, n. 3 (Summer, 1969), pp. 158-159; Colin McArthur, 500
       wds., pt. cr.

6142 SUPPOSE THEY GAVE A WAR AND NOBODY CAME (Hy Averback)
    Films & F: v. 17, n. 6 (Mar., 1971), p. 57; John Francis, 200 wds., cp. cr.

    SUR LA ROUTE DE SALINA (see: Road To Salina)

6143 SURF BEACH (Bern Gandy)
    Interntl F G: v. 4 (1967), p. 49; 75 wds., pt. cr.

6144 SURF PARTY (Maury Dexter)
        Filmf: v. VII (1964), p. 181; comp., cp. cr.
        Films & F: v. 10, n. 8 (May, 1964), pp. 25-26; David Rider, 300 wds., cp.
            cr.

6145 SURFACING ON THE THAMES (Dave Rimmer)
        Take One: v. 2, n. 11 (1971), p. 29; Kirk Tougas, 700 wds., no cr.

6146 SURFARI (Milton Blair)
        Filmf: v. X (1967), p. 206; comp., cp. cr.

6147 SURPRISE PACKAGE (Stanley Donen)
        Filmf: v. III (1960), p. 273; comp., cp. cr.
        Films & F: v. 7, n. 2 (Nov., 1960), p. 31; Raymond Durgnat, 400 wds., cp.
            cr.

6148 SURRENDER — HELL! (John Barnwell)
        Filmf: v. II (1959), p. 286; comp., cp. cr.

      SURVIVAL (Tad Danielewski/see: The Guide)

      SURVIVAL (Jules Dassin/see: Survival 1967)

6149 SURVIVAL 1967 (Jules Dassin)
        (also: Survival)
        Filmf: v. XI (1968), p. 282; comp., cp. cr.
        Films & F: v. 15, n. 2 (Nov., 1968), p. 43; Gordon Gow, 350 wds., cp. cr.

6150 SUSAN SLADE (Delmer Daves)
        Filmf: v. IV (1961), p. 281; comp., cp. cr.
        Films & F: v. 8, n. 7 (Apr., 1962), pp. 32-33; Philip Strick, 400 wds., cp. cr.
        Films in R: v. XII, n. 9 (Nov., 1961), pp. 557-558; Ellen Fitzpatrick, 150
            wds., no cr.

      SUZANNE SIMONIN, LA RELIGIEUSE DE DIDEROT (see: La Religieuse)

      SVEGLIATI E UCCIDI (see: Wake Up and Die)

6151 SVENGALI (Noel Langley)
        Films & F: v. 1, n. 5 (Feb., 1955), p. 18; Catherine De La Roche, 300 wds.,
            cp. cr.

      SVENSKA FLICKOR I PARIS (see: The Flamboyant Sex)

      SVEZIA, INFERNO E PARADISO (see: Sweden: Heaven and Hell)

6152 SWAMP WATER (Jean Renoir)
        (also: The Man Who Came Back)
        F Soc Rev: Dec. (1967), pp. 17-19; Alexander Sesonske, 800 wds., cp. cr.

6153 SWAN, THE (Charles Vidor)
        Films & F: v. 2, n. 8 (May, 1956), pp. 20-21; Peter G. Baker, 425 wds., cp.
            cr.
        Films in R: v. VII, n. 4 (Apr., 1956), pp. 172-174; Henrietta Lehman, 450
            wds., no cr.

6154 SWAN LAKE (Z. Tulubyeva)
        Filmf: v. III (1960), p. 23; comp., cp. cr.
        Films & F: v. 15, n. 1 (Oct., 1968), pp. 53-54; Gordon Gow, 500 wds., cp.
            cr.
        Films & F: v. 15, n. 2 (Nov., 1968), p. 44; Gordon Gow, 650 wds., cp. cr.
        Films in R: v. XI, n. 3 (Mar., 1960), pp. 171-172; Tatiana Balkoff Drowne,
            250 wds., no cr.

6155 SWEDEN — HEAVEN AND HELL (Luigi Scattini)
        (also: Svezia, Inferno E Paradiso)
        Filmf: v. XII (1969), p. 405; comp., cp. cr.

      SWEDISH FLY GIRLS (see: Christa)

SWEDISH LOVE STORY, A (see: En Kärlekshistoria)

SWEDISH SIN, THE (see: Barnvagnen)

6156 SWEET BIRD OF YOUTH (Richard Brooks)
     F Quarterly: v. XV, n. 4 (Summer, 1962), p. 64; R. M. Hodgens, 100 wds.,
        no cr.
     Filmf: v. V (1962), p. 65; comp., cp. cr.
     Films & F: v. 8, n. 9 (June, 1962), p. 35; John Cutts, 600 wds., cp. cr.
     Films in R: v. XIII, n. 4 (Apr., 1962), pp. 233-234; Elaine Rothschild, 300
        wds., no cr.

6157 SWEET BODY OF DEBORAH, THE (Romolo Guerrieri)
     (also: Il Dolce Corpo di Deborah)
     Filmf: v. XII (1969), p. 175; comp., cp. cr.
     Films & F: v. 15, n. 7 (Apr., 1969), p. 46; Brian Murphy, 400 wds., pt. cr.

6158 SWEET CHARITY (Bob Fosse)
     Filmf: v. XII (1969), p. 131; comp., cp. cr.
     Films & F: v. 15, n. 7 (Apr., 1969), pp. 39-40; Robin Bean, 1300 wds., cp.
        cr.
     Sight & S: v. 38, n. 2 (Spring, 1969), p. 98; Tom Milne, 650 wds., pt. cr.

6159 SWEET ECSTASY (Max Pecas)
     (also: Douce Violence)
     Filmf: v. VI (1963), p. 11; comp., cp. cr.

6160 SWEET HUNTERS (Ruy Guerra)
     Movie: n. 17 (Winter, 1969-1970), p. 37; Ian Cameron, 200 wds., no cr.

SWEET LADIES, THE (see: Anyone Can Play)

SWEET LIFE, THE (see: La Dolce Vita)

SWEET LIGHT IN A DARK ROOM (see: Romeo, Juliet and Darkness)

6161 SWEET LOVE, BITTER (Herbert Danska)
     (also: It Won't Rub Off Baby)
     Filmf: v. X (1967), p. 55; comp., cp. cr.

6162 SWEET NOVEMBER (Robert Ellis Miller)
     Filmf: v. XI (1968), p. 29; comp., cp. cr.
     Films & F: v. 15, n. 12 (Sept., 1969), pp. 64-65; Richard Davis, 500 wds.,
        cp. cr.
     Films in R: v. XIX, n. 3 (Mar., 1968), pp. 180-181; Irene Kamsler, 200
        wds., no cr.

6163 SWEET RIDE, THE (Harvey Hart)
     Filmf: v. XI (1968), p. 228; comp., cp. cr.
     Films & F: v. 15, n. 5 (Feb., 1969), pp. 47-48; David Rider, 400 wds., cp.
        cr.

6164 SWEET SAVIOUR (Bob Roberts)
     Filmf: v. XIV (1971), p. 618; comp., cp. cr.

6165 SWEET SINS OF SEXY SUSAN, THE (Francois Legrand)
     Films & F: v. 15, n. 3 (Dec., 1968), pp. 40-41; David Austen, 350 wds., cp.
        cr.

6166 SWEET SKIN (Jacques Poitrenaud)
     (also: Strip-Tease)
     Filmf: v. IX (1966), p. 383; comp., cp. cr.

6167 SWEET SMELL OF SUCCESS (Alexander Mackendrick)
     F Culture: v. 3, n. 3 (1957), p. 16; Carol Rittgers, 600 wds., pt. cr.
     Films & F: v. 3, n. 12 (Sept., 1957), pp. 25-26; John Cutts, 400 wds., cp.
        cr.
     Films in R: v. VIII, n. 7 (Aug.-Sept., 1957), p. 354; Ellen Fitzpatrick, 150
        wds., no cr.
     Sight & S: v. 27, n. 2 (Autumn, 1957), pp. 89-90; Derek Prouse, 1000 wds.,
        pt. cr.

6168 SWEET SWEETBACK'S BAADASSSSS SONG (Melvin Van Peebles)
         Filmf: v. XIV (1971), p. 228; comp., cp. cr.

6169 SWIMMER, THE (Frank Perry)
         Filmf: v. XI (1968), p. 166; comp., cp. cr.
         Films & F: v. 15, n. 3 (Dec., 1968), pp. 36-37; Gordon Gow, 1200 wds., cp.
            cr.
         Films in R: v. XIX, n. 6 (June-July, 1968), pp. 377-379; Irene Kamsler, 200
            wds., no cr.
         Sight & S: v. 37, n. 4 (Autumn, 1968), pp. 206-207; Jan Dawson, 700 wds.,
            pt. cr.

      SWINDLE, THE (see: Il Bidone)

   . SWINDLERS, THE (see: Il Bidone)

6170 SWINGER, THE (George Sidney)
         Filmf: v. IX (1966), p. 341; comp., cp. cr.
         Films & F: v. XIII, n. 6 (Mar., 1967), pp. 33-34; Mike Sarne, 500 wds., cp.
            cr.

6171 SWINGIN'ALONG (Charles Barton)
         Filmf: v. V (1962), p. 172; comp., cp. cr.
         Films & F: v. 8, n. 12 (Sept., 1962), p. 39; John Cutts, 300 wds., cp. cr.

6172 SWINGIN' MAIDEN, THE
         Filmf: v. VII (1964), p. 49; comp., cp. cr.

6173 SWISS FAMILY ROBINSON (Ken Annakin)
         Filmf: v. III (1960), p. 331; comp., cp. cr.
         Films & F: v. 7, n. 4 (Jan., 1961), p. 33; Robin Bean, 350 wds., cp. cr.

6174 SWITCH, THE (Peter Maxwell)
         Films & F: v. 10, n. 8 (May, 1964), p. 27; Allen Eyles, 225 wds., cp. cr.

      SWITCHBOARD OPERATOR (see: Love Affair, or the Case of the Missing
         Switchboard Operator)

6175 SWORD AND THE CROSS, THE (Guido Brignone)
         Filmf: v. III (1960), p. 138; comp., cp. cr.

6176 SWORD AND THE DRAGON, THE (Alexander Ptushko)
         (also: Ilya Muromets)
         Filmf: v. III (1960), p. 284; comp., cp. cr.
         Films & F: v. 9, n. 8 (May, 1963), p. 34; Raymond Durgnat, 300 wds., cp.
            cr.

6177 SWORD IN THE STONE, THE (Wolfgang Reitherman and Walt Disney)
         Filmf: v. VI (1963), p. 286; comp., cp. cr.
         Films & F: v. 10, n. 4 (Jan., 1964), pp. 25-26; David Rider, 850 wds., cp.
            cr.

6178 SWORD OF ALI BABA (Virgil Vogel)
         Filmf: v. VIII (1965), p. 43; comp., cp. cr.

6179 SWORD OF DOOM, THE (Kihachi Okamoto)
         (also: Daibosatsu Pass; Daibosatsu Toge)
         Filmf: v. X (1967), p. 138; comp., cp. cr.

6180 SWORD OF LANCELOT (Cornel Wilde)
         (also: Lancelot and Guinevere)
         Filmf: v. VI (1963), p. 211; comp., cp. cr.
         Films & F: v. 9, n. 10 (July, 1963), p. 24; Raymond Durgnat, 500 wds., cp.
            cr.

6181 SWORD OF SHERWOOD FOREST (Terence Fisher)
         Filmf: v. IV (1961), p. 4; comp., cp. cr.

6182 SWORD OF THE CONQUEROR (Carlo Campogalliani)
        (also: Rosmund e Alboino)
        Filmf: v. V (1962), p. 348; comp., cp. cr.
        Films & F: v. 10, n. 4 (Jan., 1964), p. 32; Meredith Lawrence, 325 wds., cp.
          cr.

      SWORDS OF BLOOD (see: Cartouche)

6183 SWORDSMAN OF SIENA (Etienne Perier)
        Filmf: v. V (1962), p. 298; comp., cp. cr.
        Films & F: v. 9, n. 9 (June, 1963), p. 35; Richard Whitehall, 300 wds., cp.
          cr.

6184 SYLVIA (Gordon Douglas)
        F Quarterly: v. XVIII, n. 3 (Spring, 1965), p. 61; Ernest Callenbach, 100
          wds., no cr.
        Filmf: v. VIII (1965), p. 14; comp., cp. cr.
        Films & F: v. 11, n. 10 (July, 1965), p. 26; Allen Fyles 525 wds., cp. cr.
        Films in R: v. XVI, n. 2 (Feb., 1965), p. 114; Elaine Rothschild, 275 wds.,
          no cr.

      SYLVIE ET LE FANTOME (Claude Autant-Lara)
        Sequence: n. 12 (Autumn, 1950), p. 19; P.H., 350 wds., no cr.

      SYMPATHY FOR THE DEVIL (see: One Plus One)

6185 SYMPHONIE PASTORALE, LA (Jean Delannoy)
        Sight & S: v. 15, n. 60 (Winter, 1946-1947; Peter Streuli, 250 wds., pt. cr.

6186 SYNANON (Richard Quine)
        (also: Get Off My Back)
        F Quarterly: v. XVIII, n. 4 (Summer, 1965), p. 61; R. M. Hodgens, 200
          wds., no cr.
        Filmf: v. VIII (1965), p. 126; comp., cp. cr.
        Films & F: v. 12, n. 8 (May, 1966), p. 11; David Shipman, 650 wds., cp. cr.
        Films in R: v. XVI, n. 6 (June-July, 1965), pp. 384-385; Harvey S. Abbott,
          350 wds., no cr.

6187 SYNDICATE, THE (Frederic Goode)
        Films & F: v. 15, n. 3 (Dec., 1968), p. 48; David Austen, 225 wds., cp. cr.

      SYSKONBADD 1782 (see: My Sister, My Love)

      SYSTEM, THE (see: The Girl-Getters)

      SYTTEN (see: Eric Soya's "17")

6188 SYUZHET DLYA NEBOLSHOGO RASKAZA (Sergei Yutkevitch)
        (also: Theme for A Short Story)
        Interntl F G: v. 8 (1971), p. 270; Nina Hibbin, 250 wds., pt. cr.

      SZEGNYLEGENYEK (see: The Round-Up)

T

6189 T.A.M.I. SHOW, THE (Steve Binder)
        Filmf: v. VIII (1965), p. 94; comp., cp. cr.

6190 T-BIRD GANG
        Filmf: v. II (1959), p. 344; comp., cp. cr.

6191 T. R. BASKIN (Herbert Ross)
        Filmf: v. XIV (1971), p. 562; comp., cp. cr.
        Films in R: v. XXII, n. 9 (Nov., 1971), pp. 570-571; Hubbell Robinson, 400
          wds., no cr.

TABLE AUX CREVES, LA (see: The Village Feud)

6192 TABU (F. W. Murnau)
F Comment: v. 7, n. 2 (Summer, 1971), pp. 23-27; Robin Wood, 3800 wds., cp. cr.
F Heritage: v. 1, n. 3 (Spring, 1966), pp. 35-37; Gary L. Davis, 1000 wds., pt. cr.
F Soc Rev: Sept. (1967), pp. 15-16; Linda Lucas, 375 wds., no cr.

TABU II (see: Macabro)

6193 TAGGART (R. G. Springsteen)
Films & F: v. 11, n. 8 (May, 1965), p. 32; Allen Eyles, 275 wds., cp. cr.

6194 TAIGA (Wolfgang Liebeneiner)
Filmf: v. II (1959), p. 60; comp., cp. cr.

TAIHEIYO HITORIBOTCHI (see: Alone on the Pacific)

6195 TAILOR'S MAID, THE (Mario Monicelli)
(also: Like Father, Like Son: Padri E. Figli)
Filmf: v. II (1959), p. 232; comp., cp. cr.
Films & F: v. 5, n. 9 (June, 1959), p. 24; Dai Vaughan, 150 wds., cp. cr.

TAIYO NO HAKABA (see: The Sun's Burial)

6196 TAKE A GIANT STEP (Philip Leacock)
F Quarterly: v. XIII, n. 3 (Spring, 1960), p. 60; 50 wds., no cr.
Filmf: v. III (1960), p. 311; comp., cp. cr.
Films & F: v. 7, n. 6 (Mar., 1961), pp. 28-29; John Cutts, 350 wds., cp. cr.

6197 TAKE HER, SHE'S MINE (Henry Koster)
Filmf: v. VI (1963), p. 254; comp., cp. cr.
Films & F: v. 10, n. 4 (Jan., 1964), pp. 29-30; Richard Whitehall, 450 wds., cp. cr.
Films in R: v. XIV, n. 9 (Nov., 1963), pp. 566-567; Adelaide Comerford, 200 wds., no cr.

TAKE IT ALL (see: A Tout Prendre)

6198 TAKE THE HIGH GROUND (Richard Brooks)
Films in R: v. IV, n. 9 (Nov., 1953), pp. 484-485; 250 wds., pt. cr.

6199 TAKE THE MONEY AND RUN (Woody Allen)
F Quarterly: v. XXIII, n. 2 (Winter, 1969-1970), pp. 63-64; Michael Shedlin, 350 wds., no cr.
Filmf: v. XII (1969), p. 470; comp., cp. cr.
Films & F: v. 17, n. 4 (Jan., 1971), p. 53; Richard Davis, 350 wds., cp. cr.
Films in R: v. XX, n. 8 (Oct., 1969), p. 512; Harold Van Pelt, 150 wds., no cr.

6200 TAKING OFF (Milos Forman)
Filmf: v. XIV (1971), p. 61; comp., cp. cr.
Interntl F G: v. 9 (1972), pp. 263-264; Susan Rice, 200 wds., pt. cr.
Sight & S: v. 40, n. 4 (Autumn, 1971), pp. 221-222; David Wilson, 1200 wds., pt. cr.

6201 TALE OF TWO CITIES, A (Ralph Thomas)
F Quarterly: v. XII, n. 1 (Fall, 1958), p. 50; William Bernhardt, 400 wds., no cr.
Filmf: v. I (1958), p. 150; comp., cp. cr.
Films & F: v. 4, n. 6 (Mar., 1958), p. 25; Rupert Butler, 425 wds., cp. cr.
Films in R: v. IX, n. 7 (Aug.-Sept., 1958), pp. 398-399; Carolyn Harrow, no cr.

TALES OF BEATRIX POTTER (see: Peter Rabbit and Tales of Beatrix Potter)

6202 TALES OF HOFFMANN (Michael Powell and Emeric Pressburger)
        Films in R: v. II, n. 5 (May, 1951), pp. 44-46; Mary Ellis Peltz, 650 wds.,
              pt. cr.
        Sight & S: v. 20, n. 1 (May, 1951), pp. 17-18; Catherine de la Roche, 800
              wds., pt. cr.

6203 TALES OF MYSTERY AND IMAGINATION (Federico Fellini, Louis Malle,
              Roger Vadim)
        (also: Histoires Extraordinaires; Spirits of the Dead)
        Take One: v. 1, n. 12 (1968), p. 23; Ronald Blumer, 450 wds., pt. cr.

6204 TALES OF PARIS (Jacques Poitrenaud, Michel Boisrond, Claude Barma)
        Filmf: v. V (1962), p. 247; comp., cp. cr.

6205 TALES OF TERROR (Roger Corman)
        Filmf: v. V (1962), p. 135; comp., cp. cr.
        Films & F: v. 9, n. 8 (May, 1963), p. 30; John Cutts, 350 wds., cp. cr.
        Movie: n. 9, p. 35; 100 wds., no cr.

6206 TALK OF THE DEVIL (Francis Searle)
        Films & F: v. 15, n. 8 (May, 1969), pp. 42-43; David Rider, 275 wds., cp.
              cr.

6207 TALL MEN, THE (Raoul Walsh)
        Films & F: v. 2, n. 3 (Dec., 1955), p. 17; John Carroll, 150 wds., cp. cr.
        Sight & S: v. 25, n. 3 (Winter, 1955-1956), p. 150; Penelope Houston, 125
              wds., pt. cr.

6208 TALL STORY (Joshua Logan)
        Filmf: v. III (1960), p. 77; comp., cp. cr.
        Films & F: v. 6, n. 10 (July, 1960), p. 26; Robin Bean, 300 wds., cp. cr.
        Films in R: v. XI, n. 5 (May, 1960), p. 288; Ellen Fitzpatrick, 200 wds., no
              cr.

6209 TALL WOMEN, THE (Cechet Grooper)
        (also: Donne Alla Frontiera; The Seven Magnificent Women; Las Siete
              Magnificas; Women At the Frontier)
        Filmf: v. X (1967), p. 439; comp., cp. cr.

6210 TAMAHINE (Phillip Leacock)
        Filmf: v. VII (1964), p. 247; comp., cp. cr.
        Films & F: v. 9, n. 12 (Sept., 1963), p. 25; Robin Bean, 100 wds., cp. cr.

6211 TAMANGO (John Berry)
        Filmf: v. II (1959), p. 219; comp., cp. cr.
        Films & F: v. 6, n. 6 (Mar., 1960), p. 25; Ian Moss, 175 wds., cp. cr.

6212 TAMING, THE (Robert Arkless)
        Filmf: v. XI (1968), p. 508; comp., cp. cr.

6213 TAMING OF THE SHREW, THE (Franco Zeffirelli)
        F Quarterly: v. XXI, n. 1 (Fall, 1967), p. 61; Stephen Farber, 300 wds., no
              cr.
        Filmf: v. X (1967), p. 35; comp., cp. cr.
        Films & F: v. 13, n. 9 (June, 1967), p. 24-25; Peter Davalle, 550 wds., cp.
              cr.
        Films in R: v. XVIII, n. 4 (Apr., 1967), p. 238; Adelaide Comerford, 200
              wds., no cr.
        Sight & S: v. 36, n. 2 (Spring, 1967), pp. 97-98; Carey Harrison, 400 wds.,
              pt. cr.

6214 TAMMY AND THE DOCTOR (Harry Keller)
        Filmf: v. VI (1963), p. 137; comp., cp. cr.
        Films & F: v. 10, n. 10 (July, 1964), p. 25; David Rider, 250 wds., cp. cr.

6215 TAMMY AND THE MILLIONAIRE (Sidney Miller, Ezra Stone, Leslie Good-
              wins)
        Filmf: v. X (1967), p. 415; comp., cp. cr.

6216 TAMMY TELL ME TRUE (Harry Keller)
        Filmf: v. IV (1961), p. 201; comp., cp. cr.

6217 TANGA TIKA (Dwight Long)
      Films in R: v. IV, n. 9 (Nov., 1953), p. 485; 100 wds., no cr.

      TANIN NO KAO (see: The Face of Another)

6218 TANK BATTALION (Sherman A. Rose)
      Filmf: v. I (1958), p. 200; comp., cp. cr.

6219 TANK COMMANDOS (Burt Topper)
      Filmf: v. II (1959), p. 80; comp., cp. cr.

6220 TANK FORCE! (Terence Young)
      (also: No Time To Die)
      Filmf: v. I (1958), p. 255; comp., cp. cr.
      Films & F: v. 4, n. 9 (June, 1958), p. 27; John Cutts, 275 wds., cp. cr.

6221 TANKS ARE COMING, THE (Lewis Seiler)
      Films in R: v. II, n. 10 (Dec., 1951), p. 58; 75 wds., no cr.

      TANT QU'ON A LA SANTE (see: As Long As You're Healthy)

      TANTE ZITA (see: Zita)

      TANTSI I PYESNI NAD DNEPROM (see: Songs Over the Dnieper)

      TANZENDE HERZ, DAS (see: The Dancing Heart)

6222 TAR BABIES (Alexandre Jodorowski)
      Films & F: v. 17, n. 8 (May, 1971), pp. 101, 104-105; Raymond Durgnat,
          3000 wds., cp. cr.

6223 TARANTOS, LOS (Rovira-Beleta)
      Filmf: v. VII (1964), p. 324; comp., cp. cr.

6224 TARAS BULBA (J. Lee Thompson)
      F Quarterly: v. XVII, n. 2 (Winter, 1963-1964), p. 62; R. M. Hodgens, 150
          wds., no cr.
      Filmf: v. V (1962), p. 326; comp., cp. cr.
      Films & F: v. 9, n. 7 (Apr., 1963), pp. 28-29; Richard Whitehall, 500 wds.,
          cp. cr.
      Films in R: v. XIV, n. 1 (Jan., 1963), p. 49; Arthur B. Clark, 225 wds., no
          cr.

6225 TARAWA BEACHHEAD (Paul Wendkos)
      Filmf: v. I (1958), p. 278; comp., cp. cr.

6226 TARGETS (Peter Bogdanovich)
      F Heritage: v. 4, n. 4 (Summer, 1969), pp. 1-8; Brian Henderson, 3000
          wds., pt. cr.
      F Heritage: v. 5, n. 1 (Fall, 1969), pp. 1-8; Brian Henderson, 2000 wds., no
          cr.
      F Quarterly: v. XXI, n. 4 (Summer, 1968), pp. 61-62; Stephen Farber, 650
          wds., no cr.
      Filmf: v. XI (1968), p. 306; comp., cp. cr.
      Films & F: v. 16, n. 2 (Nov., 1969), p. 50; Gordon Gow, 800 wds., cp. cr.
      Movie: n. 15 (Spring, 1968), p. 32; 150 wds., pt. cr.

6227 TARNISHED ANGELS, THE (Douglas Sirk)
      Filmf: v. I (1958), p. 1; comp., cp. cr.
      Films & F: v. 4, n. 5 (Feb., 1958), p. 24; Ken Gay, 350 wds., cp. cr.
      Screen: v. 12, n. 2 (Summer, 1971), pp. 68-93; Fred Camper, 14000 wds.,
          cp. cr.

6228 TARTARS, THE (Richard Thorpe)
      Filmf: v. V (1962), p. 121; comp., cp. cr.

6229 TARZAN AND THE GREAT RIVER (Robert Day)
      Filmf: v. X (1967), p. 326; comp., cp. cr.

6230 TARZAN AND THE JUNGLE BOY (Robert Gordon)
      Filmf: v. XI (1968), p. 242; comp., cp. cr.

6231 TARZAN AND THE VALLEY OF GOLD (Robert Day)
      Filmf: v. X (1967), p. 114; comp., cp. cr.
      Films & F: v. 13, n. 5 (Feb., 1967), p. 34; David Adams, 600 wds., cp. cr.

6232 TARZAN GOES TO INDIA (John Guillermin)
      F Quarterly: v. XVI, n. 3 (Spring, 1963), pp. 59-60; R. M. Hodgens, 100
          wds., no cr.
      Filmf: v. V (1962), p. 186; comp., cp. cr.
      Films & F: v. 8, n. 12 (Sept., 1962), p. 35; John Cutts, 200 wds., cp. cr.

6233 TARZAN THE APE MAN (Joseph Newman)
      F Quarterly: v. XIII, n. 3 (Spring, 1960), p. 60; 50 wds., no cr.
      Filmf: v. II (1959), p. 322; comp., cp. cr.

6234 TARZAN THE MAGNIFICENT (Robert Day)
      Filmf: v. III (1960), p. 155; comp., cp. cr.

      TARZANA SMRT (see: The Death of Tarzan)

6235 TARZAN'S FIGHT FOR LIFE (Bruce Humberstone)
      Filmf: v. I (1958), p. 140; comp., cp. cr.

6236 TARZAN'S GREATEST ADVENTURE (John Guillermin)
      Filmf: v. II (1959), p. 137; comp., cp. cr.

6237 TARZAN'S THREE CHALLENGES (Robert Day)
      Filmf: v. VI (1963), p. 185; comp., cp. cr.
      Films & F: v. 11, n. 1 (Oct., 1964), p. 34; David Rider, 350 wds., cp. cr.

6238 TASK FORCE (Delmer Daves)
      Sequence: n. 11 (Summer, 1950), pp. 10-11; Lindsay Anderson, 1000 wds.,
          no cr.

6239 TASTE OF FEAR (Seth Holt)
      Films & F: v. 7, n. 8 (May, 1961), p. 26; John Cutts, 250 wds., cp. cr.

6240 TASTE OF HONEY, A (Tony Richardson)
      Film: n. 30 (Winter, 1961), p. 15; Peter Armitage, 400 wds., no cr.
      Filmf: v. V (1962), p. 95; comp., cp. cr.
      Films & F: v. 8, n. 2 (Nov., 1961), p. 22; Peter Baker, 1000 wds., cp. cr.
      Films in R: v. XIII, n. 6 (June-July, 1962), p. 366; Helen Weldon Kuhn,
          225 wds., no cr.
      Sight & S: v. 30, n. 4 (Autumn, 1961), p. 196; George Stonier, 800 wds.,
          pt. cr.

      TASTE OF MACKEREL, THE (see: An Autumn Afternoon)

6241 TASTE THE BLOOD OF DRACULA (Peter Sasdy)
      Films & F: v. 16, n. 10 (July, 1970), pp. 47-48; John Walker, 450 wds., cp.
          cr.

      TATOWIERUNG (see: Tatto)

6242 TATTO (Johannes Schaaf)
      (also: Tatowierung)
      F Quarterly: v. XXII, n. 2 (Winter, 1968-1969), p. 59; Harriet R. Polt, 200
          wds., no cr.
      Interntl F G: v. 6 (1969), p. 76; 250 wds., pt. cr.

6243 TATTOOISTS, 8, 9 AND TEN (Denis Postle and Dick Fontaine)
      Films & F: v. 16, n. 8 (May, 1970), pp. 45-46; Peter Buckley, 350 wds., cp.
          cr.

6244 TAXI DRIVER, THE (George Tzavellas)
      (also: To Soferaki)
      Filmf: v. I (1958), p. 38; comp., cp. cr.

6245 TAXI FOR TOBRUK (Denys De La Patellière)
      (also: Un Taxi Pour Tobrouk)
      Filmf: v. VIII (1965), p. 97; comp., cp. cr.

      TAXI POUR TOBROUK, UN (see: Taxi for Tobruk)

      TCHISTOE NEBO (see: Clear Skies)

6246 TEA AND SYMPATHY (Vincente Minnelli)
      F Culture: v. 2, n. 4 (1956), pp. 25-26; Arlene Croce, 1000 wds., pt. cr.
      Films & F: v. 3, n. 11 (Aug., 1957), p. 23; Peter Baker, 700 wds., cp. cr.
      Films in R: v. VII, n. 9 (Nov., 1956), pp. 464-465; Veronica Hume, 550
      wds., no cr.

6247 TEACHER AND THE MIRACLE, THE (Aldo Fabrizi)
      (also; Il Maestro)
      Filmf: v. IV (1961), p. 170; comp., cp. cr.

6248 TEACHER'S PET (George Seaton)
      Filmf: v. I (1958), p. 37; comp., cp. cr.
      Films & F: v. 4, n. 9 (June, 1958), p. 24; Richard Roud, 150 wds., cp. cr.
      Films in R: v. IX, n. 3 (Mar., 1958), p. 145; Ellen Fitzpatrick, 125 wds., no
      cr.

6249 TEAHOUSE OF THE AUGUST MOON (Daniel Mann)
      Films & F: v. 3, n. 7 (Apr., 1957), pp. 23-24; Peter G. Baker, 450 wds., cp.
      cr.
      Films in R: v. VII, n. 10 (Dec., 1956), p. 525; Courtland Phipps, 125 wds.,
      no cr.
      Sight & S: v. 26, n. 4 (Spring, 1957), pp. 208-290; Derek Prouse, 600 wds.,
      pt. cr.

6250 TEAM FROM OUR STREET, THE (A. Maslyukov)
      Films & F: v. 1, n. 5 (Feb., 1955), p. 18; Patrick Goldring, 150 wds., cp. cr.

      TECHNIQUE OF A MURDER (see: The Hired Killer)

      TECNICA DI UN OMICIDIO (see: The Hired Killer)

      TEEN KANYA (see: Two Daughters)

6251 TEENAGE BAD GIRL (Herbert Wilcox)
      (also: My Teenage Daughter)
      Filmf: v. II (1959), p. 335; comp., cp. cr.
      Films & F: v. 2, n. 10 (July, 1956), p. 22; Rodney Giesler, 125 wds., cp. cr.

6252 TEENAGE CAVEMAN (Roger Corman)
      Filmf: v. I (1958), p. 249; comp., cp. cr.

6253 TEENAGE COMMAND PERFORMANCE (Steven Binder)
      Films & F: v. 12, n. 2 (Nov., 1965), p. 33; David Rider, 500 wds., cp. cr.

6254 TEENAGE MILLIONAIRE (Lawrence F. Doheny)
      Filmf: v. IV (1961), p. 336; comp., cp. cr.

6255 TEENAGE MOTHER (Jerry Gross)
      Filmf: v. XI (1968), p. 358; comp., cp. cr.

6256 TEENAGE REBEL (Edmund Goulding)
      Films & F: v. 3, n. 4 (Jan., 1957), pp. 24-25; Rupert Butler, 350 wds., cp.
      cr.

      TEENAGE REBELLION (see: Mondo Teeno)

6257 TEENAGE WOLF PACK (Georg Tressler)
      (also: Halbstarken)
      Filmf: v. II (1959), p. 343; comp., cp. cr.

6258 TEENAGE ZOMBIES (Jerry Warren)
      Filmf: v. III (1960), p. 356; comp., cp. cr.

6259 TEENAGERS (Pierre Roustang)
Films & F: v. 15, n. 10 (July, 1969), p. 45; David Austen, 400 wds., cp. cr.

6260 TEENAGERS FROM OUTER SPACE (Tom Graeff)
Filmf: v. II (1959), p. 268; comp., cp. cr.

TEJANO, EL (see: The Texican)

TELEFTEO PSEMMA, TO (see: A Matter of Dignity)

6261 TELEPHONE BOOK, THE (Nelson Lyon)
Filmf: v. XIV (1971), p. 617; comp., cp. cr.

6262 TELL ME IN THE SUNLIGHT (Steve Cochran)
Filmf: v. X (1967), p. 378; comp., cp. cr.

6263 TELL ME LIES (Peter Brook)
Filmf: v. XI (1968), p. 60; comp.; cp. cr.
Films & F: v. 14, n. 7 (Apr., 1968), pp. 25-26; Raymond Durgnat, 1200
wds., cp. cr.
Films in R: v. XIX, n. 3 (Mar., 1968), pp. 183-184; 150 wds., no cr.
Sight & S: v. 37, n. 2 (Spring, 1968), pp. 98-99; David Wilson, 900 wds., pt.
cr.
Take One: v. 1, n. 10 (1968), pp. 31-32; Joe Medjuck, 450 wds., pt. cr.

6264 TELL ME THAT YOU LOVE ME, JUNIE MOON (Otto Preminger)
Focus: n. 7 (Spring, 1972), pp. 26-30; Charles Flynn, 1300 wds., no cr.
Movie: n. 18 (Winter, 1970-1971), p. 40; Ian Cameron, 250 wds., no cr.

6265 TELL NO TALES (Leslie Fenton)
Focus on F: n. 5 (Winter/Nov.-Dec., 1970), p. 35; Don Miller, 300 wds., pt.
cr.

6266 TELL-TALE HEART, THE (Ernest Morris)
Filmf: v. VI (1963), p. 90; comp., cp. cr.

6267 TELL THEM WILLIE BOY IS HERE (Abraham Polonsky)
Cinema: v. 6, n. 1, pp. 51-52; Paul Schrader, 1100 wds., no cr.
F Quarterly: v. XXIII, n. 3 (Spring, 1970), pp. 60-61; Dennis Hunt, 500
wds., no cr.
F Soc Rev: v. 6, n. 8 (Apr., 1971), pp. 32-34; Dan Georgakas, 1000 wds.,
cp. cr.
Films & F: v. 16, n. 6 (Mar., 1970), pp. 35-36; Gordon Gow, 650 wds., cp.
cr.
Focus: n. 6 (Spring, 1970), pp. 31-33; Terry Curtis Fox, 1200 wds., no cr.
Sight & S: v. 39, n. 2 (Spring, 1970), pp. 101-102; Tom Milne, 1000 wds.,
pt. cr.

6268 TEMPEST (Alberto Lattuada)
(also: La Tempesta)
Filmf: v. II (1959), p. 69; comp., cp. cr.
Films & F: v. 5, n. 12 (Sept., 1959), p. 22; Dai Vaughan, 225 wds., cp. cr.
Films in R: v. X, n. 3 (Mar., 1959), pp. 159-162; Tatiana Balkoff Drowne,
1000 wds., no cr.

6269 TEMPEST, THE (David Snasdell)
Films & F: v. 15, n. 10 (July, 1969), pp. 51-52; Brian Murphy, 500 wds.,
cp. cr.

TEMPESTA, LA (see: Tempest)

6270 TEMPESTUOUS LOVE (Falk Harnack)
(also: Wie Ein Sturmwind)
Filmf: v. I (1958), p. 260; comp., cp. cr.

6271 TEMPETE SE LEVE, LA (Huy Thanh and Le Ba Huyen)
(also: The Rising Storm)
F Comment: v. IV, n. 1 (Fall, 1966), p. 22; 400 wds., no cr.

TEMPI NOSTRI (see: Slice of Life)

6272 TEMPLE OF THE WHITE ELEPHANT (Umberto Lenzi)
        Films & F: v. 12, n. 11 (Aug., 1966), p. 58; Kevin Gough-Yates, 350 wds.,
           cp. cr.

      TEMPO DI MASSACRO (see: The Brute and the Beast)

      TEMPO SE'FERMATO, IL (see: Time Stood Still)

      TEMPS DU GHETTO, LE (see: The Witnesses)

6273 TEMPTATION (Edmond T. Greville)
        (also: L'Ile du Bout du Monde)
        Filmf: v. V (1962), p. 353; comp., cp. cr.

6274 TEMPTATION ISLAND (Edmond T. Greville)
        Films & F: v. 6, n. 1 (Oct., 1959), p. 24; Robin Bean, 200 wds., cp. cr.

      TEMPTATION OF DR. ANTONIO, THE (see: Boccaccio '70)

6275 TEMPTRESS, THE (Fred Niblo)
        Focus: n. 8 (Autumn, 1972), pp. 19-23; William D. Routt, 2400 wds., no
           cr.

6276 TEN COMMANDMENTS, THE (Cecil B. DeMille)
        F Quarterly: v. XX, n. 1 (Fall, 1966), pp. 59-60; R. M. Hodgens, 300 wds.,
           no cr.
        Films & F: v. 4, n. 4 (Jan., 1958), pp. 23-24; Peter G.Baker, 625 wds., cp.
           cr.
        Films in R: v. VII, n. 9 (Nov., 1956), pp. 461-463; Henrietta Lehman, 600
           wds., no cr.
        Sight & S: v. 27, n. 3 (Winter, 1957-1958), pp. 148-149; Laurence Kitchin,
           750 wds., pt. cr.

      TEN DAYS THAT SHOOK THE WORLD (see: October)

      TEN DAYS TO DIE (see: The Last Ten Days)

6277 TEN DAYS TO TULARA (George Sherman)
        Filmf: v. I (1958), p. 273; comp., cp. cr.

6278 TEN LITTLE INDIANS (George Pollock)
        Filmf: v. IX (1966), p. 13; comp., cp. cr.
        Films & F: v. 12, n. 6 (Mar., 1965), p. 12; Nicholas Gosling, 400 wds., cp.
           cr.

6279 TEN NORTH FREDERICK (Philip Dunne)
        Filmf: v. I (1958), p. 77; comp., cp. cr.
        Films & F: v. 4, n. 11 (Aug., 1958), pp. 24-25; Derek Conrad, 550 wds., cp.
           cr.
        Films in R: v. IX, n. 5 (May, 1958), pp. 265-266; Henry Hart, 500 wds., no
           cr.

6280 10 RILLINGTON PLACE (Richard Fleischer)
        Filmf: v. XIV (1971), p. 278; comp., cp. cr.
        Films & F: v. 17, n. 8 (May, 1971), pp. 94, 96; Gordon Gow, 650 wds., cp.
           cr.
        Films in R: v. XXII, n. 6 (June-July, 1971), pp. 371-372; B. F. Leedom,
           300 wds., no cr.

6281 TEN SECONDS TO HELL (Robert Aldrich)
        Filmf: v. II (1959), p. 193; comp., cp. cr.
        Films & F: v. 5, n. 9 (June, 1959), p. 25; Derek Conrad, 200 wds., cp. cr.

6282 10:30 P.M. SUMMER (Jules Dassin)
        F Quarterly: v. XX, n. 4 (Summer, 1967), p. 80; Raymond Banacki, 250
           wds., no cr.
        Filmf: v. IX (1966), p. 288; comp., cp. cr.
        Films & F: v. 13, n. 8 (May, 1967), pp. 31-32; David Adams, 800 wds., cp.
           cr.
        Films in R: v. XVII, n. 9 (Nov., 1966), pp. 587-588; 225 wds., no cr.

6283 TEN THOUSAND BEDROOMS (Richard Thorpe)
      Films & F: v. 3, n. 8 (May, 1957), p. 28; Rupert Butler, 250 wds., cp. cr.

      TEN THOUSAND DAYS (see: The Ten Thousand Suns)

6284 10,000 DOLLARS BLOOD MONEY (Romolo Guerrieri)
      Films & F: v. 14, n. 8 (Apr., 1968), pp. 28-29; David Austen, 1300 wds.,
      cp. cr.

6285 TEN THOUSAND SUNS, THE (Ferenc Kósa)
      (also: Ten Thousand Days; Tizezer Nap)
      Interntl F G: v. 5 (1968), p. 100; György Fenyves, 250 wds., pt. cr.
      Sight & S: v. 38, n. 4 (Autumn, 1969), pp. 213-214; David Wilson, 550
      wds., no cr.

6286 TEN WHO DARED (William Beaudine)
      Filmf: v. III (1960), p. 331; comp., cp. cr.

      TENDA ROSSA, LA (see: The Red Tent)

6287 TENDER IS THE NIGHT (Henry King)
      F Quarterly: v. XV, n. 3 (Spring, 1962), p. 72; R. M. Hodgens, 100 wds., no
      cr.
      Filmf: v. V (1962), p. 11; comp., cp. cr.
      Films in R: v. XIII, n. 2 (Feb., 1962), pp. 106-107; Ellen Fitzpatrick, 350
      wds., no cr.
      Sight & S: v. 31, n. 2 (Spring, 1962), pp. 92-93; Francis Wyndham, 1200
      wds., pt. cr.

6288 TENDER MOMENT, THE (Michel Boisrond)
      (also: La Lecon Particuliere; The Private Lesson)
      Filmf: v. XIV (1971), p. 267; comp., cp. cr.
      Films & F: v. 15, n. 11 (Aug., 1969), p. 47; Brian Murphy, 725 wds., cp. cr.

6289 TENDER SCOUNDREL (Jean Becker)
      (also: Tendre Voyou)
      Filmf: v. X (1967), p. 369; comp., cp. cr.

6290 TENDER TRAP, THE (Charles Walters)
      Films & F: v. 2, n. 4 (Jan., 1956), p. 24; Peter G. Baker, 200 wds., cp. cr.
      Films in R: v. VI, n. 10 (Dec., 1955), pp. 530-531; Robert Downing, 250
      wds., pt. cr.

      TENDERNESS (see: Niejnosti)

      TENDRE VOYOU (see: Tender Scoundrel)

6291 TENEMENT, THE (CBS News)
      F Lib Quarterly: v. 1, n. 3 (Summer, 1968), pp. 48-49; Naomi S. Weiss, 350
      wds., pt. cr.

      TENGOKU TO JIGOKU (see: High and Low)

      TENTACION DESNUDA, LA (see: Woman and Temptation)

6292 TENTH VICTIM, THE (Elio Petri)
      (also: La Decima Vittima)
      F Quarterly: v. XIX, n. 3 (Spring, 1966), p. 53; William Johnson, 100 wds.,
      no cr.
      Films & F: v. 14, n. 5 (Feb., 1968), p. 25; Raymond Durgnat, 1200 wds.,
      cp. cr.
      Films in R: v. XVII, n. 1 (Jan., 1966), pp. 46-47; Henry Hart, 500 wds., no
      cr.

      TEODORA, IMPERATRICE DI BISANZIO (see: Theodora, Slave Empress)

6293 TEOREMA (Pier Paolo Pasolini)
      (also: Theorem)
      F Quarterly: v. XXIII, n. 1 (Fall, 1969), pp. 24-29; Robert Chappetta, 2200
      wds., pt. cr.

F Soc Rev: v. 4, n. 7, pp. 35-40; John Bragin, 3000 wds., cp. cr.
Filmf: v. XII (1969), p. 204; comp., cp. cr.
Films & F: v. 15, n. 9 (June, 1969), pp. 38-39; Peter Whitehead, 1450 wds.,
    cp. cr.
Films in R: v. XX, n. 6 (June-July, 1969), pp. 376-377; Henry Hart, 550
    wds., no cr.
Interntl F G: v. 7 (1970), pp. 147-148; Peter Cowie, 375 wds., pt. cr.
Take One: v. 2, n. 2 (1969), p. 23; Dominique Noguez, 550 wds., pt. cr.

6294 TERESA (Fred Zinnemann)
        Films in R: v. II, n. 4 (Apr., 1951), pp. 43-45; Hermine Rich Isaacs, 600
            wds., pt. cr.
        Sight & S: v. 20, n. 1 (May, 1951), pp. 18-19; Gavin Lambert, 800 wds., pt.
            cr.

6295 TERM OF TRIAL (Peter Glenville)
        Cinema: v. 1, n. 4, p. 45; R.G., 300 wds., pt. cr.
        Filmf: v. VI (1963), p. 5; comp., cp. cr.
        Films & F: v. 9, n. 1 (Oct., 1962), p. 32; Gordon Gow, 850 wds., cp. cr.
        Films in R: v. XIV, n. 2 (Feb., 1963), pp. 111-112; Adelaide Comerford,
            200 wds., no cr.

      TERMINAL STATION (see: Indiscretion of an American Wife)

6296 TERRA TREMA, LA (Luchino Visconti)
        F Comment: v. 1, n. 6 (Fall, 1963), pp. 34-38; Robert Connelly, 2800 wds.,
            no cr.
        Sequence: n. 12 (Autumn, 1950), pp. 38-40; Karel Reisz, 1300 wds., pt. cr.
        Sight & S: v. 26, n. 4 (Spring, 1957), pp. 213-216; Alain Tanner, 3000 wds.,
            pt. cr.

6297 TERRACE, THE (Leopoldo Torre Nilsson)
        (also: The Roof Garden; La Terraza)
        Filmf: v. VII (1964), p. 345; comp., cp. cr.

      TERRAZA, LA (see: The Terrace)

      TERRIBLE BEAUTY, A (see: The Night Fighters)

6298 TERROR, THE (Roger Corman)
        Filmf: v. VI (1963), p. 256; comp., cp. cr.
        Films & F: v. 10, n. 6 (Mar., 1964), p. 32; John Cutts, 350 wds., cp. cr.

6299 TERROR AT BLACK FALLS (Richard C. Sarafian)
        Filmf: v. V (1962), p. 369; comp., cp. cr.

6300 TERROR-CREATURES FROM THE GRAVE (Ralph Zuker)
        (also: Cinque Tombe Per Un Medium; Five Graves for a Medium)
        Filmf: v. X (1967), p. 437; comp., cp. cr.
        Films & F: v. 15, n. 10 (July, 1969), p. 56; David Austen, 150 wds., cp. cr.

6301 TERROR FROM THE YEAR 5000
        Filmf: v. I (1958), p. 233; comp., cp. cr.

6302 TERROR IN A TEXAS TOWN (Joseph H. Lewis)
        Filmf: v. I (1958), p. 259; comp., cp. cr.

6303 TERROR IN THE CITY (Allen Baron)
        (also: Pie in the Sky)
        Filmf: v. IX (1966), p. 317; comp., cp. cr.

6304 TERROR IN THE HAUNTED HOUSE (Harold Daniels)
        (also: My World Dies Screaming)
        Filmf: v. II (1959), p. 306; comp., cp. cr.

6305 TERROR IS A MAN (Gerry De Leon)
        Filmf: v. III (1960), p. 158; comp., cp. cr.

6306 TERROR OF DR. MABUSE, THE (Werner Klinger)
        F Quarterly: v. XIX, n. 1 (Fall, 1965), p. 63; R. M. Hodgens, 100 wds., no
            cr.

6307 TERROR OF THE BLOODHUNTERS (Jerry Warren)
        Filmf: v. V (1962), p. 372; comp., cp. cr.

6308 TERROR OF THE TONGS, THE (Anthony Bushell)
        Filmf: v. IV (1961), p. 81; comp., cp. cr.

        TERRORE DEI BARBARI, IL (see: Goliath and the Barbarians)

        TERRORE NELLO SPAZIO (see: Planet of the Vampires)

6309 TERRORNAUTS, THE (Montgomery Tully)
        Filmf: v. X (1967), p. 410; comp., cp. cr.

        TESORO DE MAKUBA, EL (see: The Treasure of Makuba)

6310 TESS OF THE STORM COUNTRY (Paul Guilfoyle)
        Filmf: v. IV (1961), p. 352; comp., cp. cr.
        Films in R: v. XII, n. 2 (Feb., 1961), pp. 107-108; Flavia Wharton, 150
            wds., no cr.

        TESTAMENT D'ORPHEUS, LE (see: The Testament of Orpheus)

6311 TESTAMENT OF DR. CORDELIER (Jean Renoir)
        (also: Experiment in Evil)
        F Journal: n. 21 (Apr., 1963), pp. 102-105; R. G. Howard, 1600 wds., no
            cr.
        Movie: n. 10, p. 35; 150 wds., no cr.

6312 TESTAMENT OF DR. MABUSE, THE (Werner Klingler)
        Films & F: v. 11, n. 4 (Jan., 1965), p. 39; Paul Brewer, 500 wds., cp. cr.

6313 TESTAMENT OF ORPHEUS, THE (Jean Cocteau)
        (also: Le Testament D'Orpheus)
        F Comment: v. 7, n. 4 (Winter, 1971-1972), pp. 23-27; George Amberg,
            3000 wds., cp. cr.
        Filmf: v. V (1962), p. 91; comp., cp. cr.
        Films & F: v. 6, n. 10 (July, 1960), p. 21; Roger Manvell, 800 wds., cp. cr.
        Films in R: v. XIII, n. 2 (Feb., 1962), pp. 108-109; Louise Corbin, 600
            wds., no cr.
        Sight & S: v. 29, n. 3 (Summer, 1960), pp. 143-144; Peter John Dyer, 850
            wds., pt. cr.

6314 TETE CONTRE LES MURS, LA (Georges Franju)
        (also: Head Against the Walls; The Keepers)
        F Journal: n. 15 (Mar., 1960), pp. 51-54; Ian Jarvie, 1200 wds., no cr.
        F Quarterly: v. XII, n. 4 (Summer, 1959), pp. 56-57; John Adams, 400
            wds., no cr.
        F Soc Rev: Sept. (1967), pp. 11-12; John Thomas, 650 wds., pt. cr.
        Films & F: v. 7, n. 11 (Aug., 1961), pp. 25-26; Raymond Durgnat, 650
            wds., cp. cr.
        Sight & S: v. 30, n. 4 (Autumn, 1961), pp. 196-197; Peter John Dyer, 850
            wds., pt. cr.

6315 TETTO, IL (Vittorio De Sica)
        (also: The Roof)
        F Culture: v. 2, n. 3 (1956), p. 24; Guido Aristarco, 1200 wds., pt. cr.
        F Quarterly: v. XIII, n. 2 (Winter, 1959), pp. 49-50; Arlene Croce, 700
            wds., no cr.
        Filmf: v. II (1959), p. 117; comp., cp. cr.
        Films & F: v. 7, n. 1 (Oct., 1960), p. 26; Gordon Gow, 500 wds., cp. cr.
        Films in R: v. IX, n. 1 (Jan., 1958), p. 33; Romano V. Tozzi, 200 wds., no
            cr.

6316 TEXAS ACROSS THE RIVER (Michael Gordon)
        Filmf: v. IX (1966), p. 32l; comp., cp. cr.

6317 TEXICAN, THE (Lesley Selander)
        (also: El Tejano)
        Filmf: v. IX (1966), p. 385; comp., cp. cr.
        Films & F: v. 13, n. 5 (Feb., 1967), p. 32; Allen Eyles, 200 wds., cp. cr.

THANK HEAVEN FOR SMALL FAVORS (see: Un Drôle de Paroissien)

6318 THANK YOU ALL VERY MUCH (Waris Hussein)
(also: A Touch of Love)
Filmf: v. XII (1969), p. 429; comp., cp. cr.
Films & F: v. 16, n. 3 (Dec., 1969), p. 52; Richard Davis, 550 wds., cp. cr.

THANKS, AUNT (see: Zia Grazie)

THAT CAT (see: Cassandra Cat)

6319 THAT CERTAIN FEELING (Norman Panama and Melvin Frank)
Films & F: v. 3, n. 3 (Dec., 1956), p. 26; P. L. Mannock, 150 wds., cp. cr.

6320 THAT COLD DAY IN THE PARK (Robert Altman)
F Quarterly: v. XXIII, n. 1 (Fall, 1969), p. 56; Michael Dempsey, 400 wds.,
no cr.
Filmf: v. XII (1969), p. 277; comp., cp. cr.
Films & F: v. 16, n. 9 (June, 1970), pp. 85, 88; David Hutchison, 850 wds.,
cp. cr.

6321 THAT DANGEROUS AGE (Gregory Ratoff)
Sight & S: v. 18, n. 70 (Summer, 1949), p. 90; Arthur Vesselo, 100 wds., no
cr.

6322 THAT DARN CAT (Robert Stevenson)
Films in R: v. XVI, n. 10 (Dec., 1965), pp. 642-643; Albertine Ross, 150
wds., no cr.

THAT JANE FROM MAINE (see: It Happened To Jane)

6324 THAT KIND OF WOMAN (Sidney Lumet)
Filmf: v. II (1959), p. 213; comp., cp. cr.
Films & F: v. 6, n. 2 (Nov., 1959), p. 24; Ian Moss, 250 wds., cp. cr.
Sight & S: v. 29, n. 1 (Winter, 1959-1960), p. 40; Richard Roud, 350 wds.,
pt. cr.

6325 THAT LADY (Terence Young)
Films & F: v. 1, n. 9 (June, 1955), p. 20; Jill Hardy, 125 wds., cp. cr.
Films in R: v. VI, n. 6 (June-July, 1955), p. 290; Diana Willing, 225 wds.,
pt. cr.

6326 THAT MAN FROM RIO (Philippe De Broca)
(also: L'Homme de Rio)
F Quarterly: v. XVIII, n. 2 (Winter, 1964), p. 59; James Michael Martin,
250 wds., no cr.
Filmf: v. VII (1964), p. 152; comp., cp. cr.
Films & F: v. 11, n. 9 (June, 1965), p. 24; Gordon Gow, 1050 wds., cp. cr.
Sight & S: v. 34, n. 3 (Summer, 1965), pp. 147-148; J. H. Fenwick, 650
wds., pt. cr.

6327 THAT MAN GEORGE (Jacques Deray)
(also: L'Homme de Marrakech; The Man from Marrakech)
Filmf: v. XI (1968), p. 354; comp., cp. cr.

6328 THAT MAN IN ISTANBUL (Anthony Isasi)
(also: L'Homme D'Istanbul)
Filmf: v. IX (1966), p. 146; comp., cp. cr.

THAT NAUGHTY GIRL (see: Mam'zelle Pigalle)

6329 THAT NIGHT (John Newland)
Films & F: v. 3, n. 12 (Sept., 1957), pp. 23-24; Peter G. Baker, 300 wds.,
cp. cr.
Films in R: v. VIII, n. 8 (Oct., 1957), p. 407; John Springer, 150 wds., no
cr.

6330 THAT RIVIERA TOUCH (Cliff Owen)
Films & F: v. 12, n. 3 (Dec., 1965), pp. 56-57; David Rider, 350 wds., cp.
cr.

6331 THAT SPLENDID NOVEMBER (Mauro Bolognini)
(also: Un Bellissimo Novembre)
Filmf: v. XIV (1971), p. 326; comp., cp. cr.

THAT TENDER AGE (see: The Adolescents)

6332 THAT TENNESSEE BEAT (Richard Brill)
Filmf: v. IX (1966), p. 384; comp., cp. cr.

6333 THAT TOUCH OF MINK (Delbert Mann)
Filmf: v. V (1962), p. 125; comp., cp. cr.
Films & F: v. 8, n. 9 (June, 1962), p. 37; Richard Whitehall, 375 wds., cp.
cr.

6334 THAT WOMAN (Will Tremper)
(also: Berlin 1st Eine Suende Wert; Berlin Is Worth a Sin)
Filmf: v. XI (1968), p. 280; comp., cp. cr.

THAT WOMAN OPPOSITE (see: City After Midnight)

6335 THAT'S THE WAY IT IS (Denis Sanders)
Films in R: v. XXII, n. 1 (Jan., 1971), p. 46; Tatiana Balkoff Drowne, 150
wds., no cr.

THEATRE OF DEATH (see: Blood Fiend)

THEIR FIRST TRIP TO TOKYO (see: Tokyo Story)

THEIR SECRET AFFAIR (see: Top Secret Affari)

THELMA JORDAN (see: The File on Thelma Jordan)

6336 THEM (Gordon Douglas)
Films in R: v. V, n. 5 (May, 1954), pp. 244-245; Nicolas Monju, 450 wds.,
no cr.

THEME FOR A SHORT STORY (see: Syuzhet Dlya Nebolshogo Raskaza)

6337 THEN THERE WERE THREE (Alex Nicol)
Filmf: v. V (1962), p. 64; comp., cp. cr.

6338 THEODORA GOES WILD (Richard Boleslawski)
F Soc Rev: Oct. (1965), p. 29; David Mallery, 125 wds., pt. cr.

6339 THEODORA, SLAVE EMPRESS (Riccardo Freda)
(also: Teodora, Imperatrice di Bisanzio)
Films & F: v. 1, n. 8 (May, 1955), p. 18; John Simmons, 200 wds., cp. cr.

THEOREM (see: Teorema)

6340 THERE LIVED AN OLD MAN AND AN OLD WOMAN (Grigori Chukhrai)
(also: Zhili-Byli Starik So Starukhoi)
Interntl F G: v. 3 (1966), p. 149; 250 wds., pt. cr.

6341 THERE WAS A CROOKED MAN (Stuart Burge)
Films & F: v. 7, n. 2 (Nov., 1960), p. 32; John Cutts, 250 wds., cp. cr.

6342 THERE WAS A CROOKED MAN . . . (Joseph L. Mankiewicz)
Films & F: v. 17, n. 4 (Jan., 1971), p. 60; Gordon Gow, 550 wds., cp. cr.

6343 THERE WAS A DOOR (Derek Williams)
Sight & S: v. 27, n. 3 (Winter, 1957-1958), p. 149; David Robinson, 450
wds., no cr.

6344 THERE WAS AN OLD COUPLE (Grigory Choukhrai)
(also: Gili-Bili Starik So Staroukhoi)
Filmf: v. X (1967), p. 158; comp., cp. cr.

6345 THERE'S A GIRL IN MY SOUP (Roy Boulting)
Films & F: v. 17, n. 9 (June, 1971), p. 68; Margaret Tarratt, 200 wds., cp.
cr.

6346 THERE'S ALWAYS A PRICE TAG (Denys De La Patelliere)
      (also: Retour de Manivelle)
      Filmf: v. I (1958), p. 93; comp., cp. cr.

6347 THERE'S NO BUSINESS LIKE SHOW BUSINESS (Walter Lang)
      Films & F: v. 1, n. 6 (Mar., 1955), p. 21; Dennis Millmore, 250 wds., cp. cr.
      Films in R: v. VI, n. 1 (Jan., 1955), pp. 33-34; Robert Downing, 600 wds.,
        pt. cr.

6348 THERESE (Georges Franju)
      (also: Thérèse Desqueyroux)
      F Soc Rev: Feb. (1966), pp. 20-21; Bernard Oesch, 425 wds., cp. cr.
      Filmf: v. VI (1963), p. 318; comp., cp. cr.
      Films & F: v. 11, n. 6 (Mar., 1965), pp. 29-30; Gordon Gow, 925 wds., cp.
        cr.
      Movie: n. 12 (Spring, 1965), p. 45; 75 wds., no cr.
      Movie: n. 13 (Summer, 1965), pp. 34-35; James Leahy, 1500 wds., no cr.
      Sight & S: v. 34, n. 2 (Spring, 1965), pp. 93-94; Tom Milne, 900 wds., pt.
        cr.

6349 THERESE AND ISABELLE (Radley Metzger)
      F Quarterly: v. XXII, n. 1 (Fall, 1968), pp. 63-67; Richard Corliss, 2600
        wds., pt. cr.
      Filmf: v. XI (1968), p. 181; comp., cp. cr.
      Films & F: v. 16, n. 2 (Nov., 1969), pp. 44-45; Gordon Gow, 550 wds., cp.
        cr.

      THERESE DESQUEYROUX (see: Thérèse)

6350 THERESE RAQUIN (Marcel Carné)
      Films & F: v. 2, n. 10 (July, 1956), p. 23; Peter John Dyer, 300 wds., cp.
        cr.
      Sight & S: v. 26, n. 1 (Summer, 1956), p. 34; Derek Prouse, 600 wds., pt.
        cr.

6351 THERMIDOR (Tinto Brass)
      (also: Ca Ira-Il Fiume Della Rivolta; Ca Ira-River of Revolt)
      Filmf: v. XIV (1971), p. 515; comp., cp. cr.

6352 THESE ARE MY PEOPLE (George Stoney)
      F Quarterly: v. XXIV, n. 1 (Fall, 1970), p. 62; Ernest Callenbach, 450 wds.,
        no cr.

6353 THESE ARE THE DAMNED (Joseph Losey)
      (also: The Damned)
      F Quarterly: v. XIX, n. 1 (Fall, 1965), p. 63; R. M. Hodgens, 225 wds., no
        cr.
      Films & F: v. 9, n. 8 (May, 1963), pp. 24-25; Raymond Durgnat, 850 wds.,
        cp. cr.
      Movie: n. 9, pp. 32-34; Paul Mayersberg, 2300 wds., pt. cr.
      Sight & S: v. 32, n. 3 (Summer, 1963), pp. 143-144; Eric Rhode, 750 wds.,
        pt. cr.

      THESE DANGEROUS YEARS (see: Dangerous Youth)

6354 THESE FOUR COSY WALLS (John Clayton)
      F Lib Quarterly: v. 2, n. 3 (Summer, 1969), pp. 37, 39; Kathryn Dean, 450
        wds., pt. cr.

      THESE GHOSTS (see: Ghosts - Italian Style)

6355 THESE THOUSAND HILLS (Richard Fleischer)
      Filmf: v. II (1959), p. 79; comp., cp. cr.
      Films & F: v. 5, n. 7 (Apr., 1959), p. 23; Peter G. Baker, 125 wds., cp. cr.

      THEY ALL DIED LAUGHING (see: A Jolly Bad Fellow)

6356 THEY ALL DO IT (Knud Leif Thomsen)
      Films & F: v. 15, n. 10 July, 1964), p. 55; David Hutchison, 250 wds., cp.
        cr.

6357 THEY CALL ME MR. TIBBS (Gordon Douglas)
        Films & F: v. 17, n. 7 (Apr., 1971), pp. 50-51; David Rider, 400 wds., cp.
            cr.

6358 THEY CAME FROM BEYOND SPACE (Freddie Francis)
        Filmf: v. X (1967), p. 424; comp., cp. cr.

6359 THEY CAME TO CORDURA (Robert Rossen)
        Filmf: v. II (1959), p. 241; comp., cp. cr.
        Films & F: v. 6, n. 3 (Dec., 1959), pp. 22-23; Peter John Dyer, 500 wds.,
            cp. cr.
        Films in R: x. X, n. 9 (Nov., 1959), pp. 557-558; Logan MacDonald, 325
            wds., no cr.

6360 THEY CAME TO ROB LAS VEGAS (Antonio Isasi)
        (also: Las Vegas, 500 Millones)
        Filmf: v. XII (1969), p. 44; comp., cp. cr.
        Films & F: v. 16, n. 1 (Oct., 1969), p. 51; Richard Davis, 200 wds., cp. cr.

6361 THEY LIVE BY NIGHT (Nicholas Ray)
        Sequence: n. 7 (Spring, 1949), pp. 39-41; Gavin Lambert, 1000 wds., pt. cr.

        THEY LOVE AS THEY PLEASE (see: Greenwich Village Story)

6362 THEY MADE ME A FUGITIVE (Alberto Cavalcanti)
        (also: I Became a Criminal)
        Sight & S: v. 16, n. 63 (Autumn, 1947), p. 120; Arthur Vesselo, 300 wds.,
            no cr.

6363 THEY MIGHT BE GIANTS (Anthony Harvey)
        Filmf: v. XIV (1971), p. 172; comp., cp. cr.
        Films in R: v. XXII, n. 5 (May, 1971), p. 314; Gwenneth Britt, 100 wds.,
            no cr.

6364 THEY SHOOT HORSES, DON'T THEY? (Sydney Pollack)
        Cinema: v. 6, n. 1, pp. 11-15; Stephen Farber, 2800 wds., no cr.
        F Quarterly: v. XXIII, n. 4 (Summer, 1970), pp. 42-47; Paul Warshow,
            3000 wds., pt. cr.
        F Soc Rev: v. 5, n. 9 (May, 1970), pp. 32-37; Jonathan Benair, 2000 wds.,
            cp. cr.
        Filmf: v. XII (1969), p. 457; comp., cp. cr.
        Films & F: v. 16, n. 11 (Aug., 1970), p. 40; Gordon Gow, 800 wds., cp. cr.
        Films in R: v. XXI, n. 1 (Jan., 1970), pp. 48-49; Henry Hart, 550 wds., no
            cr.
        Focus: n. 6 (Spring, 1970), pp. 40-42; Myron Meisel and Charles Flynn,
            1500 wds., no cr.
        Focus on F: n. 3 (May-Aug., 1970), pp. 3-6; Allen Eyles, 750 wds., cp. cr.

6365 THEY WERE EXPENDABLE (John Ford)
        Sequence: n. 11 (Summer, 1950), pp. 19-24; Lindsay Anderson, 3500 wds.,
            no cr.

6366 THEY WERE NOT DIVIDED (Terence Young)
        Sequence: n. 11 (Summer, 1950), pp. 10-11; Lindsay G. Anderson, 1000
            wds., no cr.

6367 THEY WERE TEN (Baruch Dienar)
        Filmf: v. IV (1961), p. 204; comp., cp. cr.

6368 THEY WHO DARE (Lewis Milestone)
        Films & F: v. 15, n. 11 (Aug., 1969), p. 80; Kingsley Canham, 550 wds., no
            cr.

        THEY WHO TREAD ON THE TIGER'S TAIL (see: The Men Who Tred on the
            Tiger's Tail)

6369 THICK PUCKER (Robert Nelson)
        F Culture: n. 48-49 (Winter-Spring, 1970), p. 25; Robert Nelson, 400 wds.,
            pt. cr.
        F Quarterly: v. XX, n. 3 (Spring, 1967), pp. 50-52; Earl Bodien, 1400 wds.,
            no cr.

6370 THIEF, THE (Russell Rouse)
        Films in R: v. III, n. 9 (Nov., 1952), pp. 470-471; Terence Anderson, 450
          wds., pt. cr.
        Sight & S: v. 22, n. 3 (Jan.-Mar., 1953), p. 130; Penelope Houston, 200
          wds., no cr.

6371 THIEF OF BAGDAD (Raoul Walsh)
        F Soc Rev: Sept. (1965), pp. 13-14; J.T., 175 wds., no cr.

6372 THIEF OF BAGHDAD (Arthur Lubin)
        Filmf: v. IV (1961), p. 180; comp., cp. cr.
        Films & F: v. 9, n. 5 (Feb., 1963), pp. 40-41; Richard Whitehall, 400 wds.,
          cp. cr.

6373 THIEF OF PARIS, THE (Louis Malle)
        (Le Voleur)
        F Quarterly: v. XXIII, n. 1 (Fall, 1969), pp. 47-48; Tony Reif, 650 wds., pt.
          cr.
        Filmf: v. X (1967), p. 253; comp., cp. cr.
        Films in R: v. XVIII, n. 8 (Oct., 1967), p. 507-508; Hartley Ramsay, 350
          wds., no cr.

6374 THIN RED LINE, THE (Andrew Marton)
        Filmf: v. VII (1964), p. 292; comp., cp. cr.
        Films & F: v. 16, n. 4 (Jan., 1970), pp. 43-44; David Hutchison, 600 wds.,
          cp. cr.

6375 THING, THE (Christian Nyby)
        Films in R: v. II, n. 6 (June-July, 1951), pp. 38-39; Thomas T. Foose, 350
          wds., pt. cr.

6376 THING THAT COULDN'T DIE, THE (Will Cowan)
        Filmf: v. I (1958), p. 104; comp., cp. cr.

6377 THINGS OF LIFE, THE (Claude Sautet)
        (also: Les Choses de la Vie)
        Films & F: v. 17, n. 7 (Apr., 1971), pp. 56-57; Gordon Gow, 400 wds., cp.
          cr.
        Films in R: v. XXI, n. 8 (Oct., 1970), pp. 508-509; Joanne Chandler, 150
          wds., no cr.

6378 THIRD DAY, THE (Jack Smight)
        Films & F: v. 12, n. 1 (Oct., 1965), p. 26; Gordon Gow, 600 wds., cp. cr.

      THIRD KEY, THE (see: The Long Arm)

6379 THIRD LOVER, THE (Claude Chabrol)
        (also: L'Oeil du Malin)
        F Culture: n. 31 (Winter, 1963-1964), pp. 53-54; Robert Giard, 700 wds.,
          no cr.
        Filmf: v. VI (1963), p. 194; comp., cp. cr.
        Movie: n. 10, pp. 10-11; Jean-Andre Fieschi, 400 wds., no cr.

6380 THIRD MAN, THE (Carol Reed)
        Films & F: v. 15, n. 6 (Mar., 1969), pp. 87-88; Kingsley Canham, 600 wds.,
          no cr.
        Films in R: v. I, n. 2 (Mar., 1950), pp. 25-27; Ferencz Gunczy, 400 wds.,
          pt. cr.
      ● Sequence: n. 10 (New Year, 1950), pp. 176-177; Derick Grigs, 900 wds., pt.
          cr.

6381 THIRD MAN ON THE MOUNTAIN (Ken Annakin)
        Filmf: v. II (1959), p. 279; comp., cp. cr.
        Films & F: v. 6, n. 3 (Dec., 1959), p. 23; Robin Bean, 550 wds., cp. cr.

6382 THIRD OF A MAN (Robert Lewin)
        Filmf: v. V (1962), p. 353; comp., cp. cr.

      THIRD PART OF THE NIGHT, THE (see: Trecia Czesc Nocy)

6383 THIRD SECRET, THE (Charles Crichton)
      Filmf: v. VII (1964), p. 79; comp., cp. cr.
      Films & F: v. 11, n. 3 (Dec., 1964), pp. 24-25; Richard Davis, 700 wds., cp.
          cr.

6384 THIRD SEX, THE (Veit Harlan)
      (also: Anders Als du und Ich)
      Filmf: v. II (1959), p. 83; comp., cp. cr.
      Films & F: v. 5, n. 8 (May, 1959), p. 23; Peter G. Baker, 600 wds., cp. cr.

6385 THIRD VOICE, THE (Hubert Cornfield)
      Filmf: v. III (1960), p. 41; comp., cp. cr.
      Films & F: v. 6, n. 8 (May, 1960), p. 25; R. E. Durgnat, 100 wds., cp. cr.
      Films in R: v. XI, n. 3 (Mar., 1960), p. 171; Don Miller, 150 wds., no cr.

6386 13 FIGHTING MEN (Harry Gerstad)
      Filmf: v. III (1960), p. 59; comp., cp. cr.

6387 13 FRIGHTENED GIRLS (William Castle)
      Filmf: v. VI (1963), p. 182; comp., cp. cr.

6388 13 GHOSTS (William Castle)
      Filmf: v. III (1960), p. 175; comp., cp. cr.

6389 13 WEST STREET (Philip Leacock)
      Filmf: v. V (1962), p. 122; comp., cp. cr.

6390 13th LETTER, THE (Otto Preminger)
      Films in R: v. II, n. 3 (Mar., 1951), p. 44; Stephen Lewis, 300 wds., pt. cr.

6391 — 30 — (Jack Webb)
      (also: Deadline Midnight)
      Filmf: v. II (1959), p. 256; comp., cp. cr.
      Films & F: v. 6, n. 3 (Dec., 1959), p. 25; Derek Conrad, 350 wds., cp. cr.

6392 30 FOOT BRIDE OF CANDY ROCK, THE (Sidney Miller)
      Filmf: v. II (1959), p. 269; comp., cp. cr.

6393 30 IS A DANGEROUS AGE, CYNTHIA (Joseph McGrath)
      Filmf: v. XI (1968), p. 74; comp., cp. cr.
      Films & F: v. 15, n. 3 (Dec., 1968), p. 36; David Austen, 550 wds., cp. cr.

6394 39 STEPS, THE (Ralph Thomas)
      Filmf: v. III (1960), p. 261; comp., cp. cr.
      Films & F: v. 5, n. 7 (Apr., 1959), pp. 23-25; Peter G. Baker, 200 wds., cp.
          cr.
      Films in R: v. XI, n. 7 (Aug.-Sept., 1960),   p. 429-430; Maude McGlashan,
          200 wds., no cr.
      Sight & S: v. 28, n. 2 (Spring, 1959), p. 94; Penelope Houston, 300 wds.,
          pt. cr.

6395 36 HOURS (George Seaton)
      F Quarterly: v. XVIII, n. 3 (Spring, 1965), p. 61; R. M. Hodgens, 100 wds.,
          no cr.
      Filmf: v. VIII (1965), p. 27; comp., cp. cr.
      Films & F: v. 11, n. 5 (Feb., 1965), p. 35; Richard Davis, 450 wds., cp. cr.
      Sight & S: v. 34, n. 1 (Winter, 1964-1965), p. 41; John Russell Taylor, 300
          wds., pt. cr.

6396 30 YEARS OF FUN (Robert Youngson)
      Filmf: v. VI (1963), p. 327; comp., cp. cr.
      Films & F: v. 9, n. 11 (Aug., 1963), pp. 25-26; Ian Johnson, 400 wds., cp.
          cr.
      Films in R: v. XIV, n. 2 (Feb., 1963), pp. 110-111; Romano Tozzi, 250
          wds., no cr.

6397 THIS ANGRY AGE (René Clément)
      (also: Barrage Contre le Pacifique; La Diga Sul Pacifico; The Sea Wall)
      F Quarterly: v. XII, n. 1 (Fall, 1958), pp. 53-54; A.M.Z. 400 wds., no cr.
      Filmf: v. I (1958-1959), p. 138; comp., cp. cr.
      Films & F: v. 4, n. 7 (Apr., 1958), p. 24; Peter G. Baker, 400 wds., cp. cr.

Films in R: v. IX n. 9 (Nov., 1958), pp. 519-520; Mariana North, 600 wds., no cr.
Sight & S: v. 27, n. 4 (Spring, 1958), pp. 198; Penelope Houston, 750 wds., pt. cr.

6398 THIS COULD BE THE NIGHT (Robert Wise)
Films & F: v. 3, n. 10 (July, 1957), p. 33; Derek Conrad, 300 wds., cp. cr.

6399 THIS EARTH IS MINE (Henry King)
Filmf: v. II (1959), p. 143; comp., cp. cr.

6400 THIS HAPPY FEELING (Blake Edwards)
Filmf: v. I (1958), p. 100; comp., cp. cr.
Films & F: v. 4, n. 12 (Sept., 1958), pp. 23-24; Peter John Dyer, 200 wds., cp. cr.

6401 THIS IS EDWARD STEICHEN (Merrill Brockway, prod.)
F Lib Quarterly: v. 1, n. 1 (Winter, 1967-1968), p. 46; John Lunsford, 300 wds., pt. cr.

6402 THIS IS MY LOVE (Stuart Heisler)
Films & F: v. 1, n. 5 (Feb., 1955), p. 24; Clayton Cole, 450 wds., cp. cr.

6403 THIS IS MY STREET (Sidney Hayers)
Films & F: v. 10, n. 6 (Mar., 1964), p. 28; Allen Eyles, 500 wds., cp. cr.

6404 THIS IS THE B.B.C. (Richard Cawston)
Sight & S: v. 29, n. 1 (Winter, 1959-1960), p. 39; Derek Hill, 500 wds., no cr.

6405 THIS MAN MUST DIE (Claude Chabrol)
(also: Killer; Que la Bête Meure)
F Heritage: v. 6, n. 3 (Spring, 1971), pp. 26-31; Robert Giard, 2500 wds., no cr.
Films & F: v. 16, n. 9 (June, 1970), pp. 79-80; Gordon Gow, 1000 wds., cp. cr.

6406 THIS PROPERTY IS CONDEMNED (Sydney Pollack)
Cinema: v. 3, n. 3 (July, 1966), p. 47; Rory Guy, 700 wds., pt. cr.
F Quarterly: v. XX, n. 2 (Winter, 1966-1967), p. 61; Stephen Farber, 450 wds., no cr.
Filmf: v. IX (1966), p. 206; comp., cp. cr.
Films & F: v. 13, n. 2 (Nov., 1966), p. 6, 8; Raymond Durgnat, 1500 wds., cp. cr.

THIS REBEL AGE (see: The Beat Generation)

6407 THIS REBEL BREED (Richard L. Bare)
Filmf: v. III (1960), p. 35; comp., cp. cr.

6408 THIS RUGGED LAND (Arthur Hiller)
Films & F: v. 11, n. 10 (July, 1965), p. 32; Allen Eyles, 450 wds., cp. cr.

6409 THIS SHOCKING WORLD (Gianni Proia)
Filmf & F: v. 11, n. 4 (Jan., 1965), p. 35; Allen Eyles, 450 wds., cp. cr.

6410 THIS SPECIAL FRIENDSHIP (Jean Delannoy)
(also: Les Amities Particulieres)
Filmf: v. X (1967), p. 336; comp., cp. cr.

6411 THIS SPORTING LIFE (Lindsay Anderson)
Cinema: v. 1, n. 6 (Nov.-Dec., 1963), p. 44; James Silke, 250 wds., pt. cr.
F Quarterly: v. XVII, n. 4 (Summer, 1964), pp. 45-48; Ernest Callenbach, 1700 wds., pt. cr.
Filmf: v. VI (1963), p. 139; comp., cp. cr.
Films & F: v. 9, n. 6 (Mar., 1963), p. 32; Peter Baker, 900 wds., cp. cr.
Films in R: v. XIV, n. 7 (Aug.-Sept., 1963), pp. 437-438; Ivor Howard, 250 wds., no cr.
Interntl F G: v. 1 (1964), p. 76, 150 wds., pt. cr.
Movie: n. 7, p. 33; Gavin Millar, 1000 wds., pt. cr.
Movie: n. 10, pp. 21-22; 1800 wds., no cr.

THIS STRANGE AWAKENING (see: Female Fiends)

6412 THIS STUFF'LL KILL YA! (Herschell Gordon Lewis)
        Filmf: v. XIV (1971), p. 754; comp., cp. cr.

6413 THIS TIME THE WORLD (Marlin Johnson)
        F Quarterly: v. XXI, n. 3 (Spring, 1968), pp. 61-62; Albert Johnson, 700
            wds., no cr.

6414 THIS TRANSIENT LIFE (Akio Jissoji)
        (also: Mujo; Vanity of Life)
        Filmf: v. XIV (1971), p. 187; comp., cp. cr.

6415 THOMAS CROWN AFFAIR, THE (Norman Jewison)
        F Quarterly: v. XXII, n. 4 (Summer, 1969), pp. 60-61; Leo Braudy, 400
            wds., no cr.
        Filmf: v. XI (1968), p. 232; comp., cp. cr.
        Films & F: v. 15, n. 7 (Apr., 1969), pp. 41-42; David Rider, 800 wds., cp.
            cr.
        Films in R: v. XIX, n. 7 (Aug.-Sept., 1968), p. 455; Ellen Fitzpatrick Mc-
            Hugh, 250 wds., no cr.
        Movie: n. 16 (Winter, 1968-1969), p. 39; Mark Shivas, 75 wds., no cr.

6416 THOMAS ER FREDLOS (Sven Gronlykke)
        Interntl F G: v. 6 (1969), p. 62; Peter Cowie, 150 wds., pt. cr.

THOMAS L'IMPOSTEUR (see: Thomas the Imposter)

6417 THOMAS THE IMPOSTER (Georges Franju)
        (also: Thomas l'Imposteur)
        Films & F: v. 12 (May, 1966), pp. 18, 51; Peter Whitehead, 1120 wds., cp.
            cr.
        Sight & S: v. 35, n. 2 (Spring, 1966), pp. 87-89; Tom Milne, 2500 wds., pt.
            cr.

6418 THOROUGHLY MODERN MILLIE (George Roy Hill)
        F Quarterly: v. XXI, n. 1 (Fall, 1967), pp. 61-62; Stephen Farber, 200 wds.,
            no cr.
        Filmf: v. X (1967), p. 83; comp., cp. cr.
        Films in R: v. XVIII, n. 4 (Apr., 1967), p. 243; Page Cook, 250 wds., no cr.

THOSE BLASTED KIDS (see: De Pokkers Unger)

6419 THOSE CALLOWAYS (Norman Tokar)
        Filmf: v. VIII (1965), p. 131; comp., cp. cr.
        Films & F: v. 11, n. 8 (May, 1965), pp. 27-28; John Cutts, 375 wds., cp. cr.
        Films in R: v. XVI, n. 2 (Feb., 1965), pp. 115-116; Nanda Ward Haynes,
            150 wds., no cr.

6420 THOSE DARING YOUNG MEN IN THEIR JAUNTY JALOPIES (Ken
            Annakin)
        (also: Monte Carlo or Bust)
        Filmf: v. XII (1969), p. 323; comp., cp. cr.
        Films & F: v. 16, n. 1 (Oct., 1969), p. 40; Verrina Glaessner, 300 wds., cp.
            cr.

6421 THOSE FANTASTIC FLYING FOOLS (Don Sharp)
        (also: Blast-Off; Jules Verne's Rocket to the Moon)
        Filmf: v. X (1967), p. 301; comp., cp. cr.

6422 THOSE MAGNIFICENT MEN IN THEIR FLYING MACHINES (Ken Anna-
            kin)
        (also: How I Flew From London To Paris in 25 Hours and 11 Minutes)
        Cinema: v. 3, n. 1 (Dec., 1965), p. 48; Janice May, 450 wds., pt. cr.
        F Quarterly: v. XIX, n. 1 (Fall, 1965), p. 63; R. M. Hodgens, 100 wds., no
            cr.
        Filmf: v. VIII (1965), p. 123; comp., cp. cr.
        Films & F: v. 11, n. 11 (Aug., 1965), p. 31; Robin Bean, 400 wds., cp. cr.
        Films in R: v. XVI, n. 7 (Aug.-Sept., 1965), p. 451; Wilfred Mifflin, 200
            wds., no cr.

6423 THOU SHALT NOT KILL (Claude Autant-Lara)
(also: Tu Ne Tueras Point)
Films & F: v. 8, n. 7 (Apr., 1962), p. 28; Paul Rotha, 1000 wds., cp. cr.

6424 THOUSAND CLOWNS, A (Fred Coe)
Film: n. 47 (Winter, 1966), pp. 26-27; Bernard Hrusa, 150 wds., no cr.
Films & F: v. 13, n. 5 (Feb., 1967), p. 33; Richard Davis, 400 wds., cp. cr.
Films in R: v. XVI, n. 10 (Dec., 1965), pp. 641-642; Henry Hart, 275 wds.,
no cr.
Sight & S: v. 36, n. 1 (Winter, 1966-1967), pp. 46-47; John Russell Taylor,
400 wds., pt. cr.

6425 THOUSAND EYES OF DR. MABUSE, THE (Fritz Lang)
Films & F: v. 9, n. 2 (Nov., 1962), p. 40; Raymond Durgnat, 650 wds., cp.
cr.
Movie: n. 4 (Nov., 1962), p. 6; Mark Shivas, 800 wds., pt. cr.

6426 THREAT, THE (Charles R. Rondeau)
Filmf: v. III (1960), p. 45; comp., cp. cr.

6427 THREATENING SKY, THE (Joris Ivens)
(also: Le Ciel, La Terre)
Films & F: v. 13, n. 12 (Sept., 1967), p. 26; Raymond Durgnat, 800 wds.,
cp. cr.

6428 THREE (Aleksandar Petrovic)
(also: Tri; Trio)
Filmf: v. X (1967), p. 201; comp., cp. cr.
Films & F: v. 16, n. 4 (Jan., 1970), pp. 44, 49; Mark Powell, 700 wds., cp.
cr.

6429 THREE AVENGERS, THE (Gianfranco Parolini)
Films & F: v. 12, n. 1 (Oct., 1965), p. 31; Richard Davis, 250 wds., cp. cr.

6430 THREE BITES OF THE APPLE (Alvin Ganzer)
Filmf: v. X (1967), p. 159; comp., cp. cr.
Films & F: v. 13, n. 11 (Aug., 1967), p. 28; Richard Davis, 350 wds., cp. cr.

6431 THREE BLONDES IN HIS LIFE (Leon Chooluck)
Filmf: v. IV (1961), p. 2; comp., cp. cr.

6432 THREE BRAVE MEN (Philip Dunne)
Films & F: v. 3, n. 7 (Apr., 1957), p. 24; P. L. Mannock, 200 wds., cp. cr.
Films in R: v. VIII, n. 2 (Feb., 1957), p. 82; E.D.M., 150 wds., no cr.

6433 THREE CABALLEROS, THE (Norman Ferguson)
Films & F: v. 9, n. 9 (June, 1963), p. 37; Ian Johnson, 350 wds., cp. cr.

6434 THREE CAME HOME (Jean Negulesco)
Films in R: v. I, n. 3 (Nov., 1950), pp. 29-30, 48; Arthur Knight, 550 wds.,
pt. cr.

6435 THREE CAME TO KILL (Edward L. Cahn)
Filmf: v. III (1960), p. 64; comp., cp. cr.

6436 THREE COINS IN THE FOUNTAIN (Jean Negulesco)
Films & F: v. 1, n. 1 (Oct., 1954), p. 29; Sergio Viotti, 150 wds., cp. cr.
Films in R: v. V, n. 6 (June-July, 1954), pp. 303-304; Robert Kass, 350
wds., no cr.

THREE DAUGHTERS (see: Tri Dcery)

THREE DAYS AND A CHILD (see: Not Mine To Love)

THREE DAYS OF VICTOR CHERNISHES (see: Tri Dnya Viktora Cherniskeva)

6437 THREE FABLES OF LOVE (Rene Clair)
(also: Les Quatre Verites)
Filmf: v. VI (1963), p. 196; comp., cp. cr.

Films & F: v. 9, n. 11 (Aug., 1963), pp. 26; 31; Brian O'Brien, 500 wds., cp. cr.

Films in R: v. XIV, n. 8 (Oct., 1963), p. 493; Louise Corbin, 200 wds., no cr.

6438 THREE FACES OF EVE, THE (Nunnally Johnson)
Films & F: v. 4, n. 3 (Dec., 1957), p. 22; Peter G. Baker, 400 wds., cp. cr.
Films in R: v. VIII, n. 8 (Oct., 1957), pp. 404-405; Diana Willing, 250 wds., no cr.

THREE FACES OF LOVE (see: Sekishun)

6439 THREE GIRLS FROM ROME (Luciano Emmer)
Films in R: v. IV, n. 7 (Aug.-Sept., 1953), p. 368; 200 wds., pt. cr.

6440 THREE GODFATHERS (John Ford)
Film: n. 44 (Winter, 1965-1966), pp. 26-27; Douglas McVay, 500 wds., no cr.
Movie: n. 13 (Summer, 1965), p. 45; 125 wds., no cr.

6441 THREE GUNS FOR TEXAS (David Lowell Rich, Paul Stanley, Earl Bellamy)
Filmf: v. XI (1968), p. 532; comp., cp. cr.

6442 THREE HATS FOR LISA (Sidney Hayers)
Films & F: v. 11, n. 10 (July, 1965), pp. 34-35; Richard Davis, 525 wds., cp. cr.

6443 300 SPARTANS, THE (Rudolph Mate)
Filmf: v. V (1962), p. 223; comp., cp. cr.
Films & F: v. 9, n. 3 (Dec., 1962), p. 47; 250 wds., cp. cr.

6444 THREE IN THE ATTIC (Richard Wilson)
Cinema: v. 6, n. 1, p. 45; Patrick Ferrell, 500 wds., no cr.
F Quarterly: v. XXIII, n. 1 (Fall, 1969), pp. 56-57; Albert Johnson, 800 wds., no cr.
Filmf: v. XII (1969), p. 52; comp., cp. cr.
Films & F: v. 15, n. 12 (Sept., 1969), p. 68; Peter Buckley, 850 wds., cp. cr.

6445 3 INTO 2 WON'T GO (Peter Hall)
Filmf: v. XII (1969), p. 356; comp., cp. cr.
Films & F: v. 16, n. 2 (Nov., 1969), pp. 45-46; Gordon Gow, 550 wds., cp. cr.

6446 THREE LIVES (Kate Millett, Louva Irvine, Susan Klechner, Robin Mide)
F Lib Quarterly: v. 5, n. 1 (Winter, 1971-1972), pp. 53-54; Kristina Nordstrom, 500 wds., pt. cr.
Filmf: v. XIV (1971), p. 750; comp., cp. cr.

6447 THREE LIVES OF THOMASINA, THE (Don Chaffey)
Filmf: v. VII (1964), p. 59; comp., cp. cr.
Films & F: v. 10, n. 11 (Aug., 1964), pp. 25-26; Allen Eyles, 250 wds., cp. cr.

6448 THREE MEN IN A BOAT (Ken Annakin)
Filmf: v. II (1959), p. 199; comp., cp. cr.
Films & F: v. 3, n. 5 (Feb., 1957), p. 25; Peter G. Baker, 300 wds., cp. cr.

THREE MOVES TO FREEDOM (see: Brainwashed)

THREE MURDERESSES (see: Women Are Weak)

6449 3 NUTS IN SEARCH OF A BOLT (Tommy Noonan)
Filmf: v. VII (1964), p. 333; comp., cp. cr.

6450 THREE ON A COUCH (Jerry Lewis)
Cahiers in Eng: n. 11 (Sept., 1967), pp. 57-59; Jean-Louis Comolli, 1500 wds., cp. cr.
Cinema: v. 3, n. 4 (Dec., 1966), p. 50; Curtis Lee Hanson, 500 wds., no cr.
Filmf: v. IX (1966), p. 185; comp., cp. cr.
Films & F: v. 13, n. 3 (Dec., 1966), pp. 13-16; Raymond Durgnat, 800 wds., cp. cr.

6451 THREE ON A SPREE (Sidney J. Furie)
      Filmf: v. IV (1961), p. 304; comp., cp. cr.

6452 THREE ON LSD (Max Miller, David W. Parker, Paul Burnford, prods.)
      F Lib Quarterly: v. 1, n. 4 (Fall, 1968), p. 39; Janice Galbavy, 900 wds., pt.
      cr.

      THREE PENNY OPERA (see: The Threepenny Opera)

6453 THREE PLUS TWO (Genrikh Organisyan)
      Films & F: v. 12, n. 10 (July, 1966), pp. 13, 16; Allen Eyles, 450 wds., cp.
      cr.

6454 THREE SECRETS (Robert Wise)
      Films & F: v. 15, n. 10 (July, 1969), p. 86; Kingsley Canham, 500 wds., no
      cr.

6455 THREE SISTERS, THE (Samson Samsonov)
      (also: Tri Sestri)
      Filmf: v. XII (1969), p. 30; comp., cp. cr.

6456 THREE STOOGES GO AROUND THE WORLD IN A DAZE, THE (Norman
      Maurer)
      Filmf: v. VI (1963), p. 302; comp., cp. cr.

6457 THREE STOOGES IN ORBIT, THE (Edward Bernds)
      Filmf: v. V (1962), p. 164; comp., cp. cr.

6458 THREE STOOGES MEET HERCULES, THE (Edward Bernds)
      Filmf: v. V (1962), p. 4; comp., cp. cr.

6459 THREE TO GO (Peter Weir)
      Interntl F G: v. 9 (1972), pp. 53-54; David J. Statton, 200 wds., pt. cr.

6460 THREE TRUTHS IN THE WELL (Francois Villiers)
      (also: Le Puits Aux Trois Verites)
      Films & F: v. 9, n. 7 (Apr., 1963), pp. 34-35; Peter G. Baker, 350 wds., cp.
      cr.

6461 THREE VIOLENT PEOPLE (Rudolph Maté)
      Films & F: v. 3, n. 5 (Feb., 1957), pp. 22-23; P L. Mannock, 150 wds., cp.
      cr.

      THREE WOMEN (see: Trois Femmes)

6462 3 WORLDS OF GULLIVER, THE (Jack Sher)
      Filmf: v. III (1960), p. 322; comp., cp. cr.
      Films & F: v. 7, n. 3 (Dec., 1960), pp. 30-31; Dai Vaughan, 400 wds., cp.
      cr.
      Films in R: v. XI, n. 10 (Dec., 1960), pp. 616-617; R.S.T., 200 wds., no cr.

6463 THREEPENNY OPERA, THE (G.W. Pabst)
      (also: Die Dreigroschenoper; The Beggar's Opera)
      F Quarterly: v. XIV, n. 1 (Fall, 1960), pp. 43-45; Arlene Croce, 1100 wds.,
      pt. cr.
      Filmf: v. III (1960), p. 202; comp., cp. cr.
      Films & F: v. 7, n. 7 (Apr., 1961), pp. 15-17, 38; 3500 wds., cp. cr.
      Films in R: v. XI, n. 7 (Aug.-Sept., 1960), p. 433; Mark Seitling, 250 wds.,
      no cr.

6464 THRILL OF IT ALL, THE (Norman Jewison)
      Filmf: v. VI (1963), p. 163; comp., cp. cr.
      Films & F: v. 10, n. 3 (Dec., 1963), p. 27; Richard Whitehall, 550 wds., cp.
      cr.

6465 THRONE OF BLOOD (Akira Kurosawa)
      (also: Cobweb Castle; Kumonso-jo)
      Cinema: v. 1, n. 1, p. 44; 125 wds., pt. cr.
      Film: n. 15 (Jan.-Feb., 1958), pp. 22-23; Charles Fox, 700 wds., no cr.
      F Journal: n. 8 (July, 1957), pp. 3-4; Motoji Suda, 450 wds., no cr.

F Soc Rev: Feb. (1967), pp. 25-27; Alexander Sesonske, 800 wds., pt. cr.
Filmf: v. IV (1961), p. 318; comp., cp. cr.
Films & F: v. 4, n. 9 (June, 1958), p. 23; Peter John Dyer, 600 wds., cp. cr.
Films in R: v. XII, n. 10 (Dec., 1961), p. 622; Carlos Clarens, 275 wds., no cr.
Sight & S: v. 27, n. 2 (Summer, 1958), p. 250; Kenneth Cavander, 600 wds., pt. cr.

6466 THROUGH A GLASS DARKLY (Ingmar Bergman)
(also: Sasom I En Spegel)
Cinema: v. 1, n. 2, p. 33; 150 wds., pt. cr.
F Quarterly: v. XV, n. 4 (Summer, 1962), pp. 50-53; Vernon Young, 1400 wds., pt. cr.
Filmf: v. V (1962), p. 59; comp., cp. cr.
Films & F: v. 9, n. 4 (Jan., 1963), pp. 47-48; Peter Cowie, 900 wds., cp. cr.
Films in R: v. XIII, n. 4 (Apr., 1962), pp. 230-231; Henry Hart, 750 wds., no cr.
Movie: n. 6, pp. 30-31; Goran Persson, 1050 wds., pt. cr.
Sight & S: v. 32, n. 1 (Winter, 1962-1963), pp. 38-39; Peter Harcourt, 850 wds., no cr.

THROUGH THE SOUND BARRIER (see: Breaking the Sound Barrier)

6467 THUNDER ALLEY (Richard Rush)
Filmf: v. X (1967), p. 266; comp., cp. cr.
Films & F: v. 14, n. 10 (July, 1968), p. 38; Richard Davis, 300 wds., cp. cr.

6468 THUNDER BAY (Anthony Mann)
Films in R: v. IV, n. 6 (June-July, 1953), pp. 297-298; 300 wds., no cr.

6469 THUNDER IN CAROLINA (Paul Helmick)
Filmf: v. III (1960), p. 333; comp., cp. cr.

6470 THUNDER IN THE EAST (Nicholas Farkas)
(also: La Bakaille)
F Heritage: v. 4, n. 1 (Fall, 1968), pp. 19-28; Herman G. Weinberg, 3500 wds., pt. cr.

6471 THUNDER IN THE SUN (Russell Rouse)
Filmf: v. II (1959), p. 67; comp., cp. cr.

6472 THUNDER ISLAND (Jack Leewood)
Filmf: v. VI (1963), p. 309; comp., cp. cr.

6473 THUNDER OF DRUMS, A (Joseph Newman)
Film: n. 31 (Sept., 1962), p. 14; Ian Cameron, 350 wds., no cr.
Filmf: v. IV (1961), p. 249; comp., cp. cr.
Films & F: v. 8, n. 5 (Feb., 1962), p. 32; Robin Bean, 300 wds., cp. cr.

6474 THUNDER ROAD (Arthur Ripley)
Filmf: v. I (1958), p. 96; comp., cp. cr.
Films in R: v. IX, n. 6 (June-July, 1958), p. 336; Nancy Wharton, 150 wds., no cr.

6475 THUNDERBALL (Terence Young)
Cinema: v. 3, n. 2 (Mar., 1966), p. 45; Curtis Lee Hanson, 650 wds., pt. cr.
F Quarterly: v. XIX, n. 3 (Spring, 1966), pp. 53-54; R. M. Hodgens, 200 wds., no cr.
Films in R: v. XVII, n. 1 (Jan., 1966), pp. 46-47; Henry Hart, 500 wds., no cr.

6476 THUNDERBIRD 6 (David Lane)
Films & F: v. 14, n. 11 (Aug., 1968), p. 25; David Rider, 300 wds., cp. cr.

6477 THUNDERBIRDS ARE GO (David Lane)
Filmf: v. XI (1968), p. 527; comp., cp. cr.
Films & F: v. 13, n. 8 (May, 1967), p. 31; Richard Davis, 650 wds., cp. cr.

6478 THUNDERBOLT (Josef Von Sternberg)
Focus on F: n. 2 (Mar.-Apr., 1970), pp. 54-56; Claire Johnston, 1800 wds., cp. cr.

6479 THUNDERHOOF (Phil Karlson)
    (also: Fury)
    Focus on F: n. 5 (Winter/Nov.-Dec., 1970), p. 45; Don Miller, 350 wds., pt. cr.

6480 THUNDERING JETS (Helmut Dantine)
    Filmf: v. I (1958), p. 53; comp., cp. cr.

6481 THURSDAY'S CHILDREN (Lindsey Anderson and Guy Brenton)
    Films & F: v. 1, n. 3 (Dec., 1954), p. 20; Peter Barnes, 75 wds., cp. cr.
    Sight & S: v. 25, n. 1 (Summer, 1955), p. 36; Gavin Lambert, 300 wds., pt. cr.

6482 THX 1138 (George Lucas)
    (also: THX 1138-4EB)
    Cineaste: v. II, n. 1 (Summer, 1968), p. 25; Gary Crowdus, 600 wds., no cr.
    F Quarterly: v. XXIV, n. 4 (Summer, 1971), p. 67; Ernest Callenbach, 525 wds., no cr.
    F Soc Rev: May (1968), p. 20; William A. Starr, 300 wds., pt. cr.
    Filmf: v. XIV (1971), p. 143; comp., cp. cr.
    Interntl F G: v. 9 (1972), p. 266; Susan Rice, 200 wds., pt. cr.

THX 1138-4EB (see: THX 1138)

TI-KOYO ET IL SUO PESCECANE (see: Tiko and the Shark)

6483 TIA TULA, LA (Miguel Picazo)
    Films in R: v. XVI, n. 7 (Aug.-Sept., 1965), pp. 447-448; Rene H. Jordan, 150 wds., no cr.

6484 TIARA TAHITI (William T. Kotcheff)
    Filmf: v. VI (1963), p. 280; comp., cp. cr.
    Films & F: v. 8, n. 11 (Aug., 1962), pp. 29-30; Michael Ratcliffe, 500 wds., cp. cr.

6485 TICKLE ME (Norman Taurog)
    Films & F: v. 11, n. 11 (Aug., 1965), p. 33; Franki Owen, 400 wds., cp. cr.

6486 TICKLISH AFFAIR, A (George Sidney)
    Filmf: v. VI (1963), p. 178; comp., cp. cr.
    Films & F: v. 10, n. 3 (Dec., 1963), pp. 27, 28; Gordon Gow, 600 wds., cp. cr.

6487 TIGER AND THE PUSSYCAT, THE (Dino Risi)
    (also: Il Tigre)
    F Quarterly: v. XXI, n. 2 (Winter, 1967-1968), p. 64; Raymond Banacki, 150 wds., no cr.
    Filmf: v. X (1967), p. 272; comp., cp. cr.

6488 TIGER BAY (J. Lee Thompson)
    F Quarterly: v. XIII, n. 4 (Summer, 1960), pp. 51-52; Norman C. Moser, 650 wds., pt. cr.
    Filmf: v. II (1959), p. 334; comp., cp. cr.
    Films & F: v. 5, n. 8 (May, 1959), p. 25; Peter G. Baker, 200 wds., cp. cr.
    Films in R: v. XI, n. 1 (Jan., 1960), p. 43; Colley Williams, 200 wds., no cr.

TIGER BY THE TAIL (see: Cross-Up)

6489 TIGER IN THE SMOKE (Roy Baker)
    Films & F: v. 3, n. 4 (Jan., 1957), p. 27; Rodney Giesler, 175 wds., cp. cr.

6490 TIGER MAKES OUT, THE (Arthur Hiller)
    Filmf: v. X (1967), p. 267; comp., cp. cr.
    Films & F: v. 14, n. 6 (Mar., 1968), p. 29; David Austen, 500 wds., cp. cr.

TIGER VON ESCHNAPUR, DER (see: Tigress of Bengal)

6491 TIGER WALKS, A (Norman Tokar)
    Filmf: v. VII (1964), p. 220; comp., cp. cr.
    Films & F: v. 10, n. 8 (May, 1964), p. 26; John Cutts, 125 wds., cp. cr.
    Films in R: v. XV, n. 4 (Apr., 1964), p. 244; Romano Tozzi, 200 wds., no cr.

6492 TIGHT LITTLE ISLAND (Alexander Mackendrick)
         (also: Whiskey Galore)
         Films in R: v. I, n. 1 (Feb., 1950), pp. 29-30; Mary Britton Miller, 500 wds.,
               pt. cr.

         TIGRE, IL (see: The Tiger and the Pussycat)

6493 TIGRESS OF BENGAL (Fritz Lang)
         (also: Der Tiger von Eschnapur)
         Film: n. 33 (Autumn, 1962), p. 18; Nicholas Bartlett, 250 wds., no cr.
         Films & F: v. 8, n. 9 (June, 1962), p. 39; Raymond Durgnat, 550 wds., cp.
               cr.

         TIKHII DON (see: Quiet Flows the Don)

6494 TIKO AND THE SHARK (Folco Quilici)
         (also: Ti-Koyo et il Suo Pescecane)
         Filmf: v. IX (1966), p. 280; comp., cp. cr.

6495 TILL DEATH US DO PART (Norman Cohen)
         Films & F: v. 15, n. 6 (Mar., 1969), pp. 54-55; Raymond Durgnat, 1100
               wds., cp. cr.

         TILLSAMMANS MED GUNILLA MONDAG KVALL OCH TISDAG (see:
               Guilt)

6496 TILT TO THE SUN (Ronald Bowie)
         Interntl F G: v. 5 (1968), p. 123; 90 wds., pt. cr.

6497 TIMBUKTU (Jacques Tourneur)
         Filmf: v. II (1959), p. 272; comp., cp. cr.

6498 TIME BOMB (Yves Ciampi)
         (also: Le Vent Se Leve)
         Filmf: v. V (1962), p. 14; comp., cp. cr.

6499 TIME FOR BURNING, A (Barbara Connell and William Jersey)
         F Comment: v. IV, n. 2 & 3 (Fall-Winter, 1967), pp. 54-56; 500 wds., cp.
               cr.
         F Quarterly: v. XX, n. 2 (Winter, 1966-1967), pp. 51-53; Harland Nelson,
               800 wds., pt. cr.
         Filmf: v. X (1967), p. 61; comp., cp. cr.
         Films in R: v. XVII, n. 8 (Oct., 1966), p. 524; 100 wds., no cr.

6500 TIME FOR DYING, A (Budd Boetticher)
         F Quarterly: v. XXIII, n. 2 (Winter, 1969-1970), p. 64; Dan Bates, 450
               wds., no cr.

6501 TIME FOR KILLING, A (Phil Karlson)
         (also: The Long Ride Home)
         Filmf: v. XI (1968), p. 425; comp., cp. cr.
         Films & F: v. 14, n. 12 (Sept., 1968), p. 45; David Austen, 400 wds., cp. cr.

6502 TIME, GENTLEMEN, PLEASE (Lewis Gilbert)
         Sight & S: v. 22, n. 2 (Oct.-Dec., 1952), pp. 78-79; Edgar Anstey, 1000
               wds., no cr.

6503 TIME IS (Don Levy)
         F Lib Quarterly: v. 1, n. 1 (Winter, 1967-1968), pp. 46, 60; David Wade
               Chambers, 325 wds., pt. cr.

6504 TIME LIMIT (Karl Malden)
         Films & F: v. 4, n. 4 (Jan., 1958), p. 24; Gordon Gow, 650 wds., cp. cr.
         Films in R: v. VIII, n. 9 (Nov., 1957), pp. 463-464; John M. Bassett, 400
               wds., no cr.

6505 TIME LOCK (Gerald Thomas)
         Filmf: v. II (1959), p. 28; comp., cp. cr.
         Films & F: v. 4, n. 1 (Oct., 1957), pp. 23-24; Gordon Gow, 300 wds., cp.
               cr.

6506 TIME LOST AND TIME REMEMBERED (Desmond Davis)
        (also: I Was Happy Here)
        F Quarterly: v. XX, n. 3 (Spring, 1967), p. 63; Albert Johnson, 350 wds.,
             no cr.
        Filmf: v. IX (1966), p. 232; comp., cp. cr.
        Films & F: v. 12, n. 12 (Sept., 1966), pp. 18, 59, 60; Raymond Durgnat,
             1100 wds., cp. cr.
        Interntl F G: v. 4 (1967), p. 91; 250 wds., pt. cr.

6507 TIME MACHINE, THE (George Pal)
        F Quarterly: v. XIV, n. 1 (Fall, 1960), p. 62; 50 wds., no cr.
        Filmf: v. III (1960), p. 193; comp., cp. cr.
        Films & F: v. 6, n. 12 (Sept., 1960), p. 25; Peter G. Baker, 300 wds., cp. cr.

6508 TIME OF INDIFFERENCE (Francesco Maselli)
        (also: Gli Indifferenti; The Indifferent Ones)
        Filmf: v. IX (1966), p. 264; comp., cp. cr.

        TIME OF MASSACRE (see: The Brute and the Beast)

6509 TIME OF THE HEATHEN, THE (Peter Kass)
        Films & F: v. 10, n. 6 (Mars., 1964), pp. 30-31; Raymond Durgnat, 750
             wds., cp. cr.

6510 TIME OF THE LOCUST (Peter Gessner)
        F Comment: v. IV, n. 1 (Fall, 1966), p. 39; 100 wds., no cr.
        F Soc Rev: Apr. (1967), p. 19; Patrick MacFadden, 350 wds., pt. cr.

6511 TIME OUT FOR LOVE (Jean Valere)
        (also: Les Personnes Grandes)
        Filmf: v. VI (1963), p. 189; comp., cp. cr.

6512 TIME OUT OF WAR (Denis Sanders)
        Films & F: v. 1, n. 2 (Nov., 1954), p. 20; John Simmons, 100 wds., cp. cr.
        Sight & S: v. 24, n. 4 (Spring, 1955), pp. 197-198; Lindsay Anderson, 500
             wds., no cr.

6513 TIME STOOD STILL (Ermanno Olmi)
        (also: Il Tempo Se'Fermato)
        Sight & S: v. 32, n. 2 (Spring, 1963), p. 94; John Gillett, 700 wds., no cr.

        TIME TO LIVE AND A TIME TO DIE (Louis Malle/see: Le Feu Follet)

6514 TIME TO LOVE AND A TIME TO DIE, A (Douglas Sirk)
        Filmf: v. I (1958), p. 124; comp., cp. cr.
        Films & F: v. 4, n. 12 (Sept., 1958), p. 24; 500 wds., cp. cr.
        Screen: v. 12, n. 2 (Summer, 1971), pp. 95-98; Jean Luc-Godard, 1800
             wds., no cr.
        Sight & S: v. 27, n. 6 (Autumn, 1958), pp. 318-319; Richard Roud, 500
             wds., pt. cr.

6515 TIME TO SING, A (Arthur Dreifuss)
        Filmf: v. XI (1968), p. 535; comp., cp. cr.

6516 TIME TRAVELLERS, THE (Ib Melchior)
        Films & F: v. 12, n. 3 (Dec., 1965), p. 34; Richard Davis, 325 wds., cp. cr.

6517 TIME WITHOUT PITY (Joseph Losey)
        Films & F: v. 3, n. 9 (June, 1957), pp. 21-22; Peter G. Baker, 600 wds., cp.
             cr.

6518 TIMES FOR (Steve Dwoskin)
        Films & F: v. 17, n. 7 (Apr., 1971), pp. 51-53; Peter Buckley, 750 wds., cp.
             cr.

6519 TIMES GONE BY (Alessandro Blasetti)
        Films in R: v. IV, n. 7 (Aug.-Sept., 1953), p. 366; 160 wds., pt. cr.

6520 TIN STAR, THE (Anthony Mann)
        Silms & F: v. 4, n. 4 (Jan., 1958), p. 27; Gordon Gow, 250 wds., cp. cr.

6521 TINGLER, THE (William Castle)
         Filmf: v. II (1959), p. 332; comp., cp. cr.

         TINI ZABUTIKH PREDKIV (see: Shadows of Forgotten Ancestors)

6522 TIPS FOR TODAY (Jerzy Hoffman and Edward Skorzewski)
         (also: Typy Na Dzis)
         F Quarterly: v. XV, n. 1 (Fall, 1961), pp. 51-54; Roger Sandall, 1250 wds.,
            no cr.

         TIREZ SUR LE PIANISTE (see: Shoot the Piano Player)

6523 TITAN: THE STORY OF MICHELANGELO, THE (Richard Lyford)
         Films in R: v. I, n. 2 (Mar., 1950), pp. 23-25; Henry Hart, 600 wds., pt. cr.

         TITANI, I (see: Sons of Thunder)

6524 TITANIC (Jean Negulesco)
         Films in R: v. IV, n. 5 (May, 1953), pp. 241-242; 200 wds., pt. cr.

6525 TITFIELD THUNDERBOLT (Charles Crichton)
         Sight & S: v. 22, n. 2 (Apr.-June, 1953), p. 196; Penelope Houston, 400
            wds., pt. cr.

6526 TITICUT FOLLIES (Frederick Wiseman)
         Cinema: v. 6, n. 1, pp. 33-34; Stephen Mamber, 750 wds., no cr.
         F Comment: v. 5, n. 3 (Fall, 1969), pp. 60-61; Paul Bradlow, 1300 wds., no
            cr.
         F Lib Quarterly: v. 4, n. 2 (Spring, 1971), pp. 29-33; E. Michael Desilets,
            1500 wds., no cr.
         F Quarterly: v. XXI, n. 2 (Winter, 1967-1968), p. 55; Ernest Callenbach,
            125 wds., no cr.
         F Soc Rev: Oct. (1967), pp. 17-19; John L. Reilly, 600 wds., pt. cr.
         Filmf: v. X (1967), p. 314; comp., cp. cr.
         Films in R: v. XVIII, n. 9 (Nov., 1967), p. 580; 100 wds., no cr.
         N Y Rev of Books: v. XVII, n. 6 (21 Oct., 1971), pp. 19-22; Edgar Z.
            Friedenberg, 3000 wds., no cr.

         TIZEZER NAP (see: The Ten Thousand Suns)

         TO (see: Two People)

6527 TO BE A CROOK (Claude LeLouch)
         (also: The Decadent Influence; Une Fille et des Fusils; A Girl and Guns)
         Cineaste: v. I, n. 1 (Summer, 1967), p. 10; Andrew Lugg, 400 wds., no cr.
         F Quarterly: v. XXI, n. 1 (Fall, 1967), p. 60; Margot S. Kernan, 225 wds.,
            no cr.
         Filmf: v. X (1967), p. 32; comp., cp. cr.
         Films in R: v. XVIII, n. 2 (Feb., 1967), p. 117; Louise Corbin, 200 wds.,

         TO BE A MAN (see: Cry of Battle)

6528 TO BED OR NOT TO BED (Gian Luigi Polidoro)
         F Quarterly: v. XVII, n. 4 (Summer, 1964), p. 59; Ernest Callenbach, 225
            wds., no cr.
         Filmf: v. VI (1963), p. 305; comp., cp. cr.

6529 TO CATCH A THIEF (Alfred Hitchcock)
         F Culture: v. 1, n. 5-6 (Winter, 1955), p. 31; Andrew Sarris, 1000 wds., pt.
            cr.
         Films & F: v. 2, n. 3 (Dec., 1955), p. 16; Peter G. Baker, 250 wds., cp. cr.
         Films in R: v. VI, n. 7 (Aug.-Sept., 1955), p. 346; 375 wds., no cr.
         Sight & S: v. 25, n. 3 (Winter, 1955-1956), p. 150; Penelope Houston, 250
            wds., pt. cr.

6530 TO DIE IN MADRID (Frederic Rossif)
         (also: Mourir a Madrid)
         F Quarterly: v. XIX, n. 4 (Summer, 1966), pp. 55-56; Cesar Grana, 700
            wds., pt. cr.
         F Soc Rev: Feb. (1966), p. 12; Harvey Deneroff, 150 wds., pt. cr.

F Soc Rev: v. 6, n. 6 (Feb., 1971), pp. 41-46; Leonard Rubenstein, 2000 wds., cp. cr.

Films & F: v. 13, n. 8 (May, 1967), pp. 30-31; Ken Gay, 400 wds., cp. cr.

TO EACH HIS OWN (see: We Still Kill the Old Way)

6531 TO GRAB THE RING (Nikolai van der Heyde)
Interntl F G: v. 6 (1969), p. 131; Peter Cowie, 200 wds., pt. cr.

6532 TO HELL AND BACK (Jesse Hibbs)
Films in R: v. VI, n. 8 (Oct., 1955), p. 408; George Mitchell, 300 wds., pt. cr.

6533 TO KILL A MOCKINGBIRD (Robert Mulligan)
F Quarterly: v. XVI, n. 3 (Spring, 1963), p. 60; R. M. Hodgens, 150 wds., no cr.
Filmf: v. VI (1963), p. 13; comp., cp. cr.
Films & F: v. 9, n. 9 (June, 1963), p. 27; Gordon Gow, 900 wds., cp. cr.
Films in R: v. XIV, n. 3 (Mar., 1963), pp. 172-173; Henry Hart, 500 wds., no cr.
Movie: n. 9, p. 35; 75 wds., no cr.
Sight & S: v. 32, n. 3 (Summer, 1963), p. 147; John Russell Taylor, 350 wds., pt. cr.

TO LIVE (see; Ikuru)

6534 TO LOVE (Jorn Donner)
(also: Att Alska)
F Quarterly: v. XIX, n. 3 (Spring, 1966), pp. 34-36; Ernest Callenbach, 1300 wds., pt. cr.
Sight & S: v. 35, n. 4 (Autumn, 1966), pp. 200-201; Philip Strick, 300 wds., pt. cr.

6535 TO PARIS WITH LOVE (Robert Hamer)
Films & F: v. 1, n. 5 (Feb., 1955), p. 19; Derek Hill, 150 wds., cp. cr.

6536 TO SIR, WITH LOVE (James Clavell)
F Quarterly: v. XXI, n. 2 (Winter, 1967-1968), pp. 50-52; Stephen Farber, 1100 wds., pt. cr.
Filmf: v. X (1967), p. 139; comp., cp. cr.
Films & F: v. 14, n. 2 (Nov., 1967), p. 25; Robin Bean, 600 wds., cp. cr.

TO SOFERAKI (see: Taxi Driver)

6537 TO TRAP A SPY (Don Medford)
Filmf: v. IX (1966), p. 76; comp., cp. cr.

6538 TOBRUK (Arthur Hiller)
Filmf: v. X (1967), p. 52; comp., cp. cr.
Films & F: v. 13, n. 12 (Sept., 1967), p. 24; Richard Davis, 250 wds., cp. cr.
Films in R: v. XVIII, n. 1 (Jan., 1967), pp. 52-53; Page Cook, 200 wds., no cr.

6539 TOBY TYLER (Charles Barton)
Filmf: v. III (1960), p. 81; comp., cp. cr.
Films & F: v. 6, n. 8 (May, 1960), pp. 24-25; John Cutts, 150 wds., cp. cr.

6540 TOCCATA (Herman van der Horst)
Interntl F G: v. 6 (1969), p. 121; Peter Cowie, 125 wds., pt. cr.

6541 TODAY IT'S ME, TOMORROW YOU (Tonio Cervi)
Films & F: v. 15, n. 12 (Sept., 1969), p. 72; David Hutchison, 400 wds., cp. cr.

6542 TODD KILLINGS, THE (Barry Shear)
Filmf: v. XIV (1971), p. 560; comp., cp. cr.

TOI LE VENIN (see: The Night Is Not for Sleep)

6543 TOILEANACH A DFHILL, AN (Jim Mulkerns)
(also: The Return of the Islander)
Interntl F G: v. 9 (1972), p. 99; Anthony Slide, 200 wds., pt. cr.

6544 TOKYO AFTER DARK (Norman Herman)
Filmf: v. II (1959), p. 17; comp., cp. cr.

TOKYO MONOGATARI (see: Tokyo Story)

6545 TOKYO OLYMPIAD (Kon Ichikawa)
F Comment: v. 3, n. 3 (Summer, 1965), pp. 38-40; Cid Corman, 1800 wds., no cr.
F Quarterly: v. XIX, n. 3 (Spring, 1966), p. 50; John Thomas, 450 wds., pt. cr.
Filmf: v. IX (1966), p. 374; comp., cp. cr.
Films & F: v. 12, n. 2 (Nov., 1965), p. 25; Peter Cowie, 1000 wds., cp. cr.
Interntl F G: v. 3 (1966), p. 103; 300 wds., pt. cr.
Movie: n. 14 (Autumn, 1965), p. 40; Mark Shivas, 125 wds., no cr.
Sight & S: v. 34, n. 4 (Autumn, 1965), p. 199; John Gillett, 800 wds., no cr.

6546 TOKYO STORY (Yasujiro Ozu)
(also: Their First Trip to Tokyo; Tokyo Monogatari)
Film: n. 13 (Sept.-Oct., 1957), pp. 20-21; John Gillett, 500 wds., no cr.
Films & F: v. 11, n. 10 (July, 1965), p. 33; Gordon Gow, 700 wds., cp. cr.
Movie: n. 13 (Summer, 1965), pp. 32-33; Robin Wood, 1600 wds., no cr.

TOLLDREISTEN GESCHICHTEN DES HONORE DE BALZAC, DIE (see: The Brazen Women of Balzac)

TOLLER HECHT AUF KRUMMER TOUR (see: The Phony American)

6547 TOM JONES (Tony Richardson)
Filmf: v. VI (1963), p. 205; comp., cp. cr.
Films & F: v. 9, n. 11 (Aug., 1963), pp. 21-22; Peter Baker, 700 wds., cp. cr.
Films in R: v. XIV, n. 8 (Oct., 1963), pp. 496-497; Angus Buchanan, 325 wds., no cr.
Interntl F G: v. 1 (1964), p. 74; 150 wds., pt. cr.

6540 TOM THUMB (George Pal)
Filmf: v. I (1958), p. 255; comp., cp. cr.
Films & F: v. 5, n. 4 (Jan., 1959), p. 23; Peter G. Baker, 125 wds., cp. cr.
Films in R: v. X, n. 1 (Jan., 1959), p. 40; Prudence Ashton, 200 wds., no cr.

6549 TOMB OF LIGEIA, THE (Roger Corman)
F Quarterly: v. XVIII, n. 3 (Spring, 1965), pp. 61-62; John Thomas, 200 wds., no cr.
Films & F: v. 11, n. 6 (Mar., 1965), p. 38; Robin Bean, 325 wds., cp. cr.

6550 TOMB OF TURTURE (William Grace)
Filmf: v. IX (1966), p. 388; comp., cp. cr.

6551 TOMBOY AND THE CHAMP (Francis D. Lyon)
Filmf: v. IV (1961), p. 373; comp., cp. cr.
Films & F: v. 9, n. 5 (Feb., 1963), David Rider, 300 wds., cp. cr.

6552 TOMMY STEELE STORY, THE (Gerard Bryant)
(also: Rock Around the World)
Sight & S: v. 27, n. 1 (Summer, 1957), p. 43; David Robinson, 300 wds., pt. cr.

TOMORROW AT MIDNIGHT (see: For Love or Money)

6553 TOMORROW IS MY TURN (Andre Cayatte)
Cinema: v. 1, n. 3, p. 34; 200 wds., pt. cr.
Filmf: v. V (1962), p. 80; comp., cp. cr.
Films in R: v. XIII, n. 3 (Mar., 1962), pp. 173-174; Louise Corbin, 225 wds., no cr.

TON OMBRE A LA MIENNE (see: Your Shadow Is Mine)

6554 TONIGHT IN BRITAIN (Gerry Bryant)
Films & F: v. 1, n. 3 (Dec., 1954), p. 20; Ivan Pattison, 300 wds., cp. cr.

6555 TONIGHT LET'S ALL MAKE LOVE IN LONDON (Peter Whitehead)
        Films & F: v. 14, n. 5 (Feb., 1968), pp. 23-24; Raymond Durgnat, 1100
          wds., cp. cr.

6556 TONIO DROGER (Rolf Thiele)
        Filmf: v. XI (1968), p. 13; comp., cp. cr.
        Films in R: v. XIX, n. 2 (Feb., 1968), pp. 108-109; Henry Hart, 375 wds.,
          no cr.

6557 TONKA (Lewis R. Foster)
        Filmf: v. II (1959), p. 48; comp., cp. cr.

6558 TONY DRAWS A HORSE (John Paddy Carstairs)
        Films in R: v. II, n. 7 (Aug.-Sept., 1951), p. 40-41; Margaret I. Lamont, 450
          wds., pt. cr.

6559 TONY ROME (Gordon Douglas)
        Filmf: v. X (1967), p. 349; comp., cp. cr.
        Films & F: v. 14, n. 5 (Feb., 1968), p. 22; David Austen, 600 wds., cp. cr.

      TOO HOT TO HANDLE (see: Playgirls After Dark)

6560 TOO LATE BLUES (John Cassavetes)
        F Quarterly: v. XV, n. 1 (Winter, 1961-1962), pp. 49-51; Albert Johnson,
          1200 wds., pt. cr.
        Filmf: v. V (1962), p. 33; comp., cp. cr.
        Films & F: v. 8, n. 3 (Dec., 1961), pp. 29-31; Raymond Durgnat, 700 wds.,
          cp. cr.
        Sight & S: v. 31, n. 1 (Winter 1961-1962), pp. 40-41; Philip Oakes, 900
          wds., pt. cr.

6561 TOO LATE THE HERO (Robert Aldrich)
        Films & F: v. 17, n. 1 (Oct., 1970), p. 44; Gordon Gow, 550 wds., cp. cr.

6562 TOO MANY CROOKS (Mario Zampi)
        Filmf: v. II (1959), p. 102; comp., cp. cr.
        Films & F: v. 5, n. 7 (Apr., 1959), p. 23; Peter G. Baker, 175 wds., cp. cr.

      TOO MUCH TALK (see: Ohayo)

6563 TOO MUCH, TOO SOON (Art Napoleon)
        Filmf: v. I (1958), p. 69; comp., cp. cr.
        Films & F: v. 4, n. 11 (Aug., 1958), p. 27; John Cutts, 300 wds., cp. cr.
        Films in R: v. IX, n. 5 (May, 1958), pp. 268-269; William K. Everson, 400
          wds., no cr.

      TOO SOON TO DIE (see: Wake Up and Die)

6564 TOO SOON TO LOVE (Richard Rush)
        Filmf: v. III (1960), p. 33; comp., cp. cr.

6565 TOO YOUNG FOR LOVE (Erica Balque)
        (also: Zu Jung fur Die Liebe)
        Films & F: v. 11, n. 2 (Nov., 1964), p. 28; David Rider, 500 wds., cp. cr.

6566 TOO YOUNG TO LOVE (Muriel Box)
        Films & F: v. 6, n. 7 (Apr., 1960), p. 25; R. E. Durgnat, 150 wds., cp. cr.

6567 TOO YOUNG, TOO IMMORAL (Raymond Phelan)
        Filmf: v. V (1962), p. 218; comp., cp. cr.

6568 TOP, THE (Jimmy Murakami)
        F Quarterly: v. XIX, n. 4 (Summer, 1966), pp. 65-66; Ernest Callenbach,
          800 wds., pt. cr.

6569 TOP SECRET AFFAIR (H. C. Potter)
        (also: Their Secret Affair)
        Films & F: v. 3, n. 8 (May, 1957), p. 26; Leo Harris, 400 wds., cp. cr.
        Films in R: v. VIII, n. 2 (Feb., 1957), p. 85; V.H., 125 wds., no cr.

6570 TOPAZ (Alfred Hitchcock)
  F Heritage: v. 5, n. 2 (Winter, 1969-1970), pp. 17-23; Joseph McBride,
    2000 wds., no cr.
  F Quarterly: v. XXIII, n. 3 (Spring, 1970), pp. 41-44; Richard Corliss, 2100
    wds., pt. cr.
  Films & F: v. 16, n. 4 (Jan., 1970), pp. 39-40; Gordon Gow, 750 wds., cp.
    cr.
  Films in R: v. XXI, n. 2 (Feb., 1970), pp. 119-120; Elaine Rothschild, 300
    wds., no cr.
  Focus: n. 6 (Spring, 1970), pp. 26-27; Z. Samuel Bernstein, 1100 wds., no
    cr.
  Movie: n. 18 (Winter, 1970-1971), pp. 10-13; Michael Walker, 2500 wds.,
    no cr.
  N Y Rev of Books: v. XIV, n. 4 (Feb. 26, 1970), pp. 27-31; Robert
    Mazzocco, 3500 wds., no cr.
  Sight & S: v. 39, n. 1 (Winter, 1969-1970), p. 49; Philip Strick, 800 wds.,
    pt. cr.

6571 TOPKAPI (Jules Dassin)
  F Quarterly: v. XVIII, n. 2 (Winter, 1964), pp. 59-60; R. M. Hodgens, 200
    wds., no cr.
  Filmf: v. VII (1964), p. 216; comp., cp. cr.
  Films & F: v. 11, n. 3 (Dec., 1964), p. 24; Gordon Gow, 500 wds., cp. cr.
  Films in R: v. XV, n. 8 (Oct., 1964), pp. 498-499; Nanda Ward Haynes, 300
    wds., no cr.

  TORA NO O O FUMU OTOKOTACHI (see: The Men Who Tread on the
    Tiger's Tail)

6572 TORA! TORA! TORA! (Richard Fleischer, Toshio Masuda, Kinji Fukasaku)
  Cineaste: v. IV, n. 2 (Fall, 1970), pp. 40-41; John Pyros, 1200 wds., pt. cr.
  Films & F: v. 17, n. 3 (Dec., 1970), pp. 50-51; Gordon Gow, 750 wds., cp.
    cr.
  Films in R: v. XXI, n. 8 (Oct., 1970), pp. 503-505; Henry Hart, 500 wds.,
    no cr.

6573 TORERO! (Carlos Velo)
  F Culture: v. 3, n. 3 (1957), pp. 14-15; Barry Sussman, 1200 wds., pt. cr.
  Films in R: v. VIII, n. 5 (May, 1957), pp. 224-225; R. V. Tozzi, 400 wds.,
    no cr.

6574 TORMENT (Robert Hossein)
  Films & F: v. 7, n. 7 (Apr., 1961), pp. 29-30; Raymond Durgnat, 400 wds.,
    cp. cr.

  TORMENT (Alf Sjoberg/see: Frenzy)

6575 TORMENTED (Bert I. Gordon)
  Filmf: v. III (1960), p. 350; comp., cp. cr.

6576 TORN CURTAIN (Alfred Hitchcock)
  Cahiers in Eng: n. 10 (May, 1967), p. 51; Jean Narboni, 1000 wds., no cr.
  Cahiers in Eng: n. 10 (May, 1967), pp. 51-55; Jean-Louis Comolli, 2000
    wds., no cr.
  Cahiers in Eng: n. 10 (May, 1967), pp. 55-56; Sylvain Godet, 600 wds., no
    cr.
  Cahiers in Eng: n. 10 (May, 1967), pp. 58-59; Andrew Sarris, 1700 wds., no
    cr.
  Cahiers in Eng: n. 10 (May, 1967), pp. 59-60; Stephen Gottlieb, 600 wds.,
    no cr.
  F Quarterly: v. XX, n. 2 (Winter, 1966-1967), p. 63; R. M. Hodgens, 75
    wds., no cr.
  Filmf: v. IX (1966), p. 188; comp., cp. cr.
  Films & F: v. 13, n. 1 (Oct., 1966), pp. 9, 12; Gordon Gow, 1050 wds., cp.
    cr.
  Films in R: v. XVII, n. 7 (Aug.-Sept., 1966), p. 451; Adelaide Comerford,
    250 wds., no cr.
  Sight & S: v. 35, n. 4 (Autumn, 1966), p. 198; Penelope Houston, 500 wds.,
    pt. cr.
  Take One: v. 1, n. 1 (Sept.-Oct., 1966), pp. 16-17; Bob Huber, 675 wds., pt.
    cr.

6577 TORPEDO RUN (Joseph Pevney)
       Filmf: v. I (1958), p. 199; comp., cp. cr.

6578 TORPEDO ZONE (Duilio Coletti)
       (also: La Grande Speranza)
       Filmf: v. II (1959), p. 343; comp., cp. cr.

6579 TORTURE GARDEN (Freddie Francis)
       Filmf: v. XI (1968), p. 291; comp., cp. cr.
       Films & F: v. 14, n. 6 (Mar., 1968), p. 26; Richard Davis, 800 wds., cp. cr.

6580 TOSCA, LA (Jean Renoir, Luchino Visconti, Carl Koch)
       Sight & S: v. 35, n. 2 (Spring, 1966), p. 91; Tom Milne, 1200 wds., pt. cr.

6581 TOSCA (Carmine Gallone)
       Filmf: v. I (1958), p. 220; comp., cp. cr.
       Films in R: v. IX, n. 6 (June-July, 1958), pp. 337-338; Louise Corbin, 175
          wds., no cr.

6582 TOTE VON BEVERLY HILLS, DIE (Michaël Pfleghar)
       Interntl F G: v. 2 (1965), p. 78; Peter Graham, 200 wds., pt. cr.

6583 TOTEM (Ed Emshwiller)
       F Quarterly: v. XX, n. 3 (Spring, 1967), pp. 46-50; Richard Whitehall, 2200
          wds., no cr.

       TOTEN AUGEN VON LONDON, DIE (see: Dead Eyes of London)

6584 TOUCH, THE (Ingmar Bergman)
       (also: Beroringen)
       F Quarterly: v. XXV, n. 2 (Winter, 1971-1972), pp. 58-59; Ernest Callen-
          bach, 500 wds., no cr.
       Filmf: v. XIV (1971), p. 507; comp., cp. cr.
       Sight & S: v. 40, n. 4 (Autumn, 1971), p. 224; Philip Strick, 1100 wds., pt.
          cr.

6585 TOUCH AND GO (Michael Truman)
       Films & F: v. 2, n. 2 (Nov., 1955), pp. 16-17; Catherine de la Roche, 200
          wds., cp. cr.

6586 TOUCH OF DEATH (Lance Comfort)
       Films & F: v. 9, n. 5 (Feb., 1963), pp. 41-42; Ian Johnson, 550 wds., cp. cr.

6587 TOUCH OF EVIL (Orson Welles)
       F Comment: v. 7, n. 2 (Summer, 1971), pp. 51-53; Terry Comito, 1800
          wds., cp. cr.
       F Culture: n. 20 (1959), pp. 80-82; Herman G. Weinberg, 1100 wds., pt. cr.
       Filmf: v. I (1958), p. 89; comp., cp. cr.
       Films & F: v. 4, n. 10 (July, 1958), pp. 25-26; John Cutts, 550 wds., cp. cr.
       Films in R: v. IX, n. 4 (Apr., 1958), p. 206; Jeremy Browne, 250 wds., no
          cr.
       Sight & S: v. 27, n. 5 (Summer, 1958), pp. 251-252; Penelope Houston, 550
          wds., pt. cr.

6588 TOUCH OF FLESH, THE (R. John Hugh)
       Filmf: v. III (1960), p. 356; comp., cp. cr.

6589 TOUCH OF LARCENY, A (Guy Hamilton)
       Filmf: v. III (1960), p. 64; comp., cp. cr.
       Films & F: v. 6, n. 5 (Feb., 1960), p. 24; Ian Moss, 300 wds., cp. cr.
       Films in R: v. XI, n. 2 (Feb., 1960), p. 101; Norman Cecil, 275 wds., no cr.

       TOUCH OF LOVE, A (see: Thank You All Very Much)

6590 TOUCHABLES, THE (Robert Freeman)
       F Quarterly: v. XXIII, n. 1 (Fall, 1969), pp. 56-57; Albert Johnson, 800
          wds., no cr.
       Filmf: v. XI (1968), p. 475; comp., cp. cr.
       Films & F: v. 16, n. 4 (Jan., 1970), p. 44; John Walker, 450 wds., cp. cr.

TOUCHEZ-PAS AU GRISBI (see: Grisbi)

6591 TOUGHEST GUN IN TOMBSTONE (Earl Bellamy)
Filmf: v. I (1958), p. 224; comp., cp. cr.

TOUHA ZUANA ANADA (see: Adrift)

6592 TOUS LES GARCONS S'APELLENT PATRICK (Jean-Luc Godard)
(also: Charlotte et Veronique)
Movie: n. 12 (Spring 1965), p. 45; 75 wds., no cr.

TOUT L'OR DU MONDE (see: All the Gold in the World)

6593 TOUT PRENDRE, A (Claude Jutra)
(also: The Way It Goes; Take It All)
F Quarterly: v. XVII, n. 2 (Winter, 1963-1964), pp. 39-42; Colin Young,
1400 wds., pt. cr.
Filmf: v. IX (1966), p. 101; comp., cp. cr.

6594 TOUTE LA MEMOIRE DU MONDE (Alain Resnais)
F Quarterly: v. XIII, n. 1 (Fall, 1959), pp. 56-61; Noel Burch, 2900 wds.,
no cr.

TOWARD THE UNKNOWN (see: Brink of Hell)

6595 TOWER OF LONDON (Roger Corman)
Filmf: v. VI (1963), p. 345; comp., cp. cr.
Films & F: v. 14, n. 1 (Oct., 1967), p. 23; David Austen, 400 wds., cp. cr.

6596 TOWER OF LUST (Abel Gance)
Films & F: v. 7, n. 11 (Aug., 1961), p. 26; Raymond Durgnat, 250 wds., cp.
cr.

6597 TOWERS OPEN FIRE (Anthony Balch)
Movie: n. 11, p. 33; Ian Cameron, 950 wds., pt. cr.

TOWN CALLED BASTARD, A (see: A Town Called Hell)

6598 TOWN CALLED HELL, A (Robert Parrish)
(also: A Town Called Bastard)
Filmf: v. XIV (1971), p. 597; comp., cp. cr.
Films & F: v. 17, n. 10 (July, 1971), p. 58; Peter Buckley, 400 wds., cp. cr.

6599 TOWN LIKE ALICE, A (Jack Lee)
(also: The Rape of Malaya)
Filmf: v. I (1958), p. 184; comp., cp. cr.
Films & F: v. 2, n. 7 (Apr., 1956), p. 14; Peter G. Baker, 250 wds., cp. cr.

6600 TOWN ON TRIAL (John Guillerman)
Films & F: v. 3, n. 6 (Mar., 1957), p. 24; P. L. Mannock, 200 wds., cp. cr.

6601 TOWN WITHOUT PITY (Gottfried Reinhardt)
(also: Stadt Ohne Mitleid)
Filmf: v. IV (1961), p. 267; comp., cp. cr.
Films & F: v. 8, n. 4 (Jan., 1962), pp. 33-34; Robin Bean, 800 wds., cp. cr.
Films in R: v. XII, n. 9 (Nov., 1961), pp. 554-555; Elaine Rothschild, 250
wds., no cr.

6602 TOYS IN THE ATTIC (George Roy Hill)
Cinema: v. 1, n. 5, p. 46; R. G., 400 wds., pt. cr.
Filmf: v. VI (1963), p. 151; comp., cp. cr.
Films & F: v. 10, n. 3 (Dec., 1963), p. 38; Gordon Gow, 500 wds., cp. cr.
Films in R: v. XIV, n. 7 (Aug.-Sept., 1963), p. 439; Adelaide Comerford,
200 wds., no cr.

6603 TRACK OF THE CAT (William Wellman)
Films in R: v. VI, n. 1 (Jan., 1955), pp. 37-38; 350 wds., pt. cr.

6604 TRACK OF THUNDER (Joseph Kane)
Filmf: v. XI (1968), p. 17; comp., cp. cr.

6605 TRADER HORN (W. S. Van Dyke)
        Focus on F: n. 10 (Summer, 1972), pp. 57-58; John Gillett, 700 wds., cp.
           cr.
        Views & Rev: v. 3, n. 1 (Summer, 1971), pp. 35-45; Ray Cabana Jr. 4000
           wds., no cr.
        Views & Rev: v. 3, n. 1 (Summer, 1971), pp. 51-58; Jon Tuska, 2000 wds.,
           cp. cr.

        TRADITA (see: Night of Love)

6606 TRAFFIC (Jacques Tati)
        Focus on F: n. 8 (Oct., 1971), p. 8; Allen Eyles, 250 wds., cp. cr.

6607 TRAIL DRIVE (Alan James)
        Views & Rev: v. 2, n. 2 (Fall, 1970), pp. 30-35; 1400 wds., cp. cr.

6608 TRAIN, THE (John Frankenheimer)
        Cinema: v. 2, n. 6 (Aug., 1965), pp. 48-49; Harlan Ellison, 1500 wds., pt.
           cr.
        Filmf: v. VIII (1965), p. 75; comp., cp. cr.
        Films & F: v. 11, n. 3 (Dec., 1964), p. 25; Robin Bean, 600 wds., cp. cr.
        Films in R: v. XVI, n. 3 (Mar., 1965), pp. 179-180; Joan Horvath, 350 wds.,
           no cr.
        Sight & S: v. 34, n. 1 (Winter, 1964-1965), p. 40; Penelope Houston, 750
           wds., pt. cr.

6609 TRAIN ROBBERS, THE (Roberto Farias)
        (also: O Assalto Ao Trem Pagador)
        Films & F: v. 10, n. 2 (Nov., 1963), p. 31; Robin Bean, 350 wds., cp. cr.

6610 TRAITOR, THE (Michael McCarthy)
        Films & F: v. 3, n. 8 (May, 1957), pp. 26-27; Peter G. Baker, 200 wds., cp.
           cr.

6611 TRAITORS, THE (Robert Tronson)
        Filmf: v. VI (1963), p. 126; comp., cp. cr.
        Films & F: v. 8, n. 12 (Sept., 1962), pp. 36-37; David Rider, 400 wds., cp.
           cr.

6612 TRAITOR'S GATE (Freddie Francis)
        Filmf: v. IX (1966), p. 387; comp., cp. cr.

        TRAMP, THE (see: Magnificent Tramp)

6613 TRAMPLERS, THE (Albert Band)
        Filmf: v. IX (1966), p. 358; comp., cp. cr.
        Films & F: v. 15, n. 1 (Oct., 1968), p. 48; David Austen, 250 wds., cp. cr.

        TRANQUILLO POSTO DI CAMPAGNA, UN (see: A Quiet Place in the Coun-
           try)

6614 TRANS-EUROPE EXPRESS (Alain Robbe-Grillet)
        Filmf: n. 50 (Winter, 1967), pp. 31-32; Langdon Dewey, 500 wds., no cr.
        F Quarterly: v. XXII, n. 3 (Spring, 1969), pp. 40-44; Judith Gollub, 3000
           wds., pt. cr.
        Filmf: v. XI (1968), p. 193; comp., cp. cr.
        Films & F: v. 15, n. 9 (June, 1969), pp. 41-42; Brian Murphy, 800 wds., cp.
           cr.
        Films in R: v. XIX, n. 6 (June-July, 1968), p. 377; Louise Corbin, 150 wds.,
           no cr.

6615 TRANSPORT FROM PARADISE (Zbynek Brynych)
        (also: Transport Z Raje)
        F Soc Rev: May (1968), pp. 29-33; Patrick MacFadden, 1700 wds., pt. cr.
        Filmf: v. X (1967), p. 44; comp., cp. cr.

        TRANSPORT Z RAJE (see: Transport from Paradise)

6616 TRAP, THE (Norman Panama)
        (also: The Baited Trap)
        Filmf: v. II (1959), p. 10, comp., cp. cr.
        Films & F: v. 5, n. 7 (Apr., 1959), p. 22; Peter G. Baker, 120 wds., cp. cr.

6617 TRAP, THE (Sidney Hayers)
Filmf: v. XI (1968), p. 56; comp., cp. cr.
Take One: v. 1, n. 2 (Nov.-Dec., 1966), pp. 28-29; Tony Reif, 500 wds., pt.
cr.

6618 TRAPEZE (Carol Reed)
Films & F: v. 2, n. 11 (Aug., 1956), pp. 23-24; P. L. Mannock, 250 wds.,
cp. cr.
Films in R: v. VII, n. 6 (June-July, 1956), pp. 286-287; Robert Anck, 300
wds., no cr.
Sight & S: v. 26, n. 1 (Summer, 1956), pp. 32-33; John Wilcox, 575 wds.,
pt. cr.

6619 TRAPP FAMILY, THE (Wolfgang Liebeneiner)
Filmf: v. IV (1961), p. 195; comp., cp. cr.
Films & F: v. 7, n. 12 (Sept., 1961), p. 28; Richard Whitehall, 350 wds., cp.
cr.
Films in R: v. XII, n. 4 (Apr., 1961), pp. 241-242; Gunther von Lemnitz,
225 wds., no cr.

6620 TRAPPED IN TANGIERS (Antonio Cervi)
Filmf: v. III (1960), p. 161; comp., cp. cr.

6621 TRASH (Andy Warhol and Paul Morrissey)
N Y Rev of Books: v. XV, n. 12 (Jan. 7, 1971), pp. 3-4, 6; Elizabeth
Hardwick, 3300 wds., no cr.
Take One: v. 2, n. 9 (1970), p. 22; John Hofsess, 225 wds., pt. cr.

6622 TRAUMA (Robert Malcolm Young)
Filmf: v. V (1962), p. 365; comp., cp. cr.

TRAUMENDE MUND, DIE (see: Dreaming Lips)

6623 TRAVERSEE DE PARIS, LA (Claude Autant-Lara)
(also: Pig Across Paris)
Films & F: v. 3, n. 7 (Apr., 1957), p. 23; Paul Rotha, 800 wds., cp. cr.
Sight & S: v. 26, n. 4 (Spring, 1957), pp. 207-208; Jean Queval, 850 wds.,
pt. cr.

6624 TRAVIATA, LA (Mario Lanfranchi)
Filmf: v. XI (1968), p. 38; comp., cp. cr.
Films & F: v. 13, n. 12 (Sept., 1967), pp. 24-25; Gordon Gow, 900 wds.,
cp. cr.

TRE VOLTI DELLA PAURA, I (see: Black Sabbath)

6625 TREAD SOFTLY STRANGER (Gordon Parry)
Filmf: v. II (1959), p. 341; comp., cp. cr.
Films & F: v. 4, n. 10 (July, 1958), pp. 28, 35; John Cutts, 150 wds., cp. cr.

6626 TREASURE ISLAND (Byron Haskins)
Films in R: v. I, n. 6 (Sept., 1950), p. 34; 150 wds., pt. cr.

6627 TREASURE OF MAKUBA, THE (Joe Lacy)
(also: El Tesoro de Makuba)
Filmf: v. X (1967), p. 439; comp., cp. cr.

6628 TREASURE OF SAN GENNARO (Dino Risi)
(also: Operation San Gennaro; Operazione San Gennaro)
Filmf: v. XI (1968), p. 49; comp., cp. cr.

TREASURE OF SAN TERESA, THE (see: Hot Money Girl)

6629 TREASURE OF THE SIERRA MADRE (John Huston)
Sequence: n. 7 (Spring, 1949), pp. 34-36; Peter Ericsson, 1500 wds., pt. cr.

6630 TRECIA CZESC NOCY (Andrzej Zulawski)
(also: The Third Part of the Night)
Interntl F G: v. 9 (1972), p. 219; Ryszard Koniczek, 175 wds., pt. cr.

6631 TREE, THE (Robert Guenette)
        Filmf: v. XII (1969), p. 244; comp., cp. cr.
        Take One: v. 2, n. 4 (1969), p. 20; George Lellis, 800 wds., pt. cr.

      TRESPASSER, THE (see: Night Editor)

      TRI (see: Three)

6632 TRI DCERY (Stefan Uher)
        (also: Three Daughters)
        Interntl F G: v. 6 (1969), p. 56; Felix Bucher, 200 wds., pt. cr.

6633 TRI DNYA VIKTORA CHERNISKEVA (Mark Ossepian)
        (also: Three Days of Victor Chernishas)
        Interntl F G: v. 7 (1970), p. 236; 250 wds., pt. cr.

      TRI SESTRI (see: The Three Sisters)

6634 TRIAL (Mark Robson)
        Films in R: v. VI, n. 8 (Oct., 1955), pp. 414-415; Courtland Phipps, 400
            wds., pt. cr.

6635 TRIAL, THE (Orson Welles)
        (also: Le Proces)
        F Quarterly: v. XVI, n. 4 (Summer, 1963), pp. 40-43; Ernest Callenbach,
            1100 wds., pt. cr.
        F Soc Rev: Jan. (1967), pp. 21-22; John Thomas, 350 wds., pt. cr.
        Filmf: v. VI (1963), p. 25; comp., cp. cr.
        Films & F: v. 10, n. 3 (Dec., 1963), pp. 25-26; John Cutts, 825 wds., cp. cr.
        Films in R: v. XIV, n. 3 (Mar., 1963), p. 178; Henry Hart, 225 wds., no cr.
        Movie: n. 7, pp. 9-10; Mark Shivas, 1200 wds., pt. cr.
        Take One: v. 1, n. 1 (Sept.-Oct., 1966), p. 26; Brian Nevitt, 225 wds., pt. cr.

6636 TRIAL AND ERROR (James Hill)
        (also: The Dock Brief)
        F Quarterly: v. XVI, n. 3 (Spring, 1963), p. 60; R. M. Hodgens, 150 wds.,
            no cr.
        Filmf: v. V (1962), p. 304; comp., cp. cr.
        Films & F: v. 9, n. 2 (Nov., 1962), p. 37; Richard Whitehall, 250 wds., cp.
            cr.
        Films in R: v. XIII, n. 10 (Dec., 1962), p. 628; Wilfred Mifflin, 100 wds., no
            cr.

6637 TRIAL OF JOAN OF ARC, THE (Robert Bresson)
        (also: Le Proces de Jeanne D'Arc)
        Filmf: v. VIII (1965), p. 70; comp., cp. cr.
        Films & F: v. 9, n. 5 (Feb., 1963), p. 36; Gordon Gow, 750 wds., cp. cr.
        Films in R: v. XVI, n. 3 (Mar., 1965), p. 176; Henry Hart, 200 wds., no cr.
        Movie: n. 7, pp. 30-32; Paul Mayersberg, 2600 wds., pt. cr.
        Movie: n. 8, pp. 29-30; 500 wds., no cr.
        Sight & S: v. 32, n. 1 (Winter, 1962-1963), pp. 37-38; Robert Vas, 1000
            wds., no cr.

      TRIAL OF SERGEANT RUTLEDGE, THE (see: Sergeant Rutledge)

6638 TRIALS OF OSCAR WILDE, THE (Ken Hughes)
        (also: The Green Carnation)
        Filmf: v. III (1960), p. 184; comp., cp. cr.
        Films & F: v. 6, n. 10 (July, 1960), p. 23; Peter Baker, 1000 wds., cp. cr.
        Films in R: v. XI, n. 7 (Aug.-Sept., 1960), pp. 432-433; Henry Hart, 400
            wds., no cr.
        Sight & S: v. 29, n. 3 (Summer, 1960), p. 146; Derek Hill, 750 wds., pt. cr.

6639 TRIBES (Joseph Sargent)
        Filmf: v. XIV (1971), p. 475; comp., cp. cr.

      TRIBULATIONS D'UN CHINOIS EN CHINE, LES (see: Up To His Ears)

      TRICETJEDNA VE STINU (see: 90 Degrees in the Shade)

6640 TRICHEURS, LES (Marcel Carné)
      (also: The Adulteress; The Cheaters; Youthful Sinners)
      Filmf: v. I (1958), p. 18; comp., cp. cr.
      Films & F: v. 7, n. 5 (Feb., 1961), p. 28; Raymond Durgnat, 600 wds., cp.
          cr.
      Films in R: v. IX, n. 2 (Feb., 1958), pp. 90-91; Louise Corbin, 125 wds., no
          cr.

      TRIGGER HAPPY (see: The Deadly Companions)

6641 TRILOGY (Frank Perry)
      Films in R: v. XX, n. 10 (Dec., 1969), pp. 636-638; Henry Hart, 450 wds.,
          no cr.

6642 TRIO (Ken Annakin and Harold French)
      Films in R: v. I, n. 8 (Nov., 1950), pp. 19-21; Arthur Knight, 750 wds., pt.
          cr.

      TRIO (Aleksandar Petrovic/see: Three)

6643 TRIO BALLET (G. Rappaport)
      Films in F: v. 1, n. 2 (Nov., 1954), pp. 18-19; Peter Brinson, 325 wds., cp.
          cr.

      TRIONFO DI ERCOLE, IL (see: The Triumph of Hercules)

6644 TRIP, THE (Roger Corman)
      Cinema: v. 3, n. 6 (Winter, 1967), p. 47; Guy Sternwood, 400 wds., pt. cr.
      F Quarterly: v. XXI, n. 2 (Winter, 1967-1968), p. 64; Seu Do Nim; 200
          wds., no cr.
      Filmf: v. X (1967), p. 270; comp., cp. cr.
      Films & F: v. 15, n. 9 (June, 1969), pp. 51-52; Colin Heard, 1500 wds., cp.
          cr,
      Films & F: v. 17, n. 12 (Sept., 1971), pp. 56-57; Peter Buckley, 550 wds.,
          cp. cr.
      Sight & S: v. 38, n. 1 (Winter, 1968-1969), pp. 47-48; Philip Strick, 1200
          wds., pt. cr.
      Take One: v. 1, n. 7 (1967), p. 26; John Hofsess, 350 wds., pt. cr.

      TRIP DOWN THE RIVER, A (see: Rejs)

6645 TRIPLE CROSS (Terence Young)
      Filmf: v. X (1967), p. 206; comp., cp. cr.
      Films & F: v. 14, n. 3 (Dec., 1967), pp. 24-25; Peter Davalle, 400 wds., cp.
          cr.
      Films in R: v. XVIII, n. 5 (May, 1967), pp. 308-309; Wilfred Mifflin, 250
          wds., no cr.

6646 TRISTANA (Luis Bunuel)
      F Quarterly: v. XXIV, n. 2 (Winter, 1970-1971), pp. 52-55; Joan Mellen,
          2000 wds., pt. cr.
      Interntl F G: v. 8 (1971), p. 240; Peter Cowie, 200 wds., pt. cr.
      Movie: n. 18 (Winter, 1970-1971), p. 40; Ian Cameron, 50 wds., no cr.
      Sight & S: v. 40, n. 2 (Spring, 1971), p. 103; Julian Jebb, 900 wds., pt. cr.

6647 TRIUMPH OF HERCULES, THE (Alberto de Martino)
      (also: Il Trionfo di Ercole)
      Films & F: v. 12, n. 2 (Nov., 1965), pp. 31-32; Raymond Durgnat, 550
          wds., cp. cr.

6648 TRIUMPH OF THE WILL (Leni Riefenstahl)
      F Comment: v. 3, n. 1 (Winter, 1965), pp. 22-23; Marshall Lewis, 900 wds.,
          pt. cr.
      F Comment: v. 3, n. 1 (Winter, 1965), pp. 28-31; Robert Gardner, 2400
          wds., no cr.

6649 TRIUMPH OVER VIOLENCE (Mikhail Romm)
      (also: Obiknovenni Fashizm; Ordinary Fascism)
      Filmf: v. XI (1968), p. 308; comp., cp. cr.
      Interntl F G: v. 4 (1967), p. 170; 225 wds., pt. cr.

6650 TROG (Freddie Francis)
        Films & F: v. 17, n. 11 (Aug., 1971), pp. 54-55, 59; Eric Braun, 1000 wds.,
        cp. cr.

6651 TROIS FEMMES (Andre Michel)
        (also: Three Women)
        Films & F: v. 1, n. 7 (Apr., 1955), p. 20; Derek Hill, 200 wds., cp. cr.

6652 317E SECTION, LA (Pierre Schoendoerffer)
        F Quarterly: v. XIX, n. 3 (Spring, 1966), pp. 48-50; Peter Graham, 1100
        wds., pt. cr.
        Interntl F G: v. 3 (1966), p. 71; Peter Graham, 300 wds., pt. cr.
        Movie: n. 14 (Autumn, 1965), p. 41; Mark Shivas, 150 wds., no cr.

6653 TROJAN HORSE, THE (Giorgio Ferroni)
        Filmf: v. V (1962), p. 370; comp., cp. cr.

6654 TROJAN WOMEN, THE (Michael Cacoyannis)
        Filmf: v. XIV (1971), p. 620; comp., cp. cr.
        Films in R: v. XXII, n. 9 (Nov., 1971), pp. 569-570; Charles F. Reilly, 300
        wds., no cr.

      TROLLENBERG TERROR, THE (see: The Crawling Eye)

      TROPIC HUNGER (see: Corinna Darling)

6655 TROPIC OF CANCER (Joseph Strick)
        F Heritage: v. 6, n. 1 (Fall, 1970), pp. 27-29; Louis Delpino, 800 wds., no
        cr.
        Films & F: v. 17, n. 3 (Dec., 1970), pp. 51-52; Margaret Tarratt, 450 wds.,
        cp. cr.
        Films in R: v. XXI, n. 3 (Mar., 1970), pp. 175-176; Henry Hart, 350 wds.,
        no cr.

      TROPICI (see: Tropics)

6656 TROPICS (Gianni Amico)
        (also: Tropici)
        Filmf: v. XII (1969), p. 112; comp., cp. cr.

6657 TROTTIE TRUE (Brian Desmond Hurst)
        (also: The Gay Lady)
        Sequence: n. 10 (New Year, 1950), p. 154; D.V., 150 wds., no cr.

      TROU, LE (see: The Night Watch)

      TROU NORMAND, LE (see: Crazy for Love)

      TROUBLE AT SIXTEEN (see: Platinum High School)

6658 TROUBLE FOR FATHER (A. Sakelarios)
        (also: Delistavro Kai Gios)
        Filmf: v. I (1958), p. 1; comp., cp. cr.

      TROUBLE IN BAHAI FOR O.S.S. 117 (see: O.S.S. 117 — Mission for a Killer)

6659 TROUBLE IN MOLOPOLIS (Phillippe Mora)
        Interntl F G: v. 8 (1971), p. 125; Anthony Slide, 250 wds., pt. cr.

6660 TROUBLE IN PARADISE (Ernst Lubitsch)
        F Comment: v. 6, n. 3 (Fall, 1970), pp. 47-48; Richard Koszarski, 1300
        wds., cp. cr.

6661 TROUBLE IN STORE (John Paddy Carstairs)
        Films in R: v. VII, n. 2 (Feb., 1956), p. 86; Eileen Kelly, 200 wds., no cr.

6662 TROUBLE IN THE SKY (Charles Frend)
        (also: Cone of Silence)
        Filmf: v. IV (1961), p. 162; comp., cp. cr.
        Films & F: v. 6, n. 9 (June, 1960), p. 22; 300 wds., cp. cr.

6663 TROUBLE WITH ANGELS, THE (Ida Lupino)
       Filmf: v. IX (1966), p. 99; comp., cp. cr.
       Films & F: v. 12, n. 10 (July, 1966), p. 57; David Rider, 350 wds., cp. cr.

6664 TROUBLE WITH GIRLS, THE (Peter Tewksbury)
       (also: The Chautauqua)
       Films & F: v. 16, n. 5 (Feb., 1970), p. 40; David Austen, 250 wds., cp. cr.

6665 TROUBLE WITH HARRY, THE (Alfred Hitchcock)
       F Culture: v. 1, n. 5-6 (Winter, 1955), p. 31; Andrew Sarris, 1000 wds., pt.
           cr.
       Films & F: v. 2, n. 8 (May, 1956), p. 21; P. L. Mannock, 225 wds., cp. cr.
       Films in R: v. VI, n. 9 (Nov., 1955), pp. 465-466; Henry Hart, 350 wds., pt.
           cr.
       Sight & S: v. 26, n. 1 (Summer, 1956), pp. 30-31; Penelope Houston, 900
           wds., pt. cr.

6666 TROUBLE MAKER, THE (Theodore J. Flicker)
       Filmf: v. VII (1964), p. 322; comp., cp. cr.
       Films & F: v. 11, n. 5 (Feb., 1965), p. 32; Allen Eyles, 500 wds., cp. cr.

6667 TROUBLE MAKERS (Robert Machover and Norm Fruchter)
       F Comment: v. IV, n. 2 & 3 (Fall-Winter, 1967), pp. 54-56; William Sloan,
           500 wds., cp. cr.

6668 TRUE AS A TURTLE (Wendy Toye)
       Films & F: v. 3, n. 7 (Apr., 1957), p. 24; Peter G. Baker, 200 wds., cp. cr.

6669 TRUE GRIT (Henry Hathaway)
       Filmf: v. XII (1969), p. 241; comp., cp. cr.
       Films & F: v. 16, n. 3 (Dec., 1969), pp. 37-38; David Austen, 850 wds., cp.
           cr.
       Films in R: v. XX, n. 7 (Aug.-Sept., 1969), pp. 445-446; Robert
           Marmorstein, 200 wds., no cr.
       Focus: n. 5 (Oct., 1969), pp. 31-32; James Jubak, 700 wds., no cr.
       Focus: n. 6 (Spring, 1970), pp. 3-6; Barbara Bernstein, 2000 wds., no cr.
       Focus on F: n. 1 (Jan.-Feb., 1970), pp. 3-6; Allen Eyles, 1600 wds., cp. cr.

6670 TRUE PATRIOT LOVE (Joyce Wieland)
       F Culture: n. 52 (Spring, 1971), pp. 64-73; Joyce Wieland, 2200 wds., no
           cr.

6671 TRUE STORY OF JESSE JAMES (Nicholas Ray)
       (also: The James Brothers)
       Films & F: v. 3, n. 8 (May, 1957), p. 25; 300 wds., cp. cr.
       Films in R: v. VIII, n. 5 (May, 1957), p. 225; Joseph E. Rickards, 75 wds.,
           no cr.

6672 TRUE STORY OF LYNN STUART, THE (Lewis Seiler)
       Filmf: v. I (1958), p. 24; comp., cp. cr.

6673 TRUNK, THE (Donovan Winter)
       Filmf: v. IV (1961), p. 372; comp., cp. cr.

6674 TRUNK TO CAIRO (Menahem Golan)
       Filmf: v. IX (1966), p. 376; comp., cp. cr.

6675 TRUTH, THE (Henry-Georges Clouzot)
       (also: La Verite)
       F Quarterly: v. XV, n. 3 (Spring, 1962), pp. 65-68; Herbert Feinstein, 1800
           wds., pt. cr.
       Filmf: v. IV (1961), p. 157; comp., cp. cr.
       Films & F: v. 8, n. 4 (Jan., 1962), pp. 29-31; Gordon Gow, 900 wds., cp. cr.
       Films in R: v. XII, n. 2 (Feb., 1961), pp. 104-105; Peter Lennon, 450 wds.,
           no cr.

6676 TRUTH ABOUT OUR MARRIAGE, THE (Henri Decoin)
       (also: La Verite sur le Bebe Donge)
       Films & F: v. 1, n. 9 (June, 1955), p. 22; Timothy Bungey, 100 wds., cp. cr.

6677 TRUTH ABOUT SPRING, THE (Richard Thorpe)
Films & F: v. 11, n. 10 (July, 1965), p. 35; Robin Bean, 400 wds., cp. cr.

6678 TRUTH ABOUT WOMEN, THE (Muriel Box)
Filmf: v. I (1958), p. 178; comp., cp. cr.
Films & F: v. 4, n. 7 (Apr., 1958), p. 23; Derek Conrad, 300 wds., cp. cr.

6679 TRYGON FACTOR, THE (Cyril Frankel)
Filmf: v. XII (1969), p. 70; comp., cp. cr.

6680 TSAR'S BRIDE, THE (Vladimir Gorikker)
Filmf: v. IX (1966), p. 60; comp., cp. cr.
Films in R: v. XVII, n. 4 (Apr., 1966), p. 253; Tatiana Balkoff Drowne, 150
wds., no cr.

TU NE TUERAS POINT (see: Thou Shaft Not Kill)

TU SERAS TERRIBLEMENT GENTILLE (see: You Only Love Once)

TULIPE NOIRE, LA (see: The Black Tulip)

6681 TUMBLEWEEDS (King Baggot)
Views & Rev: v. I, n. 4 (Spring, 1970), pp. 18-22; 1200 wds., cp. cr.

TUMULT (see: Relations)

6682 TUNES OF GLORY (Ronald Neame)
Filmf: v. III (1960), p. 346; comp., cp. cr.
Films & F: v. 7, n. 3 (Dec., 1960), pp. 29-30; Richard Whitehall, 950 wds.,
cp. cr.
Films in R: v. XII, n. 1 (Jan., 1961), pp. 37-38; Ellen Fitzpatrick, 250 wds.,
no cr.
Sight & S: v. 30, n. 1 (Winter, 1960-1961), p. 37; Terence Kelly, 500 wds.,
pt. cr.

6683 TUNNEL OF LOVE, THE (Gene Kelly)
Filmf: v. I (1958), p. 225; comp., cp. cr.
Films & F: v. 5, n. 10 (July, 1959), p. 23; Brenda Davies, 250 wds., cp. cr.

TUNNEL 28 (see: Escape from East Berlin)

6684 TURNING POINT, THE (F. Ermler)
Sight & S: v. 15, n. 60 (Winter, 1946-1947), p. 154; Roger Manvell, 100
wds., no cr.

TUTTI A CASA (see: Everybody Go Home)

6685 TWELFTH NIGHT (Yan Fried)
Films & F: v. 2, n. 9 (June, 1956), pp. 23-24; Michael Winner, 250 wds., cp.
cr.
Sight & S: v. 26, n. 1 (Summer, 1956), p. 35; John Gillett, 300 wds., pt. cr.

6686 TWELVE ANGRY MEN (Sidney Lumet)
F Culture: v. 3, n. 2 (1957), pp. 14-15; Jonathan Baumbach, 1200 wds., pt.
cr.
Films & F: v. 3, n. 9 (June, 1957), p. 23; Peter G. Baker, 225 wds., cp. cr.
Films in R: v. VIII, n. 5 (May, 1957), pp. 221-222; Marshall Ainslee, 400
wds., no cr.

6687 TWELVE HOURS TO KILL (Edward L. Cahn)
Filmf: v. III (1960), p. 93; comp., cp. cr.

TWELVE MILLIONS (see: The Human Dutch)

6688 TWELVE O'CLOCK HIGH (Henry King)
Films in R: v. I, n. 2 (Mar., 1950), pp. 29-31; Frances Taylor Patterson,
1000 wds., pt. cr.
Sequence: n. 11 (Summer, 1950), pp. 10-11; Lindsay Anderson, 1000 wds.,
no cr.
Sight & S: v. 19, n. 3 (May, 1950), pp. 125-126; Frank Hauser, 900 wds.,
pt. cr.

6689 12 TO THE MOON (David Bradley)
    Filmf: v. III (1960), p. 186; comp., cp. cr.

6690 12-12-42 (Bernard Stone, Tom McDonough, Dick Gerendasy, prods.)
    F Lib Quarterly: v. 1, n. 2 (Spring, 1968), p. 37; G. William Jones, 200
        wds., pt. cr.

6691 25th HOUR, THE (Henri Verneuil)
    (also: La Vingt — Cinquieme Heure)
    Filmf: v. X (1967), p. 50; comp., cp. cr.
    Films & F: v. 13, n. 8 (May, 1967), pp. 28-29; Richard Davis, 400 wds., cp.
        cr.
    Films in R: v. XVIII, n. 3 (Mar., 1967), pp. 175-176; Flavia Wharton, 175
        wds., no cr.

6692 20 HOURS (Zoltan Fabri)
    (also: Husz Ora)
    Films & F: v. 13, n. 5 (Feb., 1967), pp. 28-29; Richard Davis, 900 wds., cp.
        cr.

6693 21-87 (Arthur Lipsett)
    Interntl F G: v. 2 (1965), p. 59; 100 wds., pt. cr.

6694 TWENTY PLUS TWO (Joseph M. Newman)
    (also: It Started in Tokyo)
    Filmf: v. V (1962), p. 238; comp., cp. cr.
    Films & F: v. 9, n. 3 (Dec., 1962), p. 45; Tony Mallerman, 200 wds., cp. cr.

6695 23rd PSALM (Stan Brakhage)
    (also: Song XXIII)
    F Culture: n. 46 (Autumn, 1967), pp. 14-18; Jerome Hill, Bob Lamberton,
        Fred Camper, 3000 wds., no cr.
    F Quarterly: v. XX, n. 4 (Summer, 1967), pp. 73-76; Judith Shatnoff, 1500
        wds., no cr.

6696 20,000 EYES (Jack Leewood)
    Filmf: v. IV (1961), p. 122; comp., cp. cr.

6697 20,000 LEAGUES UNDER THE SEA (Richard Fleischer)
    Films & F: v. 1, n. 11 (Aug., 1955), p. 17; Derek Hill, 150 wds., cp. cr.
    Films in R: v. VI, n. 1 (Jan., 1955), pp. 34-35; Ralph Gerstle, 450 wds., pt.
        cr.
    Sight & S: v. 25, n. 1 (Summer, 1955), p. 36; Ray Edwards, 600 wds., pt.
        cr.

6698 £20,000 KISS, THE (John Moxley)
    Films & F: v. 9, n. 8 (May, 1963), p. 31; Tony Mallerman, 150 wds., cp. cr.

6699 23 PACES TO BAKER STREET (Henry Hathway)
    Films & F: v. 2, n. 12 (Sept., 1956), p. 23; Peter G. Baker, 175 wds., cp. cr.

6700 23 SKIDOO (Julian Biggs)
    Interntl F G: v. 3 (1966), p. 55; 100 wds., pt. cr.

6701 TWICE A MAN (Gregory Markopoulos)
    Cinema: v. 3, n. 4 (Dec., 1966), p. 49; Richard Whitehall, 1000 wds., pt. cr.
    F Culture: n. 31 (Winter, 1963-1964), pp. 10-11; Ken Kelman, 750 wds.,
        cp. cr.
    F Culture: n. 32 (Spring, 1964), p. 9; Robert Brown, 350 wds., no cr.
    F Culture: n. 37 (1965), p. 15; Robert Kelly, 600 wds., no cr.

6702 TWICE ROUND THE DAFFODILS (Gerald Thomas)
    Films & F: v. 8, n. 8 (May, 1962), p. 36; John Cutts, 150 wds., cp. cr.

6703 TWICE TOLD TALES (Sidney Salkow)
    Filmf: v. VI (1963), p. 320; comp., cp. cr.

6704 TWILIGHT FOR THE GODS (Joseph Pevney)
    Filmf: v. I (1958), p. 141; comp., cp. cr.

6705 TWILIGHT OF HONOR (Boris Sagal)
      (also: The Charge Is Murder)
      Filmf: v. VI (1963), p. 255; comp., cp. cr.
      Films & F: v. 10, n. 7 (Apr., 1964), p. 31; Raymond Durgnat, 500 wds., cp.
          cr.

6706 TWINKY (Richard Donner)
      Films & F: v. 16, n. 6 (Mar., 1970), p. 36; Peter Buckley, 550 wds., cp. cr.

6707 TWIST ALL NIGHT (William J. Hole)
      Filmf: v. V (1962), p. 368; comp., cp. cr.

6708 TWIST AROUND THE CLOCK (Oscar Rudolph)
      Filmf: v. V (1962), p. 10; comp., cp. cr.

6709 TWIST OF SAND, A (Don Chaffey)
      Filmf: v. XII (1969), p. 55; comp., cp. cr.
      Films & F: v. 15, n. 7 (Apr., 1969), pp. 44-45; Richard Davis, 200 wds., cp.
          cr.

6710 TWISTED GIRLS (Silvio Amadio)
      (also: L Isola delle Svedesi)
      Films & F: v. 17, n. 3 (Dec., 1970), p. 60; Richard Weaver, 350 wds., cp. cr.

6711 TWISTED NERVE (Roy Boulting)
      Filmf: v. XII (1969), p. 65; comp., cp. cr.
      Films & F: v. 15, n. 5 (Feb., 1969), pp. 34-36; Gordon Gow, 650 wds., cp.
          cr.
      Films in R: v. XX, n. 4 (Apr., 1969), p. 254; Page Cook, 250 wds., no cr.

6712 "2" (Mac Ahlberg)
      (also: I, A Woman — Part II; Jeg-En Kvinde, II)
      Filmf: v. XII (1969), p. 92; comp., cp. cr.
      Films & F: v. 15, n. 5 (Feb., 1969), p. 47; Richard Davis, 225 wds., cp. cr.

6713 TWO ACRES OF LAND (Bimal Roy)
      Films & F: v. 3, n. 1 (Oct., 1956), p. 23; Shirley Cobham, 225 wds., cp. cr.
      Sight & S: v. 25, n. 3 (Winter, 1955-1956), pp. 145-146; John Gillett, 700
          wds., pt. cr.

6714 TWO AND TWO MAKE SIX (Freddie Francis)
      Filmf: v. VI (1963), p. 264; comp., cp. cr.
      Films & F: v. 8, n. 10 (July, 1962), p. 38; David Gerrard, 375 wds., cp. cr.

6715 TWO APENNY (James F. Collier)
      Films & F: v. 14, n. 12 (Sept., 1968), p. 46; David Austen, 350 wds., cp. cr.

6716 TWO ARE GUILTY (Andre Cayette)
      (also: Le Glaive et la Balance)
      Filmf: v. VII (1964), p. 30; comp., cp. cr.
      Films & F: v. 10, n. 11 (Aug., 1964), p. 27; Allen Eyles, 450 wds., cp. cr.

6717 TWO BEFORE ZERO (William D. Farella)
      Filmf: v. V (1962), p. 296; comp., cp. cr.

6718 TWO BY NOYES
      F Lib Quarterly: v. 1, n. 3 (Summer, 1968), p. 48; Robert Wersan, 350
          wds., pt. cr.

6719 TWO CENTS WORTH OF HOPE (Renato Castellani)
      Films in R: v. III, n. 10 (Dec., 1952), pp. 529-530; 350 wds., no cr.

6720 TWO DAUGHTERS (Satyajit Ray)
      (also: Teen Kanya)
      F Journal: n. 20 (Aug., 1962), p. 81; R. J. Garlick, 350 wds., no cr.
      Filmf: v. VI (1963), p. 117; comp., cp. cr.
      Films & F: v. 9, n. 9 (June, 1963), pp. 29-30; Tony Mallerman, 650 wds.,
          cp. cr.
      Films in R: v. XIV, n. 6 (June-July, 1963), p. 365; Ellen Fitzpatrick, 150
          wds., no cr.
      Sight & S: v. 30, n. 3 (Summer, 1961), p. 148; Eric Rhode, 600 wds., pt. cr.

TWO FACES OF DR. JEKYLL, THE (see: House of Fright)

6721 TWO FLAGS WEST (Robert Wise)
    Sight & S: v. 19, n. 8 (Dec., 1950), pp. 333-334; Lindsay Anderson, 750
        wds., pt. cr.

6722 TWO FOR THE ROAD (Stanley Donen)
    F Quarterly: v. XX, n. 4 (Summer, 1967), pp. 79-80; Raymond Banacki,
        200 wds., no cr.
    F Quarterly: v. XXI, n. 1 (Fall, 1967), pp. 37-42; Stephen Farber, 2600
        wds., pt. cr.
    Filmf: v. X (1967), p. 107; comp., cp. cr.
    Films & F: v. 13, n. 12 (Sept., 1967), p. 20; Mike Sarne, 500 wds., cp. cr.
    Films in R: v. XVIII, n. 5 (May, 1967), pp. 307-308; Flavia Wharton, 350
        wds., no cr.
    Sight & S: v. 36, n. 4 (Autumn, 1967), pp. 206; Jan Dawson, 450 wds., pt.
        cr.

6723 TWO FOR THE SEESAW (Robert Wise)
    F Quarterly: v. XVI, n. 3 (Spring, 1963), p. 60; R. M. Hodgens, 150 wds.,
        no cr.
    Filmf: v. V (1962), p. 291; comp., cp. cr.
    Films & F: v. 9, n. 8 (May, 1963), p. 27; Tony Mallerman, 800 wds., cp. cr.
    Films in R: v. XIII, n. 10 (Dec., 1962), p. 625; Prudence Ashton, 150 wds.,
        no cr.
    Movie: n. 9, p. 35; 50 wds., no cr.
    Sight & S: v. 32, n. 2 (Spring, 1963), p. 93; Brenda Davies, 700 wds., pt. cr.

6724 TWO GENTLEMEN SHARING (Ted Kotcheff)
    Filmf: v. XII (1969), p. 475; comp., cp. cr.

6725 TWO GIRLS AND A SAILOR
    Films & F: v. 15, n. 6 (Mar., 1969), pp. 86-87; Kingsley Canham, 300 wds.,
        no cr.

6726 TWO-HEADED SPY, THE (Andre de Toth)
    Filmf: v. II (1959), p. 42; comp., cp. cr.
    Films & F: v. 5, n. 4 (Jan., 1959), p. 24; Peter G. Baker, 350 wds., cp. cr.

6727 200 MOTELS (Frank Zappa)
    Filmf: v. XIV (1971), p. 719; comp., cp. cr.

TWO IN LOVE (see: A Ballad of Love)

6728 TWO-LANE BLACKTOP (Monte Hellman)
    F Quarterly: v. XXV, n. 2 (Winter, 1971-1972), pp. 53-55; Greg Ford, 1100
        wds., pt. cr.
    Filmf: v. XIV (1971), p. 343; comp., cp. cr.

6729 TWO LEFT FEET (Roy Baker)
    Films & F: v. 11, n. 10 (July, 1965), p. 28; Richard Davis, 250 wds., cp. cr.

6730 TWO LITTLE BEARS, TWO (Randall Hood)
    Filmf: v. V (1962), p. 128; comp., cp. cr.

6731 TWO LOVES (Charles Walters)
    (also: Spinster)
    Filmf: v. IV (1961), p. 131; comp., cp. cr.
    Films & F: v. 7, n. 12 (Sept., 1961), pp. 29-30; Phillip Riley, 700 wds., cp.
        cr.
    Films in R: v. XII, n. 6 (June-July, 1961), pp. 357-358; Mary T. McGiffert,
        125 wds., no cr.

TWO MARINES AND A GENERAL (see: War, Italian Style)

6732 TWO MEN AND A WARDROBE (Roman Polanski)
    F Quarterly: v. XII, n. 3 (Spring, 1959), pp. 53-55; Jonathan Harker, 700
        wds., pt. cr.

6733 TWO NIGHTS WITH CLEOPATRA (Mario Mattoli)
      (also: Due Notti con Cleopatra)
      Filmf: v. VI (1963), p. 344; comp., cp. cr.

6734 TWO OF US, THE (Claude Berri)
      (also: The Old Man and the Child; Le Vieil Homme Et L'Enfant)
      Filmf: v. XI (1968), p. 47; comp., cp. cr.
      Films & F: v. 14, n. 8 (Apr., 1968), p. 29; David Austen, 350 wds., cp. cr.
      Films in R: v. XIX, n. 3 (Mar., 1968), pp. 175-176; Louise Corbin, 200
      wds., no cr.

6735 TWO ON A GUILLOTINE (William Conrad)
      Filmf: v. VIII (1965), p. 12; comp., cp. cr.

6736 TWO OR THREE THINGS I KNOW ABOUT HER (Jean-Luc Godard)
      (also: Deux ou Trois Choses que Je Sais d'Elle)
      F Heritage: v. 3, n. 3 (Spring, 1968), pp. 23-26; Molly Haskell, 1100 wds.,
      no cr.
      F Soc Rev: v. 4, n. 2, pp. 38-44; Jon Rosenbaum, 2500 wds., cp. cr.
      Films & F: v. 17, n. 4 (Jan., 1971), pp. 51-52; Peter Buckley, 750 wds., cp.
      cr.

6737 TWO PEOPLE (Palle Kjaerulff-Schmidt)
      (also: To)
      F Quarterly: v. XIX, n. 3 (Spring, 1966), pp. 34-36; Ernest Callenbach,
      1300 wds., pt. cr.

6738 TWO RODE TOGETHER (John Ford)
      F Quarterly: v. XV, n. 1 (Fall, 1961), p. 56; R. M. Hodgens, 75 wds., no cr.
      Filmf: v. IV (1961), p. 159; comp., cp. cr.
      Films & F: v. 7, n. 11 (Aug., 1961), pp. 26-27; Gordon Gow, 200 wds., cp.
      cr.
      Films in R: v. XII, n. 7 (Aug.-Sept., 1961), p. 428; Robert Anck, 125 wds.,
      no cr.

6739 2001: A SPACE ODYSSEY (Stanley Kubrick)
      Cineaste: v. II, n. 1 (Summer, 1968), pp. 10-11; H. Mark Gasser, 1200 wds.,
      no cr.
      Cineaste: v. II, n. 1 (Summer, 1968), pp. 12-14; Gary Crowdus, 1500 wds.,
      no cr.
      Cinema: v. 4, n. 2 (Summer, 1968), p. 58; Norman Spinrad, 800 wds., no
      cr.
      Cinema: v. 4, n. 2 (Summer, 1968), p. 59; Axel Madsen, 700 wds., pt. cr.
      F Comment: v. 5, n. 4 (Winter, 1969), pp. 6-8; Elie Flatto, 1200 wds., cp. cr.
      F Comment: v. 5, n. 4 (Winter, 1969), pp. 10-14; F. A. Macklin, 2100 wds.,
      no cr.
      F Culture: n. 48-49 (Winter-Spring, 1970), pp. 53-56; Max Kozloff, 2500
      wds., no cr.
      F Heritage: v. 3, n. 4 (Summer, 1968), pp. 1-9; Don Daniels, 1700 wds., no
      cr.
      F Heritage: v. 3, n. 4 (Summer, 1968), pp. 12-20 Tim Hunter, Stephen
      Kaplan and Peter Jaszi, 2000 wds., no cr.
      F Quarterly: v. XXII, n. 1 (Fall, 1968), pp. 56-62; Judith Shatnoff, 3900
      wds., pt. cr.
      F Soc Rev: v. 5, n. 5 (Jan., 1970), pp. 23-26; Michael Sragow, 1500 wds.,
      cp. cr.
      F Soc Rev: v. 5, n. 5 (Jan., 1970), pp. 27-34; Clive James, 2000 wds., cp. cr.
      F Soc Rev: v. 5, n. 6 (Feb., 1970), pp. 23-27; Frederik Pohl, 1500 wds., no
      cr.
      Filmf: v. XI (1968), p. 95; comp., cp. cr.
      Films & F: v. 14, n. 10 (July, 1968), pp. 24-27; David Austen, 3700 wds.,
      cp. cr.
      Films in R: v. XIX, n. 5 (May, 1968), pp. 308-309; Logan Westover, 225
      wds., no cr.
      Interntl F G: v. 6 (1969), pp. 84-85; Peter Cowie, 250 wds., pt. cr.
      Journal of P C: v. II, n. 1 (Summer, 1968), pp. 167-171; John J. Fritscher,
      2000 wds., no cr.

Journal of P C: v. IV, n. 4 (Spring, 1971), pp. 961-965; David G. Hoch,
    3200 wds., no cr.
Screen: v. 10 n. 1 (Jan.-Feb., 1969), pp. 104-112; Robert O'Meara, 2800
    wds., cp. cr.
Sight & S: v. 35, n. 2 (Spring, 1966), pp. 57-60; David Robinson, 2500
    wds., pt. cr.
Sight & S: v. 37, n. 3 (Summer, 1968), pp. 153-154; Philip Strick, 1100
    wds., pt. cr.

6740 2000 YEARS LATER (Bert Tenzer)
      Filmf: v. XII (1969), p. 164; comp., cp. cr.

6741 TWO TICKETS TO PARIS (Greg Garrison)
      Filmf: v. V (1962), p. 274; comp., cp. cr.

      TWO TIMID PEOPLE (see: Les Deux Timides)

6742 TWO VIRGINS (Yoko Ono)
      F Culture: n. 48-49 (Winter-Spring, 1970), p. 32-33; Yoko Ono, 500 wds.,
          no cr.

6743 TWO-WAY STRETCH (Robert Day)
      Filmf: v. IV (1961), p. 39; comp., cp. cr.
      Films & F: v. 6, n. 6 (Mar., 1960), pp. 23-24; Dai Vaughan, 250 wds., cp.
          cr.

6744 TWO WEEKS IN ANOTHER TOWN (Vincente Minnelli)
      F Culture: n. 26 (Fall, 1962), pp. 53-54; Peter Bogdanovich, 750 wds., cp.
          cr.
      F Quarterly: v. XVI, n. 3 (Spring, 1963), p. 60; R. M. Hodgens, 150 wds.,
          no cr.
      Filmf: v. V (1962), p. 177; comp., cp. cr.
      Films & F: v. 9, n. 1 (Oct., 1962), p. 36; Richard Whitehall, 700 wds., cp.
          cr.
      Films in R: v. XIII, n. 7 (Aug.-Sept,, 1962), pp. 427 620, Ellen Fitzpatrick,
          600 wds., no cr.
      Movie: n. 2 (Sept., 1962), p. 35; Paul Mayersberg, 100 wds., no cr.
      Movie: n. 3 (Oct., 1962), pp. 10-12; Paul Mayersberg, 2800 wds., pt. cr.
      Sight & S: v. 31, n. 4 (Autumn, 1962), pp. 196-197; John Russell Taylor,
          450 wds., pt. cr.

6745 TWO WEEKS IN SEPTEMBER (Serge Bourguignon)
      (also: A Coeur Joie; With Joyous Heart)
      Cinema: v. 3, n. 6 (Winter, 1967), p. 47; Axel Madsen, 400 wds., no cr.
      Filmf: v. XI (1968), p. 66; comp., cp. cr.

6746 TWO WOMEN (Vittorio De Sica)
      (also: La Ciociara)
      Cinema: v. 1, n. 1, p. 43; 175 wds., pt. cr.
      Filmf: v. IV (1961), p. 113; comp., cp. cr.
      Films & F: v. 7, n. 12 (Sept., 1961), p. 27; Peter Baker, 600 wds., cp. cr.
      Films in R: v. XII, n. 5 (May, 1961), pp. 297-298; Louise Corbin, 400 wds.,
          no cr.

      TYOMEHEN PAIVAK KIRJA (see: A Worker's Diary)

      TYPHON SUR NAGASAKI (see: Typhoon Over Nagasaki)

6747 TYPHOON OVER NAGASAKI (Yves Ciampi)
      (also: Typhon sur Nagasaki)
      Films & F: v. 3, n. 10 (July, 1957), p. 25; Derek Conrad, 250 wds., cp. cr.

      TYPY NA DZIS (see: Tips for Today)

      TYSTNADEN (see: The Silence)

UCCELLACCI E UCCELLINI (see: Hawks and Sparrows)

UCCIDI O MUORI (see: Kill or Be Killed)

6748 UGETSU MONOGATARI (Kenji Mizoguchi)
     Films & F: v. 8, n. 8 (May, 1962), p. 30; Paul Rotha, 900 wds., cp. cr.
     Sight & S: v. 31, n. 2 (Spring, 1962), pp. 97-99; Eric Rhode, 2000 wds., pt.
        cr.

6749 UGLY AMERICAN, THE (George Englund)
     Filmf: v. VI (1963), p. 61; comp., cp. cr.
     Films & F: v. 9, n. 10 (July, 1963), pp. 21-22; Raymond Durgnat, 850
        wds., cp. cr.
     Films in R: v. XIV, n. 5 (May, 1963), pp. 305-306; Henry Hart, 400 wds.,
        no cr.

6750 UGLY DACHSHUND, THE (Norman Tokar)
     Filmf: v. IX (1966), p. 89; comp., cp. cr.
     Films & F: v. 12, n. 3 (Dec., 1965), p. 16; Richard Davis, 250 wds., cp. cr.
     Films in R: v. XVII, n. 2 (Feb., 1966), pp. 115-116; Astrid Hurlick, 200
        wds., no cr.

6751 UGLY ONES, THE (Eugenio Martin)
     (also: The Bonty Killer; El Precio De Un Hombre)
     Filmf: v. XI (1968), p. 484; comp., cp. cr.

     ULTIMA PREDA DEL VAMPIRO (see: Playgirls and the Vampire)

     ULTIMO CZAR, L' (see: The Night They Killed Rasputin)

     ULTIMO DEI VICHINGHI (see: Last of the Vikings)

6752 ULYSSES (Mario Camerini)
     Films & F: v. 1, n. 12 (Sept., 1955), p. 20; Dennis Millmore, 225 wds., cp.
        cr.
     Films in R: v. VI, n. 7 (Aug.-Sept., 1955), p. 346; Harrison Galbraith, 120
        wds., pt. cr.

6753 ULYSSES (Joseph Strick)
     Filmf: v. X (1967), p. 71; comp., cp. cr.
     Films & F: v. 13, n. 11 (Aug., 1967), pp. 21-22; Raymond Durgnat, 1200
        wds., cp. cr.
     Films in R: v. XVIII, n. 4 (Apr., 1967), pp. 236-238; Henry Hart, 450 wds.,
        no cr.
     Interntl F G: v. 5 (1968), pp. 90-91; 200 wds., pt. cr.
     N Y Rev of Books: v. VIII, n. 11 (15 June, 1967), pp. 12-13; Richard
        Ellman, 1100 wds., no cr.
     Sight & S: v. 36, n. 3 (Summer, 1967), pp. 144-145; James Price, 700 wds.,
        pt. cr.

6754 UMBERTO D (Vittorio De Sica)
     Filmf: n. 4 (Mar., 1955), pp. 19-20; Larry Semmens, 250 wds., no cr.
     Film: n. 4 (Mar., 1955), pp. 20-21; Jon Evans, 400 wds., no cr.
     F Culture: v. 1, n. 5-6 (Winter, 1955), pp. 30-31; George N. Fenin, 1100
        wds., pt. cr.
     Films & F: v. 1, n. 3 (Dec., 1954), p. 21; Catherine De La Roche, 250 wds.,
        cp. cr.
     Films in R: v. III, n. 9 (Nov., 1952), p. 472; 250 wds., pt. cr.
     Sight & S: v. 23, n. 2 (Oct.-Dec., 1953), pp. 87-88; Karel Reisz, 1600 wds.,
        pt. cr.

6755 UMBRELLAS OF CHERBOURG, THE (Jacques Demy)
      (also: Les Parapluies de Cherbourg)
      Cinema: v. 2, n. 5 (Mar.-Apr., 1965), p. 49; Michael Caen, 700 wds., pt. cr.
      Film: n. 41 (1964), p. 12; Douglas McVay, 150 wds., no cr.
      F Comment: v. 3, n. 2 (Spring, 1965), pp. 62-63; Stephen Chodes, 650
          wds., pt. cr.
      Filmf: v. VII (1964), p. 330; comp., cp. cr.
      Films & F: v. 11, n. 4 (Jan., 1965), p. 28; Gordon Gow, 900 wds., cp. cr.
      Films in R: v. XVI, n. 1 (Jan., 1965), p. 49; Adelaide Comerford, 225 wds.,
          no cr.
      Interntl F G: v. 2 (1965), p. 69; Peter Graham, 200 wds., pt. cr.
      Sight & S: v. 34, n. 1 (Winter, 1964-1965), p. 37; J. H. Fenwick, 750 wds.,
          no cr.

      UN, DEUX, TROIS, QUATRE! (see: Black Tights)

6756 UNCHAINED (Hall Bartlett)
      Films & F: v. 1, n. 8 (May, 1955), p. 21; Derek Hill, 150 wds., cp. cr.
      Films in R: v. V, n. 9 (Nov., 1954), p. 483; 250 wds., no cr.

6757 UNCLE, THE (Desmond Davis)
      Filmf: v. IX (1966), p. 209; comp., cp. cr.

6758 UNCLE VANYA (Franchot Tone and John Goetz)
      Filmf: v. I (1958), p. 87; comp., cp. cr.
      Films in R: v. IX, n. 6 (June-July, 1958), p. 333; Helen Weldon Kuhn, 300
          wds., no cr.

6759 UNCOMMON CLAY (Thomas Craven)
      Films in R: v. III, n. 4 (Apr., 1952), p. 201; 125 wds., pt. cr.

6760 UNCOMMON THIEF, AN (Eldar Ryazanov)
      (also: Berogis Automobilya; Watch Your Automobile)
      Filmf: v. X (1967), p. 401; comp., cp. cr.

6761 UNCONQUERED, THE (Nancy Hamilton)
      Films in R: v. V, n. 6 (June-July, 1954), pp. 309-310; Elspeth Hart, 250
          wds., no cr.

6762 UNDEFEATED, THE (Paul Dickson)
      Sight & S: v. 19, n. 8 (Dec., 1950), pp. 329-330; Richard Winnington, 900
          wds., pt. cr.

6763 UNDEFEATED, THE (Andrew V. McLaglen)
      Films & F: v. 16, n. 2 (Nov., 1969), pp. 51-52; David Austen, 400 wds., cp.
          cr.
      Films in R: v. XX, n. 8 (Oct., 1969), pp. 511-512; Arthur B. Clark, 125
          wds., no cr.

6764 UNDELIVERED LETTER, THE (Mikhail Kalatozov)
      (also: Nyeotpravlyenniye Pismo)
      F Quarterly: v. XV, n. 1 (Fall, 1961), pp. 49-51; Edward Drew, 800 wds.,
          pt. cr.

6765 UNDER CAPRICORN (Alfred Hitchcock)
      Sequence: n. 10 (New Year, 1950), pp. 154-155; Lindsay G. Anderson, 100
          wds., no cr.
      Sight & S: v. 18, n. 71 (Dec., 1949), p. 21; 30 wds., pt. cr.

6766 UNDER TEN FLAGS (Duilio Coletti)
      Filmf: v. III (1960), p. 208; comp., cp. cr.
      Films & F: v. 7, n. 4 (Jan., 1961), p. 35; Clayton Cole, 225 wds., cp. cr.
      Films in R: v. XI, n. 8 (Oct., 1960), pp. 493-494; Arthur B. Clark, 200
          wds., no cr.

6767 UNDER THE CARIBBEAN (Hans Hass)
      Films & F: v. 1, n. 5 (Feb., 1955), p. 19; Jill Hardy, 200 wds., cp. cr.

6768 UNDER THE PARIS SKY (Julien Duvivier)
      Films in R: v. III, n. 2 (Feb., 1952), p. 88; B. G. Marple, 175 wds., no cr.

6769 UNDER THE RED SEA (Hans Hass)
      Films in R: v. III, n. 8 (Oct., 1952), p. 416; 180 wds., no cr.

6770 UNDER THE SOUTHERN CROSS (Armand Denis)
      Sight & S: v. 24, n. 4 (Spring, 1955), p. 200; Catherine de la Roche, 400
      wds., pt. cr.

6771 UNDER THE YUM-YUM TREE (David Swift)
      F Quarterly: v. XVII, n. 3 (Spring, 1964), p. 63; R. M. Hodgens, 50 wds.,
      no cr.
      Filmf: v. VI (1963), p. 243; comp., cp. cr.
      Films & F: v. 10, n. 6 (Mar., 1964), pp. 31-32; Allen Eyles, 375 wds., cp. cr.
      Films in R: v. XIV, n. 9 (Nov., 1963), p. 565; Ellen Fitzpatrick, 200 wds.,
      no cr.

6772 UNDERSTANDING MOVIES (National Council of Teachers of English)
      Films in R: v. II, n. 3 (Mar., 1951), pp. 42-43; Edward Gordon, 300 wds.,
      pt. cr.

6773 UNDERWATER (John Sturges)
      Films & F: v. 1, n. 8 (May, 1955), p. 18; Peter Barnes, 150 wds., cp. cr.

6774 UNDERWATER CITY, THE (Frank McDonald)
      Filmf: v. V (1962), p. 170; comp., cp. cr.

6775 UNDERWATER WARRIOR (Andrew Marton)
      Filmf: v. I (1958), p. 42; comp., cp. cr.
      Films in R: v. IX, n. 5 (May, 1958), p. 271; E. Dexter Charles, 100 wds., no
      cr.

      UNDERWORLD INFORMERS (see: The Informers)

6776 UNDERWORLD, U.S.A. (Samuel Fuller)
      F Quarterly: v. XV, n. 1 (Fall, 1961), p. 56; R. M. Hodgens, 150 wds., no
      cr.
      Filmf: v. IV (1961), p. 94; comp., cp. cr.
      Films & F: v. 9, n. 1 (Oct., 1962), pp. 38-39; Raymond Durgnat, 800 wds.,
      cp. cr.
      Movie: n. 5 (Dec., 1962), pp. 3-6; V. F. Perkins, 2300 wds., no cr.

6777 UNE ET L'AUTRE, L' (Rene Allio)
      (also: The Other One: Skin Deep)
      Sight & S: v. 37, n. 1 (Winter, 1967-1968), pp. 11-12; Tom Milne, 800 wds.,
      pt. cr.

6778 UNEARTHLY STRANGER (John Krish)
      Films & F: v. 10, n. 3 (Dec., 1963), pp. 30-31; David Rider, 350 wds., cp.
      cr.

6779 UNEXPECTED, THE (Alberto Lattuada)
      (also: L'Imprevisto)
      Films & F: v. 9, n. 3 (Dec., 1962), pp. 44-45; Gordon Gow, 325 wds., cp.
      cr.

6780 UNFAITHFUL NIGHT, THE (Antoine d'Ormesson)
      (also: La Nuit Infidele)
      Films & F: v. 15, n. 5 (Feb., 1969), p. 40; David Hutchison, 300 wds., cp.
      cr.

6781 UNFAITHFULS, THE (Mario Monicelli and Steno)
      (also: Le Infedeli)
      Filmf: v. IV (1961), p. 367; comp., cp. cr.

6782 UNFORGIVEN, THE (John Huston)
      F Quarterly: v. XIII, n. 4 (Summer, 1960), p. 61; 75 wds., no cr.
      Filmf: v. III (1960), p. 73; comp., cp. cr.
      Films & F: v. 6, n. 10 (July, 1960), pp. 21-22; Gordon Gow, 650 wds., cp.
      cr.
      Films in R: v. XI, n. 5 (May, 1960), pp. 287-288; Albert "Hap" Turner, 275
      wds., no cr.

Sight & S: v. 29, n. 3 (Summer, 1960), p. 142; Penelope Houston, 900 wds., pt. cr.

UNGEHEUER VON LONDON CITY, DAS (see: The Monster of London City)

6783 UNHOLY WIFE, THE (John Farrow)
Films & F: v. 3, n. 10 (July, 1957), p. 25; Kay Collier, 300 wds., cp. cr.

6784 UNIDENTIFIED FLYING OBJECTS (Winston Jones)
Films & F: v. 3, n. 2 (Nov., 1956), pp. 26-27; Peter G. Baker, 250 wds., cp. cr.
Films in R: v. VII, n. 7 (Aug.-Sept., 1956), pp. 345-346; Courtland Phipps, 450 wds., no cr.

6785 UNINHIBITED, THE (Juan-Antonio Bardem)
(also: Los Pianos Mecanicos; The Player Pianos)
Filmf: v. XI (1968), p. 235; comp., cp. cr.

6786 UNKNOWN, THE (Tod Browning)
Films in R: v. XXI, n. 7 (Aug.-Sept., 1970), pp. 452-454; Ted Zehender, 1200 wds., no cr.

6787 UNKNOWN REASONS (Fred Mogubgub)
Interntl F G: v. 9 (1972), p. 266; Margot S. Kernan, 150 wds., no cr.

6788 UNKNOWN SOLDIER, THE (Edvin Laine)
F Journal: n. 18 (Oct., 1961), pp. 20-21; James D. Merralls, 150 wds., no cr.
Films & F: v. 4, n. 12 (Sept., 1958), pp. 21-22; Gordon Gow, 300 wds., cp. cr.
Sight & S: v. 27, n. 6 (Autumn, 1958), p. 315; Dai Vaughan, 650 wds., no cr.

6789 UNLUCKY COUNTRY, THE (Donald Murray)
Interntl F G: v. 5 (1968), p. 47; 100 wds., pt. cr.

6790 UNMAN, WITTERING AND ZIGO (John MacKenzie)
Filmf: v. XIV (1971), p. 311; comp., cp. cr.
Focus on F: n. 7 (Summer, 1971), pp. 3-4; Peter Cowie and Derek Elley, 350 wds., cp. cr.

UNRECONCILED (see: Nicht Versohnt)

UNSEEN HEROES (see: Missile from Hell)

6791 UNSENT LETTER, THE (Michael Kalatovoz)
Films in R: v. XV, n. 3 (Mar., 1964), pp. 172-173; Steven P. Hill, 300 wds., no cr.

6792 UNSINKABLE MOLLY BROWN, THE (Charles Walters)
Cinema: v. 2, n. 2 (July, 1964), p. 48; Rory Guy, 325 wds., pt. cr.
Filmf: v. VII (1964), p. 128; comp., cp. cr.
Filmf & F: v. 10, n. 12 (Sept., 1964), p. 16; John Cutts, 725 wds., cp. cr.
Films in R: v. XV, n. 6 (June-July, 1964), pp. 373-374; 175 wds., no cr.
Sight & S: v. 33, n. 4 (Autumn, 1964), pp. 197-198; J. H. Fenwick, 650 wds., pt. cr.

6793 UNSTOPPABLE MAN, THE (Terry Bishop)
Filmf: v. IV (1961), p. 364; comp., cp. cr.

6794 UNSTRAP ME (George Kuchar)
Filmf: v. XI (1968), p. 500, comp., cp. cr.

UNTER GEIERN (see: Frontier Hellcat)

6795 UNTIL THEY SAIL (Robert Wise)
Films & F: v. 4, n. 4 (Jan., 1958), p. 27; Kay Collier, 200 wds., cp. cr.
Films in R: v. VIII, n. 9 (Nov., 1957), p. 464; Ellen Fitzpatrick, 250 wds., no cr.

UNTO A GOOD LAND (see: Nvbyggarna)

6796 UNTOUCHED AND PURE (Mort Ransen)
        Take One: v. 2, n. 7 (1970), pp. 22-23; Ronald Blumer, 750 wds., pt. cr.

        UNVANQUISHED, THE (see: Aparajito)

        UNWANTED WOMEN (see: Donne Senza Nome)

6797 UNWED MOTHER (Walter Doniger)
        Filmf: v. I (1958), p. 271; comp., cp. cr.

        UNWORTHY OLD WOMAN, THE (see: The Shameless Old Lady)

6798 UOMINI CONTRO (Francesco Rosi)
        Movie: n. 18 (Winter, 1970-1971), p. 40; Ian Cameron, 125 wds., no cr.

6799 UOMO A META, UN (Vittorio De Seta)
        F Quarterly: v. XX, n. 3 (Spring, 1967), pp. 37-39; Margot, S. Kernan, 1200
            wds., pt. cr.

        UOMO A UOMO, DA (see: Death Rides a Horse)

        UOMO DAI CINQUE PALLONI, L' (see: The Man with the Balloons)

        UOMO DI PAGLIA, L' (see: Man of Straw)

        UOMO, UN CAVALLO, E UNA PISTOLA, UN (see: The Stranger Returns)

6800 UP FRONT (Alexander Hall)
        Films in R: v. II, n. 6 (June-July, 1951), pp. 40-41; Arthur Knight, 400
            wds., pt. cr.

6801 UP IN THE WORLD (John Paddy Carstairs)
        Films & F: v. 3, n. 4 (Jan., 1957), pp. 25-26; Rodney Giesler, 150 wds., cp.
            cr.

6802 UP JUMPED A SWAGMAN (Christopher Miles)
        Films & F: v. 12, n. 6 (Mar., 1965), p. 54; David Rider, 250 wds., cp. cr.

6803 UP PERISCOPE (Gordon Douglas)
        Filmf: v. II (1959), p. 36; comp., cp. cr.
        Films & F: v. 5, n. 8 (May, 1959), p. 24; Dai Vaughan, 175 wds., cp. cr.

6804 UP THE CREEK! (Val Guest)
        Filmf: v. I (1958), p. 238; comp., cp. cr.
        Films & F: v. 4, n. 9 (June, 1958), p. 27; Derek Conrad, 200 wds., cp. cr.

6805 UP THE DOWN STAIRCASE (Robert Mulligan)
        Cinema: v. 3, n. 6 (Winter, 1967), p. 50; Harlan Ellison, 2500 wds., no cr.
        F Quarterly: v. XXI, n. 2 (Winter, 1967-1968), pp. 50-52; Stephen Farber,
            1100 wds., pt. cr.
        Filmf: v. X (1967), p. 219; comp., cp. cr.
        Films & F: v. 13, n. 11 (Aug., 1967), p. 20; Raymond Durgnat, 850 wds.,
            cp. cr.
        Films in R: v. XVIII, n. 6 (June-July, 1967), p. 367; Adelaide Comerford,
            175 wds., no cr.

6806 UP THE JUNCTION (Peter Collinson)
        Filmf: v. XI (1968), p. 83; comp., cp. cr.
        Films & F: v. 14, n. 6 (Mar., 1968), pp. 29-30; David Austen, 650 wds., cp.
            cr.
        Films in R: v. XIX, n. 4 (Apr., 1968), p. 245; Helen Weldon Kuhn, 200
            wds., no cr.

6807 UP THE MacGREGORS (Frank Garfield)
        (also: Sette Donne Per I MacGregor; Seven Women for the MacGregors)
        Filmf: v. XI (1968), p. 536; comp., cp. cr.

        UP TIGHT (see: Uptight)

6808 UP TO HIS EARS (Philippe De Broca)
        (also: Les Tribulations d'un Chinois en Chine; Up To His Neck)
        F Quarterly: v. XX, n. 2 (Winter, 1966-1967), p. 63; Dan Bates, 75 wds., no
            cr.
        Filmf: v. IX (1966), p. 131; comp., cp. cr.
        Films in R: v. XVII, n. 6 (June-July, 1966), p. 383; Henry Hart, 300 wds.,
            no cr.

      UP TO HIS NECK (see: Up To His Ears)

6809 UPPER HAND, THE (Denys de la Patelliere)
        (also: Du Rififi A Paname; Rififi in Paris)
        Filmf: v. X (1967), p. 224; comp., cp. cr.

6810 UPSTAIRS AND DOWNSTAIRS (Ralph Thomas)
        Filmf: v. III (1960), p. 345; comp., cp. cr.
        Films & F: v. 6, n. 1 (Oct., 1959), p. 24; Robin Bean, 250 wds., cp. cr.

6811 UPTHRONE STONE, THE (Sandor Sara)
        (also: Feldobott Ko)
        Film: n. 57 (Winter, 1970), pp. 27-28; Peter Cargin, 150 wds., pt. cr.

6812 UPTIGHT (Jules Dassin)
        Cineaste: v. II, n. 4 (Spring, 1969), pp. 2-3, 34; Ruthe B. Stein, 2000 wds.,
            pt. cr.
        Cinema: v. 5, n. 1, pp. 42-43; 1500 wds., pt. cr.
        F Quarterly: v. XXII, n. 3 (Spring, 1969), p. 64; William Roth, 400 wds., no
            cr.
        Filmf: v. XI (1968), p. 494; comp., cp. cr.
        Films & F: v. 15, n. 9 (June, 1969), p. 50; Richard Davis, 400 wds., cp. cr.
        Films in R: v. XX, n. 2 (Feb., 1969), p. 118; Arthur B. Clark, 125 wds., no
            cr.

6813 UPTURNED GLASS, THE (Lawrence Huntington)
        Sight & S: v. 16, n. 63 (Autumn, 1947), p. 120; Arthur Vesselo, 150 wds.,
            no cr.

6814 URSULA (Reni Mertens and Walter Marti)
        (also: Oder das Unwerte Leben)
        Interntl F G: v. 5 (1968), p. 149; 150 wds., pt. cr.

6815 URSUS IN THE LAND OF FIRE (Giorgio Simonelli)
        (also: Ursus Nella Terra di Fuoco)
        Films & F: v. 10, n. 10 (July, 1964), p. 26; David Rider, 150 wds., cp. cr.

6816 URSUS IN THE VALLEY OF THE LIONS (Carlo Bagaglia)
        (also: Ursus Nelle Valle Dei Leoni)
        Films & F: v. 9, n. 10 (July, 1963), p. 28; Raymond Durgnat, 400 wds., cp.
            cr.

      URSUS NELLA TERRA DI FUOCO (see: ursus in the Land of Fire)

      URSUS NELLA VALLE DEI LEONI (see: Ursus in the Valley of the Lions)

6817 URTAIN (Manuel Summers)
        Movie: n. 18 (Winter, 1970-1971), p. 40; Ian Cameron, 175 wds., no cr.

      UTVANDRARNA (see: The Emigrants)

6818 V.I.P.'S, THE (Anthony Asquith)
        Cinema: v. 1, n. 6 (Nov.-Dec., 1963), p. 46; Rory Guy, 200 wds., pt. cr.
        F Quarterly: v. XVII, n. 2 (Winter, 1963-1964), pp. 62-63; R. M. Hodgens,
            200 wds., no cr.

Filmf: v. VI (1963), p. 187; comp., cp. cr.
Films & F: v. 10, n. 1 (Oct., 1963), pp. 21-22; Raymond Durgnat, 600
wds., cp. cr.
Films in R: v. XIV, n. 8 (Oct., 1963), pp. 492-493; Wilfred Mifflin, 250
wds., no cr.

V GORODYE S (see: In the Town of S)

V TIKHOM OKEANE (see: In the Pacific)

VACANCES DE M. HULOT, LES (see: Mr. Hulot's Holiday)

6819 VAGABOND KING, THE (Michael Curtiz)
Films & F: v. 2, n. 8 (May, 1956), p. 21; Peter G. Baker, 400 wds., cp. cr.

VAGHE STELLE DELL'ORSA (see: Of a Thousand Delights)

YAGYU BUGEICHO (see: Secret Scrolls)

VAKHTANG VRONSKY (see: Lileia)

6820 VALDEZ IS COMING (Edwin Sherin)
Filmf: v. XIV (1971), p. 59; comp., cp. cr.

VALERIE A TYDEN DIVU (see: Valerie and Her Week of Wonders)

6821 VALERIE AND HER WEEK OF WONDERS (Jaromil Jires)
(also: Valerie A Tyden Divu)
Films & F: v. 17, n. 11 (Aug., 1971), p. 54; Gordon Gow, 700 wds., cp. cr.
Interntl F G: v. 8 (1971), pp. 103-105; Jan Zalman, 350 wds., pt. cr.

6822 VALI (Sheldon and Diane Rochlin)
(also: Vali — The Witch of Positano)
Filmf: v. X (1967), p. 178; comp., cp. cr.

VALI — THE WITCH OF POSITANO (see: Vali)

6823 VALIANT, THE (Roy Baker)
Filmf: v. V (1962), p. 197; comp., cp. cr.
Films & F: v. 8, n. 5 (Feb., 1962), pp. 31-32; Gordon Gow, 450 wds., cp.
cr.

VALLEY OF FURY (see: Chief Crazy Horse)

6824 VALLEY OF GWANGI, THE (James O'Connolly)
Filmf: v. XII (1969), p. 401; comp., cp. cr.
Films & F: v. 16, n. 3 (Dec., 1969), p. 56; David Hutchison, 600 wds., cp.
cr.

6825 VALLEY OF MYSTERY (Joseph Leytes)
Filmf: v. X (1967), p. 425; comp., cp. cr.

6826 VALLEY OF THE DOLLS (Mark Robson)
Filmf: v. X (1967), p. 416; comp., cp. cr.
Films & F: v. 14, n. 6 (Mar., 1968), pp. 31-32; Raymond Durgnat, 1100
wds., cp. cr.
Films in R: v. XIX, n. 1 (Jan., 1968), pp. 52-53; Page Cook, 400 wds., no
cr.

6827 VALLEY OF THE DRAGONS (Edward Bernds)
Filmf: v. V (1962), p. 100; comp., cp. cr.

6828 VALLEY OF THE EAGLES (Terence Young)
Films in R: v. III, n. 4 (Apr., 1952), pp. 199-200; 180 wds., no cr.

6829 VALLEY OF THE KINGS (Robert Pirosh)
Films & F: v. 1, n. 1 (Oct., 1954), p. 30; Clayton Cole, 150 wds., cp. cr.
Films in R: v. V, n. 7 (Aug.-Sept., 1954), p. 368; 75 wds., no cr.

6830 VALLEY OF THE REDWOODS (William Witney)
Filmf: v. III (1960), p. 82; comp., cp. cr.

6831 VALPARAISO . . . VALPARAISO! (Pascal Aubier)
        Interntl F G: v. 9 (1972), p. 135; Peter Cowie, 200 wds., pt. cr.

6832 VALUE FOR MONEY (Ken Annakin)
        Films & F: v. 2, n. 1 (Oct., 1955), p. 19; Derek Hill, 175 wds., cp. cr.

6833 VAMPIRE LOVERS, THE (Roy Ward Baker)
        Filmf: v. XIV (1971), p. 14; comp., cp. cr.
        Films & F: v. 17, n. 3 (Dec., 1970), pp. 56, 59; Richard Weaver, 400 wds.,
          cp. cr.

6834 VAMPIRES, LES (Louis Feuillade)
        F Quarterly: v. XXIV, n. 2 (Winter, 1970-1971), pp. 56-60; Ellen Mandel,
          2700 wds., pt. cr.
        Sight & S: v. 33, n. 2 (Spring, 1964), pp. 96-97; Richard Roud, 800 wds.,
          no cr.

      VAMPIRI, I (see: The Devil's Commandment)

6835 VAMPYR (Carl Dreyer)
        Focus: n. 7 (Spring, 1972), pp. 2-3; David Bordwell, 1400 wds., no cr.

      VANGELO SECONDO MATTEO, IL (see: The Gospel According to St.
          Matthew)

      VANINA VANINI (see: The Betrayer)

      VANISHING CORPORAL, THE (see: The Elusive Corporal)

6836 VANISHING LEGION, THE (B. Reeves Eason)
        Views & Rev: v. 3, n. 2 (Fall, 1971), pp. 16-32; Jon Tuska, 4500 wds., cp.
          cr.

6837 VANISHING POINT (Richard C. Sarafian)
        Filmf: v. XIV (1971), p. 130; comp., cp. cr.

6838 VANISHING PRAIRIE (James Algar and Walt Disney)
        Films & F: v. 1, n. 9 (June, 1955), p. 21; Jill Hardy, 150 wds., cp. cr.
        Films in R: v. V, n. 8 (Oct., 1954), pp. 432-433; Elspeth Hart, 400 wds., no
          cr.

      VANITY OF LIFE (see: This Transient Life)

      VAR ENGANG EN KRIG, DER (see: Once There Was a War)

6839 VARAN THE UNBELIEVABLE (Jerry A. Baerwitz)
        (also: Daikaiju Baran)
        Filmf: v. VI (1963), p. 52; comp., cp. cr.

      VARGTIMMEN (see: Hour of the Wolf)

6840 VARIATIONS ON A CELLOPHANE WRAPPER (Dave Rimmer)
        Take One: v. 2, n. 11 (1971), p. 29; Kirk Tougas, 700 wds., no cr.

      VARIETY LIGHTS (see: Lights of Variety)

6841 VASILI'S RETURN (V. I. Pudovkin)
        (also: Vozvrashchenie Vasilya Bortnikova)
        Films in R: v. IV, n. 9 (Nov., 1953), p. 482; 75 wds., no cr.

      VAXDOCKAN (see: The Doll)

6842 VELVET VAMPIRE, THE (Stephanie Rothman)
        Filmf: v. XIV (1971), p. 500; comp., cp. cr.

6843 VENDEMIARE (Otar Iosseliani)
        (also: When Leaves Fall)
        Interntl F G: v. 6 (1969), p. 179; Peter Cowie, 200 wds., pt. cr.

      VENDETTA DELLA SIGNORA (see: The Visit)

VENERE DI CHEROHEA, LA (see: The Goddess of Love)

6844 VENETIAN AFFAIR, THE (Jerry Thorpe)
      Filmf: v. X (1967), p. 5; comp., cp. cr.
      Films & F: v. 13, n. 5 (Feb., 1967), p. 32; Ian Johnson, 450 wds., cp. cr.

6845 VENGEANCE (Freddie Francis)
      Films & F: v. 10, n. 3 (Dec., 1963), p. 38; Meredith Lawrence, 250 wds.,
           cp. cr.

6846 VENGEANCE IN TIMBER VALLEY (Paul May)
      Films & F: v. 9, n. 7 (Apr., 1963), pp. 33-34; Ian Johnson, 300 wds., cp. cr.

6847 VENGEANCE OF FU MANCHU, THE (Jeremy Summers)
      Filmf: v. XI (1968), p. 57; comp., cp. cr.

6848 VENGEANCE OF SHE, THE (Cliff Owen)
      Filmf: v. XI (1968), p. 187; comp., cp. cr.
      Films & F: v. 14, n. 9 (June, 1968), p. 28; Michael Armstrong, 200 wds.,
           cp. cr.

6849 VENGEANCE OF THE GLADIATORS (Herbert Wise)
      Films & F: v. 9, n. 6 (Mar., 1963), p. 39; David Rider, 250 wds., cp. cr.

      VENNE UN UOMO, E (see: A Man Named John)

6850 VENOM (Knud Lief Thomsen)
      (also: Gift)
      Filmf: v. XI (1968), p. 12, 46; comp., cp. cr.
      Films & F: v. XIII, n. 6 (Mar., 1967), pp. 35-36; Raymond Durgnat, 800
           wds., cp. cr.

      VENT D'EST (see: Wind from the East)

      VENT SE LEVE, LE (see: Time Bomb)

6851 VERA CRUZ (Robert Aldrich)
      Films & F: v. 1, n. 7 (Apr., 1955), p. 20; Derek Hill, 200 wds., cp. cr.

6852 VERBOTEN! (Samuel Fuller)
      Filmf: v. II (1959), p. 239; comp., cp. cr.

6853 VERDI (Raffaello Matarazzo)
      Films & F: v. 1, n. 3 (Dec., 1954), p. 21; Derwent May, 100 wds., cp. cr.

6854 VERDICT, THE (David Eady)
      Filmf & F: v. 10, n. 8 (May, 1964), pp. 26-27; David Rider, 225 wds., cp.
           cr.

      VERDUGO, EL (Not on Your Life)

      VERGINE DI NORIMBERGA, LE (see: The Castle of Terror)

      VERGINE PER IL PRINCIPE, UNA (see: A Maiden for the Prince)

      VERITE, LA (see: The Truth)

      VERITE SUR LE BEBE DONGE, LA (see: The Truth About Our Marriage)

6855 VERLORENE, DER (Peter Lorre)
      (also: The Lost One)
      Sight & S: v. 36, n. 1 (Winter, 1966-1967), p. 45; Peter John Dyer, 600
           wds., pt. cr.

      VERSAILLES (see: Royal Affairs in Versailles)

      VERSPAETUNG IN MARIENBORN (see: Stop Train 349)

6856 VERTIGO (Alfred Hitchcock)
      Filmf: v. I (1958), p. 85; comp., cp. cr.

Films & F: v. 4, n. 12 (Sept., 1958), p. 25; Derek Conrad, 450 wds., cp. cr.
Films in R: v. IX, n. 6 (June-July, 1958), pp. 333-335; Jeremy Browne, 325 wds., no cr.
Journal of P C: v. II, n. 2 (Fall, 1968), pp. 321-331; Francis M. Nevins, Jr., 3500 wds., no cr.
Sight & S: v. 27, n. 6 (Autumn, 1958), p. 319; Penelope Houston, 350 wds., pt. cr.

VERY CURIOUS GIRL, A (see: La Fiancee du Pirate)

6857 VERY EDGE, THE (Cyril Frankel)
Films & F: v. 9, n. 9 (June, 1963), p. 37; John Cutts, 250 wds., cp. cr.

6858 VERY HANDY MAN, A (Alessandro Blasetti)
(also: Liola)
Filmf: v. IX (1966), p. 356; comp., cp. cr.

VERY HAPPY ALEXANDER (see: Alexander)

VERY IMPORTANT PERSON (see: A Coming-Out Party)

6859 VERY NICE, VERY NICE (Arthur Lipsett)
Interntl F G: v. 1 (1964), p. 117; 75 wds., pt. cr.

6860 VERY PRIVATE AFFAIR, A (Louis Malle)
(also: Vie Privee)
F Quarterly: v. XVI, n. 3 (Spring, 1963), p. 60; R. M. Hodgens, 50 wds., no cr.
Filmf: v. V (1962), p. 229; comp., cp. cr.
Films & F: v. 9, n. 2 (Nov., 1962), pp. 32-33; Roger Manvell, 950 wds., cp. cr.
Films in R: v. XIII, n. 8 (Oct., 1962), p. 491; Jean Cambon, 200 wds., no cr.
Movie: n. 3 (Oct., 1962), p. 36; 75 wds., no cr.

6861 VERY SPECIAL FAVOR, A (Michael Gordon)
Films & F: v. 12, n. 3 (Dec., 1965), pp. 32-33; David Rider, 500 wds., cp. cr.
Films in R: v. XVI, n. 7 (Aug.-Sept., 1965), pp. 450-451; Constance Levering, 175 wds., no cr.

6862 VESUVIUS EXPRESS
Films in R: v. V, n. 4 (Apr., 1954), p. 193; 125 wds., no cr.

VIA MARGUTTA (see: Run with the Devil)

6863 VIACCIA, LA (Mauro Bolognini)
(also: The Love Makers)
Filmf: v. V (1962), p. 309; comp., cp. cr.
Films & F: v. 11, n. 9 (June, 1965), p. 32; Raymond Durgnat, 700 wds., cp. cr.

6864 VIBRATIONS (Barry Gerson)
Take One: v. 2, n. 7 (1970), p. 27; Bob Cowan, 400 wds., no cr.

6865 VICE AND VIRTUE (Roger Vadim)
(also: Le Vice et la Vertu)
F Quarterly: v. XX, n. 1 (Fall, 1966), p. 60; R. M. Hodgens, 125 wds., no cr.
Filmf: v. VIII (1965), p. 46; comp., cp. cr.
Films & F: v. 9, n. 12 (Sept., 1963), p. 26; Peter G. Baker, 275 wds., cp. cr.

VICE ET LA VERTU, LE (see: Vice and Virtue)

6866 VICE RAID (Edward L. Cahn)
Filmf: v. III (1960), p. 3; comp., cp. cr.

6867 VICE VERSA (Peter Ustinov)
Sight & S: v. 17, n. 65 (Spring, 1948), p. 42; Arthur Vesselo, 150 wds., no cr.

6868 VICIOUS CIRCLE (Jacqueline Audry)
(also: Huis Clos)
Films & F: v. 6, n. 5 (Feb., 1960), pp. 22-23; Peter John Dyer, 500 wds.,
cp. cr.
Sight & S: v. 29, n. 1 (Winter, 1959-1960), pp. 39-40; Eric Rhode, 375
wds., pt. cr.

VICIOUS CIRCLE, THE (Gerald Thomas/see: The Circle)

VICOMTE REGLE SES COMPTES, LE (see: The Viscount)

6869 VICTIM (Basil Dearden)
Filmf: v. V (1962), p. 29; comp., cp. cr.
Films & F: v. 8, n. 1 (Oct., 1961), p. 26; Peter Baker, 600 wds., cp. cr.
Films in R: v. XIII, n. 2 (Feb., 1962), pp. 107-108; 250 wds., no cr.
Sight & S: v. 30, n. 4 (Autumn, 1961), pp. 198-199; Terence Kelly, 600
wds., pt. cr.

6870 VICTORS, THE (Carl Foreman)
Cinema: v. 2, n. 1 (Feb., 1964), p. 47; James Silke, 200 wds., pt. cr.
F Quarterly: v. XVII, n. 3 (Spring, 1964), p. 63; R. M. Hodgens, 200 wds.,
no cr.
Filmf: v. VI (1963), p. 273; comp., cp. cr.
Films & F: v. 10, n. 4 (Jan., 1964), p. 26; Peter Baker, 925 wds., cp. cr.
Films in R: v. XIV, n. 10 (Dec., 1963), pp. 624-626; Henry Hart, 950 wds.,
no cr.
Sight & S: v. 33, n. 1 (Winter, 1963-1964), pp. 40-41; John Gillett, 650
wds., pt. cr.

6871 VICTORY AT SEA (Isaac Kleinerman, editor)
Films in R: v. V, n. 7 (Aug.-Sept., 1954), p. 362; Nicolas Monjo, 125 wds.,
no cr.

6872 VIDAS SECAS (Nelson Pereira dos Santos)
(Barren Lives)
F Quarterly: v. XXIV, n. 3 (Spring, 1971), pp. 49-50; Randall Conrad, 1000
wds., pt. cr.
Filmf: v. XII (1969), p. 293; comp., cp. cr.
Interntl F G: v. 2 (1965), p. 108; Peter Graham, 200 wds., pt. cr.

VIE, UNE (see: End of Desire)

VIE A DEUX, LA (see: Life Together)

VIE A L'ENVERS, LA (see: Life Upside Down)

6873 VIE COMMENCE DEMAIN, LA (Nicole Vedres)
Sequence: n. 13 (New Year, 1951), p. 15; Lindsay G. Anderson, 350 wds.,
no cr.
Sight & S: v. 19, n. 10 (Feb., 1951), p. 414; Gavin Lambert, 500 wds., pt.
cr.

6874 VIE DE DHATEAU, LA (Jean Philippe Rappeneau)
(also: Chateau Life; A Matter of Resistance)
F Quarterly: v. XXI, n. 3 (Spring, 1968), pp. 62-63; Stephen Farber, 200
wds., no cr.
Filmf: v. X (1967), p. 79; comp., cp. cr.

VIE, L'AMOUR, LA MORT, LA (see: Life, Love, Death)

VIE PRIVEE (see: A Very Private Affair)

VIEIL HOMME ET L'ENFANT, LE (see: The Two of Us)

VIEILLE DAME INDIGNE, LA (see: The Shameless Old Lady)

VIERGES, LES (see: The Virgins)

6875 VIEW FROM POMPEY'S HEAD, THE (Philip Dunne)
Films in R: v. VI, n. 10 (Dec., 1955), p. 528; Edith Gordon, 350 wds., pt.
cr.

6876 VIEW FROM THE BRIDGE, A (Sidney Lumet)
      Film: n. 32 (Summer, 1962), pp. 17-18; Bernard Hrusa, 300 wds., no cr.
      Filmf: v. V (1962), p. 5; comp., cp. cr.
      Films & F: v. 8, n. 7 (Apr., 1962), p. 29; Peter Baker, 500 wds., cp. cr.
      Films in R: v. XIII, n. 2 (Feb., 1962), pp. 102-103; Henry Hart, 500 wds.,
          no cr.
      Sight & S: v. 31, n. 2 (Spring, 1962), pp. 95-96; Norm Fruchter, 600 wds.,
          pt. cr.

6877 VIJANDEN, DE (Hugo Claus)
      (also: The Enemies)
      Interntl F G: v. 6 (1969), p. 127; Peter Cowie, 200 wds., pt. cr.

6878 VIKING QUEEN, THE (Don Chaffey)
      Filmf: v. X (1967), p. 400; comp., cp. cr.

6879 VIKING WOMEN AND THE SEA SERPENT (Roger Corman)
      Filmf: v. I (1958), p. 10; comp., cp. cr.

6880 VIKINGS, THE (Richard Fleischer)
      Filmf: v. I (1958), p. 101; comp., cp. cr.
      Films & F: v. 4, n. 11 (Aug., 1958), p. 25; Gordon Gow, 350 wds., cp. cr.
      Films in R: v. IX, n. 7 (Aug.-Sept., 1958), p. 402; Hakon Margesson, 200
          wds., no cr.

6881 VILLA! (James B. Clark)
      Filmf: v. I (1958), p. 258; comp., cp. cr.

6882 VILLA BORGHESE (Gianni Franciolini)
      Films & F: v. 2, n. 4 (Jan., 1956), pp. 21-22; P. L. Mannock, 150 wds., cp.
          cr.

6883 VILLA RIDES (Buzz Kulik)
      Filmf: v. XI (1968), p. 264; comp., cp. cr.
      Films & F: v. 14, n. 12 (Sept., 1968), p. 44; Allen Eyles, 400 wds., cp. cr.

6884 VILLAGE, THE (Leopold Lindtberg)
      Films & F: v. 2, n. 2 (Nov., 1955), p. 18; John Carroll, 100 wds., cp. cr.
      Films in R: v. IV, n. 9 (Nov., 1953), p. 485; 175 wds., no cr.
      Sight & S: v. 23, n. 1 (July-Sept., 1953), p. 34; Penelope Houston, 250
          wds., pt. cr.

      VILLAGE FAIR, THE (see: Jour de Fete)

6885 VILLAGE FEUD, THE (Henri Verneuil)
      (also: La Table aux Creves)
      Films & F: v. 1, n. 12 (Sept., 1955), p. 20; Michell Roper, 200 wds., cp. cr.

6886 VILLAGE OF THE DAMNED (Wolf Rilla)
      Filmf: v. III (1960), p. 289; comp., cp. cr.
      Films & F: v. 6, n. 11 (Aug., 1960), pp. 24-25; John Cutts, 300 wds., cp. cr.
      Films in R: v. XII, n. 1 (Jan., 1961), p. 39; Jack Jacobs, 175 wds., no cr.

6887 VILLAGE ON THE RIVER
      F Journal: n. 18 (Oct., 1961), p. 20; Brian J. Davies, 100 wds., no cr.

6888 VILLAIN (Michael Tuchner)
      Filmf: v. XIV (1971), p. 211; comp., cp. cr.

      VINGT — CINQUIEME HEURE, LA (see: The 25th Hour)

6889 VIOL, LE (Jacques Doniol-Valcroze)
      (also: Overgreppet; A Question of Rape; The Rape)
      Filmf: v. XI (1968), p. 381; comp., cp. cr.
      Films & F: v. 15, n. 6 (Mar., 1969), p. 44; Claire Johnston, 350 wds., cp. cr.
      Sight & S: v. 37, n. 4 (Autumn, 1968), p. 209; David Wilson, 400 wds., pt.
          cr.

6890 VIOL D'UNE JEUNE FILLE DOUCE (Gilles Carle)
      Take One: v. 2, n. 1 (1969), p. 21; Gabriel Breton, 700 wds., pt. cr.

6891 VIOLENCE AT HIGH NOON (Nagisa Oshima)
        (also: Hakucho No Torima)
        Film: n. 58 (Spring, 1970), p. 5; 100 wds., pt. cr.

6892 VIOLENT AND THE DAMNED, THE (Carlos Hugo Christensen)
        (also: Assassinos)
        Filmf: v. V (1962), p. 366; comp., cp. cr.

6893 VIOLENT ENEMY, THE (Don Sharp)
        Films & F: v. 15, n. 11 (Aug., 1969), pp. 43; 46; David Adams, 650 wds.,
        cp. cr.

6894 VIOLENT FOUR, THE (Carlo Lizzani)
        (also: Banditi A Milano)
        Filmf: v. XI (1968), p. 352; comp., cp. cr.

      VIOLENT JOURNEY, A (see: The Fool Killer)

      VIOLENT MEN, THE (see: Rough Company)

6895 VIOLENT ONES, THE (Fernando Lamas)
        Filmf: v. X (1967), p. 392; comp., cp. cr.
        Films & F: v. 15, n. 12 (Sept., 1969), pp. 70-71; David Hutchison, 300
        wds., cp. cr.

6896 VIOLENT PLAYGROUND (Basil Dearden)
        Films & F: v. 4, n. 6 (Mar., 1958), pp. 23-24; Ken Gay, 450 wds., cp. cr.
        Sight & S: v. 27, n. 4 (Spring, 1958), p. 203; Derek Hill, 500 wds., pt. cr.

6897 VIOLENT ROAD (Howard Koch)
        Filmf: v. I (1958), p. 74; comp., cp. cr.

6898 VIOLENT SATURDAY (Richard Fleischer)
        Films & F: v. 1, n. 10 (July, 1955), p. 15; Peter Barnes, 150 wds., cp. cr.
        Films in R: v. VI, n. 5 (May, 1955), pp. 239-240; John Springer, 600 wds.,
        pt. cr.

6899 VIOLENT SUMMER (Valerio Zurlini)
        Filmf: v. IV (1961), p. 126; comp., cp. cr.
        Films in R: v. XI, n. 10 (Dec., 1960), pp. 614-615; Carlos Clarens, 175
        wds., no cr.

6900 VIOLENT WOMEN (Barry Mahon)
        Filmf: v. II (1959), p. 343; comp., cp. cr.

6901 VIOLETTES IMPERIALES (Richard Pottier)
        Films & F: v. 1, n. 12 (Sept., 1955), p. 19; Derek Hill, 200 wds., cp. cr.

6902 VIOLINIST, THE (Ernest Pintoff)
        F Quarterly: v. XIII, n. 3 (Spring, 1960), p. 60; 50 wds., no cr.

6903 VIRGIN AND THE GYPSY, THE (Christopher Miles)
        Films & F: v. 16, n. 12 (Sept., 1970), pp. 59, 62; Gordon Gow, 950 wds.,
        cp. cr.
        Sight & S: v. 39, n. 4 (Autumn, 1970), pp. 220-221; Nigel Andrews, 700
        wds., pt. cr.

      VIRGIN FOR THE PRINCE, A (see: A Maiden for the Prince)

6904 VIRGIN ISLAND (Pat Jackson)
        F Quarterly: v. XIII, n. 4 (Summer, 1960), p. 61; 50 wds., no cr.
        Filmf: v. III (1960), p. 52; comp., cp. cr.
        Films & F: v. 5, n. 3 (Dec., 1958), pp. 22-23; Peter John Dyer, 400 wds.,
        cp. cr.
        Sight & S: v. 28, n. 1 (Winter, 1958-1959), p. 40; Derek Hill, 300 wds., pt.
        cr.

6905 VIRGIN SACRIFICE (Fernando Wagner)
        Filmf: v. II (1959), p. 346; comp., cp. cr.

6906 VIRGIN SOLDIERS, THE (John Dexter)
        Films & F: v. 16, n. 3 (Dec., 1969), p. 42; John Walker, 650 wds., cp. cr.

6907 VIRGIN SPRING, THE (Ingmar Bergman)
         (also: Jungfrukallan; Well of the Virgin)
         F Heritage: v. 2, n. 2 (Winter, 1966-1967), pp. 2-20; David Madden, 5000
             wds., no cr.
         F Quarterly: v. XIII, n. 4 (Summer, 1960), pp. 43-47; Vernon Young, 1800
             wds., pt. cr.
         Filmf: v. III (1960), p. 277; comp., cp. cr.
         Films & F: v. 7, n. 10 (July, 1961), pp. 26-27; Gordon Gow, 450 wds., cp.
             cr.
         Films in R: v. XI, n. 9 (Nov., 1960), pp. 556-557; Helen Weldon Kuhn, 400
             wds., no cr.

6908 VIRGIN QUEEN, THE (Henry Koster)
         Films & F: v. 2, n. 2 (Nov., 1955), p. 17; Peter G. Baker, 100 wds., cp. cr.
         Films in R: v. VI, n. 8 (Oct., 1955), pp. 408-409; Robert Downing, 500
             wds., pt. cr.
         Films & F: v. 15, n. 5 (Feb., 1969), pp. 45-46; David Hutchison, 250 wds.,
             cp. cr.

6909 VIRGINIA WOOLF: THE MOMENT WHOLE (Janet Sternburg, prod.)
         F Lib Quarterly: v. 5, n. 1 (Winter, 1971-1972), p. 54; Janet Handelman,
             200 wds., pt. cr.

6910 VIRGINS, THE (Jean-Pierre Mocky)
         (also: Les Vierges)
         Films & F: v. 13, n. 11 (Aug., 1967), p. 23; Raymond Durgnat, 700 wds.,
             cp. cr.

6911 VIRIDIANA (Luis Bunuel)
         Cinema: v. 1, n. 3, p. 33; 250 wds., pt. cr.
         Film: n. 33 (Autumn, 1962), pp. 20-21; Philip Strick, 450 wds., no cr.
         F Culture: n. 24 (Spring, 1962), pp. 76-82; Emilio G. Riera, 2000 wds., pt.
             cr.
         F Quarterly: v. XV, n. 2 (Winter, 1961-1962), pp. 55-56; David Stewart
             Hull, 500 wds., pt. cr.
         Filmf: v. V (1962), p. 83; comp., cp. cr.
         Films & F: v. 8, n. 9 (June, 1962), p. 32; Paul Rotha, 1100 wds., cp. cr.
         Films in R: v. XIII, n. 2 (Feb., 1962), pp. 110-111; Elaine Rothschild, 475
             wds., no cr.
         Movie: n. 1 (June, 1962), pp. 14-16; Andrew Sarris, 2300 wds., no cr.

6912 VIRINEYA (V. Fetin)
         Interntl F G: v. 7 (1970), pp. 240-241; Nina Hibbln, 300 wds., pt. cr.

6913 VIRTUOUS BIGAMIST, THE (Mario Soldati)
         (also: Sous le Ciel de Provence)
         Filmf: v. II (1959), p. 152; comp., cp. cr.

6914 VIRTUOUS SCOUNDREL, THE (Sacha Guitry)
         Filmf in R: v. VIII, n. 9 (Nov., 1957), pp. 465-466; Louise Corbin, 150
             wds., no cr.

6915 VISCOUNT, THE (Maurice Cloche)
         (also: Le Vicomte Regle Ses Comptes; The Viscount Settles Accounts)
         Filmf: v. X (1967), p. 131; comp., cp. cr.

         VISCOUNT SETTLES ACCOUNTS, THE (see: The Viscount)

6916 VISIT, THE (Bernhard Wicki)
         (also: Der Besuch; La Rancune; Vendetta dell Signora)
         Filmf: v. VII (1964), p. 254; comp., cp. cr.
         Films & F: v. 12, n. 1 (Oct., 1965), p. 30; Allen Eyles, 750 wds., cp. cr.
         Films in R: v. XV, n. 7 (Aug.-Sept., 1964), pp. 445-446; Henry Hart, 450
             wds., no cr.
         Interntl F G: v. 2 (1965), p. 77; Peter Graham, 200 wds., pt. cr.

6917 VISIT TO A SMALL PLANET (Norman Taurog)
         Filmf: v. III (1960), p. 70; comp., cp. cr.
         Films & F: v. 6, n. 9 (June, 1960), p. 24; Peter G. Baker, 250 wds., cp. cr.

6918 VISITA, LA (Antonio Pietrangeli)
        Filmf: v. IX (1966), p. 192; comp., cp. cr.

6919 VISTRIL V GORACH (Bolot Shamshiev)
        (also: Karash-Karash; A Shot in the Mountains)
        Interntl F G: v. 8 (1971), pp. 269-270; Nina Hibbin, 225 wds., pt. cr.

6920 VITELLONI, I (Federico Fellini)
        (also: The Young and the Passionate)
        F Culture: v. 2, n. 4 (1956), pp. 24-25; Eugene Archer, 1800 wds., pt. cr.
        F Soc Rev: v. 5, n. 9 (May, 1970), pp. 42-45; Mark Sufrin, 1200 wds., cp.
          cr.
        Films & F: v. 1, n. 3 (Dec., 1954), p. 21; Louis Marks, 325 wds., cp. cr.
        Films in R: v. VII, n. 10 (Dec., 1956), p. 527-528; Diana Willing, 350 wds.,
          no cr.

      VIVA AND LOUIS (see: Blue Movie)

6921 VIVA LA MUERTE (Fernando Arrabal)
        Interntl F G: v. 9 (1972), p. 137; Amos Vogel, 200 wds., pt. cr.

6922 VIVA LAS VEGAS (George Sidney)
        (also: Love in Las Vegas)
        Filmf: v. VII (1964), p. 65; comp., cp. cr.
        Films & F: v. 10, n. 7 (Apr., 1964), p. 31; Robin Bean, 200 wds., cp. cr.

      VIVA LAS VEGAS (Roy Rowland/see: Meet Me in Las Vegas)

6923 VIVA MARIA! (Louis Malle)
        Cahiers in Eng: n. 6 (Dec., 1966), pp. 53-54; Jean Louis Camolli, 500 wds.,
          cp. cr.
        Cinema: v. 3, n. 2 (Mar., 1966), p. 48; Richard Whitehall, 500 wds., pt. cr.
        F Quarterly: v. XIX, n. 3 (Spring, 1966), p. 54; R. M. Hodgens, 150 wds.,
          no cr.
        Films & F: v. 12, n. 6 (Mar., 1965), p. 6; Gordon Gow, 700 wds., cp. cr.
        Films in R: v. XVII, n. 1 (Jan., 1966), pp. 46-47; Henry Hart, 500 wds., no
          cr.
        Interntl F G: v. 4 (1967), p. 70; 200 wds., pt. cr.
        Sight & S: v. 35, n. 2 (Spring, 1966), p. 90; Penelope Houston, 1500 wds.,
          pt. cr.

6924 VIVA ZAPATA! (Elia Kazan)
        Films in R: v. III, n. 3 (Mar., 1952), pp. 132-134; Henry Hart, 900 wds., pt.
          cr.
        Sight & S: v. 21, n. 4 (Apr.-June, 1952), p. 170; Catherine de la Roche, 600
          wds., pt. cr.

6925 VIVE MONSIEUR BLAIREAU (Yves Robert)
        Films & F: v. 4, n. 12 (Sept., 1958), p. 23; Derek Conrad, 225 wds., cp. cr.

      VIVRE POUR VIVRE (see: Live for Life)

6926 VIVRE SA VIE (Jean-Luc Godard)
        (also: It's My Life; My Life To Live)
        Film: n. 35 (Spring, 1963), pp. 30, 32; 500 wds., no cr.
        Filmf: v. VI (1963), p. 268; comp., cp. cr.
        Films & F: v. 9, n. 4 (Jan., 1963), p. 44; Peter Baker, 500 wds., cp. cr.
        Movie: n. 3 (Oct., 1962), p. 30; Mark Shivas, 350 wds., pt. cr.
        Movie: n. 6, pp. 23-25: Jean-Andre Fieschi, trans. by Garry Broughton,
          2100 wds., pt. cr.
        Movie: n. 8, pp. 28-29; 1200 wds., no cr.

6927 VIXEN, THE (Alberto Lattuada)
        (also: La Lupa; The She-Wolf)
        Films & F: v. 5, n. 8 (May, 1959), p. 23; Derek Conrad, 225 wds., cp. cr.

      VIXEN (Russ Meyer/ see: Russ Meyer's Vixen)

6928 VIXENS, THE (Harvey Cort)
        (also: Friends And Lovers)
        Filmf: v. XII (1969), p. 69; comp., cp. cr.

6929 VLADIMIR AND ROSA (Jean-Luc Godard)
      Cineaste: v. IV, n. 3 (Winter, 1970-1971), p. 39; Joan Mellen, 500 wds., pt.
        cr.
      Filmf: v. XIV (1971), p. 632; comp., cp. cr.
      Take One: v. 2, n. 11 (1971), p. 14; Susan Rice, 650 wds., no cr.

      VLCI JAMA (see: The Wolf Trap)

      VO VLASTI ZOLOTA (see: Lust for Gold)

      VOCI BIANCHE (see: White Voices)

      VOGLIA MATTA, LA (see: Crazy Desire)

6930 VOICE IN THE MIRROR (Harry Keller)
      Filmf: v. I (1958), p. 132; comp., cp. cr.

      VOICE IN THE WATER, THE (see: De Stem Van Het Water)

6931 VOICE OF SILENCE, THE (G. W. Pabst)
      Films in R: v. V, n. 8 (Oct., 1954), p. 436; 175 wds., no cr.

6932 VOICES (Richard Mordaunt)
      Films & F: v. 16, n. 10 (July, 1970), p. 48; Ken Gay, 250 wds., cp. cr.

      VOICI LE TEMPS DES ASSASSINS (see: Murder a la Carte)

      VOIE LACTEE, LA (see: The Milky Way)

6933 VOLCANO (Haroun Tazieff)
      (also: Les Rendezvous du Diable)
      F Journal: n. 20 (Aug., 1962), p. 82; R. J. Garlick, 150 wds., no cr.

6934 VOLCANO SURTSEY (Barrie McLean)
      F Lib Quarterly: v. 2, n. 2 (Spring, 1969), pp. 53-54; John S. Robotham,
        200 wds., pt. cr.

      VOLEUR, I F (see: The Thief of Paris)

      VOLNITSA (see: Flames on the Volga)

      VOLSHEVNOYE ZERKALO (see: The Enchanted Mirror)

6935 VON RICHTHOFEN AND BROWN (Roger Corman)
      Filmf: v. XIV (1971), p. 334; comp., cp. cr.

6936 VON RYAN'S EXPRESS (Mark Robson)
      Cinema: v. 2, n. 6 (Aug., 1965), pp. 49-50; Harlan Ellison, 850 wds., pt. cr.
      Films & F: v. 11, n. 11 (Aug., 1965), p. 24; Gordon Gow, 550 wds., cp. cr.

      VORETZ E KLOUN (see: The Wrestler and the Clown)

      VOULEZ-VOUS DANSER AVEC MOI? (see: Come Dance With Me)

      VOYAGE DU SILENCE, LE (see: Voyage of Silence)

6937 VOYAGE OF SILENCE (Christian de Chalonge)
      (also: O Salto; Le Voyage du Silence)
      Filmf: v. XI (1968), p. 348; comp., cp. cr.

6938 VOYAGE OF THE BRIGANTINE YANKEE, THE (National Geographic
        Society)
      F Lib Quarterly: v. 1, n. 4 (Fall, 1968), p. 56; Elsie H. Vandale, 500 wds.,
        pt. cr.

6939 VOYAGE SURPRISE (Pierre Prevert)
      Films & F: v. 15, n. 5 (Feb., 1969), p. 36; Richard Davis, 350 wds., cp. cr.

6940 VOYAGE TO THE BOTTOM OF THE SEA (Irwin Allen)
      Filmf: v. IV (1961), p. 189; comp., cp. cr.
      Films & F: v. 7, n. 12 (Sept., 1961), pp. 28-29; Phillip Riley, 450 wds., cp.
        cr.

6941 VOYAGE TO THE END OF THE UNIVERSE (Jindrich Pollak)
        (also: Ikaria XB1)
        Films & F: v. 12, n. 2 (Nov., 1965), p. 33; Richard Davis, 350 wds., cp. cr.

        VOYOU, LE (see: The Crook)

        VOZVRASHCHENIE VASILYA BORTNIKOVA (see: Vasili's Return)

        VRASDA PO NASEM (see: Murder Czech Style)

        VREDENS DAG (see: Day of Wrath)

6942 VULTURE, THE (Lawrence Huntington)
        Filmf: v. X (1967), p. 152; comp., cp. cr.

6943 WR: MYSTERIES OF THE ORGANISM (Dusan Makavejev)
        (also: WR — Misterije Organisma)
        Cineaste: v. V, n. 1 (Winter, 1971-1972), pp. 18-21; Joan Mellen, 2600
            wds., pt. cr.
        F Soc Rev: v. 7, n. 3 (Nov., 1971), pp. 20-21; Gary Crowdus, 400 wds., pt.
            cr.
        Filmf: v. XIV (1971), p. 608; comp., cp. cr.
        Interntl F G: v. 9 (1972), pp. 285-286; Peter Cowie, 200 wds., pt. cr.

6944 WUSA (Stuart Rosenberg)
        F Quarterly: v. XXIV, n. 3 (Spring, 1971), pp. 58-59; Robert G. Michels,
            500 wds., no cr.
        Films in R: v. XXI, n. 10 (Dec., 1970), p. 647; William Herron, 125 wds.,
            no cr.

6945 WACKIEST SHIP IN THE ARMY, THE (Richard Murphy)
        Filmf: v. IV (1961), p. 26; comp., cp. cr.
        Films & F: v. 7, n. 6 (Mar., 1961), pp. 26-27; Robin Bean, 250 wds., cp. cr.

6946 WACO (R. G. Springsteen)
        Filmf: v. IX (1966), p. 235; comp., cp. cr.

6947 WAGES OF FEAR, THE (Henri-Georges Clouzot)
        (also: Le Salaire de la Peur)
        Films & F: v. 11, n. 9 (June, 1965), p. 34; Allen Eyles, 700 wds., cp. cr.
        Films in R: v. VI, n. 2 (Feb., 1955), p. 85; Henrietta Lehman, 450 wds., no
            cr.
        Sight & S: v. 23, n. 4 (Apr.-June, 1954), pp. 197-198; Karel Reisz, 800
            wds., pt. cr.

6948 WAGONMASTER (John Ford)
        Sequence: n. 13 (New Year, 1951), p. 17; Lindsay G. Anderson, 450 wds.,
            no cr.
        Sight & S: v. 19, n. 8 (Dec., 1950), pp. 333-334; Lindsay Anderson, 750
            wds., pt. cr.

        WAHRHEIT UBER ROSEMARIE, DIE (see: She Walks by Night)

6949 WAIT UNTIL DARK (Terence Young)
        F Quarterly: v. XXI, n. 3 (Spring, 1968), p. 63; Stephen Farber, 300 wds.,
            no cr.
        Filmf: v. X (1967), p. 324; comp., cp. cr.
        Films & F: v. 14, n. 11 (Aug., 1968), p. 33; David Austen, 450 wds., cp. cr.
        Films in R: v. XVIII, n. 10 (Dec., 1967), pp. 644-645; Page Cook, 300 wds.,
            no cr.

        WAITING WOMEN (see: Secrets of Women)

6950 WAKE ME WHEN IT'S OVER (Mervyn LeRoy)
     F Quarterly: v. XIII, n. 4 (Summer, 1960), p. 61; 75 wds., no cr.
     Filmf: v. III (1960), p. 89; comp., cp. cr.
     Films & F: v. 6, n. 9 (June, 1960), pp. 23-24; John Cutts, 250 wds., cp. cr.

6951 WAKE UP AND DIE (Carlo Lizzani)
     (also: Lutring; Svegliati E Uccidi; Too Soon To Die)
     Filmf: v. XI (1968), p. 331; comp., cp. cr.

6952 WALK, DON'T RUN (Charles Walters)
     Filmf: v. IX (1966), p. 227; comp., cp. cr.
     Films & F: v. 12, n. 12 (Sept., 1966), pp. 6-7; Richard Davis, 450 wds., cp. cr.
     Films in R: v. XVII, n. 7 (Aug.-Sept., 1966), p. 453; 50 wds., no cr.

6953 WALK IN THE SHADOW (Basil Dearden)
     (also: Life for Ruth)
     Filmf: v. IX (1966), p. 242; comp., cp. cr.

6954 WALK IN THE SPRING RAIN, A (Guy Green)
     Films & F: v. 17, n. 3 (Dec., 1970), p. 56; John Francis, 200 wds., cp. cr.

6955 WALK IN THE SUN, A (Lewis Milestone)
     Sight & S: v. 19, n. 12 (Apr., 1951), pp. 472-473; Gavin Lamberg, 1650 wds., pt. cr.

6956 WALK LIKE A DRAGON (James Clavel)
     Filmf: v. III (1960), p. 189; comp., cp. cr.

6957 WALK ON THE WILD SIDE (Edward Dmytryk)
     Cinema: v. 1, n. 2, p. 33; 50 wds., pt. cr.
     Film: n. 32 (Summer, 1962), p. 20; Peter Armitage, 100 wds., no cr.
     Filmf: v. V (1962), p. 57; comp., cp. cr.
     Films & F: v. 8, n. 7 (Apr., 1962), p. 32; John Cutts, 350 wds., cp. cr.
     Films in R: v. XIII, n. 3 (Mar., 1962), pp. 171-172; Ellen Fitzpatrick, 375 wds., no cr.

6958 WALK TALL (Maury Dexter)
     Filmf: v. III (1960), p. 262; comp., cp. cr.

6959 WALK WITH LOVE AND DEATH, A (John Huston)
     F Heritage: v. 6, n. 2 (Winter, 1970-1971), pp. 14-18; Michael Dempsey, 2000 wds., pt. cr.
     F Soc Rev: v. 6, n. 2 (Oct., 1970), pp. 44-46; Michael Sragow, 1000 wds., cp. cr.
     Filmf in R: v. XX, n. 8 (Oct., 1969), p. 511; Norman Cecil, 175 wds., no cr.

6960 WALKABOUT (Nicolas Roeg)
     Filmf: v. XIV (1971), p. 250; comp., cp. cr.
     Interntl F G: v. 9 (1972), p. 106; Peter Cowie, 250 wds., pt. cr.

6961 WALKING (Ryan Larkin)
     F Lib Quarterly: v. 4, n. 3 (Summer, 1971), p. 42; Nadine Covert, 150 wds., pt. cr.

6962 WALKING DOWN BROADWAY (Erich von Stroheim)
     (also: Hello, Sister)
     Screen: v. 11, n. 4-5 (Aug.-Sept., 1970), pp. 89-96; Joel W. Finlander, 2500 wds., cp. cr.
     Sight & S: v. 39, n. 4 (Autumn, 1970), pp. 208-210; Richard Koszarski, 2500 wds., pt. cr.

6963 WALKING STICK, THE (Eric Till)
     Films & F: v. 17, n. 1 (Oct., 1970), pp. 42, 44; Gordon Gow, 650 wds., cp. cr.

6964 WALKING TARGET (Edward L. Cahn)
     Filmf: v. III (1960), p. 353; comp., cp. cr.

6965 WALKOVER (Jerzy Skolimowski)
     Movie: n. 14 (Autumn, 1965), p. 41; Ian Cameron, 125 wds., no cr.

6966 WALL OF NOISE (Richard Wilson)
        Filmf: v. VI (1963), p. 197; comp., cp. cr.
        Films & F: v. 10, n. 2 (Nov., 1963), p. 33; David Rider, 325 wds., cp. cr.

      WALLS (see: Falak)

6967 WALLS OF MALAPAGA, THE (Rene Clement)
        Films in R: v. I, n. 4 (May-June, 1950), pp. 26-28; Jacqueline Clark, 750
          wds., pt. cr.

6968 WALTZ KING, THE (Steve Previn)
        Films & F: v. 10, n. 7 (Apr., 1964), pp. 31-32; Allen Eyles, 425 wds., cp. cr.

6969 WALTZ OF SEX (Ake Falck)
        Films & F: v. 15, n. 8 (May, 1969), pp. 43-44; David Rider, 500 wds., cp.
          cr.

6970 WALTZ OF THE TOREADORS (John Guillermin)
        (also: The Amorous General)
        Filmf: v. V (1962), p. 189; comp., cp. cr.
        Films & F: v. 8, n. 8 (May, 1962), p. 34; Richard Whitehall, 400 wds., cp.
          cr.
        Films in R: v. XIII, n. 8 (Oct., 1962), pp. 485-486; Louise Corbin, 200
          wds., no cr.

6971 WANDA (Barbara Loden)
        F Quarterly: v. XXV, n. 1 (Fall, 1971), pp. 49-51; Estelle Changas, 700
          wds., pt. cr.
        Filmf: v. XIV (1971), p. 179; comp., cp. cr.
        Films & F: v. 17, n. 7 (Apr., 1971), pp. 49-50; 550 wds., cp. cr.
        Movie: n. 18 (Winter, 1970-1971), p. 40; Ian Cameron, 100 wds., no cr.
        Sight & S: v. 40, n. 1 (Winter, 197-1971), p. 15; John Russell Taylor, 800
          wds., pt. cr.

6972 WANDERER, THE (Jean-Gabriel Albicocco)
        (also: Le Grand Meaulnes)
        Filmf: v. XII (1969), p. 128; comp., cp. cr.

      WANTON, THE (see: Maneges)

      WANTON COUNTESS, THE (see: Senso)

6973 WAR AND PEACE (King Vidor)
        Films & F: v. 3, n. 3 (Dec., 1956), pp. 21-22; Peter John Dyer, 500 wds.,
          cp. cr.
        Films in R: v. VII, n. 7 (Aug.-Sept., 1956), pp. 314-316; Arthur Mayer,
          1200 wds., no cr.
        Films in R: v. VII, n. 8 (Oct., 1956), pp. 408-409; Herbert G. Luft, 500
          wds., no cr.
        Films in R: v. VII, n. 8 (Oct., 1956), pp. 409-410; Tatiana Balkoff Downe,
          300 wds., no cr.
        Films in R: v. VII, n. 8 (Oct., 1956), pp. 410-411; Henry Hart, 750 wds., no
          cr.
        Sight & S: v. 26, n. 3 (Winter, 1956-1957), p. 152; Penelope Houston, 750
          wds., pt. cr.

6974 WAR AND PEACE (Sergei Bondarchuk)
        (also: Woina I Mir)
        Filmf: v. XI (1968), p. 127; comp., cp. cr.
        Films & F: v. 15, n. 8 (May, 1969), pp. 60-63; Uran Guralnik, 2800 wds.,
          no cr.
        Films & F: v. 15, n. 9 (June, 1969), pp. 47, 50; David Austen, 1000 wds.,
          cp. cr.
        Films in R: v. XIX, n. 6 (June-July, 1968), pp. 373-375; Henry Hart, 700
          wds., no cr.
        Interntl F G: v. 4 (1967), pp. 166-167; Felix Bucher, 300 wds., pt. cr.
        Interntl F G: v. 5 (1968), p. 159; 200 wds., pt. cr.
        Sight & S: v. 38, n. 2 (Spring, 1969), pp. 97-98; James Price, 1000 wds., no
          cr.
        Take One: v. 1, n. 10 (1968), pp. 28-29; David Patrick, 550 wds., pt. cr.

6975 WAR BETWEEN THE PLANETS (Anthony Dawson)
         (also: Missione Pianeta Errante; Mission: Planet Erring)
         Filmf: v. XIV (1971), p. 538; comp., cp. cr.

6976 WAR GAME, THE (Peter Watkins)
         F Comment: v. 3, n. 4 (Fall, 1965), pp. 5-12; 6000 wds., no cr.
         F Quarterly: v. XXI, n. 1 (Fall, 1967), pp. 45-47; Kristin Young, 1000 wds.,
              pt. cr.
         F Soc Rev: Jan. (1968), pp. 10-12; Claire Clouzot, 1200 wds., no cr.
         Filmf: v. X (1967), p. 90; comp., cp. cr.
         Sight & S: v. 35, n. 2 (Spring, 1966), pp. 92-93; Penelope Houston, 1500
              wds., no cr.
         Take One: v. 1, n. 5 (June, 1967), pp. 31-32; Patrick MacFadden, 1500
              wds., pt. cr.

         WAR GODS OF THE DEEP (see: City Under the Sea)

6977 WAR HUNT (Denis Sanders)
         F Quarterly: v. XV, n. 4 (Summer, 1962), pp. 53-55; Basil Wright, 700
              wds., pt. cr.
         Filmf: v. V (1962), p. 237; comp., cp. cr.
         Films & F: v. 10, n. 2 (Nov., 1963), p. 25; Robin Bean, 300 wds., cp. cr.

6978 WAR IS HELL (Burt Topper)
         Filmf: v. VII (1964), p. 35; comp., cp. cr.

6979 WAR IS HELL (Robert Nelson)
         F Culture: n. 48-49 (Winter-Spring, 1970), pp. 29-30; Robert Nelson, 500
              wds., pt. cr.

         WAR IS OVER, THE (La Guerre Est Finie)

6980 WAR, ITALIAN STYLE (Luigi Scattini)
         (also: Due Marinos E Un Generale; Two Marines and a General)
         Filmf: v. X (1967), p. 125; comp., cp. cr.
         Films in R: v. XVIII, n. 3 (Mar., 1967), pp. 177-178; Henry Hart, 200 wds.,
              no cr.

6881 WAR LORD, THE (Franklin Schaffner)
         Cinema: v. 3, n. 1 (Dec., 1965), p. 49; Harlan Ellison, 450 wds., pt. cr.
         F Quarterly: v. XIX, n. 3 (Spring, 1966), p. 54; William Johnson, 150 wds.,
              no cr.
         Films & F: v. 12, n. 5 (Feb., 1966), p. 6; Gordon Gow, 650 wds., cp. cr.
         Films in R: v. XVI, n. 9 (Nov., 1965), p. 583; Henry Hart, 175 wds., no cr.

6982 WAR LOVER, THE (Phillip Leacock)
         Filmf: v. VI (1963), p. 20; comp., cp. cr.
         Films & F: v. 9, n. 11 (Aug., 1963), p. 26; John Cutts, 500 wds., cp. cr.
         Films in R: v. XIII, n. 9 (Nov., 1962), pp. 554-555; Adelaide Comerford,
              150 wds., no cr.

6983 WAR OF THE BUTTONS, THE (Yves Robert)
         (also: La Guerre des Boutons)
         Filmf: v. VI (1963), p. 333; comp., cp. cr.
         Films & F: v. 11, n. 5 (Feb., 1965), pp. 36-37; Mike Sarne, 525 wds., cp. cr.

6984 WAR OF THE COLOSSAL BEAST (Bert I. Gordon)
         Films: v. I (1958), p. 166; comp., cp. cr.

6985 WAR OF THE SATELLITES (Roger Corman)
         Filmf: v. I (1958), p. 180; comp., cp. cr.

6986 WAR OF THE TROJANS (Albert Band)
         (also: La Leggenda di Enea)
         Films & F: v. 11, n. 4 (Jan., 1965), p. 33; Allen Eyles, 450 wds., cp. cr.

6987 WAR ON THE WORLDS, THE (Byron Haskins)
         Films in R: v. IV, n. 5 (May, 1953), p. 241; 120 wds., pt. cr.

6988 WAR PARTY (Lesley Selander)
         Filmf: v. VIII (1965), p. 97; comp., cp. cr.

6989 WAR WAGON, THE (Burt Kennedy)
         Filmf: v. X (1967), p. 235; comp., cp. cr.
         Films & F: v. 14, n. 5 (Feb., 1968), p. 24; Allen Eyles, 600 wds., cp. cr.

6990 WARKILL (Ferde Grofe, Jr.)
         Filmf: v. XI (1968), p. 140; comp., cp. cr.
         Films & F: v. 15, n. 7 (Apr., 1969), p. 50; David Hutchison, 500 wds., cp.
            cr.

6991 WARLOCK (Edward Dmytryk)
         Filmf: v. II (1959), p. 97; comp., cp. cr.
         Films & F: v. 5, n. 9 (June, 1959), pp. 22-23; Peter John Dyer, 450 wds.,
            cp. cr.

6992 WARNING SHOT (Buzz Kulik)
         Filmf: v. X (1967), p. 163; comp., cp. cr.
         Films & F: v. 13, n. 6 (Mar., 1967), p. 32; David Adams, 450 wds., cp. cr.
         Films in R: v. XVIII, n. 2 (Feb., 1967), pp. 114-115; Roi Frumkes, 150
            wds., no cr.

6993 WARRENDALE (Allan King)
         Cinema: v. 5, n. 1, p. 45; Toby Meikeljohn, 550 wds., no cr.
         F Comment: v. 5, n. 3 (Fall, 1969), pp. 60-61; Paul Bradlow, 1300 wds., no
            cr.
         F Quarterly: v. XXI, n. 2 (Winter, 1967-1968), pp. 52-55; Ernest
            Callenbach, 1600 wds., pt. cr.
         Filmf: v. XI (1968), p. 375; comp., cp. cr.
         Films & F: v. 15, n. 2 (Nov., 1968), pp. 52, 54; Gordon Gow, 800 wds., cp.
            cr.
         Interntl F G: v. 5 (1968), p. 53; 120 wds., pt. cr.
         Sight & S: v. 37, n. 1 (Winter, 1967-1968), pp. 44-46; Jan Dawson, 2500
            wds., no cr.
         Take One: v. 1, n. 7 (1967), p. 23; Antony Lorraine, 800 wds., pt. cr.

6994 WARRIOR AND THE SLAVE GIRL, THE (Vittorio Cottafavi)
         (also: La Rivolta del Gladiatori)
         Filmf: v. II (1959), p. 338; comp., cp. cr.

6995 WARRIOR EMPRESS, THE (Pietro Francisci)
         (also: Saffo, Venere di Lesbo)
         Filmf: v. IV (1961), p. 176; comp., cp. cr.

      WARRIORS, THE (see: The Dark Avenger)

6996 WARRIORS FIVE (Leopoldo Savona)
         Filmf: v. V (1962), p. 369; comp., cp. cr.
         Films & F: v. 9, n. 5 (Feb., 1963), p. 42; David Rider, 600 wds., cp. cr.

      WARRIOR'S REST (see: Love on a Pillow)

6997 WARSAW GHETTO (Hugh Burnett, prod.)
         F Lib Quarterly: v. 2, n. 2 (Spring, 1969), pp. 24, 26; Lewis Archibald, 300
            wds., pt. cr.

      WARUI YATSU HODO YOKU NEMURU (see: The Bad Sleep Well)

6998 WASP WOMAN, THE (Roger Corman)
         Filmf: v. II (1959), p. 346; comp., cp. cr.

6999 WASTREL, THE (Michael Cacoyannis)
         (also: Il Relitto)
         Filmf: v. VI (1963), p. 336; comp., cp. cr.

      WATAGHI WA KAI NY NEARITAI (see: I Want To Be a Shellfish)

      WATCH YOUR AUTOMOBILE (see: An Uncommon Thief)

7000 WATCH YOUR STERN (Gerald Thomas)
         Filmf: v. V (1962), p. 212; comp., cp. cr.

7001 WATER BIRDS (Walt Disney, prod.)
      Films in R: v. III, n. 7 (Aug.-Sept., 1952), p. 356; 200 wds., no cr.

7002 WATERFRONT (Michael Anderson)
      (also: Waterfront Women)
      Sequence: n. 12 (Autumn, 1950), p. 18; J.C., 225 wds., no cr.

      WATERFRONT WOMEN (see: Waterfront)

7003 WATERHOLE No. 3 (William Graham)
      F Quarterly: v. XXI, n. 3 (Spring, 1968), p. 63; Stephen Farber, 400 wds.,
            no cr.
      Filmf: v. X (1967), p. 297; comp., cp. cr.

7004 WATERLOO (Sergei Bondarchuk)
      Filmf: v. XIV (1971), p. 70; comp., cp. cr.
      Films & F: v. 17, n. 4 (Jan., 1971), pp. 48-49; Gordon Gow, 900 wds., cp.
            cr.
      Films in R: v. XXI, n. 5 (May, 1971), pp. 311-312; Sigmund Glaubmann,
            250 wds., no cr.

7005 WATERMELON MAN (Melvin Van Peebles)
      Films & F: v. 16, n. 12 (Sept., 1970), pp. 63, 68; Gordon Gow, 700 wds.,
            cp. cr.

      WATERMELONS (see: O Dem Watermelons)

7006 WATERSMITH (Will Hindle)
      F Quarterly: v. XXII, n. 3 (Spring, 1969), pp. 47-50; Richard Corliss, 1700
            wds., no cr.

7007 WATUSI (Kurt Neuman)
      Filmf: v. II (1959), p. 132; comp., cp. cr.

7008 WAVELENGTH (Michael Snow)
      F Culture: n. 46 (Autumn, 1967), pp. 5-6; Bob Lamberton, 500 wds., no cr.
      F Quarterly: v. XXI, n. 4 (Summer, 1968), pp. 50-52; Jud Yalkut, 1000
            wds., pt. cr.
      Films & F: v. 15, n. 3 (Dec., 1968), pp. 76-77; Philip Strick, 1100 wds., no
            cr.

      WAY IT GOES, THE (see: A Tout Prendre)

7009 WAY OUT (Irvin S. Yeaworth, Jr.)
      Filmf: v. X (1967), p. 332; comp., cp. cr.

7010 WAY TO THE GOLD, THE (Robert D. Webb)
      Films & F: v. 3, n. 11 (Aug., 1957), p. 25; Rodney Giesler, 200 wds., cp. cr.

7011 WAY . . . WAY OUT (Gordon Douglas)
      Filmf: v. IX (1966), p. 296; comp., cp. cr.
      Films & F: v. 13, n. 10 (July, 1967), p. 26; Gordon Gow, 450 wds., cp. cr.

7012 WAY WEST, THE (Andrew V. McLaglen)
      Filmf: v. X (1967), p. 146; comp., cp. cr.
      Films & F: v. 13, n. 11 (Aug., 1967), pp. 20-21; David Austin, 750 wds., cp.
            cr.
      Films in R: v. XVIII, n. 6 (June-July, 1967), pp. 370-371; Henry Hart, 225
            wds., no cr.

7013 WAYWARD BUS, THE (Victor Vicas)
      Films & F: v. 3, n. 12 (Sept., 1957), p. 24; John Cutts, 400 wds., cp. cr.

7014 WAYWARD WIFE, THE (Mario Soldati)
      (also: La Provinciale)
      Films & F: v. 2, n. 4 (Jan., 1956), p. 22: P.L. Mannock, 150 wds., cp. cr.

7015 WE ARE ALL MURDERERS (Andre Cayatte)
      (also: Are We All Murderers?; Nous Sommes Tous des Assassins)
      F Culture: v. 3, n. 1 (1957), pp. 15-16; Arlene Croce, 2000 wds., pt. cr.

Films in R: v. VII, n. 2 (Feb., 1957), pp. 83-84; Louise Corbin, 150 wds., no cr.
Sight & S: v. 23, n. 3 (Jan.-Mar., 1954), pp. 144-145; David Fisher, 750 wds., no cr.

WE DIE ALONE (see: Nine Lives)

7016 WE DON'T BURY ON SUNDAY (Michel Drach)
F Journal: n. 18 (Oct., 1961), p. 17; Brian Davies, 500 wds., no cr.

7017 WE HAVE NO ART, WE DO EVERYTHING AS WELL AS WE CAN (Baylis Glascock Films, prod.)
F Lib Quarterly: v. 3, n. 2 (Spring, 1970), pp. 44-45; Rual Askew, 550 wds., pt. cr.

7018 WE JOINED THE NAVY (Wendy Toye)
Films & F: v. 9, n. 4 (Jan., 1963), p. 50; John Cutts, 250 wds., cp. cr.

7019 WE MAY EAT OF THE FRUIT OF THE TREES OF THE GARDEN (see: Le Fruit du Paradis)

7020 WE SHALL RETURN (Philip Goodman)
Filmf: v. VI (1963), p. 344; comp., cp. cr.

7021 WE STILL KILL THE OLD WAY (Elio Petri)
(also: A Ciascuno II Suo; To Each His Own)
F Soc Rev: v. VII, n. 4 (Dec., 1971), pp. 37-40; Maria-Teresa Ravage, 850 wds., pt. cr.
Filmf: v. XI (1968), p. 59; comp., cp. cr.

7022 WE, THE WOMEN (Gianni Franciolini, Roberto Rossellini, Luigi Zampa, Luchino Visconti)
(also: Siamo Donne)
Films & F: v. 1, n. 3 (Dec., 1954), p. 18; John Minchinton, 200 wds., cp. cr.

7023 WE WERE STRANGERS (John Huston)
Sequence: n. 9 (Autumn, 1949), pp. 127-129; Gavin Lambert, 1200 wds., pt. cr.

7024 WEAPON, THE (Val Guest)
Films & F: v. 3, n. 2 (Nov., 1956), p. 27; Shirley Cobham, 200 wds., cp. cr.

7025 WEB OF EVIDENCE (Jack Cardiff)
(also: Beyond This Place)
Filmf: v. II (1959), p. 239; comp., cp. cr.
Films & F: v. 5, n. 10 (July, 1959), p. 25; Brenda Davies, 200 wds., cp. cr.

7026 WEB OF FEAR (Francois Villiers)
(also: Constance Aux Enfers; Constance in Hell)
Filmf: v. X (1967), p. 58; comp., cp. cr.

WEB OF PASSION (see: A Double Tour)

7027 WEBSTER BOY, THE (Don Chaffey)
Films & F: v. 8, n. 11 (Aug., 1962), p. 33; David Gerrard, 375 wds., cp. cr.

WEDDING BREAKFAST (see: The Catered Affair)

7028 WEDDING IN MONACO, THE (Jean Mason, photog.)
Films in R: v. VII, n. 6 (June-July, 1956), pp. 282-283; Henry Hart, 750 wds., no cr.

7029 WEDDING NIGHT (Rene Jayet)
Films & F: v. 1, n. 2 (Nov., 1954), p. 19; R. E. Durgnat, 50 wds., cp. cr.

7030 WEDDING NIGHT (Piers Haggard)
(also: I Can't . . . I Can't)
Filmf: v. XIV (1971), p. 723; comp., cp. cr.

7031 WEDDING PARTY, THE (Cynthia Munroe, Brian De Palma, Wilford Leach)
Filmf: v. XII (1969), p. 213; comp., cp. cr.

7032 WEDDING — SWEDISH STYLE (Ake Falck)
    Films & F: v. 13, n. 9 (June, 1967), p. 25; Richard Davis, 200 wds., cp. cr.

7033 WEDDINGS AND BABIES (Morris Engel)
    Filmf: v. III (1960), p. 315; comp., cp. cr.
    Films in R: v. XI, n. 9 (Nov., 1960), p. 558; Adelaide Comerford, 75 wds.,
        no cr.

7034 WEDLOCK HOUSE: AN INTERCOURSE (Stan Brakhage)
    F Quarterly: v. XIV, n. 3 (Spring, 1961), pp. 47-48; Ernest Callenbach,
        1200 wds., no cr.

7035 WEE GEORDIE (Frank Launder)
    (also: Geordie)
    Films & F: v. 2, n. 1 (Oct., 1955), p. 18; Derek Hill, 250 wds., cp. cr.
    Films in R: v. VII, n. 10 (Dec., 1956), pp. 525-526; Jim Scovotti, 100 wds.,
        no cr.

7036 WEEKEND (Palle Kjaerulff-Schmidt)
    Filmf: v. VII (1964), p. 85; comp., cp. cr.
    Films & F: v. 10, n. 3 (Dec., 1963), p. 38; John Cutts, 150 wds., cp. cr.

7037 WEEKEND (Jean-Luc Godard)
    F Soc Rev: v. 4, n. 2, pp. 38-44; Jon Rosenbaum, 2500 wds., cp. cr.
    Filmf: v. XI (1968), p. 255; comp., cp. cr.
    Films & F: v. 15, n. 5 (Feb., 1969), p. 34; Peter Whitehead, 850 wds., cp.
        cr.
    Movie: n. 16 (Winter, 1968-1969), pp. 29-33; Robin Wood, 4000 wds., no
        cr.
    Sight & S: v. 37, n. 3 (Summer, 1968), pp. 151-152; Jan Dawson, 1200
        wds., pt. cr.
    Take One: v. 1, n. 11 (1968), p. 23; Joe Medjuck, 500 wds., pt. cr.

    WEEKEND A ZUYDCOOTE (see: Weekend at Dunkirk)

7038 WEEKEND AT DUNKIRK (Henri Verneuil)
    (also: Week-end a Zuydcoote)
    Filmf: v. IX (1966), p. 140; comp., cp. cr.
    Films & F: v. 12, n. 11 (Aug., 1966), pp. 7, 10; David Rider, 475 wds., cp.
        cr.

7039 WEEKEND, ITALIAN STYLE (Dino Risi)
    (also: The Beach Umbrella; L'Ombrellone)
    Filmf: v. XI (1968); comp., cp. cr.

7040 WEEKEND WITH LULU, A (John Paddy Carstairs)
    Filmf: v. V (1962), p. 118; comp., cp. cr.

    WEIRD, WICKED WORLD (see: Go! Go! Go! World)

7041 WELCOME MR. MARSHALL (Luis G. Berlanga)
    Films & F: v. 1, n. 8 (May, 1955), p. 20; Peter Brinson, 300 wds., cp. cr.

7042 WELCOME TO HARD TIMES (Burt Kennedy)
    (Killer on a Horse)
    Cinema: v. 3, n. 5 (Summer, 1967), p. 50; Curtis Lee Hanson, 500 wds., no
        cr.
    F Quarterly: v. XXI, n. 1 (Fall, 1967), pp. 49-58; Stephen Farber, 5000
        wds., pt. cr.
    Filmf: v. X (1967), p. 111; comp., cp. cr.
    Films in R: v. XVIII, n. 5 (May, 1967), p. 310; Gwenneth Britt, 175 wds.,
        no cr.

7043 WELL, THE (Leo Popkin and Russell Rouse)
    Sight & S: v. 21, n. 4 (Apr.-June, 1952), pp. 171-172; Penelope Houston,
        800 wds., pt. cr.

7044 WE'LL BURY YOU! (Jack Leewood and Jack Thomas, prods.)
    Filmf: v. V (1962), p. 262; comp., cp. cr.
    Films in R: v. XIII, n. 9 (Nov., 1962), pp. 556-557; Elaine Rothschild, 400
        wds., no cr.

WELL OF THE VIRGIN (see: The Virgin Spring)

WELL . . . WELL . . . (see: Oj Oj Oj)

7045 WE'RE NO ANGELS (Michael Curtiz)
      Films & F: v. 2, n. 1 (Oct., 1955), p. 21; Peter Barnes, 225 wds., cp. cr.

7046 WEREWOLF IN A GIRLS' DORMITORY (Richard Benson)
      Filmf: v. VI (1963), p. 96; comp., cp. cr.

7047 WEREWOLVES ON WHEELS (Michael Levesque)
      Filmf: v. XIV (1971), p. 604; comp., cp. cr.

7048 WEST II (Michael Winner)
      Films & F: v. 10, n. 2 (Nov., 1963), p. 26; Robin Bean, 275 wds., cp. cr.

7049 WEST END JUNGLE (Arnold Louis Miller)
      Filmf: v. VI (1963), p. 35; comp., cp. cr.

      WEST OF MONTANA (see: Mail Order Bride)

7050 WEST SIDE STORY (Robert Wise and Jerome Robbins)
      Cinema: v. 1, n. 1, p. 44; 25 wds., pt. cr.
      Film: n. 32 (Summer, 1962), pp. 13-14; Bernard Hrusa, 200 wds., no cr.
      F Quarterly: v. XV, n. 4 (Summer, 1962), pp. 58-60; Albert Johnson, 1100
           wds., pt. cr.
      Filmf: v. IV (1961), p. 245; comp., cp. cr.
      Films & F: v. 8, n. 7 (Apr., 1962), p. 30; Peter Baker, 525 wds., cp. cr.
      Films & F: v. 15, n. 12 (Sept., 1969), p. 72; Chris Jones, 600 wds., cp. cr.
      Films in R: v. XII, n. 9 (Nov., 1961), pp. 549-552; Henry Hart, 900 wds.,
           no cr.
      Sight & S: v. 31, n. 2 (Spring, 1962), pp. 94-95; John Russell Taylor, 1200
           wds., pt. cr.

7051 WESTBOUND (Budd Boetticher)
      Filmf: v. II (1959), p. 120; comp., cp. cr.

7052 WESTERN HERO, THE (CBS Films)
      F Lib Quarterly: v. 3, n. 1 (Winter, 1969-1970), p. 41; Mimi Ritti, 400
           wds., pt. cr.

7053 WESTERNER, THE (William Wyler)
      F Journal: n. 6 (Dec., 1956), pp. 12-13; Joel Greenberg, 750 wds., pt. cr.

7054 WESTWARD HO, THE WAGONS! (William Beaudine)
      Films & F: v. 3, n. 9 (June, 1957), p. 21; P. L. Mannock, 175 wds., cp. cr.

7055 WHAT A CRAZY WORLD (Michael Carreras)
      Films & F: v. 10, n. 4 (Jan., 1964), pp. 27-28; Allen Eyles, 550 wds., cp. cr.

      WHAT A WAY TO DIE! (see: Beyond Control)

7056 WHAT A WAY TO GO! (J. Lee Thompson)
      F Quarterly: v. XVIII, n. 1 (Fall, 1964), p. 62; R. M. Hodgens, 100 wds., no
           cr.
      Filmf: v. VII (1964), p. 134; comp., cp. cr.
      Films & F: v. 10, n. 11 (Aug., 1964), pp. 22-23; John Cutts, 900 wds., cp.
           cr.
      Films in R: v. XV, n. 6 (June-July, 1964), pp. 372-373; Patricia Mills, 250
           wds., no cr.

      WHAT A WOMAN (see: Lucky To Be a Woman)

7057 WHAT AM I BID? (Gene Nash)
      Filmf: v. X (1967), p. 422; comp., cp. cr.

7058 WHAT DID YOU DO IN THE WAR, DADDY? (Blake Edwards)
      Filmf: v. IX (1966), p. 251; comp., cp. cr.
      Films & F: v. 13, n. 2 (Nov., 1966), pp. 54-55; 750 wds., cp. cr.

7059 WHAT DO YOU SAY TO A NAKED LADY? (Allen Funt)
Films & F: v. 17, n. 8 (May, 1971), p. 101; Margaret Tarratt, 450 wds., cp.
cr.

7060 WHAT EVER HAPPENED TO AUNT ALICE? (Lee H. Katzin)
Filmf: v. XII (1969), p. 390; comp., cp. cr.
Films & F: v. 16, n. 2 (Nov., 1969), p. 53; Gordon Gow, 400 wds., cp. cr.

7061 WHAT EVER HAPPENED TO BABY JANE? (Robert Aldrich)
Cinema: v. 1, n. 3, p. 32; 250 wds., pt. cr.
F Quarterly: v. XVI, n. 3 (Spring, 1963), pp. 60-61; R. M. Hodgens, 150
wds., no cr.
Filmf: v. V (1962), p. 256; comp., cp. cr.
Films & F: v. 9, n. 7 (Apr., 1963), p. 28; Roger Manvell, 750 wds., cp. cr.
Films in R: v. XIII, n. 10 (Dec., 1962), pp. 622-623; Arthur B. Clark, 375
wds., no cr.
Movie: n. 8, p. 6-7; Andrew Sarris, 1700 wds., no cr.

7062 WHAT HARVEST FOR THE REAPER? (Morton Silverstein)
F Lib Quarterly: v. 2, n. 2 (Spring, 1969), p. 54; Eugene King, 625 wds., pt.
cr.

WHAT LOLA WANTS (see: Damn Yankees)

7063 WHAT PRICE GLORY? (John Ford)
Sight & S: v. 22, n. 3 (Jan.-Mar., 1953), p. 131; Lindsay Anderson, 300
wds., pt. cr.

7064 WHAT PRICE MURDER (Henri Verneuil)
(also: A Kiss for a Killer)
Filmf: v. I (1958), p. 247; comp., cp. cr.
Films in R: v. IX, n. 10 (Dec., 1958), p. 596; Robert B. Kreis, 225 wds., no
cr.

7065 WHAT'S GOOD FOR THE GOOSE (Menahem Golan)
Films & F: v. 15, n. 12 (Sept., 1969), p. 62; David Hutchison, 300 wds., cp.
cr.

WHAT'S IN IT FOR HARRY? (see: How To Make It)

7066 WHAT'S NEW PUSSYCAT? (Clive Donner)
Cahiers in Eng: n. 2 (1966), pp. 75-76; Michel Mardore, 1700 wds., cp. cr.
Films & F: v. 12, n. 1 (Oct., 1965), pp. 27-28; Raymond Durgnat, 850
wds., cp. cr.
Films in R: v. XVI, n. 7 (Aug.-Sept., 1965), pp. 446-447; Adelaide
Comerford, 175 wds., no cr.
Sight & S: v. 34, n. 4 (Autumn, 1965), p. 201; J. H. Fenwick, 600 wds., pt.
cr.

7067 WHAT'S SO BAD ABOUT FEELING GOOD? (George Seaton)
Filmf: v. XI (1968), p. 218; comp., cp. cr.

7068 WHAT'S THE MATTER WITH HELEN? (Curtis Harrington)
Filmf: v. XIV (1971), p. 214; comp., cp. cr.

7069 WHAT'S UP, DOC? (Peter Bogdanovich)
Focus on F: n. 10 (Summer, 1972), p. 11; Allen Eyles, 200 wds., cp. cr.

7070 WHAT'S UP, TIGER LILY? (Original Japanese version by Senkichi Tanig-
zuchi; American adaptation by Woody Allen)
(also: Kizino Kizi; Key of Keys)
Filmf: v. IX (1966), p. 354; comp., cp. cr.

7071 WHEEL OF FIRE (Julio Coll)
Films & F: v. 11, n. 2 (Nov., 1964), pp. 28-29; Richard Davis, 350 wds., cp.
cr.

7072 WHEELCHAIR, THE (Marco Ferreri)
Films & F: v. 10, n. 8 (May, 1964), p. 24; Gordon Gow, 600 wds., cp. cr.

7073 WHEELER DEALERS, THE (Arthur Hiller)
      (also: Separate Beds)
      Filmf: v. VI (1963), p. 259; comp., cp. cr.
      Films & F: v. 10, n. 12 (Sept., 1964), pp. 21-22; Allen Eyles, 250 wds., cp.
      cr.
      Films in R: v. XIV, n. 9 (Nov., 1963), pp. 563-564; Wilfred Mifflin, 200
      wds., no cr.

7074 WHEN A WOMEN ASCENDS THE STAIRS (Mikio Naruse)
      Filmf: v. VI (1963), p. 174; comp., cp. cr.

      WHEN ANGELS DON'T FLY (see: The Last Temptation)

      WHEN ANGELS FALL (see: Quand les Anges Tombent)

7075 WHEN COMEDY WAS KING (Robert Youngson)
      Filmf: v. III (1960), p. 68; comp., cp. cr.
      Films & F: v. 6, n. 7 (Apr., 1960), p. 25; John Cutts, 150 wds., cp. cr.
      Films in R: v. XI, n. 3 (Mar., 1960), pp. 169-170; Henry Hart, 275 wds., no
      cr.

7076 WHEN DINOSAURS RULED THE EARTH (Val Guest)
      Filmf: v. XIV (1971), p. 29; comp., cp. cr.
      Films & F: v. 17, n. 4 (Jan., 1971), p. 60; Margaret Tarratt, 150 wds., cp.
      cr.

7077 WHEN EIGHT BELLS TOLL (Etienne Perier)
      Filmf: v. XIV (1971), p. 136; comp., cp. cr.
      Films & F: v. 17, n. 8 (May, 1971), p. 94; Gordon Gow, 400 wds., cp. cr.

7078 WHEN HELL BROKE LOOSE (Kenneth G. Crane)
      Filmf: v. I (1958), p. 272; comp., cp. cr.

      WHEN I'M DEAD AND WHITE (see: Kada Budem Mrtav I Beo)

      WHEN LEAVES FALL (see: Vendemiare)

7079 WHEN STRANGERS MEET (William Castle)
      Focus on F: n. 5 (Winter/Nov.-Dec., 1970), p. 42; Don Miller, 500 wds., pt.
      cr.

7080 WHEN THE BOYS MEET THE GIRLS (Alvin Ganzer)
      Filmf: v. IX (1966), p. 5; comp., cp. cr.
      Films & F: v. 13, n. 6 (Mar., 1967), p. 37; David Adams, 250 wds., cp. cr.

      WHEN THE CAT COMES (see: Cassandra Cat)

7081 WHEN THE CLOCK STRIKES (Edward L. Cahn)
      Filmf: v. IV (1961), p. 188; comp., cp. cr.
      Films & F: v. 9, n. 6 (Mar., 1963), pp. 39-40; Ian Johnson, 300 wds., cp. cr.

7082 WHEN THE GIRLS TAKE OVER (Russell Hayden)
      Filmf: v. V (1962), p. 363; comp., cp. cr.

7083 WHEN THIS YOU SEE, REMEMBER ME (Perry Miller Adato)
      F Lib Quarterly: v. 5, n. 1 (Winter, 1971-1972), pp. 54-57; Lillian Gerard,
      1200 wds., pt. cr.

7084 WHEN TOMORROW DIES (Larry Kent)
      Interntl F G: v. 4 (1967), pp. 56-57; 300 wds., pt. cr.
      Take One: v. 1, n. 1 (Sept.-Oct., 1966), p. 24; Joe Medjuck, 400 wds., pt.
      cr.

7085 WHEN WORLDS COLLIDE (Rudolph Mate)
      Films in R: v. II, n. 8 (Oct., 1951), pp. 51-52; Roscoe Davis, 35 wds., pt. cr.

7086 WHERE ANGELS GO — TROUBLE FOLLOWS (James Neilsen)
      Filmf: v. XI (1968), p. 132; comp., cp. cr.

7087 WHERE EAGLES DARE (Brian C. Hutton)
      Filmf: v. XII (1969), p. 107; comp., cp. cr.
      Films & F: v. 15, n. 7 (Apr., 1969), p. 40; Chris Jones, 300 wds., cp. cr.

7088 WHERE HAS POOR MICKEY GONE? (Gerry Levy)
      Films & F: v. 10, n. 9 (June, 1964), p. 27; Allen Eyles, 250 wds., cp. cr.

7089 WHERE IT'S AT (Garson Kanin)
      Filmf: v. XII (1969), p. 222; comp., cp. cr.
      Films in R: v. XX, n. 6 (June-July, 1969), pp. 380-381; Eunice Sinkler, 100
          wds., no cr.

7090 WHERE LOVE HAS GONE (Edward Dmytryk)
      Filmf: v. VII (1964), p. 284; comp., cp. cr.
      Films & F: v. 11, n. 5 (Feb., 1965), pp. 29-30; Mike Sarne, 775 wds., cp. cr.
      Films in R: v. XV, n. 9 (Nov., 1964), pp. 572-573; Adelaide Comerford,
          450 wds., no cr.

7091 WHERE THE ACTION IS (Max Pecas)
      Films & F: v. 15, n. 5 (Feb., 1969), p. 49; Richard Davis, 150 wds., pt. cr.

7092 WHERE THE BOYS ARE (Henry Levin)
      Filmf: v. IV (1961), p. 5; comp., cp. cr.
      Films & F: v. 7, n. 8 (May, 1961), p. 30; Robin Bean, 150 wds., cp. cr.
      Films in R: v. XII, n. 2 (Feb., 1961), pp. 110-111; Robert C. Roman, 200
          wds., no cr.

7093 WHERE THE BULLETS FLY (John Gilling)
      Filmf: v. X (1967), p. 262; comp., cp. cr.

7094 WHERE THE HOT WIND BLOWS (Jules Dassin)
      (also: The Law; La Loi)
      Filmf: v. III (1960), p. 267; comp., cp. cr.
      Films & F: v. 7, n. 5 (Feb., 1961), pp. 32-33; Peter G. Baker, 550 wds., cp.
          cr.

7095 WHERE THE SPIES ARE (Val Guest)
      Filmf: v. IX (1966), p. 14; comp., cp. cr.

7096 WHERE THE TRUTH LIES (Henri Decoin)
      (also: Malefices)
      Filmf: v. V (1962), p. 242; comp., cp. cr.

      WHERE VULTURES FLY (see: Prisoners of the Congo)

7097 WHERE WERE YOU WHEN THE LIGHTS WENT OUT? (Hy Averback)
      Filmf: v. XI (1968), p. 285; comp., cp. cr.
      Films & F: v. 14, n. 12 (Sept., 1968), p. 42; David Rider, 250 wds., cp. cr.

7098 WHERE'S JACK? (James Clavell)
      Films & F: v. 15, n. 10 (July, 1969), pp. 44-45; Chris Jones, 600 wds., cp.
          cr.
      Films in R: v. XX, n. 6 (June-July, 1969), p. 380; Gwenneth Britt, 175
          wds., no cr.

7099 WHERE'S POPPA? (Carl Reiner)
      F Quarterly: v. XXIV, n. 4 (Summer, 1971), pp. 60-63; Stephen Farber,
          1550 wds., pt. cr.
      Focus on F: n. 8 (Oct., 1971), pp. 5-6; Richard Combs and Pat Billings, 350
          wds., cp. cr.

7100 WHILE BRAVE MEN DIE (Fulton Lewis III)
      F Comment: v. IV, n. 1 (Fall, 1966), pp. 25-26; 400 wds., no cr.

7101 WHILE THE CITY SLEEPS (Fritz Lang)
      Films & F: v. 2, n. 8 (May, 1956), p. 25; John Carroll, 225 wds., cp. cr.

7102 WHIRLWIND (Hiroshi Inagaki)
      (also: Dai Tatsumaki)
      Filmf: v. XI (1968), p. 334; comp., cp. cr.

WHISKEY GALORE (see: Tight Little Island)

7103 WHISPERERS, THE (Bryan Forbes)
Filmf: v. X (1967), p. 187; comp., cp. cr.
Films & F: v. 14, n. 2 (Nov., 1967), p. 27; Gordon Gow, 700 wds., cp. cr.
Films in R: v. XVIII, n. 7 (Aug.-Sept., 1967), p. 441; Henry Hart, 200 wds.,
no cr.
Sight & S: v. 36, n. 4 (Autumn, 1967), pp. 205-206; Brenda Davies, 500
wds., pt. cr.
Take One: v. 1, n. 7 (1967), pp. 25-26; Clive Denton, 350 wds., pt. cr.

7104 WHISPERING FOOTSTEPS (Howard Bretherton)
Focus on F: n. 5 (Winter/Nov.-Dec., 1970), pp. 40-41; Don Miller, 350
wds., pt. cr.

7105 WHISTLE AT EATON FALLS, THE (Robert Siodmak)
(also: Richer Than the Earth)
Sight & S: v. 21, n. 4 (Apr.-June, 1952), pp. 171-172; Penelope Houston,
800 wds., pt. cr.

7106 WHISTLE DOWN THE WIND (Bryan Forbes)
Filmf: v. V (1962), p. 103; comp., cp. cr.
Films & F: v. 7, n. 12 (Sept., 1961), pp. 27-28; Peter G. Baker, 750 wds.,
cp. cr.
Films in R: v. XIII, n. 5 (May, 1962), p. 295; Flavia Wharton, 125 wds., no
cr.
Sight & S: v. 30, n. 4 (Autumn, 1961), p. 199; Penelope Houston, 450 wds.,
pt. cr.

7107 WHITE BUS, THE (Lindsay Anderson)
Films & F: v. 14, n. 12 (Sept., 1968), p. 42; Gordon Gow, 700 wds., cp. cr.
Sight & S: v. 37, n. 4 (Autumn, 1968), pp. 205-206; Daniel Millar, 800
wds., pt. cr.

7108 WHITE CHRISTMAS (Michael Curtiz)
Films & F: v. 1, n. 3 (Dec., 1954), p. 18; 200 wds., cp. cr.
Films in R: v. V, n. 10 (Dec., 1954), p. 543; Henry Hart, 200 wds., no cr.

7109 WHITE CORRIDORS (Pat Jackson)
Films in R: v. III, n. 7 (Aug.-Sept., 1952), p. 359; 175 wds., pt. cr.
Sight & S: v. 21, n. 1 (Aug.-Sept., 1951), pp. 20-21; Gavin Lambert, 1200
wds., pt. cr.

7110 WHITE FEATHER (Robert Webb)
Films & F: v. 1, n. 8 (May, 1955), p. 19; Catherine De La Roche, 275 wds.,
cp. cr.

7111 WHITE GAME, THE (Bo Widerberg)
Movie: n. 17 (Winter, 1969-1970), p. 37; Ian Cameron, 100 wds., no cr.

WHITE LADDER, THE (see: Secret World)

7112 WHITE MANE (Albert Lamorisse)
Films in R: v. V, n. 2 (Feb., 1954), pp. 91-92; Ralph Gerstle, 200 wds., no
cr.

7113 WHITE NIGHTS (Luchino Visconti)
(also: Notti Bianche)
F Journal: n. 18 (Oct., 1961), p. 18; R. J. Garlick, 400 wds., no cr.
F Quarterly: v. XII, n. 2 (Winter, 1958), pp. 58-59; James Kerans, 350 wds.,
no cr.
Filmf: v. IV (1961), p. 227; comp., cp. cr.
Films & F: v. 4, n. 10 (July, 1958), p. 27; John Francis Lane, 950 wds., cp.
cr.
Films in R: v. XII, n. 6 (June-July, 1961), p. 361; 150 wds., no cr.
Sight & S: v. 27, n. 5 (Summer, 58), p. 249; Peter John Dyer, 800 wds., pt.
cr.

7114 WHITE SLAVE SHIP (Silvio Amadio)
(also: L'Ammutinamento; The Mutiny)

Filmf: v. V (1962), p. 365; comp., cp. cr.
Films & F: v. 9, n. 2 (Nov., 1962), p. 42; Robin Bean, 200 wds., cp. cr.

7115 WHITE SLAVERY (Michael Steel)
Filmf: v. III (1960), p. 351; comp., cp. cr.

7116 WHITE SLAVES OF CHINATOWN (Joseph A. Mawra)
Films & F: v. 11, n. 4 (Jan., 1965), p. 34; Raymond Durgnat, 650 wds., cp. cr.

WHITE STALLION, THE (see: Crin Blanc, Le Cheval Sauvage)

7117 WHITE VOICES (Pasquale Festa Campanile)
(also: Voci Bianche)
Filmf: v. VIII (1965), p. 121; comp., cp. cr.

7118 WHITE WARRIOR, THE (Riccardo Freda)
Filmf: v. IV (1961), p. 10; comp., cp. cr.

7119 WHITE WILDERNESS (James Algar and Walt Disney)
Filmf: v. I (1958), p. 190; comp., cp. cr.
Films & F: v. 6, n. 5 (Feb., 1960), p. 23; Robin Bean, 125 wds., cp. cr.
Films in R: v. IX, n. 9 (Nov., 1958), p. 518; Elspeth Hart, 200 wds., no cr.

7120 WHO ARE YOU, POLLY MAGGOO? (William Klein)
(also: Qui Etes-vous Polly Magoo?
Sight & S: v. 37, n. 1 (Winter, 1967-1968), p. 42; Jan Dawson, 400 wds., pt. cr.

7121 WHO IS HARRY KELLERMAN AND WHY IS HE SAYING THOSE
TERRIBLE THINGS ABOUT ME? (Ulu Grosbard)
Filmf: v. XIV (1971), p. 256; comp., cp. cr.

7122 WHO KILLED MARY WHATS' ERNAME? (Ernie Pintoff)
Filmf: v. XIV (1971), p. 623; comp., cp. cr.

WHO KNOWS? (see: A Bullet for the General)

WHO RIDES WITH KANE? (see: Young Billy Young)

WHO SAW HIM DIE: (see: Ole Dole Doff)

7123 WHO SAYS I CAN'T RIDE A RAINBOW? (Edward Mann)
Filmf: v. XIV (1971), p. 716; comp., cp. cr.

7124 WHO WAS MADDOX? (Geoffrey Nethercott)
Films & F: v. 10, n. 12 (Sept., 1964), p. 22; Richard Davis, 175 wds., cp. cr.

7125 WHO WAS THAT LADY? (George Sidney)
Filmf: v. III (1960), p. 82; comp., cp. cr.
Films & F: v. 6, n. 9 (June, 1960), p. 22; Peter G. Baker, 200 wds., cp. cr.

7126 WHOLE TRUTH, THE (John Guillermin)
Filmf: v. I (1958), p. 183; comp., cp. cr.

7127 WHOLLY COMMUNION (Peter Whitehead)
F Lib Quarterly: v. 2, n. 2 (Spring, 1969), p. 55; Wiley Hampton, 300 wds.,
pt. cr.
Films & F: v. 12, n. 3 (Dec., 1965), pp. 53, 56; Raymond Durgnat, 700
wds., cp. cr.

7128 WHO'S AFRAID OF VIRGINIA WOOLF? (Mike Nichols)
F Quarterly: v. XX, n. 1 (Fall, 1966), pp. 45-48; Ernest Callenbach, 2000
wds., pt. cr.
Filmf: v. IX (1966), p. 149; comp., cp. cr.
Films & F: v. 12, n. 12 (Sept., 1966), p. 6; Gordon Gow, 1150 wds., cp. cr.
Films in R: v. XVII, n. 7 (Aug.-Sept., 1966), pp. 448-450; Henry Hart, 450
wds., no cr.
Sight & S: v. 35, n. 4 (Autumn, 1966), pp. 198-199; James Price, 500 wds.,
pt. cr.

7129 WHO'S BEEN SLEEPING IN MY BED? (Daniel Mann)
　　　Filmf: v. VI (1963), p. 300; comp., cp. cr.
　　　Films & F: v. 10, n. 6 (Mar., 1964), pp. 28-29; Gordon Gow, 650 wds., cp.
　　　　　cr.

7130 WHO'S GOT THE ACTION? (Daniel Mann)
　　　Filmf: v. V (1962), p. 311; comp., cp. cr.
　　　Films & F: v. 9, n. 6 (Mar., 1963), p. 41; John Cutts, 250 wds., cp. cr.

7131 WHO'S MINDING THE MINT? (Howard Morris)
　　　Filmf: v. X (1967), p. 398; comp., cp. cr.

7132 WHO'S MINDING THE STORE? (Frank Tashlin)
　　　F Quarterly: v. XVII, n. 3 (Spring, 1964), p. 63; R. M. Hodgens, 100 wds.,
　　　　　no cr.
　　　Filmf: v. VI (1963), p. 293; comp., cp. cr.
　　　Films & F: v. 10, n. 5 (Feb., 1964), p. 31; Raymond Durgnat, 500 wds., cp.
　　　　　cr.

7133 WHO'S THAT KNOCKING AT MY DOOR? (Martin Scorsese)
　　　(also: I Call First; J. R.)
　　　Filmf: v. XII (1960), p. 439; comp., cp. cr.
　　　Take One: v. 2, n. 4 (1969), p. 20; George Lellis, 800 wds., pt. cr.

　　　WHY BOTHER TO KNOCK? (see: Don't Bother To Knock)

7134 WHY MUST I DIE? (Roy Del Ruth)
　　　Filmf: v. III (1960), p. 210; comp., cp. cr.

7135 WICKED AS THEY COME (Ken Hughes)
　　　Films & F: v. 2, n. 10 (July, 1956), p. 26; P. L. Mannock, 175 wds., cp. cr.

7136 WICKED DREAMS OF PAULA SCHULTZ, THE (George Marshall)
　　　Filmf: v. XI (1968), p. 8; comp., cp. cr.

7137 WICKED GO TO HELL, THE (Robert Hossein)
　　　Filmf: v. IV (1961), p. 9; comp., cp. cr.
　　　Films & F: v. 3, n. 1 (Oct., 1956), p. 24; Peter John Dyer, 350 wds., cp. cr.
　　　Sight & S: v. 26, n. 2 (Autumn, 1956), pp. 98-99; Derek Hill, 525 wds., pt.
　　　　　cr.

7138 WICKED WOMEN (Russell Rouse)
　　　Films in R: v. IV, n. 10 (Dec., 1953), p. 540; 200 wds., pt. cr.

　　　WIDOWER, THE (see: An Autumn Afternoon)

　　　WIE EIN STURMWIND (see: Tempestuous Love)

7139 WIFE FOR A NIGHT (Mario Camerini)
　　　(also: Moglie per una Notte)
　　　Filmf: v. I (1958), p. 128; comp., cp. cr.

7140 WIFESWAPPERS, THE (Derek Ford)
　　　Films & F: v. 17, n. 1 (Oct., 1970), p. 46; John Francis, 250 wds., cp. cr.

7141 WILD AFFAIR, THE (John Krish)
　　　Filmf: v. IX (1966), p. 382; comp., cp. cr.
　　　Films & F: v. 12, n. 4 (Jan., 1966), pp. 27-28; David Adams, 600 wds., cp.
　　　　　cr.

7142 WILD AND THE INNOCENT, THE (Jack Sher)
　　　Filmf: v. II (1959), p. 154; comp., cp. cr.

7143 WILD AND THE WILLING, THE (Ralph Thomas)
　　　Filmf: v. VII (1964), p. 32; comp., cp. cr.
　　　Films & F: v. 9, n. 2 (Nov., 1962), pp. 36-37; Robin Bean, 450 wds., cp. cr.

7144 WILD AND WONDERFUL (Michael Anderson)
　　　Filmf: v. VII (1964), p. 178; comp., cp. cr.
　　　Films & F: v. 11, n. 3 (Dec., 1964), pp. 25-26; Allen Eyles, 450 wds., cp. cr.

7145 WILD ANGELS, THE (Roger Corman)
         F Quarterly: v. XX, n. 2 (Winter, 1966-1967), p. 63; Ernest Callenbach, 300
              wds., no cr.
         Filmf: v. IX (1966), p. 372; comp., cp. cr.
         Films & F: v. 15, n. 10 (July, 1969), p. 53; Colin Heard, 1000 wds., cp. cr.
         Sight & S: v. 38, n. 1 (Winter, 1968-1969), pp. 47-48; Philip Strick, 1500
              wds., pt. cr.
         Take One: v. 1, n. 2 (Nov.-Dec., 1966), pp. 27-28; Alan Collins, 950 wds.,
              pt. cr.

7146 WILD BUNCH, THE (Sam Peckinpah)
         Cineaste: v. III, n. 3 (Winter, 1969-1970), pp. 18-20, 28; Kenneth R.
              Brown, 2000 wds., pt. cr.
         F Comment: v. 6, n. 3 (Fall, 1970), pp. 55-57; William Pechter, 1500 wds.,
              cp. cr.
         F Heritage: v. 5, n. 2 (Winter, 1969-1970), pp. 1-10, 32; John Alan
              McCarty, 3000 wds., no cr.
         F Soc Rev: v. 5, n. 3 (Nov., 1969), pp. 31-37; Michael Sragow, 2500 wds.,
              pt. cr.
         Filmf: v. XII (1969), p. 217; comp., cp. cr.
         Films & F: v. 16, n. 1 (Oct., 1969), pp. 39-40; David Austen, 1300 wds., cp.
              cr.
         Films in R: v. XX, n. 7 (Aug.-Sept., 1969), pp. 446-447; Arthur B. Clark,
              275 wds., no cr.
         Focus: n. 5 (Oct., 1969), pp. 5-8; Myron Meisel, 2700 wds., no cr.
         Focus: n. 5 (Oct., 1969), p. 8; Charles Flynn, 500 wds., no cr.
         Focus: n. 5 (Oct., 1969), p. 9; James Jubak, 500 wds., no cr.
         Sight & S: v. 38, n. 4 (Autumn, 1969), pp. 208-209; Tom Milne, 1100 wds.,
              pt. cr.

7147 WILD CHILD, THE (Francois Truffaut)
         (also: L'Enfant Sauvage)
         F Quarterly: v. XXIV, n. 3 (Spring, 1971), pp. 42-45; Harriett R. Polt, 800
              wds., pt. cr.
         Films & F: v. 17, n. 5 (Feb., 1971), pp. 48-49; Margaret Tarratt, 1000 wds.,
              cp. cr.
         Films in R: v. XXI, n. 9 (Nov., 1970), pp. 570-571; Hubbell Robinson, 400
              wds., no cr.
         Interntl F G: v. 8 (1971), pp. 247-248; Felix Bucher, 200 wds., pt. cr.
         Movie: n. 18 (Winter, 1970-1971), p. 38; Ian Cameron, 150 wds., pt. cr.
         Sight & S: v. 40, n. 1 (Winter, 1970-1971), p. 46; David Wilson, 1200 wds.,
              pt. cr.

7148 WILD COUNTRY, THE (Robert Totten)
         Filmf: v. XIV (1971), p. 149; comp., cp. cr.
         Films in R: v. XXII, n. 2 (Feb., 1971), pp. 108-109; Arthur B. Clark, 175
              wds., no cr.

7149 WILD EYE, THE (Paolo Cavara)
         (also: L'Occhio Selvaggio)
         Filmf: v. XI (1968), p. 367; comp., cp. cr.

7150 WILD FOR KICKS (Edmond T. Greville)
         (also: 'Beat' Girl)
         Filmf: v. IV (1961), p. 312; comp., cp. cr.

7151 WILD HARVEST (Jerry A. Baerwitz)
         Filmf: v. IV (1961), p. 371; comp., cp. cr.

      WILD HEART, THE (see: Gone To Earth)

7152 WILD HERITAGE (Charles Haas)
         Filmf: v. I (1958), p. 243; comp., cp. cr.

      WILD HORSES OF FIRE (see: Shadows of Forgotten Ancestors)

7153 WILD IN THE COUNTRY (Philip Dunne)
         Filmf: v. IV (1961), p. 145; comp., cp. cr.
         Films & F: v. 7, n. 11 (Aug., 1961), p. 28; Peter G. Baker, 225 wds., cp. cr.

7154 WILD IN THE STREETS (Barry Shear)
    F Soc Rev: May (1968), pp. 22-25; Patrick MacFadden, 1100 wds., pt. cr.
    Filmf: v. XI (1968), p. 191; comp., cp. cr.

7155 WILD IS THE WIND (George Cukor)
    Films & F: v. 4, n. 6 (Mar., 1958), p. 28; Gordon Gow, 450 wds., cp. cr.
    Sight & S: v. 27, n. 4 (Spring, 1958), p. 202; Derek Prouse, 475 wds., pt. cr.

7156 WILD LOVE (Mauro Bolognini)
    (also: Gli Inamorati)
    Filmf: v. IV (1961), p. 75; comp., cp. cr.

7157 WILD 90 (Norman Mailer)
    Filmf: v. XI (1968), p. 24; comp., cp. cr.

7158 WILD ONE, THE (Lazlo Benedek)
    (also: Hot Blood)
    Films & F: v. 1, n. 6 (Mar., 1955), p. 24; Clayton Cole, 200 wds., cp. cr.
    Films & F: v. 1, n. 9 (June, 1955), p. 22; Peter Brinson, 275 wds., cp. cr.
    Films & F: v. 14, n. 7 (Apr., 1968), p. 24; Raymond Durgnat, 1000 wds.,
        cp. cr.
    Films in R: v. IV, n. 10 (Dec., 1953), pp. 533-535; Henry Hart, 1300 wds.,
        pt. cr.
    Sight & S: v. 25, n. 1 (Summer, 1955), pp. 30-31; Gavin Larbert, 1200
        wds., pt. cr.

7159 WILD PARTY, THE (Dorothy Arzner)
    F Soc Rev: Mar. (1966), p. 18; Davis S. Hull, 100 wds., pt. cr.

7160 WILD RACERS, THE (Daniel Haller)
    Filmf: v. XI (1968), p. 222; comp., cp. cr.
    Take One: v. 1, n. 10 (1968), pp. 30-31; Alan Collins, 600 wds., pt. cr.

7161 WILD REBELS, THE (William Grefe)
    Filmf: v. X (1967), p. 420; comp., cp. cr.

7162 WILD RIDE, THE (Harvey Berman)
    Filmf: v. III (1960), p. 353; comp., cp. cr.

7163 WILD RIDERS (Richard Kanter)
    Filmf: v. XIV (1971), p. 333; comp., cp. cr.

7164 WILD RIVER (Elia Kazan)
    (also: The Woman and the Wild River)
    F Quarterly: v. XIII, n. 4 (Summer, 1960), pp. 50-51; Henry Goodman, 800
        wds., pt. cr.
    Filmf: v. III (1960), p. 127; comp., cp. cr.
    Films & F: v. 6, n. 11 (Aug., 1960), p. 32; R. E. Durgnat, 400 wds., cp. cr.
    Films in R: v. XI, n. 6 (June-July, 1960), pp. 356-357; Henry Hart, 650
        wds., no cr.

7165 WILD ROVERS (Blake Edwards)
    Filmf: v. XIV (1971), p. 198; comp., cp. cr.

7166 WILD SEED (Brian G. Hutton)
    F Quarterly: v. XVIII, n. 4 (Summer, 1965), pp. 56-57; Ernest Callenbach,
        600 wds., pt. cr.

7167 WILD STRAWBERRIES (Ingmar Bergman)
    (also: Smultronstallet)
    F Journal: n. 17 (Apr., 1961), pp. 120-121; Beverly O'Donnell, 800 wds.,
        no cr.
    F Quarterly: v. XIII, n. 1 (Fall, 1959), pp. 44-47; Eugene Archer, 2000
        wds., no cr.
    Filmf: v. II (1959), p. 157; comp., cp. cr.
    Films & F: v. 5, n. 3 (Dec., 1958), p. 24; Peter John Dyer, 600 wds., cp. cr.
    Films in R: v. X, n. 4 (Apr., 1959), pp. 231-232; Henry Hart, 650 wds., no
        cr.
    Sight & S: v. 28, n. 1 (Winter, 1958-1959), p. 35; Kenneth Cavander, 1000
        wds., pt. cr.

7168 WILD WESTERNERS, THE (Oscar Rudolph)
        Filmf: v. V (1962), p. 230; comp., cp. cr.
        Films & F: v. 9, n. 3 (Dec., 1962), p. 40; Tony Mallerman, 200 wds., cp. cr.

7169 WILD, WILD PLANET (Anthony Dawson)
        (also: I Criminali Della Galassia)
        Filmf: v. X (1967), p. 255; comp., cp. cr.
        Films & F: v. 14, n. 7 (Apr., 1968), p. 27; Raymond Durgnat, 500 wds., cp.
        cr.

7170 WILD WILD WINTER (Len Weinrib)
        Filmf: v. IX (1966), p. 3; comp., cp. cr.

7171 WILD WINGS (Edgar Anstey, prod.)
        F Lib Quarterly: v. 2, n. 2 (Spring, 1969), pp. 55-56; William Vickrey, 400
        wds., pt. cr.

7172 WILD WOMEN OF WONGO (James L. Wolcott)
        Filmf: v. II (1959), p. 345; comp., cp. cr.

7173 WILD YOUTH (John Schreyer)
        Filmf: v. IV (1961), p. 367; comp., cp. cr.

        WILL OF THE WISP (see: Le Feu Follet)

7174 WILL PENNY (Tom Gries)
        Filmf: v. XI (1968), p. 136; comp., cp. cr.
        Films & F: v. 14, n. 6 (Mar., 1968), p. 28; Richard Davis, 250 wds., cp. cr.
        Films in R: v. XIX, n. 4 (Apr., 1968), pp. 240-241; Page Cook, 250 wds.,
        no cr.

        WILL SUCCESS SPOIL ROCK HUNTER? (see: Oh! For a Man!)

7175 WILL THE REAL NORMAL MAILER PLEASE STAND UP? (Dick Fontaine)
        Films & F: v. 15, n. 10 (July, 1969), p. 56; Brian Murphy, 700 wds., cp. cr.

7176 WILLARD (Daniel Mann)
        Filmf: v. XIV (1971), p. 208; comp., cp. cr.
        Journal of P C: v. V n. 2 (Fall, 1971), p. 473; Albert E. Kalson, 350 wds.,
        no cr.

7177 WILLIAM FAULKNER (Robert Saudek Associates)
        F Lib Quarterly: v. 2, n. 2 (Spring, 1969), pp. 16, 18; Marsha R. Porte,
        1400 wds., pt. cr.

7178 WILLIAM FAULKNER'S MISSISSIPPI (Robert Guenette, prod.)
        F Lib Quarterly: v. 2, n. 2 (Spring, 1969), pp. 16, 18; 1400 wds., pt. cr.

7179 WILLIAM: FROM GEORGIA TO HARLEM (Bert Salzman, prod.)
        F Lib Quarterly: v. 4, n. 4 (Fall, 1971), p. 55; Hannah Miller, 300 wds., pt.
        cr.

        WILLST DU EWIG JUNGFRAU BLEIBEN? (see: Do You Want To Be a
        Virgin Forever?)

7180 WILLY WONKA AND THE CHOCOLATE FACTORY (Mel Stuart)
        Filmf: v. XIV (1971), p. 286; comp., cp. cr.
        Focus on F: n. 8 (Oct., 1971), pp. 9-10; Ivan Butter and Allen Eyles, 300
        wds., cp. cr.

7181 WINCHESTER '73 (Anthony Mann)
        Sequence: n. 12 (Autumn, 1950), pp. 18-19; C.H., 300 wds., no cr.

7182 WIND, THE (Charles Crichton)
        Sight & S: v. 17, n. 65 (Spring, 1948), p. 43; Arthur Vesselo, 75 wds., no cr.

7183 WIND ACROSS THE EVERGLADES (Nicholas Ray)
        Filmf: v. I (1958), p. 165; comp., cp. cr.
        Focus: n. 8 (Autumn, 1972), pp. 55-57; Terry Curtis Fox, 1600 wds., no cr.

7184 WIND CANNOT READ, THE (Gilbert Thomas)
      Filmf: v. III (1960), p. 47; comp., cp. cr.
      Films & F: v. 4, n. 11 (Aug., 1958), pp. 25-26; Peter G. Baker, 250 wds.,
      cp. cr.

7185 WIND FROM THE EAST (Jean-Luc Godard)
      (also: Vent D'Est)
      F Comment: v. 7, n. 3 (Fall, 1971), pp. 65-57; Joan Mellen, 3000 wds., cp.
      cr.
      Movie: n. 18 (Winter, 1970-1971), p. 40; Ian Cameron, 100 wds., no cr.
      Take One: v. 2, n. 10 (1971), p. 14; Jules Lorkin, 250 wds., no cr.

7186 WIND OF HATE (N. Tsiforos)
      (also: Anemos Tou Missous)
      Filmf: v. I (1958), p. 224; comp., cp. cr.

7187 WINDFALL IN ATHENS (Michael Cacoyannis)
      Filmf: n. 24 (Mar.-Apr., 1960), pp. 16-19; Alan Stanbrook, 1200 wds., no
      cr.
      Sight & S: v. 24, n. 3 (Jan.-Mar., 1955), p. 146; Penelope Houston, 275
      wds., pt. cr.

7188 WINDFLOWERS (Adolfas Mekas)
      Filmf: v. XI (1968), p. 35; comp., cp. cr.

7189 WINDJAMMER (Louis de Rochemont and Bill Colleran)
      Filmf: v. I (1958), p. 65; comp., cp. cr.
      Films & F: v. 4, n. 10 (July, 1958), p. 26; Peter G. Baker, 325 wds., cp. cr.

7190 WINDOM'S WAY (Ronald Neame)
      Filmf: v. I (1958), p. 187; comp., cp. cr.
      Films & F: v. 4, n. 5 (Feb., 1958), pp. 25-26; Gordon Gow, 475 wds., cp.
      cr.

7191 WINDOW, THE (Ted Tetzlaff)
      Sequence: n. 7 (Spring, 1949), pp. 39-41; Gavin Lambert, 1000 wds., pt. cr.

7192 WINDOW WATER BABY MOVING (Stan Brakhage)
      F Quarterly: v. XIV, n. 3 (Spring, 1961), pp. 47-48; Ernest Callenbach,
      1200 wds., no cr.

7193 WINGS OF CHANCE (Edward Dew)
      Filmf: v. IV (1961), p. 373; comp., cp. cr.

7194 WINGS OF EAGLES, THE (John Ford)
      Films & F: v. 3, n. 8 (May, 1957), p. 23; Paul Rotha, 950 wds., cp. cr.
      Films in R: v. VIII, n. 3 (Mar., 1957), pp. 132-133; Ellen Fitzpatrick, 300
      wds., no cr.

7195 WINK OF AN EYE (Winston Jones)
      Filmf: v. I (1958), p. 250; comp., cp. cr.

7196 WINNERS OF THE WILDERNESS (W. S. Van Dyke)
      Views & R: v. 3, n. 2 (Fall, 1971), pp. 43-51; 2000 wds., cp. cr.

7197 WINNETOU THE WARRIOR (Harald Reinl)
      Films & F: v. 11, n. 7 (Apr., 1965), pp. 29-30; Allen Eyles, 600 wds., cp. cr.

7198 WINNING (James Goldstone)
      F Quarterly: v. XXIII, n. 1 (Fall, 1969), pp. 57-58; Stephen Farber, 700
      wds., no cr.
      Filmf: v. XII (1969), p. 230; comp., cp. cr.
      Films & F: v. 16, n. 3 (Dec., 1969), pp. 46, 52; David Hutchison, 950 wds.,
      cp. cr.

7199 WINNING WAY, THE (Jesse Hibbs)
      (also: The All American)
      Films & F: v. 1, n. 9 (June, 1955), p. 22; Derek Hill, 125 wds., cp. cr.

7200 WINSLOW BOY, THE (Anthony Asquith)
      Films in R: v. I, n. 3 (Nov., 1950), pp. 25-27; Ann Griffith, 600 wds., pt. cr.
      Sight & F: v. 17, n. 68 (Winter, 1948-1949), p. 182; Arthur Vesselo, 225
         wds., pt. cr.

7201 WINTER KEPT US WARM (David Secter)
      Filmf: v. XI (1968), p. 18; comp., cp. cr.
      Take One: v. 1, n. 1 (Sept.-Oct., 1966), p. 24; Joe Medjuck, 250 wds., pt.
         cr.

7202 WINTER LIGHT (Ingmar Bergman)
      (also: Nattvardsgasterna; Communicants)
      Filmf: v. VI (1963), p. 85; comp., cp. cr.
      Films & F: v. 9, n. 9 (June, 1963), p. 27-28; Peter Cowie, 450 wds., cp. cr.
      Films in R: v. XIV, n. 5 (May, 1963), pp. 299-301; Henry Hart, 650 wds.,
         no cr.
      Interntl F G: v. 1 (1964), p. 85; 200 wds., pt. cr.
      Sight & S: v. 32, n. 3 (Summer, 1963), p. 146; Eric Rhode, 350 wds., pt. cr.

7203 WINTER MEETING (Bretaigne Windust)
      Sequence: n. 10 (New Year, 1950), p. 157; Lindsay G. Anderson, 225 wds.,
         no cr.

7204 WINTER OF THE WITCH (Gerald Herman)
      F Lib Quarterly: v. 4, n. 1 (Winter, 1970-1971), p. 50; Irene Wood, 200
         wds., pt. cr.
      F Lib Quarterly: v. 4, n. 1 (Winter, 1970-1971), p. 51; Marsha R. Porte, 250
         wds., pt. cr.

      WINTER WIND (see: Sirocco D'Hiver)

7205 WINTERSET (Alfred Santell)
      Film: n. 5 (Sept.-Oct., 1955), pp. 21-22; Graham Greene, 400 wds., no cr.

      WIR WONDERKINDER (see: Aren't We Wonderful)

7206 WIR-SWEI (Ulrich Schamoni)
      Interntl F G: v. 8 (1971), p. 151; 175 wds., pt. cr.

      WIRTSHAUS IM SPESSART, DAS (see: The Spessart Inn)

7207 WISHING MACHINE, THE (Josef Pinkava)
      (also: Autonat Na Prani)
      Filmf: v. XIV (1971), p. 567; comp., cp. cr.

7208 WITCH IN LOVE, THE (Damiano Damiani)
      (also: The Strange Obsession; La Strega in Amore)
      Films & F: v. 15, n. 3 (Dec., 1968), pp. 45, 48; Chris Jones, 1000 wds., cp.
         cr.

7209 WITCH WITHOUT A BROOM, A (Joe Lacy)
      (also: Un Bruja Sin Escoba)
      Filmf: v. X (1967), pp. 395; 442, comp., cp. cr.

7210 WITCHCRAFT (Don Sharp)
      Filmf: v. VIII (1965), p. 38; comp., cp. cr.

7211 WITCHCRAFT THROUGH THE AGES (Benjamin Christensen)
      (also: Haxan)
      Films & F: v. 15, n. 5 (Feb., 1969), p. 48; Gordon Gow, 150 wds., cp. cr.

7212 WITCHES, THE (Luchino Visconti, Mauro Bolognine, Franco Rossi, Pierre
         Paolo Pasolini, Vittorio De Sica)
      (also: Le Streghe)
      Filmf: v. XIV (1971), p. 740; comp., cp. cr.

      WITCHES, THE (Cyril Frankel/see: The Devil's Own)

7213 WITCHES OF SALEM (Raymond Rouleau)
        (also: The Crucible; Les Sorcieres de Salem)
        Filmf: v. I (1958), p. 292; comp., cp. cr.
        Films & F: v. 4, n. 1 (Oct., 1957), pp. 25, 27; Peter John Dyer, 550 wds.,
            cp. cr.
        Sight & S: v. 27, n. 2 (Autumn, 1957), pp. 91-92; Derick Grigs, 700 wds.,
            pt. cr.

        WITCHFINDER GENERAL (see: The Conqueror Worm)

7214 WITCH'S CRADLE, THE (Maya Deren)
        F Culture: n. 39 (Winter, 1965), pp. 1-2; Maya Deren, 150 wds., pt. cr.

        WITH GUNILLA ON MONDAY EVENING AND TUESDAY (see: Guilt)

        WITH JOYOUS HEART (see: Two Weeks in September)

7215 WITH NO ONE TO HELP US
        F Lib Quarterly: v. 2, n. 2 (Spring, 1969), p. 55; Kenneth W. Axthelm, 325
            wds., pt. cr.

7216 WITH SIX YOU GET EGGROLL (Howard Morris)
        Filmf: v. XI (1968), p. 415; comp., cp. cr.
        Films & F: v. 15, n. 4 (Jan., 1969), pp. 53-54; Chris Jones, 600 wds., cp. cr.

        WITHOUT END (see: Sin Fin)

7217 WITNESS FOR THE PROSECUTION (Billy Wilder)
        Films & F: v. 4, n. 6 (Mar., 1958), pp. 25-26; John Cutts, 500 wds., cp. cr.
        Films & F: v. 9, n. 6 (Mar., 1963), p. 42; John Cutts, 500 wds., cp. cr.
        Films in R: v. IX, n. 3 (Mar., 1958), pp. 144-145; Robert Downing, 250
            wds., no cr.

7218 WITNESSES, THE (Frederic Rossif)
        (also: Le Temps du Ghetto)
        F Soc Rev: v. 6, n. 4 (Dec., 1970), pp. 43-47; Leonard Rubenstein, 2000
            wds., pt. cr.
        Filmf: v. X (1967), p. 368; comp., cp. cr.

7219 WIVES AND LOVERS (John Rich)
        Filmf: v. VI (1963), p. 191; comp., cp. cr.
        Films & F: v. 10, n. 2 (Nov., 1963), p. 22; Raymond Durgnat, 650 wds., cp.
            cr.

7220 WIZARD OF BAGHDAD THE (George Sherman)
        Filmf: v. IV (1961), p. 32; comp., cp. cr.

        WOINA I MIR (see: War and Peace)

7221 WOLF DOG (Sam Newfield)
        Films & F: v. I (1958), p. 297; comp., cp. cr.

7222 WOLF LARSEN (Harmon Jones)
        Filmf: v. I (1958), p. 188; comp., cp. cr.

7223 WOLF TRAP, THE (Jiri Weiss)
        (also: Vlci Jama)
        Films & F: v. 10, n. 7 (Apr., 1964), p. 33; John Crome, 500 wds., cp. cr.

7224 WOMAN AND TEMPTATION (Armando Bo)
        (also: The Nude Temptation; La Tentacion Desnuda)
        Filmf: v. XII (1969), p. 24; comp., cp. cr.

        WOMAN AND THE WILD RIVER, THE (see: Wild River)

7225 WOMAN EATER, THE
        Filmf: v. II (1959), p. 205; comp., cp. cr.

7226 WOMAN FOR JOE, THE (George More O'Ferrall)
        Films & F: v. 2, n. 1 (Oct., 1955), p. 18; Peter G. Baker, 150 wds., cp. cr.

7227 WOMAN IN A DRESSING GOWN (J. Lee Thompson)
        Films & F: v. 4, n. 1 (Oct., 1957), p. 24; John Cutts, 500 wds., cp. cr.
        Films in R: v. VIII, n. 9 (Nov., 1957), pp. 462-463; Nigel Ames, 125 wds.,
            no cr.
        Sight & S: v. 27, n. 2 (Autumn, 1957), p. 92; John Gillett, 650 wds., pt. cr.

        WOMAN IN THE DUNES (see: Woman of the Dunes)

7228 WOMAN IN THE HALL, THE (Jack Lee)
        Sight & S: v. 16, n. 64 (Winter, 1947-48), p. 137; Arthur Vesselo, 150 wds.,
            pt. cr.

7229 WOMAN IN THE PAINTING, THE (Franco Rossi)
        (also: Amici per la Pelle; Friends for Life)
        F Quarterly: v. XII, n. 3 (Spring, 1959), pp. 48-49; William Bernhardt, 600
            wds., no cr.
        Filmf: v. II (1959), p. 30; comp., cp. cr.
        Films & F: v. 3, n. 8 (May, 1957), p. 27; Peter G. Baker, 250 wds., cp. cr.
        Films in R: v. X, n. 2 (Feb., 1959), pp. 110-111; Romano Tozzi, 200 wds.,
            no cr.
        Sight & S: v. 27, n. 1 (Summer, 1957), p. 42; Roy Edwards, 550 wds., pt.
            cr.

7230 WOMAN IN THE WINDOW (Luciano Emmer)
        (also: La Ragazza in Vetrina)
        Films & F: v. 8, n. 8 (May, 1962), p. 35; Gordon Gow, 350 wds., cp. cr.

        WOMAN IN WHITE, A (see: Le Journal d'une Femme en Blanc)

7231 WOMAN IS A WOMAN, A (Jean-Luc Godard)
        (also: Une Femme Est une Femme)
        F Quarterly: v. XVIII, n. 2 (Winter, 1964), pp. 56-57; Henry Heifetz, 500
            wds., pt. cr.
        F Soc Rev: Sept. (1965), p. 12; John Thomas, 300 wds., pt. cr.
        Films & F: v. 13, n. 8 (May, 1967), p. 30; Peter Whitehead, 300 wds., cp.
            cr.
        Movie: n. 7, p. 26; Mark Shivas, 500 wds., no cr.

7232 WOMAN LIKE SATAN, A (Julien Duvivier)
        (also: The Female; Le Femme et le Pantin)
        Filmf: v. III (1960), p. 84; comp., cp. cr.
        Films & F: v. 6, n. 7 (Apr., 1960), p. 23; Robin Bean, 150 wds., cp. cr.

7233 WOMAN OBSESSED (Henry Hathaway)
        Filmf: v. II (1959), p. 115; comp., cp. cr.

7234 WOMAN OF DARKNESS (Arne Mattsson)
        (also: Yngsjomordet)
        Films & F: v. 16, n. 1 (Oct., 1969), pp. 51-52; Brian Murphy, 650 wds., cp.
            cr.

        WOMAN OF DOLWYN (see: The Last Days of Dolwyn)

7235 WOMAN OF STRAW (Basil Dearden)
        Filmf: v. VII (1964), p. 304; comp., cp. cr.
        Films & F: v. 10, n. 9 (June, 1964), pp. 23-24; Allen Eyles, 650 wds., cp.
            cr.

        WOMAN OF SUMMER (see: The Stripper)

7236 WOMAN OF THE DUNES (Hiroshi Teshigahara)
        (also: Suna No Onna; Woman in the Dunes)
        Cinema: v. 2, n. 5 (Mar.-Apr., 1965), p. 49; James Silke, 225 wds., pt. cr.
        Film: n. 41 (1964), pp. 19-20; Bernard Hrusa and Ian Jarvie, 500 wds., no
            cr.
        F Comment: v. 3, n. 1 (Winter, 1965), pp. 56-60; Adrienne Johnson
            Mancia, 2400 wds., no cr.
        F Comment: v. 3, n. 1 (Winter, 1965), pp. 64-65; Kirk Bond, 1000 wds., pt.
            cr.
        F Comment: v. 3, n. 1 (Winter, 1965), p. 66; Clara Hoover, 600 wds., no cr.

F Quarterly: v. XVIII, n. 2 (Winter, 1964), pp. 43-46; Judith Shatnoff, 1400 wds., pt. cr.
Filmf: v. VII (1964), p. 294; comp., cp. cr.
Films & F: v. 11, n. 9 (June, 1965), pp. 32-33; Gordon Gow, 800 wds., cp. cr.
Films in R: v. XV, n. 10 (Dec., 1964), pp. 631-632; Charles A. Butler, 175 wds., no cr.
Interntl F G: v. 2 (1965), pp. 104-105; Peter Graham, 200 wds., pt. cr.
Sight & S: v. 34, n. 3 (Summer, 1965), pp. 145-146; Michael Kustow, 1200 wds., no cr.

7237 WOMAN OF THE RIVER (Mario Soldati)
(also: La Donna del Fiume)
Films & F: v. 2, n. 10 (July, 1956), p. 25; P. L. Mannock, 200 wds., cp. cr.
Films & F: v. 9, n. 5 (Feb., 1963), pp. 43-44; Robin Bean, 350 wds., cp. cr.

7238 WOMAN TIMES SEVEN (Vittorio De Sica)
Filmf: v. X (1967), p. 196; comp., cp. cr.
Films & F: v. 14, n. 9 (June, 1968), p. 24; Raymond Durgnat, 950 wds., cp. cr.

WOMAN WITHOUT A FACE (see: Mister Buddwing)

7239 WOMANHUNT
Filmf: v. V (1962), p. 68; comp., cp. cr.

7240 WOMAN'S FILM (Judy Smith, Louise A'aimo, Ellen Sorrin)
Cineaste: v. IV, n. 3 (Winter, 1970-1971), pp. 40-41; Ruth McCormick, 700 wds., pt. cr.
F Lib Quarterly: v. 5, n. 1 (Winter, 1971-1972), pp. 57-58; Shirley McPherson, 600 wds., pt. cr.
F Quarterly: v. XXV, n. 1 (Fall, 1971), pp. 48-49; Siew Hwa Beh, 850 wds., pt. cr.

7241 WOMAN'S WORLD (Jean Negulesco)
Films in R: v. V, n. 10 (Dec., 1954), p. 544; 100 wds., no cr.

7242 WOMEN ARE WEAK (Michel Boisrond)
(also: Three Murderesses; Faibles Femmes)
Filmf: v. II (1959), p. 173; comp., cp. cr.
Films in R: v. XI, n. 3 (Mar., 1960), pp. 170-171; George Malko, 250 wds., no cr.

WOMEN AT THE FRONTIER (see: The Tall Women)

7243 WOMEN BY NIGHT (Mino Ley)
Films & F: v. 9, n. 5 (Feb., 1963), p. 43; Raymond Durgnat, 350 wds., cp. cr.

7244 WOMEN IN CAGES (Gerry De Leon)
Filmf: v. XIV (1971), p. 703; comp., cp. cr.

WOMEN IN CHAINS (see: La Prisonniere)

7245 WOMEN IN LOVE (Ken Russell)
Cinema: v. 6, n. 1, pp. 48-49; Paul Schrader, 1450 wds., no cr.
Film: n. 57 (Winter, 1970), p. 29; Pat Hodgson, 500 wds., pt. cr.
F Heritage: v. 6, n. 4 (Summer, 1971), pp. 1-6; Robert F. Knoll, 2000 wds., pt. cr.
F Lib Quarterly: v. 3, n. 4 (Fall, 1970), pp. 6-12; Lillian N. Gerard, 1700 wds., no cr.
F Quarterly: v. XXIV, n. 1 (Fall, 1970), pp. 43-47; Elliott Sirkin, 2400 wds., pt. cr.
Films & F: v. 16, n. 4 (Jan., 1970), pp. 49-50; Gordon Gow, 600 wds., cp. cr.
Films in R: v. XXI, n. 4 (Apr., 1970), pp. 241-243; Helen Weldon Kuhn, 175 wds., no cr.
Interntl F G: v. 8 (1971), pp. 125-128; Russell Campbell, 450 wds., pt. cr.
Sight & S: v. 39, n. 1 (Winter, 1969-1970), pp. 49-50; Jan Leslie Christie, 700 wds., pt. cr.

7246 WOMEN OF RUSSIA (Julien Bryan, prod.)
 F Lib Quarterly: v. 2, n. 2 (Spring, 1969), pp. 18-20; Alan Clark, 1300
  wds., pt. cr.

7247 WOMEN OF THE PREHISTORIC PLANET (Arthur Pierce)
 Filmf: v. IX (1966), p. 350; comp., cp. cr.

7248 WOMEN OF THE WORLD (Gualtiero Jacopetti)
 (also: La Donna del Monde Eva Sconoscuita)
 Cinema: v. 1, n. 6 (Nov.-Dec., 1963), p. 46; Edwin Schnepf, 250 wds., pt.
  cr.
 Filmf: v. VI (1963), p. 153; comp., cp. cr.
 Films & F: v. 10, n. 3 (Dec., 1963), p. 38; Raymond Durgnat, 600 wds., cp.
  cr.
 Films in R: v. XIV, n. 7 (Aug.-Sept., 1963), pp. 435-436; Estelle Slocum,
  400 wds., no cr.

7249 WOMEN ON THE MARCH: PARTS I AND II (Douglas Tunstell, prod.)
 F Lib Quarterly: v. 5, n. 1 (Winter, 1971-1972), pp. 42-45; Madeline
  Friedlander, 650 wds., pt. cr.

7250 WOMEN UP IN ARMS (United Nations)
 F Lib Quarterly: v. 5, n. 1 (Winter, 1971-1972), pp. 42-45; Madeline
  Friedlander, 650 wds., pt. cr.

7251 WOMEN WITHOUT HOPE (Raoul Andre)
 Films & F: v. 1, n. 4 (Jan., 1955), p. 20; Derwent May, 125 wds., cp. cr.

 WOMEN'S DREAMS (see: Dreams)

7252 WONDER OF LOVE, THE (F. J. Gottlieb)
 Films & F: v. 15, n. 10 (July, 1969), pp. 50-51; David Hutchison 150 wds.,
  cp. cr.

7253 WONDERFUL ADVENTURES OF NILS, THE (Kenne Fant)
 Interntl F G: v. 1 (1964), p. 88; 150 wds., pt. cr.

7254 WONDERFUL COUNTRY, THE (Robert Parrish)
 Filmf: v. II (1959), p. 249; comp., cp. cr.
 Films & F: v. 6, n. 3 (Dec., 1959), p. 23; Derek Conrad, 250 wds., cp. cr.

7255 WONDERFUL LIFE (Sidney J. Furie)
 (also: Singer's Paradise)
 Films & F: v. 10, n. 11 (Aug., 1964), p. 26; Peter G. Baker, 300 wds., cp.
  cr.

7256 WONDERFUL TO BE YOUNG (Sidney J. Furie)
 (also: The Young Ones)
 Filmf: v. VI (1963), p. 30; comp., cp. cr.
 Films & F: v. 8, n. 5 (Feb., 1962), p. 34; Robin Bean, 200 wds., cp. cr.

7257 WONDERFUL WORLD OF THE BROTHERS GRIMM, THE (Henry Levin)
 Filmf: v. V (1962), p. 201; comp., cp. cr.
 Films & F: v. 9, n. 11 (Aug., 1963), p. 25; Raymond Durgnat, 500 wds., cp.
  cr.
 Films in R: v. XIII, n. 8 (Oct., 1962), pp. 490-491; Elaine Rothschild, 200
  wds., no cr.

7258 WONDERS OF ALADDIN, THE (Henry Levin)
 Filmf: v. IV (1961), p. 316; comp., cp. cr.
 Films & F: v. 9, n. 4 (Jan., 1963), p. 54; Robin Bean, 200 wds., cp. cr.

7259 WONDERWALL (Joe Massot)
 Films & F: v. 15, n. 6 (Mar., 1969), p. 44; Gordon Gow, 600 wds., cp. cr.

7260 WOO WHO? MAY WILSON (Amalie R. Rothschild, prod.)
 F Lib Quarterly: v. 5, n. 1 (Winter, 1971-1972), pp. 58-59; Nadine Covert,
  600 wds., pt. cr.

7261 WOODEN HORSE, THE (Jack Lee)
    Sequence: n. 12 (Autumn, 1950), p. 18; K.R., 225 wds., no cr.
    Sight & S: v. 19, n. 7 (Nov., 1950), pp. 286-288; Gavin Lambert, 2200
        wds., pt. cr.

7262 WOODSTOCK (Michael Wadleigh)
    Cinema: v. 6, n. 1, pp. 49-51; Stephen Mamber, 1600 wds., no cr.
    F Quarterly: v. XXIII, n. 4 (Summer, 1970), p. 61; Ernest Callenbach, 50
        wds., no cr.
    F Quarterly: v. XXIV, n. 3 (Spring, 1971), pp. 54-56; Foster Hirsch, 1400
        wds., pt. cr.
    Films & F: v. 16, n. 11 (Aug., 1970), pp. 46-47; Margaret Tarratt, 550 wds.,
        cp. cr.
    Films in R: v. XXI, n. 5 (May, 1970), pp. 304-305; Tatiana Balkoff
        Drowne, 550 wds., pt. cr.
    Interntl F G: v. 8 (1971), pp. 262-263; Margot S. Kernan, 300 wds., pt. cr.
    Journal of P C: v. IV, n. 3 (Winter, 1971), pp. 769-776; Lawrence J.
        Dessner, 2800 wds., no cr.
    Sight & S: v. 39, n. 3 (Summer, 1970), pp. 159-1960; David Pirie, 800 wds.,
        pt. cr.

    WORD, THE (see: Ordet)

7263 WORK IS A FOUR LETTER WORD (Peter Hall)
    Films & F: v. 14, n. 10 (July, 1968), pp. 29, 32; Raymond Durgnat, 600
        wds., cp. cr.

7264 WORKER'S DIARY, A (Rista Jarva)
    (also: Tyomehen Paivakirja)
    Movie: n. 16 (Winter, 1968-1969), pp. 37-38; Peter von Bagh, 400 wds., no
        cr.

7265 WORLD BY NIGHT (Luigi Vanzi)
    (also: Il Mondo di Notte)
    Filmf: v. IV (1961), p. 327; comp., cp. cr.

7266 WORLD BY NIGHT NO. 2 (Gianni Proia)
    (also: Mondo di Notte Numero Due)
    Films & F: v. 9, n. 4 (Jan., 1963), pp. 53-54; Tony Mallerman, 350 wds.,
        cp. cr.
    Sight & S: v. 32, n. 1 (Winter, 1962-1963), pp. 39-40; John Russell Taylor,
        700 wds., no cr.

    WORLD CUP 1966 (see: Goal!)

7267 WORLD DANCES, THE (L. Derbysheva)
    (also: Iskusstvo Druzei)
    Filmf: v. I (1958), p. 102; comp., cp. cr.

7268 WORLD IN FLAMES (Hans Gnamm)
    (also: Inflamed World)
    Films & F: v. 10, n. 7 (Apr., 1964), pp. 30-31; Raymond Durgnat, 400
        wds., cp. cr.

7269 WORLD IN MY POCKET (Alvin Rakoff)
    (also: On Friday at Eleven)
    Filmf: v. V (1962), p. 86; comp., cp. cr.
    Films in R: v. XIII, n. 2 (Feb., 1962), p. 104; Arthur B. Clark, 225 wds., no
        cr.

7270 WORLD OF ABBOTT AND COSTELLO, THE (Max J. Rosenberg)
    Films & F: v. 12, n. 8 (May, 1966), pp. 10-11; Allen Eyles, 500 wds., cp. cr.

7271 WORLD OF APU, THE (Satyajit Ray)
    (also: Apur Sansar)
    Film: n. 24 (Mar.-Apr., 1960), pp. 20-24; Douglas McVay, 1200 wds., no cr.
    F Culture: n. 21 (Summer, 1960), pp. 62-65; Arlene Croce, 1000 wds., pt.
        cr.
    F Journal: n. 16 (Aug., 1960), pp. 83-85; John Burgess, 800 wds., no cr.

F Quarterly: v. XIII, n. 3 (Spring, 1960), pp. 53-54; Jonathan Harker, 600
    wds., pt. cr.
Filmf: v. III (1960), p. 223; comp., cp. cr.
Films & F: v. 7, n. 8 (May, 1961), p. 29; Raymond Durgnat, 650 wds., cp.
    cr.
Films in R: v. XI, n. 3 (Mar., 1960), pp. 166-167; Henry Hart, 450 wds., no
    cr.
Sight & S: v. 30, n. 1 (Winter, 1960-1961), pp. 35-36; John Gillett, 900
    wds., pt. cr.

7272 WORLD OF FASHION, THE (Robert Freeman)
    (also: Mini-Midi)
    Films & F: v. 15, n. 7 (Apr., 1969), p. 52; Ken Gay, 350 wds., cp. cr.

7273 WORLD OF HANS CHRISTIAN ANDERSEN, THE (Kimio Yabuki)
    (also: Hansu Kurishitan Anderusan; No Sekai)
    Filmf: v. XIV (1971), p. 759; comp., cp. cr.

7274 WORLD OF HENRY ORIENT, THE (George Roy Hill)
    F Quarterly: v. XVIII, n. 1 (Fall, 1964), p. 62; R. M. Hodgens, 125 wds., no
        cr.
    Filmf: v. VII (1964), p. 63; comp., cp. cr.
    Films & F: v. 10, n. 10 (July, 1964), pp. 20-21; Allen Eyles, 600 wds., cp.
        cr.
    Films in R: v. XV, n. 4 (Apr., 1964), pp. 242-243; Elaine Rothschild, 300
        wds., no cr.

7275 WORLD OF SUZIE WONG, THE (Richard Quine)
    Filmf: v. III (1960), p. 285; comp., cp. cr.
    Films & F: v. 7, n. 5 (Feb., 1961), pp. 30-31; Gordon Gow, 400 wds., cp.
        cr.
    Films in R: v. XI, n. 10 (Dec., 1960), p. 615; Adelaide Comerford, 175
        wds., no cr.

7276 WORLD TEN TIMES OVER, THE (Wolf Rilla)
    Films & F: v. 10, n. 3 (Dec., 1963), p. 28; Allen Eyles, 750 wds., cp. cr.

7277 WORLD, THE FLESH, AND THE DEVIL, THE (Ranald MacDougall)
    Filmf: v. II (1959), p. 105; comp., cp. cr.
    Films & F: v. 5, n. 12 (Sept., 1959), p. 22; Dai Vaughan, 200 wds., cp. cr.

7278 WORLD WAS HIS JURY, THE (Fred F. Sears)
    Filmf: v. I (1958), p. 4; comp., cp. cr.

7279 WORLD WITHOUT END (Basil Wright and Paul Rotha)
    Films in R: v. V, n. 4 (Apr., 2954), pp. 196-197; 100 wds., no cr.
    Sight & S: v. 23, n. 3 (Jan.-Mar., 1954), p. 147; Forsyth Hardy, 575 wds.,
        no cr.

7280 WORLD WITHOUT SUN (Jacques-Yves Cousteau)
    (also: Le Monde Sans Soleil)
    Filmf: v. VII (1964), p. 342; comp., cp. cr.
    Films in R: v. XVI, n. 1 (Jan., 1965), pp. 44-45; Henry Hart, 300 wds., no
        cr.

7281 WOULD-BE GENTLEMAN, THE (Jean Meyer)
    Filmf: v. III (1960), p. 88; comp., cp. cr.
    Films in R: v. XI, n. 4 (Apr., 1960), pp. 232-233; George Malko, 450 wds.,
        no cr.

7282 WOW (Claude Jutra)
    Take One: v. 2, n. 5 (1970), p. 28; Ronald Blumer, 500 wds., pt. cr.

7283 WOZZECK (George C. Klaren)
    Filmf: v. V (1962), p. 200; comp., cp. cr.
    Sequence: n. 13 (New Year, 1951), pp. 37-38; Alan Bowness and Graham
        Woodford, 1000 wds., pt. cr.

7284 WRECK OF THE MARY DEARE, THE (Michael Anderson)
Filmf: v. II (1959), p. 267; comp., cp. cr.
Films & F: v. 6, n. 6 (Mar., 1960), p. 23; Tony Keniston, 225 wds., cp. cr.
Films in R: v. X, n. 10 (Dec., 1959), pp. 622-623; Arthur B. Clark, 150
wds., no cr.

7285 WRECKING CREW, THE (Phil Karlson)
Filmf: v. XII (1969), p. 46; comp., cp. cr.
Films & F: v. 15, n. 7 (Apr., 1969), p. 46; David Rider, 250 wds., cp. cr.

7286 WRESTLER AND THE CLOWN, THE (Ki Yudin and B. Barnet)
(also: Voretz E Kloun)
Filmf: v. I (1958), p. 288; comp., cp. cr.

7287 WRONG ARM OF THE LAW, THE (Cliff Owen)
Filmf: v. VI (1963), p. 71; comp., cp. cr.
Films & F: v. 9, n. 8 (May, 1963), p. 30; Ian Johnson, 400 wds., cp. cr.
Sight & S: v. 32, n. 2 (Spring, 1963), p. 94; Tom Milne, 450 wds., pt. cr.

7288 WRONG BOX, THE (Bryan Forbes)
F Quarterly: v. XX, n. 2 (Winter, 1966-1967), p. 63; Stephen Farber, 200
wds., no cr.
Filmf: v. IX (1966), p. 190; comp., cp. cr.
Films in R: v. XVII, n. 7 (Aug.-Sept., 1966), p. 450; Ivor Howard, 225
wds., no cr.
Sight & S: v. 35, n. 3 (Summer, 1966), p. 149; Philip Strick, 350 wds., pt.
cr.

7289 WRONG MAN, THE (Alfred Hitchcock)
Films & F: v. 3, n. 7 (Apr., 1957), p. 26; Ken Gay, 300 wds., cp. cr.
Films in R: v. VIII, n. 1 (Jan., 1957), pp. 33-34; Veronica Hume, 350 wds.,
no cr.
Sight & S: v. 26, n. 4 (Spring, 1957), p. 211; Penelope Houston, 600 wds.,
pt. cr.

WSZYSTKO NA SPRZEDAZ (see: Everything for Sale)

WUNDER DER LIEBE, DAS (see: The Miracle of Love)

7290 WUNDER DES MALACHIAS, DAS (Bernard Wicki)
(also: Malachias; The Miracle of Father Malachias)
F Quarterly: v. XV, n. 2 (Winter, 1961-1962), pp. 59-60; Donald Richie,
450 wds., pt. cr.

7291 WUTHERING HEIGHTS (Robert Fuest)
Filmf: v. XIV (1971), p. 85; comp., cp. cr.
Films & F: v. 17, n. 10 (July, 1971), pp. 50-51; Eric Braun, 1500 wds., cp.
cr.
Films in R: v. XXII, n. 2 (Feb., 1971), pp. 105-106; Gloria Ives, 400 wds.,
no cr.

7292 WYETH PHENOMENON, THE (Harry Morgan)
F Lib Quarterly: v. 2, n. 2 (Spring, 1969), p. 56; Patricia Del Mar, 200 wds.,
pt. cr.

7293 X-15 (Richard Donner)
Filmf: v. V (1962), p. 56; comp., cp. cr.

7294 X — THE MAN WITH THE X-RAY EYES (Roger Corman)
(also: The Man with the X-Ray Eyes)
F Quarterly: v. XVII, n. 2 (Winter, 1963-1964), p. 63; R. M. Hodgens, 150
wds., no cr.

Filmf: v. VI (1963), p. 240; comp., cp. cr.
Films & F: v. 10, n. 12 (Sept., 1964), p. 18; Peter Cowie, 225 wds., cp. cr.

7295 X — THE UNKNOWN (Leslie Norman)
Films & F: v. 3, n. 2 (Nov., 1956), p. 24; P. L. Mannock, 200 wds., cp. cr.

Y

7296 YUL 871 (Saul Bass)
Take One: v. 1, n. 1 (Sept.-Oct., 1966), p. 25; 150 wds., pt. cr.

YA IDE PO MOSKVE (see: Meet Me in Moscow)

YA KOPIEL PAPO (see: Dimka)

YABU NO NAKA NO KURONEKO (see: Kuroneko)

YAGYA BUGEICHO (see: Secret Scrolls)

7297 YANCO (Servando Gonzalez)
F Journal: n. 20 (Aug., 1962), pp. 84; 89; R. J. Garlick, 200 wds., no cr.
Filmf: v. VII (1964), p. 142; comp., cp. cr.

7298 YANGTSE INCIDENT (Michael Anderson)
(also: Battle Hell)
Films & F: v. 3, n. 8 (May, 1957), p. 24; Ken Gay, 250 wds., cp. cr.
Films in R: v. VIII, n. 8 (Oct., 1957), pp. 407-408; Courtland Phipps, 150
    wds., no cr.
Sight & S: v. 26, n. 4 (Spring, 1957), p. 209; John Gillett, 650 wds., pt. cr.

7299 YANK IN VIET-NAM, A (Marshall Thompson)
Filmf: v. VII (1964), p. 328; comp., cp. cr.

YANKEE, THE (see: Janken)

YAWAR MALLKU (see: Blood of the Condor)

7300 YEAR OF THE YAMOO (Herschell Gordon Lewis)
Filmf: v. XIV (1971), p. 758; comp., cp. cr.

7301 YEARS OF LIGHTNING, DAY OF DRUMS (Bruce Herschenson)
(also: John F. Kennedy: Years of Lightning, Day of Drums)
F Comment: v. IV, n. 2-3 (Fall-Winter, 1967), pp. 39-44; 4000 wds., no cr.
Filmf: v. IX (1966), p. 85; comp., cp. cr.
Films & F: v. 13, n. 2 (Nov., 1966), pp. 13; 16; Sheridan Morley, 450 wds.,
    cp. cr.
Films in R: v. XVII, n. 3 (Mar., 1966), pp. 186-187; Henry Hart, 300 wds.,
    no cr.

7302 YELLOW CANARY, THE (Buzz Kulik)
F Quarterly: v. XVII, n. 2 (Winter, 1963-1964), p. 63; Ernest Callenbach,
    150 wds., no cr.
Filmf: v. VI (1963), p. 99; comp., cp. cr.
Films & F: v. 9, n. 9 (June, 1963), p. 29; Ian Johnson, 350 wds., cp. cr.

7303 YELLOW ROLLS-ROYCE, THE (Anthony Asquith)
F Quarterly: v. XVIII, n. 3 (Spring, 1965), p. 62; William Johnson, 125
    wds., no cr.
Films & F: v. 11, n. 5 (Feb., 1965), p. 30; Robin Bean, 800 wds., cp. cr.
Films in R: v. XVI, n. 6 (June-July, 1965), pp. 385-386; Elaine Rothschild,
    450 wds., no cr.

7304 YELLOW SUBMARINE (George Dunning)
    Filmf: v. XI (1968), p. 335; comp., cp. cr.
    Films & F: v. 14, n. 12 (Sept., 1968), pp. 46-47; David Rider, 900 wds., cp.
      cr.
    Films in R: v. XIX, n. 10 (Dec., 1968), pp. 650-651; Henry Hart, 550 wds.,
      no cr.
    Sight & S: v. 37, n. 4 (Autumn, 1968), p. 204; Gavin Millar, 800 wds., no
      cr.

7305 YELLOW TEDDYBEARS, THE (Robert Hartford-Davis)
    Films & F: v. 9, n. 12 (Sept., 1963), pp. 25-26; Raymond Durgnat, 250
      wds., cp. cr.

7306 YELLOWSTONE KELLY (Gordon Douglas)
    Films: v. II (1959), p. 260; comp., cp. cr.
    Films & F: v. 6, n. 1 (Oct., 1959), p. 24; Derek Conrad, 150 wds., cp. cr.

7307 YESTERDAY AND TODAY
    Films in R: v. IV, n. 9 (1953), p. 484; 200 wds., pt. cr.

7308 YESTERDAY GIRL (Alexander Kluge)
    (also: Abschied von Gestern)
    Films & F: v. 13, n. 8 (May, 1967), pp. 27-28; Raymond Durgnat, 1000
      wds., cp. cr.
    Interntl F G: v. 5 (1968), p. 78; 200 wds., pt. cr.
    Sight & S: v. 36, n. 2 (Spring, 1967), p. 95; David Wilson, 600 wds., no cr.

7309 YESTERDAY, TODAY AND TOMORROW (Vittorio De Sica)
    Cinema: v. 2, n. 2 (July, 1964), p. 49; James Silke, 225 wds., pt. cr.
    F Comment: v. 2, n. 1 (Winter, 1964), pp. 43-44; Gordon Hitchens, 900
      wds., pt. cr.
    F Quarterly: v. XVII, n. 4 (Summer, 1964), pp. 59-60; Neal Oxenhandler,
      200 wds., no cr.
    Filmf: v. VII (1964), p. 57; comp., cp. cr.
    Films & F: v. 11, n. 1 (Oct., 1964), pp. 29-30; Michael Sarne, 950 wds., cp.
      cr.
    Films in R: v. XV, n. 3 (Mar., 1964), pp. 174-175; Flavia Wharton, 225
      wds., no cr.

7310 YESTERDAY'S ENEMY (Val Guest)
    Filmf: v. II (1959), p. 318; comp., cp. cr.
    Films & F: v. 5, n. 12 (Sept., 1959), p. 24; Peter Baker, 450 wds., cp. cr.

    YEUX SANS VISAGE, LES (see: The Horror Chamber of Dr. Faustus)

7311 YIELD TO THE NIGHT (J. Lee Thompson)
    (also: Blonde Sinner)
    Films & F: v. 2, n. 10 (July, 1956), p. 22; Peter John Dyer, 225 wds., cp.
      cr.
    Sight & S: v. 26, n. 1 (Summer, 1956), p. 35; Alberta Marlow, 200 wds., pt.
      cr.

    YNGSJOMORDET (see: Woman of Darkness)

    YO YO (see: Yoyo)

7312 YOG — MONSTER FROM SPACE (Inoshiro Honda)
    (also: Space Amoeba)
    Filmf: v. XIV (1971), p. 502; comp., cp. cr.

7313 YOJIMBO (Akira Kurosawa)
    Filmf: v. V (1962), p. 275; comp., cp. cr.
    Films & F: v. 16, n. 11 (Aug., 1970), p. 46; Gordon Gow, 600 wds., cp. cr.
    Films in R: v. XIII, n. 9 (Nov., 1962), p. 561; Harold Dillingham, 100 wds.,
      no cr.

    YOTSUYA KWAIDAN (see: Illusion of Blood)

7314 YOU ARE ON INDIAN LAND (George Stoney)
    F Quarterly: v. XXIV, n. 1 (Fall, 1970), p. 62; Ernest Callenbach, 450 wds.,
      no cr.

7315 YOU ARE WHAT YOU EAT (Barry Feinstein)
        Filmf: v. XI (1968), p. 423; comp., cp. cr.
        Films & F: v. 15, n. 7 (Apr., 1969), pp. 53-54; Hugh Witt, 650 wds., cp. cr.

7316 YOU CAN'T RUN AWAY FROM IT (Dick Powell)
        Films & F: v. 3, n. 2 (Nov., 1956), p. 24; P. L. Mannock, 175 wds., cp. cr.

7317 YOU CAN'T WIN 'EM ALL (Peter Collinson)
        Films & F: v. 17, n. 5 (Feb., 1971), p. 56; Margaret Tarratt, 200 wds., cp.
            cr.

7318 YOU DIG IT? (Richard Mason)
        Journal of P C: v. IV, n. 3 (Winter, 1971), pp. 675-676; Charles D. Peavy,
            300 wds., no cr.

       YOU DON'T NEED PYJAMAS AT ROSIE'S (see: The First Time)

7319 YOU HAVE TO RUN FAST (Edward L. Cahn)
        Filmf: v. IV (1961), p. 250; comp., cp. cr.

7320 YOU MUST BE JOKING (Michael Winner)
        Films & F: v. 12, n. 1 (Oct., 1965), pp. 28-29; Robin Bean, 500 wds., cp.
            cr.

7321 YOU ONLY LIVE TWICE (Lewis Gilbert)
        F Quarterly: v. XXI, n. 1 (Fall, 1967), p. 62; Stephen Farber, 225 wds., no
            cr.
        Filmf: v. X (1967), p. 166; comp., cp. cr.
        Films in R: v. XVIII, n. 7 (Aug.-Sept., 1967), pp. 441-442; Adelaide
            Comerford, 300 wds., no cr.

7322 YOU ONLY LOVE ONCE (Dirk Sanders)
        (also: A Gentle Love; Tu Seras Terriblement Gentille; You Will Be Terribly
            Nice)
        Filmf: v. XII (1969), p. 274; comp., cp. cr.
        Films & F: v. 15, n. 11 (Aug., 1969), p. 46; Gordon Gow, 800 wds., cp. cr.

       YOU WILL BE TERRIBLY NICE (see: You Only Love Once)

7323 YOUNG AMERICANS (Alex Grasshoff)
        Filmf: v. XII (1969), pp. 263, 336; comp., cp. cr.
        Films in R: v. XVIII, n. 8 (Oct., 1967), pp. 505-506; Alice Bradford Shaw,
            275 wds., no cr.

       YOUNG AND EAGER (see: Claudelle Inglish)

7324 YOUNG AND THE BRAVE, THE (Francis D. Lyon)
        Filmf: v. VI (1963), p. 306; comp., cp. cr.

7325 YOUNG AND THE COOL, THE (William J. Hole, Jr.)
        Films & F: v. 9, n. 4 (Jan., 1963), p. 51; Raymond Durgnat, 250 wds., cp.
            cr.

       YOUNG AND THE DAMNED, THE (see: Los Olvidados)

       YOUNG AND THE PASSIONATE, THE (see: I Vitelloni)

7326 YOUNG AND WILD (William Witney)
        Filmf: v. I (1958), p. 49; comp., cp. cr.

7327 YOUNG AND WILLING (Ralph Thomas)
        Filmf: v. VII (1964), p. 32; comp., cp. cr.

       YOUNG ANIMALS, THE (see: Born Wild)

7328 YOUNG APHRODITES (Nikos Koundouros)
        Filmf: v. X (1967), p. 3; comp., cp. cr.
        Films & F: v. 13, n. 10 (July, 1967), pp. 25-26; Raymond Durgnat, 500
            wds., cp. cr.

7329 YOUNG AT HEART (Gordon Douglas)
 Films & F: v. 1, n. 6 (Mar., 1955), p. 22; Paul Vaughan, 150 wds., cp. cr.

7330 YOUNG BESS (George Sidney)
 Films in R: v. IV, n. 6 (June-July, 1953), p. 300; 200 wds., pt. cr.

7331 YOUNG BILLY YOUNG (Burt Kennedy)
 (also: Who Rides with Kane?)
 Filmf: v. XII (1969), p. 453; comp., cp. cr.
 Films & F: v. 16, n. 2 (Nov., 1969), p. 46; David Austen, 200 wds., cp. cr.

7332 YOUNG CAPTIVES, THE (Irvin Kershner)
 Filmf: v. II (1959), p. 37; comp., cp. cr.
 Sight & S: v. 28, n. 3-4 (Summer-Autumn, 1959), p. 174; Peter John Dyer,
   225 wds., no cr.

7333 YOUNG CASSIDY (John Ford and Jack Cardiff)
 Filmf: v. VIII (1965), p. 56; comp., cp. cr.
 Films & F: v. 11, n. 7 (Apr., 1965), pp. 24-26; Mike Sarne, 2300 wds., cp.
   cr.
 Films in R: v. XVI, n. 4 (Apr., 1965), pp. 247-248; Henry Hart, 350 wds.,
   no cr.
 Sight & S: v. 34, n. 2 (Spring, 1965), p. 97; Brenda Davies, 550 wds., pt. cr.

7334 YOUNG COUPLE, A (Rene Gainville)
 (also: Un Jeune Couple)
 Filmf: v. XIV (1971), p. 727; comp., cp. cr.

7335 YOUNG DOCTORS, THE (Phil Karlson)
 Film: n. 30 (Winter, 1961), p. 16; Peter Armitage, 150 wds., no cr.
 F Quarterly: v. XV, n. 2 (Winter, 1961-1962), p. 62; R. M. Hodgens, 50
   wds., no cr.
 Filmf: v. IV (1961-1962), p. 191; comp., cp. cr.
 Filmf & F: v. 8, n. 3 (Dec., 1961), pp. 32-33; John Cutts, 475 wds., cp. cr.
 Films in R: v. XII, n. 8 (Oct., 1961), pp. 486-487; Wilfred Mifflin, 300
   wds., no cr.

7336 YOUNG GIRLS BEWARE (Yves Allegret)
 (also: Good Girls Beware; Mefiez Vous, Fillettes)
 Filmf: v. II (1959), p. 236; comp., cp. cr.

7337 YOUNG GIRLS OF ROCHEFORT, THE (Jacques Demy)
 (also: Les Demoiselles de Rochefort)
 F Quarterrly: v. XXI, n. 4 (Summer, 1968), pp. 45-48; Albert Johnson,
   1300 wds., pt. cr.
 Filmf: v. XI (1968), p. 152; comp., cp. cr.
 Sight & S: v. 36, n. 4 (Autumn, 1967), p. 204; Carey Harrison, 400 wds., no
   cr.

7338 YOUNG GO WILD, THE (Alfred Vohrer)
 Filmf: v. VI (1963), p. 345; comp., cp. cr.

7339 YOUNG GRADUATES, THE (Robert Anderson)
 Filmf: v. XIV (1971), p. 412; comp., cp. cr.

7340 YOUNG GUARD (Sergei Gerasimov)
 Sequence: n. 7 (Spring, 1949), pp. 37-38; Gavin Lambert, 700 wds., pt. cr.

7341 YOUNG GUNS OF TEXAS (Maury Dexter)
 Filmf: v. VI (1963), p. 22; comp., cp. cr.

 YOUNG HAVE NO MORALS, THE (see: The Chasers)

7342 YOUNG HAVE NO TIME, THE (Johannes Allen)
 Filmf: v. II (1959), p. 304; comp., cp. cr.
 Films & F: v. 5, n. 6 (Mar., 1959), p. 23; Derek Conrad, 225 wds., cp. cr.

 YOUNG HELLIONS, THE (see: High School Confidential)

 YOUNG INVADERS, THE (see: Darby's Rangers)

7343 YOUNG JESSE JAMES (William Claxton)
     Filmf: v. III (1960), p. 192; comp., cp. cr.

7344 YOUNG LAND, THE (Ted Tetzlaff)
     Filmf: v. II (1959), p. 326; comp., cp. cr.
     Films in R: v. X, n. 6 (June-July, 1959), pp. 361-362; Claudia Belmont, 350
       wds., no cr.

7345 YOUNG LIONS, THE (Edward Dmytryk)
     F Quarterly: v. XII, n. 1 (Fall, 1958), pp. 45-50; Colin Young, 2100 wds.,
       no cr.
     Filmf: v. I (1958), p. 51; comp., cp. cr.
     Films & F: v. 4, n. 9 (June, 1958), p. 23; Paul Rotha, 750 wds., cp. cr.
     Films in R: v. IX, n. 4 (Apr., 1958), pp. 204-205; Helen Weldon Kuhn, 450
       wds., no cr.
     Sight & S: v. 27, n. 5 (Summer, 1958), pp. 248-249; Penelope Houston,
       1200 wds., pt. cr.

7346 YOUNG LOVE (Roland Hallstrom)
     (also: Poika Eli Kesaansa)
     Filmf: v. IV (1961), p. 369; comp., cp. cr.

7347 YOUNG LOVERS, THE (Anthony Asquith)
     (also: Chance Meeting)
     Films & F: v. 1, n. 2 (Nov., 1954), p. 18; Catherine De La Roche, 300 wds.,
       cp. cr.
     Films in R: v. VI, n. 3 (Mar., 1955), p. 134; 180 wds., no cr.
     Sight & S: v. 24, n. 2 (Oct.-Dec., 1954), p. 90; Penelope Houston, 400 wds.,
       pt. cr.

7348 YOUNG LOVERS, THE (Samuel Goldwyn, Jr.)
     Filmf: v. VIII (1965), p. 83; comp., cp. cr.
     Films in R: v. XV, n. 8 (Oct., 1964), pp. 501-502; Joan Horvath, 225 wds.,
       no cr.

7349 YOUNG MAN OF MUSIC (Michael Curtiz)
     (also: Young Man With a Horn)
     Sequence: n. 11 (Summer, 1950), pp. 14-15; K.R., 350 wds., no cr.

     YOUNG MAN WITH A HORN (see: Young Man of Music)

7350 YOUNG MR. LINCOLN (John Ford)
     F Heritage: v. 6, n. 4 (Summer, 1971), pp. 13-18; Joseph McBride and
       Michael Wilmington, 2200 wds., pt. cr.

7351 YOUNG ONE, THE (Luis Bunuel)
     (also: Island of Shame; La Joven)
     Filmf: v. IV (1961), p. 18; comp., cp. cr.
     Films & F: v. 8, n. 5 (Feb., 1962), p. 32; Philip Strick, 400 wds., cp. cr.
     Films in R: v. XII, n. 2 (Feb., 1961), pp. 111-112; Louise Corbin, 375 wds.,
       no cr.

     YOUNG ONE, THE (Jack Garfein/see: End As a Man)

     YOUNG ONES, THE (see: Wonderful To Be Young)

7352 YOUNG PHILADELPHIANS, THE (Vincent Sherman)
     (also: The City Jungle; The Philadelphians)
     Filmf: v. II (1959), p. 101; comp., cp. cr.
     Films & F: v. 5, n. 10 (July, 1959), pp. 24-25; Ian Moss, 400 wds., cp. cr.
     Films in R: v. X, n. 6 (June-July, 1959), pp. 355-357; Diana Willing Cope,
       400 wds., no cr.

7353 YOUNG RACERS, THE (Roger Corman)
     Filmf: v. VI (1963), p. 198; comp., cp. cr.
     Films & F: v. 10, n. 8 (May, 1964), p. 26; Raymond Durgnat, 500 wds., cp.
       cr.

7354 YOUNG RUNAWAYS, THE (Arthur Dreifuss)
     Filmf: v. XI (1968), p. 398; comp., cp. cr.

7355 YOUNG SAVAGES, THE (John Frankenheimer)
    F Quarterly: v. XV, n. 1 (Fall, 1961), p. 56; R. M. Hodgens, 150 wds., no
        cr.
    Filmf: v. IV (1961), p. 107; comp., cp. cr.
    Films & F: v. 7, n. 11 (Aug., 1961), p. 29; Peter G. Baker, 250 wds., cp. cr.
    Films in R: v. XII, n. 5 (May, 1961), p. 296; Arthur B. Clark, 200 wds., no
        cr.
    Sight & S: v. 30, n. 3 (Summer, 1961), pp. 146-147; Peter John Cyer, 800
        wds., pt. cr.

    YOUNG SCARFACE (see: Brighton Rock)

7356 YOUNG STRANGER, THE (John Frankenheimer)
    F Culture: v. 3, n. 5 (Dec., 1957), p. 15; Colinette Leitch, 700 wds., pt. cr.
    Films & F: v. 3, n. 7 (Apr., 1957), p. 24; Peter John Dyer, 650 wds., pt. cr.
    Films in R: v. VIII, n. 5 (May, 1957), p. 225; Diana Willing, 150 wds., no
        cr.
    Sight & S: v. 26, n. 4 (Spring, 1957), p. 212; Derek Prouse, 550 wds., pt. cr.

7357 YOUNG SWINGERS, THE (Maury Dexter)
    Filmf: v. VI (1963), p. 344; comp., cp. cr.

7358 YOUNG, THE EVIL AND THE SAVAGE, THE (Anthony Dawson)
    (also: Sette Vergini per il Diavolo; Seven Virgins for the Devil)
    Filmf: v. XI (1968), p. 366; comp., cp. cr.

7359 YOUNG TORLESS (Volker Schloendorff)
    (also: Der Junge Torless)
    F Quarterly: v. XX, n. 2 (Winter, 1966-1967), pp. 42-44; Ernest Callenbach,
        800 wds., pt. cr.
    Filmf: v. XI (1968), p. 289; comp., cp. cr.
    Films & F: v. 14, n. 10 (July, 1968), pp. 27-28; Michael Armstrong, 1300
        wds., cp. cr.
    Interntl F G: v. 4 (1967), p. 78; 150 wds., pt. cr.

7360 YOUNG WARRIORS, THE (John Peyser)
    Filmf: v. X (1967), p. 270; comp., cp. cr.

7361 YOUNG, WILLING AND EAGER (Lance Comfort)
    (also: Rag Doll)
    Filmf: v. VI (1963), p. 342; comp., cp. cr.

7362 YOUNG WOLVES, THE (Marcel Carne)
    (also: Les Jeunes Loups)
    Films & F: v. 16, n. 4 (Jan., 1970), pp. 50-51; David McGillivray, 250 wds.,
        cp. cr.

7363 YOUNG WORLD, A (Vittorio De Sica)
    (also: Un Monde Nouveau)
    Filmf: v. IX (1966), p. 124; comp., cp. cr.
    Films in R: v. XVII, n. 6 (June-July, 1966), pp. 380-381; Gwenneth Britt,
        350 wds., no cr.

7364 YOUNGBLOOD HAWKE (Delmer Daves)
    Filmf: v. VII (1964), p. 270; comp., cp. cr.
    Films & F: v. 11, n. 2 (Nov., 1964), pp. 29-30; Allen Eyles, 850 wds., cp.
        cr.

7365 YOUR CHEATIN' HEART (Gene Nelson)
    Films & F: v. 12, n. 8 (May, 1966), p. 14; Richard Davis, 400 wds., cp. cr.
    Films in R: v. XV, n. 10 (Dec., 1964), pp. 636-637; Eloise Carpenter, 75
        wds., no cr.

    YOUR MONEY OR YOUR LIFE (see: La Bourse et la Vie)

7366 YOUR PAST IS SHOWING (Mario Zampi)
    (also: The Naked Truth)
    Filmf: v. I (1958), p. 129; comp., cp. cr.
    Films & F: v. 4, n. 4 (Jan., 1958), p. 24; Peter G. Baker, 500 wds., cp. cr.

7367 YOUR SHADOW IS MINE (Andre Michel)
         (also: Ton Ombre a la Mienne)
         Filmf: v. VI (1963), p. 161; comp., cp. cr.

7368 YOUR WITNESS (Robert Montgomery)
         (also: Eye Witness)
         Sequence: n. 11 (Summer, 1950), pp. 15-16; A.M., 300 wds., no cr.

7369 YOU'RE A BIG BOY NOW (Francis Ford Coppola)
         F Quarterly: v. XX, n. 4 (Summer, 1967), p. 80; Stephen Farber, 450 wds.,
              no cr.
         Filmf: v. X (1967), p. 74; comp., cp. cr.
         Films & F: v. 13, n. 11 (Aug., 1967), p. 23; Raymond Durgnat, 1000 wds.,
              cp. cr.
         Films in R: v. XVIII, n. 5 (May, 1967), p. 309; Page Cook, 300 wds., no cr.
         Interntl F G: v. 5 (1968), p. 154; 330 wds., pt. cr.
         Sight & S: v. 36, n. 3 (Summer, 1967), p. 148; David Wilson, 450 wds., pt.
              cr.
         Take One: v. 1, n. 5 (June, 1967), pp. 29-30; Tony Reif, 550 wds., pt. cr.

7370 YOU'RE IN THE NAVY NOW (Henry Hathaway)
         Films in R: v. II, n. 5 (May, 1951), pp. 43-44; J. R. Coolidge, 150 wds., pt.
              cr.

7371 YOU'RE MY EVERYTHING (Walter Lang)
         Sequence: n. 11 (Summer, 1950), p. 14; Peter Ericsson, 200 wds., no cr.

7372 YOU'RE NO GOOD (George Kaczender)
         Interntl F G: v. 4 (1967), p. 57; 100 wds., pt. cr.

7373 YOU'RE ONLY YOUNG TWICE
         Sight & S: v. 22, n. 2 (Oct.-Dec., 1952), pp. 78-79; Edgar Anstey, 1000
              wds., no cr.

7374 YOURS, MINE AND OURS (Melville Shavelson)
         Filmf: v. XI (1968), p. 141; comp., cp. cr.
         Films & F: v. 14, n. 8 (Apr., 1968), pp. 27-28; Raymond Durgnat, 1100
              wds., cp. cr.
         Films in R: v. XIX, n. 5 (May, 1968), p. 312; Wilfred Mifflin, 150 wds., no
              cr.

7375 YOUTH RUNS WILD (Mark Robson)
         Focus on F: n. 5 (Winter/Nov.-Dec., 1970), pp. 41-42; Don Miller, 300
              wds., pt. cr.

       YOUTHFUL SINNERS (see: Les Tricheurs)

7376 YOU'VE GOT TO BE SMART (Ellis Kadison)
         Filmf: v. X (1967), p. 439; comp., cp. cr.

7377 YOU'VE GOT TO WALK IT LIKE YOU TALK IT OR YOU'LL LOSE THAT
              BEAT (Peter Locke)
         Filmf: v. XIV (1971), p. 684; comp., cp. cr.

7378 YOYO (Pierre Etaix)
         (also: Yo Yo)
         Cinema: v. 3, n. 2 (Mar., 1966), p. 48; Saul Kahan, 225 wds., pt. cr.
         F Quarterly: v. XVIII, n. 4 (Summer, 1965), p. 58; Ginette Billard, 400
              wds., pt. cr.
         Filmf: v. X (1967), p. 69; comp., cp. cr.
         Films & F: v. 12, n. 2 (Nov., 1965), p. 27; Peter Cowie, 450 wds., cp. cr.
         Interntl F G: v. 3 (1966), pp. 67-68; Peter Graham, 200 wds., pt. cr.
         Sight & S: v. 34, n. 4 (Autumn, 1965), p. 197; John Russell Taylor, 600
              wds., no cr.

       YUKINOJO HENGE (see: An Actor's Revenge)

Z

7379 Z (Costa-Gavras)
F Quarterly: v. XXIII, n. 2 (Winter, 1969-1970), p. 64; Lawrence
Loewinger, 300 wds., no cr.
F Soc Rev: v. 5, n. 4 (Dec., 1969), pp. 28-35; Dan Georgakas, 2200 wds.,
cp. cr.
Films & F: v. 16, n. 3 (Dec., 1969), pp. 38-39; 600 wds., cp. cr.
Films in R: v. XXI, n. 1 (Jan., 1970), p. 50; Aline Derain, 75 wds., no cr.
Focus: n. 6 (Spring, 1970), pp. 45-46; Charles Flynn, 800 wds., no cr.
Interntl F G: v. 7 (1970), p. 116; Felix Bucher, 125 wds., pt. cr.
Movie: n. 17 (Winter, 1969-1970), p. 37, Ian Cameron, 100 wds., no cr.
Sight & S: v. 39, n. 1 (Winter, 1969-1970), pp. 47-48; Gavin Millar, 1200
wds., pt. cr.
Take One: v. 2, n. 4 (1969), pp. 20-21; Joseph Kostolefsky, 300 wds., pt.
cr.

7380 ZABRISKIE POINT (Michelangelo Antonioni)
F Heritage: v. 5, n. 3 (Spring, 1970), pp. 22-25; Anthony Macklin, 1000
wds., no cr.
F Heritage: v. 6 n. 1 (Fall, 1970), pp. 7-24; Stephen Handzo, 5000 wds., pt.
cr.
F Quarterly: v. XXIII, n. 3 (Spring, 1970), pp. 35-38; Ernest Callenbach,
1600 wds., pt. cr.
F Soc Rev: v. 5, n. 8, pp. 37-42; Foster Hirsch, 3000 wds., cp. cr.
Films & F: v. 16, n. 8 (May, 1970), pp. 36-37; Gordon Gow, 800 wds., cp.
cr.
Films in R: v. XXI, n. 3 (Mar., 1970), pp. 177-179; Arlene Kramborg, 400
wds., no cr.
Focus: n. 6 (Spring, 1970), pp. 36-37; Charles Flynn, 800 wds., no cr.
Interntl F G: v. 8 (1971), pp. 263-264; Margot S. Kernan, 300 wds., pt. cr.
Movie: n. 18 (Winter, 1970-1971), pp. 21-23; Robin Wood, 1600 wds., no
cr.
Sight & S: v. 39, n. 3 (Summer, 1970), pp. 124-126; Julian Jebb, 2000
wds., no cr.

7381 ZACHARIAH (George Englund)
Filmf: v. XIV (1971), p. 78; comp., cp. cr.
Take One: v. 2, n. 11 (1971), pp. 24-25; Tim Bay, 600 wds., pt. cr.

ZACHAROVANAYA DESNA (see: The Enchanted Desna)

7382 ZARAK (Terence Young)
Films & F: v. 3, n. 5 (Feb., 1957), p. 23; Rodney Giesler, 150 wds., cp. cr.

7383 ZATOICHI (Kimiyoshi Yasuda)
(also: Zatoichi Kenkatabi; Zatoichi's Gambling Feber)
Filmf: v. XI (1968), p. 258; comp., cp. cr.
Interntl F G: v. 5 (1968), p. 106; 200 wds., pt. cr.

ZATOICHI JIGOKUTABI (see: Showdown for Zatoichi)

ZATOICHI KENKATABI (see: Zatoichi)

ZATOICHI'S GAMBLING FEVER (see: Zatoichi)

7384 ZAZIE (Louis Malle)
(also: Zazie Dans le Metro)
F Quarterly: v. XVI, n. 4 (Summer, 1963), pp. 38-40; James Stroller, 1000
wds., pt. cr.
Filmf: v. IV (1961), p. 333; comp., cp. cr.
Films & F: v. 9, n. 4 (Jan., 1963), pp. 45-46; Gordon Gow, 800 wds., cp. cr.
Movie: n. 4 (Nov., 1962), p. 35; 150 wds., no cr.
Sight & S: v. 32, n. 1 (Winter, 1962-1963), p. 37; Geoffrey Newell-Smith,
800 wds., no cr.

ZAZIE DANS LE METRO (see: Zazie)

7385 ZEPPELIN (Etienne Perier)
      Filmf: v. XIV (1971), p. 55; comp., cp. cr.
      Films & F: v. 17, n. 12 (Sept., 1971), p. 52; Peter Buckley, 300 wds., cp. cr.

7386 ZERO DE CONDUITE (Jean Vigo)
      (also: Zero for Conduct)
      Sight & S: v. 15, n. 59 (Autumn, 1946), p. 96; Roger Manvell, 400 wds., no
          cr.

      ZERO FOR CONDUCT (see: Zero de Conduite)

7387 ZERO HOUR (Hall Bartlett)
      Films in R: v. VIII, n. 10 (Dec., 1957), p. 524; Hy Arnold, 175 wds., no cr.

7388 ZERO IN THE UNIVERSE (George Moorse)
      Filmf: v. IX (1966), p. 342; comp., cp. cr.

7389 ZERO THE FOOL (Morley Markson)
      Take One: v. 2, n. 5 (1970), pp. 28-29; Kay Armatage, 500 wds., pt. cr.

      ZERT (see: The Joke)

      ZHENITBA BALZAMINOVA (see: The Marriage of Balzaminov)

      ZHILI-BYLI STARIK SO STARUKHOI (see: There Lived an Old Man and an
          Old Woman)

      ZHURBINS, THE (see: The Big Family)

7390 ZIA GRAZIE (Salvatore Samperi)
      (also: Come Play with Me; Thanks, Aunt)
      Filmf: v. XII (1969), p. 20; comp., cp. cr.

7391 ZIG-ZAG (Richard A. Colla)
      Take One: v. 2, n. 8 (1970), p. 23; Howard Curle, 75 wds., no cr.

      ZIGEUNERBARON, DER (see: The Gypsy Baron)

7392 ZITA (Robert Enrico)
      (also: Tante Zita)
      Cinema: v. 4, n. 4 (Dec., 1968), p. 34; Morgan Gleason, 950 wds., no cr.
      Filmf: v. XI (1968), p. 312; comp., cp. cr.
      Films & F: v. 15, n. 5 (Feb., 1969), p. 44; Gordon Gow, 400 wds., cp. cr.

      ZOMBIES (see: I Eat Your Skin)

      ZOO (Bert Haanstra)
      Interntl F G: v. 1 (1964), p. 113; 75 wds., pt. cr.

      ZOO, THE (Satyajit Ray/see: Chidiakhana)

7393 ZORBA, THE GREEK (Michael Cacoyannis)
      F Quarterly: v. XVIII, n. 4 (Summer, 1965), p. 61; Ernest Callenbach, 150
          wds., no cr.
      Films & F: v. 11, n. 8 (May, 1965), pp. 26-27; George Angell, 1300 wds.,
          cp. cr.
      Films in R: v. XVI, n. 1 (Jan., 1965), pp. 46-47; Romano Tozzi, 400 wds.,
          no cr.
      Films in R: v. XVI, n. 3 (Mar., 1965), p. 182; Malvin Wald, 250 wds., no cr.
      Interntl F G: v. 3 (1966), p. 144; 300 wds., pt. cr.

7394 ZORNS LEMMA (Hollis Frampton)
      F Culture: n. 52 (Spring, 1971), pp. 88-95; Mark Segal, 1500 wds., no cr.
      Take One: v. 2, n. 8 (1970), pp. 26-27; Bob Cowan, 700 wds., no cr.

7395 ZORRO (J. R. Marchent)
      Films & F: v. 9, n. 10 (July, 1963), p. 25; Ian Johnson, 200 wds., cp. cr.

ZORRO CONTRO MACISTE (see: Samson and the Slave Queen)

7396 ZOTZ! (William Castle)
    Filmf: v. V (1962), p. 248; comp., cp. cr.

ZU JUNG FUR DIE LIEBE (see: Too Young for Love)

7397 ZUCKERKANDL (John and Faith Hubley)
    F Lib Quarterly: v. 3, n. 1 (Winter, 1969-1970), pp. 41, 44; Lewis
        Archibald, 600 wds., pt. cr.

7398 ZULU (Cy Endfield)
    F Quarterly: v. XVIII, n. 1 (Fall, 1964), p. 62; R. M. Hodgens, 100 wds., no
        cr.
    Filmf: v. VII (1964), p. 158; comp., cp. cr.
    Films & F: v. 10, n. 5 (Feb., 1964), p. 30; Gordon Gow, 850 wds., cp. cr.
    Films in R: v. XV, n. 6 (June-July, 1964), p. 373; Brian Sandenbergh, 200
        wds., no cr.

7399 ZUR SACHE, SCHATZCHEN (May Spils)
    Interntl F G: v. 6 (1969), p. 76; 225 wds., pt. cr.

ZURCHER VERLOGUNG, DIE (see: The Affairs of Julie)

ZVONYAT, OTKROYTE DVER (see: The Girl and the Burgler)

ZWISCHEN ZEIT UND EWIGKEIT (see: Between Time and Eternity)

7400 ZYCIE RODZINNE (Krzysztof Zanussi)
    (also: Family Life)
    Interntl F G: v. 9 (1972), p. 216; Peter Cowie, 200 wds., pt. cr.

ZYRAFIATKO (see: The Little Giraffe)

INDEX
TO CRITICAL
REVIEWS OF
BOOKS ABOUT FILM

Together With:
INDEX TO CRITICAL FILM REVIEWS
      In British and American Film Periodicals

Compiled and Edited by Stephen E. Bowles
University of Northern Colorado

VOLUME III: CRITICAL REVIEWS OF BOOKS ABOUT FILM A–Z

Burt Franklin & Co., Inc.   NEW YORK

A

7401 ABC OF FILM AND TV WORKING TERMS (Oswald Skilbeck)
       Am Cinematog: v. 41, n. 10 (Oct., 1960), p. 588; 100 wds., pt. pub.

7402 A-Z OF MOVIE MAKING (Wolf Rilla)
       F Comment: v. 7, n. 4 (Winter, 1971-1972), p. 80; Norman Kagan, 200
           wds., cp. pub.
       Interntl F G: v. 8 (1971), p. 435; 50 wds., pt. pub.

7403 AARON COPLAND (Julia Smith)
       Films in R: v. VII, n. 5 (May, 1956), p. 233; Edward Jablonski, 275 wds.,
           cp. pub.

7404 *ABSCHIED VON GESTERN (Alexander Kluge)
       Interntl F G: v. 5 (1968), p. 159; 20 wds., pt. pub.

7405 ACADEMY AWARDS, THE (Paul Michael)
       Films & F: v. 13, n. 3 (Dec., 1966), pp. 42-43; Sheridan Morley, 100 wds.,
           no pub.

7406 ACTING: A HANDBOOK OF THE STANISLAVSKI METHOD (Toby Cole)
       Hollywood Q: v. III, n. 3 (Spring, 1948), pp. 333-335, William W. Melnitz,
           1200 wds., cp. cr.

7407 ACTOR GUIDE TO THE TALKIES, AN (Richard B. Dimmit, comp.)
       Screen: v. 11, n. 4-5 (July-Oct., 1970), p. 134; Gillian Hartnoll, 50 wds., cp.
           pub.

7408 ACTORS ON ACTING (Toby Cole and Helen Krich Chinoy, eds.)
       Hollywood Q: v. IV, n. 3 (Spring, 1950), p. 316; Franklin Fearing, 280
           wds., cp. cr.

7409 ACTOR'S WAYS AND MEANS, THE (Michael Redgrave)
       Sight & S: v. 23, n. 3 (Jan.-Mar., 1954), p. 164; Philip Hope-Wallace, 400
           wds., cp. pub.

7410 ADDITIONAL DIALOGUE: LETTERS OF DALTON TRUMBO (Helen
           Manfull, ed.)
       F Comment: v. 7, n. 1 (Spring, 1971), pp. 83-84; Howard Suber, 1000 wds.,
           cp. pub.
       F Soc Rev: v. 7, n. 2 (Oct., 1971), pp. 48-49; Gary Crowdus, 800 wds., cp.
           pub.
       Films in R: v. XXII, n. 7 (Aug.-Sept., 1971), pp. 432-433; 150 wds., cp.
           pub.,
       Sight & S: v. 40, n. 3 (Summer, 1971), p. 157; Philip French, 1600 wds.,
           cp. pub.

7411 *AGE INGRAT DU CINEMA, L' (Léon Moussinac)
       Sight & S: v. 16, n. 63 (Autumn, 1947), pp. 128-129; Ruth Partington, 600
           wds., pt. pub.

7412 AGEE ON FILM: VOLUME I: CRITICISM AND REVIEWS (James Agee)
    F Quarterly: v. XII, n. 3 (Spring, 1959), pp. 58-61; Jonathan Harker, 1500
    wds., cp. pub.

7413 AGEE ON FILM: VOLUME II: FIVE FILM SCRIPTS (James Agee)
    F Quarterly: v. XIV, n. 1 (Fall, 1960), p. 58; Henry Breitrose, 500 wds., cp.
    pub.
    Interntl F G: v. 3 (1966), p. 257; 250 wds., cp. cr.
    Sight & S: v. 30, n. 1 (Winter, 1960-1961), pp. 46-47; John Russell Taylor,
    1000 wds., cp. pub.

7414 AGEE ON FILM: VOLUMES I AND II (James Agee)
    F Heritage: v. 3, n. 1 (Fall, 1967), pp. 12-19; Joel Siegel, 1800 wds., no
    pub.

7415 ALAIN RESNAIS, OR THE THEME OF TIME (John Ward)
    Films & F: v. 14, n. 12 (Sept., 1968), p. 50; Sheridan Morley, 150 wds., cp.
    cr.
    Interntl F G: v. 6 (1969), p. 278; 50 wds., pt. pub.

7416 ALAN DWAN: THE LAST PIONEER (Peter Bogdanovich)
    Films & F: v. 17, n. 8 (May, 1971), p. 136; Sheridan Morley, 200 wds., pt.
    pub.
    Focus on F: n. 6 (Spring, 1971), p. 60; Allen Eyles, 175 wds., cp. pub.
    Interntl F G: v. 9 (1972), p. 455; 75 wds., pt. pub.

7417 ALEC GUINNESS (Kenneth Tynan)
    Films in R: v. V, n. 4 (Apr., 1954), pp. 200-201; Elspeth Hart, 550 wds.,
    cp. pub.
    Sight & S: v. 23, n. 3 (Jan.-Mar., 1954), p. 164; Philip Hope-Wallace, 400
    wds., cp. pub.

7418 ALEXANDER KORDA (Paul Tabori)
    Sight & S: v. 29, n. 1 (Winter, 1959-1960), p. 48; Brenda Davies, 350 wds.,
    cp. pub.

7419 ALL-AMERICAN BOY, THE (Charles Eastman)
    Interntl F G: v. 9 (1972), p. 455; 50 wds., pt. pub.

7420 ALL TALKING! ALL SPRING! ALL DANCING! —A PICTORIAL HIS-
    TORY OF THE MOVIE MUSICAL (John Springer)
    F Comment: v. 5, n. 3 (Fall, 1969), p. 78; William K. Everson, 200 wds., cp.
    pub.
    Films in R: v. XVIII, n. 3 (Mar., 1967), p. 173; Henry Hart, 125 wds., cp.
    cr.
    Interntl F G: v. 5 (1968), p. 259; 50 wds., pt. pub.

7421 AMERICAN CINEMA: DIRECTORS AND DIRECTIONS; 1929-1968, THE
    (Andrew Sarris)
    Cinema: v. 5, n. 1, p. 46; Robert Joseph, 250 wds., pt. pub.
    Cinema J: v. VIII, n. 2 (Spring, 1969), pp. 33-35; Michael Budd, 1250 wds.,
    cp. cr.
    F Comment: v. 5, n. 4 (Winter, 1969), p. 78; 150 wds., cp. pub.
    F Quarterly: v. XXII, n. 3 (Spring, 1969), p. 57; Ernest Callenbach, 200
    wds., cp. pub.
    F Soc Rev: v. 4, n. 5, pp. 41-44; Jonathan Rosenbaum, 1200 wds., cp. pub.
    Take One: v. 2, n. 3 (1969), pp. 26-27; David Dorfman, 1200 wds., cp. pub.

7422 AMERICAN CINEMATOGRAPHER MANUAL (Joseph V. Mascelli and
    Arthur C. Miller)
    Am Cinematog: v. 41, n. 12 (Dec., 1960), p. 718; 300 wds., pt. cr.
    Cineaste: v. II, n. 1 (Summer, 1968), p. 27; Gary Crowdus, 100 wds., pt.
    pub.
    Films in R: v. XII, n. 5 (May, 1961), pp. 306-307; George Mitchell, 350
    wds., cp. pub.
    Films in R: v. XVIII, n. 3 (Mar., 1967), pp. 171-172; George J. Mitchell,
    350 wds., cp. pub.
    Take One: v. 1, n. 12 (1968), p. 29; Wally Gentleman, 250 wds., cp. pub.

7423 *AMERICAN CINEMATOGRAPHY — D. W. GRIFFITH (S. M. Eisenstein and S. J. Yutkevich, eds.)
Hollywood Q: v. I, n. 1 (Oct., 1945), pp. 126-127; Boris Ingster, 450 wds., cp. pub.

7424 AMERICAN FILM INSTITUTE CATALOG OF MOTION PICTURES PRODUCED IN THE UNITED STATES: FEATURE FILMS; 1921-1930, THE (Kenneth W. Munden, gen. ed.)
Cinema J. v. XI, n. 1 (Fall, 1971), pp. 63-65; Timothy J. Lyons, 1100 wds., cp. cr.
F Comment: v. 7, n. 4 (Winter, 1971-1972), pp. 76-77; Andrew C. McKay, 1800 wds., cp. pub.
F Quarterly: v. XXV, n. 2 (Winter, 1971-1972), pp. 59-65; Herman G. Weinberg, 3200 wds., cp. pub.
F Quarterly: v. XXV, n. 4 (Summer, 1972), pp. 44-46; Francis Jones, Sam Kula, Steve Zito, 1600 wds., cp. pub.
Focus on F: n. 10 (Summer, 1972), p. 59; Allen Eyles, 900 wds., cp. pub.
Interntl F G: v. 9 (1972), p. 455; 50 wds., pt. pub.
Take One: v. 2, n. 12 (1971), p. 30; Foster Stackhouse, 250 wds., cp. pub.

7425 AMERICAN MOTION PICTURE DIRECTORS (Robert Haller)
F Soc Rev: Nov. (1965), pp. 27-28; David Stewart Hull, 350 wds., cp. pub.

7426 AMERICAN MOVIE, THE (William K. Everson)
F Comment: v. 2, n. 1 (Winter, 1964), pp. 46-47; Stuart Selby, 1200 wds., cp. cr.
F Quarterly: v. XVI, n. 4 (Summer, 1963), p. 61; 50 wds., cp. pub.

7427 AMERICAN MOVIES REFERENCE BOOK: THE SOUND ERA (Paul Michael, gen. ed.)
Cinema: v. 5, n. 3, p. 40; 800 wds., cp. pub.
Cinema J: v. IX, n. 1 (Fall, 1969), pp. 47-48; John L. Fell, 200 wds., cp. pub.
Films in R: v. XX, n. 8 (Oct., 1969), pp. 496-501; Earl Anderson, 2100 wds., cp. pub.
Films in R: v. XX, n. 9 (Nov., 1969), pp. 580-584; C. Hoyt, M. Kreuger, J. Nolan, 1600 wds., no pub.
Screen: v. 11, n. 4-5 (July-Oct., 1970), pp. 135-136; Gillian Hartnoll, 100 wds., cp. pub.
Views & Rev: v. I, n. 2 (Fall, 1969), pp. 67-70; Karl Thiede, 1500 wds., cp. pub.

7428 AMERICAN MUSICAL, THE (Tom Vallance)
Films & F: v. 17, n. 8 (May, 1971), p. 136; Sheridan Morley, 200 wds., pt. pub.
Interntl F G: v. 8 (1971), p. 435; 50 wds., pt. pub.

7429 *AMOUR, EROTISME ET CINEMA (Ado Kyrou)
F Culture: v. 3, n. 2 (1957), p. 22; Herman G. Weinberg, 700 wds., cp. pub.
Interntl F G: v. 5 (1968), p. 259; 25 wds., pt. pub.
Sight & S: v. 27, n. 1 (Summer, 1957), p. 51; Richard Roud, 800 wds., cp. pub.

7430 ANAGRAM OF IDEAS ON ART, FORM AND FILM, AN (Maya Daren)
Sight & S: v. 16, n. 61 (Spring, 1947), p. 7; J. M. Smithells, 400 wds., cp. pub.

7431 ANATOMY OF THE FILM (H. H. Wollenberg)
Sight & S: v. 17, n. 65 (Spring, 1948), p. 51; John Huntley, 650 wds., pt. pub.

7432 ANDY WARHOL (John Coplans, Jonas Mekas, Calvin Tomkins)
Films & F: v. 17, n. 7 (Apr., 1971), p. 16; Sheridan Morley, 300 wds., pt. pub.

7433 ANDY WARHOL: FILMS AND PAINTINGS (Peter Gidal)
Sight & S: v. 40, n. 2 (Spring, 1971), p. 110; Richard Roud, 1000 wds., cp. pub.

7434 ANIMAL FARM (George Orwell)
Films & F: v. 1, n. 7 (Apr., 1955), p. 30; Louis Marks, 125 wds., pt. pub.

7435 ANIMATED FILM, THE (Roger Manvell)
Films & F: v. 1, n. 7 (Apr., 1955), p. 30; Bernard Orna, 25 wds., pt. pub.

7436 ANIMATED FILM: CONCEPTS, METHODS, USES (Roy Madsen)
Interntl F G: v. 8 (1971), p. 435; 50 wds., pt. pub.

7437 ANIMATED FILM MAKING (Anthony Kinsey)
Films & F: v. 16, n. 10 (July, 1970), p. 64; Sheridan Morley, 100 wds., pt. pub.
Interntl F G: v. 8 (1971), p. 435; 75 wds., pt. pub.

7438 ANIMATION ART IN THE COMMERCIAL FILM (Eli L. Levitan)
Am Cinematog: v. 41, n. 11 (Nov., 1960), p. 646; 150 wds., pt. pub.

7439 ANIMATION IN THE CINEMA (Ralph Stephenson)
Films & F: v. 13, n. 11 (Aug., 1967), p. 47; Sheridan Morley, 75 wds., pt. pub.
Interntl F G: v. 5 (1968), p. 259; 25 wds., pt. cr.

7440 *ANTHOLOGIE DU CINEMA (various series)
Interntl F G: v. 5 (1968), p. 259; 25 wds., pt. pub.
Interntl F G: v. 6 (1969), p. 271; 50 wds., pt. pub.
Interntl F G: v. 7 (1970), pp. 393, 395; 75 wds., pt. pub.
Interntl F G: v. 8 (1971), p. 435; 50 wds., pt. pub.

7441 *ANTHONY MANN (J. C. Missiaen)
Interntl F G: v. 3 (1966), p. 263; 200 wds., cp. pub.

7442 ANTI-TRUST IN THE MOTION PICTURE INDUSTRY: ECONOMIC AND
LEGAL ANALYSIS (Michael Conant)
Cinema Studies: v. I, n. 7 (June, 1963), pp. 180-182; N.M.H., 100 wds., cp. pub.
F Quarterly: v. XIV, n. 3 (Spring, 1961), pp. 62-63; Ernest Callenbach, 900 wds., cp. pub.

7443 *ANTONIONI (Roger Tailleur and Paul-Louis Thirard)
Interntl F G: v. 2 (1965), p. 253; 75 wds., pt. pub.

7444 ANTONIONI (Ian Cameron and Robin Wood)
F Comment: v. 6, n. 1 (Spring, 1970), p. 68; Donald Staples, 100 wds., cp. pub.
Films & F: v. 15, n. 9 (June, 1969), p. 68; Sheridan Morley, 150 wds., pt. pub.

7445 ANTONIONI: A MONOGRAPH (Philip Strick)
F Comment: v. 1, n. 6 (Fall, 1963), pp. 56-68; Harry Feldman, 1200 wds., cp. pub.
Sight & S: v. 32, n. 3 (Summer, 1963), pp. 153-154; Geoffrey Nowell-Smith, 600 wds., cp. cr.

7446 APU TRILOGY, THE (Robin Wood)
F Quarterly: v. XXV, n. 4 (Summer, 1972), p. 37; 75 wds., cp. pub.
Focus on F: n. 10 (Summer, 1972), p. 62; Allen Eyles, 275 wds., cp. pub.

7447 *ARBETARNA LAMNAR FABRIKEN (Carl Henrik Svenstedt)
Interntl F G: v. 9 (1972), pp. 455, 459; 50 wds., pt. pub.

7448 ARCHAEOLOGY OF THE CINEMA (C. W. Ceram)
F Heritage: v. 1, n. 4 (Summer, 1966), pp. 39-40; R. C. Dale, 475 wds., cp. pub.
F Soc Rev: Mar. (1966), p. 23; Edwin Jahiel, 275 wds., cp. pub.
Films in R: v. XVII, n. 1 (Jan., 1966), pp. 43-44; Walter H. Stainton, 300 wds., cp. pub.
Sight & S: v. 35, n. 1 (Winter, 1965-1966), pp. 49-50; David Robinson, 600 wds., cp. pub.

7449 AROUND CINEMAS: SECOND SERIES (James Agate)
Sight & S: v. 17, n. 68 (Winter, 1948-1949), p. 197; Roger Smithells, 200 wds., cp. pub.

7450 ART AND DESIGN IN THE BRITISH FILM (Edward Carrick, comp.)
        Sight & S: v. 17, n. 68 (Winter, 1948-1949), p. 196; George Haslam, 325
          wds., cp. pub.

7451 ART AND VISUAL PERCEPTION (Rudolph Arnheim)
        Quarterly of FR TV: v. IX, n. 1 (Fall, 1954), pp. 209-211; Franklin
          Fearing, 550 wds., cp. pub.

7452 *ART DU CINEMA, L' (Pierre Lherminier)
        F Culture: n. 31 (Winter, 1963-1964), p. 68; Herman G. Weinberg, 100
          wds., cp. pub.

7453 *ART DU COSTUME DANS LE FILM, L' (Jacques Manuel)
        Sequence: n. 12 (Autumn, 1950), pp. 45-47; Laurence Irving, 1700 wds.,
          pt. pub.

7454 ART IN MOVEMENT (John Halas and Roger Manvell)
        Interntl F G: v. 9 (1972), p. 459; 50 wds., pt. pub.

7455 ART OF ACTING, THE (John Dolman, Jr.)
        Hollywood Q: v. IV, n. 1 (Fall, 1949), p. 104; Franklin Fearing, 50 wds.,
          cp. pub.

7456 ART OF ANIMATION, THE (Ralph Stephenson)
        Cinema J. v. VIII, n. 2 (Spring, 1969), pp. 32-33; John Tibbetts, 750 wds.,
          cp. pub.

7457 ART OF THE FILM, THE (Ernest Lindgren)
        F Culture: n. 34 (Fall, 1964), pp. 66-67; 400 wds., cp. pub.
        F Quarterly: v. XVII, n. 4 (Summer, 1964), p. 64; 75 wds., cp. pub.
        F Soc Rev: v. 6, n. 2 (Oct., 1970), pp. 48-49; Michael Sragow, 800 wds., cp.
          pub.
        Films & F: v. 16, n. 12 (Sept., 1970), p. 94; Sheridan Morley, 100 wds., pt.
          pub.
        Films in R: v. XV, n. 1 (Jan., 1964), p. 39; Norman Cecil, 100 wds., cp.
          pub.
        Hollywood Q: v. IV, n. 1 (Fall, 1949), p. 101; Franklin Fearing, 200 wds.,
          cp. pub.
        Interntl F G: v. 1 (1964), p. 232; 50 wds., pt. pub.
        Sight & S: v. 17, n. 66 (Summer, 1948), pp. 104-105; Arthur Vesselo, 500
          wds., cp. pub.

7458 ART OF THE MOTION PICTURES, THE (Jean Benoit-Levy, trans. by
          Theodore R. Jaeckel)
        F Comment: v. 7, n. 4 (Winter, 1971-1972), p. 79; Lewis Jacobs, 200 wds.,
          cp. pub.
        Hollywood Q: v. II, n. 2 (Jan., 1947), pp. 212-213; Irving Pichel, 600 wds.,
          cp. pub.
        Sight & S: v. 15, n. 59 (Autumn, 1946), p. 108; Herman G. Weinberg, 500
          wds., pt. pub.

7459 ART OF THE MOVING PICTURE, THE (Vachel Lindsay)
        Films in R: v. XXI, n. 5 (May, 1970), p. 292; Diana Willing Cope, 100 wds.,
          cp. pub.

7460 ART OF W. C. FIELDS, THE (William K. Everson)
        Films & F: v. 15, n. 4 (Jan., 1969), p. 72; Sheridan Morley, 1050 wds., pt.
          pub.
        Films in R: v. XIX, n. 2 (Feb., 1968), p. 106; A.H.W., 175 wds., cp. pub.
        Interntl F G: v. 6 (1969), p. 271; 50 wds., pt. pub.

7461 ARTHUR PENN (Robin Wood)
        Films & F: v. 15, n. 7 (Apr., 1969), p. 68; Sheridan Morley, 125 wds., pt.
          pub.
        Interntl F G: v. 7 (1970), p. 395; 50 wds., pt. pub.

7462 AUDIO-VISUAL MAN, THE (Pierre Babin, ed.)
        Interntl F G: v. 9 (1972), p. 459; 50 wds., pt. pub.

7463 AUDIO-VISUAL METHODS IN TEACHING (Edgar Dale)
        Sight & S: v. 16, n. 63 (Autumn, 1947), p. 129; Margaret Simpson, 600
        wds., cp. pub.

7464 AUDIO-VISUAL SCHOOL LIBRARY SERVICE: A HANDBOOK FOR
        LIBRARIANS (Margaret I. Rufsvold)
        Hollywood Q: v. IV, n. 2 (Winter, 1949), p. 213; Franklin Fearing, 150
        wds., cp. pub.

7465 AUDIOVISUAL AIDS TO INSTRUCTION (William Exton, Jr.)
        Sight & S: v. 17, n. 66 (Summer, 1948), p. 105; S. Oreanu, 450 wds., cp.
        pub.

7466 AUSTRALIAN CINEMA, THE (John Baxter)
        Focus on F: v. 10 (Summer, 1972), p. 61; Allen Eyles, 150 wds., cp. pub.
        Interntl F G: v. 9 (1972), p. 459; 50 wds., pt. pub.

7467 AUTHORS OF SWEDISH FEATURE FILMS AND SWEDISH TV THEATRE
        (Sven G. Winquist)
        Interntl F G; v. 7 (1970), p. 395; 50 wds., pt. pub.

7468 AUTOBIOGRAPHY of CECIL B. DeMILLE, THE (Donald Hayne, ed.)
        Films in R: v. XI, n. 5 (May, 1960), pp. 299-301; Jack Spears, 800 wds., cp.
        pub.
        Sight & S: v. 29, n. 4 (Autumn, 1960), pp. 203-204; David Robinson, 700
        wds., cp. pub.

7469 *AUTOUT DES DAMES DU BOIS DE BOULOGNE (Paul Guth)
        Hollywood Q: v. I, n. 4 (July, 1946), pp. 441-442; G.S., 200 wds., cp. pub.

B

7470 BAD GUYS — A PICTORIAL HISTORY OF THE MOVIE VILLAIN, THE
        (William K. Everson)
        F Comment: v. 6, n. 1 (Spring, 1970), p. 75; 75 wds., cp. pub.
        F Soc Rev: Sept. (1966), pp. 37-38; Edwin Jahiel, 425 wds., cp. pub.
        Films in R: v. XIX, n. 10 (Dec., 1968), pp. 640-641; Stephen G. Handzo,
        200 wds., cp. pub.

7471 BARRYMORES, THE (Hollis Alpert)
        Sight & S: v. 34, n. 2 (Spring, 1965), p. 101; Elizabeth Sussex, 600 wds.,
        cp. pub.

7472 BASHFUL BILLIONAIRE (Albert B. Gerber)
        Films in R: v. XIX, n. 1 (Jan., 1968), p. 46; E.H.N., 225 wds., cp. pub.

7473 BATTLE OF BRITAIN: THE MAKING OF A FILM, THE (Leonard Mosley)
        Films & F: v. 16, n. 2 (Nov., 1969), p. 70; Sheridan Morley, 450 wds., pt.
        pub.

7474 BEGINNINGS OF THE BIOGRAPH: THE STORY OF THE MUTOSCOPE
        AND THE BIOGRAPH AND THEIR SUPPLYING CAMERA
        (Gordon Hendricks)
        F Soc Rev: Dec. (1965), pp. 22-23; Harvey Deneroff, 450 wds., cp. pub.
        Films in R: v. XVI, n. 5 (May, 1965), p. 308; Gerald D. McDonald, 250
        wds., cp. pub.

7475 BEHIND THE CAMERA (William Kuhns and Thomas F. Giardino)
        Interntl F G: v. 9 (1972), p. 459; 25 wds., pt. pub.

7476 BEHIND THE SCREEN — THE HISTORY AND TECHNIQUES OF THE
        MOTION PICTURE (Kenneth MacGowan)
        F Comment: v. 5, n. 4 (Winter, 1969), p. 80; 150 wds., cp. pub.

N Y Rev of Books: v. III, n. 10 (Dec. 3, 1964), pp. 16-18; A. Alvarez, 2000
wds., pt. pub.
Sight & S: v. 35, n. 2 (Spring, 1966), p. 102; David Wilson, 550 wds., cp.
pub.

7477 BELLOCCHIO: CHINA IS NEAR AND WRITINGS ON FILM (Marco
Bellocchio)
Cineaste: v. III, n. 2 (Fall, 1969), p. 30; Gary Crowdus, 500 wds., cp. pub.

7478 BENNETT PLAYBILL, THE (Joan Bennett and Lois Kibbee)
Films in R: v. XXII, n. 7 (Aug.-Sept., 1971), p. 435; Eleanor H. Nash, 300
wds., cp. pub.

7479 *BERGMAN OM BERGMAN (Stig Bjorkman, Torsen Manns, Jonas Sima)
Interntl F G: v. 9 (1972), p. 459; 50 wds., pt. pub.

7480 BEST FILM PLAYS OF 1943-1944 (John Gassner and Dudley Nichols, eds.)
Hollywood Q: v. I, n. 1 (Oct., 1945), pp. 116-118; E. N. Hooker, 950 wds.,
cp. pub.

7481 BEST FILM PLAYS, 1945 (John Gassner and Dudley Nichols, eds.)
Hollywood Q: v. II, n. 3 (Apr., 1947), pp. 308-309; John Paxton, 750 wds.,
cp. pub.

7482 BEST MOVIE STORIES (Guy Slater, ed.)
Films & F: v. 15, n. 9 (June, 1969), p. 69; Sheridan Morley, 200 wds., pt.
pub.

7483 BEST REMAINING SEATS: THE STORY OF THE GOLDEN AGE OF THE
MOVIE PALACE, THE (Ben M. Hall)
F Quarterly: v. XVI, n. 4 (Summer, 1963), p. 61; Ernest Callenbach, 250
wds., cp. pub.
Films in R: v. XIII, n. 6 (June-July, 1962), pp. 372-373; Arthur B. Clark,
400 wds., cp. pub.

7484 BEVERLY HILLS IS MY BEAT (Clinton H. Anderson)
Films in R: v. XI, n. 9 (Nov., 1960), p. 565; Arthur B. Clark, 325 wds., cp.
pub.

7485 BIG MAN: THE JOHN WAYNE STORY, THE (Mike Tomkies)
Focus on F: v. 7 (Summer, 1971), p. 60; Allen Eyles, 300 wds., cp. pub.

7486 BILLY WILDER (Axel Madsen)
Cinema J: v. X, n. 1 (Fall, 1970), pp. 59-60; Howard Suber, 700 wds., cp.
pub.
Views & Rev: v. I, n. 4 (Spring, 1970), pp. 71-72; 500 wds., cp. pub.

7487 BING AND OTHER THINGS (Kathryn Crosby)
Films & F: v. 15, n. 2 (Nov., 1968), pp. 72-73; Sheridan Morley, 1200 wds.,
pt. pub.

7488 BIOGRAPH BULLETINS 1896-1908 (Kemp R. Niver, comp.)
Films in R: v. XXII, n. 7 (Aug.-Sept., 1971), p. 431; Henry Hart, 200 wds.,
cp. pub.

7489 BIOGRAPHY OF DRACULA — THE LIFE STORY OF BRAM STOKER, A
(Harry Ludlam)
Films in R: v. XVII, n. 7 (Aug.-Sept., 1966), pp. 435-437; George J.
Mitchell, 750 wds., cp. pub.

7490 BLACKS IN AMERICAN FILMS: TODAY AND YESTERDAY (Edward
Mapp)
F Quarterly: v. XXV, n. 4 (Summer, 1972), p. 42; 75 wds., cp. pub.

7491 BLOND VENUS: A LIFE OF MARLENE DIETRICH (Leslie Frewin)
F Culture: v. 2, n. 1 (1956), p. 30; H. G. Weinberg, 100 wds., cp. pub.
Films & F: v. 2, n. 3 (Dec., 1955), p. 26; Rod Hume, 100 wds., pt. pub.
Films in R: v. VIII, n. 1 (Jan., 1957), p. 35; Elspeth Hart, 300 wds., cp.
pub.

7492 BLUFF YOUR WAY IN THE CINEMA (Ken Wlaschin)
        Films & F: v. 15, n. 11 (Aug., 1969), p. 61; Sheridan Morley, 100 wds., pt.
        pub.

7493 BOGIE — THE BIOGRAPHY OF HUMPHREY BOGART (Joe Hyams)
        F Comment: v. IV, n. 2-3 (Fall-Winter, 1967), p. 114; Daniel Talbot, 11
        wds., cp. pub.
        Films in R: v. XVIII, n. 2 (Feb., 1967), pp. 101-103, 111; Clifford
        McCarty, 1150 wds., cp. pub.

7494 BOOK OF FILM, THE (Jerzy Gizycki)
        Films & F: v. 1, n. 3 (Dec., 1954), p. 29; Roger Manvell, 200 wds., pt. pub.

7495 BORIS KARLOFF AND ERROL FLYNN (James Robert Parish)
        Interntl F G: v. 7 (1970), p. 395; 50 wds., pt. pub.

7496 *BOULEVARD DU CINEMA A L'EPOQUE DE GEORGES MELIES (Jacques
        Deslandes)
        Interntl F G: v. 2 (1965), p. 257; 75 wds., pt. pub.
        Sight & S: v. 33, n. 1 (Winter, 1963-1964), pp. 48-49; David Robinson, 475
        wds., pt. pub.

7497 BOUND AND GAGGED (Kalton C. Lahue)
        Interntl F G: v. 7 (1970), p. 395; 50 wds., pt. cr.

7498 BRIGHT SIDE OF BILLY WILDER, THE (Tom Wood)
        Cinema J: v. X, n. 1 (Fall, 1970), pp. 59-60; Howard Suber, 700 wds., cp.
        pub.
        Films in R: v. XXI, n. 5 (May, 1970), pp. 290-291; George Baring, 175
        wds., cp. pub.

7499 BRITISH CINEMA — AN ILLUSTRATED GUIDE (Denis Gifford)
        F Comment: v. 6, n. 1 (Spring, 1970), p. 73; 50 wds., cp. pub.
        Interntl F G: v. 6 (1969), p. 271; 50 wds., pt. pub.
        Screen: v. 11, n. 2 (Mar.-Apr., 1970), p. 97; Gillian Hartnoll, 50 wds., cp.
        pub.

7500 BRITISH FILM INDUSTRY: A REPORT BY P.E.P. (Political and Economic
        Planning)
        Films in R: v. III, n. 8 (Oct., 1952), pp. 418-421; Terry Ramsaye, 1500
        wds., cp. pub.
        Quarterly of FR TV: v. VII, n. 3 (Spring, 1953), pp. 313-314; Franklin
        Fearing, 550 wds., cp. pub.

7501 BRITISH FILM INDUSTRY YEARBOOK, THE (John Sullivan, ed.)
        Sight & S: v. 17, n. 67 (Autumn, 1948), p. 152; 125 wds., cp. pub.

7502 BRITISH FILM MUSIC (John Huntley)
        Hollywood Q: v. III, n. 2 (Winter, 1947-1948); Lawrence Morton, 1200
        wds., cp. pub.
        Sight & S: v. 16, n. 63 (Autumn, 1947), p. 111; Stuart Keen, 700 wds., cp.
        pub.

7503 BRITISH FILM YEAR BOOK, THE (Peter Novle, comp.)
        Sight & S: v. 15, n. 59 (Autumn, 1946), p. 107; 250 wds., cp. pub.

        BROADS (see: Dames)

7504 BROADWAY HEARTBEAT (Bernard Sobel)
        Films in R: v. V, n. 2 (Feb., 1954), pp. 102-104; Robert Downing, 700
        wds., cp. pub.

7505 BULLS, BALLS, BiCYCLES AND ACTORS (Charles Bickford)
        Films in R: v. XVII, n. 1 (Jan., 1966), p. 45; Jeanne Stein, 225 wds., cp.
        pub.

7506 *BUNUEL (Carlos Rebolledo and Frédéric Grange)
        Interntl F G: v. 3 (1966), p. 262; 175 wds., cp. pub.

7507 *BUSTER KEATON (Marcel Oms)
        Cinema Studies: v. II, n. 1 (June, 1965), pp. 9-12; N.M.H., 1600 wds., cp.
        pub.

7508 *BUSTER KEATON (David Turconi and Francesco Savio)
        Cinema Studies: v. II, n. 1 (June, 1965), pp. 9-12; N.M.H., 1600 wds., cp.
        pub.

7509 *BUSTER KEATON (J. P. Lebel)
        Cinema Studies: v. II, n. 1 (June, 1965), pp. 9-12; N.M.H., 1600 wds., cp.
        pub.

7510 BUSTER KEATON (J. P. Lebel, trans. by P. D. Stovin)
        Cinema J: v. IX, n. 1 (Fall, 1969), pp. 53 55; John Tibbetts, 900 wds., cp.
        pub.
        F Comment: v. 6, n. 1 (Spring, 1970), p. 73; 75 wds., cp. pub.
        Interntl F G: v. 3 (1966), p. 261; 200 wds., cp. pub.

7511 BUSTER KEATON (David Robinson)
        Cinema J: v. IX, n. 1 (Fall, 1969), pp. 53-55; John Tibbetts, 900 wds., cp.
        pub.
        Films & F: v. 15, n. 6 (Mar., 1969), pp. 72-73; Sheridan Morley, 100 wds.,
        pt. pub.
        Interntl F G: v. 7 (1970), p. 395; 50 wds., pt. pub.

C

7512 CALL ME LUCKY (Bing Crosby and Pete Martin)
        Films in R: v. IV, n. 8 (Oct., 1953), pp. 437-438; Elspeth Chapin, 650 wds.,
        cp. pub.

7513 CAME THE DAWN: MEMORIES OF A FILM PIONEER (Cecil M. Hepworth)
        Films in R: v. III, n. 3 (Mar., 1952), pp. 138-140; Theodore Huff, 1500
        wds., cp. pub.
        Sight & S: v. 21, n. 1 (Aug.-Sept., 1951), p. 45; 400 wds., cp. pub.

7514 CAMERA AND I, THE (Joris Ivens)
        Cineaste: v. III, n. 4 (Spring, 1970), pp. 26-27; Bob Summers, 800 wds., cp.
        pub.
        Cinema J: v. XI, n. 1 (Fall, 1971), pp. 65-66; Peter Harcourt, 800 wds., cp.
        pub.
        F Comment: v. 7, n. 1 (Spring, 1971), p. 86; Willard Van Dyke, 750 wds.,
        cp. pub.
        F Soc Rev: v. 5, n. 6 (Feb., 1970), pp. 44-48; Gary Crowdus, 1200 wds., cp.
        pub.
        Films & F: v. 16, n. 8 (May, 1970), p. 64; Sheridan Morley, 100 wds., pt.
        pub.
        Interntl F G: v. 8 (1971), p. 435; 50 wds., pt. pub.

7515 *CARL'Z SPENSER CAPLIN (G. A. Avenarius)
        F Quarterly: v. XV, n. 1 (Fall, 1961), p. 63; Steven P. Hill, 300 wds., cp.
        pub.

7516 CASE HISTORY OF A MOVIE, A (Dore Schary, with Charles Palmer)
        Films in R: v. I, n. 8 (Nov., 1950), pp. 26-27; Henry Hart, 450 wds., cp.
        pub.
        Hollywood Q: v. V (1950-1951), pp. 420-422; Franklin Fearing, 480 wds.,
        cp. pub.

7517 CASEBOOK ON FILM, A (Charles Samuels)
        Films & F: v. 16, n. 11 (Aug., 1970), p. 64; Sheridan Morley, 75 wds., pt.
        pub.

7518 CATALOGING AND CLASSIFICATION OF CINEMA LITERATURE, THE
(Robert Steele)
F Soc Rev: Apr. (1968), pp. 39-40; Sam Kula, 600 wds., cp. pub.
Films & F: v. 14, n. 5 (Feb., 1968), p. 54; Sheridan Morley, 150 wds., pt.
pub.

7519 *CATALOGO BOLAFFI DEL CINEMA ITALIANO (Giulio Bolaffi)
Films & F: v. 13, n. 7 (Apr., 1967), p. 41; Sheridan Morley, 25 wds., pt.
pub.
Sight & S: v. 36, n. 2 (Spring, 1967), p. 104; Richard Roud, 225 wds., cp.
pub.

7520 CATALOGUE OF COPYRIGHT ENTRIES: MOTION PICTURES, 1912-1939
(Library of Congress)
Screen: v. 11, n. 4-5 (July-Oct., 1970), p. 135; Gillian Hartnoll, 75 wds., cp.
pub.

7521 CECIL B. DE MILLE (Michael Mourlet)
Interntl F G: v. 7 (1970), p. 395; 50 wds., pt. pub.

7522 CELLULOID MISTRESS, THE (Rodney Ackland and Elspeth Grant)
Films & F: v. 1, n. 4 (Jan., 1955), p. 30; John Minchinton, 100 wds., pt.
pub.
Films in R: v. VI, n. 4 (Apr., 1955), p. 200; L.V., 200 wds., cp. pub.

7523 CELLULOID MUSE: HOLLYWOOD DIRECTORS SPEAK, THE (Charles
Higham and Joel Greenberg, eds.)
Films & F: v. 16, n. 5 (Feb., 1970), p. 70; Sheridan Morley, 200 wds., pt.
pub.
Interntl F G: v. 8 (1971), p. 435; 75 wds., pt. pub.
Screen: v. 11, n. 3 (Summer, 1970), pp. 112-114; Margaret Tarratt, 1100
wds., cp. pub.
Sight & S: v. 38, n. 4 (Autumn, 1969), pp. 217-218; John Russell Taylor,
400 wds., cp. pub.

7524 CELLULOID SACRIFICE: ASPECTS OF SEX IN THE MOVIES (Alexander
Walker)
Cineaste: v. II, n. 4 (Spring, 1969), p. 23; Gary Crowdus, 150 wds., pt. pub.
Cinema: v. 4, n. 2 (Summer, 1968), p. 60; Alice Kuhns, 450 wds., cp. pub.
F Soc Rev: May (1968), p. 39; Frank Manchel, 50 wds., cp. pub.
Films & F: v. 13, n. 3 (Dec., 1966), p. 42; Sheridan Morley, 450 wds., no
pub.
Interntl F G: v. 5 (1968), p. 259; 25 wds., pt. pub.
Sight & S: v. 36, n. 1 (Winter, 1966-1967), pp. 50-51; David Robinson, 800
wds., cp. pub.

7525 CENSOR MARCHES ON: RECENT MILESTONES IN THE ADMINISTRA-
TION OF THE OBSCENITY LAW IN THE UNITED STATES
(Morris L. Ernst and Alexander Lindsey)
Sight & S: v. 16, n. 64 (Winter, 1947-1948), p. 160; John M. Smithells, 700
wds., cp. pub.

7526 CENSOR, THE DRAMA, AND THE FILM, 1900-1934, THE (Dorothy
Knowles)
Sight & S: v. 16, n. 64 (Winter, 1947-1948), p. 160; John M. Smithells, 700
wds., cp. pub.

7527 CENSORSHIP OF THE MOVIES: THE SOCIAL AND POLITICAL CON-
TROL OF A MASS MEDIUM (Richard S. Randall)
Cinema J: v. IX, n. 2 (Spring, 1970), pp. 53-55; Richard Dyer MacCann,
1200 wds., cp. pub.
F Comment: v. 5, n. 2 (Spring, 1969), p. 90; Robert Steele, 650 wds., cp.
pub.

7528 CENSORSHIP: THE SEARCH FOR THE OBSCENE (Morris L. Ernst and
Alan U. Schwartz)
F Quarterly: v. XVIII, n. 1 (Fall, 1964), p. 58; Ernest Callenbach, 125 wds.,
cp. pub.

7529 *CENSURE DES FILMS ET L'ADMISSION DES ENFANTS AU CINEMA A
         TRAVERS LE MONDE, LA (L. Lunders)
         Cinema Studies: v. I, n. 5 (Sept., 1962), pp. 114-115; N.M.H., 800 wds., cp.
         pub.

7530 *CENT VISAGES DU CINEMA, LES (Marcel Lapierre)
         Sight & S: v. 18, n. 70 (Summer, 1949), pp. 96-97; Colin Borland, 300
         wds., cp. pub.

7531 CHAPLIN: LAST OF THE CLOWNS (Parker Tyler)
         Sight & S: v. 17, n. 66 (Summer, 1948), p. 106; Herman G. Weingerg, 400
         wds., cp. pub.

7532 CHAPLIN, THE IMMORTAL TRAMP (R. J. Minney)
         Sight & S: v. 24, n. 2 (Oct.-Dec., 1954), p. 106; David Robinson, 400 wds.,
         cp. pub.

       CHARLES LAUGHTON STORY, THE (see: The Laughton Story)

7533 CHARLIE (Ben Hecht)
         Films in R: v. IX, n. 4 (Apr., 1958), pp. 214-215; Jack Spears, 450 wds., cp.
         pub.

7534 CHARLIE CHAPLIN (Theodore Huff)
         Films in R: v. II, n. 4 (Apr., 1951), pp. 39-41; Gilbert Seldes, 1000 wds.,
         cp. pub.
         Quarterly of FR TV: v. VI, n. 1 (Fall, 1951), pp. 103-104; Franklin
         Fearing, 250 wds., cp. pub.
         Sight & S: v. 21, n. 2 (Oct.-Dec., 1951), pp. 95-96; H. D. Waley, 600 wds.,
         cp. pub.

7535 CHARLIE CHAPLIN (Marcel Martin)
         F Quarterly: v. XXI, n. 4 (Summer, 1968), pp. 55-56; Claire Clouzot, 325
         wds., cp. pub.
         Films & F: v. 13, n. 4 (Jan., 1967), p. 57; Sheridan Morley, 100 wds., pt.
         pub.
         Interntl F G: v. 5 (1968), p. 259; 25 wds., pt. pub.

7536 *CHARLOT (Jean Mitry)
         F Culture: v. 3, n. 2 (1957), p. 22; Herman G. Weinberg, 700 wds., cp. pub.

7537 CHILD OF THE CENTURY, A (Ben Hecht)
         Films in R: v. V, n. 7 (Aug.-Sept., 1954), pp. 374-375; Isaac Bickerstaff,
         400 wds., cp. pub.

7538 CHILD STARS, THE (Norman Zierald)
         Films & F: v. 13, n. 3 (Dec., 1966), p. 42; Sheridan Morley, 250 wds., no
         pub.
         Films in R: v. XVII, n. 7 (Aug.-Sept., 1966), p. 437; Robert Downing, 200
         wds., cp. pub.
         Sight & S: v. 36, n. 1 (Winter, 1966-1967), pp. 50-51; David Robinson, 800
         wds., pt. pub.

7539 CHILDREN AND FILMS (Mary Field)
         Sight & S: v. 24, n. 1 (July-Sept., 1954), p. 49; Janet Hills, 900 wds., cp.
         pub.

7540 CHILDREN AS FILM MAKERS (John Lidstone and Don McIntosh)
         Films & F: v. 17, n. 3 (Dec., 1970), p. 64; Sheridan Morley, 100 wds., pt.
         pub.

7541 CHILDREN'S ATTENDENCE AT MOTION PICTURES (Edgar Dale)
         F Comment: v. 7, n. 2 (Summer, 1971), pp. 70-72; Garth Jowett, 2200
         wds., cp. pub.

7542 CHILDREN'S SLEEP (Samuel Renshaw, Vernon L. Miller and Dorothy P.
         Marquis)
         F Comment: v. 7, n. 2 (Summer, 1971), pp. 70-72; Garth Jowett, 2200
         wds., cp. pub.

7543 CINE-FILM PROJECTION (Cecil A. Hill)
      Sight & S: v. 18, n. 70 (Summer, 1949), p. 98; C. R. Gibbs, 650 wds., cp.
      pub.

7544 *CINE FRANCES: ORIGEN, HISTORIA, CRITICA (Manuel Villegas Lopez)
      Sight & S: v. 17, n. 65 (Spring, 1948), p. 52; Norah Lewis, 400 wds., cp.
      pub.

7545 CINEMA, THE (Stanley Reed)
      Sight & S: v. 22, n. 1 (July-Sept., 1952), E. Francis Mills, 350 wds., cp. pub.

7546 CINEMA (Thomas Wiseman)
      Sight & S: v. 33, n. 4 (Autumn, 1964), p. 44; Brenda Davies, 275 wds., cp.
      pub.

7547 *CINEMA, LE (J Segers and J. Dereymaeker)
      Interntl F G: v. 9 (1972), p. 461; 50 wds., pt. pub.

7548 CINEMA AS ART, THE (Ralph Stephenson and J. R. Debrix)
      F Soc Rev: Dec. (1966), p. 36; Michael Budd, 400 wds., cp. pub.
      Interntl F G: v. 4 (1967), p. 273; 100 wds., pt. pub.

7549 *CINEMA BURLESQUE AMERICAIN 1912-1930, LE (Jacques Chevallier)
      Cinema Studies: v. II, n. 1 (June, 1965), pp. 9-12; N.M.H., 1600 wds., cp.
      pub.

7550 *CINEMA CATTOLICO: DOCUMENTI DELLA SANTA SEDE SUL CINEMA
      (Enrico Baragli, S. J., comp.)
      Cinema Studies: v. I, n. 3 (Aug., 1961), pp. 63-64; N.M.H., 900 wds., cp.
      pub.

7551 *CINEMA DELLA REALTA (Giuseppe Ferrara and Giancarlo Tesi)
      F Culture: v. 1, n. 4 (Summer, 1955), p. 29; George N. Fenin, 325 wds., cp.
      pub.

7552 *CINEMA DEVIENT UN ART, LE (Georges Sadoul)
      Films in R: v. III, n. 6 (June-July, 1952), pp. 298-299; Monica Stirling, 650
      wds., cp. pub.

7553 *CINEMA DOPO LA GUERRA A VENEZIA, IL (Flavia Paulon, ed.)
      F Culture: v. 3, n. 1 (1957), p. 33; G. N. Fenin, 250 wds., cp. pub.

7554 *CINEMA DU FRANCE (Roger Regent)
      Hollywood Q: v. IV, n. 2 (Winter, 1949), pp. 213; Franklin Fearing, 100
      wds., cp. pub.
      Sequence: n. 7 (Spring, 1949), pp. 43-44; Gavin Lambert, 1200 wds., pt.
      pub.

7555 *CINEMA E RESISTENZA (Giovanni Vento and Massimo Mida)
      F Quarterly: v. XIII, n. 2 (Winter, 1959), p. 63; Letizia Ciotti Milier, 250
      wds., cp. pub.

7556 *CINEMA ENCYCLOPEDIE, LE (Georges Charensol)
      F Heritage: v. 2, n. 1 (Fall, 1966), pp. 30-32; Herman G. Weinberg, 900
      wds., cp. pub.

7557 *CINEMA ET LE SACRE, LE (Henri Agel and the Abbé Ayfre)
      Interntl F G: v. 2 (1965), p. 256; 75 wds., pt. pub.

7558 *CINEMA ET LITTERATURE (Etienne Fuzellier)
      Interntl F G: v. 3 (1966), pp. 261-262; 175 wds., cp. pub.

7559 CINEMA EYE, CINEMA EAR—SOME KEY FILM MAKERS OF THE
      SIXTIES (John Russell Taylor)
      F Comment: v. 3, n. 3 (Summer, 1965), pp. 76-78; Adrienne Mancia, 1300
      wds., cp. pub.
      F Quarterly: v. XVIII, n. 1 (Fall, 1964), p. 59; Ernest Callenbach, 150 wds.,
      cp. pub.
      F Soc Rev: May (1966), p. 21; Stuart A. Selby, 850 wds., cp. pub.
      Interntl F G: v. 2 (1965), p. 250; 175 wds., pt. pub.

N Y Rev of Books: v. III, n. 10 (Dec. 3, 1964), pp. 16-18; A. Alvazer, 2000 wds., pt. pub.
Sight & S: v. 33, n. 4 (Autumn, 1964), pp. 208-209; Jacques Brunius, 1000 wds., cp. pub.

7560 CINEMA IN PAKISTAN, THE (Alamgir Kabir)
    Interntl F B: v. 8 (1971), p. 435; 50 wds., pt. pub.

7561 *CINEMA ITALIANO, OGGI (Alessandro Blasetti and Gian Luigi Rondi)
    Films in R: v. II, n. 7 (Aug.-Sept., 1951), p. 47; Lauro Venturi, 400 wds., cp. pub.

7562 *CINEMA ITALIANO, IL (Carlo Lizzani)
    Films in R: v. IV, n. 9 (Nov., 1953), pp. 489-490; Lauro Venturi, 450 wds., cp. pub.

7563 *CINEMA ITALIEN, LE (Pierre Leprohon)
    Interntl F G: v. 5 (1968), p. 259; 25 wds., pt. pub.

7564 *CINEMA ITALIEN, LE (Freddy Buache)
    Interntl F G: v. 8 (1971), pp. 435; 437; 50 wds., pt. pub.

7565 *CINEMA JAPONAIS, LE
    F Culture: v. 1, n. 5-6 (Winter, 1955), p. 38; H. G. Weinberg, 150 wds., cp. pub.

7566 *CINEMA MODERNE, LE (Gilles Jacob)
    Sight & S: v. 33, n. 3 (Summer, 1964), p. 154; Tom Milne, 700 wds., cp. pub.

7567 *CINEMA MUTO SOVIETICO, IL (Nikolàj Lébedev)
    Cinema Studies: v. I, n. 9 (June, 1964), pp. 233-235; N.M.H., 1100 wds., cp. pub.

7568 *CINEMA NEOREALISTICO ITALIANO, IL (Giulio Cesare Castello)
    F Culture: v. 2, n. 2 (1956), p. 32; G. N. Fenin, 200 wds., cp. pub.

7569 CINEMA 1950 (Roger Manvell, ed.)
    Films in R: v. I, n. 7 (Oct., 1950), pp. 27-29; Richard Griffith, 900 wds., cp. pub.
    Sight & S: v. 19, n. 5 (July, 1950), p. 222; James Morgan, 400 wds., cp. pub.

7570 CINEMA 1951 (Roger Manvell and R. K. Neilson-Baxter, eds.)
    Sight & S: v. 20, n. 2 (June, 1951), p. 64; Alan Brien, 550 wds., cp. pub.

7571 CINEMA 1952 (Roger Manvell, ed.)
    Films in R: v. IV, n. 2 (Feb., 1953), pp. 102-103; Gerald Weales, 600 wds., cp. pub.

7572 CINEMA OF ALAIN RESNAIS, THE (Roy Armes)
    F Comment: v. 6, n. 1 (Spring, 1970), p. 73; 100 wds., cp. pub.
    Films & F: v. 14, n. 9 (June, 1968), p. 42; 150 wds., pt. pub.
    Interntl F G: v. 6 (1969), p. 271; 50 wds., pt. pub.

7573 CINEMA OF ALFRED HITCHCOCK, THE (Peter Bogdanovich)
    F Quarterly: v. XVI, n. 4 (Summer, 1963), p. 63; 50 wds., cp. pub.
    Interntl F G: v. 1 (1964), p. 228; 30 wds., pt. pub.

7574 CINEMA OF CARL DREYER, THE (Tom Milne)
    F Comment: v. 7, n. 3 (Fall, 1971), pp. 71-73; David Bordwell, 1600 wds., cp. pub.
    Interntl F G: v. 8 (1971), p. 437; 50 wds., pt. pub.

7575 CINEMA OF FRANCOIS TRUFFAUT, THE (Graham Petrie)
    Films & F: v. 17, n. 5 (Feb., 1971), p. 64; Sheridan Morley, 150 wds., pt. pub.
    Interntl F G: v. 8 (1971), p. 437; 50 wds., pt. pub.

7576 CINEMA OF FRITZ LANG, THE (Paul Jensen)
     Films & F: v. 16, n. 2 (Nov., 1969), pp. 70-71; Sheridan Morley, 150 wds.,
          cp. pub.
     Interntl F G: v. 7 (1970), p. 396; 50 wds., pt. pub.

7577 CINEMA OF JOHN FRANKENHEIMER, THE (Gerald Pratley)
     Films & F: v. 16, n. 9 (June, 1970), p. 124; Sheridan Morley, 650 wds., pt.
          pub.
     Interntl F G: v. 7 (1970), p. 396; 50 wds., pt. pub.
     Take One: v. 2, n. 9 (1970), p. 29; Joe Medjuck, 200 wds., cp. pub.

7578 CINEMA OF JOSEF VON STERNBERG, THE (Al Milgrom, ed.)
     F Comment: v. IV, n. 2-3 (Fall-Winter, 1967), pp. 118-122; Kirk Bond,
          1100 wds., cp. pub.

7579 CINEMA OF JOSEF VON STERNBERG, THE (John Baxter)
     Interntl F G: v. 9 (1972), p. 459; 50 wds., pt. pub.

7580 CINEMA OF JOSEPH LOSEY, THE (James Leahy)
     F Culture: n. 50-51 (Fall-Winter, 1970), p. 62; 100 wds., cp. pub.
     F Soc Rev: v. 4, n. 4; pp. 40-41; Frank Manchel, 900 wds., cp. pub.
     Interntl F G: v. 5 (1968), p. 261; 25 wds., pt. pub.

7581 CINEMA OF OTTO PREMINGER, THE (Gerald Pratley)
     Interntl F G: v. 9 (1972), p. 459; 50 wds., pt. pub.

7582 CINEMA OF ROMAN POLANSKI, THE (Ivan Butler)
     Interntl F G: v. 8 (1971), p. 437; 50 wds., pt. pub.
     Screen: v. 12, n. 1, pp. 59-60; Colin McArthur, 800 wds., cp. pub.

7583 *CINEMA — PAR CEUX QUI LE FONT, LE (Denis Marion)
     Sight & S: v. 18, n. 71 (Dec., 1949), p. 30; Colin Borland, 350 wds., cp.
          pub.

7584 *CINEMA SELON HITCHCOCK, LE (Francois Truffaut)
     Interntl F G: v. 5 (1968), p. 261; 25 wds., pt. pub.

7585 *CINEMATOGRAFIA NELLA GIURISPRUDENZA, LA (Augusto Fragola)
     Cinema Studies: v. II, n. 5 (Sept., 1967), p. 90; N.M.H., 230 wds., cp. pub.

7586 *CINQUANTE ANS DE CINEMA FRANCAIS (Pierre Leprohon)
     Films in R: v. V, n. 10 (Dec., 1954), p. 548; Gerald D. McDonald, 200 wds.,
          cp. pub.

7587 CLASSICS OF HORROR—AN ILLUSTRATED HISTORY OF THE
          HORROR FILM (Carlos Clarens)
     Cineaste: v. I, n. 2 (Fall, 1967), pp. 26-27; Timothy Bay, 1000 wds., pt.
          pub.

7588 CLASSICS OF THE FILM (Arthur Lennig, ed.)
     F Heritage: v. 1, n. 4 (Summer, 1966), pp. 38-39; Frank Manchel, 300 wds.,
          cp. pub.

7589 CLASSICS OF THE FOREIGN FILM (Parker Tyler)
     F Quarterly: v. XVII, n. 2 (Winter, 1963-1964), p. 60; Ernest Callenbach,
          250 wds., cp. pub.

7590 CLASSICS OF THE SILENT SCREEN: A PICTORIAL TREASURY (Joe
          Franklin)
     Films in R: v. XI, n. 3 (Mar., 1960), pp. 179-180; Gerald D. McDonald, 600
          wds., cp. pub.

7591 CLAUDE CHABROL (Robin Wood and Michael Walker)
     Focus on F: n. 6 (Spring, 1971), p. 61; Allen Eyles, 75 wds., cp. pub.
     Interntl F G: v. 9 (1972), pp. 459, 461; 50 wds., pt. pub.
     Sight & S: v. 40, n. 2 (Spring, 1971), p. 110; Tom Milne, 1200 wds., cp.
          pub.

7592 CLEOPATRA PAPERS, THE (Jack Brodsky and Nathan Weiss)
        F Comment: v. 2, n. 3 (Summer, 1964), p. 62; Harry Feldman, 350 wds.,
            cp. pub.
        F Culture: n. 31 (Winter, 1963-1964), p. 68; Herman G. Weinberg, 75 wds.,
            cp. pub.

7593 CLOSE UP (1927-1933)
        Take One: v. 2, n. 12 (1971), p. 30; Herman G. Weinberg, 500 wds., cp.
            pub.

7594 CLOWN PRINCES AND COURT JESTERS (Kalton C. Lahue and Samuel Gill)
        Interntl F G: v. 8 (1971); 50 wds., pt. pub.

7595 *COCKATRICE (Wolf Mankowitz)
        Films in R: v. XIV, n. 9 (Nov., 1963), p. 559; Flavia Wharton, 200 wds., cp.
            pub.

7596 COCTEAU (Francis Steegmuller)
        N Y Rev of Books: v. XVI, n. 1 (Jan. 28, 1971), pp. 29-33; Robert
            Mazzocco, 4500 wds., pt. pub.

7597 COCTEAU ON THE FILM: A CONVERSATION RECORDED BY ANDRE
            FRAIGNEAU (Jean Cocteau and Andre Fraigneau)
        Sight & S: v. 23, n. 4 (Apr.-Juen, 1954), pp. 218-219; Alexander
            Mackendrick, 950 wds., co. pub.

7598 *CODICE DELLO SPETTACOLO (Enzo Capaccioli and Pasquale Russe)
        Cinema Studies: v. I, n. 9 (June, 1964), pp. 243-244; N.M.H., 725 wds., cp.
            pub.

7599 COLDITZ STORY, THE (P. R. Reid)
        Films & F: v. 1, n. 6 (Mar., 1955), p. 30; John Minchinton, 100 wds., pt.
            pub.

7600 COLLECTING CLASSIC FILMS (Kalton C. Lahue)
        Films In R: v. XXI, n. 8 (Oct., 1970), pp. 501-502; Samuel A. Peeples, 150
            wds., cp. pub.

7601 COLOUR CINEMATOGRAPHY (Adrian Cornwell-Clyne)
        Films in R: v. III, n. 2 (Feb., 1952), p. 91; Joseph V. Noble, 350 wds., cp.
            pub.

7602 COMEDY FILMS (John Montgomery)
        Sight & S v. 23, n. 4 (Apr.-June, 1954), p. 219; Liam O'Laoghaire, 300
            wds., cp. pub.

7603 COMMENTAIRES (Chris Marker)
        Sight & S: v. 31, n. 3 (Summer, 1962), pp. 152-153; Jean Queval, 1000
            wds., cp. pub.

7604 COMMUNICATING IDEAS TO THE PUBLIC (Stephen E. Fitzgerald)
        Hollywood Q: v. V (1950-1951), pp. 316-317; Franklin Fearning, 140 wds.,
            cp. pub.

7605 COMPETITIVE CINEMA, A (Terence Kelly with Graham Norton and George
            Perry)
        F Quarterly: v. XXI, n. 1 (Fall, 1967), pp. 62-64; Peter Cowie, 1000 wds.,
            cp. pub.
        Interntl F G: v. 5 (1968), p. 261; 10 wds., pt. pub.
        Sight & S: v. 35, n. 4 (Autumn, 1966), p. 205; Ian Wright, 650 wds., cp.
            pub.

7606 COMPLETE TECHNIQUE OF MAKING FILMS, THE (Pierre Monier)
        Am Cinematog: v. 41, n. 11 (Nov., 1960), p. 646; 125 wds., pt. pub.

7607 COMPLETE WORKS OF AKIRA KUROSAWA, THE (Kinema Jumpo Sha
            Co.)
        F Quarterly: v. XXV, n. 4 (Summer, 1972), pp. 39-40; Donald Richie, 250
            wds., cp. pub.

7608 COMPOSERS IN AMERICA (Claire R. Reis)
Hollywood Q: v. III, n. 1 (Fall, 1947), pp. 101-104; Lawrence Morton, 1200 wds., cp. pub.

7609 COMPOSING FOR THE FILMS (Hanns Eisler)
Hollywood Q: v. III, n. 2 (Winter, 1947-1948), pp. 208-211; Lawrence Morton, 1200 wds., cp. pub.
Sight & S: v. 21, n. 4 (Apr.-June, 1952), pp. 182-183; Antony Hopkins, 700 wds., cp. pub.

7610 CONCISE HISTORY OF THE CINEMA, A (Peter Cowie)
Interntl F G: v. 9 (1972), p. 461; 50 wds., pt. pub.

7611 CONFESSIONS OF A CULTIST: ON THE CINEMA, 1955-1969 (Andrew Sarris)
F Quarterly: v. XXIV, n. 3 (Spring, 1971), pp. 25-26; Ernest Callenbach, 300 wds., cp. pub.
F Soc Rev: v. 6, n. 6 (Feb., 1971), pp. 47-49; Michael Sragow, 1000 wds., cp. pub.
Sight & S: v. 40, n. 1 (Winter, 1970-1971), p. 54; Penelope Houston, 700 wds., cp. pub.

7612 CONTEMPORARY CINEMA, THE (Penelope Houston)
F Comment: v. 2, n. 3 (Summer, 1964), pp. 61-62; James Blue, 450 wds., cp. pub.
F Quarterly: v. XVII, n. 4 (Summer, 1964), p. 63; Ernest Callenbach, 75 wds., cp. pub.

7613 CONTEMPORARY POLISH CINEMATOGRAPHY (Wladislaw Banaszkiewicz)
Cinema Studies: v. I, n. 8 (Dec., 1963), pp. 205-207; John Minchinton, 1300 wds., cp. pub.
F Quarterly: v. XVIII, n. 2 (Winter, 1964), pp. 60-61; Michael Klein, 800 wds., cp. pub.

7614 CONTINUED NEXT WEEK: A HISTORY OF THE MOVING PICTURE SERIAL (Kalton C. Lahue)
Cinema Studies: v. II, n. 1 (June, 1965), pp. 12-13; N.M.H., 850 wds., cp. pub.
F Comment: v. 3, n. 2 (Spring, 1965), pp. 79-80; William K. Everson, 1100 wds., cp. pub.
Films in R: v. XVI, n. 5 (May, 1965), pp. 306-307; Edward Connor, 525 wds., cp. pub.

7615 CONTINUITY GIRL (Angela Mack)
Films & F: v. 4, n. 7 (Apr., 1958), p. 33; Martin Gray, 50 wds., pt. pub.

7616 CONTROL TECHNIQUES IN FILM PROCESSING (Society of Motion Picture and Television Engineers)
Am Cinematog: v. 41, n. 10 (Oct., 1960), p. 588; 150 wds., pt. pub.

7617 CONVERSATIONS (Don Shay)
Films in R: v. XXI, n. 5 (May, 1970), p. 291; Alice H. Witham, 250 wds., cp. pub.

7618 *CONVERSION AUX IMAGES? (Amédée Ayfre)
Interntl F G: v. 3 (1966), p. 261; 200 wds., cp. pub.

7619 COPINGER AND SKONE JAMES ON COPYRIGHT (F. E. Skone James and E. P. Skone James)
Cinema Studies: v. II, n. 2 (June, 1966), pp. 41-42; N.M.H., 750 wds., cp. pub.

7620 COPYRIGHT AND ANTITRUST (Joseph Taubman)
Cinema Studies: v. I, n. 7 (June, 1963), pp. 180-182; N.M.H., 1000 wds., cp. pub.

7621 COUNTLESS TREASURES ACQUIRED FROM METRO-GOLDWYN-MAYER, THE (5 catalogues)
F Comment: v. 6, n. 3 (Fall, 1970), pp. 73-74; Herman G. Weinberg, 1000 wds., cp. pub.

7622 CRAFT OF FILM, THE (J. David Fisher)
      Films & F: v. 16, n. 10 (July, 1970), p. 64; Sheridan Morley, 150 wds., pt.
        pub.
      Interntl F G: v. 8 (1971), p. 437; 75 wds., pt. pub.

7623 CRAZY MIRROR: HOLLYWOOD COMEDY AND THE AMERICAN IMAGE
      (Raymond Durgnat)
      F Soc Rev: v. 6, n. 3 (Nov., 1970), pp. 47-48; Jeff Sweet, 600 wds., cp.
        pub.
      Films & F: v. 15, n. 8 (May, 1969), p. 74; Sheridan Morley, 150 wds., pt.
        pub.
      Interntl F G: v. 7 (1970), p. 395; 50 wds., pt. pub.
      Screen: v. 11, n. 2 (Mar.-Apr., 1970), pp. 92-95; Donald W. McCaffrey,
        1600 wds., pt. pub.

7624 CRAZY SUNDAYS: F. SCOTT FITZGERALD IN HOLLYWOOD (Aaron
      Latham)
      Interntl F G: v. 9 (1972), p. 461; 50 wds., pt. pub.

7625 CREATIVE FILM-MAKING (Kirk Smallman)
      Films & F: v. 16, n. 6 (Mar., 1970), p. 74; Sheridan Morley, 100 wds., pt.
        pub.

7626 CRISIS OF A BRITISH FILM, THE
      Sight & S: v. 18, n. 70 (Summer, 1949), p. 97; Peter Plaskitt, 250 wds., cp.
        pub.

7627 CRITICISM AND CENSORSHIP (Walter Kerr)
      Films in R: v. VIII, n. 6 (June-July, 1957), pp. 289-290; Henry Hart, 175
        wds., cp. pub.

7628 CUKOR AND CO. (Gary Carey)
      F Quarterly: v. XXV, n. 1 (Fall, 1971), pp. 57-58; Joseph McBride, 900
        wds., cp. pub.

7629 CULTURAL REVOLUTION: A MARXIST ANALYSIS, THE (Irwin Silber)
      Cineaste: v. IV, n. 4 (Spring, 1971), pp. 31-32; Bill Nichols, 1100 wds., cp.
        pub.

D

7630 D. W. GRIFFITH, FILM MASTER (Iris Barry)
      F Comment: v. 3, n. 3 (Summer, 1965), pp. 78-79; Lewis Jacobs, 700 wds.,
        cp. pub.
      F Soc Rev: Dec. (1965), pp. 22-23; Harvey Deneroff, 475 wds., cp. pub.

7631 D. W. GRIFFITH: HIS LIFE AND WORK (Robert M. Henderson)
      F Quarterly: v. XXV, n. 4 (Summer, 1972), pp. 37-38; 150 wds., cp. pub.

7632 D. W. GRIFFITH: THE YEARS AT BIOGRAPHY (Robert M. Henderson)
      F Comment: v. 7, n. 1 (Spring, 1971), pp. 84, 86; David Shephard, 600
        wds., cp. pub.
      Films in R: v. XXI, n. 8 (Oct., 1970), p. 499; Alice H. Witham, 200 wds.,
        cp. pub.

7633 DAM BUSTERS, THE (Paul Brickhill)
      Films & F: v. 1, n. 6 (Mar., 1955), p. 30; John Minchinton, 100 wds., pt.
        pub.

7634 DAMES (Ian and Elisabeth Cameron)
      F Comment: v. 6, n. 1 (Spring, 1970), p. 68; Donald Staples, 250 wds., cp.
        pub.
      Films & F: v. 15, n. 9 (June, 1969), p. 68; Sheridan Morley, 175 wds., pt.
        pub.

7635 DANCE TO THE PIPER (Agnes De Mille)
        Films in R: v. III, n. 6 (June-July, 1952), pp. 293-295; Theordore Huff,
        1100 wds., cp. pub.

7636 DAYS OF THRILLS AND ADVENTURE (Alan G. Barbour)
        Films & F: v. 17, n. 5 (Feb., 1971), p. 64; Sheridan Morley, 200 wds., pt.
        pub.
        Focus on F: n. 8 (Oct., 1971), p. 61; 150 wds., cp. pub.
        Interntl F G: v. 9 (1972), p. 461; 50 wds., pt. pub.

7637 DAYS WERE TOO SHORT (Marcel Pagnol, trans. by Rita Barisse)
        Sight & S: v. 30, n. 1 (Winter, 1960-1961), p. 47; Isabel Quigly, 300 wds.,
        cp. pub.

7638 DAY WITH THE FILM MAKERS, A (Francis Rodker)
        Films in R: v. IV, n. 8 (Oct., 1953), p. 438; 100 wds., cp. pub.

7639 DECLINE OF THE CINEMA: AN ECONOMIST'S REPORT, THE (John
        Spraos)
        Cinema Studies: v. I, n. 8 (Dec., 1963), pp. 203-205; F.J.D., 1200 wds., cp.
        pub.
        F Quarterly: v. XVI, n. 4 (Summer, 1963), pp. 62-63; 50 wds., cp. pub.
        Films & F: v. 8, n. 7 (Apr., 1962), p. 45; Martin Gray, 230 wds., cp. pub.
        Sight & S: v. 31, n. 2 (Spring, 1962), pp. 100-101; Duncan Crow, 750 wds.,
        cp. pub.

7640 *DECOUVERTE DU CINEMA GREC (Aglae Mitropoulos)
        Interntl F G: v. 7 (1970), p. 395; 50 wds., pt. pub.

7641 *DEFENSE DU COURT-METRAGE FRANCAIS (Francois Porcile)
        Interntl F G: v. 4 (1967), p. 277; 100 wds., pt. pub.

7642 *DEFENSE ET ILLUSTRATION DE LA MUSIQUE DANS LE FILM (Henry
        Colpi)
        F Culture: n. 31 (Winter, 1963-1964), p. 69; Herman G. Weinberg, 100
        wds., cp. pub.

7643 DESIGN IN MOTION (John Halas and Roger Manvell)
        Sight & S: v. 31, n. 3 (Summer, 1962), p. 153; Bernard Orna, 225 wds., cp.
        pub.

7644 DESIGNING FOR FILMS (Edward Carrick)
        Films in R: v. I, n. 5 (July-Aug., 1950), pp. 38-39; Lewis Jacobs, 400 wds.,
        cp. pub.
        Sequence: n. 12 (Autumn, 1950), pp. 45-47; Laurence Irving, 1700 wds.,
        pt. pub.
        Sight & S: v. 19, n. 2 (Apr., 1950), p. 90; Catherine de la Roche, 500 wds.,
        cp. pub.

7645 DESIGNING MALE (Howard Greer)
        Films in R: v. III, n. 1 (Jan., 1952), pp. 44-45; Elspeth Chapin, 300 wds.,
        cp. pub.

7646 *DESSIN ANIME, LE (Lo Duca)
        Sequence: n. 9 (Autumn, 1949), p. 139; Peter Ericsson, 350 wds., cp. pub.

7647 *DESSIN ANIME APRES WALT DISNEY, LE (Robert Benayoun)
        Sight & S: v. 30, n. 4 (Autumn, 1961), pp. 204-205; David Robinson, 750
        wds., cp. pub.

7648 *DEUTSCHER FILM KATALOG
        F Quarterly: v. XX, n. 3 (Spring, 1967), pp. 59-60; David Stewart Hull, 325
        wds., cp. pub.

7649 *DEUTSCHER NACHKRIEGSFILM (Peter Pleyer)
        F Quarterly: v. XX, n. 3 (Spring, 1967), pp. 59-60; David Stewart Hull, 325
        wds., cp. pub.

7650 DIARY AND SUNDRY OBSERVATIONS OF THOMAS A. EDISON, THE
       (Dagobert D. Runes, ed.)
       Films in R: v. I, n. 6 (Sept., 1950), pp. 39-40; Henry Hart, 300 wds., cp.
       pub.

7651 DIARY OF A FILM (Jean Cocteau, trans, by Ronald Duncan)
       Films in R: v. I, n. 9 (Dec., 1950), pp. 44-46; Henry Hart, 750 wds., cp.
       pub.
       Sight & S: v. 19, n. 7 (Nov., 1950), pp. 300-301; Derick Grigs, 700 wds., cp.
       pub.

7652 DICTIONARY OF PHOTOGRAPHY AND MOTION PICTURE ENGINEER-
       ING (Wolfgang Grau)
       Films in R: v. IX, n. 9 (Nov., 1958), p. 532; Bradner Lacy, 200 wds., cp.
       pub.

7653 DICTIONARY OF THE CINEMA, A (Peter Graham)
       Cinema J: v. IX, n. 1 (Fall, 1969), pp. 46-47; John L. Fell, 350 wds., cp.
       pub.
       F Quarterly: v. XIX, n. 2 (Winter, 1965-1966), p. 59; 50 wds., cp. pub.
       Interntl F G: v. 6 (1969), p. 271; 50 wds., pt. pub.
       Screen: v. 11, n. 2 (Mar.-Apr., 1970), p. 97; Gillian Hartnoll, 50 wds., cp.
       pub.

7654 *DICTIONNAIRE DES CINEASTES (Georges Sandoul)
       Cinema J: v. IX, n. 1 (Fall, 1969), pp. 46-47; John L. Fell, 400 wds., cp.
       pub.
       F Soc Rev: Mar. (1966), pp. 20-21; Edwin Jahiel, 625 wds., cp. pub.

7655 *DICTIONNAIRE DES FILMS (Georges Sadoul)
       F Soc Rev: Apr. (1966), p. 8; Harvey Deneroff, 125 wds., cp. pub.

7656 *DICTIONNAIRE DU CINEMA
       Cinema Studies: v. I, n. 6 (Dec., 1962), pp. 153-154; N.M.H., 550 wds., cp.
       pub.
       Sight & S: v. 31, n. 4 (Autumn, 1962), p. 205; John Gillett, 300 wds., cp.
       pub.

7657 *DICTIONNAIRE DU CINEMA (Maurice Bessy and Jean-Louis Chardans)
       Films in R: v. XVIII, n. 8 (Oct., 1967), pp. 501-502; Jack Spears, 225 wds.,
       cp. pub.

7658 *DICTIONNAIRE DU CINEMA ET DE LA TELEVISION (Maurice Bessy and
       Jean-Louis Chardans)
       F Heritage: v. 2, n. 1 (Fall, 1966), pp. 30-32; Herman G. Weinberg, 900
       wds., cp. pub.
       Sight & S: v. 35, n. 1 (Winter, 1965-1966), p. 50; John Gillett, 450 wds.,
       cp. pub.

7659 DIETRICH — THE STORY OF A STAR (Leslie Frewin)
       F Comment: v. 5, n. 4 (Winter, 1969), p. 80; 100 wds., cp. pub.
       Films & F: v. 14, n. 9 (June, 1968), p. 42; 150 wds., pt. pub.

7660 *DIEU AU CINEMA (Amedée Ayfre)
       F Soc Rev: v. IV, n. 7 (Aug.-Sept., 1953), p. 373; Monica Stirling, 160 wds.,
       cp. pub.
       Sight & S: v. 23, n. 3 (Jan.-Mar., 1954), p. 163; Lindsay Anderson, 1000
       wds., cp. pub.

7661 DIRECTING FOR MOTION PICTURES (Terence Marner, ed.)
       Interntl F G: v. 9 (1972), p. 461; 50 wds., pt. pub.

7662 DIRECTOR — A GUIDE TO MODERN THEATRE PRACTICE, THE (W. A.
       Gregory)
       Cineaste: v. II, n. 2 (Fall, 1968), pp. 18-19; Gary Crowdus, 200 wds., pt.
       pub.

7663 DISCIPLE AND HIS DEVIL, THE (Valerie Pascal)
       Focus on F: n. 10 (Summer, 1972), p. 62; Allen Eyles, 100 wds., cp. pub.

7664 DISCOVERY IN FILM (Robert Heyer and Anthony Meyer)
      Screen: v. 11, n. 4-5 (July-Oct., 1970), pp. 131-132; Jim Hillier, 600 wds.,
         cp. pub.

7665 DISCOVERY OF CINEMA, A (Thorold Dickinson)
      F Quarterly: v. XXV, n. 4 (Summer, 1972), pp. 38-39; Clyde Smith, 200
         wds., cp. pub.
      Films & F: v. 17, n. 10 (July, 1971), p. 64; Sheridan Morley, 100 wds., pt.
         pub.
      Focus on F: n. 7 (Summer, 1971), p. 59; Allen Eyles, 125 wds., cp. pub.
      Interntl F G: v. 9 (1972), pp. 461, 463; 75 wds., pt. pub.

7666 DISENCHANTED, THE (Budd Schulberg)
      Hollywood Q: v. V (1950-1951), pp. 420-421; Franklin Fearing, 360 wds.,
         cp. pub.

7667 DISNEY VERSION, THE (Richard Schickel)
      Cinema J: v. VIII, n. 2 (Spring, 1969), pp. 32-33; John Tibbetts, 750 wds.,
         cp. pub.
      F Comment: v. 5, n. 3 (Fall, 1969), p. 74; Cecile Starr, 1000 wds., cp. pub.
      F Quarterly: v. XXI, n. 4 (Summer, 1968), p. 56; 50 wds., cp. pub.
      F Soc Rev: v. 4, n. 1 Sept., 1968), pp. 44-45; Frank Manchel, 1000 wds.,
         cp. pub.
      Films & F: v. 15, n. 3 (Dec., 1968), p. 65; Sheridan Morley, 150 wds., pt.
         pub.
      Films & F: v. 15, n. 4 (Jan., 1969), p. 56; David Rider, 900 wds., no pub.
      Films in R: v. XIX, n. 10 (Dec., 1968), p. 643; 75 wds., cp. pub.
      Sight & S: v. 38, n. 1 (Winter, 1968-1969), p. 52; Penelope Houston, 600
         wds., cp. pub.

7668 *DIVISMO: MITOLOGIA DEL CINEMA, IL (Giulio Cesare Castello)
      F Culture: v. IV, n. 1 (Jan., 1958), p. 22; George N. Fenin, 275 wds., cp.
         pub.
      Films in R: v. IX, n. 2 (Feb., 1958), p. 99; Romano V. Tozzi, 250 wds., cp.
         pub.

7669 DO YOU SLEEP IN THE NUDE? (Rex Reed)
      Films & F: v. 16, n. 6 (Mar., 1970), p. 74; Sheridan Morley, 200 wds., pt.
         pub.
      Screen: v. 11, n. 2 (Mar.-Apr., 1970), p. 95; 100 wds., cp. pub.

7670 DOCTOR AND THE DEVILS, THE (Dylan Thomas)
      Sight & S: v. 23, n. 2 (Oct.-Dec., 1953), p. 108; James Hanley, 900 wds.,
         cp. pub.

7671 DOCUMENTARY FILM (Paul Rotha, with Richard Griffith and Sinclair Read)
      Films: v. I, n. 1 (Nov., 1939), pp. 106-109; Arthur Rosenheimer, Jr., 1100
         wds., cp. pub.
      Sight & S: v. 22, n. 2 (Oct.-Dec., 1952), p. 93; John Grierson, 1600 wds.,
         cp. pub.

7672 DOCUMENTARY IN AMERICAN TELEVISION (A. William Bluem)
      Am Cinematog: v. 46, n. 1 (Jan., 1965), p. 24; 125 wds., cp. pub.
      F Comment: v. 3, n. 4 (Fall, 1965), p. 75; Willard Van Dyke, 200 wds., cp.
         pub.
      F Lib Quarterly: v. 1, n. 1 (Winter, 1967-1968), p. 56; Richard Dyer
         MacCann, 1400 wds., pt. pub.
      F Quarterly: v. XIX, n. 2 (Winter, 1965-1966), p. 58; Ernest Callenbach,
         400 wds., cp. pub.

7673 DOCUMENTARY TRADITION, THE (Lewis Jacobs)
      F Quarterly: v. XXV, n. 4 (Summer, 1972), p. 39; 125 wds., cp. pub.

7674 *DOCUMENTS DE CINEMA
      Interntl F G: v. 1 (1964), p. 233; 75 wds., pt. pub.

7675 *DOLCE VITA, LA (Federico Fellini and Lo Duca)
      Sight & S: v. 30, n. 1 (Winter, 1960-1961), p. 47; John Gillett, 125 wds.,
         cp. pub.

7676 DON CAMILLO'S DILEMMA (Giovanni Guareschi)
      Films & F: v. 1, n. 2 (Nov., 1954), p. 30; John Minchinton, 75 wds., pt.
      pub.

7677 DON'T FALL OFF THE MOUNTAIN (Shirley MacLaine)
      Films & F: v. 17, n. 8 (May, 1971), p. 136; Sheridan Morley, 75 wds., pt.
      pub.
      Films & F: v. 17, n. 10 (July, 1971), p. 64; Sheridan Morley, 125 wds., pt.
      pub.

7678 DON'T SAY YES UNTIL I FINISH TALKING: A BIOGRAPHY OF
      DARRYL F. ZANUCK (Mel Gussow)
      F Soc Rev: v. VII, n. 4 (Dec., 1971), pp. 45, 48, 50; Foster Hirsch, 1200
      wds., cp. pub.
      Films in R: v. XXII, n. 7 (Aug.-Sept., 1971), pp. 435-436; Clark Davidson,
      150 wds., cp. pub.

7679 DOUGLAS FAIRBANKS: THE FOURTH MUSKETEER (Ralph Hancock and
      Letitia Fairbanks)
      Films in R: v. IV, n. 6 (June-July, 1953), pp. 308-310; Robert Downing,
      800 wds., cp. pub.
      Quarterly of FR TV: v. VIII, n. 2 (Winter, 1953), pp. 208-209; Franklin
      Fearing, 200 wds., cp. pub.
      Sight & S: v. 23, n. 3 (Jan.-Mar., 1954), pp. 163-164; David Robinson, 600
      wds., cp. pub.

7680 DOVJENKO (Luda and Jean Schnitzer)
      Interntl F G: v. 5 (1968), p. 201, 25 wds., pt. pub.

7681 DRAWN AND QUARTERED (Richard Winnington)
      Sequence: n. 7 (Spring, 1949), pp. 43-44; Gavin Lambert, 1200 wds., pt.
      pub.
      Sight & S: v. 17, n. 68 (Winter, 1948-1949), p. 197; Alan A. Richardson,
      275 wds., cp. pub.

7682 DREAMS AND THE DREAMERS, THE (Hollis Alpert)
      F Comment: v. 1, n. 6 (Fall, 1963), pp. 55-56; Gordon Hitchens, 225 wds.,
      cp. pub.
      F Quarterly: v. XVI, n. 4 (Summer, 1963), p. 62; Ernest Callenbach, 150
      wds., cp. pub.

7683 DREAMS FOR SALE (Kalton C. Lahue)
      Interntl F G: v. 9 (1972), p. 463; 50 wds., pt. pub.

7684 DRESS DOCTOR, THE (Edith Head, with Jane Kesner Ardmore)
      Films & F: v. 9, n. 2 (Nov., 1962), p. 73; Martin Gray, 50 wds., pt. pub.
      Films in R: v. X, n. 3 (Mar., 1959), p. 180; Diana Willing Cope, 200 wds.,
      cp. pub.

7685 *DREYER (Jean Sémolué)
      Interntl F G: v. 1 (1964), p. 228; 50 wds., pt. pub.

7686 DWIGHT MACDONALD ON MOVIES (Dwight Macdonald)
      Cinema J: v. IX, n. 2 (Spring, 1970), pp. 55-56; Richard Geary, 900 wds.,
      cp. pub.
      F Comment: v. 6, n. 3 (Fall, 1970), p. 72; Foster Hirsch, 1200 wds., cp.
      pub.
      F Quarterly: v. XXIV, n. 3 (Spring, 1971), p. 26; Ernest Callenbach, 250
      wds., cp. pub.
      F Soc Rev: v. 5, n. 4 (Dec., 1969), pp. 45-46; Michael Sragow, 400 wds., cp.
      pub.
      Screen: v. 11, n. 6 (Nov.-Dec., 1970), pp. 90-92; Jim Hillier, 1200 wds., pt.
      pub.
      Sight & S: v. 39, n. 2 (Spring, 1970), pp. 108-109; Philip French, 850 wds.,
      cp. pub.
      Take One: v. 2, n. 12 (1971), pp. 29-30; Glen Henter, 150 wds., cp. pub.

7687 DYNAMICS OF THE FILM (Joseph and Harry Feldman)
      Films in R: v. III, n. 4 (Apr., 1952), p. 202; Henry Hart, 200 wds., cp. pub.
      Quarterly of FR TV: v. VII, n. 2 (Winter, 1952), pp. 213-214 300 wds., cp.
      pub.

E

7688 EARLY AMERICAN CINEMA (Anthony Slide)
  Films & F: v. 17, n. 9 (June, 1971), p. 92; Sheridan Morley, 250 wds., pt.
    pub.
  Interntl F G: v. 8 (1971), p. 437; 50 wds., pt. pub.

7689 EASTERN EUROPE (Nina Hibbin)
  Screen: v. 11, n. 2 (Mar.-Apr., 1970), p. 98; Gillian Hartnoll, 50 wds., cp.
    pub.
  Interntl F G: v. 7 (1970), p. 395; 50 wds., pt. pub.

7690 EASY THE HARD WAY (Joe Pasternak with David Chandler)
  Films in R: v. VII, n. 10 (Dec., 1956), p. 535; Jack Spears, 250 wds., cp.
    pub.

7691 ECONOMIC CONTROL OF THE MOTION PICTURE INDUSTRY (Mae D.
    Huettig)
  Hollywood Q: v. I, n. 1 (Oct., 1945), pp. 127-128; Howard Estabrook, 330
    wds., cp. pub.

7692 *ECRAN DEMONIAQUE, L' (Lotte H. Eisner)
  F Comment: v. 6, n. 1 (Spring, 1970), p. 66; Kirk Bond, 450 wds., cp. pub.
  Films in R: v. III, n. 8 (Oct., 1952), pp. 422-423; Arthur Knight, 475 wds.,
    cp. pub.
  Interntl F G: v. 4 (1967), pp. 275-276; 200 wds., pt. pub.
  Quarterly of F R TV: v. VII, n. 3 (Spring, 1953), pp. 315-316; Franklin
    Fearing, 550 wds., cp. pub.
  Sight & S: v. 23, n. 1 (July-Sept., 1953), p. 50; Basil Wright, 700 wds., cp.
    pub.

7693 ED WYNN'S SON (Keenan Wynn)
  Films in R: v. XI, n. 5 (May, 1960), pp. 303-304; Robert C. Roman, 600
    wds., cp. pub.

7694 EDISON (Matthew Josephson)
  Cinema Studies: v. I, n. 4 (Dec., 1961), pp. 80-82; Brian Coe, 1100 wds.,
    cp. pub.

7695 EDISON MOTION PICTURE MYTH, THE (Gordon Hendricks)
  Cinema Studies: v. I, n. 9 (June, 1964), pp. 235-237; Brian Coe, 1000 wds.,
    cp. pub.
  F Quarterly: v. XVI, n. 2 (Winter, 1962-1963), pp. 51-52; George Pratt, 800
    wds., cp. pub.
  Films & F: v. 9, n. 2 (Nov., 1962), p. 73; Martin Gray, 200 wds., pt. pub.
  Films in R: v. XIII, n. 5 (May, 1962), pp. 307-308; Raymond Fielding, 650
    wds., cp. pub.
  Sight & S: v. 32, n. 1 (Winter, 1962-1963), p. 48; R. A. Rudorff, 500 wds.,
    cp. pub.

7696 EDUCATIONAL AND CULTURAL FILMS: EXPERIMENTS IN EUROPEAN
    CO-PRODUCTION (S. I. Van Nooten)
  Interntl F G: v. 4 (1967), p. 275; 150 wds., pt. pub.

7697 EDUCATIONAL FILMS: WRITING, DIRECTING AND PRODUCING FOR
    CLASSROOM, TELEVISION AND INDUSTRY (Lewis Herman)
  F Comment: v. 3, n. 3 (Summer, 1965), pp. 76-76; Donald E. Staples, 700
    wds., cp. pub.
  F Lib Quarterly: v. 1, n. 1 (Winter, 1967-1968), p. 56; 125 wds., pt. pub.

7698 ELECTRONIC MOTION PICTURES (Albert Abramson)
  Quarterly of F R TV: v. X, n. 2 (Winter, 1955), pp. 213-214; Franklin
    Fearing, 200 wds., cp. pub.

7699 ELEMENTS OF COLOR IN PROFESSIONAL MOTION PICTURES (Special
        Committee of the Society of Motion Pictures and Television
        Engineers)
        Films in R: v. IX, n. 4 (Apr., 1958), pp. 215-216; Henry Hart, 200 wds., cp.
        pub.

7700 ELEMENTS OF FILM (Lee Bobker)
        Films & F: v. 16, n. 4 (Jan., 1970), p. 72; Sheridan Morley, 75 wds., pt.
        pub.

7701 ELINOR GLYN (Anthony Glyn)
        Films in R: v. VII, n. 4 (Apr., 1956), pp. 186-187; Lawrence J. Quirk, 650
        wds., cp. pub.

7702 ELIZABETH TAYLOR: HER LIFE, HER LOVES, HER FUTURE (Ruth
        Waterbury)
        Films in R: v. XV, n. 8 (Oct., 1964), pp. 496-497; Flavia Wharton, 200
        wds., cp. pub.

7703 ELVIS, A BIOGRAPHY (Jerry Hopkins)
        Journal of P C: v. V, n. 3 (Winter, 1971), pp. 622-623; R. Serge Denisoff,
        750 wds., cp. pub.

7704 EMERGENCE OF FILM ART, THE (Lewis Jacobs, ed.)
        Cineaste: v. II, n. 4 (Spring, 1969), p. 23; Gary Crowdus, 200 wds., pt. pub.
        Cinema: v. 5, n. 2, p. 42; 500 wds., cp. pub.
        Cinema J: v. IX, n. 1 (Fall, 1969), p. 55-56; Richard Dyer MacCann, 400
        wds., cp. pub.
        F Comment: v. 6, n. 1 (Spring, 1970), p. 69; Herman G. Weinberg, 125
        wds., cp. pub.
        F Lib Quarterly: v. 2, n. 3 (Summer, 1969), p. 29; Paul Falkenberg, 550
        wds., pt. pub.
        Films & F: v. 16, n. 5 (Feb., 1970), p. 70; Sheridan Morley, 125 wds., pt.
        pub.
        Interntl F G: v. 7 (1970), p. 395; 50 wds., pt. pub.

7705 EMOTIONAL RESPONSES OF CHILDREN TO THE MOTION PICTURE
        SITUATION, THE (Wendell S. Dysinger and Christian A.
        Ruckmick)
        F Comment: v. 7, n. 2 (Summer, 1971), pp. 70-72; Garth Jowett, 2200
        wds., cp. pub.

7706 ENCYCLOPEDIA OF FILM AND TELEVISION TECHNIQUES (Raymond
        Spottiswoode, ed.)
        Screen: v. 11, n. 2 (Mar.-Apr., 1970), pp. 90-92; Douglas Lowndes, 900
        wds., cp. pub.

7707 *ENCYCLOPEDIE DU CINEMA PAR L'IMAGE: TOME II, L' (Roger
        Boussinot)
        Sight & S: v. 40, n. 2 (Spring, 1971), pp. 111; John Russell Taylor, 800
        wds., cp. pub.

7708 END TO COMEDY, AN (Robert Carson)
        Films in R: v. XV, n. 1 (Jan., 1964), p. 41; Alice H. Witham, 125 wds., cp.
        pub.

7709 *ENTR'ACTE (Glauco Viazzi, ed.)
        Sight & S: v. 18, n. 70 (Summer, 1949), p. 97; Muriel Grindrod, 400 wds.,
        cp. pub.

7710 *ERHOBENE ZEIGEFINGER, DER (George Bose)
        Sight & S: v. 19, n. 2 (Apr., 1950), p. 90; Egon Larsen, 275 wds., cp. pub.

7711 *ERIC VON STROHEIM (Bob Bergut)
        Sight & S: v. 30, n. 2 (Spring, 1961), pp. 98-99; Lotte H. Eisner, 900 wds.,
        cp. pub.

7712 EROS IN THE CINEMA (Raymond Durgnat)
        Cinema J: v. VIII, n. 2 (Spring, 1969), pp. 38-40; John L. Fell, 850 wds.,
            cp. pub.
        F Quarterly: v. XXI, n. 1 (Fall, 1967), p. 64; Ernest Callenbach, 250 wds.,
            cp. pub.
        Films & F: v. 13, n. 3 (Dec., 1966), p. 42; Sheridan Morley, 125 wds., no
            pub.
        Interntl F G: v. 5 (1968), p. 261; 25 wds., pt. pub.

7713 *EROTIK FOR MILLIONER (Ove Brusen Dorff and Poul Heinningsen)
        Films & F: v. 4, n. 7 (Apr., 1958), p. 33; Martin Gray, 100 wds., pt. pub.

7714 *EROTISME AU CINEMA, L' (Lo Duca)
        F Culture: v. 3, n. 2 (1957), p. 22; Herman G. Weinberg, 700 wds., cp. pub.
        Films in R: v. VIII, n. 8 (Oct., 1957), p. 422; Jack Spears, 200 wds., cp.
            pub.
        Sight & S: v. 27, n. 1 (Summer, 1957), p. 51; Richard Roud, 800 wds., cp.
            pub.

7715 *ESSENZA DEL FILM: A CURA DI FERNALDO DI GIAMMATTEO
            (Fernaldo di Giammatteo, ed.)
        Sight & S: v. 17, n. 66 (Summer, 1948), p. 105; M. K. Grindrod, 250 wds.,
            cp. pub.

7716 *ESTHETIQUE ET PSYCHOLOGIE DU CINEMA (Jean Mitry)
        F Comment: v. 5, n. 3 (Fall, 1969), p. 81; Herman G. Weinberg, 350 wds.,
            cp. pub.

7717 EXPANDED CINEMA (Gene Youngblood)
        Cineaste: v. IV, n. 2 (Fall, 1970), pp. 43-45; Noe Goldwasser, 2500 wds.,
            cp. pub.
        Cinema J: v. X, n. 2 (Spring, 1971), pp. 60-64; Donald Crafton, 2700 wds.,
            cp. pub.
        F Comment: v. 7, n. 1 (Spring, 1971), pp. 82-83; Norman Kagan, 1700
            wds., cp. pub.
        F Quarterly: v. XXIV, n. 3 (Spring, 1971), pp. 28-31; Ernest Callenbach,
            1900 wds., cp. pub.
        Films & F: v. 17, n. 8 (May, 1971), p. 136; Sheridan Morley, 50 wds., pt.
            pub.
        Interntl F G: v. 9 (1972), p. 463; 50 wds., pt. pub.

7718 EXPERIMENT IN THE FILM (Roger Manvell, ed.)
        Films in R: v. II, n. 3 (Mar., 1951), pp. 45-46; Arthur Knight, 750 wds., cp.
            pub.
        Hollywood Q: v. IV, n. 1 (Fall, 1949), p. 98; Franklin Fearing, 200 wds.,
            pt. pub.
        Sequence: n. 9 (Autumn, 1949), pp. 138-139; Lindsay Anderson, 1200
            wds., pt. pub.

7719 EXPERIMENTAL CINEMA: A FIFTY-YEAR EVOLUTION (David Curtis)
        F Quarterly: v. XXV, n. 4 (Summer, 1972), pp. 31-34; William Moritz,
            1900 wds., cp. pub.
        Interntl F G: v. 9 (1972), p. 463; 50 wds., pt. pub.

7720 EXPERIMENTS ON MASS COMMUNICATION (Fred D. Sheffield, Carl I.
            Horland, Arthur A. Lumsdaine)
        Hollywood Q: v. IV, n. 1 (Fall, 1949), pp. 98-99; Franklin Fearing, 300
            wds., cp. pub.

7721 EXPLORING THE FILM (William Kuhns and Robert Stanley)
        Cineaste: v. III, n. 1 (Summer, 1969), pp. 24, 26; Gary Crowdus, 500 wds.,
            pt. pub.

7722 EYE, FILM, AND CAMERA IN COLOR PHOTOGRAPHY
        F Quarterly: v. XIII, n. 3 (Spring, 1960), pp. 62-63; Raymond Fielding, 600
            wds., cp. pub.

F

7723 *F. W. MURNAU (Lotte H. Eisner)
 F Comment: v. 6, n. 1 (Spring, 1970), p. 66; Kirk Bond, 600 wds., cp. pub.
 Interntl F G: v. 3 (1966), p. 263; 175 wds., cp. pub.
 Sight & S: v. 34, n. 3 (Summer, 1965), pp. 153-154; David Robinson, 1100
  wds., cp. pub.

7724 FABULOUS FANNY, THE (Norman Katkov)
 Films in R: v. IV, n. 3 (Mar., 1953), pp. 153-154; Robert Downing, 350
  wds., cp. pub.

7725 FABULOUS TOM MIX, THE (Olive Stokes Mix with Eric Heath)
 Films in R: v. IX, n. 2 (Feb., 1958), pp. 99-101; William K. Everson, 500
  wds., cp. pub.

7726 FACE ON THE CUTTING ROOM FLOOR: THE STORY OF MOVIE AND
  TELEVISION CENSORSHIP, THE (Murray Schumach)
 Cinema Studies: v. II, n. 3 (Mar., 1967), pp. 59-60; N.M.H., 850 wds., cp.
  pub.

7727 FACTUAL FILM: A SURVEY, THE (The Arts Enquiry)
 Hollywood Q: v. II, n. 4 (July, 1947), pp. 427-429; Philip Dunne, 1200
  wds., cp. pub.

7728 *FANTASTIQUE AU CINEMA, LE (Michel Laclos)
 Films & F: v. 4, n. 8 (May, 1958), p. 35; Martin Gray, 100 wds., pt. pub.
 Sight & S: v. 27, n. 6 (Autumn, 1958), p. 326; Roy Edwards, 1000 wds.,
  cp. pub.

7729 FEAR ON TRIAL (John Henry Faulk)
 F Comment: v. 3, n. 4 (Fall, 1965), pp. 70-73; F. William Howton, 2500
  wds., cp. pub.

7730 FEDERICO FELLINI (Gilbert Salachas, trans. by Rosalie Siegel)
 Cineaste: v. II, n. 4 (Spring, 1969), p. 22; Gary Crowdus, 250 wds., pt. pub.
 Cinema: v. 5, n. 2, p. 43; Stephen Mamber, 300 wds., cp. pub.
 Cinema J: v. IX, n. 2 (Spring, 1970), pp. 48-51; Peter Harcourt, 1600 wds.,
  cp. pub.
 Interntl F G: v. 7 (1970), pp. 395-396; 50 wds., pt. pub.

7731 FELLINI (Suzanne Budgen)
 F Quarterly: v. XX, n. 3 (Spring, 1967), pp. 56-57; Ernest Callenbach, 150
  wds., cp. pub.
 F Soc Rev: Dec. (1966), p. 35; A. W. Hodgkinson, 175 wds., cp. pub.
 Sight & S: v. 35, n. 4 (Autumn, 1966), p. 205; John Russell Taylor, 400
  wds., cp. pub.

7732 FELLINI (Angelo Solmi, trans. by Elizabeth Greenwood)
 Cinema J: v. IX, n. 2 (Spring, 1970), pp. 48-51; Peter Harcourt, 1600 wds.,
  cp. pub.
 F Comment: v. 6, n. 1 (Spring, 1970), p. 75; 125 wds., cp. pub.
 F Quarterly: v. XXI, n. 4 (Summer, 1968), p. 56; 50 wds., cp. pub.
 F Soc Rev: v. 4, n. 8, pp. 42-43; Frank Manchel, 600 wds., cp. pub.
 Films & F: v. 13, n. 12 (Sept., 1967), p. 46; Sheridan Morley, 50 wds., pt.
  pub.

7733 *FEMME DANS LE CINEMA FRANCAIS, LA (Jacques Siclier)
 Films in R: v. X, n. 1 (Jan., 1959), p. 52; Jack Spears, 250 wds., cp. pub.

7734 FESTIVAL DEATH (Ralph Stephenson)
 Interntl F G: v. 4 (1967), p. 275; 125 wds., pt. pub.

7735 FIFTY YEAR DECLINE AND FALL OF HOLLYWOOD, THE (Ezra
     Goodman)
     F Quarterly: v. XIV, n. 3 (Spring, 1961), p. 64; Ernest Callenbach, 125
     wds., cp. pub.

7736 FIFTY YEARS OF GERMAN FILM (H. H. Wollenberg)
     Sequence: n. 7 (Spring, 1949), pp. 44-45; Peter Ericsson, 450 wds., pt. pub.
     Sight & S: v. 17, n. 68 (Winter, 1948); C. A. Laurentzsch, 200 wds., pt.
     pub.

7737 FIGURES OF LIGHT: FILM CRITICISM AND COMMENT (Stanley
     Kauffmann)
     F Quarterly: v. XXIV, n. 3 (Spring, 1971), p. 26; Ernest Callenbach, 250
     wds., cp. pub.
     F Soc Rev: v. 6, n. 7 (Mar., 1971), pp. 49-50; Michael Sragow, 1000 wds.,
     cp. pub.

7738 FILM (Roger Manvell)
     Quarterly of FR TV: v. X, n. 2 (Winter, 1955), pp. 210-212; Franklin
     Fearing, 350 wds., cp. pub.

7739 FILM, THE (Andrew Sarris, ed.)
     F Comment: v. 6, n. 1 (Spring, 1970), p. 75; 75 wds., cp. pub.

7740 FILM: A MONTAGE OF THEORIES (Richard Dyer MacCann)
     F Soc Rev: Dec. (1966), p. 37; Anthony W. Hodgkinson, 350 wds., cp. pub.

7741 FILM ACTOR, THE (Michael Pate)
     Interntl F G: v. 8 (1971), p. 437, 439; 50 wds., pt. pub.

7742 FILM: AN ANTHOLOGY (Daniel Talbot)
     F Quarterly: v. XIII, n. 3 (Spring, 1960), p. 61; Jonathan Harker, 500 wds.,
     cp. pub.
     F Soc Rev: Apr. (1966), p. 23-24; Alexander Sesonske, 450 wds., cp. pub.
     Interntl F G: v. 4 (1967), p. 273; 100 wds., pt. pub.
     Sight & S: v. 29, n. 2 (Spring, 1960), pp. 101-102; Jay Leyda, 500 wds., cp.
     pub.

7743 FILM AND EDUCATION (Ernest Lindgren, ed. by Godfrey M. Elliott)
     Films in R: v. I, n. 5 (July-Aug., 1950), pp. 41-42; Gloria Waldron Grover,
     350 wds., cp. pub.
     Hollywood Q: v. IV, n. 1 (Fall, 1949), pp. 101-102; Franklin Fearing, 200
     wds., cp. pub.

7744 FILM AND ITS TECHNIQUES (Raymond Spottiswoode)
     Films in R: v. II, n. 7 (Aug.-Sept., 1951), pp. 44-46; Lewis Jacobs, 650
     wds., cp. pub.
     Quarterly of FR TV: v. VI (1951-1952), pp. 102-103; Franklin Fearning,
     700 wds., cp. pub.
     Sight & S: v. 22, n. 1 (July-Sept., 1952), p. 44; H. D. Waley, 600 wds., cp.
     pub.

7745 FILM AND SOCIETY (Richard Dyer MacCann, ed.)
     F Comment: v. 5, n. 4 (Winter, 1969), p. 80; 50 wds., cp. pub.
     F Soc Rev: Oct. (1966), pp. 37-38; David J. Powell, 450 wds., cp. pub.
     Take One: v. 1, n. 3 (Feb., 1967), p. 29; Patrick MacFadden, 400 wds., cp.
     pub.

7746 FILM AND THE FUTURE (Andrew Buchanan)
     Hollywood Q: v. I, n. 3 (Apr., 1946), pp. 339-340; Irving Lerner, 550 wds.,
     cp. pub.

7747 FILM AND THE LIBERAL ARTS (T. J. Ross)
     Cinema J: v. X, n. 2 (Spring, 1971), pp. 58-60; Marvin Felheim, 650 wds.,
     cp. pub.

7748 FILM AND THE PUBLIC, THE (Roger Manvell)
     Films & F: v. 2, n. 1 (Oct., 1955), p. 28; Werdon Anglin, 150 wds., pt. pub.
     Sight & S: v. 25, n. 2 (Autumn, 1955), p. 107; John Wilcox, 350 wds., cp.
     pub.

7749 FILM AND TV GRAPHICS (John Halas)
        Films & F: v. XIV, n. 1 (Oct., 1967), p. 32; Sheridan Morley, 100 wds., pt.
            pub.
        Interntl F G: v. 5 (1968), p. 261; 25 wds., pt. pub.

7750 FILM AS ART (Rudolf Arnheim)
        F Culture: v. 3, n. 5 (Dec., 1957), p. 22; Peter Walsh, 250 wds., cp. pub.
        Films & F: v. 4, n. 8 (May, 1958), p. 3; Martin Gay, 250 wds., pt. pub.
        Films & F: v. 16, n. 5 (Feb., 1970), p. 70; Sheridan Morley, 100 wds., pt.
            pub.
        Sight & S: v. 27, n. 5 (Summer, 1958), p. 260; Kenneth Cavander, 650
            wds., cp. pub.

7751 FILM AS FILM: CRITICAL RESPONSES TO FILM ART (Joy Gould Boyum
            and Adrienne Scott)
        Focus on F: n. 7 (Summer, 1971), p. 59; Allen Eyles, 100 wds., cp. pub.

7752 FILM: BOOK I (Robert Hughes, ed.)
        F Quarterly: v. XII, n. 3 (Spring, 1959), pp. 61-62; Ernest Callenbach, 500
            wds., cp. pub.
        F Quarterly: v. XII, n. 4 (Summer, 1959), pp. 61-64; Robert Hughes and
            Ernest Callenbach, 1500 wds., cp. pub.
        Sight & S: v. 29, n. 1 (Winter, 1959-1960), p. 49; Derek Hill, 375 wds., cp.
            pub.

7753 FILM: BOOK 2: FILMS OF WAR AND PEACE (Robert Hughes, ed.)
        F Comment: v. 1, n. 3 (1962), pp. 39-40; Robert Windeler, 650 wds., cp.
            pub.
        F Quarterly: v. XVII, n. 2 (Winter, 1963-1964), p. 58; Ernest Callenbach,
            550 wds., cp. pub.

7754 *FILM CECOSLOVACCO, IL (Ernesto G. Laura, ed.)
        F Quarterly: v. XIV, n. 3 (Spring, 1961), p. 64; Letizia Ciotti Miller, 400
            wds., cp. pub.

7755 FILM CENSORS AND THE LAW (Neville March Hunnings)
        Interntl F G: v. 6 (1969), p. 271; 50 wds., pt. pub.
        Sight & S: v. 37, n. 1 (Winter, 1967-1968), pp. 50-51; John Mortimer, 1700
            wds., cp. pub.

7756 FILM COMPOSERS IN AMERICA (Clifford McCarty, ed.)
        Films in R: v. IV, n. 7 (Aug.-Sept., 1953), p. 375; 150 wds., cp. pub.

7757 FILM CULTURE READER (P. Adams Sitney, ed.)
        Cineaste: v. IV, n. 3 (Winter, 1970-1971), pp. 47-48; Marco Pinares, 1000
            wds., cp. pub.
        Cinema J: v. X, n. 2 (Spring, 1971), pp. 60-64; Donald Crafton, 2700 wds.,
            cp. pub.
        F Comment: v. 7, n. 3 (Fall, 1971), pp. 73-74; Bill Simon, 1000 wds., cp.
            pub.
        F Soc Rev: v. 6, n. 4 (Dec., 1970), pp. 48-50; Foster Hirsch, 600 wds., cp.
            pub.
        Focus on F: n. 7 (Summer, 1971), p. 60; Allen Eyles, 150 wds., cp. pub.

7758 FILM DAILY YEAR BOOK OF MOTION PICTURES (Jack Alicoate, ed.)
        Films in R: v. IV, n. 7 (Aug.-Sept., 1953), p. 372; Bradner Lacey, 200 wds.,
            cp. pub.
        Films in R: v. VI, n. 7 (Aug.-Sept., 1955), p. 354; Bradner Lacy, 300 wds.,
            cp. pub.
        Films in R: v. VIII, n. 6 (June-July, 1957), p. 289; Bradner Lacy, 200 wds.,
            cp. pub.
        Films in R: v. IX, n. 9 (Nov., 1958), p. 527; Bradner Lacy, 225 wds., cp.
            pub.
        Films in R: v. XIV, n. 9 (Nov., 1963), pp. 558-559; Bradner Lacy, 200
            wds., cp. pub.
        Screen: v. 11, n. 4-5 (July-Oct., 1970), p. 134; Gillian Hartnoll, 100 wds.,
            cp. pub.

7759 FILM DIRECTOR AS SUPERSTAR, THE (Joseph Gelmis)
      Cinema J: v. X n. 2 (Spring, 1971), pp. 58-60; Marvin Felheim, 650 wds.,
          cp. pub.
      Films & F: v. 17, n. 10 (July, 1971), p. 64; Sheridan Morley, 125 wds., pt.
          pub.
      Interntl F G: v. 9 (1972), p. 463; 75 wds., pt. pub.

7760 FILM ESSAYS AND A LECTURE (Sergei Eisenstein, trans. by Jay Leyda)
      Cineaste: v. IV, n. 2 (Fall, 1970), pp. 42-43; Bill Nichols, 1000 wds., cp.
          pub.
      Films & F: v. 14, n. 11 (Aug., 1968), p. 56; Sheridan Morley, 600 wds., pt.
          pub.
      Sight & S: v. 38, n. 1 (Winter, 1968-1969), pp. 52-53; D.R., 100 wds., cp.
          pub.

7761 FILM EXPERIENCE — ELEMENTS OF MOTION PICTURE ART, THE (Roy
          Huss and Norman Silverstein)
      Cineaste: v. I, n. 4 (Spring, 1968), p. 34; Gary Crowdus, 75 wds., pt. pub.
      F Comment: v. 6, n. 1 (Spring, 1970), p. 74; 150 wds., cp. pub.
      F Soc Rev: May (1968), p. 38; Frank Manchel, 50 wds., cp. pub.

7762 FILM FORM AND FILM SENSE (Sergei Eisenstein, trans. and ed. by Jay
          Leyda)
      F Culture: v. 3, n. 5 (Dec., 1957), p. 22; Herman G. Weinberg, 275 wds., cp.
          pub.
      Hollywood Q: v. IV, n. 1 (Fall, 1949), p. 102; Franklin Fearing, 200 wds.,
          pt. pub.
      Sight & S: v. 21, n. 1 (Aug.-Sept., 1951), pp. 44-45; Karel Reisz, 1600 wds.,
          cp. pub.

7763 FILM 'HAMLET': A RECORD OF ITS PRODUCTION, THE (Brenda Cross)
      Sight & S: v. 17, n. 66 (Summer, 1948), p. 107; 150 wds., cp. pub.

7764 *FILM IN UNDERGROUND (Brigit Hein)
      F Quarterly: v. XXV, n. 4 (Summer, 1972), pp. 31-34; William Moritz,
          1900 wds., cp. pub.

7765 FILM IN EDUCATION, THE (Andrew Buchanan)
      Films in R: v. III, n. 8 (Oct., 1952), p. 421-422; Walter H. Stainton, 400
          wds., cp. pub.

7766 FILM IN FRANCE (Roy Fowler)
      Hollywood Q: v. II, n. 3 (Apr., 1947), pp. 321-322; Harold Salemson, 500
          wds., pt. pub.

7767 FILM IN THE THIRD REICH: A STUDY OF THE GERMAN CINEMA,
          1933-1945 (David Stewart Hull)
      Cineaste: v. III, n. 4 (Spring, 1970), pp. 24-25; Calvin Green, 2000 wds., cp.
          pub.
      Cinema J: v. X, n. 1 (Fall, 1970), pp. 60-64; Richard B. Byrne, 1800 wds.,
          cp. pub.
      F Comment: v. 6, n. 2 (Summer, 1970), p. 60; George Amberg, 650 wds.,
          cp. pub.
      F Heritage: v. 5, n. 4 (Summer, 1970), pp. 31-32; Herman G. Weinberg, 400
          wds., cp. pub.
      Films & F: v. 16, n. 10 (July, 1970), p. 64; Sheridan Morley, 250 wds., pt.
          pub.
      Films in R: v. XXI, n. 5 (May, 1970), pp. 291-292; Eleanor H. Nash, 75
          wds., cp. pub.
      Interntl F G: v. 8 (1971), p. 439; 75 wds., pt. pub.
      Journal of P C: v. IV, n. 3 (Winter, 1971), pp. 827-829; Edgar F. Daniels,
          600 wds., cp. pub.
      Sight & S: v. 39, n. 4 (Autumn, 1970), pp. 223-224; David Wilson, 700
          wds., cp. pub.
      Take One: v. 2, n. 8 (1970), p. 28; Glen Hunter, 100 wds., cp. pub.

7768 FILM INDEX: A BIBLIOGRAPHY: VOLUME I, THE FILM AS ART, THE
      (Harold Leonard, gen. ed.)
      Cinema: v. 4, n. 3 (Fall, 1968), p. 46; Timothy J. Lyons, 250 wds., pt. pub.
      F Comment: v. IV, n. 2-3 (Fall-Winter, 1967), pp. 106-107; Herman G.
            Weinberg, 700 wds., cp. pub.
      Screen: v. 11, n. 4-5 (July-Oct., 1970), p. 134; Gillian Hartnoll, 75 wds., cp.
            pub.

7769 FILM: ITS ECONOMIC, SOCIAL, AND ARTISTIC PROBLEMS, THE (Georg
            Schmidt, Werner Schmalenbach, Peter Bachlin, trans. by Hugo
            Weber and Roger Manvell)
      Hollywood Q: v. V (1950-1951), p. 102; Franklin Fearing, 250 wds., cp.
            pub.

7770 *FILM-KUNST, FILM-KOHN, FILM KORRUPTION (Carl Neumann, Kurt
            Belling, Hans-Walther Betz)
      Hollywood Q: v. I, n. 1 (Oct., 1945), pp. 124-126; William Dieterele, 800
            wds., cp. pub.

7771 *FILM LITTERATUR I DEBATTEN: EN BIBLIOGRAFI SAMMANSTALLD
            OCH KOMMENTERAD (Gosta Werner)
      Cinema Studies: v. I, n. 5 (Sept., 1962), pp. 115-116; Glynne Parker, 900
            wds., cp. pub.

7772 FILM-MAKER'S ART, THE (Haig P. Manoogian)
      Cinema: v. 4, n. 2 (Summer, 1968), p. 60; Thomas B. Markus, 500 wds., pt.
            pub.
      F Comment: v. IV, n. 2-3 (Fall-Winter, 1967), pp. 112-113; Ray Sipherd,
            450 wds., cp. pub.
      F Quarterly: v. XIX, n. 4 (Summer, 1966), p. 69; Ernest Callenbach, 175
            wds., cp. pub.
      F Soc Rev: Nov. (1966), pp. 36-37; Robert W. Goggin, 450 wds., cp. pub.
      Films & F: v. 13, n. 3 (Dec., 1966), p. 42; Sheridan Morley, 75 wds., no
            pub.

7773 FILM MAKERS ON FILM MAKING (Harry M. Geduld, ed.)
      Cinema J: v. VII (Winter, 1967-1968), pp. 36-37; Richard Dyer MacCann,
            850 wds., cp. pub.
      F Lib Quarterly: v. 2, n. 1 (Winter, 1968-1969), p. 53; 500 wds., pt. pub.
      F Quarterly: v. XXI, n. 3 (Spring, 1968), p. 55; Ernest Callenbach, 150
            wds., cp. pub.
      F Soc Rev: Dec. (1967), pp. 33-36; Frank Manchel, 1200 wds., cp. pub.
      Films & F: v. 16, n. 7 (Apr., 1970), p. 72; Sheridan Morley, 450 wds., pt.
            pub.
      Interntl F G: v. 6 (1969), p. 271; 50 wds., pt. pub.

7774 FILM-MAKING FROM SCRIPT TO SCREEN (Andrew Buchanan)
      Films in R: v. III, n. 2 (Feb., 1952), p. 92; 100 wds., cp. pub.
      Quarterly of FR TV: v. VI, n. 1 (Fall, 1951), p. 102; Franklin Fearing, 100
            wds., cp. pub.

7775 FILM MUSIC (Marie L. Hamilton)
      Films & F: v. 1, n. 8 (May, 1955), p. 30; Michael Facer, 100 wds., pt. pub.

7776 *FILM NEI PROBLEMI DELL'ARTE, IL (Luigi Chiarini)
      Films in R: v. I, n. 7 (Oct., 1950), pp. 30-32; Nadir Giannitrapani, 1100
            wds., pt. pub.
      Hollywood Q: v. IV, n. 3 (Spring, 1950), p. 315; Franklin Fearing, 125
            wds., cp. pub.

7777 FILM, 1962 (Vittorio Spinazzola, ed.)
      F Comment: v. 1, n. 4 (1963), pp. 47-48; Robert Connolly, 550 wds., cp.
            pub.

7778 FILM 67/68: AN ANTHOLOGY OF CRITICISM BY THE NATIONAL
            SOCIETY OF FILM CRITICS (Richard Schickel and John Simon,
            eds.)
      Cinema J: v. VIII, n. 2 (Spring, 1969), pp. 35-38; Richard Dyer MacCann,
            1600 wds., cp. pub.

7779 FILM 68/69: AN ANTHOLOGY BY THE NATIONAL SOCIETY OF FILM
CRITICS (Hollis Alpert and Andrew Sarris, eds.)
Cinema J: v. IX, n. 2 (Spring, 1970), pp. 55-56; Richard Geary, 900 wds.,
cp. pub.
F Soc Rev: v. 5, n. 7, pp. 44-47; Michael Sragow, 1200 wds., cp. pub.

7780 FILM NOTES (Arthur Lenning, ed.)
F Quarterly: v. XIV, n. 3 (Spring, 1961), pp. 59-50; Ernest Callenbach, 750
wds., cp. pub.

7781 FILM NOTES (Eileen Bowser)
F Quarterly: v. XXIV, n. 3 (Spring, 1971), pp. 59-60; Jay Leyda, 500 wds.,
pt. pub.
Films & F: v. 17, n. 6 (Mar., 1971), p. 64; Sheridan Morley, 200 wds., pt.
pub.
Films in R: v. XXI, n. 8 (Oct., 1970), p. 500; 75 wds., cp. pub.

7782 FILM OF MURDER IN THE CATHEDRAL, THE (George Hoellering)
Quarterly of FR TV: v. VII, n. 4 (Summer, 1953), pp. 429-430; Franklin
Fearing, 225 wds., cp. pub.
Sight & S: v. 22, n. 1 (July-Sept., 1952), pp. 43-44; Lindsay Anderson, 500
wds., cp. pub.

7783 FILM REVIEW (F. Maurice Speed, ed.)
Films & F: v. 4, n. 3 (Dec., 1957), p. 29; Martin Gray, 75 wds., pt. pub.
Interntl F G: v. 5 (1968), p. 261; 25 wds., pt. pub.
Interntl F G: v. 6 (1969), p. 275; 50 wds., pt. pub.
Interntl F G: v. 7 (1970), p. 396; 75 wds., pt. pub.
Interntl F G: v. 8 (1971), p. 439; 75 wds., pt. pub.
Interntl F G: v. 9 (1972), p. 463; 50 wds., pt. pub.
Screen: v. 11, n. 1, p. 100; Christopher Wicking, 300 wds., cp. pub.
Screen: v. 11, n. 4-5 (July-Oct., 1970), p. 136; Gillian Hartnoll, 50 wds., cp.
pub.

7784 FILM SCRIPT (Adrian Brunel)
Sequence: n. 7 (Spring, 1949), p. 45; John Boud, 300 wds., pt. pub.
Sight & S: v. 17, n. 68 (Winger, 1948-1949), p. 196; Paul Sheridan, 250
wds., cp. pub.

7785 FILM SOCIETY PRIMER, THE (Cecile Starr)
Quarterly of FR TV: v. XI, n. 1 (Fall, 1956), p. 107; Franklin Fearing, 100
wds., cp. pub.

7786 FILM STUDY IN HIGHER EDUCATION (David C. Stewart, ed.)
F Comment: v. IV, n. 2-3 (Fall-Winter, 1967), pp. 109-110; George
Bouwman, 400 wds., cp. pub.
F Quarterly: v. XX, n. 1 (Fall, 1966), p. 63; Ernest Callenbach, 50 wds., cp.
pub.
F Soc Rev: Sept. (1966), pp. 35-36; Anthony Hodgkinson, 550 wds., cp.
pub.

7787 FILM SURVEY 2 (Federation of Film Societies)
Interntl F G: v. 5 (1968), p. 261; 25 wds., pt. pub.

7788 FILM TECHNIQUE AND FILM ACTING (V. I. Pudovkin, trans. by Ivor
Montagu)
Hollywood Q: v. IV, n. 1 (Fall, 1949), pp. 102-103; Franklin Fearing, 200
wds., cp. pub.
Quarterly of FR TV: v. IX, n. 1 (Fall, 1954), p. 214; Franklin Fearing, 100
wds., cp. pub.

7789 FILM: THE CREATIVE EYE (David A. Sohn)
Interntl F G: v. 9 (1972), p. 466; 50 wds., pt. pub.

7790 FILM: THE CREATIVE PROCESS (John Howard Lawson)
F Comment: v. 3, n. 3 (Summer, 1965), pp. 72-75; George Bluestone, 2900
wds., cp. pub.
F Heritage: v. 1, n. 2 (Winter, 1965-1966), pp. 37-40; Jackson G. Barry,
1200 wds., cp. pub.
Interntl F G: v. 3 (1966), p. 257; 200 wds., cp. pub.

N Y REV of Books: v. III, n. 10 (Dec. 3, 1964), pp. 16-18; A. Alvarez, 2000 wds., pt. pub.
Sight & S: v. 34, n. 4 (Autumn, 1965), p. 206; Elizabeth Sussex, 600 wds., cp. pub.

7791 FILM TILL NOW, THE (Paul Rotha, with Richard Griffith)
Films in R: v. I, n. 5 (July-Aug., 1950), pp. 29-35; Gilbert Seldes, 1500 wds., cp. pub.
Films in R: v. I, n. 8 (Nov., 1950), pp. 4-6; Herman G. Weinberg, 1000 wds., no pub.
Films in R: v. I, n. 8 (Nov., 1950), pp. 7-8, 32; Richard Griffith, 850 wds., no pub.
Hollywood Q: v. V (1950-1951), pp. 201-202; Franklin Fearing, 575 wds., pt. pub.
Sequence: n. 11 (Summer, 1950), p. 45; Lindsay Anderson, 650 wds., pt. pub.
Sight & S: v. 19, n. 1 (Mar., 1950), p. 40; Penelope Houston, 1000 wds., cp. pub.

7792 *FILM UND FILMWIRTSCHAFT IN DER SCHWEIZ
Interntl F G: v. 6 (1969), p. 275; 50 wds., pt. pub.

7793 FILM WORLD (Ivor Montagu)
Sight & S: v. 34, n. 2 (Spring, 1965), pp. 100-101; Peter Harcourt, 800 wds., cp. pub.

7794 FILMED BOOKS AND PLAYS (A. G. S. Enser)
Films & F: v. 17, n. 8 (May, 1971), p. 136; Sheridan Morley, 50 wds., pt. pub.

7795 *FILMENS HVEM HVAD HVOR (Bjorn Rasmussen)
Interntl F G: v. 6 (1969), p. 271; 50 wds., pt. pub.
Interntl F G: v. 7 (1970), p. 396; 75 wds., pt. pub.
Interntl F G: v. 9 (1972), p. 463; 50 wds., pt. pub.

7796 FILMGOER'S COMPANION, THE (Leslie Halliwell, comp.)
F Comment: v. 3, n. 4 (Fall, 1965), pp. 79-80; Robert Steele, 1300 wds., cp. pub.
Films & F: v. 16, n. 10 (July, 1970), p. 64; Sheridan Morley, 350 wds., pt. pub.
Films & F: v. 14, n. 1 (Oct., 1967), p. 32; Sheridan Morley, 600 wds., pt. pub.
Films in R: v. XIX, n. 3 (Mar., 1968), pp. 170-171; E.H.N., 100 wds., cp. pub.
Films in R: v. XXI, n. 8 (Oct., 1970), p. 499; 50 wds., cp. pub.
Screen: v. 11, n. 4-5 (July-Oct., 1970); Gillian Hartnoll, 100 wds., cp. pub.

7797 FILMS: A REPORT ON THE SUPPLY OF FILMS FOR EXHIBITION IN CINEMAS (The Monopolies Commission)
F Quarterly: v. XXI, n. 1 (Fall, 1967), pp. 62-64; Peter Cowie, 1000 wds., cp. pub.

7798 FILMS AND FEELINGS (Raymond Durgnat)
Cinema J: v. VIII, n. 2 (Spring, 1969), pp. 38-40; John L. Fell, 850 wds., cp. pub.
F Quarterly: v. XXII, n. 3 (Spring, 1969), pp. 55-56; Ernest Callenbach, 500 wds., cp. pub.
F Soc Rev: v. 7, n. 3 (Nov., 1971), pp. 45-50; Foster Hirsch, 1500 wds., cp. pub.
Films & F: v. 13, n. 11 (Aug., 1967), p. 47; Sheridan Morley, 250 wds., pt. pub.
Interntl F G: v. 6 (1969), p. 275; 50 wds., pt. pub.
Sight & S: v. 36, n. 4 (Autumn, 1967), pp. 210-211; Philip French, 1200 wds., cp. pub.

7799 FILMS AND FILM-MAKERS (Jan Zalman)
Interntl F G: v. 6 (1969), p. 275; 50 wds., pt. pub.

7800 FILMS BEGET FILMS (Jan Zaiman)
        F Comment: v. IV, n. 2-3 (Fall-Winter, 1967), p. 114; Gary Carey, 350
          wds., cp. pub.
        Interntl F G: v. 3 (1966), p. 257; 200 wds., cp. pub.
        Sight & S: v. 34, n. 1 (Winter, 1964-1965), p. 49; John Gillett, 600 wds.,
          cp. pub.

7801 FILMS FOR PERSONNEL MANAGEMENT (Louis Goodman)
        F Lib Quarterly: v. 2, n. 3 (Summer, 1969), p. 54; 50 wds., pt. pub.

7802 FILMS IN AMERICA, 1929-1969 (Martin Quigley and Richard Gertner)
        Films & F: v. 17, n. 5 (Feb., 1971), p. 64; Sheridan Morley, 850 wds., pt.
          pub.
        Films in R: v. XXII, n. 7 (Aug.-Sept., 1971), p. 434; Alice H. Whitham, 250
          wds., cp. pub.
        Sight & S: v. 40, n. 2 (Spring, 1971), p. 111; John Russell Taylor, 800 wds.,
          cp. pub.

7803 FILMS IN BUSINESS AND INDUSTRY (Henry Clay Gipson)
        Hollywood Q: v. III, n. 2 (Winter, 1947-1948), p. 216; Robert Rahtz, 400
          wds., cp. pub.

7804 FILMS IN DEPTH
        Interntl F G: v. 9 (1972), p. 463; 50 wds., pt. pub.

7805 FILMS IN FOCUS (Richard Auty)
        Sight & S: v. 18, n. 70 (Summer, 1949), p. 97; Peter Plaskitt, 250 wds., cp.
          pub.

7807 FILMS OF AKIRA KUROSAWA, THE (Donald Richie)
        Am Cinematog: v. 47, n. 9 (Sept., 1966), pp. 599, 645-646; 1200 wds., cp.
          pub.
        F Comment: v. 3, n. 4 (Fall, 1965), pp. 75-79; George Bluestone, 3000
          wds., cp. pub.
        F Soc Rev: Jan. (1966), p. 25; John Thomas, 225 wds., cp. pub.
        F Soc Rev: Mar. (1966), pp. 21-22; Gordon Hitchens, 350 wds., cp. pub.
        Films in R: v. XXII, n. 7 (Aug.-Sept., 1971), p. 436; Herbert Lee, 150 wds.,
          cp. pub.
        Interntl F G: v. 4 (1967), p. 271; 200 wds., pt. pub.
        Sight & S: v. 35, n. 2 (Spring, 1966), p. 101; John Gillett, 750 wds., cp.
          pub.

7808 FILMS OF ALFRED HITCHCOCK, THE (George Perry)
        F Comment: v. IV, n. 2-3 (Fall-Winter, 1967), pp. 116-117; Edwin Jahiel,
          200 wds., cp. pub.
        F Heritage: v. 1, n. 4 (Summer, 1966), pp. 37-38; Robert Haller, 400 wds.,
          cp. pub.
        Sight & S: v. 35, n. 1 (Winter, 1965-1966), p. 49; Penelope Houston, 750
          wds., cp. pub.

7809 FILMS OF CECIL B. DE MILLE, THE (Gene Ringgold and DeWitt Bodeen)
        F Soc Rev: v. 5, n. 2 (Oct., 1969), pp. 45-56; Harvey Deneroff, 400 wds.,
          cp. pub.
        Films in R: v. XX, n. 7 (Aug.-Sept., 1969), pp. 427-428; John Grosvenor,
          125 wds., cp. pub.
        Interntl F G: v. 8 (1971), p. 439; 75 wds., pt. pub.

7810 FILMS OF CHARLIE CHAPLIN, THE (Gerald D. McDonald, Michael
          Conway, and Mark Ricci)
        Films in R: v. XVII, n. 4 (Apr., 1966), p. 246; Jack Spears, 275 wds., cp.
          pub.

7811 FILMS OF CLARK GABLE, THE (Gabe Essoe)
        Focus on F: n. 8 (Oct., 1971), p. 60; 200 wds., cp. pub.

7812 FILMS OF FRANK SINATRA, THE (Gene Ringgold and Clifford McCarty)
        Focus on F: n. 10 (Summer, 1972), p. 64; Allen Eyles, 200 wds., cp. pub.

7813 FILMS OF FREDERIC MARCH, THE (Lawrence J. Quirk)
        Focus on F: n. 10 (Summer, 1972), p. 64; Allen Eyles, 200 wds., cp. pub.

7814 FILMS OF GARY COOPER, THE (Homer Dickens)
        Focus on F: n. 8 (Oct., 1971), p. 60; 200 wds., cp. pub.

7815 FILMS OF HAL ROACH, THE (William K. Everson)
        F Comment: v. 7, n. 3 (Fall, 1971), pp. 75-76; Leonard Maltin, 500 wds.,
          cp. pub.

7816 FILMS OF JEAN-LUC GODARD, THE (Ian Cameron, ed.)
        Cineaste: v. IV, n. 1 (Summer, 1970), pp. 29-30; Calvin Green, 1500 wds.,
          cp. pub.
        Screen: v. 11, n. 2 (Mar.-Apr., 1970), pp. 86-88; David Spiers, 300 wds., pt.
          pub.

7817 FILMS OF JOSEF VON STERNBERG, THE (Andrew Sarris)
        F Comment: v. IV, n. 2-3 (Fall-Winter, 1967), pp. 118-122; Kirk Bond,
          1100 wds., cp. pub.
        F Quarterly: v. XX, n. 3 (Spring, 1967), pp. 55-56; Ernest Callenbach, 500
          wds., cp. pub.
        F Soc Rev: Jan. (1967), pp. 36-37; A. W. Hodgkinson, 275 wds., cp. pub.
        Interntl F G: v. 5 (1968), p. 261; 25 wds., pt. pub.
        Sight & S: v. 36, n. 2 (Spring, 1967), pp. 103-104; Tom Milne, 700 wds.,
          cp. pub.

7818 FILMS OF JAMES STEWART, THE (Arthur McClure, Ken Jones, Alfred
          Twoney)
        Films & F: v. 17, n. 6 (Mar., 1971), p. 64; Sheridan Morley, 450 wds., pt.
          pub.
        Interntl F G: v. 8 (1971), p. 439; 50 wds., pt. pub.

7819 FILMS OF LAUREL AND HARDY, THE (William K. Everson)
        F Comment: v. 5, n. 4 (Winter, 1969), pp. 76-77; Kirk Bond, 1200 wds., cp.
          pub.
        F Quarterly: v. XXI, n. 2 (Winter, 1967-1968), p. 59; Ernest Callenbach,
          225 wds., cp. pub.
        Films in R: v. XVIII, n. 8 (Oct., 1967), p. 501; Alice H. Witham, 100 wds.,
          cp. pub.

7820 FILMS OF MARLENE DIETRICH, THE (Homer Dickens)
        Cineaste: v. II, n. 1 (Summer, 1968), pp. 27-28; Gary Crowdus, 100 wds.,
          pt. pub.
        F Comment: v. 5, n. 4 (Winter, 1969), p. 80; 125 wds., cp. pub.

7821 FILMS OF MARILYN MONROE, THE (Michael Conway and Mark Ricci,
          eds.)
        F Comment: v. 5, n. 4 (Winter, 1969), p. 79; 100 wds., cp. pub.

7822 FILMS OF NANCY CARROLL, THE (Paul Nemcek)
        Films In R: v. XXI, n. 8 (Oct., 1970), p. 502; John R. Chester, 225 wds.,
          cp. pub.

7823 FILMS OF ORSON WELLES, THE (Charles Higham)
        Cinema J: v. XI, n. 2 (Spring, 1972), pp. 42-44; Linda Provinzano, 700
          wds., cp. pub.
        Films & F: v. 17, n. 3 (Dec., 1970), p. 63; Sheridan Morley, 250 wds., pt.
          pub.
        Focus on F: n. 5 (Winter/Nov.-Dec., 1970), p. 60; Allen Eyles, 350 wds.,
          cp. pub.
        Interntl F G: v. 9 (1972), p. 463; 50 wds., pt. pub.
        Journal of P C: v. IV, n. 1 (Summer, 1970), pp. 265-267; Robert J. Lyons,
          700 wds., pt. pub.
        Sight & S: v. 40 n. 1 (Winter, 1970-1971), pp. 53-54; Gavin Millar, 700
          wds., cp. pub.

7824 FILMS OF ROBERT BRESSON, THE (Ian Cameron, ed.)
        F Comment: v. 7, n. 2 (Summer, 1971), pp. 73-75; Andrée Hayum, 1300
          wds., cp. pub.
        Interntl F G: v. 8 (1971), p. 439; 50 wds., pt. pub.
        Screen: v. 11, n. 3 (Summer, 1970), pp. 114-115; Suzanne Budgen, 750
          wds., pt. pub.

7825 FILMS OF ROBERT ROSSEN, THE (Alan Casty)
        Films & F: v. 16, n. 1 (Oct., 1969), p. 70; Sheridan Morley, 150 wds., pt.
          pub.

7826 FILMS OF SPENCER TRACY, THE (Donald Deschner)
        Cineaste: v. II, n. 3 (Winter, 1968-1969), p. 19; Gary Crowdus, 200 wds.,
          pt. pub.
        Interntl F G: v. 7 (1970), p. 396; 50 wds., pt. pub.

7827 FILMS OF W. C. FIELDS, THE (Donald Deschner)
        Interntl F G: v. 5 (1968), p. 261; 25 wds., pt. pub.

7828 FILMS ON ART: A SPECIALIZED STUDY, AN INTERNATIONAL CATA-
          LOGUE (William McK. Chapman)
        Films in R: v. III, n. 7 (Aug.-Sept., 1952), pp. 361-361; Annabelle Forsch,
          650 wds., cp. pub.
        Quarterly of FR TV: v. VI (1951-1952), p. 212; Franklin Fearing, 90 wds.,
          pt. pub.
        Sight & S: v. 19, n. 1 (Mar., 1950), pp. 41-42; Gavin Lambert, 1000 wds.,
          cp. pub.

7829 FILMS ON THE CAMPUS (Thomas Fensch)
        Interntl F G: v. 8 (1971), p. 439; 50 wds., pt. pub.

7830 FILMSTRIP AND SLIDE PROJECTION (M. K. Kidd and C. W. Long)
        Sight & S: v. 18, n. 70 (Summer, 1949), p. 97; F. E. Farley, 300 wds., cp.
          pub.

7831 FILMSTRIPS (Vera M. Falconer)
        Sight & S: v. 17, n. 67 (Autumn, 1948), p. 151; F. E. Farley, 400 wds., cp.
          pub.

7832 *FILMTRILOGI, EN (Ingmar Bergman)
        Sight & S: v. 34, n. 1 (Winter, 1964-1965), pp. 48-49; Neville March
          Hunnings, 700 wds., cp. pub.

7833 FILMVIEWER'S HANDBOOK, THE (Emile G. McAnany and Robert Wil-
          liams)
        F Soc Rev: Mar. (1966), pp. 9-10; Edwin Jahiel, 950 wds., cp. pub.

7834 *FIRE FILM (Carl Th. Dreyer, ed. by Ole Storm)
        Sight & S: v. 34, n. 2 (Spring, 1965), pp. 101; Frederic Fleischer, 650 wds.,
          cp. pub.

7835 FIRST PERSON PLURAL (Dagmar Godowsky)
        Films in R: v. IX, n. 9 (Nov., 1958), pp. 529-531; Romano Tozzi, 600 wds.,
          cp. pub.
        Sight & S: v. 28, n. 3-4; (Summer-Autumn, 1959), p. 187; Philip Oakes, 800
          wds., cp. pub.

7836 FIRST TWENTY YEARS: A SEGMENT OF FILM HISTORY, THE (Kemp
          R. Niver)
        Am Cinematog: v. 50, n. 3 (Mar., 1969), pp. 342-343; 347; George J.
          Mitchell, 1000 wds., cp. pub.
        F Quarterly: v. XXII, n. 3 (Spring, 1969), pp. 57-58; Ernest Callenbach,
          100 wds., cp. pub.
        Films in R: v. XX, n. 3 (Mar., 1969), pp. 176, 182; Robert Giroux, 375
          wds., cp. pub.

7837 FIRST YEAR OF SESAME STREET, THE (Samuel Ball and Gerry Ann
          Bogatz)
        Interntl F G: v. 9 (1972), p. 465; 50 wds., pt. pub.

7838 FIT FOR THE CHASE: CARS AND THE MOVIES (Raymond Lee)
        Interntl F G: v. 7 (1970), p. 396; 50 wds., pt. pub.

7839 FIVE C'S OF CINEMATOGRAPHY, THE (Joseph V. Mascelli)
        Am Cinematog: v. 47, n. 2 (Feb., 1966), pp. 214-215, 220, 222; 1400 wds.,
          cp. pub.
        Cineaste: v. I, n. 4 (Spring, 1968), p. 24; Gary Crowdus, 150 wds., pt. pub.

F Quarterly: v. XIX, n. 4 (Summer, 1966), pp. 69-70; Ernest Callenbach, 175 wds., cp. pub.
Films in R: v. XVII, n. 4 (Apr., 1966), pp. 245-246; George J. Mitchell, 350 wds., cp. pub.
Take One: v. 1, n. 12 (1968), p. 29; Wally Gentleman, 225 wds., cp. pub.

7840 FLASHBACK (George Pearson)
Films & F: v. 4, n. 3 (Dec., 1957), p. 29; Martin Gray, 125 wds., pt. pub.
Films in R: v. X, n. 1 (Jan., 1959), pp. 52-54; William K. Everson, 500 wds., cp. pub.
Sight & F: v. 27, n. 3 (Winter, 1957-1958), pp. 156-157; Ernest Lindgren, 850 wds., cp. pub.

7841 FOCUS ON CITIZEN KANE (Ronald Gottesman, ed.)
Focus on F: n. 8 (Oct., 1971), p. 60; 150 wds., cp. pub.

7842 FOCUS ON FAME (Anthony Beauchamps)
Films & F: v. 4, n. 7 (Apr., 1958), p. 33; Martin Gray, 100 wds., pt. pub.

7843 *FOI ET LES MONTAGNES, OU LE SEPTIEME ART AU PASSE, LA (Henri Fescourt)
Cinema Studies: v. I, n. 5 (Sept., 1962), pp. 107-110; Tom Milne, 1800 wds., cp. pub.

7844 FONDAS: THE FILMS AND CAREERS OF HENRY, JANE AND PETER FONDA, THE (John Springer)
Films in R: v. XXII, n. 7 (Aug.-Sept., 1971), pp. 433-434; I.B., 75 wds., cp. pub.

7845 *FONDEMENTS DE L'ART CINEMATOGRAPHIQUE, LES (Jean R. Debrix)
Films in R: v. XIV, n. 1 (Jan., 1963), p. 53; Jack Edmund Nolan, 300 wds., cp. pub.

7846 FOOTNOTES TO THE FILM (Charles Davy, ed.)
Interntl F G: v. 9 (1972), p. 466; 50 wds., pt. pub.

7847 FOREIGN FILMS ON AMERICAN SCREENS (Michael F. Mayer)
F Soc Rev: Mar. (1966), p. 19; Gordon Hitchens, 200 wds., cp. pub.

7848 FORTY YEARS OF SCREEN CREDITS (John T. Weaver, comp.)
Films in R: v. XXI, n. 8 (Oct., 1970), pp. 500-501; 150 wds., cp. pub.
Films in R: v. XXI, n. 10 (Dec., 1970), p. 648; Earl Anderson (a letter), 250 wds., no pub.

7849 FOUR ASPECTS OF THE FILM (James Limbacher)
F Soc Rev: v. 5, n. 1 (Sept., 1969), pp. 47-48; Dennis Kawicki, 400 wds., cp. pub.
Films & F: v. 16, n. 2 (Nov., 1969), p. 71; 100 wds., pt. pub.
Take One: v. 2, n. 8 (1970), pp. 27-28; Glen Hunter, 125 wds., cp. pub.

7850 FOUR FABULOUS FACES (Larry Carr)
Films & F: v. 17, n. 10 (July, 1971), p. 64; Sheridan Morley, 100 wds., pt. pub.

7851 FOUR GREAT COMEDIANS (Donald McCaffrey)
Cinema J: v. IX, n. 1 (Fall, 1969), pp. 53-55; John Tibbetts, 900 wds., cp. pub.
Interntl F G: v. 6 (1969), p. 275; 50 wds., pt. pub.

7852 FOUR SCREENPLAYS OF INGMAR BERGMAN (trans. by Lars Malmstrom and David Kushner)
Cinema Studies: v. I, n. 3 (Aug., 1961), pp. 61-63; Grete Selby, 1200 wds., cp. pub.
F Quarterly: v. XIV, n. 3 (Spring, 1961), pp. 61-62; R. H. Turner, 1000 wds., cp. pub.
Sight & S: v. 30, n. 2 (Spring, 1961), pp. 97-98; John Russell Taylor, 1200 wds., cp. pub.

7853 FOX GIRLS, THE (James Robert Parish)
Focus on F: n. 10 (Summer, 1972), pp. 60-61; Allen Eyles, 300 wds., cp. pub.

7854 FRAGMENTS: JANET HILLS, 1919-1956 (Janet Hills)
      Sight & S: v. 26, n. 3 (Winter, 1956-1957), p. 162; Stanley Reed, 300 wds.,
      cp. pub.

7855 *FRANCE (Marcel Martin)
      Interntl F G: v. 9 (1972), p. 466; 50 wds., pt. pub.

7856 FRANCOIS TRUFFAUT (C. G. Crisp)
      Focus on F: n. 10 (Summer, 1972), p. 62; Allen Eyles, 275 wds., cp. pub.

7857 FRANJU (Raymond Durgnat)
      F Quarterly: v. XXII, n. 3 (Spring, 1969), p. 58; Ernest Callenbach, 100
      wds., cp. pub.
      Films & F: v. 15, n. 3 (Dec., 1968), p. 65; Sheridan Morley, 200 wds., pt.
      pub.
      Interntl F G: v. 6 (1969), p. 275; 50 wds., pt. pub.

      FRANK CAPRA: THE NAME ABOVE THE TITLE (see: The Name Above
      the Title)

7858 FRED ASTAIRE AND HIS WORK (Alfonso Hackl)
      Films & F: v. 16, n. 10 (July, 1970), p. 64; Sheridan Morley, 75 wds., pt.
      pub.

7859 FREEDOM OF THE MOVIES: A REPORT ON SELF-REGULATION FROM
      THE COMMISSION ON FREEDOM OF THE PRESS (Ruth A.
      Inglis)
      Sight & S: v. 16, n. 64 (Winter, 1947-1948), p. 160; John M. Smithells, 700
      wds., cp. pub.

7860 *FREIWILLIGE SELBSKONTROLLE DER FILMWIRTSCHAFT UND DAS
      ZENSURVERBOT DES GRUNDGES, DIE (Johanne Noltenius)
      Cinema Studies: v. I, n. 1 (Mar., 1960), pp. 19-20; F. Munch, 600 wds., cp.
      pub.

7861 FRENCH CINEMA SINCE 1946 (Roy Armes)
      Cinema J: v. X, n. 2 (Spring, 1971), pp. 56-58; Judith Gollub, 1150 wds.,
      cp. pub.
      F Lib Quarterly: v. 1, n. 3 (Summer, 1968), p. 54; Harvey Deneroff, 350
      wds., pt. pub.
      F Quarterly: v. XXI, n. 1 (Fall, 1967), pp. 64-65; James Michael Martin,
      300 wds., cp. pub.
      Films & F: v. 13, n. 3 (Dec., 1966), p. 42; Sheridan Morley, 200 wds., no
      pub.
      Interntl F G: v. 5 (1968), p. 261; 25 wds., pt. pub.

7862 FRENCH CINEMA TODAY, THE (Gordon Reid and Raymond Lefevre)
      Interntl F G: v. 1 (1964), p. 231; 30 wds., pt. pub.

7863 FRENCH FILM (Georges Sadoul)
      Quarterly of FR TV: v. IX, n. 1 (Fall, 1954), pp. 106-107; Franklin
      Fearing, 125 wds., cp. pub.
      Sight & S: v. 23, n. 3 (Jan.-Mar., 1954), p. 162; Ernest Lindgren, 750 wds.,
      cp. pub.

7864 FRIESE-GREENE, CLOSE-UP OF AN INVENTOR (Ray Allister)
      Sequence: n. 7 (Spring, 1949), p. 44; Lindsay Anderson, 500 wds., pt. pub.
      Sight & S: v. 17, n. 68 (Winter, 1948-1949), p. 198, T. D. Griffin-Beale, 275
      wds., cp. pub.

7865 FRITZ LANG (Alfred Eibel, ed.)
      Interntl F G: v. 3 (1966), p. 259; 175 wds., cp. pub.

7866 FRITZ LANG IN AMERICA (Peter Bogdanovich)
      Cinema J: v. VIII, n. 1 (Fall, 1968), pp. 46-47; John Fell, 800 wds., cp.
      pub.
      F Comment: v. 6, n. 1 (Spring, 1970), p. 68; Donald Staples, 125 wds., cp.
      pub.
      Films & F: v. 15, n. 7 (Apr., 1969), p. 68; Sheridan Morley, 125 wds., pt.
      pub.

7867 FROM CALIGARI TO HITLER: A PSYCHOLOGICAL HISTORY OF THE
        GERMAN FILM (Siegfried Kracauer)
        Hollywood Q: v. II, n. 4 (July, 1947), pp. 422-427; Franklin Fearing, 2500
            wds., cp. pub.
        Screen: v. 12, n. 3 (Summer, 1971), pp. 143-150; Andrew Tudor, 3500
            wds., pt. pub.

7868 FROM CAVE PAINTING TO COMIC STRIP (Lancelot Hogben)
        Films in R: v. I, n. 2 (Mar., 1950), pp. 37-39; Jules V. Schwerin, 700 wds.,
            cp. pub.

7869 FROM SCRIPT TO SCREEN (Bruce Woodhouse)
        Sight & S: v. 17, n. 68 (Winter, 1948-1949), p. 198; Peter Plaskitt, 325
            wds., cp. pub.

7870 FROM UNDER MY HAT (Hedda Hopper)
        Films in R: v. IV, n. 1 (Jan., 1953), pp. 40-41; Elspeth Chapin, 750 wds.,
            cp. pub.
        Sight & S: v. 23, n. 1 (July-Sept., 1953), p. 51; Araminta Teas, 550 wds.,
            cp. pub.

7871 FUN IN A CHINESE LAUNDRY (Josef von Sternberg)
        F Heritage: v. 1, n. 3 (Spring, 1966), pp. 38-40; Herman G. Weinberg, 1200
            wds., cp. pub.
        Films & F: v. 13, n. 4 (Jan., 1967), p. 56; Sheridan Morley, 600 wds., pt.
            pub.
        Films in R: v. XVI, n. 5 (May, 1965), pp. 305-306; Eleanor H. Nash, 500
            wds., cp. pub.
        Sight & S: v. 34, n. 4 (Autumn, 1965), pp. 202-205; Elliott Stein, 3500
            wds., cp. pub.

7872 FUTURE OF BRITISH FILMS, THE (Richard Winnington and Nicholas
        Davenport)
        Sight & S: v. 20, n. 2 (June, 1951), pp. 63-64; Duncan Crow, 350 wds., cp.
            pub.

7873 *GAG, LE (Francois Mars)
        Cinema Studies: v. II, n. 1 (June, 1965), pp. 9-12; N.M.H., 1600 wds., cp.
            pub.
        Interntl F G: v. 3 (1966), p. 262; 175 wds., cp. pub.

7874 GANGSTER FILM, THE (John Baxter)
        Films & F: v. 17, n. 8 (May, 1971), p. 136; Sheridan Morley, 200 wds., pt.
            pub.

7875 GARBO (Fritiof Billquist)
        Sight & S: v. 30, n. 2 (Spring, 1961), pp. 99-100; Margaret Hinxman, 600
            wds., cp. pub.

7876 GARBO (John Bainbridge)
        F Culture: v. 1, n. 3 (May-June, 1955), p. 32; G. N. Fenin, 375 wds., cp.
            pub.
        Films & F: v. 2, n. 2 (Nov., 1955), p. 26; Michell Raper, 100 wds., pt. pub.
        Films in R: v. VI, n. 7 (Aug.-Sept., 1955), p. 355-357; Elspeth Hart, 1000
            wds., cp. pub.
        Quarterly of FR TV: v. X, n. 1 (Fall, 1955), p. 103; Franklin Fearing, 150
            wds., cp. pub.
        Sight & S: v. 25, n. 2 (Autumn, 1955), p. 107; Penelope Houston, 550 wds.,
            cp. pub.

7877 GARBO (Norman Zierold)
      Films & F: v. 16, n. 10 (July, 1970), p. 64; Sheridan Morley, 100 wds., pt.
          pub.
      Interntl F G: v. 8 (1971), p. 439; 25 wds., pt. pub.

7878 GARBO AND THE NIGHT WATCHMEN (Alistair Cooke, ed.)
      Focus on F: n. 8 (Oct., 1971), p. 63; 175 wds., cp. pub.

7879 *GARY COOPER, LE CAVALIER DE L'OUEST (Lucienne Escoube)
      Interntl F G: v. 4 (1967), p. 277; 75 wds., pt. pub.

7880 GARY COOPER STORY, THE (George Carpozi, Jr.,)
      Focus on F: n. 7 (Summer, 1971), p. 60; Allen Eyles, 300 wds., cp. pub.

7881 *GEORG WILHELM PABST (Barthelemy Amengual)
      Interntl F G: v. 4 (1967), p. 276; 100 wds., pt. pub.

7882 GEORGE STEVENS: AN AMERICAN ROMANTIC (Donald Richie)
      F Comment: v. 6, n. 3 (Fall, 1970), pp. 75-77; Charles Silver, 1600 wds.,
          cp. pub.

7883 *GEORGES FRANJU (Gabriel Vialle)
      Interntl F G: v. 6 (1969), p. 275; 50 wds., pt. pub.

7884 *GEORGES MELIES (Georges Sadoul, ed.)
      Sight & S: v. 31, n. 2 (Spring, 1962), p. 100; David Robinson, 800 wds., cp.
          pub.

7885 *GEORGES MELIES, MAGE (Maurice Bessy and Lo Duca)
      Sight & S: v. 31, n. 2 (Spring, 1962), p. 100; David Robinson, 800 wds., cp.
          pub.

7886 *GERARD PHILIPE (Georges Sadoul)
      Interntl F G: v. 6 (1969), pp. 277-278; 50 wds., pt. pub.

7887 GERMAN CINEMA, THE (Roger Manvell and Heinrich Fraenkel)
      F Quarterly: v. XXV, n. 4 (Summer, 1972), p. 42; 100 wds., cp. pub.
      Films & F: v. 17, n. 11 (Aug., 1971), p. 14; Sheridan Morley, 175 wds., pt.
          pub.

7888 GERMANY (Felix Bucher)
      Films & F: v. 17, n. 8 (May, 1971), p. 136; Sheridan Morley, 150 wds., pt.
          pub.
      Interntl F G: v. 7 (1970), p. 399; 50 wds., pt. pub.

7889 GERSHWIN YEARS, THE (Edward Jablonski and Lawrence D. Stewart)
      Films in R: v. X, n. 3 (Mar., 1959), pp. 178-179; Don Miller, 375 wds., cp.
          pub.

7890 *GESCHICHTE DES FILMS (Ulrich Gregor and Enno Patalas)
      F Quarterly: v. XVIII, n. 1 (Fall, 1964), pp. 57-58; Colin Young, 225 wds.,
          cp. pub.

7891 *GESCHICHTE DES MODERNEN FILMS (Ulrich Gregor and Enno Patalas)
      F Quarterly: v. XX, n. 3 (Spring, 1967), pp. 58-59; Harriet R. Polt, 350
          wds., cp. pub.

7892 *GESTALT DER FILMKUNST VON ASTA NIELSEN BIS WALT DISNEY
          (Ludwig Gesek)
      Sight & S: v. 17, n. 68 (Winter, 1948-1949), p. 196; Narah Lewis, 300 wds.,
          cp. pub.

7893 GETTING IDEAS FROM THE MOVIES (Perry W. Holaday and George D.
          Stoddard)
      F Comment: v. 7, n. 2 (Summer, 1971), pp. 70-72; Garth Jowett, 2200
          wds., cp. pub.

7894 GIFT HORSE, THE (Hildegard Neff)
      Focus on F: n. 8 (Oct., 1971), pp. 59-60; P.D.C. 225 wds., cp. pub.

7895 GIRL LIKE I, A (Anita Loos)
    Films in R: v. XVIII, n. 3 (Mar., 1967), pp. 172-173; Robert Downing, 250
    wds., cp. pub.

7896 GLASS TEAT, THE (Harlan Ellison)
    Cineaste: v. III, n. 4 (Spring, 1970), pp. 27, 32; Noe Goldwasser, 1000 wds.,
    cp. pub.

7897 GLOSSARY OF MOTION PICTURE TERMINOLOGY (Thurston C. Jordan,
    Jr.)
    Films in R: v. XIX, n. 10 (Dec., 1968), p. 640; L.W., 75 wds., cp. pub.

7898 GODARD (Richard Roud)
    Cineaste: v. IV, n. 1 (Summer, 1970), pp. 29-30; Calvin Green, 1500 wds.,
    cp. pub.
    F Quarterly: v. XXI, n. 4 (Summer, 1968), p. 55; 125 wds., no pub.
    F Soc Rev: May (1968), p. 39; Frank Manchel, 50 wds., cp. pub.
    Films & F: v. 16, n. 12 (Sept., 1970), p. 94; Sheridan Morley, 100 wds., pt.
    pub.
    Interntl F G: v. 5 (1968), p. 263; 25 wds., pt. pub.

7899 *GOETHE UND DER FILM (Heinrich Heining)
    Sight & S: v. 19, n. 1 (Mar., 1950), p. 42; Muriel Grindrod, 350 wds., cp.
    pub.

7900 GOING STEADY (Pauline Kael)
    Cineaste: v. III, n. 4 (Spring, 1970), p. 23; Ruth McCormick, 1000 wds., cp.
    pub.
    F Heritage: v. 5, n. 4 (Summer, 1970), pp. 29-31; Robert Moss, 900 wds.,
    cp. pub.
    F Soc Rev: v. 5, n. 6 (Feb., 1970), pp. 40-44; Michael Sragow, 500 wds.; cp.
    pub.
    Focus on F: n. 5 (Winter/Nov.-Dec., 1970), p. 61; P.D.C., 200 wds., cp.
    pub.
    Sight & S: v. 40, n. 1 (Winter, 1970-1971), p. 54; Penelope Houston, 700
    wds., cp. pub.

7901 GOING TO THE CINEMA (Andrew Buchanan)
    Sight & S: v. 16, n. 62 (Summer, 1947), p. 85; Mary Field, 500 wds., pt.
    pub.

7902 GOLDEN WEB: A HISTORY OF BROADCASTING IN THE UNITED
    STATES, 1933-1953, THE (Eric Barnouw)
    Cineaste: v. V, n. 1 (Winter, 1971-1972), pp. 23-25; Tom Brom, 2000 wds.,
    cp. pub.
    F Comment: v. 5, n. 2 (Spring, 1969), pp. 91-94; Richard J. Meyer, 1700
    wds., cp. pub.
    F Lib Quarterly: v. 3, n. 2 (Spring, 1970), p. 39; George Wallach, 400 wds.,
    cp. pub.

7903 GOOD COMPANY (Mary Field)
    Sight & S: v. 22, n. 1 (July-Sept., 1952), p. 43; Stanley Reed, 750 wds., cp.
    pub.

7904 GOODNESS HAD NOTHING TO DO WITH IT (Mae West)
    Films in R: v. XI, n. 1 (Jan., 1960), pp. 50-52; Robert Downing, 700 wds.,
    cp. pub.

7905 GOTTA SING, GOTTA DANCE (John Kobal)
    Films & F: v. 17, n. 12 (Sept., 1971), p. 66; Sheridan Morley, 500 wds., pt.
    pub.

7906 GRAMMAR OF THE FILM, A (Raymond Spottiswoode)
    Am Cinematog: v. 41, n. 11 (Nov., 1960), p. 646; 75 wds., pt. pub.
    Films & F: v. 2, n. 1 (Oct., 1955), p. 28; Peter Brinson, 150 wds., pt. pub.
    Films in R: v. I, n. 4 (May-June, 1950), pp. 35-36; Arthur Knight, 550 wds.,
    cp. pub.
    Quarterly of FR TV: v. VI (1951-1952), p. 103; Franklin Fearing, 80 wds.,
    pt. pub.
    Sight & S: v. 25, n. 2 (Autumn, 1955), pp. 106-107; Pauline Kael, 900 wds.,
    cp. pub.

7907 *GRANDE AVENTURE DU CINEMA SUEDOIS, LA (Jean Béranger)
       Sight & S: v. 30, n. 2 (Spring, 1961), pp. 97-98; John Russell Taylor, 1200
       wds., cp. pub.

7908 *GRANDE AVENTURE DU WESTERN, LA (J. L. Rieupeyrout)
       Interntl F G: v. 4 (1967), p. 276; 75 wds., pt. pub.

7909 *GRANDS CINEASTES, LES (Henri Agel)
       F Quarterly: v. XV, n. 1 (Fall, 1961), pp. 58-60; Steven P. Hill, 900 wds.,
       cp. pub.

7910 GREAT ACTING (British Broadcasting Company)
       Films & F: v. 14, n. 5 (Feb., 1968), p. 54; Sheridan Morley, 150 wds., pt.
       pub.

7911 GREAT AUDIENCE, THE (Gilbert Seldes)
       Films in R: v. II, n. 1 (Jan., 1951), pp. 44-45; Quincy Howe, 800 wds., cp.
       pub.
       Hollywood Q: v. V (1950-1951), pp. 418-419; Franklin Fearing, 550 wds.,
       cp. pub.

7912 GREAT CHARLIE, THE (Robert Payne)
       Sight & S: v. 22, n. 3 (Jan.-Mar., 1953), p. 143; Jeffrey Bernard, 375 wds.,
       cp. pub.

7913 GREAT COMPANIONS (Max Eastman)
       Films in R: v. XI, n. 1 (Jan., 1960), p. 52; A.H.W., 250 wds., cp. pub.

7914 GREAT FILMS: FIFTY GOLDEN YEARS OF MOTION PICTURES, THE
       (Bosley Crowther)
       Cinema J: v. VIII, n. 2 (Spring, 1969), pp. 35-38; Richard Dyer MacCann,
       1600 wds., cp. pub.
       F Comment: v. 5, n. 4 (Winter, 1969), p. 78; 125 wds., cp. pub.
       F Quarterly: v. XXII, n. 1 (Fall, 1968), pp. 79-80; Ernest Callenbach, 300
       wds., cp. pub.
       F Soc Rev: Mar. (1968), pp. 35-37; Frank Manchel, 1500 wds., cp. pub.

7915 GREAT FUNNIES — A HISTORY OF FILM COMEDY, THE (David
       Robinson)
       Cineaste: v. III, n. 1 (Summer, 1969), pp. 23-24; Gary Crowdus, 500 wds.,
       cp. pub.
       Cinema: v. 5, n. 2, pp. 42-43; 200 wds., cp. pub.
       Cinema J: v. IX, n. 1 (Fall, 1969), pp. 53-55; John Tibbetts, 900 wds., cp.
       pub.

7916 GREAT GOD PAN, THE (Robert Payne)
       Films in R: v. III, n. 6 (June-July, 1952), pp. 297-298; H. G. Weinberg, 550
       wds., cp. pub.
       Quarterly of FR TV: v. VII, n. 1 (Fall, 1952), pp. 90-92; Franklin Fearing,
       400 wds., cp. pub.

7917 GREAT MOVIE STARS: THE GOLDEN YEARS, THE (David Shipman)
       Cinema J: v. XI, n. 1 (Fall, 1971), pp. 68-71; Kent R. Brown, 1300 wds.,
       cp. pub.
       Films & F: v. 17, n. 4 (Jan., 1971), p. 66; Sheridan Morley, 400 wds., pt.
       pub.
       Focus on F: n. 5 (Winter/Nov.-Dec., 1970), pp. 59-60; Allen Eyles, 200
       wds., cp. pub.
       Journal of P C: v. IV, n. 3 (Winter, 1971), pp. 822-824; Ralph Haven Wolfe,
       700 wds., cp. pub.
       Sight & S: v. 40, n. 2 (Spring, 1971), p. 111; John Russell Taylor, 800 wds.,
       cp. pub.

7918 GRETA GARBO (Raymond Durgnat and John Kobal)
       F Heritage: v. 2, n. 2 (Winter, 1966-1967), p. 33; 250 wds., cp. pub.

7919 GRIERSON ON DOCUMENTARY (John Grierson, ed. by Forsyth Hardy)
       F Comment: v. IV, n. 2-3 (Fall-Winter, 1967), p. 117; Jack C. Ellis, 650
       wds., cp. pub.
       F Soc Rev: Dec. 1966), pp. 34-35; D. J. Powell, 350 wds., cp. pub.

Hollywood Q: v. III, n. 2 (Winter, 1947-1948), pp. 202-207; Arthur Knight,
    2500 wds., cp. pub.
Sight & S: v. 15, n. 59 (Autumn, 1946), pp. 106-107; Roger Manvell, 2000
    wds., cp. pub.

7920 GRIFFITH AND THE RISE OF HOLLYWOOD (Paul O'Dell)
    Films & F: v. 17, n. 9 (June, 1971), p. 92; Sheridan Morley, 250 wds., pt.
        pub.
    Interntl F G: v. 8 (1971), p. 439; 25 wds., pt. pub.

7921 GROUCHO (Arthur Marx)
    Films & F: v. 1, n. 3 (Dec., 1954), p. 29; John Minchinton, 200 wds., pt.
        pub.

7922 GROUCHO AND ME (Groucho Marx)
    Films & F: v. 6, n. 4 (Jan., 1960), p. 32; Martin Gray, 100 wds., pt. pub.
    Sight & S: v. 29, n. 1 (Winter, 1959-1960), pp. 47-48; Penelope Gilliatt, 750
        wds., cp. pub.

7923 GROUCHO LETTERS, THE (Groucho Marx)
    Films & F: v. 16, n. 3 (Dec., 1969), p. 72; Sheridan Morley, 500 wds., pt.
        pub.

7924 GUIDE FOR FILM TEACHERS TO FILM-MAKING BY TEENAGERS, A
        (Rodger Larson)
    F Comment: v. 6, n. 1 (Spring, 1970), p. 72; 175 wds., cp. pub.

7925 GUIDE TO DEVELOPMENT FILMS, A (Jean Marie Ackerman)
    F Lib Quarterly: v. 1, n. 1 (Winter, 1967-1968), p. 56; B. Penny Northern,
        50 wds., pt. pub.

7926 GUIDE TO FILMMAKING (Edward Pincus)
    F Comment: v. 6, n. 3 (Fall, 1970), p. 78; Hubert Smith, 750 wds., cp. pub.
    Take One: v. 2, n. 4 (1969), pp. 23-24; Ronald H. Blumer, 500 wds., cp.
        pub.

H

7927 HALL OF FAME OF WESTERN STARS, THE (Ernest N. Corneau)
    Interntl F G: v. 8 (1971), p. 439; 50 wds., pt. pub.
    Journal of P C: v. IV, n. 1 (Summer, 1970), pp. 263-265; Michael T.
        Marsden, 800 wds., cp. pub.
    Views & Rev: v, I, n. 3 (Winter, 1970), pp. 73-74; 600 wds., cp. pub.

7928 HAMLET: THE FILM AND THE PLAY (Alan Dent, ed.)
    Sight & S: v. 17, n. 67 (Autumn, 1948), p. 152; 175 wds., cp. pub.

7929 HANDBOOK OF BASIC MOTION-PICTURE TECHNOLOGY (Emil E.
        Brodbeck)
    Films in R: v. I, n. 3 (Nov., 1950), pp. 36-37; Lewis Jacobs, 550 wds., cp.
        pub.

7930 HANDBOOK OF TV AND FILM TECHNIQUE, THE (Charles W. Curran)
    Quarterly of FR TV: v. VIII, n. 3 (Spring, 1954), p. 317; Franklin Fearing,
        125 wds., cp. pub.

7931 HARLOW: AN INTIMATE BIOGRAPHY (Irving Shulman)
    F Comment: v. 2, n. 3 (Summer, 1964), pp. 59-61; Harry Feldman, 2100
        wds., cp. pub.
    F Culture: n. 40 (Spring, 1966), p. 67; Taylor Mead, 800 wds., cp. pub.
    Films in R: v. XV, n. 8 (Oct., 1964), p. 496; 225 wds., cp. pub.

7932 HAROLD LLOYD'S WORLD OF COMEDY (William Cahn)
Cinema Studies: v. II, n. 1 (June, 1965), pp. 9-12; N.M.H., 1600 wds., cp. pub.
Sight & S: v. 35, n. 3 (Summer, 1966), p. 154; John Gillett, 450 wds., cp. pub.

7933 HARPO SPEAKS! (Harpo Marx, with Rowland Barber)
Sight & S: v. 31, n. 1 (Winter, 1961-1962), pp. 49-50; David Robinson, 1500 wds., cp. pub.

7934 HAUNTED SCREEN: EXPRESSIONISM IN THE GERMAN CINEMA AND THE INFLUENCE OF MAX REINHARDT (Lotte H. Eisner, trans. by Roger Greaves)
Cinema J: v. X, n. 1 (Fall, 1970), pp. 60-64; Richard B. Byrne, 1800 wds., cp. pub.
F Comment: v. 6, n. 2 (Summer, 1970), pp. 60-62; Herman G. Weinberg, 1200 wds., cp. pub.
F Soc Rev: v. 5, n. 6 (Feb., 1970), p. 48; Harvey Deneroff, 400 wds., cp. pub.
Films & F: v. 16, n. 4 (Jan., 1970), p. 72; Sheridan Morley, 125 wds., pt. pub.
Films in R: v. XXI, n. 5 (May, 1970), p. 292; Ruth Kramborg, 100 wds., cp. pub.
Interntl F G: v. 8 (1971), pp. 439; 441; 50 wds., pt. pub.
Journal of P C: v. IV, n. 3 (Winter, 1971), pp. 824-827; Edgar F. Daniels, 1200 wds., cp. pub.
Screen: v. 12, n. 3 (Summer, 1971), pp. 143-150; Andrew Tudor, 3200 wds., pt. pub.
Sight & S: v. 39, n. 1 (Winter, 1969-1970), p. 52; Thorold Dickinson, 700 wds., cp. pub.
Take One: v. 2, n. 8 (1970), p. 28; Glen Hunter, 100 wds., cp. pub.

7935 HAVE TUX, WILL TRAVEL: BOB HOPE'S OWN STORY (Bob Hope, with Pete Martin)
Films in R: v. VI, n. 6 (June-July, 1955), pp. 297-298; Eleanor H. Nash, 500 wds., cp. pub.

7936 HAYS OFFICE, THE (Raymond Morley)
Hollywood Q: v. I, n. 1 (Oct., 1945), pp. 120-121; John Elliott Williams, 640 wds., cp. pub.
Sight & S: v. 16, n. 64 (Winter, 1947-1948), p. 160; John M. Smithells, 700 wds., pt. pub.

7937 HEAVIES, THE (Ian and Elisabeth Cameron)
F Comment: v. 6, n. 1 (Spring, 1970), p. 68; Donald Staples, 250 wds., cp. pub.
F Soc Rev: Mar. (1968), pp. 38-39; Edwin Jahiel, 400 wds., pt. pub.

7938 HELEN HAYES: ON REFLECTION (W. H. Allen)
Films & F: v. 15, n. 8 (May, 1969), p. 74; Sheridan Morley, 150 wds., pt. pub.

7939 HELLO, HOLLYWOOD! THE STORY OF THE MOVIES BY THE PEOPLE WHO MAKE THEM (Allen Rivkin and Laura Kerr)
F Quarterly: v. XVI, n. 2 (Winter, 1962-1963), pp. 58-59; Ernest Callenbach, 150 wds., cp. pub.

7940 *HENRI-GEORGES CLOUZOT (Pietro Bianchi)
Films in R: v. III, n. 4 (Apr., 1952), p. 204; Robert F. Hawkins, 200 wds., cp. pub.

7941 HER TWELVE MEN (Louise Baker)
Films & F: v. 1, n. 4 (Jan., 1955), p. 30; Jill Hardy, 25 wds., pt. pub.

7942 HILLS OF BEVERLY, THE (Libbie Block)
Films in R: v. IX, n. 4 (Apr., 1958), p. 215; Eleanor H. Nash, 225 wds., cp. pub.

7943 HIS EYE IS ON THE SPARROWS (Ethel Waters, with Charles Samuels)
Sight & S: v. 21, n. 3 (Jan.-Mar., 1952), p. 138; Harold Lang, 450 wds., cp. pub.

7944 *HISTOIRE DU CINEMA (Giuseppe Lo Duca)
        Hollywood Q: v. III, n. 4 (Spring, 1948), pp. 454-456; Jacques Queval, 800
           wds., cp. pub.

7945 *HISTOIRE DU CINEMA (Maurice Bardèche and Robert Brasillach)
        Sequence: n. 8 (Summer, 1949), p. 91; Peter Ericsson, 600 wds., cp. pub.

7946 *HISTOIRE DU CINEMA (René Jeanne and Charles Ford)
        Sight & S: v. 23, n. 1 (July-Sept., 1953), p. 51; James Morgan, 450 wds., cp.
           pub.

7947 *HISTOIRE DU CINEMA (Pierre Leprohon)
        Interntl F G: v. 1 (1964), p. 226; 50 wds., cp. pub.

7948 *HISTOIRE DU CINEMA (Jean Mitry)
        F Quarterly: v. XXV, n. 1 (Fall, 1971), pp. 58-63; Lee Atwell, 2800 wds.,
           no pub.
        Films & F: v. 14, n. 11 (Aug., 1968), p. 56; Sheridan Morley, 150 wds., pt.
           pub.

7949 *HISTOIRE DU CINEMA AMERICAIN, 1926-1947 (Pierre Artis)
        Sight & S: v. 17, n. 65 (Spring, 1948), p. 52; Ragna Jackson, 350 wds., cp.
           pub.

7950 *HISTOIRE DU WESTERN (Charles Ford)
        Films in R: v. XVI, n. 2 (Feb., 1965), pp. 107-108; Jack Edmund Nolan,
           475 wds., cp. pub.

7951 *HISTOIRE D'UN ART: LE CINEMA DES ORIGINES A NOS JOURS
           (Georges Sadoul)
        Sight & S: v. 18, n. 72 (Jan., 1950), pp. 37-38; Rachael Low, 1000 wds., cp.
           pub.

7952 *HISTOIRE ENCYCLOPEDIQUE DU CINEMA (René Jeanne and Charles
           Ford)
        Cinema Studies: v. I, n. 1 (Mar., 1960), pp. 16-18; Tom Milne, 1400 wds.,
           cp. pub.
        Films in R: v. V, n. 3 (Mar., 1954), pp. 149-150; Gerald D. McDonald, 550
           wds., cp. pub.
        Films in R: v. VIII, n. 7 (Aug.-Sept., 1957), pp. 357-359; Gerald D.
           McDonald, 850 wds., cp. pub.
        Films in R: v. XIV, n. 7 (Aug.-Sept., 1963), p. 426; Gerald D. McDonald,
           350 wds., cp. pub.
        Sight & S: v. 17, n. 66 (Summer, 1948), p. 106; Ragna Jackson, 500 wds.,
           cp. pub.

7953 *HISTOIRE EN MILLE IMAGES DU CINEMA (Maurice Bessy)
        Interntl F G: v. 3 (1966), p. 264; 200 wds., cp. pub.

7954 *HISTORIA DEL CINE ARGENTINO (Domingo di Nubila)
        Cinema Studies: v. I, n. 7 (June, 1963), pp. 177-179; Alfredo Roffe, 1000
           wds., cp. pub.

7955 *HISTORIA DO CINEMA (Fernando Duarte)
        F Culture: v. 3, n. 5 (Dec., 1957), p. 22; George N. Fenin, 125 wds., cp.
           pub.

7956 HISTORICAL STUDY OF THE COLOR MOTION PICTURE, A (James L.
           Limbacher)
        Am Cinematog: v. 45, n. 3 (Mar., 1964), p. 136; 150 wds., pt. pub.

7957 *HISTORIEN OM DANSK FILM (Ebbe Neergaard)
        Cinema Studies: v. I, n. 2 (Dec., 1960), pp. 43-44; Bent Grasten, 900 wds.,
           cp. pub.

7958 HISTORY OF MOTION PICTURES, THE (Maurice Bardèche and Robert
           Brasillach)
        Interntl F G: v. 9 (1972), p. 466; 50 wds., pt. pub.

7959 HISTORY OF PHOTOGRAPHY (Joseph Maria Edler, trans. by Edward Epstean)
Hollywood Q: v. I, n. 1 (Oct., 1945), pp. 118-120; 800 wds., cp. pub.

7960 HISTORY OF THE AMERICAN FILM INDUSTRY: FROM ITS BEGINN-INGS TO 1931 (Benjamin Hampton)
Films & F: v. 16, n. 11 (Aug., 1970), p. 64; Sheridan Morley, 100 wds., pt. pub.
Sight & S v. 39, n. 4 (Autumn, 1970), p. 223; David Robinson, 1000 wds., cp. pub.

7961 HISTORY OF THE BRITISH FILM, THE (Rachael Low)
Films & F: v. 17, n. 10 (July, 1971), p. 64; Sheridan Morley, 225 wds., pt. pub.
Films in R: v. II, n. 6 (June-July, 1951), pp. 42-44; Theodore Huff, 1400 wds., cp. pub.
Films in R: v. II, n. 8 (Oct., 1951), pp. 54-56; Theodore Huff, 1100 wds., cp. pub.
Focus on F: n. 8 (Oct., 1971), p. 59; 400 wds., cp. pub.
Hollywood Q: v. IV, n. 2 (Winter, 1949), p. 213; Franklin Fearing, 100 wds., cp. pub.
Interntl F G: v. 9 (1972), pp. 466; 469; 50 wds., pt. pub.
Quarterly of FR TV: v. VI, n. 1 (Fall, 1951), pp. 104-105; Franklin Fearing, 550 wds., cp. pub.
Sequence: n. 7 (Spring, 1949), p. 44; Lindsay Anderson, 500 wds., pt. pub.
Sequence: n. 11 (Summer, 1950), p. 47; Penelope Houston, 250 wds., pt. pub.
Sight & S: v. 18, n. 71 (Dec., 1949), p. 28; Paul Rotha, 1200 wds., cp. pub.
Sight & S: v. 20, n. 1 (May, 1951), pp. 28-29; Michael Powell, 1300 wds., cp. pub.
Sight & S: v. 40, n. 3 (Summer, 1971), pp. 169-170; Michael Balcon, 1200 wds., cp. pub.

7962 HISTORY OF THE KINETOGRAPH, KINETOSCOPE AND KINETOPHONO-GRAPH (W.K.L. and Antonia Dickson)
F Comment: v. 7, n. 4 (Winter, 1971-1972), pp. 78-79; Lewis Jacobs, 350 wds., cp. pub.

7963 *HITCHCOCK (Eric Rohmer and Claude Chabrol)
F Culture: v. IV, n. 2 (Feb., 1958), p. 22; Herman G. Weinberg, 175 wds., cp. pub.

7964 *HITCHCOCK (Francois Truffaut, with Helen G. Scott)
F Lib Quarterly: v. 1, n. 2 (Spring, 1968), p. 39; Lillian Gerhardt, 400 wds., pt. pub.
F Quarterly: v. XXI, n. 4 (Summer, 1968), pp. 21-27; Leo Braudy, 3600 wds., no pub.
F Soc Rev: May (1968), p. 39; Frank Manchel, 50 wds., cp. pub.
Films & F: v. 15, n. 3 (Dec., 1968), p. 64; Sheridan Morley, 900 wds., pt. pub.
Films in R: v. XIX, n. 1 (Jan., 1968), pp. 44-45; Diana Willing Cope, 600 wds., cp. pub.
N Y Rev of Books, v. XIV, n. 4 (Feb. 26, 1970), pp. 27-31; Robert Mazzocco, 3500 wds., pt. pub.
Take One: v. 2, n. 5 (1970), p. 22; Susan Steinberg, 1100 wds., no pub.

7965 *HITCHCOCK (Noel Simsolo)
Interntl F G: v. 7 (1970), p. 396; 50 wds., pt. pub.

7966 HITCHCOCK'S FILMS (Robin Wood)
F Comment: v. 7, n. 4 (Winter, 1971-1972), pp. 74-75; Foster Hirsch, 2200 wds., cp. pub.
F Heritage: v. 1, n. 4 (Summer, 1966), pp. 37-38; Robert Haller, 400 wds., cp. pub.
F Quarterly: v. XX, n. 1 (Fall, 1966), pp. 62-63; James Michael Martin, 650 wds., cp. pub.
F Soc Rev: v. 5, n. 2 (Oct., 1969), pp. 44-45; Harvey Deneroff, 500 wds., cp. pub.
Sight & S: v. 35, n. 1 (Winter, 1965-1966), p. 49; Penelope Houston, 750 wds., cp. pub.

7967 HOLLYWOOD CAMERAMEN (Charles Higham)
    Films & F: v. 16, n. 11 (Aug., 1970), p. 64; Sheridan Morley, 125 wds., pt.
        pub.
    Interntl F G: v. 8 (1971), pp. 441; 50 wds., pt. pub.
    Take One: v. 2, n. 8 (1970), pp. 23-24; Herman G. Weinberg, 400 wds., cp.
        pub.

7968 *HOLLYWOOD D'HIER ET D'AUJOURD'HUI (Robert Florey)
    Films in R: v. I, n. 3 (Nov., 1950), pp. 31-32; Theodore Huff, 700 wds., cp.
        pub.
    Sight & S: v. 18, n. 71 (Dec., 1949), p. 28; Adam Helmer, 400 wds., cp.
        pub.

7969 HOLLYWOOD HALLUCINATION, THE (Parker Tyler)
    Cinema: v. 6, n. 2 (Fall, 1970), pp. 42-44; Margaret Bach, 2600 wds., cp.
        pub.

7970 HOLLYWOOD IN THE FIFTIES (Gordon Gow)
    Interntl F G: v. 9 (1972), p. 469; 50 wds., pt. pub.

7971 HOLLYWOOD IN THE FORTIES (Charles Higham and Joel Greenberg)
    Cinema J: v. IX, n. 1 (Fall, 1969), pp. 48-50; Howard Suber, 1300 wds., cp.
        pub.
    F Lib Quarterly: v. 2, n. 3 (Summer, 1969), pp. 30-31; Don Walker, 200
        wds., pt. pub.
    F Quarterly: v. XXIII, n. 1 (Fall, 1969), pp. 59-61; R. C. Dale, 1600 wds.,
        pt. pub.
    Interntl F G: v. 6 (1969), p. 275; 50 wds., pt. pub.

7972 HOLLYWOOD IN THE THIRTIES (John Baxter)
    Cinema J: v. IX, n. 1 (Fall, 1969), pp. 48-50; Howard Suber, 1300 wds., cp.
        pub.
    F Lib Quarterly: v. 2, n. 3 (Summer, 1969), pp. 30-31; Don Walker, 200
        wds., pt. pub.
    F Quarterly: v. XXIII, n. 1 (Fall, 1969), pp. 59-61; R. C. Dale, 1600 wds.,
        pt. pub.
    F Soc Rev: v. 4, n. 5, pp. 40-41; Frank Manchel, 650 wds., cp. pub.
    Films in R: v. XXI, n. 3 (Mar., 1970), p. 185; William Thomaier (a letter),
        200 wds., no pub.
    Interntl F G: v. 6 (1969), p. 275; 50 wds., pt. pub.

7973 HOLLYWOOD IN THE TWENTIES (David Robinson)
    Cinema J: v. IX, n. 1 (Fall, 1969), pp. 48-50; Howard Suber, 1300 wds., cp.
        pub.
    F Lib Quarterly: v. 2, n. 3 (Summer, 1969), pp. 30-31; Don Walker, 250
        wds., pt. pub.
    F Quarterly: v. XXIII, n. 1 (Fall, 1969), pp. 59-61; R. C. Dale, 1600 wds.,
        pt. pub.
    Interntl F G: v. 6 (1969), p. 275; 50 wds., pt. pub.

7974 HOLLYWOOD IN TRANSITION (Richard Dyer MacCann)
    F Comment: v. 1, n. 3 (1962), p. 38; Robert Windeler, 350 wds., cp. pub.
    F Quarterly: v. XVI, n. 4 (Summer, 1963), p. 62; Ernest Callenbach, 250
        wds., cp. pub.

7975 HOLLYWOOD LOOKS AT ITS AUDIENCE: A REPORT OF FILM AUDI-
        ENCE RESEARCH (Leo A. Handel)
    Films in R: v. I, n. 8 (Nov., 1950), pp. 25-26; M. R. Werner, 600 wds., cp.
        pub.
    Hollywood Q: v. V (1950-1951), p. 420; Franklin Fearing, 360 wds., cp.
        pub.
    Sight & S: v. 20, n. 1 (May, 1951), pp. 29-30; Penelope Houston, 1300
        wds., cp. pub.

7976 HOLLYWOOD MUSICAL, THE (John Russell Taylor and Arthur Jackson)
    Focus on F: v. 8 (Oct., 1971), p. 59; 350 wds., cp. pub.

7977 HOLLYWOOD ON TRIAL: THE STORY OF THE TEN WHO WERE
        INDICTED (Gordon Kahn)
    Hollywood Q: v. III, n. 3 (Spring, 1948), pp. 328-332; Max Radin, 3000
        wds., cp. pub.

7978 HOLLYWOOD PILOT: THE BIOGRAPHY OF PAUL MANTZ (Don Dwig-
gens)
Films in R: v. XVIII, n. 8 (Oct., 1967), p. 502; Philip Kensing, 175 wds.,
cp. pub.

7979 HOLLYWOOD RAJAH: THE LIFE AND TIMES OF LOUIS B. MAYER
(Bosley Crowther)
Films in R: v. XI, n. 4 (Apr., 1960), pp. 238-239; Eleanor H. Nash, 225
wds., cp. pub.

7980 HOLLYWOOD SAGA (William C. de Mille)
Films: v. I, n. 1 (Nov., 1939), pp. 109-111; Norman Lusk, 650 wds., cp.
pub.

7981 HOLLYWOOD SCAPEGOAT: THE BIOGRAPHY OF ERICH VON STOHEIM
(Peter Noble)
Films in R: v. I, n. 5 (July-Aug., 1950), pp. 35-38; Herman G. Weinberg,
700 wds., cp. pub.
Sequence: n. 12 (Autumn, 1950), pp. 47-48; Alberta Marlow, 1000 wds.,
pt. pub.
Sight & S: v. 19, n. 6 (Aug., 1950), p. 262; Catherine de la Roche, 750
wds., cp. pub.

7982 HOLLYWOOD: THE DREAM FACTORY (Hortense Powdermaker)
Films in R: v. I, n. 9 (Dec., 1950), pp. 42-43; Alice Penfield, 500 wds., cp.
pub.
Hollywood Q: v. V (1950-1951), pp. 313-315; Franklin Fearing, 750 wds.,
cp. pub.
Sight & S: v. 21, n. 3 (Jan.-Mar., 1952), p. 137; Penelope Houston, 1200
wds., cp. pub.

7983 HOLLYWOOD, THE HAUNTED HOUSE (Paul Mayersberg)
Interntl F G: v. 6 (1969), p. 277; 50 wds., pt. pub.
Sight & S: v. 37, n. 2 (Spring, 1968), pp. 104-105; Carl Foreman, 1500
wds., cp. pub.

7984 HOLLYWOOD TODAY (Allen Eyles and Pat Billings)
Interntl F G: v. 9 (1972), p. 469; 50 wds., pt. pub.

7985 HOLLYWOOD TYCOONS, THE (Norman Zierold)
Films & F: v. 16, n. 6 (Mar., 1970), p. 74; Sheridan Morley, 400 wds., pt.
pub.

7986 HOLLYWOOD, U.S.A.: FROM SCRIPT TO SCREEN (Alice Evans Field)
Films in R: v. III, n. 2 (Feb., 1952), p. 90; Eleanor H. Nash, 300 wds., cp.
pub.
Quarterly of FR TV: v. VII, n. 1 (Fall, 1952), pp. 93-94; Franklin Fearing,
200 wds., cp. pub.

7987 HONEYCOMB, THE (Adela Rogers St. John)
Films in R: v. XX, n. 9 (Nov., 1969), pp. 621-624; Christopher North, 1250
wds., cp. pub.

7988 HORIZONS WEST: STUDIES OF AUTHORSHIP WITHIN THE WESTERN
(Jim Kitses)
F Comment: v. 6, n. 2 (Summer, 1970), pp. 63-66; Thomas R. Atkins, 1500
wds., cp. pub.
Interntl F G: v. 8 (1971), p. 441; 50 wds., pt. pub.
Screen: v. 11, n. 1, pp. 95-96; Christopher Wicking, 800 wds., cp. pub.

7989 HORROR! (Drake Douglas)
F Comment: v. 5, n. 3 (Fall, 1969), p. 79; William K. Everson, 225 wds., cp.
pub.
F Quarterly: v. XX, n. 3 (Spring, 1967), pp. 57-58; R. D. Dale, 750 wds.,
cp. pub.
Films & F: v. 13, n. 12 (Sept., 1967), p. 46; Sheridan Morley, 50 wds., pt.
pub.
Films in R: v. XIX, n. 3 (Mar., 1968), p. 170; F. K. Schliemann, 175 wds.,
cp. pub.

7990 HORROR FILM, THE (Ivan Butler)
        F Quarterly: v. XXII, n. 3 (Spring, 1969), pp. 56-57; R. C. Dale, 500 wds.,
            cp. pub.
        Films & F: v. 13, n. 12 (Sept., 1967), p. 46; Sheridan Morley, 550 wds., pt.
            pub.
        Interntl F G: v. 5 (1968), p. 263; 25 wds., pt. pub.

7991 HORROR IN THE CINEMA (Ivan Butler)
        Interntl F G: v. 8 (1971), p. 441; 50 wds., pt. pub.
        Screen: v. 12, n. 1, pp. 59-60; Colin McArthur, 800 wds., cp. pub.

7992 HORROR MOVIES (Carlos Clarens)
        Interntl F G: v. 6 (1969), p. 277; 50 wds., pt. pub.
        Sight & S: v. 37, n. 4 (Autumn, 1968), pp. 212-213; Peter John Dyer, 800
            wds., cp. pub.

7993 HOW FILMS ARE MADE (Stanley Reed and John Huntley)
        Films & F: v. 2, n.1 (Oct., 1955), p. 28; Peter G. Baker, 50 wds., pt. pub.
        Films In R: v. VII, n. 10 (Dec., 1956), pp. 535-536; Gerald Pratley, 150
            wds., cp. pub.

7994 HOW HOLLYWOOD RATES (George Raborn)
        Films in R: v. VI, n. 8 (Oct., 1955), pp. 420-422; John Springer, 1000 wds.,
            cp. pub.

7995 HOW IT HAPPENED HERE, THE MAKING OF A FILM (Kevin Brownlow)
        F Comment: v. 5, n. 4 (Winter, 1969), p. 79; 125 wds., cp. pub.
        Films & F: v. 14, n. 12 (Sept., 1968), p. 50; Sheridan Morley, 150 wds., pt.
            pub.
        Interntl F G: v. 6 (1969), p. 277; 50 wds., pt. pub.

7996 HOW TO APPRECIATE MOTION PICTURES (Edgar Dale)
        F Comment: v. 7, n. 2 (Summer, 1971), pp. 70-72; Garth Jowett, 2200
            wds., cp. pub.

7997 HOW TO FILM AS AN AMATEUR (G. Wain)
        Sight & S: v. 18, n. 70 (Summer, 1949), p. 98; C. R. Gibbs, 650 wds., cp.
            pub.

7998 HOW TO MAKE A JEWISH MOVIE (Melville Shavelson)
        Focus on F: n. 7 (Summer, 1971), p. 59; Allen Eyles, 225 wds., cp. pub.

7999 HOW TO MAKE OR NOT TO MAKE A CANADIAN FILM (André Paquet,
            ed.)
        Cineaste: v. II, n. 3 (Winter, 1968-1969), p. 19; Gary Crowdus, 100 wds.,
            pt. pub.

8000 HOW TO RUN A FILM LIBRARY (Encyclopedia Britannica)
        Hollywood Q: v. I, n. 4 (July, 1946), pp. 442-443; Arthur Rosenheimer, Jr.,
            350 wds., cp. pub.

8001 HOW TO SCRIPT AMATEUR FILMS (Oswell Blakeston)
        Sight & S: v. 18, n. 70 (Summer, 1949), p. 98; Gavin Lambert, 250 wds.,
            cp. pub.

8002 *HOWARD HAWKS (J-C Missaien)
        Interntl F G: v. 4 (1967), p. 279; 100 wds., pt. pub.

8003 HOWARD HAWKS (Robin Wood)
        F Comment: v. 7, n. 4 (Winter, 1971-1972), pp. 74-75; Foster Hirsch, 2200
            wds., cp. pub.
        F Quarterly: v. XXII, n. 3 (Spring, 1969), p. 58; 50 wds., cp. pub.
        Films & F: v. 14, n. 12 (Sept., 1968), p. 50; Sheridan Morley, 150 wds., pt.
            pub.
        Interntl F G: v. 6 (1969), p. 275; 50 wds., pt. pub.

8004 HOWARD HUGHES (John Keats)
        Films & F: v. 13, n. 8 (May, 1967), p. 44; Sheridan Morley, 25 wds., pt.
            pub.

8005 HUMAN NATURE OF PLAYWRITING, THE (Samson Raphaelson)
          Hollywood Q: v. IV, n. 3 (Spring, 1950), p. 317; Franklin Fearing, 150
          wds., cp. pub.

8006 HUMPHREY BOGART (Bernard Eisenschitz)
          Films in R: v. XIX, n. 10 (Dec., 1968), p. 641; Clifford McCarty, 225 wds.,
          cp. pub.

8007 HUMPHREY BOGART — THE MAN AND HIS FILMS (Paul Michael)
          F Soc Rev: Mar. (1966), pp. 7-8; Gordon Hitchens, 400 wds., cp. pub.

I

8008 I AM CURIOUS (Vilgot Sjoman)
          Interntl F G: v. 7 (1970), p. 396; 50 wds., pt. pub.

8009 I BLEW MY HORN (Jesse Lasky)
          Films & F: v. 4, n. 4 (Jan., 1958), p. 33; Martin Gray, 150 wds., pt. pub.
          Films in R: v. VIII, n. 10 (Dec., 1957), pp. 536-537; William K. Everson,
          600 wds., cp. pub.
          Sight & S: v. 27, n. 3 (Winter, 1957-1958), pp. 155-156; John Cutts, 500
          wds., cp. pub.

8010 I COULDN'T SMOKE THE GRASS ON MY FATHER'S LAWN (Michael
          Chaplin)
          Films in R: v. XVII, n. 6 (June-July, 1966), p. 378; Henry Hart, 225 wds.,
          cp. pub.

8011 I LOST IT AT THE MOVIES (Pauline Kael)
          F Heritage: v. 1, n. 1 (Fall, 1965), pp. 45-47; David Madden, 1200 wds., cp.
          pub.
          F Quarterly: v. XVIII, n. 3 (Spring, 1965), pp. 57-58; Ernest Callenbach,
          1100 wds., cp. pub.
          F Soc Rev: May (1966), p. 21; Stuart A. Selby, 850 wds., cp. pub.
          Sight & S: v. 34, n. 3 (Summer, 1965), p. 155; Geoffrey Nowell-Smith, 525
          wds., cp. pub.

8012 I WAS CURIOUS — DIARY OF THE MAKING OF A FILM (Vilgot Sjoman,
          trans. by Alan Blair)
          Cineaste: v. II, n. 3 (Winter, 1968-1969), p. 18; Gary Crowdus, 250 wds.,
          pt. pub.
          F Comment: v. 6, n. 2 (Summer, 1970), p. 66; 150 wds., cp. pub.
          Interntl F G: v. 7 (1970), pp. 396; 399; 50 wds., pt. pub.

8013 IDEAS ON FILM (Cecile Starr, ed.)
          Films in R: v. II, n. 9 (Nov., 1951), p. 43; Marie L. Hamilton, 200 wds., cp.
          pub.
          Quarterly of FR TV: v. VI, n. 4 (Summer, 1952), p. 426; Franklin Fearing,
          150 wds., cp. pub.

8014 I'LL CRY TOMORROW (Lillian Roth)
          Films in R: v. V, n. 7 (Nov., 1954), pp. 488-489; Robert Downing, 400
          wds., cp. pub.

8015 ILLUSTRATED HISTORY OF THE HORROR FILM, AN (Carlos Clarens)
          F Comment: v. 5, n. 3 (Fall, 1969), p. 79; William K. Everson, 300 wds., cp.
          pub.
          F Quarterly: v. XXI, n. 3 (Spring, 1968), pp. 52-54; R. C. Dale, 1100 wds.,
          cp. pub.
          F Soc Rev: v. 4, n. 7, pp. 41-42; Frank Manchel, 700 wds., cp. pub.
          Films in R: v. XIX, n. 3 (Mar., 1968), p. 170; F. K. Schliemann, 175 wds.,
          cp. pub.

8016 IMAGE EMPIRE: A HISTORY OF BROADCASTING IN THE UNITED
        STATES FROM 1953, THE (Erik Barnouw)
      Cineaste: v. V, n. 1 (Winter, 1971-1972), pp. 23-25; Tom Brom, 2000 wds.,
        cp. pub.

8017 IMAGE INDUSTRIES: A CONSTRUCTIVE ANALYSIS OF FILMS AND
        TELEVISION, THE (William Lynch)
      Films in R: v. XII, n. 5 (May, 1961), p. 308; Robert C. Roman, 200 wds.,
        cp. pub.

8018 IMAGE MAKERS, THE (William F. Lynch)
      F Quarterly: v. XIII, n. 2 (Winter, 1959), pp. 61-63; Hugh Gray, 900 wds.,
        cp. pub.

8019 *IMAGES DU CINEMA FRANCAIS (Nicole Vedrés)
      Hollywood Q: v. I, n. 2 (Jan., 1946), pp. 240-241; Man Ray, 550 wds., cp.
        pub.

8020 IMMEDIATE EXPERIENCE: MOVIES, COMICS, THEATRE AND OTHER
        ASPECTS OF MODERN CULTURE, THE (Robert Warshow)
      F Culture: n. 31 (Winter, 1963-1964), p. 68; Herman G. Weinberg, 50 wds.,
        cp. pub.
      F Quarterly: v. XVI, n. 2 (Winter, 1962-1963), p. 56; Ernest Callenbach,
        400 wds., cp. pub.
      Sight & S: v. 31, n. 4 (Autumn, 1962), pp. 204-205; Peter Harcourt, 800
        wds., cp. pub.

8021 IMMORTALS OF THE SCREEN (Ray Stuart)
      F Quarterly: v. XX, n. 1 (Fall, 1966), p. 63; Earl Bodien, 50 wds., cp. pub.
      Films & F: v. XIV, n. 1 (Oct., 1967), p. 32; Sheridan Morley, 150 wds., pt.
        pub.

8022 IMPERSONATION OF ANGELS, AN (Frederick Brown)
      Films & F: v. 16, n. 3 (Dec., 1969), p. 72; Sheridan Morley, 75 wds., pt.
        pub.

8023 IMPROVISATION FOR THE THEATRE (Viola Spolin)
      F Quarterly: v. XVII, n. 2 (Winter, 1963-1964), pp. 58-59; Tung, 600 wds.,
        cp. pub.

8024 IN THE BEGINNING: PROGRAM NOTES TO ACCOMPANY ONE HUN-
        DRED EARLY MOTION PICTURES (Kemp Niver)
      Cineaste: v. I, n. 4 (Spring, 1968), p. 23; Robert Steele, 300 wds., pt. pub.
      F Soc Rev: v. 4, n. 2, p. 47; John Bragin, 200 wds., cp. pub.

8025 INCIDENTAL MUSIC IN THE SOUND FILM (Gerald Cockshott)
      Hollywood Q: v. III, n. 2 (Winter, 1947-1948), pp. 211-214; Lawrence
        Morton, 1200 wds., cp. pub.

8026 INDEPENDENT FILMMAKING (Lenny Lipton)
      F Quarterly: v. XXV, n. 4 (Summer, 1972), pp. 36-37; Ernest Callenbach,
        650 wds., cp. pub.

8027 *INDEX DE LA CINEMATOGRAPHIE FRANCAISE 1963
      Interntl F G: v. 1 (1964), p. 226; 30 wds., pt. pub.

8028 INDIAN FILM, THE (Panna Shah)
      Quarterly of FR TV: v. VI, n. 1 (Fall, 1951), pp. 100-101; Franklin
        Fearing, 300 wds., cp. pub.

8029 INDIAN FILM (Erik Barnouw and S. Krishnaswamy)
      Cinema Studies: v. I, n. 9 (June, 1964), pp. 241-242; N.M.H., 500 wds., cp.
        pub.
      F Comment: v. 2, n. 2 (1964), pp. 57-58; Stuart Selby, 700 wds., cp. pub.
      F Culture: n. 31 (Winter, 1963-1964), p. 68; Herman G. Weinberg, 100
        wds., cp. pub.
      F Quarterly: v. XVII, n. 4 (Summer, 1964), pp. 61-62; Edward Harrison,
        600 wds., cp. pub.
      Films in R: v. XIV, n. 9 (Nov., 1963), p. 559; Harold Singh, 100 wds., cp.
        pub.
      Sight & S: v. 33, n. 1 (Winter, 1963-1964), p. 48; John Gillett, 475 wds.,
        cp. pub.

8030 INFLUENCE OF THE CINEMA ON CHILDREN AND ADOLESCENTS: AN
ANNOTATED INTERNATIONAL BIBLIOGRAPHY, THE
(UNESCO)
Cinema Studies: v. I, n. 6 (Dec., 1962), pp. 143-145; Mary Field, 1100
wds., cp. pub.

8031 INFORMATION FILM: A REPORT OF THE PUBLIC LIBRARY INQUIRY,
THE (Gloria Waldron, with Cecile Starr)
Films in R: v. I, n. 1 (Feb., 1950), pp. 39-40; Richard Griffith, 650 wds.,
cp. pub.
Hollywood Q: v. IV, n. 2 (Winter, 1949), pp. 212-213; Franklin Fearing,
200 wds., cp. pub.

8032 INFORMATIONAL FILM YEAR BOOK
Sight & S: v. 17, n. 67 (Autumn, 1948), p. 152; 175 wds., cp. pub.

8033 INGMAR BERGMAN (Birgitta Steene)
F Comment: v. 6, n. 2 (Summer, 1970), p. 66; 250 wds., cp. pub.
F Heritage: v. 3, n. 4 (Summer, 1968), pp. 35-36; Erik Sandberg-Diment,
550 wds., cp. pub.
F Lib Quarterly: v. 3, n. 4 (Fall, 1970), pp. 17-28; Gordon Hitchens, 200
wds., cp. pub.
Interntl F G: v. 7 (1970), p. 399; 50 wds., pt. pub.

8034 INGMAR BERGMAN (Robin Wood)
F Comment: v. 6, n. 1 (Spring, 1970), p. 68; Donald Staples, 150 wds., cp.
pub.
F Comment: v. 7, n. 4 (Winter, 1971-1972), pp. 74-75; Foster Hirsch, 2200
wds., cp. pub.
F Quarterly: v. XXIII, n. 4 (Summer, 1970), pp. 61-62; Ernest Callenbach,
175 wds., cp. pub.
Interntl F G: v. 7 (1970), p. 399; 50 wds., pt. pub.
Sight & S: v. 39, n. 1 (Winter, 1969-1970), pp. 53-54; Philip Strick, 700
wds., cp. pub.

8035 INGMAR BERGMAN: A MOTION MONOGRAPH (Peter Cowie)
Cinema Studies: v. I, n. 5 (Sept., 1962), pp. 117-118; N.M.H., 650 wds., cp.
pub.
F Comment: v. 1, n. 4 (1963), pp. 46-47; Harry Feldman, 1800 wds., cp.
pub.
Sight & F: v. 31, n. 2 (Spring, 1962), p. 101; Peter Harcourt, 400 wds., cp.
pub.

8036 *INGMAR BERGMAN ET SES FILMS (Jean Bérenger)
Cinema Studies: v. I, n. 1 (Mar., 1960), pp. 18-19; Liam O'Laoghaire, 450
wds., cp. pub.

8037 *INGMAR BERGMAN: LA TRILOGIE (Michel Esteve, ed.)
Interntl F G: v. 5 (1968), p. 259; 25 wds., pt. pub.

8038 *INGMAR BERGMAN: TEATERMANNEN OCH FILMSKAPAREN (Fritiof
Billquist)
Cinema Studies: v. I, n. 3 (Aug., 1961), pp. 61-63; Grete Selby, 1200 wds.,
cp. pub.

8039 INGRID BERGMAN: AN INTIMATE PORTRAIT (Joseph Henry Steele)
F Quarterly: v. XII, n. 4 (Summer, 1959), pp. 58-60; C. Cameron Macauley,
700 wds., cp. pub.
Films in R: v. XI, n. 2 (Feb., 1960), p. 113; Eleanor H. Nash, 175 wds., cp.
pub.
Sight & S: v. 29, n. 3 (Summer, 1960), p. 152; Isabel Quigly, 500 wds., cp.
pub.

8040 INNOCENT EYE, THE (Arthur Calder-Marshall)
F Comment: v. 2, n. 2 (1964), pp. 56-57; George Amberg, 1000 wds., cp.
pub.
F Quarterly: v. XX, n. 4 (Summer, 1967), p. 76; Ernest Callenbach, 200
wds., cp. pub.
Films in R: v. XIV, n. 9 (Nov., 1963), p. 558; Eleanor H. Nash, 200 wds.,
cp. pub.
Sight & S: v. 32, n. 4 (Autumn, 1963), pp. 205-206; Brenda Davies, 700
wds., cp. pub.

8041 INQUISITION IN EDEN (Alvah Bessie)
      Films in R: v. XVI, n. 5 (May, 1965), pp. 308-309; Warren Locke, 250
          wds., cp. pub.

8042 INTELLIGENT EYE, THE (Richard L. Gregory)
      Cinema J: v. X, n. 1 (Fall, 1970), pp. 51-54; John L. Fell, 1600 wds., cp.
          pub.

8043 INTERNATIONAL FILM ANNUAL, NO. 1 (Campbell Dixon, ed.)
      Films & F: v. 4, n. 5 (Feb., 1958), p. 35; Martin Gray, 150 wds., pt. pub.
      Sight & S: v. 27, n. 3 (Winter, 1957-1958), p. 157; John Gillett, 200 wds.,
          cp. pub.

8044 INTERNATIONAL FILM ANNUAL, NO. 2 (William Whitebait, ed.)
      Films & F: v. 6, n. 5 (Feb., 1960), p. 35; Martin Gray, 100 wds., pt. pub.
      Sight & S: v. 28, n. 1 (Winter, 1958-1959), pp. 47-48; Derick Grigs, 500
          wds., cp. pub.

8045 INTERNATIONAL FILM GUIDE (Peter Cowie, ed.)
      F Soc Rev: Jan. (1957), p. 38; John Thomas, 300 wds., cp. pub.
      Screen: v. 11, n. 2 (Mar.-Apr., 1970), pp. 96-97; Gillian Hartnoll, 250 wds.,
          cp. pub.
      Sight & S: v. 33, n. 1 (Winter, 1963-1964), p. 49; Brenda Davies, 200 wds.,
          cp. pub.

8046 INTERNATIONAL FILM INDUSTRY: WESTERN EUROPE AND AMERICA
          SINCE 1945, THE (Thomas H. Guback)
      Cineaste: v. V, n. 1 (Winter, 1971-1972), pp. 26-27; Gary Crowdus, 1000
          wds., cp. pub.
      Cinema J: v. X, n. 1 (Fall, 1970), pp. 54-59; Calvin Pryluck, 1900 wds., cp.
          pub.
      Sight & S: v. 39, n. 3 (Summer, 1970), p. 165; Neville Hunnings, 700 wds.,
          cp. pub.

8047 INTERNATIONAL MOTION PICTURE ALMANAC (Charles B. Aaronson,
          ed.)
      Films in R: v. IX, n. 3 (Mar., 1958), pp. 152-154; Roi A. Uselton, 850 wds.,
          cp. pub.

8048 *INTERNATIONALE FILMBIBLIOGRAPHIE 1952-1962 (H. P. Manz, ed.)
      Cinema Studies: v. I, n. 9 (June, 1964), pp. 242-243; Glynne Parker, 750
          wds., cp. pub.

8049 INTERVIEWS WITH FILM DIRECTORS (Andrew Sarris, ed.)
      Cinema J: v. VIII, n. 2 (Spring, 1969), pp. 33-35; Michael Budd, 1250 wds.,
          cp. pub.
      F Lib Quarterly: v. 2, n. 1 (Winter, 1968-1969), pp. 53; 63; Wayne T.
          Campbell, Jr., 600 wds., pt. pub.
      F Quarterly: v. XXI, n. 3 (Spring, 1968), pp. 54-55; Ernest Callenbach, 300
          wds., cp. pub.
      F Soc Rev: May (1968), p. 39; Frank Manchel, 50 wds., cp. pub.

8050 INTRODUCTION TO CINEMATOGRAPHY, AN (John Mercer)
      Cineaste: v. II, n. 1 (Summer, 1968), pp. 26-27; Gary Crowdus, 150 wds.,
          pt. pub.

8051 INTRODUCTION TO THE AMERICAN UNDERGROUND FILM, AN (Shel-
          don Renan)
      Cinema J: v. VII (Winter, 1967-1968), pp. 37-38; Kirk Bond, 650 wds., cp.
          pub.
      F Heritage: v. 5, n. 2 (Winter, 1969-1970), pp. 30-31; 350 wds., cp. pub.
      F Lib Quarterly: v. 1, n. 2 (Spring, 1968), pp. 39-40; Robert Steele, 300
          wds., pt. pub.
      F Quarterly: v. XXI, n. 2 (Winter, 1967-1968), p. 59; Ernest Callenbach,
          200 wds., cp. pub.
      F Soc Rev: Jan. (1968), pp. 17-20; Emory Menefee, 1300 wds., cp. pub.
      Interntl F G: v. 6 (1969), p. 277; 50 wds., pt. pub.

8052 INTRODUCTION TO THE ART OF THE MOVIES (Lewis Jacobs, ed.)
F Quarterly: v. XIII, n. 3 (Spring, 1960), pp. 61-62; Ernest Callenbach, 200 wds., cp. pub.
Films in R: v. XI, n. 5 (May, 1960), pp. 301-303; Eleanor H. Nash, 950 wds., cp. pub.

8053 INTRODUCTION TO THE EGYPTIAN CINEMA, AN (M. Khan)
F Comment: v. 7, n. 4 (Winter, 1971-1972), p. 80; Norman Kagan, 300 wds., cp. pub.
Films & F: v. 16, n. 5 (Feb., 1970), p. 70; Sheridan Morley, 75 wds., pt. pub.
Interntl F G: v. 8 (1971), p. 441; 50 wds., pt. pub.

8054 INTRODUCTION TO 3-D (H. Dewhurst)
Films & F: v. 1, n. 2 (Nov., 1954), p. 30; Louis Marks, 75 wds., pt. pub.

8055 *INVENTION DU CINEMA, L' (Georges Sadoul)
Sight & S: v. 15, n. 58 (Summer, 1946), p. 64; R.L., 250 wds., cp. pub.

8056 *ISKUSSTVO MILLONOV (D. S. Pisarevsky, ed.)
F Quarterly: v. XV, n. 1 (Fall, 1961), pp. 63-64; Steven P. Hill, 300 wds., cp. pub.

8057 IT TAKES MORE THAN TALENT (Mervyn LeRoy, with Alice Canfield)
Quarterly of FR TV: v. VIII, n. 2 (Winter, 1953), pp. 207-208; Franklin Fearing, 200 wds., cp. pub.

8058 ITALIAN CINEMA, THE (Vernon Jarratt)
Films in R: v. III, n. 5 (May, 1952), pp. 246-249; Theodore Huff, 1300 wds., cp. pub.

8059 ITALIAN CINEMA TODAY (Gian Luigi Rondi)
F Comment: v. IV, n. 2-3 (Fall-Winter, 1967), pp. 110-111; Robert Connelly, 900 wds., cp. pub.
F Heritage: v. 2, n. 3 (Spring, 1967), pp. 35-36; Robert Haller, 500 wds., cp. pub.
F Quarterly: v. XX, n. 3 (Spring, 1967), p. 58; Ernest Callenbach, 125 wds., cp. pub.
Films & F: v. 13, n. 11 (Aug., 1967), p. 47; Sheridan Morley, 75 wds., pt. pub.
Interntl F G: v. 5 (1968), p. 263; 10 wds., pt. pub.

8060 IT'S ONLY A MOVIE (Clark McKowen and William Sparke)
F Quarterly: v. XXV, n. 4 (Summer, 1972), p. 39; 100 wds., cp. pub.

8061 IVAN THE TERRIBLE (Sergei M. Eisenstein, trans. by Ivor Montagu and Herbert Marshall)
Sight & S: v. 32, n. 2 (Spring, 1963), p. 100; David Robinson, 800 wds., cp. pub.

J

8062 *JACQUES PREVERT (Jean Queval)
Sight & S: v. 26, n. 1 (Summer, 1956), p. 53; Roy Edwards, 600 wds., cp. pub.

8063 JAPAN (Arne Svensson)
Interntl F G: v. 8 (1971), pp. 441, 443; 50 wds., pt. pub.

8064 JAPANESE FILM: ART AND INDUSTRY, THE (Joseph L. Anderson and Donald Richie)
Cinema Studies: v. I, n. 2 (Dec., 1960), pp. 36-38; Tom Milne, 1100 wds., cp. pub.
F Quarterly: v. XIII, n. 1 (Fall, 1959), pp. 61-63; Colin Young, 1300 wds., cp. pub.

Films in R: v. XI, n. 4 (Apr., 1960), p. 238; Alice H. Witham, 200 wds., cp. pub.
Sight & S: v. 29, n. 1 (Winter, 1959-1960), p. 47; Derek Prouse, 900 wds., cp. pub.

8065 JAPANESE MOVIES (Donald Ritchie)
F Quarterly: v. XVI, n. 2 (Winter, 1962-1963), p. 58; Ernest Callenbach, 400 wds., cp. pub.
Sight & S: v. 31, n. 4 (Autumn, 1962), p. 205; David Robinson, 600 wds., cp. pub.

8066 JAZZ IN THE MOVIES (David Meeker)
Focus on F: n. 10 (Summer, 1972), p. 62; Allen Eyles, 250 wds., cp. pub.

8067 JEAN COCTEAU (Margaret Crosland)
Films & F: v. 1, n. 6 (Mar., 1955), p. 30; John Minchinton, 150 wds., pt. pub.
Sight & S: v. 24, n. 4 (Spring, 1955), p. 217; James Morgan, 225 wds., cp. pub.

8068 JEAN COCTEAU (René Gilson)
Cineaste: v. II, n. 4 (Spring, 1969), p. 22; Denis Kawicki, 200 wds., pt. pub.
Cinema: v. 5, n. 2, p. 43; Stephen Mamber, 300 wds., cp. pub.
F Quarterly: v. XXIII, n. 1 (Fall, 1969), p. 61; 100 wds., cp. pub.

8069 *JEAN GREMILLON (Henri Agel)
Interntl F G: v. 8 (1971), p. 443; 50 wds., pt. pub.

8070 JEAN-LUC GODARD: A CRITICAL ANTHOLOGY (Toby Mussman, ed.)
F Soc Rev: v. 4, n. 4, pp. 42-43; Jonathan Rosenbaum, 750 wds., cp. pub.

8071 JEAN-LUC GODARD: AN INVESTIGATION OF HIS FILMS AND PHILOS-OPHY (Jean Collet)
Cineaste: v. IV, n. 1 (Summer, 1970), pp. 29-30; Calvin Green, 1500 wds., cp. pub.
Films & F: v. 17, n. 1 (Oct., 1970), p. 72; Sheridan Morley, 125 wds., pt. pub.
Interntl F G: v. 9 (1972), p. 473; 50 wds., pt. pub.

8072 *JEAN-PIERRE MELVILLE (Jean Wagner)
Cinema Studies: v. II, n. 1 (June, 1965), p. 14; Tom Milne, 600 wds., cp. pub.

8073 *JEAN RENOIR (Armand-Jean Cauliez)
Cinema Studies: v. I, n. 6 (Dec., 1962), pp. 148-151; Tom Milne, 2000 wds., cp. pub.

8074 *JEAN RENOIR (Bernard Chardère, ed.)
Cinema Studies: v. I, n. 6 (Dec., 1962), pp. 148-151; Tom Milne, 2000 wds., cp. pub.
Sight & S: v. 32, n. 1 (Winter, 1962-1963), p. 48; Tom Milne, 700 wds., cp. pub.

8075 *JEAN RENOIR (Pierre Leprohon)
Interntl F G: v. 6 (1969), p. 278; 50 wds., pt. pub.

8076 *JEAN RENOIR (Andre Bazin)
Interntl F G: v. 9 (1972), p. 469; 50 wds., pt. pub.

8077 JEAN RENOIR: THE WORLD OF HIS FILMS (Leo Braudy)
F Quarterly: v. XXV, n. 4 (Summer, 1972), p. 37; 200 wds., cp. pub.

8078 *JEAN VIGO (P. E. Sales Gomes)
Sight & S: v. 27, n. 2 (Autumn, 1957), pp. 102-103; Roy Edwards, 500 wds., cp. pub.

8079 *JEAN VIGO (Pierre Lherminier)
Interntl F G: v. 6 (1969), p. 278; 50 wds., pt. pub.

8080 JEAN VIGO (John M. Smith)
      F Quarterly: v. XXV, n. 4 (Summer, 1972), p. 39; 75 wds., cp. pub.
      Focus on F: n. 10 (Summer, 1972), p. 62; Allen Eyles, 275 wds., cp. pub.

8081 *JOHN FORD (Jean Mitry)
      Films in R: v. VI, n. 9 (Nov., 1955), p. 474; Ralph Gerstlé, 200 wds., cp.
          pub.
      Quarterly of FR TV: v. X, n. 1 (Fall, 1955), pp. 102-103; Franklin Fearing,
          150 wds., cp. pub.

8082 *JOHN FORD (Philippe Haudiquet)
      Films & F: v. 13, n. 8 (May, 1967), p. 44; Sheridan Morley, 25 wds., pt.
          pub.
      Interntl F G: v. 5 (1968), p. 261; 25 wds., pt. pub.

8083 JOHN FORD (Peter Bogdanovich)
      Cineaste: v. II, n. 3 (Winter, 1968-1969), pp. 18-19; Gary Crowdus, 550
          wds., pt. pub.
      F Quarterly: v. XXII, n. 3 (Spring, 1969), p. 58; 50 wds., cp. pub.
      Films & F: v. 14, n. 8 (Apr., 1968), p. 60; Sheridan Morley, 200 wds., pt.
          pub.
      Interntl F G: v. 6 (1969), p. 275; 50 wds., pt. pub.

8084 JOHN GIELGUD (Ronald Hayman)
      Films & F: v. 17, n. 12 (Sept., 1971), p. 66; Sheridan Morley, 50 wds., pt.
          pub.

8085 *JOHN HUSTON (Robert Benayoun)
      Interntl F G: v. 5 (1968), p. 263; 25 wds., pt. pub.

8086 JOHN HUSTON: KING REBEL (William F. Nolan)
      Films in R: v. XVII, n. 1 (Jan., 1966), p. 45; Alice H. Witham, 125 wds., cp.
          pub.

8087 JOHN STEINBECK AND HIS FILMS (Michael Borrows)
      Interntl F G: v. 9 (1972), p. 469; 50 wds., pt. pub.

8088 JOSEF VON STERNBERG — A CRITICAL STUDY OF A GREAT FILM
          DIRECTOR (Herman G. Weinberg)
      Cineaste: v. I, n. 4 (Spring, 1968), p. 24; Gary Crowdus, 150 wds., pt. pub.
      Cinema J: v. IX, n. 1 (Fall, 1969), p. 56; Richard Dyer MacCann, 550 wds.,
          cp. pub.
      F Comment: v. IV, n. 2-3 (Fall-Winter, 1967), pp. 118-122; Kirk Bond,
          1100 wds., cp. pub.
      F Heritage: v. 2, n. 3 (Spring, 1967), pp. 33-35; Robert Hammond, 800
          wds., cp. pub.
      F Quarterly: v. XX, n. 3 (Spring, 1967), pp. 55-56; Ernest Callenbach, 500
          wds., cp. pub.
      F Quarterly: v. XXI, n. 4 (Summer, 1968), p. 56; 75 wds., cp. pub.
      F Soc Rev: Jan. (1968), pp. 30-32; Frank Manchel, 1100 wds., cp. pub.
      Interntl F G: v. 5 (1968), p. 265; 25 wds., pt. pub.
      Sight & F: v. 36, n. 2 (Spring, 1967), pp. 103-104; Tom Milne, 700 wds.,
          cp. pub.

8089 *JOSEF VON STERNBERG — EINE DARSTELLUNG (Alice Goetz; Helmut
          W. Banz, Otto Kellner, eds.)
      F Comment: v. IV, n. 2-3 (Fall-Winter, 1967), pp. 118-122; Kirk Bond,
          1100 wds., cp. pub.

8090 JUDY (Joe Morella and Edward Epstein)
      Films & F: v. 16, n. 5 (Feb., 1970), p. 70; Sheridan Morley, 150 wds., pt.
          pub.

8091 JULIE ANDREWS (John Cottrell)
      Films & F: v. 15, n. 10 (July, 1969), pp. 71-72; Sheridan Morley, 450 wds.,
          pt. pub.

8092 JULIE ANDREWS (Robert Windeler)
      Films & F: v. 16, n. 12 (Sept., 1970), p. 94; Sheridan Morley, 375 wds., pt.
          pub.

K

8093 KARLOFF (Alan Barbour, Alvin Marill and James Parish)
Views & Rev: v. I, n. 1 (Summer, 1969), p. 62; Earl Atwell, 150 wds., cp.
pub.

8094 KEATON (Rudi Blesh)
F Comment: v. 5, n. 3 (Fall, 1969), p. 78; William K. Everson, 125 wds., cp.
pub.
F Quarterly: v. XX, n. 1 (Fall, 1966), pp. 60-61; Hugh Kenner, 800 wds.,
cp. pub.
Films & F: v. 13, n. 10 (July, 1967), p. 42; Sheridan Morley, 800 wds., pt.
pub.
Sight & S: v. 36, n. 3 (Summer, 1967), p. 157; Penelope Houston, 800 wds.,
cp. pub.

8095 *KEATON AND COMPANY: LES BURLESQUES AMERICAINS DU
"MUET" (Jean-Pierre Coursodon)
Cinema Studies: v. II, n. 1 (June, 1965), pp. 9-12; N.M.H., 1600 wds., cp.
pub.

8096 KING COHN: THE LIFE AND TIMES OF HARRY COHN (Bob Thomas)
Films in R: v. XVIII, n. 8 (Oct., 1967), pp. 500-501; 175 wds., cp. pub.
Sight & S: v. 37, n. 2 (Spring, 1968), pp. 104-105; Carl Foreman, 1500
wds., cp. pub.

8097 KING OF COMEDY (Mack Sennett, with Cameron Shipp)
Films & F: v. 2, n. 1 (Oct., 1955), p. 28; Peter Brinson, 125 wds., pt. pub.
Films In R: v. VI, n. 4 (Apr., 1955), pp. 198-200; William K. Everson, 1100
wds., cp. pub.
Sight & S: v. 24, n. 4 (Spring, 1955), p. 217; William K. Everson, 600 wds.,
cp. pub.

8098 KING OF HOLLYWOOD, THE (Charles Samuels)
Films & F: v. 9, n. 2 (Nov., 1962), p. 73; Martin Gray, 125 wds., pt. pub.

8099 KINO: A HISTORY OF THE RUSSIAN AND SOVIET FILM (Jay Leyda)
F Quarterly: v. XIV, n. 2 (Winter, 1960), pp. 59-60; David Stewart Hull,
900 wds., cp. pub.
Sight & S: v. 29, n. 4 (Autumn, 1960), pp. 202-203; Thorold Dickinson,
1200 wds., cp. pub.

8100 KISS KISS BANG BANG (Pauline Kael)
Cineaste: v. I, n. 4 (Spring, 1968), pp. 23-24; Gary Crowdus, 200 wds., pt.
pub.
Cinema J: v. VIII, n. 2 (Spring, 1969), pp. 35-38; Richard Dyer Mac Cann,
1600 wds., cp. pub.
F Comment: v. 5, n. 4 (Winter, 1969), p. 78; 200 wds., cp. pub.
F Quarterly: v. XXI, n. 4 (Summer, 1968), p. 54; Ernest Callenbach, 650
wds., cp. pub.
Films & F: v. 16, n. 6 (Mar., 1970), p. 74; Sheridan Morley, 300 wds., pt.
pub.
Screen: v. 11, n. 3 (Summer, 1970), pp. 115-117; Edward Buscombe, 1100
wds., pt. pub.
Sight & S: v. 39, n. 2 (Spring, 1970), pp. 108-109; Philip French, 850 wds.,
cp. pub.

8101 *KLEINES FILMLEXIKON: KUNST, TECHNIK, GESCHICHTE BIOGRAPH-
IE, SCHRIFTUM
Sight & S: v. 15, n. 58 (Summer, 1946), p. 64; M.E.C., 100 wds., pt. pub.

8102 KNIGHT ERRANT (Brian Connell)
Quarterly of FR TV: v. X, n. 2 (Winter, 1955), p. 209; Franklin Fearing,
150 wds., cp. pub.

8103 *KUROSAWA (Sacha Ezratty)
Interntl F G: v. 2 (1965), p. 225; 300 wds., pt. pub.

L

8104 *L 136: DAGBOK MED INGMAR BERGMAN (Vilgot Sjoman)
Sight & F: v. 34, n. 1 (Winter, 1964-1965), pp. 48-49; Neville March Hunnings, 700 wds., cp. pub.

8105 LANDSCAPE OF CONTEMPORARY CINEMA (Leon Lewis and William David Sherman)
Films & F: v. 13, n. 11 (Aug., 1967), p. 47; Sheridan Morley, 50 wds., pt. pub.
Interntl F G: v. 5 (1968), p. 263; 10 wds., pt. pub.

8106 *LANGUAGE CINEMATOGRAPHIQUE, LE (Francois Chevassu and Marcel Martin)
Interntl F G: v. 1 (1964), p. 225; 50 wds., pt. pub.

8107 LANGUAGES OF CRITICISM AND THE SCIENCES OF MAN: THE STRUCTURALIST CONTROVERSY, THE (Richard Macksey and Eugenio Donato)
Screen: v. 12, n. 1, pp. 49-58; Ben Brewster, 5500 wds., cp. pub.

8108 LAUGHTER IS A WONDERFUL THING (Joe E. Brown)
Films in R: v. IX, n. 1 (Jan., 1958), pp. 39-40; Robert Downing, 525 wds., cp. pub.

8109 LAUGHTON STORY, THE (Kurt Singer)
Films & F: v. 1, n. 4 (Jan., 1955), p. 30; John Minchinton, 100 wds., pt. pub.
Films in R: v. V, n. 10 (Dec., 1954), pp. 548-549; Robert Downing, 150 wds., cp. pub.

8110 LAUREL AND HARDY (Raymond Borde and Charles Perrin)
Cinema Studies: v. II, n. 1 (June, 1965), pp. 9-12; N.M.H., 1600 wds., cp. pub.
F Quarterly: v. XXI!, n. 3 (Spring, 1969), p. 58; 50 wds., cp. pub.
Films & F: v. 14, n. 8 (Apr., 1968), p. 60; Sheridan Morley, 200 wds., pt. pub.
Interntl F G: v. 6 (1969), p. 277; 50 wds., pt. pub.

8111 LAURETTE (Marguerite Courtney)
Films in R: v. VI, n. 7 (Aug.-Sept., 1955), pp. 358-359; Robert Downing, 800 wds., cp. pub.

8112 LESSONS WITH EISENSTEIN (Vladimir Nizhny, trans. and ed. by Ivor Montagu and Jay Leyda)
Sight & S: v. 32, n. 2 (Spring, 1963), p. 100; David Robinson, 800 wds., cp. pub.

8113 LET EM ROLL (Charles M. Daugherty)
Films in R: v. I, n. 6 (Sept., 1950), p. 38; Elspeth Burke Chapin, 150 wds., cp. pub.

8114 LIBRARY USES OF THE NEW MEDIA OF COMMUNICATION (C. Walter Stone, ed.)
F Lib Quarterly: v. 1, n. 2 (Spring, 1968), pp. 40-41; Madeleine M. Nichols, 350 wds., pt. pub.

8115 LIFE OF MAYAKOVSKY, THE (Wiktor Woroszylski, trans. by Boleslaw Taborski)
Cineaste: v. V, n. 1 (Winter, 1971-1972), pp. 25-26; Dan Georgakas, 1000 wds., cp. pub.

8116 LIFE STORY OF DANNY KAY, THE (Dick Richards)
   Sight & S: v. 18, n. 70 (Summer, 1949), p. 98; Daphne Turrell, 100 wds.,
    cp. pub.

8117 LIFE WITH GROUCHO (Arthur Marx)
   Films in R: v. VI, n. 4 (Apr., 1955), pp. 200-201; Robert Downing, 700
    wds., cp. pub.

8118 LIGHT OF A STAR (Gwen Robyns)
   Films & F: v. 15, n. 7 (Apr., 1969), p. 68; Sheridan Morley, 250 wds., pt.
    pub.

   LILLIAN GISH: THE MOVIES, MR. GRIFFITH AND ME (see: The Movies,
    Mr. Griffith and Me)

8120 LIMELIGHTERS (Oriana Fallaci)
   Films & F: v. 14, n. 7 (Apr., 1968), p. 38; Sheridan Morley, 850 wds., pt.
    pub.

8121 LINDSAY ANDERSON (Elizabeth Sussex)
   Films & F: v. 16, n. 4 (Jan., 1970), p. 72; Sheridan Morley, 850 wds., pt.
    pub.
   Interntl F G: v. 8 (1971), p. 443; 50 wds., pt. pub.
   Screen: v. 11, n. 2 (Mar.-Apr., 1970), pp. 88-90; David Spiers, 1000 wds.,
    pt. pub.
   Sight & S: v. 39, n. 2 (Spring, 1970), p. 109; Daniel Millar, 450 wds., cp.
    pub.

8122 *LINGUAGGIO DEL FILM, IL (Renato May)
   Sight & S: v. 17, n. 67 (Autumn, 1948), p. 151; Arthur Vesselo, 300 wds.,
    cp. pub.

8123 LION'S SHARE, THE (Bosley Crowther)
   Films in R: v. VIII, n. 6 (June-July, 1957), pp. 288-289; Robert Downing,
    400 wds., cp. pub.
   Sight & S: v. 27, n. 2 (Autumn, 1957), p. 102; Penelope Houston, 900 wds.,
    cp. pub.

8124 LITERATURE AND FILM (Robert Richardson)
   Cineaste: v. III, n. 3 (Winter, 1969-1970), p. 22; Noe Goldwasser, 600 wds.,
    cp. pub.
   Cinema J. v. IX, n. 2 (Spring, 1970), pp. 51-53; Christian Koch, 1300 wds.,
    cp. pub.
   F Heritage: v. 6, n. 3 (Spring, 1971), pp. 32-36; Charles L. P. Silet, 2000
    wds., cp. pub.
   Films & F: v. 16, n. 8 (May, 1970), p. 64; Sheridan Morley, 150 wds., pt.
    pub.

8125 LITERATURE OF CINEMA, THE (Martin S. Dworkin)
   Interntl F G: v. 8 (1971), p. 443; 75 wds., pt. pub.

8126 LITTLE FELLOW: THE LIFE AND WORK OF CHARLIE CHAPLIN, THE
    (Peter Cotes and Thelma Niklaus)
   Films in R: v. II, n. 9 (Nov., 1951), pp. 40-42; Theodore Hoff, 1000 wds.,
    cp. pub.
   Quarterly of FR TV: v. VI, n. 4 (Summer, 1952), pp. 426-427; Franklin
    Fearing, 150 wds., cp. pub.
   Sight & S: v. 21, n. 2 (Oct.-Dec., 1951), pp. 95-96; H. D. Waley, 600 wds.,
    cp. pub.

8127 *LIUDI I FILMY RUSSKOVO DOREVOLIUTSIONNOVO KINO (Romil P.
    Sobolev)
   F Culture: n. 34 (Fall, 1964), pp. 62-65; Stephen P. Hill, 1800 wds., cp.
    pub.

8128 LIVELIEST ART, THE (Arthur Knight)
   F Culture: v. IV, n. 1 (Jan., 1958), p. 23; Herman G. Weinberg, 1500 wds.,
    cp. pub.
   Films in R: v. IX, n. 9 (Nov., 1958), pp. 531-532; Henry Hart, 200 wds., cp.
    pub.
   Sight & S: v. 27, n. 3 (Winter, 1957-1958), p. 155; William Whitebait, 650
    wds., cp. pub.

8129 LON CHANEY PORTFOLIO, THE (Bill Nelson)
        Focus on F: n. 7 (Summer, 1971), pp. 59-60; Allen Eyles, 125 wds., cp.
        pub.

8130 LONDON (Sergei Obraztsov)
        Films & F: v. 4, n. 7 (Apr., 1958), p. 33; Martin Gray, 100 wds., pt. pub.

8131 LONELY ARTIST: A CRITICAL INTRODUCTION TO THE FILMS OF
        LESTER JAMES PERIES, THE (Philip Coorey)
        Sight & S: v. 40, n. 2 (Spring, 1971), p. 111; John Gillett, 600 wds., cp.
        pub.

8132 LONELY LIFE: AN AUTOBIOGRAPHY, THE (Bette Davis)
        Films in R: v. XIII, n. 8 (Oct., 1962), pp. 498-499; Flavia Wharton, 525
        wds., cp. pub.

8133 LONG LOOK AT SHORT FILMS, A (Derrick Knight and Vincent Porter)
        Interntl F G: v. 5 (1968), p. 263; 10 wds., pt. pub.

8134 *LOSEY (Pierre Rissient)
        Interntl F G: v. 5 (1968), p. 263; 20 wds., pt. pub.

8135 LOSEY ON LOSEY (Tom Milne, ed.)
        Cinema J: v. VIII, n. 1 (Fall, 1968), pp. 46-47; John Fell, 800 wds., cp.
        pub.
        F Culture: n. 50-51 (Fall-Winter, 1970), p. 62; 125 wds., cp. pub.
        F Quarterly: v. XXI, n. 4 (Summer, 1968), p. 55; 75 wds., no pub.
        F Soc Rev: May (1968), p. 38; Frank Manchel, 50 wds., cp. pub.
        Interntl F G: v. 5 (1968), p. 263; 20 wds., pt. pub.

8136 LOST FILMS (Gary Carey)
        F Quarterly: v. XXIV, n. 3 (Spring, 1971), pp. 59-60; Jay Leyda, 500 wds.,
        pt. pub.
        Films & F: v. 17, n. 6 (Mar., 1971), p. 64; Sheridan Morley, 200 wds., pt.
        pub.

8137 *LOUIS FEUILLADE (Francis Lacassin)
        Cinema Studies: v. II, n. 1 (June, 1965), pp. 12-13; N.M.H., 850 wds., cp.
        pub.

8138 *LOUIS LUMIERE, INVENTEUR (Maurice Bessy and Lo Duca)
        Hollywood Q: v. V (1950-1951), p. 201; Franklin Fearing, 125 wds., cp.
        pub.
        Sight & S: v. 17, n. 67 (Autumn, 1948), p. 151; Norah Lewis, 320 wds., cp.
        pub.

8139 LOVE AND DEATH: A STUDY OF CENSORSHIP (G. Legman)
        Films in R: v. I, n. 6 (Sept., 1950), pp. 37-38; Arthur Knight, 350 wds., cp.
        pub.

8140 LUBITSCH TOUCH — A CRITICAL STUDY OF A GREAT FILM DIREC-
        TOR, THE (Herman G. Weinberg)
        Cineaste: v. II, n. 3 (Winter, 1968-1969), p. 19; Gary Crowdus, 200 wds.,
        pt. pub.
        Cinema: v. 5, n. 1, pp. 46-47; Robert Joseph, 300 wds., pt. pub.
        Cinema J: v. IX, n. 1 (Fall, 1969), p. 56; Richard Dyer MacCann, 550 wds.,
        cp. pub.
        F Comment: v. 5, n. 3 (Fall, 1969), p. 83; Frank Manchel, 600 wds., cp.
        pub.
        F Heritage: v. 5, n. 2 (Winter, 1969-1970), pp. 31-32; R. A. Haller, 450
        wds., cp. pub.
        F Soc Rev: v. 4, n. 5, pp. 44-45; A. D. Malmfelt, 800 wds., cp. pub.
        Films & F: v. 15, n. 6 (Mar., 1969), p. 72; Sheridan Morley, 150 wds., pt.
        pub.
        Interntl F G: v. 7 (1970), p. 399; 50 wds., pt. pub.

8141 LUCKY STAR (Margaret Lockwood)
        Films & F: v. 2, n. 3 (Dec., 1955), p. 26; Peter G. Baker, 75 wds., pt. pub.

8142   *LUIS BUÑUEL (Ado Kyrou)
Interntl F G: v. 2 (1965), p. 251; 100 wds., pt. pub.

8143   LUIS BUÑUEL (Raymond Durgnat)
Cineaste: v. II, n. 3 (Winter, 1968-1969), pp. 18-19; Gary Crowdus, 550 wds., pt. pub.
Cinema J. v. VIII, n. 2 (Spring, 1969), pp. 38-40; John L. Fell, 850 wds., cp. pub.
F Quarterly: v. XXI, n. 4 (Summer, 1968), p. 55; 75 wds., no pub.
F Soc Rev: v. 4, n. 6, pp. 41-43; Frank Manchel, 1000 wds., cp. pub.
Interntl F G: v. 9 (1972), p. 469; 50 wds., pt. pub.

8144   LYING IN STATE (Stanton Griffis, ed.)
Films In R: v. IV, n. 7 (Aug.-Sept., 1953), pp. 374-375; Eleanor H. Nash, 400 wds., cp. pub.

8145   *MACK SENNETT: IL "RE DELLE COMICHE" (David Turconi)
Cinema Studies: v. I, n. 7 (June, 1963), pp. 175-177; N.M.H., 1200 wds., cp. pub.
F Quarterly: v. XVI, n. 2 (Winter, 1962-1963), pp. 53-54; Lowry Nelson, Jr., 450 wds., cp. pub.
Interntl F G: v. 5 (1968), p. 265; 25 wds., pt. pub.

8146   MADE FOR MILLIONS: A CRITICAL STUDY OF THE NEW MEDIA OF INFORMATION AND ENTERTAINMENT (Frederick Laws, ed.)
Sight & S: v. 16, n. 63 (Autumn, 1947), p. 129; 450 wds., cp. pub.

8147   MADE IN U.S.A. (Jean-Luc Godard)
Films & F: v. 14, n. 5 (Feb., 1968), p. 54; Sheridan Morley, 150 wds., pt. pub.

8148   MAGIC AND MYTH OF THE MOVIES (Parker Tyler)
Cinema: v. 6, n. 2 (Fall, 1970), pp. 42-44; Margaret Bach, 2600 wds., cp. pub.
Focus on F: n. 8 (Oct., 1971), p. 63; 175 wds., cp. pub.
Hollywood Q: v. II, n. 4 (July, 1947), pp. 434-436; Herman G. Weinberg, 750 wds., cp. pub.

8149   MAGIC LANTERN, THE (Robert Carson, ed.)
Films in R: v. IV, n. 1 (Jan., 1953), pp. 41-43; Elspeth Chapin, 300 wds., cp. pub.

8150   MAGIC SHADOWS: THE STORY OF THE ORIGINS OF MOTION PIC-TURES (Martin Quigley, Jr.)
Cinema Studies: v. I, n. 6 (Dec., 1962), pp. 145-148; Hermann Hecht, 1600 wds., cp. pub.
F Quarterly: v. XIV, n. 1 (Fall, 1960), pp. 58-59; 100 wds., cp. pub.
Films in R: v. I, n.2 (Mar., 1950), p. 40; B.G., 75 wds., cp. pub.
Films in R: v. XII, n. 1 (Jan., 1961), p. 54; Henry Hart, 125 wds., cp. pub.
Hollywood Q: v. IV, n. 1 (Fall, 1949), p. 103; Franklin Fearing, 100 wds., cp. pub.
Sight & S: v. 17, n. 65 (Spring, 1948), p. 52; Ernest Lindgren, 250 wds.,

8151   MAKING A FILM: THE STORY OF "SECRET PEOPLE" (Lindsay Anderson)
Films in R: v. III, n. 7 (Aug.-Sept., 1952), pp. 360-361; Stephen Lewis, 500 wds., cp. pub.
Quarterly of FR TV: v. VII, n. 2 (Winter, 1952), pp. 211-213; Franklin Fearing, 400 wds., cp. pub.
Sight & S: v. 21, n. 4 (Apr.-June, 1952), p. 182; Frank Hauser, 650 wds., cp. pub.

8152 MAKING AND SHOWING YOUR OWN FILMS (George H. Sewell)
      Films & F: v. 1, n. 6 (Mar., 1955), p. 30; John Minchinton, 50 wds., pt.
      pub.

8153 MAKING AND UNMAKING OF "QUE VIVA MEXICO! ", THE (Harry M.
      Geduld and Ronald Gottesman)
      Films & F: v. 17, n. 1 (Oct., 1970), p. 72; Sheridan Morley, 550 wds., pt.
      pub.

8154 MAKING LANTERN SLIDES AND FILMSTRIPS (C. Douglas Milner)
      Sight & S: v. 18, n. 70 (Summer, 1949), p. 97; F. E. Farley, 300 wds., cp.
      pub.

8155 MAKING OF FEATURE FILMS — A GUIDE, THE (Ivan Butler)
      Films & F: v. 17, n. 9 (June, 1971), p. 92; Sheridan Morley, 150 wds., pt.
      pub.
      Interntl F G: v. 9 (1972), p. 469; 50 wds., pt. pub.

8156 MAKING OF KUBRICK'S "2001", THE (Jerome Agel, ed.)
      Interntl F G: v. 8 (1971), p. 443; 50 wds., pt. pub.

8157 MAKING THE MOVIES (Jeanne Bendick)
      Hollywood Q: v. I, n. 3 (Apr., 1946), pp. 340-341; Sondra K. Gorney, 300
      wds., cp. pub.

8158 MAMOULIAN (Tom Milne)
      Films & F: v. 16, n. 8 (May, 1970), p. 64; Sheridan Morley, 750 wds., pt.
      pub.
      Interntl F G: v. 8 (1971), p. 443; 50 wds., pt. pub.
      Screen: v. 11, n. 1, pp. 96-99; Philip Johns, 1500 wds., pt. pub.
      Take one: v. 2, n. 8 (1970), p. 29; Thomas R. Atkins, 300 wds., cp. pub.

8159 MAN AND THE MOVIES (W. R. Robinson, ed.)
      Cineaste: v. II, n. 4 (Spring, 1969), pp. 22-23; Gary Crowdus, 200 wds., pt.
      pub.
      Cinema J: v. VII (Winter, 1967-1968), pp. 36-37; Richard Dyer MacCann,
      850 wds., cp. pub.
      F Soc Rev: Dec. (1967), pp. 31-33; Charles D. Peavy, 1100 wds., cp. pub.

8160 MAN OF ARAN (Pat Mullen)
      F Comment: v. 7, n. 2 (Summer, 1971), pp. 76-77; Jack C. Ellis, 700 wds.,
      cp. pub.

8161 *MANIFESTE D'UN ART NOUVEAU LA POLYVISION (Nelly Kaplan)
      F Culture: v. 2, n. 2 (1956), p. 31; Herman G. Weinberg, 800 wds., cp. pub.

8162 MANIPULATOR, THE (Diane Cilento)
      Films & F: v. 13, n. 11 (Aug., 1967), p. 47; Sheridan Morley, 50 wds., pt.
      pub.

8163 MANUAL ON FILM EVALUATION (Emily S. Jones)
      F Lib Quarterly: v. 1, n. 4 (Fall, 1968), p. 47; 100 wds., pt. pub.

8164 *MARCEL CARNE (Jean Quéval)
      Sight & S: v. 23, n. 1 (July-Sept., 1953), pp. 50-51; Gavin Lambert, 700
      wds., cp. pub.

8165 MARGARET RUTHERFORD (Eric Keown)
      Films in R: v. IX, n. 2 (Feb., 1958), p. 101; Robert Downing, 400 wds., cp.
      pub.

8166 MARILYN MONROE (Maurice Zolotow)
      Am Cinematog: v. 41, n. 12 (Dec., 1960), p. 718; 300 wds., pt. pub.
      F Culture: n. 31 (Winter, 1963-1964), p. 68; Herman G. Weinberg, 75 wds.,
      cp. pub.
      Sight & S: v. 30, n. 2 (Spring, 1961), pp. 99-100; Margaret Hinxman, 600
      wds., cp. pub.

8167 MARLENE DIETRICH (John Kobal)
      Cineaste: v. II, n. 1 (Summer, 1968), p. 27; Gary Crowdus, 75 wds., pt.
      pub.

F Comment: v. 5, n. 3 (Fall, 1969), p. 80; Herman G. Weinberg, 100 wds., cp. pub.
Films & F: v. 14, n. 9 (June, 1968), p. 42; 150 wds., pt. pub.
Interntl F G: v. 6 (1969), p. 271; 50 wds., pt. pub.

8168 MARLENE DIETRICH'S ABC (Marlene Dietrich)
Films in R: v. XIII, n. 8 (Oct., 1962), pp. 497-498; Diana Willing Cope, 375 wds., cp. pub.

8169 MARX BROTHERS, THE (Kyle Crichton)
Films in R: v. I, n. 5 (July-Aug., 1950), pp. 25-29; James Agee, 1200 wds., cp. pub.

8170 MARX BROTHERS, THE (Raymond Durgnat)
Cinema J: v. VIII, n. 2 (Spring, 1969), pp. 38-40; John L. Foll, 850 wds., cp. pub.

8171 MARX BROTHERS AT THE MOVIES, THE (Paul D. Zimmerman and Burt Goldblatt)
F Comment: v. 6, n. 1 (Spring, 1970), p. 71; 100 wds., cp. pub.

8172 MARX BROTHERS: THEIR WORLD OF COMEDY, THE (Allen Eyles)
F Heritage: v. 3, n. 1 (Fall, 1967), p. 36; Robert Steele, 275 wds., cp. pub.
Films & F: v. 16, n. 3 (Dec., 1969), p. 72; Sheridan Morley, 250 wds., pt. pub.
Sight & S: v. 35, n. 3 (Summer, 1966), p. 154; John Gillett, 450 wds., cp. pub.

8173 MARY PICKFORD: COMEDIENNE (Kemp R. Niver, ed. by Bebe Bergsten)
Am Cinematog: v. 51, n. 6 (June, 1970), pp. 587-588; George J. Mitchell, 500 wds., cp. pub.
Films in R: v. XXI, n. 5 (May, 1970), p. 287; Robert Giroux, 250 wds., cp. pub.
Interntl F G: v. 8 (1971), p. 443; 50 wds., pt. pub.

8174 MASCULINE-FEMININE (Jean-Luc Godard)
Screen: v. 11, n. 2 (Mar.-Apr., 1970), pp. 86-88; David Spiers, 750 wds., pt. pub.

8175 MASS COMMUNICATIONS AND AMERICAN EMPIRE (Herbert Schiller)
Cineaste: v. III, n. 3 (Winter, 1969-1970), pp. 22-24; Ruth McCormick, 2000 wds., cp. pub.

8176 MASS MEDIA AND MASS MAN (Alan Casty, ed.)
F Comment: v. 5, n. 4 (Winter, 1969), p. 78; 75 wds., cp. pub.

8177 MASS MEDIA IN THE SOVIET UNION (Mark W. Hopkins)
Cineaste: v. IV, n. 2 (Fall, 1970), pp. 45-46; Ruth McCormick, 700 wds., cp. pub.

8178 *MAURITZ STILLER OCH HANS FILMER 1912-1916 (Gosta Werner)
Sight & S: v. 39, n. 4 (Autumn, 1970), pp. 224-225; Neville Hunnings, 450 wds., cp. pub.

8179 *MAX LINDER (Charles Ford)
Sight & S: v. 35, n. 3 (Summer, 1966), p. 154; John Gillett, 450 wds., cp. pub.

8180 MELVILLE ON MELVILLE (Rue Nogueira, ed.)
Focus on F: n. 8 (Oct., 1971), p. 63; 125 wds., cp. pub.

8181 MEMOIRS OF A PROFESSIONAL CAD (George Sanders)
Films in R: v. XII, n. 1 (Jan., 1961), pp. 49-51; Eleanor H. Nash, 450 wds., cp. pub.

8182 MEMOIRS OF A STAR (Pola Negri)
Films in R: v. XXI, n. 8 (Oct., 1970), p. 500; Joanne Chandler, 125 wds., cp. pub.
Interntl F G: v. 8 (1971), p. 443; 75 wds., pt. pub.

8183 MEMOIRS OF WILL H. HAYS, THE (Will H. Hays)
      Films in R: v. VII, n. 5 (May, 1956), pp. 232-233; Jack Spears, 350 wds.,
         cp. pub.
      Quarterly of FR TV: v. X, n. 2 (Winter, 1955), pp. 209-210; Franklin
         Fearing, 250 wds., cp. pub.

8184 MEMORIES (Ethel Barrymore)
      Films in R: v. VI, n. 7 (Aug.-Sept., 1955), pp. 357-358; R. Downing, 300
         wds., cp. pub.

8185 MERELY COLOSSAL: THE STORY OF THE MOVIES FROM THE LONG
         CHASE TO THE CHAISE LOUNGE (Arthur Mayer)
      Films in R: v. IV, n. 3 (Mar., 1953), p. 152; Eleanor A. Nash, 275 wds., cp.
         pub.
      Quarterly of FR TV: v. VIII, n. 2 (Winter, 1953), p. 208; Franklin Fearing,
         150 wds., cp. pub.

8186 MICHAEL BALCON PRESENTS . . . A LIFETIME OF FILMS (Sir Michael
         Balcon)
      Cinema J: v. X, n. 1 (Fall, 1970), pp. 54-59; Calvin Pryluck, 1900 wds., cp.
         pub.
      Films & F: v. 15, n. 8 (May, 1969), p. 74; Sheridan Morley, 500 wds., pt.
         pub.
      Interntl F G: v. 7 (1970), p. 399; 75 wds., pt. pub.
      Sight & S: v. 38, n. 2 (Spring, 1969), p. 108; Penelope Houston, 325 wds.,
         cp. pub.

8187 MICHELANGELO ANTONIONI (Ian Cameron)
      Sight & S: v. 32, n. 3 (Summer, 1963), pp. 153-154; Geoffrey Nowell-
         Smith, 600 wds., cp. pub.

8188 *MICHELANGELO ANTONIONI (Pierre Leprohon)
      Interntl F G: v. 2 (1965), p. 251; 100 wds., pt. pub.

8189 *MILLE ET UN METIERS DU CINEMA, LES (Pierre Leprohon)
      Sight & S: v. 17, n. 68 (Winter, 1948-1949), p. 196; Ragna Jackson, 350
         wds., cp. pub.

8190 MILLION AND ONE NIGHTS: A HISTORY OF THE MOTION PICTURE
         THROUGH 1925, A (Terry Ramsaye)
      F Comment: v. 3, n. 1 (Winter, 1965), p. 69; William Sloan, 75 wds., cp.
         pub.
      F Quarterly: v. XVII, n. 4 (Summer, 1964), p. 64; Ernest Callenbach, 125
         wds., cp. pub.
      Films in R: v. XV, n. 3 (Mar., 1964), p. 165; Henry Hart, 300 wds., cp. pub.
      Sight & S: v. 33, n. 2 (Spring, 1964), pp. 101-102; John Russell Taylor, 550
         wds., cp. pub.

8191 *MINNELLI (Francois Truchand)
      Interntl F G: v. 5 (1968), p. 263; 25 wds., pt. pub.

8192 MINUTES OF THE LAST MEETING (Gene Fowler)
      Films in R: v. V, n. 8 (Oct., 1954), pp. 439-440; Robert Downing, 450
         wds., cp. pub.

8193 MIRACLE OF THE MOVIES, THE (Leslie Wood)
      Sight & S: v. 16, n. 64 (Winter, 1947-1948), p. 180; 150 wds., cp. pub.

8194 *MIRAGE DU CINEMA, LE (Sammy Beracha)
      Sight & S: v. 17, n. 66 (Summer, 1948), p. 107; Ragna Jackson, 200 wds.,
         cp. pub.

8195 MIRROR FOR ENGLAND, A (Raymond Durgnat)
      F Quarterly: v. XXV, n. 4 (Summer, 1972), p. 38; 50 wds., cp. pub.
      Films & F: v. 17, n. 2 (Nov., 1970), p. 64; Sheridan Morley, 350 wds., pt.
         pub.
      Films & F: v. 17, n. 9 (June, 1971), p. 92; Sheridan Morley, 500 wds., pt.
         pub.
      Interntl F G: v. 9 (1972), p. 469; 50 wds., pt. pub.

8196 MR. LAUREL AND MR. HARDY (John McCabe)
       Cinema Studies: v. I, n. 7 (June, 1963), pp. 175-177; N.M.H., 1200 wds.,
          cp. pub.
       F Comment: v. 5, n. 4 (Winter, 1969), pp. 76-77; Kirk Bond, 1200 wds., cp.
          pub.
       F Quarterly: v. XV, n. 1 (Fall, 1961), pp. 57-58; Carlos Clarens, 950 wds.,
          cp. pub.
       Films in R: v. XII, n. 6 (June-July, 1961), pp. 367-369; Robert Downing,
          750 wds., cp. pub.
       Sight & S: v. 31, n. 1 (Winter, 1961-1962), pp. 49-50; David Robinson,
          1500 wds., cp. pub.

8197 MR. RANK: A STUDY OF J. ARTHUR RANK AND BRITISH FILMS (Alan
          Wood)
       Films in R: v. IV, n. 6 (June-July, 1953), pp. 310-311; Alice H. Witham,
          300 wds., cp. pub.
       Sight & S: v. 22, n. 2 (Oct.-Dec., 1952), p. 93; Duncan Crow, 1000 wds.,
          cp. pub.

8198 *MIZOGUCHI (Vê-Hô)
       Interntl F G: v. 2 (1965), p. 225; 300 wds., pt. pub.

8199 MOGULS, THE (Norman Zierold)
       Films in R: v. XX, n. 7 (Aug.-Sept., 1969), pp. 428-429; Alice H. Whitman,
          200 wds., cp. pub.

8200 *MONSIEUR CHAPLIN, OU LE RIRE DANS LA NUIT (Maurice Bessy)
       Films in R: v. IV, n. 4 (Apr., 1953), pp. 202-203; Herman G. Weinberg, 525
          wds., cp. pub.

8201 MOON'S A BALLOON, THE (David Niven)
       Focus on F: n. 8 (Oct., 1971), p. 59; 200 wds., cp. pub.

8202 *MOSFILM: ARTICLES, DOCUMENTS, PICTURES (Iskusstvo)
       Cinema Studies: v. I, n. 5 (Sept., 1962), pp. 110-114; Jay Leyda, 2000
          wds., cp. pub.

8203 MOTION PICTURE: A SELECTED BOOKLIST, THE (American Library
          Association)
       Hollywood Q: v. II, n. 2 (Jan., 1947), p. 219; Lewis Jacobs, 100 wds., cp.
          pub.

8204 MOTION PICTURE AGREEMENTS (Morris Ernst and Alexander Lindey)
       Hollywood Q: v. IV, n. 3 (Spring, 1950), p. 317; Franklin Fearing, 80 wds.,
          cp. pub.

8205 MOTION PICTURE EMPIRE (Gertrude Jobes)
       Cineaste: v. V, n. 1 (Winter, 1971-1972), p. 28; Ruth McCormick, 650 wds.,
          cp. pub.
       F Soc Rev: Nov. (1967), pp. 34-36; Frank Manchel, 800 wds., cp. pub.
       F Soc Rev: Nov. (1967), p. 36; Anthony W. Hodgkinson, 400 wds., cp. pub.

8206 MOTION PICTURE PRODUCTION FOR INDUSTRY (Jay E. Gordon)
       Am Cinematog: v. 42, n. 7 (July, 1961), p. 406; 250 wds., pt. pub.

8207 MOTION-PICTURE WORK (David S. Hulfish)
       F Comment: v. 7, n. 4 (Winter, 1971-1972), p. 79; Lewis Jacobs, 250 wds.,
          cp. pub.

8208 MOTION PICTURES (Samuel Beckoff)
       Films in R: v. V, n. 4 (Apr., 1954), p. 201; Marilyn Adams, 50 wds., cp.
          pub.

8209 MOTION PICTURES AND STANDARDS OF MORALITY (Charles C. Peters)
       F Comment: v. 7, n. 2 (Summer, 1971), pp. 70-72; Garth Jowett, 2200
          wds., cp. pub.

8210 MOTION PICTURES AND THE SOCIAL ATTITUDES OF CHILDREN (Ruth
          C. Peterson and L. L. Thurstone)
       F Comment: v. 7, n. 2 (Summer, 1971), pp. 70-72; Garth Jowett, 2200
          wds., cp. pub.

8211 MOTION PICTURES AND YOUTH (W. W. Charters)
      F Comment: v. 7, n. 2 (Summer, 1971), pp. 70-72; Garth Jowett, 2200
      wds., cp. pub.

8212 MOTION PICTURES AS A MEDIUM OF INSTRUCTION AND COMMUNI-
      CATION: AN EXPERIMENTAL ANALYSIS OF THE EFFECTS
      OF TWO FILMS (Franklin Fearing)
      Hollywood Q: v. V (1950-1951), p. 103; Franklin Fearing, 125 wds., cp.
      pub.

8213 MOTION PICTURES FROM THE LIBRARY OF CONGRESS PAPER PRINT
      COLLECTION, 1894-1912 (Kemp R. Niver, ed. by Bebe Bergsten)
      Am Cinematog: v. 48, n. 7 (July, 1967), p. 499; 250 wds., cp. pub.
      Cinema Studies: v. II, n. 5 (Sept., 1967), pp. 88-89; N.M.H., 550 wds., cp.
      pub.
      F Soc Rev: Jan. (1968), p. 20; H.P., 900 wds., cp. pub.
      Films in R: v. XVIII, n. 8 (Oct., 1967), p. 500; Henry Hart, 200 wds., cp.
      pub.
      Interntl F G: v. 6 (1969), p. 277; 50 wds., pt. pub.
      Sight & S: v. 37, n. 1 (Winter, 1967-1968), p. 51; David Robinson, 450
      wds., cp. pub.

8214 MOTION PICTURES IN THE DOCTRINE OF THE CATHOLIC CHURCH
      F Culture: v. 2, n. 2 (1956), p. 32; 325 wds., cp. pub.

8215 MOTION PICTURES 1894-1912: IDENTIFIED FROM U.S. COPYRIGHT
      OFFICE (Howard Lamarr Walls, ed.)
      Films in R: v. V, n. 2 (Feb., 1954), pp. 101-102; Henry Hart, 400 wds., cp.
      pub.
      Quarterly of FR TV: v. VIII, n. 4 (Summer, 1954), pp. 426-427; Franklin
      Fearing, 250 wds., cp. pub.

8216 MOTION PICTURES 1912-1939: CATALOG OF COPYRIGHT ENTRIES,
      CUMULATIVE SERIES (Copyright Office)
      Films in R: v. III, n. 2 (Feb., 1952), p. 92; Henry Hart, 125 wds., cp. pub.
      Quarterly of FR TV: v. VI, n. 4 (Summer, 1952), p. 424; Franklin Fearing,
      150 wds., cp. pub.

8217 MOTION PICTURES 1940-1949: CATALOG OF COPYRIGHT ENTRIES,
      CUMULATIVE SERIES (Copyright Office)
      Films in R: v. V, n. 2 (Feb., 1954), pp. 101-102; Henry Hart, 400 wds., cp.
      pub.
      Quarterly of FR TV: v. VIII, n. 4 (Summer, 1954), pp. 426-427; Franklin
      Fearing, 250 wds., cp. pub.

8218 MOTION PICTURES 1950-1959: CATALOG OF COPYRIGHT ENTRIES,
      CUMULATIVE SERIES (Copyright Office)
      Films in R: v. XII, n. 5 (May, 1961), p. 306; Henry Hart, 200 wds., cp. pub.

8219 MOTION PICTURES 1960-1969: CATALOG OF COPYRIGHT ENTRIES,
      CUMULATIVE SERIES (Copyright Office)
      Films in R: v. XXII, n. 7 (Aug.-Sept., 1971), pp. 431-432; Bradner Lacy,
      125 wds., cp. pub.

8220 MOTION PICTURES: THE DEVELOPMENT OF AN ART FROM SILENT
      FILMS TO THE AGE OF TELEVISION (A. R. Fulton)
      Cinema Studies: v. I, n. 7 (June, 1963), pp. 179-180; R. A. Rudorff, 750
      wds., cp. pub.
      Films in R: v. XII, n. 6 (June-July, 1961), pp. 366-367; Robert C. Roman,
      400 wds., cp. pub.

8221 MOVEMENT IN TWO DIMENSIONS: A STUDY OF THE ANIMATED AND
      PROJECTED PICTURES WHICH PRECEDED THE INVENTION
      OF CINEMATOGRAPHY (Olive Cook)
      Cinema Studies: v. I, n. 9 (June, 1964), pp. 237-241; R. A. Heaword, 2500
      wds., cp. pub.
      Sight & S: v. 33, n. 1 (Winter, 1963-1964), pp. 48-49; David Robinson, 475
      wds., cp. pub.

8222 MOVIE COMEDY TEAMS (Leonard Maltin)
        Focus on F: n. 6 (Spring, 1971), p. 61; Allen Eyles, 200 wds., cp. pub.
        Views & Rev: v. 3, n. 1 (Summer, 1971), pp. 77-80; Karl Thiede, 1200
          wds., cp. pub.

8223 MOVIE LOT TO BEACHHEAD (editors of Look Magazine)
        Hollywood Q: v. I, n. 1 (Oct., 1945), p. 115; John Larkin, 550 wds., cp.
          pub.

8224 MOVIE MAN (David Robinson)
        F Soc Rev: May (1968), p. 39; Frank Manchel, 50 wds., cp. pub.
        Films & F: v. 14, n. 1 (Oct., 1967), p. 32; Sheridan Morley, 175 wds., pt.
          pub.

8225 MOVIE MOGULS, THE (Philip French)
        Films & F: v. 15, n. 11 (Aug., 1969), p. 61; Sheridan Morley, 550 wds., pt.
          pub.
        Sight & S: v. 38, n. 4 (Autumn, 1969), pp. 216-217; Gavin Millar, 600 wds.,
          cp. pub.

8226 MOVIE PARADE 1888-1949: A PICTORIAL SURVEY OF WORLD CINEMA
        (Paul Rotha and Roger Manvell)
        Films in R: v. I, n. 7 (Oct., 1950), pp. 29-30; Siegfried Kracauer, 200 wds.,
          cp. pub.
        Sequence: n. 11 (Summer, 1950), pp. 46-47; Alberta Marlow, 650 wds., pt.
          pub.
        Sight & S: v. 19, n. 4 (June, 1950), p. 175; Penelope Houston, 650 wds., cp.
          pub.

8227 MOVIE STARS, THE (Richard Griffith)
        Cinema J: v. XI, n. 1 (Fall, 1971), pp. 68-71; Kent R. Brown, 1300 wds.,
          cp. pub.
        F Comment: v. 7, n. 1 (Spring, 1971), pp. 78, 80, 82; Gary Carey, 2600
          wds., cp. pub.
        Films in R: v. XXII, n. 1 (Jan., 1971), p. 30; Alice H. Witham, 250 wds., cp.
          pub.
        Journal of P C: v. IV, n. 3 (Winter, 1971), pp. 822-824; Ralph Haven Wolfe,
          700 wds., cp. pub.

8228 MOVIES, THE (Richard Griffith and Arthur Mayer)
        Films & F: v. 4, n. 6 (Mar., 1958), p. 35; Paul Rotha, 700 wds., pt. pub.

8229 MOVIES: A PSYCHOLOGICAL STUDY (Martha Wolfenstein and Nathan
        Leites)
        Films in R: v. I, n. 5 (July-Aug., 1950), pp. 40-41; Hortense Powdermaker,
          300 wds., cp. pub.
        Hollywood Q: v. V (1950-1951), pp. 101-102; Franklin Fearing, 450 wds.,
          cp. pub.

8230 MOVIES AND CONDUCT (Herbert Blumer)
        F Comment: v. 7, n. 2 (Summer, 1971), pp. 70-72; Garth Jowett, 2200
          wds., cp. pub.

8231 MOVIES AND HOW THEY ARE MADE (Frank Manchel)
        Screen: v. 11, n. 4-5 (July-Oct., 1970), pp. 130-131; R. C. Vanndey, 550
          wds., cp. pub.

8232 MOVIES AND SOCIETY (Ian C. Jarvie)
        F Comment: v. 7, n. 2 (Summer, 1971), pp. 72-73; Garth Jowett, 750 wds.,
          cp. pub.

8233 MOVIES AS MEDIUM, THE (Lewis Jacobs)
        Interntl F G: v. 9 (1972), p. 469; 50 wds., pt. pub.

8234 MOVIES, CENSORSHIP AND THE LAW (Ira H. Carmen)
        Cinema Studies: v. II, n. 3 (Mar., 1967), pp. 59-60; N.M.H., 850 wds., cp.
          pub.

8235 MOVIES, DELINQUENCY, AND CRIME (Herbert Blumer and Philip M. Hauser)
F Comment: v. 7, n. 2 (Summer, 1971), pp. 70-72; Garth Jowett, 2200 wds., cp. pub.

8236 MOVIES FOR TV (John H. Battison)
Films in R: v. II, n. 2 (Feb., 1951), pp. 44-45; Henry Hart, 300 wds., cp. pub.
Hollywood Q: v. V (1950-1951), pp. 417-418; Franklin Fearing, 160 wds., cp. pub.

8237 MOVIES IN THE AGE OF INNOCENCE, THE (Edward Wagenknecht)
Cinema Studies: v. I, n. 8 (Dec., 1963), p. 207; Liam O'Leary, 350 wds., cp. pub.
F Quarterly: v. XVI, n. 2 (Winter, 1962-1963), pp. 52-53; Ernest Callenbach, 550 wds., cp. pub.
Films in R: v. XIV, n. 7 (Sept.-Aug., 1963), pp. 425-426; Gerald D. McDonald, 425 wds., pt. pub.

8238 MOVIES INTO FILM: FILM CRITICISM (John Simon)
F Comment: v. 7, n. 3 (Fall, 1971), pp. 74-75; John W. Locke, 900 wds., cp. pub.
F Soc Rev: v. 6, n. 8 (Apr., 1971), pp. 49-50; Michael Sragow, 1000 wds., cp. pub.

8239 MOVIES, MR. GRIFFITH AND ME, THE (Lillian Gish, with Ann Pinchot)
Cineaste: v. II, n. 4 (Spring, 1969), p. 21; Ernest Burns, 150 wds., pt. pub.
Cinema J: v. IX, n. 1 (Fall, 1969), pp. 50-52; Thomas R. Cripps, 1200 wds., cp. pub.
F Comment: v. 5, n. 4 (Winter, 1969), p. 77; Kirk Bond, 600 wds., cp. pub.
F Heritage: v. 4, n. 4 (Summer, 1969), pp. 32-34; Joseph McBride, 1000 wds., cp. pub.
F Heritage: v. 5, n. 1 (Fall, 1969), pp. 32-34; Joseph McBride, 850 wds., cp. pub.
Films & F: v. 16, n. 1 (Oct., 1969), p. 70; Sheridan Morley, 850 wds., pt. pub.
Films in R: v. XX, n. 7 (Aug.-Sept., 1969), pp. 430-431; Henry Hart, 400 wds., cp. pub.
Interntl F G: v. 7 (1970), p. 399; 50 wds., pt. pub.
Sight & S: v. 38, n. 4 (Autumn, 1969), p. 216; Bessie Love, 700 wds., cp. pub.
Take One: v. 2, n. 4 (1969), p. 23; Robert Steele, 500 wds., cp. pub.

8240 MOVIES ON TV (Steven H. Scheuer)
Focus on F: n. 10 (Summer, 1972), p. 60; Allen Eyles, 275 wds., cp. pub.
Take One: v. 2, n. 7 (1970), p. 30; Douglas Sharples, 1000 wds., cp. pub.

8241 MOVIES THAT TEACH (Charles F. Hoban, Jr.)
Hollywood Q: v. II, n. 3 (Apr., 1947), pp. 323-325; Robert Rahtz, 950 wds., cp. pub.

8242 MOVIES: THE HISTORY OF AN ART AND AN INSTITUTION (Richard Schickel)
F Quarterly: v. XVIII, n. 3 (Spring, 1965), p. 59; Ernest Callenbach, 150 wds., cp. pub.
F Soc Rev: Mar. (1966), p. 25; Adrienne Mancia, 300 wds., cp. pub.

8243 MOVING IMAGE: A GUIDE TO CINEMATIC LITERACY, THE (Robert Gessner)
Cinema J: v. IX, n. 1 (Fall, 1969), pp. 52-53; Robert Steele, 600 wds., cp. pub.
F Heritage: v. 4, n. 1 (Fall, 1968), pp. 35-36; Robert Steele, 500 wds., cp. pub.
F Soc Rev: v. 4, n. 3, pp. 46-47; Frank Manchel, 850 wds., cp. pub.
Take One: v. 1, n. 12 (1968), pp. 29-30; Herman G. Weinberg, 1100 wds., cp. pub.

8244 *MURNAU (Charles Jameux)
Interntl F G: v. 4 (1967), pp. 277-278; 75 wds., pt. pub.

8245 MUSICAL FILM, THE (Douglas McVay)
    Interntl F G: v. 5 (1968), p. 263; 25 wds., pt. pub.

8246 MY AUTOBIOGRAPHY (Charles Chaplin)
    Cinema Studies: v. II, n. 1 (June, 1965), pp. 9-12; N.M.H., 1600 wds., cp.
        pub.
    F Comment: v. IV, n. 1 (Fall, 1966), pp. 85-88; Harry Feldman, 1100 wds.,
        cp. pub.
    F Quarterly: v. XIX, n. 2 (Winter, 1965-1966), pp. 54-58; David Madden,
        3000 wds., cp. pub.
    Films & F: v. 11, n. 2 (Nov., 1964), pp. 11-13; Peter Cotes, 2800 wds., pt.
        pub.
    Films in R: v. XV, n. 10 (Dec., 1964), pp. 606-607; A.M.W., 400 wds., no
        pub.
    Films in R: v. XV, n. 10 (Dec., 1964), pp. 607-610; Jack Spears, 1300 wds.,
        no cr.
    N Y Rev of Books: v. III, n. 5 (Oct. 22, 1964), pp. 1-4; F. W. Dupee, 3500
        wds., pt. pub.
    Sight & S: v. 33, n. 4 (Autumn, 1964), pp. 206-207; David Robinson, 1400
        wds., cp. pub.

8247 MY FATHER AND I (Joseph Schildkraut, with Leo Lania)
    Films in R: v. X, n. 7 (Aug.-Sept., 1959), pp. 427-428; Robert C. Roman,
        350 wds., cp. pub.

8248 MY FATHER, CHARLIE CHAPLIN (Charles Chaplin, Jr., with N. and M.
        Rau)
    Cinema Studies: v. II, n. 1 (June, 1965), pp. 9-12; N.M.H., 1600 wds., cp.
        pub.
    Films in R: v. XII, n. 1 (Jan., 1961), pp. 51-54; Robert Downing, 1300
        wds., cp. pub.

8249 MY FIRST HUNDRED YEARS IN HOLLYWOOD (Jack L. Warner, with Dean
        Jennings)
    Films in R: v. XVII, n. 1 (Jan., 1966), p. 44; Alice H. Witham, 350 wds., cp.
        pub.

8250 MY LIFE WITH CHAPLIN: AN INTIMATE MEMOIR (Lita Grey Chaplin,
        with Morton Cooper)
    F Heritage: v. 2, n. 4 (Summer, 1967), pp. 34-35; Robert Steele, 450 wds.,
        cp. pub.
    Films in R: v. XVII, n. 8 (Oct., 1966), p. 515; Henry Hart, 200 wds., cp.
        pub.

8251 MY STORY (Mary Astor)
    Films in R: v. X, n. 3 (Mar., 1959), p. 177; Robert Downing, 225 wds., cp.
        pub.
    Sight & S: v. 28, n. 3-4 (Summer-Autumn, 1959), p. 187; Philip Oakes, 800
        wds., cp. pub.

8252 MY WAYWARD PARENT: A BOOK ABOUT IRVIN S. COBB (Elisabeth
        Cobb)
    Hollywood Q: v. I, n. 2 (Jan., 1946), pp. 241-242; E. N. Hooker, 550 wds.,
        cp. pub.

8253 MY WICKED, WICKED WAYS (Errol Flynn)
    Films in R: v. XI, n. 3 (Mar., 1960), pp. 180-181; Anthony Thomas, 400
        wds., cp. pub.

8254 MY WONDERFUL WORLD OF SLAPSTICK (Buster Keaton, with Charles
        Samuels)
    Cinema Studies: v. I, n. 8 (Dec., 1963), pp. 201-203; John Gillett, 1100
        wds., cp. pub.
    F Quarterly: v. XIII, n. 3 (Spring, 1960), p. 62; Ernest Callenbach, 200
        wds., cp. pub.
    Films & F: v. 13, n. 12 (Sept., 1967), p. 46; Sheridan Morley, 150 wds., pt.
        pub.
    Films in R: v. XI, n. 8 (Oct., 1960), pp. 500-502; William K. Everson, 800
        wds., cp. pub.

8255 NAME ABOVE THE TITLE: AN AUTOBIOGRAPHY, THE (Frank Capra)
Cinema J: v. XI, n. 2 (Spring, 1972), pp. 37-40; Russell Merritt, 1500 wds.,
cp. pub.
F Comment: v. 7, n. 4 (Winter, 1971-1972), pp. 77-78; Jean-Loup Bourget,
1300 wds., cp. pub.
Films in R: v. XXII, n. 7 (Aug.-Sept., 1971), p. 433; Henry Hart, 200 wds.,
cp. pub.

8256 *NAR FILMEN KOM TILL SVERIGE: CHARLES MAGNUSSON OCH
SVENSKA BIO (Bengt Idestam-Almquist)
Cinema Studies: v. I, n. 2 (Dec., 1960), pp. 38-41; Rune Waldekranz, 1800
wds., cp. pub.

8257 NATIONAL FILM ARCHIVE CATALOGUE, PART III: SILENT FICTION
FILMS 1895-1930 (British Film Institute)
Cinema Studies: v. II, n. 3 (Mar., 1967), pp. 57-59; Liam O'Leary, 1000
wds., cp. pub.
Interntl F G: v. 5 (1968), p. 263; 25 wds., pt. pub.

8258 'NEATH THE MASK: THE STORY OF THE EAST FAMILY (John M. East)
Sight & S: v. 36, n. 4 (Autumn, 1967), p. 211; David Robinson, 500 wds.,
cp. pub.

8259 NEGATIVE SPACE: MANNY FARBER ON THE MOVIES (Manny Farber)
Cinema: v. 6, n. 3 (Spring, 1971), pp. 54-56; Richard Thompson, 1600
wds., cp. pub.
Cinema J: v. XI, n. 2 (Spring, 1972), pp. 34-37; John L. Fell, 1500 wds., cp.
pub.
F Comment: v. 7, n. 3 (Fall, 1971), pp. 70-71; Jim Kitses, 1800 wds., cp.
pub.
F Quarterly: v. XXIV, n. 3 (Spring, 1971), pp. 26-28; Ernest Callenbach,
950 wds., cp. pub.
F Soc Rev: v. 6, n. 9 (May, 1971), pp. 49-50; Foster Hirsch, 1000 wds., cp.
pub.
Films & F: v. 17, n. 10 (July, 1971), p. 64; Sheridan Morley, 75 wds., pt.
pub.
Interntl F G: v. 9 (1972), p. 469; 50 wds., pt. pub.
Screen: v. 12, n. 3 (Summer, 1971), pp. 161-164; Jim Hillier, 1500 wds.,
cp. pub.
Sight & S: v. 40, n. 4 (Autumn, 1971), pp. 227-228; Philip French, 900
wds., cp. pub.
Take One: v. 2, n. 12 (1971), p. 29; Glen Hunter, 200 wds., cp. pub.

8260 NEGRO IN FILMS, THE (Peter Noble)
F Comment: v. 7, n. 4 (Winter, 1971-1972), pp. 79-80; Lewis Jacobs, 350
wds., cp. pub.
Hollywood Q: v. IV, n. 1 (Fall, 1949), pp. 99-100; Franklin Fearing, 300
wds., pt. pub.
Sequence: n. 7 (Spring, 1949), p. 45; Adam Helmer, 175 wds., pt. pub.

8261 NEW AMERICAN CINEMA: A CRITICAL ANTHOLOGY, THE (Gregory
Battcock, ed.)
Cinema J: v. VII (Winter, 1967-1968), pp. 37-48; Kirk Bond, 650 wds., cp.
pub.
F Quarterly: v. XXI, n. 4 (Summer, 1968), p. 56; 50 wds., cp. pub.
F Soc Rev: Jan. (1968), pp. 17-20; Emory Menefee, 1300 wds., cp. pub.
Interntl F G: v. 6 (1969), p. 277; 50 wds., pt. pub.

8262 NEW CINEMA IN BRITAIN (Roger Manvell)
Cineaste: v. III, n. 1 (Summer, 1969), pp. 23-24; Gary Crowdus, 500 wds.,
cp. pub.
Cinema: v. 5, n. 2 pp. 42-43; 200 wds., cp. pub.
Interntl F G: v. 7 (1970), pp. 399, 401; 50 wds., pt. pub.

8263 NEW CINEMA IN EUROPE (Roger Manvell)
        Interntl F G: v. 4 (1967), pp. 273, 275; 100 wds., pt. pub.

8264 NEW CINEMA IN THE USA (Roger Manvell)
        Cineaste: v. II, n. 1 (Summer, 1968), p. 27; Gary Crowdus, 100 wds., pt.
            pub.
        Films & F: v. 14, n. 9 (June, 1968), p. 42; 150 wds., pt. pub.
        Interntl F G: v. 6 (1969), p. 277; 50 wds., pt. pub.

8265 NEW DOCUMENTARY IN ACTION: A CASE-BOOK IN FILM MAKING,
            THE (Alan Rosenthal)
        Cinema J: v. XI, n. 2 (Spring, 1972), pp. 40-42; Peter Harcourt, 900 wds.,
            cp. pub.

8266 NEW PICTORIAL HISTORY OF THE TALKIES, A (Daniel Blum and John
            Kobal)
        F Comment: v. 6, n. 1 (Spring, 1970), p. 68; 75 wds., cp. pub.
        Journal of P C: v. IV, n. 3 (Winter, 1971), pp. 822-824; Ralph Haven Wolfe,
            700 wds., cp. pub.

8267 NEW SCREEN TECHNIQUES (Martin Quigley, Jr., ed.)
        Films in R: v. V, n. 1 (Jan., 1954), p. 40; Christopher North, 325 wds., cp.
            pub.
        Quarterly of FR TV: v. VIII, n. 3 (Spring, 1954), pp. 316-317; Franklin
            Fearing, 125 wds., cp. pub.

8268 NEW SPIRIT IN THE CINEMA, THE (Huntley Carter)
        F Comment: v. 7, n. 4 (Winter, 1971-1972), p. 79; Lewis Jacobs, 250 wds.,
            cp. pub.

8269 NEW WAVE, THE (Peter Graham)
        Cinema J: v. X, n. 2 (Spring, 1971), pp. 56-58; Judith Gollub, 1150 wds.,
            cp. pub.
        F Soc Rev: v. 4, n. 7, pp. 42-44; James N. MacDonald, 800 wds., cp. pub.
        Films & F: v. 14, n. 12 (Sept., 1968), p. 50; Sheridan Morley, 150 wds., pt.
            pub.
        Interntl F G: v. 6 (1969), p. 277; 50 wds., pt. pub.

8270 NEW YORK TIMES FILM REVIEWS, 1913-1968, THE
        Cinema J: v. X, n. 2 (Spring, 1971), pp. 51-56; Howard Suber, 2200 wds.,
            cp. pub.
        F Comment: v. 6, n. 3 (Fall, 1970), pp. 74-75; Herman G. Weinberg, 1000
            wds., cp. pub.
        Films in R: v. XXII, n. 8 (Oct., 1971), pp. 457-467; Henry Hart, 3800 wds.,
            no pub.

8271 NEWSREELS ACROSS THE WORLD (Peter Baechlin and Maurice Muller-
            Strauss)
        Sight & S: v. 22, n. 3 (Jan.-Mar., 1953), p. 142; Duncan Crow, 500 wds., cp.
            pub.

8272 NEXT TIME DRIVE OFF THE CLIFF (Gene Fernett)
        Views & Rev: v. I, n. 2 (Fall, 1969), pp. 70-71; 800 wds., cp. pub.

8273 NICE WORK (Adrian Brunel)
        Sight & S: v. 18, n. 72 (Jan., 1950), p. 38; Penelope Houston, 350 wds., cp.
            pub.

8274 *NICHOLAS RAY (Francois Truchaud)
        Interntl F G: v. 4 (1967), p. 278; 100 wds., pt. pub.

8275 *NOMOTHESIA KINEMATOGRAPHOU (Dem. Ath. Stergianopoulos)
        Cinema Studies: v. I, n. 9 (June, 1964), pp. 243-244; N.M.H., 725 wds., cp.
            pub.

8276 NORMA JEAN: IN SEARCH OF MARILYN MONROE (Fred Lawrence
            Guiles)
        Films & F: v. 15, n. 12 (Sept., 1969), pp. 78-79; Sheridan Morley, 550
            wds., pt. pub.

Films & F: v. 17, n. 7 (Apr., 1971), pp. 14, 16; Sheridan Morley, 600 wds., pt. pub.

Films in R: v. XX, n. 7 (Aug.-Sept., 1969), p. 429; Eleanor H. Nash, 200 wds., cp. pub.

8277 NOT SO LONG AGO (Lloyd Morris)
Films in R: v. I, n. 1 (Feb., 1950), pp. 40-42; Quincy Howe, 450 wds., cp. pub.

8279 NOTES ON A FILM DIRECTOR (Sergei Eisenstein, trans. by X. Danko, ed. by R. Yurenev)
Films & F: v. 17, n. 6 (Mar., 1971), p. 64; Sheridan Morley, 50 wds., pt. pub.
Sight & S: v. 28, n. 3-4 (Summer-Autumn, 1959), p. 188; Jay Leyda, 400 wds., cp. pub.

8280 NOTES OF A SOVIET ACTOR (Nicoloi Cherkassov)
Sight & S: v. 27, n. 2 (Autumn, 1957), p. 103; David Robinson, 350 wds., cp. pub.

8281 NOTES ON A COWARDLY LION (John Lahr)
Films & F: v. 16, n. 5 (Feb., 1970), p. 70; Sheridan Morldy, 150 wds., pt. pub.

8282 *NOUVEAU CINEMA HONGROIS, LE (Michel Estève, ed.)
Interntl F G: v. 8 (1971), p. 443; 50 wds., pt. pub.

8283 *NOUVEAU CINEMA SCANDINAVE, LE (Jean Béranger)
Interntl F G: v. 7 (1970), p. 401; 50 wds., pt. pub.

8284 *NOUVEAUX CINEASTES POLONAIS (Philippe Haudiquet)
Cinema Studies: v. I, n. 8 (Dec., 1963), pp. 205-207; John Minchinton, 1300 wds., cp. pub.

8285 *NOUVEL ART, LE CINEMA SONORE, UN (Jean Keim)
Hollywood Q: v. III, n. 4 (Spring, 1948), pp. 454-456; Jacques Queval, 800 wds., cp. pub.

8286 NOUVELLE VAGUE: THE FIRST DECADE (Raymond Durgnat)
F Quarterly: v. XVI, n. 4 (Summer, 1963), pp. 61-62; Ernest Callenbach, 100 wds., cp. pub.

8287 NOVELS INTO FILM (George Bluestone)
F Culture: v. 3, n. 4 (Oct., 1957), p. 22; Peter Walsh, 225 wds., cp. pub.
F Quarterly: v. XII, n. 1 (Fall, 1958), pp. 54-55; Lester Asheim, 750 wds., cp. pub.
Films & F: v. 4, n. 4 (Jan., 1958), p. 33; Martin Gray, 150 wds., pt. pub.
Sight & S: v. 27, n. 3 (Winter, 1957-1958), p. 155; Richard Roud, 500 wds., cp. pub.

8288 *NUOVO CINEMA ITALIANO, IL (Giuseppe Ferrara)
F Culture: v. 3, n. 4 (Oct., 1957), p. 22; George N. Fenin, 125 wds., cp. pub.
Sight & S: v. 27, n. 4 (Spring, 1958), p. 210; Alain Tanner, 500 wds., cp. pub.

O

8289 ODYSSEY OF A FILM-MAKER: ROBERT FLAHERTY'S STORY, THE (Francis Hubbard Flaherty)
F Quarterly: v. XIII, n. 4 (Summer, 1960), p. 62; 125 wds., cp. pub.

8290 OKAY FOR SOUND (Frederic M. Thrasher, ed.)
Hollywood Q: v. II, n. 2 (Jan., 1947), pp. 218-219; Lewis Jacobs, 550 wds., cp. pub.

8291 OLIVIERS, THE (Felix Barker)
      Films in R: v. IV, n. 10 (Dec., 1953), pp. 546-547; Marilyn Adams, 800
            wds., cp. pub.
      Sight & S: v. 23, n. 2 (Oct.-Dec., 1953), p. 109; Jeffrey Bernard, 400 wds.,
            cp. pub.

8292 *OM FILMEN: ARTIKLER OG INTERVIEWS (Carl Th. Dryer, ed. by Erik
            Ulrichsen)
      Cinema Studies: v. I, n. 2 (Dec., 1960), pp. 41-43; Bent Grasten, 900 wds.,
            cp. pub.
      Sight & S: v. 34, n. 2 (Spring, 1965), p. 101; Frederic Fleisher, 650 wds.,
            cp. pub.

      ON MOVIES (see: Dwight Macdonald On Movies)

8294 120 DANCE FILMS (Peter Brinson)
      Films & F: v. 1, n. 1 (Oct., 1954), p. 28; John Minchinton, 150 wds., pt.
            pub.

8295 ONE REEL A WEEK (Fred J. Balshofer and Arthur C. Miller)
      Am Cinematog: v. 49, n. 4 (Apr., 1968), p. 293; George Mitchell, 300 wds.,
            cp. pub.
      Cinema J. v. VIII, n. 1 (Fall, 1968), pp. 47-48; Kirk Bond, 750 wds., cp.
            pub.
      F Lib Quarterly: v. 1, n. 4 (Fall, 1968), p. 47; 550 wds. pt. pub.
      F Quarterly: v. XXI, n. 3 (Spring, 1968), pp. 50-52; Hugh Kenner, 1100
            wds., cp. pub.
      F Soc Rev: Apr. (1968), pp. 38-39; Harriet R. Polt, 500 wds., cp. pub.
      Films & F: v. 14, n. 9 (June, 1968), p. 42; 150 wds., pt. pub.
      Films in R: v. XIX, n. 3 (Mar., 1968), pp. 169-170; Graham Primrose, 200
            wds., cp. pub.

8296 OPPORTUNITIES IN MOTION PICTURES (Pincus W. Tell)
      Hollywood Q: v. IV, n. 1 (Fall, 1949), p. 104; Franklin Fearing, 50 wds.,
            pt. pub.

8297 ORIENT: A SURVEY OF FILMS PRODUCED IN COUNTRIES OF ARAB
            AND ASIAN CULTURE (Winifred Holmes, comp.)
      Sight & S: v. 29, n. 2 (Spring, 1960), p. 102; Penelope Houston, 325 wds.,
            cp. pub.

8298 ORSON WELLES (Maurice Bessy, trans. by Ciba Vaughn)
      Cinema J: v. XI, n. 2 (Spring, 1972), pp. 42-44, Linda Provinzano, 700
            wds., cp. pub.

8299 ORSON WELLES (Joseph McBride)
      Focus on F: n. 10 (Summer, 1972), p. 64; Allen Eyles, 200 wds., cp. pub.

8300 *OSCENO E IL DIRITTO PENALE, L' (Manlio Mazzanti)
      Cinema Studies: v. I, n. 8 (Dec., 1963), pp. 208-209; N.H.M., 1100 wds.,
            cp. pub.

8301 OTHER HOLLYWOOD, THE (Edward Thorpe)
      Focus on F: n. 5 (Winter/Nov.-Dec., 1970), pp. 60-61; Allen Eyles, 100
            wds., cp. pub.

8302 OUR MODERN ART THE MOVIES (Ernest Callenbach)
      Quarterly of FR TV: v. X, n. 2 (Winter, 1955), p. 212; Franklin Fearing,
            200 wds., cp. pub.

8303 OUR MOVIE MADE CHILDREN (Henry James Forman)
      F Comment: v. 7, n. 2 (Summer, 1971), pp. 70-72; Garth Jowett, 2200
            wds., cp. pub.

8304 OUR WILL ROGERS (Homer Croy)
      Films in R: v. V, n. 5 (May, 1954), pp. 248-249; Robert Downing, 700
            wds., cp. pub.

8305 OUTLINE OF CZECHOSLOVAKIAN CINEMA (Landon Dewey)
 F Comment: v. 7, n. 4 (Winter, 1971-1972), p. 80; Norman Kogan, 300 wds., cp. pub.
 Films & F: v. 17, n. 9 (June, 1971), p. 92; Sheridan Morley, 75 wds., pt. pub.
 Focus on F: n. 6 (Spring, 1971), p. 60; Allen Eyles, 150 wds., cp. pub.

8306 PAINTING WITH LIGHT (John Alton)
 Hollywood Q: v. IV, n. 1 (Fall, 1949), p. 104; Franklin Fearing, 50 wds., cp. pub.
 Sequence: n. 11 (Summer, 1950), p. 48; Walter Lassally, 300 wds., pt. pub.

8307 *PANORAMA DU CINEMA (Georges Charensol)
 Hollywood Q: v. III, n. 4 (Spring, 1948), pp. 454-456; Jacques Queval, 800 wds., cp. pub.
 Sight & S: v. 16, n. 64 (Winter, 1947-1948), p. 179; Norah K. Lewis, 200 wds., cp. pub.

8308 *PANORAMA DU FILM NOIR AMERICAN (Raymond Borde and Etienne Chaumeton)
 Sight & S: v. 25, n. 4 (Spring, 1956), p. 162; Lindsay Anderson, 350 wds., cp. pub.

8309 *PAPPA SANDREW (Eric Wennerholm)
 Cinema Studies: v. II, n. 2 (June, 1966), pp. 42-43; N.M.H., 650 wds., cp. pub.

8310 PARADE'S GONE BY, THE (Kevin Brownlow)
 Am Cinematog: v. 50, n. 2 (Feb., 1969), pp. 242-243; Robert V. Kerns, 450 wds., cp. pub.
 Cinema: v. 4, n. 4 (Dec., 1968), p. 46; Robert Joseph, 300 wds., pt. pub.
 Cinema J: v. IX, n. 1 (Fall, 1969), pp. 50-52; Thomas R. Cripps, 1200 wds., cp. pub.
 F Comment: v. 7, n. 4 (Winter, 1971-1972), pp. 80-81; Howard Suber, 1200 wds., cp. pub.
 F Heritage: v. 4, n. 4 (Summer, 1969), pp. 35-36; Stephen Mamber, 500 wds., cp. pub.
 F Heritage: v. 5, n. 1 (Fall, 1969), pp. 35-36; Stephen Mamber, 450 wds., cp. pub.
 F Lib Quarterly: v. 2, n. 3 (Summer, 1969), p. 29; 200 wds., pt. pub.
 F Soc Rev: v. 4, n. 4, pp. 41-42; John Bragin, 700 wds., cp. pub.
 Films & F: v. 15, n. 10 (July, 1969), p. 71; Sheridan Morley, 550 wds., pt. pub.
 Films in R: v. XX, n. 3 (Mar., 1969), pp. 174-175; Robert Giroux, 750 wds., cp. pub.
 Films in R: v. XX, n. 4 (Apr., 1969), pp. 257-258; Kevin Brownlow, (a response), 800 wds., no pub.
 Interntl F G: v. 7 (1970), p. 401; 75 wds., pt. pub.
 Sight & S: v. 38, n. 3 (Summer, 1969), p. 160; Rodney Ackland, 900 wds., cp. pub.

8311 PARE LORENTZ AND THE DOCUMENTAFY FILM (Robert L. Snyder)
 F Lib Quarterly: v. 2, n. 3 (Summer, 1969), pp. 53-54; Harris N. Liechti, 850 wds., pt. pub.
 F Quarterly: v. XXII, n. 1 (Fall, 1968), p. 80; Ernest Callenbach, 350 wds., cp. pub.
 F Soc Rev: v. 4, n. 2, pp. 45-46; Frank Manchel, 900 wds., cp. pub.
 Films & F: v. 15, n. 7 (Apr., 1969), p. 56; Ken Gay, 600 wds., pt. pub.

8312 PASOLINI ON PASOLINI: INTERVIEWS WITH OSWALD STACK (Oswald
   Stack)
  Cineaste: v. IV, n. 3 (Winter, 1970-1971), pp. 43-44; Calvin Green, 1200
   wds., cp. pub.
  F Lib Quarterly: v. 3, n. 4 (Fall, 1970), p. 17; Thomas Atkins, 400 wds., cp.
   pub.
  Interntl F G: v. 8 (1971), p. 443; 50 wds., pt. pub.
  Screen: v. 11, n. 1 p. 99; Tom Gale, 150 wds., pt. pub.

8313 PASSPORT TO PARIS (Vernon Duke)
  Films in R: v. VI, n. 8 (Oct., 1955), pp. 422-423; R. B. Tozzi, 750 wds., cp.
   pub.

8314 PATTERNS OF REALISM (Roy Armes)
  Interntl F G: v. 9 (1972), p. 473; 50 wds., pt. pub.

8315 PAYNE FUND STUDIES OF MOTION PICTURES AND SOCIAL VALUES
   (Arno Press and N. Y. Times)
  F Comment: v. 7, n. 2 (Summer, 1971), pp. 70-72; Garth Jowett, 2200
   wds., pt. pub.

8316 PEARL WHITE, THE PEERLESS FEARLESS GIRL (Manuel Weltman and
   Raymond Lee)
  Films & F: v. 17, n. 2 (Nov., 1970), p. 64; Sheridan Morley, 100 wds., pt.
   pub.

8317 PEOPLE WHO MAKE MOVIES (Theodore Taylor)
  Films in R: v. XIX, n. 2 (Feb., 1968), p. 107; Diana Willing Cope, 175 wds.,
   cp. pub.

8318 PERSISTENCE OF VISION: A COLLECTION OF FILM CRITICISM (Joseph
   McBride, ed.)
  Cinema: v. 5, n. 2, p. 42; 500 wds., cp. pub.
  F Comment: v. 6, n. 3 (Fall, 1970), pp. 77-78; Richard Koszarski, 450 wds.,
   cp. pub.
  F Quarterly: v. XXII, n. 3 (Spring, 1969), p. 58; 50 wds., cp. pub.

8319 PERSONAL VISION OF INGMAR BERGMAN, THE (Jorn Donner, trans. by
   Holger Lundberg)
  F Comment: v. 2, n. 2 (1964), pp. 58-59; Birgitta Steene, 1500 wds., cp.
   pub.
  F Quarterly: v. XVII, n. 4 (Summer, 1964), p. 62; Ernest Callenbach, 200
   wds., cp. pub.
  Interntl F G: v. 2 (1965), p. 249; 250 wds., pt. pub.
  Sight & S: v. 33, n. 3 (Summer, 1964), p. 154; 350 wds., cp. pub.

8320 PETIT SOLDAT, LE (Jean-Luc Godard)
  Films & F: v. 14, n. 5 (Feb., 1968), p. 54; Sheridan Morley, 150 wds., pt.
   pub.

8321 PHOTOGRAPHIC THEORY FOR THE MOTION PICTURE CAMERAMAN
   (Russell Campbell, ed.)
  Interntl F G: v. 8 (1971), p. 447; 75 wds., pt. pub.

8322 PICTORIAL CONTINUITY: HOW TO SHOOT A MOVIE STORY (Arthur L.
   Gaskell and David A. Englander)
  Hollywood Q: v. III, n. 1 (Fall, 1947), p. 105; Richard Collins, 300 wds.,
   cp. pub.
  Sight & S: v. 17, n. 65 (Spring, 1948), pp. 52-53; Peter Plaskitt, 250 wds.,
   cp. pub.

8323 PICTORIAL HISTORY OF THE MOVIES, A (Deems Taylor, Bryant Hale,
   Marcelene Peterson)
  Films in R: v. I, n. 6 (Sept., 1950), pp. 35-37; Theodore Huff, 900 wds., cp.
   pub.

8324 PICTORIAL HISTORY OF THE SILENT SCREEN, A (Daniel Blum)
  Films & F: v. 9, n. 2 (Nov., 1962), p. 73; Martin Gray, 225 wds., pt. pub.
  Films in R: v. IV, n. 10 (Dec., 1953), pp. 547-549; Gerald D. McDonald,
   1800 wds., cp. pub.

8325 PICTORIAL HISTORY OF THE TALKIES, A (Daniel Blum)
         Films in R: v. X, n. 3 (Mar., 1959), pp. 176-177; Don Miller, 450 wds., cp.
             pub.

8326 PICTURE: A STORY ABOUT HOLLYWOOD (Lillian Ross)
         Films in R: v. IV, n. 7 (Aug.-Sept., 1953), p. 373; N. Hope Wilson, 170
             wds., cp. pub.
         Quarterly of FR TV: v. VII, n. 4 (Summer, 1953), pp. 431-432; Franklin
             Fearing, 250 wds., cp. pub.
         Quarterly of FR TV: v. XI, n. 4 (Summer, 1957), p. 427; Franklin
             Fearing, 75 wds., cp. pub.
         Sight & S: v. 22, n. 4 (Apr.-June, 1953), pp. 200-201; Penelope Houston,
             1500 wds., cp. pub.

8327 PICTURE HISTORY OF THE CINEMA, A (Ernest Lindgren)
         Cinema Studies: v. I, n. 4 (Dec., 1961), pp. 87-88; N.M.H., 1000 wds., cp.
             pub.
         Sight & S: v. 29, n. 4 (Autumn, 1960), p. 204; William Whitebait, 250 wds.,
             cp. pub.

8328 PICTURE MAKER OF THE OLD WEST: WILLIAM H. JACKSON (Clarence
             S. Jackson)
         Hollywood Q: v. III, n. 3 (Spring, 1948), p. 332; K.M., 160 wds., cp. pub.

8329 PICTURE PALACE, THE (Dennis Sharp)
         Films & F: v. 15, n. 12 (Sept., 1969), p. 79; Sheridan Morley, 150 wds., no
             pub.
         Interntl F G: v. 7 (1970), p. 401; 100 wds., pt. pub.
         Sight & S: v. 38, n. 3 (Summer, 1969), pp. 161-162; Nathan Silver, 1500
             wds., cp. pub.

8330 PIERROT LE FOU (Jean Luc-Godard, trans. by Peter Whitehead)
         Screen: v. 11, n. 2 (Mar.-Apr., 1970), pp. 86-88; David Spiers, 500 wds., pt.
             pub.

8331 *PIONNIERS DU CINEMA, 1897-1909, LES (Georges Sadoul)
         Sight & S: v. 17, n. 65 (Spring, 1948), pp. 51-52; Rachel Low, 750 wds., cp.
             pub.

8332 PLAN FOR FILM STUDIOS (H. Junge)
         Hollywood Q: v. I, n. 4 (July, 1946), pp. 450-451; W. L. Pereidra, 700 wds.,
             pt. pub.

8333 PLAYER: A PROFILE OF AN ART, THE (Lillian Ross and Helen Ross)
         F Quarterly: v. XVI, n. 2 (Winter, 1962-1963), pp. 56-58; Ernest
             Callenbach, 600 wds., cp. pub.
         Sight & S: v. 32, n. 2 (Spring, 1963), pp. 100-101; Penelope Houston, 400
             wds., cp. pub.

8334 POLITICS AND FILM (Leif Furhammar and Folke Isaksson)
         F Quarterly: v. XXV, n. 4 (Summer, 1972), pp. 29-31; David Degener, 1000
             wds., cp. pub.
         Focus on F: n. 8 (Oct., 1971), pp. 61, 63; 150 wds., cp. pub.

8335 *PORPORA E IL NERO, LA (Guido Aristarco, ed.)
         Cinema Studies: v. I, n. 6 (Dec., 1962), pp. 151-153; N.M.H., 1000 wds.,
             cp. pub.

8336 PORTRAIT OF A DIRECTOR: SATYAJIT RAY (Marie Seton)
         F Quarterly: v. XXV, n. 4 (Summer, 1972), p. 37; 75 wds., cp. pub.
         Films & F: v. 17, n. 10 (July, 1971), p. 64; Sheridan Morley, 100 wds., pt.
             pub.
         Focus on F: n. 7 (Summer, 1971), p. 58; P.D.C., 250 wds., cp. pub.
         Interntl F G: v. 9 (1972), p. 473; 50 wds., pt. pub.

8337 PORTRAIT OF A FLYING YORKSHIREMAN (Paul Rotha, ed.)
         Films in R: v. IV, n. 7 (Aug.-Sept., 1953), p. 373; Elspeth Chapin, 500
             wds., cp. pub.

8338 PORTRAIT OF JOAN: A BIOGRAPHY, A (Joan Crawford, with Jane Kesner
      Ardmore)
      Films in R: v. XIII, n. 8 (Oct., 1962); E. H. N., 200 wds., cp. pub.
      Interntl F G: v. 8 (1971), p. 447; 75 wds., pt. pub.

8339 *PRAXIS DU CINEMA (Noel Burch)
      Interntl F G: v. 8 (1971), p. 447; 50 wds., pt. pub.

8340 PREFACE TO FILM (Raymond Williams and Michael Orrom)
      Quarterly of FR TV: v. X, n. 1 (Fall, 1955), pp. 103-105; Franklin Fearing,
      300 wds., cp. pub.
      Sight & S: v. 24, n. 3 (Jan.-Mar., 1955), p. 160; Liam O'Laoghaire, 600
      wds., cp. pub.

8341 *PREMIER PLAN (Bernard Chardère, gen. ed.) (Includes monographs on: Luis
      Buñel, Jacques Prévert, Michelangelo Antonioni, Orson Welles,
      Luchino Visconti, Alain Resnais)
      Cinema Studies: v. I, n. 4 (Dec., 1961), pp. 83-85; Tom Milne, 1600 wds.,
      cp. pub.

8342 PRESENTING SCOTLAND: A FILM SURVEY (Norman Wilson)
      Hollywood Q: v. I, n. 4 (July, 1946), pp. 444-446; Joseph Krumgold, 1200
      wds., cp. pub.

8343 PRESERVATION OF MOTION PICTURE FILM, THE (The International
      Center of the Audio-Visual Arts and Sciences)
      F Comment: v. 2, n. 4 (Fall, 1965), p. 61; Joanne Godbout, 600 wds., cp.
      pub.

8344 *PREVERT, LES (Gérard Guillot)
      Films & F: v. 13, n. 8 (May, 1967), p. 44; Sheridan Morley, 25 wds., pt.
      pub.
      Interntl F G: v. 5 (1968), p. 263; 25 wds., pt. pub.

8345 PRIMER OF PLAYWRITING, A (Kenneth Macgowan)
      Films in R: v. II, n. 10 (Dec., 1951), p. 59; Henry Hart, 300 wds., cp. pub.

8346 PRINCESS OF MONACO: THE STORY OF GRACE KELLY (Grant Gaither)
      Films in R: v. VIII, n. 9 (Nov., 1957), p. 467; Diana Willing, 175 wds., cp.
      pub.

8347 PRINCIPLES OF CINEMATOGRAPHY (Lester J. Wheeler)
      Am Cinematog: v. 40, n. 6 (June, 1959), pp. 380, 382; 125 wds., pt. pub.
      Am Cinematog: v. 44, n. 9 (Sept., 1963), p. 516; 150 wds., pt. pub.

8348 PRIVATE EYE, THE COWBOY, AND THE VERY NAKED GIRL, THE
      (Judith Crist)
      Cinema: v. 4, n. 4 (Dec., 1968), p. 46; Robert Joseph 600 wds., pt. pub.
      Cinema J: v. VIII, n. 2 (Spring, 1969), pp. 35-38; Richard Dyer MacCann,
      1600 wds., cp. pub.
      F Comment: v. 5, n. 2 (Spring, 1969), pp. 90-91; Robert Steele, 850 wds.,
      pt. pub.
      F Soc Rev: v. 5, n. 4 (Dec., 1969), pp. 44-45; Michael Sragow, 450 wds., cp.
      pub.

8349 PRIVATE SCREENINGS: VIEWS OF THE CINEMA OF THE SIXTIES (John
      Simon)
      Cinema J: v. VIII, n. 2 (Spring, 1969), pp. 35-38; Richard Dyer MacCann,
      1600 wds., cp. pub.
      F Quarterly: v. XXI, n. 2 (Winter, 1967-1968), pp. 57-59; Ernest
      Callenbach, 800 wds., cp. pub.

8350 PRODUCER, THE (Richard Brooks)
      Films in R: v. III, n. 1 (Jan., 1952), p. 43; Alice H. Witham, 500 wds., cp.
      pub.

8351 PROFESSIONAL CINEMATOGRAPHY (Charles G. Clark)
      Am Cinematog: v. 45, n. 3 (Mar., 1964), p. 136; 150 wds., pt. pub.
      Films in R: v. XV, n. 3 (Mar., 1964), pp. 164-165; George J. Mitchell, 350
      wds., cp. pub.

8352 PROJECTIONISTS' FAULT FINDING CHART (Cecil A. Hill)
   Sight & S: v. 18, n. 70 (Summer, 1949), p. 98; C. R. Gibbs, 650 wds., cp. pub.

8353 PROPER JOB, A (Brian Aherne)
   Films in R: v. XXI, n. 5 (May, 1970), pp. 287-290; Henry Hart, 900 wds., cp. pub.

8354 *PROTECTION DE LA JEUNESSE PAR LA CENSURE CINEMATOGRAPHIQUE EN FRANCE ET A L'ETRANGER, LA (Constantine Matthéos)
   Cinema Studies: v. II, n. 3 (Mar., 1967), pp. 59-60; N.M.H., 850 wds., cp. pub.

8355 PUBLIC ARTS, THE (Gilbert Seldes)
   Films in R: v. VII, n. 10 (Dec., 1956), p. 536; Robert Downing, 325 wds., cp. pub.
   Quarterly of FR TV: v. XI, n. 2 (Winter, 1956), pp. 210-213; Franklin Fearing, 800 wds., cp. pub.

8356 PUBLIC IS NEVER WRONG, THE (Adolph Zukor, with Dale Kramer)
   Films & F: v. 1, n. 1 (Oct., 1954), p. 28; John Minchinton, 200 wds., pt. pub.
   Films in R: v. IV, n. 9 (Nov., 1953), pp. 488-489; Robert Downing, 600 wds., cp. pub.
   Quarterly of FR TV: v. IX, n. 1 (Fall, 1954), p. 107; Franklin Fearing, 150 wds., cp. pub.
   Sight & S: v. 24, n. 2 (Oct.-Dec., 1954), pp. 105-106; James Morgan, 400 wds., cp. pub.

8357 PUBLISHED SCREENPLAYS: A CHECKLIST (Clifford McCarty)
   F Quarterly: v. XXV, n. 4 (Summer, 1972), p. 40; Steven P. Hill, 250 wds., cp. pub.
   Films in R: v. XXII, n. 7 (Aug.-Sept., 1971), pp. 434-435; Christopher North, 75 wds., cp. pub.

8358 PUT MONEY IN THE PURSE: THE DIARY OF THE FILM OF "OTHELLO" (Micheál MacLiammóir)
   Films in R: v. IV, n. 5 (May, 1953), pp. 248-249; Eleanor H. Nash, 500 wds., cp. pub.
   Sight & S: v. 22, n. 2 (Oct.-Dec., 1952), p. 93; James Morgan, 450 wds., cp. pub.

Q

8359 QUE VIVA MEXICO! (S. M. Eisenstein)
   Films in R: v. IV, n. 4 (Apr., 1953), p. 202; Alice M. Witham, 275 wds., cp. pub.

   *QU'EST-CE QUE LE CINEMA? (see: What is Cinema?)

8361 QUITE REMARKABLE FATHER: THE BIOGRAPH OF LESLIE HOWARD, A (Leslie Ruth Howard)
   Films in R: v. XI, n. 1 (Jan., 1960), pp. 49-50; Homer Dickens, 200 wds., cp. pub.

R

8362 RADIO DRAMA ACTING AND PRODUCTION: A HANDBOOK (Walter Kingson and Rome Cowgill)
   Hollywood Q: v. V (1950-'51), p. 205; Franklin Fearing, 200 wds., cp. pub.

8363 RAILWAYS IN THE CINEMA (John Huntley)
       Films & F: v. 16, n. 3 (Dec., 1969), p. 72; 350 wds., pt. pub.

8364 *RAIMU, OU LA VIE DE CESAR: SOUVENIRS SUR L'ILLUSTRE
       COMEDIEN (Paul Olivier)
       Sight & S: v. 17, n. 67 (Autumn, 1948), p. 152; 200 wds., cp. pub.

8365 READINGS IN NONBOOK LIBRARIANSHIP (Jean Kujoth)
       F Lib Quarterly: v. 2, n. 3 (Summer, 1969), p. 29; 150 wds., pt. pub.

8366 REAL TINSEL, THE (Bernard Rosenberg)
       Films & F: v. 17, n. 10 (July, 1971), p. 64; Sheridan Morley, 125 wds., pt.
       pub.
       Sight & S: v. 40, n. 4 (Autumn, 1971), p. 228; John Gillett, 600 wds., cp.
       pub.

8367 *REFLEXION FAITE (René Clair)
       Films in R: v. III, n. 6 (June-July, 1952), pp. 295-296; Monica Stirling, 800
       wds., cp. pub.

8368 REFLECTIONS ON THE CINEMA (René Clair)
       Sight & S: v. 23, n. 4 (Apr.-June, 1954), pp. 218-219; Alexander Macken-
       drick, 950 wds., cp. pub.

8369 *REGARDS SUR LE CINEMA INDIEN (Philippe Parrain)
       Interntl F G: v. 8 (1971), p. 447; 50 wds., pt. pub.

8370 RELIGION IN THE CINEMA (Ivan Butler)
       Interntl F G: v. 7 (1970), p. 401; 50 wds., pt. pub.

8371 RENE CLAIR ET LES BELLES-DE-NUIT (Georges Charensol)
       Sight & S: v. 23, n. 1 (July-Sept., 1953), pp. 50-51; Gavin Lambert, 700
       wds., cp. pub.

8372 *RENE CLEMENT (André Farwagi)
       Films & F: v. 13, n. 12 (Sept., 1967), p. 46; Sheridan Morley, 50 wds., pt.
       pub.

8373 RENOIR, MY FATHER (Jean Renoir)
       F Quarterly: v. XVI, n. 2 (Winter, 1962-1963), p. 59; Ernest Callenbach, 75
       wds., cp. pub.

8374 REPORTING (Lillian Ross)
       Films & F: v. 15, n. 11 (Aug., 1969), p. 61; Sheridan Morley, 175 wds., pt.
       pub.

8375 REST OF THE STORY, THE (Sheilah Graham)
       Films in R: v. XV, n. 8 (Oct., 1964), pp. 495-496; Harold Longwell, 350
       wds., cp. pub.

8376 *REVISIONE DEI FILM E DEI LAVORI TEATRALI
       Cinema Studies: v. I, n. 6 (Dec., 1962), pp. 151-153; N.M.H., 1000 wds.,
       cp. pub.

8377 RISE OF THE AMERICAN FILM: A CRITICAL HISTORY, THE (Lewis
       Jacobs)
       Cinema J: v. IX, n. 1 (Fall, 1969), pp. 55-56; Richard Dyer MacCann, 400
       wds., cp. pub.
       Films: v. I, n. 1 (Nov., 1939), pp. 104-106; Jay Leyda, 1700 wds., cp. pub.
       Interntl F G: v. 9 (1972), p. 464; 50 wds., pt. pub.

8378 ROAD TO MILTOWN, OR UNDER THE SPREADING ATROPHY, THE (S.
       J. Pearlman)
       Films in R: v. VIII, n. 7 (Aug.-Sept., 1957), p. 359; Richard Kraft, 250
       wds., cp. pub.

8379 ROBERT BENCHLEY (Nathaniel Benchley)
       Films in R: v. VII, n. 1 (Jan., 1956), pp. 40-41; Robert Downing, 200 wds.,
       cp. pub.

8380 *ROBERT BRESSON (René Briot)
        Sight & S: v. 27, n. 3 (Winter, 1957-1958), p. 156; Derick Grigs, 525 wds.,
        cp. pub.

8381 ROBERT DONAT (J. C. Trewin)
        Films & F: v. 15, n. 3 (Dec., 1968), pp. 64-65; Sheridan Morley, 650 wds.,
        pt. pub.

8382 *ROBERT FLAHERTY (Wolfgang Klaue and Jay Leyda, comp.)
        F Comment: v. 3, n. 3 (Summer, 1965), p. 78; Walter Talmon-Gros, 300
        wds., cp. pub.

8383 ROBERT MORLEY, RESPONSIBLE GENTLEMEN (Robert Morley)
        Films & F: v. 13, n. 4 (Jan., 1967), p. 57; Robin Bean, 450 wds., pt. pub.

8384 *ROBERTO ROSSELLINI (José Luis Guarner)
        Interntl F G: v. 9 (1972), p. 473; 50 wds., pt. pub.

8385 ROGER CORMAN: THE MILLENIC VISION (David Will and Paul Willemen)
        Interntl F G: v. 8 (1971), p. 447; 50 wds., pt. pub.

8386 *ROMANCE AMERICAINE (Henri Agel)
        Interntl F G: v. 2 (1965), p. 256; 100 wds., pt. pub.

8387 ROSE TATTOO, THE (Tennessee Williams)
        Films & F: v. 1, n. 8 (May, 1955), p. 30; Eve Robin, 100 wds., pt. pub.

8388 ROTHA ON THE FILM (Paul Rotha)
        Films & F: v. 4, n. 7 (Apr., 1958), p. 33; Peter Cotes, 600 wds., pt. pub.
        Sight & S: v. 27, n. 4 (Spring, 1958), pp. 209-210; John Maddison, 1000
        wds., cp. pub.

8389 ROYAL BALLET ON STAGE AND SCREEN, THE (Maurice Moiseiwitsch
        and Eric Warman, eds.)
        Films & F: v. 6, n. 9 (June, 1960), p. 34; Martin Gray, 75 wds. pt. pub.

8390 RUN-THROUGH: A MEMOIR (John Houseman)
        F Quarterly: v. XXV, n. 4 (Summer, 1972), p. 38; Charles Higham, 500
        wds., cp. pub.

8391 RUNNING AWAY FROM MYSELF: A DREAM PORTRAIT OF AMERICA
        DRAWN FROM THE FILMS OF THE '40's (Barbara Deming)
        Cineaste: v. IV, n. 4 (Spring, 1971), pp. 30-31; Joan Mellen, 750 wds., cp.
        pub.
        Cinema J: v. XI, n. 2 (Spring, 1972), pp. 34-37; John L. Fell, 1500 wds., cp.
        pub.
        F Heritage: v. 6, n. 1 (Fall, 1970), pp. 31-37; David Madden, 3000 wds., cp.
        pub.

8392 *RYSK FILM: EN KONSTART BLIR TILL (Bengt Idestam-Almquist)
        Cinema Studies: v. I, n. 9 (June, 1964), pp. 233-235; N.M.H., 1100 wds.,
        cp. pub.

S

8393 *S. M. EISENSTEIN (Jean Mitry)
        F Culture: v. 3, n. 2 (1957), p. 22; Herman G. Weinberg, 700 wds., cp. pub.

8394 SACHA GUITRY — THE LAST BOULEVARDIER (James Harding)
        F Comment: v. 5, n. 3 (Fall, 1969), p. 80; Herman G. Weinberg, 650 wds.,
        cp. pub.
        Films & F: v. 15, n. 2 (Nov., 1968), pp. 72-73; Sheridan Morley, 1200 wds.,
        pt. pub.

8395 SAINT CINEMA: SELECTED WRITINGS 1929-1970 (Herman G. Weinberg)
       F Comment: v. 7, n. 1 (Spring, 1971), p. 88; George Amberg, 200 wds., cp.
          pub.
       F Culture: n. 50-51 (Fall-Winter, 1970), pp. 81-82; Harry M. Geduld, 1300
          wds., cp. pub.
       F Heritage: v. 6, n. 4 (Summer, 1971), pp. 30-31; Herbert I. Cohen, 800
          wds., cp. pub.
       F Quarterly: v. XXIV, n. 3 (Spring, 1971), pp. 60-61; Charles Higham, 550
          wds., cp. pub.
       F Soc Rev: v. 6, n. 4 (Dec., 1970), pp. 48-50; Foster Hirsh, 700 wds., cp.
          pub.
       Films & F: v. 17, n. 3 (Dec., 1970), p. 63; Sheridan Morley, 100 wds., pt.
          pub.
       Focus on F: n. 6 (Spring, 1971), p. 61; Allen Eyles, 125 wds., cp. pub.
       Interntl F G: v. 9 (1972), p. 473; 50 wds., pt. pub.
       Sight & S: v. 40, n. 1 (Winter, 1970-1971), p. 54; Penelope Houston, 700
          wds., cp. pub.
       Take One: v. 2, n. 10 (1971), pp. 37-38; Glen Hunter, 150 wds., cp. pub.

8396 SALT OF THE EARTH (Herbert Biberman)
       F Comment: v. IV, n. 1 (Fall, 1966), pp. 89-90; Emile De Antonio, 500
          wds., cp. pub.
       F Quarterly: v. XIX, n. 2 (Winter, 1965-1966), p. 60; Ernest Callenbach,
          125 wds., cp. pub.

8397 *SAMTAL I HOLLYWOOD (Nils Petter Sundgren)
       Interntl F G: v. 9 (1972), p. 473; 50 wds., pt. pub.

8398 SAMUEL FULLER (David Will and Peter Wollen, ed.)
       F Quarterly: v. XXV, n. 4 (Summer, 1972), pp. 34-35; Bill Nichols, 800
          wds., cp. pub.
       Films & F: v 16, n. 2 (Nov., 1969), p. 70; Sheridan Morley, 250 wds., pt.
          pub.

8399 SAMUEL FULLER (Phil Hardy)
       Cineaste: v. IV, . 4 (Spring, 1971), pp. 32-33; Calvin Green, 1200 wds., cp.
          pub.
       F Quarterly: v. XXV, n. 4 (Summer, 1972), pp. 34-35; Bill Nichols, 800
          wds., cp. pub.
       Films & F: v. 17, n. 3 (Dec., 1970), p. 63; Sheridan Morley, 125 wds., pt.
          pub.
       Focus on F: n. 6 (Spring, 1971), p. 61; Allen Eyles, 75 wds., cp. pub.
       Screen: v. 11, n. 6 (Nov.-Dec., 1970), pp. 88-90; Edward Buscombe, 1100
          wds., cp. pub.

8400 SAMUEL FULLER (Nicholas Garnham)
       Focus on F: n. 8 (Oct., 1971), p. 63; 100 wds., cp. pub.

8401 SAMUEL GOLDWYN: THE PRODUCER AND HIS FILMS (Richard Griffith)
       F Culture: v. 2, n. 3 (1956), p. 32; A. Croce, 300 wds., cp. pub.
       Sight & S: v. 26, n. 1 (Summer, 1956), p. 53; John Wilcox, 350 wds., cp.
          pub.

8402 SARABAND FOR DEAD LOVERS: THE FILM AND ITS PRODUCTION
       Sequence: n. 7 (Spring, 1949), p. 45; John Caldwell, 175 wds., cp. pub.

8403 *SATYAJIT RAY (Uma Krupanidhi, ed.)
       Interntl F G: v. 5 (1968), p. 263; 25 wds., pt. pub.

8405 SAY . . . DIDN'T YOU USED TO BE GEORGE MURPHY? (George Murphy,
          with Victor Lasky)
       Films in R: v. XXI, n. 8 (Oct., 1970), p. 501; Eleanor H. Nash, 200 wds.,
          cp. pub.

8406 SCANDINAVIAN FILM (Forsyth Hardy)
       Films in R: v. IV, n. 4 (Apr., 1953), pp. 201-202; Charles L. Turner, 575
          wds., cp. pub.
       Sight & S: v. 23, n. 1 (July-Sept., 1953), p. 49; Ebbe Neergaard, 900 wds.,
          cp. pub.

8407 *SCEAL NA SCANNAN (Proinsias O'Conlvain, ed.)
        Sight & S: v. 24, n. 1 (July-Sept., 1954), p. 49; Liam O'Laoghaire, 250
        wds., cp. pub.

8408 *SCHATTEN EROBERN DIE WELT: WIE FILM UND KINO WURDEN
        (Freiedrich Porges)
        Sight & S: v. 17, n. 66 (Summer, 1948), p. 106; Norah Lewis, 200 wds., cp.
        pub.

8409 SCIENCE FICTION FILM (Denis Gifford)
        Focus on F: n. 6 (Spring, 1971), pp. 60-61; Allen Eyles, 100 wds., cp. pub.
        Interntl F G: v. 9 (1972), p. 473; 50 wds., pt. pub.

8410 SCIENCE FICTION IN THE CINEMA (John Baxter)
        F Soc Rev: v. 5, n. 5 (Jan., 1970), pp. 45-46; Michael Sragow, 350 wds., cp.
        pub.
        Films & F: v. 16, n. 9 (June, 1970), p. 124; Sheridan Morley, 200 wds., pt.
        pub.
        Interntl F G: v. 7 (1970), p. 401; 50 wds., pt. pub.

8411 SCRATCH AN ACTOR (Sheliah Graham)
        Films & F: v. 15, n. 9 (June, 1969), p. 68; Sheridan Morley, 650 wds., pt.
        pub.

8412 SCREEN AND AUDIENCE (John E. Cross and Arnold Rattenbury, eds.)
        Sight & S: v. 16, n. 64 (Winter, 1947-1948), p. 179; 200 wds., cp. pub.

8413 SCREEN ARTS: A GUIDE TO FILM AND TELEVISION APPRECIATION
        THE (Edward Fischer)
        Films in R: v. XI, n. 8 (Oct., 1960), p. 502; 50 wds., cp. pub.

8414 SCREEN LOVERS: KISSES AND CLINCHES, 1896-1956 (John Springer)
        Films in R: v. VII, n. 1 (Jan., 1956), p. 40; Alice H. Witham, 175 wds., cp.
        pub.

8415 SCREEN WORLD (Daniel Blum, ed.)
        Films in R: v. VI, n. 9 (Nov., 1955), p. 474; Elspeth Hart, 200 wds., cp.
        pub.
        Screen: v. 11, n. 4-5 (July-Oct., 1970), p. 133; Gillian Hartnoll, 100 wds.,
        pt. pub.

8416 SCREENPLAYS OF MICHELANGELO ANTONIONI (Michelangelo Antoni-
        oni)
        Sight & S: v. 34, n. 1 (Winter, 1964-1965), p. 49; Penelope Houston, 400
        wds., cp. pub.

8417 SEASTROM AND STILLER IN HOLLYWOOD (Hans Pensel)
        F Comment: v. 7, n. 1 (Spring, 1971), pp. 86, 88; Herman G. Weinberg, 200
        wds., cp. pub.
        Films & F: v. 16, n. 11 (Aug., 1970), p. 64; Sheridan Morley, 75 wds., pt.
        pub.
        Interntl F G: v. 8 (1971), p. 447; 50 wds., pt. pub.

8418 SEAT AT THE CINEMA, A (Roger Manvell)
        Sight & S: v. 21, n. 1 (Aug.-Sept., 1951), p. 45; 250 wds., cp. pub.

8419 SECOND WAVE (Ian Cameron, ed.)
        Films & F: v. 16, n. 12 (Sept., 1970), p. 94; Sheridan Morley, 100 wds., pt.
        pub.
        Focus on F: n. 6 (Spring, 1971), p. 61; Allen Eyles, 75 wds., cp. pub.
        Interntl F G: v. 8 (1971), p. 447; 50 wds., pt. pub.

8420 SEE NO EVIL: LIFE INSIDE A HOLLYWOOD CENSOR (Jack Vizzard)
        Films in R: v. XXII, n. 1 (Jan., 1971), pp. 29-30; Christopher North, 325
        wds., cp. pub.

8421 SEEN ANY GOOD MOVIES LATELY? (William K. Zinsser)
        Films in R: v. X, n. 3 (Mar., 1959), p. 179; Eleanor H. Nash, 150 wds., cp.
        pub.
        Sight & S: v. 29, n. 3 (Summer, 1960), p. 152; Derek Hill, 400 wds., cp.
        pub.

8422 SELF-ENCHANTED, MAE MURRAY: IMAGE OF AN ERA, THE (Jane
     Ardmore)
          Films in R: v. XI, n. 7 (Aug.-Sept., 1960), pp. 434-435; Gerald D.
          McDonald, 750 wds., cp. pub.

8423 SELF PORTRAIT (Man Ray)
          F Culture: n. 31 (Winter, 1963-1964), p. 68; Herman G. Weinberg, 100
          wds., cp. pub.

8424 SELZNICK (Bob Thomas)
          F Comment: v. 6, n. 3 (Fall, 1970), p. 79; Donald Staples, 350 wds., cp.
          pub.
          Films in R: v. XXII, n. 1 (Jan., 1971), p. 31; 125 wds., cp. pub.

8425 *SEPT ANS DE CINEMA FRANCAIS (Henri Agel, et al.)
          Sight & S: v. 23, n. 1 (July-Sept., 1953), pp. 50-51; Gavin Lambert, 700
          wds., cp. pub.

8426 SERGEI EISENSTEIN: AN INVESTIGATION INTO HIS FILMS AND
     PHILOSOPHY (Léon Moussinac, trans. by D. Sandy Petry)
          F Comment: v. 6, n. 2 (Summer, 1970), pp. 62-63; Herman G. Weinberg,
          500 wds., cp. pub.
          F Lib Quarterly: v. 3, n. 4 (Fall, 1970), p. 18; Robert Steele, 500 wds., cp.
          pub.
          F Soc Rev: v. 5, n. 9 (May, 1970), pp. 46-47; Harvey Deneroff, 1000 wds.,
          cp. pub.
          Films & F: v. 17, n. 1 Oct., 1970), p. 72; Sheridan Morley, 250 wds., pt.
          pub.
          Interntl F G: v. 9 (1972), p. 473; 50 wds., pt. pub.
          Screen: v. 12, n. 4 (Winter, 1971-1972), pp. 168-171; T. Ryall, 1200 wds.,
          cp. pub.

8427 SERGEI EISENSTEIN AND UPTON SINCLAIR: THE MAKING AND
     UNMAKING OF "QUE VIVA MEXICO! " (Harry M. Geduld and
     Ronald Gottesman)
          F Comment: v. 7, n. 1 (Spring, 1971), pp. 86, 88; Herman G. Weinberg, 200
          wds., cp. pub.
          F Soc Rev: v. 6, n. 5 (Jan., 1971), pp. 48-50; Thomas Benson, 1000 wds.,
          cp. pub.
          Sight & S: v. 40, n. 1 (Winter, 1970-1971), p. 53; Ivor Montagu, 1700 wds.,
          cp. pub.

8428 SERGEI M. EISENSTEIN (Marie Seton)
          Films in R: v. III, n. 9 (Nov., 1952), pp. 473-476; Seymour Stern, 1750
          wds., cp. pub.
          Films in R: v. III, n. 10 (Dec., 1952), pp. 534-539; Seymour Stern, 3000
          wds., cp. pub.
          Sight & S: v. 22, n. 3 (Jan.-Mar., 1953), pp. 140-141; Thorold Dickinson,
          2000 wds., cp. pub.

8429 SERIALS: SUSPENSE AND DRAMA BY INSTALLMENT, THE (Raymond
     William Stedman)
          F Comment: v. 7, n. 3 (Fall, 1971), p. 76; Miles Kreuger, 850 wds., cp. pub.

8430 SERPENT'S EYE: SHAW AND THE CINEMA, THE (Donald Costello)
          F Comment: v. IV, n. 2-3 (Fall-Winter, 1967), p. 115; Anthony Hodg-
          kinson, 450 wds., cp. pub.

8431 SEVENTY YEARS OF CINEMA (Peter Cowie)
          Cinema: v. 5, n. 2, p. 42; 300 wds., cp. pub.
          F Comment: v.5, n. 3 (Fall, 1969), p. 81; Herman G. Weinberg, 225 wds.,
          cp. pub.
          Films & F: v. 15, n. 12 (Sept., 1969), p. 79; Sheridan Morley, 150 wds., pt.
          pub.
          Films in R: v. XX, n. 7 (Aug.-Sept., 1969), pp. 429-430; Bebe Bergsten, 300
          wds., cp. pub.
          Interntl F G: v. 7 (1970), p. 401; 50 wds., pt. pub.

8432 SEX EDUCATION FILM (Laura J. Singer and Judith Buskin)
          Interntl F G: v. 9 (1972), p. 465; 50 wds., pt. pub.

SEX IN THE MOVIES (see: The Celluloid Sacrifice)

8433 SEX, PSYCHE, ETCETERA IN THE FILM (Parker Tyler)
Cinema: v. 6, n. 2 (Fall, 1970), pp. 42-44; Margaret Bach, 2600 wds., cp.
pub.
Sight & S: v. 40, n. 3 (Summer, 1971), p. 170; John Taylor Russell, 900
wds., cp. pub.

8434 SHADOW PUPPETS (Olive Blackham)
Cinema Studies: v. I, n. 3 (Aug., 1961), pp. 59-61; Eric Walter White 800
wds., cp. pub.

8435 SHAKESPEARE ON SILENT FILM (Robert Hamilton Ball)
Cinema J: v. IX, n. 2 (Spring, 1970), pp. 53-55; Richard Dyer MacCann,
1200 wds., cp. pub.
F Comment: v. 6, n. 1 (Spring, 1970), p. 74; 150 wds., cp. pub.
F Lib Quarterly: v. 2, n. 3 (Summer, 1969); p. 54; 200 wds., pt. pub.
F Soc Rev: v. 4, n. 6, pp. 43-44; Betty Bandel, 750 wds., cp. pub.
Sight & S: v. 37, n. 4 (Autumn, 1968), pp. 213-214; Philip Hope-Wallace,
500 wds., cp. pub.

8436 *SHAKESPEARE, TIME AND CONSCIENCE (Grigori Kozintsev)
Sight & S: v. 37, n. 3 (Summer, 1968), p. 159; Michael Kustow, 1200 wds.,
cp. pub.

8437 SHATTERING OF THE IMAGE, THE (Richard G. Hubler)
Films in R: v. X, n. 3 (Mar., 1959), pp. 179-180; Eleanor H. Nash, 175
wds., cp. pub.

8438 SHORT HISTORY OF THE MOVIES, A (Gerald Mast)
Cinema J: v. XI, n. 1 (Fall, 1971), pp. 67-68; Donald E. Staples, 900 wds.,
cp. pub.

8439 SHOTS IN THE DARK (Edgar Anstey, Roger Manvell, Ernest Lindgren, Paul
Rotha, eds.)
Quarterly of FR TV: v. VII, n. 1 (Fall, 1952), pp. 92-93; Franklin Fearing,
150 wds., cp. pub.
Sight & S: v. 21, n. 4 (Apr.-June, 1952), p. 182; Robert Hamer, 400 wds.,
cp. pub.

8440 SIGHT, SOUND AND SOCIETY (David Manning White and Richard Averson,
eds.)
Sight & S: v. 38, n. 1 (Winter, 1968-1969), p. 52; Colin McArthur, 500
wds., cp. pub.

8441 SIGNS AND MEANING IN THE CINEMA (Peter Wollen)
Cineaste: v. III, n. 2 (Fall, 1969), pp. 27-29; A. D. Malmfelt, 2200 wds., cp.
pub.
Cinema J: v. IX, n. 2 (Spring, 1970), pp. 51-53; Christian Koch, 1300 wds.,
cp. pub.
F Comment: v. 7, n. 2 (Summer, 1971), pp. 75-76; Brian Henderson, 1400
wds., cp. pub.
Films & F: v. 15, n. 6 (Mar., 1969), p. 73; Sheridan Morley, 150 wds., pt.
pub.
Interntl F G: v. 7 (1970), p. 401; 75 wds., pt. pub.

8442 SILENT CINEMA, THE (Liam O'Leary)
Sight & S: v. 34, n. 3 (Summer, 1965), p. 154; Tom Milne, 325 wds., cp.
pub.

8443 SILENT STAR (Colleen Moore)
Cinema J: v. VIII, n. 1 (Fall, 1968), pp. 47-48; Kirk Bond, 750 wds., cp.
pub.
F Comment: v. 5, n. 3 (Fall, 1969), p. 80; Herman G. Weinberg, 125 wds.,
cp. pub.
Films in R: v. XIX, n. 10 (Dec., 1968), pp. 641-643; Eleanor H. Nash, 450
wds., cp. pub.

8444 SILENT VOICE — A TEXT, THE GOLDEN AGE OF THE CINEMA, THE
(Arthur Lennig)
F Comment: v. 5, n. 4 (Winter, 1969), p. 78; 250 wds., cp. pub.

8445 SIMPLE ART OF MAKING FILMS, THE (Tony Rose)
      Sight & S: v. 27, n. 2 (Autumn, 1957), p. 103; Derek Hill, 300 wds., cp.
      pub.

8446 SINATRA: A BIOGRAPHY (Arnold Shaw)
      Films & F: v. 15, n. 2 (Nov., 1968), pp. 72-73; Sheridan Morley, 1200 wds.,
      pt. pub.

8447 *SJOSTROM (René Jeanne and Charles Ford)
      Interntl F G: v. 2 (1965), p. 256; 100 wds., pt. pub.

8448 SKY AND THE STARS, THE (Albert Préjean, trans. by Virginia Graham)
      Sight & S: v. 26, n. 3 (Winter, 1956-1957), p. 161; David Robinson, 700
      wds., cp. pub.

8449 SLIDE AREA: SCENES OF HOLLYWOOD LIFE, THE (Gavin Lambert)
      Sight & S: v. 28, n. 3-4 (Summer-Autumn, 1959), pp. 186-187; Dilys
      Powell, 600 wds., cp. pub.

8450 SOCIAL CONDUCT AND ATTITUDES OF MOVIE FANS, THE (Frank K.
      Shuttleworth and Mark A. May)
      F Comment: v. 7, n. 2 (Summer, 1971), pp. 70-72; Garth Jowett, 2200
      wds., cp. pub.

8451 SOCIOLOGY OF FILM ART, THE (George Huaco)
      F Comment: v. 3, n. 4 (Fall, 1965), pp. 80-81; David Stewart Hull, 100
      wds., cp. pub.
      F Comment: v. 3, n. 4 (Fall, 1965), pp. 81-82; Joseph Goldberg, 550 wds.,
      cp. pub.
      F Quarterly: v. XIX, n. 2 (Winter, 1965-1966), p. 59; Ernest Callenbach,
      600 wds., cp. pub.
      F Soc Rev: Nov. (1966), pp. 37-38; Anthony W. Hodgkinson, 400 wds., cp.
      pub.
      Sight & S: v. 34, n. 4 (Autumn, 1965), pp. 205-206; Penelope Houston, 625
      wds., cp. pub.

8452 SOULS IN TORMENT (Ronald Searle)
      Films & F: v. 1, n. 4 (Jan., 1955), p. 30; Jill Hardy, 75 wds., pt. pub.

8453 SOUND AND THE DOCUMENTARY FILM (Ken Cameron)
      Sight & S: v. 16, n. 64 (Winter, 1947-1948), p. 178; Ernest Lindgren, 250
      wds., cp. pub.

8454 SOUNDS FOR SILENTS (Charles Hofmann)
      F Lib Quarterly: v. 3, n. 2 (Spring, 1970), p. 39; 100 wds., cp. pub.
      Films & F: v. 16, n. 9 (June, 1970), p. 124; Sheridan Morley, 100 wds., pt.
      pub.
      Films in R: v. XXII, n. 1 (Jan., 1971), pp. 30-31; Page Cook, 350 wds., cp.
      pub.
      Interntl F G: v. 8 (1971), pp. 447, 449; 50 wds., pt. pub.

8455 SOVIET CINEMA (Thorold Dickinson and Catherine De La Roche)
      Sequence: n. 7 (Spring, 1949), pp. 44-45; Peter Ericsson, 450 wds., pt. pub.
      Sight & S: v. 17, n. 68 (Winter, 1948-1949), p. 198; Barbara Petrovskaia,
      500 wds., cp. pub.

8456 SOVIET FILM INDUSTRY, THE (Paul Babitsky and John Rimberg)
      Quarterly of FR TV: v. XI, n. 1 (Fall, 1956), pp. 104-105; Franklin
      Fearing, 275 wds., cp. pub.

8457 *SOZIALGESCHICTE DER STARS (Enno Patalas, ed.)
      Interntl F G: v. 3 (1966), p. 259; 200 wds., cp. pub.

8458 SPEAKING CANDIDLY: FILMS AND PEOPLE IN NEW ZEALAND (Gordon
      Mirams)
      Sight & S: v. 15, n. 60 (Winter, 1946-1947), p. 156; M. E. Cohen, 600 wds.,
      cp. pub.

8459 SPELLBOUND IN DARKNESS (George C. Pratt, ed.)
      F Quarterly: v. XXI, n. 1 (Fall, 1967), p. 64; Ernest Callenbach, 150 wds.,
      cp. pub.

8460 SPENCER TRACY: A BIOGRAPHY (Larry Swindell)
      Views & Rev: v. I, n. 3 (Winter, 1970), pp. 72-73; 600 wds., cp. pub.

8461 SPLINTERS FROM HOLLYWOOD TRIPODS (Virgil E. Miller)
      Am Cinematog: v. 46, n. 1 (Jan., 1965), p. 24; 150 wds., cp. pub.
      Films in R: v. XVI, n. 2 (Feb., 1965), pp. 108-109; George J. Mitchell, 450
          wds., cp. pub.

8462 SPLIT FOCUS (Peter Hopkinson)
      Sight & S: v. 39, n. 1 (Winter, 1969-1970), pp. 52-53; Kevin Brownlow, 600
          wds., cp. pub.

8463 SPOTLIGHT ON FILMS (Egon Larsen)
      Sequence: n. 13 (New Year, 1951), pp. 46-47; Alberta Marlow, 600 wds.,
          pt. pub.
      Sight & S: v. 19, n. 9 (Jan., 1951), p. 379; Alan Brien, 1000 wds., cp. pub.

8464 STAGE TO SCREEN (Nicolas A. Vardac)
      Films in R: v. I, n. 3 (Nov., 1950), pp. 33-34; George Freedley, 500 wds.,
          cp. pub.
      Hollywood Q: v. IV, n. 3 (Spring, 1950), p. 314; Franklin Fearing, 150
          wds., cp. pub.

8465 STANDARDS OF PHOTOPLAY APPRECIATION (William Lewin and Alex-
          ander Frazier)
      Films in R: v. VIII, n. 6 (June-July, 1957), p. 289; Prudence Underwood,
          100 wds., cp. pub.

8466 STAR MAKER: THE STORY OF D. W. GRIFFITH (Homer Croy)
      F Quarterly: v. XII, n. 4 (Summer, 1959), p. 60; Ernest Callenbach, 100
          wds., cp. pub.

8467 STARDOM: THE HOLLYWOOD PHENOMENON (Alexander Walker)
      Cinema J: v. XI, n. 1 (Fall, 1971), pp. 68-71; Kent R. Brown, 1300 wds.,
          cp. pub.
      Films & F: v. 16, n. 11 (Aug., 1970), p. 64; Sheridan Morley, 450 wds., pt.
          pub.
      Interntl F G: v. 8 (1971), p. 449; 75 wds., pt. pub.

8468 STARS, THE (Richard Schickel)
      F Quarterly: v. XVI, n. 2 (Winter, 1962-1963), pp. 56-58; Ernest
          Callenbach, 600 wds., cp. pub.

8469 STARS: AN ACCOUNT OF THE STAR-SYSTEM IN MOTION PICTURES,
          THE (Edgar Morin)
      F Quarterly: v. XIII, n. 4 (Summer, 1960), pp. 61-62; Ernest Callenbach,
          500 wds., cp. pub.

8470 STEPS IN TIME (Fred Astaire)
      Films in F: v. 6, n. 9 (June, 1960), p. 34; Martin Gray, 100 wds., pt. pub.
      Films in R: v. X, n. 7 (Aug.-Sept., 1959), pp. 426-427; Don Miller, 300
          wds., cp. pub.
      Sight & S: v. 29, n. 3 (Summer, 1960), p. 152; Isabel Quigly 500 wds., cp.
          pub.

8471 *STORIA DEL CINEMA (Benedetti, Radius, Giovetti, Ricas)
      Films in R: v. IV, n. 2 (Feb., 1953), pp. 103-104; Herman G. Weinberg, 125
          wds., cp. pub.

8472 *STORIA DELLE TEORICHE DEL FILM (Guido Aristarco Turini)
      Films in R: v. III, n. 1 (Jan., 1952), p. 44; Robert F. Hawkins, 250 wds., cp.
          pub.

8473 STORIES THEY WOULDN'T LET ME DO ON TV (Alfred Hitchcock, ed.)
      Films in R: v. VIII, n. 8 (Oct., 1957), p. 420; Alice H. Witham, 100 wds.,
          cp. pub.

8474 STORY OF CUDDLES, THE (S. Z. Sakall)
      Films & F: v. 1, n. 3 (Dec., 1954), p. 29; Ivan Pattison, 200 wds., pt. pub.

8475 STORY OF "THE MISFITS", THE (James Goode)
     F Comment: v. 1, n. 6 (Fall, 1963), p. 54; 100 wds., cp. pub.
     F Culture: n. 34 (Fall, 1964), pp. 65-66; Andrew Sarris, 1200 wds., cp. pub.
     Films in R: v. XV, n. 1 (Jan., 1964), p. 39; Alice H. Witham, 125 wds., cp.
          pub.

8476 STORY OF WALT DISNEY, THE (Diane Disney Miller)
     Films in R: v. IX, n. 9 (Nov., 1958), pp. 527-529; Elspeth Hart, 800 wds.,
          cp. pub.

8477 STRAUB (Richard Roud)
     Focus on F: n. 10 (Summer, 1972), p. 64; Allen Eyles, 200 wds., cp. pub.

8478 STROHEIM (Joel Finler)
     Cineaste: v. II, n. 3 (Winter, 1968-1969), pp. 18-19; Gary Crowdus, 550
          wds., pt. pub.
     F Quarterly: v. XXI, n. 4 (Summer, 1968), p. 55; 75 wds., no pub.
     Interntl F G: v. 5 (1968), p. 265; 25 wds., pt. pub.
     Take One: v. 2, n. 1 (1969), pp. 28-29; Joe Claener, 100 wds., cp. pub.

8479 STUDIES IN THE ARAB THEATRE AND CINEMA (Jacob M. Landau)
     F Quarterly: v. XII, n. 4 (Summer, 1959), p. 60; Ernest Callenbach, 100
          wds., cp. pub.

8480 STUDIO, THE (John Gregory Dunne)
     Cineaste: v. III, n. 1 (Summer, 1969), p. 23; Gary Crowdus, 600 wds., cp.
          pub.
     F Comment: v. 6, n. 1 (Spring, 1970), pp. 75-76; 125 wds., cp. pub.
     F Soc Rev: v. 5, n. 1 (Sept., 1969), pp. 45-47; Gary Crowdus, 600 wds., cp.
          pub.
     Films & F: v. 16, n. 7 (Apr., 1970), p. 72; Sheridan Morley, 650 wds., pt.
          pub.
     Films in R: v. XX, n. 7 (Aug.-Sept., 1969), p. 428; Henry Hart, 225 wds.,
          cp. pub.
     Interntl F G: v. 8 (1971), p. 449; 50 wds., pt. pub.
     Sight & S: v. 39, n. 3 (Summer, 1970), pp. 165-166; Gavin Millar, 500 wds.,
          cp. pub.

8481 *STUMME SCENE: DANSK BIOGRAFTEATER INDTIL LYDFILMENS
          GENNEMBRUD, DEN (Gunnar Sandfeld)
     Cinema Studies: v. II, n. 5 (Sept., 1967), pp. 89-90; N.M.H., 500 wds.,

8482 STYLES OF RADICAL WILL (Susan Sontag)
     Cineaste: v. III, n. 1 (Summer, 1969), p. 22; Gary Crowdus, 1100 wds., cp.
          pub.
     Screen: v. 11, n. 3 (Summer, 1970), pp. 115-117; Edward Buscombe, 1100
          wds., pt. pub.

8483 *SUCKSDORFF (Mauritz Edstrom)
     Interntl F G: v. 7 (1970), p. 401; 50 wds., pt. pub.

8484 *SUMA DE LEGISLACION DEL ESPECTACULO (Fernando Vizcaino Casas)
     Cinema Studies: v. I, n. 9 (June, 1964), pp. 243-244; N.M.H., 725 wds., cp.
          pub.

8485 SUNSHINE AND SHADOW (Mary Pickford)
     F Culture: v. 1, n. 4 (Summer, 1955), p. 29; Richard Kraft, 475 wds., cp.
          pub.
     Films in R: v. VI, n. 6 (June-July, 1955), pp. 295-297; Gerald D.
          McDonald, 1200 wds., cp. pub.
     Quarterly of FR TV: v. X, n. 2 (Winter, 1955), pp. 208-209; Franklin
          Fearing, 50 wds., cp. pub.
     Sight & S: v. 26, n. 2 (Winter, 1956-1957), p. 161; David Robinson, 700
          wds., cp. pub.

8486 SUPPLEMENT TO THE 16MM INDEX (Guy Coté)
     Films in R: v. X, n. 3 (Mar., 1959), p. 180; Bradner Lacy, 75 wds., cp. pub.

8487 *SURREALISME AU CINEMA, LE (Ado Kyrou)
     Sight & S: v. 23, n. 2 (Oct.-Dec., 1953), p. 109; Roy Edwards, 700 wds., cp.
          pub.

8488 *SURREALISME ET CINEMA (Yves Kovacs, ed.)
Sight & S: v. 35, n. 2 (Spring, 1966), pp. 101-102; Geoffrey Nowell-Smith,
500 wds., cp. pub.

8489 SUSPENSE IN THE CINEMA (Gordon Gow)
F Comment: v. 6, n. 1 (Spring, 1970), p. 73; 75 wds., cp. pub.
F Soc Rev: v. IV, n. 9 (May, 1969), pp. 41-43; Frank Manchel, 1000 wds.,
cp. pub.
Films & F: v. 14, n. 9 (June, 1968), p. 42; 150 wds., cp. pub.
Interntl F G: v. 6 (1969), p. 278; 25 wds., pt. pub.

8490 *SVENSK FILM PA VAG (Kenne Fant)
Interntl F G: v. 6 (1969), p. 278; 50 wds., pt. pub.

8491 *SVENSKA SJUDFILMER 1929-1966 OCH DERAS REGISSORER (Sven G.
Winquist)
Interntl F G: v. 1 (1969), p. 278; 50 wds., pt. pub.

8492 SWEDEN I AND II (Peter Cowie)
Interntl F G: v. 7 (1970), pp. 401, 403; 75 wds., pt. pub.
Screen: v. 11, n. 2 (Mar.-Apr., 1970), p. 98; Gillian Hartnoll, 50 wds., pt.
pub.
Sight & S: v. 40, n. 2 (Spring, 1971), pp. 111-112; Neville Hunnings, 700
wds., cp. pub.

8493 SWEDISH CINEMA (Peter Cowie)
Films & F: v. 13, n. 3 (Dec., 1966), p. 42; Sheridan Morley, 100 wds., no
pub.
Interntl F G: v. 5 (1968), p. 265; 25 wds., pt. pub.

8494 SYMBOL, THE (Alvah Bessie)
F Comment: v. IV, n. 2-3 (Fall-Winter, 1967), pp. 111-112; Donald Skoller,
600 wds., cp. pub.

T

8495 TV MOVIES (Leonard Maltin, ed.)
Focus on F: n. 5 (Winter/Nov.-Dec., 1970), pp. 61-62; Allen Eyles, 250
wds., cp. pub.
Interntl F G: v. 8 (1971), p. 449; 50 wds., pt. pub.
Take One: v. 2, n. 7 (1970), p. 30; Douglas Sharples, 1000 wds., cp. pub.
Views & Rev: v. I, n. 4 (Spring, 1970), p. 72; 400 wds., cp. pub.

8496 TV MOVIE ALMANAC AND RATINGS (Steven H. Scheuer, gen. ed.)
Films in R: v. X, n. 3 (Mar., 1959), pp. 177-178; Henry Hart, 150 wds., cp.
pub.

8497 *TABLEAU BLANC, LE (André Lang, ed.)
Sight & S: v. 17, n. 68 (Winter, 1948-1949), p. 197; Colin Borland, 375
wds., cp. pub.

8498 TAKE IT FOR A FACT (Ada Reeve)
Sight & S: v. 24, n. 4 (Spring, 1955), p. 217; David Robinson, 450 wds., cp.
pub.

8499 TALKING ABOUT CINEMA (Jim Kitses, with Ann Mercer)
F Soc Rev: Oct. (1966), pp. 35-37; Anthony W. Hodgkinson, 800 wds., cp.
pub.

8500 TALKING OF SHAKESPEARE (John Garrett, ed.)
Films in R: v. VI, n. 9 (Nov., 1955), pp. 472-473; Robert Downing, 800
wds., cp. pub.

8501 TULLULAH (Tullulah Bankhead)
        Films in R: v. IV, n. 1 (Jan., 1953), pp. 42-43; Robert Downing, 475 wds.,
              cp. pub.
        Sight & S: v. 22, n. 3 (Jan.-Mar., 1953), p. 143; Harold Lang, 450 wds., cp.
              pub.

8502 TARZAN OF THE MOVIES (Gabe Essoe)
        Cineaste: v. II, n. 3 (Winter, 1968-1969), p. 19; Gary Crowdus, 200 wds.,
              pt. pub.

8503 TEACHING ABOUT FILM (J. M. L. Peters)
        F Quarterly: v. XVI, n. 4 (Summer, 1963), p. 63; Ernest Callenbach, 200
              wds., cp. pub.

8504 TEACHING ANIMATION TO CHILDREN (Yvonne Anderson)
        Take One: v. 2, n. 11 (1971), p. 38; Sandra Arioli, 300 wds., cp. pub.

8505 TECHNIQUE OF DOCUMENTARY FILM PRODUCTION, THE (W. Hugh
              Baddeley)
        Cineaste: v. I, n. 4 (Spring, 1968), pp. 24, 35; Gary Crowdus, 150 wds., pt.
              pub.
        F Comment: v. IV, n. 2-3 (Fall-Winter, 1967), p. 113; Austin F. Lamont,
              500 wds., cp. pub.

8506 TECHNIQUE OF EDITING 16MM FILMS, THE (John Burder)
        Am Cinematog: v. 51, n. 5 (May, 1970), p. 477; George J. Mitchell, 350
              wds., cp. pub.
        Cineaste: v. II, n. 1 (Summer, 1968), p. 26; Gary Crowdus, 150 wds., pt.
              pub.
        F Comment: v. 6, n. 1 (Spring, 1970), p. 71; 75 wds., cp. pub.

8507 TECHNIQUE OF FILM AND TELEVISION MAKE-UP, THE (Vincent J. R.
              Kehoe)
        Films & F: v. 4, n. 5 (Feb., 1958), p. 35; Martin Gray, 175 wds., pt. pub.

8508 TECHNIQUE OF FILM ANIMATION, THE (John Halas and Roger Manvell)
        Am Cinematog: v. 40, n. 6 (June, 1959), p. 380; 125 wds., pt. pub.
        F Quarterly: v. XIII, n. 1 (Fall, 1959), pp. 63-64; Benjamin Jackson, 450
              wds., cp. pub.
        Sight & S: v. 28, n. 3-4 (Summer-Autumn, 1959), p. 188; Richard Williams,
              550 wds., cp. pub.

8509 TECHNIQUE OF FILM EDITING, THE (Karel Reisz and Gavin Millar)
        Cineaste: v. II, n. 1 (Summer, 1968), p. 26; Gary Crowdus, 200 wds., pt.
              pub.
        Cinema: v. 4, n. 3 (Fall, 1968), p. 46; Timothy J. Lyons, 225 wds., pt. pub.
        F Comment: v. 5, n. 4 (Winter, 1969), pp. 78-79; 100 wds., cp. pub.
        F Quarterly: v. XXII, n. 3 (Spring, 1969), pp. 50-55; C. Cameron Macauley,
              4000 wds., cp. pub.
        Films in R: v. IV, n. 10 (Dec., 1953), pp. 543-544; Victor Volmar, 600
              wds., cp. pub.
        Quarterly of FR TV: v. VIII, n. 3 (Spring, 1954), p. 312; Franklin Fearing,
              350 wds., cp. pub.
        Sight & S: v. 22, n. 4 (Apr.-June, 1953), pp. 199-200; Seth Holt, 1000 wds.,
              cp. pub.

8510 TECHNIQUE OF FILM MUSIC, THE (John Huntley and Roger Manvell)
        Films & F: v. 4, n. 4 (Jan., 1958), p. 33; Martin Gray, 250 wds., pt. pub.
        Sight & S: v. 27, n. 4 (Spring, 1958), pp. 210-211; Arthur Jacobs, 600 wds.,
              cp. pub.

8511 TECHNIQUE OF FILM MUSIC, THE (Alec Nesbitt)
        F Comment: v. 1, n. 6 (Fall, 1963), p. 55; Mark Dichter, 125 wds., cp. pub.

8512 TECHNIQUE OF SPECIAL EFFECTS CINEMATOGRAPHY, THE (Raymond
              Fielding)
        Am Cinematog: v. 47, n. 1 (Jan., 1966), p. 19; Charles G. Clarke, 350 wds.,
              cp. pub.
        Films in R: v. XVII, n. 6 (June-July, 1966), pp. 377-378; George J.
              Mitchell, 425 wds., cp. pub.
        Films in R: v. XVII, n. 7 (Aug.-Sept., 1966), p. 461; Raymond Fielding (a
              reply), 400 wds., no pub.

8513 TECHNIQUE OF THE DOCUMENTARY FILM, THE (W. Hugh Baddeley)
Am Cinematog: v. 44, n. 9 (Sept., 1963), p. 516; 125 wds., pt. pub.

8514 TECHNIQUE OF THE FILM CUTTING ROOM, THE (Ernest Walter)
Am Cinematog: v. 51, n. 4 (Apr., 1970), pp. 361, 365; George J. Mitchell,
600 wds., cp. pub.

8515 TECHNIQUE OF THE MOTION PICTURE CAMERA, THE (H. Mario
Kaimonde Souto, ed. by Raymond Spottiswoode)
Cineaste: v. II, n. 2 (Fall, 1968), p. 19; Gary Crowdus, 200 wds., pt. pub.
Films in R: v. XIX, n. 1 (Jan., 1968), pp. 45-46; George J. Mitchell, 250
wds., cp. pub.

8516 TECHNOLOGICAL HISTORY OF MOTION PICTURES AND TELEVISION,
A (Raymond Fielding, ed.)
Am Cinematog: v. 49, n. 3 (Mar., 1968), pp. 222-223, 225; Joseph V.
Mascelli, 900 wds., cp. pub.
F Soc Rev: Apr. (1968), pp. 36-38; Frank Manchel, 1100 wds., cp. pub.
Films & F: v. 14, n. 11 (Aug., 1968), p. 57; Sheridan Morley, 200 wds., pt.
pub.
Films in R: v. XIX, n. 3 (Mar., 1968), p. 169; Henry Hart, 175 wds., cp.
pub.
Sight & S: v. 38, n. 1 (Winter, 1968-1969), p. 53; D.R., 125 wds., cp. pub.

8517 TELEVISION WRITER, THE (Erik Barnouw)
F Comment: v. 1, n. 3 (1962), pp. 38-39; Robert Windeler, 600 wds., cp.
pub.

8518 TELL IT TO LOUELLA (Louella Parsons)
Films in R: v. XIII, n. 6 (June-July, 1962), p. 371; Diana Willing Cope, 300
wds., cp. pub.

8519 THALBERG: LIFE AND LEGEND (Bob Thomas)
Cinema: v. 5, n. 1, p. 46; Robert Joseph, 700 wds., pt. pub.
F Quarterly: v. XXIII, n. 1 (Fall, 1969), p. 62; Ernest Callenbach, 250 wds.,
cp. pub.
F Soc Rev: v. IV, n. 9 (May, 1969), pp. 43-45; Gary Crowdus, 1000 wds.,
cp. pub.
Films & F: v. 17, n. 11 (Aug., 1971), p. 14; Sheridan Morley, 150 wds., pt.
pub.
Films in R: v. XX, n. 3 (Mar., 1969), pp. 175-196; Alice H. Whitham, 150
wds., cp. pub.
Films in R: v. XX, n. 4 (Apr., 1969), pp. 258-259; Earl Anderson (a letter),
600 wds., no pub.
Focus on F: n. 7 (Summer, 1971), p. 58; Allen Eyles, 250 wds., cp. pub.
Interntl F G: v. 9 (1972), pp. 473, 475; 50 wds., pt. pub.

8520 THANK YOU FOR HAVING ME (Caroline Lejeune)
Sight & S: v. 33, n. 2 (Spring, 1964), p. 101; Penelope Houston, 600 wds.,
cp. pub.

8521 *THEATER UND FILM IM DRITTEN REICH (Joseph Wulf Gutersloh)
F Comment: v. IV, n. 2-3 (Fall-Winter, 1967), p. 116; George Amberg, 350
wds., cp. pub.
F Quarterly: v. XIX, n. 2 (Winter, 1965-1966), p. 60; J. M. Svendsen, 100
wds., pt. pub.

8522 THEATRE ARTS ANTHOLOGY (Rosamond Gilder, et al., eds.)
Films in R: v. II, n. 2 (Feb., 1951), pp. 43-44; Walter Stainton, 500 wds.,
cp. pub.

8523 *THEATRE-FILM: DAS LEBEN UND ICH (Emil Jannings)
Films in R: v. IV, n. 10 (Dec., 1953), pp. 549-550; Herman G. Weinberg,
750 wds., cp. pub.

8524 THEATRICAL COMPANION TO COWARD (Raymond Mander and Joe
Mitchenson)
Films & F: v. 4, n. 2 (Nov., 1957), p. 39; Martin Gray, 450 wds., pt. pub.

8525 THEMES — SHORT FILMS FOR DISCUSSION (William Kuhns)
     Cineaste: v. III, n. 1 (Summer, 1969), pp. 24, 26; Gary Crowdus, 500 wds.,
     pt. pub.

8526 *THEORIE DER MASSENMEDIEN (Erich Feldman)
     F Quarterly: v. XVII, n. 4 (Summer, 1964), pp. 62-63; George Amberg, 200
     wds., cp. pub.

8527 THEORY AND TECHNIQUE OF PLAYWRITING AND SCREENWRITING
     (John Howard Lawson)
     Hollywood Q: v. IV, n. 1 (Fall, 1949), p. 100; Franklin Fearing, 200 wds.,
     cp. pub.
     Sequence: n. 11 (Summer, 1950), pp. 45-46; Peter Ericsson, 700 wds., pt.
     pub.
     Sight & S: v. 18, n. 72 (Jan., 1950), p. 37; Ernest Lindgren, 700 wds., cp.
     pub.

8528 THEORY OF FILM: THE REDEMPTION OF PHYSICAL REALITY (Sieg-
     fried Kracauer)
     Am Cinematog: v. 41, n. 10 (Oct., 1960), p. 588; 125 wds., pt. pub.
     F Quarterly: v. XIV, n. 2 (Winter, 1960), pp. 56-58; Ernest Callenbach,
     1200 wds., cp. pub.

8529 THEORY OF STEROSCOPIC TRANSMISSION AND ITS APPLICATION TO
     THE MOTION PICTURE, THE (Raymond and Nigel Spottis-
     woode)
     Quarterly of FR TV: v. VIII, n. 3 (Spring, 1954), pp. 315-316; Franklin
     Fearing, 350 wds., cp. pub.

8530 THEORY OF THE FILM (Béla Balázs)
     Films in R: v. IV, n. 7 (Aug.-Sept., 1953), pp. 371-372; Henry Hart, 550
     wds., cp. pub.
     Quarterly of FR TV: v. VIII, n. 2 (Winter, 1953), pp. 206-207; Franklin
     Fearing, 600 wds., cp. pub.

8531 THINGS I HAD TO LEARN, THE (Loretta Young)
     Films In R: v. XIV, n. 1 (Jan., 1963), pp. 52-53; Robert C. Roman, 350
     wds., cp. pub.

8532 THIS IS ON ME (Bob Hope)
     Films & F: v. 1, n. 2 (Nov., 1954), p. 30; Peter Brinson, 70 wds., pt. pub.

8533 THOUSAND AND ONE DELIGHTS, A (Alan G. Barbour)
     Focus on F: n. 10 (Summer, 1972), pp. 61-62; Allen Eyles, 200 wds., cp.
     pub.

8534 THREE BRITISH SCREENPLAYS: "BRIEF ENCOUNTER", "ODD MAN
     OUT", "SCOTT OF THE ANTARCTIC" (Roger Manvell, ed.)
     Sequence, n. 13 (New Year, 1951), pp. 45-46; Lindsay Anderson, 1300
     wds., pt. pub.
     Sight & S: v. 19, n. 9 (Jan., 1951), pp. 379-380; James Morgan, 550 wds.,
     cp. pub.

8535 THREE FACES OF THE FILM: THE ART, THE DREAM, THE CULT, THE
     (Parker Tyler)
     F Quarterly: v. XIV, n. 2 (Winter, 1960), pp. 58-59; Ernest Callenbach, 500
     wds., cp. pub.
     Films & F: v. 14, n. 8 (Apr., 1968), p. 60; Sheridan Morley, 200 wds., pt.
     pub.
     Sight & S: v. 30, n. 3 (Summer, 1961), pp. 153-154; John Russell Taylor,
     600 wds., cp. pub.

8536 3434 US GOVERNMENT FILMS (Seerley Reid and Virginia Wilkins)
     Films in R: v. IV, n. 1 (Jan., 1953), p. 42; Eleanor H. Nash, 200 wds., cp.
     pub.

8537 TITLE GUIDE TO THE TALKIES, A (Richard B. Dimmit, comp.)
     Screen: v. 11, n. 4-5 (July-Oct., 1970), pp. 133-134; Gillian Hartnoll, 50
     wds., cp. pub.

8538 TO BE CONTINUED (Ken Weiss and Ed Goodgold)
      Focus on F: n. 10 (Summer, 1972), p. 60; Allen Eyles, 175 wds., cp. pub.

8539 TO ENCOURAGE THE ART OF THE FILM: THE STORY OF THE BRITISH
          FILM INSTITUTE (Ivan Butler)
      Focus on F: n. 10 (Summer, 1972), p. 62; Allen Eyles, 125 wds., cp. pub.

8540 TO SEE THE DREAM (Jessamyn West)
      Films & F: v. 4, n. 8 (May, 1958), p. 35; Martin Gray, 100 wds., pt. pub.
      Films in R: v. VIII, n. 9 (Nov., 1957), pp. 467-468; Elspeth Hart, 450 wds.,
          cp. pub.
      Quarterly of FR TV: v. XI, n. 4 (Summer, 1957), pp. 427-428; Franklin
          Fearing, 250 wds., cp. pub.
      Sight & S: v. 27, n. 5 (Summer, 1958), pp. 260-261; Derek Hill, 400 wds.,
          cp. pub.

8541 TOO MUCH, TOO SOON (Diana Barrymore and Gerold Frank)
      Films in R: v. VIII, n. 8 (Oct., 1957), pp. 420-422; R. V. Tozzi, 700 wds.,
          cp. pub.

8542 TOTAL RECOIL (Kyle Crichton)
      Films in R: v. XII, n. 6 (June-July, 1961), p. 369; 175 wds., cp. pub.

8543 TOWARDS A SOCIOLOGY OF THE CINEMA (I. C. Jarvie)
      Films & F: v. 16, n. 12 (Sept., 1970), p. 94; Sheridan Morley, 100 wds., pt.
          pub.
      Interntl F G: v. 8 (1971), p. 449; 50 wds., pt. pub.

8544 TOWER IN BABEL: A HISTORY OF BROADCASTING IN THE UNITED
          STATES TO 1933, A (Erik Barnouw)
      Cineaste: v. V, n. 1 (Winter, 1971-1972), pp. 23-25; Tom Brom, 2000 wds.,
          cp. pub.
      F Comment: v. IV, n. 2-3 (Fall-Winter, 1967), pp. 107-108; Richard J.
          Meyer, 850 wds., cp. pub.

8545 TOWER OF BABEL, SPECULATIONS ON THE CINEMA (Eric Rhode)
      F Comment: v. 5, n. 3 (Fall, 1969), pp. 78-79; William K. Everson, 150
          wds., cp. pub.
      F Quarterly: v. XX, n. 4 (Summer, 1967), p. 76; Ernest Callenbach, 150
          wds., cp. pub.
      F Soc Rev: May (1968), pp. 38-39; Frank Manchel, 50 wds., cp. pub.
      Interntl F G: v. 4 (1967), p. 273; 100 wds., pt. pub.
      Sight & S: v. 35, n. 3 (Summer, 1966), p. 153; Geoffrey Nowell-Smith, 725
          wds., cp. pub.

8546 TRACY AND HEPBURN: AN INTIMATE MEMOIR (Garson Kanin)
      Focus on F: n. 10 (Summer, 1972), p. 64; Allen Eyles, 200 wds., cp. pub.

8547 TRAINING AIDS — OVERUSE IS ABUSE (Major Donald P. Blake)
      F Lib Quarterly: v. 1, n. 4 (Fall, 1968), p. 47; 50 wds., pt. pub.

8548 *TRAITE GENERAL DE TECHNIQUE DU CINEMA (Jean Vivié)
      Sight & S: v. 17, n. 67 (Autumn, 1948), p. 151; Colin Borland, 300 wds.,
          cp. pub.

8549 TREE IS A TREE, A (King Vidor)
      Films & F: v. 1, n. 3 (Dec., 1954), p. 29; Peter Brinson, 200 wds., pt. pub.
      Films in R: v. IV, n. 10 (Dec., 1953), pp. 544-546; Frank Daugherty, 800
          wds., cp. pub.
      Quarterly of FR TV: v. VIII, n. 3 (Spring, 1954), pp. 318-319; Franklin
          Fearing, 150 wds., cp. pub.
      Sight & S: v. 23, n. 4 (Apr.-June, 1954), pp. 217-218; Lindsay Anderson,
          2000 wds., cp. pub.

8550 *TRENTE ANS DE CINEMA AMERICAIN (Jean-Piere Coursodon)
      Films & F: v. 16, n. 10 (July, 1970), p. 64; Sheridan Morley, 100 wds., pt.
          pub.
      Interntl F G: v. 8 (1971), p. 449; 50 wds., pt. pub.

8551 *TU N'AS RIEN VU A HIROSHIMA (Raymond Ravar, gen. director)
      Interntl F G: v. 1 (1964), p. 224; 50 wds., cp. pub.

8552 *TUTELA PENALE DEL PUDORE E DELLA PUBBLICA DECENZA, LA
         (Rodolfo Venditti)
      Cinema Studies: v. I, n. 8 (Dec., 1963), pp. 208-209; N.M.H., 1100 wds.,
         cp. pub.

8553 TWENTY FIVE THOUSAND SUNSETS: THE AUTOBIOGRAPHY OF
         HERBERT WILCOX (Herbert Wilcox)
      Films in R: v. XIX, n. 10 (Dec., 1968), pp. 639-640; Alan A. Coulson, 400
         wds., cp. pub.

8554 TWENTY-FOUR TIMES A SECOND: FILMS AND FILM-MAKERS (William
         S. Pechter)
      F Comment: v. 7, n. 3 (Fall, 1971), p. 74; Robert Chappetta, 800 wds., cp.
         pub.
      F Quarterly: v. XXIV, n. 3 (Spring, 1971), pp. 23-25; Ernest Callenbach,
         1200 wds., cp. pub.
      F Soc Rev: v. 7, n. 1 (Sept., 1971), pp. 47-50; Michael Sragow, 1200 wds.,
         cp. pub.
      Sight & S: v. 40, n. 4 (Autumn, 1971), p. 228; Gilberto Perez-Guillermo,
         1000 wds., cp. pub.

8555 TWENTY YEARS OF BRITISH FILM: 1925-1945 (Michael Balcon, Ernest
         Lindgren, Forsyth Hardy, Roger Manvell)
      Hollywood Q: v. II, n. 3 (Apr., 1947), pp. 319-320; John Collier, 500 wds.,
         cp. pub.

8556 TWENTY YEARS OF CINEMA IN VENICE (International Exhibition of
         Cinematography)
      Films in R: v. IV, n. 2 (Feb., 1953), p. 104; H.T., 300 wds., cp. pub.

8557 TWO REELS AND A CRANK (Albert E. Smith, with Phil A. Koury)
      Films in R: v. IV, n. 2 (Feb., 1953), pp. 99-102; Theordore Huff, 1500
         wds., cp. pub.

U

8558 UNDERGROUND FILM: A CRITICAL HISTORY, THE (Parker Tyler)
      Cinema: v. 6, n. 2 (Fall, 1970), pp. 42-44; Margaret Bach, 2600 wds., cp.
         pub.
      F Comment: v. 7, n. 1 (Spring, 1971), pp. 76-78; Regina Cornwall, 2500
         wds., cp. pub.
      F Heritage: v. 5, n. 2 (Winter, 1969-1970), pp. 30-31; 350 wds., cp. pub.
      Films & F: v. 17, n. 10 (July, 1971), p. 64; Sheridan Morley, 75 wds., pt.
         cr.
      Interntl F G: v. 8 (1971), p. 449; 50 wds., pt. pub.
      Sight & S: v. 40, n. 3 (Summer, 1971), p. 170; John Russell Taylor, 900
         wds., cp. pub.

8559 UNDERSTANDING MEDIA (Marshall McLuhan)
      F Quarterly: v. XIX, n. 3 (Spring, 1966), pp. 58-64; Stephen Taylor, 3500
         wds., cp. pub.

8560 UNEMBARRASSED MUSE: THE POPULAR ARTS IN AMERICA, THE
         (Russel B. Nye)
      Journal of P C: v. IV, n. 3 (Winter, 1971), pp. 737-741; Ray B. Browne,
         1500 wds., cp. pub.

8561 UPTON SINCLAIR PRESENTS WILLIAM FOX (Upton Sinclair)
      Cineaste: v. V, n. 1 (Winter, 1971-1972), pp. 27-28; Bob Summers, 500
         wds., cp. pub.

8562 USE OF THE FILM, THE (Basil Wright)
      Sequence: n. 8 (Summer, 1949), p. 91; Lindsay Anderson, 150 wds., pt.
         pub.

8563 USING FILMS: A HANDBOOK FOR THE PROGRAM PLANNER (James
      Limbacher, ed.)
      F Lib Quarterly: v. 1, n. 1 (Winter, 1967-1968), p. 56; 75 wds., pt. pub.

8564 USTINOV IN FOCUS (Tony Thomas, ed.)
      Interntl F G: v. 9 (1972), p. 475; 50 wds., pt. pub.

8565 VAGRANT VIKING (Peter Freuchen)
      Films in R: v. V, n. 1 (Jan., 1954), p. 41; Elspeth Hart, 350 wds., cp. pub.

8566 VALENTINO (Alan Arnold)
      Films in R: v. V, n. 10 (Dec., 1954), pp. 549-551; Elspeth Hart, 1000 wds.,
      cp. pub.

8567 VALENTINO (Irving Shulman)
      F Comment: v. 5, n. 3 (Fall, 1969), pp. 75-77; Robert Steele, 3500 wds.,
      cp. pub.
      Films & F: v. 15, n. 7 (Apr., 1969), p. 68; Sheridan Morley, 75 wds., pt.
      pub.
      Films in R: v. XIX, n. 2 (Feb., 1968), pp. 104-106; Robert Giroux, 650
      wds., cp. pub.

8568 VAMPYR, LETRANGE AVENTURE DE DAVID GRAY (Aldo Buzzi, ed.)
      Sight & S: v. 18, n. 70 (Summer, 1949), p. 97; Muriel Grindrod, 400 wds.,
      cp. pub.

8569 VERSATILES, THE (Alfred Twomey and Arthur McClure)
      Films & F: v. 16, n. 1 (Oct., 1969), p. 70; Sheridan Morley, 100 wds., pt.
      pub.
      Interntl F G: v. 7 (1970), p. 403; 50 wds., pt. pub.

8570 VIEW FROM THE SIXTIES, THE (George Oppenheimer)
      Films in R: v. XVII, n. 8 (Oct., 1966), p. 516; Robert Downing, 250 wds.,
      cp. pub.

8571 VIKING EGGELING, 1880-1925, ARTIST AND FILMMAKER, LIFE AND
      WORK (Louise O'Konor)
      F Quarterly: v. XXV, n. 4 (Summer, 1972), pp. 31-34; William Moritz,
      1900 wds., cp. pub.

8572 *VINGT ANS DE CINEMA SOVIETIQUE (Luda and Jean Schnitzer)
      Interntl F G: v. 2 (1965), p. 253; 75 wds., pt. pub.

8573 VIOLENCE AND THE MASS MEDIA (Otto N. Larsen, ed.)
      F Quarterly: v. XXII, n. 1 (Fall, 1968), pp. 77-79; Ernest Callenbach, 1100
      wds., cp. pub.

8574 VIOLENCE ON THE SCREEN (André Glucksmann)
      Screen: v. 12, n. 3 (Summer, 1971), pp. 152-156; Ashley Pringle, 2000
      wds., cp. pub.

8575 VIRGIN SPRING, THE (Ulla Isaksson, ed.)
      Sight & S: v. 30, n. 2 (Spring, 1961), pp. 97-98; John Russell Taylor, 1200
      wds., cp. pub.

8576 *VISCONTI (Yves Guillaume)
      Interntl F G: v. 5 (1968), p. 265; 25 wds., pt. pub.

8577 VISCONTI (Geoffrey Nowell-Smith)
      F Quarterly: v. XXI, n. 4 (Summer, 1968), p. 55; 50 wds., no pub.
      F Soc Rev: May (1968), p. 38; Frank Manchel, 50 wds., cp. pub.

8578 VISITATION: THE FILM STORY OF THE MEDICAL MISSIONARIES OF
         MARY (Andrew Buchanan)
         Sight & S: v. 17, n. 67 (Autumn, 1948), p. 152; Raymond Garlick, 300
            wds., cp. pub.

8579 VISUAL THINKING (Rudolf Arnheim)
         Cinema J: v. X, n. 1 (Fall, 1970), pp. 51-54; John L. Fell, 1600 wds., cp.
            pub.

8580 *VITEZNY FILM (Svet Sovietu, pub.)
         Sequence: n. 13 (New Year, 1951), pp. 44-45; Quentin Rogers, 1500 wds.,
            cp. pub.

8581 *VOM WERDEN DEUTSCHER FILM-KUNST (Dr. Oskar Kalbus)
         Hollywood Q: v. I, n. 1 (Oct., 1945), pp. 124-216; William Dieterele, 800
            wds., cp. pub.

8582 *VON ROSSELLINI ZU FELLINI (Martin Schlappner, ed.)
         Sight & S: v. 28, n. 2 (Spring, 1959), p. 101; Wihelm Viola, 350 wds., cp.
            pub.

8583 VON STROHEIM (Thomas Quinn)
         Interntl F G: v. 9 (1972), p. 475; 50 wds., pt. pub.

8584 W. C. FIELDS: HIS FOLLIES AND FORTUNES (R. L. Taylor)
         F Culture: n. 31 (Winter, 1963-1964), p. 68; Herman G. Weinberg, 25 wds,
            cp. pub.

8585 WALL-TO-TALL TRAP, THE (Morton Freedgood)
         Films in R: v. VIII, n. 6 (June-July, 1957), p. 290; Eleanor H. Nash, 200
            wds., cp. pub.

       WALT DISNEY (see: The Disney Version)

8586 WALT DISNEY TREASURY (Steffi Fletcher and Jane Werner, arrangers)
         Films in R: v. V, n. 2 (Feb., 1954), p. 104; 175 wds., cp. pub.

8587 WANDERER: AN AUTOBIOGRAPHY (Sterling Hayden)
         Films in R: v. XV, n. 1 (Jan., 1964), pp. 39-40; Henry Hart, 400 wds., cp.
            pub.

8588 WARM THRILL OF PLEASURE PAPERS, THE (David Gale)
         Films & F: v. 16, n. 11 (Aug., 1970), p. 64; Sheridan Morley, 150 wds., pt.
            pub.

8589 WE BARRYMORES (Lionel Barrymore, with Cameron Ship)
         Films in R: v. II, n. 8 (Oct., 1951), pp. 56-57; Elspeth Chapin, 300 wds., cp.
            pub.
         Sight & S: v. 21, n. 3 (Jan.-Mar., 1952), p. 138; Harold Lang, 450 wds., cp.
            pub.

8590 WE MADE A FILM IN CYPRESS (Laurie Lee and Ralph Keene)
         Sight & S: v. 16, n. 64 (Winter, 1947-1948), p. 179; 200 wds., cp. pub.

8591 *WEG DES FILMS, DER (Friedrich V. Zglinicki, ed.)
         F Culture: v. 3, n. 4 (Oct., 1957), pp. 21-22; Gordon Hendricks, 800 wds.,
            cp. pub.

8592 WESTERN: AN ILLUSTRATED GUIDE, THE (Allen Eyles, comp.)
         Interntl F G: v. 5 (1968), p. 265; 25 wds., pt. pub.
         Screen: v. 11, n. 2 (Mar.-Apr., 1970), p. 97; Gillian Hartnoll, 50 wds., cp.
            pub.

8593 WESTERN: FROM SILENTS TO CINERAMA, THE (George N. Fenin and
William K. Everson)
F Culture: n. 27 (Winter, 1962-1963), p. 74; Herman G. Weinberg, 300
wds., cp. pub.
F Quarterly: v. XVII, n. 2 (Winter, 1963-1964), pp. 54-57; Robert C.
Roman, 2300 wds., cp. pub.
F Soc Rev: Sept. (1966), pp. 37-38; Edwin Jahiel, 425 wds., cp. pub.
Interntl F G: v. 2 (1965), p. 250; 125 wds., pt. pub.
Sight & S: v. 32, n. 3 (Summer, 1963), p. 153; Peter Harcourt, 750 wds.,
cp. pub.

8594 WHAT IS CINEMA? (André Bazin, trans. by Hugh Gray)
F Comment: v. 5, n. 3 (Fall, 1969), pp. 81-82; J. Dudley Andrew, 1400
wds., cp. pub.
F Heritage: v. 3, n. 2 (Winter, 1967-1968), pp. 34-36; Norman Hartweg,
800 wds., cp. pub.
F Lib Quarterly: v. 1, n. 3 (Summer, 1968), pp. 53-54; Donald E. Staples,
200 wds., pt. pub.
F Soc Rev: Oct. (1967), pp. 30-33; John Thomas, 1500 wds., cp. pub.
Interntl F G: v. 1 (1964), p. 225; 50 wds., pt. pub.
Interntl F G: v. 6 (1969), p. 278; 50 wds., pt. pub.
Sight & S: v. 30, n. 3 (Summer, 1961), p. 153; Jean Queval, 900 wds., cp.
pub.

8595 WHEN MOVIES BEGAN TO SPEAK (Frank Manchel)
Screen: v. 11, n. 4-5 (July-Oct., 1970), pp. 130-131; R. C. Vanndey, 550
wds., pt. pub.

8596 WHEN PICTURES BEGAN TO MOVE (Frank Manchel)
Screen: v. 11, n. 4-5 (July-Oct., 1970), pp. 130-131; R. C. Vanndey, 550
wds., pt. pub.

8597 WHEN THE MOVIES WERE YOUNG (Mrs. D. W. Griffith)
Sight & S: v. 39, n. 4 (Autumn, 1970), p. 223; David Robinson, 1000 wds.,
cp. pub.

8598 WHERE WE CAME IN: SEVENTY YEARS OF THE BRITISH FILM
INDUSTRY (C. A. Oakley)
Cinema Studies: v. II, n. 1 (June, 1965), pp. 15-16; N.M.H., 650 wds., cp.
pub.
Interntl F G: v. 2 (1965), p. 251; 175 wds., pt. pub.
Sight & S: v. 34, n. 1 (Winter, 1964-1965), pp. 49-50; David Robinson, 400
wds., cp. pub.

8599 WHITE RUSSIAN — RED FACE (Monja Danischewsky)
Films & F: v. 13, n. 4 (Jan., 1967), p. 56; Sheridan Morley, 350 wds., pt.
pub.

8600 WHO COULD ASK FOR ANYTHING MORE? (Ethel Merman)
Quarterly of FR TV: v. X, n. 2 (Winter, 1955), p. 210; Franklin Fearing,
125 wds., cp. pub.

8601 WHO IS THAT? (Personality Posters, pub.)
Films & F: v. 14, n. 5 (Feb., 1968), p. 54; Sheridan Morley, 150 wds., pt.
pub.

8602 WHO WROTE THE MOVIES AND WHAT ELSE DID THEY WRITE? AN
INDEX OF SCREEN WRITERS AND THEIR FILM WORKS,
1936-1969 (Leonard Spigelgass, comp.)
Cinema J: v. X, n. 2 (Spring, 1971), pp. 51-56; Howard Suber, 2200 wds.,
cp. pub.
Films in R: v. XXII, n. 7 (Aug.-Sept., 1971), p. 432; Christopher North,
200 wds., cp. pub.
Focus on F: n. 6 (Spring, 1971), pp. 59-60; Allen Eyles, 300 wds., cp. pub.

8603 WHY A DUCK? VISUAL AND VERBAL GEMS FROM THE MARX
BROTHERS' MOVIES (Richard J. Anobile, ed.)
Focus on F: n. 10 (Summer, 1972), p. 62; Allen Eyles, 250 wds., cp. pub.

8604 WHY ME? AN AUTOBIOGRAPHY (William Gargan)
      Films in R: v. XX, n. 7 (Aug.-Sept., 1969), p. 427; Alice H. Witham, 225
         wds., cp. pub.

8605 *WIE SIE FILMEN (Ulrich Gregor, ed.)
      F Comment: v. IV, n. 2-3 (Fall-Winter, 1967), pp. 114-115; Paul
         Falkenberg, 300 wds., cp. pub.
      Interntl F G: v. 4 (1967), p. 271; 150 wds., pt. pub.

8606 WILL ACTING SPOIL MARILYN MONROE? (Pete Martin)
      Films in R: v. VII, n. 8 (Oct., 1956), p. 421; Robert Downing, 450 wds., cp.
         pub.

8607 WILLOWBROOK CINEMA STUDY PROJECT (Ralph Amelio)
      Cineaste: v. III, n. 1 (Summer, 1969), pp. 24, 26; Gary Crowdus, 500 wds.,
         pt. pub.

8608 WINCHESTER'S SCREEN ENCYCLOPEDIA (Maud M. Miller, ed.)
      Hollywood Q: v. IV, n. 1 (Fall, 1949), pp. 104-105; Franklin Fearing, 350
         wds., pt. pub.
      Sight & S: v. 17, n. 67 (Autumn, 1948), p. 152; 225 wds., cp. pub.

8609 WINNERS OF THE WEST: THE SAGEBRUSH HEROES OF THE SILENT
         SCREEN (Kalton C. Lahue)
      Interntl F G: v. 9 (1972), p. 475; 50 wds., pt. pub.
      Views & Rev: v. 3, n. 2 (Fall, 1971), pp. 71-75; Jon Tuska, 2500 wds., pt.
         pub.

8610 WITH A CAST OF THOUSANDS: A HOLLYWOOD CHILDHOOD (Jill
         Schary Zimmer)
      Films in R: v. XIV, n. 9 (Nov., 1963), p. 560; Alice H. Witham, 150 wds.,
         cp. pub.

8611 WITH EISENSTEIN IN HOLLYWOOD: A CHAPTER OF AUTOBIOGRAPHY
         (Ivor Montagu)
      Cineaste: v. II, n. 4 (Spring, 1969), p. 21; Gary Crowdus, 200 wds., pt. pub.
      F Comment: v. 5, n. 3 (Fall, 1969), p. 81; Herman G. Weinberg, 250 wds.,
         cp. pub.
      F Soc Rev: v. 4, n. 8, pp. 43-45; Gary Crowdus, 1200 wds., cp. pub.
      Films & F: v. 15, n. 6 (Mar., 1969), p. 72; Sheridan Morley, 600 wds., pt.
         pub.
      Interntl F G: v. 7 (1970), p. 403; 50 wds., pt. pub.
      Sight & S: v. 38, n. 2 (Spring, 1969), p. 107; David Robinson, 750 wds., cp.
         pub.

8612 WORD AND IMAGE: A HISTORY OF THE HUNGARIAN CINEMA (Istvan
         Nemeskurty)
      Films & F: v. 15, n. 2 (Nov., 1968), p. 73; Sheridan Morley, 200 wds., pt.
         pub.
      Interntl F G: v. 6 (1969), p. 278; 50 wds., pt. pub.
      Sight & S: v. 38, n. 2 (Spring, 1969), p. 107; Jay Leyda, 500 wds., cp. pub.

8613 WORK OF THE FILM DIRECTOR, THE (A. J. Reynertson)
      Films & F: v. 17, n. 3 (Dec., 1970), pp. 63-64; Sheridan Morley, 100 wds.,
         pt. pub.

8614 WORKING FOR THE FILMS (Oswell Blakeston, ed.)
      Hollywood Q: v. III, n. 3 (Spring, 1948), pp. 332-333; K.M., 100 wds., cp.
         pub.

8615 WORLD OF ROBERT FLAHERTY, THE (Richard Griffith)
      Films in R: v. IV, n. 6 (June-July, 1953), pp. 307-308; Richard Leacock,
         600 wds., cp. pub.
      Quarterly of FR TV: v. VIII, n. 1 (Fall, 1953), pp. 100-102; Franklin
         Fearing, 550 wds., cp. pub.
      Sight & S: v. 23, n. 2 (Oct.-Dec., 1953), p. 109; Herman G. Weinberg, 750
         wds., cp. pub.

8616 WORLD ON FILM: CRITICISM AND COMMENT, A (Stanley Kauffmann)
        F Comment: v. IV, n. 2-3 (Fall-Winter, 1967), pp. 108-109; Lewis Jacobs,
            1000 wds., cp. pub.
        F Quarterly: v. XX, n. 3 (Spring, 1967), pp. 54-55; Ernest Callenbach, 750
            wds., cp. pub.
        F Soc Rev: Mar. (1968), pp. 37-38; 450 wds., cp. pub.
        Screen: v. 11, n. 6 (Nov.-Dec., 1970), pp. 90-92; Jim Hillier, 1200 wds., pt.
            pub.
        Sight & S: v. 36, n. 4 (Autumn, 1967), pp. 210-211; Philip French, 1200
            wds., cp. pub.

8617 WORLD VIEWED, THE (Stanley Cavell)
        F Quarterly: v. XXV, n. 4 (Summer, 1972), pp. 28-29; Leo Braudy, 1300
            wds., cp. pub.

8618 WORLD-WIDE INFLUENCE OF THE CINEMA: A STUDY OF OFFICIAL
            CENSORSHIP AND THE INTERNATIONAL CULTURAL AS-
            PECTS OF MOTION PICTURES (John Eugene Harley)
        Sight & S: v. 16, n. 64 (Winter, 1947-1948), John M. Smithells, 700 wds.,
            cp. pub.

8619 WRITING FOR THE SCREEN (Clara Beranger)
        Films in R: v. II, n. 6 (June-July, 1951), pp. 45-46; Frances Taylor
            Patterson, 450 wds., cp. pub.
        Hollywood Q: v. V (1950-1951), p. 205; Franklin Fearing, 80 wds., cp.
            pub.

Y

8620 YEAR IN THE DARK: JOURNAL OF A FILM CRITIC, 1968-1969, A (Ren-
            ata Adler)
        F Soc Rev: v. 6, n. 1 (Sept., 1970), pp. 47-48; Michael Sragow, 650 wds.,
            cp. pub.

8621 YES, MR. DeMILLE (Phil A. Koury)
        Films in R: v. XI, n. 2 (Feb., 1960), p. 114; Jack Spears, 300 wds., cp. pub.

8622 YOUR CAREER IN FILM MAKING (George N. Gordon and Irving A. Falk)
        F Comment: v. 6, n. 3 (Fall, 1970), pp. 78-79; Ernest D. Rose, 500 wds.,
            cp. pub.

8623 YOUTH, COMMUNICATION AND LIBRARIES (Frances Henne, Alice
            Brooks and Ruth Ersted, eds.)
        Hollywood Q: v. IV, n. 3 (Spring, 1950), pp. 314-315; Franklin Fearing,
            150 wds., pt. pub.

Z

8624 ZSA ZSA GABOR (Gerold Frank)
        Films in R: v. XII, n. 1 (Jan., 1961), pp. 48-49; Penelope Holmes, 575 wds.,
            cp. pub.

8625 ZUIDERZEE (Corrado Terzi, ed.)
        Sight & S: v. 18, n. 70 (Summer, 1949), p. 97; Muriel Grindrod, 400 wds.,
            cp. pub.

INDEX TO DIRECTORS

INDEX TO DIRECTORS

ABBAS, Khwaji Ahmad, 3257, 4276
ABBOTT, George, 1355, 3477, 4760
ABEL, Jeanne and Alan, 3134
ABRAMSON, Hans (var. sp.: Hans Abrahamson), 5232, 5380, 5628, 5799
ADAMSON, Al, 747, 1680, 2037, 2731, 2860, 5501
ADATO, Perry Miller, 7083
ADDISS, Jus, 1305
ADIDGE, Pierre, 3818
ADREON, Franklin, 1578, 4554
AGRANENKO, Zakhar 3541
AHLBERG, Mac 2960, 4373, 6712
AINSWORTH, John, 425
ALAIMO, Louise 7240
ALAZRAKI, Benito 5148
ALBERTSON, Eric 5650
ALBICOCCO, Jean-Gabriel, 2369, 6972
ALBIN, Hans, 2233, 2265
ALCOCER, Santos (see: Edward Mann)
ALDRICH, Robert, 191, 299, 313, 550, 1587, 2088, 2160, 2535, 2954, 3348, 3465, 3487, 3532, 5871, 6281, 6561, 6851, 7061
ALEA, Tomas Gutierrez, 4075
ALEXANDRESCO, M., 3822
ALEXEIFF, Alexander, 4527
ALGAR, James, 67, 3285, 3531, 3645, 6838, 7119
ALLAN, Elkan, 3729
ALLAND, William, 3684
ALLEGRET, Marc, 625, 634, 1482, 1922, 3428, 3902, 4943, 5537
ALLEGRET, Yves, 3972, 4567, 4711, 4977, 5639, 5742, 7336
ALLEN, Irwin, 196, 2057, 3709, 5555, 6031, 6940
ALLEN, Johannes, 7342
ALLEN, Lewis, 209, 6098
ALLEN, Woody, 369, 6199, 7070
ALLIO, René, 5692, 6777
ALMOND, Paul, 18, 3135
ALOV, Alexander 109, 4837

ALTMAN, Herbert S., 1592
ALTMAN, Robert, 771, 1223, 3031, 3198, 3795, 3806, 6320
ALVAREZ, Santiago, 5667
ALVENTOSA, Ricardo, 2749
ALVEY, Glenn, 2734
AMADIO, Silvio, 114, 4128, 6710, 7114
AMATEAU, Rod, 5994
AMERO, John and Lem, 1571
AMICO, Gianni, 6656
AMYES, Julian, 2794, 4133
ANDERSON, James M., 1258
ANDERSON, John Murray, 3365
ANDERSON, Lindsay, 3013, 6411, 6481, 7107
ANDERSON, Madeline, 2967
ANDERSON, Sr., Michael, 111, 251, 1028, 2084, 4358, 4480, 4691, 5133, 5684, 5726, 7002, 7144, 7284
ANDERSON, Robert, 1082, 7339
ANDERSOON, Roy, 3305
ANDRE, Raoul, 1105, 2766, 7251
ANENT, Walton C., 1995
ANGEL, Suzanne, 3530
ANGER, Kenneth, 1729, 3123, 5543
ANGHELOPOULOS, Thodoros, 159
ANKER, 6099
ANNAKIN, Ken, 15, 416, 567, 1164, 1291, 1936, 2726, 2820, 2886, 3079, 3672, 3682, 3693, 4143, 5104, 6033, 6173, 6381, 6420, 6422, 6448, 6642, 6832
ANNENSKY, A., 199
ANNENSKY, Isidore, 5455
ANSTEY, Edgar, 5152, 7171
ANTHONY, Joseph, 107, 901, 907, 4041, 5157
ANTON, Amerigo, 3338
ANTONIONI, Michelangelo, 151, 315, 657, 1734, 2529, 3731, 4539, 5207, 7380
ARCHIMBAUD, George, 3707
ARDAVIN, Cesar, 3517
ARGENTO, Dario, 579, 969

ARKIN, Alan, 3627
ARKLESS, Robert, 6212
ARLISS, Leslie, 3012, 3903
ARMSTRONG, Michael, 2670, 3028
ARNOLD, Jack, 333, 2396, 2728, 2782, 3072, 3152, 3436, 3643, 3929, 4221, 4263, 4498, 5926
ARNOLD, Newton, 2618
ARNOLD, Steve, 3784
ARNSHTAM, Lev, 365, 5363
ARRABAL, Fernando, 6921
ARSHAM, Miriam, 1761
ARTHUR, Robert Alan, 3704
ARZNER, Dorothy, 7159
ASHBY, Hal, 2656, 3448
ASHCROFT, Ronnie, 287
ASHER, Robert, 1718, 2107, 3097, 3870, 3887, 4630, 5010, 6012
ASHER, William, 430, 569, 2019, 3235, 3523, 4303
ASQUITH, Anthony, 806, 1236, 1632, 2575, 3040, 3570, 4120, 4628, 4705, 6818, 7200, 7303, 7347
ASTRUC, Alexandre, 1281, 1791, 5288, 5676
ATTENBOROUGH, Richard, 4599
AUBIER, Pascal. 6831
AUDLEY, Michael, 4003
AUDRY, Jacquiline, 590, 2271, 2361, 3052, 4177, 6868
AUREL, Jean, 1424, 2171, 4742
AUTANT-LARA, Claude, 307, 1526, 1804, 2523, 3255, 3736, 3993, 4572, 4612, 5318, 5391, 5639, 6035, 6423, 6623
AVAKIAN, Aram, 1794, 3424
AVELLANA, Lamberto V., 1309
AVERBACH, Llya, 6004
AVERBACK, Hy, 1003, 2491, 2985, 6142, 7097
AVILDSEN, John G., 1317, 2542, 3224
AXEL, Gabriel, 1261, 1372, 2373, 2593
AXELMAN, Torbjörn, 4603
AXELROD, George, 3689, 5580
AYRES, Lew, 128

BACON, Lloyd, 2211
BADER, Alfred, 3851
BADZIAN, Teresa; 3623
BAERWITZ, Jerry A., 6839, 7151
BAGGOT, King, 6681
BAILLIE, Bruce, 961, 5126
BAKER, Anthony (pseud. for Helmut Fornbacher) 520
BAKER, Robert, 2725, 3191, 5745
BAKER, Roy, 206, 2050, 2062, 3077, 3194, 4230, 4462, 4575, 4669, 4693, 4808, 5531, 5792, 6489, 6729, 6833
BALABAN, Burt, 2296, 2776, 3817, 4291

BALCH, Anthony, 6597
BALCHIN, Brian Desmond, 3896
BALCON, Michael, 1303
BALDI, Ferdinando, 1392, 1707
BALDI, Gian Vittorio, 39, 3501
BALDI, Marcello, 5508, 6085
BALDWIN, Gerald H., 976
BALIK, Jaroslav, 1456
BALLARD, Carroll, 4902
BALQUE, Erica, 6565
BAND, Albert, 1889, 6613, 6986
BANK STREET COLLEGE OF EDUCATION, 5185
BANOVICH, Tamás, 1837
BARAN, Jack, 5373
BARATIER, Jacques, 2417, 4990
BARBERA, Joseph, 2761, 3910
BARDEM, Juan A., 78, 1451, 2481, 3752, 6785
BARE, Richard L., 6407
BARMA, Claude, 6204
BARNET, B., 7286
BARNWELL, John, 6148
BARON, Allen, 626, 6303
BARRETO, Lima, 881, 4486
BARRIS, George, 3274
BARRON, Arthur, 585, 1897, 4316
BARRY, Wesley, 1264
BARTLETT, Hall, 118, 912, 1009, 1685, 1886, 6756, 7387
BARTLETT, Richard, 4208, 5122
BARTLETT, Scott, 4091, 4226
BARTON, Charles, 5683, 6171, 6539
BASILICO, René, 4270
BASOV, Vladimir, 4501
BASS, Jules, 1420
BASS, Saul, 7296
BASTID, J.L., 5093
BATALOV, Aleksei, 4744
BATCHELOR, Joy, 195, 2809
BATTERSBY, Roy, 678
BAVA, Mario (occasional pseud. is John Hold) 611, 615, 1363, 1619, 1815, 1855, 2743, 3336, 3403, 4929
BAYLIS, Peter, 2012
BEALL, Dewitt, 3691
BEAN, Robert E., 3831
BEARDSLEY, Keith, 5222
BEATTY, Edgar, 2798
BEAUDINE, William, 575, 1595, 3058, 3210, 3454, 6386, 7054
BEAVER, Lee W. (see: Carlo Lizzani)
BEAVERS, Robert, 1220, 6010
BECKER, Harold, 5753
BECKER, Jacques, 57, 135, 216, 950, 1903, 2533, 4467, 5244
BECKER, Jean, 342, 6289
BECKER, Vernon P., 2240
BEEBE, Ford, 3475
BELGARD, Arnold, 1722
BELLACHIO, Marco (var. sp.: Mario Bellochio) 1050, 2034

DIRECTORS

BELLAMY, Earl, 343, 3067, 4277, 5972, 6441, 6591
BELLAMY, Edward, 2569
BELSON, Jordan, 121, 4193, 4881, 5220, 5470
BANAYOUN, Robert, 4792
BENDER, Erich F., 2705, 4095
BENE, Carmel (var. sp.: Carmelo Bene) 885, 4528
BENEDEK, Laslo (var. sp.: Lazlo Benedek) 1376, 1454, 3892, 4371, 4465, 7158
BENEDICK, Robert, 1083
BENEDICT, Richard, 3039
BENNATI, Giuseppe, 1823, 5213
BENNETT, Compton, 71, 522, 1097, 3372, 5867
BENNETT, Spencer, 297, 6087
BENSON, Leon, 2093, 2094
BENSON, Richard, 7046
BERCOVICI, Leonardo, 5965, 6025
BERGENSTRAHLE, Johan, 3834
BERGLUND, Per, 3855
BERGMAN, Ingmar, 792, 1542, 1548, 1691, 2890, 3550, 3854, 4440, 4543, 4812, 4862, 4976, 5323, 5516, 5598, 5664, 5689, 5761, 5851, 6108, 6115, 6466, 6584, 6907, 7167, 7202
BERKE, Lester W., 3705
BERKE, William, 1199, 3147, 4269
BERKOVIC, Zvonimir, 5369
BERLANGA, Luis Garcia, 4531, 5353, 7041
BERMAN, Harvey, 7162
BERMAN, Monty, 2725, 3191, 5583, 5745
BERNARD, Raymond 2231, 5660
BERNDS, Edward, 91, 1832, 2783, 3267, 5100, 5113, 5260, 5927, 6457, 6458, 6827
BERNELS, Peter, 2223, 2265
BERNHARDT, Curtis, 443, 1358, 2252, 3103, 3389, 4088, 4148
BERNIER, George, 4135
BERRI, Claude, 4017, 6734
BERRY, John, 1647, 4053, 6211
BERTANDAUBERT, Claude, 1145
BERTOLUCCI, Bernardo, 467, 1166, 1178, 4801, 6061
BERTUCELLI, Jean-Luis, 5164
BERWICK, Irvin, 4220, 6066
BEVERIDGE, James, 589
BEYER, Frank, 4352
BIBERMAN, Abner, 2095
BIBERMAN, Herbert, 5465, 5836
BIELINSKA, Helena (var. sp.: Halina Bielska) 3780, 4702
BIGGS, Julian, 6700
BILLINGTON, Kevin, 3099, 3589
BILLITTERI, Salvatore, 5443
BILLON, Pierre, 2835, 4197

BINDER, Steve, 6189, 6253
BIRCH, Dudley, 2085
BIRDWELL, Russell, 2352
BISHOP, Terry, 1245, 4181, 6793
BJORKMAN, Stig, 3196
BLACK, Noel, 1246, 3208, 5014
BLAIR, George, 2957, 5768
BLAIR, Milton, 6146
BLAND, Edward, 1313
BLASETTI, Alessandro, 3779, 5842, 6519, 6858
BLISTENE, Marcel, 2018
BLOOMFIELD, George, 3209
BLUE, James, 4615
BLUEMKE, Ralph C., 5345
BLUWAL, Marcel, 4795
BO, ARMANDO, 7224
BOBROVSKY, Anatoli, 4274
BOCAN, Hynek, 4492, 5036
BOETTGER, Fritz, 3179
BOETTICHER, Budd, 813, 825, 1147, 5282, 5319, 5607, 6500, 7051
BOGART, Paul, 2602, 4005, 5822
BOGDANOVICH, Peter, 3840, 6226, 7069
BOGIN, Mikhail, 360
BOHDZIEWICZ, Antoni, 2546
BOIKOV, Bi, 1419
BOISROND, Michel, 1154, 3901, 4118, 4798, 6204, 6288, 7242
BOISSET, Yves, 1198
BOISSOL, Claude, 3278
BOLESLAWSKI, Richard, 6338
BOLOGNINI, Mauro (var. sp.: Mauro Bolognine) 489, 2165, 2213, 4540, 4612, 5119, 5610, 6331, 6863, 7156, 7212
BOND, Jack, 5614
BONDARCHUK, Sergei, 1947, 6974, 7004
BONNARD, Mario, 3464, 4447
BONNIERE, René, 132
BONUCCI, Alberto, 5670
BONZI, Leonardo, 2520, 3699
BOORMAN, John, 974, 2497, 2712, 3544, 4959
BOOTH, Harry, 631, 3377
BORDERIC, Fritz, 1107
BORDERIE, Bernard, 187
BOROWCZYK, Walerian, 624, 1643, 2473, 3218, 5242
BORZAGE, Frank, 541, 1049, 4234
BOSTAN, Elisabeta, 4349
BOULTENHOUSE, Charles, 1583, 2615
BOULTING, John (also see: John and Roy Boulting), 2700, 3026, 3776, 3846, 5045, 5390
BOULTING, John and Roy, 789, 1913, 1918, 2550, 5322, 5638
BOULTING, Roy, (also see: John and Roy Boulting) 803, 2200, 2640, 3252, 3921, 5410, 6345, 6711

BOURGUIGNON, Serge, 5273, 6130, 6745
BOURNE, Peter, 2148
BOURSEILLER, Antoine, 3997
BOWIE, Ronald, 6496
BOX, Muriel, 432, 716, 1878, 5174, 5779, 6092, 6566, 6678
BOYD, Arthur, 603
BOYER, Jacques, 5609
BOYER, Jean, 1260, 1720, 1971, 2804, 2980
BOYKO, Eugene, 2706
BRABANT, Charles, 4749, 4817
BRADLEY, David, 1684, 3280, 6689
BRADY, Hal (pseud. for Alfonso Brescia) 278
BRAGAGLIA, Carlo L., 2625, 4107, 6816
BRAHM, John, 1893, 2881
BRAKHAGE, Stan, 213, 262, 665, 980, 1637, 1876, 3766, 4069, 4328, 5003, 5804, 6695, 7034, 7192
BRAMBLE, A.V., 5731
BRAND, Albert, 2970
BRANDO, Marlon, 4648
BRANDON, Liane, 225
BRANDT, Henry, 3692, 4038
BRANNON, Fred C., 4150, 5502
BRASS, Tinto, 6351
BRAULT, Michel, 39, 4991, 5632
BRAUN, Harold, 2393, 3358
BRAUNBERGER, Pierre, 824, 4793
BRAZZI, Rossano (Occasional pseud. is Edward Ross) 1065, 5076
BREAKSTON, George, 730, 3979
BRECHER, Irving 5451
BREER, ROBERT, 978, 3029, 3199, 3906
BRENNER, Joseph, 4368
BRENTON, Guy, 6481
BRESCIA, Alfonso (see: Hal Brady)
BRESLER, Jerry, 5956
BRESLOW, Mark, 3434
BRESSON, Robert, 306, 1352, 1565, 1968, 3916, 4257, 4890, 5105, 6637
BRETHERTON, Howard, 7104
BRICKEN, Jules, 1685, 1865
BRIDGES, Alan, 17, 3110
BRIGNONE, Guido, 1369, 4354, 6175
BRILL, Richard, 6332
BRITTAIN, Donald, 512, 4074
BROCKWAY, Merrill, 6401
BROMBERGER, Herve, 1357, 2232
BROMLY, Alan, 183, 2110
BROOK, Paul, 4184
BROOK, Peter, 470, 3361, 3690, 3985, 6263
BROOKE, Ralph, 653
BROOKS, Mel, 5051
BROOKS, Richard, 405, 623, 805, 968, 975, 1284, 1642, 1767, 2639, 3045, 3469, 3491, 3688, 5052, 5892,

6022, 6156, 6198
BROOKS, Thor, 259, 3536
BROUGHTON, James, 457, 4946
BROWER, Otto, 1524
BROWN, Bruce, 1795, 4625
BROWN, Clarence, 3108
BROWN, Howard, 4043
BROWN, Karl, 5987
BROWN, Lawrence, 4906
BROWNING, Tod, 2192, 6786
BROWNLOW, Kevin, 3154
BRUCKMAN, Clyde, 2287
BRUSATI, Franco, 1596
BRYAN, Julian (var. sp.: Julien Bryan) 165, 3538, 5235, 5429, 5431, 7246
BRYANT, Gerard, 6552, 6554
BRYANT, William A., 4737
BRYNCH, Zbynek, 1993, 5819, 6615

BUCHANAN, Larry, 2195
BUCHS, Julio, 821, 4555
BUCKALEW, Bethel G., 492
BUCKNELL, Robert G., 4239
BULAJIC, Velijko, 415, 2795, 4520
BULLINS, Ed., 614
BUÑUEL, LUIS, 52, 480, 809, 1279, 1564, 1868, 4114, 4247, 4389, 4619, 5250, 5781, 6646, 6911, 7351
BURGE, Stuart, 3282, 4111, 4720, 6341
BURNETT, Hugh, 6997
BURNFORD, Paul, 6452
BURSTALL, Tim, 4757, 5047
BURTON, John Nelson, 4400
BURTON, Richard, 1616, 2606
BUSHELL, Anthony, 184, 6308
BUSHELMAN, John, 795, 5766, 5858
BUTE, Mary Ellen, 2015
BUTLER, David, 1123, 1149, 2345, 3371, 5296
BUTLER, Robert, 389, 2573, 5525
BUZZELL, Edward, 4023

CBS NEWS, 1813, 2303, 2659, 2942, 2981, 5957, 6291, 7052
CACOYANNIS, Michael, 1414, 1762, 2348, 4046, 4723, 6001, 6654, 6999, 7187, 7393
CADEC, Paul, 649
CAGNEY, James, 5734
CAHN, Edward L., 449, 735, 858, 1118, 1327, 1638, 2048, 2168, 2226, 2258, 2555, 2558, 2565, 2572, 2842, 3068, 3093, 3120, 3167, 3214, 4304, 4522, 4606, 4687, 4963, 5316, 5582, 6101, 6435, 6687, 6866, 6964, 7081, 7319
CAIANO, Mario, 258, 1705, 1996
CALEF, Henri, 1943
CAMERINI, Mario, 169, 316, 2823, 3297, 3488, 5418, 5601, 6752, 7139

DIRECTORS

CAMIEL, Eric, 5292
CAMMELL, Donald, 4858
CAMPANILE, Pasquale Festa, 44, 1031, 2341, 3572, 3872, 7117
CAMPOGALLIANI, Carlo, 2442, 3810, 4109, 5899, 6182
CAMUS, Marcel, 607, 1682, 2235
CAP, Franz, 3100
CAPOLINO, Eduardo, 1722
CAPRA, Frank, 2819, 4139, 4958
CAPRIOLI, Vittorio, 3617
CAPUANO, Luigi, 3610, 4347, 5259
CARAYANNIS, Costas, 2293
CARBONNAUX, Norbert, 879
CARDIFF, Jack, 1381, 2359, 3098, 3607, 3612, 3680, 4322, 5534, 5906, 7025, 7333
CARLE, Gilles, 5197, 6890
CARLISLE, Robert, 5872
CARLSEN, Henning, 979, 2941, 4849
CARLSON, Richard, 237, 3331, 5450
CARNE, Marcel, 1799, 2884, 3254, 6350, 6640, 7362
CARR, James, 212
CARR, Thomas, 954, 2582, 6104
CARRAS, Anthony, 4686
CARRERAS, Enrique, 4033
CARRERAS, Michael, 1330, 3700, 3975, 4819, 5002, 5510, 5832, 5997, 7055
CARRIER, Rick, 6055
CARSTAIRS, John Paddy, 552, 1047, 1532, 3290, 3939, 4653, 5966, 6558, 6661, 6801, 7040
CARTIER, Rudolph, 4818
CASS, Henry, 648, 2610, 2637, 3468
CASSAVETES, John, 1043, 1895, 2953, 4127, 5679, 6560
CASTELLANI, Renato, 859, 2320, 4130, 5362, 6719
CASTELLARI, Enzio G., 3340
CASTLE, William, 150, 844, 2834, 2905, 2993, 3555, 3799, 4168, 4466, 4607, 5054, 5946, 6042, 6387, 6388, 6521, 7079, 7396
CATES, Gil, 5309
CATES, Joseph, 1941, 2358
CAVALCANTI, Alberto, 2027, 2126, 6362
CAVALIER, Alain, 1002
CAVANI, Liliana, 882
CAVARA, Paolo, 3893, 7149
CAWSTON, Richard, 6404
CAYETTE, André, 136, 162, 1871, 3291, 4144, 4807, 6553, 6716, 7015
CECCHINI, Giogio, 4203
CERCHIO, Fernando, 1112, 2410, 2686, 5117
CEREO, Ferrucio, 4755
CERVI, Antonio, 4191, 6620
CHABROL, Claude, 1, 314, 446, 449, 529, 692, 718, 1004, 1242, 1969, 2411, 3449, 4700, 4796, 5424, 5634, 6379, 6405
CHABUKIANI, Vakhtang, 364
CHAFFEY, Don, 767, 1267, 1289, 1483, 2083, 2528, 2865, 3201, 3202, 3248, 3947, 4050, 4391, 4658, 5023, 5121, 6447, 6709, 6878, 7027
CHAITIN, Norman, 5846
CHAMPION, Gower, 4335
CHANDLER, John, 5835
CHAPLIN, Charles, 1010, 1089, 1098, 1230, 1639, 2426, 3357, 3605, 4185, 4217, 4904, 5736
CHARON, Jacques, 2073
CHENAL, Pierre, 4459, 4474, 5798
CHERCHIO, Fernando, 1494
CHERTOK, Harvey, 5650
CHIAVRELI, Mikhail, 1908
CHKEIDZE, Rezo, 1950
CHMIELEWSKI, Tadevsz, 1843
CHOMSKY, Marvin, 1844
CHOOLUCK, Leon, 6431
CHRISTENSEN, Benjamin, 1537, 4180, 7211
CHRISTENSEN, Carlos Hugo, 6892
CHRISTENSEN, Nils Reinhardt, 4815
CHRISTIAN-JAQUE, 41, 276, 324, 619, 720, 887, 1433, 1588, 1666, 1778, 1920, 3511, 3781, 3824, 4372, 5140, 5913, 5925
CHRISTOPHE, Jean, 4649
CHUKHRAI, Grigori (var. sp.: Grigory Choukhrai), 356, 1109, 6340, 6344
CHYTILOVA, Vera, 1349, 2229, 4839
CIAMPI, Yves, 2752, 4045, 5830, 6498, 6747
CLAIR, René, 112, 451, 486, 1517, 1976, 2483, 3168, 3719, 4978, 5763, 6437
CLARK, Bruce, 5816
CLARK, James B., 166, 557, 1636, 1701, 2092, 3144, 4176, 4332, 4651, 5439, 5752, 6881
CLARK, Kenneth, 1101
CLARKE, Robert, 2765
CLARKE, Shirley, 784, 1181, 1197, 4984, 5532, 5828
CLAUS, Hugo, 6877
CLAVELL, James, 2045, 3494, 6536, 6956, 7098
CLAXTON, William F., 1498, 3512, 5970, 7343
CLAYTON, Jack, 506, 3088, 4726, 5079, 5371
CLAYTON, John, 6354
CLAYTON, William, 3188
CLEARY, William, 2825
CLEMENT, Dick, 4721, 5668
CLEMENT, René, 305, 1400, 2308, 3133, 3219, 3265, 3758, 4051, 5086, 5290, 6397, 6967

CLOCHE, Maurice (var. sp.: Maurke Cloche) 2379, 6915
CLOUZOT, Henri-Georges, 1201, 1551, 2208, 4888, 5035, 5098, 6675, 6947
CLOWES, St. John L., 4500
COCHRAN, Steve, 6262
COCTEAU, Jean, 84, 481, 4713, 6313
COE, Fred, 4059, 6424
COE, Peter, 3650
COGHILL, Neville, 1616
COHEN, Nathan, 5900
COHEN, Norman, 1345, 3657, 6495
COHEN, Robert Carl, 4201
COLEMAN, Herbert, 402, 4986
COLETTI, Duilio, 2689, 2717, 2896, 6578, 6766
COLL, Julio, 4376, 5097, 7071
COLLA, Richard A., 7391
COLLERAN, Bill, 7189
COLLIER, James F., 6715
COLLINS, Gunther, 3268
COLLINS, Warren, 4308
COLLINSON, Peter, 3670, 4846, 6806, 7317
COLPI, Henri, 1130, 3667
COMENCINI, Luigi, 453, 761, 817, 1850, 2165, 2701
COMFORT, Lance, 427, 762, 1545, 2490, 3641, 3923, 4081, 4285, 5790, 6586, 7361
COMMONS, David, 190
CONDE, Manuel, 2291
CONNELL, Barbara, 6499
CONNER, Bruce, 1214, 4265, 5245
CONRAD, William, 749, 3918, 4314, 6735
CONYERS, Darcy, 3886
COOK, Fielder, 544, 2831, 2927, 4827, 5069
COOKE, Alan, 4122
COOPER, Kenneth, 2474
COOPER, Merian C., 2158
COPELAND, Jack L., 1463, 2732
COPELAND, Jodie, 140
COPPOLA, Francis Ford, 1478, 2014, 2412, 5156, 7369
CORBUCCI, Sergio, 1457, 1709, 2721, 4126, 4385, 5831
CORMAN, Roger, 295, 654, 814, 1265, 2278, 2671, 2902, 2923, 3107, 3498, 3632, 3809, 4030, 4919, 5005, 5175, 5203, 5459, 5579, 5706, 5818, 6205, 6252, 6298, 6549, 6595, 6644, 6879, 6935, 6985, 6998, 7145, 7294, 7353
CORNELIUS, Henry, 2290, 2963, 3507, 4418, 4820
CORNFIELD, Hubert, 4450, 5011, 6385
CORNELL, Jonas, 2534, 2934, 3597
CORT, Harvey, 2495, 6928
COSTA, Mario, 423, 596, 992, 5118, 5146, 5794
COSTA-GAVRAS, 1174, 5725, 5840, 7379
COTTAFAVI, Vittorio, 1075, 2443, 2741, 2742, 3537, 6994
COUFFER, Jack, 3363, 4475, 5305
COURNOT, Michel, 2281
COUSTEAU, Jacques-Yves, 5774, 7280
COUTARD, Raoul, 2814
COWAH, Will, 533, 6376
COYLE, John, 1409
COYNE, James, 923
CRABTREE, Arthur, 1989, 2861, 5104, 6046
CRANE, Kenneth, 2597, 3979, 4218, 7078
CRAVEN, Thomas, 6759
CRAVERI, M., 3699
CRICHTON, Charles, 404, 419, 736, 1600, 2096, 2683, 3506, 3507, 3930, 6383, 6525, 7182
CRISP, Donald, 1649
CROMWELL, John, 2409, 4049
CRONENBERG, David, 1278, 6007
CROSLAND, Alan, 4379, 4637
CRUM, Jim, 4546
CRUMP, Owen, 988, 1218
CRUZE, James, 1244
CUKOR, George, 24, 526, 710, 871, 1011, 1394, 1742, 2723, 3163, 3292, 3556, 4018, 4320, 4822, 4883, 5984, 7155
CUNHA, Richard, 2186, 2323, 2350, 4151, 5702
CUNY, Louis, 485
CURNICK, David, 3577
CURREY, Jack, 5416
CURTEIS, Ian, 5055
CURTIS, Dan, 4446
CURTIS, Jack, 2081
CURTIZ, Michael, 50, 511, 715, 765, 768, 1015, 1148, 1746, 2178, 2624, 3356, 2937, 4346, 4517, 5067, 5530, 6819, 7045, 7108, 7349
CUSHMAN, Ralph, 5577
CZINNER, Paul, 684, 1646, 5364, 5384, 5400

DA COSTA, Morton, 308, 3142, 4306
DAALDER, Renee, 679
DABAT, Ghisha M., 5499
DADIRAS, Dimis, 4601
D'AILLY, Diederik, 3792
DALIANIDIS, Yiannis, 5999
DALLAMANO, Massimo (see: Max Dillman)
DAMIANI, Damiano, 265, 822, 1784, 2339, 7208
DANELIA, Georgy (var. sp: Georgi Danielewski) 563, 2547, 4491
DANIELEWSKI, Ted (var. sp.: Tad

Danielewski) 563, 2547, 4491
DANIELS, Harold, 1386, 6304
DANIELS, Marc, 4995
DANSKA, Herbert, 5297, 6161
DANTINE, Helmut, 6480
DARCNE, Robert, 503
DARCUS, Jack, 2499
DASSIN, Jules, 2682, 4356, 4401, 4430, 4872, 5059, 5293, 6149, 6282, 6571, 6812, 7094
DAUGHERTY, Herschel, 3590
DAVES, Delmer, 349, 420, 1248, 1479, 1698, 2623, 3373, 3496, 4799, 5361, 5938, 6112, 6150, 6238, 7364
DAVID, Harold, 908
DAVIES, Valentine, 499
DAVIS, Allan, 1121
DAVIS, Charles, 2311
DAVIS, Desmond, 2367, 4421, 4809, 5850, 6506, 6757
DAVIS, Eddie, 4770
DAVIS, Hassoldt, 5910
DAVIS, Peter, 5606, 6073
DAWSON, Anthony (pseud. for Antonio Margheriti) 421, 959, 2403, 2429, 3592, 3674, 5833, 6975, 7169, 7358
DAY, Robert, 674, 865, 1207, 2029, 2672, 3581, 4699, 5699, 6231, 6234, 6237, 6743
DE AGOSTINI, Fabio, 548
DE ANTONIO, Emile, 145, 3062, 4116, 4960, 5425
DE BROCA, Philippe, 134, 941, 1522, 2384, 3245, 3364, 3723, 3894, 4612, 5634, 6326, 6808
DE CHALONGE, Christian, 6937
DE CORDOVA, Frederick, 2187, 3021
DE FELICE, Linello, 77, 1188, 1189
DE FEO, Francesco, 5031
DE FILIPPO, Eduardo, 2147, 5639, 5728
DE FINA, Don, 6073
DE HIRSCH, Storm, 2465
DE LA CERDA, Clemente, 5784
DE LA PARRA, Pim, 4571
DE LA PATELLIERE, Denys, 918, 3989, 4717, 4987, 5405, 6245, 6346, 6809
DE LACY, Philippe, 1083
DE LEON, Gerardo (var. sp.: Gerry De Leon) 1332, 6305, 7244
DE MARTINO, Alberto, 1591, 2853, 4695, 5593, 5934, 6647
DE MILLE, Cecil B. 2515, 5754, 6276
DE PALMA, Brian, 2527, 4279, 7031
DE PAOLA, Alessio, 1030
DE POTIER, Adrian, 1686
DE RENZY, ALEX, 2808
DE ROCHEMONT, Richard, 2436, 7189
DE SANTIS, Giuseppe, 592, 3169, 5333
DE SETA, Vittorio, 375, 6799
DE SICA, Vittorio, 72, 530, 676, 1172,

2275, 2424, 3076, 4011, 4141, 4921, 5542, 6132, 6315, 6746, 6754, 7212, 7238, 7309, 7363
DE TOTH, André, 1407, 2423, 2903, 3942, 4209, 4213, 4242, 4933, 6726
DEARDEN, Basil, 279, 663, 2206, 2968, 3326, 3519, 3926, 3953, 4031, 4121, 4681, 4731, 4923, 4966, 5495, 5589, 5721, 5848, 6869, 6896, 6953, 7235
DECOIN, Henri, 456, 962, 1023, 1057, 2106, 3719, 6676, 7096
DEIN, Edward, 1331, 3526, 5643
DEL RUTH, Roy, 120, 7134
DELANNOY, Jean, 393, 456, 2408, 2939, 3096, 3719, 4190, 4569, 6185, 6410
DELGADO, Luis M., 1575
DELL, Jeffrey, 3921
DELVAUX, André, 3949
DEMICHELLI, Tulio, 5895
DEMING, Norman, 4745
DEMY, Jacques, 424, 3653, 4183, 5634, 6755, 7337
DENHAM, Reginald, 1935
DENIS, Armand, 6770
DERAY, Jacques, 711, 5295, 5797, 6327
DERBYSHEVA, L., 7267
DEREK, John, 4638
DEREN, Maya, 290, 1060, 4062, 4090, 5325, 7214
DEVENISH, Ross, 2407
DEVILLE, Michel, 433, 498, 985
DEW, Edward, 6084, 7193
DEXTER, John, 4901, 6906
DEXTER, Maury, 85, 709, 1403, 2020, 2647, 2778, 2900, 4024, 4125, 4964, 5085, 6144, 6958, 7341, 7357
DHERY, Robert, 479, 1224
DHOMME, Sylvan, 5634
DICKINSON, Thorold, 2796, 4994, 5116, 5590
DICKSON, Paul, 1390, 5504, 6762
DIENAR, Baruch, 6367
DIETERLE, William, 1766, 3848, 4622, 5566
DILLMAN, Max (pseud. for Massimo Dallamano), 373
DIMOPOULOS, Dino (var. sp.: Dinos Dimopoulos) 286, 2862, 5165
DINO, Abidine, 2407
DINOR, Todor, 1350
DISNEY, Walt, 67, 245, 1078, 3284, 3285, 3427, 3531, 3888, 4620, 4646, 4866, 5838, 5862, 6177, 6838, 7001, 7119
DITVOORST, Adriaan, 4781
DIZIKIRIKIS, George, 330
DMYTRYK, Edward, 129, 226, 660, 794, 860, 921, 1748, 1792, 2385, 2812, 3527, 4142, 4259, 5159,

(cont.)
5238, 5688, 5869, 6957, 6991,
7090, 7345
DOHENY, Lawrence F., 6254
DOLIN, Boris, 1084, 4412, 5428, 5517
DOMNICK, Ottomar, 3249
DONAN, Martin (see: Mario Donen)
DONEHUE, Vincent, 3665, 6134
DONEN, Mario (occasional pseud. is
Martin Donan), 5573
DONEN, Stanley, 242, 461, 1013, 1355,
1469, 2241, 2382, 2485, 3075,
3176, 3388, 4635, 4640, 4760,
5633, 5793, 5975, 6147, 6722
DONIGER, Walter, 2904, 5446, 6797
DONIOL-VALCROZE, Jacques, 2199,
2260, 3879, 6889
DONNER, Clive, 98, 2545, 2691, 2748,
3790, 4535, 5591, 5888, 7066
DONNER, Jorn (var. sp.: John Donner),
198, 605, 2645, 4350, 6534
DONNER, Richard, 5464, 6706, 7293
DONOHUE, Jack, 282, 323, 4015
DONOVAN, King, 5062
DONSKOI, Mark, 2468, 2471, 2692
DORFMAN, Ron, 2538
D'ORMESSON, Antoine, 6780
DOS SANTOS, Nelson Pereira, 6872
DOUCHET, Jean, 4796
DOUGHTEN Jr., Russell, 1979, 2871
DOUGLAS, Gordon, 394, 864, 1072,
1108, 1512, 1988, 2109, 2140,
2425, 2654, 3048, 3430, 5311,
5348, 5788, 5800, 5971, 5980,
6184, 6336, 6357, 6559, 6803,
7011, 7306, 7329
DOUGLAS, Robert, 4464
DOVSHENKO, Alexander, 1719, 1786
DOWNEY, Robert, 998, 4496, 5094
DRACH, Michel, 143, 7016
DRAKE, Oliver, 3789
DRASIN, Dan, 6122
DRASKOVIC, Boro, 2851
DREIFUSS, Arthur, 2123, 3275, 3457,
3579, 3732, 5101, 5317, 6515, 7354
DREVILLE, Jean, 857, 1635, 3441,
4524, 5639, 5940
DREYER, Carl (TH.), 1410, 2307,
4034, 4706, 4813, 6835
DROMGOOLE, Patrick, 1429
DU BOIS, Alberto, 4910
DUARTE, Anselmo, 2386
DUCHESNE, Louis, 5802
DUDKO, Apollinariy, 5839
DUDLEY, Carl, 5932
DUDREMET, Jean Charles, 3761
DUFFELL, Peter, 2907
DUHOUR, Clement, 3586
DUNLOP, Ian, 366, 1492
DUNN, Willie, 358
DUNNE, Philip, 628, 661, 2791, 3049,
3613, 5026, 6279, 6432, 6875, 7153

DUNNING, George, 7304
DUPONT, Frans, 4983, 5061
DURSTON, David, 2976
DUVIVIER, Julien, 200, 721, 835,
1520, 1550, 2821, 3635, 3928,
3995, 3996, 4278, 4988, 5257,
5258, 6768, 7232
DWAN, Allan, 1787, 3129, 4251, 5332,
5486
DWOSKIN, Steve, 6518
DYMON, Frankie, 1450
DZIEDZINA, Julian, 725

EADY, David, 1896, 3061, 6854
EAGLE, Arnold, 1724
EASON, B. Reeves, 3475, 6836
EASTMAN, Gordon, 2787
EASTWOOD, Clint, 4935
EDWARDS, Blake, 764, 1384, 1422,
1864, 2505, 2568, 2680, 2786,
4698, 4802, 4857, 4909, 5735,
6400, 7058, 7165
EISENSTEIN, Sergei, 525, 3182, 3183,
4574, 6072
EKK, Nikolai, 5337
ELDRIDGE, John, 752, 5544
ELFSTROM, Robert, 3233
ELKINS, Robert, 3823
ELORRIETA, Jose Maria (see: Joe
Lacy)
EMMER, Luciano, 565, 870, 1644,
3546, 4252, 4887, 5326, 6439, 7230
EMMETT, E.V.H., 152
EMSHWILLER, Ed., 2300, 3030, 5233,
5546, 6583
ENDFIELD, Cy., 1042, 1425, 2711,
2764, 3216, 4344, 5487, 5556,
5917, 7298
ENGEL, Morris, 3622, 3755, 7033
ENGLUND, George, 5760, 6749, 7381
ENRICO, Robert, 484, 3066, 3455,
7392
EPHRON, Henry, 5791
ERIKSEN, Dan, 4105
ERMAN, John, 3890
ERMLER, F., 6684
ERSKINE, Chester, 174
ESPINA, Jose Maria Font, 1554
ETAIX, Pierre, 268, 6103, 7378
EUSTACHE, Jean, 345
EVERNGAM, Howard, 5114

FABRI, Zoltan, 744, 3466, 4087, 6692
FABRIZI, Aldo, 4586, 6247
FAENZA, Roberto, 1824
FAINTSIMMER, Alexander, 2365
FAIRCHILD, William, 5767
FALCK, Ake, 6969, 7032
FANT, Kenne, 7253
FARALLA, William D. (var. sp.: William

D. Farella), 5209, 6717
FARELLA, William D. (see: William D. Farella)
FARIAS, Roberto, 6609
FARKAS, Nicholas, 6470
FARRAR, Anthony, 5787
FARROW, John, 337, 823, 2836, 3232, 6783
FASSBINDER, Rainer Werner, 3310
FEENEY, John, 3317
FEHER, Imre, 6128
FEINSTEIN, Barry, 7315
FEJER, Tamas, 1216
FELDHAUS-WEBER, Mary, 1561
FELIU, Jorge, 1554
FELIX, Louis, 2696
FELLINI, Federico, 531, 676, 1119, 1640, 1747, 1962, 1963, 3279, 3595, 3731, 4541, 6040, 6203, 6920
FELSENSTEIN, Walter, 1986
FELTHAM, Kerry, 2496
FENTON, Leslie, 6265
FERGUSON, Graeme, 3725, 5600
FERGUSON, Norman, 6433
FERNANDEZ, Emilio, 5387
FERNO, John, 5825
FERRER, Jose, 1128, 2503, 2774, 2961, 5264, 5740, 5991
FERRER, Mel, 1846, 2522
FERRERI, Marco, 235, 1180, 1576, 3501, 3964, 5108, 7072
FERRONI, Giorgio, 247, 4115, 6653
FETIN, V., 6912
FEUILLADE, Louis, 6834
FEVER, Mark, 2554
FILIPPO, Eduardo, 3387
FINLEY, George (pseud. for Giorgio Stegani), 33
FINNEY, Albert, 1019
FISCHER, O.W., 269
FISHER, Terence, 777, 1324, 1333, 1534, 1679, 2182, 2184, 2470, 2856, 2858, 2888, 2895, 3143, 3948, 4271, 4448, 4875, 5266, 6181
FLAHERTY, Robert, 3714
FLEISCHER, Richard, 372, 382, 516, 542, 714, 1032, 1169, 1250, 1615, 1925, 2353, 2644, 3483, 4377, 5602, 6280, 6355, 6572, 6697, 6880, 6898
FLEISCHMANN, Peter, 2949
FLEMING, Victor, 2448
FLEMYNG, Gordon, 1351, 1629, 2056, 2494, 3288, 3467, 5950
FLICKER, Theodore J., 5008, 6666
FLOREY, Robert, 1883
FLORIO, Aldo, 2046
FLYNN, John, 5620
FONDA, Peter, 2800
FONTAINE, Dick, 1672, 6243, 7175
FORBES, Bryan, 1435, 3370, 3423, 3668, 3842, 5561, 7103, 7106, 7288

FORD, Alexander (var. sp.: Aleksander Ford), 1753, 2026, 2039, 3402
FORD, Charles Henri, 3237
FORD, Derek, 2537, 7140
FORD, John, 1036, 1653, 2864, 2916, 2917, 3673, 3958, 4026, 4167, 4187, 5130, 5312, 5321, 5565, 5622, 5654, 6121, 6365, 6440, 6738, 6948, 7063, 7194, 7333, 7350
FORDE, Walter, 904, 4032
FOREMAN, Carl, 6870
FORLONG, Michael, 2519, 6019
FORMAN, Milos, 609, 2022, 3762, 6200
FORNBACHER, Helmut (see: Anthony Baker)
FORSBERG, Lars, 3200
FOSSE, Bob, 854, 6158
FOSTER, Harry, 3557
FOSTER, Harv, 2544
FOSTER, Lewis R., 5758, 6557
FOSTER, Norman, 790, 1398, 1399, 4384, 5758
FOWLER, Jr., Gene., 2267, 2747, 4708, 5191, 5738
FOWLER, Kell, 4654
FOWLEY, Douglas, 3815
FOX, Wallace, 4998
FRACASSI, Clemente, 83, 1809
FRAKER, William A., 4223
FRAMPTON, Hollis, 7394
FRANCIOLINI, Gianni, 456, 2376, 3158, 6882, 7022
FRANCIS, Coleman, 5827
FRANCIS, Freddie, 1438, 1628, 1678, 1856, 4273, 4469, 4783, 5075, 6358, 6579, 6612, 6650, 6714, 6845
FRANCISCI, Pietro, 304, 2740, 2744, 2746, 5748, 6995
FRANCO, Jesus (var. sp.: Jess Franco), 319, 1549, 4483, 6094
FRANJU, Georges, 1953, 2478, 2854, 3269, 5490, 6314, 6348, 6417
FRANK, Charles, 3106
FRANK, Hubert, 1608
FRANK, Melvin, 7, 831, 1235, 1898, 3203, 3405, 3598, 6044, 6319
FRANK, Robert, 441, 4057, 5078, 5785
FRANK, T.C. (pseud. for Tom Laughlin) 573, 704, 5064
FRANKEL, Cyril, 102, 1546, 1654, 3178, 3885, 3936, 4405, 4512, 5703, 6679, 6857
FRANKENHEIMER, John, 105, 578, 1870, 2058, 2480, 2591, 2866, 2997, 3967, 5572, 5637, 6608, 7355, 7356
FRANKLIN, James Wendell, 838
FRANKLIN, Sidley, 395
FRAZER, John, 4557
FREDA, Riccardo (occasional pseud. is Robert Hampton) 868, 1538, 1869,

(cont.)
2315, 2852, 5474, 6339, 7118
FREEDLAND, George, 4229
FREEDMAN, Joel E., 5815
FREEMAN, Robert, 5596, 6590, 7272
FREGONESE, Hugo, 231, 439, 1462, 2660, 3988, 5512
FRENCH, Harold, 1789, 3956, 4315, 5104, 5342, 6642
FREND, Charles, 104, 3521, 3669, 3856, 5411, 6662
FREUND, Karl, 3820
FREZ, Ilya, 1579
FRIED, Yan, 6685
FRIEDKIN, David, 2617
FRIEDKIN, William, 587, 741, 2197, 2457, 4460
FRIEDMAN, Serge, 1670
FRIEDMANN, Anthony, 396
FRIENDLY, Fred W., 5503
FRUCHTER, Norm, 6667
FUEST, Robert, 5, 168, 3289, 7291
FUKASAKA, Kinji (var. sp.: Finji Fukasaku), 2525, 6572
FUKI, Lugio, 4598
FUKUDA, Jun, 1731, 5897
FULCI, Lucio, 808
FULLER, Samuel, 1282, 2708, 2894, 4085, 4363, 5414, 5697, 5723, 6776, 6852
FUNT, Allen, 7059
FURIE, Sidney J., 236, 739, 1365, 1612, 1714, 3124, 3515, 3522, 3621, 4366, 5857, 6451, 7255, 7256

GAAL, Istvan, 3844
GAFFNEY, Robert, 2183
GAINVILLE, Rene, 7334
GAISSEAU, Pierre Dominique, 2060, 4678, 5394, 5824
GALLONE, Carmine, 940, 1645, 1944, 2805, 3826, 4096, 6581
GALLU, Samuel, 643, 3946
GANCE, Abel, 411, 6596
GANDY, Bern, 6143
GANNAWAY, Albert C., 3945, 4503, 4956
GANZER, Alvin, 1233, 3524, 6430, 7080
GARDNER, David., 4776
GARDNER, Robert, 713, 1426
GARFEIN, Jack, 1790, 5893
GARFIELD, Frank (pseud. for Franco Giraldi), 4129, 5642, 6807
GARNETT, Tay, 982, 1477, 3877, 4435, 5657
GARRETT, Oliver H.P., 910
GARRETT, Otis., 3431
GARRISON, Greg, 2760, 6741
GARY, Romain, 583
GASPARD-HUIT, Pierre, 2362, 4595

GAST, Michael, 2994
GATTI, Armand, 4618
GAURAS, 1174
GAVALDON, Robert, 519, 3637, 3802, 5698
GAYSON, Godfrey, 3443
GAZCON, Gilberto, 5145
GEALLIS, Jim, 3274
GEISSENDOERFER, Hans W., 3250
GENERO, Jack, 1945
GENOINO, Arnaldo, 2751
GENTILOMO, Giacomo, 1014, 2445, 3478
GEORGE, G.W., 3198
GEORGIADIS, Vassilis, 5211
GERARD, Charles, 1347, 1482
GERASIMOV, Sergei, 5129
GERENDASY, Dick, 6690
GERMI, Pietro, 584, 1113, 1603, 3938, 5599
GERONIMI, Clyde, 4655, 5838
GERRONE, Sergio, 4507
GERSHFIELD, Burton, 4547
GERSON, Barry, 6864
GERSTAD, Harry, 6386
GESSNER, Nicolas, 5890
GESSNER, Peter, 2007, 6510
GETINO, Octavio, 2848
GIANCHIUI, Paolo (see: Paul Maxwell)
GIANNETTI, Alfredo, 1801
GIANNINI, Ettore, 4390
GIBSON, Alan, 1269, 2464
GIBSON, Bill, 2115
GIELGUD, John, 2606
GIL, Rafael, 4138
GILBERT, Lewis, 36, 46, 97, 942, 952, 1310, 1354, 1973, 2209, 3694, 5183, 5559, 5662, 5796, 6502, 7321
GILBERT, Philip, 636
GILES, David, 1360
GILLIAT, Sidney, 1187, 2521, 3529, 3656, 4680, 5708, 5992, 6028
GILLING, John, 374, 641, 787, 1280, 1294, 2248, 2775, 3102, 3166, 3933, 3974, 4272, 4768, 4916, 4924, 5248, 5678, 7093
GILROY, Frank, 1504
GIMBEL, Peter, 668
GIRALDI, Franco (see: Frank Garfield)
GIRARD, Bernard, 271, 1428, 3821, 4803, 5283
GIROLAMI, Enzo (see: E.G. Rowland)
GIROSI, Marcello, 4222
GIST, Robert, 147
GLASCOCK, Baylis, 7017
GLASSER, Bernard, 5413, 5624
GLENVILLE, Peter, 455, 1159, 2885, 4058, 5030, 6105, 6295
GLEYZER, Raymundo, 4093
GLUECK, Wolfgang, 2054
GNAMM, Hans, 7268
GOBBI, Sergio, 5671

GODARD, Jean-Luc, 127, 371, 449, 769, 793, 903, 1054, 1190, 1928, 1970, 2002, 2253, 3835, 4028, 4612, 4662, 4796, 4869, 4898, 5634, 6079, 6592, 6736, 6926, 6929, 7037, 7185, 7231
GODFREY, Bob, 1605
GOETZ, John, 6758
GOLAN, Menahem, 3785, 3992, 6674, 7065
GOLD, Jack, 682, 3646, 5195
GOLDMAN, Peter Emmanuel, 1732
GOLDSTONE, James, 800, 2266, 3131, 3222, 3911, 5217, 7198
GOLDSTONE, Richard, 4494, 5923
GOLDWYN Jr., Samuel, 7348
GOLIK, Kresco, 2222
GOMEZ, Manuel Octavio, 5020
GONZALEZ, Servando, 2113, 7297
GOODE, Frederic, 2614, 4970, 6187
GOODMAN, Philip, 7020
GOODWINS, Leslie, 6215
GORDON, Bert I., 303, 729, 3853, 4894, 6575, 6984
GORDON, Lewis H., 5554
GORDON, Michael, 743, 1339, 2121, 2911, 3043, 4264, 4905, 4979, 6316, 6861
GORDON, Robert, 621, 1353, 5178
GORG, Alan, 5515
GORIKKER, Vladimir, 6680
GORLING, Lars, 2549
GOSLING, Nicholas, 1688
GOSSAGE, John, 1915
GOTTLIEB, Carl, 989
GOTTLIEB, Franz Josef, 4134, 4874, 7252
GOTTSCHALK, Robert, 1366
GOULD, Terry, 3748
GOULDER, Stanley, 5769
GOULDING, Edmund, 3990, 6256
GRACE, William, 6550
GRAEFF, Tom., 6260
GRAHAM, Peter, 4169
GRAHAM, William A., 2843, 6088, 7003
GRANGIER, Gilles, 2277, 3863, 4206, 4339, 4426, 4608, 5935
GRANIER-DE FERRE, Pierre, 1115, 4790
GRAS, E., 3699
GRASSHOFF, Alexander, 3197, 7323
GRAU, Jorge, 3745
GRAUMAN, Walter, 2975, 3429, 5147, 5812
GRAVER, Gary, 1774
GRAY, John, 366
GRAY, Mike, 4294
GRAYSON, Godfrey, 5943
GREAVES, William, 3054, 4997
GREDE, Kjell, 2661, 2933
GREEN, Guy, 194, 1491, 1555, 3591, 3695, 3867, 4002, 4047, 4823, 5434, 6954
GREEN, Joseph, 748
GREEN, Walon, 2733, 5953
GREENE, David Allen, 1151, 2995, 5569, 5741, 6043
GREENE, Felix, 1048, 1319, 3092
GREENE, Herbert, 1212
GREENE, Philip, 2676
GREENSPAN, Henry, 5231
GREFE, William, 1446, 6011, 7161
GREGORETTI, Ugo, 448, 4407
GREMILLON, Jean, 3783, 5241
GREVILLE, Edmond T., 846, 2619, 2906, 6273, 6274, 7150
GRIECO, Sergio, 2943, 3765, 4473, 4915
GRIES, Tom., 2354, 2947, 4035, 4553, 4656, 7174
GRIFFI, Giuseppe Patroni, 3991
GRIFFITH, Charles B., 2130
GRIFFITH, D.W., 586, 1907, 2694, 6078
GRIMALDI, Hugo, 284, 2333, 2936, 2969, 4310
GRINTER, Brad F., 2082
GROFE, Jr., Ferde, 6990
GRONLYKKE, Sven, 6416
GROOPER, Cechet, 6209
GROSBARD, Ula, 6086, 7121
GROSS, Jerry, 6255
GROSSMAN, Richard, 5222
GROULX, Gilles, 967
GRUNEWALD, Allan, 4471
GRZIMEK, Bernhard (also see: Bernhard and Michael Grzimek), 4506
GRZIMEK, Bernhard and Michael (also see: Bernhard Grzimek), 5619
GUARNIERI, Mauro, 2679
GUENETTE, Robert, 6631, 7178
GUERRA, Ruy, 1516, 6160
GUERRIERI, Romolo, 3243, 6157, 6284
GUERRINI, Mino, 3718
GUEST, Val, 283, 452, 873, 924, 949, 1412, 1750, 1867, 2713, 3173, 3221, 3582, 5102, 5103, 6016, 6804, 7024, 7076, 7095, 7310
GUGGENHEIM, Charles, 2506
GUILFOYLE, Paul, 6310
GUILLERMIN, John, 664, 780, 1418, 1756, 2570, 3001, 4398, 4748, 5167, 6232, 6236, 6600, 6970, 7126
GUITRY, Sacha, 3757, 5399, 6914
GUNN, Gilbert, 1213, 2374
GURNEY, Robert, 1739
GUTHRIE, Tyrone, 4580

HAANSTRA, Bert, 1921, 2937, 5327, 6002
HAAS, Charles, 440, 555, 2381, 4932,

(cont.)
6109, 7152
HAAS, Hugo, 706, 3648, 4456
HABIB, Ralph, 456, 3652
HACKENSCHMIED, Alexander, 4090
HAECHLER, Horst, 270
HAEDRICH, Rolf, 6018
HAESAERTS, Paul, 2427
HAGGARD, Piers, 650, 7030
HAGMANN, Stuart, 476, 6064
HAGUET, Andre, 6026
HAIG, Roul, 4604
HALAS, John, 195, 2809
HALDANE, Don, 4475
HALE, Jeffrey, 2509
HALE, William, 2563, 3260
HALEY, Jack, 3737
HALL, Alexander, 2136, 2419, 6800
HALL, Peter, 4106, 4856, 6445, 7263
HALLDOFF, Jan, 1697, 3412, 3644, 5389
HALLENBECK, E. Darrell, 4661
HALLER, Daniel, 1533, 4896, 7160
HALLSTROM, Roland, 7346
HAMEIRI, Y., 5811
HAMER, Robert, 1511, 3151, 3350, 5526, 5538, 5942, 6535
HAMILTON, Guy, 413, 509, 1018, 1136, 1540, 1557, 2239, 2437, 3925, 3981, 4286, 4805, 5308, 6589
HAMILTON, Nancy, 6761
HAMMID, Alexander, 4064, 4994
HAMMOND, Peter, 5954
HAMPTON, Robert (see: Riccardo Freda)
HANCOCK, John, 3558
HANDEL, Leo A., 5690
HAN-HSIANG, Li, 1783
HANI, Susumu, 775, 4374, 5700
HANNA, Nancy, 1605
HANNA, William, 2761, 3910
HANOUN, Marcel, 5782
HARLAN, Viet, 3845, 6384
HARLING, Don, 1911
HARLOW, John, 238
HARNACK, Falk, 161, 3132, 6270
HARRINGTON, Curtis, 2262, 4461, 5112, 7068
HARRIS, Hilary, 2790, 4479
HARRIS, James B., 462
HARRISON, Norman, 3065
HARRYHAUSEN, Roy, 3202
HART, Harvey, 839, 2145, 6104, 6163
HART, Malcolm, 254
HARTFORD-DAVIS, Robert, 618, 1209, 2449, 5488, 5507, 7305
HARTL, Karl, 3576
HARTOG, Simon, 3891
HARVEY, Anthony, 1716, 3608, 6363
HARVEY, Herk, 917
HARVEY, Laurence, 994, 1362
HAS, Wojciech, 2918, 3793, 5496

HASHIMOTO, Shinobu, 2998
HASKIN, Byron, 249, 712, 896, 1185, 2218, 3215, 3630, 3676, 4993, 5349, 5615, 6626, 6987
HASS, Hans, 6767, 6769
HATHAWAY, Henry, 1094, 1488, 2041, 2172, 2215, 2274, 2916, 3484, 3533, 4396, 4420, 4526, 4563, 5027, 5141, 5149, 5651, 5729, 5907, 6669, 6699, 7233, 7370
HATHAWAY, Terence, 2219
HATTON, Maurice, 4999
HAWKS, Howard, 558, 559, 1757, 2299, 2666, 3445, 3977, 4211, 4563, 5310, 5313
HAYDEN, Russell, 7082
HAYERS, Sidney, 834, 1091, 2008, 4162, 4835, 5924, 6403, 6442, 6617
HEARD, Paul, 2841
HECHT, Ben, 22, 1276
HECKFORD, Michael, 1298
HEIFITZ, Joseph, 540, 1404, 3060, 3438
HEINZ, Richard, 4755
HEISLER, Stuart, 836, 2811, 3140, 5981, 6402
HELLER, Anthony, 1311
HELLMAN, Monte, 336, 434, 6728
HELLSTROM, Gunnar, 4370
HELMICK, Paul, 6469
HEMENWAY, Carl, 5222
HENDRICKS, William L., 3230
HENNING-JENSEN, Astrid and Bjarne, 1599, 4831, 4962
HENREID, Paul, 671, 1432, 2380, 3639
HENRIKSON, Anders, 4588
HERBST, I., 5811
HERD, David, 5862
HERMAN, Gerald, 7204
HERMAN, Jean, 6126
HERMAN, Norman, 4204, 6544
HERRINGTON, Ramsey, 2122
HERSCHENSON, Bruce, 7301
HERSKO, Janos, 1553, 3127
HERTZ, Nathan, 300
HERZ, Juraj, 1268
HERZOG, Werner, 1845, 1942, 3525
HESSLER, Gordon, 971, 3485, 4568, 5547
HEUSCH, Paolo, 1415
HEYER, John, 338
HEYERDAHL, Thor, 3409
HEYES, Douglas, 444, 3393
HEYNOWSKI, Walter, 3503
HIBBS, Jesse, 5279, 6532, 7199
HIBLER, Winston, 1021
HICKOX, Douglas, 1808, 3175
HIKEN, Nat, 3724, 3741
HILL, Colin, 1380
HILL, Dennis, 6023
HILL, George Roy, 847, 2677, 4860, 6418, 6602, 7274

HILL, Jack, 539, 640
HILL, James, 595, 703, 894, 1208, 1764, 1848, 3391, 6083, 6636
HILL, Jerome, 93, 2484, 4682, 5480
HILLER, Arthur, 149, 911, 2870, 3746, 4137, 4733, 4843, 4941, 4971, 5060, 6408, 6491, 6538, 7073
HILLIARD, Richard, 3664, 6118
HILLYER, Lambert, 400
HINDLE, Will, 1053, 7006
HINDS, Anthony, 1677, 6059
HINKLE, Robert, 4614
HISAMATSU, Seija, 4614
HITCHCOCK, Alfred, 580, 1552, 2972, 3437, 3651, 3954, 4006, 4525, 4536, 5072, 5188, 5302, 5376, 5436, 5968, 6056, 6529, 6570, 6576, 6665, 6765, 6856, 7289
HNIZDOVSKY, Jacques, 5713
HOBBS, C. Fredric, 5381
HOBL, Pavel, 1606
HOCKMAN, Ned, 5986
HODGES, Mike, 2310
HOELLERING, George, 2868, 4290
HOEY, Michael, 4388
HOFBAUER, Ernst, 5208
HOFFMAN, David, 3362
HOFFMAN, Jerzy, 1141, 6522
HOFFMANN, Kurt, 244, 1177, 2102, 5939
HOFSEES, John, 4762, 4950
HOGLAND, Gunnar, 4326, 4570
HOLD, JOHN (see: Mario Bava)
HOLDEN, Anton, 255
HOLE, Jr., William J., 1544, 2157, 2318, 5936, 6707, 7325
HOLMES, Cecil, 3712
HOLT, Joel, 3304
HOLT, Seth, 1364, 4375, 4548, 5548, 5993, 6239
HOMOKI-NAGY, I., 2135
HONDA, Inoshiro, 298, 408, 1508, 2181, 2414, 2415, 2592, 2597, 3359, 3360, 4256, 4342, 5355, 7312
HOOD, Randall, 6730
HOPPER, Dennis, 1727, 3473
HOPPER, Jerry, 670, 1852, 3841, 4156, 4351, 5043
HORIUCHI, Manao, 604
HORMAND, Annelise, 5605
HORN, Leonard J., 3701, 3849, 5356
HORNER, Harry, 4408, 5214
HOSBERG, Rolf, 3889
HOSSEIN, Robert, 4434, 4441, 4549, 6574, 7137
HOST, Per, 3476
HOUGH, John, 6097
HOUWER, Rob, 3323
HOVEN, Adrian, 3681
HOVING, Hattum, 5452
HOWARD, Cy, 3756
HOWARD, Noel, 3989

HOWE, James Wong, 3119
HU, Sang, 3569, 5693
HUBLEY, John (also see: John and Faith Hubley), 1744, 4590
HUBLEY, John and Faith (also see: John Hubley), 7397
HUGH, R. John, 3614, 6588
HUGHES, Ken, 257, 949, 1056, 1287, 3204, 3226, 4458, 4585, 5847, 6045, 6638, 7135
HUGHES, Robert, 5347
HUILLET, Daniele, 4424
HULTEN, 1346
HUMBERSTONE, Bruce, 3840, 6235
HUMBERT, Humphrey, 54
HUME, Kenneth, 3185
HUNDT, Charles J., 5786
HUNNEBELLE, Andre (var. sp.: André Hunnebelle), 890, 1926, 4343, 4566, 5677
HUNT, Peter, 4627
HUNTER, Max (see: Massimo Pupillo)
HUNTINGTON, Lawrence, 4166, 6813, 6942
HURST, Brian Desmond, 473, 616, 1063, 1368, 4937, 5778, 6657
HURWITZ, Harry, 5056
HUSSEIN, Waris, 4072, 6318
HUSTON, John, 68, 275, 384, 442, 527, 949, 2205, 2697, 3324, 3417, 3616, 3898, 4146, 4179, 4258, 4454, 5201, 5223, 5375, 5789, 6629, 6782, 6959, 7023
HUTTON, Brian, 1932, 2755, 3315, 4753, 5873, 7087, 7166
HUTTON, Robert, 5843
HUYEN, Le Ba, 6271
HYATT, Donald, 3510

IANZELO, Tony, 217
ICHAC, Marcell, 202
ICHIKAWA, Kon, 23, 125, 832, 1803, 2023, 4578, 6545
IMAMURA, Shohei, 3090, 4484, 4975
INAGAKI, Hiroshi, 376, 1074, 1375, 3406, 5136, 5301, 5592, 7102
INDOVINA, F., 4612
INGRAMS, Michael, 4763
INGSTER, Boris, 6053
INTRATOR, Jerald, 5498
IOSSELIANI, Otar, 6843
IRELAND, O'Dale, 1385, 2781
IRVINE, Louva, 6446
IRVING, John, 920
IRVING, Richard, 3149
ISAAC, Alberto, 4621
ISAMENDI, Antonio, 53
ISASI-ISASMENDI, J. Antonio, 5275, 6328, 6360
ISHIHARA, Shintaro, 3720
ISHMUHAMEDOV, Elier, 4425

IVENS, Joris, 1928, 5659, 6427
IVORY, James, 687, 2583, 2910, 5686

JACK, Del, 1167
JACKSON, Larry E., 1217, 5334
JACKSON, Pat, 588, 1665, 1789, 1967, 4502, 5645, 6904, 7109
JACKSON, Wilfred, 1080
JACOB, Kurt, 4559
JACOBS, Jimmy, 3535
JACOBS, Werner, 469, 2551, 2702
JACOBSEN, Johan, 6051
JACOPETTI, Gualtiero, 63, 4200, 7248
JAEGER, Kobi, 3298
JAGLOM, Henry, 5447
JAKUBISKO, Jufo, 1496
JAMES, Alan, 3778, 6607
JANCSO, Miklos, 1179, 1745, 4338, 5199, 5395, 5762, 5803
JANIC, Tomo, 608
JARROTT, Charles, 204
JARVA, Risto, 500, 7264
JASNY, Vojtech (var. sp.: Voltech Jasny), 951, 1851, 4912
JASON, Leigh, 1059
JAYET, René, 7029
JEDRYKO, Stanislaw, 5967
JEFFRIES, Lionel, 5154
JENNINGS, Humphrey, 2024
JERSEY, William, 6499
JESSUA, Alain, 3347, 3587
JEWISON, Norman, 260, 1077, 1984, 2150, 2254, 3057, 5432, 5608, 6464
JIRES, Jaromil, 1304, 2025, 3244, 4839, 6821
JISSOJI, Norman, 6415
JOANNON, Leo, 1474
JODOROWSKY, Alexandro, 1760, 6222
JOFFE, Alex, 280, 686, 1919, 2144, 3042, 5291, 5294
JOHNSON, Floch, 3871
JOHNSON, Lamont, 1243, 2559, 3410, 3812
JOHNSON, Marlin, 6413
JOHNSON, Nunnally, 185, 620, 2919, 3924, 3959, 4457, 4596, 6438
JONES, Chuck, 4877
JONES, Eugene, 1891
JONES, Harmon C., 437, 827, 1667, 7222
JONES, Le Roi, 614
JONES, Robert, 923
JONES, Winston, 6784, 7195
JORDAN, Larry, 2792
JOSIPOVICI, Jean, 2079
JOURDAN, Erven, 2599
JUGERT, Rudolf, 3744, 5709
JULIANO, Joseph R., 302
JUNG-ALSEN, Kurt, 6032
JURACEK, Pavel, 1849, 3251, 5029
JURAN, Nathan, 1723, 2030, 2087,

2451, 3190, 3446, 5666, 5749
JUTRA, Claude, 4196, 6593, 7282

KACHYNA, Karel, 1124
KACZENDER, George, 1660, 4884, 7372
KADAR, Jan, 42, 5733
KADISON, Ellis, 963, 7376
KALATOZOV, Mikhail, 1253, 5218, 6764, 6791
KANE, Joseph, 3950, 4538, 6604
KANIN, Garson, 7089
KANTER, Hal, 4642
KANTER, Richard, 7163
KAPLAN, Nelly, 3, 1981, 2360
KAPLAN, Richard, 1761
KAPLUNOVSKY, V., 897
KAPOOR, Raj., 699
KARABASZ, Kazimierz, 4850
KARDAR, Oaejay, 1411
KARDISH, Larry, 5845
KARDOS, Ferenc, 2530
KARLSON, Phil, 2566, 2719, 2850, 3325, 3329, 4880, 5163, 5527, 5595, 5765, 6479, 6501, 7285, 7335
KARMEN, Roman, 1084, 1419, 2501, 3137, 5428
KARN, Bill, 2051, 3797
KASS, Peter, 6509
KAST, Pierre, 475, 5567
KASTLE, Leonard, 2839
KATANIAN, Vassily, 1084, 5428, 5626
KATZIN, Lee H., 2699, 3518, 7060
KAUFMAN, Millard, 1191
KAUFMAN, Philip, 2438, 2504
KAUTNER, Helmut, 61, 892, 1543, 3458, 4215, 5982, 5253, 5254, 6049
KAWALEROWICZ, Jerzy (var sp.: Jerry Kawalerowicz) 3830, 4255, 4463, 4878
KAY, Gilbert, 5576
KAY, Roger, 855, 5732
KAYE, Stanton, 753
KAYLOR, Robert, 1485
KAZAN, Elia, 144, 256, 326, 1721, 1884, 3943, 4636, 4771, 4911, 5949, 6070, 6924, 7164
KAZAN, Mrs. Elia (see: Barbara Loden)
KAZANSKY, G., 2101
KEATON, Buster, 2287
KEIGHLEY, William, 6069
KELLER, Harry, 754, 1405, 1964, 3046, 5653, 5809, 6003, 6214, 6216, 6930
KELLINO, Roy, 5776
KELLOGG, Ray, 2324, 2517, 3341, 4319
KELLY, Gene., 2335, 2642, 2727, 3122, 3176, 4635, 5793, 6683
KELLY, James, 435
KELLY, Ron, 991, 3367

DIRECTORS

KEMENY, John, 512
KENDALL, Nancy, 122
KENNEDY, Burt, 1495, 1586, 2452, 3874, 4207, 5263, 5396, 6141, 6989, 7042, 7331
KENT, Larry, 7084
KENT, Laurence, 2768
KENWORTH, Jr., N. Paul, 4861
KERSHNER, Irvin, 1885, 2010, 2091, 2844, 3767, 3775, 5977, 7332
KESLER, Henry S., 5902
KESSLER, Bruce, 189, 2282, 3345, 5780
KETSON, Daniel, 2669
KIDD, Michael, 4086
KIMBALL, Ward, 3922
KIMMINS, Anthony, 154, 898, 4123, 5852, 5853
KING, Allan, 4016, 6993
KING, Henry, 96, 491, 755, 919, 1391, 2564, 3735, 4563, 5025, 5865, 6119, 6287, 6399, 6688
KING, John, 3161
KING, Louis, 1020, 2945, 4080, 4864
KINNEY, Jack, 4670
KINOSHITA, Keisuke, 361, 914, 5710
KINOSHITA, Ryo, 5540
KINUGASA, Teinosuke, 2279
KISHON, Ephraim, 5462
KIVIKOSKI, Erkko, 3321
KJAERULFF-SCHMID, Palle, 4641, 6737, 7036
KJELLIN, Alf, 3814, 4099
KLAREN, George C., 7283
KLECHNER, Susan, 6446
KLEIN, William, 1928, 4159, 7120
KLEINERMAN, Isaac, 6871
KLEINSINGER, George, 5772
KLINE, Benjamin, 3593
KLINGER, Werner, 4704, 6306, 6312
KLOS, Elmar, 5733
KLUGE, Alexander, 263, 7308
KLUSHANTSEY, P. (var. sp.: P. Klushentsev) 2510, 5341
KLUSHENTSEV, P. (see: P. Klushantsey)
KNEELAND, Ted, 1613, 5076
KNIGHT, Arthur, 4313
KNIGHT, Castleton, 5110, 5120, 5403
KNIGHT, Christopher, 923
KNIGHT, John, 3876, 4189
KNOWLES, Bernard, 2227
KOBAYASHI, Masaki, 2646, 3422, 4485, 5193
KOCH, Carl, 6580
KOCH, Howard, W., 177, 705, 2138, 2185, 3472, 6897
KOELER, Manfred, 2893
KOENIG, Hans H., 532
KOENIG, Wolf, 3662
KOGAN, Soloman, 1084, 5428
KOLM-VELTEE, H.W., 1648

KOMISSARJEVSKY, V., 1788
KONCHALOVSKY-MIKHALKOV, Andrei, 1717
KONWICKI, Tadeusz (var. sp.: Thaddeus Konwicki), 3462, 5467
KORDA, Alexander, 3008, 4000
KORDA, Zoltan, 1315, 6021
KORTY, John, 1262, 2245, 5331
KOSA, Ferenc, 6285
KOSTER, Henry, 1340, 1442, 1500, 2097, 2190, 2454, 2663, 3913, 4160, 4318, 4327, 4364, 4563, 5346, 5795, 6034, 6197, 6908
KOTCHEFF, Ted, 3578, 4734, 6724
KOTCHEFF, William T., 6484
KOUNDOUROS, Nikos, 7328
KOVACS, Andras, 1132, 1902
KOWALSKI, Bernard L., 638, 2325, 2874, 3416, 4449, 6009
KOZINTSEV, Grigory (var. sp.: Grigori Kozintsev) 1650, 2607, 3306
KOZOMARA, Ljubisa, 1300
KRAMER, Frank (pseud. for Gianfranco/Giancarlo Parclini), 34, 35, 5435, 6429
KRAMER, Stanley, 627, 1473, 1736, 2543, 3081, 3172, 3270, 3381, 4529, 4629, 5016, 5135, 5585, 5720
KRANCER, Burt, 3588
KRASNA, Norman, 139
KRISH, John, 1466, 3952, 6778, 7141
KRISTY, Leonid (var. sp.: L. Kristie), 1084, 1093, 1788, 5428
KROITER, Roman, 3662
KROLL, Nathan, 2574
KRONICK, William, 724
KRSKA, Vaclav, 2370
KUBELKA, Peter, 4727, 5541
KUBRICK, Stanley, 1114, 1626, 3343, 3346, 3655, 4825, 5933, 6739
KURY, Erich, 5382
KUCHAR, George, 6794
KULIJANOV, Lev, 2891
KULIK, Buzz, 1866, 5186, 5314, 5623, 6883, 6992, 7302
KULLE, Jarl, 696
KUMEL, Harry, 1389, 4216
KUNERT, Joachim, 4, 55
KUNZ, Werner, 3148, 4551, 4952
KUPER, Jack, 5409
KURI, Yogi, 82
KURODA, Yoshio, 2552
KUROKI, Kazuo, 5764
KUROSAWA, Akira, 348, 1634, 1703, 2762, 2770, 2984, 3017, 3771, 4079, 5170, 5204, 5491, 5648, 6065, 6465, 7313
KUTZ, Kazimierz, 5874

LABRO, Maurice, 5406
LACOMBE, Georges, 5639

LACY, Joe (pseud. for José María Elorrieta), 2064, 6627, 7209
LAINE, Edvin, 6788
LAMAS, Fernando, 6895
LAMB, John, 4084
LAMBART, Evelyn, 4780
LAMBERT, Gavin, 208
LAMORISSE, Albert, 1283, 5202, 6039, 7112
LAMOTHE, Arthur, 987, 4992
LAMPIN, Georges, 1270, 3009
LANCASTER, Burt, 3318
LANDAU, Saul, 1985
LANDERS, Lew, 2879
LANDIS, James, 86, 5976
LANDOR, Jo, 4778
LANDOW, George, 386, 5240
LANDRES, Paul, 2061, 2224, 2404, 3239, 3659, 3919, 4136, 4707, 5894
LANE, David, 6476, 6477
LANFRANCHI, Mario, 6624
LANG, Fritz, 545, 1106, 2935, 3263, 4092, 4231, 4671, 5750, 6425, 6493, 7101
LANG, Walter, 845, 866, 875, 1501, 3192, 3355, 4010, 4633, 5863, 6347, 7371
LANGLEY, Noel, 4891, 5563, 6151
LANZA, Anthony, 2400, 3073
LAPOKNYSH, Vasili, 3600
LARKIN, Ryan, 6961
LARSEN, Keith, 4152
LASKOS, Orestis, 2439
LASKOWSKI, Jan, 3462
LATTUADA, Alberto, 38, 197, 428, 2191, 2539, 3595, 3731, 3843, 3970, 4040, 4743, 6006, 6268, 6779, 6927
LAUGHLIN, Tom (see: T.C. Frank)
LAUGHTON, Charles, 4453
LAUNDER, Frank, 487, 667, 772, 891, 2112, 2507, 2521, 2631, 3227, 5082, 7035
LAUTNER, Georges, 1293, 2255, 2508, 5339, 5663
LAVAGNINO, F.A., 3699
LAVEN, Arnold, 201, 2306, 2399, 5143, 5393, 5469
LAVROVSKY, Leonid (var. sp.: Leonid Lavrosky), 365, 685, 5363, 5586
LAVUT, Martin, 289
LAWRENCE, Marc, 4472
LAWRENCE, Quentin, 947, 1256, 3951, 4936
LAZAGA, Pedro, 2388
LE BORG, Reginald, 613, 1441, 1568, 1877, 2089
LE CHANOIS, Jean-Paul, 945, 2982, 4773
LE ROY, Mervyn, 347, 791, 1521, 1880, 2586, 2828, 3634, 3882, 4025, 4167, 4192, 4511, 5134, 5378, 6950
LEACH, Wilford, 7031
LEACOCK, Philip, 757, 1825, 2611, 2785, 3085, 3552, 3626, 5138, 5182, 5929, 6196, 6210, 6389, 6982
LEADER, Anton M., 1045
LEAF, Caroline, 5482
LEAF, Paul, 331
LEAN, David, 766, 781, 1631, 2816, 3514, 3836, 4617, 5433, 6116
LEAR, Norman, 1134
LEARNER, Keith, 1605
LEBEDEV, Oleg, 1084, 5428
LEDER, Herbert J., 2228, 5012
LEDERER, Charles, 4404
LEE, Jack, 899, 1086, 5344, 6599, 7228, 7261
LEENHARDT, Roger, 1348, 5243
LEEWOOD, Jack, 6472, 6696, 7044
LEFRANC, Guy, 3772
LEFTWICH, Ed., 5964
LEGRAND, Francois, 6165
LEHTINEN, Virke, 4312
LEIBENEIHER, Wolfgang, 240
LEISEN, Mitchell, 2355, 4101, 5953
LEISER, Erwin, 1058, 2304, 4070, 4284
LEITNER, Herman, 2103, 4063, 4382
LELOUCH, Claude, 1288, 1928, 3583, 3640, 3734, 3905, 4791, 6527
LEMM, Staffan, 6073
LEMMON, Jack, 3413
LEMONT, Jack, 2210, 3411, 5685
LENICA, Jan, 1643, 3240
LENZER, Don, 2675
LENZI, Umberto, 2709, 3117, 4782, 5475, 5483, 6272
LEON, Jean, 1607
LEONARD, Herbert, 4859
LEONARD, Herman, 2420
LEONARD, Robert Z., 447, 2739, 3314
LEONE, Sergio, 1144, 2035, 2117, 2456, 4644
LERNER, Carl, 602
LERNER, Irving, 1099, 1312, 1739, 4283, 5402, 6082
LERNER, Murray, 1974
LESCHENKO, N., 2510
LESIEWICZ, Witold, 4810
LESLIE, Alfred, 441, 5078
LESTER, Richard, 460, 2244, 2649, 2735, 2736, 2913, 3396, 4262, 4870, 5303
LETERRIER, Francois, 4355
LEVESQUE, Michael, 7047
LEVIN, Henry, 142, 504, 1155, 1158, 1378, 1502, 2292, 2822, 2838, 3014, 3262, 3386, 3553, 3663, 4299, 4422, 4433, 5009, 5239, 7092, 7257, 7258
LEVITOW, Abe, 2283, 4877
LEVKOYEV, G., 3087

LEVY, Don, 2757, 6503
LEVY, Gerry, 680, 4899, 7088
LEVY, Ralph, 464
LEVY, Raoul, J., 1471, 2594
LEWIN, Robert, 6382
LEWIS III, Fulton, 7100
LEWIS, Herschell Gordon, 642, 6090, 6412, 7300
LEWIS, Jay, 325, 2833, 3114, 3642
LEWIS, Jerry, 478, 553, 1822, 3425, 4560, 4826, 6450
LEWIS, Joseph, 2553, 4330, 5866, 6302
LEWIS, Robert, 224
LEWIS, Vance, (pseud. for Luigi Vanzi), 6050, 6054, 7265
LEY, Mino, 7243
LEYTES, Joseph, 1225, 6825
LIBERATORE, Ugo, 700
LIEBENEINER, Wolfgang, 1361, 6194, 6619
LIGHT, Mike, 2653
LIMBACH, Russell T., 4557
LINDER, Maud Max, 3502
LINDGREN, Lars Magnus, 1444
LINDSAY-HOGG, Michael, 3551
LINDTBERG, Leopold, 6884
LINNECAR, Vera, 1605
LIPSCOMB, James, 668
LIPSETT, Arthur, 6693, 6859
LIPSKY, Oldrich, 2638, 3539
LITTIN, Miguel, 1754
LITTLEWOOD, Joan, 5932
LITVAK, Anatole, 16, 160, 1464, 1467, 2049, 2460, 3256, 3678, 4451, 5856
LIZZANI, Carlo (occasional pseud. is Lee W. Beaver) 472, 1588, 2797, 2940, 3731, 6894, 6951
LLOYD, Harold, 2243, 2657, 3327
LOACH, Kenneth, 3319, 4968
LOCKE, Peter, 7377
LODEN, Barbara (Mrs. Elia Kazan), 6971
LOGAN, Joshua, 840, 869, 1805, 1923, 4756, 4892, 5520, 5922, 6208
LOGERAU, Edwourd, 5588
LONG, Dwight, 6217
LONG, Richard, 3884
LONGYEL, Ivan, 1117
LOPEZ-PORTILLO, Jorge, 2038
LORENZ, Pare, 5328
LORRE, Peter, 6855
LOSEY, Joseph, 12, 697, 1006, 1171, 1601, 1841, 1998, 2402, 2587, 3353, 3794, 4186, 5575, 5629, 6052, 6353, 6517
LOURIE, Eugene, 1143, 2322, 2469
LOW, Colin, 1088, 1205, 2956
LOWELL, David, 5611
LOY, Nanni, 2155, 2687, 3832
LUBIN, Arthur, 1827, 2116, 2818, 3070, 6372
LUBITSCH, Ernst, 178, 1122, 6660

LUCAS, George, 6482
LUDWIG, Edward, 2556
LUKINSKY, I., 1071
LUMET, Sidney, 173, 853, 1437, 1901, 2236, 2536, 2793, 3352, 3671, 4832, 5557, 5969, 6686, 6876
LUNTZ, Edouard, 2475, 4360
LUPINO, Ida, 564, 6663
LUPO, Michele, 1447, 2444
LUSKE, Hamilton, 1595, 4655
LYE, Len, 2194
LYFORD, Richard, 6523
LYNN, Robert, 1008, 1125, 1614, 3078, 4267
LYON, Francis D., 673, 958, 1506, 1509, 1835, 2502, 4205, 5923, 6551, 7324
LYON, Nelson, 6261

MABE, Byron, 5705
MAC ARTHUR, Charles, 1276
MC BRIDE, Jim., 1396, 2394, 4323
MC CAREY, Leo, 59, 320, 482, 3715, 4336, 5162, 5500
MC CARTHY, Frank, 2548
MC CARTHY, Michael, 13, 3180, 4685, 6610
MC CLORY, Kevin, 728
MC COY, Denys, 3482
MC DERMOTT, Gerald, 133, 158
MAC DONALD, David, 2434, 4233
MC DONALD, Frank, 2560, 3983, 5083, 5180, 6774
MAC DONALD, Wallace, 2567
MC DONOUGH, Tom., 4381, 6690
MAC DOUGALL, Elspeth, 1957
MAC DOUGALL, Ranald, 2405, 3944, 5107, 6089, 7277
MC EVEETY, Bernard, 802, 2021, 4117, 5281
MC GRATH, Joseph, 630, 949, 3847, 6393
MC GOWAN, Dorrell, 397
MC GOWAN, Stuart, 397
MC GOWAN, Tom, 3973
MC GUIRE, Don, 1476, 3234
MAC KENDRICK, Alexander, 1540, 1663, 2769, 2788, 3440, 3931, 3971, 5472, 6030, 6167, 6492
MAC KENZIE, John, 6790
MC LAGLEN, Andrew V., 359, 377, 1055, 1535, 2114, 2193, 2724, 3631, 3813, 4214, 4659, 5715, 6763, 7012
MC LAREN, Norman, 629, 4806
MC LEAN, Barrie, 6934
MC LEOD, Norman Z., 99, 4210
MC NAUGHT, Bob, 5560
MAC NEILL, Ian, 1096
MAC TAGGART, James, 117
MACCHI, Guilio, 1472, 3501

MACHOVER, Robert, 6667
MACK, Russell, 4639
MACKENZIE, Kent, 1861, 5505
MACKEY, Clarke, 4679
MACNEICE, Louis, 1184
MADDEN, Lee, 2730
MADDOW, Ben, 58, 5509
MAETZIG, Kurt, 2031
MAFFEI, Mario, 4203
MAGNUSON, John, 3542
MAHON, Barry, 1320, 1431, 5352, 6900
MAILER, Norman, 523, 3873, 7157
MAJANO, Anton Giulio, 296
MAKAVEJEV, Dusan, 3084, 3716, 3934, 6943
MALAPARTE, Curzio, 1285
MALASOMMA, Nunzio, 5270
MALATESTA, Guido, 1142, 2249, 2441
MALDEN, Karl, 6504
MALENOTTI, Roberto, 5834
MALLE, Louis, 862, 1977, 2188, 3754, 4301, 5774, 6203, 6373, 6860, 6923, 7384
MALOUF, Yusuf, 796
MAMOULIAN, Rouben, 5109, 5775, 6106
MANASTER, Benjamin, 2438
MANDY, 1255
MANFREDI, Nino, 5670
MANKIEWICZ, Henry, 820
MANKIEWICZ, Joseph L., 103, 388, 1111, 1683, 1828, 2044, 2585, 2837, 2898, 3281, 3352, 3562, 4515, 4851, 5128, 6100, 6342
MANN, Anthony, 1076, 1362, 1503, 1755, 1909, 2119, 2246, 2395, 2413, 2754, 3940, 4077, 5617, 6062, 6468, 6520, 7181
MANN, Daniel, 6, 25, 849, 1152, 1689, 2043, 2882, 3018, 3271, 3456, 4260, 4724, 5379, 6249, 7129, 7130, 7176
MANN, Delbert, 335, 1377, 1395, 1443, 1499, 2036, 2280, 3753, 4021, 4100, 4158, 4741, 4907, 5125, 5613, 6333
MANN, Edward (pseud. for Santos Alcocer), 984, 2604, 7123
MANOUSSAKIS, Costas, 1954
MANTHOULIS, Robert, 1894
MARCELLINI, Romolo, 2479, 3800, 5367
MARCELLINI, Siro, 5581
MARCH, Alex, 534, 1367, 4775
MARCHENT, J.R., 7395
MARGETTS, Mike, 254
MARGHERITI, Antonio (see: Anthony Dawson)
MARIN, Edwin L., 948
MARISCHKA, Ernst, 1773, 2137, 6037
MARKER, Chris, 1318, 1486, 3217, 3247, 3414, 3565, 5813
MARKLE, Fletcher, 3069
MARKOPOULOS, Gregory, 1819, 3022, 6701
MARKSON, Morley, 7389
MARNER, Eugene and Carol, 4886
MARQUAND, Christian, 880, 4584
MARSHALL, Frank, 2268, 2297, 2584
MARSHALL, George, 45, 731, 1308, 1382, 1706, 1749, 2284, 2643, 2846, 2916, 3033, 3165, 4042, 4397, 4774, 5440, 5714, 7136
MARSHALL, William, 4876
MART, Paul, 450
MARTENS, Reni, 6814
MARTI, Walter, 6814
MARTIN, Charles, 1455, 3015
MARTIN, Eugenio, 6751
MARTIN, Jay, 5691
MARTIN, William, 3193
MARTINO, Sergio, 4417
MARTINSON, Leslie H., 401, 600, 1879, 1951, 2127, 3424, 4175, 4750
MARTON, Andrew, 64, 252, 582, 1251, 1528, 2518, 3155, 3372, 3682, 4078, 5033, 5657, 6374, 6775
MARVI, Renato, 2403
MARYAMOV, E., 1090
MASELLI, Francesco, 2011, 3501, 3563, 3731, 6508
MASINI, Guiseppe, 215
MASLYUKOV, A., 6250
MASON, Bill, 4754
MASON, Jean, 7028
MASON, Richard, 310, 2221, 2314, 7318
MASSOT, Joe, 7259
MASTROCINQUE, Camillo, 203, 1752
MASUDA, Toshio, 6572
MASUMURA, Yasuzo, 4811, 5200
MATARAZZO, Raffaello, 6853
MATE, Rudolph, 612, 1470, 2124, 4508, 5392, 5649, 5747, 6443, 6461, 7085
MATHLING, Sven, 4688
MATHOT, Leon, 683
MATSUBAYASHI, Shue, 2969
MATSUYAMA, Zenzo, 2634
MATTER, Axel, 1693
MATTHAU, Walter, 2269
MATTOLI, Mario, 6733
MATTSSON, Arne, 222, 1641, 4243, 4470, 4668, 7234
MAURER, Norman, 4738, 6456
MAWRA, Joseph A., 7116
MAXWELL, Paul (pseud. for Paolo Gianchiui), 6138
MAXWELL, Peter, 5616, 6174
MAY, Elaine, 4411
MAY, Paul, 6846
MAYBERRY, Russ, 3213
MAYER, Gerald, 788, 1556

DIRECTORS

MAYO, Archie, 4428
MAYSLES, David and Albert, 2336, 5461
MAZIERRE, Francis, 5814
MAZURSKY, Paul, 672
MAZZETTI, Lorenzo, 3501
MEDAK, Peter, 4393
MEDFORD, Don, 1211, 2948, 4709, 6537
MEDFORD, Harold, 3998
MEDVECZKY, Diurka, 4829
MEHBOOB, 2616, 4254
MEINECHE, Annelise, 1814, 2076
MEISEL, Kurt, 1237, 4362
MEKAS, Adolfas, 1168, 2600, 7188
MEKAS, Jonas, 785, 2581
MELCHOIR, Ib, 193, 6516
MELENDEZ, Bill, 733
MELVILLE, Jean-Pierre, 248, 993, 1518, 1675, 1800, 1978, 3545, 5476
MENDEZ, Ferdinand, 610
MENOTTI, Giancarlo, 4064
MENZEL, Jiri, 888, 1116, 4839
MERINO, Jose Luis, 5549
MERRICK, Laurence, 594, 2541
MERRIWEATHER, Nicholas, 1743
MERUSI, Renzo, 1388
MESSINA, Philip, 2422, 5815
METZGER, Radley, 872, 913, 6349
MEYER, Andy, 5674
MEYER, Jean, 4014, 7281
MEYER, Otto, 5636
MEYER, Russ, 1035, 1820, 1924, 1937, 2009, 2453, 2914, 5426, 5647
MEYERING, Kees, 3003
MEYERS, Richard, 1203
MEYERS, Sidney, 5131, 5509
MICHEL, André, 5492, 5911, 6651, 7367
MIDE, Robin, 6446
MIHIC, Gordon, 1300
MIKELS, Ted V., 288, 2974
MILES, Bernard, 1007
MILES, Christopher, 5277, 6802, 6903
MILESTONE, Lewis, 110, 2223, 2603, 3302, 4311, 4573, 4974, 5084, 5155, 6368, 6955
MILFORD, Gene, 5091
MILLAND, Ray, 3904, 4772, 5448
MILLER, Arnold Louis, 5021, 5821, 7049
MILLER, David, 340, 895, 1560, 2609, 2635, 3661, 4103, 4701, 4728, 6027
MILLER, Max, 6452
MILLER, Robert Ellis, 221, 848, 2690, 6162
MILLER, Sidney, 2312, 6215, 6392
MILLER, Warren, 5817
MILLETT, Kate, 6446
MILLIGAN, Andy, 3383
MILLIN, David, 5285
MILLS, John, 2590

MILLS, Reginald, 4867
MILNER, Allen H., 5280
MIMICA, Vatroslav, 4542
MINDLIN, Jr., Michael, 3259
MINER, Allen H., 1070, 4367
MINGOZZI, Gian Franco, 3501
MINNELLI, Vincente, 148, 344, 370, 490, 786, 1127, 1240, 1497, 2161, 2334, 2461, 2830, 3379, 3677, 3788, 3825, 4624, 4913, 5237, 5484, 5883, 6036, 6246, 6744
MIR, Ezra, 4766
MISHIMA, 5324
MISHURIN, A., 5904
MISUMI, Kenji, 816, 5739
MITCHELL, Denis, 1037
MITROVIK, Zika, 1992
MITTA, Alexander, 2340
MIZOGUCHI, Kenji, 5493, 5718, 6068, 6748
MIZUTANI, Hiroshi, 3023
MOCKY, Jean Pierre, 723, 1029, 1696, 3747, 4703, 5859, 5881, 6910
MOFFA, Paolo, 2212
MOGUBGUB, Fred, 6787
MOGUY, Leonide, 1563
MOLINARO, Edouard (var. sp.: Edward Molinaro), 341, 2375, 3895, 4814, 5634
MOMPLET, Anthony, 3116
MONICELLI, Mario, 2512, 4710, 5119, 5880, 6195, 6781
MONKS, Jr., John, 4494
MONTAGNE, Edward J., 3807, 5236
MONTALDO, Giuliano, 2482, 5438
MONTERO, Roberto Bianchi, 4199
MONTGOMERY, George, 5471, 5998
MONTGOMERY, Robert, 2256, 7368
MONTGOMERY, Thomas, 3360
MOORE, Michael, 815, 1872, 1938, 3335, 4779
MOORSE, George, 3419, 3543, 7388
MORA, Phillippe, 6659
MORAHAN, Christopher, 1558
MORASSI, Mauro, 6093
MORDAUNT, Richard, 6932
MOREAN, Richard, 4043
MORGAN, Harry, 7292
MORGENSTERN, Janusz, 5603
MORIN, Edgar, 1068
MORRIS, Ernest, 1239, 6266
MORRIS, Howard, 7131, 7216
MORRISSEY, Paul, 2078, 6621
MORROW, Vic, 1460, 3914
MORSE, Terry, 2414
MOSER, G., 3699
MOSES, Milton, 1163
MOULLET, Luc, 5855
MOUSSY, Marcel, 5458
MOXEY, John, 1459, 2174, 2855, 5073, 6060, 6698
MOYNIHAN, Frank, 2825

MUIR, Dalton, 1740
MULKERNS, Jim, 6543
MULLIGAN, Andy, 2005
MULLIGAN, Robert, 329, 1157, 1956, 2500, 3091, 3749, 5089, 5172, 5945, 5978, 6111, 6533, 6805
MUNK, Andrzej, 1817, 4810
MUNROE, Cynthia, 7031
MURAKAMI, Jimmy, 6568
MURIEL, Emilio Gomez, 1785
MURNAU, F.W., 4722, 6133, 6192
MURPHY, Dudley, 1780
MURPHY, Richard, 6945
MURRAY, Donald, 6789
MURROW, Edward R., 5503
MUSSO, Carlo, 3501
MUSY, Vittorio, 5755
MUTRUX, Floyd, 1715
MYERS, David, 2676
MYERS, Frank, 3703

NET, 380
NADEL, Arthur, 1104
NAKAHIRA, Jasushi, 3294, 4930
NAKAMURA, Noboru, 5604
NAPOLEON, Art, 6563
NAPOLITANO, Gian Gaspare, 2520
NARIZZANO, Silvio, 658, 1574, 2302, 3687
NARUSAWA, Masashibe, 677
NARUSE, Mikio, 7074
NARZISI, Gianni, 1604
NASH, Gene, 1580, 7057
NATIONAL COUNCIL OF TEACHERS OF ENGLISH, 6772
NATIONAL FILM BOARD OF CANADA, 546, 689, 4068, 4854
NATIONAL GEOGRAPHIC SOCIETY, 6938
NAUD, William, 2880
NAUMOV, Vladimir, 109, 4837
NAZARRO, Ray, 229, 5265
NEAME, Ronald, 1000, 1834, 2257, 2435, 2867, 2973, 3915, 3957, 3962, 4165, 5018, 5063, 5069, 5553, 5665, 6682, 7190
NEGULESCO, Jean, 510, 734, 996, 1222, 1342, 2332, 2924, 3118, 3211, 4268, 4563, 4951, 5158, 6434, 6436, 6524, 7241
NEILSON, James, 48, 688, 1627, 2032, 2071, 2295, 4227, 4228, 5261, 7086
NELLI, Piero, 3501
NELSON, Gene, 1196, 2613, 2652, 2847, 3390, 7365
NELSON, Gunvor, 5535
NELSON, Mervyn, 5886
NELSON, Ralph, 1022, 1228, 1704, 1946, 1949, 2086, 3602, 5252, 5876, 5877
NELSON, Robert, 318, 1175, 2487, 2492, 2598, 2876, 4562, 4591, 4602, 4844, 4931, 6139, 6369, 6979
NELSON, Sam, 4745
NEMEC, Jan, 1559, 4022, 4839, 5247
NETHERCOTT, Geoffrey, 7124
NEUMANN, Kurt, 1092, 1227, 2100, 3808, 7007
NEVARD, Peter, 2538
NEVE, Alexis, 1966
NEW YORK NEWSREEL, 1401
NEW YORK TIMES, 2950
NEWFIELD, Sam, 2067, 7221
NEWLAND, John, 5963, 6329
NEWLEY, Anthony, 876, 6117
NEWMAN, David, 4667
NEWMAN, Joseph, 536, 2141, 2301, 2561, 3368, 3369, 6233, 6473, 6694
NEWMAN, Paul, 5142
NEWMEYER, Fred, 1934, 2204
"NEWSREEL, THE", 1146, 4317, 4847
NEWSREEL FOOTAGE, 4684, 4690
NIBLO, Fred, 4345, 6275
NICHOLS, Dudley, 4261, 5805
NICHOLS, Mike, 916, 973, 2476, 7128
NICHOLSON, Jack, 1695, 2090
NICOL, Alex, 5551, 6337
NICOLAESCU, Sergiu, 3461
NIELSON, James, 6110
NIEVES-CONDE, José Antonio, 5918
NISKANEN, Mikko, 5823
NOEL, Alexander, 351
NOELTE, Rudolf, 956
NOONAN, Tommy, 6449
NORDSTROM, 1346
NORMAN, Leslie, 1713, 3286, 4178, 4444, 5568, 5722, 5931, 7295
NOSSECK, Martin, 4229
NOSSECK, Max, 2273
NUSSGRUBER, Rudolph (var. sp.: Rudolf Nussgruber), 2103, 4063
NYBERG, Borje, 2958
NYBY, Christian, 2033, 4689, 6375

OBOLER, Arch, 811, 850
O'BRIEN, Edmund, 3980
O'CONNELL, Jack, 1061, 2526, 5271
O'CONNOLLY, Jim, 505, 1290, 3629, 6824
ODETS, Clifford, 6038
O'FERRALL, George More, 2524, 2693, 7226
O'HANLON, George, 5370
O'HARA, Gerry, 115, 4007, 4947
O'HERLIHY, Michael, 1997, 4645
OKAMOTO, Kihachi, 1779, 3334, 5477, 6179
OLD, John M., 4442
OLDEN, John, 2493
OLIVIER, Laurence, 2605, 5024, 5278
OLMI, Ermanno, 170, 1982, 4650, 5530, 5921, 6513

OLSSON, Stellan, 4716
O'NEIL, Robert Vincent, 645, 5074
ONO, Yoko, 2003, 2004, 5166, 6742
OONK, Jan, 3407
OPHULS, Marcel, 368, 983, 3720, 5912
OPHULS, Max, 3560, 3574, 3654, 3827, 4926, 5194, 5368
ORGANISYAN, Genrikh, 6453
ORKIN, Ruth, 3622
ORROM, Michael, 4985
ORSINI, Valentino, 4739
OSCO, Bill, 4198
O'SHAUGHNESEY, John, 5919
OSHIMA, Nagisa, 726, 995, 1445, 1570, 2105, 3955, 4369, 4953, 5717, 6135, 6891
OSONE, Tatsuo, 3044
OSSEPIAN, Mark, 6633
OSTROVSKI, Grisha, 1515
OSWALD, Gerd, 79, 750, 830, 1275, 3380, 4788, 5550
OTI, Manuel Mur, 6005
OTTEN, Malcolm, 4777
OURY, Gerard, 745, 1273, 1662, 1838, 2294, 6096
OVE, Horace, 5225
OWEN, Cliff, 3864, 5049, 6330, 6848, 7287
OWEN, Don, 1816, 4518, 5421
OZEP, Fedor, 804
OZU, Yasujiro, 311, 4600, 6546

PABST, G.W., 62, 363, 3299, 3489, 3566, 6463, 6931
PADGET, Calvin Jackson, 2143, 4665, 5574
PADULA, Fred, 1810
PAGE, Anthony, 3063
PAGLIERO, Marcel, 4749
PAGNOL, Marcel, 997, 2662, 3564
PAKKASVIRTA, Jaakko, 2261, 3320
PAKULA, Alan J., 3395, 6008
PAL, George, 294, 5640, 6507, 6548
PALTENGHI, David, 3311
PANAMA, Norman, 7, 1235, 2920, 3405, 3897, 4532, 5336, 6319, 6616
PAOLELLA, Domenico, 1859, 2578, 2667
PAPAS, Michael, 5042
PAPATAKIS, Nico, 10
PAPIC, Krsto, 3615
PAPOUSEK, Jaroslav, 4250
PARADJANOV, Sergey, 5681
PARIS, Jerry, 1664, 2915, 5985
PARKER, Ben, 722
PARKER, Chris, 1337
PARKER, David W., 6452
PARKER, Joe, 2873
PARKER, Robert, 1170
PARKS, Gordon, 3520, 5682
PAROLINI, Gianfranco/Giancarlo (see:

Frank Kramer)
PARRISH, Robert, 675, 949, 1668, 1711, 2016, 3056, 3782, 5087, 5442, 6598, 7254
PARRY, Gordon, 689, 4387, 5453, 6625
PASOLINI, Pier Paolo, 11, 1461, 2472, 2678, 3900, 4060, 4582, 4903, 6293, 7212
PASSENDORFER, Jerzy, 211
PASSER, Ivan, 701, 708, 3105
PASTINA, Giorgio, 4586
PATRICK, Nigel, 2925
PATRONI-GRIFFI, Giuseppe, 4660
PAUL, Byron, 3575
PAUL, John, 2628
PAVLOVIC, Zivojin, 3295, 5173
PECAS, Max, 6159, 7091
PECKINPAH, Sam, 357, 1439, 3881, 5284, 7146
PEERCE, Larry, 561, 2462, 3064, 4664, 5952
PEETERS, Barbara, 837
PELISSIER, Anthony, 1789, 2807, 4863
PENN, Arthur, 101, 694, 1027, 3528, 3619, 4098, 4140
PENN, Leo, 3908
PENNEBAKER, D.A., 1661, 4224, 4663
PENNINGTON-RICHARDS, C.M., 1001, 1669, 3082, 3426, 4348
PERGAMENT, André, 4495, 4784
PERIER, Etienne, 782, 4281, 6183, 7077, 7385
PERRAULT, Pierre, 4991, 5228
PERRY, Frank, 1393, 1567, 1609, 3439, 3486, 6169, 6641
PERRY, Gordon, 4545
PERRY, Peter, 4202
PETERS, Brooke L., 164
PETRI, Elio, 281, 3115, 5132, 6292, 7021
PETRIE, Daniel, 751, 3011, 3875, 5160, 5962, 6013
PETROFF, Boris, 4736
PETROFF, Hamil, 863, 5420
PETRONI, Guilio, 1458
PETROV, Vladmir, 3095
PETROVIC, Alexander (var. sp.: Aleksandar Petrovic), 528, 2979, 6428
PEVNEY, Joseph, 317, 946, 1297, 3935, 4452, 4955, 4980, 5810, 6577, 6704
PEYSER, John, 4292, 7360
PFLEGHAR, Michael, 2928, 4612, 5618, 6582
PHELAN, Raymond, 6567
PHILIPP, Harold, 576, 6041
PICAZO, Miguel, 6483
PICHEL, Irving, 1409, 1507, 4020
PIERCE, Arthur C., 3453, 7247

PIEROTTI, Piero, 4914
PIETRANGELI, Antonio, 43, 3157, 3859, 4873, 5119, 6918
PIGAUT, Roger, 3852
PINCUS, Ed, 4667
PINK, Sidney, 1064, 2013, 3264, 5249
PINKAVA, Josef, 7207
PINTILIE, Lucian, 5196
PINTOFF, Ernest, 2664, 6902, 7122
PIRES, Gérard, 1821
PIROSH, Robert, 2364, 6829
PITT, George, 4414
PIWOWSKI, Marek, 5230
PLACE, Lou, 1343
PLATTS-MILLS, Barne, 797
POGOSTIN, S. Lee, 2648
POHLAND, Hansjurgen, 3309
POITRENAUD, Jacques, 4009, 6166, 6204
POLANSKI, Roman, 448, 1322, 1940, 1958, 3399, 3805, 5099, 5251, 5383, 6732
POLIDORO, Gian Luigi, 4994, 5412, 6528
POLLACK, Sydney, 957, 5521, 5841, 6364, 6406
POLLAK, Jinfrich, 6941
POLLET, Jean-Daniel, 362, 4796
POLLOCK, George, 799, 3339, 4280, 4282, 4293, 4298, 4957, 5374, 5463, 6278
POLONSKY, Abraham, 2133, 5359, 6267
POOLE, Wakefield, 742
PONTECORVO, Gillo, 410, 833, 3303
POPKIN, Leo, 7043
PORTER, Edwin S., 3585
POST, Ted, 494, 2621, 3534
POSTLE, Denis, 6243
POTTER, H.C., 6569
POTTERTON, Gerald, 4321, 5153
POTTIER, Richard, 1392, 6901
POWELL, Dick, 1182, 1797, 2946, 5951, 7316
POWELL, Michael, 74, 1769, 2447, 4048, 4597, 4841, 5090, 5216, 6202
PRAEGER, Stanley, 378
PRAVOV, I., 3787
PREMINGER, Otto, 56, 163, 181, 691, 829, 906, 915, 1238, 1863, 2952, 3047, 3505, 3965, 4225, 4973, 5330, 5456, 5820, 6095, 6264, 6390
PRESSBURGER, Emeric, 2447, 4048, 4597, 5090, 5216, 6202
PREVERT, Pierre, 6939
PREVIN, Steve, 123, 707, 1826, 6968
PRICE, Bamlet L., 4674
PRINCE, Harold, 5891
PRIVETT, Bob, 4996
PROIA, Gianni, 6409, 7266
PRONIN, Vasili, 3257
PROSPERI, Franco (see: Frank Shannon)
PRUNAS, Pasquale, 497 .
PTUSHKO, Alexander, 1811, 5444, 6176
PUCCINI, Gianni, 3718
PUDOVKIN, V.I., 4253, 6841
PUPILLO, Massimo (occasional pseud. are Max Hunter and Ralph Zuker), 655, 6300
PYRIEV, Ivan, 3010

QUESTI, Guilio, 3501
QUILICI, Folco, 3479, 5630, 5834, 6494
QUINE, Richard, 477, 1694, 2237, 2883, 2926, 3159, 3523, 4333, 4537, 4593, 4696, 4797, 5092, 5669, 5868, 5879, 6057, 6186, 7275
QUINN, Anthony, 812
QUINN, Gordon, 2829, 3089
QUINTERO, José, 5358

RABENALT, Arthur Maria, 517, 2588, 2799, 3497, 3722
RADEMAKERS, Fons, 1623, 3398
RADEV, Veulo, 4838
RADOK, Alfred, 4610
RAFELSON, Bob, 2042, 2685
RAFKIN, Alan, 182, 2316, 2921, 4519, 5287, 5687
RAIHAN, Zahir, 3220
RAKOFF, Alvin, 1160, 2817, 2878, 5372, 5518, 7269
RAMATI, Alexander, 5485
RANODY, Laszlo, 426, 2128, 4752
RANSEN, Mort, 1067, 4504, 6796
RAPP, Joel, 412, 2780
RAPPAPORT, G., 6643
RAPPENEAU, Jean Philippe, 6874
RAPPER, Irving, 758, 1062, 2390, 4001, 4132, 6029
RATOFF, Gregory, 1210, 4715, 5401, 6321
RATONY, Akos V., 986, 1539
RAVN, Jens, 3969
RAWLINS, John, 3702
RAY, Nicholas, 566, 593, 1994, 3366, 3404, 4804, 5192, 5511, 6361, 6671, 7183
RAY, Satyajit, 232, 1026, 1038, 1519, 3868, 4307, 4824, 5000, 6720, 7271
RAYMOND, Bob, 3773
REED, Carol, 80, 1910, 2072, 3322, 3328, 3777, 3907, 4616, 4725, 4735, 5423, 5990, 6380, 6618
REEK, Edmund, 1931, 2826
REEVES, Michael, 1183, 5267, 5701, 5909
REGAMEY, Maurice, 2595
REGNOLI, Piero, 4939

DIRECTORS

REGUEIRO, Francisco, 131
REICHENBACH, Francois, 146, 1131, 4061
REICHMAN, Thomas, 4124
REID, Alastair, 328, 4432
REINER, Carl, 1806, 7099
REINHARDT, Gottfried, 513, 5189, 5808, 6036, 6601
REINL, Harald, 3492, 7197
REIS, Irving, 1904, 2167, 4589
REISNER, Allen, 108, 1417, 5457
REISZ, Karel, 3763, 4241, 4443, 5506
REITHERMAN, Wolfgang, 245, 3284, 4655, 6177
REITMAN, Ivan, 4712
REITZ, Edgar, 905, 2309, 3869
RELPH, Michael, 1397, 1490, 2968, 3819, 4731, 5721
RENOIR, Jean, 719, 1041, 1274, 1475, 1768, 2196, 2430, 3633, 4019, 4787, 4800, 5227, 5329, 6152, 6311, 6580
RESNAIS, Alain, 1928, 2540, 2803, 3206, 3499, 4300, 4429, 6594
REVESZ, György, 3444
REYNOLDS, Sheldon, 285, 4920
REYNOLDS, William, 1025
RICCI, Luciano, 960, 6029
RICE, Ron, 1073, 2098, 5114
RICH, David Lowell, 1874, 2674, 2759, 3751, 3828, 4925, 5386, 6441
RICH, John, 681, 1725, 4409, 5397, 7219
RICHARD, Jean-Louis, 4039
RICHARDSON, Ralph, 4295
RICHARDSON, Tony, 1016, 1807, 2608, 3504, 3660, 3683, 3750, 3838, 4392, 5198, 5454, 5479, 6240, 6547
RICHIE, Donald, 2053
RICHTER, Hans, 1751
RIEFENSTAHL, Leni, 501, 6648
RILLA, Wolf, 334, 861, 1793, 4751, 4889, 5522, 6886, 7276
RIM, Carlo, 3649
RIMMER, David, 1359, 3450, 6145, 6840
RIPLEY, Arthur, 6474
RISI, Dino, 1726, 1991, 2165, 2347, 3717, 3731, 4164, 4967, 5017, 5524, 5757, 6487, 6628, 7039
RISI, Nelo, 1430, 3501
RITCHIE, Michael, 1676
RITELIS, Viktors, 1301
RITT, Martin, 606, 801, 1741, 2040, 2513, 2737, 2827, 2932, 3675, 4188, 4489, 4740, 4786, 5916, 5961
RIVALTA, Giorgio, 1215, 4879
RIVER, Fernand, 3878
RIVETTE, Jacques, 155, 4794, 5234
ROACH, Hal, 1263
ROBBE-GRILLET, Alain, 3038, 6614

ROBBINS, Jerome, 7050
ROBERT SAUDEK ASSOCIATES, 7177
ROBERT, Yves, 94, 2824, 6925, 6983
ROBERTS, Bob, 6164
ROBINSON, David, 2758
ROBINSON, Tom Scott, 3770
ROBSON, Mark, 783, 1005, 1344, 1737, 2220, 2636, 2651, 2832, 3083, 3596, 3624, 3698, 4477, 4871, 4882, 5048, 5050, 6634, 6826, 6936, 7375
ROCHA, Glauber, 218, 599, 3547
ROCHLIN, Sheldon and Diane, 6822
RODE, Alfred, 2017
RODRIGUEZ, Ismael, 1321, 3041
ROEG, Nicolas, 4858, 6960
ROEMER, Michael, 4534
ROFFMAN, Julian, 4029
ROGELL, Albert S., 2120, 5215
ROGERS, Peter, 4816
ROGOSIN, Lionel, 1150, 2459, 4631
ROHMER, Eric, 1103, 1138, 3798, 4796, 5759
ROLEY, Sutton, 2930
ROMAN, Barbro, 2059
ROMAR, Mikhail, 6649
ROMERO, Eddie, 436, 438, 3696, 4245, 5151
ROMERO, George A., 4455
ROMM, Mikhail, 37, 4476
RONDEAU, Charles R., 1547, 2349, 3636, 6426
RONDI, Brunello, 1481
ROOKS, Conrad, 1012
ROOM, Abram, 2276
ROONEY, Mickey, 5038
ROOS, Ole, 4097
ROSE, Sherman A., 6218
ROSE, William L., 4765
ROSENBERG, Max J., 7270
ROSENBERG, Stuart, 239, 1194, 4291, 5123, 6944
ROSHAL, Grigory, 2065, 5806
ROSI, Francesco, 2620, 4191, 4240, 5468, 6798
ROSS, Charles, 4778
ROSS, Edward (see: Rossano Brazzi)
ROSS, Herbert, 2466, 4747, 6191
ROSSELLINI, Roberto, 514, 2288, 2305, 2514, 3720, 4131, 4439, 4759, 5320, 5639, 5870, 6076, 7022
ROSSEN, Robert, 95, 113, 756, 2955, 3139, 3603, 3899, 6359
ROSSI, Franco, 1452, 2165, 4550, 5377, 7212, 7229
ROSSIF, Frederic, 6530, 7218
ROTHA, Paul, 964, 3584, 4505, 5770, 7279
ROTHMAN, Benjamin and Lawrence, 3460
ROTHMAN, Stephanie, 640, 3171, 6842

ROTHSCHILD, Amalie R., 3160, 7260
ROTSLER, William, 81, 2368
ROUCH, Jean, 39, 1068, 4796, 4868, 5096
ROULEAU, Raymond, 3760, 7213
ROULLET, Serge, 496
ROUQUIER, Georges, 1933
ROUSE, Russell, 884, 1939, 2892, 2897, 4415, 4714, 6370, 6471, 7043, 7138
ROUSSEAU, Jean-Pierre, 1940
ROUSSEL, Mick, 5673
ROUSTANG, Pierre, 6259
ROUVE, Pierre, 1200
ROVIRA-BELETA, 6223
ROW, Alexander, 1079, 3187
ROWE, Peter, 4394
ROWLAND, E.G. (pseud. for Enzo Girolami), 4834
ROWLAND, Roy, 2055, 2346, 2810, 3982, 4066, 5558, 5644, 5829
ROY, Bimal, 6713
ROZIER, Willy, 137, 2351, 5034, 5783
RUBBO, Michael, 5441
RUDOLPH, Oscar, 1659, 6708, 7168
RUGGLES, Wesley, 3027
RUSH, Richard, 1983, 2313, 2729, 3909, 4587, 5070, 5514, 6467, 6564
RUSSELL, Ken, 571, 732, 1531, 2198, 4305, 7245
RUTTMANN, Walther, 502
RYAN, Frank, 867
RYAZANOV, Eldar, 6760
RYCHMAN, Ladislav, 3435
RYDELL, Mark, 2173, 5229

SACHA, Jean, 4565
SAGAL, Boris, 1277, 1577, 2344, 2576, 2707, 3833, 4249, 4623, 6705
SAGAN, Leontine, 3829
SAKELLARIOS, Alekos (var. sp.: Alekos Sakelarios), 2951, 6658
SAKS, Gene, 390, 856
SAKS, George, 4577
SALA, Vittorio, 1382, 5960
SALAM, Shadi Abdel, 4445
SALCE, Luciano, 1259, 1758, 3387, 3628, 5119
SALE, Richard, 2298, 5652
SALERNO, Enrico Maria, 207
SALKOW, Sidney, 554, 651, 3471, 4288, 5127, 5807, 6703
SALZMAN, Bert, 4110, 7179
SAMPERI, Salvatore, 2488, 7390
SAMSONOV, Samson, 4112, 6455
SAMSONOV, Sergei, 2486
SANDERS, Denis, 1271, 1771, 4657, 5724, 5915, 6335, 6512, 6977
SANDERS, Dirk, 7322
SANDOR, Pál, 352
SANGSTER, Jimmy, 2857, 3786

SANJINES, Jorge, 647
SANTELL, Alfred, 7205
SARA, Sandor, 6811
SARAFIAN, Richard C., 176, 2176, 3932, 5417, 6299, 6837
SARGENT, Joseph, 2132, 2720, 4666, 5958, 6639
SARKKA, Toivo, 4113, 5004
SARNE, Michael, 3223, 4340, 5338
SARNO, Joseph W., 3080, 3740, 4232
SARTRE, Jean-Paul, 1589
SASDY, Peter, 1229, 6241
SASLAVSKY, Luis, 1480, 5006, 5711, 5973
SASSY, Jean-Paul, 4056
SAUDEK ASSOCIATES, Robert (see: Robert Saudek Associates)
SAUNDERS, Charles, 1387, 3337, 4297, 4383
SAURA, Carlos, 2272, 2440, 2944
SAUTET, Claude, 6377
SAVILLE, Philip, 507, 4581, 6017
SAVILLE, Victor, 3349, 5777
SAVONA, Leopoldo, 6996
SBARGE, Stephen, 3125
SCANDELARI, Jacques, 521
SCARPELLI, Umberto, 2327
SCARZA, Vince, 1594
SCATTINI, Luigi, 2392, 6155, 6980
SCAVOLINI, Romana, 2
SCHAAF, Johannes, 6242
SCHACH, Leonard, 1311
SCHAEFER, Armand, 3593
SCHAEFER, George, 1633, 3804, 4842
SCHAFFNER, Franklin J., 508, 1671, 4423, 4828, 4928, 6075, 6981
SCHAIN, Don, 2337
SCHAMONI, Peter, 5536, 7206
SCHAMONI, Ulrich, 3150
SCHARY, Dore, 20, 414
SCHATZBERG, Jerry, 4769, 5095
SCHECHNER, Richard, 1584
SCHELL, Maximilian, 2028
SCHEUMANN, Gerhard, 3503
SCHINDEL, Morton, 1700, 2641
SCHLESINGER, John, 574, 1383, 1927, 3351, 4102, 6123
SCHLONDORFF, Volker, 4095, 4236, 4954, 7359
SCHMIDT, 3251
SCHNEIDER, Alan, 2001
SCHOEDSACK, Ernest B., 2158, 4108
SCHOENDORFFER, Pierre, 172, 6652
SCHORM, Ewald, 1234, 4839, 5262
SCHREIBER, Paulbruno, 4341
SCHREYER, John, 7173
SCHROEDER, Robert, 4237
SCHROTH, Carl Heinz, 5184
SCHWARTZ, Douglas, 4836
SCHWEITZER, Mikhail, 5255
SCOLA, Ettore, 1525, 3559
SCORSESE, Martin, 7133

SCOTESE, Giuseppe Maria, 5205
SCOTT, Peter Graham, 591, 1252, 1948, 2688, 3554, 4431, 4989
SCULLY, Denis, 3258
SEARLE, Francis, 6206
SEARS, Fred F., 350, 990, 1254, 2319, 2421, 7278
SEATON, George, 87, 551, 1226, 1232, 2845, 3620, 4949, 5065, 6248, 6395, 7067
SECTER, David, 4592, 7201
SEGAL, Alex, 116, 2655, 3266
SEGEL, Yakov, 1416, 1929
SEILER, Lewis, 6221, 6672
SEKELY, Steve, 1408, 3316
SEKIGAWA, Hideo, 738, 2802
SELANDER, Lesley, 246, 2139, 2142, 3658, 6317, 6988
SELLERS, Peter, 2983, 5422
SELTZER, Leo, 3195
SEMBENE, Ousmane, 598, 3968
SEN, Mrinal, 88, 353
SENFT, Haro, 5489
SEQUENS, Jiri, 277
SEQUI, Mario, 1126
SERDARIS, Vangelis, 3618
SERGEYEV, Konstantin, 5839
SERRADOU, Narcisco Ibanez, 2908
SETO, Javier, 955, 1702
SEVEN, Johnny, 4386
SEVERAC, Jacques, 1338
SEWELL, Vernon, 1325, 4044, 4149, 6071, 6077
SHA, Huang, 3569, 5693
SHAMSHIEV, Bolot, 6919
SHANE, Maxwell, 4468
SHANIN, Ronald E., 69
SHANNON, Frank (pseud. for Franco Prosperi), 63, 2801
SHAPIRO, Mikhail, 3307
SHARITS, Paul, 4533, 4895, 5179, 5181
SHARP, Don, 379, 778, 1328, 1529, 1687, 1890, 3174, 3385, 5171, 5354, 6421, 6893, 7210
SHARPE, Robert K., 466
SHARPSTEEN, Ben, 1712
SHAVELSON, Melville, 445, 953, 2052, 2909, 3164, 4410, 4632, 4900, 5646, 7374
SHEA, Jack, 1423
SHEAR, Barry, 6542, 7154
SHEBIB, Don, 2418, 2458
SHELDON, James, 759, 1536
SHELDON, Sidney, 843
SHELENKOV, Alexander, 685, 5586
SHELLEY, Joshua, 4859
SHEPARD, Gerald S., 2753
SHER, Jack, 3308, 3728, 6462, 7142
SHERIDAN, Jay J., 4378
SHERIN, Edwin, 2397, 6820
SHERMAN, George, 547, 1039, 1221, 1371, 1798, 1990, 2104, 2125, 2710, 3474, 5854, 5898, 6277, 7220
SHERMAN, Lowell, 5704
SHERMAN, Vincent, 57, 1980, 2665, 3004, 3019, 4357, 5571, 7352
SHINDO, Kaneto, 1044, 3136, 3421, 3706, 4675
SHINODA, Masahiro, 1673, 5727
SHOLEM, Lee, 972, 1775, 3713
SHONTEFF, Lindsay, 1523, 4119, 5570
SHUEN, Shu, 243
SIDNEY, George, 852, 1735, 2596, 3207, 3287, 3382, 4761, 4852, 5206, 6170, 6486, 6922, 7125, 7330
SIEGEL, Donald, 327, 471, 560, 1192, 1590, 1738, 2069, 2557, 2622, 2714, 2887, 3112, 3342, 3606, 3839, 4510, 5315, 5928, 5983
SIEGEL, Yakov, 2891
SIELMANN, Heinz, 3692, 4038
SILVERSTEIN, Elliott, 483, 965, 2630, 3912
SILVERSTEIN, Morton, 7062
SIMMONS, Anthony, 644, 2164, 6124
SIMON, Frank, 5106
SIMONELLI, Giorgio, 6815
SINATRA, Frank, 4521
SINGER, Alexander, 889, 1135, 3726, 5071
SINHA, Tapan, 5419
SIODMAK, Curt, 3857
SIODMAK, Robert, 1335, 1336, 1530, 1830, 2000, 2080, 3862, 4981, 7105
SIRK, Douglas, 407, 3035, 5756, 6227, 6514
SJOBERG, Alf, 2202, 4147
SJOBERG, Tore, 1892, 5597
SJOMAN, Vilgot, 1692, 2166, 2964, 2965, 2966, 3791, 4172, 4334
SKALENAKIS, George, 1302
SKOLIMOWSKI, Jerzy, 49, 1468, 1484, 6965
SKORZEWSKI, Edward, 6522
SKOUEN, Arne, 4478
SLATZER, Robert F., 2722
SLEDGE, John, 2159, 3119, 4413
SLUIZER, George, 1102
SLUTSKY, Mikhail, 1975
SMART, Ralph, 841, 5104
SMIGHT, Jack, 2658, 3007, 3025, 3296, 4516, 5137, 5594, 6063, 6378
SMIT, Bout, 241
SMITH, Jack, 2066
SMITH, Judy, 7240
SMITHEE, Allen, 1453
SNASDELL, David, 6269
SNOW, Edgar, 4652
SNOW, Michael, 5226, 7008
SOLANAS, Fernando, 2848
SOLAS, Humberto, 3774
SOLDATI, Mario, 4586, 6913, 7014, 7237

SOLITO, Giacinto, 2338
SOLLIMA, Sergio (see: Sergio Sollina)
SOLLINA, Sergio (var. sp.: Sergio Sollima), 543, 5670
SOLNTSEVA, Yulia, 2070
SOLOMOS, George Paul, 4380
SOLWAY, Clifford, 4163
SONE, John, 3727
SONTAG, Susan, 1710
SORRIN, Ellen, 7240
SOULANES, Louis, 2214, 2230
SOYUZMULTFILM, 5861
SPAFFORD, Robert, 2698
SPARR, Robert, 4238
SPECTRA PICTURES, 3710
SPERLING, Karen, 3883
SPIEKER, Franz Josef, 3418
SPILS, May, 7399
SPINOLA, Paolo, 2234
SPOTTON, John, 842, 4074
SPRING, Sylvia, 3837
SPRINGSTEEN, R.G., 230, 406, 818, 1137, 1156, 2681, 2872, 3238, 4694, 5219, 5268, 5737, 6193, 6946
SPRY, Robin, 5057
STAHL, John M., 339
STANLEY, Paul, 1316, 4153, 6441
STARRETT, Jack, 1306, 5409
STAUDTE, Wolfgang, 130, 5385, 5801
STEEG, Ted, 4830
STEEL, June, 3313, 3333
STEEL, Michael, 7115
STEGANI, Giorgio (see: George Finley)
STENO, 943, 1402, 5077, 6781
STEPHEN, A.C., 6091
STEPHENS, Peter, 4309
STERN, Bert, 3205
STERN, Steven Hillard, 322
STERNBURG, Janet, 6909
STEVENS, George, 100, 1572, 2321, 2516, 4677, 4922, 5694
STEVENS, Leslie, 2756, 3447, 5041
STEVENS, Mark, 6136
STEVENS, Robert, 2996, 3055, 4399
STEVENSON, Robert, 9, 463, 622, 1373, 2401, 3051, 3242, 3332, 3721, 4027, 4145, 4611, 5896, 6322
STIGLIC, France, 4487
STIX, John, 2506
STOLL, Jerry, 5905
STOLOFF, Ben, 1510
STOLOFF, Victor, 3104
STONE, Andrew L., 1314, 1465, 3277, 3495, 4402, 4438, 4821, 5584, 5901
STONE, Barbara and David, 1168
STONE, Bernard, 6690
STONE, David (see: Barbara and David Stone)
STONE, Ezra, 6215
STONEY, George C., 312, 3109, 6352, 7314
STOOKEY, N. Paul, 4523

STORCK, Henri, 5404
STOUMEN, Louis Clyde, 597, 3032, 4359, 4692
STOYANOV, Todor, 1515
STRAND, Chick, 4248
STRANGERUP, Henrik, 2383
STRAUB, Jean-Marie, 1069, 4424
STRICK, Joseph, 355, 5509, 6655, 6753
STROCK, Herbert L., 646, 1257, 2416, 2922, 3000, 5289
STROYEVA, Vera, 702
STUART, Mel, 3016, 7180
STURGES, John, 346, 851, 1831, 2356, 2498, 2562, 2601, 2889, 3005, 3493, 3508, 3861, 3865, 4008, 4403, 4609, 5497, 5625, 6773
STURGES, Preston, 2201
STURLIS, Edward, 1916
SUCKSDORFF, Arne, 2099, 2489, 4324, 4848, 4961
SUDGE, Joel, 2433
SUMMERS, Jeremy, 1292, 1842, 1972, 2893, 5080, 5478, 6847
SUMMERS, Manuel, 3273, 6817
SURD, Iona, 727
SURIN, Fred, 774
SUTHERLAND, A. Edward, 1847
SWERIN, Charlotte, 5461
SWIFT, David, 2455, 2931, 3101, 3733, 4965, 6771
SWIMMER, Sal (var. sp.: Saul Swimmer), 1162, 2134, 4173
SYLBERT, Paul, 5996
SZABO, Istvan, 75, 76, 227

TAKAMURA, Takeji, 5246
TALAMO, Gino, 4382
TALANKIN, Igor, 5948, 6114
TALLAS, Gregg, 387, 570
TAMBURELLA, Paolo W., 5304
TANIGZUGHI, Senkichi, 7070
TANNER, Alain, 1017
TAO, Hsu, 2357
TARADASH, Daniel, 6020
TARKOVSKY, Andrei, 4329
TASHLIN, Frank, 126, 332, 886, 1081, 1597, 2285, 2342, 2389, 3181, 3920, 4594, 5039, 5351, 5519, 7132
TATI, Jacques, 3253, 4161, 4195, 4940, 6606
TAUROG, Norman, 106, 581, 662, 828, 1618, 1656, 1674, 2250, 2251, 2377, 3153, 3638, 4676, 4764, 5621, 5937, 5944, 6485, 6917
TAVELLO, Dino, 1772
TAVIANI, Paolo and Vittorio, 5914
TAYLOR, Don, 1833, 1854, 3189
TAYLOR, Gordon, 5286
TAYLOR, Sam, 1862, 2204
TAZIEFF, Haroun, 6933
TEGSTROM, Rickard, 1299

TELFORD, Frank, 367
TEMANER, Gerald, 2829, 3089
TENNY, Del, 1329, 2859, 2977
TENZER, Bert, 6740
TESHIGAHARA, Hiroshi, 1888, 5407, 7236
TESSARI, Duccio, 515, 4337, 4918, 5908
TETERIN, Yevgeni, 4274
TETUNiC, Louis, 3312
TETZLAFF, Ted, 5657, 7191, 7344
TEWKSBURY, Peter, 1630, 1777, 5995, 6125, 6664
THANH, Huy, 6271
THIELE, Rolf, 1759, 2363, 2531, 4499, 5382, 6556
THOM, Robert, 179
THOMAS, Gerald, 518, 549, 925, 926, 927, 928, 929, 930, 931, 932, 933, 934, 935, 936, 937, 938, 939, 1085, 3128, 4558, 4945, 5161, 6505, 6702, 7000
THOMAS, Gilbert, 7184
THOMAS, Jack, 7044
THOMAS, Leland R., 4331
THOMAS, Lowell, 4732, 5564
THOMAS, Ralph, 8, 874, 1033, 1186, 1436, 1610, 1611, 1621, 1622, 1624, 2772, 2773, 2875, 3130, 3146, 3816, 4493, 4497, 4758, 4855, 5884, 6201, 6394, 6810, 7143, 7327
THOMAS, Robert, 693
THOMPSON, Francis, 4416
THOMPSON, J. Lee., 119, 267, 468, 883, 999, 1231, 1487, 1875, 2063, 2118, 2450, 2577, 2962, 3231, 3374, 3811, 4514, 5256, 6224, 6488, 7056, 7227, 7311
THOMPSON, Marshall, 7299
THOMPSON, Palmer, 3884
THOMPSON, Walter, 5923
THOMSEN, Knud Leif, 6356, 6850
THORPE, Jerry, 1406, 6844
THORPE, Richard, 51, 292, 2111, 2238, 2431, 2840, 2849, 2901, 3184, 3344, 3401, 3459, 6081, 6228, 6283, 6323, 6677
TIEN, Hsieh, 1960
TIKHOMIREV, Roman (var. sp.: Roman Tikhomirov), 1840, 5115
TILL, Eric, 2877, 6963
TINAYRE, Daniel, 2264
TOBALINA, Carlos, 5221
TOGNAZZI, Ugo, 2806
TOKAR, Norman, 556, 2108, 2632, 2863, 5473, 5513, 6419, 6491, 6750
TONE, Franchot, 6758
TOPPER, Burt, 1541, 1566, 2650, 2718, 6058, 6219, 6978
TORRE-NILSSON, Leopoldo, 1730, 1905, 2006, 2170, 2612, 2899, 6113, 6297
TORRES, Miguel Contreras, 3481
TORRES, Pepe, 3998
TORS, Ivan, 5276
TOTTEN, Robert, 5124, 7148
TOURJANSKY, W., 2410, 5032
TOURNEUR, Jacques, 970, 1100, 1161, 1326, 1959, 2326, 3549, 5989, 6497
TOUSSAINT, Carlos, 2477
TOYE, Wendy, 6668, 7018
TOYODA, Shiro, 3024, 4171
TRATZCENKO, Konstantin, 6120
TRAVERS, Alfred, 5022
TREMPER, Will, 1796, 6334
TRESSKER, George, 4089
TRESSLER, Georg, 3860, 6257
TREVOR, Simon, 66
TRINTIGNANT, Nadine Marquand, 3162, 4194
TRIVAS, Victor, 2684
TRNKA, Jiri, 1781, 4104
TROELL, Jan, 1776, 2750, 4613
TRONSON, Robert, 5307, 6611
TRUFFAUT, Francois, 458, 776, 1900, 2162, 3276, 3720, 4155, 4170, 4840, 5730, 6014, 7147
TRUMAN, Michael, 2406, 4182, 6585
TRUMBO, Dalton, 3236
TRUMBULL, Douglas, 5771
TSIFOROS, N., 7186
TUCHNER, Michael, 6888
TULLY, Montgomery, 403, 737, 740, 1763, 1829, 1965, 4037, 5015, 5545, 5773, 6309
TULYBIYEVA, Z., (var. sp.: Z. Tulubyeva), 2938, 6154
TUNSTELL, Douglas, 7249
TURMAN, Lawrence, 4012
TURRELL, Saul J., 3725
TUTTLE, Frank W., 2715, 3141
TZAVELLAS, George, 214, 3604, 6244

UCHIKAWA, Seiichiro, 3272
UHER, Stefan, 6632
ULMER, Edgar C., 138, 215, 524, 1514, 2625
UNITED NATIONS, 3994, 7250
UNIVERSITY OF ARIZONA, 1120
UNIVERSITY OF MISSISSIPPI, 1952
URQUIZA, Zacarius Gomez, 5298
USTINOV, Peter, 572, 3433, 5360, 5539, 6867
UYS, Jamie, 73, 1581

VADIM, Roger, 171, 383, 637, 1087, 2259, 3567, 3742, 4437, 4509, 4944, 5013, 5634, 6203, 6865
VAJDA, Ladislao (var. sp.: Ladislas Vajda), 2432, 3156, 3960, 3976, 3986, 4853, 5680

VALERE, Jean, 6511
VAN DER HEYDE, Nikolai, 5028, 6531
VAN DER HOEVEN, Jan, 6129
VAN DER HORST, Herman, 157, 4767, 6540
VAN DER LINDEN, Charles, 537
VAN DEUSEN, Pieter, 3392
VAN DYKE, W.S., 6605, 7196
VAN PEEBLES, Melvin, 6024, 6168, 7005
VANCINI, Florestano, 3501
VANE, Norman, 2077
VANZI, Luigi (see: Vance Lewis)
VARDA, Agnès, 690, 1110, 1928, 3611, 4683
VARLAMOV, L., 3053
VARLUCKWELL, Max, 4289
VARNEL, Max, 2511, 4174
VAS, Robert, 5224
VEDRES, Nicole, 3580, 6873
VELO, Carlos, 6573
VENTO, Giovanni, 4395
VERHOEVEN, Michael, 4564
VERHOEVEN, Paul, 1133, 1839, 1961
VERNEUIL, Henri, 220, 354, 535, 1247, 1857, 2129, 2571, 3759, 4052, 4212, 4789, 5007, 5712, 5744, 6691, 6885, 7038, 7064
VERTOV, Dziga, 3963
VESELY, Herbert, 798
VESOTA, Bruno, 746, 3113
VICARIO, Marco, 2403, 4361, 5641
VICAS, Victor, 1219, 7013
VIDOR, Charles, 2627, 3738, 5274, 5903, 6153
VIDOR, King, 1930, 2151, 2633, 3966, 5882, 6973
VIGO, Jean, 291, 7386
VILLIERS, David, 878
VILLIERS, Francois, 1728, 6460, 7026
VIOLA, Albert T., 5001
VISCONTI, Luchino, 488, 676, 1356, 1448, 3545, 4583, 4586, 5350, 5612, 6048, 6296, 6580, 7022, 7113, 7212
VLACIL, Frantisek, 4004
VOGEL, Virgil, 3111, 6178
VOHRER, Alfred, 70, 1266, 1427, 1585, 2068, 2225, 7338
VOLNOV, Konstantine, 4013
VON BAKY, Josef, 1173, 1690, 2738, 4275, 6000
VON BORSODY, Eduard (var. sp.: Edward von Borsody), 1202, 3568
VON CZIFFRA, Geza, 2075
VON PODMANITSKY, Felix, 2813
VON PRAUNHEIM, Rosa, 5388
VON RADVANYI, Geza, 1652
VON RATHONY, Akos, 4885
VON STERNBERG, Josef, 659, 1527, 1593, 2971, 3801, 4246, 5449, 5528, 5695, 6478

VON STROHEIM, Erich, 5111, 6962
VORHAUS, Bernard, 60
VRIJMAN, Jan, 5187
VRONSKY, A., 5904
VUKOTIC, Dusan, 5661

WGBH-TV, 261
WADLEIGH, Michael, 7262
WAGNER, Fernando, 6905
WAJDA, Andrzei, 272, 273, 810, 1853, 2289, 3086, 3301, 3415, 3711, 3720, 5743
WALKER, Peter, 1195, 3941, 6074
WALKER, Robert, 6067
WALSH, Raoul, 562, 893, 1379, 1598, 1836, 3354, 3394, 3609, 3999, 4353, 5044, 5269, 5716, 6207, 6371
WALTERS, Charles, 274, 2391, 2784, 3283, 3601, 4942, 6290, 6731, 6792, 6952
WANAMAKER, Sam, 977, 1858, 1999
WARDENBURG, Fred, 2675
WARDL, Al, 2745
WARHOL, Andy, 568, 656, 666, 1034, 1782, 2078, 2169, 2959, 3034, 3666, 3764, 4325, 4552, 5552, 5837, 6621
WARNER, Jr., Jack, 807
WARREN, Charles Marquis, 639, 981, 1024, 1489
WARREN, Jerry, 3071, 3111, 6258, 6307
WARREN, Norman J., 3769
WATERS, Charles, 1657
WATKINS, Peter, 1323, 2387, 5046, 5081, 6976
WATT, Harry, 2156, 3186, 4746, 5746
WATT, Nate, 1987
WAXMAN, Albert S., 1296
WAYNE, John, 90, 2517
WEBB, Jack, 1341, 1681, 3490, 4865, 6391
WEBB, Robert, 495, 2398, 2580, 3739, 4634, 4917, 5066, 5635, 5656, 7010, 7110
WEBSTER, Nicholas, 1434, 2446, 4154
WECHSLER, David, 5299
WEIDENMAN, Alfred, 40, 167, 266, 1307, 1440, 5523
WEINBERG, Maxwell, 3400
WEINRIB, Lennie, 429, 4730, 7170
WEIR, Peter, 6459
WEIS, Don, 1286, 1573, 1699, 2286, 2317, 3375, 3686
WEISENBORN, Gordon, 5019
WEISS, Adrian, 773
WEISS, Jiri, 4287, 4481, 5366, 7223
WEISS, Peter, 2059
WEISZ, Frans, 2270, 6127
WELLES, Mel, 1129, 3145
WELLES, Orson, 1095, 3037, 3803,

3858, 4157, 4718, 6047, 6587, 6635
WELLMAN, William, 422, 635, 1374, 2467, 2771, 3138, 3442, 4419, 6603
WENDKOS, Paul, 180, 301, 418, 454, 944, 1887, 2329, 2330, 2331, 2579, 3241, 4083, 6225
WERKER, Alfred, 3177, 3697, 5190
WERNER, Peter, 2177
WERTMULLER, Lina, 3647
WEXLER, Haskell, 4065
WHALE, James, 2179
WHITE, Douglas, 309
WHITE, Jules, 6015
WHITEHEAD, Peter, 6555, 7127
WHITNEY, James, 3452
WHITTAKER, Roger, 1051
WICKI, Bernard, 779, 3682, 4244, 6916, 7290
WICKMAN, Torgny, 3451
WIDERBERG, Bo, 26, 392, 1770, 3225, 5176, 7111
WIELAND, Joyce, 6670
WIESEN, Bernard, 1955
WILBUR, Crane, 399
WILCOX, Fred McLeod, 2131, 5578, 5675
WILCOX, Herbert, 1370, 3376, 3432, 3599, 3961, 4055, 5955, 6251
WILDE, Cornel, 431, 3984, 4365, 4488, 6180
WILDE, Ted, 3327
WILDER, Billy, 14, 233, 2146, 3126, 3384, 3708, 3730, 4672, 5037, 5437, 5658, 5885, 5947, 5979, 6137, 7217
WILDER, W. Lee, 669, 5959
WILEY, Dorothy, 5535
WILLIAMS, Derek, 6343
WILLIAMS, Dick, 3625
WILLIAMS, Elmo, 1249
WILLIAMS, Emlyn, 3463
WILLIAMS, Paul, 4729, 5272
WILLIS, Allen, 2676
WILLIS, Jack, 3516
WILSON, John David, 5719
WILSON, Richard, 89, 3121, 4833, 5177, 6444, 6966
WINDUST, Bretaigne, 1893, 7203
WINNER, Michael, 2263, 2343, 2626, 3020, 3246, 3513, 4296, 4934, 7048, 7320
WINSTON, Ron, 141, 381, 1658
WINTER, Donovan, 4845, 5058, 6673
WIODZIMIERZ, Haupe, 3780
WIRTH, Franz Peter, 250
WISBAR, Frank, 409, 1165
WISE, Herbert, 124, 6849
WISE, Robert, 175, 900, 1413, 1493, 1860, 2673, 2704, 2999, 4579, 5415, 5481, 5631, 5889, 5920, 5982, 6398, 6454, 6721, 6723, 6795, 7050

WISEMAN, Frederick, 398, 2779, 2869, 3509, 6526
WISHMAN, Doris, 1569
WITNEY, William, 228, 695, 966, 1193, 2149, 3293, 3679, 4036, 4785, 5587, 6830, 7326
WITT, Claus Peter, 2493
WOLCOTT, James L., 7172
WOLF, Fred, 577
WOLF, Konrad, 5053, 5988
WOLFF, Perry, 3300, 5849, 6102
WOLK, Lazarusl, 2767
WOLPER, David, 1052, 2154
WOOD, Duncan, 391
WOOD, Edward, 4927
WOOD, Peter, 3050
WOODRUFF, Frank, 1334
WOODS, Jack, 1812
WORTH, Frank, 2629
WORTH, Howard, 5144
WRANGELL, Basil, 5923
WREDE, Caspar, 385, 4647, 5040
WRIGHT, Basil, 3036, 5974, 7279
WRIGHT, Ralph, 4861
WUEST, Harry, 2695
WYLER, William, 493, 538, 922, 1046, 1139, 1505, 1513, 2207, 2242, 2703, 2929, 3571, 5357, 7053

YABLONSKY, Yabo, 321
YABUKI, Kimio, 7273
YARBROUGH, Jean, 5460
YASUDA, Kimiyoshi, 3880, 7383
YATES, Peter, 826, 3228, 4302, 4673, 5343, 6107
YEAWORTH, Irwin S., 633, 1582, 2153, 7009
YERSIN, Yves, 186
YORKIN, Bud, 1153, 1602, 3094, 4406
YOSHIDA, Yoshishige, 1818
YOUNG, Harold, 4490
YOUNG, Jeff, 465
YOUNG, Robert Malcolm, 6622
YOUNG, Terence, 21, 153, 617, 1066, 1206, 1588, 1625, 2217, 4054, 4938, 4972, 5398, 5445, 5627, 6021, 6220, 6325, 6366, 6475, 6645, 6828, 6949, 7382
YOUNG, Tony, 2763
YOUNGER, Tom, 4513
YOUNGSON, Robert, 1421, 2152, 2247, 2428, 3796, 6396, 7075
YOUTKEVICH, Sergei (see: Sergei Yutkevitch)
YUDIN, Ki, 7286
YUTKEVITCH, Sergei (var. sp.: Sergei Youtkevich), 770, 3540, 4719, 6188

ZACHER, Josef, 760
ZADEK, Peter, 3006

ZAGNI, Giancarlo, 5707
ZAKHAROV, Rostislav, 1079
ZAMPA, Luigi, 205, 223, 3743, 7022
ZAMPI, Mario, 717, 2047, 4544, 6562, 7366
ZANUSSI, Krzysztof, 6080, 7400
ZAPHIRATOS, Henri, 4561
ZAPPA, Frank, 6727
ZBONEK, Edwin, 4219
ZEFFIRELLI, Franco, 5365, 6213
ZEMAN, Karel, 1881, 1882, 3212, 3261
ZENS, Will, 902, 2716
ZETTERLING, Mai, 156, 1617, 2372, 3768, 4436
ZGURIDI, A., 3059
ZIEHM, Howard, 2653
ZINNEMANN, Fred, 19, 474, 2216, 2668, 2777, 3330, 3917, 4073, 4076, 4556, 4605, 5562, 6131, 6294
ZOHAR, Uri, 4530
ZUGSMITH, Albert, 1140, 1176, 1651, 4266, 4626, 5038, 5672
ZUKER, Ralph (see: Massimo Pupillo)
ZULAWSKI, Andrzej, 6630
ZURLINI, Valerio, 601, 1914, 2366, 5875, 6899
ZWERIN, Charlotte, 2336, 5347

INDEX TO FILM REVIEWERS

INDEX TO FILM REVIEWERS

A.M., 740, 846, 3634, 3825, 4515, 5578, 7368
A.M.Z., 6397
A.P.H., 2390, 3108, 5742
AARONS, Marion, 2999
ABBOTT, Harvey S., 6186
ABRAMS, Sandra R., 4559
ADAMS, David, 1367, 1602, 1630, 2194, 2837, 2952, 3105, 3259, 3838, 3949, 4169, 5052, 5305, 5481, 5799, 5884, 5958, 6088, 6231, 6282, 6314, 6893, 6992, 7080, 7141
ADAMSON, Joe, 4210
ADDISON, Montague, 2192
ADRIAN, Allan Aaron, 4898
AGEE, James, 6137A, 6137B
AGUIRRE, José, 474, 5402, 5781
AIGNER, Hal, 3784, 5225
AINSLEE, Marshall, 6686
ALLEN, Campbell, 772, 1656, 3216, 5838
ALLEN, Don, 4075, 6014
ALLEN, Roderic, 1640, 4358
ALTHOUSE, Eliot, 1178
AMBERG, George, 6313
AMES, Nigel, 5183, 5374, 7227
ANCK, Robert, 5284, 6618, 6738
ANDERSON, Lindsay G. (also see: L.G.A.), 113, 148, 422, 442, 451, 545, 586, 950, 1007, 1047, 1152, 1284, 1601, 1644, 1694, 1903, 2435, 2553, 2807, 2832, 2935, 3350, 3470, 3697, 3714, 3827, 4108, 4131, 4167, 4430, 4693, 4759, 4911, 5092, 5130, 5194, 5206, 5244, 5411, 5542, 5565, 5942, 6121, 6238, 6365, 6366, 6512, 6688, 6721, 6765, 6873, 6948A, 6948B, 7063, 7203
ANDERSON, Terence, 922, 4318, 4336, 6370
ANDREWS, Nigel, 49, 797, 2953, 3115, 3361, 3767, 4188, 4223, 6903

ANDREWS, Warren, 660
ANGELL, George, 1383, 7393
ANSTEY, Caleb, 2946
ANSTEY, Edgar, 757, 6502, 7373
ANTONIO, Emile De, 4960
APPEL, Jr., Alfred, 3205, 5598
APPLETON, William W., 5278
ARANA, José, 3986
ARCHER, Eugene, 1467, 3328, 3357, 3505, 4453, 4529, 4605, 4711, 5192, 5889, 6920, 7167
ARCHIBALD, Lewis, 133, 1744, 3452, 4074, 5152, 5753, 6997, 7397
ARISTARCO, Guido, 315, 4539, 6315
ARMES, Roy, 529
ARMITAGE, Peter, 3086, 3270, 3499, 3882, 4322, 4539, 4578, 4958, 5350, 5949, 6105, 6240, 6957, 7335
ARMSTAGE, Kay, 3837, 7389
ARMSTRONG, Michael, 206, 226, 285, 480, 622, 930, 1056, 1159, 1534, 1749, 2242, 2387, 2571, 2757, 3700, 4106, 4154, 4340, 4581, 4593, 4681, 4695, 4878, 4968, 5058, 5356, 5365, 5808, 5823, 5832, 5946, 6848, 7359
ARNOLD, Hy, 4489, 5892, 7387
ARTHYR, Lew, 3500
ASHTON, Dudley Shaw, 3916
ASHTON, Prudence, 510, 782, 1797, 1882, 3051, 3439, 5138, 5666, 5916, 6548, 6723
ASKEW, Rual, 7017
ATWELL, Lee, 906, 1968, 4329
AUSTEN, David, 46, 74, 142, 187, 301, 403, 413, 461, 601, 680, 745, 780, 801, 820, 826, 869, 917, 960, 1022, 1070, 1104, 1142, 1183, 1194, 1228, 1335, 1336, 1360, 1362, 1371, 1376, 1406, 1433, 1457, 1661, 1676, 1731, 1795, 1875, 1927, 1951, 2041, 2071, 2091, 2115, 2143, 2262, 2476, 2573, 2596, 2621, 2707, 2748, 2755,

(cont.)
2893, 2927, 3045, 3338, 3381,
3492, 3790, 3839, 4095, 4421,
4507, 4616, 4627, 4638, 4644,
4748, 4870, 4907, 4928, 4959,
4993, 5106, 5343, 5459, 5521,
5569, 5594, 5618, 5671, 5897,
5909, 5975, 5995, 6011, 6074,
6165, 6187, 6259, 6284, 6300,
6393, 6490, 6501, 6559, 6595.
6613, 6664, 6669, 6715, 6734,
6739, 6763, 6806, 6949, 6974,
7012, 7146, 7331
AUSTEN, Olive, 5276
AXTHELM, Kenneth, 217, 351, 4546,
5835, 7215

BACHMANN, Gideon, 2, 467, 1475,
1747, 1863, 2034, 4424
BAIRD, Naomi, 1504
BAKER, Augusta, 158
BAKER, Peter C., 15, 43, 89, 95, 96,
102, 119, 149, 153, 160, 171, 177,
194, 201, 251, 299, 304, 333, 384,
395, 439, 477, 491, 493, 504, 506,
514, 516, 522, 538, 542, 580, 606,
607, 616, 623, 661, 728, 734, 755,
758, 761, 781, 832, 840, 874, 877,
899, 919, 964, 968, 975, 1006,
1028, 1033, 1094, 1111, 1164,
1182, 1191, 1219, 1338, 1368,
1397, 1411, 1412, 1465, 1467,
1487, 1490, 1491, 1540, 1728,
1747, 1863, 1867, 1884, 1898,
1921, 1973, 1988, 1994, 2045,
2063, 2083, 2096, 2100, 2103,
2107, 2116, 2147, 2207, 2217,
2252, 2273, 2285, 2298, 2334,
2367, 2372, 2374, 2414, 2450,
2585, 2587, 2649, 2691, 2711,
2774, 2782, 2785, 2786, 2803,
2916, 2919, 2925, 2939, 2955,
2961, 2963, 3018, 3026, 3049,
3081, 3088, 3102, 3139, 3176,
3198, 3207, 3234, 3252, 3256,
3270, 3276, 3290, 3294, 3318,
3346, 3380, 3388, 3391, 3399,
3423, 3427, 3440, 3445, 3456,
3464, 3502, 3514, 3519, 3522,
3529, 3548, 3561, 3586, 3625,
3660, 3675, 3694, 3730, 3735,
3819, 3921, 3930, 3940, 3944,
3957, 3965, 3981, 3990, 4041,
4157, 4167, 4184, 4195, 4263,
4291, 4320, 4333, 4353, 4357,
4364, 4367, 4428, 4489, 4514,
4525, 4541, 4548, 4567, 4594,
4597, 4605, 4629, 4673, 4680,
4685, 4701, 4715, 4749, 4751,
4760, 4784, 4816, 4825, 4832,
4841, 4871, 4989, 5011, 5072,

5079, 5090, 5121, 5140, 5157,
5158, 5182, 5237, 5250, 5344,
5374, 5379, 5500, 5560, 5565,
5568, 5612, 5627, 5629, 5644,
5652, 5657, 5684, 5698, 5716,
5774, 5775, 5796A, 5796B, 5829,
5842, 5871, 5882, 5883, 5885,
5922, 5923, 5929, 5931, 5977,
6020, 6021, 6027, 6031, 6059,
6100, 6105, 6119, 6131, 6153,
6240, 6246, 6249, 6276, 6290,
6329, 6355, 6384, 6394, 6397,
6411, 6438, 6448, 6460, 6488,
6507, 6517, 6529, 6547, 6548,
6562, 6599, 6610, 6616, 6638,
6668, 6686, 6699, 6726, 6746,
6784, 6819, 6865, 6869, 6870,
6876, 6908, 6917, 6926, 7050,
7094, 7106, 7125, 7153, 7184,
7189, 7226, 7229, 7255, 7310,
7355, 7366
BALDE, Gibril, 647
BALLAN, Lewis, 860
BANACKI, Raymond, 886, 2021, 2173,
2262, 3296, 3833, 4240, 6282,
6487, 6722
BANNING, Bradford, 5128
BANNING, Griswold, 6134
BARKER, Raleigh, 1341
BARNES, Clive, 684
BARNES, Peter, 783, 809, 870, 1010,
1232, 1369, 1600, 1809, 2518,
2524, 3129, 3458, 3609, 4231,
4743, 4946, 5087, 5244, 5648,
5658, 6481, 6773, 6898, 7045
BARR, Charles, 1274, 2742, 3353,
3863, 4802, 5251
BARSY, Kalman, 2848
BARTHOLOMEW, David, 101
BARTLETT, Louise, 256, 2058, 3319,
3795, 5271, 6008
BARTLETT, Nicholas, 6493
BASSETT, John M., 6504
BATES, Dan, 383, 1003, 1013, 2160,
2242, 2399, 2517, 2655, 2754,
2923, 3047, 3126, 3144, 3689,
4011, 4238, 4272, 4959, 5051,
6500, 6808
BATTCOCK, Gregory, 656, 1782, 5552
BATTEN, Mary, 1747
BAUMBACH, Jonathan, 1741, 4825,
6686
BAXTER, Brian, 135, 1963
BAY, Tim, 7381
BAZELON, David T., 4960
BEACHAM, Rod, 1874
BEAN, Robin, 11, 38, 70, 105, 111,
118, 144, 146, 180, 215, 220, 244,
266, 355, 385, 390, 416, 419, 423,
427, 430, 527, 557, 574, 578, 619,
657, 658, 662, 721, 798, 865, 921,
974, 1251, 1272, 1280, 1308, 1312,

1354, 1392, 1545, 1555, 1598,
1614, 1615, 1627, 1699, 1701,
1768, 1796, 1824, 1826, 1836,
1866, 1901, 1909, 1914, 1932,
2008, 2057, 2069, 2087, 2111,
2155, 2160, 2213, 2238, 2251,
2289, 2306, 2343, 2366, 2377,
2431, 2440, 2580, 2593, 2601,
2626, 2632, 2719, 2830, 3020,
3043, 3126, 3165, 3172, 3246,
3285, 3332, 3358, 3385, 3390,
3411, 3513, 3554, 3680, 3682,
3698, 3719A, 3719B, 3720, 3728,
3810, 3892, 3900, 3967, 4027,
4036, 4121, 4137, 4160, 4186,
4228, 4283, 4314, 4361, 4387,
4477, 4497, 4521, 4561, 4698,
4699, 4750, 4764, 4799, 4809,
4871, 4872, 4885, 4945, 4955,
4979, 5005, 5023, 5034, 5046,
5080, 5083, 5189, 5286,
5319, 5361, 5468, 5499, 5572,
5585, 5595, 5616, 5622, 5637,
5720, 5850, 5895, 5938, 5945,
5959, 6041, 6057, 6075, 6130,
6158, 6173, 6208, 6210, 6274,
6381, 6422, 6473, 6536, 6549,
6601, 6608, 6609, 6677, 6810,
6922, 6945, 6977, 7048, 7092,
7114, 7119, 7143, 7232, 7237,
7256, 7257, 7303, 7320
BECK, James M., 6065
BECKMAN, T.S., 2654, 2655
BEDFORD, Richard H., 4826
BEH, Sieu Hwa, 7240
BEHLMER, Rudy, 4875
BELL, Aaron, 195
BELMONT, Claudia, 606, 892, 3083,
3665, 5613, 7344
BELTON, John, 4211
BELZ, Carl J., 1214, 4265, 5245
BENAIR, Jonathan, 6364
BERG, Marilyn, 3434, 4646
BERGMAN, Ingmar, 4543
BERNARD, Jeffrey, 3986
BERNHARDT, William, 3017, 4170,
5382, 6201, 7229
BERNSTEIN, Barbara, 1032, 3763,
5424, 6669
BERNSTEIN, Judith, 1757, 5310, 5313
BERNSTEIN, Samuel, 2203, 6570
BIBBY, Anne, 546
BIBERMAN, Karl, 5877
BICKNELL, Sam, 5347
BILLARD, Ginette, 2540, 7378
BILLINGS, Pat, 2197, 7099
BISHOP, Christopher, 4070
BLADES, John, 559
BLAIR, Salley Ann, 690
BLAKESTON, Oswell, 3645, 3816,
5712
BLAND, Edward, 1313
BLANDFORD, Mark, 2706, 4754
BLUMENBERG, Richard, 3499
BLUMER, Ronald, 18, 101, 132, 4016,
4564, 4806, 5070, 5496, 6203,
6796, 7282
BODIEN, Earl, 1175, 1203, 4562, 4727,
4931, 5541, 6369
BOELKER, Dudley, 4526
BOGDANOVICH, Peter, 580, 1587,
1757, 2505, 2666, 4006, 5484, 6744
BOLAS, Terry, 3528, 4599
BOND, Kirk, 1710, 2307, 2890, 4862,
5761, 7236
BONTEMPS, Jacques, 3997, 5099
BORDWELL, David, 1089, 1095, 3958,
4536, 6835
BORNEMAN, Ernest, 1236, 5188, 6040
BORSHELL, Allen, 629
BOWEN, Clarissa, 68, 4891
BOWNESS, Alan, 7283
BOWSER, Eileen, 5493
BOYAJIAN, Cecile Starr (also see:
Cecile Starr), 1700, 2641
BOYS, Barry, 446, 1240, 4869
BRADFORD, Walton, 712
BRADLOW, Paul, 6526, 6993
BRAGIN, John, 1050, 1054, 1970,
2472, 2678, 4019, 4300, 5207, 6293
BRAUDY, Leo, 1102, 3619, 5142, 6415
BRAUN, Eric, 322, 1345, 1771, 2086,
3518, 3812, 4072, 4855, 5435,
6650, 7291
BREEN, James, 764
BREHM, Randi, 574
BREITROSE, Henry, 784, 4074, 5532,
5828
BRENDER, Jacobo, 5784
BRENNAN, K.G., 2603
BRETON, Gabriel, 987, 4992, 6890
BREWER, Paul, 1972, 2847, 3686,
5277, 6312
BRIGG, Peter, 1278, 2496, 3577
BRINSON, Peter, 860, 915, 1500, 1698,
2196, 2427, 3622, 4390, 4636,
5026, 5363, 5400, 5633, 6643,
7041, 7158
BRITT, Gwenneth, 206, 389, 1428,
1602, 2060, 2091, 2108, 2591,
2690, 2927, 3099, 3209, 3284,
3668, 4214, 4332, 4340, 4695,
4729, 5059, 5089, 5217, 5229,
6363, 7042, 7098, 7363
BROUGHTON, James, 5422
BROWN, Constance, 4720
BROWN, Kenneth R., 357, 7146
BROWN, Peter G., 2775
BROWN, Robert, 6701
BROWNE, Jeremy, 6587, 6856
BROWNLOW, Kevin, 5987
BROWNSON, Carol, 3217
BRUCE, Louise, 3680, 4825
BRUCKMAN, Adolf, 382, 3041, 5824

BRUSTEIN, Robert, 1626, 3279
BUCHANAN, Angus, 6547
BUCHER, Felix, 186, 528, 1017, 1349, 4022, 6632, 6974, 7147, 7379
BUCK, Tony, 2557, 4096, 5067, 5266, 5463
BUCKLEY, Peter, 115, 515, 876, 932, 1062, 1778, 1853, 2184, 2254, 2462, 2537, 2639, 2679, 2885, 3315, 3340, 3446, 3451, 3485, 3486, 3741, 3867, 4162, 4188, 4240, 4273, 4325, 4393, 4747, 5380, 5557, 5789, 5876, 6243, 6444, 6518, 6598, 6644, 6706, 6736, 7385
BUCKNER, Garth, 3462, 4813
BUDGEN, Suzanne, 3206, 5227A, 5227B
BUNGEY, Timothy, 1378, 6679
BURCH, Nöel, 978, 3029, 3199, 3565, 3906, 6594
BURGESS, Jackson, 1393, 1626, 2536, 3391, 3690, 3775, 3806, 4710, 5781
BURGESS, John, 315, 672, 1279, 3619, 4389, 4539, 5480, 7271
BURNETT, Ron, 1034
BURROUGHS, Archie, 1148, 4974
BUTCHER, Maryvonne, 2472
BUTLER, Charles A., 126, 171, 279, 988, 1455, 2017, 2256, 3163, 3840, 3922, 4063, 4295, 4632, 4725, 4943, 5162, 5494, 6037, 7236
BUTLER, Ivan, 7180
BUTLER, Rupert, 59, 104, 347, 526, 565, 566, 715, 990, 1473, 1501, 1797, 1827, 2237A, 2237B, 2680, 2682, 2794, 3496, 3901, 3916, 4133, 4861, 5024, 5556, 5708, 5947, 5980, 6005, 6201, 6256, 6283
BYRON, Stuart, 2661

C.H., 2246, 7181
CABANA, Jr., Ray, 6605
CADBURY, Alison, 2369
CADWALADER, R.C., 2782
CAEN, Michel, 2540, 4898, 5251, 6755
CALDWELL, William E., 3516
CALLENBACH, Earnest, 1, 116, 144, 194, 213, 358, 457, 577, 580, 607, 753, 916, 941, 980, 1027, 1034, 1036, 1048, 1074, 1313, 1426, 1634, 2676, 1653, 1661, 1676, 1716, 1754, 1770, 1783, 1795, 1810, 1817, 1985, 2007, 2026, 2074, 2205, 2244, 2245, 2437, 2505, 2581, 2792, 2793, 2825, 2829, 2854, 3090, 3091, 3217, 3364, 3370, 3515, 3746, 3868, 3881, 3958, 3985, 4004, 4046, 4224, 4248, 4255, 4323, 4436, 4479, 4609, 4629, 4778, 4823,

4881, 4886, 4960, 4984, 5052, 5072, 5126, 5220, 5246, 5272, 5301, 5331, 5396, 5461, 5470, 5480, 5484, 5535, 5575, 5594, 5629, 5689, 5804, 5921, 6103, 6113, 6122, 6184, 6352, 6411, 6482, 6526, 6528, 6534, 6568, 6584, 6635, 6737, 6993, 7034, 7128, 7145, 7166, 7192, 7262, 7302, 7314, 7359, 7380, 7393
CAMBON, Jean, 4492, 6860
CAMERON, Ian, 1, 11, 446, 496, 691, 692, 696, 718, 769, 770, 817, 826, 905, 1022, 1242, 1318, 1424, 1468, 1576, 1768, 1864, 1953, 1962, 1981, 2411, 2586, 2949, 3269, 3273, 3544, 3547, 3597, 3608, 3798, 3954, 4006, 4225, 4445, 4543, 4868, 4903, 5057, 5142, 5264, 5472, 5476, 5496, 5676, 5718, 5803, 5870, 5914, 6061, 6160, 6264, 6473, 6597, 6646, 6798, 6817, 6965, 6971, 7111, 7147, 7185, 7376
CAMPBELL, Russell, 3319, 4188, 6064, 7245
CAMPER, Fred, 262, 1073, 4328, 5114, 5240, 6227, 6695
CANHAM, Kingsley, 52, 103, 749, 852, 1070, 1223, 1471, 1920, 2342, 2812, 3254, 3707, 3949, 4026, 4075, 4270, 4338, 4827, 5009, 5066, 5084, 5193, 5302, 5414, 5805, 5951, 5983, 6368, 6380, 6454, 6725
CAREY, Gary, 983, 2633, 4300, 6014
CARGIN, Peter, 1017, 2851, 2949, 3774, 4250, 6811
CARPENTER, Eloise Hart, 703, 2092, 4176, 4365
CARPENTER, Helen, 323, 2109, 4655, 5568, 7365
CARRENO, Richard D., 480, 3835
CARROLL, John, 1128, 1648, 2136, 2391, 2651, 2791, 3226, 3469, 3527, 3924, 4020, 4718, 5278, 5387, 5635, 6116, 6207, 6884, 7101
CARTER, Caroline, 2890
CARUSO, Settimio, 1050, 2339, 4582
CASE, John P., 3262
CASTELLO, Casare, 3279
CASTY, Alan, 4028, 4832
CAVANDER, Kenneth, 163, 2867, 3036, 4401, 4418, 4556, 5041, 5568, 5906, 6465, 7167
CAWELTI, John G., 694A, 694B
CECIL, Norman, 194, 480, 1019, 1287, 1356, 1632, 1713, 1923, 2063, 2191, 2402, 3001, 3013, 3016, 3322, 3417, 3690, 4120, 4787, 5051, 5569, 6589, 6959
CHADBOURNE, Eric, 847

CHAMBERLIN, Philip, 451, 467, 574, 637, 1048, 1868, 5561
CHAMBERS, Wade, 4316, 6503
CHANAN, Michael, 2591
CHANDLER, Joanne, 3050, 6377
CHANGAS, Estelle, 2476, 3763, 4726, 6971
CHAPIN, Elspeth Burke (also see: Elspeth Hart), 1078, 1391, 3372, 3622, 4866
CHAPPETTA, Robert, 26, 2412, 5383, 6293
CHARLES, E. Dexter, 6775
CHAUTEMPS, Yvonne, 2384, 5320
CHIMNEY, Ernest, 2826
CHODES, Stephen, 6755
CHOMONT, Tom S., 1220, 1819
CHRISTIE, Jan L., 605, 5781, 7245
CHUKHRAI, Grigori, 4178
CLARENS, Carlos, 1, 446, 1242, 2188, 3995, 5353, 6465, 6899
CLARK, Alan, 3538, 5235, 5429, 5431, 7246
CLARK, Arthur B., 89, 180, 356, 416, 578, 670, 745, 751, 776, 853, 883, 923, 1036, 1077, 1169, 1354, 1653, 1804, 1805, 1879, 1891, 2155, 2288, 2358, 2480, 2482, 2493, 2512, 2601, 2811, 2827, 3064, 3091, 3224, 3225, 3270, 3721, 3881, 3942, 3967, 3978, 4121, 4291, 4627, 4691, 4694, 4750, 4769, 4959, 5008, 5052, 5313, 5396, 5425, 5428, 5432, 5461, 5479, 5625, 5654, 5688, 5744, 5949, 6018, 6224, 6763, 6766, 6812, 7061, 7146, 7148, 7269, 7284, 7355
CLARK, Harold Ormesby, 104
CLARK, Jacqueline, 6967
CLARK, Joan, 1052
CLARK, Penelope, 4942
CLOUZOT, Claire, 1050, 1895, 2910, 2959, 3105, 3762, 5106, 5234, 6976
COBHAM, Shirley, 372, 6713, 7024
COCKS, Jay, 657, 776, 826, 1958, 3608, 5459
COCKS, Jr., John C., 531
COE, Paul-Etienne, 5164
COHEN, Hubert I., 657
COHEN, Jules, 5207
COHN, Emma, 3710
COLE, Clayton, 513, 612, 786, 794, 823, 1706, 1721, 2935, 3371, 4351, 5026, 5633, 5868, 6081, 6402, 6766, 6829, 7158
COLE, Mary Howland, 976
COLLIDGE, Joseph R., 5917
COLLIER, Kay, 335, 445, 588, 924, 1270, 1476, 2250, 2640, 3961, 4512, 4569, 4622, 5440, 5522, 6783, 6795

COLLINS, Alan, 2579, 7145, 7160
COMBS, Richard, 957, 2699, 2997, 4921, 5154, 5173, 5203, 6111, 7099
COMERFORD, Adelaide, 390, 464, 875, 895, 906, 1043, 1240, 1362, 1546, 2010, 2161, 2476, 2522, 2577, 2611, 2658, 2931, 3055, 3124, 3271, 3384, 3607, 3750, 4322, 4401, 4406, 4521, 4585, 4860, 5060, 5119, 5133, 5480, 5622, 5765, 5945, 6075, 6197, 6213, 6295, 6576, 6602, 6755, 6805, 6982, 7033, 7066, 7090, 7275, 7321
COMITO, Terry, 6587
COMOLLI, Jean-Louis, 127, 362, 1900, 4862, 6450, 6576, 6923
CONNELLY, Robert, 2155, 3548, 5921, 6296
CONNER, Edward, 493, 2500, 3366
CONOVER, Shirley, 2220, 4573, 5072, 5651, 5880
CONRAD, Derek, 21, 99, 308, 341, 349, 473, 510, 552, 667, 738, 812, 1222, 1373, 1857, 1880, 2201, 2375, 2417, 2623, 2888, 3001, 3019, 3096, 3098, 3301, 3432, 3488, 3493, 3533, 3649, 3947, 3959, 3976, 4144, 4156, 4271, 4327, 4404, 4437, 4579, 4670, 4788, 4981, 4988, 5260, 5301, 5310, 5321, 5351, 5353, 5372, 5457, 5613, 5665, 5997, 6092, 6279, 6281, 6391, 6398, 6678, 6747, 6804, 6856, 6925, 6927, 7254, 7306, 7342
CONRAD, Randall, 11, 5905, 6872
CONROY, Frank, 694, 3045
COOK, Christopher, 938, 957, 4230
COOK, Jim, 694
COOK, Page, 221, 236, 505, 694, 1056, 1615, 2014, 2021, 2517, 2596, 2952, 3246, 3608, 4111, 4593, 4616, 4624, 4726, 5014, 5142, 5364, 5365, 5572, 5575, 5850, 5978, 6418, 6538, 6711, 6826, 6949, 7174, 7369
COOLIDGE, J.R., 7370
CORBIN, Louise, 220, 316, 324, 498, 593, 637, 693, 945, 996, 1138, 1250, 1461, 1475, 1758, 1768, 1784, 1900, 1977, 2162, 2201, 2308, 2460, 2983, 3211, 3441, 3449, 3499, 3550, 3567, 3583, 3742, 3760, 3775, 3788, 3905, 3928, 4144, 4212, 4357, 4364, 4372, 4541, 4705, 4788, 4978, 4987, 4988, 5069, 5086, 5140, 5227, 5234, 5399, 5526, 5634, 5664, 5692, 5735, 5801, 6014, 6039, 6313, 6437, 6528, 6553, 6581, 6614, 6640, 6734, 6746, 6914, 6970, 7015, 7351

CORLISS, Richard, 59, 339, 410, 585, 903, 951, 1053, 1928, 2223, 2890, 2913, 2960, 3030, 3715, 4065, 4862, 6349, 6570, 7006
CORMAN, Cid, 2646, 6545
COTE, Guy, 4574
COURCEY, Nigel de, 404
COVERT, Nadine, 466, 1561, 3160, 3420, 5164, 6961, 7260
COWAN, Bob, 122, 6864, 7394
COWIE, Peter, 10, 198, 248, 281, 352, 479, 500, 502, 529, 605, 611, 624, 696, 719, 776, 807, 882, 995, 1019, 1026, 1103, 1174, 1179, 1207, 1274, 1291, 1293, 1356, 1448, 1516, 1519, 1542, 1559, 1697, 1745, 1776, 1818, 1902, 1958, 1962, 1969, 2022, 2042, 2383, 2386, 2473, 2534, 2607, 2661, 2890, 2899, 2933, 2964, 3013, 3084, 3115, 3196, 3200, 3225, 3295, 3305, 3412, 3587, 3597, 3690, 3696, 3798A, 3798B, 3834, 3844, 3855, 3920, 3955, 3969, 4206, 4216, 4312, 4350, 4352, 4425, 4613, 4716, 4810, 4812, 4838, 4940, 5007, 5199, 5247, 5262, 5323, 5389, 5395, 5430, 5461, 5664, 5733, 6014, 6293, 6416, 6466, 6531, 6540, 6545, 6646, 6739, 6790, 6831, 6843, 6877, 6943, 6960, 7202, 7294, 7378, 7400
COX, Douglas, 5511
CRADDOCK, John, 1015, 1016, 2779, 3013
CRAMER, Alex, 3832
CRANDALL, Maya, 4740
CRAWFORD, Edward, 4960
CRAWFORD, Hugh, 2479
CRAWFORD, Pamela, 1034
CRAWFORD, Stanley, 1786, 2307, 3154, 3762, 6986, 4191, 4534, 5204, 5686
CREELEY, Robert, 4069
CRICK, Philip, 5931
CROCE, Arlene, 232, 384, 684, 769, 805, 919, 1181, 1807, 2162, 2308, 3346, 3550, 3655, 4146, 4824, 5202, 5375, 6134, 6246, 6315, 6463, 7015, 7271
CROME, John, 3780, 3918, 4607, 7223
CROOKS, Harold, 1038
CROWDUS, Gary, 708, 847, 1356, 1634, 3002, 3225, 3480, 4301, 5081, 5365, 5447, 5912, 6064, 6130, 6482, 6739, 6943
CURLE, Howard, 833, 7391
CUTTS, John, 50, 90, 107, 110, 138, 160, 233, 323, 340, 382, 391, 425, 478, 490, 503, 572, 593, 617, 637, 736, 739, 782, 851, 852, 895, 931, 942, 1011, 1045, 1086, 1095, 1133, 1148, 1247, 1370, 1377, 1418, 1422, 1432, 1568, 1603, 1631, 1657, 1669, 1755, 1767, 1787, 1830, 1838, 1841, 1864, 1885, 1919, 1956, 2014, 2040, 2043, 2097, 2150, 2161, 2178, 2188, 2218, 2241, 2260, 2301, 2328, 2332, 2352, 2405, 2469, 2485, 2519, 2545, 2611, 2619, 2666, 2697, 2714, 2804, 2840, 2844, 2845, 2849, 2854, 2882, 2895, 2931, 2955, 3052, 3082, 3085, 3132, 3205, 3242, 3283, 3360, 3366A, 3366B, 3426, 3441, 3487, 3490, 3495, 3498, 3556, 3654, 3730, 3742, 3753, 3776, 3813, 3875, 3925, 3957, 4030, 4050, 4086, 4233, 4264, 4306, 4358, 4401, 4405, 4431, 4443, 4493, 4537, 4761, 4827, 4852, 4875, 4883, 4909, 4919, 4938, 4949, 4958, 4973, 4995, 5160, 5163, 5172, 5174, 5264, 5280, 5284, 5289, 5294, 5303, 5349, 5415, 5423, 5458, 5472, 5503, 5520, 5571, 5626, 5669, 5703, 5711, 5714, 5722, 5792, 5812, 5893, 5896, 5933, 5969, 5991, 6017, 6072, 6082, 6134, 6156, 6167, 6171, 6196, 6205, 6220, 6232, 6239, 6298, 6341, 6419, 6491, 6539, 6563, 6587, 6625, 6635, 6702, 6792, 6857, 6886, 6950, 6957, 6982, 7013, 7018, 7036, 7056, 7075, 7130, 7217A, 7217B, 7227, 7337

D.G., 2409
D.V., 6657
DALE, R.C., 5407
DANCYGER, Ken, 2869, 3062
DANIELS, Don, 6739
DART, Michael, 1039
DAVALLE, Peter, 64, 258, 1072, 1200, 1304, 2480, 3864, 4047, 4111, 4360, 4365, 4790, 5060, 5393, 5428, 5462, 6213, 6645
DAVIDSON, Sara, 703
DAVIES, Brenda, 26, 112, 334, 799, 996, 1066, 1356, 1409, 1914, 2367, 2583, 2737, 2828, 3060, 3608, 3749, 3917, 4306, 4338, 4720, 4817, 4838, 4860, 4968, 5162, 5195, 5239, 5916, 6683, 6723, 7025, 7103, 7333
DAVIES, Brian, 1, 1565, 2789, 3136, 3397, 3398, 3595, 3683, 4831, 5603, 6887
DAVIS, Daniel S., 953, 1901
DAVIS, Fitzroy, 4710
DAVIS, Gary L., 6192
DAVIS, Richard, 55, 147, 221, 239,

283, 394, 424, 431, 505, 549, 571,
628, 651, 737, 831, 894, 925, 937,
958, 971, 1001, 1003, 1031, 1160,
1211, 1224, 1290, 1325, 1364,
1384, 1443, 1532, 1546, 1573,
1578, 1586, 1628, 1629, 1663,
1858, 1859, 1894, 1996, 1997,
2035, 2050, 2117, 2176, 2182,
2245, 2313, 2396, 2491, 2507,
2568, 2670, 2681, 2690, 2709,
2720, 2730, 2745, 2795, 2833,
2838, 2892, 2975, 3046, 3227,
3248, 3296, 3297, 3422, 3448,
3449, 3459, 3575, 3672, 3721,
3729, 3756, 3834, 3876, 3941,
3952, 4007, 4019, 4119, 4129,
4145, 4168, 4173, 4272, 4386,
4400, 4402, 4409, 4483, 4532,
4661, 4714, 4721, 4768, 4782,
4802, 4811, 4823, 4929, 4933,
5010, 5071, 5127, 5168, 5204,
5211, 5256, 5354, 5396, 5413,
5417, 5547, 5603, 5628, 5662,
5688, 5833, 5840, 5877, 5907,
5944, 6097, 6141, 6162, 6199,
6318, 6360, 6383, 6395, 6424,
6429, 6430, 6442, 6467, 6477,
6516, 6538, 6579, 6691, 6692,
6709, 6712, 6729, 6750, 6812,
6939, 6941, 6952, 7016, 7032,
7071, 7091, 7124, 7174, 7365

DAVIS, Roscoe, 1413, 7085

DAWSON, Jan, 459, 1138, 1468, 2313,
2476, 2758, 3621, 3795, 3806,
4102, 4662, 4999, 5057, 5272,
5689, 6123, 6169, 6722, 6993,
7037, 7120

DAY, Hugh de Sola, 6031

DE LA ROCHE, Catherine, 195, 199,
387, 451, 915, 1187, 1339, 1342,
1825, 2163, 2196, 2279, 2810,
3219, 3328, 3782, 3899, 3904,
3913, 3939, 3956, 3986, 4021,
5107, 6151, 6202, 6585, 6754,
6770, 6924, 7110, 7347

DE LAUROT, Edouard, 6040

DE VARIS, Anna, 1762

DEAN, Kathryn, 6354

DEBRIX, Jean R., 4713

DEGNAN, James P., 727

DEL MAR, Patricia, 7292

DELAHAYE, Michel, 1900, 2472, 2545,
3768, 4363

DELPINO, Louis, 6655

DEMME, Jonathan, 3135

DEMPSEY, Michael, 888, 2504, 5035,
5575, 6320, 6959

DENBY, David, 666, 801, 4102, 4971,
5305

DENEROFF, Harvey, 1907, 4275, 4531,
6530

DENTON, Clive, 306, 3045, 7103

DERAIN, Aline, 7379

DEREN, Maya, 290, 1060, 4062, 4090,
5325, 7214

DERR, William B., 3368

DERR, Wilson, 5789

DESCH, Bernard, 5686

DESILETS, E. Michael, 1897, 6526

DESKEY, Michael, 2197, 3894

DESSNER, Lawrence J., 7262

DETWEILER, Robert, 672

DEWEY, Lang (Langdon), 23, 424,
1138, 1444, 1786, 1888, 2472,
2607, 2678, 3170, 3414, 3548,
3587, 4191, 4903, 4984, 5369,
5686, 6614

DIAMANT, Ralph, 4663

DIAZ, Rodolfo, 3640

DICKSON, Robert G., 5723

DILLINGHAM, Harold, 348, 7313

DONIOL-VALEROZE, Jacques, 315

DOOLEY, Roger B., 269, 456, 783,
1600, 1792, 1997, 4142

DOUGLAS, Peter, 4008

DOWNING, Robert, 395, 869, 968,
1156, 3207, 3877, 4718, 5026,
5278, 6290, 6347, 6908, 7217

DOYLE, Neil, 3591, 3753

DREW, Edward, 6764

DROWNE, Tatiana Balkoff, 64, 66, 160,
365, 684, 702, 805, 989, 1093,
1103, 1253, 1579, 1646, 1647,
1650, 1840, 1929, 1947, 2336,
2863, 2891, 3010, 3233, 3285,
3307, 3363, 3818, 3852, 4488,
4719, 4867, 5129, 5169, 5384,
5417, 5444, 5553, 5557, 6048,
6114, 6154, 6268, 6335, 6680,
6973, 7262

DRUMMOND, Gordon, 1587

DUNCAN, Catherine, 2003

DUNHAM, Harold, 3154, 3351, 5506

DUPERLY, Denis, 5605

DURGNAT, Raymond, 9, 135, 187,
295, 306, 332, 336, 375, 400, 409,
444, 446, 471, 480, 481, 489, 508,
541, 590, 671, 723, 743, 768, 781,
805, 861, 864, 879, 883, 994, 1027,
1029, 1034, 1076, 1135, 1145,
1155, 1167, 1173, 1181, 1250,
1252, 1261, 1279, 1311, 1322,
1329, 1330, 1357, 1394, 1428,
1435, 1436, 1450, 1452, 1482,
1484, 1509, 1536, 1564, 1565,
1574, 1585, 1587, 1607, 1620,
1631, 1640, 1641, 1662, 1716,
1750, 1759, 1767, 1791, 1799,
1822, 1823, 1849, 1855, 1869,
1918, 1924, 1925, 1926, 1928,
1935, 1940, 1976, 2004, 2036,
2062, 2144, 2173, 2192, 2256,
2259, 2294, 2346, 2359, 2361,
2369, 2456, 2460, 2470, 2472,
2516, 2523, 2536, 2540, 2578,
2600, 2620, 2657, 2673, 2683,

(cont.)
2700, 2705, 2723, 2742, 2764,
2766, 2772, 2793, 2799, 2811,
2859, 2884, 2926, 2934, 2938,
2940, 3004, 3032, 3056, 3057,
3065, 3099, 3107, 3112, 3181,
3185, 3221, 3269, 3342, 3384,
3396, 3402, 3405, 3425, 3429,
3454, 3466, 3499, 3501, 3567,
3582, 3588, 3595, 3612, 3616,
3640, 3647, 3655, 3670, 3674,
3725, 3747, 3750, 3768, 3822,
3828, 3926, 3934, 3937, 3938,
3975, 3991, 4011, 4014, 4022,
4056, 4172, 4241, 4243, 4255,
4262, 4278, 4326, 4334, 4398,
4407, 4436, 4442, 4448, 4461,
4499, 4517, 4518, 4524, 4531,
4540, 4550, 4560, 4578, 4675,
4700, 4703, 4713, 4726, 4786,
4791, 4807, 4845, 4862, 4869,
4890, 4923, 4925, 4934, 4975,
5004, 5022, 5042, 5093, 5101,
5118, 5165, 5243, 5251, 5267,
5275, 5307, 5308, 5360, 5376,
5385, 5478, 5488, 5496, 5507,
5510, 5538, 5561, 5588, 5599,
5651, 5679, 5699, 5707, 5730,
5749, 5761, 5769, 5847, 5857,
5859, 5948, 6042, 6043, 6048,
6103, 6107, 6147, 6176, 6180,
6222, 6263, 6292, 6314, 6353,
6385, 6406, 6425, 6427, 6450,
6493, 6495, 6506, 6509, 6555,
6560, 6566, 6574, 6596, 6640,
6647, 6705, 6749, 6753, 6776,
6805, 6816, 6818, 6826, 6850,
6863, 6910, 7029, 7066, 7116,
7127, 7132, 7158, 7164, 7169,
7219, 7238, 7243, 7248, 7257,
7263, 7268, 7271, 7305, 7308,
7325, 7328, 7353, 7369, 7374
DUVAL-CLAIR, Anne, 41
DYER, Peter John, 36, 62, 151, 161,
232, 233, 273A, 273B, 274, 280,
307, 313, 317, 326, 332, 572, 606,
613, 660, 691, 693, 739, 828, 873,
1042, 1097, 1169, 1253, 1281,
1305, 1324, 1365, 1388, 1452,
1474, 1535, 1572, 1632, 1645,
1677, 1691, 1741, 1765, 1790,
1843, 1867, 1871, 1915, 1925,
1971, 2006, 2016, 2271, 2277,
2308, 2347, 2348, 2486, 2503,
2521, 2533, 2595, 2662, 2666,
2668, 2723, 2738, 2752, 2819,
2844, 2868, 2897, 2909, 2933,
2954, 2971, 3017, 3072, 3130,
3194, 3262A, 3262B, 3322, 3354,
3373, 3398, 3428, 3470, 3489,
3524, 3550, 3624, 3652, 3663,
3665, 3854, 3900, 3929, 3935,

3967, 3993, 4006, 4046, 4058,
4100, 4177, 4222, 4247, 4254,
4259, 4418, 4485, 4705, 4719,
4761, 4818, 4824, 4853, 4869,
4872, 4974, 4978, 5016, 5065,
5072, 5086, 5103, 5129, 5148,
5175, 5190, 5251, 5269, 5298,
5371, 5410, 5506, 5524, 5561,
5563, 5579, 5613, 5654, 5664A,
5664B, 5722, 5757, 5776, 5791,
5848, 5851, 5885, 5933, 5956,
5966, 5977, 6001, 6068, 6115,
6128, 6313, 6314, 6350, 6359,
6400, 6465, 6855, 6868, 6904,
6973, 6991, 7113, 7137, 7167,
7213, 7311, 7332, 7355, 7356

E.D.M., 6432
"EDITORS, THE", 1379
EDLEN, Arvid, 3699
EDWARDS, Roy, 4064, 6697, 7229
EHRENSTEIN, David, 1034
EISENSCHER, Judith, 5465
EISNER, Lotte H., 2483
ELEY, Michael, 1668
ELLEY, Derek, 3031, 5726, 6790
ELLISON, Harlan, 416, 444, 623, 903,
3279, 4031, 4098, 5383, 6608,
6805, 6936, 6981
ELLISTON, Maxine Hall, 2119, 2543
ELLMAN, Richard, 6753
ELMORE, Martius L., 6130
EMMENS, Carol A., 2967
ENLEY, Frank, 663
ENNIS, Paul, 2244
ERICSSON, Peter, 216, 592, 663, 1201,
2385, 2898, 3324, 3574, 3783,
4848, 4913, 5098, 5116, 5856,
6106, 6629, 7371
EVANS, Jon, 6754
EVANS, Mary, 1040
EVERSON, William K., 843, 2428,
3935, 4658, 4816, 6563
EYLES, Allen, 17, 97, 129, 167, 173,
231, 242, 282, 329, 371, 377, 379,
544, 567, 618, 630, 664, 681, 693,
776, 839, 903, 906, 912, 916, 953,
959, 1043, 1077, 1100, 1116, 1161,
1287, 1442, 1478, 1481, 1513,
1696, 1704, 1705, 1707, 1821,
1890, 1958, 1970, 2021, 2084,
2092, 2127, 2198, 2204, 2225,
2233, 2243, 2254, 2287, 2302,
2315, 2423, 2559, 2562, 2564,
2570, 2622, 2646, 2652, 2654,
2754, 2788, 2827, 2853, 2883,
2889, 2948, 2993, 3047, 3060,
3079, 3091, 3097, 3110, 3121,
3140, 3201, 3235, 3238, 3260,
3377, 3512, 3603, 3543, 3751,
3756, 3792, 4126, 4161, 4188,

4223, 4299, 4343, 4375, 4380,
4396, 4454, 4469, 4472, 4535,
4577, 4664, 4805, 4828, 4873,
4940, 4952, 4972, 5021, 5142,
5175, 5203, 5223, 5261, 5263,
5311, 5397, 5432, 5476, 5497,
5513, 5579, 5584, 5597, 5608,
5682, 5760, 5765, 5770, 5841,
5934, 5970, 6012, 6044, 6069,
6174, 6184, 6193, 6317, 6364,
6403, 6408, 6409, 6447, 6453,
6066, 6666, 6669, 6716, 6771,
6883, 6916, 6947, 6968, 6986,
6989, 7055, 7069, 7073, 7088,
7144, 7180, 7197, 7235, 7270,
7274, 7276, 7364
EYRE, John, 1543

F. DE ST. E., 691
FAIRSERVICE, Donald, 4140
FARBER, Stephen, 72, 97, 129, 147,
    544, 826, 949, 973, 1019, 1262,
    1362, 1587, 1757, 1806, 1870,
    1886, 1899, 1918, 2072, 2146,
    2462, 2476, 2639, 2712, 2748,
    2827, 2837, 2883, 2929, 2931,
    2952, 2985, 3348, 3486, 3532,
    3603, 3858, 3912, 4340, 4532,
    4553, 4577, 4616, 4858, 4870,
    4928, 5018, 5133, 5521, 5569,
    5572, 5692, 6008, 6043, 6213,
    6226, 6364, 6406, 6418, 6536,
    6722, 6805, 6874, 6949, 7003,
    7042, 7099, 7198, 7288, 7321, 7369
FARMER, James, 1197
FARQUHAR, Hobart M., 4827
FARSON, Daniel, 2112
FEDERMAN, Raymond, 2001
FEIGENBAUM, Sandra, 5331
FEINSTEIN, Herbert, 764, 4058, 4648,
    6675
FENIN, G.N., 346, 623, 781, 2424,
    2651, 3673, 3730, 4880, 5658,
    6020, 6754
FENWICK, J.H., 829, 2536, 3384, 4407,
    5670, 6326, 6755, 6792, 7066
FENYVES, György, 224, 6285
FERGENSON, Ruth L., 893
FERGUSON, Ian, 5197
FERRELL, Patrick, 6444
FIELD, Simon, 3292
FIELD, Sydney, 3056, 3661
FIELDING, Raymond, 5310, 5838
FIESCHI, Jean-André, 314, 1077, 3279,
    3449, 4535, 6379, 6926
FILMER, Paul, 105, 578, 3967
FINLANDER, Joel W., 6962
FISCHER, Eleanor, 4045
FISHER, David, 2972, 4161, 7015
FISHKO, Sara, 5461
FITZPATRICK, Ellen, 105, 233, 274,

308, 315, 335, 542, 661, 676, 699,
764, 849, 852, 1011, 1186, 1498,
2178, 2205, 2335, 2405, 2635,
2713, 2882, 4539, 4548, 2932,
3056, 3075, 3130, 3195, 3423,
3733, 3861, 4041, 4042, 4156,
4525, 4640, 4798, 4852, 5016,
5157, 5358, 5371, 5448, 5520,
5767, 5885, 6038, 6089, 6112,
6130, 6150, 6167, 6208, 6248,
6287, 6415, 6682, 6720, 6744,
6771, 6795, 6957, 7194
FLATTO, Elie, 6739
FLAUS, John, 1640, 3276, 5350
FLUGG, Darrell E., 1348, 1744
FLYNN, Charles, 847, 1727, 1873,
    1874, 1969, 2229, 2639, 3037,
    3469, 3654, 4065, 4599, 4933,
    5156, 5975, 6264, 6364, 7146,
    7379, 7380
FOOSE, Thomas T., 765, 2211, 2663,
    3192, 3794, 4589, 5312, 5329,
    5989, 5992, 6375
FOOTE, Sterling De. G., 580, 1611
FORBES, Bryan, 1626
FORD, Greg, 6728
FOTHERGILL, Robert, 4679
FOWNES, Effingham, 3159
FOX, Charles, 6465
FOX, Terry Curtis, 5359, 6267, 7183
FRAGOSO, Joao De., 607
FRANCHI, R.M., 1640
FRANCIS, John, 222, 1055, 1672,
    1865, 6142, 6954, 7140
FRANCOVICH, Allen, 599
FRANKENHEIMER, John, 5637
FRASER, Graham, 3762
FRAZER, John, 3968
FREEMAN, Ethel Cutler, 5607
FREEMAN, Joseph, 2581
FRENCH, Philip, 101, 1192, 1587,
    1970, 2088, 2505, 3091, 3619,
    4065, 4599, 4858, 4959, 5978
FRIEDENBERG, Edgar Z., 398, 2476,
    2779, 2869, 3509, 6526
FRIEDLANDER, Madeline, 1957, 2222,
    2659, 2825, 3994, 7249, 7250
FRIEDLICH, Ruth K., 710, 2390, 4268
FRIESEMANN, Paul, 1543
FRITSCHER, John J., 6739
FRUCHTER, Norm, 371, 6876
FRUMKES, Roi, 658, 2748, 4993, 6992

G.A.W., 305
GALBAVY, Janice, 6452
GALBRAITH, Harrison, 6753
GALLASCH, Peter F., 263, 2949, 3006,
    3250, 3310, 3418, 3419, 3525
GALT, Isobel, 4031
GANIS, Alma, 898
GARDNER, Robert, 6648

GARGA, B.D., 3183
GARGIN, Peter, 4792
GARLICK, R.J., 3183, 3438, 3854, 5129, 5227, 6720, 6933, 7113, 7297
GASSER, H. Mark, 6739
GAY, Ken, 63, 67, 196, 338, 597, 632, 862, 1298, 1340, 1398, 2135, 2407, 2502, 2937, 3033, 3036, 3069, 3085, 3584, 3637, 3657, 3692, 3770, 4070, 4227, 4284, 4414, 4429, 4462, 4475, 4506, 4621, 4763, 4804, 5066, 5299, 5355, 5480, 5504, 5824, 5892, 6026, 6102, 6227, 6530, 6896, 6932, 7274, 7289, 7298
GAYNOR, Julie, 225
GEDULD, Carolyn, 694
GEIST, Kenneth, 922
GELDZAHLER, Henry, 5837
GEORGAKAS, Dan, 1985, 6267, 7379
GEORGIADOU, Mirella, 159, 330, 2293, 3618, 4601, 5196
GERALD, Yvonne, 4195
GERARD, Lillian N., 701, 916, 3105, 3806, 6123, 7083, 7245
GERRARD, David, 393, 688, 779, 1068, 1277, 1595, 2360, 2434, 3264, 3860, 4899, 5460, 5645, 6714, 7027
GERSTEIN, Evelyn, 3182
GERSTLE, Ralph, 202, 1184, 1721, 2947, 4732, 5357, 5774, 6697, 7112
GESSNER, Robert, 3585
GIARD, Robert, 6379, 6402
GIBBS, Harriet, 4577
GIESLER, Rodney, 511, 803, 1451, 1735, 2131, 2342, 2467, 2642, 2784, 3178, 3277, 3379, 3553, 3669, 3693, 4480, 4544, 4634, 5143, 5183, 5332, 5445, 6251, 6489, 6801, 7010, 7382
GILCHRIST, John, 540, 1825, 3564, 3913, 4817
GILLETT, John, 199, 411, 527, 839, 859, 881, 1036, 1037, 1136, 1180, 1186, 1437, 1653, 1757, 1863, 1982, 2023, 2070, 2235, 2239, 2413, 2577, 2692A, 2692B, 2910, 2916, 2953, 3081, 3083, 3095, 3133, 3270, 3413, 3540, 3569, 3646, 3861, 4101, 4183, 4240, 4276, 4283, 4305, 4307, 4560, 4578, 5105, 5183, 5327, 5353, 5528, 5796, 5851, 5880, 5906, 5947, 5974, 6068, 6513, 6545, 6546, 6605, 6685, 6713, 6870, 7227, 7271, 7298
GILLIOTT, Penelope, 1181, 3353
GILSON, René, 306
GINENSKY, Richard, 623, 1409, 4697
GLADWELL, David, 3013
GLAESSNER, Verina, 2078, 6420

GLAUBMAN, Sigmund, 415, 3494, 4647, 5218, 7004
GLEASON, Morgan, 7392
GLENVILLE, Peter, 455
GLUSHANOK, Paul, 694, 3716, 3868
GODARD, Jean-Luc, 6514
GODET, Sylvain, 6576
GOFFE, Louise, 1512
GOLDFARB, Peter, 4200
GOLDRING, Patrick, 5794, 6250
GOLDWASSER, Noe, 3835, 4644
GOLLUB, Judith, 5323, 6614
GOODE, Peter, 2155, 4329
GOODMAN, Henry, 1540, 1632, 2867, 5880, 7164
GOODWIN, Michael, 2848, 3034, 3806, 4722
GORDON, Edith, 6875
GORDON, Edward, 6772
GORETTA, Claude, 5202
GOSLING, Nicholas, 901, 1008, 2671, 4406, 5248, 5259, 6278
GOTTLIEB, Stephen, 3353, 6576
GOUGH-YATES, Kevin, 420, 731, 896, 1027, 1125, 1139, 2263, 2449, 3117, 3370, 4015, 4142, 4476, 5839, 6083, 6096, 6272
GOULD, Arlene, 3611, 5020
GOULD, Diana, 242
GOW, Gordon, 1, 71, 80, 87, 98, 112, 127, 134, 143, 170, 204, 214, 236, 256, 265, 268, 315, 327, 328, 357, 383, 401, 458, 467, 474, 498, 529, 583, 587, 605, 609, 654, 672, 687, 690, 692, 694, 697, 711, 714, 741, 769, 771, 833, 848, 849, 875, 886, 918, 965, 973, 1002, 1019, 1023, 1036, 1087, 1124, 1141, 1172, 1174, 1179, 1230, 1231, 1240, 1248, 1268, 1321, 1344, 1349, 1355, 1393, 1408, 1425, 1448, 1468, 1512, 1531, 1550, 1558, 1567, 1570, 1653, 1673, 1692, 1710, 1713, 1733, 1734, 1770, 1808, 1870, 1895, 1900, 1912, 1946, 1962, 1968, 1969, 1977, 1982, 1998, 2012, 2022, 2034, 2070, 2076, 2119, 2170, 2239, 2244, 2253, 2424, 2448, 2455, 2461, 2466, 2494, 2505, 2517, 2562, 2583, 2591, 2609, 2612, 2630, 2658, 2727, 2762, 2773, 2817, 2824, 2864, 2890, 2910, 2931, 2946, 2997, 3013, 3025, 3037, 3050, 3051, 3083, 3115, 3124, 3136, 3154, 3203, 3206, 3211, 3223, 3228, 3247, 3279, 3289, 3303, 3319, 3326, 3351, 3353, 3364, 3455, 3504, 3515, 3544, 3545, 3552, 3583, 3590, 3608, 3619, 3650, 3653, 3667, 3668A, 3668B, 3671, 3687, 3688,

3745, 3762, 3763, 3795, 3798,
3804, 3879, 3905, 3912, 3958,
3985, 4005, 4025, 4031, 4039,
4065, 4098, 4140, 4159, 4165,
4183, 4216, 4244, 4260, 4293,
4300, 4302, 4305A, 4305B, 4307,
4329, 4366, 4389, 4410, 4450,
4463, 4467, 4492, 4539, 4583,
4599, 4609, 4648, 4669, 4677,
4710, 4720, 4723, 4740, 4756,
4783, 4801, 4812, 4826, 4828,
4839, 4840, 4856, 4858A, 4858B,
4888, 4900, 4903, 4905, 4987,
4990, 5008, 5018, 5051, 5057,
5059, 5132, 5133, 5138, 5198,
5207, 5238, 5247, 5252, 5273,
5290, 5323, 5336, 5338, 5375,
5383, 5395, 5402, 5433, 5476,
5484, 5487, 5491, 5506, 5518,
5520, 5553, 5575, 5585, 5586,
5610, 5654, 5660, 5668, 5676,
5681, 5689, 5700, 5715, 5734,
5797, 5820, 5853, 5880, 5888,
5891, 5932, 5954, 5971, 5978,
5982, 5993, 6006, 6008, 6014,
6040, 6111, 6123A, 6123B, 6126,
6149, 6154A, 6154B, 6169, 6226,
6267, 6280, 6295, 6315, 6326,
6342, 6348, 6349, 6364, 6377,
6378, 6405, 6445, 6486, 6504,
6505, 6520, 6533, 6546, 6561,
6570, 6571, 6572, 6576, 6602,
6624, 6637, 6675, 6711, 6738,
6755, 6779, 6782, 6788, 6821,
6823, 6880, 6903, 6907, 6923,
6936, 6763, 6981, 6993, 7004,
7005, 7011, 7060, 7072, 7077,
7103, 7107, 7128, 7129, 7155,
7190, 7211, 7230, 7236, 7245,
7259, 7275, 7313, 7322, 7380,
7384, 7392, 7398
GRAHAM, Penelope, 5901
GRAHAM, Peter, 10, 125, 484, 985,
    1130, 1564, 1747, 1868, 1977,
    2025, 2166, 2171, 2646, 2749,
    2932, 3218, 3247, 3255, 3548,
    4300, 4752, 4840, 5079, 5176,
    5242, 5692, 5875, 6103, 6582,
    6652A, 6652B, 6755, 6872, 6916,
    7236, 7378
GRANA, Cesar, 6530
GRATZ, Arthur, 3913
GRAUMAN, Jr., Lawrence, 4146, 6082
GRAY, Hugh, 1762
GRAY, Martin, 3564, 5889
GRAYSON, Anne, 1299
GREEN, Calvin, 833
GREEN, Guy, 3867
GREEN, Harris, 1270
GREEN, O.O., 659, 1527, 1593, 4246,
    5528, 5695
GREENBERG, Joel, 3708, 7053

GREENE, Graham, 7205
GREENSPUN, Roger, 3276
GREER, Herb, 3063
GREGERSEN, Halfdan, 4147
GREGOR, Ulrich, 218
GRENIER, Cynthia, 1947, 4307, 4609
GRENIER, Richard, 4615
GRIFFITH, Ann, 103, 7200
GRIFFITH, Richard, 855, 3594
GRIGS, Derick, 275, 4147, 4574, 6380,
    7213
GRISCOM, Julia Howard, 3081
GROOMS, Roger, 3047
GUARNER, José Luis, 1075
GUERLAIN, Quentin, 3835, 4984
GUILLAUME, Jean, 664
GUNCZY, Ferencz, 6380
GUPTA, Chidananda das, 1026, 5000
GURALNIK, Uran, 6974
GUY, Rory, 455, 474, 677, 895, 1993,
    2673, 2838, 3007, 3422, 3433,
    3796, 4264, 4365, 4823, 5163,
    5273, 5637, 5654, 5669, 5921,
    5961, 6406, 6792, 6818

HAGEN, Ray, 2649
HALL, Janet, 880, 2877, 6086
HALL, John, 4766
HALPRIN, Elinor, 3124, 5961
HAMALIAN, Leo, 4662
HAMEL, David, 3927
HAMMER, Gregory, 826, 3532
HAMPTON, Wiley, 7127
HANDELMAN, Janet, 5606, 6909
HANDZO, Stephen, 7380
HANFORD, Davidson, 4010
HANSON, Curtis Lee, 652, 1194, 2536,
    2658, 3023, 3047, 3241, 4363,
    4930, 6450, 6475, 7042
HARCOURT, Peter, 574, 2736, 3522,
    3660, 4680, 4812, 6466
HARCOURT-SMITH, Simon, 4926,
    5170, 5968
HARDWICK, Elizabeth, 2336, 2538,
    3002, 6621
HARDY, Forsyth, 7279
HARDY, Jill, 354, 443, 620, 1185,
    1746, 4882, 4887, 5315, 5378,
    5392, 5630, 5693, 6325, 6767, 6838
HARKER, Jonathan, 6732, 7271
HARRIS, Leo, 407, 843, 943, 1057,
    1275, 1497, 2345, 3314, 4595,
    4596, 5414, 6569
HARRIS, Michael, 1016, 4862
HARRISON, Ben, 935
HARRISON, Carey, 657, 6213, 7337
HARRISON, Patricia, 153
HARROW, Carolyn, 1373, 1746, 2467,
    4148, 6201
HART, Dennis, 5008
HART, Elspeth (also see: Elspeth

(cont.)
Chapin), 792, 1399, 2391, 2502, 2628, 2666, 3242, 3924, 4611, 4871, 4965, 5838, 6838, 7119
HART, Henry, 7, 18, 56, 68, 80, 90, 93, 101, 116, 144, 162, 163, 176, 204, 232, 251, 326, 329, 388, 455, 459, 472, 477, 493, 508, 527, 572, 587, 657, 733, 766, 769, 781, 805, 847, 851, 921, 975, 999, 1007, 1012, 1022, 1083, 1101, 1119, 1139, 1174, 1226, 1232, 1236, 1249, 1295, 1377, 1422, 1440, 1448, 1471, 1488, 1531, 1542, 1548, 1589, 1616, 1626, 1631, 1640, 1710, 1734, 1751, 1753, 1760, 1761, 1860, 1863, 1884, 1892, 1927, 1930, 1931, 1962, 1995, 2015, 2035, 2040, 2088, 2154, 2241, 2307, 2353, 2367, 2437, 2448A, 2448B, 2474, 2483, 2545, 2605, 2607, 2677, 2717, 2723, 2737, 2803, 2830, 2890, 2903, 2926, 2941, 2944, 2955, 3026, 3037, 3045, 3053, 3076, 3098, 3115, 3133, 3135, 3172, 3279A, 3279B, 3312, 3326, 3377, 3388, 3447, 3470, 3514, 3522, 3551, 3603, 3616, 3671, 3682, 3683, 3688, 3739, 3752, 3798, 3803, 3838, 3842, 3854, 3916, 3959, 3985, 4020, 4054, 4146, 4157, 4179, 4186, 4187, 4200, 4213, 4241, 4255, 4258, 4320, 4419, 4451, 4453, 4462, 4477, 4478, 4480, 4493, 4515, 4518, 4529, 4556, 4599, 4605, 4609, 4617, 4631, 4634, 4648, 4672, 4684, 4690, 4714, 4715, 4717, 4735, 4824, 4828, 4832, 4851, 4862, 4890, 4928, 4946, 4973, 5018, 5030, 5041, 5046, 5090, 5110, 5123, 5130, 5134, 5170, 5207, 5278, 5321, 5330, 5346, 5350, 5382, 5383, 5391, 5433, 5437, 5481, 5615, 5686, 5689, 5720, 5726, 5761, 5865, 5906, 5947, 5984, 6017, 6056, 6062, 6100, 6111, 6119, 6131, 6132, 6141, 6279, 6292, 6293, 6364, 6424, 6466, 6475, 7523, 6533, 6556, 6572, 6635, 6637, 6638, 6641, 6655, 6665, 6749, 6753, 6761, 6806, 6870, 6876, 6916, 6923, 6924, 6973, 6974, 6980, 6981, 7012, 7028, 7050, 7075, 7103, 7108, 7128, 7158, 7164, 7167, 7202, 7271, 7280, 7301, 7304, 7333
HARTNOLL, Gillian, 173
HASKELL, Molly, 5968, 6133, 6736
HAUSER, Frank, 422, 4633, 6688
HAUSER, Robert T., 1980

HAYCOCK, Joel, 2336
HAYNES, Nanda Ward, 4027, 6419, 6571
HAZLITT, Justin, 4786, 6034
HEARD, Colin, 999, 1458, 2712, 6644, 7145
HEIFETZ, Henry, 1166, 7231
HEIMER, Esther, 4100
HELLER, Paul, 2416
HELMER, Adam, 2305
HENDERSON, Brian, 6226A, 6226B
HENDRICKS, Gordon, 4631
HENSTELL, Bruce, 529, 3627
HERRON, William, 357, 463, 711, 1032, 1089, 2132, 2152, 3352, 3480, 3806, 4008, 4122, 5017, 5156, 5585, 6944
HEUER, Kenneth, 1507
HIBBIN, Nina, 1717, 3306, 6004, 6188, 6912, 6919
HIGHAM, Charles, 3566
HILL, Derek, 15, 77, 267, 346, 428, 1210, 1365, 1540, 1802, 2274, 2503, 2752, 3075, 3625, 3759, 3947, 3966, 3981, 3982, 4415, 4444, 4458, 4480, 4715, 4731, 4808, 5043, 5138, 5224, 5375, 5516, 5721, 5777, 5807, 5810, 5929, 6062, 6404, 6535, 6638, 6651, 6697, 6756, 6832, 6851, 6896, 6901, 6904, 7035, 7137, 7199
HILL, Jerome, 1876, 6695
HILL, Steven P., 3086, 3963, 4461, 5467, 5743, 6791
HILLIER, Jim, 3798, 4183
HINES, T.S., 5648
HINXMAN, Margaret, 9, 2528, 4655
HIRSCH, Foster, 672, 2042, 3827, 4450, 4858, 5217, 5697, 6111, 7262, 7380
HIRSCHMAN, Jack, 1747
HITCHCOCK, Alfred, 580, 5188
HITCHCOCK, Peggy, 113, 551
HITCHENS, Dolores, 424
HITCHENS, Gordon, 1197, 2386, 4467, 4615, 4960, 5465, 7309
HOCH, David G., 6739
HODGENS, R.M., 25, 180, 236, 332, 333, 382, 455, 462, 611, 615, 626, 628, 637, 676, 839, 883, 921, 1011, 1046, 1087, 1108, 1111, 1144, 1148, 1161, 1171, 1240, 1312, 1597, 1864, 1866, 1923, 1925, 1946, 1973, 1994, 2010, 2043, 2097, 2155, 2161, 2217, 2335, 2346, 2389, 2405, 2446, 2498, 2545, 2575, 2577, 2586, 2601, 2654, 2664, 2844, 2926, 2954, 2955, 3088, 3121, 3181, 3265, 3366, 3384, 3385, 3429, 3465, 3487, 3602, 3603, 3684, 3726, 3749, 3813, 3817, 3967, 3977,

4025, 4030, 4031, 4306, 4358,
4363, 4365, 4375, 4477, 4521,
4675, 4741, 4750, 4786, 4797,
4799, 4909, 4986, 5011, 5112,
5160, 5163, 5212, 5252, 5311,
5358, 5423, 5479, 5497, 5595,
5765, 5841, 5920, 5949, 6125,
6156, 6186, 6224, 6232, 6276,
6287, 6306, 6353, 6395, 6422,
6475, 6533, 6571, 6576, 6636,
6723, 6738, 6744, 6771, 6776,
6818, 6860, 6865, 6870, 6923,
7056, 7061, 7132, 7274, 7294,
7335, 7355, 7398
HODGKINSON, Tony, 4751
HODGSON, Pat, 1710, 7245
HOELLERING, George, 4290
HOFSESS, John, 1296, 1356, 1584,
1695, 1808, 2418, 2808, 3224,
4712, 4950, 4984, 5433, 5891,
6123, 6621, 6644
HOLDEN, James, 1041
HOLLISTER, Sidney, 1396
HOLLOWAY, Ron, 1300, 3615, 4542
HOLTAN, Orley I., 101, 1727, 3849,
4065A, 4065B, 4102A, 4102B
HOOPS, Jonathan, 2890, 3611, 5689
HOOVER, Clara, 7236
HOPE-WALLACE, Philip, 148, 470,
2816, 3803, 4966, 6028
HORVATH, Joan, 45, 467, 1383, 1909,
1949, 3070, 4534, 5599, 6608, 7348
HOUSTON, Beverle, 5383
HOUSTON, Penelope, 14, 56, 194, 205,
274, 315, 388, 477, 481, 599, 623,
710, 765, 803, 806, 964, 1013,
1026, 1111, 1383, 1625, 1676,
1734, 1789A, 1789B, 1807, 1860,
1862, 1898, 1900, 1901, 2167,
2172, 2244, 2287, 2290, 2321,
2682, 2693, 2703, 2793, 2809,
2913, 2973, 3088A, 3088B, 3152,
3225, 3228, 3347, 3357, 3370,
3440, 3499, 3556, 3567, 3596,
3616, 3683, 3788, 3878, 3907,
3954, 3987, 4021, 4076, 4157,
4300, 4450, 4537, 4548, 4563,
4629, 4636, 4648, 4650, 4672,
4705, 4725, 4822, 4851, 4940,
4958, 5024, 5048, 5133, 5214,
5357, 5456, 5479, 5567, 5622,
5638, 5676, 5759, 5879, 5984,
6001, 6020, 6022, 6131, 6207,
6370, 6394, 6397, 6525, 6529,
6576, 6587, 6608, 6665, 6782,
6856, 6884, 6923, 6973, 6976,
7043, 7105, 7106, 7187, 7289,
7345, 7347
HOUWER, Rob, 4236
HOVING, George, 2840
HOW, Quincy, 2436
HOWARD, Ivor, 6411, 7288

HOWARD, R.G., 4800, 6311
HOWLAND, McClure M., 5486
HOWSTON, F. William, 785, 4534
HOWTON, Louise, 5543
HRUSA, Bernard, 1564, 1755, 3353,
3366, 3655, 3868, 4306, 4590,
5625, 6424, 6876, 7050, 7236
HUBER, Bob, 6576
HUEBEL, Harry Russell, 3224
HUFF, Theodore, 3280, 3605
HUGESSON, Vivienne, 98, 4038
HUGH, Elydr Ap, 1910, 4217
HUGHES, Harrison, 87
HUGHES, Robert, 892
HULL, David Stewart, 1276, 1847,
1934, 2151, 3560, 3595, 4637,
5436, 6911, 7159
HUME, Veronica, 347, 6246, 7289
HUNT, David, 1079, 3122, 3848, 5903
HUNT, Dennis, 847, 1022, 1512, 1587,
2119, 2313, 2513, 2543, 3057,
3092, 3704, 3818, 3867, 6267
HUNTER, Tim, 6739
HUNTLEY, John, 1083
HURLICK, Astrid, 6750
HUTCHINS, Lavinia, 617
HUTCHINS, Patricia, 1686
HUTCHINSON, David, 278, 373, 1302,
1363, 1446, 1502, 1591, 1604,
1678, 2046, 2081, 2296, 2452,
2579, 3015, 3572, 3773, 3811,
4470, 4656, 5314, 6050, 6085,
6320, 6356, 6374, 6541, 6780,
6824, 6895, 6908, 6990, 7065,
7198, 7252
HYATT, Hannah, 312, 4349, 5300

IBBERSON, Jack, 826, 3319, 5014,
6043
INOBRAN, Jean, 3353
IRONS, James, 2462
ISAAC, Dan, 1054
ISAACS, Hermine Rich, 4076, 4771,
6070, 6294
IVES, Gloria, 4175, 4465, 7291

J.A., 1152
J.C., 1922, 7002
J.G., 2164, 4752
J.H., 2762
J.M., 3428
J.T., 424
JABLONSKI, Edward, 148, 370, 413,
511, 787, 1342, 1355, 1735, 2334,
2372, 2810, 3355, 4760, 4761,
4865, 5775, 5793, 5922
JACKSON, Benjamin T., 1135, 1861,
5041, 5509
JACKSON, Don, 3131
JACKSON, Ragna, 1599, 4962

JACOB, Gilles, 306, 498, 4840
JACOBS, Arthur, 1646
JACOBS, Jack, 6886
JACOBSON, Herbert L., 530
JAFFE, Ira S., 1119
JAHIEL, Edwin, 346, 360, 1548, 1900, 3829, 4476, 4837, 5255, 5650
JAMES, Clive, 6739
JAMESON, Richard T., 5725
JARVIE, Ian, 273, 467, 1242, 1923, 2770, 3088, 3154, 4389, 4675, 6314, 7236
JASZI, Peter, 6739
JEBB, Julian, 916, 3206, 6646, 7380
JEFFEREY, Penny, 4523
JEFFERY, Richard, 4006
JEFFREY, Penelope S., 1463
JENSEN, Paul, 2179, 4092
JOHNSON, Albert, 201, 232, 356, 493, 679, 694, 968, 1169, 1355, 1473, 1572, 1663, 2053, 3013, 3269, 3322, 3407, 4098, 4556, 4878, 5014, 5251, 5333, 5338, 5679, 6051, 6100, 6127, 6413, 6444, 6506, 6560, 6590, 7050, 7337
JOHNSON, Elsie, 3749
JOHNSON, Ian, 452, 649, 676, 1014, 1107, 1112, 1239, 1292, 1440, 2030, 2085, 2257, 2560, 2686, 2806, 2929, 2954, 3128, 3231, 3339, 3401, 3733, 3749, 3775, 3824, 4115, 4212, 4313, 4658, 4944, 5117, 5147, 5293, 5348, 5473, 5474, 5517, 5858, 6110, 6396, 6433, 6586, 6844, 6846, 7081, 7287, 7302, 7395
JOHNSON, M. Elizabeth, 4161
JOHNSON, William, 176, 306, 329, 410, 461, 474, 574, 583, 697, 869, 903, 1616, 1803, 1928, 2913, 3037, 3795, 4006, 4535, 5487, 5771, 6292, 6981, 7303
JOHNSTON, Claire, 682, 725, 1141, 1673, 3430, 4551, 4613, 5580, 6478, 6889
JONES, Chris, 279, 584, 1711, 1846, 2014, 2073, 2307, 2614, 2667, 2915, 2966, 3348, 3359, 4158, 4460, 5814, 5950, 7050, 7087, 7098, 7208, 7216
JONES, Dufre, 3958, 5284
JONES, G. William, 6690
JORDAN, René, 1567, 2472, 4191, 4436, 6483
JUBAK, James, 1969, 3206, 3292, 3654, 4624, 6669, 7146

K.R., 4130, 5562, 7261, 7349
KABIR, Alamgir, 3220
KAEL, Pauline, 572, 965, 2737, 4672, 5730

KAGEN, Norman, 3640
KAHAN, Saul, 1671, 3124, 3762, 3768, 5641, 7378
KAHLENBERG, Richard, 599
KALSON, Albert E., 1833, 2513, 3627, 7176
KAMSLER, Irene, 6162, 6169
KANE, Joe, 1760
KAPLAN, Stephen, 6739
KASS, Robert, 716, 761, 866, 1285, 1303, 1505, 1893, 2216, 2693, 2771, 2972, 3281, 3382, 3401, 3440, 3620, 5063, 6436
KATZ, William, 2303, 3313
KAVANAGH, Thomas M., 2253
KEHOE, William, 470
KELLY, Eileen, 1128, 6661
KELLY, Robert, 262, 6701
KELLY, Terence, 6682, 6870
KELMAN, Ken, 386, 1719, 5320, 5543, 6701
KENISTON, Tony, 717, 1811, 2635, 3598, 4403, 4942, 5527, 7284
KENNEDY, Eileen, 3458
KENNEDY, Ellen C., 3158, 5456
KERANS, James, 4541, 7113
KERBEL, Michael, 3560
KERNAN, Margot S., 12, 357, 480, 694, 826, 1895, 1927, 1969, 2245, 2476, 3246, 3716, 3795, 3835, 4224, 4460, 5042, 5126, 5223, 5383, 6527, 6787, 6799, 7262, 7380
KINDER, Marsha, 3396, 5383
KINEMATOGRAPH COMMITTEE, THE, 3746
KING, Eugene, 3054, 7062
KING, Pamela Ann, 3519
KISBEY, John, 1880
KITCHIN, Lawrence, 2882, 6276
KLEIN, Michael, 833, 4898
KNIGHT, Arthur, 275, 657, 1098, 2484, 2665, 2790, 2832, 3108, 3856, 4416, 4508, 4793, 5968, 6434, 6642, 6800
KNIGHT, Peter, 801
KNOLL, Robert F., 7245
KOHAN, Saul, 1471
KONICZEK, Ryszard, 810, 5230, 5874, 6080, 6630
KORTY, John, 4590
KOSTOLEFSKY, Joseph, 2819, 3026, 4520, 4829, 5064, 5366, 5916, 7379
KOSZARSKI, Richard, 1780, 3327, 3365, 3820, 4139, 4346, 4722, 6660, 6962
KOZLOFF, Max, 410, 657, 690, 903, 1928, 2913, 3045, 6048, 6739
KRAFT, Richard, 3535
KRAMBORG, Arlene, 1567, 4072, 5037, 7380
KRAMER, Leonie, 2867
KREIS, Robert B., 7064

KREUGER, Miles, 3177
KRUUS, Alar, 380
KUHN, Helen Weldon, 58, 1172, 1572, 1747, 2012, 2236, 3136, 3154, 3578, 3882, 4105, 4657, 4812, 5808, 6051, 6240, 6758, 6806, 6907, 7245, 7345
KUIPER, John B., 6072
KULA, Sam, 1418, 4640
KUSTOW, Michael, 371, 1716, 2607, 3247, 3251, 4241, 4796, 5761, 7236

L.G.A. (also see: Lindsay G. Anderson), 3836, 4771, 6137
L.R., 4518
L.W., 4960
LACEY, Bradner, 3186, 5902
LAMBERT, Gavin, 174, 275, 370, 486, 752, 766, 850, 922, 1005, 1054, 1127, 1284, 1352, 1390, 1467, 1473, 1511, 1526, 1600, 1652, 1753, 1800, 1933, 2151, 2279, 2483, 2603, 2629, 2703, 2903, 3076, 3270, 3281, 3343, 3346, 3506, 3605, 3665, 3673, 3683, 3783, 3801, 3916, 3923, 3931, 3971, 4234, 4258, 4290, 4356, 4367, 4389, 4453, 4505, 4572, 4619, 4635, 4713A, 4713B, 4728, 4771, 4825, 5026, 5045, 5201, 5227, 5241, 5329, 5363, 5590, 5631, 5633, 5675, 5868, 6116, 6294, 6361, 6481, 6873, 6955, 7023, 7109, 7158, 7191, 7261, 7340
LAMBERT, Linda, 4183
LAMBERTON, Bob, 6695, 7008
LAMONT, Margaret I., 3865, 6558
LANDESMAN, Rocco, 916, 5272
LANDSBERGIS, A., 5362, 6116
LANE, John Francis, 2867, 7113
LAREAU, Normand, 2673
LARSON, Angelica, 78
LASKY, Betty, 128
LAWRENCE, Meredith, 1877, 3717, 4182, 6182, 6845
LAWSON, Sylvia, 210, 3712, 5819
LEADER, Bill, 1646
LEAHY, James, 3881, 6348
LEEDOM, B.F., 714, 1833, 6280
LEHMAN, Henrietta, 860, 2408, 2489, 3106, 3489, 3758, 5639, 6153, 6276, 6947
LEISER, Erwin, 2304, 4862
LEITCH, Colinette, 7356
LEJEUNE, C.A., 792, 2983, 3286, 4146
LEJOUS-VARGAS, Adrian, 4093
LELLIS, George, 1016, 1617, 5870, 6631, 7133
LENNING, Arthur, 5111
LENNON, Peter, 475, 769, 2260, 6675
LESTER, Richard, 3396

LETNER, Kenneth J., 419, 426, 608, 3026, 3921, 4263
LEVERING, Constance, 6861
LEVERING, Philip C., 698, 4068, 4806, 5088, 5210, 5515, 5887
LEVINE, Rashelle, 2044
LEVY, Jacques, 967
LEWIS, Marshall, 6648
LEWIS, Stephen, 1454, 4064, 4922, 6390
LEYDA, Jay, 702, 1639, 4179, 4904, 5278, 5648, 5736
LIFTON, Mitchell, 1253
LIMBACHER, James L., 1780, 5408
LINCOLN, Rae, 4344
LINDGREN, Ernest, 3846
LINDSAY, Bryan, 3224
LITHGOW, James, 1034, 2066
LIVINGSTON, Howard, 5733
LOBELL, George, 4639
LOEB, Emily, 5938, 6125
LOEWINGER, Larry, 3003, 4792, 5813, 7379
LOKIN, Jules, 1163
LONGWELL, Howard, 491
LORD, George, 4359
LORKIN, Jules, 7185
LORRAINE, Antony, 6993
LOSANO, Wayne A., 1035, 2914, 5426
LOUTZENHISER, James K., 5882
LOWELL, Constance, 63, 1414, 1437, 2302, 2883
LUCAS, Christopher, 5764
LUCAS, Linda, 3517, 6192
LUDDY, Tom, 793, 2002
LUDWIG, Paul, 4696
LUFT, Herbert G., 855, 6973
LUGG, Andrew, 2540, 6527
LUMET, Sidney, 4832
LUNSFORD, John, 1120, 6401

MC ARTHUR, Colin, 1853, 6141
MAC BEAN, James Roy, 5320
MC BRIDE, Joseph, 256, 654, 1095, 2917, 3037, 5037, 6570, 7350
MAC CANN, Richard Dyer, 4100
MC CARTY, John Man, 7146
MC CARTY, Mark, 713, 2128, 2458
MC CLURE, Michael, 1637
MC CORMICK, Ruth, 763, 4317, 4847, 7240
MC CORT, Harry, 801, 2462
MC CRACKEN III, Hugh, 1790
MAC DONALD, Dwight, 2606
MAC DONALD, Logan, 6359
MC FADDEN, Patrick (also see: Patrick Mac Fadden), 903, 1174, 1626, 1900
MAC FADDEN, Patrick (also see: Patrick Mc Fadden), 410, 1770, 2336, 2517, 2678, 2768, 2827, 3775, 4869, 4960, 5461A, 5461B,

(cont.)
6510, 6615, 6976, 7154
MC GIFFERT, Mary T., 6731
MC GILLIVRAY, David, 1449, 1671, 2181, 2219, 2744, 3011, 4044, 4059, 4624, 4665, 5960, 6060, 7362
MC GLASHAN, Maude, 1807, 5322, 6394
MC KEGNEY, Michael, 529
MC LEOD, Constance, 4763
MC MANIGAL, Rod, 968, 4100
MC PHERSON, Ian, 446
MC PHERSON, Shirley, 1401, 4997, 7240
MC VAY, Douglas, 232, 311, 970, 2586, 3276, 3399, 3545, 4255, 4786, 4824, 5079, 5320, 5655, 5921, 6106, 6440, 6755, 7271
MACKLIN, F. Anthony, 694, 1383, 1626, 2042, 4862, 6739, 7380
MADDEN, David, 6907
MADDISON, John, 4619
MADSEN, Axel, 431, 527, 1230, 1484, 1770, 1895, 1977, 2173, 3414, 4201, 4451, 5223, 6739, 6745
MAHERN, Michael, 35, 2621
MALCOLM, Derek, 4114
MALKO, George, 7242, 7281
MALLERMAN, Tony, 154, 600, 1165, 1258, 1441, 1447, 1459, 1665, 1879, 1936, 2268, 2280, 2311, 2584, 3137, 3288, 3988, 4189, 4494, 4551, 4876, 5581, 5965, 6032, 6694, 6698, 6720, 6723, 7168, 7266
MALLERY, David, 178, 320, 3898, 6338
MALLORY, James, 690
MALLOY, James, 3057
MALMFELT, A.D., 2527, 4898, 5689
MAMBER, Stephen, 2779A, 2779B, 2869, 3509, 6526, 7262
MANCIA, Adrienne Johnson, 7236
MANDEL, Ellen, 6834
MANDER, Kay, 3699
MANES, Stephen, 753, 1900, 2035, 2146, 2244, 2480, 3724, 5426, 5572
MANILLA, James, 501
MANN, Delbert, 1499
MANNOCK, P.L., 51, 139, 224, 325, 337, 581, 791, 836, 952, 1235, 1417, 1775, 1852, 1878, 1939, 2106, 2232, 2805, 2894, 2980, 3173, 3180, 3355, 3376, 3695, 3772, 3902, 3954, 4066, 4372, 4438, 4865, 4892, 5102, 5453, 5591, 5617, 5788, 5879, 6040, 6319, 6432, 6461, 6600, 6618, 6665, 6882, 7014, 7054, 7135, 7237, 7295, 7316
MANTUELLA, José, 5148
MANVELL, Roger, 56, 291, 683, 804, 855, 857, 1110, 1122, 1242, 1410, 1521, 1632, 1683, 1762, 1807, 1834, 1933, 2202, 2577, 2694, 2999, 3086, 3087, 3168, 3182, 3254, 3299, 3438, 3651, 3678, 3683, 3882, 3888, 4120, 4253, 4341, 4813, 5040, 5227, 5350, 5404, 5566, 5731, 5750, 5921, 6047, 6313, 6684, 6860, 7061, 7386
MARCORELLES, Louis, 326, 769, 1242, 4794, 4978, 5425, 5759
MARCUS, Robert D., 2548
MARDORE, Michel, 7066
MARGESSON, Hakon, 6880
MARKE, Louis, 1792
MARKIOS, Constantine, 2682
MARKOPOULOS, Gregory, 1583, 2066, 2465, 5543, 5674, 6010
MARKOWITZ, Ruth, 3392
MARKS, Louis, 183, 388, 887, 2118, 2739, 3076, 3781, 4185, 4653, 5318, 6920
MARLOW, Alberta, 19, 2133, 2605, 3404, 4617, 7311
MARMORSTEIN, Robert, 6669
MARPLE, B.G., 14, 442, 756, 825, 1464, 2172, 2503, 2886, 3469, 3506, 3931, 4258, 5201, 6768
MARSHALL, George, 779
MARTIN, Bruce, 12, 1322, 3057, 5046
MARTIN, James, 829, 895, 1784, 2259, 3539, 4186, 4959, 5840, 6326
MARTIN, Paul-Louis, 1900, 4518
MASON, Ronald, 5664
MAST, Gerald, 2287, 2426
MASTERMAN, Len, 1322
MAWDSLEY, J.A., 5053
MAXWELL, Hal, 2131, 3018, 3777
MAY, Derwent, 1479, 1552, 5188, 6853, 7251
MAY, Janice, 6422
MAYER, Arthur, 6973
MAYERSBERG, Paul, 181, 514, 623, 915, 1111, 1422, 1767, 2192, 2321, 3528, 3688, 3967, 3978, 4140A, 4140B, 4772, 4794, 4973, 5223, 5243, 5456, 5500, 6353, 6637, 6744A, 6744B
MAZZOCCO, Robert, 127, 2307, 6570
MEADE, Osgood, 414
MEDJUCK, Joe, 97, 101, 289, 1181, 1246, 1587, 1655, 2035, 4019, 4308, 4776, 5231, 5781, 6007, 6263, 7037, 7084, 7201
MEEKER, Hubert, 657
MEIER, David, 562
MEIKELJOHN, Toby, 6993
MEISEL, Myron, 101, 1453, 1998, 2953, 3348, 3486, 5018, 5789, 6095, 6364, 7146
MEKAS, Jonas, 2668, 3123, 4706, 5321
MELLEN, Joan, 145, 1174, 1448, 3002,

6646, 6929, 6943, 7185
MELTON, Hollis, 2177
MELVILLE, Jean-Pierre, 3653
MENEFEE, Emory, 4004
MERRALLS, James D., 146, 426, 603,
  1486, 1807, 2128, 2196A, 2196B,
  2463, 3127, 3254, 3408, 5047,
  5328, 6788
MERSON, John, 54, 247
MEYERS, Arthur S., 4969
MICCICHE, Lino, 1576, 3563, 4801
MICHAELS, Robert, 6064
MICHELS, Robert G., 6944
MIFFLIN, Wilfred, 20, 431, 953, 956,
  1009, 1111, 1194, 1755, 1925,
  2049, 2498, 2505, 2474, 2793,
  2885, 3047, 3353, 3429, 3925,
  3958, 4188, 4306, 4443, 5252,
  5459, 5637, 5662, 5854, 5921,
  5961, 6422, 6636, 6645, 6818,
  7073, 7335, 7374
MILLAR, Daniel, 7107
MILLAR, Gavin, 718, 1011, 1969,
  3002, 3013, 3567, 5580, 6014,
  6411, 7304, 7379
MILLAU, Georges, 994, 1914, 2847,
  3843, 4467, 4710, 4909, 5048
MILLER, Don, 60, 812, 867, 910, 1010,
  1334, 1503, 1514, 1883, 2120,
  2945, 3330, 3431, 3523, 3549,
  3689, 4070, 4330, 4333, 4433,
  4864, 5768, 5866, 6053, 6265,
  6385, 6479, 7079, 7104, 7375
MILLER, Earl, 811
MILLER, Hannah, 4110, 4780, 5185,
  7179
MILLER, Henry, 243
MILLER, Jonathan, 574, 3172, 3399,
  5785
MILLER, Letizia Ciotti, 281, 4439
MILLER, Logan, 3544
MILLER, Mary Britton, 2689, 3349,
  6492
MILLMORE, Dennis, 3599, 5050, 6347,
  6752
MILLS, Patricia, 7056
MILLS, Peter, 212, 928, 933, 3581,
  4383
MILLS, W.E., 4718, 5170, 5648
MILNE, Tom, 12, 155, 355, 357, 529,
  654, 694, 847, 965, 1004, 1068,
  1190, 1322, 1424, 1518, 1626,
  1727, 1768, 1953, 2014, 2192,
  2310, 2540, 2690, 2934, 3025,
  3037, 3121, 3269, 3395, 3449,
  3619, 3689, 3690, 3711, 3881,
  4028, 4257, 4443, 4516, 4543,
  4898, 5008, 5203, 5234, 5424,
  5476, 5682, 5891, 5932, 6009,
  6158, 6268, 6348, 6417, 6580,
  6777, 7146, 7287
MILVERTON, C.A., 3462

MINCHINTON, John, 1136, 1821,
  2039, 2489, 3095, 3936, 5257,
  5315, 5778, 5842, 7022
MINISH, Geoffrey, 459, 993, 1103,
  1174, 3774, 5881
MITCHELL, George J., 2916, 4311,
  6532
MONOHAN, James, 4867
MONJO, Nicolas, 6336, 6871
MONTAGU, Ivor, 6072
MORAVIA, Alberto, 1962
MORGAN, James, 6, 65, 104, 344, 506,
  900, 1044, 1106, 1187, 2414, 2644,
  2796, 3163, 3318, 3601, 3965,
  4018, 4261, 4377, 4628, 5793,
  5917, 5981
MORISON, Abner, 3232
MORITSUGU, Frank, 3905
MORLEY, Ronald, 724
MORLEY, Sheridan, 3917, 7301
MORRISSETTE, Bruce, 3038
MOSELEY, Roy, 2543
MOSEN, David, 5245
MOSER, Norman C., 5603, 6488
MOSS, Ian, 845, 1636, 2329, 2624,
  2822, 2901, 3159, 3232, 3927,
  3974, 6211, 6324, 6589, 7352
MOSS, Robert F., 357, 2313
MOWAT, David, 3416
MUNDY, Robert, 2042, 5037
MURPHY, Anne F., 2697, 3648
MURPHY, Brian, 109, 254, 468, 507,
  880, 920, 1138, 1146, 2341, 3028,
  3084, 3149, 3421, 3769, 4153,
  4194, 4641, 4667, 4999, 5036,
  5200, 5262, 5762, 5781, 6073,
  6157, 6269, 6289, 6614, 7175, 7234
MURRAY, Brian, 257, 2401
MUSSMAN, Toby, 1034
MYHERS, John, 1962

NARBONI, Jean, 6576
NASH, Eleanor H., 1315, 3755, 5143,
  6070
NELSON, Harlan S., 4720, 6499
NELSON, Paul, 3172
NELSON, Robert, 318, 1175, 2487,
  2492, 2598, 2876, 4562, 4591,
  4602, 4844, 4931, 6139, 6369, 6979
NEUFELD, Max, 555, 2831, 4441,
  4976, 5598, 6108
NEVILLE, Tove, 4641
NEVINS, Jr., Francis M., 6856
NEVITT, Brian, 6635
NICHOLS, Bill, 1178, 4564, 5164, 6079
NIM, Seu Do, 6644
NOQUEZ, Dominique, 6293
NORDSTROM, Kristina, 6446
NORRIS, Daphne, 175, 4305, 5505
NORTH, Christopher, 1487, 3378
NORTH, Mariana, 6397

NOWELL-SMITH, Geoffrey, 11, 2155, 2620, 2649, 3124, 4389, 4539, 4801, 5468, 7384

OAKES, Philip, 2955, 6560
O'BRIEN, Brian, 890, 1153, 1520, 1709, 1992, 2441, 4282, 4292, 4335, 4348, 4774, 5124, 5601, 5907, 6437
ODDIE, Alan G., 1770
O'DONNELL, Beverly, 7167
OESCH, Bernard, 6348
O'HARA, Charles, 4693
OHIRA, Kazuto, 2023
OHLIN, Peter, 5037
O'LAOGHAIRE, Liam, 3183, 4453
O'MEARA, Robert, 6739
ONO, Yoko, 2003, 2004, 5166, 6742
ORMISTON, W.F., 1201
ORNA, Bernard, 195, 2357, 2510, 2628, 3866, 4610, 4996
OWEN, Franki, 260, 2292, 3021, 6323, 6485
OXENHANDLER, Neal, 1962, 6048, 6130, 7309

P.C., 442, 4518, 4534, 4991, 5109
P.D.C., 3415
PALETZ, David, 3750, 4241
PANIAQUA, Cita, 4114
PARTINGTON, Ruth, 5763
PASKAL, Merrily, 1816
PATRICK, David, 6974
PATTERSON, Frances Taylor, 806, 1339, 1773, 2516, 3917, 4290, 4629, 6070, 6688
PATTISON, Barri, 1673
PATTISON, Ivan, 794, 2935, 3673, 3676, 5830, 6554
PAUL, William, 5194, 6014
PAZ, Octavio, 4389
PEARSON, Alice Canby, 2173
PEARSON, Gabriel, 1817
PEARSON, Maisie K., 5383
PEAVY, Charles D., 614, 2314, 6024, 7318
PECHTER, William, 7146
PELTIER, Euclid J., 165, 261
PELTZ, Mary Ellis, 6202
PENN, Arthur, 694
PERIER, Martin, 2162
PERKINS, V.F., 1994, 2321, 2666, 3366, 3965, 4085, 5330, 5376, 5888, 6776
PERRY, John, 1244
PERSSON, Goran, 6466
PETERSON, Rolfe, 4132
PETRIE, Graham, 3798, 4257
PETROWSKI, Minou, 4028
PETRUCCI, Antonio, 4141

PHELPS, Donald, 4718
PHIPPS, Courtland, 445, 1497, 1685, 1741, 2321, 2342, 2413, 2867, 3139, 3675, 3730, 3738, 4077, 4580, 5159, 5192, 5375, 5564, 5565, 5883, 5969, 6249, 6634, 6784, 7298
PIERSON, Howard, 2028
PILE, Susan, 1034
PINGA, Ben, 2279, 3044
PIRIE, David, 2336, 4224, 7262
PITTMAN, Bruce, 4340, 4394
PLOTKIN, Frederick, 4718
POHL, Frederik, 6739
POLLOCK, Robert, 1221, 1943, 2208, 3311, 4197, 5779
POLT, Harriet R., 172, 525, 719, 997, 1069, 1109, 1197, 1456, 1517, 1727, 1881, 1922, 2022, 2288, 2600, 3212, 3269, 3438, 3893, 3905, 3976, 4000, 4028, 5129, 5686, 6242, 7147
POPESCU, Dagmar, 3461
PORTE, Masha R., 331, 1813, 1952, 3510, 5185, 7177, 7204
PORTER, Irene, 5482
POWELL, Mark, 2920, 3716, 6428
PRATLEY, Gerald, 18, 1660, 2239, 2418, 2544, 3400, 4196, 4776, 4828, 5197
PRATT, James Reece, 219
PRATT, John, 150, 1793, 4384
PREMINGER, Otto, 906
PRICE, James, 383, 1034, 1770, 1912, 1927, 3422, 3763, 4721, 4810, 4870, 5961, 6753, 6974, 7128
PRIMA, Jesse, 3013
PROUSE, Derek, 531, 871, 1551, 1721, 1790, 1792, 2236, 2308, 2409, 2734, 3854, 4333, 4408, 4719, 4892, 5278, 5350, 5379, 5679, 6167, 6249, 6350, 7155, 7356
PURDY, Strother, 1868
PYHALA, Mikko, 5020
PYROS, John, 6572

Q.R., 1769, 2447
QUEVAL, Jean, 3253, 6623

R.D., 2585, 5379
R.G., 6602
R.K., 3415, 6124
R.S.T., 6462
R.W., 3088, 4242
RABINOWITZ, Mark, 2668, 4001, 4058
RACKLEY, Edward, 1939
RACZ, Juan-Andres, 1754
RAFFETTO, Francis, 2497
RAMSEY, Hartley, 95, 377, 550, 965, 3734, 4263, 5024, 5141, 6373

FILM REVIEWERS

RANEY, William V., 3793, 5324
RAPER, Michell, 456, 786, 2982, 5646
RAPPAPORT, Mark, 3456
RATCLIFFE, Michael, 707, 3642, 4821,
   5049, 6484
RAVAGE, Alan, 2488
RAVAGE, Maria-Teresa, 2488, 3843,
   5468, 7021
RAWLINS, Adrian, 5679
READE, Millicent, 2454
REAL, Jere, 265
REEVES, Penelope, 5401
REGNIER, Michel, 1088
REIF, Tony, 3013, 3792, 6373, 6617,
   7369
REILLY, Charles, 1984, 3361, 6654
REILLY, John L., 6526
REINER, Eric, 1747
REISZ, Karel, 1451, 1884, 2216, 2348,
   2769, 3040, 3622, 3758, 3943,
   4073, 4922, 5315, 5368, 5437,
   6070, 6296, 6754, 6947
RENAN, Sheldon, 4226
REYNOLDS, Michael, 1988, 5384
RHAWN, Flavia Wharton (also see:
   Flavia Wharton), 1764, 2114, 2733,
   5154, 5602
RHODE, Eric, 1272, 1519, 1640, 1747,
   2162, 3351, 4890, 5509, 6105,
   6353, 6720, 6748, 6868, 7202
RICE, Susan, 101, 2253, 3292, 3520,
   3621A, 3621B, 4305, 4828, 5094,
   6200, 6482, 6929
RICHARDS, Jeffrey, 2158
RICHARDSON, Boyce, 2913
RICHARDSON, Tony, 975, 2430, 2489,
   4179, 4711, 5449, 5648
RICHIE, Donald, 726, 775, 1445, 1673,
   2770, 4374, 4484, 4600, 4975, 7290
RICKARDS, Joseph E., 6671
RIDER, David, 44, 126, 211, 230, 245,
   252, 429, 449, 464, 543, 596, 729,
   754, 759, 844, 927, 929, 939, 1080,
   1263, 1307, 1347, 1351, 1372,
   1429, 1466, 1493, 1529, 1575,
   1581, 1597, 1658, 1664, 1712,
   1718, 1777, 1805, 1848, 1856,
   1916, 1948, 1949, 1960, 1979,
   1999, 2049, 2056, 2089, 2093,
   2187, 2226, 2240, 2283, 2297,
   2389, 2477, 2576, 2637, 2724,
   2736, 2756, 2761, 2850, 2863,
   2865, 2875, 2900, 2930, 2975,
   3005, 3094, 3143, 3144, 3155,
   3174, 3175, 3284, 3375, 3424,
   3443, 3531, 3610, 3629, 3704,
   3726, 3910, 3934, 3978, 3980,
   4054, 4280, 4281, 4474, 4566,
   4584, 4608, 4630, 4689, 4779,
   4842, 4936, 4947, 4951, 4970,
   4985, 5014, 5069, 5151, 5209,
   5276, 5281, 5390, 5469, 5483,
   5534, 5593, 5633, 5640, 5670,
   5862, 5937, 6071, 6144, 6163,
   6177, 6206, 6214, 6237, 6253,
   6330, 6357, 6415, 6476, 6551,
   6565, 6611, 6663, 6778, 6802,
   6815, 6849, 6854, 6861, 6966,
   6969, 6996, 7038, 7097, 7285, 7304
RIERA, Emilio G., 6911
RILEY, Phillip, 134, 604, 824, 1654,
   1980, 1990, 2047, 2174, 2376,
   2500, 2528, 2902, 2962, 3205,
   3723, 3747, 4103, 4298, 4632,
   4694, 5161, 5306, 5589, 5746,
   5943, 5988, 6016, 6731, 6940
RITTGER, Carol, 3440, 6167
RITTI, Mimi, 7052
RITTS, Morton, 2473
ROBIN, Eve, 4078
ROBINSON, David, 163, 487, 644,
   1900, 1905, 2628, 2864, 2963,
   3154, 3183, 3198, 3548, 3570,
   3654, 3850, 4718, 4723, 4725,
   4909, 4990, 5128, 5526, 6103,
   6343, 6552, 6739
ROBINSON, Hubbell, 973, 3746, 4733,
   5891, 6191, 7147
ROBOTHAM, John, 2981, 6934
RODRIGUEZ, Juan, 1067, 5008
ROHMER, Eric, 1238
ROMAN, Robert C., 50, 1540, 2640,
   2831, 3017, 3694, 4104, 4298,
   4670, 4799, 4937, 5684, 6082, 7092
ROPER, Michell, 6885
ROSE, William, 3172
ROSENBAUM, Jon, 6736, 7037
ROSENFIELD, Tony, 4762
ROSENTHAL, Stuart, 3806
ROSS, Albertine, 6322
ROSS, Harry, 2052
ROSS, Michael, 2685, 3608
ROSS, T.J., 852, 3767, 4186, 5035
ROSS, Veronica, 4397
ROTH, William, 6812
ROTHA, Paul, 472, 531, 1007, 1150,
   1464, 1930, 2162, 2321, 2409,
   2481, 3462A, 3462B, 3699, 3754,
   3788, 4179, 4556, 4994, 5456,
   5509, 5526, 6423, 6623, 6748,
   6911, 7194, 7345
ROTHSCHILD, Elaine, 149, 239, 574,
   627, 697, 708, 916, 949, 1159,
   1230, 1384, 1574, 1633, 2043,
   2146, 2242, 2466, 2540, 2543,
   2602, 2727, 2929, 2953, 3020,
   3292, 3413, 3438, 3504, 3517,
   3548, 3698, 3762, 4411, 4454,
   4677, 4747, 4823, 4941, 4958,
   5079, 5147, 5223, 5256, 5484,
   5594, 5841, 5982, 6042, 6156,
   6184, 6570, 6601, 6911, 7044,
   7257, 7274, 7303
ROUD, Richard, 47, 127, 151, 306, 634,

(cont.)
906, 1069, 1110, 1171, 1499, 1730, 2235, 2253, 2402, 2660, 3075, 3276, 3528, 3924, 3949, 4028, 4489, 4583, 5782, 5859, 5969, 5973, 6248, 6324, 6514, 6834
ROUTT, William D., 1537, 3089, 3691, 4180, 4345, 6275
RUBENSTEIN, Leonard, 497, 597, 1048, 1051, 1174, 2813, 3002, 3584, 4070, 4074, 4429, 4652, 5246, 5441, 5667, 5912, 6530, 7218
RUBENSTEIN, Roberta, 771
RUBIN, Elizabeth, 690
RUFF, Penelope, 856, 2639
RUSSELL, Elizabeth, 5925
RYALL, Tom, 1993

SAINTSBURY, B.T., 4353, 5796
SALVATORE, Dominic, 1313
SANDALL, Roger, 315, 1068, 1150, 1916, 2099, 3240, 3514, 3623, 4429, 4702, 4850, 5096, 5967, 6522
SANDENBERGH, Brian, 4535, 7398
SARGO, Tino Mendes, 3548
SARNE, Mike, 12, 1437, 2010, 2077, 2344, 2437, 2677, 3881, 4192, 4451, 4585, 4691, 5176, 5735, 5920, 6170, 6722, 6983, 7090, 7309, 7333
SARRIS, Andrew G., 56, 95, 326, 635, 719, 1231, 1342, 1721, 1884, 1928, 2321, 2489, 2540, 2585, 3738, 3916, 3958, 3967, 4028, 4541, 4668, 4892, 5379, 5565, 5664, 6001, 6062, 6078, 6529, 6576, 6665, 6911, 7061
SAWYCKY, Roman, 5713
SAWYER, Paul, 2162
SCHAFFNER, Franklin, 508
SCHELLING, Otto, 67
SCHMITT, Richard, 1900
SCHNEEMAN, Carolee, 5543
SCHNEPF, Edwin, 7248
SCHRADER, John, 1994, 2049, 2155, 2369, 2973, 3126, 3514, 3602, 3824, 5938, 6065, 6130
SCHRADER, Paul, 2022, 2462, 2527, 3013, 3504, 4102, 6267, 7245
SCHWERIN, Jules V., 1781, 3350
SCOVOTTI, Jim, 499, 2520, 2651, 3256, 4066, 4701, 5889, 7035
SEELYE, John, 277, 1726, 2649, 2735, 3522, 4562, 5496, 5681, 5733, 5878
SEGAL, Mark, 7394
SEITLING, Mark, 6463
SELZ, Thalia, 441, 2899, 4994
SEMMENS, Larry, 6754
SENNETT, Ted, 2819
SESONSKE, Alexander, 2196, 2307, 3802, 6152, 6465

SEYDOR, Paul, 2476, 4102
SHADOIAN, Jack, 3140
SHARITS, Paul, 4533, 4895, 5179, 5181
SHATNOFF, Judith, 665, 776, 961, 998, 1034, 1732, 4065, 4091, 4928, 5292, 6695, 6739, 7236
SHAW, Alice Bradford, 7323
SHEDLIN, Michael, 6199
SHERATSKY, Rodney E., 3, 5222
SHERMAN, Susan, 1168, 1319, 1985
SHERWIN, Sally, 6065
SHIPMAN, Graham, 5092, 6045
SHIPMAN, David, 5621, 5795, 6186
SHIVAS, Mark, 56, 131, 163, 392, 424, 580, 697, 1019, 1068, 1110, 1130, 1131, 1139, 1286, 1393A, 1393B, 1444, 1747, 1768, 1982, 2014, 2600, 2646, 2916, 2918, 3013, 3154, 3217, 3247, 3270, 3283, 3342, 3449, 3548, 3653, 3671, 3690, 4191, 4576, 4618, 4700, 4796, 4799, 4821, 4991, 5086, 5383, 5575, 5632, 5982, 6126, 6415, 6425, 6545, 6635, 6652, 6926, 7231
SIEGAL, Joel E., 3653
SILKE, James, 144, 906, 921, 1013, 1747, 1784, 1909, 2160, 2217, 2386, 2455, 2616, 2770, 3090, 3202, 3399, 3439, 3548, 3688, 3749, 3881, 4011, 4454, 5423, 5599, 5754, 5761, 5877, 6125, 6411, 6870, 7236, 7309
SILVER, Charles, 3037
SILVERMAN, Michael, 5912
SIMMONS, John, 487, 1071, 6339, 6512
SIMON, John, 1054
SINGER, Alexander, 486, 5027
SINGH, Harold, 4307
SINKLER, Eunice, 368, 1617, 2042, 2254, 2313, 2583, 3228, 4011, 4083, 4102, 4114, 4155, 4192, 4673, 4721, 4756, 4856, 4896, 5290, 5561, 5975, 7089
SIRKEN, Elliott, 100, 3395, 3767, 7245
SISKIND, Miriam, 3373
SITNEY, P. Adams, 213, 1060, 1637, 1729, 2098, 2615, 3123, 5003, 5785
SKOLLER, Donald, 2307, 2540
SLIDE, Anthony, 1380, 1688, 3891, 5844, 6543, 6659
SLOAN, William, 6667
SLOAT, Warren, 4124
SLOCUM, Estelle, 7248
SMITH, Clyde B., 2965, 2966, 3062
SMITH, Jesse, 430, 4443, 5724
SMITH, John M., 256, 1512
SMITH, Lily N.L., 2244, 5840
SMITH, Rachel, 4948
SMITH, W.G., 5906

SMITHEE, Alan, 672, 1453
SNODING, Clifton, 2042, 2839
SNOW, Michael, 5226
SOMMERS, Janet, 1000, 1432, 1442, 2788, 3266
SONDHEIM, Steve, 1552, 2585, 2784, 4636, 5188
SONTAG, Susan, 4300, 4862
SPAIN, Louise, 1350, 2942
"SPARTACUS", 480, 1396, 4599
SPEED, William, 4854
SPIERS, David, 3013
SPILKA, Mark, 3746
SPINRAD, Norman, 2593, 6739
SPRINGER, John, 919, 2963, 4167, 4892, 6329, 6898
S RAGOW, Michael, 204, 357, 455, 1174, 1794, 3514, 3608, 3806, 3917, 4828, 6739, 6959, 7146
STACKHOUSE, J. Foster, 1054
STANBROOK, Alan, 1649, 2348, 3350, 3437, 3714, 4046, 4813, 7187
STARR, Cecile (also see: Cecile Starr Boyajian), 1150, 3109, 4527
STARR, Francis, 1928
STARR, Wiliam A., 1337, 2422, 3115, 3236, 3333, 5122, 6482
STECKLER, Roy P., 2138
STEELE, Robert, 1724, 2099, 4479, 4828
STEIN, Elliott, 2307, 4455
STEIN, Ruthe, 3763, 6812
STEINBERY, Betty, 4902
STENZEL, Robert, 5772
STERN, Michael A., 4560
STERN, Nina Weiss, 5694
STERNWOOD, Guy, 3057, 3064, 6644
STEWART, Alastair, 832
STOLLER, James, 1650, 2199, 6055, 7384
STONE, Marvin, 4557
STONE, Shelby, 3851
STONIER, George, 6240
STRARAM, Patrick, 156, 2837
STRATTON, David J., 4734, 6459
STRAZZULLA, Gaetano, 235, 453, 2472, 4191, 4739, 5207, 5599
STREULI, Peter, 276, 2835, 3009, 5913, 6185
STRICK, Philip, 56, 125, 726, 1320, 1285, 1448, 1484, 1548, 1634, 1734, 1755, 1868, 2024, 2058, 2287, 2288, 2406, 2480, 2890, 3253, 3292, 3544, 3690, 3960, 4016, 4389, 4440, 4487, 4794, 4812, 4903, 5193, 5323, 5366, 5533, 6019, 6150, 6534, 6570, 6584, 6644, 6739, 6911, 7008, 7145, 7288, 7351
SUDA, Motoji, 6465
SUFRIN, Mark, 4988, 6920
SUGY, Catherine, 2543

SUMMERS, Bob, 3125
SUNSHINE, Adrian, 4640
SUSSEX, Elizabeth, 329, 474, 690, 1393, 1631, 2010, 2205, 2472, 2941, 3126, 3647, 3775, 3868, 4454, 4476, 5176, 6075, 6125
SUSSMAN, Barry, 3458, 6573
SUTHERLAND, Elizabeth, 5506
SUTLIFFE, Virgil, 1473
SVENSSON, Arne, 1673, 3037, 4812
SWISS, Patrick, 3364
SWYKER, Betty, 5911
SZOGYI, Alex, 5438

TANAKA, I., 384
TANNER, Alain, 307, 5612, 6296
TARRATT, Margaret, 101, 168, 175, 396, 460, 599, 726, 1288, 1356, 1496, 1633, 1689, 1821, 2015, 2078, 2371, 2473, 2608, 2857, 2995, 3224, 3282, 3467, 3666, 3746, 3767, 3821, 3847, 4017, 4035, 4057, 4099, 4114, 4223, 4237, 4249, 4363, 4392, 4571, 4733, 4867, 5037, 5154, 5229, 5313, 5383, 5531, 5692, 5723, 5901, 5994, 6048, 6345, 6655, 7059, 7076, 7147, 7262, 7317
TAYLOR, Basil, 4887
TAYLOR, Brian, 3491, 3521, 3885
TAYLOR, John Russell, 105, 143, 146, 676, 792, 1019, 1135, 1139, 1466, 1841, 1890, 1963, 1977, 2146, 2242, 2545, 2658, 3099, 3396, 3417, 3750, 4039, 4200, 4445, 4535, 5223, 5243, 5360, 5629, 6083, 6395, 6424, 6533, 6744, 6971, 7050, 7266, 7378
TAYLOR, Stephen, 1012, 1626, 4454, 5079, 5761
TECHINE, Andre, 2438
TEPLE, James R., 2299
THEVOZ, Michel, 1970
THOMAS, Eleanor Lansing, 1467, 3176, 3957
THOMAS, John, 127, 467, 580, 842, 1970, 2192, 2472, 2540, 3247, 3353, 3422, 3655, 3661, 4034, 4960, 5153, 5207, 5468, 5629, 6113, 6314, 6545, 6635, 7231
THOMPSON, Kenneth, 292, 2433, 4020, 4408, 5559, 5756
THOMPSON, Richard, 5654
THORNTON, Jr., Harold R., 3409
THORPE, Edward, 4529
TOIVIAINEN, Sakari, 3320, 3321
TOLAND, Helen, 2608
TOUGAS, Kirk, 1359, 2499, 3450, 6145, 6840
TOZZI, Romano, 135, 169, 375, 816, 941, 1087, 1501, 1519, 1554, 1703,

(cont.)
1841, 2080, 2196, 2348, 2424,
2586, 2657, 2954, 3122, 3374,
3511, 3531, 3654, 3717, 3720,
3731, 3796, 3813, 4228, 4817,
5238, 5307, 5310, 5919, 5920,
5991, 6001, 6115, 6315, 6396,
6491, 6573, 7229, 7393
TREVOR-ROPER, H.R., 1906, 1908
TUNG, 311
TUPPER, Lucy, 2328, 2864, 3776, 3819
TURNER, Albert "Hap", 1248, 5714,
6782
TURNER, John B., 6076
TURNER, R.H., 792, 1242, 3802
TUSKA, Jon, 1524, 3475, 3593A,
3593B, 4998, 5155, 6605, 6836
TUTEN, Frederic, 1727
TYLER, Parker, 1643, 2236, 3276,
3499, 3766, 4683, 4794, 5078, 5679

UBELL, Earl, 4629
UDOFF, Yale M., 1977, 3396, 3843,
4184, 4710

V.H. 6569
VALENTIN, Gregory, 3183
VALLANCE, Tom, 854, 2097, 2244,
3753
VAN PELT, Harold, 6199
VANCE, James S., 3771
VANDALE, Elsie H., 6938
VAS, Robert, 768, 1179, 2363, 2854,
3086, 3127, 3438, 3584, 4467,
4794, 5385, 6128, 6637
VAUGHAN, Dai, 191, 536, 540, 767,
859, 907, 1186, 1543, 1621, 2052,
2200, 2284, 2358, 2522, 2740,
3709, 3887, 4042, 4046, 4526,
4651, 4655, 4965, 5082, 5434,
5466, 5494, 5685, 5746, 6089,
6112, 6195, 6268, 6462, 6743,
6788, 6803, 7277
VAUGHAN, David, 2241, 2334, 2372,
3176, 4086, 4635, 4760, 5922
VAUGHAN, Paul, 3287A, 3287B, 7329
VAUGHN, Susan Beach, 579
VENTURI, Lauro, 2430, 2514, 4141,
5362
VERMILYE, Jerry, 1006, 1173, 5167,
5212, 5264
VESSELO, Arthur, 200, 238, 625, 689,
789, 841, 891, 904, 1206, 1742,
1828, 1910, 1913, 2027, 2126,
2206, 2432, 2550, 2605, 2820,
3008, 3012, 3151, 3463, 3656,
3903, 4032, 4048, 4055, 4123,
4143, 4166, 4315, 4500, 4545,
4575, 4617, 4746, 4820, 5104,
5116, 5216, 5495, 5539, 5869,

5955, 6321, 6362, 6813, 6867,
7182. 7200, 7228
VICKREY, William, 7171
VIOTTI, Sergio, 432, 5330, 6436
VOGEL, Amos, 1942, 3731, 6921
VON BAUG, Peter, 776, 2261, 5251,
7264
VON CLEMNITZ, Elsa, 5923
VON LEMNITZ, Gunther, 2137, 2962,
3301, 6619
VON THUNA, Ulrich, 2309, 2543, 4954

WADDY, Stacy, 3868, 4516, 5614
WAGNER, Geoffrey, 659
WAHL, Jan, 3357
WALD, Malvin, 7393
WALKER, Don, 4381
WALKER, Jesse, 1197
WALKER, John, 117, 1190, 1269,
1287, 1395, 1576, 1624, 1756,
2464, 2527, 4332, 4971, 5331,
6241, 6590, 6906
WALKER, Michael, 4098, 5689, 6570
WALLINGTON, Mike, 218, 1998
WALSH, Gabriel, 1895, 2359
WALSH, Peter, 5520, 6119
WALTERS, Wilson, 494
WANTZ, Susan, 417
WARD, Frank, 4813
WARSHOW, Paul, 1727, 6008, 6364
WASHBURN, Colton, 1767
WEAVER, Hortense, 1127
WEAVER, Richard, 189, 797, 1089,
1195, 1229, 1608, 1966, 2310,
2488, 2953, 3571, 3748, 3814,
4122, 4164, 4175, 4455, 6710, 6833
WEBSTER, Carol, 2088
WEINBERG, Gretchen, 3654
WEINBERG, Herman G., 3, 195, 892,
1448, 1981, 2963, 3183, 3633,
3963, 4097, 4157, 4195, 5148,
6470, 6587
WEINER, Bernard, 1760, 4828, 5081
WEINTRAUB, Stanley, 3514
WEISBROD, Rachel, 4870
WEISS, Naomi, 4830, 5957, 6291
WELLINGTON, Frederick, 690, 1970,
4840
WERSAN, Robert, 6718
WESTOVER, Logan, 6739
WHARTON, Flavia (also see: Flavia
Wharton Rhawn), 97, 214, 364, 461,
468, 829, 912, 1016, 1086, 1108,
1113, 1393, 1762, 1770, 2099,
2536, 2547, 2632, 2648, 2700,
2736, 2837, 2844, 3048, 3063,
3088, 3126, 3162, 3348, 3364,
3370, 3396, 3433, 3556, 3771,
4002, 4006, 4025, 4140, 4165,
4358, 4516, 4543, 4842, 4872,
4951, 4968, 5629, 5733, 5893,

6103, 6105, 6310, 6691, 6722, 7106, 7309
WHARTON, Nancy, 911, 6474
WHITE, Francis, 5465
WHITEBAIT, William, 1475, 4185, 4946
WHITEHALL, Richard, 25, 356, 475, 509, 556, 591, 751, 982, 1000, 1013, 1046, 1171, 1189, 1286, 1475, 1623, 1625, 1896, 1923, 2010, 2109, 2121, 2161, 2205, 2220, 2236, 2300, 2321, 2356, 2472, 2498, 2529, 2575, 2586, 2713, 2725, 2737, 2932, 2973, 2996, 3014, 3055, 3101, 3123, 3153, 3164, 3326, 3329, 3374, 3398, 3578, 3591, 3607, 3613, 3641, 3661, 3723, 3840, 3861, 3874, 3954, 3985, 3998, 4002, 4006, 4010, 4132, 4174, 4191, 4311, 4322, 4456, 4547, 4573, 4587, 4720, 4833, 4835, 4860, 4889, 5048, 5227, 5233, 5399, 5479, 5511, 5546, 5625, 5649, 5800, 5831, 5990, 6013, 6034, 6038, 6125, 6183, 6197, 6224, 6333, 6372, 6464, 6583, 6619, 6636, 6682, 6701, 6744, 6923, 6970
WHITEHEAD, Peter, 1192, 4582, 4796, 4898, 5364, 5620, 6293, 6417, 7037, 7231
WHITMAN, Gregg E., 5822
WICKING, Chris, 2367
WIELAND, Joyce, 6670
WILCOX, John, 67, 5293, 6618
WILLIAM, Forrest, 88, 353
WILLIAMS, Bonnie E., 589, 1323
WILLIAMS, Colley, 6488
WILLIAMS, David, 23
WILLIAMS, F.D., 694, 3560
WILLIAMS, Gordon, 947, 2331, 3951, 5295
WILLIAMS, Peter, 5400
WILLING, Diana, 15, 504, 526, 734, 1469, 1622, 1956, 2207, 2704, 3422, 3427, 3521, 3673, 3965, 4021, 4222, 5202, 5454, 5657, 5829, 6040, 6116, 6325, 6438, 6920, 7352, 7356
WILMINGTON, Michael, 2917, 5037, 7350
WILSON, David, 263, 1027, 1132, 1174, 1356, 1444, 1445, 2022, 2630, 2712, 3057, 3433, 3603, 4828, 4928, 5369, 5416, 5572, 6200, 6263, 6285, 6889, 7147, 7308, 7369
WILSON, J.A., 1283, 2478, 5288
WILSON, N. Hope, 6, 240, 1462, 2290, 2291, 3677, 4071, 5940
WINDSOR, Helen J., 3103
WINFIELD, George, 1076
WINGE, John H., 4217
WINKLER, Richard, 1928

WINNER, Michael, 1018, 1105, 1399, 1967, 2231, 2364, 2483, 2715, 4453, 4468, 4773, 4827, 5391, 5530, 5852, 6685
WINNINGTON, Richard, 103, 113, 530, 756, 825, 4076, 5368, 6056, 6762
WINOGURA, Dale, 204
WISE, Naomi, 4722
WITHAM, Alice H., 196, 443
WITONSKI, Peter, 2035, 2117
WITT, Hugh, 7315
WITTMAN, George, 566
WOLCOTT, Joel, 338, 2520
WOLFE, Wallace D., 224
WOLL, Susan, 3873
WOOD, Eloise, 840
WOOD, Irene, 82, 1605, 7204
WOOD, Robin, 56, 424, 480, 1036, 1653, 1863, 2363, 2890, 4862, 5207, 5310, 5654, 5761, 6192, 6546, 7037, 7380
WOODFORD, Graham, 7283
WOODSIDE, Harold G., 4662
WORTH, Martin, 3972
WRAY, Wendell, 2950
WRIGHT, Basil, 1181, 1279, 2471, 3322, 3357, 3645, 4631, 4735, 5346, 6997
WRIGHT, Elsa Gress, 2307
WYNDHAM, Francis, 508, 3423, 3591, 3671, 5358, 6287

YALKUT, Jud, 7008
YAS, Robert, 2770
YATES, Anna, 5040
YORDAN, Philip, 755
YOUNG, Colin, 244, 273, 781, 1346, 1982, 2828, 2999, 4353, 4578, 5207, 5253, 5347, 5664, 6593, 7345
YOUNG, Kristin, 6976
YOUNG, Vernon, 3854, 4961, 6466, 6907
YOUNGBLOOD, Gene, 121, 4193, 4881, 5220, 5470
YOUNGSON, Robert G., 344, 1864

ZALMAN, Jan, 1268, 1851, 2229, 3244, 5029, 6821
ZANUCK, Darryl F., 3682
ZEHENDER, Ted, 6786
ZEMAN, Marvin, 3633

INDEX TO AUTHORS

INDEX TO AUTHORS

AARONSON, Charles B., 8047
ABRAMSON, Albert, 7698
ACKERMAN, Jean Marie, 7925
ACKLAND, Rodney, 7522
ADLER, Renata, 8620
AGATE, James, 7449
AGEE, James, 7412, 7413, 7414
AGEL, Henri, 7557, 7909, 8069, 8386, 8424
AGEL, Jerome, 8156
AHERNE, Brian, 8353
ALICOATE, Jack, 7758
ALLEN, W.H., 7938
ALLISTER, Ray, 7864
ALPERT, Hollis, 7471, 7682, 7779
ALTON, John, 8306
AMELIO, Ralph, 8607
AMENGUAL, Barthelemy, 7881
AMERICAN LIBRARY ASSOCIATION, 8203
ANDERSON, Clinton H., 7484
ANDERSON, Joseph L., 8064
ANDERSON, Lindsay, 8151
ANDERSON, Yvonne, 8504
ANOBILE, Richard J., 8603
ANSTEY, Edgar, 8439
ANTONIONI, Michelangelo, 8416
ARDMORE, Jane Kesner, 7684, 8338, 8422
ARISTARCO, Guido, 8335
ARMES, Roy, 7572, 7861, 8314
ARNHEIM, Rudolph, 7451, 7750, 8579
ARNOLD, Alan, 8566
ARTIS, Pierre, 7949
ARTS ENQUIRY, THE, 7727
ASTAIRE, Fred, 8470
ASTOR, Mary, 8251
AUTY, Richard, 7805
AVENARIUS, G.A., 7515
AVERSON, Richard, 8440
AYFRE, Abbé, 7557
AYFRE, Amédée, 7618, 7660

BABIN, Pierre, 7462
BABITSKY, Paul, 8456
BACHLIN, Peter, 7769
BADDELEY, W. Hugh, 8505, 8513
BAECHLIN, Peter, 8271
BAINBRIDGE, John, 7876
BAKER, Louise, 7941
BALAZS, Béla, 8530
BALCON, Sir Michael, 8186, 8555
BALL, Robert Hamilton, 8435
BALL, Samuel, 7837
BALSHOFER, Fred J., 8295
BANASZKIEWICZ, Wladislaw, 7613
BANKHEAD, Tallulah, 8501
BANZ, Helmut W., 8089
BARAGLI, Enrico, S.J., 7550
BARBER, Rowland, 7933
BARBOUR, Alan G., 7636, 8093, 8533
BARDECHE, Maurice, 7945, 7958
BARISSE, Rita, 7637
BARKER, Felix, 8291
BARNOUW, Erik, 7902, 8016, 8029, 8517, 8544
BARRY, Iris, 7630
BARRYMORE, Diana, 8541
BARRYMORE, Ethel, 8184
BARRYMORE, Lionel, 8589
BATTCOCK, Gregory, 8261
BATTISON, John H., 8236
BAXTER, John, 7466, 7579, 7874, 7972, 8410
BAZIN, André, 8076, 8594
BEAUCHAMPS, Anthony, 7842
BECKOFF, Samuel, 8208
BELLING, Kurt, 7770
BELLOCCHIO, Marco, 7477
BENAYOUN, Robert, 7647, 8085
BENCHLEY, Nathaniel, 8379
BENDICK, Jeanne, 8157
BENNETT, Joan, 7478
BENOIT-LEVY, Jean, 7458
BERACHA, Sammy, 8194
BERANGER, Clara, 8619
BERANGER, Jean, 7907, 8036, 8283

BERGMAN, Ingmar, 7832
BERGSTEN, Bebe, 8173, 8213
BERGUT, Bob, 7711
BESSIE, Alvah, 8041, 8494
BESSY, Maurice, 7657, 7658, 7885, 7953, 8138, 8200, 8298
BETZ, Hans-Walther, 7770
BIANCHI, Pietro, 7940
BIBERMAN, Herbert, 8396
BICKFORD, Charles, 7505
BILLINGS, Pat, 7984
BILLQUIST, Fritiof, 7875, 8038
BJORKMAN, Stif, 7479
BLACKMAN, Olive, 8434
BLAIR, Alan, 8012
BLAKE, Donald P., 8547
BLAKESTON, Oswell, 8001, 8614
BLASETTI, Alessandro, 7561
BLESH, Rudi, 8094
BLOCK, Libbie, 7942
BLUEM, A. William, 7672
BLUESTONE, George, 8287
BLUM, Daniel, 8266, 8324, 8325, 8415
BLUMER, Herbert, 8230, 8235
BOBKER, Lee, 7700
BODEEN, De Witt, 7809
BOGATZ, Gerry Ann, 7837
BOGDANOVICH, Peter, 7416, 7573, 7865, 8083
BOLAFFI, Giulio, 7519
BORDE, Raymond, 8110, 8308
BORROWS, Michael, 8087
BOUSSINOT, Roger, 7707
BOWSER, Eileen, 7781
BOYUM, Joy Gould, 7751
BRASILLACH, Robert, 7945, 7958
BRAUDY, Leo, 8077
BRICKHILL, Paul, 7633
BRINSON, Peter, 8294
BRIOT, René, 8380
BRITISH BROADCASTING COMPANY, 7910
BRITISH FILM INSTITUTE, 8257
BRODBECK, Emil E., 7929
BRODSKY, Jack, 7592
BROOKS, Alice, 8623
BROOKS, Richard, 8350
BROWN, Frederick, 8022
BROWN, Joe E., 8108
BROWNLOW, Kevin, 7995, 8310
BRUNEL, Adrian, 7784, 8273
BUACHE, Freddy, 7564
BUCHANAN, Andrew, 7746, 7765, 7774, 7901, 8578
BUCHER, Felix, 7888
BUDGEN, Suzanne, 7731
BURCH, Nöel, 8339
BURDER, John, 8506
BUSKIN, Judith, 8432
BUTLER, Ivan, 7582, 7990, 7991, 8155, 8370, 8539
BUZZI, Aldo, 8568

CAHN, William, 7932
CALDER-MARSHALL, Arthur, 8040
CALLENBACH, Ernest, 8302
CAMERON, Ian, 7444, 7816, 7824, 8187, 8419
CAMERON, Ian and Elisabeth, 7634, 7937
CAMERON, Ken, 8453
CAMPBELL, Russell, 8321
CANFIELD, Alice, 8057
CAPACCIOLI, Enzo, 7598
CAPRA, Frank, 8255
CAREY, Gary, 7628, 8136
CARMEN, Ira H., 8234
CARPOZI, Jr., George, 7880
CARR, Larry, 7850
CARRICK, Edward, 7450, 7644
CARSON, Robert, 7708, 8149
CARTER, Huntley, 8268
CASAS, Fernando Vizcaino, 8484
CASTELLO, Giulio Cesare, 7568, 7668
CASTY, Alan, 7825, 8176
CAULIEZ, Armand-Jean, 8073
CAVELL, Stanley, 8617
CERAM, C.W., 7448
CHABROL, Claude, 7963
CHANDLER, David, 7690
CHAPLIN, Charles, 8246
CHAPLIN, Jr., Charles, 8248
CHAPLIN, Lita Grey, 8250
CHAPLIN, Michael, 8010
CHAPMAN, William McK., 7828
CHARDANS, Jean-Louis, 7657, 7658
CHARDERE, Bernard, 8074, 8341
CHARENSOL, Georges, 7556, 8307, 8371
CHARTERS, W.W., 8211
CHAUMETON, Etienne, 8308
CHERKASSOV, Nicoloi, 8280
CHEVALLIER, Jacques, 7549
CHEVASSU, Francois, 8106
CHIARINI, Luigi, 7776
CHINOY, Helen Krich, 7408
CILENTO, Diane, 8162
CLAIR, René, 8367, 8368
CLARENS, Carlos, 7587, 7992, 8015
CLARK, Charles G., 8351
COBB, Elisabeth, 8252
COCKSHOTT, Gerald, 8025
COCTEAU, Jean, 7597, 7651
COLE, Toby, 7406, 7408
COLLET, Jean, 8071
COLPI, Henri, 7642
CONANT, Micnael, 7442
CONNELL, Brian, 8102
CONWAY, Michael, 7810, 7821
COOK, Olive, 8221
COOKE, Alistair, 7878
COOPER, Morton, 8250
COOREY, Philip, 8131
COPLANS, John, 7432
COPYRIGHT OFFICE (UNITED

STATES), 8215, 8216, 8217, 8218, 8219
CORNEAU, Ernest N., 7927
CORNWELL-CLYNE, Adrian, 7601
COSTELLO, Donald, 8430
COTE, Guy, 8486
COTES, Peter, 8126
COTTRELL, John, 8091
COURSODON, Jean-Pierre, 8095, 8550
COURTNEY, Marguerite, 8111
COWGILL, Rome, 8362
COWIE, Peter, 7610, 8035, 8045, 8431, 8492, 8493
CRAWFORD, Joan, 8338
CRICHTON, Kyle, 8169, 8542
CRISP, C.G., 7856
CRIST, Judith, 8348
CROSBY, Bing, 7512
CROSBY, Kathryn, 7487
CROSLAND, Margaret, 8067
CROSS, Brenda, 7763
CROSS, John E., 8412
CROWTHER, Bosley, 7914, 7979, 8123
CROY, Homer, 8304, 8466
CURRAN, Charles W., 7930
CURTIS, David, 7719

DALE, Edgar, 7463, 7541, 7996
DANISCHEWSKY, Monja, 8599
DANKO, X., 8279
DAREN, Maya, 7430
DAUGHERTY, Charles M., 8113
DAVENPORT, Nicholas, 7872
DAVIS, Bette, 8132
DE LA ROCHE, Catherine, 8455
DE MILLE, Agnes, 7635
DE MILLE, William C., 7980
DEBRIX, J.R., 7548, 7845
DEMING, Barbara, 8391
DENT, Alan, 7928
DEREYMAEKER, J., 7547
DESCHNER, Donald, 7826, 7827
DESLANDES, Jacques, 7496
DEWEY, Lang (Langdon), 8305
DEWHURST, H., 8054
DI GIAMMATTO, Fernaldo, 7715
DI NUBILA, Domingo, 7954
DICKENS, Homer, 7814, 7820
DICKINSON, Thorold, 7665, 8455
DICKSON, W.K.L. and Antonia, 7962
DIETRICH, Marlene, 8168
DIMMIT, Richard B., 7407, 8537
DIXON, Campbell, 8043
DOLMAN, Jr., John, 7455
DONATO, Eugenio, 8107
DONNER, Jorn, 8319
DORFF, Ove Brusen, 7713
DOUGLAS, Drake, 7989
DREYER, Carl (TH.), 7834, 8292
DUARTE, Fernando, 7955
DUCA, (Giuseppe) Lo, 7646, 7675, 7714, 7885, 7944, 8138
DUKE, Vernon, 8313
DUNCAN, Ronald, 7651
DUNNE, John Gregory, 8480
DURGNAT, Raymond, 7623, 7712, 7798, 7857, 7918, 8143, 8170, 8195, 8286
DWIGGINS, Don, 7978
DWORKIN, Martin S., 8125
DYSINGER, Wendell S., 7705

EAST, John M., 8258
EASTMAN, Charles, 7419
EASTMAN, Max, 7913
EDLER, Joseph Maria, 7959
EDSTROM, Mauritz, 8483
EIBEL, Alfred, 7865
EISENSCHITZ, Bernard, 8006
EISENSTEIN, Sergei M., 7423, 7760, 7762, 8061, 8279, 8359
EISLER, Hanns, 7609
EISNER, Lotte H., 7692, 7723, 7934
ELLIOTT, Godfrey, M., 7743
ELLISON, Harlan, 7896
ENCYCLOPEDIA BRITANNICA, 8000
ENGLANDER, David A., 8322
ENSER, A.G.S., 7794
EPSTEAN, Edward, 7959
EPSTEIN, Edward, 8090
ERNST, Morris L., 7525, 7528, 8204
ERSTED, Ruth, 8623
ESCOUBE, Lucienne, 7879
ESSOE, Gabe, 7811, 8502
ESTEVE, Michel, 8037, 8282
EVERSON, William K., 7426, 7460, 7470, 7815, 7819, 8593
EXTON, Jr., William, 7465
EYLES, Allen, 7984, 8172, 8592
EZRATTY, Sacha, 8103

FAIRBANKS, Letitia, 7679
FALCONER, Vera M., 7831
FALK, Irving A., 8622
FALLACI, Oriana, 8120
FANT, Kenne, 8490
FARBER, Manny, 8259
FARWAGI, Audré, 8372
FAULK, John Henry, 7729
FEARING, Franklin, 8212
FEDERATION OF FILM SOCIETIES, 7787
FELDMAN, Erich, 8526
FELDMAN, Joseph and Harry, 7687
FELLINI, Federico, 7675
FENIN, George N., 8593
FENSCH, Thomas, 7829
FERNETT, Gene, 8272
FERRARA, Giuseppe, 7551, 8288
FESCOURT, Henri, 7843
FIELD, Alice Evans, 7986

FIELD, Mary, 7539, 7903
FIELDING, Raymond, 8512, 8516
FINLER, Joel, 8378
FISCHER, Edward, 8413
FISHER, J. David, 7622
FITZGERALD, Stephen E., 7604
FLAHERTY, Francis Hubbard, 8289
FLETCHER, Steffi, 8586
FLOREY, Robert, 7968
FLYNN, Errol, 8253
FORD, Charles, 7946, 7950, 7952, 8179, 8447
FORMAN, Henry James, 8303
FOWLER, Gene, 8192
FOWLER, Roy, 7766
FRAENKEL, Heinrich, 7887
FRAGOLA, Augusto, 7585
FRAIGNEAU, André, 7597
FRANK, Gerold, 8541, 8624
FRANKLIN, Joe, 7590
FRAZIER, Alexander, 8465
FREEDGOOD, Morton, 8585
FRENCH, Philip, 8225
FREUCHEN, Peter, 8565
FREWIN, Leslie, 7491, 7659
FULTON, A.R., 8220
FURHAMMAR, Leif, 8334
FUZELLIER, Etienne, 7558

GAITHER, Grant, 8346
GALE, David, 8588
GARGAN, William, 8604
GARNHAM, Nicholas, 8400
GARRETT, John, 8500
GASKELL, Arthur L., 8322
GASSNER, John, 7481
GEDULD, Harry M., 7773, 8153, 8427
GELMIS, Joseph, 7759
GERBER, Albert B., 7472
GERTNER, Richard, 7802
GESEK, Ludwig, 7892
GESSNER, Robert, 8243
GIARDINO, Thomas F., 7475
GIDAL, Peter, 7433
GIFFORD, Denis, 7499, 8409
GILDER, Rosamond, 8522
GILL, Samuel, 7594
GILSON, René, 8068
GIPSON, Henry Clay, 7803
GISH, Lillian, 8239
GIZYCKI, Jerzy, 7494
GLUCKSMANN, André, 8574
GLYN, Anthony, 7701
GODARD, Jean-Luc, 8147, 8174, 8320, 8330
GODOWSKY, Dagmar, 7835
GOETZ, Alice, 8089
GOLDBLATT, Burt, 8171
GOMES, P.E. SALES, 8078
GOODE, James, 8475
GOODGOLD, Ed., 8538

GOODMAN, Ezra, 7735
GOODMAN, Louis, 7801
GORDON, George N., 8622
GORDON, Jay E., 8206
GOTTESMAN, Ronald, 7841, 8153, 8427
GOW, Gordon, 7970, 8489
GRAHAM, Peter, 7653, 8269
GRAHAM, Sheilah, 8375, 8411
GRAHAM, Virginia, 8448
GRANGE, Frédéric, 7506
GRANT, Elspeth, 7522
GRAU, Wolfgang, 7652
GREAVES, Roger, 7934
GREENBERG, Joel, 7523, 7971
GREENWOOD, Elizabeth, 7732
GREER, Howard, 7645
GREGOR, Ulrich, 7890, 7891, 8605
GREGORY, Richard L., 8042
GREGORY, W.A., 7662
GRIERSON, John, 7917
GRIFFIS, Stanton, 8144
GRIFFITH, Mrs., D.W., 8597
GRIFFITH, Richard, 7671, 7791, 8227, 8228, 8401, 8615
GUARESCHI, Giovanni, 7676
GUARNER, José Luis, 8384
GUBECK, Thomas H., 8046
GUILES, Fred Lawrence, 8276
GUILLAUME, Yves, 8576
GUILLOT, Gérard, 8344
GUSSOW, Mel, 7678
GUTERSLOH, Joseph Wulf, 8521
GUTH, Paul, 7469

HACKL, Alfonso, 7858
HALAS, John, 7454, 7643, 7749, 8508
HALE, Bryant, 8323
HALL, Ben M., 7483
HALLER, Robert, 7425
HALLIWELL, Leslie, 7796
HAMILTON, Marie L., 7775
HAMPTON, Benjamin, 7960
HANCOCK, Ralph, 7679
HANDEL, Leo A., 7975
HARDING, James, 8394
HARDY, Forsyth, 7919, 8406, 8555
HARDY, Phil, 8399
HARLEY, John Eugene, 8618
HAUDIQUET, Philippe, 8082, 8284
HAUSER, Philip M., 8235
HAYDEN, Sterling, 8587
HAYMAN, Ronald, 8084
HAYNE, Donald, 7468
HAYS, Will H., 8183
HEAD, Edith, 7684
HEATH, Eric, 7725
HECHT, Ben, 7533, 7537
HEIN, Brigit, 7764
HEINING, Heinrich, 7899
HENDERSON, Robert M., 7631, 7632

AUTHORS

HENDRICKS, Gordon, 7474, 7695
HENNE, Frnaces, 8623
HENNINGSEN, Poul, 7713
HEPWORTH, Cecil M., 7513
HERMAN, Lewis, 7697
HEYER, Robert, 7664
HIBBIN, Nina, 7689
HIGHAM, Charles, 7523, 7823, 7967, 7971
HILL, Cecil A., 7543, 8352
HILLS, Janet, 7854
HITCHCOCK, Alfred, 8473
HOBAN, Charles F., 8241
HOELLERING, George, 7782
HOFMANN, Charles, 8454
HOGBEN, Lancelot, 7868
HOLADAY, Perry W., 7893
HOLMES, Winifred, 8297
HOPE, Bob, 7935, 8532
HOPKINS, Jerry, 7703
HOPKINS, Mark W., 8177
HOPKINSON, Peter, 8462
HOPPER, Hedda, 7870
HORLAND, Carl I., 7720
HOUSEMAN, John, 8390
HOUSTON, Penelope, 7612
HOWARD, Leslie Ruth, 8361
HUACO, George, 8451
HUBLER, Richard G., 8437
HUETTIG, Mae D., 7691
HUFF, Theodore, 7534
HUGHES, Robert, 7752, 7753
HULFISH, David S., 8207
HULL, David Stewart, 7767
HUNNINGS, Neville March, 7755
HUNTLEY, John, 7502, 7993, 8363, 8510
HUSS, Roy, 7761
HYAMS, Joe, 7493

IDESTAM-ALMQUIST, Bengt, 8256, 8392
INGLIS, Ruth A., 7859
INTERNATIONAL CENTER OF THE AUDIO-VISUAL ARTS AND SCIENCES, 8343
INTERNATIONAL EXHIBITION OF CINEMATOGRAPHY, 8556
ISAKSSON, Folke, 8334
ISAKSSON, Ulla, 8575
ISKUSSTVO, 8202
IVENS, Joris, 7514

JABLONSKI, Edward, 7889
JACKSON, Arthur, 7976
JACKSON, Clarence S., 8328
JACOB, Gilles, 7566
JACOBS, Lewis, 7673, 7704, 8052, 8233, 8377
JAECKEL, Theodore R., 7458

JAMES, F.E. and E.P. Skone, 7619
JAMEUX, Charles, 8244
JANNINGS, Emil, 8523
JARRATT, Vernon, 8058
JARVIE, Ian C., 8232, 8543
JEANNE, René, 7946, 7952, 8447
JENNINGS, Dean, 8249
JENSEN, Paul, 7576
JOBES, Gertrude, 8205
JONES, Emily S., 8163
JONES, Ken, 7818
JORDAN, Jr., Thurston, 7897
JOSEPHSON, Matthew, 7694
JUNGE, H., 8332

KABIR, Alamgir, 7560
KAEL, Pauline, 7900, 8011, 8100
KAHN, Gordon, 7977
KALBUS, Oskar, 8581
KANIN, Garson, 8546
KAPLAN, Nelly, 8161
KATKOV, Norman, 7724
KAUFFMANN, Stanley, 7737, 8616
KEATON, Buster, 8254
KEATS, John, 8004
KEENE, Ralph, 8590
KEHOE, Vincent J.R., 8507
KEIM, Jean, 8285
KELLNER, Otto, 8089
KELLY, Terence, 7605
KEOWN, Eric, 8165
KERR, Laura, 7939
KERR, Walter, 7627
KHAN, M., 8053
KIBBEE, Lois, 7478
KIDD, M.K., 7830
KINEMA JUMPO SHA Co., 7607
KINGSON, Walter, 8362
KINSEY, Anthony, 7437
KITSES, Jim, 7988, 8499
KLAUE, Wolfgang, 8382
KLUGE, Alexander, 7404
KNIGHT, Arthur, 8128
KNIGHT, Derrick, 8133
KNOWLES, Dorothy, 7526
KOBAL, John, 7905, 7918, 8167, 8266
KOURY, Phil A., 8557, 8621
KOVACS, Yves, 8488
KOZINTSEV, Grigori, 8436
KRACAUER, Siegfried, 7867, 8528
KRAMER, Dale, 8356
KRISHNASWAMY, S., 8029
KRUPANIDHI, Uma, 8403
KUHNS, William, 7475, 7721, 8525
KUJOTH, Jean, 8365
KUSHNER, David, 7852
KYROU, Ado, 7429, 8142, 8487

LACASSIN, Francis, 8137
LACLOS, Michel, 7728

LAHR, John, 8281
LAHUE, Kalton C., 7497, 7594, 7600, 7614, 7683, 8609
LAMBERT, Gavin, 8449
LANDAU, Jacob, M., 8479
LANG, André, 8497
LANIA, Leo, 8247
LAPIERRE, Marcel, 7530
LARSEN, Egon, 8463
LARSEN, Otto N., 8573
LARSON, Rodger, 7924
LASKY, Jesse, 8009
LASKY, Victor, 8405
LATHAM, Aaron, 7624
LAURA, Ernesto G., 7754
LAWS, Frederick, 8146
LAWSON, John Howard, 7790, 8527
LE ROY, Mervyn, 8057
LEAHY, James, 7580
LEBEDEV, Nikolaj, 7567
LEBEL, J.P., 7509, 7510
LEE, Laurie, 8590
LEE, Raymond, 7838, 8316
LEGMAN, G., 8139
LEITES, Nathan, 8229
LEJEUNE, Caroline, 8520
LENNIG, Arthur, 7588, 7780, 8444
LEONARD, Harold, 7768
LEPROHON, Pierre, 7563, 7586, 7947, 8075, 8188, 8189
LEVITAN, Eli L., 7438
LEWIN, William, 8465
LEWIS, Leon, 8105
LEYDA, Jay, 7760, 7762, 7800, 8099, 8112, 8382
LHERMINIER, Pierre, 7452, 8079
LIBRARY OF CONGRESS, 7520
LIDSTONE, John, 7540
LIMBACHER, James, 7849, 7956, 8563
LINDGREN, Ernest, 7457, 7743, 8327, 8439, 8555
LINDSAY, Vachel, 7459
LINDSEY, Alexander, 7525, 8204
LIPTON, Lenny, 8026
LIZZANI, Carlo, 7562
LOCKWOOD, Margaret, 8141
LONG, C.W., 7830
LOOK MAGAZINE, 8223
LOOS, Anita, 7895
LOPEZ, Manuel Villegas, 7544
LOW, Rachael, 7961
LUDLAM, Harry, 7489
LUMSDAINE, Arthur A., 7720
LUNDBERG, Holger, 8319
LUNDERS, L., 7529
LYNCH, William F., 8017, 8018

MC ANANY, Emile G., 7833
MC BRIDE, Joseph, 8299, 8318
MC CABE, John, 8196
MC CAFFREY, Donald, 7851

MAC CANN, Richard Dyer, 7740, 7745, 7974
MC CARTY, Clifford, 7756, 7812, 8357
MC CLURE, Arthur, 7818, 8569
MAC DONALD, Dwight, 7686
MC DONALD, Gerald, 7810
MAC GOWAN, Kenneth, 7476, 8345
MC INTOSH, Don, 7540
MC KOWEN, Clark, 8060
MAC LAINE, Shirley, 7677
MAC LIAMMOIR, Micheal, 8358
MC LUHAN, Marshall, 8559
MC VAY, Douglas, 8245
MACK, Angela, 7615
MACKSEY, Richard, 8107
MADSEN, Axel, 7486
MADSEN, Roy, 7436
MALMSTROM, Lars, 7852
MALTIN, Leonard, 8222, 8495
MANCHEL, Frank, 8231, 8595, 8596
MANDER, Raymond, 8524
MANFULL, Helen, 7410
MANKOWITZ, Wolf, 7595
MANNS, Torsen, 7479
MANOOGIAN, Haig P., 7772
MANUEL, Jacques, 7453
MANVELL, Roger, 7435, 7454, 7569, 7570, 7571, 7643, 7718, 7738, 7748, 7887, 8226, 8262, 8263, 8264, 8418, 8439, 8508, 8510, 8534, 8555
MANZ, H.P., 8048
MAPP, Edward, 7490
MARILL, Alvin, 8093
MARION, Denis, 7583
MARKER, Chris, 7603
MARNER, Terence, 7661
MARQUIS, Dorothy P., 7542
MARS, Francois, 7873
MARSHALL, Herbert, 8061
MARTIN, Marcel, 7535, 7855, 8106
MARTIN, Pete, 7512, 7935, 8606
MARX, Arthur, 7921, 8117
MARX, Groucho, 7922, 7923
MARX, Harpo, 7933
MASCELLI, Joseph V., 7422, 7839
MAST, Gerald, 8438
MATTHEOS, Constantine, 8354
MAY, Mark A., 8450
MAY, Renato, 8122
MAYER, Arthur, 8185, 8228
MAYER, Michael F., 7847
MAYERSBERG, Paul, 7983
MAZZANTI, Manlio, 8300
MEEKER, David, 8066
MEKAS, Jonas, 7432
MERCER, Ann, 8499
MERCER, John, 8050
MERMAN, Ethel, 8600
MEYER, Anthony, 7664
MICHAEL, Paul, 7405, 7427, 8007
MIDA, Massimo, 7555

AUTHORS

MILGROM, Al, 7578
MILLAR, Gavin, 8509
MILLER, Arthur C., 7422, 8295
MILLER, Diane Disney, 8476
MILLER, Maud M., 8608
MILLER, Vernon L., 7542
MILLER, Virgil E., 8461
MILNE, Tom, 7574, 8135, 8158
MILNER, C. Douglas, 8154
MINNEY, R.J., 7532
MIRAMS, Gordon, 8458
MISSIAEN, J.C., 7441, 8002
MITCHENSON, Joe, 8524
MITROPOULOS, Aglae, 7640
MITRY, Jean, 7536, 7716, 7948, 8081, 8393
MIX, Olive Stokes, 7725
MOISEIWITSCH, Maurice, 8389
MONIER, Pierre, 7606
MONOPOLIES COMMISSION, THE, 7797
MONTAGU, Ivor, 7788, 7793, 8061, 8112, 8611
MONTGOMERY, John, 7602
MOORE, Collene, 8443
MORELLA, Joe, 8090
MORIN, Edgar, 8469
MORLEY, Raymond, 7930
MORLEY, Robert, 8383
MORRIS, Lloyd, 8277
MOSLEY, Leonard, 7473
MOURLET, Michael, 7521
MOUSSINAC, Léon, 7411, 8426
MULLEN, Pat, 8160
MULLER-STRAUSS, Maurice, 8271
MUNDEN, Kenneth W., 7424
MURPHY, George, 8405
MUSSMAN, Toby, 8070

NEERGAARD, Ebbe, 7957
NEFF, Hildegard, 7894
NEGRI, Pola, 8182
NEILSON-BAXTER, R.K., 7570
NELSON, Bill, 8129
NEMCEK, Paul, 7822
NEMESKURTY, Istvan, 8612
NESBITT, Alec, 8511
NEUMANN, Carl, 7770
NEW YORK TIMES, THE, 8270, 8315
NICHOLS, Dudley, 7481
NIKLAUS, Thelma, 8126
NIVEN, David, 8201
NIVER, Kemp R., 7488, 7836, 8024, 8173, 8213
NIZHNY, Vladimir, 8112
NOBLE, Peter, 7503, 7981, 8260
NOGUEIRA, Rue, 8180
NOLAN, William F., 8086
NOLTENIUS, Johanne, 7860
NORTON, Graham, 7605
NOWELL-SMITH, Geoffrey, 8577

NYE, Russell B., 8560

OAKLEY, C.A., 8598
OBRAZTSOV, Sergei, 8130
O'CONLVAIN, Proinsias, 8407
O'DELL, Paul, 7920
O'KONOR, Louise, 8571
O'LEARY, Liam, 8442
OLIVIER, Paul, 8364
OMS, Marcel, 7507
OPPENHEIMER, George, 8570
ORROM, Michael, 8340
ORWELL, George, 7434

PAGNOL, Marcel, 7637
PALMER, Charles, 7516
PAQUET, André, 7999
PARISH, James Robert, 7495, 7853, 8093
PARRAIN, Philippe, 8369
PARSONS, Louella, 8518
PASCAL, Valerie, 7663
PASTERNAK, Joe, 7690
PATALAS, Enno, 7890, 7891, 8457
PATE, Michael, 7741
PAYNE, Robert, 7912, 7916
PEARLMAN, S.J., 8378
PEARSON, George, 7840
PECHTER, William S., 8554
PENSEL, Hans, 8417
PERRIN, Charles, 8110
PERRY, George, 7605, 7808
PERSONALITY POSTERS, 8601
PETERS, Charles C., 8209
PETERS, J.M.L., 8503
PETERSON, Marcelone, 8323
PETERSON, Ruth C., 8210
PETRIE, Graham, 7575
PETRY, D. Sandy, 8426
PICKFORD, Mary, 8485
PINCHOT, Ann, 8239
PINCUS, Edward, 7926
PISAREVSKY, D.S., 8056
PLEYER, Peter, 7649
PORCILE, Francois, 7641
PORGES, Freidrich, 8408
PORTER, Vincent, 8133
POULON, Flavia, 7553
POWDERMAKER, Hortense, 7982
PRATLEY, Gerald, 7577, 7581
PRATT, George C., 8459
PREJEAN, Albert, 8448
PUDOVKIN, V.I., 7788

QUEVAL, Jean, 8062, 8164
QUIGLEY, Jr., Martin, 7802, 8150, 8267
QUINN, Thomas, 8583
QUIRK, Lawrence J., 7813

RABORN, George, 7994
RAMSAYE, Terry, 8190
RANDALL, Richard S., 7527
RAPHAELSON, Samson, 8005
RASMUSSEN, Bjorn, 7795
RATTENBURY, Arnold, 8412
RAU, N. and M., 8248
RAVAR, Raymond, 8551
RAY, Man, 8423
READ, Sinclair, 7671
REBOLLEDO, Carlos, 7506
REDGRAVE, Michael, 7409
REED, Rex, 7669
REED, Stanley, 7545, 7993
REEVE, Ada, 8498
REGENT, Roger, 7554
REID, Gordon, 7862
REID, P.R., 7599
REID, Seerley, 8536
REIS, Claire R., 7608
REISZ, Karel, 8509
RENAN, Sheldon, 8051
RENOIR, Jean, 8373
RENSHAW, Samuel, 7542
REYNERTSON, A.J., 8613
RHODE, Eric, 8545
RICCI, Mark, 7810, 7821
RICHARDS, Dick, 8116
RICHARDSON, Robert, 8124
RICHIE, Donald, 7807, 7882, 8064, 8065
RIEUPEYROUT, J.L., 7908
RILLA, Wolf, 7402
RIMBERG, John, 8456
RINGGOLD, Gene, 7809, 7812
RISSIENT, Pierre, 8134
RIVKIN, Allen, 7939
ROBINSON, David, 7511, 7915, 7973, 8224
ROBINSON, W.R., 8159
ROBYNS, Gwen, 8118
RODKER, Francis, 7638
ROHMER, Eric, 7963
RONDI, Gian Luigi, 7561, 8059
ROSE, Tony, 8445
ROSENBERG, Bernard, 8366
ROSENTHAL, Alan, 8265
ROSS, Helen, 8333
ROSS, Lillian, 8326, 8333, 8374
ROSS, T.J., 7747
ROTH, Lillian, 8014
ROTHA, Paul, 7671, 7791, 8226, 8337, 8388, 8439
ROUD, Richard, 7898, 8477
RUCKMINK, Christian A., 7705
RUFSVOLD, Margaret I., 7464
RUNES, Dagobert D., 7650
RUSSE, Pasquale, 7598

SADOUL, Georges, 7552, 7654, 7655, 7863, 7886, 7951, 8055, 8331

ST. JOHN, Adela Rogers, 7987
SAKALL, S.Z., 8474
SALACHAS, Gilbert, 7730
SAMUELS, Charles, 7517, 7943, 8098, 8254
SANDERS, George, 8181
SANDFELD, Gunnar, 8481
SARRIS, Andrew, 7421, 7611, 7739, 7779, 7817, 8049
SAVIO, Francesco, 7508
SCHARY, Dore, 7516
SCHEUER, Steven H., 8240, 8496
SCHICKEL, Richard, 7667, 7778, 8242, 8468
SCHILDKRAUT, Joseph, 8247
SCHILLER, Herbert, 8175
SCHLAPPNER, Martin, 8582
SCHMALENBACH, Werner, 7769
SCHMIDT, Georg, 7769
SCHNITZER, Luda and Jean, 7680, 8572
SCHULBERG, Budd, 7666
SCHUMACH, Murray, 7726
SCHWARTZ, Alan U., 7528
SCOTT, Adrienne, 7751
SCOTT, Helen G., 7964
SEARLE, Ronald, 8452
SEGERS, J., 7547
SELDES, Gilbert, 7911, 8355
SEMOLUE, Jean, 7685
SENNETT, Mack, 8097
SETON, Marie, 8336, 8404, 8428
SEWELL, George H., 8152
SHAH, Panna, 8028
SHARP, Dennis, 8329
SHAVELSON, Melville, 7998
SHAW, Arnold, 8446
SHAY, Don, 7617
SHEFFIELD, Fred D., 7720
SHERMAN, William David, 8105
SHIPMAN, David, 7917
SHIPP, Cameron, 8097, 8589
SHULMAN, Irving, 7931, 8567
SHUTTLEWORTH, Frank K., 8450
SICLIER, Jacques, 7733
SIEGEL, Rosalie, 7730
SILBER, Irwin, 7629
SILVERSTEIN, Norman, 7761
SIMA, Jonas, 7479
SIMON, John, 7778, 8238, 8349
SIMSOLO, Noel, 7965
SINCLAIR, Upton, 8561
SINGER, Kurt, 8109
SINGER, Laura J., 8432
SITNEY, P. Adams, 7757
SJOMAN, Vilgot, 8008, 8012, 8104
SKILBECK, Oswald, 7401
SLATER, Guy, 7482
SLIDE, Anthony, 7688
SMALLMAN, Kirk, 7625
SMITH, Albert E., 8557
SMITH, John M., 8080

AUTHORS

SMITH, Julia, 7403
SNYDER, Robert L., 8311
SOBEL, Bernard, 7504
SOBOLEV, Romil P., 8127
SOCIETY OF MOTION PICTURE AND TELEVISION ENGINEERS, 7616, 7699
SOHN, David A., 7789
SOLMI, Angelo, 7732
SONTAG, Susan, 8482
SOUTO, H. Mario Kaimonde, 8515
SPARKE, William, 8060
SPEED, F. Maurice, 7783
SPIGELGASS, Leonard, 8602
SPINAZZOLA, Vittorio, 7777
SPOLIN, Viola, 8023
SPOTTISWOODE, Nigel, 8529
SPOTTISWOODE, Raymond, 7706, 7744, 7906, 8515, 8529
SPRAOS, John, 7639
SPRINGER, John, 7420, 7844, 8414
STACK, Oswald, 8312
STANLEY, Robert, 7721
STARR, Cecile, 7785, 8013, 8031
STEDMAN, Raymond William, 8429
STEEGMULLER, Francis, 7596
STEELE, Joseph Henry, 8039
STEELE, Robert, 7518
STEENE, Brigitta, 8033
STEPHENSON, Ralph, 7439, 7456, 7548, 7734
STERGIANOPOULOS, DEM. ATH., 8275
STEWART, David C., 7786
STEWART, Lawrence D., 7889
STODDARD, George D., 7893
STONE, C. Walter, 8114
STORM, Ole, 7834
STOVIN, P.D., 7510
STRICK, Philip, 7445
STUART, Ray, 8021
SULLIVAN, John, 7501
SUNDGREN, Nils Petter, 8397
SUSSEX, Elizabeth, 8121
SVENSSON, Arne, 8063
SVENSTEDT, Carl Henrik, 7447
SVET SOVIETU, 8580
SWINDELL, Larry, 8460

TABORI, Paul, 7418
TABORSKI, Boleslaw, 8115
TAILLEUR, Roger, 7443
TALBOT, Daniel, 7742
TAUBMAN, Joseph, 7620
TAYLOR, Deems, 8323
TAYLOR, John Russell, 7559, 7976
TAYLOR, R.L., 8584
TAYLOR, Theodore, 8317
TELL, Pincus W., 8296
TERZI, Corrado, 8625
TESI, Giancarlo, 7551

THIRARD, Paul-Louis, 7443
THOMAS, Bob, 8096, 8424, 8519
THOMAS, Dylan, 7670
THOMAS, Tony, 8564
THORPE, Edward, 8301
THRASHER, Frederic M., 8290
THURSTONE, L.L., 8210
TOMKIES, Mike, 7485
TOMKINS, Calvin, 7432
TREWIN, J.C., 8381
TRUCHAND, Francois, 8191, 8274
TRUFFAUT, Francois, 7584, 7964
TRUMBO, Dalton, 7410
TURCONI, David, 7508, 8145
TURINI, Guido Aristarco, 8472
TWONEY, Alfred, 7818, 8569
TYLER, Parker, 7531, 7589, 7969, 8148, 8433, 8535, 8558
TYNAN, Kenneth, 7417

U N E S C O, 8030
ULRICHSEN, Erik, 8292

VALLANCE, Tom, 7428
VAN NOOTEN, S.I., 7696
VARDAC, Nicolas A., 8464
VAUGHN, Ciba, 8298
VE-HO, 8198
VEDRES, Nicole, 8019
VENDITTI, Rodolfo, 8552
VENTO, Giovanni, 7555
VIALLE, Gabriel, 7883
VIAZZI, Glauco, 7709
VIDOR, King, 8549
VIVIE, Jean, 8548
VIZZARD, Jack, 8420
VON STERNBERG, Josef, 7871

WAGENKNECHT, Edward, 8237
WAGNER, Jean, 8072
WAIN, G., 7997
WALDRON, Gloria, 8031
WALKER, Alexander, 7524, 8467
WALKER, Michael, 7591
WALLS, Howard Lamarr, 8215
WALTER, Ernest, 8514
WARD, John, 7415
WARMAN, Eric, 8389
WARNER, Jack L., 8249
WARSHOW, Robert, 8020
WATERBURY, Ruth, 7702
WATERS, Ethel, 7943
WEAVER, John T., 7848
WEBER, Hugo, 7769
WEINBERG, Herman G., 8088, 8140, 8395
WEISS, Ken, 8538
WEISS, Nathan, 7592
WELTMAN, Manuel, 8316

749

WENNERHOLM, Eric, 8309
WERNER, Gosta, 7771, 8178
WERNER, Jane, 8586
WEST, Jessamyn, 8540
WEST, Mae, 7904
WHEELER, Lester J., 8347
WHITE, David Manning, 8440
WHITEBAIT, William, 8044
WHITEHEAD, Peter, 8330
WILCOX, Herbert, 8553
WILKINS, Virginia, 8536
WILL, David, 8385, 8598
WILLEMEN, Paul, 8385
WILLIAMS, Raymond, 8340
WILLIAMS, Robert, 7833
WILLIAMS, Tennessee, 8387
WILSON, Norman, 8342
WINDELER, Robert, 8092
WINDQUIST, Sven G., 7467, 8491
WINNINGTON, Richard, 7681, 7872
WISEMAN, Thomas, 7546
WLASCHIN, Ken, 7492
WOLFENSTEIN, Martha, 8229
WOLLEN, Peter, 8398, 8441
WOLLENBERG, H.H., 7431, 7736
WOOD, Alan, 8197
WOOD, Leslie, 8193
WOOD, Robin, 7444, 7446, 7461, 7591,
    7966, 8003, 8034
WOOD, Tom, 7498
WOODHOUSE, Bruce, 7869
WOROSZYLSKI, Wiktor, 8115
WRIGHT, Basil, 8562
WYNN, Keenan, 7693

YOUNG, Loretta, 8531
YOUNGBLOOD, Gene, 7717
YURENEV, R., 8279
YUTKEVICH, S.J., 7423

ZALMAN, Jan, 7799
ZGLINICKI, Friedrich V., 8591
ZIERALD, Norman, 7538, 7877, 7985,
    8199
ZIMMER, Jill Schary, 8610
ZIMMERMAN, Paul D., 8171
ZINSSER, William K., 8421
ZOLOTOW, Maurice, 8166
ZUKOR, Adolph, 8356

INDEX TO BOOK REVIEWERS

INDEX TO BOOK REVIEWERS

A.H.W., 7460, 7913, 8247
ACKLAND, Rodney, 8310
ADAMS, Marilyn, 8208, 8291
AGEE, James, 8169
ALVAREZ, A., 7476, 7559, 7790
AMBERG, George, 7767, 8040, 8395, 8521, 8526
ANDERSON, Earl, 7427, 7848, 8519
ANDERSON, Lindsay, 7660, 7718, 7782, 7791, 7864, 7961, 8308, 8534, 8549, 8562
ANDREW, J. Dudley, 8594
ANGLIN, Werdon, 7748
ARIOLI, Sandra, 8504
ASHEIM, Lester, 8287
ATKINS, Thomas R., 7988, 8158, 8312
ATWELL, Lee, 7948, 8093

BACH, Margaret, 7969, 8148, 8433, 8558
BAKER, Peter G., 7993, 8141
BALCON, Michael, 7961
BANDEL, Betty, 8435
BARING, George, 7498
BARRY, Jackson G., 7790
BAY, Timothy, 7587
BEAN, Robin, 8383
BENSON, Thomas, 8427
BERGSTEN, Bebe, 8431
BERNARD, Jeffrey, 7912, 8291
BICKERSTAFF, Isaac, 7537
BLUE, James, 7612
BLUESTONE, George, 7790, 7807
BLUMER, Ronald H., 7926
BODIEN, Earl, 8021
BOND, Kirk, 7578, 7692, 7723, 7817, 7819, 8051, 8088, 8089, 8196, 8239, 8261, 8295, 8443
BORDWELL, David, 7574
BORLAND, Colin, 7530, 7583, 8497, 8548
BOUD, John, 7784
BOURGET, Jean-Loup, 8255

BOUWMAN, George, 7786
BRAGIN, John, 8024, 8310
BRAUDY, Leo, 7964, 8617
BREITROSE, Henry, 7413
BREWSTER, Ben, 8107
BRIEN, Alan, 7570, 8463
BRINSON, Peter, 7906, 8097, 8532, 8549
BROM, Tom, 7902, 8016, 8544
BROWN, Kent R., 7917, 8227, 8467
BROWNE, Ray B., 7560
BROWNLOW, Kevin, 8310, 8462
BRUNIUS, Jacques, 7559
BUDD, Michael, 7421, 7548, 8049
BUDGEN, Suzanne, 7024
BURNS, Ernest, 8239
BUSCOMBE, Edward, 8100, 8399, 8482
BYRNE, Richard B., 7767, 7934

CALDWELL, John, 8402
CALLENBACH, Ernest, 7421, 7442, 7483, 7528, 7559, 7589, 7611, 7612, 7672, 7682, 7686, 7712, 7717, 7731, 7735, 7737, 7752A, 7752B, 7753, 7772, 7773, 7780, 7786, 7798, 7817, 7819, 7836, 7839, 7857, 7914, 7939, 7974, 8011, 8020, 8026, 8034, 8040, 8049, 8051, 8052, 8059, 8065, 8088, 8100, 8190, 8237, 8242, 8254, 8259, 8286, 8311, 8319, 8333, 8349, 8373, 8396, 8451, 8459, 8466, 8468, 8469, 8479, 8503, 8519, 8528, 8535, 8545, 8554, 8573, 8616
CAMPBELL, Jr., Wayne T., 8049
CAREY, Gary, 7800, 8227
CAVANDER, Kenneth, 7750
CECIL, Norman, 7457
CHANDLER, Joanne, 8182
CHAPIN, Elspeth Burke (also see: Elspeth Hart) 7512, 7645, 7870, 8113, 8149, 8337, 8589

CHAPPETTA, Robert, 8554
CHESTER, John R., 7822
CLAENER, Joe, 8478
CLARENS, Carlos, 8196
CLARK, Arthur B., 7483, 7484
CLARKE, Charles G., 8512
CLOUZOT, Claire, 7535
COE, Brian, 7694, 7695
COHEN, Hubert I., 8395
COHEN, M.E., 8458
COLLIER, John, 8555
COLLINS, Richard, 8322
CONNOLLY, Robert, 7777, 8059
CONNOR, Edward, 7614
COOK, Page, 8454
COPE, Diana Willing (also see: Diana Willing), 7459, 7684, 7964, 8168, 8317, 8518
CORNWALL, Regina, 8558
COTES, Peter, 8246, 8388
COULSON, Alan A., 8553
COWIE, Peter, 7605, 7797
CRAFTON, Donald, 7717, 7757
CRIPPS, Thomas R., 8239, 8310
CROCE, A., 8401
CROW, Duncan, 7639, 7872, 8197, 8271
CROWDUS, Gary, 7410, 7422, 7477, 7514, 7524, 7662, 7704, 7721, 7730, 7761, 7820, 7825, 7839, 7915, 7999, 8012, 8046, 8050, 8083, 8088, 8100, 8140, 8143, 8159, 8167, 8262, 8264, 8478, 8480A, 8480B, 8482, 8502, 8505, 8506, 8509, 8519, 8525, 8607, 8611A, 8611B
CUTTS, John, 8009

D.R., 7760, 8516
DALE, R.C., 7448, 7971, 7972, 7973, 7989, 7990, 8015
DANIELS, Edgar F., 7767, 7934
DAUGHERTY, Frank, 8549
DAVIDSON, Clark, 7678
DAVIES, Brenda, 7418, 7546, 8040, 8045
DE ANTONIO, Emile, 8396
DE LA ROCHE, Chatherine, 7644, 7981
DEGENER, David, 8334
DENEROFF, Harvey, 7474, 7630, 7655, 7809, 7861, 7934, 7966, 8426
DENISOFF, R. Serge, 7703
DICHTER, Mark, 8511
DICKENS, Homer, 8361
DICKINSON, Thorold, 7934, 8099, 8428
DIETERELE, William, 7770, 8581
DORFMAN, David, 7421
DOWNING, Robert, 7504, 7538, 7679, 7724, 7895, 7904, 8014, 8108, 8109, 8111, 8117, 8123, 8165, 8184, 8192, 8196, 8248, 8251, 8304, 8355, 8356, 8379, 8500, 8501, 8570, 8606
DUNNE, Philip, 7727
DUPEE, F.W., 8246
DYER, Peter John, 7992

E.H.N. (also see: Eleanor H. Nash), 7472, 7796, 8338
EDWARDS, Roy, 7728, 8062, 8078, 8487
EISNER, Lotte H., 7711
ELLIS, Jack C., 7919, 8160
ERICSSON, Peter, 7646, 7736, 7945, 8455, 8527
ESTABROOK, Howard, 7691
EVERSON, William K., 7420, 7614, 7725, 7840, 7989, 8009, 8015, 8094, 8097A, 8097B, 8254, 8545
EYLES, Allen, 7416, 7424, 7446, 7466, 7485, 7591, 7663, 7665, 7751, 7757, 7812, 7813, 7823, 7853, 7856, 7880, 7917, 7998, 8066, 8080, 8129, 8222, 8240, 8299, 8301, 8305, 8395, 8399, 8409, 8419, 8477, 8495, 8519, 8533, 8538, 8539, 8546, 8602, 8603

F.J.D., 7639
FALKENBERG, Paul, 7704, 8605
FARLEY, F.E., 7830, 7831, 8154
FEARING, Franklin, 7408, 7451, 7455, 7457, 7464, 7500, 7516, 7534, 7554, 7604, 7666, 7679, 7692, 7698, 7718, 7720, 7738, 7743, 7744, 7762, 7769, 7774, 7776, 7782, 7785, 7788A, 7788B, 7791, 7828, 7863, 7867, 7876, 7906, 7911, 7916, 7930, 7961A, 7961B, 7975, 7982, 7986, 8005, 8013, 8028, 8031, 8057, 8081, 8102, 8126, 8138, 8150, 8151, 8183, 8185, 8204, 8212, 8215, 8216, 8217, 8229, 8236, 8306, 8267, 8296, 8302, 8306, 8326A, 8326B, 8340, 8355, 8356, 8362, 8439, 8456, 8464, 8485, 8509, 8527, 8529, 8530, 8540, 8549, 8600, 8608, 8615, 8619, 8623
FELDMAN, Harry, 7445, 7592, 7931, 8035, 8246
FELHEIM, Marvin, 7747, 7759
FELL, John L., 7427, 7653, 7654, 7712, 7798, 7866, 8042, 8135, 8143, 8170, 8259, 8391, 8579
FENIN, George N., 7551, 7553, 7568, 7668, 7876, 7955, 8288
FIELD, Mary, 7901, 8030
FIELDING, Raymond, 7695, 7722, 8512

BOOK REVIEWERS

FLEISHER, Frederic, 7834, 8292
FOREMAN, Carl, 7983, 8096
FORSCH, Annabelle, 7828
FREEDLEY, George, 8464
FRENCH, Philip, 7410, 7686, 7798, 8100, 8259, 8616

GALE, Tom, 8312
GARLICK, Raymond, 8578
GAY, Ken, 8311
GEARY, Richard, 7686, 7779
GEDULD, Harry M., 8395
GENTLEMAN, Wally, 7422, 7839
GEORGAKAS, Dan, 8115
GERHARDT, Lillian, 7964
GERSTLE, Ralph, 8081
GIANNITRAPANI, Nadir, 7776
GIBBS, C.R., 7543, 7997, 8352
GILLETT, John, 7656, 7658, 7675, 7800, 7807, 7932, 8029, 8043, 8131, 8172, 8179, 8254, 8366
GILLIAT, Penelope, 7922
GIROUX, Robert, 7836, 8173, 8310, 8567
GODBOUT, Joanne, 8343
GOGGIN, Robert W., 7772
GOLDBERG, Joseph, 8451
GOLDWASSER, Noe, 7717, 7896, 8124
GOLLUB, Judith, 7861, 8269
GORNEY, Sondra K., 8157
GRASTEN, Bent, 7957, 8292
GRAY, Hugh, 8018
GRAY, Martin, 7615, 7639, 7684, 7695, 7713, 7728, 7750, 7783, 7840, 7842, 7922, 8009, 8043, 8044, 8098, 8130, 8287, 8324, 8389, 8470, 8507, 8510, 8524, 8540
GREEN, Calvin, 7767, 7816, 7898, 8071, 8312, 8399
GRIERSON, John, 7671
GRIFFIN-BEALE, T. D., 7864
GRIFFITH, Richard, 7569, 7791, 8031
GRIGS, Derick, 7651, 8044, 8380
GRINDROD, Muriel K., 7709, 7715, 7899, 8568, 8625
GROSVENOR, John, 7809
GROVER, Gloria Waldron, 7743

H.P., 8213
H.T., 8556
HALLER, Robert A., 7808, 7966, 8059, 8140
HAMER, Robert, 8439
HAMILTON, Marie L., 7775, 8013
HAMMOND, Robert, 8088
HANDZO, Stephen G., 7470
HANLEY, James, 7670
HARCOURT, Peter, 7514, 7730, 7732, 7793, 8020, 8035, 8265, 8593
HARDY, Jill, 7941, 8452

HARKER, Jonathan, 7412, 7742
HARRISON, Edward, 8029
HART, Elspeth (also see: Elspeth Burke Chapin), 7417, 7491, 7876, 8415, 8476, 8540, 8565, 8566
HART, Henry, 7420, 7488, 7516, 7627, 7650, 7651, 7687, 7699, 8010, 8128, 8150, 8190, 8213, 8215, 8216, 8217, 8218, 8236, 8239, 8250, 8255, 8270, 8345, 8353, 8480, 8496, 8516, 8530, 8587
HARTNOLL, Gillian, 7407, 7427, 7499, 7520, 7653, 7689, 7758, 7768, 7783, 7796, 8045, 8415, 8492, 8537, 8592
HARTWEG, Norman, 8594
HASLAM, George, 7450
HAUSER, Frank, 8151
HAWKINS, Robert F., 7940, 8472
HAYUM, Andrée, 7824
HEAWORD, R.A., 8221
HECHT, Hermann, 8150
HELMER, Adam, 7968, 8260
HENDERSON, Brian, 8441
HENDRICKS, Gordon, 8591
HIGHAM, Charles, 8390, 8395
HILL, Derek, 7752, 8421, 8445, 8540
HILL, Steven (Stephen) P., 7515, 7909, 8056, 8127, 8357
HILLIER, Jim, 7664, 7686, 8259, 8616
HILLS, Janet, 7539
HINXMAN, Margaret, 7875, 8166
HIRSCH, Foster, 7678, 7686, 7757, 7798, 7966, 8003, 8034, 8259, 8395
HITCHENS, Gordon, 7682, 7807, 7847, 8007, 8033
HODGKINSON, Anthony W., 7731, 7739, 7786, 7817, 8205, 8430, 8451, 8499
HOLMES, Penelope, 8624
HOLT, Seth, 8509
HOOKER, E.N., 7480, 8252
HOPE-WALLACE, Philip, 7409, 7417, 8435
HOPKINS, Anthony, 7609
HOUSTON, Penelope, 7611, 7667, 7791, 7808, 7876, 7900, 7961, 7966, 7975, 7982, 8094, 8123, 8186, 8226, 8273, 8297, 8326, 8333, 8395, 8416, 8451, 8520
HOWE, Quincy, 7911, 8277
HOWTON, F. William, 7729
HOYT, C., 7427
HUFF, Theodore, 7513, 7635, 7961A, 7961B, 7968, 8058, 8126, 8323, 8557
HUGHES, Robert, 7752
HULL, David Stewart, 7425, 7648, 7649, 8099, 8451
HUME, Rod, 7491
HUNNINGS, Neville March, 7823, 8046, 8104, 8178, 8492

HUNTER, Glen, 7686, 7767, 7849, 7934, 8259, 8395
HUNTLEY, John, 7431

I.B., 7844
INGSTER, Boris, 7423
IRVING, Laurence, 7453, 7644

JABLONSKI, Edward, 7403
JACKSON, Benjamin, 8508
JACKSON, Ragna, 7949, 7952, 8189, 8194
JACOBS, Arthur, 8510
JACOBS, Lewis, 7458, 7630, 7644, 7744, 7929, 7962, 8203, 8207, 8260, 8268, 8290, 8616
JAHIEL, Edwin, 7448, 7470, 7654, 7808, 7833, 7937, 8593
JOHNS, Philip, 8158
JONES, Francis, 7424
JOSEPH, Robert, 7421, 8140, 8310, 8348, 8519
JOWETT, Garth, 7541, 7542, 7705, 7893, 7996, 8209, 8210, 8211, 8230, 8232, 8235, 8303, 8315, 8450

K.M., 8328, 8614
KAEL, Pauline, 7906
KAGAN, Norman, 7402, 7717, 8053, 8305
KAWICKI, Dennis, 7849, 8068
KEEN, Stuart, 7502
KENNER, Hugh, 8094, 8295
KENSING, Philip, 7978
KERNS, Robert V., 8310
KITSES, Jim, 8259
KLEIN, Michael, 7613
KNIGHT, Arthur, 7692, 7718, 7906, 7919, 8139
KOCH, Christian, 8124, 8441
KOSZARSKI, Richard, 8318
KRACAUER, Siegfried, 8226
KRAFT, Richard, 8378, 8485
KRAMBORG, Ruth, 7934
KREUGER, Miles, 7427, 8429
KRUMGOLD, Joseph, 8342
KUHNS, Alice, 7524
KULA, Sam, 7424, 7518
KUSTOW, Michael, 8436

L.V., 7522
L.W., 7897
LACY, Bradner, 7652, 7758A, 7758B, 7758C, 7758D, 7758E, 8219, 8486
LAMBERT, Gavin, 7554, 7681, 7828, 8001, 8164, 8371, 8425
LAMONT, Austin F., 8505
LANG, Harold, 7943, 8501, 8589

LARKIN, John, 8223
LARSEN, Egon, 7710
LASSALLY, Walter, 8306
LAURENTZSCH, C.A., 7736
LEACOCK, Richard, 8615
LEE, Herbert, 7807
LERNER, Irving, 7746
LEWIS, Norah, 7544, 7892, 8138, 8307, 8408
LEWIS, Stephen, 8151
LEYDA, Jay, 7742, 7781, 8136, 8202, 8279, 8377, 8612
LIECHTI, Harris N., 8311
LINDGREN, Ernest, 7840, 7863, 8150, 8453, 8527
LOCKE, John W., 8238
LOCKE, Warren, 8041
LONGWELL, Harold, 8375
LOVE, Bessie, 8239
LOW, Rachael, 7951, 8331
LOWNDES, Douglas, 7706
LUSK, Norman, 7980
LYONS, Robert J., 7823
LYONS, Timothy J., 7424, 7768, 8509

M.E.C., 8101
MC ARTHUR, Colin, 7582, 7991, 8440
MC BRIDE, Joseph, 7628, 8239, 8239
MC CAFFREY, Donald W., 7623
MAC CANN, Richard Dyer, 7527, 7672, 7704, 7773, 7778, 7914, 8088, 8100, 8140, 8159, 8348, 8349, 8377, 8435
MC CARTY, Clifford, 7493, 8006
MC CORMICK, Ruth, 7900, 8175, 8177, 8205
MC DONALD, Gerald D., 7474, 7586, 7590, 7957A, 7952B, 7952C, 8237, 8324, 8422, 8485
MAC DONALD, James N., 8269
MAC FADDEN, Patrick, 7745
MC KAY, Andrew C., 7424
MACAULEY, C. Cameron, 8039, 8509
MACKENDRICK, Alexander, 7597, 8368
MADDEN, David, 8011, 8246, 8391
MADDISON, John, 8388
MALMFELT, A.D., 8140, 8441
MALTIN, Leonard, 7815
MAMBER, Stephen, 7730, 8068, 8310, 8310
MANCHEL, Frank, 7524, 7580, 7588, 7667, 7732, 7761, 7773, 7898, 7914, 7964, 7972, 8015, 8049, 8088, 8135, 8140, 8143, 8205, 8224, 8243, 8311, 8489, 8516, 8545, 8577
MANCIA, Adrienne, 7559, 8242
MANVELL, Roger, 7494, 7919
MARKS, Louis, 7434, 8054
MARKUS, Thomas B., 7772

MARLOW, Alberta, 7981, 8226, 8463
MARSDEN, Michael T., 7927
MARTIN, James Michael, 7861, 7966
MASCALLI, Joseph V., 8516
MAZZOCCO, Robert, 7596, 7964
MEAD, Taylor, 7931
MEDJUCK, Joe, 7577
MELLEN, Joan, 8391
MELNITZ, William W., 7406
MENEFEE, Emory, 8051, 8261
MERRITT, Russell, 8255
MEYER, Richard J., 7902, 8544
MILLAR, Daniel, 8121
MILLAR, Gavin, 7823, 8225, 8480
MILLER, Don, 7889, 8325, 8470
MILLER, Letizia Ciotti, 7555, 7754
MILLS, E. Francis, 7545
MILNE, Tom, 7566, 7591, 7817, 7843, 7952, 8064, 8072, 8073, 8074A, 8074B, 8088, 8341, 8442
MINCHINTON, John, 7522, 7599, 7613, 7633, 7676, 7921, 8067, 8109, 8152, 8284, 8294, 8356
MITCHELL, George J., 7422A, 7422B, 7489, 7836, 7839, 8173, 8295, 8351, 8461, 8506, 8512, 8514, 8515
MONTAGU, Ivor, 8427
MORGAN, James, 7569, 7946, 8067, 8356, 8358, 8534
MORITZ, William, 7719, 7764, 8571
MORLEY, Sheridan, 7405, 7415, 7416, 7428, 7432, 7437, 7439, 7444, 7457, 7460, 7461, 7473, 7482, 7487, 7492, 7511, 7514, 7517, 7518, 7519, 7523, 7524, 7535, 7538, 7540, 7575, 7576, 7577, 7622, 7623, 7625, 7634, 7636, 7665, 7667, 7669, 7677A, 7677B, 7688, 7700, 7704, 7712, 7717, 7732, 7749, 7750, 7759, 7760, 7767, 7772, 7773, 7781, 7794, 7796A, 7796B, 7798, 7802, 7818, 7823, 7825, 7850, 7857, 7858, 7861, 7866, 7871, 7874, 7877, 7887, 7888, 7898, 7905, 7910, 7917, 7920, 7923, 7934, 7938, 7960, 7961, 7964, 7967, 7985, 7989, 7990, 7995, 8003, 8004, 8021, 8022, 8053, 8059, 8071, 8082, 8083, 8084, 8090, 8091, 8092, 8094, 8100, 8105, 8110, 8118, 8121, 8124, 8136, 8140, 8147, 8153, 8155, 8158, 8162, 8172, 8186, 8195A, 8195B, 8224, 8225, 8239, 8254, 8259, 8269, 8276A, 8276B, 8279, 8281, 8305, 8310, 8316, 8320, 8329, 8344, 8366, 8372, 8374, 8381, 8394, 8395, 8398, 8399, 8404, 8410, 8411, 8417, 8419, 8426, 8431, 8441, 8446, 8454, 8467, 8480, 8493, 8516, 8519, 8535, 8543,

8550, 8558, 8567, 8569, 8588, 8599, 8601, 8611, 8612, 8613
MORTIMER, John, 7755
MORTON, Lawrence, 7502, 7608, 7609, 8025
MOSS, Robert, 7900
MUNCH, F., 7860

N.M.H., 7442, 7507, 7508, 7509, 7529, 7549, 7550, 7567, 7585, 7598, 7614, 7619, 7620, 7656, 7726, 7873, 7932, 8029, 8035, 8095, 8110, 8137, 8145, 8196, 8213, 8234, 8246, 8248, 8275, 8300, 8309, 8327, 8335, 8354, 8376, 8392, 8481, 8484, 8552, 8598
NASH, Eleanor H. (also see: E.H.N.), 7478, 7767, 7871, 7935, 7942, 7979, 7986, 8039, 8040, 8052, 8144, 8181, 8185, 8276, 8358, 8405, 8421, 8437, 8443, 8536, 8585
NEERGAARD, Ebbe, 8406
NELSON, Jr., Lowry, 8145
NICHOLS, Bill, 7629, 7760, 8398, 8399
NICHOLS, Madeleine M., 8114
NOBLE, Joseph V., 7601
NOLAN, Jack Edmund, 7427, 7845, 7950
NORTH, Christopher, 7987, 8267, 8357, 8420, 8602
NOWELL-SMITH, Geoffrey, 7445, 8011, 8187, 8488, 8545

OAKES, Philip, 7835, 8251
O'LAOGHAIRE, Liam, 7602, 8036, 8340, 8407
O'LEARY, Liam, 8237, 8257
OREANU, S., 7465
ORNA, Bernard, 7435, 7643

P.D.C., 7894, 7900, 8404
PARKER, Glynne, 7771, 8048
PARTINGTON, Ruth, 7411
PATTERSON, Frances Taylor, 8619
PATTISON, Ivan, 8474
PAXTON, John, 7481
PEAVY, Charles D., 8159
PEEBLES, Samuel A., 7600
PENFIELD, Alice, 7982
PEREIDRA, W.L., 8332
PEREZ-GUILLERMO, Gilberto, 8554
PETROVSKAIA, Barbara, 8455
PICHEL, Irving, 7458
PINARES, Marco, 7757
PLASKITT, Peter, 7626, 7805, 7869, 8322
POLT, Harriet R., 7891, 8295
POWDERMAKER, Hortense, 8229
POWELL, David J., 7745, 7919

POWELL, Dilys, 8449
POWELL, Michael, 7961
PRATLEY, Gerald, 7993
PRATT, George, 7695
PRIMROSE, Graham, 8295
PRINGLE, Ashley, 8574
PROUSE, Derek, 8064
PROVINZANO, Linda, 7823, 8298 `
PRYLUCK, Calvin, 8046, 8186

QUEVAL, Jean (Jacques), 7603, 7944,
  8285, 8307, 8594
QUIGLY, Isabel, 7637, 8039, 8470
QUIRK, Lawrence J., 7701

R.L., 8055
RADIN, Max, 7977
RAHTZ, Robert, 7803, 8241
RAMSAYE, Terry, 7500
RAPER, Mitchell, 7876
RAY, Man, 8019
REED, Stanley, 7854, 7903
REISZ, Karel, 7762
RICHARDSON, Alan A., 7681
RICHIE, Donald, 7607
RIDER, David, 7667
ROBIN, Eve, 8387
ROBINSON, David, 7448, 7468, 7496,
  7524, 7532, 7538, 7647, 7679,
  7723, 7884, 7885, 7933, 7960,
  8061, 8065, 8112, 8196, 8213,
  8221, 8246, 8258, 8280, 8448,
  8485, 8498, 8597, 8598, 8611
ROFFE, Alfredo, 7954
ROGERS, Quentin, 8580
ROMAN, Robert C., 7693, 8017, 8220,
  8247, 8531, 8593
ROSE, Ernest D., 8622
ROSENBAUM, Jonathan, 7421, 8070
ROSENHEIMER, Arthur, 7671, 8000
ROTHA, Paul, 7961, 8228
ROUD, Richard, 7429, 7433, 7519,
  7714, 8287
RUDORFF, R.A., 7695, 8220
RYALL, T., 8426

SALEMSON, Harold, 7766
SANDBERG-DIMENT, Erik, 8033
SARRIS, Andrew, 8475
SCHLIEMANN, F.K., 7989, 8015
SCHWERIN, Jules V., 7868
SELBY, Grete, 8038
SELBY, Stuart, 7426, 7559, 7852,
  8011, 8029
SELDES, Gilbert, 7534, 7791
SESONSKE, Alexander, 7742
SHARPLES, Douglas, 8240, 8495
SHEPHARD, David, 7632
SHERIDAN, Paul, 7784

SIEGEL, Joel, 7414
SILET, Charles L.P., 8124
SILVER, Charles, 7882
SILVER, Nathan, 8329
SIMON, Bill, 7757
SIMPSON, Margaret, 7463
SINGH, Harold, 8029
SIPHERD, Ray, 7772
SKOLLER, Donald, 8494
SLOAN, William, 8190
SMITH, Clyde, 7665
SMITH, Hubert, 7926
SMITHELLS, John M., 7430, 7449,
  7525, 7526, 7859, 7936, 8618
SPEARS, Jack, 7468, 7533, 7657, 7690,
  7714, 7733, 7810, 8183, 8246, 8621
SPIERS, David, 7816, 8121, 8174, 8330
SPRINGER, John, 7994
SRAGOW, Michael, 7457, 7611, 7686,
  7737, 7779, 7900, 8238, 8348,
  8410, 8554, 8620
STACKHOUSE, Foster, 7424
STAINTON, Walter H., 7448, 7765,
  8522
STAPLES, Donald, 7444, 7634, 7697,
  7866, 7937, 8034, 8424, 8438, 8594
STARR, Cecile, 7667
STEELE, Robert, 7527, 7796, 8024,
  8051, 8172, 8239, 8243A, 8243B,
  8250, 8348, 8426, 8567
STEENE, Birgitta, 8319
STEIN, Elliott, 7871
STEIN, Jeanne, 7505
STEINBERG, Susan, 7964
STERN, Seymour, 8428A, 8428B
STIRLING, Monica, 7552, 7660, 8367
STRICK, Philip, 8034
SUBER, Howard, 7410, 7486, 7498,
  7971, 7972, 7973, 8270, 8310, 8602
SUMMERS, Bob, 7514, 8561
SUSSEX, Elizabeth, 7471, 7790
SVENDSEN, J.M., 8521
SWEET, Jeff, 7623

TALBOT, Daniel, 7493
TALMON-GROS, Walter, 8382
TANNER, Alain, 8288
TARRATT, Margaret, 7523
TAYLOR, John Russell, 7413, 7523,
  7707, 7731, 7802, 7852, 7907,
  7917, 8190, 8433, 8535, 8558, 8575
TAYLOR, Stephen, 8559
TEAS, Araminta, 7870
THIEDE, Karl, 7427, 8222
THOMAIER, William, 7972
THOMAS, Anthony, 8253
THOMAS, John, 7807, 8045, 8594
THOMPSON, Richard, 8259
TIBBETTS, John, 7456, 7510, 7511,
  7667, 7851, 7915
TOZZI, Romano V., 7668, 7835, 8313,
  8541

BOOK REVIEWERS

TUDOR, Andrew, 7867, 7934
TUNG, 8023
TURNER, Charles L., 8406
TURNER, R.H., 7852
TURRELL, Daphne, 8116
TUSKA, Jon, 8609

UNDERWOOD, Prudence, 8465
USELTON, Roi A., 8047

VAN DYKE, Willard, 7514, 7672
VANNDEY, R.C., 8231, 8595, 8596
VENTURI, Lauro, 7561, 7562
VESSELO, Arthur, 7457, 8122
VIOLA, Wilhelm, 8582
VOLMAR, Victor, 8509

WALDEKRANZ, Rune, 8256
WALEY, H.D., 7534, 7744, 8126
WALKER, Don, 7971, 7972, 7973
WALLACH, George, 7902
WALSH, Peter, 7750, 8287
WEALES, Gerald, 7571
WEINBERG, Herman G., 7424, 7429,
    7452, 7458, 7491, 7531, 7536,
    7556, 7565, 7592, 7593, 7621,
    7642, 7658, 7704. 7714, 7716,
    7762, 7767, 7768, 7791, 7871,
    7916, 7934, 7963, 7967, 7981,
    8020, 8029, 8128, 8148, 8161,
    8166, 8167, 8200, 8243, 8270,
    8393, 8394, 8417, 8423, 8426,
    8427, 8431, 8443, 8471, 8523,
    8584, 8593, 8611, 8615
WERNER, M.R., 7975
WHARTON, Flavia, 7595, 7702, 8132
WHITE, Eric Walter, 8434
WHITEBAIT, William, 8128, 8327
WICKING, Christopher, 7783, 7988
WILCOX, John 7748, 8401
WILLIAMS, John Elliott, 7936
WILLIAMS, Richard, 8508
WILLING, Diana (also see: Diana Willing
    Cope), 8346
WILSON, David, 7476, 7767
WILSON, N. Hope, 8326
WINDELER, Robert, 7753, 7974, 8517
WITHAM, Alice H., 7617, 7632, 7708,
    7802, 7819, 8064, 8086, 8197,
    8199, 8227, 8249, 8350, 8359,
    8414, 8473, 8475, 8519, 8604, 8610
WOLFE, Ralph Haven, 7917, 8227,
    8266
WRIGHT, Basil, 7692
WRIGHT, Ian, 7605

YOUNG, Colin, 7890, 8064

ZITO, Steve, 7424

SUBJECT INDEX TO BOOKS

SUBJECT INDEX TO BOOKS

GENERAL REFERENCE SOURCES
General Encyclopedic Sources, 7427, 7492, 7556, 7796, 7952, 8101, 8608
Bibliographic Sources and Research Guides, 7407, 7518, 7519, 7768, 7771,
8027, 8030, 8048, 8203, 8357
Film Information: Sources and Reviews, 7424, 7488, 7520, 7550, 7621, 7648,
7655, 7674, 7794, 7828, 8213, 8215, 8216, 8217, 8218, 8219, 8240, 8257,
8270, 8294, 8357, 8486, 8495, 8496, 8536, 8537
Film Personalities: Sources and Reviews, 7424, 7488, 7520, 7550, 7621, 7648,
7655, 7674, 7794, 7828, 8213, 8215, 8216, 8217, 8218, 8219, 8240, 8257,
8270, 8294, 8357, 8486, 8495, 8496, 8536, 8537
Film Personalities: Sources and Credits, 7407, 7467, 7654, 7756, 7848, 7909,
7917, 7927, 7984, 8021, 8569, 8592, 8602
Glossaries and Dictionaries, 7401, 7653, 7656, 7657, 7658, 7897, 8106, 8122
Annuals and Periodicals, 7440, 7503, 7569, 7570, 7571, 7593, 7758, 7776, 7783,
7795, 8032, 8043, 8044, 8045, 8047, 8415

CENSORSHIP, AND LEGAL ASPECTS
7525, 7526, 7527, 7528, 7529, 7726, 7755, 7859, 7860, 8139, 8204, 8234, 8300,
8420, 8618, 8484, 8552

GENERAL INTRODUCTORY BOOKS
7517, 7622, 7687, 7700, 7738, 7739, 7761, 7789, 7793, 7833, 8052, 8060,
8208, 8233, 8302, 8340, 8355, 8413

FILM HISTORY
General Histories of World Cinema, 7476, 7546, 7610, 7665, 7704, 7791, 7890,
7944, 7945, 7946, 7947, 7948, 7951, 7952, 7955, 7958, 8185, 8193, 8205,
8220, 8242, 8307, 8327, 8408, 8431, 8438, 8463, 8471, 8591
Pre-History of the Cinema, 7448, 7496, 8055, 8149, 8150, 8190, 8221, 8434,
8464
History of the Silent Cinema, 7836, 8190, 8331, 8442, 8444, 8459, 8481
National Cinemas,
Asia, 8297
Australia and New Zealand, 7466, 8458
Eastern Europe (Austria, Hungary, Czechoslovakia, Poland), 7613, 7689,
7754, 8282, 8284, 8305, 8419, 8612
France, 7544, 7554, 7586, 7641, 7733, 7766, 7855, 7861, 7862, 7863, 8019,
8269, 8286, 8354, 8425
Germany and Switzerland, 7736, 7649, 7767, 7792, 7867, 7887, 7888, 7934,
8521, 8981
Great Britain (including Scotland and Ireland), 7499, 7500, 7872, 7961,
8195, 8262, 8342, 8418, 8555, 8598
India, 8029, 8369

(**Film History** cont.)

Italy and Greece, 7553, 7555, 7561, 7562, 7563, 7564, 7568, 7585, 7598, 7640, 8058, 8059, 8288, 8314

Japan, 7565, 8063, 8064, 8065

Near-East (Egypt, Arabia, Pakistan), 7560, 8053, 8297, 8479

Scandinavia (Denmark, Norway, Sweden), 7907, 7957, 8283, 8406, 8490, 8491, 8492, 8493

South America, 7954

Soviet Union, 7567, 8099, 8127, 8202, 8455, 8456, 8572, 8580

United States

General Histories, 7476, 8128, 8228, 8377, 8550

Pre-History, 7695, 7762

The Silent Era, 7474, 7549, 7688, 7920, 7973, 8136, 8237, 8310, 8596, 8597, 8609

From Silent to Sound, 7949, 7960, 7968, 7973, 8290, 8595

The Sound Era, 7421, 7426, 7735, 7802, 7970, 7971, 7972, 8277, 8308, 8391

Specialized Histories

Anti-Trust, 7442

Cars, 7838

Film Noir, 8308

Foreign Films, 7847

Hays Office, 7936

Railroads, 8363

Religion, 8370

Television, 7672

Blacklisting, 7977, 8041

Sociology and Psychology (including The Payne Foundation series), 7541, 7705, 7745, 7752, 7893, 7911, 7974, 7975, 7982, 7996, 8017, 8018, 8209, 8210, 8211, 8229, 8230, 8232, 8235, 8315, 8412, 8450, 8543

Studios and Moguls, 7985, 8123, 8199, 8225, 8332, 8480

Stars and Hollywood, 7850, 8227, 8301, 8397, 8467, 8468, 8469

Academy Awards, 7405

Censorship, and Legal Aspects, 7525, 7526, 7527, 7528, 7529, 7726, 7755, 7859, 7860, 8139, 8204, 8234, 8300, 8420, 8618, 8484, 8552

Contemporary Cinema, 7566, 7605, 7612, 7639, 7649, 7696, 7717, 7891, 7892, 7984, 8046, 8105, 8263, 8264, 8269, 8282, 8283, 8284, 8286, 8288, 8419

Technological Histories, 7849, 8516

Specialized Histories

Censorship, 7529, 8618

Color, 7956

Influence, 8618

Moving-Picture Theatre, 7483, 8329

Realism, 7551

Sociological Comparisons, 8451

Picture Histories, 7590, 7707, 7953, 8226, 8266, 8323, 8324, 8325, 8327

FILM CLASSIFICATIONS

Documentary Film, 7671, 7672, 7673, 7727, 7919, 8265, 8271, 8311, 8513

Experimental Film, 7718, 7719, 7757, 7764, 8051, 8261, 8558

Genre Studies

Comedy, 7549, 7602, 7623, 7873, 8222, 8364

Drama and Suspense, 8489

Gangster and Crime, 7874

Horror and Science-Fiction, 7587, 7692, 7728, 7989, 7990, 7991, 7992, 8015, 8409, 8410

Musical and Musical Comedy, 7420, 7428, 7905, 7915, 8245

Western, 7908, 7927, 7950, 7988, 8592, 8593, 8609

Animated Film, 7435, 7439, 7454, 7456, 7646, 7647

Erotic Film, 7429, 7524, 7712, 7713, 7714

Compilation Film, 7800

Surrealism, 8487, 8488

(**Film Classifications** cont.)
   Serials and Shorts, 7497, 7614, 7636, 8295, 8429, 8538
   Themes in Films
      Goethe, 7899
      Jazz, 8066
      Politics, 8334
      Shakespeare, 8435, 8436, 8500
      Violence, 8574
      War, 7753
   Types and Groups
      Blacks, 7490, 8260
      Child Stars, 7538
      Comics, 7594
      Lovers, 8414
      Tarzan, 8502
      Villains, 7470, 7937
      Women, 7634, 7853
   Religious Orientation, 7557, 7660, 8214
   Short Films, 7721, 7804, 8133, 8525

FILM THEORY AND AESTHETICS
   Theories of Film Art, 7452, 7457, 7458, 7459, 7548, 7583, 7716, 7750, 7770,
      7776, 7790, 7798, 7845, 7906, 8224, 8441, 8472, 8526, 8528, 8530, 8594,
      8617
   Related Works on Film Art, 7430, 7451, 7642, 7643, 7772, 8243, 8535, 8579
   Specialized Perspectives on Film Art
      Critical Appraisals and Readings, 7740, 7742, 7751, 7159
      Film and Related Arts, 7558, 8124, 8287

FILM CRITICISM
   Studies on Selected Films, 7588, 7589, 7590, 7780, 7781, 7914, 8024
   Varied Critics: Anthologies of Criticism, 7778, 7779, 7878, 8318, 8439
   Individual Critics: Collected Writings,
      Adler, Renata, 8620
      Agate, James, 7449
      Agee, James, 7412, 7414
      Alpert, Hollis, 7682
      Crist, Judith, 8348
      Farber, Manny, 8259
      Kael, Pauline, 7900, 8011, 8100
      Kauffmann, Stanley, 7737, 8616
      Macdonald, Dwight, 7686
      Pechter, William, 8554
      Sarris, Andrew, 7611
      Simon, John, 8238, 8349
      Sontag, Susan, 8482
      Tyler, Parker, 7969, 8148, 8433
      Warshow, Robert, 8020
      Weinberg, Herman G., 8395
      Winnington, Richard, 7681
      Zinsser, William K., 8421

FILM PERSONALITIES
   Gossips, Scandals, Anecdotes, 7870, 8411, 8518
   Compilations: Interviews, Articles and Studies
      Performers, 7408, 7669, 7850, 7851, 8155, 8333, 8457
      Film-Makers, 7475, 7523, 7759, 7773, 7939, 7967, 8049, 8155, 8265, 8310,
         8317, 8366
      Directorial Studies: Varied Directors, 7421, 7559, 8341, 8545
   Individual Studies: Writings By Film Personalities
      Aherne, Brian, 8353
      Astaire, Fred, 8470

(**Film Personalities**; Individual Studies; Writings By Film Personalities, cont.)

Astor, Mary, 8251
Balcon, Sir Michael, 8186
Bankhead, Tullulah, 8501
Barrymore, Diana, 8541
Barrymore, Ethel, 8184
Barrymore, Lionel, 8589
Beauchamps, Anthony, 7842
Bergman, Ingmar, 7479
Bickford, Charles, 7505
Brown, Frederick, 8022
Brown, Joe E., 8108
Brunel, Adrian, 8273
Capra, Frank, 8255
Chaplin, Charles, 8246
Cherkassov, Nicoloi, 8280
Cilento, Diane, 8162
Clair, René, 8367, 8368
Cocteau, Jean, 7597
Crichton, Kyle, 8542
Danischewsky, Monja, 8599
Daren, Maya, 7430
Davis, Bette, 8132
De Mille, Agnes, 7635
De Mille, Cecil B., 7468
De Mille, William C., 7980
Dietrich, Marlene, 8168
Dreyer, Carl Th., 8292
Eastman, Max, 7913
Eisenstein, Sergei, 7760, 7762, 8279
Fernett, Gene, 8272
Field, Mary, 7903
Flynn, Errol, 8253
Fowler, Gene, 8192
Gargan, William, 8604
Gish, Lillian, 8239
Godowsky, Dagmar, 7835
Greer, Howard, 7645
Grierson, John, 7919
Hayden, Sterling, 8587
Hays, Will, 8183
Head, Edith, 7684
Hecht, Ben, 7537
Hepworth, Cecil M., 7513
Hills, Janet, 7854
Hitchcock, Alfred, 7964
Hope, Bob, 7935, 8532
Houseman, John, 8390
Ivens, Joris, 7514
Jannings, Emil, 8523
Keaton, Buster, 8254
Lasky, Jesse, 8009
Le Roy, Mervyn, 8057
Lejeune, Caroline, 8520
Lockwood, Margaret, 8141
Loos, Anita, 7895
Losey, Joseph, 8135
Mack, Angela, 7615
Mac Laine, Shirley, 7677
Marker, Chris, 7603
Marx, Groucho, 7922, 7923
Marx, Harpo, 7933

Melville, Jean-Pierre, 8180
Merman, Ethel, 8600
Miller, Vergil E., 8461
Montagu, Ivor, 8611
Moore, Colleen, 8443
Morley, Robert, 8383
Murphy, George, 8405
Neff, Hildegard, 7894
Negri, Pola, 8182
Niven, David, 8201
Oppenheimer, George, 8570
Pagnol, Marcel, 7637
Pasolini, Pier-Paolo, 8312
Pasternak, Joe, 7690
Pearson, George, 7840
Pickford, Mary, 8485
Pudovkin, V.I., 7788
Ray, Man, 8423
Redgrave, Michael, 7409
Renoir, Jean, 8373
Robyns, Gwen, 8118
Roth, Lillian, 8014
Rotha, Paul, 8337, 8388
St. John, Adela Rogers, 7987
Sanders, George, 8181
Schildkraut, Joseph, 8247
Schulberg, Budd, 7666
Smith, Albert E., 8557
Vidor, King, 8549
Von Sternberg, Josef, 7871
Warner, Jack L., 8249
West, Mae, 7904
Wilcox, Herbert, 8553
Wright, Basil, 8562
Wynn, Keenan, 7693
Young, Loretta, 8531
Zimmer, Jill Schary, 8610
Zukor, Adolph, 8356

Individual Studies: Writings About Film
    Personalities

Anderson, Lindsay, 8121
Andrews, Julie, 8091, 8092
Antonioni, Michelangelo, 7443, 7444,
    7445, 8187, 8188
Astaire, Fred, 7858
Barrymore (Lionel, Ethel, John), 7471
Bennett, Joan, 7478
Bergman, Ingmar, 8033, 8034, 8035,
    8036, 8038, 8319
Bergman, Ingrid, 8039
Bogart, Humphrey, 7493, 8006, 8007
Bresson, Robert, 7824, 8380
Buñuel, Luis, 7506, 8142, 8143
Cahn, Harry, 8096
Carné, Marcel, 8164
Carroll, Nancy, 7822
Chabrol, Claude, 7591
Chaney, Lon, 8129
Chaplin, Charles, 7515, 7531, 7532,
    7533, 7534, 7535, 7810, 7912,
    7916, 8010, 8126, 8200, 8248, 8250

SUBJECT INDEX TO BOOKS

(**Film Personalities**; Individual Studies; Writings About Film Personalities, cont.)

Clement, René, 8372
Clouzot, Henri-Georges, 7940
Cobb, Irving S., 8252
Cocteau, Jean, 7596, 8067, 8068
Cooper, Gary, 7814, 7879, 7880
Corman, Roger, 8385
Crawford, Joan, 8338
Crosby, Bing, 7487, 7512
"Cuddles", 8474
Cukor, George, 7628
De Mille, Cecil B., 7521, 7809, 8621
Dietrich, Marlene, 7491, 7659, 7820, 8167
Disney, Walt, 7667, 8476, 8586
Donat, Robert, 8381
Dovzhenko, Alexander, 7680
Dreyer, Carl Th., 7574, 7685
Dwan, Alan, 7416
Eggeling, Viking, 8571
Eisenstein, Sergei, 8112, 8393, 8426, 8427, 8428, 8611
Fairbanks, Douglas, 7679
Fairbanks, Jr., Douglas, 8102
Fellini, Federico, 7730, 7731, 7732, 8582
Feuillade, Louis, 8137
Fields, W.C., 7460, 7827, 8584
Flaherty, Robert, 8040, 8289, 8382, 8615
Flynn, Errol, 7495
Fonda (Henry, Jane, Peter), 7844
Ford, John, 8081, 8082, 8083
Fox, William, 8561
Franju, Georges, 7857, 7883
Frankenheimer, John, 7577
Friese-Greene, William, 7864
Fuller, Samuel, 8398, 8399, 8400
Gable, Clark, 7811
Gabor, Zsa, Zsa, 8624
Garbo, Greta, 7875, 7876, 7877, 791
Garland, Judy, 8090
Gielgud, John, 8084
Glyn, Elinor, 7701
Godard, Jean-Luc, 7816, 7898, 8070, 8071
Goldwyn, Samuel, 8401
Gremillon, Jean, 8069
Griffith, D.W., 7423, 7630, 7631, 7632, 8466
Guinness, Alec, 7417
Guitry, Sacha, 8394
Harlow, Jean, 7931
Hawks, Howard, 8002, 8003
Hayes, Helen, 7938
Hepburn, Katherine, 8546
Hitchcock, Alfred, 7573, 7584, 7808, 7963, 7964, 7965, 7966
Howard, Leslie, 8361
Huston, John, 8085, 8086
Karloff, Boris, 7495, 8093
Kaye, Danny, 8116

Keaton, Buster, 7507, 7508, 7509, 7510, 7511, 8094, 8095
Kelly, Grace, 8346
Korda, Alexander, 7418
Kurosawa, Akira, 7607, 7807, 8103
Lahr, Burt, 8281
Lang, Fritz, 7576, 7865, 7866
Laughton, Charles, 8109
Laurette, 8111
Laurel and Hardy, 7819, 8110, 8196
Leigh, Vivien, 8291
Linder, Max, 8179
Lloyd, Harold, 7932
Lorenz, Pare, 8311
Losey, Joseph, 7581, 8134, 8135
Lubitsch, Ernst, 8140
Lumière, Louis, 8138
Magnusson, Charles, 8256
Mamoulian, Rouben, 8158
Mann, Anthony, 7441
Mantz, Paul, 7978
March, Fredric, 7813
Marx Brothers, 8169, 8170, 8171, 8172, 8603
Marx, Groucho, 7921, 8117
Mayer, Louis B., 7979
Méliès, Georges, 7884, 7885
Melville, Jean-Pierre, 8072, 8180
Minnelli, Vincente, 8191
Mix, Tom, 7725
Mizoguchi, Kenji, 8198
Monroe, Marilyn, 7821, 8166, 8276, 8606
Murnau, F.W., 7723, 8244
Murray, Mae, 8422
Olivier, Laurence, 8291
Pabst, G.W., 7881
Pascal, Gabriel, 7663
Pasolini, Pier-Paolo, 8312
Penn, Arthur, 7461
Peries, Lester James, 8131
Philipe, Gérard, 7886
Pickford, Mary, 8173
Polanski, Roman, 7582
Preminger, Otto, 7581
Prévert, Jacques, 8062
Rank, J. Arthur, 8197
Ray, Nicholas, 8274
Ray, Satyajit, 8336, 8403
Renoir, Jean, 8073, 8074, 8075, 8076, 8077
Resnais, Alain, 7415, 7572
Roach, Hal, 7815
Rossellini, Roberto, 8384, 8582
Rossen, Robert, 7825
Rutherford, Margaret, 8165
Seastrom, Victor (var. sp.: Victor Sjostrom), 8417, 8447
Selznick, David O., 8424
Sennett, Mack, 8097, 8145
Sinatra, Frank, 7812

(**Film Personalities**; Individual Studies; Writings About Film Personalities, cont.)

Sjostrom, Victor (see: Victor Seastrom)
Steinbeck, John, 8087
Stevens, George, 7882
Stewart, James, 7818
Stiller, Mauritz, 8178, 8417
Straub, Jean-Marie, 8477
Sucksdorff, Arne, 8483
Taylor, Elizabeth, 7702
Thalberg, Irving, 8519
Tracy, Spencer, 7826, 8460, 8546
Truffaut, Francois, 7575, 7856
Ustinov, Peter, 8564
Valentino, Rudolph, 8566, 8567
Vigo, Jean, 8078, 8079, 8080
Visconti, Luchino, 8576, 8577
Von Sternberg, Josef, 7578, 7579, 7817, 8088, 8089
Von Stroheim, Erich, 7711, 7981, 8478, 8583
Warhol, Andy, 7432, 7433

Wayne, John, 7485
Welles, Orson, 7823, 8298, 8299
White, Pearl, 8316
Wilder, Billy, 7486, 7498
Zanuck, Darryl F., 7678
Film-Related Personalities
Benchley, Robert, 8379
Brice, Fanny, 7724
Copland, Aaron, 7403
Coward, Noel, 8524
Edison, Thomas, 7650
Fitzgerald, F. Scott, 7624
Gershwin, George, 7889
Graham, Sheilah, 8375
Hughes, Howard, 7472, 8004
Pearlman, S.J., 8378
Presley, Elvis, 7703
Rogers, Will, 8304
Shaw, George Bernard, 8430
Trumbo, Dalton, 7410

INDIVIDUAL FILMS

Scripts and Stories
Anthology Scripts, 7413, 7414, 7480, 7481, 7482, 7832, 7852, 8037, 8416, 8534
Individual Scripts,
All-American Boy, The, 7419
China is Near, 7477
Doctor and the Devils, The, 7670
Dolce Vita, La, 7675
Entr'Acte, 7709
I Am Curious, 8008
Ivan the Terrible, 8061
L-136 (The Passion of Anna), 8104
Made in U.S.A., 8147
Masculine-Feminine, 8174
Petit Soldat, Le, 8320
Pierrot le Fou, 8330
Que Viva Mexico! , 8359
Rose Tattoo, The, 8387
Salt of the Earth, 8396
Vampyr, 8568
Virgin Spring, The, 8575
Studies and Production Descriptions
Apu Trilogy (Pather Panchali, Aparajito, The World of Apu), 7446
Battle of Britain, The, 7473
Beauty and the Beast, 7651
Belles-de-Nuit, Les, 8371
Citizen Kane, 7841
Cleopatra, 7592
Dam Busters, The, 7633
Friendly Persuasion, 8540
Hamlet, 7763, 7928
It Happened Here, 7995
I Am Curious, 8012
Man of Aran, 8160
Misfits, The, 8475
Murder in the Cathedral, 7782
Next Voice You Hear, The, 7516
Othello, 8358
Que Viva Mexico! , 8153, 8427

(Individual Films cont.)
    Red Badge of Courage, The, 8326
    Saraband for Dead Lovers, 8402
    Secret People, 8151
    2001: A Space Odyssey, 8156

FILM-MAKING

Reference and General Sources, 7422, 7652, 7706
Film-Making Techniques and Processes
    Acting, 7406, 7408, 7455, 7741
    Art Designing, 7450, 7644
    Cinematography, 7601, 7722, 7839, 8050, 8321, 8347, 8351, 8515
    Color, 7699
    Costuming, 7453
    Directing, 7661, 8613
    Editing, 8376, 8506, 8509, 8514
    Film-Making, 7606, 7744, 7772, 7774, 7792, 7869, 7929, 7993, 8155, 8189,
        8194, 8231, 8267, 8339, 8505, 8513, 8548
    Lighting, 8306
    Make-Up, 8507
    Music, 7609, 7642, 7756, 7775, 8025, 8510, 8511
    Processing, 7616
    Sound, 8285, 8453
    Special Effects, 8512
    Writing, 7784, 8243, 8527, 8619
Professional Film-Making: Hollywood Style, 7402, 7638, 7772, 7983, 7993,
    8155, 8231
Amateur Film-Making: Independent Style, 7540, 7625, 7924, 7926, 7997, 8001,
    8026, 8152, 8322, 8445
Animation, 7436, 7437, 7438, 7749, 8508
Specialized Film-Making Techniques and Sources, 7697, 7698, 7801, 7803, 7828,
    7998, 7999, 8054, 8161, 8206, 8432, 8505, 8529
Film-Making and Business Practices, 7442, 7620, 7691, 7769, 7797

FILM-RELATED BOOKS

General Interest, 7489, 7504, 7604, 7608, 7629, 7662, 7720, 7830, 7831, 7868,
    7910, 7952, 8005, 8023, 8107, 8115, 8130, 8146, 8154, 8258, 8328, 8345,
    8362, 8465, 8473, 8517, 8522, 8559, 8560, 8573, 8578, 8601, 8623
Audio-Visual and Educational Works, 7462, 7463, 7464, 7465, 7543, 7743,
    7747, 7765, 7786, 7829, 7924, 8114, 8163, 8212, 8241, 8343, 8352, 8365,
    8499, 8503, 8504, 8547, 8607, 8622, 8623
Film Societies and Collecting, 7600, 7785, 7787, 8000, 8539, 8556, 8563
Mass Communications and Broadcasting, 7720, 7868, 7902, 8016, 8175, 8176,
    8177, 8544

UNION LIST OF PERIODICALS

CHECKLIST OF LIBRARY ABBREVIATIONS

UNION LIST OF PERIODICALS

The following list of periodicals treated in this volume locates all holdings recorded by the Library of Congress at the time of publication. Expansion of the Library of Congress location symbols in this list follows at the end.

American Cinematographer
v. 1- 1920- monthly

CLSU	CaOOND
DLC	MiEM
IU	ICRL
DSI	InLP
NN	ICJ
PP	OC
CLU	KyU
MB	IaU
CL	IEN
CU	MH
WaS	MiU
CSdNEL	NNC
NB	MtBC
OU	KU
OrP	AzU
CSt	CoU

Cahiers du Cinema in English
defunct; New York
n. 1 (Jan., 1966) to n. 12 (Dec., 1967)
US ISSN 0575-0954

ArU 1-	NjP 1-
C 1-	OAU 1-
CaBVaU 1-	OrU 1-
CaNBSaM 1-	TxHR 7-
CaOTU 1-	ViU 1-
CaOWA 1-	
CaQML 1-	
CLSU 1-	
CPT 2-	
CSt 1-	
CU-SB 1-	
IaU 1-	
ICA 1-	
IEN 1-	
InNd 7-	
KU 7-	
MA 1-	
MBU 1-	
MdBJ 1-	
MiU 7-	
MNS 1-	
NIC 1-	

Cineaste
quarterly; New York
v. 1, n. 1 (Fall, 1967)
US ISSN 0009-7004

CaOWtU [3]-
CLSU [1]-
CU 3-
DLC [1]-
FTaSU [3]-
IaU [1]-
ICarbS [2]-
LU-NO 1-
MH 3-
OrU [1]-
VtU 2-
WaU 1-

Cinema
3 issues/year; Beverly Hills, Calif.
v. 1, n. 1 (1962)
US ISSN 0009-7047

CLSU [2]-
CLU [3]-
IaAS 4-
ICU 2-
LNHT 1-
MH 1-
MiDU 4-
MnSSC 3-
NIC [2]-
OrU 1-

Cinema Journal
formerly: Society of Cinematologists
v. 1, n. 1 (1961-1962)
US ISSN 0009-7101

CaOKQ 7-	KU 7-
CL I-	MB 6-
CLSU 4/5-	MiDW 6-
CLU 7-	NSyU 3-
CU 3-	OrU 3-
CU-SB 7-	
DLC 1/2-	
IaU 6-	
IU 1/2-	

Cinema Studies
Society for Film History Research
defunct; London
v. 1, n. 1 (Mar., 1960) to v. II, n. 3
(Mar., 1967)
UK ISSN 0578-2996
CaAEU [2]-
CLSU 1-
CLU [1]-
CoU 1-
CSt 1-
DLC [1]-
IaU 1-
ICU 1-
IEN [1]-
KU [1]
MH 1-
MiDW 2-
NN [1]-

Film
British Federation of Film Societies
quarterly
n. 1 (Oct., 1954)
UK ISSN 0015-1025

AzU 27-	IaAS 53-
CaBVa 1-	MiD 1-
CaBViV 49-	MiEM 31
CaOHM [2-17]-	MNS 19-
CaOOU 53-	MtBC 52-
CaOPAL 1970-	NcU 44-
CaOWtU [19-49]-	NhD 2-
CaQMG 47-	NN 1-
CaSRU 50-	OAU 29-
CLU	OrU 29-
CNoS 27-	UU 1970-
CoFS 41	VtU 57-
CU-SB 35-	WaU 47-
DLC 12-	WU 41-

Film Comment
formerly: Vision (first two issues)
quarterly; New York
v. 1, n. 1 (Spring, 1962)
US ISSN 0015-119X

ArU 5-	DLC [1]-
CaBViV 4-	FTaSU 6-
CaOKQ 1-	GU 1-3
CaOOCC [3]-	IaAS 4-
CaOOU 5-	IEN 4-
CaOTER 5-	InLP 6-
CaOTY 5-	InNd 4-
CaOWA 1-[6]	InU 1-4
CaOWtU 1-	IU [1]-
CaQMG 1-	KU 3-
CaQMU 1-	MA [6]-
CaSRU [6]-	MBU 5-
CaSSU (4) -	MdBJ 1-
CLSU [1]-	MH [4]-
CLU [1]-	MNS [1]-
CoFS 5-	MnSSC 6-
CoU [1]-	MnU 5-
CSfSt 3-	MoU 5-
CSt 1-	MsSM 6-
CtY 5-	MWalB 1-
CU [1]-	NcGU 5-
CU-Riv 5-	NhU 6-
CU-S (4)-	NIC 3-
CU-SB (4)-	NN 1-
DeU 6-	NNC 1-

(Film Comment cont.)
NNStJ 1-
NSyU [1]-
OAU 1-
OC 1-
OCIW 1-
OCU 5-
OO 3-
OrU 1-
PPiCI 3-
PSC 6-
PSt 1-
SdU [3]-
ViLxW [3]-
VtU 6-
WU 1-3

Film Culture
quarterly; New York
v. 1, n. 1 (Jan., 1965)
US ISSN 0015-1211

AAP 46-	MCM 44-
ArU 46-	MH [1]
AzU 19-	MiD 1-
CaAEU 47-	MiEM 22-
CaBVa [1]-	MNS [2]-
CaBVaS [1-41]-	MnSSC 40
CaNSHD 34-	MnU [9-30]-
CaOKQ 45-	MoSW 36-
CaOTU 44-	MoU 46-
CaOTY 1-	MtBC 20-
CaOWA 1-	MWelC 47-
CaOWtU 48-	NBu [1]-
CaQML 24-	NcD 1-
CaQMU 40-	NcU 40-
CaSSU 42-	NhD 1-
CL 11-	NhU 47-
CLSU [1]-	NIC 4-
CLU 1-	NjP 28-
CoFS 34-	NjR 35-
CoU 45, 48/49-	NN
CSf NO. [9-42]	NNC 1-
CtU [1]-	NNC-T 39-
CtY 1-	NNF 19-
CU 1-	NRU 44-
CU-SB 9-	NSyU 34-
DLC [1]-	NTRS 37-
FBrU 42-	OC 1-
FMU [3]-	OU 24-

Filmfacts
24 issues/year; New York
v. 1 (1953)
US ISSN 0015-153X

ArU 1-	CU 3-
C 3-	CU-Riv 1-
CaBVa 1-	CU-SB 10-
CaOKQ 1-	DeU 1-
CaOTER 13-	FTaSU 12-
CaOTY 11-	IEdS 1-
CaOWA 12-	IEN 1-
CaQML 1965-	InLP 1-
CLS 3-	InNd 1-
CLSU 1-	IU 1-
CLU 1-	LU 1-
CoFS 10-	MA 1-
CoU 1-	MB 3-
CSfSt 1-	MBU [9]-
CSt 3-	MH [10]-
CtY 1-	MiDW 12

(Filmfacts cont.)
MNS 11-
MnSSC 12-
MoS 6-
MoSW 12-
MoU 1-
MtBC [10]-
MWeIC 1-
NB 1-
NcD 11-
NhD 1-
NhU [11]-
NIC 10-
NN 1-
OAU 6-
OCl 1-
OkS 10-

OrU 6-
OU 3-
PPD 10-
PSt 1-
TxCM 1-
UPB 11-
WaU 7-

Film Journal
New Melbourne Film Group
quarterly
n. 9 (Feb., 1958) to n. 23 (July, 1954)
AT ISSN 0430-4322
CLU 1963-
IaU [1957,59]-
NIC [1955-65]
NNC [1956]-

Film Library Quarterly
quarterly; New York
n. 1, n. 1 (Winter, 1967-1968)
US ISSN 0015-1327
ArU 2-
C 1-
CaAE 1-
CaBVa 1-
CaBVaU [1]-
CaNSHD 1-
CaOONF [1]-
CaOONG [1]-
CaOPAL 2-
CaOTC [1]-
CaOTER 1-
CaOTY 1-
CaOWA [1]-
CaOWtU 1-
CaQMG [2]-
CLU 1-
CoD 1-
CoU [1]-
CU 1-
DLC 1-
FBrU 1-
GU [1]-
IaAS 1-
IaU 1-
ICarbS [1]-
ICU 1-
IEN [1]-
InLP 2-
InNd 1-
IU [1]-
KPT 1-
KU-M 2-
KyU 1-
LU 1-
MB 1-
MBU 1-
MdU 1-
MiDU 1-

MiDW [2]-
MiU [3]-
MNS 1-
MnSSC 1-
MnU [1]-
MoU 1-
MtBC 1-
MtU 1-
N 1-
NcGU 1-
NcU 1-
NhD 1-
NhU 3-
NIC 1-
NjR 1-
NN 1-
NNC 1-
NNC-T 2-
NNStJ 1-
NSyU 1-
OCU 1-
OrCS 1-
OrU 1-
OSW 1-
OU 1-
P 1-
PBL 1-
PPD 1-
PPiU 1-
PSt 1-
PV 2-
ScU 1-
UU 1-
ViBlbV 1-
Wa [1]-
WaU 1-
WU 1-

Film Heritage
quarterly
v. 1, n. 1 (Autumn, 1965)
US ISSN 0015-1270
ArU [4]-
AU 1-
AzTcS 1-
CaOLU 1-
CaOTY 4-
CaOWA 1-
CaQML 1-
CLSU 4-
CLU 1-
CNoS 2-
CoFS 1-
CoU 6-
CSfSt 1-
CSt 1-
CU 6-
CU-SB [2]-
DLC 1-
FTaSU 5-
IaGG 1-
IaU 1-
IEN [3]-
InLP 1-
IU 1-
KAS [4]-
MB 5-
MBU 1-

MdBJ 1-
MH 1-
MiEM 1-
MiU [1]-
MNS [1]-
MnSSC 1-
MtBC 3-
NIC 1-
NjP 1-
NmLcU [1]-
NN 1-
NNC 1-
NRU 1-
OAU 1-
OO [1]-
OrCS 1-
OrU 1-
OSW 1-
OU 4-
P 2-
PPT 1-
PSC 1-
UPB [2]-
VtU 1-
WaU 2
WU 1-

Films in Review
National Board of Review of Motion
Pictures
10 issues/year
v. 1, n. 1 (Feb., 1950)
US ISSN 0015-1688
ArU [4] -
AzU 4-
C 1-
CaBViV 18-
CaOHM 5-
CaOKQ 1-
CaOOU [12] -
CaOTU [5-6] -
CaSSU 18-
CL 1-
CLS [10] -
CLSU 1-
CLU 1-
CoD [20] -
CoFS 16-
CoU 1-
CSf 14
CSfSt 13-
CSt 1-
CtHT 17-
CtY 1-
CU 1-
CU-Riv 18-
DeU 1-
DLC 1-
FBrU 18-
FM 5-
FMU [1] -
FU [1-2] 3-
GU 1-
IaAS 21-
IaU [1] -
ICU 1-

IEN 1-
In 1-
InLP 1-
INS 1-
IU 1-
KU 5-
KyU 9-
LNHT 13-
MB 1-
MBU [2-18] -
MdU 9-
McU 2-
MH 1-
Mi 8, 10
MiDW 21-
MiU 1-
MNS 1-
MnSSC 17-
MoS 1-
MsU 16-
MtBC [19] -
MWalB [6] -
N [1] -
NBu [3-4] -
NcU 3-
NdU 9-
NhD 1-
NIC 1-
NjR 1-
NN 1-
NNC 6-
NNCoCi 1-
NNF 10-

(**Films in Review** cont.)

NNU 9-	TxETW 1-
OAU 18-	TxHR 21-
OCl 1-	TxLT 1-
OCU [18]-	TxSaT 21-
OrCS 20-	TxU 5-
PBL 20-	UU 21-
PPi 6-	ViW [4]-
PPiU 17-	VtNN 20
PSC 1-	WaT 4-
PSt 1-	WaU 1-
PU 1-	WM 1-
TNJ 1-	WU 13-
TxCM 19-	WyU 1-

Film Quarterly
formerly: Hollywood Quarterly;
formerly: Quarterly of Film,
    Radio and Television
quarterly
v. 12, p. 1 (Fall, 1958)

AU 1[2]+	MiEM [2]+
ArU 1+	MiU 1+
AzU 1+	MnNC 1+
C 1+	MnSJ 1+
CSJC 2+	MnU 1+
CSmH 1+	MoS 1+
CSt 1+	MoSW 1+
CU 1+	MoU 1+
CaB 1+	N 1+
CoD 1+	NB 2+
CoFS 1+	CCC 1+
CoU 1+	CL 1+
CoDU 1+	CLU 1+
CtY 1+	CSf 4+
DCU 3+	NBC 1+
DHU 1[2-3]+	NBuG 1+
DLC 1+	NBuU 1+
DeU 3+	NCH 1-3
FMU [2]+	NCaS [2]+
FJ 2+	NIC 1+
FTS 1+	NNCoCi 1+
GAT 1+	NJQ 1+
IC 1+	NFQC 1+
ICA 1+	NNU [1]+
ICarbS 2+	NPV 1+
ICU 1+	NRU 1+
IEN 1+	NbU 1+
IGK 1+	NcGU 1+
IRA 1+	NcU 3+
IU 1+	NhD 1+
IaAS 1+	NhU 1+
IaU 1+	NjP 1+
In 1+	NjR [2]+
InLP 1+	OAkU [2-4]
InU 1+	OCl 1+
K 1+	OCIW 1+
KU [2]+	OO 1+
KyLoU 1+	OU 1+
LNHT [1]-[3]+	Ok 1+
LU 1+	OkS 1+
MA 1+	OkTU 4+
MBU [3]+	OrPR 1+
MH 1+	PBm 1+
MMeT 1+	PLF 1+
MNS 1+	PPD 4+
MdBE 1+	PPT 1+
MdBJ 1+	PPiCl 1+
MiD 1+	PPiU 1+
MiDW 1+	PRA 2-3

(**Film Quarterly** cont.)

PSt 1-[3]+	
PU 2+	
RPB 1+	
ScU 1+	
SdU 1+	
TNJ 1+	
TU 1+	
TxDW 1+	
TxDaM 1+	
TxHR 5+	
TxU 1+	
WM 1+	
WU 1+	
WaS 1+	
WaT 1+	
WaU 1+	
WaWW 1-3	
WvU [2]+	
WyU 1+	

Film Society Review
American Federation of Film So-
    cieties
monthly (Sept-May 1964)

AzU 1964	MB 5-
CaAEU 5-	MBU 5-
CaOPAL 6-	MiEM [1966]-
CLSU 1968-	MNS 1969-
CNoS [1966]-	MtBC [1967]-
CoU [1965]-	NbU 6-
CStclU 5-	NcU [1964]-
CU 6-	NIC [1965]-
CU-Riv [1968]-	NmLcU [1966]
DeU 5-	NN 1-
DLC [1964]-	NSyU
FU [1965]-	OCIW 1968-
IaU [1965]-	OCU 1967-
ICarbS [1968]-	OU 1964-
ICU [1966]-	PSC [1968]-
IEN 5-	TxLT 5-
InLP [1968-	VtU 6-
InNd [1967]-	WaU [1966]-

**Films: A Quarterly of Discussion and
        Analysis**
defunct
v. 1, n. 1 (Nov., 1939) to v. 1, n. 4
    (Summer, 1940)

CU
DLC
ICA
MH
MiD
MiU
NBuG
CLSU no2-4
CtY no2-4
NN
NhD no1-3
NNC
NNU
NjP
PPPM
ViW
WaU
NjP
PPi
WaU no2-4

Films and Filming
monthly; London
v. 1, n. 1 (Oct., 1954)
UK ISSN 0015-167X

CaAEU [16]-	INS 15-
CaBVaS 13-	IU [9]-
CaBVaU 10-	KU [15]-
CaBViV [14]-	KyU [5]-
CaNBFU [14]-	MA [12]-
CaNSHD 11-	MB [16]-
CaOKQ 14-	MBU [11]-
CaOOCC [12]-	MiD 3-
CaOONL [8-14],16-	MiDW [16]-
CaOTY 16-	MiEM [13]
CaOW 15-	MiU [16]-
CaOWA [14]-	MNS [8]-
CaQMG [13]-	MsSM 16-
CaQMU [13]-	MtBC [6]-
CaSSU [13]-	NcU 7-
CL 9-	NIC 8-
CLSU 1-	NjP [12]-
CLU 6-	NmLcU [9]-
CoFS [15]-	NN [2]-[4]-
CoU 1-	NNC 15-
CSf [11]	OAU 12-
CSfSt 8-	OC 1-
CSt [14-15]	OCI 1-
CtY 8-	OCU [14]-
CU-S [14]-	OU [11]-
CU-SB [10]-	PBL 15-
DLC 1-	PPt 11-
FTaSU [16]-	PSC [14]-
FU 1-	PU 10-
IaAS [16]-	TxHR 14-
IaU [12]-	TxU 16-
IEN [14]-	WaU [6]-
InLP 1-	WU 11-
InNd 5-	

Focus
Documentary Film Group
irregular
n. 1 (Feb., 1967)
US ISSN 0015-4989
DLC [1969]-

Focus on Film
quarterly; London
n. 1 (Jan.,-Feb., 1970)

CaBVaU [1970]-	MBU 2-
IaAS 1-	OrU-S 9-
CU 1-	TxSaT 1-
CaQML 1-	
ICarbS 6-	
IU 1-	
MNS 1-	
MiU 1-	

Hollywood Quarterly. See Film Quarterly

International Film Guide
annual; London
v. 1 (1964)
UK ISSN 0074-6053

AAP 1966-	AzU 1965-
AU 1964-	CaBVa 1964
AzTeS 1966-	CaBVaS 1968-

(International Film Guide cont.)

CaBViV 1967-	MdBJ 1966-
CaMWU 1968-	MH 1965-
CaNBFU 1965-66	MiDW 1966-
CaOH 1964-	MiEM 1966-
CaOHM 1966	MiU 1967
CaOTER 1968-	MnM 1965-
CaOTU 1968-	MNS 1967-
CaOTY 1964-	MoU 1968
CaQML 1967-	MWalB 1968-
CaSRU 1968	NB 1964-
CL 1964-	NbU 1964, 67-
CLSU 1963-	NcD 1964-
CoD 1964-	NcU 1964-
CoFS 1964-	NhD 1964-
CoU 1964-	NIC 1964-
CSf 1964, 65	NjP 1964-
CSt 1964-	NNC 1964-
CtY 1968	NNC-T 1965-
CU-Riv 1964, 67-	NNU 1964
CU-S 1964-1967	NRRI 1964-
DeU 1966-	OCI 1964-
DLC 1964-	OkU 1969-
FTaSU 1964	OO 1966-
FU 1965	OrU 1964, 66-
GU 1967-	OU 1968-
IaAS 1968-	P 1965-
IaU 1964-	PPT 1966-
ICU 1964-	PSt 1964-
IEN 1969-	PU 1967
InLP 1969	ScU 1965
IU 1964-	TxCM 1970-
KyU 1968-	UPB 1964
LNHT 1967-	UU 1964, 69-
MA 1965-	ViU 1966
MB 1967-	WyU 1964-
MBU 1964	

Journal of Popular Culture
Modern Language Association of
America
quarterly
v. 1, n. 1 (Summer, 1967)
US ISSN 0022-3840

AAP 1-	CU-S 1-
AU 1-	CU-SB 1-
AzTeS 1-	DeU 3-
C 1-	DLC 1-
CaAEU [1]-	FBrU 1-
CaBVaS 1-	FMU 1-
CaBVaU 1-	FTaSU 2-
CaNSHD 1-	GEU 1-
CaOOCC 1-	GU 1-
CaOONM 1-	IaAS 1-
CaOTU 1-	IaGG 1-
CaOTY 3-	IaU 1-
CaOWtU 1-	ICarbS 1-
CaQMG [1]-	ICU 1-
CaSRU 4-	IEdS 1-
CaSSU 1-	IEN 1-
CCC 1-	InLP 1-
CL 1-	InNd 1-
CLU 1-	InU 1-
CoFS [1]-	IU 1-
CoU 1-	KMK 1-
CPT [1]	KPT 3-
CSt	KyU 1-
CtY 1-	LNHT 1-
CU 1-	LNL 1-
CU-Riv 1-	LU 1-

(Journal of Popular Culture cont.)

MA 1-	OC 1-
MdBJ 1-	OCIW 1-
MdU 1-	OkS 1-
McB 1-	OrCS 1-
McU 1-	OrU 1-
MH 1-	OU 1-
MiDW 1-	PPiU
MiEM 1-	PSC 1-
MiU [1] -	PSt 1-
MnU 1-	PU 1-
MoU [1] -	PV 2-
MShM 3-	RPB 1-
MsSM [1] -	ScCleU 1-
MtBC 1-	ScU 1-
MtU 1-	TNJ 1-
MWalB 1-	TxDaM 1-
N 1-	TxHR 1-
NcGU 1-	TxLT 1-
NcU 1-	TxSaT 3-
NhD 1-	ULA [3] -
NhU 1-	UPB [2] -
NIC 1-	UU 1-
NjP 1-	ViU 1-
NjR 1-	VtMiM 1-
NmLcU 1-	VtU 3-
NN 1-	WaU [2] -
NNC 1-	WBB [3] -
NRU 1-	WU 1-
NSoaS 3-	WyU 2-

Movie
  irregular/quarterly; London
  n. 1 (June, 1962) — n. 18 (Winter,
  1970-1971)
  UK ISSN 0027-268X
CaQMG 16-
CaQML 7-
CLSU 12-
CSfSt 12-
CSt 10-
CU 16-
CU-SB 16-
DLC 1-
ICarbS 15-
IEN 1-
IU 15-
NIC 1-
NjP 12-
NN 1-
OrU 1-
OU 12-
PU 4-
UU 9-
WU 8-

New York Review of Books
  24 issues/year; New York
  v. 1, n. 1 (Jan., 1963)
  US ISSN 0028-7504

AAP [2] -	CaMWU 4-
AMAU [1] -	CaNBFU [2] -
ArU [1] -	CaNBSaM [1] -
AU 1-	CaNSHD [1] -
AzTeS 4-	CaNSHPL 1-
C 1-	CaOKQ 1-
CaAEU 1-	CaOKQH 15-
CaBVa 1-	CaOLU
CaBVaS 1-	CaOOCC 1-
CaBVaU 1-	CaOONL 1-[4-5] -

(New York Review of Books cont.)

CaOOSS [6] -	MiEM 5-
CaOOU 6-	MiMtpT 1-
CaOTC [12] -	MiU [1] -
CaOTU 1-	MiU-L 11-
CaOTV [1] -[3] -	MMeT 1-
CaOTY 1-	MNF 1-
CaOW 1-	MNS 1-
CaOWtU [1] -	MnSSC 1-
CaQMaC [7] -	MnU 1-
CaQML [1-]	MoRM [1] -
CaQMM [15] -	MoSW 1-
CaQStJ 8-	MoU 1-
CaSRL 1-	MsSM 1-
CaSSU 4-	MsU 1-
CL 1-	MtBC [6] -
CLSU [1] -	MWalB 1-
CoD 1-	MWelC [1] -
CoFS 1-	MWiW 1-
CoU 1-	N 1-
CPT [1] -	NAIfC 6-
CSf 1-	NB 2, 3-
CSfSt 1-	NbU 1-
CSjC	NBu 2-
CSt 1-	NcD 1-
CStclU 1-	NcGU 1-
CtNIC 1-	NcRS [1] -
CtW 1-	NcU 2-
CtY [1] -	NhD 1-
CtY-M 11-	NjP 1-
CU-Riv [1] -	NjPE 2-
CU-SB [1] -	NjR 1-
DLC 1-	NmLcU [2] -
FMU [1] -	NN 1-
FTaSU 1-	NNC 1-
FU 1-	NNStJ 1-
GAT 1-	NNU 1-
GEU 1-	NNU-L [8] -
GU [2] -	NRU 1-
IaAS [1] -	NSyU 1-
IaGG 1-	NTRS 5-
IaU 1-	OC 1-
ICN [1] -	OCl 1-
ICU 1-	OCIW 2-
IdU 2-	OCU 1-
IEdS 6-	OkS [1] -
IEN 1-	OkU [2] -
In [1] -	OO [1] -
InLP [1] -	OrCS 1-
InU 1-	OrPU 8-
IU 1-	OrU 2-
KMK 1-	OU [1] -
KPT 1-	P 1-
KU 1-	PPi 1-
KU-M 3-	PPiD 1-
LNHT 1-	PPiPT 9-
LNL 1-	PSC 1-
LU [1]	PU 1-
MA 1-	PV 2-
MBCo 1-[3] -	RPB 1-
MBU 1-	ScCleU 6-
MCM 1-	SdU 6-
MdBJ [3] -	TNJ 1-
MdU 1-	TxDaM 1-
MeLB [1] -	TxHR 1-
MH 1-	TxSaT 2-
Mi 1-8	ULA
MiD 1-	UU 2-
MiDU 1-	ViBlbV 1-
MiDW [1] -	ViU [1] -

(New York Review of Books cont.)
VtNN 1-
Wa [1]-
WaU [1]-
WBB 1-
WHi 11-
WU [1]-
WyU 1-

Quarterly of Film, Radio and Television.
See **Film Quarterly**

Screen
formerly: Screen Education
Society for Education in Film and
Television
quarterly; London
v. 10, n. 1 (Jan.-Feb., 1969)
UK ISSN 0036-9543

AAP 1968-	ICarbS [10]-
ArU 12-	ICU 10-
CaBVaS 10-	IEN 10-
CaNSHD [1968]-	InLP [10]-
CaOKQH 10-	InU 10-
CaOTER 10	IU 10-
CaOTY 10-	KU 10
CaQMG 1968-	KyU 10-
CaQML 1967-	MA 1968-
CaSSU 10-	MH 10-
CLSU [10]-	NIC 10-
CoU 10-	OCIW [10]-
CSt [11]	OrU [1967]-
DLC [10]-	PSt 11-
IaU 10-	WU 10-

Sequence
defunct; London
n. 1 (Dec., 1946) — n. 14 (New Year,
1952)
CLU 3+
ICA 10+
IEN 4-5, 7+
InNd 4-14
MH 2+
MdBE 13+
MiD 2+
NN 4-5, 7+
TxDa 10+
ICA 10-14

Sight and Sound
British Film Institute
quarterly; London
v. 15, n. 58 (Summer, 1946)

C [1-3]+	NRE 1[2]+
CLSU [5-6] 8+	NjP 7+
CSt [1]+	OCl 1
CaM 1-7	PBm 5+
CtY 1+	
DHEW 1+	
IC 23, 25+	
IEN 1+	
IU [1-2]+	
MiD 1940+	
MnU 3-[7]	
NbU 24-28	
NN 1+	
NNC-T 4+	

(Sight and Sound cont.)
—Index series. no1, Je 1943+
At head of title: Special supplement
to Sight and Sound. 3 repeated in
numbering
CLSU 18
CLU 1-4, 7, 11+
CaH no[1+]
CaV 1-3, 6-8, 10+
CtY 1-18
DLC 1-3
ICA 1+
MdBE 1-3, 5-11, 13-18
NN 1-3, 5, 7, 9-15, 17, 18
NNC 13+

Take One
bi-monthly; Montreal, Canada
v. 1, n. 2 (Sept., 1966)
CN ISSN 0039-9132
CaAEU 1-
CaBVa 1-
CaBVaU 1-
CaOOCC 1-
CaOONF 1-
CaOONL 1-
CaOOP 1-
CaOOSS [1]-
CaOTU 1-
CaOW 1-
CaOWA [1]-
CaOWtU [2]-
CaQMaC 1-
CaQMG 1-
CaSRU [1]-
CLSU [1]-
CLU 1-
CoU 1-
CSt 1-
CtU 2-
CtY 1-
CU [1]-
CU-SB [2]-
DLC 1-
IaU [2]-
ICarbS [2]
ICU 1-
IU [1]-
MH 1-
OrU [1]-
VtU 2-

Views & Reviews
quarterly; Milwaukee, Wisc.
v. 1, n. 1 (Summer, 1969)
US ISSN 0042-5923
AzTeS 2-
CoFS 1-
CU-SB 1-
ICU 1-
IEN 1-
InNd 1-
KyU 1-
MH 1-
OrU 1-
WaU 1-
WM 1-

CHECKLIST OF LIBRARY ABBREVIATIONS

The symbols L, L*, P, and M following the name of a library refer to the library's facilities for lending serials and for furnishing photocopies and microfilms

L = The library lends serials
L*= The library restricts its lending of serials. Applications should be made in each case
P = The library can furnish photocopies *(usually for a fee)*
M = The library can furnish microfilms *(usually for a fee)*

ALABAMA
AAP   Auburn University, Auburn (formerly Alabama Polytechnic Institute) (L*, P, M)
AMAU   Air University Library, Maxwell Air Force Base (L*, P)
AU   University of Alabama, University (P)

ARKANSAS
ArU   University of Arkansas (L*, P)

ARIZONA
AzTeS   Arizona State University (formerly Arizona State College) Tempe (L*)
AzU   University of Arizona, Tucson (L*, P, M)

CALIFORNIA
C   California State Library, Sacramento (L, P)
CCC   Honnold Library, Claremont. (Housing the libraries of Pomona College, Claremont Men's College, Claremont Graduate School, Harvey Mudd College, and serving Scripps College) (L*, P)
CL   Los Angeles Public Library, Rufus B. von KleinSmid Central Library, Los Angeles (L*, P)
CLSU   University of Southern California, Los Angeles (L, P, M)
CLU   University of California, Los Angeles (L*, P, M)
CNoS   San Fernando Valley State College, Northridge (L*)
CPT   California Institute of Technology, Pasadena (P, M)
CSdNEL   U.S. Navy Electronics Laboratory Library, San Diego (L)
CSf   San Francisco Public Library, San Francisco (L*, P)
CSfSt   San Francisco State College, San Francisco (L*)
CSjC   San Jose State College, San Jose (P)
CSmH   Henry E. Huntington Library and Museum, San Marino
CSt   Stanford University Libraries, Stanford (L*, P, M)

(CALIFORNIA cont.)

CStclU	University of Santa Clara, Santa Clara (L*, P)
CU	University of California, Berkeley (L*, P, M)
CU-Riv	—University of California, Riverside (L, P)
CU-S	—University of California, San Diego, La Jolla. (Includes Biomedical Library and Scripps Institution of Oceanography Library) (P)
CU-SB	University of California, Santa Barbara

CANADA

CaAE	Edmonton Public Library, Edmonton, Alta. (L*, P)
CaAEU	University of Alberta, Edmonton, Alta. (L*, P)
CaB	University of British Columbia
CaBVa	Vancouver Public Library, Vancouver, B.C. (L*, P)
CaBVaS	Simon Fraser University, Vancouver
CaBVaU	University of British Columbia, Vancouver, B.C. (L*, P, M)
CaBViV	University of Victoria Library, Victoria, B.C. (P)
CaH	Hamilton Public Library
CaM	McGill University, Montreal
CaMWU	University of Manitoba, Wimmipeg, Man. (L*, P)
CaNBFU	University of New Brunswick Library, Fredericton, N.B. (L*, P, M)
CaNBSaM	Mount Allison University Library, Sackville, N.B. (L, P)
CaNSHD	Dalhousie University, Halifax, N.S. (P)
CaNSHPL	Nova Scotia Provincial Library, Halifax, N.S. (L*, P)
CaOH	Hamilton Public Library, Hamilton, Ont. (L*, P)
CaOHM	McMaster University, Hamilton, Ont. (L*, P, M)
CaOKQ	Queen's University Library, Kingston, Ont. (L*, P, M)
CaOKQH	—Health Sciences Library
CaOLU	University of Western Ontario, London, Ont. (L*, P, M)
CaOOCC	Carleton College Library, Ottawa, Ont. (L*, P)
CaOOND	Dept. of National Defence, Departmental Library, Ottawa, Ont. (L, P)
CaOONF	National Film Board Library, Montreal, Que. (L, P)
CaOONG	National Gallery of Canada Library, Ottawa, Ont. (L*, P)
CaOONL	National Library of Canada, Ottawa, Ont. (L, P, M)
CaOONM	National Museum of Canada, Ottawa, Ont. (L, P)
CaOOP	Library of Parliament, Ottawa, Ont. (L*, P)
CaOOSS	Department of Secretary of State, Ottawa
CaOOU	Université d'Ottawa Library, Ottawa, Ont. (L*, P)
CaOPAL	Lakehead University Library, Thunder Bay, Ont. (L*, P, M)
CaOTC	Ontario College of Education, Toronto, Ont. (L*, P)
CaOTER	Ontario Institute for Studies in Education, Toronto (P)
CaOTU	University of Toronto, Toronto, Ont. (L, P, M)
CaOTV	Victoria University, Toronto, Ont.
CaOTY	York University Library, Toronto, Ont. (L*, P)
CaOW	Windsor Public Library, Windsor, Ont.
CaOWA	University of Windsor Library, Windsor, Ont. (L*, P)
CaOWtU	University of Waterloo, Waterloo, Ont. (L)
CaQMG	Sir George Williams University, Montreal, Que.
CaQML	Loyola College, Montreal, Que. (L*, P)
CaQMM	McGill University, Montreal, Que. (L*, P, M)
CaQMU	Université de Montréal, Montreal, Que. (L*, P, M)
CaQMaC	McDonald College Library, Ste-Anne de Bellevue, Montreal Que. (L*, P)
CaQStJ	College Militaire royal de St-Jean, St. Jean, Que. (L)
CaSRL	Legislative Library of Saskatchewan, Regina, Sask. (L, P)
CaSRU	University of Saskatchewan Regina Campus, Regina (P)
CaSSU	University of Saskatchewan, Saskatoon, Sask. (L, P)
CaV	Vancouver Public Library

COLORADO
CoD	The Public Library, The City and County of Denver (P)
CoDu	University of Denver
CoFS	Colorado State University, Fort Collins (L*, P, M)
CoU	University of Colorado, Boulder (L*, P, M)

CONNECTICUT
CtHT	Trinity College, Hartford (L*, P)
CtNIC	Connecticut College, New London (L*, P)
CtU	University of Connecticut, Storrs (L*, P)
CtW	Wesleyan University, Middletown (L*, P)
CtY	Yale University, New Haven (L*, P, M)
CtY-M	—Medical School (L, P, M)

DISTRICT OF COLUMBIA
DCU	Catholic University Library (L*, P, M)
DHEW	U.S. Department of Health, Education and Welfare Library (L*)
DHU	Howard University (L*)
DLC	Library of Congress (P, M)
DSI	Smithsonian Institution Library (L, P, M)

DELAWARE
DeU	University of Delaware, Newark (L*, P)

FLORIDA
FBrU	Florida Atlantic University, Boca Raton (L*, P)
FJ	Jacksonville Public Library System
FM	Miami Public Library, Miami (L*, P, M)
FMU	University of Miami Library, Coral Gables (L*, P)
FTS	University of South Florida, Tampa
FTaSU	Florida State University, Tallahassee (L*, P, M)
FU	University of Florida, Gainesville (L*, P, M)

GEORGIA
GAT	Georgia Institute of Technology, Atlanta (L*, P, M)
GEU	Emory University, Emory University (L*, P, M)
GU	University of Georgia, Athens (L*, P, M)

ILLINOIS
IC	Chicago Public Library, Chicago (L*, P, M)
ICA	Art Institute of Chicago, Chicago (L*, P, M)
ICJ	John Crerar Library, Chicago (L*, P, M)
ICN	Newberry Library, Chicago (L, P, M)
ICRL	Center for Research Libraries, Chicago (L, P, M)
ICU	University of Chicago, Chicago (L)
ICarbS	Southern Illinois University, Carbondale (L*, P)
IEN	Northwestern University, Evanston (L*, P)
IEN-C	Joseph Schaffner Library of Commerce, Chicago
IEdS	Southern Illinois University, Edwardsville Campus (L*, P)
IGK	Knox College, Galesburg
INS	Illinois State University, Normal (P)
IRA	Augustana College Library, Rock Island (L*, P)
IU	University of Illinois, Urbana (L*, P, M)

IOWA
IaAS	Iowa State University of Science and Technology, Ames (P, M)

(IOWA cont.)
IaGG   Grinnell College, Grinnell (L*, P)
IaU   University of Iowa, Iowa City (L, P, M)

IDAHO
IdU   University of Idaho, Moscow (L*, P)

INDIANA
In   Indiana State Library, Indianapolis (L*, P, M)
InLP   Purdue University, Lafayette (L*, P, M)
InNd   University of Notre Dame, South Bend (L, P)
InU   Indiana University, Bloomington (L, P)

KANSAS
K   Kansas State Library, Topeka
KAS   St. Benedict's College, Atchison (L*, P)
KMK   Kansas State College of Agriculture and Applied Science, Manhattan
           (L*, P)
KPT   Kansas State College of Pittsburg, Pittsburg (L*,P)
KU   University of Kansas Libraries, Lawrence (P)
KU-M   —School of Medicine Library, Kansas City, (L*, P)

KENTUCKY
KyLoU   University of Louisville, Louisville (L*, P, M)
KyU   University of Kentucky, Lexington (L*, P, M)

LOUISIANA
LNHT   Tulane University Library, New Orleans (L*, P, M)
LNL   Loyola University, New Orleans (P)
LU   Louisiana State University, Baton Rouge (L*, P, M)
LU-NO   —Louisiana State University in New Orleans (L*, P, M)

MASSACHUSETTS
MA   Amherst College, Amherst (L*, P)
MB   Boston Public Library, Boston (P, M)
MBCo   Countway Library of Medicine (Harvard-Boston Medical Libraries),
           Boston (L*, P)
MBU   Boston University, Boston
MCM   Massachusetts Institute of Technology, Cambridge (P, M)
MH   Harvard University, Cambridge (P, M)
MMeT   Tufts University, Medford (L*, P)
MNF   Forbes Public Library, Northampton (L*, P, M)
MNS   Smith College Library, Northampton (L, P)
MShM   Mount Holyoke College, South Hadley (L*, P)
MWalB   Brandeis University, Waltham (L*, P)
MWelC Wellesley College Library, Wellesley (L*, P)
MWiW   Williams College, Williamstown (L, P)

MARYLAND
MdBE   Enoch Pratt Free Library, Baltimore
MdBJ   Johns Hopkins University, Baltimore (L*, P. M)
MdU   University of Maryland, College Park (L, P. M)

MAINE
MeB   Bowdoin College, Brunswick (L, P)

(MAINE cont.)
MeLB   Bates College, Lewiston (L, P)
MeU   University of Maine, Orono (L*, P)

MICHIGAN
Mi   Michigan State Library, Lansing (L*, P)
MiD   Detroit Public Library, Detroit (L)
MiEM   Michigan State University, East Lansing (L*, P, M)
MiDU   University of Detroit, Detroit (P, M)
MiDW   Wayne State University, Detroit (L*, P, M)
MiMtpT   Central Michigan College, Mount Pleasant (L*)
MiU   University of Michigan, Ann Arbor (L, P, M)
MiU-L   —Law Library (L*, P)

MINNESOTA
MnNC   Carleton College, Northfield (L, P)
MnM   Minneapolis Public Library, Minneapolis (L*, P, M)
MnSJ   James Jerome Hill Reference Library, St. Paul (L*, P)
MnSSC   College of St. Catherine, St. Paul (L*, P)
MnU   University of Minnesota, Minneapolis (L*, P, M)

MISSOURI
MoRM   University of Missouri School of Mines and Metallurgy, Rolla
MoS   St. Louis Public Library, St. Louis (L*, P)
MoSW   Washington University, St. Louis (P)
MoU   University of Missouri, Columbia (L*, P, M)

MISSISSIPPI
MsSM   Mississippi State University, State College (L, P)
MsU   University of Mississippi Library, Oxford (L*, P)

MONTANA
MtBC   Montana State University at Bozeman (L*, P, M)
MtU   University of Montana at Missoula (L*, P, M)

NEW YORK
N   New York State Library, Albany (L*, P, M)
NAlfC   State University of New York, College of Ceramics at Alfred University, Alfred
NB   Brooklyn Public Library, Brooklyn (L*, P)
NBC   Brooklyn College, Brooklyn (L*, P, M)
NBu   Buffalo and Erie County Public Library, Buffalo (L, P)
NBuG   Grosvenor Reference Division, Buffalo and Erie County Public Library, Buffalo
NBuU   State University of New York at Buffalo
NCH   Hamilton College, Clinton (L, P)
NCaS   St. Lawrence University, Canton (L*, P)
NFQC   Queens College Library, Flushing (P)
NIC   Cornell University, Ithaca (L*, P, M)
NN   New York Public Library, New York (P, M)
NNC   Columbia University, New York (L*, P, M)
NNC-T   —Teachers College (L, P)
NNcoCi   College of the City of New York, N.Y. (L*)
NNF   Library, Fordham University, New York (L*)
NNStJ   St. John's University Libraries, New York (L*, P)

(NEW YORK cont.)

NNU	New York University Libraries, New York (P)
NNU-L	—School of Law Library (L*)
NPV	Vassar College, Poughkeepsie
NRE	Eastman Kodak Company, Rochester (P)
NRRI	Rochester Institute of Technology, Rochester (L*, P)
NRU	University of Rochester, Rochester (L*, P)
NSoaS	Long Island University, Southampton College, Southampton (P)
NSyU	Syracuse University. Syracuse (P, M)
NTRS	Russell Sage College, Troy (L*, P)

NEBRASKA

NbU	University of Nebraska, Lincoln (P)

NORTH CAROLINA

NcD	Duke University, Durham (L*, P, M)
NcRS	North Carolina State University at Raleigh (P)
NcU	University of North Carolina, Chapel Hill (P, M)
NcGU	University of North Carolina at Greensboro, Greensboro (L)

NORTH DAKOTA

NdU	University of North Dakota, Grand Forks (L, P)

NEW HAMPSHIRE

NhD	Dartmouth College, Hanover (L, P)
NhU	University of New Hampshire, Durham (L*, P)

NEW MEXICO

NmLcU	New Mexico State University, Las Cruces

NEW JERSEY

NjP	Princeton University, Princeton (L*, P, M)
NjPE	Educational Testing Service, Princeton (L*, P)
NjR	Rutgers University Library, New Brunswick (P, M)

OHIO

OAU	Ohio University, Athens (L, P)
OAkU	University of Akron, Akron (L*, P)
OC	Public Library of Cincinnati and Hamilton County, Cincinnati (L*, P)
OCU	University of Cincinnati, Cincinnati (L*, P)
OCl	Cleveland Public Library, Cleveland (L*, P, M)
OClW	Case Western Reserve University, Cleveland (P)
OO	Oberlin College, Oberlin (L*, P)
OSW	Wittenberg University, Springfield (P)
OU	Ohio State University, Columbus (L*, P, M)

OKLAHOMA

OK	Oklahoma State Library, Oklahoma City
OkS	Oklahoma State University, Stillwater (P)
OkTU	University of Tulsa, Tulsa (L*, P, M)
OkU	University of Oklahoma, Norman (L, P, M)

OREGON

OrCS	Oregon State University, Corvallis (P)
OrP	Library Association of Portland

(OREGON cont.)

OrPF	Reed College, Portland
OrPU	University of Portland, Portland (L)
OrU	University of Oregon, Eugene (L*, P, M)

PENNSYLVANIA

P	Pennsylvania State Library, Harrisburg (L*, P)
PBL	Lehigh University, Bethlehem (L*, P, M)
PBm	Bryn Mawr College Library, Bryn Mawr (L*, P)
PLF	Franklin and Marshall College, Lancaster (L, P)
PP	Free Library of Philadelphia, Philadelphia (L*, P, M)
PPD	Drexel University, Philadelphia (P)
PPPM	Philadelphia Museum of Art, Philadelphia (L*, P)
PPT	Temple University, Philadelphia (L*, P)
PPi	Carnegie Library of Pittsburgh, Pittsburgh (L*, P)
PPiCI	Carnegie Institute of Technology, Pittsburgh (L*, P)
PPiD	Duquesne University, Pittsburgh (L*, P, M)
PPiPT	Pittsburgh Theological Seminary (L*, P, M)
PPiU	University of Pittsburgh, Pittsburgh (L*, P)
PRA	Albright College, Reading
PSC	Swarthmore College, Swarthmore (L, P)
PSt	Pennsylvania State University, University Park (L*, P, M)
PU	University of Pennsylvania, Philadelphia (L*, P, M)
PV	Villanova University (P)

RHODE ISLAND

RPB	Brown University, Providence (L*, P, M)

SOUTH CAROLINA

ScCleU	Clemson University, Clemson (P)
ScU	University of Sourh Carolina, Columbia (L*)

SOUTH DAKOTA

SdU	University of South Dakota, Vermillion (P)

TENNESSEE

TNJ	Joint University Libraries (Vanderbilt University, George Peabody College for Teachers, and Scarritt College) Nashville (L*, P, M)
TU	University of Tennessee, Knoxville (L, P)

TEXAS

TxCM	Texas A & M University, College Station (L*, P)
TxDW	Texas Womans University, Denton
TxDa	Dallas Public Library, Dallas (L*, P, M)
TxDaM	Southern Methodist University, Dallas (L*, P, M)
TxETW	Texas Western College, El Paso (P)
TxHR	Rice University, Houston (L*, P)
TxLT	Texas Tech University, Lubbock (L*, P, M0
TxSaT	Trinity University, San Antonio (L*)
TxU	University of Texas, Austin (L*, P, M)

UTAH

ULA	Utah State University, Logan (L*, P)
UPB	Brigham Young University, Provo (L, P, M)
UU	University of Utah, Salt Lake City (L*, P)

VIRGINIA

ViBlbV   Virginia Polytechnic Institute, Blacksburg (L*, P, M)
ViLxW   Washington & Lee University, Lexington (L*, P)
ViU   University of Virginia, Charlottesville (L*, P, M)
ViW   College of William and Mary, Williamsburg (L*, P)

VERMONT

VtMiM   Middlebury College, Middlebury (L, P)
VtNN   Norwich University, Northfield (L*, P)
VtU   University of Vermont and State Agricultural College, Burlington (L*, P)

WISCONSIN

WBB   Beloit College, Beloit (L*)
WHi   Wisconsin State Historical Society, Madison (L*, P, M)
WM   Milwaukee Public Library, Milwaukee (L*, P, M)
WU   University of Wisconsin, Madison (L, P, M)

WASHINGTON

Wa   Washington State Library, Olympia (L, P)
WaS   Seattle Public Library
WaT   Tacoma Public Library, Tacoma (L*, P)
WaU   University of Washington, Seattle (L*, P, M)
WaWW   Whitman College, Walla Walla

WEST VIRGINIA

WvU   West Virginia University, Morgantown

WYOMING

WyU   Wyoming University, Laramie (L*, P, M)